THE PRENTICE-HALL SERIES IN MARKETING
Philip Kotler, Series Editor

third edition

Principles

Prentice/Hall International

# of Marketing

Philip Kotler

Northwestern University

Principles of Marketing, third edition by Philip Kotler
Editorial/production supervision by Esther S. Koehn
Interior/cover design by Maureen D. Eide
Cover illustration by Tcherevkoff Studios Ltd.
Photo research by Tobi Zausner
Manufacturing buyer: Ed O'Dougherty

Printed in the United States of America

10   9   8   7   6   5   4

ISBN 0-13-701830-4

Prentice-Hall International (UK) Limited, *London*
Prentice-Hall of Australia Pty. Limited, *Sydney*
Prentice-Hall Canada Inc., *Toronto*
Prentice-Hall Hispanoamericana, S.A., *Mexico*
Prentice-Hall of India Private Limited, *New Delhi*
Prentice-Hall of Japan, Inc., *Tokyo*
Prentice-Hall of Southeast Asia Pte. Ltd., *Singapore*
Editora Prentice-Hall do Brasil, Ltda., *Rio de Janeiro*
Whitehall Books Limited, *Wellington, New Zealand*
Prentice-Hall, *Englewood Cliffs, New Jersey*

*This book is dedicated to my
students who have taught me so much.*

About the Author

Philip Kotler is one of the world's leading authorities on marketing. He is the Harold T. Martin Professor of Marketing at the Kellogg Graduate School of Management, Northwestern University. He received his master's degree at the University of Chicago and his Ph.D. degree at M.I.T., both in economics. He did post-doctoral work in mathematics at Harvard and in behavioral science at the University of Chicago.

Dr. Kotler is the author of *Marketing Management: Analysis, Planning and Control* (Prentice-Hall), now in its fifth edition. This text has been translated into eleven languages, including Russian and Chinese, and is the most widely used marketing textbook in graduate schools of business. His *Marketing for Nonprofit Organizations,* now in its second edition, is the best seller in that specialized area. Dr. Kotler's other books include *The New Competition; Marketing Professional Services; Strategic Marketing for Educational Institutions,* and *Marketing Model-Building.* In addition, he has written over eighty articles for leading journals, including the *Harvard Business Review, Journal of Marketing, Journal of Marketing Research, Management Science, Journal of Business Strategy,* and *Futurist.* He is the only three-time winner of the coveted Alpha Kappa Psi award for the best annual article published in the *Journal of Marketing.*

Dr. Kotler has served as chairman of the College on Marketing of the Institute of Management Sciences (TIMS); a director of the American Marketing Association; a trustee of the Marketing Science Institute, and a director of Management Analysis Center (MAC). He has consulted many major American companies on marketing strategy.

In 1978, Dr. Kotler received the *Paul D. Converse Award* given by the American Marketing Association to honor "outstanding contributions to science in marketing." In 1983, he received the *Steuart Henderson Britt Award* as Marketer of the Year. In 1985, he was named the first recipient of the *Distinguished Marketing Educator Award,* a new award established by the American Marketing Association. In the same year, The Academy for Health Services Marketing established the *Philip Kotler Award for Excellence in Health Care Marketing* and nominated him as the first recipient. He also received the *Prize for Marketing Excellence* awarded by the European Association of Marketing Consultants and Sales Trainers.

Contents

2

The Marketing Management Process 28

two
ORGANIZING THE MARKETING PLANNING PROCESS

3

Strategic Planning and Marketing Planning 54

4

Marketing Research and Information Systems 84

three
ANALYZING MARKET OPPORTUNITIES

5
The Marketing Environment 123

6
Consumer Markets: Influences on Consumer Behavior 158

7
Consumer Markets: Buyer Decision Processes 186

four

SELECTING TARGET MARKETS

9

Measuring and Forecasting Demand 242

10

Market Segmentation, Targeting, and Positioning 260

five

DEVELOPING THE MARKETING MIX

11

Designing Products: Products, Brands, Packaging, and Services 294

15

Placing Products: Distribution Channels and Physical Distribution 408

16

Placing Products: Retailing and Wholesaling 443

17

Promoting Products: Communication and Promotion Strategy 484

18

Promoting Products: Advertising, Sales Promotion, and Publicity 508

19

Promoting Products: Personal Selling and Sales Management 542

six
MANAGING THE MARKETING EFFORT

20
Competitive Marketing Strategies 578

21
Implementing, Organizing, and Controlling Marketing Programs 606

seven
EXTENDING MARKETING

Appendix 1
Marketing Arithmetic   738

Appendix 2
Careers in Marketing   745

Glossary   753

Author Index   762

Subject Index   766

Preface

Marketing is something that we all do. "We all live by selling something," noted the writer Robert Louis Stevenson. Workers exchange their labor for income and use their income to buy wanted goods. Companies sell their goods and use the receipts to buy raw materials and equipment needed to produce more goods, making a profit along the way. Nations exchange their goods for the needed goods of other nations.

Marketing is the study of exchange processes: how transactions are initiated, motivated, facilitated, and consummated. *Marketing management* deals with how organizations and people can improve their exchange activities to produce more income for themselves and more satisfaction for others. The *marketing concept* is a philosophy of marketing that says that organizations that create genuine consumer satisfaction usually succeed in achieving their organizational goals.

Marketing consists of a set of principles for choosing target markets, identifying customer needs, developing want-satisfying products and services, and delivering value to customers and profit to the company. Most successful companies owe their success to practicing a thoroughgoing customer orientation. McDonald's owes its success to meeting people's needs for fast food service; Kodak to meeting their needs for inexpensive reliable cameras; and Apple Computer, to meeting their needs for user-friendly personal computers. Such companies as Procter & Gamble, Gillette, Sears, IBM, and Delta are exemplary practitioners of the marketing concept. They make consumer needs the basis of company opportunities.

Students are surprised to find how broadly applicable marketing is. Marketing is relevant not only to manufacturing companies, wholesalers, and retailers, but to every organization. Lawyers, accountants, physicians, and management consultants are increasingly using marketing ideas to expand their practices. Colleges, hospitals, museums, and performing arts groups are turning to marketing in the face of low or declining demand for their services. No politician can get the required votes, and no resort area can get the needed tourists without developing and carrying out marketing plans. And students, when they enter the job market, must do "marketing research" to determine the best opportunities and the best way to "market themselves" to prospective employers. Students report that their study of marketing is an "eyeopener" that leads them to see familiar things in an entirely new way.

MAJOR FEATURES OF THIS BOOK

More students than ever are studying marketing. And there are more textbooks to choose among. Each textbook reflects the author's particular mindset, style, and enthusiasm for the subject. This text is built on five principles.

Comprehensive

The student's first exposure to marketing should present the subject primarily in its breadth. This book covers the major marketing topics of interest to marketing students and practitioners. Students will read about the *major institutions* that are involved in the marketing process—manufacturers, wholesalers, retailers, advertising agencies, marketing research firms, banks, shippers, warehouses, and many others. Students will also examine the *major tools* used by modern marketers—product design, packaging, branding, ancillary services, pricing, advertising, sales promotion, publicity, and personal selling. Finally, students will examine the *major environmental forces* affecting the marketing process—demographics, economics, ecology, technology, politics, and culture.

Systematic

Marketing can easily become overwhelming in its multitude of topics, concepts, theories, and examples. The great need is to present this abundant material in a systematic framework so that readers know where they have been, where they are, and where they are going in the subject. This text utilizes a seven part structure. Part One, *Understanding Marketing,* introduces the student to the basic role marketing plays in the economy, and the way marketing is planned and managed in companies. Part Two, *Organizing the Marketing Planning Process,* shows how marketing fits into the company's strategic planning process and how companies gather the information needed to understand customers, competitors, and other actors in the marketplace. Part Three, *Analyzing Market Opportunities,* describes the marketing environment and the needs and buying patterns of consumer and organizational buyers. Part Four, *Selecting Target Markets,* presents principles and tools for measuring and forecasting demand, and for segmenting, selecting, and entering attractive markets, and providing distinctive need-fulfilling offers. Part Five, *Developing the Marketing Mix,* describes the specific principles for designing, pricing, placing, and promoting attractive products and services. Part Six, *Managing the Marketing Effort,* discusses the marketing management systems companies use to implement, organize, and control their marketing effort. Part Seven, *Extending Marketing,* describes international marketing, services marketing, and nonprofit marketing, and it concludes with a discussion of marketing's impact on society.

Scientific

This text presents concepts, generalizations, and theories of marketing that are supported by scientific research and evidence. Marketing is an applied science built on the foundations of *economic science, behavioral science, and modern management theory*. Economic science reminds us that marketing involves the use of scarce resources to satisfy competing needs and therefore these resources must be allocated carefully. Behavioral science reminds us that marketing is about people—people who buy and who run organizations—and that we must understand their needs, motivations, attitudes, and behavior. Finally, management theory reminds us that marketing seeks answers to how organizations can best manage their marketing activities to create value for themselves, their customers, and society.

Practical

Every marketing situation is unique. Managers need to know how to analyze marketing problems and apply relevant marketing theory to solving them. This book describes numerous situations in which well-known and little-known companies applied marketing to solve marketing problems—whether there was too little demand for their products or services, the wrong kind of demand, or even too much demand. The situations are illustrated in examples running through the text, in special boxed exhibits, and in longer case studies.

Lively

A textbook has to be lively lest it cheat the student of the joy of the subject. Marketing is a fascinating subject and the author hopes he has communicated his enthusiasm to the reader. Almost every chapter opens with a vignette describing a company facing a particular marketing situation that will be discussed in the chapter. Throughout the chapter, timely and interesting examples are presented to illustrate important principles.

The author's intention is to present marketing in a comprehensive, systematic, scientific, practical, and lively manner. Whether the intention has been achieved will be determined by the market—how satisfied the readers are, and how much use they can make of the book's ideas.

PEDAGOGICAL AIDS

This book employs many aids to facilitate student learning. The main ones within the book are: *opening vignettes,* beginning most chapters with a dramatic marketing story designed to arouse the student's interest; *major chapter issues,* stated immediately following the vignette; numerous *figures, tables, and photos,* illustrating important points with strong visual materials; *boxed exhibits,* containing material of unusual interest; *summaries,* wrapping up each chapter with a prose statement of major concepts; *review questions,* addressing the major points made in each chapter; *twenty case studies,* describing real companies groping with difficult marketing situations and challenging students to apply marketing principles to actual problems; *two appendices,* one on marketing arithmetic and another on marketing careers; an *extensive glossary* of terms for quick reference, and *two indices,* one by author, one by subject matter.

In addition several supplements are available to help in the teaching/learning process. They are: A *Study Guide* for students, containing questions and exercises for each textbook chapter; an Instructor's Manual with Case Commentaries, consisting of outlines and teaching suggestions for each chapter, analyses of all 20 text cases plus five additional cases with analyses, and readings of current interest; a 2,400-plus item *Test Bank,* offering both true-false and multiple choice questions; *Prentice-Hall's Computerised Testing Service; Floppy-Disk Testing for Apple and IBM;* 180 *Transparency Masters,* and 110 *Full-Color Transparencies.* A software package will also be available.

CHANGES IN THE THIRD EDITION

The third edition is being written during difficult times for many companies, industries, and nations. Many mainstay U.S. industries—steel, autos, construction equipment, textiles, shoes—are experiencing slow or no growth and facing aggressive competition from foreign firms that have lower labor and other costs. The new "high tech" industries—computers, electronics, robotics—are expanding but they also face strong quality foreign competition and offer little employment opportunity because they are not labor-intensive. Service industries—fast food restaurants, hotels, health clubs, and so on—are growing rapidly and are labor-intensive, but they do not provide great opportunities for productivity gains. Which industries represent the best hope for the future, and whether the government should favor certain industries over others, is being hotly debated. In the meantime, national unemployment is too high and hits certain groups especially hard. Consumers are buying new products, such as home computers, videorecorders, and so on, but none of them represent the income and employment frontier provided by the major industries of the past such as railroads, autos, and aircraft.

Meanwhile, two-thirds of the world's people remain underfed, underclothed, and underhoused. They have basic needs which existing industrial capacity can supply—but they don't have the necessary purchasing power. The global economy has still to solve the problem of creating trade patterns whereby those who have high need for basic goods can somehow pay for them, with cash or other goods, sooner or later. The markets of the less developed countries represent the New Frontier, if only they can be served.

Upon the shoulders of company marketers falls the task of defining what their companies can profitably make and sell, here and abroad. They must spot and appraise such developments as the emergence of the Yuppie market, the singles market, the elderly market, the Hispanic market, and their differing needs. Marketers must then steer their companies toward developing attractive products and services for these markets. Ideally, marketing's task is to get companies to produce the right products at the right price offered in the right places with the right promotion. They should do this within the framework of satisfying the consumers' needs, their own corporate needs, and their social responsibilities.

The third edition of *Principles of Marketing* adds several improvements in the way of organization, content, and writing style. The main change in organization is to describe in Chapter 3—rather than at the end of the book—what marketing planning is and how it fits into the company's overall strategic planning process, and to present an early bird's-eye view of the main elements of an effective marketing plan, with the individual elements to be examined in later chapters.

As for content, the third edition has added substantial new material on competitive marketing strategies, marketing plan implementation problems, and marketing channel behavior and conflict. The discussion has been improved and expanded in such topic areas as strategic planning, marketing's role in relation to other business functions, new marketing research approaches, organizational buying behavior, product and brand positioning, the role of prices in the marketing mix, and consumer perceptions of pricing. A substantial number of new and contemporary cases has been added, as well as many new vignette chapter openers and exhibits. The book now features five-color printing to increase its attractiveness and readability. The writing style has been improved in terms of shorter sentences, more active verbs, less redundancy, and other features that increase readability. All the supplementary materials have been revised and improved, including the Instructor's Manual, Test Item File, Study Guide, and Color Transparencies.

The third edition has been revised through a process of collecting extensive feedback from faculty adopters and student users. The book's goal is to be user-friendly, providing students with the best training in marketing so that they can master tomorrow's marketing opportunities and challenges with confidence.

ACKNOWLEDGMENT

Every textbook owes its existence to the work and wisdom of numerous predecessors and colleagues. A great debt is owed to the pioneers of marketing who first identified the field's major issues, clarified marketing's purpose and scope, and contributed major ideas to its development.

This third edition owes a major debt to my friend, colleague, and former student, Professor Gary M. Armstrong. Professor Armstrong has been a longtime reviewer and user of *Principles of Marketing* and helped me rework every page of the text in the interests of improved clarity, organization, and examples. His great pedagogic insights into the complex world of marketing helped me immeasurably in the process of preparing the third edition.

I also want to thank my longtime Northwestern colleague and friend, Professor Richard M. Clewett, for preparing fresh cases for this edition, drawing on his vast experience in teaching and writing. The cases are timely, lively, and challenging. I also want to acknowledge the past contributions of Professor Patrick E. Murphy of Notre Dame University and Professor Bruce Wrenn of Andrews University for material they prepared. A large number of able reviewers who used the second edition of *Principles of Marketing* provided invaluable suggestions for the third edition. I am indebted to the following colleagues:

Gerald Albaum
University of Oregon

Raymond F. Keyes
Boston College

David L. Appel University of Notre Dame	Jean Lefebvre University of Hartford
Boris W. Becker Oregon State University	John Martin Boston University
Michael Belch San Diego State University	Douglas W. Mellott, Jr. Louisiana Tech University
Robert L. Berl Memphis State University	Chem Narayana University of Illinois at Chicago
Paul N. Bloom University of North Carolina	Robert Olsen California State University, Fullerton
Austin Byron Northern Arizona University	Christopher P. Puto University of Michigan
Charles R. Canedy III University of Hartford	David R. Rink Northern Illinois University
Keith Cox University of Houston	Dennis W. Rook University of Southern California
Rohit Deshpande University of Texas at Austin	Dean Siewers Rochester Institute of Technology
Thomas Falcone Indiana University of Penna.	Clint B. Tankersley Syracuse University
Denise Johnson Indiana University	Peter Wilton University of California, Berkeley

My colleagues at Northwestern have always provided generous time for the discussion and evaluation of major marketing ideas. For their insights, I am indebted to Professors James C. Anderson, Bobby J. Calder, Lakshman Krishnamurthi, Stephen A. LaTour, Sidney J. Levy, Prahbakant Sinha, John F. Sherry, Louis W. Stern, Brian Sternthal, Alice M. Tybout, and Andris Zoltners.

Thanks also go to my Dean and longtime friend, Donald P. Jacobs, for his always generous support of my research and writing efforts.

A book is not a book without a publishing company. And the company that I most enjoy working with—and have since 1967—is Prentice-Hall. They are the "publishing professionals." Elizabeth Classon, my former editor, contributed strongly and imaginatively to the development of the second and third editions. Whitney Blake, my current editor, added fresh insight. I also want to acknowledge the fine editorial work of Esther Koehn, college production editor, and the creative graphic design of Maureen Eide.

Thanks are also due to our departmental secretaries at Northwestern University who helped me meet each deadline: Marion Davis, Laura Kingsley, Ruby Chan, and Tracy Ayers.

I also want to thank the Harold T. Martin family for the generous support of my chair at Northwestern University.

Finally, thanks are due to my wife Nancy, my daughters Amy, Melissa, and Jessica, and to my close friends for their continuous support and encouragement.

Principles of Marketing

one

UNDERSTANDING MARKETING

Part One of this book presents the "big picture": What is marketing? Why do we need marketing? How does marketing work?

1
Social Foundations of Marketing: Meeting Human Needs

Marketing touches all of us every day of our lives. We wake up to a Sears radio alarm clock, which begins to play a Lionel Richie song followed by a United Airlines commercial advertising a Hawaiian vacation. We enter the bathroom where we brush our teeth with Colgate, shave with Gillette, gargle with Listerine, spray our hair with Revlon, and use other toiletries and appliances produced by manufacturers around the world. We put on our Calvin Klein jeans and Bass shoes. We enter the kitchen and drink Minute Maid orange juice, and pour Borden milk into a bowl of Kellogg's Rice Krispies. Later we drink a cup of Maxwell House coffee with two teaspoons of Domino sugar while munching on a slice of Sara Lee coffee cake. We consume oranges grown in California, coffee imported from Brazil, a newspaper made of Canadian wood pulp, and radio news coming from as far away as Australia. We fetch our mail and find a Metropolitan Museum of Art shoppers' catalog, a letter from a Prudential insurance sales representative offering services, and coupons saving us money on our favorite brands. We step out of our homes and drive to the Northbrook Court Shopping Center with its Neiman-Marcus, Lord & Taylor, Sears, and hundreds of other stores filled with goods from floor to ceiling. Later we exercise at a Nautilus Fitness Center, have our hair cut at Vidal Sassoon, and plan a Carribbean trip at a Thomas Cook travel agency.

The marketing system has made all this possible, with little effort on our part. It has delivered to us a standard of living that would have been inconceivable to our ancestors.

WHAT IS MARKETING?

What does the term marketing mean? Three hundred college administrators were asked this question.[1] Ninety percent said that marketing was selling, advertising, or public relations. Only 9 percent said that marketing also included needs assessment, marketing research, product development, pricing, and distribution. Most people mistakenly identify marketing with selling and promotion.

No wonder! Americans are bombarded with television commercials, newspaper ads, direct mail, and sales calls. Someone is always trying to sell something. It seems that we cannot escape death, taxes, or selling.

Therefore many students are surprised to learn that the most important part of marketing is not selling: Selling is only the tip of the marketing iceberg. Selling is only one of several marketing functions, and often not the most important one. If the marketer does a good job of identifying consumer needs, developing appropriate products, and pricing, distributing, and promoting them effectively, these goods will sell very easily.

Everyone knows about "hot" products to which consumers flock in droves. When Eastman Kodak designed its instamatic camera, when Atari designed its first video games, and when Mazda introduced its RX-7 sports car, these manufacturers were swamped with orders because they had designed the "right" product. Not me-too products, but distinct ones offering new benefits.

Peter Drucker, one of the leading management theorists, put it this way:

> *The aim of marketing is to make selling superfluous.* The aim is to know and understand the customer so well that the product or service fits him and sells itself.[2]

This is not to say that selling and promotion are unimportant, but rather that they are part of a larger "marketing mix" or set of marketing tools that must be orchestrated for maximum impact on the marketplace.

Here is our definition of *marketing:*

> **Marketing** is human activity directed at satisfying needs and wants through exchange processes.

To enrich this definition, we will explain the following terms: *needs, wants, demands, products, exchange, transactions,* and *markets.*[3]

Needs The most fundamental concept underlying marketing is that of human needs, which we define as follows:

> A **human need** is a state of felt deprivation in a person.

Human needs are plentiful and complex. They include basic physiological needs for food, clothing, warmth, and safety; social needs for belonging, influence, and affection; and individual needs for knowledge and self-expression. These needs are not created by Madison Avenue, but are a basic part of human makeup.

When a need is not satisfied, the person is unhappy. An unhappy person will do one of two things—look for an object that will satisfy the need, or try to extinguish the desire. People in industrial societies try to find or develop objects that will satisfy their desires. People in poor societies try to reduce their desires to what is available.

Wants **Human wants** are the form human needs take as shaped by culture and individual personality. A hungry person in Bali wants mangoes, suckling pig, and beans. A hungry person in the United States wants a hamburger, French fries, and a coke. Wants are described in terms of culturally defined objects that will satisfy the need.

As a society evolves, the wants of its members expand. They are exposed to more objects that pique their curiosity, interest, and desire. Producers take specific actions to build desire for their products. They try to form a connection between what they produce and people's needs. They promote their product as a satisfier of one or more particular needs. The marketer does not create the need; it exists.

Sellers often confuse wants and needs. A manufacturer of drill bits may think that the customer needs a drill bit, but what the customer really needs is a hole. In this sense, there are no products; there are only services performed by products.

Some sellers suffer from "marketing myopia."[4] They are so taken with their products that they focus only on existing wants and lose sight of underlying customer needs. They forget that a physical product is only a tool to solve a consumer problem. These sellers are vulnerable to successor products—if a new product comes along that serves the need better or cheaper, the customer will have the same need but a new want.

Kaiser Sand & Gravel Company's marketing mission is to "find a need and fill it." *Courtesy of Kaiser Sand & Gravel Company, a subsidiary of Koppers Company, Inc.*

Demands People have almost unlimited wants but limited resources. They choose products that produce the most satisfaction for their money. *Their wants become* **demands** *when backed by purchasing power.*

It is easy to list the demands in a given society at a given point in time. In a given year, 230 million Americans might purchase 67 billion eggs, 2 billion chickens, 5 million hair dryers, 133 billion domestic air travel passenger miles, and over 20 million lectures by college English professors. These and other consumer goods and services lead in turn to a demand for more than 150 million tons of steel, 4 billion tons of cotton, and many other industrial goods. These are a few of the demands that get expressed in a $2 trillion economy.

A society could plan next year's production by using this year's mix of demand. The USSR and other centrally planned economies plan production on this basis. Demands, however, are not that reliable. People get tired of some things they are currently consuming; they seek variety for its own sake; and they make new choices in response to changing prices and incomes.

Consumers view products as bundles of benefits and choose products that give them the best bundle for their money. Thus a Toyota represents basic transportation, low purchase price, and fuel economy; a Cadillac represents comfort, luxury, and status. People choose the product whose combined attributes deliver the most satisfaction, given their wants and resources.

Products Human needs, wants and demands suggest the existence of products. We define product as follows:

> A **product** is anything that can be offered to a market for attention, acquisition, use, or consumption that might satisfy a want or need.

Suppose a person feels the need to be more attractive. We will call all the products that are capable of satisfying this need the product choice set. They may include new clothes, hair styling services, a Caribbean suntan, exercise classes, and many others. These products are not all equally desirable. The more accessible and less expensive products, such as clothing and a new haircut, are likely to be purchased first.

We can represent a specific product and a specific human want as circles and represent the product's want-satisfying ability by the degree that it covers the want circle. Figure 1-1A shows that product A has no want-satisfying ability relative to want X. Figure 1-1B shows that product B has partial want-satisfying ability. Figure 1-1C shows that product C has virtually complete want-satisfying ability. Product C would be called an ideal product.

Producers are interested in the concept of an ideal product because the closer a product matches the consumer's desire, the more successful the producer will be. Suppose an ice-cream producer asks a consumer how much "creaminess" and "sweetness" he or she likes in ice cream. And suppose the consumer's answer is represented by "ideal" in Figure 1-2. Now the consumer is asked to taste three competitive brands of ice cream and describe their levels of creaminess and sweetness. These are also represented by points in Figure 1-2.

We would predict that the consumer would prefer brand B because it comes

FIGURE 1-1
Three Degrees of Want
Satisfaction

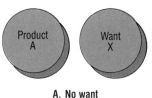

A. No want
satisfaction

B. Partial want
satisfaction

C. Complete want
satisfaction

closer than the other brands to "packaging" the ideal levels of the two attributes the consumer wants. If the producer offered an ice-cream closer to the consumer's ideal than brand B, the new brand should outsell B, providing that price, availability, and other conditions are similar. The moral is that producers should determine the consumer group they want to sell to and should provide a product that comes as close as possible to satisfying this group's wants.

The concept of product is not limited to physical objects. Anything capable of satisfying a need can be called a product. In addition to goods and services, this includes *persons, places, organizations, activities,* and *ideas.* A consumer decides which entertainers to watch on television, places to go on a vacation, organizations to contribute to, and ideas to support. From the consumer's point of view, these are alternative products. If the term product seems unnatural at times, we can substitute the term satisfier, resource, or offer. All describe something of value to someone.

Exchange Marketing occurs when people decide to satisfy needs and wants through exchange.

> **Exchange** is the act of obtaining a desired object from someone by offering something in return.

Exchange is one of four ways in which individuals can obtain a desired object. For example, hungry people can obtain food in the following ways. They can find

FIGURE 1-2
Vanilla Ice-Cream
Brands in a Brand
Space Made Up of
Creaminess and
Sweetness

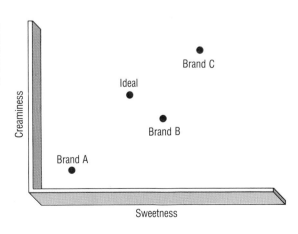

their own food by hunting, fishing, or fruit gathering (self-production). They can steal or seize food from someone else (coercion). They can beg for food (begging). Finally, they can offer some resource such as money, another good, or a service for the food (exchange).

Of these four ways of satisfying needs, exchange has much in its favor. People do not have to prey on others or depend on donations. Nor do they have to have the skills needed to produce every necessity for themselves. They can concentrate on producing the things they make best and trade them for items produced by others. A society whose members produce what they are good at producing ends up with much more total output than under any other alternative.

Specialization in production, however, does not always lead to a society that uses exchange as the major principle for distributing goods.[5] Some societies work on the principle of reciprocity. Each producer supplies goods or services to others who need them and in turn goes to others for whatever is needed. The modern family works on this principle, with each member freely providing services to the other members without formal exchange arrangements. Other societies use the principle of redistribution. Producers turn over part or all of their output to a leader or a central depot. The output is then redistributed to persons according to needs, status, or power.

But in most societies, producers sell their goods to others in exchange for money. Exchange is the core concept of the discipline of marketing. For a voluntary exchange to take place, five conditions must be satisfied:

1. There are at least two parties.
2. Each party has something that may be of value to the other party.
3. Each party is capable of communication and delivery.
4. Each party is free to accept or reject the other party's offer.
5. Each party believes it is appropriate or desirable to deal with the other party.

These five conditions set up a potential for exchange. Whether exchange actually takes place depends upon the parties' coming to an agreement on the terms. If they agree, we conclude that the act of exchange leaves all of them better off (or at least not worse off) because each was free to reject or accept the offer. In this sense, exchange is a value-creating process. Just as production creates value, so exchange creates value by enlarging the consumption possibilities facing an individual.

Exchange is a sophisticated human activity without a counterpart in the animal kingdom. Ant colonies and gorilla societies show some division of labor, but little evidence of formal exchange. Adam Smith observed that "nobody ever saw a dog make a fair and deliberate exchange of one bone for another with another dog. Nobody ever saw one animal by its gestures and natural cries signify to another, this is mine, that is yours; I am willing to give this for that."[6] But man, according to Adam Smith, has a natural "propensity to barter, truck, and exchange one thing for another." Anthropologists have cast doubt over whether exchange is a natural human propensity or a learned disposition, but exchange seems in any case to be a uniquely human activity.[7]

Transactions If exchange is the core concept of the discipline of marketing, what is the discipline's unit of measurement? The answer is a transaction. A **transaction** *consists of a trade of values between two parties.* We must be able to say A gives X to B and gets Y in return. Jones gives $400 to Smith and obtains a television set. This is a classic monetary transaction, although transactions do not require money as one of the traded values. A barter transaction would consist of Jones giving a refrigerator to Smith in return for a television set. A barter transaction can also consist of the trading of services instead of goods, as when lawyer Jones writes a will for physician Smith in return for a medical examination (see Exhibit 1-1).

A transaction involves at least two things of value, conditions that are agreed to, a time of agreement, and a place of agreement. Usually a legal system arises to support and enforce compliance by the transactors. Transactions can easily give rise to conflicts based on misinterpretation or malice. Without a law of contracts, people would approach transactions with some distrust, and everyone would lose.

Businesses keep track of their transactions and analyze them carefully. For example, sales analysis involves evaluating a company's sales transactions by product, customer, territory, and other specific variables.

EXHIBIT 1-1

GOING BACK TO BARTER

Companies usually sell their products and services for money. But in today's competitive and cash-poor economy, many are returning to the primitive practice of barter—trading the goods and services they make for other goods and services they need. Companies barter over $20 billion worth of goods and services a year, and the industry is growing at an annual rate of 25 percent. Over 65 percent of all New York Stock Exchange companies do some sort of bartering. Barter provides a way for companies to increase sales, unload excess or obsolete inventories, and conserve cash. For example, when Shell Oil found it was stuck with 5 million Can Care strips—a product like the No-Pest Strip for killing insects in garbage cans—it arranged an exchange with a Caribbean resort for a load of unrefined sugar. When Climaco Corporation was overstocked with bubble bath, it swapped the excess at full value for $300,000 worth of advertising for another one of its products.

Not surprisingly, many kinds of specialty trading companies have arisen to help companies with bartering. Retail trade exchanges and trade clubs arrange barter for small to medium-sized retailers and other smaller businesses. Larger corporations use corporate trade consultants and brokerage firms for services ranging from import-export documentation to transactional risk analysis. Media brokerage houses provide advertising in exchange for products. International barter is handled by countertrade organizations. One trading company, Barter Systems, Inc., of Oklahoma City, operates sixty-two trading centers around the United States. A letter that it recently sent to a select number of its twenty-five thousand clients contained the following statement: "Wanted: $300,000 worth of dried milk or cornflakes in exchange for an airplane of equal value." These bartering companies use computers to locate parties that may want to trade and give moneylike credits for future deals. They usually pay their employees in cash, but prefer to pay them in goods and services if the employees are willing.

Sources: Based on Linda A. Dickerson, "Barter to Gain a Competitive Edge in a Cash-Poor Economy," *Marketing News,* March 16, 1984, pp. 1–2; Jack G. Kaikati, "Marketing without Exchange of Money," *Harvard Business Review,* November–December 1982, pp. 72–74; and "Swapathon," *Time,* November 9, 1981, pp. 74–75.

A *transaction* differs from a *transfer*. In a transfer, A gives X to B but receives nothing explicit in return. Transfers include gifts, subsidies, and altruistic acts. It would seem that marketers should confine their study to transactions rather than transfers. However, transfer behavior can also be understood through the concept of exchange. The transferrer gives a gift in the expectation of some benefit, such as a good feeling, relief from a sense of guilt, or the wish to put the other party under an obligation. Professional fundraisers are acutely aware of the "reciprocal" motives underlying donor behavior and try to provide the benefits sought by the donors. If they neglect the donors or show no gratitude, they will soon lose the donors' support. As a result, marketers have recently broadened the concept of marketing to include the study of transfer behavior as well as transaction behavior.

In the broadest sense, the marketer is seeking to bring about a response to some offer, and the response is not buying or trading in the narrow sense. A political candidate wants a response called votes, a church wants a response called joining, a social action group wants a response called adopting the idea. Marketing consists of actions undertaken to elicit a desired response from a target audience toward some object.

Markets

The concept of transactions leads to the concept of a market.

> A **market** is the set of actual and potential buyers of a product.

To understand the nature of a market, imagine a primitive economy consisting of four persons: a fisherman, a hunter, a potter, and a farmer. Figure 1-3 shows three different ways in which these tradespeople could meet their needs. In the first case, self-sufficiency, they gather the needed goods for themselves. Thus the hunter spends most of the time hunting, but also takes time to fish, make pottery, and farm to obtain the other goods. The hunter is less efficient at hunting, and the same is true of the other tradespeople. In the second case, decentralized exchange, each person sees the other three as potential "buyers" who make up a market. Thus the hunter may make separate trips to trade goods with the fisherman, the potter, and the farmer to exchange meat for their goods. In the third case, centralized exchange, a new person called a merchant appears and locates in a central area called a marketplace. Each tradesperson brings goods to the merchant and trades

FIGURE 1-3
Evolution toward Centralized Exchange

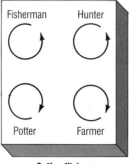

Self-sufficiency

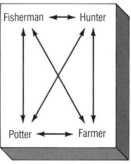

Decentralized exchange

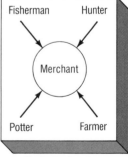

Centralized exchange

for other needed goods. Thus the hunter transacts with one "market" to obtain all the needed goods, rather than with three other persons.

The emergence of a merchant substantially reduces the total number of transactions required to accomplish a given volume of exchange. In other words, merchants and central marketplaces increase the transactional efficiency of the economy.[8]

As the number of persons and transactions increases in a society, the number of merchants and marketplaces also increases. In advanced societies, markets need not be physical places where buyers and sellers interact. With modern communications and transportation, a merchant can advertise a product on late evening television, take orders from hundreds of customers over the phone, and mail the goods to the buyers on the following day without having had any physical contact with the buyers.

A market can grow up around a product, a service, or anything else of value. For example, a labor market consists of people who are willing to offer their work in return for wages or products. Various institutions will grow up around a labor market to facilitate its functioning, such as employment agencies and job-counseling firms. The money market is another important market that emerges to meet the needs of people so that they can borrow, lend, save, and safeguard money. And the donor market emerges to meet the financial needs of nonprofit organizations.

Marketing The concept of markets finally brings us full circle to the concept of marketing. Marketing means human activity that takes place in relation to markets. Marketing means working with markets to actualize potential exchanges for the purpose of satisfying human needs and wants. Thus we return to our definition of marketing as *human activity directed at satisfying needs and wants through exchange processes.*

Exchange processes involve work. Sellers have to search for buyers, identify their needs, design appropriate products, promote them, store and transport them, negotiate prices, and so on. Such activities as product development, search, communication, distribution, pricing, and service constitute core marketing activities.

Although we normally think of marketing as being carried on by sellers, buyers also carry on marketing activities. Consumers do "marketing" when they search for the goods they need at prices they can afford. A purchasing agent who needs a commodity in short supply tracks down sellers and offers attractive terms. A seller's market is one in which sellers have more power and buyers have to be the more active "marketers." In a buyer's market, buyers have more power and sellers have to be more active "marketers."

In the early 1950s the supply of goods began to outpace the demand, and marketing became identified with sellers trying to find buyers. This book will take this point of view and examine the marketing problems of sellers in a buyers' market.

MARKETING MANAGEMENT

Those who engage in the exchange process learn how to do it better over a period of time. In particular, sellers learn how to professionalize their marketing management. We define marketing management as follows:

Marketing management is the analysis, planning, implementation, and control of programs designed to create, build, and maintain beneficial exchanges with target buyers for the purpose of achieving organizational objectives.

The popular image of the marketing manager is that of someone whose task consists primarily of finding enough customers for the company's current output. This, however, is too limited a view of the range of tasks carried out by marketing managers. Marketing managers are concerned not only with creating and expanding demand, but also with modifying and occasionally reducing it. *Marketing management seeks to influence the level, timing, and character of demand in a way that will help the organization achieve its objectives.* Simply put, marketing management is *demand management.*

The organization forms an idea of a desired level of transactions with a market. At any point in time, the actual demand level may be below, equal to, or above the desired demand level. That is, there may be no demand, weak demand, adequate demand, or excessive demand, and marketing management has to cope with these different states (see Exhibit 1-2).

EXHIBIT 1-2

VARIOUS STATES OF DEMAND AND THE CORRESPONDING MARKETING TASKS

1. *Negative demand.* A market is in a state of negative demand if a major part of the market dislikes the product and may even pay a price to avoid it. People have a negative demand for vaccinations, dental work, vasectomies, and gall bladder operations. Employers feel a negative demand for ex-convicts and alcoholic employees. The marketing task is to analyze why the market dislikes the product, and whether a marketing program can change the market's beliefs and attitudes through product redesign, lower prices, and more positive promotion.

2. *No demand.* Target consumers may be uninterested in or indifferent to the product. Thus farmers may not be interested in a new farming method, and college students may not be interested in taking foreign language courses. The marketing task is to find ways to connect the benefits of the product with the person's natural needs and interests.

3. *Latent demand.* Many consumers may share a strong desire for something that cannot be satisfied by any existing product or service. There is a strong latent demand for nonharmful cigarettes, safer neighborhoods, and more fuel-efficient cars. The marketing task is to measure the size of the potential market and develop effective goods and services that will satisfy the demand.

4. *Falling demand.* Every organization, sooner or later, faces falling demand for one or more of its products. Churches have seen their membership decline, and private colleges have seen their applications decline. The marketer must analyze the causes of market decline and determine whether demand can be restimulated by finding new target markets, changing the product's features, or developing more effective communications. The marketing task is to reverse the declining demand through creative remarketing of the product.

5. *Irregular demand.* Many organizations face demand that varies on a seasonal, daily, or even hourly basis, causing problems of idle capacity or overworked capacity. In mass transit, much of the equipment is idle during the off-peak hours and insufficient during the peak travel hours. Museums are undervisited during weekdays and overcrowded during weekends. Hospital operating rooms are overbooked early in the week and underbooked toward the end of the week. The marketing task is to find ways to alter the time pattern of demand through flexible pricing, promotion, and other incentives.

6. *Full demand.* Organizations face full demand when they are pleased with their amount of business. The marketing task is to maintain the current level of demand in the face of changing consumer preferences and increasing competition. The organization must preserve its quality and continually measure consumer satisfaction to make sure it is doing a good job.

7. *Overfull demand.* Some organizations face a demand level that is higher than they can or want to handle. Thus the Golden Gate Bridge carries a higher amount of traffic than is safe; and Yellowstone National Park is overcrowded in the summertime. The marketing task, called *demarketing,* requires finding ways to reduce the demand temporarily or permanently. General demarketing seeks to discourage overfull demand and consists of such steps as raising prices and reducing promotion and service. Selective demarketing consists of trying to reduce the demand coming from those parts of the market that are less profitable or less in need of the service. Demarketing does not aim to destroy demand, but only to reduce its level.

8. *Unwholesome demand.* Unwholesome products will attract organized efforts to discourage their consumption. Unselling campaigns have been conducted against cigarettes, alcohol, hard drugs, handguns, X-rated movies, and large families. The marketing task is to get people who like something to give it up, using such tools as fear communications, price hikes, and reduced availability.

Sources: For a fuller discussion, see Philip Kotler, "The Major Tasks of Marketing Management," *Journal of Marketing,* October 1973, pp. 42–49; and Philip Kotler and Sidney J. Levy, "Demarketing, Yes, Demarketing," *Harvard Business Review,* November–December 1971, pp. 74–80.

By **marketing managers,** we mean company personnel who are involved in marketing analysis, planning, implementation, or control activities. The group includes sales managers and salespeople, advertising executives, sales promotion specialists, marketing researchers, product managers, and pricing specialists. We will say more about these marketing jobs in Chapters 2 and 21 and in Appendix 2, "Careers in Marketing."

MARKETING MANAGEMENT PHILOSOPHIES

We have described marketing management as the conscious effort to achieve desired exchange outcomes with target markets. What philosophy should guide these marketing efforts? What weight should be given to the interests of the organization, the customers, and society? Very often these conflict. Clearly, marketing activities should be carried out under some philosophy.

There are five competing concepts under which business and other organizations conduct their marketing activity: the production, product, selling, marketing, and societal marketing concepts. These concepts are responses to different periods in American economic history. Each period presented different challenges for company survival and profitability. The evolution from a production or product concept to a selling, consumer, or even societal orientation has been fueled by major social, economic, and political changes during the past half-century.

The Production Concept

The production concept is one of the oldest philosophies guiding sellers.

> The **production concept** holds that consumers will favor those products that are available and highly affordable, and therefore management should concentrate on improving production and distribution efficiency.

The production concept is an appropriate philosophy in two types of situations. The first is where the demand for a product exceeds the supply. Here management should concentrate on finding ways to increase production. The second situation is where the product's cost is high and where improved productivity is needed to bring it down. Henry Ford's whole philosophy was to perfect the production of the Model T so that its cost could be brought down and more people could afford it. He joked about offering people any color car as long as it was black. Today Texas Instruments (TI) practices this philosophy of pursuing production volume and lower costs in order to bring down prices. It succeeded in winning a major share of the American hand-calculator market with this philosophy. However, when TI applied the same strategy in the digital watch market, it failed. Although they were priced low, customers did not find TI's watches attractive.[9]

Some service organizations also follow the production concept. Many medical and dental practices are organized on assembly-line principles, as are some government agencies such as unemployment offices and license bureaus. Although it results in handling many cases per hour, this type of management is open to charges of impersonality and consumer insensitivity.

The Product Concept

The product concept is another major concept guiding sellers.

> The **product concept** holds that consumers will favor those products that offer the most quality, performance, and features, and therefore the organization should devote its energy to making continuous product improvements.

Many manufacturers believe that if they can build a better mousetrap, the world will beat a path to their door.[10] But they are often rudely shocked. The buyers are looking for a solution to a mouse problem, but not necessarily a better mousetrap. The solution might be a chemical spray, an exterminating service, or something that works better than a mousetrap. Furthermore, a better mousetrap will not sell unless the manufacturer takes positive steps to design, package, and price this new product attractively, place it in convenient distribution channels, bring it to the attention of persons who need it, and convince them that it has superior qualities.

The product concept leads to marketing myopia. Railroad management thought that users wanted trains rather than transportation and overlooked the growing challenge of airlines, buses, trucks, and automobiles. Slide-rule manufacturers thought that engineers wanted slide rules rather than calculating capacity and overlooked the challenge of pocket calculators. Colleges assume that high school graduates want a liberal arts education and overlook the shift of preference to vocationally oriented education.

The Selling Concept

Many producers follow the selling concept.

> The **selling concept** holds that consumers will not buy enough of the organization's products unless the organization undertakes a substantial selling and promotion effort.

The selling concept is practiced most aggressively with "unsought goods," those goods that buyers normally do not think of buying, such as insurance, encyclopedias, and funeral plots. These industries have perfected various sales techniques to track down prospects and hard-sell them on the benefits of their product. Hard selling also occurs with sought goods, such as automobiles.[11]

> From the moment the customer walks into the showroom, the auto salesman "psychs him out." If the customer likes the floor model, he may be told that there is another customer about to buy it and that he should decide on the spot. If the customer balks at the price, the salesman offers to talk to the manager to get a special concession. The customer waits ten minutes and the salesman returns with "the boss doesn't like it but I got him to agree." The aim is to "work up the customer" to buy on the spot.

The selling concept is also practiced in the nonprofit area. A political party will vigorously sell its candidate to the voters as being a fantastic person for the job. The candidate stumps through voting precincts from early morning to late evening shaking hands, kissing babies, meeting donors, making breezy speeches. Countless dollars are spent on radio and television advertising, posters, and mailings. Any flaws in the candidate are concealed from the public because the aim is to get the sale, not worry about postpurchase satisfaction.

The Marketing Concept

The marketing concept is a more recent business philosophy.[12]

> The **marketing concept** holds that the key to achieving organizational goals consists in determining the needs and wants of target markets and delivering the desired satisfactions more effectively and efficiently than competitors.

The marketing concept has been expressed in colorful ways, such as "Find wants and fill them"; "Make what you can sell instead of trying to sell what you can make"; "Love the customer and not the product"; "Have it your way" (Burger King); and "You're the boss" (United Airlines). J. C. Penney's motto summarizes this attitude: "To do all in our power to pack the customer's dollar full of value, quality, and satisfaction."

The selling concept and the marketing concept are frequently confused. Levitt contrasts the two:

> Selling focuses on the needs of the seller; marketing on the needs of the buyer. Selling is preoccupied with the seller's need to convert his product into cash; marketing with the idea of satisfying the needs of the customer by means of the

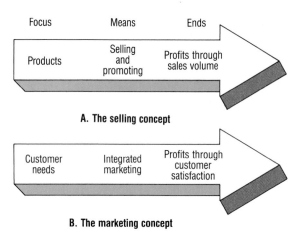

FIGURE 1-4
*The Selling and
Marketing Concepts
Contrasted*

Focus	Means	Ends
Products	Selling and promoting	Profits through sales volume

A. The selling concept

Customer needs	Integrated marketing	Profits through customer satisfaction

B. The marketing concept

product and the whole cluster of things associated with creating, delivering and finally consuming it.[13]

Figure 1-4 compares the two concepts. The selling concept starts with the company's existing products and calls for heavy selling and promoting to achieve profitable sales. The marketing concept starts with the needs and wants of the company's target customers. The company integrates and coordinates all the activities that will affect customer satisfaction and achieves its profits through creating and maintaining customer satisfaction. In essence, the marketing concept is a customer needs and wants orientation backed by integrated marketing effort aimed at generating customer satisfaction as the key to satisfying organizational goals.

The marketing concept expresses the company's commitment to *consumer sovereignty*. The company produces what consumers want, and in this way it maximizes consumer satisfaction and earns its profits.

Many companies have adopted the marketing concept. We know that Procter & Gamble, IBM, Avon, and McDonald's follow this concept faithfully (see Exhibit 1-3). We also know that the marketing concept is practiced more in consumer goods companies than in industrial goods companies, and more in large companies than in small companies.[14] Also, many companies profess the concept but do not practice it. They have the forms of marketing—such as a marketing vice-president, product managers, marketing plans, marketing research—but not the substance.[15] Several years of hard work are necessary to turn a sales-oriented company into a market-oriented company.

The Societal Marketing Concept

The societal marketing concept is the newest concept.

The **societal marketing concept** holds that the organization's task is to determine the needs, wants, and interests of target markets and to deliver the desired satisfactions more effectively and efficiently than competitors in a way that preserves or enhances the consumer's and the society's well-being.

EXHIBIT 1-3

MCDONALD'S CORPORATION APPLIES THE MARKETING CONCEPT

McDonald's Corporation, the fast-food hamburger retailer, is a master marketer. In only three decades, McDonald's has served over 45 billion hamburgers to people here and in thirty-two other countries. With over 7,900 outlets, it commands a 19 percent share of the fast-food market, far ahead of its rivals, Burger King (6.5 percent) and Wendy's (4.0 percent). Its current annual sales are running $8.7 billion. Credit for this leading position belongs to a strong marketing orientation. McDonald's knows how to serve people and adapt to changing consumer wants.

Before McDonald's, Americans could get hamburgers in restaurants or diners. In many places, the consumer encountered poor hamburgers, slow service, unattractive decor, unfriendly help, unclean conditions, and a noisy atmosphere. In 1955 Ray Kroc, a fifty-two-year-old salesman of milkshake-mixing machines, became excited about a string of seven restaurants owned by Richard and Maurice McDonald. Kroc liked their concept of a fast-food restaurant and negotiated to buy the chain and its name for $2.7 million.

Kroc decided to expand the chain by selling franchises to others. Franchisees buy a twenty-year license for $150,000. They take a ten-day training course at McDonald's "Hamburger University" in Elk Grove Village, Illinois. They emerge with a degree in "Hamburgerology," with a minor in "French Fries."

Kroc's marketing philosophy is captured in McDonald's motto of "Q.S.C. & V.," which stands for quality, service, cleanliness, and value. Customers enter a spotlessly clean restaurant, walk up to a friendly hostess, order and receive a good-tasting hamburger within no more than five minutes, and eat it there or take it out. There are no jukeboxes or telephones to create a teen-age hangout. Nor are there any cigarette machines or newspaper racks. McDonald's became a family affair, particularly appealing to the children.

As times changed, so did McDonald's. McDonald's expanded its sit-down sections, improved the decor, launched a breakfast menu, added new food items, and opened new outlets in high-traffic areas.

McDonald's has mastered the art of franchise service marketing. It chooses locations carefully, selects highly qualified franchise operators, gives complete management training at Hamburger University, supports its franchisers with a high-quality national advertising and sales promotion program, monitors product and service quality through continuous customer surveys, and puts great energy into improving the technology of hamburger production to simplify operations, bring down costs, and speed up service.

McDonald's focus on consumers has made it the world's largest food service organization.

The societal marketing concept arises from questioning whether the pure marketing concept constitutes an adequate business philosophy in an age of environmental deterioration, resource shortages, explosive population growth, worldwide inflation, and neglected social services.[16] Is the firm that senses, serves, and satisfies individual wants always acting in the best long-run interests of consumers and society? The pure marketing concept sidesteps possible conflicts between immediate consumer wants and long-run consumer welfare.

Consider the Coca-Cola Company. People see it as being a highly responsible corporation, and strong demand for its products implies that it is satisfying the wants of millions of consumers. Yet consumer and environmental groups have

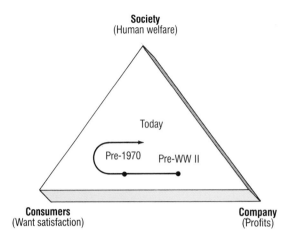

FIGURE 1-5
Three Considerations Underlying the Societal Marketing Concept

voiced the following concerns about how Coca-Cola products might harm the long-run welfare of consumers:

1. Coke delivers little nutritional benefit to its consumers.

2. Coke's sugar and phosphoric acid harm people's teeth.

3. The brominated vegetable oil in colas has been removed from the Federal Drug Administration's (FDA's) list of products "generally recognized as safe."

4. In some instances, it has been found that the caffeine in colas produces tremor, insomnia, gastrointestinal disorders, and possible cellular damage.

5. The saccharine once used in Coca-Cola's diet soft drink, Tab, has been determined to cause cancer in laboratory animals.

6. The use of one-way disposable bottles is a waste of resources and adds to the litter problem.

These and similar situations led to the formulation of the societal marketing concept.[17] The societal marketing concept calls upon marketers to balance three considerations in setting their marketing policies (see Figure 1-5). Originally, companies based their marketing decisions largely on immediate company profit calculations. Then they began to recognize the long-run importance of satisfying consumer wants, and this introduced the marketing concept. Now they are beginning to factor society's interests into their decision making. The societal marketing concept calls for balancing all three considerations. A number of companies have achieved substantial sales and profit gains by adopting and practicing the societal marketing concept.

THE GOALS OF A MARKETING SYSTEM

We know that marketing affects everyone—the buyer, the seller, the citizen. And their goals may conflict. *Buyers* want the marketplace to provide good-quality products at reasonable prices at convenient locations. They want wide brand and feature assortments; helpful, pleasant, and honest salespeople; and strong warranties backed by good follow-up service. The marketing system can make a great difference to buyer satisfaction.

Sellers face several challenging decisions when preparing an offer for the market. What features do consumers want? What consumer groups should be targeted, and how should products be designed and priced to meet consumer needs? What wholesalers and retailers should be used? And what advertising, personal selling, and sales promotion would help sell the product? The market is very demanding. Sellers must apply modern marketing thinking to develop an offer that attracts and satisfies customers.

Legislators, public interest groups, and other *citizens* have a strong interest in the marketing activities of business. Are manufacturers making safe and reliable products? Are they describing their products accurately in ads and packaging? Is competition working in the market to provide a reasonable range of quality and price choice? Are manufacturing and packaging activities hurting the environment? The marketing system has a major impact on the quality of life, and various groups of citizens want to make the system work as well as possible. They act as watchdogs of consumer interests and favor consumer education, information, and protection.

Marketing affects so many people in so many ways that it inevitably stirs controversy. Some people intensely dislike modern marketing activity, charging it with ruining the environment, bombarding the public with inane ads, creating unnecessary wants, teaching greed to youngsters, and committing several other sins. Consider the following:

> For the past 6,000 years the field of marketing has been thought of as made up of fast-buck artists, con-men, wheeler-dealers, and shoddy-goods distributors. Too many of us have been "taken" by the touts or con-men; and all of us at times have been prodded into buying all sorts of "things" we really did not need, and which we found later on we did not even want.[18]

> What does a man need—really need? A few pounds of food each day, heat and shelter, six feet to lie down in—and some form of working activity that will yield a sense of accomplishment. That's all—in a material sense. And we know it. But we are brainwashed by our economic system until we end up in a tomb beneath a pyramid of time payments, mortgages, preposterous gadgetry, playthings that divert our attention from the sheer idiocy of the charade.[19]

Others vigorously defend marketing. Consider the following:

> Aggressive marketing policies and practices have been largely responsible for the high material standard of living in America. Today through mass, low-cost marketing we enjoy products which once were considered luxuries, and which still are so classified in many foreign countries.[20]

> Advertising nourishes the consuming power of men. It creates wants for a better standard of living. It sets up before a man the goal of a better home, better clothing, better food for himself and his family. It spurs individual exertion and greater production. It brings together in fertile union those things which otherwise would not have been met.[21]

What should society seek from its marketing system? The question is timely because various governments are increasingly regulating the marketing activities of firms. Some government interventions can be quite extreme:

- Some government officials in India would like to ban the *branding* of sugar, soap, tea, rice, and other staples. They hold that branding, packaging, and advertising push up consumer prices.

- Some government officials in the Philippines favor *socialized pricing,* namely, holding down the price of staples through price control.

- Some government officials in Norway advocate banning certain "luxury" goods, such as private swimming pools, tennis courts, airplanes, and luxury automobiles. They think Norway's resources are too limited to use for these purposes. These officials favor "collective consumption" of expensive goods and services.

- The Federal Trade Commission introduced three measures in the early 1970s to promote "truth in advertising." *Advertising substantiation* required firms to stand ready to provide documentary evidence backing any claim they make in an ad. *Corrective advertising* required a firm found guilty of a false claim to spend 25 percent of its advertising budget on a corrective message. *Counter advertising* encouraged groups that oppose a product (such as an antismoking group) to have easy access to the media to present their opinion.

The increased marketing regulation throughout the world raises a fundamental question: What is the proper goal of a marketing system? Four alternative goals have been suggested: maximize consumption, maximize consumer satisfaction, maximize choice, and maximize life quality.

Maximize Consumption Many business executives believe that marketing's job should be that of facilitating and stimulating maximum consumption, which will in turn create maximum production, employment, and wealth. This view comes across in typical headlines: "Wrigley Seeks Ways to Get People to Chew More Gum"; "Opticians Introduce Fashion in Glasses to Stimulate Demand"; "Steel Industry Maps Strategy to Expand Sales"; "Car Manufacturers Try to Hypo Sales."

The underlying assumption is that the more people buy and consume, the happier they are. "More is better" is the war cry. Yet another group doubts that increased material goods mean more happiness. They see too many affluent people leading unhappy lives. Their philosophy is "less is more" and "small is beautiful."

Frederick Pohl, in a science fiction story called *The Midas Touch,* dramatizes the dire consequences of too much consumption. In his story, factories are completely automated. Goods roll out continuously, and people are required to consume as much as they can so that they will not be buried under these goods. Only the elite are excused from having to consume so much. Furthermore the elite inherit the few remaining jobs so that they will not have to face the boredom of no work.

Maximize Consumer Satisfaction Another view holds that the goal of the marketing system is to maximize consumer satisfaction, not consumption. Chewing more gum or owning more clothes counts only if this results in more consumer satisfaction.

Unfortunately, consumer satisfaction is difficult to measure. First, no economist has figured out how to add up the satisfaction of different persons on a meaningful scale so that the total satisfaction created by a particular product or marketing activity can be evaluated. Second, the direct satisfaction individual consumers obtain from particular "goods" fails to take into account the "bads," such as pollution and environmental damage. Third, the satisfaction people experience when consuming certain goods, such as status goods, depends precisely on how few other people have these goods. Thus it is difficult to evaluate a marketing system in terms of how much satisfaction it delivers to its citizens.

Maximize Choice Some marketers believe that the goal of a marketing system should be to maximize product variety and consumer choice. The system would enable consumers to find those goods that precisely satisfy their tastes. Consumers would be able to maximize their life styles and, therefore, their satisfaction.

Maximizing consumer choice, unfortunately, comes at a cost. First, goods and services will be more expensive, since great variety will call for shorter production runs and higher inventory levels. Higher prices will reduce consumers' real income and consumption. Second, the increase in product variety will require greater consumer search and effort. Consumers will have to spend more time learning about and evaluating the different products. Third, more products will not necessarily increase the consumers real choice. There are many brands of beer in the United States and most of them taste the same. When a product category contains many brands with few differences, this is called brand proliferation, and the consumer faces false choice. Finally, great product variety is not always welcomed by all consumers. Some consumers feel that there is too much choice in certain product categories, which causes frustration and anxiety.

Maximize Life Quality Many people believe that the goal of a marketing system should be to improve the "quality of life"—the quality, quantity, range, accessibility, and cost of goods; the quality of the physical environment; and the quality of the cultural environment. They would judge marketing systems not solely by the amount of direct consumer satisfaction that is created, but also by the impact of marketing activity on the quality of the physical and cultural environment. Most people would agree that quality of life is a worthwhile goal for the marketing system, but they recognize that it is not easy to measure and is subject to conflicting interpretations.

THE RAPID ADOPTION OF MARKETING

Most people think that marketing is carried on only in large companies operating in capitalistic countries. The truth is that marketing is carried on within and outside the business sector in all kinds of countries.

In the Business Sector In the business sector, different companies become interested in marketing at different times. General Electric, General Motors, Sears, Procter & Gamble, and Coca-Cola saw marketing's potentialities almost immediately. Marketing spread most rapidly in consumer packaged goods companies, consumer durables companies, and industrial equipment companies—in that order. Producers of such commodities as steel, chemicals, and paper came later to marketing consciousness, and many still have a long way to go.

Within the past decade consumer service firms, especially airlines and banks, have moved toward modern marketing. Airlines began to study travelers' attitudes toward different service features: schedule frequency, baggage handling, in-flight service, friendliness, seat comfort. They shed the notion that they were in the air carrier business and realized that they were in the total travel business. Bankers initially resisted marketing but are now embracing it enthusiastically. Marketing is also beginning to attract the interest of insurance and stock brokerage companies, although they have a long way to go in applying marketing effectively.

The latest business groups to take an interest in marketing are professional service providers, such as lawyers, accountants, physicians, and architects. Professional societies have, until recently, prohibited their members from engaging in price competition, client solicitation, and advertising. The U.S. antitrust division recently ruled that these restraints are illegal. Accountants, lawyers, and other professional groups are now allowed to advertise and to price aggressively.

> The fierce competition engendered by the new limits on corporate growth is forcing accounting firms into aggressive new postures. . . . The accountants insist on referring to their efforts to drum up business as "practice development." But many of the activities that fall under this euphemism are dead ringers for what is called "marketing" in other fields. . . . Accountants speak of "positioning" their firms and of "penetrating" unexploited new industries. They compile "hit lists" of prospective clients and then "surround" them by placing their firms' partners in close social contact with the top executives of the target companies.[22]

In the International Sector Marketing is practiced not only in the United States, but in the rest of the world. In fact, several European and Japanese multinationals—companies like Nestlé, Siemens, Toyota, and Sony—have in many cases outperformed their U.S. competitors. Multinationals have introduced and spread modern marketing practices throughout the world. As a result, management in smaller countries is beginning to ask: What is marketing? How does it differ from plain selling? How can we introduce marketing into the firm? Will it make a difference?

In socialist countries, marketing has traditionally had a bad name. However, various functions of marketing, such as marketing research, branding, advertising, and sales promotion, are now spreading rapidly. In the USSR there are now over one hundred state-operated advertising agencies and marketing research firms.[23] Several companies in Poland and Hungary have marketing departments, and several socialist universities teach marketing.

In the Nonprofit Sector Marketing is currently attracting the interest of nonprofit organizations such as colleges, hospitals, police departments, museums, and symphonies.[24] Consider the following developments:[25]

> Facing low enrollments and rising costs, many private colleges are using marketing to attract students and funds. St. Joseph's College in Renssalaer, Indiana, obtained a 40 percent increase in freshman enrollments by advertising in *Seventeen* and on several rock radio stations. Worchester Polytech offers negotiable admission to shorten the degree period for applicants based on previous study and work experience. Some other institutions are designing more complete marketing programs by analyzing their environments and markets, selecting target segments, and preparing complete marketing plans to position themselves in chosen markets.

An example of innovative hospital advertising. *Courtesy of St. Mary's Medical Center, Evansville, Indiana; art director, Greg Folz.*

As hospital costs and room rates continue to soar, many hospitals are experiencing underutilization, especially in their maternity and pediatrics sections. Many are taking steps toward marketing. A Philadelphia hospital, competing for maternity patients, offered a steak and champagne dinner with candlelight for new parents. Other hospitals, in an effort to attract physicians, have added services such as saunas, chauffeurs, and private tennis courts.

The Order of the Most Holy Trinity, a 100-member Catholic community of priests and brothers founded in 1198 and dedicated to good works in the secular world, was having trouble finding new recruits. In an effort to reach young college men, the order placed an ad in *Playboy.* The magazine claims that the ad attracted 600 new applicants.

Many cultural organizations—theatrical groups, museums, symphonies—cannot attract enough audiences and face large operating deficits. Increasingly they are turning to marketing. One concert hall, plagued by low attendance and revenues which failed to cover costs, performed a marketing audit to evaluate and improve performance. The audit resulted in recommendations that the concert hall establish a larger professional marketing staff, develop a marketing planning system, strengthen its marketing communications, raise prices, and launch an aggressive subscription campaign aimed at its different market segments.

These organizations have marketplace problems. Their administrators are struggling to keep them alive in the face of changing consumer attitudes and diminishing financial resources. Many institutions have turned to marketing as a possible answer to their problems. As a sign of the times, the Evanston Hospital of Evanston, Illinois, appointed a vice-president of marketing to develop and promote its hospital services in the community and to develop plans to attract more patients, physicians, and nurses.

U.S. government agencies are showing an increased interest in marketing. The U.S. Postal Service and Amtrak have developed marketing plans for their operations. The U.S. Army has a marketing plan to attract recruits and is one of the top advertising spenders in the country. Other government agencies are now marketing energy conservation, antismoking, and other public causes.

PLAN OF THE BOOK

The following chapters will elaborate on the themes and principles of marketing introduced in this chapter. Chapter 2, "The Marketing Management Process," provides an overview of the company marketing process, consisting of analyzing market opportunities, selecting target markets, developing the marketing mix, and managing the marketing effort.

Part Two, "Organizing the Marketing Planning Process," discusses how marketing activities are planned and integrated within the company's overall strategic plan. We will also discuss the importance of marketing research and information in preparing company and marketing plans.

Part Three, "Analyzing Market Opportunities," takes a look at the changing marketing environment and the key characteristics of consumer and organizational markets. The marketer studies these markets and the environment to better identify attractive opportunities.

Part Four, "Selecting Target Markets," describes the art of selecting appropriate markets. The process begins with demand measurement and forecasting. The marketer then segments the market, selects target segments, and positions the company's products in chosen markets.

Part Five, "Developing the Marketing Mix," examines the major marketing activities of the firm—designing, pricing, placing, and promoting products and services. We will look at the various concepts that guide marketing managers and at the techniques they use to develop attractive offers and market them successfully.

Part Six, "Managing the Marketing Effort," describes some broad competitive marketing strategies that companies can use based on their competitive positions in the market—strategies that best match company resources to environmental opportunities. We then examine how marketing plans and strategies are implemented by people in the marketing organization, others in the company, and those outside the company. This requires an effective marketing organization and marketing controls to make sure that the organization's goals are being achieved.

Part Seven, "Extending Marketing," looks at topics of current interest, including international marketing and services and nonprofit marketing. The last chapter, "Marketing and Society," returns us to the basic question of the role and purpose of marketing in society, its contributions, and its deficiencies.

The book ends with two appendixes. The first presents the marketing arithmetic used by marketing managers when making many decisions. The second discusses marketing careers and how students can apply marketing principles in the search for desirable jobs.

Exhibit 1–4 describes several approaches to the study of marketing. This book uses the managerial approach as a framework for incorporating all the others.

EXHIBIT 1-4

APPROACHES TO THE STUDY OF MARKETING

Marketing has been studied from several points of view. The following approaches are the most common:

1. *Commodity approach.* The commodity approach focuses on particular commodities and classes of products to determine how they are produced and distributed to intermediate and ultimate consumers. The major product classes studied are farm products, minerals, manufactured goods, and services.

2. *Institutional approach.* The institutional approach focuses on the nature, evolution, and functions of particular institutions in the marketing system, such as producers, wholesalers, retailers, and facilitating agencies. Institutionalists might study, say, department stores to determine how they have evolved and where they are headed.

3. *Functional approach.* The functional approach focuses on the nature and dynamics of various marketing functions, such as buying, selling, storing, financing, and promoting. A functionalist studies how these functions are carried out in various product markets and by various marketing institutions.

4. *Managerial approach.* The managerial approach focuses on the use of marketing to position organizations and products in the marketplace successfully. Managerial marketers are especially interested in marketing analysis, planning, organization, implementation, and control.

5. *Social approach.* The social approach focuses on the social contributions and costs created by various marketing activities and institutions. This approach addresses such issues as market efficiency, product obsolescence, advertising truthfulness, and the ecological impact of marketing.

■ *Summary*

Marketing touches everyone's life. It is the means by which a standard of living is developed and delivered to a people. Marketing involves a large number of activities, including marketing research, product development, distribution, pricing, advertising, and personal selling. Many people confuse marketing with selling, but marketing actually combines several activities designed to sense, serve, and satisfy consumer needs while meeting the goals of the organization. Marketing occurs long before and after the selling event.

Marketing is the study of how various parties satisfy their needs and wants through exchange processes. The key concepts in the study of marketing are needs, wants, demands, products, exchange, transactions, and markets.

Marketing management is the conscious effort to manage the exchange process to secure desired outcomes. It involves analysis, planning, implementation, and control of programs designed to create, build, and maintain beneficial exchanges with target markets for the purpose of achieving organizational objectives. Marketers must be good at managing the level, timing, and composition of demand, since demand can be in states that are at variance with what the organization wants.

Marketing management can be conducted under five different *marketing philosophies.* The production concept holds that consumers will favor products that are available at low cost, and therefore management's task is to improve production efficiency and bring down prices. The product concept holds that consumers favor quality products, and therefore little promotional effort is required. The selling concept holds that consumers will not buy enough of the company's products unless they are stimulated through a substantial selling and promotion effort. The marketing concept holds that a company should research the needs and wants of a well-defined target market and deliver the desired satis-

factions. The societal marketing concept holds that the company should generate customer satisfaction and long-run consumer and societal well-being as the key to achieving organizational goals.

Marketing practices have a major impact on people in their roles as buyers, sellers, and citizens. Different goals have been proposed for a marketing system, such as maximizing consumption, consumer satisfaction, consumer choice, or life quality. Many people believe that marketing's goal should be to enhance the quality of life and that the means should be the societal marketing concept.

Interest in marketing is intensifying as more organizations in the business sector, in the international sector, and in the nonprofit sector recognize how marketing contributes to improved performance in the marketplace.

■ Questions for Discussion

1. The historian Arnold Toynbee has criticized marketing practice in America, saying that American consumers are being manipulated into purchasing products that aren't required to satisfy the "minimum material requirements of life" or "genuine wants." What is your position? Defend it.

2. How does *marketing* differ from *selling?* Would you rather be an expert marketer or an expert seller of yourself when you are looking for a job after graduation? Explain.

3. You are planning to go to a fast-food franchise for lunch. Apply the notions of products, exchange transactions, and a market to this situation.

4. Although McDonald's Corporation has been praised as being a prime practitioner of the marketing concept, it has also been criticized for practicing a product orientation. What might have stimulated this criticism?

5. Procter & Gamble's success is often credited to the company being a good "listener." How does this relate to the marketing concept?

6. How can the marketing management philosophies of the product concept and production concept be contrasted? Give an example of each.

7. Why has the societal marketing concept superseded the marketing concept for some organizations?

8. How can marketing have an impact on each of the three aspects of the quality of life mentioned? Can you think of other qualify-of-life dimensions? How might marketing affect these?

9. Why has marketing been embraced by many nonprofit organizations in recent years? Elaborate on a specific example.

■ References

1. PATRICK E. MURPHY and RICHARD A. McGARRITY, "Marketing Universities: A Survey of Student Recruiting Activities," *College and University,* Spring 1978, pp. 249–61.
2. PETER F. DRUCKER, *Management: Tasks, Responsibilities, Practices* (New York: Harper & Row, 1973), pp. 64–65.
3. Here are some other definitions: "Marketing is the performance of business activities that direct the flow of goods and services from producer to consumer or user." "Marketing is getting the right goods and services to the right people at the right place at the right time at the right price with the right communication and promotion." "Mar-

keting is the creation and delivery of a standard of living."

4. See THEODORE LEVITT's classic article, "Marketing Myopia," *Harvard Business Review,* July–August 1960, pp. 45–56.

5. CYRIL S. BELSHAW, *Traditional Exchange and Modern Markets* (Englewood Cliffs, NJ: Prentice-Hall, 1965).

6. ADAM SMITH, *The Wealth of Nations* (New York: Crowell-Collier and Macmillan, 1909), p. 19.

7. For more discussion on marketing as an exchange process, see PHILIP KOTLER, "A Generic Concept of Marketing," *Journal of Marketing,* April 1972, pp. 46–54; and RICHARD P. BAGOZZI, "Toward a Formal Theory of Marketing Exchanges," in *Conceptual and Theoretical Developments in Marketing,* eds. O. C. FERRELL, STEPHEN W. BROWN, and CHARLES W. LAMB (Chicago: American Marketing Association, 1979), pp. 431–47.

8. For more discussion, see WROE ALDERSON, "Factors Governing the Development of Marketing Channels," in *Marketing Channels for Manufactured Products,* ed. Richard M. Clewett (Homewood, Ill.: Richard D. Irwin, 1957), pp. 211–14. The number of transactions in a decentralized exchange system is given by $N(N - 1)/2$. With four persons, this means $4(4 - 1)/2 = 6$ transactions. In a centralized exchange system, the number of transactions is given by N, here 4. Thus a centralized exchange system reduces the number of required transactions to accomplish a given volume of exchange.

9. "Texas Instruments Shows U.S. Business How to Survive in the 1980s," *Business Week,* September 18, 1978, pp. 66ff; and "The Long-Term Damage from TI's Bombshell," *Business Week,* June 15, 1981, p. 36.

10. See "So We Made a Better Mousetrap," *President's Forum,* Fall 1962, pp. 26–27.

11. See IRVING J. REIN, *Rudy's Red Wagon: Communication Strategies in Contemporary Society* (Glenview, IL: Scott, Foresman, 1972).

12. See JOHN B. MCKITTERICK, "What Is the Marketing Management Concept?" *The Frontiers of Marketing Thought and Action* (Chicago: American Marketing Association, 1957), pp. 71–82; FRED J. BORCH, "The Marketing Philosophy as a Way of Business Life," *The Marketing Concept: Its Meaning to Management,* Marketing Series, No. 99 (New York: American Management Association, 1957), pp. 3–5; and ROBERT J. KEITH, "The Market-

ing Revolution," *Journal of Marketing,* January 1960, pp. 35–38.

13. LEVITT, "Marketing Myopia."

14. CARLTON P. MCNAMARA, "The Present Status of the Marketing Concept," *Journal of Marketing,* January 1972, pp. 50–57.

15. PETER M. BANTING and RANDOLPH E. ROSS, "The Marketing Masquerade," *Business Quarterly* (Canada), Spring 1974, pp. 19–27. Also see PHILIP KOTLER, "From Sales Obsession to Marketing Effectiveness," *Harvard Business Review,* November–December 1977, pp. 67–75.

16. LAURENCE P. FELDMAN, "Societal Adaptation: A New Challenge for Marketing," *Journal of Marketing,* July 1971, pp. 54–60; and MARTIN L. BELL and C. WILLIAM EMERY, "The Faltering Marketing Concept," *Journal of Marketing,* October 1971, pp. 37–42.

17. The societal marketing concept goes by different names. See LESLIE M. DAWSON, "The Human Concept: New Philosophy for Business," *Business Horizons,* December 1969, pp. 29–38; JAMES T. ROTHE and LISSA BENSON, "Intelligent Consumption: An Attractive Alternative to the Marketing Concept," *MSU Business Topics,* Winter 1974, pp. 29–34; and GEORGE FISK, "Criteria for a Theory of Responsible Consumption," *Journal of Marketing,* April 1973, pp. 24–31.

18. RICHARD N. FARMER, "Would You Want Your Daughter to Marry a Marketing Man?" *Journal of Marketing,* January 1967, p. 1.

19. STERLING HAYDEN, *Wanderer* (New York: Knopf, 1963).

20. WILLIAM J. STANTON, *Fundamentals of Marketing,* 7th ed. (New York: McGraw-Hill, 1984), p. 9.

21. Sir Winston Churchill.

22. DEBORAH RANKIN, "How C.P.A.'s SELL THEMSELVES," *NEW YORK TIMES,* SEPTEMBER 25, 1977.

23. THOMAS V. GREER, *Marketing in the Soviet Union* (New York: Holt, Rinehart & Winston, 1973).

24. For a good review of nonprofit marketing, see CHRISTOPHER H. LOVELOCK and CHARLES B. WEINBERG, "Public and Nonprofit Marketing Comes of Age," in *Review of Marketing 1978,* eds. Gerald Zaltman and Thomas V. Bonoma (Chicago: American Marketing Association, 1978).

25. Several of these and other examples are discussed in PHILIP KOTLER, *Marketing for Nonprofit Organizations* (Englewood Cliffs, NJ: Prentice-Hall, 1982), pp. 15–17, 170–72.

2
The Marketing Management Process

Before 1970, Miller Brewing Company of Milwaukee stood as a stodgy seventh-place brewer with a 4 percent market share and flat sales. Meanwhile, Anheuser-Busch's sales were growing 10 percent a year, twice the industry's overall growth rate. Then Philip Morris, flush with cash from its successful tobacco business, decided to buy Miller as an entry into the beer market. It infused its marketing muscle into flabby Miller, took several new initiatives, and propelled Miller, in the course of five years, into the number-two spot. And by 1983, Miller held 21 percent of the beer market, short of Anheuser-Busch's 34 percent, but well ahead of Stroh's (14 percent), Heileman (10 percent), and Coors (8 percent). How did Philip Morris create this modern marketing miracle?

Essentially Philip Morris departed from the traditional approach to beer marketing—namely, working hard on production efficiency and price promotions. Philip Morris brought in classic consumer marketing techniques pioneered by Procter & Gamble and used by Philip Morris to win the number-two position in the tobacco industry and manage the most successful cigarette brand in history, Marlboro. The approach calls for studying consumer needs and wants, dividing the market into segments, identifying the best opportunity segments, producing products and packages specifically for these segments, and spending heavily to advertise and promote the new products. "Until Miller came along, the brewers operated as if there was a homogeneous market for beer that could be served by one product in one package," according to Robert S. Weinberg, a former executive with Anheuser-Busch.

Philip Morris's first step was to reposition

Miller High Life, Miller's only product. Billed as the "champagne of beers," Miller High Life attracted a disproportionate share of women and upper-income consumers who were not big beer drinkers. The Philip Morris executives commissioned marketing research and discovered that 30 percent of the beer drinkers consume 80 percent of the beer. Miller studied the characteristics of the six-pack-a-day beer drinkers—their demographic, psychological, and media profiles—and decided to develop a more "macho image" for Miller High Life. Its ads showed oil drillers drinking this beer after a major oil blowout, and young people drinking it while riding dune buggies. The ad pitch was, "If you've got the time, we've got the beer," and this campaign ran successfully for ten years.

Then Miller began to open new market segments. It noted that diet-conscious women and older people thought the standard twelve-ounce bottle of beer was too much to consume. Miller introduced the "pony-size" seven-ounce bottle and it was a great success.

This was nothing compared with its launch in 1975 of its lower-calorie beer called Lite. Lite is the most successful new beer introduced in the United States since 1900. Other low-cal beers had been marketed unsuccessfully, largely because they were promoted as diet drinks to diet-conscious consumers who do not drink much beer anyway. As a result, low-cal beers acquired a sissy image. Miller positioned Lite not as a low-calorie beer but as a less-filling beer for "real" beer drinkers. Sports personalities were featured who stated that because Lite had one-third fewer calories, they could drink more beer without feeling so filled. Even the packaging projected a masculine appeal and looked "beery."

Miller next turned to attack Anheuser-Busch's most profitable beer, Michelob, by launching its own superpremium beer, Lowenbrau. It is positioned as a beer "for good friends" during special times when buyers should "let it be Lowenbrau."

The Miller campaign revolutionized marketing in the beer industry and established Miller as an industry leader, but competitors caught on fast. By the mid-1980s, following Miller's marketing example, Budweiser was stronger than ever and Stroh's, Heileman, and Coors were growing despite a flat beer market. Miller, however, was having problems. Though sales of Miller Lite were strong, sales of the Miller High Life flagship brand were declining. The company that pioneered segmentation in the beer industry had no entries in the popular-price, superpremium, and imported segments and found itself playing catchup in these categories. No longer aiming to overtake Budweiser, Miller is trying to find the old magic—it is adding brands, trying new advertising approaches, and testing new packaging in an effort to hold its number two position.

Miller taught the industry a marketing lesson and learned one in return. And the future is still bright for the company. As one Miller wholesaler put it: "The company is a little less arrogant now and is beginning to understand things better. We'll do all right."[1]

Philip Morris acquired the Miller Brewing Company and converted it from a stodgy production-oriented company to an eminently successful marketing-oriented company. This chapter presents an overview of how successful market-oriented companies manage their marketing activities.

Every company operates in a complex and changing environment. If the company is to survive, it must offer something of value to some customer group in its environment. Through exchange, it gets back the revenues and resources it needs to survive.

The company must make sure that its corporate mission and product lines remain relevant to the market. Alert companies will reexamine their objectives, strategies, and tactics periodically. They will rely on marketing as the main system for monitoring and adapting to the changing marketplace. Marketing is not simply advertising and salesforce activity, but rather a whole process for matching the company to its best market opportunities. We define the marketing management process as follows:

> The **marketing management process** consists of (1) organizing the marketing planning process, (2) analyzing market opportunities, (3) selecting target markets, (4) developing the marketing mix, and (5) managing the marketing effort.

These steps are illustrated in Figure 2-1, along with the chapters dealing with each step. This chapter surveys the whole process.

To demonstrate the process, we will examine a well-known company, Helene Curtis:

> Helene Curtis Industries is a Chicago manufacturer of toiletries and other products. Founded over fifty years ago, the company's sales in 1983 were $243 million. Helene Curtis operates four divisions, each manufacturing several

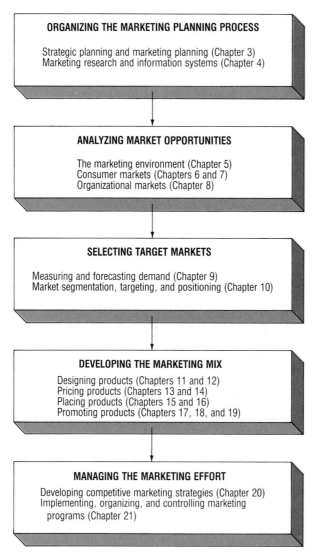

FIGURE 2-1
The Marketing Management Process

ORGANIZING THE MARKETING PLANNING PROCESS

Strategic planning and marketing planning (Chapter 3)
Marketing research and information systems (Chapter 4)

ANALYZING MARKET OPPORTUNITIES

The marketing environment (Chapter 5)
Consumer markets (Chapters 6 and 7)
Organizational markets (Chapter 8)

SELECTING TARGET MARKETS

Measuring and forecasting demand (Chapter 9)
Market segmentation, targeting, and positioning (Chapter 10)

DEVELOPING THE MARKETING MIX

Designing products (Chapters 11 and 12)
Pricing products (Chapters 13 and 14)
Placing products (Chapters 15 and 16)
Promoting products (Chapters 17, 18, and 19)

MANAGING THE MARKETING EFFORT

Developing competitive marketing strategies (Chapter 20)
Implementing, organizing, and controlling marketing
  programs (Chapter 21)

products: Consumer Products Division (shampoos, conditioners, skin-care lotions); Professional Division (shampoos, appliances); International Division; and Protective Treatments Division (sealants and adhesives).

ORGANIZING THE MARKETING PLANNING EFFORT

Every company must determine where it wants to go and how to get there. The future should not be left to chance. To meet this need, companies do strategic planning and marketing planning.

Strategic planning is a recent arrival on the company planning scene. It is companywide planning which starts with the assumption that every company con-

Helene Curtis must plan its product and business portfolio for overall company profitability. *Courtesy of Helene Curtis Industries, Inc.*

sists of several businesses. For example, Helene Curtis produces toiletries, beauty shop equipment and supplies, and sealants and adhesives. Each business consists of several products; toiletries at Helene Curtis includes shampoos, conditioners, and skin-care lotions.

Not all of these businesses or products are equally attractive. Some businesses are growing, others are stable, and still others are declining. Now if Helene Curtis consisted of only declining businesses, it would be in serious trouble. Helene Curtis must make sure that it starts enough new promising businesses (or products) to keep the company robust and growing. Helene Curtis must also know how to allocate its scarce resources to the most deserving of its current businesses. It would be a mistake to allocate its money to prop up losing businesses while starving the more promising businesses. The purpose of strategic planning is to make sure the company finds and develops strong businesses and phases down or phases out its weaker businesses.

The major tool for doing this is called *business portfolio analysis.* Basically the company grades all its current businesses in terms of which ones are worth building, maintaining, milking, and terminating; it also looks for new businesses worth adding. This is similar to managing a stock portfolio and making decisions on which stock to buy, or buy more of, or maintain, or sell some of, or sell all of. While it is much easier to make changes in a stock portfolio than in a portfolio of businesses, the analogy underlies strategic thinking.

Through strategic planning, the company decides what it wants to do with each business unit. Within this overall plan, the company must then prepare *functional* plans for each business, product or brand—plans for marketing, finance, production, and personnel. Marketing planning involves deciding on marketing strategies that will help the company to attain its overall strategic objectives. A detailed marketing plan is needed for each business. For example, suppose Helene Curtis decides that Suave shampoo should be built further because of its strong growth potential. Then the Suave brand manager will develop a marketing plan to carry out Suave's growth objective.

The Suave brand manager will actually prepare two marketing plans, a long-range plan and an annual plan. The manager will first prepare a five-year plan for Suave that describes the major factors and forces affecting this market over the next five years, the five-year objectives, the major strategies that will be used to build the brand's market share and profits, the capital required, and the profits expected. This five-year plan would be reviewed and updated each year, so that there would always be a current five-year plan.

The annual plan is then prepared, and it represents a detailed version of the first year of the five-year plan. The annual plan describes the current marketing situation, the current threats and opportunities, the objectives and issues facing the product or brand, the marketing strategy for the year, the action program, budgets, and controls. This plan is submitted to higher management for approval and becomes the basis for coordinating all the activities—production, marketing, financial—to realize the product's objectives.

In preparing marketing plans—in fact, throughout the marketing management process—managers need a plentiful supply of timely and accurate information. They need information about the past, present, and future states of the environment, target consumers, competitors, suppliers and resellers, and publics. This information is supplied by the marketing information system and marketing research. The marketing information system determines the information needs of marketing managers and obtains the needed information from several sources—internal company records, marketing intelligence, and marketing research. It then distributes this information to the right managers, in the right form, at the right time.

ANALYZING MARKET OPPORTUNITIES

Every company needs to be able to identify new market opportunities. No company can depend on its present products and markets lasting forever. We no longer hear about horse carriages, buggy whips, and slide rules—all the manufacturers either went out of business or were smart enough to switch to new businesses. In many companies, most current sales and profits come from products they did not even produce five years ago.

Some companies may think that they have few opportunities, but this means they have failed to think strategically about what business they are in and what strengths they have. In fact, every company faces an abundance of market opportunities. Suppose Helene Curtis is seeking new market opportunities. How might it identify and evaluate them?

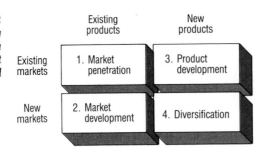

	Existing products	New products
Existing markets	1. Market penetration	3. Product development
New markets	2. Market development	4. Diversification

Market Opportunity Identification

Organizations can search for new opportunities casually or systematically. Many organizations find new ideas simply by keeping their ears and eyes open to the changing marketplace. Company executives read newspapers, attend trade shows, examine competitors' products, and gather market intelligence in other ways. Many ideas can be picked up by using informal methods.

Other organizations use formal methods of market opportunity identification. One useful device is a *product/market expansion grid.*[2] This device is shown in Figure 2-2 and will be applied to Helene Curtis's shampoo product.

Market Penetration

First, the shampoo product manager at Helene Curtis considers whether the company's major brand, Suave, can achieve deeper *market penetration*—more sales to its present customers without changing the product in any way. To do this the company might cut the list price of Suave shampoo, increase the advertising budget, improve the advertising message, get Suave into more stores, or obtain better shelf positions for Suave. Basically, the shampoo manager would like to attract customers of other brands to Suave while not losing any current customers.

Market Development

Second, the shampoo manager tries to identify new market segments for Suave. The manager reviews *demographic markets*—infants, preschoolers, teenagers, young adults, senior citizens—to see if any of these groups can be encouraged to switch to or buy more of its shampoo. Next, the manager reviews *institutional markets*—health clubs, beauty shops, hospitals—to see if sales to these buyers can be increased. Then the manager reviews *geographical markets*—France, Thailand, India—to see if these markets can be developed. All these represent market development strategies.

Product Development

Third, the shampoo manager might consider offering modified or new products to current customers. Suave shampoo could be offered in new sizes, or with new scents or ingredients, or in new packaging, all representing possible product modifications. Helene Curtis could also launch one or more new brands of shampoo to appeal to different users. It did this in 1982 and 1984 when it successfully introduced Finesse and Attune shampoos and conditioners, premium brands that complement the Suave brand aimed at the value market. Helene Curtis could also launch other hair-care products—home permanents, hair dryers—that its current customers might buy. All these represent product development strategies.

Diversification

Fourth, Helene Curtis faces a whole set of *diversification* opportunities. It could start or acquire businesses lying entirely outside of its current products and markets. It could consider entering such "hot" industries as telecommunications, word-processing equipment, personal computers, and daycare centers. Some companies try to identify the most attractive emerging industries. They feel that half the secret of success is to enter attractive industries instead of trying to be efficient in an unattractive industry.

But what constitutes an attractive industry? The Boston Consulting Group, a leading management consulting firm, says that the single best indicator of an attractive industry is the *market growth rate*.[3] According to the Boston Consulting Group, the growth rate of an attractive industry is more than 10 percent annually (this is somewhat arbitrary). Michael Porter, in his *Competitive Strategy,* offers a broader list of indicators of an attractive industry:[4]

1. *High barriers to entry.* The higher the barriers to entry (such factors as patent protection, superior location, high capital requirements, and superior reputation), the higher the firm's profits.
2. *Weak competitors.* The weaker the current competitors, the higher the firm's profits.
3. *Weak substitutes.* The fewer or less satisfactory the available substitutes, the higher the firm's profits.
4. *Weak buyers.* The weaker or less organized the buyers, the higher the firm's profits.
5. *Weak suppliers.* The weaker or less organized the suppliers, the higher the firm's profits.

This suggests that a firm should favor industries that rate high on these characteristics.[5]

Market Opportunity Evaluation It is one thing to identify opportunities and another to determine which opportunities are right for the company. We define company marketing opportunity as follows:

> A **company marketing opportunity** is an attractive arena for company marketing action in which the particular company would enjoy a competitive advantage.

For example, personal computers are an attractive industry, but we instinctively sense that they would not be appropriate for Helene Curtis. Why? The answer is suggested in Figure 2-3. A marketing opportunity must fit the company's objectives and resources. Let us consider each in turn.

Company Objectives

Every company pursues a set of objectives based on its mission and business scope. Helene Curtis, for example, primarily operates in the hair-care business and seeks a

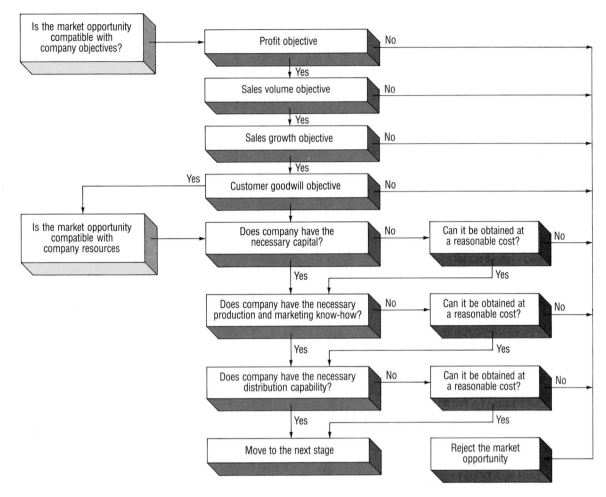

FIGURE 2-3
Evaluating a Market Opportunity in Terms of the Company's Objectives and Resources

high level of profits, sales, sales growth, and customer goodwill. Helene Curtis would probably decide that its objectives alone rule out the computer industry. Sales and profits could be volatile. Moreover, if Helene Curtis's customers view cosmetics and personal computers as being incompatible, goodwill could be diluted by this move.

Company Resources

Even if the computer industry matched Helene Curtis's objectives, Helene Curtis would probably lack the resources necessary to succeed in this industry. Each industry has certain *success requirements*. The computer industry requires a great deal of capital, technical knowhow, and effective distribution channels, all of which Helene Curtis would lack. Of course, the lack of required capabilities would not be fatal if the company could acquire them at a reasonable cost. Helene Curtis could conceivably acquire a small existing computer company. But this would be an opportunistic acquisition rather than one warranted by any resource advantage Helene Curtis could bring to this industry.

The most successful firms in an industry are those that enjoy a *differential advantage* over competitors, some superiority that results in buyer preference. IBM, for example, enjoys a differential advantage in the computer industry based on its years of manufacturing experience, its patents, its distribution strength, and its customer service. But companies can rarely find ideal, ready-made opportunities in attractive new markets that exactly fit their objectives and resources. Product development and diversification are often risky, and it may take many years before the company develops a differential advantage (see Exhibit 2-1). When evaluating market opportunities, the manager must decide whether the potential returns justify the risks.

EXHIBIT 2-1

AN ATTRACTIVE BUT RISKY MARKET OPPORTUNITY FOR JOHNSON & JOHNSON

When you think of Johnson & Johnson, you usually think of Band-Aids, Baby Shampoo, and Tylenol, or perhaps one of its other well-known consumer brands—Sine-Aid, Sundown Sunscreen, Affinity Shampoo, Tek and Reach Toothbrushes, Ortho contraceptive products, Stayfree and Carefree feminine hygiene products, and many more. J&J has been one of the most consistently successful consumer-products marketers in the world. And consumer products account for only about 40 percent of J&J's $6 billion of yearly sales. Johnson & Johnson is also very successful at selling hospital supplies and prescription drugs (it's one of the world's largest drug companies). Its marketing skill is demonstrated by the fact that more than half of its sales comes from products that are number one in their markets.

Though Johnson & Johnson's consumer products and pharmaceutical businesses have been very profitable, management felt that the growth potential in these maturing markets was limited. In the late 1970s, the company began looking for attractive new market opportunities, and decided on a bold but risky diversification into the high-growth, rapidly changing medical technology field. During the late 1970s and early 1980s, J&J acquired numerous companies in the promising high-tech health care market. Now, in addition to its more traditional products, J&J makes such exotic products as surgical lasers, synthetic vaccines, blood monitoring devices, magnetic resonance scanners, orthopedic surgical implants, and intraocular lenses (to replace natural lenses in the eye after cataract surgery). The company has even invested millions in the early stages of a venture to manufacture better medicines in outer space.

These new high-tech health care markets offer rapid growth and high profits, but J&J's move into these new fields will be difficult. Though the company has substantial financial resources, the marketing of sophisticated medical products requires very different marketing approaches, management skills, and organization structures from those Johnson & Johnson used so successfully to sell Band-Aids, shampoos, and surgical supplies. And the new markets are more volatile and competitive than J&J's traditional consumer products and pharmaceutical areas—the growth markets that attracted J&J also attracted many large and small competitors. Even a company of J&J's size will have to work long and hard to develop differential advantage.

Johnson & Johnson's move to seize a new market opportunity has been expensive.

The company has made a huge investment to establish itself in the high-tech medical business. Yet so far losses in these markets have been heavy, and management realizes that it may take many years to build a solid position in the new markets. But J&J believes that in the long run it must find and develop attractive new market opportunities to complement its businesses in maturing markets—its current products and markets will not last forever.

Sources: Based on information found in Johnson & Johnson annual reports; "Changing a Corporate Culture: Can Johnson & Johnson Go from Band-Aids to High Tech?" *Business Week,* May 14, 1984, pp. 130–38; and Henry Eason, "How a Space Venture Could Ease Suffering on Earth." *Nation's Business,* June 1984, p. 48.

SELECTING TARGET MARKETS

The process of identifying and evaluating market opportunities normally produces many new ideas. Often the real task is to choose the best ideas among several good ones that match the company's objectives and resources.

Suppose Helene Curtis evaluated a number of market opportunities and found that the "headache pain relief" market was one of the most attractive opportunities. Helene Curtis executives would then feel that the introduction of a headache remedy conformed closely to the company's objectives and resources. This type of product would relate well to the company's existing marketing strengths—a strong salesforce and distribution network, as well as extensive experience in the promotion of consumer packaged goods.

More specifically, Helene Curtis must believe that it can work effectively with the main actors in the headache-remedy marketing environment—namely, suppliers, marketing intermediaries, competitors, and publics. That is, Helene Curtis must believe that it can establish good relations with suppliers of basic chemicals, equipment, and other resources needed in this industry. It must believe that it has strong relationships with the marketing intermediaries who will carry its products to customers. It must believe that it can develop a distinctive and attractive offering. And it must believe that entry into this industry will not cause any adverse public reaction.

Each opportunity must be further studied in terms of the relevant industry's market size and market structure so that the choices can be narrowed down. This involves four steps: demand measurement and forecasting, market segmentation, market targeting, and market positioning.

Demand Measurement and Forecasting Helene Curtis would now want to make a more careful estimate of the current and future size of this market. To estimate current market size, Helene Curtis would identify all the products selling in this market—Bayer, Excedrin, Anacin, Bufferin, Tylenol, and others—and estimate their current sales. Since these products are sold through tens of thousands of outlets, the company would have to rely on data collected by some marketing research organization on a regular basis. For example, A. C. Nielsen conducts periodic store audits to estimate how much of each brand has been sold in each major product category. Helene Curtis could buy these data from A. C. Nielsen to determine whether the market is large enough.

Equally important is the future growth of the headache pain relief market.

Companies want to enter markets that show strong growth prospects. The headache pain relief market's past growth rate has been strong, but what can be said of its future growth rate? This will depend on the growth rate of certain age, income, and nationality groups, because headache remedy use is related to demographic factors. Use is also related to larger developments in the environment, such as economic conditions, the crime rate, and life style changes. Forecasting the future impact of these environmental forces is difficult, but it must be undertaken in order to make a decision about this market. It would challenge the ingenuity of Helene Curtis's marketing information specialists.

Suppose the demand forecast looks good. Helene Curtis now has to decide how to enter the market. The market consists of many types of customers, products, and needs. Helene Curtis needs to understand the market's structure and determine which segments offer the best chance to achieve its objective.

Market Segmentation

Marketers recognize that the consumers in a market are heterogeneous and can be grouped in various ways. Consumer groups can be formed on the basis of geographic variables (regions, cities), demographic variables (sex, age, income, education), psychographic variables (social classes, life styles) and behavioristic variables (purchase occasions, benefits sought, usage rates). The process of classifying customers into groups exhibiting different needs, characteristics, or behavior is called *market segmentation*. Every market is made up of market segments.

Not all ways of segmenting the market are equally useful. Distinguishing between male and female users of pain relievers, for example, is unnecessary if both respond the same way to marketing stimuli. A **market segment** consists of *consumers who respond in a similar way to a given set of marketing stimuli.* Consumers who choose the strongest pain reliever regardless of its price constitute a market segment; another market segment would be consumers who care mainly about price. It is difficult for one brand of pain reliever to be the first choice of every consumer. Companies are wise to focus their efforts on meeting the distinct needs of one or more market segments. Each target market segment should be profiled by its demographic, economic, and psychographic characteristics so that its attractiveness as a marketing opportunity can be evaluated.

Market Targeting

A company can choose to enter one or more segments of a given market. Assume that the pain reliever market can be subdivided into three *customer wants* (W1: speedy relief; W2: long-lasting relief; and W3: gentle relief) and three *customer groups* (G1: young people; G2: middle-age people; and G3: elderly people). By crossing these wants and groups, we can distinguish nine possible market segments. Helene Curtis can choose to enter this market in one of five ways, which are shown in Figure 2-4 and listed below:

1. *Concentrating on a single segment.* The company can decide to serve only one segment of the market, here making a long-lasting pain reliever for middle-age adults.

2. *Specializing on a customer want.* The company can specialize in meeting a particular customer want, here making long-lasting pain relievers for all types of buyers.

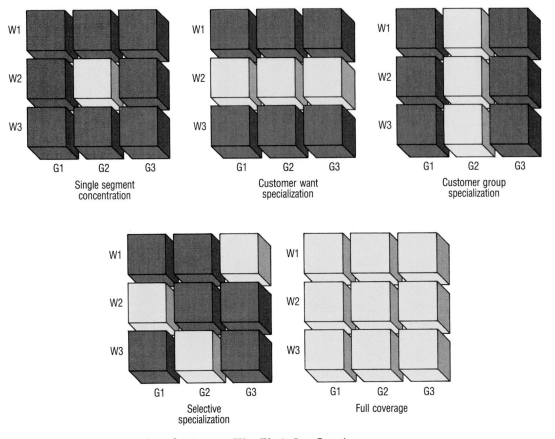

FIGURE 2-4 *Five Patterns of Market Coverage* (W = Want, G = Group)

Source: Adapted from Derek F. Abell. *Defining the Business: The Starting Point of Strategic Planning* (Englewood Cliffs, NJ: Prentic-Hall, 1980). Chap. 8.

3. *Specializing on a customer group.* The company can decide to make various pain relievers needed by a particular customer group, here middle-age adults.

4. *Serving some unrelated segments.* The company can decide to serve several market segments that have little relation to each other except that each provides an individually attractive opportunity.

5. *Covering the entire market.* The company can decide to make a complete range of pain relievers to serve all the market segments.

Most companies enter a new market by serving a single segment, and if this proves successful, they add segments and then spread vertically or horizontally. The sequence of market segments to enter should not be haphazard, but should follow a master plan. Japanese companies provide a good example of careful planning of market entry and domination. They enter a neglected part of the market, build a name by satisfying customers, and then spread to other segments. This marketing formula has won them impressive global market shares in autos, cameras, watches, consumer electronics, steel, and shipbuilding.

Large companies ultimately seek full market coverage. They want to be the

General Motors of their industry. GM says that it makes a car for every "person, purse, and personality." The leading company would normally present different offers to different market segments or would otherwise risk being outperformed in certain segments by companies that concentrate on satisfying those segments.

Market Positioning   Suppose Helene Curtis decides to go after the "heavy-user, older-adult market" for pain relievers. It would then need to identify all the products and brands currently serving customers in this market segment. These brands differ in performance characteristics, advertised appeals, prices, and in other ways. How strongly any two brands compete depends on how similar they seem to consumers. The marketer needs some way to represent how the current brands compete and the degree to which they serve important consumer desires.

The key lies in recognizing that every product is a bundle of perceived attributes. For example, Excedrin aspirin is seen as a fast-acting, ungentle pain reliever; and Tylenol is seen as a slower-acting, gentle pain reliever. This suggests that one way of comparing brands is to identify where they stand on attributes used by consumers in making their brand choice. The results can be shown on a *product position map* (see Figure 2-5A).[6]

A number of things can be observed about this map. First, it consists of only two attributes out of a larger set of possibilities (such as cost, riskiness). We could portray three dimensions at a time (in the form of a cube), but this would be cumbersome. "Gentleness" and "effectiveness" were chosen because consumers say that these are the most important attributes. Second, the attributes are rated numerically, each on a 5-point scale. Excedrin, for example, rates a 4 (good) on effectiveness and a 1 (low) on gentleness. Third, the brands are positioned according to consumer perceptions, not objective characteristics. Excedrin may actually be gentle, but what counts is how buyers perceive it. If desired, the brands could also be plotted on another map according to their objective characteristics. Fourth, the closer any two brands are in the product position map, the more they are seen by consumers as satisfying the same need. We would expect more consumer switching to occur between Bayer and Bufferin than between Excedrin and Tylenol.

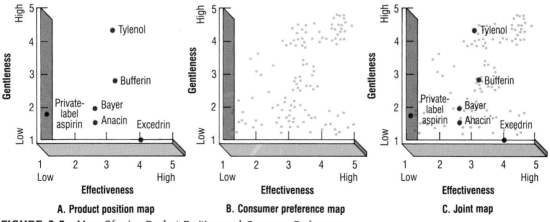

FIGURE 2-5   *Maps Showing Product Positions and Consumer Preferences*

The company must now figure out what consumers prefer with respect to the major attributes. Consumers can be asked to describe the amount of effectiveness and gentleness they want in a pain reliever. Each consumer's ideal combination of attributes can be represented as a point in a *consumer preference map.* Figure 2-5B shows a hypothetical distribution of preferences for the two pain reliever attributes.

The marketer then combines the product position map and the consumer preference map into the joint map shown in Figure 2-5C. A clear finding is that many consumers prefer a pain reliever that is both gentle and effective (upper right corner), although no current brand is perceived to offer both.

Helene Curtis can decide to go after this opportunity. To succeed, two things are necessary. First, the company must be able to manufacture a product that buyers view as combining these two attributes. Perhaps competitors have not introduced this benefit combination because they cannot find a way to produce it. Second, the company must be able to offer this product at a price that the market is willing to pay. If the cost of manufacture is extremely high, the product may be priced out of the market. But if these conditions can be fulfilled, the company will serve the market well and make a profit. In essence, the company has discovered an unsatisfied customer want and can engage in value-creating marketing.

If these conditions cannot be fulfilled, Helene Curtis will have to position itself next to an existing competitor and fight for market share. Consider the following example:[7]

> Some years ago, Bristol-Myers entered the high-gentleness segment of the pain reliever market by launching a brand called Datril against the leading brand in this segment, Tylenol. Bristol-Myers saw the high-gentleness segment as the fastest-growing segment, believed that Tylenol was a lightweight in consumer marketing, and felt that it had the resources to knock Tylenol out of the ring. Bristol-Myers priced Datril at half of Tylenol's price and advertised that all "gentle" pain relievers were identical. But it underestimated Tylenol's high consumer brand loyalty and ability to fight back. In spite of its heavy attack, Datril never managed to dethrone Tylenol. Datril had positioned itself too closely to a strong competitor.

Suppose Helene Curtis decides to go after Tylenol but wants to do it differently. It can position its brand as the "Cadillac brand" by claiming higher effectiveness than Tylenol and charging the higher price. Or it can position its brand as the "safest brand" by showing that it has the lowest record of stomach upsets of any brand. Helene Curtis can position its brand on a large number of possible attributes. The new brand should pivot on a set of attributes that enough customers consider important, desirable, and insufficiently supplied by competing brands. *Market positioning* means arranging for an offer to occupy a clear, distinctive, and desirable place in the market and in the minds of target customers.

DEVELOPING THE MARKETING MIX

Once the company has decided upon its positioning strategy, it is ready to begin planning the details of marketing mix. Marketing mix is one of the major concepts in modern marketing. We define it as follows:

Marketing mix is the set of controllable marketing variables that the firm blends to produce the response it wants in the target market.

The marketing mix consists of everything the firm can do to influence the demand for its product. The many possibilities can be collected into four groups of variables known as the "four Ps": *product, price, place,* and *promotion.*[8] The particular marketing variables under each *P* are shown in Figure 2-6.

Product stands for the "goods-and-service" combination the company offers to the target market. Thus Helene Curtis's new pain-relief "product" might consist of fifty white tablets packaged in a dark-green bottle with a childproof cap and a shelf life of three years, bearing the brand name Relief and offered with a money-back guarantee if the customer is not satisfied.

Price stands for the amount of money customers have to pay to obtain the product. Helene Curtis suggests retail and wholesale prices, discounts, allowances, and credit terms. Its "price" has to be in line with the perceived value of the offer, or else buyers will purchase competing products.

Place stands for the various company activities that make the product available to target consumers. Thus Helene Curtis chooses wholesalers and retailers, motivates them to give the product attention and exposure, checks on stock, and arranges efficient transportation and storage of the product.

Promotion stands for activities which communicate the merits of the product and persuade target customers to buy it. Thus Helene Curtis buys advertising, employs salespeople, sets up sales promotions, and arranges publicity for its product.

Designing the marketing mix involves two budgeting decisions. First, the company must decide on the total amount to spend on marketing effort *(marketing expenditure decision)*. For example, Helene Curtis might decide to spend $20 million to market a new pain reliever in the first year. Second, the company must allocate the total marketing budget to the major marketing mix tools *(marketing*

FIGURE 2-6
The Four Ps of the Marketing Mix

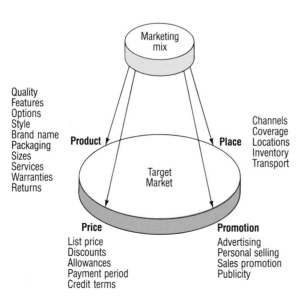

mix decision). Helene Curtis might decide to allocate most of the $20 million to advertising, with much less going to sales promotion, marketing research, and so on. Yet it would recognize that the various marketing mix tools interact and are potential substitutes.

These marketing mix decisions are heavily influenced by the company's market positioning decision. Suppose Helene Curtis decided to come out with a "Cadillac brand" for the high-gentleness market segment. This positioning decision suggests that Helene Curtis's brand must be at least as gentle as Tylenol, if not more gentle. It must use high-quality packaging, and the brand must be offered to the market in several sizes. The price should be higher than Tylenol's, and the product should be sold in quality retail outlets. The advertising budget should be large. Ads should show well-to-do users who want the best available pain reliever. The brand should avoid price cutting or promotions that would cheapen its image. Thus the positioning decision provides the basis for designing a coordinated marketing mix.

MANAGING THE MARKETING EFFORT

Managing the marketing effort involves *analysis* of markets and the marketing environment, *planning* marketing strategies and programs to take advantage of market opportunities, *implementing* these strategies and programs through an effective marketing organization, and *controlling* marketing efforts to ensure that the company operates efficiently and effectively. So far, we've examined how the company analyzes its environment, selects target markets, and plans the marketing mix to provide a market offer that meets consumer needs. But when developing a marketing strategy, managers must consider more than consumer needs—they must also consider the company's industry position relative to competitors. Marketing managers must design marketing strategies that effectively match the company's position and resources against those of competitors, and they must constantly adapt these strategies to meet changing conditions.

Further, even the best marketing strategy will be of little value unless it is implemented well. The company must mobilize its people and resources within the formal marketing organization to put the strategic plan to work. Then it must design control systems to evaluate marketing activities and performance continually to make sure that strategic marketing objectives are attained.

Competitive Marketing Strategies   To be successful, the company must do a better job than its competitors of satisfying target consumers. Thus marketing strategies must be adapted to the needs of consumers, and also to the strategies of competitors. Based on its size and industry position, the company must find the strategy that gives it the strongest possible competitive advantage.

A firm that dominates a market can adopt one or more of several *market-leader* strategies. It can try to expand the total market by looking for more usage, new users, and new uses. Because the leader has the largest market share, it gains the most when the total market is expanded. Or the company might try to increase its market share by investing heavily to attract customers away from competitors. The dominant company can also develop strategies to defend its current business against competitor attacks. It can lead the industry in innovation, competitive effec-

Market leader Crest targets broadly to parents and other adults—market nicher Pearl Drops targets smokers. *Courtesy of The Procter & Gamble Company (Crest) and Carter-Wallace, Inc. (Pearl Drops).*

tiveness, and value to consumers. It can carefully assess potential competitive threats and counterattack when necessary. The market leader may adopt a strategy of "preemptive defense"—launching new products or marketing programs to strike down competitors before they become major threats.

Market challengers are runner-up companies that aggressively attack competitors to get more market share. The challenger might attack the market leader, other firms its own size, or smaller local and regional competitors. Challengers can choose from several *market-challenger* strategies. If the challenger is strong enough, it can launch a frontal attack in which it pits its resources directly against those of competitors. A weaker challenger can launch flank attacks by concentrating its strengths against the competitor's weaknesses. Or the challenger can attack indirectly by bypassing the competitor and developing new products, new markets, or new technologies.

Some runner-up firms will choose to follow rather than challenge the market leader. Firms using *market-follower* strategies seek stable market shares and profits by following competitor's product offers, prices, and marketing programs. They may follow closely or at a distance, or they may follow closely in some ways and sometimes go their own ways. The market follower's goal is to keep current customers and to attract a fair share of new ones without drawing retaliation from the market leader or other competitors. Many market followers are more profitable than the leaders in their industries.

Smaller firms in a market, or even larger firms that lack established positions, often adopt *market-nicher* strategies. They specialize in serving market niches that major competitors overlook or ignore. Nichers avoid direct confrontations with the majors by specializing along market, customer, product, or marketing-mix lines. Through smart niching, low-share firms in an industry can be as profitable as their larger competitors.

Thus the company must choose its strategies based on its industry position and its strengths and weaknesses relative to competitors. And strategy must change to meet changes in the competitive situation. For example, Helene Curtis could enter the pain-reliever market as a nicher, offering a highly gentle and effective product to the smaller segment willing to pay a high price. Once established in this specialized segment, the company could begin challenging weaker competitors for shares in other segments. If Helene Curtis became a major competitor in the pain-reliever market, it could develop a highly differentiated product line and launch full frontal attacks against more strongly entrenched competitors.

Implementing Marketing Programs

Marketing analysis and good strategy planning are only a start toward successful company performance—the strategies must be implemented well. It is often easier to design good marketing strategies than to put them into action.

People at all levels of the marketing system must work together to implement marketing strategy and plans. People in marketing must coordinate their actions with people in finance, purchasing, manufacturing, and other departments in the company. And many people and organizations outside the company must help with implementation—suppliers, resellers, advertising agencies, research firms, the advertising media. All must coordinate their activities into an effective course of action to implement the marketing program.

Successful implementation depends on having the right people doing the right things within the right organizational structure and climate. The implementation process involves developing detailed *action programs,* constructing an effective *organization structure,* designing supporting *decision and reward systems,* finding and assigning appropriate *human resources,* and establishing a suitable *organizational climate.*

The *action program* identifies the important implementation decisions and tasks and assigns them to specific people or units in the company. It also sets a timetable for when decisions must be made and actions must be completed. The action program shows what must be done, who will do it, and how decisions and tasks will be coordinated to implement the marketing plan.

The action program will be carried out within the company's formal *organization structure.* The structure defines tasks for specific departments and people, sets lines of authority and communication, and coordinates decisions and actions across levels of the company. The organization structure should fit and support the company's marketing strategies and programs. For example, a company developing new products for rapidly changing markets might need a flexible and decentralized organization structure that encourages company people to be creative and to communicate often and informally. A more established company in more stable markets might need a centralized structure that assigns routine activities and defines more formal communication channels.

The company's *decision and reward systems* should also support marketing strategies and programs. These systems consist of operating procedures for such activities as planning, research, budgeting, recruiting, compensation, and control. Well-designed systems can encourage good implementation. For example, suppose that Helene Curtis decides to launch the new pain reliever. Much of the product's success will depend on how much attention it receives from the company's salespeople. The salesforce must convince retailers to stock the new product, give it enough shelf space, use promotional displays, and feature the product in their advertising. The salesforce compensation system can help or hinder the implementation of this new product introduction. The salespeople will want to give most of their attention to established products that are easier to sell. But if the compensation system is changed to provide higher commissions for the new product, salespeople will put more effort behind it.

Marketing programs are implemented by people, and successful implementation requires careful *human resources* planning. The company must recruit, develop, assign, and motivate people who are capable of carrying out marketing strategies and programs. And management must establish an *organizational climate* in which these people can work effectively. Strategies and programs that do not fit the firm's managerial climate and "company culture" will be hard to implement. For example, a decision by Helene Curtis to offer cut-rate products at discount prices would be resisted by salespeople who identify strongly with the company's reputation for offering quality and value.

Thus, for successful implementation all the elements of the implementation process—the action program, organization structure, decision and reward systems, people, and organizational climate—must support the marketing strategies and programs being implemented. The company must blend the five elements into a cohesive program.

Marketing Department Organization The marketing department organization provides a formal structure within which marketing analysis, planning, implementation, and control are carried out. In very small companies, one person might end up performing these management functions for all the marketing tasks: marketing research, selling, advertising, customer servicing, and so on. This person might be called the sales manager, marketing manager, or marketing director. If the company is large, several marketing specialists will be available. Thus Helene Curtis has salespeople, sales managers, marketing researchers, advertising personnel, product and brand managers, market segment managers, and customer service personnel.

Marketing organizations are typically headed by a marketing vice-president who performs two tasks. The first is to coordinate the work of all the marketing personnel. Helene Curtis's marketing vice-president must make sure, for example, that the advertising manager works closely with the salesforce manager so that the salesforce is ready to handle inquiries generated by ads that are about to be placed by the advertising department.

The marketing vice-president's other task is to work closely with the vice-presidents of finance, manufacturing, research and development, and other areas to coordinate company efforts to satisfy customers. Thus if Helene Curtis's marketing people advertise Suave as being a quality product, but R&D does not formulate it as such, or manufacturing fails to mix it properly, marketing will not deliver on its promise. The marketing vice-president's job is to make sure that all the company departments collaborate to fulfill the marketing promise made to the customers.

The marketing department's effectiveness depends not only on how it is constituted, but also on how well its personnel are selected, trained, directed, motivated, and evaluated.

Selecting able marketing personnel is critical. For example, salespeople vary greatly in their selling ability. Salespeople should not only be able to do well in the entry-level job, but should also be able to grow with the job and move up the sales ladder. Companies that pay low salaries to their salespeople, marketing researchers, brand managers, and others may end up with marketing personnel who lack the potential for greater responsibility.

Training is an essential part of every job and should lead to better performance. Each marketing job should carry a job description that defines the employee's major duties and responsibilities. Each employee needs training to understand the company's history, purpose, current situation, current goals, products, and markets.

Every employee reports to a superior who provides direction. Salespeople report to a sales manager who sets sales quotas and expenses for the current period. Each salesperson knows what is expected and how performance will be measured.

Directions are not enough. Employees must feel motivated to achieve their objectives and possibly exceed them. Their level of motivation depends on the working climate, compensation plan, attitudes of co-workers, and their boss's style of support. There is a vast difference in the performance of a "turned-on" versus "turned-off" marketing group.

Finally, marketing personnel need feedback on their performance. Managers must meet with their subordinates periodically to review their performance, praise their strengths, and point out their weaknesses and ways to correct them.

Marketing Control

Many surprises are likely to occur as marketing plans are being implemented. The company needs control procedures to make sure that its objectives will be achieved. Various manages will have to exercise control responsibilities in addition to their analysis, planning, and implementing responsibilities. Three types of marketing control can be distinguished: annual plan control, profitability control, and strategic control.

Annual Plan Control

Annual plan control is the task of making sure that the company is achieving the sales, profits, and other goals established in its annual plan. This task comprises four steps. First, management must state well-defined goals in the annual plan for each month, quarter, or other period during the year. Second, management must have ways to measure ongoing performance in the marketplace. Third, management must determine the underlying causes of any serious gaps in performance. Fourth, management must decide on the best corrective action to take to close the gaps between goals and performance. This may call for improving the ways in which the plan is being implemented, or even changing the goals.

Profitability Control

Companies need periodically to analyze the actual profitability of their different products, customer groups, trade channels, and order sizes. This is not a simple task. A company's accounting system is seldom designed to measure the real profitability of different marketing entities and activities. To measure brand profitability, for example, Helene Curtis's accountants have to estimate how much time the salesforce spends on each brand, how much advertising goes into each brand, and many other things. *Marketing profitability analysis* is the tool used to measure the profitability of different marketing activities. *Marketing efficiency studies* might also be undertaken to assess how various marketing activities can be carried on more efficiently.

Strategic Control

From time to time, companies such as Helene Curtis must stand back and critically reexamine their overall approach to the marketplace. This goes beyond carrying out annual plan control and profitability control. Marketing is one of the major areas where rapid obsolescence of objectives, policies, strategies, and programs is a constant possibility. Giant companies such as Chrysler, International Harvester, Singer, and A&P all fell on hard times because they did not watch the changing marketplace and make the proper adaptations. Because of the rapid changes in the marketing environment, each company needs to reassess its marketing effectiveness periodically. A major tool in this connection is the *marketing audit,* which is described in Chapter 21.

LOOKING AHEAD

Figure 2-7 summarizes the entire company marketing management process and the forces influencing company marketing strategy. The target customers stand in the center, and the company focuses its efforts on serving and satisfying them. The company develops a marketing mix made up of the factors under its control, the four Ps—product, price, place, and promotion. To arrive at its marketing mix, the company manages four systems: a marketing information system, a marketing planning system, a marketing organization system, and a marketing control system. These systems are interrelated in that marketing information is needed to develop marketing plans, which in turn are carried out by the marketing organization, the results of which are reviewed and controlled.

Through those systems, the company monitors and adapts to the marketing environment. The company adapts to its microenvironment, consisting of marketing intermediaries, suppliers, competitors, and publics. And it adapts to the macroenvironment, consisting of demographic/economic forces, political/legal forces, technological/ecological forces, and sociocultural forces. The company takes into

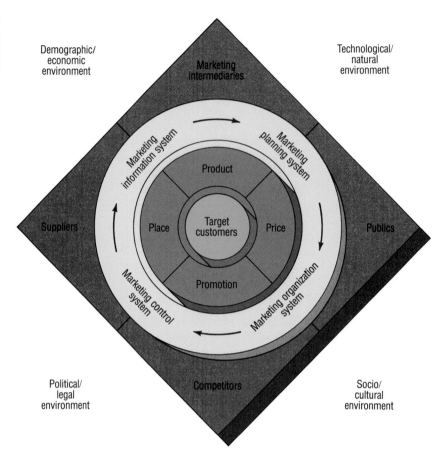

FIGURE 2-7
Factors Influencing Company Marketing Strategy

Demographic/ economic environment

Technological/ natural environment

Marketing intermediaries

Marketing information system

Marketing planning system

Product

Suppliers

Place

Target customers

Price

Publics

Promotion

Marketing control system

Marketing organization system

Political/ legal environment

Competitors

Socio/ cultural environment

account the actors and forces in the marketing environment in developing and positioning its offer to the target market.

This marketing management process will be examined in Chapters 3 through 21. Chapters 22–24 will extend marketing to additional areas, such as international marketing (Chapter 22), services and nonprofit marketing (Chapter 23), and marketing and society (Chapter 24). Chapter 24 will take us full circle, because we will then be in a better position to evaluate marketing's contributions to society.

■ *Summary*

Every company needs to manage its marketing activities effectively. Specifically, the company needs to know how to plan the marketing effort, analyze market opportunities, select appropriate target markets, develop an effective marketing mix, and manage the marketing

effort. These activities make up the marketing management process.

The marketing process starts with strategic planning and marketing planning. Strategic planning focuses on designing a robust company made up of at least some growing businesses to offset those that might be declining. Marketing planning is guided by the company's overall strategic plan and consists of long-range and annual marketing plans for specific businesses, products, and brands designed to carry out the mission identified in the strategic plan. The marketing information system provides the information needed for effective marketing planning and for the other steps in the marketing management process.

Marketing managers need to know how to identify and evaluate market opportunities. Management can identify market opportunities by working with the product/market expansion grid and paying attention to attractive new industries. Each opportunity must be evaluated as to whether it fits the company's objectives and can be handled with the company's resources.

Marketing opportunity analysis should reveal a number of attractive marketing opportunities. Each attractive opportunity will require deeper study before it can be selected as a target market. The company will want to make a more careful estimate of current and future demand to make sure that the opportunity is sufficiently attractive. If it is, the next step is to apply market segmentation to identify those customer groups and needs that the company can best serve. A *market segment* consists of customers who react in a similar way to a given set of marketing stimuli. The company might choose to serve one or more market segments. For each target market segment, the company has to determine what position it wants in that segment. It should study the positions of the competing brands in the target market with respect to the attributes consumers think are important. The company should also study the amount of demand for different possible combinations of product attributes. Then it should determine whether it wants to develop a brand to meet an unfilled need or a brand similar to an existing brand. In the latter case, it must be prepared to fight that competing brand by establishing some differentiation in the customer's mind.

Once the company has decided on its market positioning, it develops a marketing mix to support its positioning. The *marketing mix* is a blending of the four Ps—product, price, place, and promotion. The company has to decide on its total marketing budget, how the budget will be allocated to the major marketing mix categories, and how the budget within each marketing category will be allocated.

Marketing strategies must be based on consumer needs, but also on the company's industry position and resources relative to competitors. Depending on its position and strengths, the company may choose market-leader, market-challenger, market-follower, or market-nicher strategies. The company must adapt its strategies as its competitive situation changes.

Finally, the company must develop an effective implementation plan, a strong marketing department organization, and control systems to monitor activities and results. Many people and organizations must work together to implement marketing strategies and programs. Successful implementation depends on the development and blending of action programs, organization structure, decision and reward systems, human resources, and organizational climate.

The marketing department organization provides the structure for developing and implementing marketing strategies and programs. The marketing organization typically consists of a vice-president of marketing, who supervises and coordinates the work of various marketing specialists: salespeople, sales managers, advertising personnel, marketing researchers, customer service personnel, and others. The marketing vice-president's other task is to work with the vice-presidents of manufacturing, finance, research and development, and so on to coordinate the company's efforts to fulfill the company's promise to the customers. The marketing organization must be well designed and effective in selecting, training, directing, motivating, and evaluating the marketing personnel.

Implementation rarely goes as planned, so the company needs to establish some control processes. Annual plan control consists of taking steps to ensure that the annual plan objectives are reached. Profitability control consists of taking steps to identify where the company is making money and where it can improve its marketing efficiency. Strategic control consists of taking steps to evaluate and improve the company's overall marketing operation and performance.

■ Questions for Discussion

1. One marketing authority has said that "the need for the company to take account of its internal competence means that the successful company does not blindly bend its resources to the exact specifications of the marketplace." What does he mean by this? How does this relate to both the marketing concept and market opportunity evaluation?

2. In 1978 the chairman of AT&T went on intracompany TV to announce to every employee that "we will become a marketing company." What do you think he meant by that, and what company changes may be necessary for this to occur?

3. It has been reported that some Japanese manufacturers of specialized audio equipment are experiencing lagging sales and increasing competition. Using the product/market expansion grid shown in Figure 2-2, what strategies might these companies pursue?

4. Analyze the attractiveness of the beer market by using Porter's indexes.

5. A manufacturer of paraffin candles, if asked one hundred years ago what business he was in,

would have said, "I make paraffin candles." If he had been market-oriented, what would he have said?

6. Relate the five major steps in the marketing process to a service of your choice.

7. It is argued that the success of L'eggs panty hose is due to the company's understanding of the marketing mix factors. Discuss the important marketing mix variables as they relate to L'eggs.

8. If managers do a good job of organizing and implementing, they will accomplish the managing of the marketing effort step in the marketing process. Comment.

■ *References*

1. Written by the author based on "Turmoil among Brewers—Miller's Fast Growth Upsets the Beer Industry. Can It Topple U.S. Leader?" *Business Week,* November 8, 1976, pp. 58–67; Robert Reed, "Beer Makers Try New Tacks," *Advertising Age,* February 13, 1984, p. 2; and Robert Reed, "Miller No Longer a High-Flyer," *Advertising Age,* September 26, 1983, p. 4. Closing quote reprinted with permission from the September 26, 1983, issue of *Advertising Age.* Copyright 1983 by Crain Communications, Inc.

2. H. IGOR ANSOFF, "Strategies for Diversification," *Harvard Business Review,* September–October 1957, pp. 113–24.

3. For a description of the Boston Consulting Group approach, see DEREK F. ABELL and JOHN S. HAMMOND, *Strategic Market Planning* (Englewood Cliffs, NJ: Prentice-Hall, 1979), chap. 4.

4. MICHAEL E. PORTER, *Competitive Strategy: Techniques for Analyzing Industries and Competitors* (New York: Free Press, 1980), chap. 1.

5. For more details on two major approaches to evaluating industry attractiveness, see Chapter 3.

6. This example is described in technical detail in GLEN L. URBAN and JOHN R. HAUSER, *Design and Marketing of New Products* (Englewood Cliffs, NJ: Prentice-Hall, 1980), pp. 187, 221, and elsewhere.

7. See "A Painful Headache for Bristol-Myers?" *Business Week,* October 6, 1975, pp. 78–80.

8. The four P classification was first suggested by E. JEROME MCCARTHY, *Basic Marketing: A Managerial Approach* (Homewood, IL: Irwin, 1960).

two

ORGANIZING THE MARKETING PLANNING PROCESS

Part Two of this book looks at how marketers plan their activities within the company's overall strategic plan, and at the importance of marketing research and information in preparing marketing plans.

Chapter 3, STRATEGIC PLANNING AND MARKETING PLANNING

Chapter 4, MARKETING RESEARCH AND INFORMATION SYSTEMS

3
Strategic Planning and Marketing Planning

Dart & Kraft, Inc., is a huge company made up of many smaller companies, divisions, brands, and products that generate sales of almost $10 billion a year. Most consumers are familiar with the Kraft in Dart & Kraft—Kraft's retail food group sells dozens of well-known brands in more than 130 countries. Brands such as Miracle Whip, Velveeta, Kraft Salad Dressings, Parkay, Cracker Barrel, Philadelphia, Sealtest, and Breyer's are household words to most of us. And most consumers would not be surprised to learn that Kraft sells commercial and industrial food products.

Most consumers know little about the Dart in Dart & Kraft. Some of the brands are very familiar, but few of us would connect them with Dart & Kraft. They include Tupperware, Duracell batteries and flashlights, Hobart commercial food service equipment, Kitchen-Aid home appliances, and West Bend cookware and kitchen appliances. Dart & Kraft also has several less familiar products made by little-known companies such as Universal Packaging Corporation (cardboard cartons), Wilson Plastics Company (laminates and adhesives), Hospital Products Company (disposable medical and surgical products), and Absorbent Cotton Company (cotton and gauze dressings).

Planning the future of this large, diversified collection of business units is a difficult task. Each unit has special strengths and needs. Some of the companies and products are very successful in mature markets—for example, Dart & Kraft products hold almost half of the U.S. cheese market. Others are strongly positioned in smaller but faster growing markets—the recently acquired Celestial Seasonings has a 40 percent share of the growing herbal teas market and provides opportunities for expansion into natural foods products. Still others are mired in less attractive, slow-growth markets or in areas where

Dart & Kraft has less strategic advantage, areas such as bulk edible oils and cardboard cartons.

Many of these companies, products, and brands are managed independently, but each must contribute to Dart & Kraft's corporate performance. Top management must see that the company's diverse offerings combine to meet the needs of consumers and to achieve the company's overall growth and profitability goals. They do this through formal planning—planning that starts at the highest level and continues down to specific brands and functions.

First, taking into account opportunities in the marketplace and the company's relative strengths and weaknesses, top management must define Dart & Kraft's corporate mission. Will Dart & Kraft be a dairy products company, a food company, a consumer products company, or something else? Next, the company mission must be translated into specific objectives for Dart & Kraft managers. For example, the company's financial goal is to be in the top 20 percent of the consumer products industry in terms of shareholder value. Its marketing goal is to attain leadership in attractive markets by offering high-quality products that "add value" for the consumer.

Top management must then plan strategies for achieving its objectives. Dart & Kraft management has designed a "build and buy" strategy for attaining growth by increasing sales of existing products and developing or acquiring new products that complement existing lines. It wants to shed less attractive products while building or acquiring more profitable ones in more attractive markets. Accordingly, during the last several years, Dart & Kraft has pruned its product lines by 25 percent, divested several businesses (such as bulk edible oils and its fresh milk business), and used the cash to acquire more promising products (in areas such as home physical fitness equipment and natural foods).

Finally, guided by the company's overall plan, managers throughout the organization prepare marketing, financial, production, personnel and other functional plans for each company, product, and brand. These plans form an orderly hierarchy—the marketing and financial plans for Miracle Whip are part of the plan for the U.S. Retail Food Group, which is part of the Kraft Products plan, which is in turn a component of the Dart & Kraft corporate plan.

A large and complex company such as Dart & Kraft cannot survive in its fast-changing environment by making last-minute decisions and trusting to luck. Managers must use formal planning to position the company for long-run success.[1]

S ooner or later, all companies ask themselves whether they need formal planning systems, what shape such planning systems should take, and what could be done to make them work more effectively. Making continuous and miscellaneous decisions is not the same as planning. Planning is a higher-order company activity that often leads to improved profits and sales performance. In this chapter we will examine how companies plan their activities to take advantage of market opportunities and how managers assemble the marketing mix components into marketing plans. We will start with an overview of planning and then look at strategic planning, marketing planning, and the relationship between the two.

OVERVIEW OF PLANNING

Benefits of Planning Many companies operate without formal plans. In new companies, managers are so busy they have no time for planning. In mature companies, many managers argue that they have done well without formal planning and therefore it cannot be too important. They resist taking the time to prepare a written plan. They argue that the marketplace changes too fast for a plan to be useful—it would end up collecting dust. For these and other reasons, many companies have not introduced formal planning systems.

Yet formal planning can yield a number of benefits. Melville Branch lists these benefits as follows: (1) Planning encourages systematic thinking ahead by management; (2) it leads to a better coordination of company efforts; (3) it leads to the development of performance standards for control; (4) it causes the company to sharpen its guiding objectives and policies; (5) it results in better preparedness for sudden developments; (6) it brings about a more vivid sense in the participating executives of their interacting responsibilities.[2]

How Formal Planning Evolves in Organizations Rarely can an organization install an advanced planning system at the beginning. Its planning system will evolve through stages—getting better at each stage. Planning systems tend to move through the following stages.

Unplanned Stage

When companies are first organized, their managers are so busy hunting for funds, customers, equipment, and materials that they have little time to plan. Management is engrossed in the day-to-day operations required to survive.

Budgeting System Stage

The company eventually installs a budgeting system to improve its control of cash flow. Management estimates total sales for the coming year and the associated costs and cash flows. Department managers prepare budgets for their departments. These budgets are financial and do not require the kind of thought that goes into real planning. Budgets should not be confused with full-scale plans.

Annual Planning Stage

Management eventually recognizes the advantages of developing annual plans. It adopts one of three possible approaches to planning.

In the first approach, *top-down planning,* top management sets goals and plans for all the lower levels of management. This model is used in military organizations, where the generals prepare the plans and the troops carry them out. In business firms, this goes along with a Theory X view of employees—that is, they dislike responsibility and prefer to be directed.

In the opposite system, *bottom-up planning,* the various units of the organization prepare their own goals and plans based on the best they think they can do and then send them to higher levels of management for approval. This approach is based on Theory Y—that is, employees like responsibility and are more creative and committed if they participate in the planning.

Most companies use a third system known as *goals down–plans up planning.* Here top management looks at the company's opportunities and requirements and sets corporate goals for the year. The various units of the company are responsible for developing plans to help the company reach these goals. These plans, when approved by top management, become the official annual plan. A typical example is afforded by the Celanese Company:

> The annual planning process starts in late August, with top management receiving marketing research reports and sending out a guidance letter stating overall volume and profit goals. During September and October, product planning managers develop overall marketing plans in consultation with the field sales manager and the marketing vice president. In the middle of October, the marketing vice president reviews and approves the plans and submits them to the president for final approval. In the meantime, the field sales manager works with his regional sales managers and salesmen to develop field sales plans. Finally, in the fourth week in October, the controller prepares an operating budget; it goes, in early November, to top management for final approval. Thus, three months after the planning process started, a completed plan and budget are ready to be put into operation.[3]

Long-Range Planning Stage

Management realizes that a long-range plan should be prepared first and that the annual plan should be a detailed version of the first year of the long-range plan. For example, managers at the American Hospital Supply Company prepare a five-year plan for each product early in the year and an annual plan later in the year. The five-year plan is reworked each year (called *rolling planning*) because the environment changes and the long-run planning assumptions need to be reviewed.

Strategic Planning Stage

Eventually the company's managers realize that most of their planning deals only with current businesses and how to keep them going, and that they should also plan which businesses the company should stay in and which new ones it should pursue. The environment is full of surprises, and management must design the company to withstand shocks. Strategic planning involves adapting the firm to take advantage of opportunities in its constantly changing environment.

STRATEGIC PLANNING

Strategic planning sets the stage for the rest of the planning in the firm, so we will discuss it first. We define it as follows:

> **Strategic planning** is the managerial process of developing and maintaining a strategic fit between the organizations' goals and capabilities and its changing marketing opportunities. It relies on developing a clear company mission, supporting objectives and goals, a sound business portfolio, and coordinated functional strategies.

The steps in the strategic planning process are illustrated in Figure 3-1. At the corporate level, the company first defines its overall purpose and mission. This mission is then turned into a detailed set of supporting objectives that guide the whole enterprise. Next, headquarters decides what portfolio of businesses and products is best for the company, and how much resource support to give each business unit or product. Each business unit, and each product level within a business unit, must in turn develop more detailed marketing and other functional plans that support the companywide plan. Thus marketing planning occurs at the business unit, product, and market levels. It supports corporate strategic planning and involves more detailed planning for specific marketing opportunities. We discuss each of the strategic planning steps in more detail below.

Defining the Company Mission An organization exists to accomplish something in the larger environment. Its specific purpose or mission is usually clear at the beginning. Over time, its mission may become unclear as the organization grows and adds new products and markets. Or the mission may remain clear, but some managers may no longer be interested in it. Or the mission may remain clear, but may no longer be appropriate to the new conditions in the environment.

FIGURE 3-1
Steps in Strategic Planning

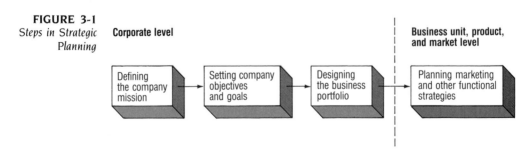

58   Two   *Organizing the Marketing Planning Process*

When management senses that the organization is drifting, it must renew its search for purpose. It is time to ask:[4] *What is our business? Who is the customer? What is value to the customer? What will our business be? What should our business be?* These simple-sounding questions are among the most difficult the company will ever have to answer. Successful companies continuously raise these questions and answer them thoughtfully and thoroughly.

Many organizations develop formal *mission statements*. A well-worked-out mission statement provides corporate personnel with a shared sense of opportunity, direction, significance, and achievement. The company mission statement acts as an "invisible hand" that guides widely dispersed employees so that they can work independently and yet collectively toward realizing the organization's potential.

Writing a formal company mission statement is not easy. Some organizations will spend a year or two trying to prepare a satisfactory statement about their firm's purpose. In the process they will discover a lot about themselves and their potential opportunities.

The mission statement should define the *business domain(s)* in which the organization will operate. Business domains can be defined in terms of *products, technologies, customer groups, customer needs,* or some combination. Companies have traditionally defined their business domains in product terms, such as "We manufacture video games," or in technological terms, such as "We are a chemical-processing firm." Some years ago, Theodore Levitt proposed that market definitions of a business are superior to product or technological definitions.[5] He argued that a business must be viewed as a *customer-satisfying* process, not a *goods-producing* process. Products and technologies eventually become obsolete, whereas basic market needs may endure forever. A market-oriented mission statement defines the business in terms of serving particular customer groups or needs. Consider these examples:

> In the early 1980s, consumers began to tire of video games. In 1983 alone, industry losses totaled over $1.5 billion. Many companies which had defined themselves as "video game producers" fell on hard times or withdrew from the market. But Bally Manufacturing, a leader in video arcade games, had defined its business as "leisure and entertainment." Guided by this definition it had diversified its portfolio to include Health and Tennis Corporation of America (a chain of health clubs) and Six Flags Corporation (entertainment parks). When the crunch hit the video games industry, the impact on Bally was minimized by the fact that video games generated less than 50% of sales.[6]

> In 1978, Sperry Rand Corporation was drifting. Its businesses included consumer appliances, hydraulic equipment, farm implements, defense electronic systems, and computers. Management then redefined Sperry as "a computer company plus." As a result, it shed its consumer appliance and hydraulic equipment businesses, cut back its emphasis on farm equipment, and increased its investments in electronic systems and computers. Six years later, Sperry was enjoying strong earnings increases and looking for acquisitions in more attractive markets such as automation equipment and robotics.[7]

In developing a market-oriented statement of mission, management should avoid making its mission too narrow or too broad. A lead pencil manufacturer that says it is in the business of making communication equipment is stating its mission too broadly. A useful approach is to move from the current product to higher levels of abstraction and then decide on the most feasible level of abstraction available to the company. Each broadening step suggests new opportunities but may also lead the company into unrealistic ventures beyond its capabilities.

A company mission statement should be motivating. Employees like to feel that their work is significant and that they are making a contribution to people's lives. If the Wrigley Company says that its mission is "to sell more gum," or "to make more money," or "to be the market leader," these are not very inspiring. Sales, profits, and market leadership should be the result of the company's successful pursuit of its mission, not the mission itself. The mission should be stated, if possible, as some good to accomplish outside the firm.

Many mission statements are written for public relations purposes and lack specific guidelines that will enable management to choose among courses of action. The statement "We want to be the leading company in this industry producing the highest-quality products with the widest distribution and the highest service at the lowest possible prices" sounds good but is full of contradictions. It will not help the company make tough decisions.

Setting Company Objectives and Goals The company's mission needs to be turned into a detailed set of supporting objectives for each level of management. Each manager should have objectives and be responsible for their accomplishment. This system is known as *management by objectives*.

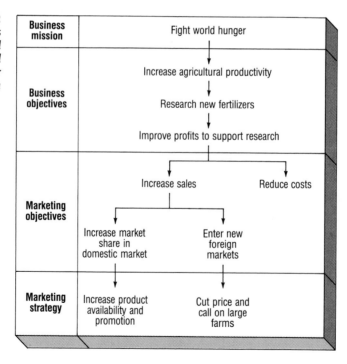

FIGURE 3-2
Hierarchy of Objectives for the International Minerals and Chemical Corporation, Fertilizer Division

As an illustration, the International Minerals and Chemical Corporation is in several businesses, including the fertilizer business. The fertilizer division does not say that its mission is to produce fertilizer. Instead, it says that its mission is "to fight world hunger." This mission leads to a hierarchy of objectives (see Figure 3-2). The mission to fight world hunger leads to the company objective of increasing agricultural productivity. Agricultural productivity can be increased by researching new fertilizers that promise higher yields. But research is expensive and requires improved profits to plow back into research programs. So a major objective becomes "profit improvement."

Profits can be improved by increasing the sales of current products, reducing current costs, or both. Sales can be increased by increasing the company's market share in the domestic market and entering new foreign markets. These become the company's current marketing objectives.

Marketing strategies must be developed to support these marketing objectives. To increase its domestic market share, the company will increase its product's availability and promotion. To enter new foreign markets, the company will cut prices and call on large farms. These are the broad marketing strategies.

Each marketing strategy would have to be spelled out in greater detail. For example, increasing the product's promotion will call for more salespeople and advertising, both of which will have to be spelled out. In this way the firm's mission is translated into a specific set of objectives for the current period. The objectives should be turned into specific quantitative goals where possible. The objective "increase our market share" is not as satisfactory as "increase our market share to 15 percent by the end of the second year." Managers use the term *goals* to describe objectives that have been made specific with respect to magnitude and time. Turning objectives into goals makes it easier to plan and control.

Designing the Business Portfolio

Guided by the company's mission statement and objectives, management must now decide what collection of businesses and products—what *business portfolio*—will best fit the company's strengths and weaknesses to opportunities in its environment. It must (1) analyze the current business portfolio and decide which businesses should receive more or less emphasis and resources, and (2) develop growth strategies for adding new products or businesses to the portfolio.

Analyzing the Current Business Portfolio

The major tool in strategic planning is *business portfolio analysis,* whereby management evaluates the businesses making up the company. The company will want to put strong resources into its more profitable businesses and phase down or withdraw from its weaker businesses. It can keep its portfolio of businesses up to date by strengthening or adding growing businesses and withdrawing from declining businesses.

Management's first step is to identify the key businesses making up the company. These can be called the strategic business units (SBUs). An SBU ideally has the following characteristics: (1) it is a single business; (2) it has a distinct mission; (3) it has its own competitors; (4) it has a responsible manager; (5) it controls certain resources; (6) it can benefit from strategic planning; and (7) it can be planned independently of the other businesses. An SBU can be one or more company divisions, a product line within a division, or sometimes a single product or brand.

Defining SBUs can be very difficult. In a large corporation, should SBUs be defined at the level of companies, divisions, product lines, or specific brands? At Dart & Kraft, is the U.S. Retail Food Division an SBU or is the Miracle Whip brand an SBU? Many companies use a hierarchy of portfolios. For example, General Electric has a five-level portfolio structure—individual products combine to make up product line portfolios, which combine to form market segment portfolios, which make up SBUs, which are combined into business sector portfolios. The corporate portfolio includes all lower-level portfolios. Thus, defining basic business units for portfolio analysis is often a complex task.

The next step calls for management to assess the attractiveness of its various SBUs in order to decide how much support each deserves. In some companies, this is done informally. Management recognizes that the company is a portfolio of different businesses or products and uses judgment to decide how each SBU should contribute to overall corporate performance and how much investment each should receive. Other companies use formal, structured portfolio planning models—customized models developed specifically for the company or standard models developed by others and adapted to the needs of the company.

The purpose of strategic planning is to find ways in which the company can best use its strengths to take advantage of attractive opportunities in the environment. So most standard portfolio analysis approaches use a matrix that assesses SBUs on two important dimensions—the attractiveness of the SBU's market or industry and the strength of the SBU's position in that market or industry. The best-known of these matrix portfolio planning approaches are those of the Boston Consulting Group and the General Electric Company.[8]

BOSTON CONSULTING GROUP APPROACH. The Boston Consulting Group (BCG), a leading management consulting firm, developed an approach in which a company classifies all its SBUs in the growth-share matrix shown in Figure 3-3. The vertical axis, *market growth rate,* refers to the annual growth rate of the market in which the product is sold and provides a measure of market attractiveness. In the figure, the market growth rate goes from a low of 0 percent to a high of 20 percent, although a larger range could be shown. Market growth is arbitrarily divided into high and low growth by a 10 percent growth line.

The horizontal axis, *relative market share,* refers to the SBU's market share relative to that of the largest competitor. It serves as a measure of company strength in the market. A relative market share of 0.1 means that the company's SBU stands at 10 percent of the leader's share; and 10 means that the company's SBU is the leader and has ten times the sales of the next-strongest company in the market. Relative market share is divided into high and low share, using 1.0 as the dividing line. Relative market share is drawn in log scale.

By dividing the growth-share matrix in the way indicated, four types of SBUs can be distinguished.

FIGURE 3-3
The BCG Growth-Share Matrix

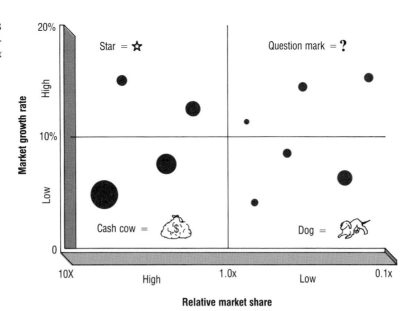

- *Stars.* Stars are high-growth, high-share SBUs. They are typically cash-using SBUs because cash is necessary to finance their rapid growth. Eventually their growth will slow down, and they will turn into cash cows and become major cash generators supporting other SBUs.
- *Cash cows.* Cash cows are low-growth, high-share SBUs. They produce a lot of cash that the company uses to pay its bills and support other SBUs that are cash using.
- *Question marks.* Question marks are low-share SBUs in high-growth markets. They require a lot of cash to maintain their share, let alone increase it. Management has to think hard about which question marks it should try to build into stars and which should be phased down or out.
- *Dogs.* Dogs are low-growth, low-share SBUs. They may generate enough cash to maintain themselves, but do not promise to be a large source of cash.

The ten circles in the growth-share matrix represent the company's ten current SBUs. The company has two stars, two cash cows, three question marks, and three dogs. The areas of the circles are proportional to the SBU's dollar sales. This company is in fair shape, although not in good shape. Fortunately it has two good-sized cash cows whose cash throw-off helps finance the company's question marks, stars, and dogs. The company should consider taking some decisive action concerning its dogs and its question marks. The picture would be worse if the company had no stars, or had too many dogs, or had only one weak cash cow.

Having arrived at this picture, the task of company portfolio planning is to determine what role to assign each SBU in the future. Four alternative objectives can be pursued:

- *Build.* Here the objective is to increase the SBU's market shares, even forgoing short-term earnings to achieve this objective. "Building" is appropriate for question marks whose share has to grow if they are to become stars.

- *Hold.* Here the objective is to preserve the SBU's market share. This objective is appropriate for strong cash cows if they are to continue to yield a large positive cash flow.
- *Harvest.* Here the objective is to increase the SBU's short-term cash flow regardless of the long-term effect. This strategy is appropriate for weak cash cows whose future is dim and from whom more cash flow is needed. It can also be used with question marks and dogs.
- *Divest.* Here the objective is to sell or liquidate the business because resources can be better used elsewhere. This is appropriate for dogs and for question marks that the company cannot finance.

As time passes, SBUs change their position in the growth-share matrix. Each SBU has a life (see Chapter 12). Many SBUs start out as question marks, move into the star category if they succeed, later become cash cows as market growth falls, and finally turn into dogs toward the end of their life cycle. The company needs to add new products and ventures continuously so that some of them will move up to star status and eventually become cash cows to help finance the other SBUs.

GENERAL ELECTRIC APPROACH.   General Electric introduced a comprehensive portfolio planning tool called a *strategic business-planning grid* (see Figure 3-4). It is similar to the BCG approach in that it uses a matrix with two dimensions—one representing industry attractiveness and one representing company strength in the industry. The best businesses are those located in highly attractive industries where the particular company has high business strength.

In Figure 3-4 *industry attractiveness* is shown on the vertical axis. In the GE approach, many factors besides market growth rate are considered. Industry attractiveness is an index made up of such factors as these:

- *Market size.* Large markets are more attractive than small markets.
- *Market growth rate.* High-growth markets are more attractive than low-growth markets.
- *Profit margin.* High profit margin industries are more attractive than low profit margin industries.
- *Competitive intensity.* Industries with many strong competitors are less attractive than industries with a few weak competitors.

FIGURE 3-4
General Electric's Strategic Business-Planning Grid

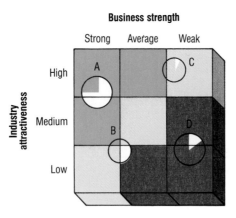

- *Cyclicality.* Industries that are less affected by the business cycle are more attractive than highly cyclical industries.

- *Seasonality.* Industries with less seasonal movement are more attractive than highly seasonal industries.

- *Scale economies.* Industries where unit costs fall with large plant size and distribution are more attractive than constant cost industries.

- *Learning curve.* Industries where unit costs fall as management accumulates experience in production and distribution are more attractive than industries where management has reached the limit of its learning.

Each of these factors is rated and combined in an index of industry attractiveness. For our purposes, an industry's attractiveness will be described as high, medium, or low.

In Figure 3-4 *business strength* is shown on the horizontal axis. Again, the GE approach uses an index rather than simply a measure of relative market share. The business strength index includes factors such as these:

- *Relative market share.* The higher the company's relative market share, the greater its business strength.

- *Price competitiveness.* The higher the company's price competitiveness, the greater its business strength.

- *Product quality.* The higher the company's product quality competitiveness, the greater its business strength.

- *Knowledge of customer/market.* The deeper the company's knowledge of customers, the greater its business strength.

- *Sales effectiveness.* The greater the company's sales effectiveness, the greater its business strength.

- *Geography.* The greater the company's geographic advantages in the market, the greater its business strength.

These factors are rated and combined in an index of business strength. Business strength can be described as strong, average, or weak.

The grid is divided into three zones. The three cells at the upper left show strong SBUs in which the company should "invest and grow." The diagonal cells stretching from the lower left to the upper right indicate SBUs that are medium in overall attractiveness. The company should maintain its level of investment in these SBUs. The three cells at the lower right indicate SBUs that are low in overall attractiveness. The company should give serious thought to harvesting or divesting them.

The circles represent four SBUs in the company. The areas of the circles are proportional to the sizes of the industries in which these SBUs compete, while the pie slices within the circles represent each SBU's market share. Thus circle A represents a company SBU with a 75 percent market share in a good-sized industry that is highly attractive and in which the company has strong business strength. Circle B represents an SBU in which the company has a 50 percent market share, but the industry is not very attractive. Circles C and D represent two other company SBUs in which the company has small market shares and not much business strength. Altogether, the company should build A, maintain B, and make some basic decision on what to do with C and D.

Management would also plot the projected positions of the SBUs with and without changes in strategies. By comparing current and projected business grids, management can identify the major strategic issues and opportunities it faces.[9]

PROBLEMS WITH MATRIX APPROACHES. The BCG, GE, and other formula-matrix approaches developed in the 1970s revolutionized strategic planning. But such approaches have limitations. They can be difficult, time-consuming, and costly to implement. Management may find it difficult to define SBUs or to decide what kinds of measures are best for the company strengths and industry effectiveness dimensions of the portfolio matrix. Also, these approaches focus on classifying current businesses, but provide little specific advice for planning an optimal portfolio—management must still use judgment to set the business objective for each SBU, to decide what resources each will be given, and to figure out which new businesses should be added to the portfolio.

The formula-matrix approaches to portfolio planning are not appropriate for every company. They can lead the company to place too much emphasis on market-share growth or growth through entry into attractive new markets. Using these approaches, many companies have ignored their current businesses and plunged into unrelated and new high-growth markets, with disastrous results.

> These overly quantitative techniques caused companies to place a great deal of emphasis on market-share growth. As a result, companies were devoting too much time to corporate portfolio planning and too little to hammering out strategies to turn sick operations into healthy ones or to ensure that a strong business remained strong. In too many instances, strategic planning degenerated into acquiring growth businesses that the buyers did not know how to manage and selling or milking to death mature ones.[10]

A company cannot rely blindly on formula approaches when analyzing and designing its business portfolio. Many companies have abandoned these formula methods in favor of more customized strategic planning approaches better suited to their specific situations. Most large, diversified companies use some form of strategic planning analysis.[11] Though such analysis is no cure-all for developing strategy, it can help management to better understand the company's overall competitive position, to assess how each business or product contributes, to better assign resources to its businesses, and to better orient the company for future success.

Developing Growth Strategies

Beyond evaluating current businesses, designing the business portfolio involves determining future businesses and business directions the company should consider. We will illustrate company growth planning with the following example:

> Modern Publishing Company issues a leading health magazine that has a monthly circulation of three hundred thousand copies. The company's marketing environment is changing rapidly in terms of consumer interests, new competitors, and rising publishing costs. It is attempting to formulate a systematic plan for company growth during the next decade.

TABLE 3-1		
Major Classes of Growth Opportunities		

I. INTENSIVE GROWTH	II. INTEGRATIVE GROWTH	III. DIVERSIFICATION GROWTH
A. Market penetration	A. Backward integration	A. Concentric diversification
B. Market development	B. Forward integration	B. Horizontal diversification
C. Product development	C. Horizontal integration	C. Conglomerate diversification

A company can develop a growth strategy by moving through three levels of analysis. The first level identifies opportunities available to the company within its current scope of operations (*intensive growth opportunities*). The second level identifies opportunities to integrate with other parts of the marketing system in the industry (*integrative growth opportunities*). The third level identifies opportunities lying outside the industry (*diversification growth opportunities*). Table 3-1 lists specific opportunities within each broad class.

INTENSIVE GROWTH. Intensive growth makes sense if the company has not fully exploited the opportunities in its current products and markets. Ansoff has proposed a useful device called a *product/market expansion grid* for identifying intensive growth opportunities.[12] This grid, shown earlier in Chapter 2, points out three major types of intensive growth opportunities:

1. *Market penetration. The company seeks increased sales for its current products in its current markets through more aggressive marketing effort.* This includes three possibilities:
   a. Modern can encourage current subscribers to increase their *purchase quantity* by giving gift subscriptions to friends.
   b. Modern can try to *attract competitor's customers* by offering lower subscription rates or promoting its magazine as being superior to other health magazines.
   c. Modern can try to *convert new prospects* who do not now read health magazines but have the same profile as current readers.

2. *Market development. The company seeks increased sales by taking its current products into new markets.* This includes three possibilities:
   a. Modern can distribute its magazine in *new geographical markets*—regional, national, or international—where it has not been available.
   b. Modern can make the magazine attractive to new consumer segments by developing appropriate features.
   c. Modern can try to sell its magazine to new institutional segments, such as hospitals, physicians' offices, and health clubs.

3. *Product development. The company seeks increased sales by developing closely related new or improved products for its current markets.* This includes three possibilities:
   a. Modern can develop *new and different magazines* that will appeal to the readers of its health magazine.
   b. Modern can create different *regional versions* of its health magazine.
   c. Modern can develop a *cassette version* of its monthly magazine for markets that prefer listening to reading.

INTEGRATIVE GROWTH. Integrative growth makes sense if the industry is strong or the company can gain by moving backward, forward, or horizontally in the industry. Three possibilities exist:

1. *Backward integration. The company seeks ownership or increased control of its supply systems.* Modern might buy a paper supply company or a printing company to increase its control over supplies.

2. *Forward integration. The company seeks ownership or increased control of its distribution systems.* Modern might see an advantage in buying some magazine wholesaler businesses or subscription agencies.

3. *Horizontal integration. The company seeks ownership or increased control of some of its competitors.* Modern might buy out other health magazines.

DIVERSIFICATION GROWTH. Diversification growth makes sense if the industry does not present much opportunity for further company growth, or if the opportunities outside the industry are superior. Diversification does not mean that the company should take just any opportunity. The company would identify fields that make use of its distinctive competences or help it overcome particular weaknesses. There are three types of diversification opportunity:

1. *Concentric diversification. The company adds new products that have technological or marketing synergies with the existing product line; these products will normally appeal to new classes of customers.* Modern, for example, might start a paperback division to take advantage of its network of magazine distributors.

2. *Horizontal diversification. The company adds new products that could appeal to its current customers though unrelated to its current product line.* For example, Modern might open up health clubs in the hope that readers of its health magazine would become club members.

3. *Conglomerate diversification. The company adds new products that have no relationship to its current technology, products, or markets; these products will normally appeal to new classes of customers.* Modern might want to enter new business areas, such as personal computers, real estate office franchising, or fast-food service.

Planning Functional Strategies

The company's strategic plan establishes the kinds of businesses the company will be in and its objectives for each SBU. Within the SBUs, more detailed planning must now take place. Each SBU must figure out what role each of its functional departments—marketing, finance, accounting, purchasing, manufacturing, personnel, and others—will play in accomplishing the objectives assigned by the company's strategic plan.

Each department specializes in dealing with different publics to obtain the inputs the business needs to accomplish its objectives—resources such as cash, labor, raw materials, research ideas, manufacturing processes, and others. For example, marketing generates revenues by negotiating exchanges with consumers. Finance arranges exchanges with lenders and stockholders to obtain cash. Thus the marketing and finance departments must work together to obtain needed funds for the business. Similarly, the personnel department supplies labor, and purchasing obtains materials needed for operations and manufacturing.

Each department plays an important role in the strategic planning process. The departments provide information about financial strategies and capabilities as inputs for strategic planning. Then management in each SBU prepares a plan that states the specific role each department will play and coordinates all the functional activities to accomplish the objectives specified for the SBU in the strategic plan.

Diversification growth: When video games sales fell, Bally diversified into health clubs and entertainment parks, both consistent with the company's leisure and entertainment mission. *Courtesy of Bally Manufacturing Corp.*

Marketing's Role in Strategic Planning

There is much overlap between overall company strategy and marketing strategy. Marketing assesses consumer needs and the company's ability to gain a competitive advantage in important markets, and these considerations guide the corporate mission and objectives. Most company strategy planning deals with marketing variables—market share, market development, growth—and it is sometimes hard to separate strategic planning from marketing planning. In fact, in some companies, strategic planning is called "strategic marketing planning."

Marketing plays a key role in developing the company's strategic plan in several ways. First, marketing provides a perspective that guides strategic planning—company strategy should revolve around obtaining competitive advantage with important groups of consumers. Second, marketing provides inputs to strategic planners by helping to identify attractive market opportunities and to assess the firm's potential for gaining competitive advantage. Finally, within individual SBUs, the marketing function designs strategies for achieving SBU objectives.[13]

Within each SBU, marketing management must figure out the best way it can contribute to achieving strategic objectives. Marketing managers in certain SBUs will find that their objective is not necessarily to build sales; their job may be to maintain the existing volume with fewer marketing dollars, or actually to reduce demand. *Thus the task of marketing management is to manage demand to the appropriate level decided by the strategic planning done at headquarters.* Marketing contributes to assessing each SBU's potential, but once the SBU's objective is set, marketing's task is to carry it out efficiently and profitably.

Marketing and the Other Business Functions

There is much confusion about marketing's importance in the firm. In some firms it is just another function. All functions count in influencing corporate strategy, and none takes leadership. This view is illustrated in Figure 3-5A. If the company faces slow growth or a sales decline, marketing may become more important for the time being (see Figure 3-5B).

Some marketers claim that marketing is the central function of the firm. They quote Drucker's statement: "The aim of the business is to create customers." They say it is marketing's job to define the company's mission, products, and markets and to direct the other functions in the task of serving customers (see Figure 3-5C).

FIGURE 3-5
Alternative Views of Marketing's Role in the Company

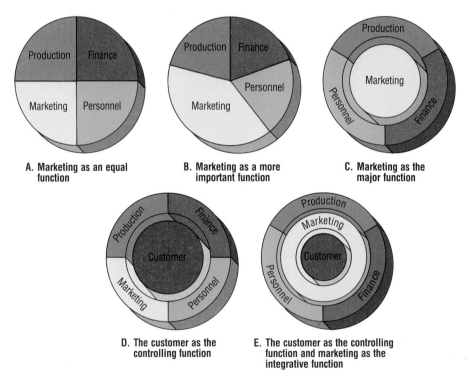

A. Marketing as an equal function

B. Marketing as a more important function

C. Marketing as the major function

D. The customer as the controlling function

E. The customer as the controlling function and marketing as the integrative function

Enlightened marketers prefer to put the customer at the center of the company. They argue for a customer orientation in which all functions work together to sense, serve, and satisfy the customer (see Figure 3-5D).

Finally, some marketers say that marketing still needs to occupy a central position in the firm if customers' needs are to be correctly interpreted and efficiently satisfied (see Figure 3-5E). These marketers argue that the assets of the firm have little value without customers. The key task of the firm is therefore to attract and hold customers. Customers are attracted through promises and held through satisfaction, and marketing's task is to define an appropriate promise and to ensure its effective delivery. But the actual satisfaction delivered to the customer is affected by the performance of the other departments, so marketing needs influence over these other departments if consumers are to be satisfied.

Interdepartmental Conflict

Each business function has a different perspective on which publics and activities are most important. Manufacturing focuses on suppliers and efficient production; finance is concerned with stockholders and sound investment; marketing emphasizes consumers and product, pricing, promotion, and distribution activities. In principle, all the functions should mesh harmoniously to achieve the firm's overall objectives. But in practice, departmental relations are often characterized by deep rivalries and misunderstandings. Some interdepartmental conflict stems from differences of opinion on what is in the best interests of the firm; some from real tradeoffs between departmental well-being and company well-being; and some from unfortunate departmental stereotypes and prejudices.

Under the marketing concept, it is desirable to coordinate all the different functions toward consumer satisfaction. The marketing department stresses the consumer's point of view. But other departments stress the importance of their own tasks, and they may resist bending their efforts to the will of the marketing department. Because departments tend to define company problems and goals from their own points of view, conflicts are inevitable. Table 3-2 summarizes the main point of view differences between marketing and other departments.

Marketing, in trying to mobilize the company's resources to develop customer satisfaction, often causes other departments to do a poorer job *in their terms.* Marketing department pressures can increase product design and material purchasing costs, disrupt production schedules, increase accounting costs, and create budget headaches. Yet the problem remains: Getting all departments to think "consumer," to look at their activities through the customer's eyes, and to put the consumer at the center of company activity.

Marketing management can best gain support for its goal of consumer satisfaction by working to understand the points of view and situations of the other functions. Marketing managers must work closely with other managers to develop a system of functional plans under which the different departments can work together to accomplish the company's overall strategic objectives.[14]

DEPARTMENT	EMPHASIS	MARKETING EMPHASIS
R&D	Basic research Intrinsic quality Functional features	Applied research Perceived quality Sales features
Engineering	Long design lead time Few models Standard components	Short design lead time Many models Custom components
Purchasing	Narrow product line Standard parts Price of material Economical lot sizes Purchasing at infrequent intervals	Broad product line Nonstandard parts Quality of material Large lot sizes to avoid stockouts Immediate purchasing for customer needs
Manufacturing	Long production lead time Long runs with few models No model changes Standard orders Ease of fabrication Average quality control	Short production lead time Short runs with many models Frequent model changes Custom orders Aesthetic appearance Tight quality control
Inventory	Fast-moving items, narrow product line Economical level of stock	Broad product line High level of stock
Finance	Strict rationales for spending Hard and fast budgets Pricing to cover costs	Intuitive arguments for spending Flexible budgets to meet changing needs Pricing to further market development
Accounting	Standard transactions Few reports	Special terms and discounts Many reports
Credit	Full financial disclosures by customers Low credit risks Tough credit terms Tough collection procedures	Minimum credit examination of customers Medium credit risks Easy credit terms Easy collection procedures

MARKETING PLANNING

The strategic plan defines the company's overall mission and sets objectives for each SBU. Within each SBU, a system of functional plans must be prepared—including marketing plans. If the SBU consists of several product lines, products, brands, and markets, plans must be written for each. Marketing plans might include product plans, brands plans, or market plans. We will now examine marketing plans and the steps involved in developing the marketing plan.

The Components of a Marketing Plan How does a marketing plan look? Our discussion will focus on product or brand plans. A product or brand plan should contain the following sections: executive summary, current marketing situation, threats and opportunities, objectives and issues, marketing strategies, action programs, budgets, and controls (see Figure 3-6).

FIGURE 3-6
*Components of
a Marketing Plan*

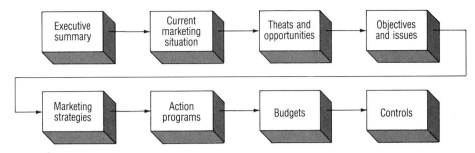

Executive Summary

The planning document should open with a short summary of the main goals and recommendations to be presented in the plan. Here is an abbreviated example:

> The 1986 Marketing Plan seeks a significant increase in company sales and profits over the preceding year. The sales target is $80 million, a planned 20 percent sales gain. This increase is deemed attainable because of the improved economic, competitive, and distribution picture. The target operating margin is $8 million, a 25 percent increase over last year. To achieve these goals, the sales promotion budget will be $1.6 million, or 2 percent of projected sales. The advertising budget will be $2.4 million, or 3 percent of projected sales. . . . [More detail follows]

The executive summary permits top management to quickly grasp the major thrust of the plan. A table of contents should follow the executive summary.

Current Marketing Situation

The first major section of the plan describes the target market and the company's position in it. The marketing planner provides information on the following topics:

- *Market description.* Here the served market is defined, including the major market segments. The size of the market (in units or dollars) is shown for several past years in total and by segment. Customer needs are reviewed, as well as factors in the marketing environment that may affect customer purchasing.
- *Product review.* Here the sales, prices, and gross margins are shown for the major products in the product line.
- *Competition.* Here the major competitors are identified and each of their strategies is described with respect to product quality, pricing, distribution, and promotion. The section also shows the market shares held by the company and each competitor.
- *Distribution.* Here recent sales trends and developments in the major distribution channels are described.

Threats and Opportunities

This section requires the manager to look ahead and visualize the major threats and opportunities facing the product. The purpose is to counter the managers' tendency to focus on current problems and fail to anticipate important developments that can have a significant impact on the firm. Managers should list as many threats and opportunities as they can imagine. Suppose the manager at a cigarette company comes up with the following list:

1. The U.S. Surgeon General is asking Congress to pass a law requiring that every cigarette brand include a skull and crossbones on the front of the package and the warning: "Scientific evidence shows that daily smoking shortens a person's life by an average of seven years."

2. An increasing number of public places are prohibiting smoking or are setting up separate sections for smokers and nonsmokers.

3. A new insect is attacking tobacco-growing areas, leading to the possibility of smaller crops in the future and larger price increases if some means cannot be found to control it.

4. The company's research lab is on the verge of finding a way to turn lettuce into benign tobacco. If successful, the new tobacco will be enjoyable and harmless.

5. Cigarette smoking is rapidly increasing in foreign markets, especially in developing nations.

Each item has implications for the cigarette business. The first three are *threats*. Not all threats warrant the same attention or concern. The manager should assess each threat according to its potential severity and its probability of occurrence. The results of assessing the three threats listed above are shown in Figure 3-7A. All three are high in potential severity, and two have a high probability of occurring.

The manager should concentrate on major threats (those in the high-severity–high-probability cell) and prepare contingency plans in advance. The manager should also keep a close watch on threats in the southwest and northeast cells, although contingency plans are not necessary. The manager can, for all practical purposes, ignore threats in the southeast cell.

The last two items in the list are *company marketing opportunities,* attractive arenas for marketing action where the company would enjoy a competitive advantage. The manager should assess each opportunity according to its potential attractiveness and the company's probability of success. The results of assessing the two opportunities are shown in Figure 3-7B. The manager will develop action plans for the opportunities falling in the northwest cell, monitor those in the southwest and northeast cells, and pay little or no attention to opportunities falling in the southeast cell.

FIGURE 3-7
Threats and Opportunities

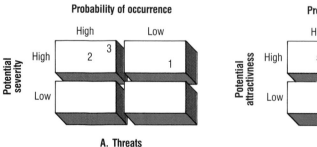

A. Threats

B. Opportunities

Objectives and Issues

Having studied the product's threats and opportunities, the manager can now set objectives and consider issues that will affect the attainment of these objectives. The objectives should be stated as goals the company would like to reach during the plan's term. For example, the manager might want to achieve a 15 percent market share, a 20 percent pretax profit on sales, and a 25 percent pretax profit on investment. Suppose the current market share is only 10 percent. This poses a key issue: How can market share be increased? The manager will want to consider the major issues involved in trying to increase market share.

Marketing Strategies

In this section, the manager outlines the broad marketing strategy or "game plan" for attaining the objectives. We define marketing strategy as follows:

> **Marketing strategy** is the marketing logic by which the business unit hopes to achieve its marketing objectives. Marketing strategy consists of specific strategies bearing on target markets, marketing mix, and marketing expenditure level.

TARGET MARKETS. Marketing strategy should spell out the market segments on which the company will focus. These segments differ in their preferences, responses to marketing effort, and profitability. The company would be smart to allocate its effort and energy to those market segments it can best serve from a competitive point of view. It should develop a marketing strategy for each targeted segment.

MARKETING MIX. The manager should outline specific strategies for such marketing mix elements as new products, field sales, advertising, sales promotion, prices, and distribution. The manager should explain how each strategy responds to the threats, opportunities, and key issues spelled out in earlier sections of the plan.

MARKETING EXPENDITURE LEVEL. The manager should also spell out the marketing budget that will be needed to carry out the various strategies. The manager knows that higher budgets will produce more sales, but is looking for the marketing budget that will produce the best profit picture.

Action Programs

The marketing strategies should be turned into specific action programs that answer the following questions: (1) *What* will be done? (2) *When* will it be done? (3) *Who* is responsible for doing it? and (4) *How much* will it cost? For example, the manager may want to intensify sales promotion as a key strategy for winning market share. A sales promotion action plan should be drawn up and should outline special offers and their dates, trade show participations, new point-of-purchase displays, and so on.

The various action plans can be tied together in a table, with twelve months (or fifty-two weeks) serving as columns and various marketing activities serving as rows. Dates show when activities or expenditures will be started, reviewed, and completed. The action plans are subject to change during the year as new problems and opportunities arise.

Budgets

The action plans allow the manager to formulate a supporting budget that is essentially a projected profit and loss statement. On the revenue side, it shows the forecasted number of units that would be sold and the average net realized price. On the expense side, it shows the cost of production, physical distribution, and marketing, broken down into finer categories. The difference is the projected profit. Higher management will review the budget and approve or modify it. Once approved, the budget is the basis for material procurement, production scheduling, manpower planning, and marketing operations.

Controls

The last section of the plan outlines the controls that will be used to monitor progress. Typically, goals and budgets are spelled out for each month or quarter. This means that higher management can review the results each period and spot businesses that are not attaining their goals. The managers of these businesses have to offer an explanation and indicate what corrective actions they will take.

Developing the Marketing Budget

We will now examine the task of constructing a marketing budget to attain a given level of sales and profits. We will first illustrate a common budget-setting approach and then describe certain improvements.

Target Profit Planning

Suppose John Smith, the ketchup product manager at Heinz, has to prepare his annual marketing plan. He will probably follow the procedure shown in Table 3-3 called *target profit planning.*

John Smith first estimates the total market for ketchup for the coming year. (We will focus on the household market.) An estimate can be formed by applying the recent growth rate of the market (6 percent) to this year's market size (23.6 million cases). This forecasts a market size of 25 million cases for next year. Smith then forecasts Heinz's sales based on the assumption that its past market share of 28 percent will continue. Thus Heinz's sales are forecasted at 7 million cases.

Next Smith sets a distributor price of $4.45 per case for the next year based mainly on expected increases in labor and material costs. Thus the planned sales revenue will be $31.15 million.

He then estimates next year's variable costs at $2.75 per case. This means that the contribution margin to cover fixed costs, profits, and marketing is $11.9 million. Suppose the company charges this brand with a fixed cost of $1 per case, or $7 million. This leaves a contribution margin of $4.9 million to cover profits and marketing.

John Smith now brings in the target profit goal. Suppose a profit level of $1.9 million will satisfy higher management. It is usually some increase, say 5 to 10

TABLE 3-3
Target Profit Plan

1. *Forecast of total market* This year's total market (23,600,000 cases) × recent growth rate (6%)	25,000,000 cases
2. *Forecast of market share*	28%
3. *Forecast of sales volume* (1 × 2)	7,000,000 cases
4. *Price to distributor*	$4.45 per case
5. *Estimate of sales revenue* (3 × 4)	$31,150,000
6. *Estimate of variable costs* Tomatoes and spices ($0.50) + bottles and caps ($1.00) + labor ($1.10) + physical distribution ($0.15)	$2.75 per case
7. *Estimate of contribution margin to cover fixed costs, profits, and marketing* ([4 − 6]3)	$11,900,000
8. *Estimate of fixed costs* Fixed charge $1 per case × 7 million cases	$7,000,000
9. *Estimate of contribution margin to cover profits and marketing* (7 − 8)	$4,900,000
10. *Estimate of target profit goal*	$1,900,000
11. *Amount available for marketing* (9 − 10)	$3,000,000
12. *Split of the marketing budget* Advertising Sales promotion Marketing research	$2,000,000 $ 900,000 $ 100,000

percent, over this year's profit. He then subtracts the target profit from what remains of the contribution margin to learn that $3 million is available for marketing.

In the final step, Smith splits the marketing budget into its mix elements, such as advertising, sales promotion, and marketing research. The split is normally in the same proportion as the preceding year's split. He decides to spend two-thirds of the money on advertising, almost one-third on sales promotion, and the remainder on marketing research.

Although this method produces a workable marketing plan and budget, several improvements are possible:

1. The product manager estimated market size and share by extrapolating past trends. He should consider changes in the marketing environment that would lead to a different demand forecast.

2. The product manager continued his past marketing strategy. But one of the reasons for the planning is to consider alternative marketing strategies and their potential impact on company sales and profits. He should not estimate the company's market share until after he develops his marketing strategy.

3. The product manager set next year's price largely to cover expected cost increases. Setting the price mainly on cost is not a market-oriented pricing method.

4. The product manager developed the marketing mix on "more-of-the-same" thinking rather than on figuring out each marketing element's potential contribution to the marketing objectives at this stage in the product's life cycle.

5. The product manager is preparing a "satisficing" plan, one that produces satisfactory profits. Instead, he should try to find the optimal profit plan.

Profit Optimization Planning

We now want to consider how to find the optimal profit plan. Profit optimization requires that the manager identify the quantitative relationship between sales volume and the various elements of the marketing mix. We will use the term *sales-response function* to describe the relationship between sales volume and one or more elements of the marketing mix.

> A **sales-response function** forecasts the likely sales volume during a specified time period associated with different possible levels of one or more marketing mix elements.

Figure 3-8 shows a hypothetical sales-response function. This function indicates that the more the company spends in a given period on marketing, the higher its sales are likely to be. The particular function is S-shaped, although other shapes are possible. The S-shaped function says that low levels of marketing expenditure are not likely to produce much sales. Too few buyers will be reached, or reached effectively, by the company's marketing. Higher levels of marketing expenditure per period will produce much higher levels of sales. Very high expenditures per period, however, might not add much more sales and would represent "marketing overkill."

The occurrence of eventually diminishing returns to increases in marketing expenditures is plausible for the following reasons. First, there is an upper limit to the total potential demand for any product. The easier sales prospects buy almost immediately, leaving the more difficult sales prospects. As the upper limit is approached, it becomes increasingly expensive to attract the remaining buyers. Second, as a company steps up its marketing effort, its competitors are likely to do the same, with the result that each company experiences increasing sales resistance. And third, if sales were to increase at an increasing rate throughout, natural monopolies would result. A single firm would take over each industry. Yet this is contrary to what we observe.

FIGURE 3-8
Sales-Response Function

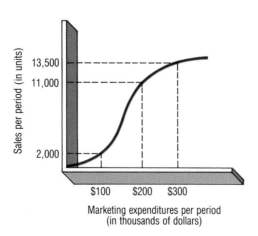

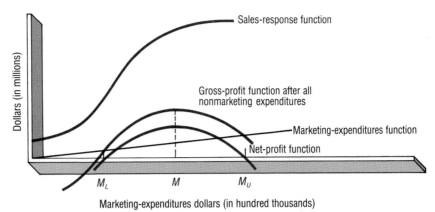

Dollars (in millions)

Sales-response function

Gross-profit function after all
nonmarketing expenditures

Marketing-expenditures function

Net-profit function

M_L M M_U

Marketing-expenditures dollars (in hundred thousands)

How can marketing managers estimate the sales-response functions that apply to their businesses? Three methods are available. The first is the *statistical method,* where the manager gathers data on past sales and levels of marketing mix variables and estimates the sales-response functions through statistical techniques.[15] The second is the *experimental method,* which calls for varying the marketing expenditure and mix levels in matched samples of geographical or other units and noting the resulting sales volume.[16] The third is the *judgmental method,* where experts are asked to make intelligent guesses about the needed relationships.[17]

Once the sales-response functions have been estimated, how are they used in profit optimization? Graphically, we introduce some further curves to find the point of optimal marketing expenditure. The analysis is shown in Figure 3-9. The key function that we start with is the sales-response function. It resembles the S-shaped sales-response function in Figure 3-8, except for two differences. First, sales response is expressed in terms of sales dollars instead of sales units so that we can find the profit-maximizing marketing expenditure. Second, the sales-response function is shown as starting above zero sales on the argument that some sales might take place even in the absence of marketing expenditures.

To find the optimal marketing expenditure, the marketing manager subtracts all nonmarketing costs from the *sales-response function* to derive the *gross-profit function.* Next, the marketing-expenditure function is represented as a straight line starting at the origin and rising at the rate of one dollar of marketing expenditure on the horizontal axis for every ten dollars on the vertical axis. The marketing-expenditure function is then subtracted from the *gross-profit curve* to derive the *net-profit curve.* The net-profit curve shows positive net profits with marketing expenditures between M_L and M_U, which could be defined as the rational range of marketing expenditure. The net-profit curve reaches a maximum of M. Therefore the marketing expenditure that would maximize net profit is $\$M$.

The graphic solution can also be carried out numerically or algebraically; indeed it has to be if sales volume is a function of more than one marketing mix variable.[18]

Eastern isn't a new airline. But we sure look like one.

Innovation is Eastern's way of meeting the challenge of deregulation. And innovation is turning Eastern into a whole new airline. One that does a better job for you.

Innovation No. 1: Owners serving customers. Better.

37,000 Eastern employees now own stock in the airline. Each has made a personal commitment to giving you better service.

Don't be surprised when Eastern people move faster, serve you better, smile a bit more. Because now they're working for *themselves* as well as you. Who's going to give you better service than the owners?

Eastern now serves 125 cities in 23 countries.

Innovation No. 2: Our new routes bring you new convenience.

If you're used to thinking of Eastern as a North-South airline, strong on vacations, Florida, and the Caribbean—well, you're only partly right. The *new* Eastern is a major East-West airline—business travelers are finding that our new hub in Kansas City makes cross-country flying easier. And travelers to Latin America will be pleased to learn that Eastern is now the *number-one* airline to South America.

Innovation No. 3: A new fleet helps us raise your comfort and hold down your costs.

New planes put Eastern ahead—planes like the A-300, a super-comfortable wide-body (Eastern was the first to fly it), and the advanced new 757, the most fuel-efficient plane flying. It's all part of Eastern's plan to give you better *value*. When you fly Eastern, you don't have to give up comfort to get efficiency. You get both. That's *value*.

Innovation No. 4: New bonuses for Eastern customers. New ways to earn awards.

Now no one makes flying pay off better or easier than Eastern. Eastern has made cooperative arrangements with other airlines, so that the new Eastern Frequent Traveler Bonus Program gives you a fast payoff and a unique choice of U.S. and international destinations.

Only Eastern has a Senior Citizens "Passport Program." Ask your Accredited Travel Agent about it. It may be the travel bonus of the decade!

Innovation No. 5: The Eastern Commitment.

Eastern people will keep working to make a trip on our airline the best value in airline travel. Our fares will be competitive, but we *won't* cut corners on equipment, maintenance, comfort, or personal service—because we don't think these things are "frills."

But find out for yourself. The next time you see a cheap fare from a cut-rate airline, call *us. Compare the fare.* We want you to see how competitive we are.

The commitment from our 37,000 owners is plain and simple: At Eastern, we will earn our wings every day by serving you better on every flight.

EASTERN
We earn our wings every day

© 1984 Eastern Air Lines, Inc.

Eastern recognizes that *all* of its people must work together to deliver air service quality to Eastern's customers. *Courtesy of Eastern Airlines.*

Some Conclusions on Marketing Planning In this chapter we have examined how companies develop strategic plans to take advantage of market opportunities, and how marketing managers design marketing plans to help the company achieve its strategic objectives. We discuss marketing planning early in the book to provide an overview of marketing's role in the company, and to introduce all the factors marketers must consider when designing effective marketing programs. This does not mean that planning is always the first marketing management activity, or that planning ends here and marketers move on to other activities. Planning is closely related to all the other marketing management activities—analysis, implementation, and control. Marketing managers must plan what to analyze and when, and marketing analysis in turn provides information for effective planning. Strategy and program implementation must be carefully planned, and control provides feedback for adjusting current strategies and planning new ones. Thus planning is a continuous process that relates to all phases of marketing management.

In Chapters 4 through 19, we will take a closer look at major marketing activities and decision areas—marketing research and analyzing marketing opportunities, selecting target markets, and developing the marketing mix. Then, in Chapters 20 and 21, we will discuss how marketing managers tie all these activities and decisions together under broad competitive marketing strategies, and how companies organize to implement and control their strategies and programs.

■ *Summary*

Not all companies use formal planning or use it well. Yet formal planning offers several benefits, including systematic thinking, better coordination of company efforts, sharper objectives, and improved performance measurement, all of which can lead to improved sales and profits. Planning in companies seems to move through several stages, including the unplanned stage, the budgeting system stage, the annual planning stage, the long-range planning stage, and the strategic planning stage.

Strategic planning sets the stage for the rest of company planning. The strategic planning process consists of developing the company's mission, objectives and goals, business portfolio, and functional plans.

Developing a sound mission statement is a challenging undertaking. The mission statement should be market-oriented, feasible, motivating, and specific if it is to direct the firm to its best opportunities. The mission statement then leads to supporting objectives and goals, in a system known as *management by objectives*.

From here, strategic planning calls for analyzing the company's business portfolio and deciding which businesses should receive more or less emphasis and resources. The company might use a formula-matrix method such as the BCG growth-share matrix or the GE strategic business grid. But most companies are now designing more customized portfolio planning approaches that better suit their unique situations.

To achieve company growth, strategic planning calls for identifying market opportunities where the company would enjoy a differential advantage over competitors.

The company can identify relevant opportunities by considering intensive growth opportunities within its present product/market scope (market penetration, market development, and product development), integrative growth opportunities within its industry (backward, forward, and horizontal integration), and diversification growth opportunities outside its industry (concentric, horizontal, and conglomerate diversification).

Each of the company's functional departments provides inputs for strategic planning. Once strategic objectives have been defined, management within each business must prepare a set of functional plans that coordinates the activities of the marketing, finance, manufacturing, and other departments. Each department has a different idea about which objectives and activities are most important. The marketing department stresses the consumer's point of view. Other functions stress different things, and this generates interdepartmental conflict.

Marketing managers must understand the points of view of the other functions and work with other functional managers to develop a system of plans that will best accomplish the firm's overall strategic objectives.

Each business has to prepare marketing plans for its products, brands, and markets. The main components of a marketing plan are: executive summary, current marketing situation, threats and opportunities, objectives and issues, marketing strategies, action programs, budgets, and controls. The marketing budget section of the plan can be developed either by setting a target profit goal or by using sales-response functions to identify the profit-optimizing marketing plan.

■ Questions for Discussion

1. Scott Paper company has faced increased competition from P&G, Georgia Pacific, Fort Howard Paper, and unbranded generics in the past decade, losing market share and being forced into developing the first strategic plan in the company's 101-year history. Discuss what you believe such a strategic plan may include.

2. Why is strategic planning such an important process for organizations moving into the 1990s?

3. Develop a mission statement for Capitol Records. Also, discuss each of the essential characteristics of this statement for Capitol.

4. Briefly describe the four types of strategic business units (SBUs) developed by the Boston Consulting Group. Classify Ford's current automobile models in each of the four categories. Defend your choices.

5. How do the major classes of growth opportunities differ? Into which class or classes would you

place the following companies—McDonald's, IBM, and Tenneco?

6. Do most businesses historically begin their marketing planning by engaging in the strategic planning process? If not, what usually happens?

7. A recently hired member of Kellogg's marketing staff was helping to put together the marketing plan for Rice Krispies. She asked, "Why is the executive summary needed?" How would you answer her?

8. Briefly discuss the aspects of the current marketing situation analysis that a marketing planner for Gallo wine would have to consider.

9. What major decisions constitute the marketing strategy phase of the marketing plan? Why is it so essential that they be well coordinated?

■ References

1. Based on information found in Dart & Kraft annual reports. Also see "Dart & Kraft Turns Back to Its Basic Business—Food," *Business Week,* June 11, 1984, pp. 100–05.
2. MELVILLE C. BRANCH, *The Corporate Planning Process* (New York: American Management Association, 1962), pp. 48–49.
3. *The Development of Marketing Objectives and Plans: A Symposium* (New York: Conference Board, 1963), p. 38.
4. See PETTER DRUCKER, *Management: Tasks, Responsibilities, Practices* (New York: Harper & Row, 1973), chap. 7.

5. THEODORE LEVITT, "Marketing Myopia," *Harvard Business Review,* July–August 1960, pp. 45–56.

6. FAYE RICE, "Guess Who's the Sultan of Sweat," *Fortune,* April 16, 1984, pp. 52–56.

7. "Sperry: Out of an Industry Crisis, a New Dedication to Electronics," *Business Week,* April 30, 1984, pp. 69–70.

8. For additional reading on these and other portfolio analysis approaches, see DEREK ABELL and JOHN S. HAMMOND, *Strategic Planning: Problems and Analytical Approaches* (Englewood Cliffs, NJ: Prentice-Hall, 1979), chap. 4; PHILIPPE HASPESLAGH, "Portfolio Planning: Limits and Uses," *Harvard Business Review,* January–February 1982, pp. 58–73; YORAM WIND and VIJAY MAHAJAN, "Designing Product and Business Portfolios," *Harvard Business Review,* January–February 1981, pp. 155–65; and YORAM WIND, VIJAY MAHAJAN, and DONALD J. SWIRE, "An Empirical Comparison of Standardized Portfolio Models," *Journal of Marketing,* Spring 1983, pp. 89–99.

9. For more reading, see ABELL and HAMMOND, *Strategic Planning,* p. 191.

10. "The New Breed of Strategic Planner," *Business Week,* September 17, 1984, p. 63.

11. See HASPESLAGH, "Portfolio Planning," p. 59.

12. H. IGOR ANSOFF, "Strategies for Diversification," *Harvard Business Review,* September–October 1957, pp. 113–24.

13. For more reading on marketing's role, see PAUL F. ANDERSON, "Marketing, Strategic Planning and the Theory of the Firm," *Journal of Marketing,* Spring 1982, pp. 15–26; and YORAM WIND and THOMAS S. ROBERTSON, "Marketing Strategy: New Directions for Theory and Research," *Journal of Marketing,* Spring 1983, pp. 12–25.

14. For more reading, see YORAM WIND, "Marketing and the Other Business Functions," in *Research in Marketing,* vol. 5, Jagdish N. Sheth, ed. (Greenwich, CT: JAI Press, 1981), pp. 237–56.

15. For examples of empirical studies using fitted sales-response functions, see DOYLE L. WEISS, "Determinants of Market Share," *Journal of Marketing Research,* August 1968, pp. 290–95; DONALD E. SEXTON, JR., "Estimating Marketing Policy Effects on Sales of a Frequently Purchased Product," *Journal of Marketing Research,* August 1970, pp. 338–47; and JEAN-JACQUES LAMBIN, "A Computer On-Line Marketing Mix Model," *Journal of Marketing Research,* May 1972, pp. 119–26.

16. See RUSSELL ACKOFF and JAMES R. EMSHOFF, "Advertising Research at Anheuser-Busch," *Sloan Management Review,* Winter 1975, pp. 1–15.

17. See PHILIP KOTLER, "A Guide to Gathering Expert Estimates," *Business Horizons,* October 1970, pp. 79–87.

18. See PHILIP KOTLER, *Marketing Decision Making: A Model Building Approach* (New York: Holt, Rinehart & Winston, 1971).

4
Marketing Research and Information Systems

In 1977, Converse was the country's largest athletic shoe producer, making two-thirds of all U.S. basketball shoes. But in the late 1970s, basketball shoes were not the hottest item. Jogging became a crusade for 25 million Americans. And joggers were not satisfied with running in battered sneakers, old shorts, and a torn T-shirt. They were rushing out to buy jogging shoes carrying such brand names as Adidas, Puma, Tiger, Nike, Brooks, New Balance, and Etonic in what had mushroomed into a $2.3 billion industry by the 1980s.

Converse's management initially chose to stay on the sidelines. "We thought jogging would be more of a fad," said one of its executives. But Converse's marketing intelligence was off. Sales of other shoe manufacturers continued to soar. For example, Nike sales increased by over thirty times between 1977 and 1983, while Converse sales increased by only 60 percent.

Converse finally decided to offer a line of jogging shoes to the market. It had to decide whether to develop shoes for the high end, low end, or both ends of the market. This required marketing research to learn what joggers wanted in shoes, how they judged shoes, and how they selected retail outlets and brands. Converse also needed to study competitors' shoes. For example, Nike introduced and touted a model called Tailwind "which rides on a cushion

of polyurethane-encapsulated air chambers" and is "the next generation of footwear."

Converse, using the marketing research data, designed several shoe models and tested them with joggers. By the mid-1980s, the company had developed several strong lines, including top-of-the-line running shoes with patented stabilizing bars to reduce knee injuries.

Research also suggested opportunities in other athletic shoe markets. Converse developed full lines of tennis and cleat shoes, and revitalized its offerings of basketball shoes to include biomechanically designed shoes featuring better support and flexibility. Even the venerable All Star canvas basketball shoe, introduced in 1916, was offered in trendy pink and purple to take advantage of the latest craze—break dancing. Converse now offers strong lines in all athletic shoe segments.

Supporting its lines with large marketing budgets, the once-stodgy company grabbed attention with ads featuring Chris Everet Lloyd and Julius Irving and snapped up the title of official athletic shoe for the 1984 Olympic Games. Though Converse still has a long race to run (a 9 percent market share vs. Nike's 35 percent), it is experiencing record sales increases in a maturing and hotly contested market. In plotting Converse's next step, the most important resource is information.[1]

In carrying out marketing analysis, planning, implementation, and control, marketing managers need information at almost every turn. They need information about customers, competitors, dealers, and other forces in the marketplace. Marion Harper put it this way: "To manage a business well is to manage its future; and to manage the future is to manage information."[2]

During the past century, most companies were small and knew their customers firsthand. Managers picked up marketing information by being around people, observing them, and asking questions. During this century, many developments have increased the need for more and better information. As companies expand to national markets, they need more information on larger, more distant markets. As incomes increase and buyers become more selective in what they buy, sellers need better information about how buyers respond to different products and appeals. As sellers use more sophisticated approaches in more competitive environments, they need information on the effectiveness of their marketing tools. Finally, companies now operate in more rapidly changing environments, and managers have a greater need for up-to-date information to make timely decisions.

The supply of information has also increased greatly. John Neisbitt suggests that the United States is undergoing a "megashift" from an industrial to an information-based economy.[3] He found that over 65 percent of the U.S. workforce is now employed in producing or processing information, compared to only 17 percent in 1950. Using improved computer systems and other technologies, companies can now provide information in great quantities. As Neisbitt points out: "Running out of information is not a problem, but drowning in it is."[4] Yet the supply of information never seems sufficient. Marketers rarely have all the information they need, and they often do not need all the information they have. They often complain that they lack enough information of the right kind or have too much of the wrong kind. Or marketing information is so dispersed throughout the company that it takes a great effort to locate simple facts. Subordinates may withhold information they believe will reflect badly on their performance. Important information often arrives too late to be useful, or timely information is not accurate.

So marketing managers need more and better information. Companies have greater capacity to provide managers with information, but often have not made good use of it. Many companies are now studying their executives' information needs and designing formal information systems to meet these needs.

THE MARKETING INFORMATION SYSTEM

We define the marketing information system as follows:[5]

> A **marketing information system (MIS)** is a continuing and interacting structure of people, equipment, and procedures to gather, sort, analyze, evaluate, and distribute pertinent, timely, and accurate information for use by marketing decision makers to improve their marketing planning, execution, and control.

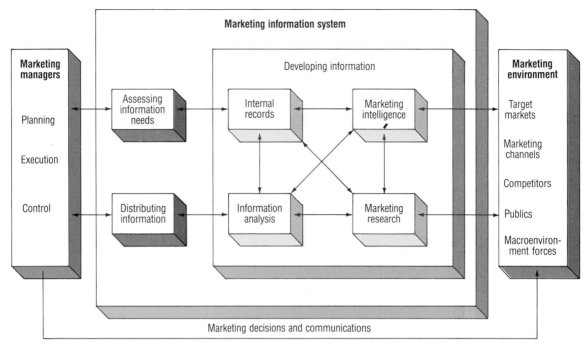

FIGURE 4-1 *The Marketing Information System*

The marketing information system concept is illustrated in Figure 4-1. The MIS begins and ends with the information user. First it interacts with marketing managers to assess their information needs. Next it develops the needed information from internal company records, marketing intelligence activities, and the marketing research process. Information analysis evaluates and processes the information to make it more useful. Finally, the MIS distributes information to managers in the right form and at the right time to help them in marketing planning, execution, and control.

We will now take a closer look at the functions of the company's marketing information system.

ASSESSING INFORMATION NEEDS

A well-designed marketing information system reconciles what information managers would *like* to have, what they really *need* and can handle, and what is *feasible* to offer. The company begins by interviewing managers to find out what information they would like. A useful set of questions is listed in Table 4-1. But managers do not always need all the information they ask for, and they may not ask for all they really need. Moreover, sometimes the MIS cannot supply all the information managers request.

TABLE 4-1
*Questionnaire for
Determining Marketing
Information Needs*

1. What types of decisions are you regularly called upon to make?
2. What types of information do you need to make these decisions?
3. What types of information do you regularly get?
4. What types of special studies do you periodically request?
5. What types of information would you like to get that you are not now getting?
6. What information would you want daily? Weekly? Monthly? Yearly?
7. What magazine and trade reports would you like to see routed to you on a regular basis?
8. What specific topics would you like to be kept informed of?
9. What types of data analysis programs would you like to see made available?
10. What do you think would be the four most helpful improvements that could be made in the present marketing information system?

Some managers will ask for whatever information they can get without thinking carefully about what they actually need and can use. With today's information technology, most companies can provide much more information—and much more complex information—than managers can realistically use. Too much information can be as harmful as too little.

Other busy managers may omit things they ought to know. Or managers may not know to ask for some types of information they should have. For example, managers might need to know that a competitor plans to introduce a new product during the coming year. Because they do not know about the new product, they do not think to ask about it. The MIS must watch the marketing environment and provide decision makers with information they should have to make key marketing decisions.

Sometimes the company cannot provide the desired information, because it is not available or because of MIS limitations. For example, a brand manager might want to know how much competitors will change their advertising budgets next year and how these changes will affect industry market shares. The information on planned budgets is probably not available. Even if it is, the company's MIS may not be sophisticated enough to forecast accurately resulting changes in market shares.

Finally, the company must decide whether the benefits of having an item of information are worth the costs of providing it, and both value and cost are often hard to assess. By itself, information has no worth—its value comes from how it is used. Though ways have been developed for calculating the value of information,[6] executives often must rely on subjective judgment. Similarly, while the company can add up the costs of the people, equipment, and facilities that make up a marketing information system, or the costs of a marketing research project, figuring the cost of a specific information item may be difficult. The costs of obtaining, processing, storing, and delivering information can mount quickly. In many cases, additional information will do little to change or improve a manager's decision, or the costs of the information will exceed the returns from the better decision that results. For example, suppose a company estimates that launching a recently developed product without any further information will yield a profit of $500,000. The manager believes that additional information will improve the marketing mix and allow the company to make $525,000. It would be foolish to pay $30,000 to obtain the additional information.

DEVELOPING INFORMATION

The information needed by marketing managers can be obtained from internal company records, marketing intelligence, and marketing research. The information analysis system then processes and transforms this information to make it more useful for marketing decision making.

Internal Records Most marketing managers use internal records and reports regularly, especially for making day-to-day planning, execution, and control decisions. The company's accounting system produces financial statements and keeps detailed records of sales and orders, costs, accounts receivable, and cash flows. Manufacturing reports on production schedules, shipments, and inventories. Salesforce call reports provide information on reseller reactions, competitive activities, and conditions in the environment. Information on customer satisfaction or service and warranty problems is reported by the Customer Service Department. Research studies done for one area may provide useful information for several other areas, and special reports purchased by one division may sometimes be used by another. Managers can use information gathered from these and other sources within the company to evaluate performance and to detect problems and opportunities.

Here are examples of how companies use internal records information in making marketing decisions:

Sears. Sears uses internal records as a powerful marketing tool. Marketing managers use computerized information on Sears' 40 million customers to promote special product and service offers to such diverse target segments as gardeners, appliance buyers, and expectant mothers. For example, Sears keeps track of the appliance purchases of each customer and promotes special service-package deals to customers who have bought several appliances but have not purchased maintenance contracts for them. Soon managers at other Sears subsidiaries—Allstate Insurance, Dean Witter Reynolds, and Coldwell Banker (real estate brokers)—will be able to develop sales leads using the same data.[7]

General Mills. Managers in the Grocery Products Division of General Mills receive sales information daily. Zone, regional, and district sales managers start their day with a teletype report on orders and shipments in their area the day before. The report also contains percentages to compare with target percentages and last year's percentages.

Mead Paper. Mead sales representatives can obtain on-the-spot answers to customers' questions about paper availability by dialing Mead Paper's computer center. The computer determines whether paper is available at the nearest warehouse and when it can be shipped; if it is not in stock, the computer checks the inventory at other nearby warehouses until one is located. If the paper is nowhere in stock, the computer determines where and when the paper can be produced. The sales representative gets an answer in seconds and thus has an advantage over competitors.

Information from internal records can usually be obtained more quickly and inexpensively than information from other sources, but it also presents some problems. Because it is often collected for other purposes, the information may be incomplete or in the wrong form for making marketing decisions. For example, accounting department sales and cost data used for financial analysis and preparing financial statements must be adapted for use in evaluating product, salesforce, or channel performance. Also, the many different areas of a large company produce great quantities of information; keeping track of it all is a difficult task. The marketing information system must gather, organize, process, and index this mountain of information so that managers can find it easily and get it quickly.

Marketing Intelligence Marketing intelligence is *happenings data,* everyday information about important environmental events—new laws, social trends, technological breakthroughs, demographic shifts, competitor maneuvers—that helps managers prepare and adjust marketing plans. The *marketing intelligence system* determines what intelligence is needed, collects it by watching and searching the environment, and delivers it to marketing managers who need it.

Defensive marketing intelligence helps avoid surprises that threaten present or future marketing plans and actions.[8] Checking patent applications can alert a company to new products being developed by competitors long before they are introduced and in time to develop strategies to defend its own product's market position. *Offensive* intelligence helps to identify opportunities. For example, intelligence information on trends in the social environment might suggest new positioning strategies or advertising approaches that take advantage of these trends.

The company's marketing intelligence system gathers information from many sources. Much valuable intelligence can be collected from the company's own personnel—executives, engineers and scientists, purchasing agents, and the salesforce. Yet company people are often busy and fail to pass on important information. The company must "sell" its people on their importance as intelligence gatherers, train them to spot new developments, and encourage them to report intelligence back to the company.

The company must also motivate suppliers, resellers, customers, and other allies to pass along important intelligence. Information on competitors can be obtained from what they say about themselves in annual reports, speeches and press releases, advertisements, and stockholder meetings. The company can learn about competitors from what others say about them in business publications, at trade shows, and in syndicated reports. Or the company can monitor what competitors do—it can buy and analyze their products, monitor their sales, watch their employment ads, and check for new patents (see Exhibit 4-1).

The company can often obtain useful information from the government under the Freedom of Information Act. For example, when the FTC asked Procter & Gamble to prove its claim that "New White Cloud bathroom tissue is the softest bathroom tissue on earth," Crown Zellerbach requested copies of all the information submitted.[9] Companies also purchase intelligence information from outside suppliers. The A. C. Nielsen Company sells bimonthly data (based on a sample of sixteen hundred stores) on brand shares, retail prices, percentage of stores stocking the item, and percentage of stockout stores. Market Research Corporation of America sells reports (based on the purchase diaries of a representative panel of seventy-five hundred households scattered throughout the country) on weekly movements of brand shares, sizes, prices, and deals. Clipping services are hired to report on competitors' ads, advertising expenditures, and media mixes.

EXHIBIT 4-1

INTELLIGENCE GATHERING: SNOOPING ON COMPETITORS

Competitive intelligence gathering has grown dramatically as more and more companies need to know what their competitors are doing. Such well-known companies as Ford, Westinghouse, General Electric, Gillette, Revlon, Del Monte, General Foods, Kraft, and J. C. Penney are known to be busy snooping on their competitors.

A recent article in *Fortune* lists over twenty techniques companies use to collect their own intelligence. The techniques fall into four major categories.

■ *Getting Information from Recruits and Competitors' Employees.* Companies can obtain intelligence through job interviews or from conversations with competitors' employees. According to *Fortune:*

When they interview students for jobs, some companies pay special attention to those who have worked for competitors, even temporarily. Job seekers are eager to impress and often have not been warned about divulging what is proprietary. They sometimes volunteer valuable information. . . . Several companies now send teams of highly trained technicians instead of personnel executives to recruit on campus.

Companies send engineers to conferences and trade shows to question competitors' technical people. Often conversations start innocently—just a few fellow technicians discussing processes and problems . . . [yet competitors'] engineers and scientists often brag about surmounting technical challenges, in the process divulging sensitive information.

Companies sometimes advertise and hold interviews for jobs that don't exist in order to entice competitors' employees to spill the beans. . . . Often applicants have toiled in obscurity or feel that their careers have stalled. They're dying to impress somebody.

In probably the hoariest tactic in corporate intelligence gathering, companies hire key executives from competitors to find out what they know.

■ *Getting Information from People Who Do Business with Competitors.* Key customers can keep the company informed about competitors—they might even be willing to request and pass along information on competitors' products.

For example, a while back Gillette told a large Canadian account the date on which it planned to begin selling its new Good News disposable razor in the U.S. . . . The Canadian distributor promptly called Bic and told it about the impending product launch. Bic put on a crash program and was able to start selling its razor shortly after Gillette did.

Intelligence can also be gathered by infiltrating customers' business operations:

Companies may provide their engineers free of charge to customers. . . . The close, cooperative relationship that the engineers on loan cultivate with the customer's design staff often enables them to learn what new products competitors are pitching.

- *Getting Information from Published Materials and Public Documents.* Keeping track of seemingly meaningless published information can provide competitor intelligence. For example, the types of people sought in help wanted ads can indicate something about a competitor's technological thrusts and new product development. Government agencies are another good source. For example:

  Although it is often illegal for a company to photograph a competitor's plant from the air . . . there are legitimate ways to get the photos. . . . Aerial photos often are on file with the U.S. Geological Survey or Environmental Protection Agency. These are public documents, available for a nominal fee.

  Companies can obtain valuable information from government agencies under the Freedom of Information Act, or they can use specialized firms to obtain such information discreetly.

- *Getting Information by Observing Competitors or Analyzing Physical Evidence.* Companies can get to know competitors better by buying their products or examining other physical evidence.

  Companies increasingly buy competitors products and take them apart to . . . determine costs of production and even manufacturing methods.

  In the absence of better information on market share and the volume of product competitors are shipping, companies have measured the rust on rails of railroad sidings to their competitors' plants or have counted the tractor-trailers leaving loading bays.

  Some companies even buy their competitors' garbage:

  Once it has left the competitor's premises, refuse is legally considered abandoned property. While some companies now shred the paper coming out of their design labs, they often neglect to do this for almost-as-revealing refuse from the marketing or public relations departments.

Though most of these techniques are legal, and some might be considered shrewd competitiveness, many involve questionable ethics. The company should take advantage of publicly available information, but responsible companies avoid practices that might be considered illegal or unethical. A company does not have to break the law or violate accepted codes of ethics to get intelligence information, and the benefits gained from using such techniques are not worth the risks.

Source: Based on Steven Flax, "How to Snoop on Your Competitors," *Fortune,* May 14, 1984, pp. 29–33. Quoted by permission of *Fortune,* © 1984 Time, Inc. All rights reserved.

Finally, some companies establish an office to collect and circulate marketing intelligence. The staff scans major publications, abstracts relevant news, and disseminates a news bulletin to marketing managers. It develops a file of relevant information. The staff assists managers in evaluating new information. These services greatly improve the quality of information available to marketing managers.

There is a vast amount of marketing intelligence information available. The marketing intelligence system must systematically scan the environment, sort out relevant and actionable information, and assist managers in evaluating and using it.

These services greatly improve the quality of information available to marketing managers.

Marketing Research Managers cannot always wait for information to arrive in bits and pieces from the marketing intelligence system. They often require formal studies of specific situations. Consider the following:

- Hewlett-Packard plans to introduce a new, lightweight portable personal computer. The brand manager wants to know how many and what kinds of people or companies will buy the product. Knowing the incomes, occupations, education, and life styles of potential customers and their reactions to the new product will help the manager develop better sales and advertising strategies.

- Pacific Stereo operates a national chain of audio equipment stores. Management wants to study the market potential of some cities in the South as locations for new stores.

- Barat College in Lake Forest, Illinois, seeks to enroll above-average women high school graduates. It needs to know what percentage of its target market has heard of Barat; what they know, how they heard about Barat, and how they feel about Barat. This information would help Barat improve its communications program.

In such situations, the marketing intelligence system will not provide the detailed information needed and managers normally do not have the skill or time to obtain the information on their own. They need formal marketing research.

We define marketing research as follows:

> **Marketing research** is the systematic design, collection, analysis, and reporting of data and findings relevant to a specific marketing situation facing the company.

Every marketer needs marketing research. A brand manager at Procter & Gamble will commission three or four major marketing research studies annually. Marketing managers in smaller companies will order fewer marketing research studies. More and more nonprofit organizations are finding that they need marketing research. A hospital wants to know whether people in its service area have a positive attitude toward the hospital. A college wants to determine what kind of image it has among high school counselors. A political organization wants to find out what voters think of the candidates.

Marketing researchers have steadily expanded their activities (see Table 4-2). The ten most common activities are measurement of market potentials, market share analysis, the determination of market characteristics, sales analysis, studies of business trends, short-range forecasting, competitive product studies, long-range forecasting, marketing information systems studies, and testing of existing products.

A company can do marketing research in its own research department or have some or all of it done outside. Small companies can ask students or professors at a local college to design and carry out the project, or they can hire a marketing research firm. Large companies—in fact, over 73 percent of them—have their own marketing research departments.[10] Marketing research departments consist of anywhere from one to several dozen researchers. The marketing research manager normally reports to the marketing vice-president. He or she performs such roles as

TABLE 4-2 *Research Activities of 599 Companies*

TYPE OF RESEARCH	PERCENT DOING IT	TYPE OF RESEARCH	PERCENT DOING IT
Advertising Research		**Product Research**	
A. Motivation research	47%	A. New product acceptance and potential	76
B. Copy research	61	B. Competitive product studies	87
C. Media research	68	C. Testing of existing products	80
D. Studies of ad effectiveness	76	D. Packaging research: design or physical	65
E. Studies of competitive advertising	67	characteristics	
Business Economics and Corporate Research		**Sales and Market Research**	
A. Short-range forecasting (up to 1 year)	89	A. Measurement of market potentials	97
B. Long-range forecasting (over 1 year)	87	B. Market share analysis	97
C. Studies of business trends	91	C. Determination of market characteristics	97
D. Pricing studies	83	D. Sales analysis	92
E. Plant and warehouse location studies	68	E. Establishment of sales quotas, territories	78
F. Acquisition studies	73	F. Distribution channel studies	71
G. Export and international studies	49	G. Test markets, store audits	59
H. MIS (Management Information System)	80	H. Consumer panel operations	63
I. Operations Research	65	I. Sales compensation studies	60
J. Internal company employees	76	J. Promotional studies of premiums, coupons,	58
Corporate Responsibility Research		sampling, deals, etc.	
A. Consumer "right to know" studies	18		
B. Ecological impact studies	23		
C. Studies of legal constraints on advertising and promotion	46		
D. Social values and policies studies	39		

Source: Dik Warren Twedt, ed., *1983 Survey of Marketing Research* (Chicago: American Marketing Association, 1983), p. 41.

study director, administrator, company consultant, and advocate. The other marketing researchers include survey designers, statisticians, behavioral scientists, and model builders.

Marketing research budgets usually range from 0.01 to 3.50 percent of company sales. Between one-half and three-quarters of this money is spent directly by the department, and the remainder is used to buy the services of outside firms. Marketing research firms fall into three groups:

1. *Syndicated-service research firms.* These firms gather periodic consumer and trade information which they sell to clients. Marketing managers can purchase reports on television audiences from the A. C. Nielsen Company or the American Research Bureau (ARB); on radio audiences from the ARB; on magazine audiences from Simmons; on warehouse movements from the Selling Areas-Marketing, Inc. (SAMI); and on retail shelf audits from Nielsen. Nielsen, the largest of these firms had estimated billings of $463 million in 1983.[11]

2. *Custom marketing research firms.* These firms are hired to carry out specific research projects. They participate in designing the study, and the report becomes the client's property. Market Facts is one of the leading custom marketing research firms, with annual billings of approximately $25 million.

3. *Specialty-line marketing research firms.* These firms provide a specialized service to other marketing research firms and company marketing research departments. The best example is the field service firm, which sells field interviewing services to other firms.

Information abounds—the problem is to give managers the *right information* at the *right time. Courtesy of Apple Computer, Inc.*

Whether a company uses such outside firms depends on the skills and resources within the company. A company with no research department will have to buy the services of research firms. But even companies with their own departments often use outside firms to do special research tasks or special studies.

The Marketing Research Process This section describes the four steps in the marketing research process (Figure 4-2): defining the problem and research objectives, developing the research plan, implementing the research plan, and interpreting and presenting the findings.

Defining the Problem and Research Objectives

The marketing manager and the researcher must work closely together to define the problem carefully and agree on the research objectives. The manager best understands the problem or decision for which information is needed; the researcher best understands marketing research and how to obtain the information.

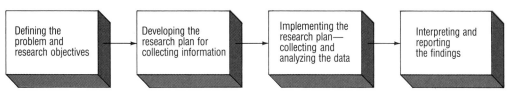

| Defining the problem and research objectives | → | Developing the research plan for collecting information | → | Implementing the research plan— collecting and analyzing the data | → | Interpreting and reporting the findings |

FIGURE 4-2 *The Marketing Research Process*

Managers must know enough about marketing research to participate in the planning and to interpret research results. If they know little about marketing research, they may obtain the wrong information, accept incorrect interpretations, or request information that costs too much. Experienced marketing researchers who understand the manager's problem should also be involved at this stage. The researcher must be able to help the manager define the problem and to suggest ways that research can help the manager make better decisions.

Defining the problem and research objectives is often the hardest step in the research process. The manager may know that something is wrong, but have trouble identifying specific causes. For example, managers of a regional discount retail chain store hastily decided that falling sales were caused by poor advertising and ordered research to test new advertising approaches. When this research showed that the current advertising was reaching the right people with the right message, the managers were puzzled. It turned out that the stores themselves were not providing what the advertising promised. More careful problem definition would have avoided the cost and delay of the advertising research and suggested research on the real problem of consumer reactions to the merchandise, products, and prices offered in the chain's stores.

The problem may also be defined too vaguely or broadly. If the managers of the retail chain had told the researchers, "Go and gather data on the retail market," they would have been disappointed in the results. Hundreds of things could be researched. To be useful, research findings must bear on specific decisions facing the company. Defining the problem vaguely or incorrectly wastes time and money. As an old adage says, a problem well defined is half solved.

When the problem has been carefully defined, the manager and researcher must set the research objectives. A marketing research project might have one of three types of objectives. Sometimes the objective is *exploratory*—to gather preliminary information that will help to better define the problem and suggest hypotheses. Sometimes the objective is *descriptive*—to describe things such as the market potential for a product, or profiles of the demographics and attitudes of consumers who buy the product. Sometimes the objective is *causal*—to test hypotheses about cause-and-effect relationships. For example, would a 10 percent decrease in tuition for a private college result in more than the 10 percent increase in enrollments needed to break even? Managers often start with exploratory research and later initiate suitable descriptive or causal research.

The statement of the problem and research objectives will govern the entire research process. The manager and researcher should put the statement in writing to be certain that they agree on the purpose and expected results of the research.

Developing the Research Plan

The second step of the marketing research process calls for determining the information needed and developing a plan for gathering it efficiently.

DETERMINING SPECIFIC INFORMATON NEEDS. The research objectives must be translated into specific information needs. For example, suppose Campbell's decides to do research to find out how consumers will react to a new bowl-shaped plastic container that costs more but allows consumers to heat the soup in a microwave oven and eat it without using and cleaning dishes. This research might call for the following specific information:

- The demographic, economic, and life style characteristics of current soup users. (Busy working couples might find the convenience of the new package worth the price; families with children might want to pay less and wash the pan and bowls.)

- Consumer usage patterns for soup—how much soup they eat, where, and when. (The new package might be ideal for adults eating lunch on the go but less convenient for parents feeding lunch to several children or restaurants serving many customers.)

- The penetration of microwave ovens in consumer and commercial markets. (The number of microwaves in homes and business lunchrooms will limit the demand for the new container.)

- Retailer reactions to the new package. (Failure to get retailer support could hurt sales of the new package.)

- Forecasts of sales of the new and current packages. (Will the new package increase Campbell's profits?)

Campbell's managers will need these and many other specific types of information to decide whether or not to introduce the new product.

SURVEYS OF SECONDARY INFORMATION. To meet the manager's information needs, the researcher can gather secondary data, primary data, or both. **Secondary data** consist of information that already exists somewhere, having been collected for

Secondary information is less costly and more quickly available; internal records are a good source. *Courtesy of Hewlett-Packard.*

TABLE 4-3

Secondary Sources of Data

A. **Internal Sources**

Internal sources include company profit and loss statements, balance sheets, sales figures, sales call reports, invoices, inventory records, and prior research reports.

B. **Government Publications**

Statistical Abstract of the U.S., updated annually, provides summary data on demographic, economic, social, and other aspects of the American economy and society.

County and City Data Book, updated every three years, presents statistical information for counties, cities, and other geographical units on population, education, employment, aggregate and median income, housing, bank deposits, retail sales, etc.

U.S. Industrial Outlook provides projections of industrial activity by industry and includes data on production, sales, shipments, employment, etc.

Marketing Information Guide provides a monthly annotated bibliography of marketing information.

Other government publications include the *Annual Survey of Manufacturers; Business Statistics; Census of Manufacturers; Census of Population; Census of Retail Trade, Wholesale Trade, and Selected Service Industries; Census of Transportation; Federal Reserve Bulletin; Monthly Labor Review; Survey of Current Business;* and *Vital Statistics Report.*

C. **Periodicals and Books**

Business Periodicals Index, a monthly, lists business articles appearing in a wide variety of business publications.

Standard and Poor's Industry Surveys provide updated statistics and analyses of industries.

Moody's Manuals provide financial data and names of executives in major companies.

Encyclopedia of Associations provides information on every major trade and professional association in the U.S.

Marketing journals include the *Journal of Marketing, Journal of Marketing Research,* and *Journal of Consumer Research.*

Useful trade magazines include *Advertising Age, Chain Store Age, Progressive Grocer, Sales and Marketing Management, Stores.*

Useful general business magazines include *Business Week, Fortune, Forbes,* and *Harvard Business Review.*

D. **Commercial Data**

A. C. Nielsen Company provides data on products and brands sold through retail outlets (Retail Index Services), data on television audiences (Media Research Services), magazine circulation data (Neodata Services, Inc.), etc.

Market Research Corporation of America provides data on weekly family purchases of consumer products (National Consumer Panel), data on home food consumption (National Menu Census), and data on 6,000 retail, drug, and discount retailers in various geographical areas (Metro Trade Audits).

Selling Areas-Marketing, Inc., provides reports on warehouse withdrawals to food stores in selected market areas (SAMI reports).

Simmons Market Research Bureau provides annual reports covering television markets, sporting goods, proprietary drugs, etc., giving demographic data by sex, income, age and brand preferences (selective markets and media reaching them).

Other commercial research houses selling data to subscribers include the *Audit Bureau of Circulation, Audits and Surveys, Dun and Bradstreet, National Family Opinion, Standard Rate and Data Service,* and *Starch.*

another purpose. **Primary data** consist of information collected for the specific purpose at hand.

Researchers usually start their investigations by gathering secondary data. Table 4-3 shows the rich variety of secondary data sources available, including *internal* and *external* sources.[12] Secondary data can usually be obtained more quickly and at a lower cost than primary data. For example, a visit to the library might provide all the information Campbell's needs on microwave oven usage at almost no cost. A study to collect primary information might take weeks or months to complete, and it would cost thousands of dollars to design data collection forms, hire interviewers, collect and analyze the data, and prepare a report of the findings. Also, secondary sources can sometimes provide data an individual company cannot collect on its own—information that is not directly available or that would be too expensive to collect. For example, it would be too expensive for Campbell's to conduct a continuing retail store audit to find out about the market shares, prices, and displays of its brands and competitors' brands. But it can buy the Nielsen Retail Index, which provides this information from regular audits of 1,300 supermarkets, 700 drug stores, and 150 mass merchandisers.[13]

Secondary data also present problems. The needed information may not exist—researchers can rarely obtain all the data they need from secondary sources. For example, Campbell's is not likely to find existing information about consumer reactions to its new package. Or the required information may be hard to locate in the mass of data available. Even when the data can be found, they might not be entirely usable. The researcher must evaluate secondary information carefully to make certain it is (1) *relevant*—that it fits or can be adapted to the needs of the research project; (2) *accurate*—it was reliably collected and accurately reported; (3) *current*—it is up to date enough for making current decisions; and (4) *impartial*—it was collected and reported in an objective way rather than to promote a special interest or point of view.

Secondary data provide a good starting point for research and often help to define the problem and research objectives. In most cases, however, secondary sources cannot provide all the needed information, and the company must collect primary data.

PLANNING PRIMARY DATA COLLECTION. Some managers collect primary data by dreaming up a few questions and finding some people to interview. Data collected this way might be useless or—even worse, misleading. The plan for primary data collection should be designed by professional marketing researchers. At the same time, marketing managers should know enough about primary data collection to approve the research design and interpret the findings.

Table 4-4 shows that designing a plan for primary data collection calls for decisions on research approaches, contact methods, sampling plan, and research instruments.

TABLE 4-4
Planning Primary Data Collection

RESEARCH APPROACHES	CONTACT METHODS	SAMPLING PLAN	RESEARCH INSTRUMENTS
Observation	Mail	Sampling unit	Questionnaire
Survey	Telephone	Sample size	Mechanical instruments
Experiment	Personal	Sampling procedure	

RESEARCH APPROACHES. Primary data can be collected through observation, surveys, and experiments.

Observational research is the gathering of primary data by observing relevant people, actions, and situations. For example:

■ An airline hires researchers to linger around airports or travel agencies to learn how travelers talk about different carriers and how agents handle flight arrangements.

■ A food products manufacturer sends researchers into supermarkets to find out the prices of competing brands or how much retailers support its brands with shelf space and displays.

■ A soft drink marketer collects competitors' ads to estimate their advertising spending and to find out about new products and marketing strategies.

■ A bank evaluates possible new branch locations by checking the locations and patronage of competing branches, traffic patterns, and neighborhood conditions.

■ A maker of personal care products pretests its ads by showing them to people and measuring eye movements, pulse rates, and other physical reactions.

■ A department store chain sends observers posing as customers to its stores to check on store conditions and customer service.

There are many different approaches to observational research.[14] The researchers can observe behavior as it occurs naturally or in artificial settings (such as a simulated grocery store). People and situations can be observed openly or through one-way mirrors, hidden cameras, or disguised observers. Observation may be highly structured (observers know exactly what to observe and record), or unstructured (observers use their own judgment about what is important). Direct observation involves watching actual behavior; indirect observation involves inferring behavior by looking at the results of that behavior. For example, a museum can check the popularity of various exhibits by noting the amount of floor wear around them.

Observational research can be used to obtain information that people are unwilling or unable to provide. For example, consumers may not know exactly what path their eyes followed through an ad or how long they lingered on the headline or illustration. They may be unwilling to tell the researcher about some aspect of their buying behavior that can be easily observed. In some cases, observation may be the only way to obtain needed information. On the other hand, some things simply cannot be observed—things such as feelings, attitudes, and motives or personal behavior. Long-run or infrequent behavior is also difficult to observe. Because of these limitations, researchers often use observation in combination with other data collection methods.

Survey research is the approach best suited for gathering descriptive information. A company that wants to know about people's knowledge, beliefs, preferences, satisfaction, or buying behavior can often find out by asking them directly. As in observation, survey research can be structured or unstructured. Structured surveys use formal lists of questions asked of all respondents in the same way. Unstructured surveys use an open format that lets the interviewer probe respondents and guide the interview, depending on their answers.

Survey research may be direct or indirect. In the direct approach, the researcher asks direct questions about the behavior or thoughts of interest—for example, "Why don't you buy clothes at K mart?" Using the indirect approach, the researcher might ask, "What kinds of people buy clothes at K mart?" From the response to this indirect question, the researcher may be able to discover why the consumer avoids K mart clothing—in fact, it may suggest reasons the consumer is not consciously aware of. (Exhibit 4-2 gives another example of the indirect survey approach.) We will say more about survey research approaches when we discuss contact methods, sampling plan, and research instruments.

EXHIBIT 4-2

WHY DID PEOPLE INITIALLY RESIST BUYING INSTANT COFFEE?

An excellent example of indirect survey research was conducted by Mason Haire to determine why housewives resisted buying instant coffee when it was first introduced. Housewives were heard to complain that it did not taste like real coffee. Yet in blindfold tests, many of these same housewives could not distinguish between a cup of instant coffee and a cup of real coffee. This indicated that much of their resistance was psychological. Haire designed the following shopping lists, the only difference being that regular coffee was on one list and instant coffee on the other:

SHOPPING LIST 1	SHOPPING LIST 2
1½ lbs. of hamburger	1½ lbs. of hamburger
2 loaves of Wonder Bread	2 loaves of Wonder Bread
Bunch of carrots	Bunch of carrots
1 can Rumford's Baking Powder	1 can Rumford's Baking Powder
Nescafé Instant Coffee	1 lb. Maxwell House coffee (drip grind)
2 cans Del Monte peaches	2 cans Del Monte peaches
5 lbs. potatoes	5 lbs. potatoes

Housewives were asked to guess the social and personal characteristics of the woman whose shopping list they saw. The comments were pretty much the same with one significant difference: A higher proportion of the housewives whose list mentioned instant coffee described the woman as "lazy, a spendthrift, a poor wife, and failing to plan well for her family." These women were attributing to the fictional housewife their own anxieties and negative images about instant coffee. The instant coffee company now knew the nature of the resistance and developed a campaign to change the image of housewives who serve instant coffee.

Source: See Mason Haire, "Projective Techniques in Marketing Research," *Journal of Marketing,* April 1950, pp. 649–56.

Survey research is the most widely used method for primary data collection, and it is often the only method used in a research study. The greatest advantage of survey research is its versatility. It can be used to obtain many different kinds of information in many different marketing situations. Depending on the survey design, it may also provide information more quickly and at lower cost than the observational or experimental research.

Survey research also presents some problems. Sometimes people are unable to answer survey questions because they cannot remember or never consciously thought about what they do and why. Or people may be unwilling to answer questions asked by unknown interviewers or about things they consider private. Busy people may not take the time. Respondents may answer survey questions even when they do not know the answer to appear smarter or more informed, or they may try to help the interviewer by giving pleasing answers. Careful survey design can help to minimize these problems.

Experimental research is best suited for gathering causal information, whereas observation is best suited for exploratory research and survey work for descriptive research. Such experimentation involves selecting matched groups of subjects, giving them different treatments, controlling unrelated factors, and checking for differences in group responses. To the extent that unrelated factors can be eliminated or controlled, differences in responses can be related to differences in the treatments. Experimental research attempts to explain cause-and-effect relationships by eliminating competing explanations of the observed findings. Observation and surveys may be used to collect information in experimental research.

Researchers at McDonald's might use experiments before adding a new sandwich to the menu to answer such questions as the following:

- How much will the new sandwich increase McDonald's sales?
- How will the new sandwich affect the sales of other menu items?
- Which advertising approach—testimonial or life style—would have the greater effect on sales of the sandwich?
- How sensitive would sales be to different prices charged for the product?
- Should the new item be targeted toward adults, children, or both?

For example, to test the effects of two different prices, McDonald's could set up the following simple experiment. It could introduce the new sandwich at one price in its restaurants in one city and at another price in restaurants in another similar city. If the cities are very similar, and if all other marketing efforts for the sandwich are the same, then differences in sales in the two cities could be related to the price charged. More elaborate experiments could be designed to include other variables and other locations.

The experimental method supplies the most convincing data if the proper controls are exercised. To the extent that the design and execution of the experiment eliminate alternative hypotheses that might explain the results, the researchers and the marketing managers can have confidence in the results.[15]

CONTACT METHODS. Information can be collected by mail, telephone, or personal interview. Table 4-5 shows the strengths and weaknesses of each of these contact methods.

Mail questionnaires can be used to collect fairly large amounts of information at a low cost per respondent. Respondents may give more honest answers, or answers to more personal questions, on a mail questionnaire than to an unknown interviewer in person or over the phone. No interviewer is involved to affect the respondent's answers. However, mail questionnaires are not very flexible—they

TABLE 4-5
*Strengths and
Weaknesses of the
Three Contact Methods*

	MAIL	TELEPHONE	PERSONAL
1. Flexibility	Poor	Good	Excellent
2. Quantity of data that can be collected	Good	Fair	Excellent
3. Control of interviewer effects	Excellent	Fair	Poor
4. Control of sample	Fair	Excellent	Fair
5. Speed of data collection	Poor	Excellent	Good
6. Response rate	Poor	Good	Good
7. Cost	Good	Fair	Poor

Source: Adapted with permission of Macmillan Publishing Company from *Marketing Research: Measurement and Method,* 3rd ed., by Donald S. Tull and Del I. Hawkins. Copyright © 1984 by Macmillan Publishing Company.

require simple and clearly worded questions; all respondents answer the same questions in a fixed order; and the researcher cannot probe or adapt the questionnaire based on earlier answers. Mail surveys usually take longer to complete, and the response rate—the number of people returning completed questionnaires—is often very low. The researcher often has little control over the mail questionnaire sample. Even with a good mailing list, it is often difficult to control *who* at the mailing address fills out the questionnaire.

Telephone interviewing is the best method for gathering information quickly, and it provides greater flexibility than mail questionnaires. Interviewers can explain questions that are not understood. They can skip some questions or probe more deeply on others, depending on the respondent's answers. Telephone interviewing allows greater sample control—interviewers can ask to speak to respondents with the desired characteristics or even by name, and response rates tend to be higher than with mail questionnaires.

Telephone interviewing also has drawbacks. The cost per respondent is higher than with mail questionnaires, and people may be reluctant to discuss personal questions with an interviewer. Using an interviewer increases flexibility, but also introduces interviewer bias. The way interviewers talk, slight differences in how they ask questions, and other differences may affect respondents' answers. Interpretations and the recording of responses may vary across interviewers, or time pressures may cause some interviewers to cheat by recording answers without asking questions.

Personal interviewing takes two forms, individual and group interviewing. *Individual interviewing* involves talking with people in their homes or offices, on the street, or in shopping malls. The interviewer must gain their cooperation, and the time involved can range from a few minutes to several hours. Sometimes a small payment or incentive is presented to people in appreciation of their time.

Group interviewing consists of inviting six to ten people to gather for a few hours with a trained interviewer to discuss a product, service, organization, or other marketing entity. To obtain worthwhile results, the interviewer needs qualifications such as objectivity, knowledge of the subject matter and industry, and some understanding of group dynamics and consumer behavior. The participants are normally paid a small sum for attending. The meeting is held in pleasant surroundings, and refreshments are served to emphasize the informality. The group inter-

Computer assisted telephone interviewing (CATI). The interviewer enters respondent's answers directly into the computer. *Courtesy of Research Triangle Institute, Research Triangle Park, NC.*

viewer starts with broad questions before moving to more specific issues, and encourages free and easy discussion, hoping that the group dynamics will bring out actual feelings and thoughts. At the same time, the interviewer "focuses" the discussion—hence the name *focus group interviewing*. The comments are recorded through note taking or on videotapes which are later studied to understand the consumers' buying process. Focus group interviewing is becoming one of the major marketing research tools for gaining insight into consumer thoughts and feelings.[16]

Personal interviewing is very flexible and can be used to collect large amounts of information. Trained interviewers can hold the respondent's attention for a long time and can explain complicated questions. They can guide interviews, explore issues, and probe respondents as the situation requires. Personal interviews can be used with any type of questionnaire. Interviewers can show subjects actual products, advertisements, or packages and observe reactions and behavior. In most cases, personal interviews can be conducted fairly quickly.

The main drawbacks of personal interviewing are costs and sampling problems. Personal interviews may cost three to four times as much as telephone interviews. Group interview studies usually use small sample sizes to keep time and costs down, and it may be hard to generalize from the results. Because interviewers have more flexibility in personal interviews, there is a greater problem of interviewer bias.

Which contact method is best depends on what information the researcher wants, and on the number and types of respondents to be contacted. Advances in computers and telecommunications will have an impact on methods of obtaining information in the future. For example, some research firms now conduct their interviewing using a combination of WATS lines and data entry terminals (called CATI—computed assisted telephone interview). The interviewer reads a set of questions from a video screen and types the respondent's answers right into the computer. This eliminates data editing and coding, reduces errors, and saves time. Other research firms have set up interactive terminals in shopping centers—respondents sit down at a terminal, read questions from a screen, and type their own answers into the computer.

SAMPLING PLAN. Marketing researchers usually draw conclusions about large groups of consumers by observing or questioning a small sample of the total consumer population. Ideally, the research sample should be representative so that the researcher can make accurate estimates of the thoughts and behaviors of the larger population. The marketing researcher must design a sampling plan, which calls for three decisions:

1. *Sampling unit: Who is to be surveyed?* The proper sampling unit is not always obvious. For example, to investigate the decision-making process for a family automobile purchase, should the researcher interview the husband, wife, other family members, dealership salespeople, or all of these? Should an industrial equipment supplier looking at how companies select its or competitors products talk to the people who use the products, those who influence the buying decision (engineers, company executives), or the purchasing agents who place the orders? Where buying roles of instigator, influencer, decider, user, or purchaser are not combined in the same person, the researcher must determine what information is needed and who is most likely to have it.

2. *Sample size: How many people should be surveyed?* Large samples give more reliable results than small samples. However, it is not necessary to sample the entire target market or even a substantial portion to achieve reliable results. Samples of less than 1 percent of a population can often provide good reliability, given a creditable sampling procedure.

3. *Sampling procedure: How should the respondents be chosen?* To obtain a representative sample, a probability sample of the population should be drawn. Probability sampling allows the calculation of confidence limits for sampling error. Thus we could conclude that "the interval five to seven trips per year has ninety-five chances in one hundred of containing the true number of trips taken annually by air travelers in the Southwest." Three types of probability sampling are described in Table 4-6A. When the cost or time involved in probability sampling is excessive, marketing researchers will take nonprobability samples. Table 4-6B describes three types of nonprobability sampling. Some marketing researchers feel that nonprobability samples can be very useful in many circumstances, even though the sampling error cannot be measured.

RESEARCH INSTRUMENTS. In collecting primary data, marketing researchers have a choice of two main research instruments—the questionnaire and mechanical devices.

The questionnaire is by far the most common instrument. Broadly speaking, a questionnaire consists of a set of questions presented to a respondent for his or her

TABLE 4-6

Types of Probability and Nonprobability Samples

A. Probability sample	
Simple random sample	Every member of the population has a known and equal chance of selection.
Stratified random sample	The population is divided into mutually exclusive groups (such as age groups), and random samples are drawn from each group.
Cluster (area) sample	The population is divided into mutually exclusive groups (such as blocks), and the researcher draws a sample of the groups to interview.
B. Nonprobability sample	
Convenience sample	The researcher selects the easiest population members from which to obtain information.
Judgment sample	The researcher uses his or her judgment to select population members who are good prospects for accurate information.
Quota sample	The researcher finds and interviews a prescribed number of people in each of several categories.

answers. The questionnaire is very flexible in that there are many ways to ask questions. Questionnaires need to be carefully developed, tested, and debugged before they can be administered on a large scale. We can usually spot several errors in a casually prepared questionnaire (see Exhibit 4-3).

In preparing a questionnaire, the marketing researcher carefully chooses the questions asked, the form of the questions, the wording of the questions, and the sequencing of the questions.

EXHIBIT 4-3

A "QUESTIONABLE" QUESTIONNAIRE

Suppose the following questionnaire had been prepared by a summer camp director to be used in interviewing parents of prospective campers. How do you feel about each question?

1. What is your income to the nearest hundred dollars?

   People don't necessarily know their income to the nearest hundred dollars nor do they want to reveal their income that closely. Futhermore, a questionnaire should never open with such a personal question.

2. Are you a strong or a weak supporter of overnight summer camping for your children?

   What do "strong" and "weak" mean?

3. Do your children behave themselves well in a summer camp?
   Yes ( ) No ( )

   "Behave" is a relative term. Besides, will people want to answer this? Furthermore, is "yes" or "no" the best way to allow a response to the question? Why is the question being asked in the first place?

4. How many camps mailed literature to you last April? This April?

  Who can remember this?

5. What are the most salient and determinant attributes in your evaluation of summer camps?

  What are "salience" and "determinant attributes"? Don't use big words on me.

6. Do you think it is right to deprive your child of the opportunity to grow into a mature person through the experience of summer camping?

  Loaded question. How can one answer "yes," given the bias?

A common type of error occurs in the *questions asked,* including questions that cannot be answered, or would not be answered, or need not be answered, and omitting questions that should be answered. Each question should be checked to determine whether it contributes to the research objectives. Questions that are merely interesting should be dropped because they lengthen the time required and try the respondent's patience.

The *form of the question* can influence the response. Marketing researchers distinguish between closed-end and open-end questions.

Closed-end questions include all the possible answers, and the respondent makes a choice among them. Table 4-7A shows the most common forms of closed-end questions as they might be used in a survey of airline users by Delta airlines.

TABLE 4-7 *Types of Questions*

A. CLOSED-END QUESTIONS

NAME	DESCRIPTION	EXAMPLE
Dichotomous	A question offering two answer choices.	"In arranging this trip, did you personally phone Delta?" Yes ☐ No ☐
Multiple choice	A question offering three or more answer choices.	"With whom are you traveling on this flight?" No one ☐ Children only ☐ Spouse ☐ Business associates/friends/relatives ☐ Spouse and children ☐ An organized tour group ☐
Likert scale	A statement with which the respondent shows the amount of agreement/disagreement.	"Small airlines generally give better service than large ones." Strongly disagree / Disagree / Neither agree nor disagree / Agree / Strongly agree 1 ☐ 2 ☐ 3 ☐ 4 ☐ 5 ☐
Semantic differential	A scale is inscribed between two bipolar words, and the respondent selects the point that represents the direction and intensity of his or her feelings.	*Delta Airlines* Large ⎯X⎯:⎯:⎯:⎯:⎯:⎯ Small Experienced ⎯:⎯:⎯:⎯:⎯X⎯:⎯ Inexperienced Modern ⎯:⎯:⎯:⎯X⎯:⎯:⎯ Old-fashioned

TABLE 4-7 (Cont.) *Types of Questions*

A. CLOSED-END QUESTIONS (Cont.)

NAME	DESCRIPTION	EXAMPLE				
Importance scale	A scale that rates the importance of some attribute from "not at all important" to "extremely important."	"Airline food service to me is"				
		Extremely important 1 ___	Very important 2 ___	Somewhat important 3 ___	Not very important 4 ___	Not at all important 5 ___
Rating scale	A scale that rates some attribute from "poor" to "excellent."	"Delta's food service is"				
		Excellent 1 ___	Very good 2 ___	Good 3 ___	Fair 4 ___	Poor 5 ___

B. OPEN-END QUESTIONS

NAME	DESCRIPTION	EXAMPLE
Completely unstructured	A question that respondents can answer in an almost unlimited number of ways.	"What is your opinion of Delta Airlines?"
Word association	Words are presented, one at a time, and respondents mention the first word that comes to mind.	"What is the first word that comes to your mind when you hear the following?" Airline _____ Delta _____ Travel _____
Sentence completion	Incomplete sentences are presented, one at a time, and respondents complete the sentence.	"When I choose an airline, the most important consideration in my decision is _____
Story completion	An incomplete story is presented, and respondents are asked to complete it.	"I flew Delta a few days ago. I noticed that the exterior and interior of the plane had very bright colors. This aroused in me the following thoughts and feelings." *Now complete the story.*
Picture completion	A picture of two characters is presented, with one making a statement. Respondents are asked to identify with the other and fill in the empty balloon.	 Fill in the empty balloon.
Thematic Apperception Tests (TAT)	A picture is presented, and respondents are asked to make up a story about what they think is happening or may happen in the picture.	 Make up a story about what you see.

Open-end questions allow the respondent to answer in his or her own words. They take various forms; the main ones are shown in Table 4-7B. Open-end questions often reveal more because respondents are not constrained in their answers. Open-end questions are especially useful in the exploratory stage of research where the investigator is trying to determine how people think and is not measuring how many people think in a certain way. Closed-end questions, on the other hand, provide answers that are easier to interpret and tabulate.

Care should be exercised in the *wording of questions.* The researcher should use simple, direct, unbiased wording. The questions should be pretested before they are used to a wide extent.

Care should also be exercised in the *sequencing of questions.* The lead question should create interest if possible. Difficult or personal questions should be asked toward the end of the interview so that respondents do not become defensive. The questions should come up in a logical order. Classificatory data on the respondent are put last because they are more personal and less interesting to the respondent.

Mechanical instruments are also used in marketing research, although questionnaires are the most common research instrument. A galvanometer is a device that measures the strength of a subject's interest or emotions aroused by an exposure to a specific ad or picture. The galvanometer picks up the minute degree of sweating that accompanies emotional arousal. The tachistoscope is a device that flashes an ad to a subject with an exposure interval that may range from less than one-hundredth of a second to several seconds. After each exposure, the respondent describes everything he or she recalls. Eye cameras are used to study respondents' eye movements to determine at what points their eyes land first, and how long they linger on a given item. The audiometer is an electronic device attached to television sets in participating homes to record when the set is on and to which channel it is tuned.[17]

PRESENTING THE RESEARCH PLAN. At this stage, the marketing researcher should summarize the plan in a written proposal. A written proposal is especially important when the research project will be large and complicated, or when an outside firm conducts the research. The proposal should cover the management problems addressed and the research objectives, specific information to be obtained, sources of secondary information or methods for collecting primary data, and how the results will help management decision making. The proposal should also include an estimate of research project costs. A written research plan or proposal ensures that all important aspects of the research project have been carefully considered and that the marketing manager and researchers agree on why and how the research will be done. The manager should review the proposal carefully before approving the project.

Implementing the Research Plan

The researcher next implements the marketing research plan. This involves collecting, processing, and analyzing the information. Data collection can be done by the company's marketing research staff or subcontracted to outside firms. The company retains greater control over the collection process and data quality by using its own staff. However, outside firms that specialize in data collection can often do the job more quickly and at lower cost.

The data collection phase of the marketing research process is generally the most expensive and the most subject to error. The researcher should monitor the fieldwork closely to make sure that the plan is correctly implemented and to guard against problems with contacting respondents, respondents who refuse to cooperate or who give biased or dishonest answers, and interviewers who make mistakes or take shortcuts. In experimental research, the researchers have to worry about matching the experimental and control groups, not influencing the participants by their presence, administering the treatments in a uniform way, and controlling for extraneous factors.

The collected data must be processed and analyzed to extract pertinent information and findings. Data from questionnaires and other instruments is checked for accuracy and completeness, and coded for computer analysis. With the help of specialists, the researcher applies standard computer programs to prepare tabulations of results and to compute averages and measures of dispersion for the major variables. The researcher may also apply advanced statistical techniques and decision models in the analytical marketing system in the hope of finding additional information.

Interpreting and Reporting the Findings

The researcher must now interpret the findings, draw conclusions about their implications, and report them to management. The researcher should not try to overwhelm managers with numbers and fancy statistical techniques—this will lose them. The researcher should present major findings that are relevant to the major decisions addressed by the research.

Interpretation should not be left only to the researchers. They are often experts in research design and statistics, but the marketing manager knows more about the problem situation and the decisions that must be made. In many cases, findings can be interpreted in different ways, and discussions between researchers and managers will help point to the best interpretations. The manager will also want to check that the research project was properly carried out, and that all the necessary analysis was done. Or, after seeing the findings, the manager may have additional questions that can be answered using the research data collected. Finally, the manager is the one who must ultimately decide what action the research suggests. The researchers may even make the data directly available to marketing managers so that they can do new analyses and test new relationships on their own.

Interpretation is a very important phase of the marketing process. The best research is meaningless if the manager blindly accepts uninformed or inaccurate interpretations from the researcher. Similarly, managers may have biased interpretations—they tend to accept research results that support their expectations and to reject those that are contrary to what they expect or hope for. Thus managers and researchers must work together closely when interpreting research results.

Marketing Research in Smaller Organizations

In this section we have looked at the marketing research process—from defining research objectives to interpreting and reporting results—as a lengthy, formal process carried out by large marketing companies. But many small businesses and nonprofit organizations also use marketing research to obtain information for making better marketing decisions. Almost any organization can find informal, low-cost alternatives to the formal and sophisticated marketing research techniques used by research experts in large firms (see Exhibit 4-4).

EXHIBIT 4-4

MARKETING RESEARCH IN SMALL BUSINESSES AND NONPROFIT ORGANIZATIONS

Managers of small businesses and nonprofit organizations often think that marketing research can be done only by experts in large companies with big research budgets. But many of the marketing research techniques discussed in this chapter can also be used less formally by smaller, less sophisticated organizations—and collecting information to improve marketing decisions need not be expensive.

Managers of small businesses and nonprofit organizations can obtain much marketing information simply by carefully *observing* the events and behavior around them. For example, retailers can evaluate new outlet locations by observing vehicle and pedestrian traffic. They can visit competing stores to check on facilities and prices. They can evaluate their customer mix by watching and recording how many and what kinds of customers shop in the store at different times of the day and different days of the week. Competitor advertising can be monitored through the systematic collection of advertisements in local media.

Managers can conduct informal *surveys* using small convenience samples that are usually adequate for exploratory research purposes. The director of an art museum can learn about patron or nonpatron reactions to new programs or exhibits by conducting informal "focus groups"—by inviting small groups to lunch and encouraging discussions on topics of interest. Retail salespeople can talk with customers visiting the store; hospital officials can interview patients. Restaurant managers might make random phone calls during slack hours to interview consumers about where they eat out and what they think of various restaurants in the area.

Managers can also conduct their own simple *experiments*. For example, by varying themes in routine fundraising mailings and tracking results, a nonprofit manager can accumulate a great deal of information about which marketing strategies work best. By varying newspaper advertisements, a store manager can learn the effects of things such as ad size and position, price coupons, and media used.

Small organizations have access to most of the secondary data available to large businesses. In addition, many associations, local media, chambers of commerce, government agencies, and others cater to the special needs of small organizations. The U. S. Small Business Administration offers dozens of free publications providing advice on topics ranging from planning small business advertising to ordering business signs. Local newspapers often provide information on the characteristics and buying patterns of area shoppers.

Sometimes volunteers and colleges are willing to help carry out research. Many nonprofit organizations have access to volunteers from local service clubs and other sources. The U. S. Small Business Administration has programs that offer assistance to small businesses. Many colleges are seeking small businesses and nonprofit organizations to serve as cases for projects in marketing research classes.

Thus secondary data collection, observation, surveys, and experiments can be used effectively by small organizations with small budgets. Though such informal research is less sophisticated and complex, it must still be done carefully. To use these informal approaches successfully, managers must carefully think through the objectives of the research, formulate questions in advance, recognize the biases introduced by smaller convenience samples and less skilled researchers, and conduct the research systematically. If carefully planned and implemented, such low-cost research can be used to obtain reliable information for improving marketing decision making.

Source: Based on information found in Alan R. Andreasen, "Cost-Conscious Marketing Research," *Harvard Business Review,* July–August, 1983, pp. 74–79, and other sources.

Information Analysis

Information gathered by the company's marketing intelligence and marketing research systems often requires more analysis, or managers need more help to apply it to marketing problems and decisions. The *analytical marketing system* includes a statistical bank and a model bank (see Figure 4-3). The *statistical bank* is a collection of advanced statistical procedures for learning more about the relationships within a set of data and their statistical reliability. These procedures allow management to go beyond frequency distributions, means, and standard deviations in the data. Managers often want to answer such questions as

- What are the major variables affecting my sales and how important is each one?
- If I raised my price 10 percent and increased my advertising expenditures 20 percent, what would happen to sales?
- What are the most discriminating predictors of consumers who are likely to buy my brand versus my competitor's brand?
- What are the best variables for segmenting my market, and how many segments exist?

The reader interested in these statistical techniques should consult a standard source.[18]

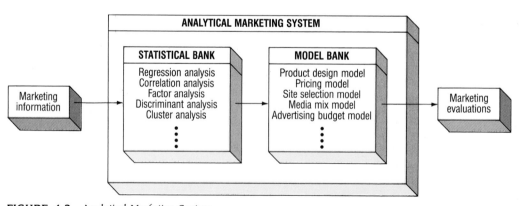

FIGURE 4-3 *Analytical Marketing System*

The *model bank* is a collection of mathematical models that will help marketers make better marketing decisions. Each model consists of a set of interrelated variables that represent some real system, process, or outcome. These models can help answer the questions *what if* and *which is best.* In the past twenty years, marketing scientists have developed a great number of models to help marketing managers make better marketing mix decisions, design sales territories and sales call plans, select sites for retail outlets, develop optimal advertising mixes, and forecast new product sales.[19]

DISTRIBUTING INFORMATION

Marketing information has no value until managers use it to make better marketing decisions. The information gathered by the marketing intelligence and marketing research systems must be distributed to the right marketing managers at the right time. Most companies have centralized marketing information systems that provide managers with regular performance reports, intelligence updates, and reports on the results of studies. Managers need these routine reports for making regular planning, execution, and control decisions. But marketing managers may also need nonroutine information or analyses for special situations and on-the-spot decisions. For example, a sales manager having trouble with a large customer wants a summary of the account's sales and profitability over the past year, or a retail store manager whose store has run out of a best-selling product wants to know the

An advanced office network ties the manager directly into the company's marketing information system. *Courtesy of AT&T Bell Laboratories.*

current inventory levels in the chain's other stores. In companies with centralized information systems, these managers must request the information from the MIS staff and wait; often the information arrives too late to be useful.

Recent developments in information handling have caused a revolution in information distribution. With recent advances in mini- and microcomputers, software for data and word processing, and telecommunications, many companies are decentralizing their marketing information systems—giving managers direct access to information stored in the system, and to programs for analyzing it and communicating the results.[20] In some companies, marketing managers can use a desk terminal to tie into the company's information network, obtain information from internal data banks or outside information services, analyze the information using statistical packages and models from the analytical marketing system, prepare reports and correspondence on a word processor, and communicate with others in the network through telecommunications (see Exhibit 4-5).

EXHIBIT 4-5

INFORMATION NETWORKS: DECENTRALIZING THE MARKETING INFORMATION SYSTEM

New information technologies are making it possible to help managers obtain, process, and send information directly through machines, rather than relying on the services of information staff specialists. The last decade's centralized information systems are evolving into distributed processing systems, taking information management out of the hands of staff specialists and putting it into the hands of managers. Many companies are developing *information networks* that use telecommunications to link information-related machines and to merge previously separate technologies such as word processing, data processing, and image processing into a single system. Marketing managers can tie into these networks and work with information stored as data on computers, text on word processors, images on microfilm, and voice on the network itself.

For example, envision the working day of a future marketing manager. On arriving at work, the manager turns to a desk terminal and reads any messages that arrived during the night, reviews the day's schedule, checks the status of an ongoing computer conference, reads several intelligence alerts, and browses through abstracts of relevant articles from the previous day's business press. To prepare for a late-morning meeting of the new products committee, the manager calls up a recent marketing research report from microfilm storage to the terminal screen, reviews relevant sections, edits them into a short report, sends copies electronically to other committee members who are also connected to the information network, and has the computer file a copy on microfilm. Before leaving for the meeting, the manager uses the terminal to make lunch reservations at a favorite restaurant and to buy airline tickets for next week's trip to Chicago. The afternoon is spent preparing sales and profit forecasts for the new product discussed at the morning meeting. The manager obtains test market data from company data banks and information on market demand, sales and shares of competing products, and projected economic conditions from external data bases to which the company subscribes. These data are used as inputs for the sales forecasting model stored in the company's model bank. The manager "plays" with the model to test the effects of different assumptions on predicted results. At home later that evening, the manager uses a portable personal computer to contact the network, prepare a report on the product, and send copies to the terminals of other involved managers who can read them first thing in the morning. When the manager logs off, the computer automatically sets the alarm clock and puts out the cat.

Modern information networks promise an exciting array of capabilities to help managers to improve performance. The costs of distributed processing systems are still prohibitive for most companies, but increasing decentralization of marketing information systems is inevitable.

Source: For more information, see Peter Nulty, "How Personal Computers Change Managers' Lives," *Fortune,* September 3, 1984, pp. 38–48.

Such *distributed processing* systems offer exciting prospects. They eliminate the intermediaries who separate the managers from needed information and allow the managers to get information quickly and tailor it to their own needs. As more managers develop the skills needed to use such systems, and as improvements in the technology make them more economical, more and more marketing companies will use decentralized marketing information systems.

■ *Summary*

In carrying out their marketing responsibilities, marketing managers need a great deal of information. Despite the growing supply of information, managers often lack enough information of the right kind or have too much of the wrong kind. To overcome these deficiencies, many companies are taking steps to improve their marketing information systems.

A well-designed marketing information system begins and ends with the user. It first *assesses information needs* by interviewing marketing managers and surveying their decision environment to determine what information is desired, needed, and feasible to offer.

The MIS next *develops information* and helps managers to use it more effectively. *Internal records* provide information on sales, costs, inventories, cash flows, and accounts receivable and payable. Such data can be obtained quickly and inexpensively, but must often be adapted for marketing decisions. The *marketing intelligence system* supplies marketing executives with everyday information about developments in the external marketing environment. Defensive intelligence helps avoid threatening surprises; offensive intelligence helps identify opportunities. Intelligence can be collected from company employees, customers, suppliers, and resellers, or by monitoring published reports, conferences, advertisements, competitor actions, and other activities in the environment.

Marketing research involves collecting information relevant to a specific marketing problem facing the company. Every marketer needs marketing research, and over three-fourths of all large companies have their own marketing research departments. Marketing research involves a four-step process. The first step consists of the manager and researcher carefully defining the problem and setting the research objectives. The objective may be exploratory, descriptive, or causal. The second step consists of developing the research plan for collecting data from primary and secondary sources. Primary data collection calls for choosing a research approach (observation, survey, experiment), choosing a contact method (mail, telephone, personal), designing a sampling plan (sampling unit, sample size, and sampling procedure), and developing research instruments (questionnaire, mechanical). The marketing manager should review the written research plan carefully before approving the project. The third step consists of implementing the marketing research plan by collecting, processing, and analyzing the information.

The fourth step consists of interpreting and reporting the findings. The analytical marketing system helps marketing managers to apply the information and provides advanced statistical procedures and models to develop more rigorous findings from information.

Finally, the marketing information system *distributes information* gathered from internal sources, marketing intelligence, and marketing research to the right managers at the right times. More and more companies are decentralizing their information systems through distributed processing networks that allow managers to have direct access to information.

■ Questions for Discussion

1. What might some research tasks be for the following areas: distribution decisions, product decisions, advertising decisions, personal selling decisions, pricing decisions?

2. In several test communities in the United States, it is possible to scan a consumer's purchases at a grocery checkout counter, beam customer-tailored commercials into this consumer's home via split cable TV, and determine if he or she later changed from buying brand A to brand B after having seen the commercials. Consumers volunteer for participation in this test. The ACLU claims that this is an invasion of privacy; marketers claim that it will revolutionize the marketing research business. What do you think?

3. How does a *marketing information system* differ from a *marketing intelligence system?*

4. What is the overriding objective of the marketing research system at Prentice-Hall?

5. Briefly describe the meaning of *analytical marketing system.* Do you feel that a men's clothing store in a small town would use this type of system? Why?

6. Once the research objectives and the problem have been defined, the researcher is then ready to begin the formal surveying of people. Comment.

7. Which type of research would be the most appropriate in the following situations, and why?

   a. Post cereals wants to investigate the effect children have on the actual purchase of its products.

   b. Your college bookstore wants to gather some preliminary information on how students feel about the merchandise and service provided by the bookstore.

   c. McDonald's is considering locating a new outlet in a fast-growing suburb.

   d. Gillette wants to test the effect of two new advertising themes for its Right Guard lime stick deodorant sales in two cities.

8. The president of a campus organization to which you belong has asked you to conduct a marketing research project on why membership is declining. Discuss how you would apply the steps in the marketing research procedure to this project.

9. List some internal company or environmental factors that would call for more marketing research by a company.

■ References

1. Based on material found in "The Jogging-Shoe Race Heats Up," *Business Week,* April 9, 1979, pp. 124–25; and "Converse: Trying a Full-Court Press in Athletic Shoes," *Business Week,* May 7, 1984, pp. 52–56.

2. MARION HARPER, JR., "A New Profession to Aid Management," *Journal of Marketing,* January 1961, p. 1.

3. JOHN NEISBITT, *Megatrends: Ten New Directions Transforming Our Lives* (New York: Warner Books, 1984).

4. NEISBITT, Megatrends, p. 16.

5. This definition is adapted from "Marketing Information Systems: An Introductory Overview," in *Readings in Marketing Information Systems,*

Samual V. Smith, Richard H. Brien, and James E. Stafford, eds. (Boston: Houghton Mifflin, 1968), p. 7.

6. DONALD S. TULL and DEL I. HAWKINS, *Marketing Research: Measurement and Method,* (3rd ed.) (New York: MacMillan, 1984), pp. 46–73.

7. See "Business Is Turning Data into a Potent Strategic Weapon," *Business Week,* August 22, 1983, p. 92.

8. DAVID B. MONTGOMERY and CHARLES B. WEINBURG, "Toward Strategic Intelligence Systems," *Journal of Marketing,* Fall 1979, pp. 41–52.

9. Ibid., p. 47.

10. DIK WARREN TWEDT, ed., *1978 Survey of Marketing Research* (Chicago: American Marketing Association, 1978).

11. See "How They Rank: 1983 Revenue Record of 35 Leading U.S. Research Companies," *Advertising Age,* May 17, 1984, p. M17. Also see JACK HONOMICHL, "First Worldwide Survey of Leading Researchers," *Advertising Age,* July 18, 1983, p. 3.

12. For an excellent annotated reference to major secondary sources of business and marketing data, see THOMAS C. KINNEAR and JAMES R. TAYLOR, *Marketing Research: An Applied Approach* (New York: McGraw-Hill, 1983), pp. 146–56, 169–84.

13. Ibid., p. 150.

14. For more information on observational research, see TULL and HAWKINS, *Marketing Research,* pp. 325–33.

15. For more information on experimental research, see SEYMOUR BANKS, *Experimentation in Marketing* (New York: McGraw-Hill, 1965).

16. BOBBY J. CALDER, "Focus Groups and the Nature of Qualitative Marketing Research," *Journal of Marketing,* August 1977, pp. 353–64.

17. For an overview of mechanical devices, see ROGER D. BLACKWELL, JAMES S. HENSEL, MICHAEL B. PHILLIPS, and BRIAN STERNTHAL, *Laboratory Equipment for Marketing Research* (Dubuque, IA: Kendall/Hunt, 1970), pp. 7–8.

18. See PAUL E. GREEN and DONALD S. TULL, *Research for Marketing Decisions,* 4th ed. (Englewood Cliffs, NJ: Prentice-Hall, 1978).

19. For a review of marketing models, see GARY L. LILIEN and PHILIP KOTLER, *Marketing Decision Making: A Model Building Approach* (New York: Harper & Row, 1983); also see JOHN D. C. LITTLE, "Decision Support Systems for Marketing Managers," *Journal of Marketing,* Summer 1979, pp. 9–26.

20. See PETER NULTY, "How Personal Computers Change Managers' Lives," *Fortune,* September 3, 1984, pp. 38–48.

CASE 1

SONY CORPORATION: WALKMAN/WATCHMAN

Sony introduced the Walkman at the end of 1979. In 1980 it shipped 550,000 of these gadgets worldwide, and by 1985 the product had become widely accepted and imitated. At least twenty companies entered the market with similar products. The Walkman provides high-quality playback through lightweight earphones attached to a lightweight cassette player worn on the belt or around the neck. Sony management must now determine whether the Walkman-type product will continue to be popular and how it should compete in this market. A first step is to determine who are the buyers, why they buy, and how the product is used.

The Walkman was created by a young engineer who made it for fun. In time it was shown to Mr. Akio Morita, Sony's chairman, who adopted it for his personal use and enthusiastically served as the product development project leader, reducing to six months the time between planning the product and its marketing instead of the usual one to two years. Product development and marketing ideas were obtained from high school and university students as they used and discussed the Walkman in a room especially equipped for observation.

In Japan the Walkman virtually sold itself following special presentations for newspaper and magazine reporters. Many articles appeared in magazines, but few in newspapers.

Special events were planned for young people, who were encouraged to try the Walkman while enjoying all kinds of activities in public places, such as skate boarding, cycling, jogging, and rope skipping.

In the United States the product has been used by people as they work, bicycle, drive, roller skate, sun themselves, ski, converse, and block out the sounds of the world. The product in use in public places was a form of promotion in itself and helped to create an ever-spiraling demand that spread worldwide, as the hula hoop had done twenty years earlier.

Competition brought imitators and price cutting. Walkman stereocassette players are being sold in mass retailing outlets for as low as $39. Competitors' products are sold for as much as 40 percent lower. Sony's response to this intense competition has been to maintain its premium prices, expand the line, and improve the products. Sony's expanded line now includes a stereocassettte player and FM stereo radio, a combination of AM/FM stereo radio with lightweight earphones, and other models.

The innovative skills of Sony in trying to keep ahead of competition are evident in the new Walkman stereocassette player. It is smaller, uses a new earphone concept, and sells for about $100 in selected retail outlets. It is as small as the plastic box that holds a standard cassette (¾″ × 2⅔″ × 4¼″) and uses one AA cell battery. Each earphone fits into the ear sideways, with the speaker facing toward the front of the ear. The earphone does not slide around on the head, sounds better than most earphones, feels comfortable, and lets the user hear more of the sounds in the environment.

In reviewing its United States marketing efforts for the Walkman, Sony is interested in knowing whether or not the product is a novelty, in which case the demand could dry up rather quickly. On the other hand, if the product serves one or more basic uses or functions, the market could be quite large and include several segments, if market segment opportunities exist. In any event, Sony will have to decide what, if any, competitive advantages it has and how best to use them in search of profit, avoiding price competition as much as possible. It could concentrate on one or two models for all parts of the market, or offer models designed especially for different segments of the market.

What groups of potential buyers exist for the Walkman, and what can Sony do to increase the sale of the product to each of these groups?

Sony's newest related innovation is its Watchman, a personal hand-held or vest-pocket black and white TV that was priced to sell for about $200, but has been advertised for as little as $149. Its 2-inch screen gives unique clarity and picture definition that rival many larger conventional sets. It brightness and luminance can easily be seen at a football game, and words are easy to read. Sony uses a miniaturized cathode-ray tube, just like most TVs. It is palm-sized (9½″ × 3″ × 6″) weighs 18 ounces, and is powered by 4 AA cell batteries or an optional voltage adapter and is equipped with a telescoping antenna and a carrying strap.

In marketing the Watchman, Sony faces the same basic marketing problems as it does with the Walkman, but in a different phase of the product life cycle. The apparent similarity of the marketing characteristics of the two products suggests that perhaps they should be marketed to consumers in the same way.

Who are the potential buyers of the Watchman? Under what circumstances would they use it? How should the Watchman be marketed?

CASE 2

QUAKER OATS COMPANY: GATORADE

Gatorade, America's number-one thirst quencher among athletes, was acquired from Stokley-Van Camp, Inc., by the Quaker Oats Company in 1983. it was seen by Quaker management as an undermarketed product with excellent potential. It is a well-known brand with a return of $5.7 million on sales of about $85 million and an annual growth rate of about 7 percent.

Quaker management sees an opportunity to expand beyond its present concentrated user base. It hopes to increase sales particularly (1) in non-Sunbelt areas; (2) in off-season periods; and (3) among a broader cut of the population. Presently 85 percent of purchases are made by "heavy users." An effort is being made to identify more clearly a wide range of thirst-quenching situations, especially those involving women and children. The management hopes to find ways to gain a share for Gatorade in the mass soft-drink market.

Gatorade, a noncarbonated beverage, was developed by Dr. Robert Cade, a professor of medicine, for use by the University of Florida football team to combat the draining effects of practice under the hot Florida sun. It was adopted by the Green Bay Packers, whose coach endorsed Gatorade. "The original product tasted like steel and salt water and made one feel like vomiting," according to Dr. Cade.

Gatorade, a cloudy, citrus-flavored drink, was introduced to the market in 1967 and quickly became the drink of champions or would-be champions. Palatability was improved by adding flavors, and product trial was achieved by mailing samples to athletic teams and coaches throughout the United States. Following these efforts, the product was an immediate success. Most sales were to sports teams. But Stokely continued to widen Gatorade's market, aiming at factory and construction workers and "anyone in a high-temperature environment." Powdered Gatorade, introduced in 1979, has been successful. Stokley marketed the product shrewdly, but it is believed there is still room for growth, including overseas, despite the opinion of one financial analyst that Gatorade may be "a product of the 70s."

The president of a food-service consulting company sees many opportunities for Quaker to do marketing experimentation with Gatorade and possibly gain a toehold in beverages. The product is available in quart bottles, 12-ounce vended cans, and powdered form. Aseptic carton packages could give Gatorade entry into the brown-bag lunch and picnic markets. Quaker has an outstanding management team and substantial business overseas, particularly in Europe and Latin America, that would make possible expansion to those areas if consumer acceptance exists for the product.

One year after acquiring the product, Quaker launched an aggressive new marketing program for Gatorade thirst quencher. The advertising campaign positioned Gatorade as a "thirst-aid" and showed the product in heavy thirst situations. It ran throughout the peak buying periods of late spring and summer. The Olympic Games were included in the advertising schedule. The campaign was created by AdCom, Quaker's advertising subsidiary. The advertising budget for Gatorade is estimated to be from $15 to $20 million a year.

The marketing effort will build on the product's strength in the Southeast and Southwest, where 60 percent of its sales are concentrated, while "reintroducing" the product in non-Sunbelt markets through heavy advertising and promotional support. Gatorade will continue its involvement with professional and college sports teams and major sports events, including NASCAR auto races, the National Football League, the National Basketball Association, and major league baseball. A youth-oriented sponsorship is the Gatorade Coach of the Year Award, in cooperation with the National Youth Sports Coaches Association.

What marketing recommendation would you make to the Quaker management, assuming you are a new management trainee who has been asked for your opinion?

three

ANALYZING MARKET OPPORTUNITIES

Part Three of this book examines the complex and changing marketplace as the source of the company's major marketing opportunities and challenges.

5

The Marketing Environment

Invented by Levi Strauss in the mid-1800s, rugged and dependable blue jeans have long been an institution in American life. But during the last decade, the $6 billion blue jean industry has fallen on hard times and flat sales. Over the years, companies such as Levi Strauss, Blue Bell (Wranglers), and V. F. Corporation (Lee's) could count on a steadily growing population and an explosion in the number of young people (caused by the baby boom) to provide 10 to 15 percent annual increases in sales. They grew complacent and internally focused. But population increases leveled off, and the baby boomers are rapidly aging out of the jeans market or looking for new features in the jeans they buy. Because of environmental trends, jeans makers must now fight for profitable shares of a stagnant market—and many are having a difficult time of it.

Levi Strauss provides the most obvious example. As the nation's largest apparel maker, the $2.5 billion company has long dominated the jeans industry; in the early 1980s, its market share stood at over 20 percent. Through the 1970s, as the demand for jeans began to shrink, Levi Strauss held fast to its basic product line of rugged denims for work and play. But tastes were changing quickly in the smaller jeans market. As the baby boom generation moved from youth toward middle age, jeans preferences shifted toward comfort, styling, and fashion. What had typically been a homogeneous mass market became more fragmented, with different segments seeking different things from their jeans.

Levi Strauss failed to adapt to the rapidly changing market environment. It responded with mass-marketing strategies by substantially increasing its advertising budget and selling through mass-market retailers such as Sears and J. C. Penney. These tactics did not work, and the company's profits plummeted.

Not all jeans producers fell victim to the changing market environment. The V. F. Corporation reacted successfully with a segmented marketing strategy for its Lee's brand. It targeted women and fashion-conscious consumers and developed new products designed to meet the special needs of these smaller segments. V. F. was rewarded for quickly adapting to the more discriminating market with steadily increasing sales. Lee's market share rose from 2.5 percent in 1980 to over 11 percent in 1984, with earnings on equity averaging over 27 percent during the period.

Recently, Levi Strauss has responded by developing strategies to reach smaller market segments with new lines that better match changing consumer preferences. By 1984, it had added over 75 new lines, including the David Hunter line (classic men's sportswear), the Perry Ellis Collection (men's, women's, and children's casual sportswear), Ralph Lauren's Polo line (high fashion), a Railsback line (corduroy and denim maternity wear), the Tourage SSE line (fashionable menswear), and many others. Yet many analysts think Levi waited too long and is doing too little to adjust to new market conditions. And the company is cutting costs and reducing operations in preparation for continued hard times.

The long-run trends are working against Levi Strauss and the other jeans makers. Success—even survival—will require that they monitor the market environment and adapt their product and marketing strategies to meet consumer needs in the fast-changing jeans market environment.[1]

Clearly, marketing success depends on developing and a sound marketing mix (the controllable variables) adapted to trends and developments in the marketing environment (the uncontrollable variables). The marketing environment represents the set of uncontrollable forces to which the company must adapt its marketing mix.

We define a company's marketing environment as follows:

> A **company's marketing environment** consists of the actors and forces that are external to the marketing management function of the firm and that impinge on the marketing management's ability to develop and maintain successful transactions with its target customers.

The changing, constraining, and uncertain marketing environment vitally affects the company. The marketing environment is in continual flux, spinning off new opportunities and new threats. Instead of changing slowly and predictably, the environment is capable of producing major surprises and shocks. Which oil companies in 1971 would have predicted the end of cheap energy so soon? How many managers at Gerber Foods foresaw the end of the baby boom? Which auto companies foresaw the tremendous impact Ralph Nader and consumers would have on their business decisions? Drucker has called this an *Age of Discontinuity,*[2] and Toffler has described it as *Future Shock.*[3]

Given that *marketing environment = opportunities and threats,* the firm must use its marketing research and marketing intelligence capabilities to monitor the changing environment. The marketing environment comprises a microenvironment and a macroenvironment. The **microenvironment** consists of the actors in the company's immediate environment that affect its ability to serve its customers—namely, the company, market channel firms, customer markets, competitors, and publics. The **macroenvironment** consists of the larger societal forces that affect all the actors in the company's microenvironment—namely, the demographic, economic, natural, technological, political, and cultural forces. We will first examine the company's microenvironment and then its macroenvironment.

THE COMPANY'S MICROENVIRONMENT

Every company's primary goal is to transact profitably with its target markets. The job of marketing management is to formulate attractive offers for its target markets. However, marketing management's success will be affected by the rest of the company, middlemen, competitors, and various publics. These actors in the company's microenvironment are shown in Figure 5-1. Marketing managers cannot simply focus on the target market's needs; also they must be conscious of all actors in the microenvironment in which the company operates. We will look at the company, suppliers, middlemen, customers, competitors, and publics—in that order. We will illustrate the role and impact of these actors by referring to the Schwinn Bicycle Company of Chicago, a major U.S. producer of bicycles.

FIGURE 5-1
Major Actors in the Company's Microenvironment

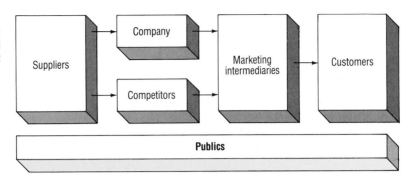

FIGURE 5-1
*Major Actors in
the Company's
Microenvironment*

Company Marketing management at Schwinn, in formulating marketing plans, must take into account the other groups in the company, such as top management, finance, R&D, purchasing, manufacturing, and accounting. All these groups constitute a company microenvironment for the marketing planners (see Figure 5-2).

Top management at Schwinn consists of the bicycle division's general manager, the executive committee, the chief executive officer, the chairman of the board, and the board of directors. These higher levels of management set the company's mission, objectives, broad strategies, and policies. Marketing managers must make decisions within the context set by top management. Furthermore, their marketing proposals must be approved by top management before they can be implemented.

Marketing managers must also work closely with the functional departments. Financial management at Schwinn is concerned with the availability of funds to carry out the marketing plan, the efficient allocation of these funds to different products and marketing activities, the likely rates of return that will be realized, and the level of risk in the sales forecast and marketing plan. Research and develop-

FIGURE 5-2
Company Microenvironment

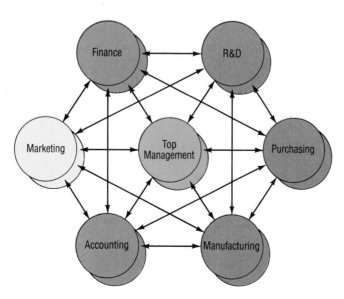

ment management focuses on the technical problems of designing safe and attractive bicycles and developing efficient methods of producing them. Purchasing worries about obtaining sufficient supplies to produce the forecasted number of bicycles. Manufacturing is responsible for acquiring sufficient production capacity and labor and meeting production targets. Accounting has to measure ongoing revenues and costs to help marketing know how well it is achieving its objectives.

All these departments have an impact on the marketing department's plans and actions. A product manager has to "sell" his or her plan to manufacturing and finance before presenting it to top management. If the manufacturing vice-president will not allocate enough production capacity, or the financial vice-president will not allocate enough money, the product manager will have to revise his or her sales targets or bring the issue before top management. The many potential conflicts between marketing and the other functions mean that marketing has to negotiate with internal groups in the company to form and implement its plans.

Suppliers

Suppliers are business firms and individuals that provide the resources needed by the company and its competitors to produce goods and services. For example, Schwinn must obtain steel, aluminum, rubber tires, gears, seats, and other materials to produce bicycles. In addition, it must obtain labor, equipment, fuel, electricity, computers, and other factors of production. Schwinn's purchasing department decides which resources to make and which to buy outside. For "buy" decisions, Schwinn's purchasing agents must develop specifications, search for suppliers, qualify them, and choose those that offer the best mix of quality, delivery reliability, credit, warranties, and low cost.

Developments in the supplier environment can have a substantial impact on the company's marketing operations. Marketing managers need to watch price trends of their key inputs. Rising supply costs may force price increases that will reduce the company's forecasted sales volume. Marketing managers are equally concerned with supply availability. Supply shortages, labor strikes, and other events can interfere with the fulfillment of delivery promises to customers and can lose sales in the short run and damage customer goodwill in the long run. Many companies prefer to buy from multiple sources to avoid overdependence on any one supplier, who might raise prices arbitrarily or limit supply. Company purchasing agents are learning how to "wine and dine" suppliers to obtain favorable treatment during periods of shortages. In other words, the purchasing department might have to "market" itself to suppliers.

Marketing Intermediaries

Marketing intermediaries are firms that aid the company in promoting, selling, and distributing its goods to final buyers. They include middlemen, physical distribution firms, marketing service agencies, and financial intermediaries.

Middlemen

Middlemen are business firms that help the company find customers or close sales with them. They fall into two types, agent middlemen and merchant middlemen. *Agent middlemen*—such as brokers and manufacturers' representatives—find customers or negotiate contracts, but do not take title to the merchandise. Schwinn, for example, might hire an agent to find customers in Venezuela and pay a commission for each bicycle sold. The agent does not own the bicycles, and Schwinn ships directly to the customers. *Merchant middlemen*—such as wholesalers and retailers—buy, take title to, and resell merchandise (they are often called *resellers*). Schwinn's primary method of marketing bicycles is to consign them to hundreds of independent dealers who try to resell them at a profit.

Why does Schwinn use middlemen at all? The answer is that middlemen help produce *place, time,* and *possession utility* for the customer more cheaply than Schwinn can by itself. Middlemen create place utility by stocking bicycles where customers are located. They create time utility by showing and delivering bicycles when consumers want them. They create possession utility by selling and transferring titles to the buyers. Schwinn would have to finance, establish, and operate a major system of national outlets if it wanted to create place, time, and possession utility on its own. Schwinn finds it better to work through a system of independent middlemen.

Middlemen help Schwinn overcome two discrepancies between output and customers' needs. The first is the *discrepancy in quantity*—Schwinn produces over a million bicycles annually, but each consumer location needs only a limited number. The second is the *discrepancy in assortment*—Schwinn produces only one brand of bicycles, but many customers want to examine an assortment of brands before making a choice. Thus discrepancies between the producer's capabilities and the market's preferences and requirements underlie the producer's use of middlemen to reach and serve its target markets effectively.

Selecting and working with middlemen, however, is not a simple task. No longer does the manufacturer face many small, independent middlemen from which to choose, but rather large and growing middlemen organizations. More and more bicycles are being sold through large corporate chains (such as Sears and K mart) and large wholesaler, retailer, and franchised-sponsored voluntary chains. These groups have great power to dictate terms or shut the manufacturer out of large-volume markets. Manufacturers must work hard to get "shelf space." In addition, they have to choose their channels carefully, because working with some channels excludes the possibility of working with others. Manufacturers have to learn how to manage their channels in the face of considerable interchannel conflict and competition.

Physical Distribution Firms

Physical distribution firms assist the company in stocking and moving goods from their origin to their destination. *Warehouses* are firms that store and protect goods before they move to the next destination. A company has to decide how much space to build itself and how much to rent from warehouse firms. *Transportation firms* consist of railroads, truckers, airlines, barges, and other freight-handling companies that specialize in moving goods from one location to another. A company has to decide on the most cost-effective modes of shipment, balancing such considerations as cost, delivery, speed, and safety.

Marketing Services Agencies

Marketing services agencies—marketing research firms, advertising agencies, media firms, and marketing consulting firms—assist the company in targeting and promoting its products to the right markets. The company faces a "make or buy" decision with respect to these services. When it decides to buy, it must choose carefully whom to hire, since these firms vary in creativity, quality, service, and price. The company has to review the performance of these firms periodically and consider replacing those that no longer perform adequately.

Financial Intermediaries

Financial intermediaries include banks, credit companies, insurance companies, and other companies that help finance transactions or insure risk associated with the buying and selling of goods. Most firms and customers depend on financial intermediaries to finance their transactions. The company's marketing performance can be seriously affected by rising credit costs or limited credit or both. For this reason, the company has to develop strong relationships with critical financial institutions.

Customers The company needs to study its customer markets closely. The company can operate in five types of customer markets. These are shown in Figure 5-3 and defined below:

1. *Consumer markets:* individuals and households that buy goods and services for personal consumption
2. *Industrial markets:* organizations that buy goods and services for their production process in order to make profits or achieve other objectives
3. *Reseller markets:* organizations that buy goods and services in order to resell them at a profit
4. *Government markets:* government agencies that buy goods and services in order to produce public services or transfer these goods and services to others who need them
5. *International markets:* buyers found abroad, including foreign consumers, producers, resellers, and governments

FIGURE 5-3
Basic Types of Customer Markets

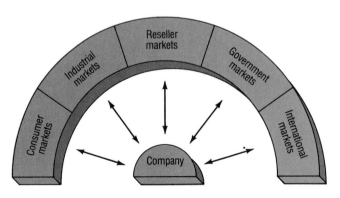

Schwinn sells bicycles in all these markets. It sells some bicycles directly to consumers through factory or retail-owned outlets. It sells bicycles to producers who use them in their operations to deliver goods or ride around the plant. It sells bicycles to bicycle wholesalers and retailers who resell them to consumer and producer markets. It could sell bicycles to government agencies. And it sells bicycles to foreign consumers, producers, resellers, and governments. Each market type has particular characteristics that call for careful study by the seller.

Competitors Every company faces a wide range of competitors. Suppose Schwinn's marketing vice-president wants to identify Schwinn's competitors. The best way to do this is to research how people make bicycle-buying decisions. The researcher can interview John Adams, a college freshman who is planning to spend some discretionary income (see Figure 5-4). John is considering several possibilities, including buying a transportation vehicle, a stereo set, or a trip to Europe. These are *desire competitors*—namely, other immediate desires the consumer might want to satisfy. Suppose John decides that he really needs better transportation. Among the possibilities are buying a car, a motorcycle, or a bicycle. These are *generic competitors*—namely, other basic ways in which the buyer can satisfy a particular desire.

If buying a bicycle turns out to be the most attractive alternative, John will next think about what type of bicycle to buy. This leads to a set of *product form competitors*—namely, other product forms that can satisfy the buyer's particular desire: here, three-speed, five-speed, or ten-speed bicycles. John may tentatively decide on a ten-speed bicycle, in which case he will want to examine several *brand competitors*—namely, other brands that can satisfy the same desire: here, Raleigh, Sears, Azuki, and Gitane.

Using this method, Schwinn's marketing vice-president can determine all the competitors standing in the way of selling more Schwinn bicycles. The manager will want to watch all four types of competitors, paying the most attention to the brand competitors because they are actively competing with Schwinn for sales. The

FIGURE 5-4 *Four Basic Types of Competitors*

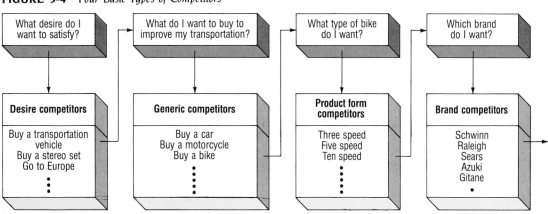

degree of competition among brand manufacturers in different industries ranges from tacit cooperation at one extreme to marketing warfare at the other.

Publics The company's marketing environment also includes various publics. We define public as follows:

> A **public** is any group that has an actual or potential interest in or impact on an organization's ability to achieve its objectives.

A company can prepare marketing plans for its major publics as well as its customer markets. Suppose the company wants some response from a particular public, such as its goodwill, favorable word of mouth, or donations of time or money. The company would have to design an offer to this public attractive enough to elicit the desired response.

Every company is surrounded by seven types of publics (see Figure 5-5):

1. *Financial publics.* Financial publics influence the company's ability to obtain funds. Banks, investment houses, stock brokerage firms, and stockholders are the major financial publics. Schwinn seeks the goodwill of these groups by issuing annual reports, answering financial questions, and satisfying the financial community that its house is in order.

2. *Media publics.* Media publics are organizations that carry news, features, and editorial opinion; specifically, newspapers, magazines, and radio and television stations. Schwinn is interested in getting more and better media coverage.

3. *Government publics.* Management must take government developments into account in formulating marketing plans. Schwinn's marketers must consult the company's lawyers about possible issues of product safety, truth-in-advertising, dealers' rights, and so on. Schwinn must consider joining with other bicycle manufacturers to lobby for better laws.

4. *Citizen action publics.* A company's marketing decisions may be questioned by consumer organizations, environmental groups, minority groups, and others. For example, parent groups are lobbying for greater safety features in bicycles, which are the nation's number-one hazardous product. Schwinn has the opportunity to achieve leadership in product safety design. Schwinn's public relations department will enable it to stay in touch with consumer groups.

5. *Local publics.* Every company comes into contact with local publics such as neighborhood residents and community organizations. Large companies usually appoint a community relations officer to deal with the community, attend meetings, answer questions, and make contributions to worthwhile causes.

FIGURE 5-5
Types of Publics

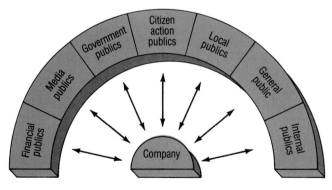

6. *General public.* A company needs to be concerned about the general public's attitude toward its products and activities. Although the general public does not act in an organized way toward the company, the public's image of the company affects its patronage. To build a strong "corporate citizen" image, Schwinn will lend its officers to community fund drives, make substantial contributions to charity, and set up systems for consumer complaint handling.

7. *Internal publics.* A company's internal publics include blue-collar workers, white-collar workers, volunteers, managers, and the board of directors. Large companies develop newsletters and other forms of communication to inform and motivate their internal publics. When employees feel good about their company, this positive attitude spills over to external publics.

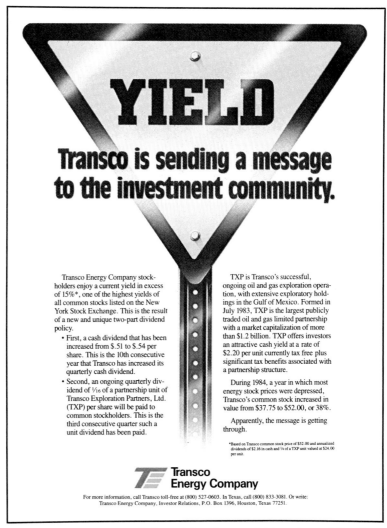

Transco communicates with financial and potential investor publics. *Reprinted with permission of Transco Energy Company.*

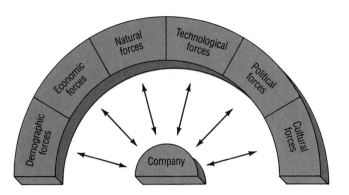

FIGURE 5-6
*Major Forces in
the Company's
Macroenvironment*

THE COMPANY'S MACROENVIRONMENT

The company and its suppliers, marketing intermediaries, customers, competitors, and publics all operate in a larger macroenvironment of forces that shape opportunities and pose threats to the company. These forces represent "uncontrollables," which the company must monitor and respond to. The macroenvironment consists of the six major forces shown in Figure 5-6. The remaining sections of this chapter will examine the trends and developments in each macroenvironment component and their implications for marketing in the coming years.

Demographic Environment

The demographic environment is of major interest to marketers because people make up markets. The most important demographic trends are described here.[4]

Changing Age Structure of the U.S. Population

The single most important demographic trend in the United States is the changing age structure of the population. The U.S. population is getting older for two reasons. First, there is a slowdown in the *birthrate,* so there are fewer young people to pull the population's average age down. Second, *life expectancy* is increasing, so there are more older people to pull the average age up.

The U.S. population stood at 234 million in 1983 and is expected to reach 300 million by the year 2020. During the baby boom that followed World War II and lasted through the early 1960s, the annual birthrate reached a peak of 4.3 million. The baby boom was followed by a "birth dearth," and by the mid-1970s the birthrate had fallen to 3.2 million. This decrease was caused by smaller family sizes resulting from the desire to improve personal living standards, the increasing desire of women to work outside the home, and improved birth control knowledge and technology. Though family sizes are expected to remain smaller, the birthrate will climb to a peak of 3.9 million by the end of the 1980s, as the baby boom generation moves through the childbearing years and creates a second but smaller baby boom. The birthrate will again decline in the 1990s. The baby boom created a large "bulge" in the U.S. age distribution, and as the baby boom generation ages, it pulls the average age up with it.

The second factor contributing to the general aging of the population is increased life expectancy. Current average life expectancy is 74 years (70 for males and 78 for females), a 25-year increase since 1900. This increasing life expectancy and the declining birthrate are producing an aging population. The U.S. median age is now 31 and is expected to reach 36 by the year 2000 and 42 by 2050.[5]

The changing age structure of the population will result in different growth rates for various age groups over the decade, and these differences will strongly affect marketers' targeting strategies. Growth trends for six age groups are summarized below.[6]

- *Children.* There will be 17 percent more preschoolers in 1990 than there were in 1980, but the growth of this group will decline in the 1990s as the baby boomers move out of childbearing years. This will mean that markets for baby's toys, clothes, furniture, and food will enjoy a temporary "boom" after years of "bust," but these markets will again decrease as the century closes.

- *Youths.* The number of 10- to 14-year-olds will drop 8 percent during the decade, and the number of 15- to 19-year-olds will drop 19 percent. Thus there will be 6 million fewer teenagers. This means a slowdown in sales growth for jeans manufacturers, movie and record companies, colleges, and others who target the teen market.

- *Young adults.* This group will decline during this and the next decade as the "birth dearth" generation moves in. Marketers who sell to the 20 to 34 age group—furniture makers, life insurance companies, sports equipment manufacturers—can no longer rely on increasing market size for increases in sales. They will have to work toward increasing shares of smaller markets.

- *Early middle age.* The baby boom generation will be moving into the 35 to 49 age group, creating huge increases. There will be increases of 41 percent in 35- to 39-year-olds, 50 percent in 40- to 44-year-olds, and 26 percent in 44- to 49-year-olds. This group is a major market for larger homes, new automobiles, clothing, entertainment, and investments.

- *Late middle age.* The 50 to 64 age group will continue to shrink until the end of the century; then it will begin to increase as the baby boomers move in. This group is a major market for eating out, travel, expensive clothing, and recreation.

- *Retirees.* The over-65 group will increase by 20 percent over the decade, and will continue to grow through the nineties and into the next century. By 2020 there will be twice as many elderly as there are teenagers. This group has a demand for retirement homes and communities, quieter forms of recreation, single-portion food packaging, and medical goods and services. Today's seniors are more self-centered, more active, and more leisure-oriented than the comparable group in past generations. They tend to spend more money on themselves and not worry about leaving money to their children.

Thus the changing age structure of the U.S. population will strongly affect future marketing decisions. In particular, the baby boom generation will continue to be a prime target for marketers (see Exhibit 5-1).

The Changing American Family

The American ideal of the two-children, two-car suburban family has been losing some of its luster. Here are the major forces at work:[7]

EXHIBIT 5-1

THE BABY BOOM "BULGE"

The baby boomers appeared between 1945 and 1959. Today there are approximately 56.6 million 25 to 39-year-olds or 24.2% of the U.S. population.

They've got:

Money: They earn about half of U.S personal income.

Jobs: Baby boomers make up 41.8% of the total U.S. civilian workforce.

Music: About 70% of stereo equipment purchases were made by boomers last year.

Demands: Especially for premium goodies to quench those upscale thirsts. But they're not as brand loyal as their parents.

Education: Half of baby boom women graduated from college.

Taste: They buy woks by the number, steam cookers by the score.

Homes: Almost 70% of the adults who purchased homes in 1983 were . . . you guessed it.

Culture: The 60's culture still lives to a degree in the minds of the 30 to 40-year-old segment, but the younger boomers are definitely '80s thinkers.

Source: Reprinted with permission from the October 18, 1984, issue of *Advertising Age.* Copyright © 1984, Crain Communications, Inc.

- *Later marriage.* Although 96 percent of all Americans will marry, the average age of couples marrying for the first time has been rising over the years and now stands at 24.8 years for males and 22.3 years for females. By 1990 over half of the 20- to 24-year-old women and one-third of the 25- to 29-year-old women will never have married. This will slow down the sales of engagement and wedding rings, bridal outfits, and life insurance.

- *Fewer children.* Couples with no children under 18 now make up 47 percent of all families. The newly married are also delaying childbearing longer. Of those families that have children, the mean number of children is 1.07, down from 3.50 in 1955. This means a slowed-down demand for baby food, toys, children's clothes, and other children's goods and services.

- *Higher divorce rate.* The United States has the world's highest divorce rate, with about 50 percent of the marriages ending in divorce. This has created over a million single-parent families and the need for additional housing units, furniture, appliances, and other household products. About 79 percent of those divorced remarry, leading to the phenomenon of the "blended" family. Currently about 69 percent of all males and 63 percent of all females are married.

- *More working mothers.* The percentage of mothers of children under age 18 who hold some kind of job has more than doubled since 1960 to over 50 percent. There is less stigma attached to working, as well as a greater number of job opportunities and new freedom resulting from birth control acceptance. Working women are a market for better clothing, day-nursery services, home-cleaning services, and more frozen dinners. The growing number of working women means less viewing of television soap operas and less reading of domestic women's magazines. Their incomes contribute 40 percent of the household's income and influence the purchase of higher-quality goods and services. Marketers of tires, automobiles, insurance, and travel service are increasingly directing their advertising to working women. All this is accompanied by a shift in the traditional roles and values of husbands and wives, with the husband assuming more domestic functions such as shopping and childcare. As a result, husbands are becoming more of a target market for food and household appliance manufacturers and retailers.[8]

The Rise of Nonfamily Households

The number of nonfamily households is increasing. These households take several forms, each of which constitutes a different market segment, complete with its own special needs:

- *Single-adult households.* Many young adults leave home and move into apartments. Other adults choose to remain single. Still others are divorced or widowed people living alone. In the United States, more than 17 million people live alone (22 percent of all households). By 1990, 45 percent of all households will be single-person or single-parent households. They are the fastest-growing category of urban home seekers. The SSWD group (single, separated, widowed, divorced) need smaller apartments; inexpensive and smaller appliances, furniture, and furnishings; and food that is packaged in smaller sizes. Their car preferences are different in that they buy half of all Mustangs and other small specialty cars, and only 8 percent of the large cars.[9] Singles are a market for various services that enable singles to meet each other, such as single bars, tours, and cruises.

- *Two-person cohabitor households.* There are about 2 million households made up of unmarried couples living together, and this number will double by 1990. Because their arrangements are more temporary, they are a market for inexpensive or rental furniture and furnishings.

- *Group households.* Group households consist of three or more persons of the same or opposite sex sharing expenses by living together. Included are college students and certain secular and religious groups who live in communes.

Marketers should consider the special needs of nonfamily households, since they are growing more rapidly than family households.

Geographic Shifts in Population

Americans are a mobile people, with approximately one out of five, or 42 million Americans, moving each year. Among the major mobility trends are the following:

- *Movement of people to the Sunbelt states.* Over the next decade the West will experience a population growth of 17 percent, and the South will experience a growth of 14 percent. The South and West now have 51 percent of the U.S. population, up from 45 percent in 1970. Major cities in the North, on the other hand, have lost population between 1970 and 1978 (New York, 7.5 percent; Pittsburgh, 5.2 percent; Jersey City, 8.9 percent; and Newark, 5.2 percent). These regional population shifts interest marketers because of marked differences in regional expenditure patterns. Consumers in the West, for example, spend relatively less on food and relatively more on automobiles than those in the Northeast. The exodus to the Sunbelt states will lessen the demand for warm clothing and home heating equipment and increase the demand for air conditioning. (For expected percentage changes in state populations during this decade, see Figure 5-7.)

- *Movement from rural to urban areas.* People have been moving from rural to urban areas for over a century. In 1880, 70 percent of the nation's population lived in rural areas; at the present time, 75 percent live in urban areas. Cities show a faster pace of living, more commuting, higher incomes, and greater variety of goods and services than can be found in the small towns and rural areas that dot America. The largest cities, such as New York, Chicago, and San Francisco, account for most of the sales of expensive furs, perfumes, luggage, and works of art; and these cities support the opera, ballet, and other forms of "high culture." Recently, however, there has been a slight shift of population back to small towns and rural areas.

- *Movement from the city to the suburbs.* Many persons live far away from their places of work, owing largely to the development of automobiles, major highways, and rapid rail and bus transit. Cities have become surrounded by suburbs, and these suburbs in turn by "exurbs." The U.S. Census Bureau has created a separate population classification for sprawling urban concentrations called MSAs (Metropolitan Statistical Areas). Very large MSAs (or supermetros) are called CMSAs (Consolidated Metropolitan Statistical Areas), which are further divided into PMSAs (Primary Metropolitan Statistical Areas).[10] These MSAs constitute the primary market focus of firms. Companies use the MSAs in researching the best geographical segments for their products, in planning their geographical rollout strategy for new products, in deciding where to purchase advertising time or space, and so on. MSA research shows, for example, that New Englanders smoke 29 percent more cigarettes than the national average; Chicagoans consume 22 percent more soft drinks; and New Yorkers use 19 percent more paper goods. The top fifty MSA markets are listed in Table 5-1 on page 138.

About 60 percent of the total population, or 39 percent of the metropolitan population, live in suburbs. Suburbs are characterized by more casual, outdoor living, greater neighbor interaction, higher incomes, and younger families. Suburbanites buy station wagons, home workshop equipment, garden furniture, lawn

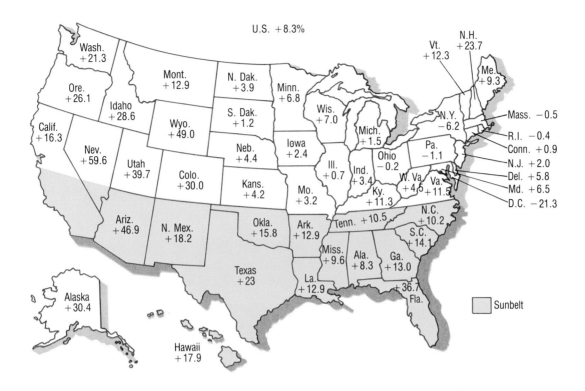

FIGURE 5-7 *Population Growth Rates: 1980–1990*

Source: U.S. Department of Commerce, Bureau of Census.

and gardening tools and supplies, and outdoor cooking equipment. Retailers have acknowledged the suburbs by building branch department stores and suburban shopping centers.

At the same time, marketers should recognize a recent countermove back to the central city, especially in cities where urban renewal has been successful. Young adults and older adults whose children have grown up are attracted by the superior cultural and recreational opportunities and less interested in suburban commuting and gardening. This has led to new high-rise apartment construction and new retail outlets within the city.

A Better-Educated and More White-Collar Population

In 1950, only half of all U.S. adults had gone beyond the ninth grade. By 1980, 70 percent of Americans over age 24 had completed high school. By 1990, the percentage of Americans over 24 who have completed college will stand at 20 percent.[11] The rising number of educated people will increase the demand for quality products, books, magazines, and travel. It portends a decline in indiscriminate television viewing, because college-educated consumers watch TV less than does the population at large.

TABLE 5-1
The Top 50 Markets in
the United States

Rank	MSA	POPULATION July 1, 1982 (thousands)	Rank	MSA	(thousands)
1	New York CMSA	17,589	26	Portland CMSA	1,332
2	Los Angeles CMSA	11,930	27	New Orleans MSA	1,300
3	Chicago CMSA	7,974	28	Columbus MSA	1,267
4	Philadelphia CMSA	5,713	29	Buffalo CMSA	1,218
5	San Francisco CMSA	5,515	30	Norfolk MSA	1,201
6	Detroit/Ann Arbor CMSA	4,630	31	Indianapolis MSA	1,182
7	Boston/Lawrence CMSA	3,988	32	Sacramento MSA	1,165
8	Houston/Galveston CMSA	3,458	33	San Antonio MSA	1,135
9	Washington, D.C.	3,339	34	Providence CMSA	1,089
10	Dallas/Fort Worth CMSA	3,143	35	Hartford CMSA	1,021
11	Cleveland/Akron CMSA	2,808	36	Charlotte/Gastonia MSA	1,003
12	Miami CMSA	2,790	37	Rochester, N.Y. MSA	979
13	Pittsburgh CMSA	2,403	38	Salt Lake City/Ogden MSA	970
14	St. Louis CMSA	2,377	39	Louisville MSA	955
15	Atlanta MSA	2,243	40	Dayton/Springfield MSA	937
16	Baltimore MSA	2,218	41	Memphis MSA	924
17	Minneapolis/St. Paul MSA	2,194	42	Oklahoma City MSA	922
18	Seattle/Tacoma CMSA	2,178	43	Birmingham MSA	890
19	San Diego MSA	1,962	44	Greensboro MSA	869
20	Tampa MSA	1,721	45	Nashville MSA	865
21	Denver/Boulder CMSA	1,721	46	Albany/Schenectady MSA	833
22	Cincinnati/Hamilton CMSA	1,672	47	Honolulu MSA	782
23	Phoenix MSA	1,609	48	Richmond MSA	773
24	Milwaukee/Racine CMSA	1,572	49	Orlando MSA	762
25	Kansas City CMSA	1,454	50	Jacksonville MSA	756

Source: Reprinted with permission from the May 21, 1984, issue of *Advertising Age.* Copyright © 1984 by Crain Communications, Inc.

In 1982, the total labor force consisted of 110 million people. Between 1960 and 1982, the proportion of white-collar workers rose from 42 to 52 percent, blue-collar workers declined from 38 to 31 percent, service workers increased from 12 to 14 percent, and farm workers declined from 8 to 3 percent. Through 1995, the most growth will come in the following occupational categories: computers, engineering, science, medicine, social service, buying, selling, secretarial, construction, refrigeration, health service, personal service, and protection.[12]

These demographic trends are highly reliable for the short and intermediate run. There is little excuse for a company's being suddenly surprised by a demographic development. The alert firm can list the major demographic trends, spell out their implications for the particular industry, and classify these implications as ranging from very positive to very negative. This is done in Table 5-2 for three industries. In the case of airlines, for example, each population trend is expected to have a positive sales and profit impact.

TABLE 5-2 *The Impact of the Changing Population Mix on Three Industries*

TRENDS	AIRLINES	APPAREL	CONSUMER ELECTRONICS
Baby boom generation matures	Many will have more money for travel as they get older. ✔✔✔	Will spend more on clothes as they age; shift from casual to higher quality. ✔✔✔	Rising incomes provide means to buy better-quality stereos, TVs, etc. ✔✔
More elderly persons	They have the time to travel but inflation may rob them of the means. ✔	Older people spend less on clothing.	Little demand from this group; often forced to make do with older products.
More working women	Second income allows more females to take trips; more single women have money. ✔✔✔	Career women need more clothing and have the money to buy it. ✔✔✔	Can buy more and higher-priced merchandise. ✔✔
Smaller family units	More disposable income per member; more economical to fly than drive. ✔✔	A shift toward higher-quality, higher-margin merchandise. ✔✔	More income per capita; electronic entertainment replaces family activities. ✔✔

✔✔✔Very positive   ✔✔Positive   ✔Mildly positive

Source: Chicago Tribune, April 8, 1979, Sec. 5, p. 1. Copyright © 1979 by Standard & Poor's Corp., 345 Hudson St., New York, N.Y. 10014 Reproduction by permission.

Economic Environment   Markets require purchasing power as well as people. Total purchasing power is a function of current income, prices, savings, and credit availability. Marketers should be aware of major trends in real income, savings, and debt, and of changing consumer expenditure patterns.

Changes in Real Income

Although money income per capita grew during the past decade, real income per capita actually declined. Real income was hurt by an inflation rate exceeding the money income growth rate, an unemployment rate between 6 and 10 percent, and an increase in the tax burden. These developments reduced *disposable personal income,* which is the amount of money people have left after taxes. Furthermore, many people have experienced reduced *discretionary income,* which is the amount they have left after paying for food, clothing, shelter, insurance, and other necessities. Reductions in discretionary income hurt sellers of discretionary goods and services, such as automobiles, large appliances, and vacations.

In response to real income decline, many Americans turned to more cautious buying. They bought more store brands and fewer national brands to save money. Many companies introduced economy versions of their products and turned to price appeals in their advertising. Some consumers postponed purchases of durable goods, while others purchased them out of fear that prices would be 10 percent higher the next year. Many families began to feel that a large home, two cars, foreign travel, and private higher education were beyond their reach.

Current projections suggest, however, that real income will rise modestly at an annual rate of 1.5 to 2 percent through the mid-1990s. This will largely result from rising affluence in certain important segments.[13] The baby boom generation will be moving into its prime wage-earning years, and the number of small families headed by dual-career couples will increase dramatically. The number of two-income families has more than tripled since 1950, and by 1990 they will represent more than 46 percent of all families. These more affluent groups will demand higher quality and better service, and they will be willing to pay for it. These consumers will buy more time-saving products and services, more travel and entertainment, more physical fitness products, more cultural activities, and more continuing education.

Marketers should pay attention to income distribution as well as average income. Income distribution in the United States is still very skewed. At the top are *upper-class consumers,* whose expenditure patterns have not been affected by current economic events and who are a major market for luxury goods (Rolls Royces starting at $100,000) and services (round-the-world cruises starting at $10,000). There is a comfortable *middle class* that exercises some expenditure restraint but is able to afford expensive clothes, minor antiques, and a small boat or second home. The *working class* must stick close to the basics of food, clothing, and shelter and must husband resources and try hard to save. Finally, the *underclass* (persons on welfare and many retirees) have to count their pennies when making purchases of even the most basic kind.

Marketers also have to take geographic income variations into account. A city like Houston is growing at a fast rate, while Detroit is languishing. Marketers must focus their efforts on the areas of greatest opportunity.

Low Savings and High Debt

Consumer expenditures are also affected by savings and debt patterns. Eighty-four percent of American spending units hold some liquid assets, the median amount being $800. Americans hold their savings in the form of bank savings accounts, bonds and stocks, real estate, insurance, money market funds, and other assets. These savings are a major source of financing major purchases.

Consumers can increase their purchasing power through borrowing. Consumer credit has been a major contributor to the rapid growth of the American economy, enabling people to buy more than their current income and savings allowed, thus creating more jobs and still more income and more demand. In 1980, outstanding consumer credit (including home mortgages) stood at $1.4 trillion, or $6,298 for every man, woman, and child in America. The cost of this credit is high, and consumers are spending around twenty-one cents of every dollar they earn to pay off existing debts. This retards the further growth of housing and other durable-goods markets that are heavily dependent on credit.

Changing Consumer Expenditure Patterns

Table 5-3 shows the percentage distribution of consumption expenditures over major goods and services categories between 1960 and 1980. Food, housing, household operations, and transportation use up most household income. Over time, however, the food, clothing, and personal care bills of households have been decreasing, while the housing, transportation, medical care, and recreational bills have been increasing. Some of these changes were observed over a century ago by Ernst Engel, a German statistician who studied how people shifted their expenditures as their income rose. He observed that as family income rises, *the percentage spent of food declines, the percentage spent on housing and household operations remains constant, and the percentage spent on other categories (clothing, transportation, recreation, health, and education) and savings increases.* Engel's "laws" have generally been validated in subsequent budget studies.

Changes in such major economic variables as money income, cost of living, interest rates, and savings and borrowing patterns have an immediate impact on the marketplace. Companies that are particularly income-sensitive are wise to invest in sophisticated economic forecasting. Businesses do not have to be wiped out by a downturn in economic activity. With adequate forewarning, they can take the necessary steps to reduce their costs and ride out the economic storm.

Natural Environment The 1960s witnessed a growing public concern over whether the natural environment was being irreparably damaged by the industrial activities of modern nations. Kenneth Boulding pointed out that the planet earth was like a spaceship in danger of running out of fuel if it failed to recycle its materials. The Meadowses, in *The Limits to Growth,*[14] raised concern about the adequacy of natural resources to sustain economic growth. Rachel Carson, in *Silent Spring,*[15] pointed out the damage to water, earth, and air caused by industrial activity of certain kinds. Watchdog groups such as the Sierra Club and Friends of the Earth sprang up, and concerned legislators proposed various measures to protect the environment.

Marketers should be aware of the threats and opportunities associated with four trends in the natural environment: impending shortages, the increased cost of energy, the increased levels of pollution, and government intervention in natural resource management.

Impending Shortages of Certain Raw Materials

The earth's materials consist of the infinite, the finite renewable, and the finite nonrenewable. An *infinite resource,* such as air, poses no immediate problem,

TABLE 5-3 *Percentage Distribution of Consumption Expenditures, 1960, 1970, 1980*			
EXPENDITURE	1960	1970	1980
Food, beverages, tobacco	27.1	23.8	21.9
Housing	14.8	15.2	16.3
Household operations	14.2	14.2	13.7
Transportation	13.1	12.6	14.5
Medical care expenses	7.2	8.1	9.9
Clothing, accessories, jewelry	9.9	9.0	7.4
Recreation	5.5	6.6	6.4
Personal business	4.4	5.1	5.4
Personal care	1.6	1.8	1.4
Other	3.3	3.7	3.2

Sources: The National Income and Product Accounts of the United States, 1929–1974 (Washington, D.C.: U.S. Bureau of Economic Analysis); and *Survey of Current Business.*

although some groups see a long-run danger. Environmental groups have lobbied for a ban on certain propellants used in aerosol cans because of their potential damage to the ozone layer. Water is already a problem in some parts of the world.

Finite renewable resources, such as forests and food, have to be used wisely. Companies in the forestry business are required to reforest timberlands in order to protect the soil and to ensure enough wood supplies to meet future demand. Food supply can be a major problem in that the amount of farmable land is relatively fixed and urban areas are constantly encroaching on farmland.

Finite nonrenewable resources, such as oil, coal, and various minerals, pose a serious problem:

> . . . it would appear at present that the quantities of platinum, gold, zinc, and lead are not sufficient to meet demands . . . silver, tin, and uranium may be in short supply even at higher prices by the turn of the century. By the year 2050, several more minerals may be exhausted if the current rate of consumption continues.[16]

The marketing implications are many. Firms using scarce minerals face substantial cost increases, even if the materials remain available. They may not find it easy to pass these cost increases on to the consumer. Firms engaged in research and development and exploration have an incredible opportunity to develop valuable new sources and materials.

Increased Cost of Energy

One finite nonrenewable resource, oil, has created the most serious problem for future economic growth. The major industrial economies of the world are heavily dependent on oil, and until cost-effective substitute forms of energy can be developed, oil will continue to dominate the world political and economic picture. The high price of oil (from $2.23 per barrel in 1970 to $34.00 per barrel in 1982) has created a frantic search for alternative forms of energy. Coal is again popular, and companies are searching for practical means to harness solar, nuclear, wind, and other forms of energy. In the solar energy field alone, hundreds of firms are putting out first-generation products to harness solar energy for heating homes and other uses.[17] Other firms are searching for ways to make a practical electric automobile, with a potential prize of billions going to the winner.

Increased Levels of Pollution

Some industrial activity will inevitably damage the quality of the natural environment. Consider the disposal of chemical and nuclear wastes, the dangerous mercury levels in the ocean, the quantity of DDT and other chemical pollutants in the soil and food supply, and the littering of the environment with nonbiodegradable bottles, plastics, and other packaging materials.

The public's concern creates a marketing opportunity for alert companies. It creates a large market for pollution control solutions such as scrubbers and recycling centers. It leads to a search for alternative ways to produce and package goods that do not cause environmental damage.[18]

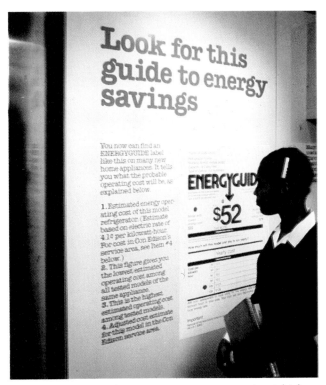

Con Edison responds to consumer concerns about high energy costs. *Courtesy of Consolidated Edison Co. of New York, Inc.*

Strong Government Intervention in Natural Resource Management

Various government agencies play an active role in environmental protection. Ironically, their effort often runs counter to the attempt to increase employment, such as when business is forced to buy expensive pollution control equipment instead of more advanced production equipment. At times, conservation has to take a back seat to economic growth.

Marketing management needs to pay attention to the natural environment for both obtaining needed resources and avoiding damage to the natural environment. Business can expect strong controls from government and pressure groups. Instead of opposing all forms of regulation, business should help develop acceptable solutions to the material and energy problems facing the nation.

Technological Environment The most dramatic force shaping people's destiny is technology. Technology has released such wonders as penicillin, open-heart surgery, and the birth control pill. It has released such horrors as the hydrogen bomb, nerve gas, and the submachine gun. It has released such mixed blessings as the automobile, television, and white bread. Our attitude toward technology depends on whether we are more impressed with its wonders or with its blunders.

Every new technology is a force for "creative destruction." Transistors hurt the vacuum-tube industry, xerography hurt the carbon-paper business, the auto hurt the railroads, and television hurt the movies. Instead of the older industries transforming into the new, they fought or ignored them, and their businesses declined.

The economy's growth rate is affected by how many major new technologies are discovered. Unfortunately, technological discoveries do not arise evenly through time—the railroad industry created a lot of investment and then there was a dearth until the auto industry emerged; later radio created a lot of investment and then there was a dearth until television appeared. In the time between major innovations, the economy can stagnate.

Small innovations in the meantime fill the gaps. Freeze-dried coffee probably made no one happier and antiperspirant deodorants probably made no one wiser, but they did create new markets and opportunities.

Each technology creates major long-run consequences that are not always foreseeable. The contraceptive pill, for example, led to smaller families, more working wives, and larger discretionary incomes—resulting in higher expenditures on vacation travel, durables, and other things.

The marketer should watch the following trends in technology.

Accelerating Pace of Technological Change

Many of today's common products were not available even a hundred years ago. Abraham Lincoln did not know of automobiles, airplanes, phonographs, radios, or the electric light. Woodrow Wilson did not know of television, aerosol cans, home freezers, automatic dishwashers, room air conditioners, antibiotics, or electronic computers. Franklin Delano Roosevelt did not know of xerography, synthetic detergents, taperecorders, birth control pills, or earth satellites. And John Kennedy did not know of personal computers, digital wristwatches, videorecorders, or word processors.

Alvin Toffler, in his book *Future Shock,* sees an accelerative thrust in the invention, exploitation, and diffusion of new technologies.[19] More ideas are being worked on; the time lag between new ideas and their successful implementation is decreasing rapidly; and the time between introduction and peak production is shortening considerably. Ninety percent of all the scientists who ever lived are alive today, and technology feeds upon itself.

In Toffler's later book, *The Third Wave,* he forecasts the emergence of the *electronic cottage* as a new way in which work and play will be organized in society.[20] The advent of word-processing typewriters, telecopiers, personal computers, and audio and video links make it possible for many people to do their work at home instead of traveling to and from offices located thirty or more minutes away. Eventually people will find that the cost of installing and operating telecommunications equipment in the home is less than the cost of commuting. The electronic cottage revolution will reduce the amount of auto pollution, bring the family closer together as a work unit, and create more home-centered entertainment and activity. It will have substantial impact on consumption patterns and marketing systems.

Unlimited Innovation Opportunities

Scientists today are working on a startling range of new technologies that will revolutionize our products and production processes. The most exciting work is being done in biotechnology, solid-state electronics, robotics, and materials science.[21] Scientists today are working on the following promising new products and services:

Practical solar energy	Commercial space shuttle	Happiness pills
Cancer cures	Lung and liver cures	Electric cars
Chemical control of mental health	Household robots that do cooking and cleaning	Electronic anesthetic for pain killing
Desalinization of seawater	Nonfattening, tasty, nutritious foods	Totally safe and effective contraceptives

In addition, scientists, speculate on fantasy products, such as small flying cars, single-person rocket belts, three-dimensional television, space colonies, and human clones. The challenge in each case is not only technical but commercial—namely, to develop practical, affordable versions of these products.

High R&D Budget

The United States leads the world in research and development spending. In 1984, R&D expenditures exceeded $97 billion and have been increasing at an average of 4.4 percent annually during this decade.[22]

The federal government supplied almost 50 percent of total R&D funds. Almost 86 percent go to applied R&D. The remainder is spent on basic research, almost half of which takes place in colleges and universities. Government research can be a rich source of new product and service ideas (see Exhibit 5-2).

The five industries spending the most R&D money are aircraft and missiles, electrical equipment and communication, chemicals and allied products, machinery, and motor vehicles and other transportation. The industries spending the least R&D money are lumber, wood products, furniture, textiles, apparel, and paper and allied products. Industries in the top range spend between 5 and 10 percent of their sales dollar on R&D, and those in the lowest range spend less than 1 percent of their sales dollar. The average company spends about 2 percent of its sales dollar on R&D.

One study showed a high correlation between R&D expenditures and company profitability. Six companies—Merck, AT&T, Dow, Eastman Kodak, IBM, and Lilly—averaged 5.7 percent in their R&D expenditures-to-sales ratio, and their profitability averaged 15.3 percent of sales. Another six companies—Boeing, Chry-

EXHIBIT 5-2

NASA: AN IMPORTANT SOURCE OF TECHNOLOGY FOR BUSINESS

Since 1958, the National Aeronautics and Space Administration has sponsored billions of dollars worth of aerospace research, and this research has inspired thousands of new industrial and consumer products. In 1962 NASA established the Technology Utilization Program to help transfer its wealth of aerospace technology to other state and federal government agencies, public institutions, and private industry. Nine NASA applications centers across the country, staffed by engineers and scientists, provide prospective users with information about existing NASA technology and help them apply this technology. NASA issues several publications aimed at increasing the use of its technology. *Tech Briefs* provides information about NASA-sponsored inventions, improvements, or innovations developed in work for NASA. NASA also publishes a summary of all NASA-patented inventions available for licensing and provides Technical Support Packages to companies seeking more specific information.

NASA-inspired aerospace research has had a dramatic impact on industrial and consumer products. For example, NASA's need for small, efficient space systems resulted in startling advances in microcircuitry, which in turn revolutionized consumer and industrial electronics with new products ranging from home computers and video games to computerized appliances and medical systems. NASA pioneered the development of communications satellites, which now carry over two-thirds of all overseas communications traffic. This satellite technology has revolutionized commercial and consumer communications services. Here are just a few of countless other applications.

- NASA's Echo project required lightweight and exceptionally thin reflective materials, and inspired research which transformed the previously small-scale plastics metalization business into a flourishing industry. Using such technology, the Metalized Products Division of King-Seeley Thermos Company now makes a large line of consumer and industrial products ranging from "insulated outdoor garments to packaging materials for frozen foods, from wall coverings to aircraft covers, from bedwarmers to window shades, labels to candy wrappings, reflective blankets to photographic reflectors."

- NASA's efforts to develop tasty, nutritional, lightweight, compactly packaged, nonperishable food for astronauts in outer space have found many applications in the industrial and consumer foods industry. A number of commercial food processing firms are now producing astronaut-type meals for public distribution—freeze-dried foods and "retort-pouch" meals that can be used for a number of purposes.

- NASA's need for a super-strong safety net to protect personnel working high in the air on space shuttles led to the invention of a new fire-resistant and ultraviolet-resistant fiber. A relatively small net made of this fiber's twine can support the average size automobile. The twine is now used to make fishing nets more than a mile long, weighing up to 60 tons, and covering more than 86 acres. The twine is smaller in diameter and denser than the conventional nylon cord, so the new nets offer less water resistance, sink faster, go deeper, and offer 30 percent productivity gains.

- A portable X-ray machine developed by NASA uses less than 1 percent of the radiation required by conventional X-ray devices. About the size of a thermos, the unit provides instant images and is ideal for use in emergency field situations such as on-the-spot scanning for bone injuries to athletes. It can also be used for instant detection of product flaws or for security uses such as examining parcels in mailrooms and business entrances.

- Special high-intensity lights developed by NASA to simulate the effect of sunlight on spacecraft resulted in several types of flashlights for professional and home use. One such hand-held light, which operates on a 12-volt auto or boat battery, is 50 times brighter than a car's highbeam headlights and projects a beam of light more than a mile—as a signal, it can be seen for over 30 miles.

- Bioengineering and physiological research to design cooling systems for astronaut space clothing has led to numerous commercial and consumer products—cooler athletic clothing, lightweight and heat-resistant clothing for firefighters, survival gear for hikers and campers, and dozens of others.

- A portable water sterilizer for purifying water aboard spacecraft has been converted into a consumer product. Smaller than a coffee pot, the unit can be attached to a faucet. It sterilizes tap water and removes objectionable tastes and odors. Another model can be used on trips by vacationers or campers.

- Medical systems developed to monitor astronauts have resulted in a portable medical monitoring and treatment system designed for use in emergencies in remote areas where hospital facilities may be hours away. The suitcase-size unit includes a vital signs monitor; a defibrillator; a scope which displays pulse rate, blood pressure, respiration rate, and temperature; and a 10-channel radio capable of transmitting vital signs to a distant physician and relaying instructions back to the scene of the emergency.

Source: Based on information found in *Spinoff* (Washington, DC: U.S. Government Printing Office), various issues between 1977 and 1983.

sler, Goodyear, McDonnell-Douglas, Signal Companies, and United Technologies—averaged 3.5 percent in their R&D expenditures-to-sales ratio and were much less profitable.[23]

Today's research is mostly carried out by laboratory teams rather than by lone inventors like Thomas Edison, Samuel Morse, or Alexander Graham Bell. Managing company scientists is a major challenge. They resent too much cost control. They are often more interested in solving scientific problems than in coming up with marketable products. Companies are adding marketing people to R&D research teams in the hope of achieving a stronger marketing orientation.

Concentration on Minor Improvements

As a result of the high cost of money, many companies are pursuing minor product improvements instead of gambling on major innovations. Even basic research companies like Du Pont, Bell Laboratories, and Pfizer are proceeding cautiously. Most companies are content to put their money into copying competitors' products and making minor feature and style improvements. Much of the research is defensive rather than offensive.

Increased Regulation

As products become more complex, the public needs to be assured of their safety. Government agencies have consequently expanded their power to investigate and ban potentially unsafe products. The Federal Food and Drug Administration has issued elaborate regulations on testing new drugs, resulting in (1) much higher industry research costs, (2) lengthening the time between idea and introduction from five to about nine years, and (3) driving much drug research to countries with fewer regulations. Safety and health regulations have also increased in the areas of food, automobiles, clothing, electrical appliances, and construction. Marketers must be aware of these regulations when proposing, developing, and launching new products.

Technological change faces opposition from those who see it as threatening nature, privacy, simplicity, and even the human race. Various groups have opposed the construction of nuclear plants, high-rise buildings, and recreational facilities in national parks. They have called for *technological assessment* of new technologies before allowing their commercialization.

Marketers need to understand the changing technological environment and how new technologies can serve human needs. They need to work closely with R&D people to encourage more market-oriented research. They must be alert to possible negative aspects of any innovation that might harm users and bring about distrust and opposition.

Political Environment   Marketing decisions are strongly affected by developments in the political and legal environment. This environment is made up of *laws, government agencies,* and *pressure groups* that influence and constrain various organizations and individuals in society. We will examine the main political trends and their implications for marketing management.

Legislation Regulating Business

Legislation affecting business has increased steadily over the years. This legislation has been enacted for a number of reasons. *The first is to protect companies from each other.* Business executives all praise competition but try to neutralize it when it touches them.

> Until recently, antitrust worries kept IBM from playing too rough in the computer industry. Through the sixties and seventies the company had fought off scores of private antitrust suits and two major federal attempts to break it up. This allowed competitors to survive profitably, or even thrive, against the industry giant. "For years, IBM's behavior was fairly predictable. It kept selling a product for four or five years and held prices stable until the end of the cycle . . . competitors could easily sneak under IBM's price umbrella. As long as they came out with products fairly soon after IBM did, they could come look forward to a few years of easy money." But in the late seventies, facing a more favorable domestic regulatory climate and more formidable international competition, IBM flexed its substantial marketing muscle. It flooded the market with innovative new products and frequent deep price cuts in all major market segments. The result was devastating. "Almost all the company's big, traditional adversaries—Burroughs, Univac, NCR, Control Data, and Honeywell, known by their initials as the "Bunch"—retreated years ago from trying to sell general-purpose computers against IBM, running for cover into specialized niches. Big Blue's more recent foray into personal computers has helped crush several rivals in that much-coveted corner of the business." Fearing total domination by IBM, competitors are screaming loudly. Charging IBM with predatory competitive practices, they are filing antitrust suits and urging federal regulators to step in and restore industry competitive balance.[24]

So laws are passed to define and prevent unfair competition. These laws are enforced by the Federal Trade Commission and the Antitrust Division of the attorney general's office.

The second purpose of government regulation is to protect consumers from unfair business practices. Some firms, if left alone, would adulterate their products, tell lies in their advertising, deceive through their packaging, and bait through their prices. Unfair consumer practices have been defined and are enforced by various agencies. Many managers see purple with each new consumer law, and yet a few have said that "consumerism may be the best thing that has happened . . . in the past 20 years."[25]

The third purpose of government regulation is to protect the larger interests of society against unbridled business behavior. It is possible for the gross national product to rise and the quality of life to fall. Most firms are not charged with the social costs of their production or products. Their prices are lower and their sales are higher than they would be if they bore these social costs. As the environment deteriorates, new laws and their enforcement will continue or increase. Business executives have to watch these developments in planning their products and marketing programs.

The marketing executive needs a good working knowledge of the major laws protecting competition, consumers, and the larger interests of society. The main federal laws are listed in Table 5-4. The earlier laws dealt mainly with protecting competition, and the later laws with protecting consumers. Marketing executives should know these federal laws and particularly the evolving court interpretations. And they should know the state and local laws that affect their local marketing activity.[26]

TABLE 5-4
Milestone U.S. Legislation Affecting Marketing

Sherman Antitrust Act (1890)
Prohibits (a) "monopolies or attempts to monopolize" and (b) "contracts, combinations, or conspiracies in restraint of trade" in interstate and foreign commerce.

Federal Food and Drug Act (1906)
Forbids the manufacture, sale, or transport of adulterated or fraudulently labeled foods and drugs in interstate commerce. Supplanted by the Food, Drug, and Cosmetic Act, 1938; amended by Food Additives Amendment in 1958 and the Kefauver-Harris Amendment in 1962. The 1962 amendment deals with pretesting of drugs for safety and effectiveness and labeling of drugs by generic name.

Meat Inspection Act (1906)
Provides for the enforcement of sanitary regulations in meat-packing establishments, and for federal inspection of all companies selling meats in interstate commerce.

Federal Trade Commission Act (1914)
Establishes the commission, a body of specialists with broad powers to investigate and to issue cease and desist orders to enforce Section 5, which declares that "unfair methods of competition in commerce are unlawful."

Clayton Act (1914)
Supplements the Sherman Act by prohibiting certain specific practices (certain types of price discrimination, tying clauses and exclusive dealing, intercorporate stockholdings, and interlocking directorates) "where the effect . . . may be to substantially lessen competition or tend to create a monopoly in any line of commerce." Provides that violating corporate officials can be held individually responsible; exempts labor and agricultural organizations from its provisions.

Robinson-Patman Act (1936)
Amends the Clayton Act. Adds the phrase "to injure, destroy, or prevent competition." Defines price discrimination as unlawful (subject to certain defenses) and provides the FTC with the right to

TABLE 5-4 (Cont.)
*Milestone U.S.
Legislation Affecting
Marketing*

establish limits on quantity discounts, to forbid brokerage allowances except to independent brokers, and to prohibit promotional allowances or the furnishing of services or facilities except where made available to all "on proportionately equal terms."

Miller-Tydings Act (1937)
Amends the Sherman Act to exempt interstate fair-trade (price fixing) agreements from antitrust prosecution. (The McGuire Act, 1952, reinstates the legality of the nonsigner clause.)

Wheeler-Lea Act (1938)
Prohibits unfair and deceptive acts and practices regardless of whether competition is injured; places advertising of foods and drugs under FTC jurisdiction.

Antimerger Act (1950)
Amends Section 7 of the Clayton Act by broadening the power to prevent intercorporate acquisitions where the acquisition may have a substantially adverse effect on competition.

Automobile Information Disclosure Act (1958)
Prohibits car dealers from inflating the factory price of new cars.

National Traffic and Safety Act (1958)
Provides for the creation of compulsory safety standards for automobiles and tires.

Fair Packaging and Labeling Act (1966)
Provides for the regulation of the packaging and labeling of consumer goods. Requires manufacturers to state what the package contains, who made it, and how much it contains. Permits industries' voluntary adoption of uniform packaging standards.

Child Protection Act (1966)
Bans sale of hazardous toys and articles. Amended in 1969 to include articles that pose electrical, mechanical, or thermal hazards.

Federal Cigarette Labeling and Advertising Act (1967)
Requires that cigarette packages contain the following statement: "Warning: The Surgeon General Has Determined That Cigarette Smoking is Dangerous to Your Health."

Truth-in-Lending Act (1968)
Requires lenders to state the true costs of a credit transaction, outlaws the use of actual or threatened violence in collecting loans, and restricts the amount of garnishments. Established a National Commission on Consumer Finance.

National Environmental Policy Act (1969)
Establishes a national policy on the environment and provides for the establishment of the Council on Environmental Quality. The Environmental Protection Agency was established by Reorganization Plan No. 3 of 1970.

Fair Credit Reporting Act (1970)
Ensures that a consumer's credit report will contain only accurate, relevant, and recent information and will be confidential unless requested for an appropriate reason by a proper party.

Consumer Product Safety Act (1972)
Establishes the Consumer Product Safety Commission and authorizes it to set safety standards for consumer products as well as exact penalties for failure to uphold the standards.

Consumer Goods Pricing Act (1975)
Prohibits the use of price maintenance agreements among manufacturers and resellers in interstate commerce.

Magnuson-Moss Warranty/FTC Improvement Act (1975)
Authorizes the FTC to determine rules concerning consumer warranties and provides for consumer access to means of redress, such as the "class action" suit. Also expands FTC regulatory powers over unfair or deceptive acts or practices.

Equal Credit Opportunity Act (1975)
Prohibits discrimination in a credit transaction because of sex, marital status, race, national origin, religion, age, or receipt of public assistance.

Fair Debt Collection Practice Act (1978)
Makes it illegal to harass or abuse any person and make false statements or use unfair methods when collecting a debt.

FTC Improvement Act (1980)
Provides the House of Representatives and Senate jointly with veto power over FTC Trade Regulation Rules. Enacted to limit FTC's powers to regulate "unfairness" issues.

Changing Government Agency Enforcement

To enforce the laws, Congress established several federal regulatory agencies—the Federal Trade Commission, the Food and Drug Administration, the Interstate Commerce Commission, the Federal Communications Commission, the Federal Power Commission, the Civil Aeronautics Board, the Consumer Products Safety Commission, the Environmental Protection Agency, and the Office of Consumer Affairs. These agencies can have a major impact on a company's marketing performance. Consider the following example:

> In 1973 the rotary-engine Mazda automobile's sales were soaring. People were impressed by its smooth ride, low repair costs, and reduced air pollution. Then the Environmental Protection Agency issued a report stating that Mazda's fuel consumption was only 11 miles per gallon in city driving. Mazda executives objected, claiming 17 to 21 miles per gallon. The charge stuck in the public's mind, however, and Mazda sales declined 39 percent in the first five months of 1974.

Government agencies have some discretion in enforcing the laws. From time to time, they appear to be overzealous and capricious. The agencies are dominated by lawyers and economists, who often lack a practical sense of how business and marketing works. In recent years the Federal Trade Commission has added staff marketing experts to achieve a better understanding of the complex issues. The degree of enforcement appears to be moderating under President Reagan, with a strong trend toward deregulation.[27]

Growth of Public Interest Groups

The number and power of public interest groups have increased during the past two decades. The most successful is Ralph Nader's Public Citizen group, which watchdogs consumer interests. Nader lifted consumerism into a major social force, first with his successful attack on unsafe automobiles (resulting in the passage of the National Traffic and Motor Vehicle Safety Act of 1962), and then through investigations of meat processing (resulting in the passage of the Wholesome Meat Act of 1967), truth-in-lending, auto repairs, insurance, and X-ray equipment. Hundreds of other consumer interest groups—private and governmental—operate at the national, state, and local levels. Other groups marketers need to consider are those seeking to protect the environment (Sierra Club, Environmental Defense); advance the "rights" of women, blacks, and senior citizens; and so on.

New laws, more active enforcement, and growing pressure groups have put restraints on marketer freedom. Marketers have to clear their plans with the company's legal and public relations departments. Private marketing transactions have moved into the public domain. Salancik and Upah put it this way:

> There is some evidence that the consumer may not be king, nor even queen. The consumer is but a voice, one among many. Consider how General Motors makes its cars today. Vital features of the motor are designed by the United States government; the exhaust system is redesigned by certain state governments; the production materials used are dictated by suppliers who control scarce material

resources. For other products, other groups and organizations may get involved. Thus, insurance companies directly or indirectly affect the design of smoke detectors; scientific groups affect the design of spray products by condemning aerosols; minority activist groups affect the design of dolls by requesting representative figures. Legal departments also can be expected to increase their importance in firms, affecting not only product design and promotion but also marketing strategies. At a minimum, marketing managers will spend less time with their research departments asking "What does the consumer want" and more and more time with their production and legal people asking "What can the consumer have."[28]

Cultural Environment

People grow up in a particular society that shapes their basic beliefs, values, and norms. They absorb, almost unconsciously, a world view that defines their relationship to themselves and others. The following cultural characteristics can affect marketing decision making.

Persistence of Core Cultural Values

People in a given society hold many beliefs and values. Their core beliefs and values have a high degree of persistence. For example, most Americans believe in work, getting married, giving to charity, and being honest. These beliefs shape and color more specific attitudes and behaviors found in everyday life. Core beliefs and values are passed on from parents to children and are reinforced by society's major institutions—schools, churches, business, and government.

People's secondary beliefs and values are more open to change. Believing in the institution of marriage is a core belief; believing that people ought to get married early is a secondary belief. Family planning marketers could argue more

Working women make up a subculture with distinctive wants and buying behavior. *Courtesy of Hewlett-Packard.*

effectively that people should get married later than that they should not get married at all. Marketers have some chance of changing secondary values, but little chance of changing core values.

Subcultures

Each society contains *subcultures*—that is, groups of people with shared value systems emerging from their common life experiences or circumstances. Episcopalians, teenagers, and Hell's Angels all represent separate subcultures whose members share common beliefs, preferences, and behaviors. To the extent that subcultural groups exhibit different wants and consumption behavior, marketers can choose subcultures as their target markets.

Shifts in Secondary Cultural Values

Although core values are fairly persistent, cultural swings do take place. Consider the impact of the Beatles, Elvis Presley, Michael Jackson, and other culture heroes on young people's hair styles, clothing, and sexual norms. Recent cultural swings are listed in a tongue-in-cheek version in Table 5-5.

Marketers have a keen interest in anticipating cultural shifts in order to spot new opportunities or threats. Several firms offer "futures" forecasts in this connection. The Monitor series of the Yankelovich marketing research firm tracks forty-one cultural values, such as "anti-bigness," "mysticism," "living for today," "away from possessions," and "sensuousness," describing the percentage of the population who share the attitude as well as the percentage who are antitrend. For example, the percentage of people who value physical fitness and well-being has been going up steadily over the years, especially in the under 30 group, the young women and upscale group, and people living in the West. Marketers will want to cater to this trend with appropriate products and communication appeals.

TABLE 5-5 *Four Decades of Cultural Change*

	1950s	1960s	1970s	1980s
Chic diseases:	Ulcers	Gonorrhea	Tennis elbow	Bed sores
Drugs of choice:	Alcohol	Marijuana	Cocaine	Alcohol
Sex symbols, female div:	Marilyn Monroe	Sophia Loren	Farrah Fawcett Majors	Bianca Jagger
Danger—men at work:	Lawyer	Communal farmer	Rock promoter	Stockbroker
Danger—women at work:	Homemaker	Executive	Lawyer	Communal farmer
Hair today:	Crewcut	Waist-length	Frizz	The bald spot
Hair tomorrow:	Ponytail	Waist-length	Frizz	The Mohawk
You were what you ate:	Steak and potatoes	Granola and sprouts	Cold soup and crepes	Instant Breakfast Baco Bits
Dancing:	The Lindy	The Frug	The Hustle	The Slump
The family:	Swiss Family Robinson	The Manson Family	The Osmond Family	The Test Tube Family
Sporting propositions:	Baseball	Football	Running	Limping

Source: Octavio Diaz, "Fickle Fads," *Miami Herald,* October 8, 1978.

The major cultural values of a society are expressed in people's relationship to themselves, others, institutions, society, nature, and the cosmos.

PEOPLE'S RELATION TO THEMSELVES.   People vary in their relative emphasis on self-gratification versus serving others. In the 1960s and 1970s, many people focused on self-gratification. Some were *pleasure seekers,* wanting fun, change, and escape. Others sought *self-realization* by joining therapeutic or religious organizations.

The marketing implications of a "me-society" are many. People use products, brands, and services as a means of self-expression. They buy their "dream cars" and "dream vacations." They spend more time outdoors in health activities (jogging, tennis), in introspection, and on arts and crafts. The leisure industry (camping, boating, arts and crafts, sports) faces good growth prospects in a society where people seek self-fulfillment.

PEOPLE'S RELATION TO OTHERS.   More recently, observers have noted a shift from a "me-society" to a "we-society" in which more people want to be with and serve others. A recent Doyle Dane Bernbach survey showed a widespread concern among adults about social isolation and a strong desire for human contact.[29] This portends a bright future for "social support" products and services that enhance direct communication between human beings, such as health clubs, vacations, and games. It also suggests a growing market for "social surrogates," things that allow a person who is alone to feel that he or she isn't alone, such as home video games and computers.

In relating to others, people desire open and easy relationships, rather than formal ones. This desire has several marketing implications. People want their homes to be more casual. They want packaging to provide more complete and honest information. They want advertising messages to be more realistic. They want salespersons to be more honest and helpful.

PEOPLE'S RELATION TO INSTITUTIONS.   People vary in their attitudes toward corporations, government agencies, trade unions, universities, and other institutions. Most people accept these institutions, although some people are highly critical of particular ones. By and large, people are willing to work for the major institutions and expect them to carry out society's work. There is, however, a *decline in institutional loyalty.* People are giving a little less to these institutions and are trusting them less. The work ethic is eroding.

Several marketing implications follow. Companies need to find new ways to win consumer confidence. They need to review their advertising communications to make sure their messages are honest. They need to review their various activities to make sure that they are coming across as "good corporate citizens." More companies are turning to *social audits*[30] and to *public relations*[31] to build a positive image with their publics.

PEOPLE'S RELATION TO SOCIETY.   People vary in their attitudes toward their society, from patriots who defend it, to reformers who want to change it, to discontents who want to leave it. The trend is toward *declining patriotism* and stronger criticism as to where the country is going. People's orientation to their society will influence their consumption patterns, levels of savings, and attitudes toward the marketplace.

PEOPLE'S RELATION TO NATURE. People vary in their attitudes toward the natural world. Some feel subjugated by it, others are in harmony with it, and still others seek mastery over it. A long-term trend has been people's growing mastery over nature through technology, and the belief that nature is bountiful. More recently, however, people have become aware of nature's fragility and finite supplies. People recognize that nature can be destroyed or spoiled by human activities.

Love of nature is leading to more camping, hiking, boating, and fishing. Business has responded with hiking boots, tenting equipment, and other gear for nature enthusiasts. Tour operators are packaging more tours to wilderness areas. Food producers have found growing markets for "natural" products such as natural cereal, natural ice-cream, and health foods. Marketing communicators are using appealing natural backgrounds in advertising their products.

PEOPLE'S RELATION TO THE UNIVERSE. People vary in their beliefs about the origin of the universe and their place in it. Most Americans are monotheistic, although their religious conviction and practice have been waning through the years. Church attendance has been falling steadily, with the exception of certain evangelical movements reaching out to bring people back to organized religion. Some of the religious impulse has not been lost but has been redirected to a growing interest in Eastern religions, mysticism, and the occult.

As people lose their religious orientation, they seek to enjoy their life on earth as fully as possible. They seek goods and experiences that offer fun and pleasure. In the meantime, religious institutions start turning to marketers for help in reworking their appeals so they can compete with the secular attractions of modern society.

In summary, cultural values are showing the following long-run trends:

"Me society"	→ "We society"
Postponed gratification	→ Immediate gratification
Hard work	→ The easy life
Formal relationships	→ Informal relationships
Religious orientation	→ Worldly, nonreligious orientation

■ *Summary*

The company must start with the marketing environment in searching for opportunities and monitoring threats. The marketing environment consists of all the actors and forces that affect the company's ability to transact effectively with the target market. The company's marketing environment can be divided into the microenvironment and the macroenvironment.

The microenvironment consists of five components. The first is the company's internal environment—its several departments and management levels—as it affects marketing management's decision making. The second component consists of the marketing channel firms that cooperate to create value: the suppliers and marketing intermediaries (middlemen, physical distribution facilitators, marketing service agencies, financial intermediaries). The third component consists of the five types of markets in which the company can sell: the consumer, producer, reseller, government, and international markets. The fourth component consists of the basic types of competitors facing any company offer: desire competitors, generic competitors, product form competitors, and brand competitors. The fifth component consists of all the publics that have an actual or potential interest in or impact on the organization's ability to achieve its objectives: financial, media, government, citizen action, and local, general, and internal publics. The company's macroenvironment consists of major forces that shape opportunities and pose threats to the company: demographic, economic, natural, technological, political, and cultural.

The demographic environment shows a changing age structure in the U. S. population, a changing American family, a rise in nonfamily households, geographic population shifts, and a better-educated and more white-collar population. The economic environment shows changing real income growth, changing savings and debt patterns, and changing consumer expenditure patterns. The natural environment shows impending shortages of certain raw materials, increased energy costs, increased pollution levels, and increasing government intervention in natural resource management. The technological environment shows accelerating technological change, unlimited innovational opportunities, high R&D budgets, concentration on minor improvements rather than major discoveries, and increased regulation of technological change. The political environment shows substantial business regulation, strong government agency enforcement, and the growth of public interest groups. The cultural environment shows long-run trends toward other-centeredness, immediate gratification, the easy life, informal relationships, and a more secular orientation.

■ Questions for Discussion

1. You are the vice-president of marketing for Walt Disney Productions. Given the changes taking place in the demographic, economic, technological, and cultural environments, what plans would you make to ensure the company's success in the next decade?

2. A major alcoholic beverage marketer is considering introducing an "adult" soft drink that would be a socially acceptable substitute for alcohol. What cultural factors could influence the introduction decision and subsequent marketing mix?

3. Life style studies conducted from 1975 to 1979 showed a positive trend in the attitude that "meal preparation should take as little time as possible." How would this affect the sales of frozen vegetables?

4. Describe the marketing channel firms that Procter & Gamble might use in marketing a new brand of laundry detergent.

5. Compare and contrast the *consumer, industrial,* and *reseller* markets, using automobiles as an illustration.

6. Discuss the four types of competitors that someone planning to open a new pizza parlor near your campus must understand.

7. How do *publics* differ from *consumers?* Explain by using a specific example.

8. It is the year A.D. 2000. The price of gasoline is $4 per gallon, the price of hamburger is $6 per pound, the average home costs $200,000, and the annual rate of inflation has been 10 percent for the past twenty years. Given this economic information, what might you speculate the market size or potential for luxury products would be?

9. The political environment has become increasingly volatile. How have Ralph Nader, the FTC, and the actions of Congress affected marketing decision making in recent years?

■ References

1. Based on information found in Laura R. Walbert, "Apparel," *Forbes,* January 2, 1984, p. 217; "Levi Strauss: A Touch of Fashion and a Dash of Humility," *Business Week,* October 24, 1983, pp. 85–86; "A Kick in the Pants for Levi's," *Business Week,* June 11, 1984, pp. 47–48; and Ruth Stroud, "Tattered Levi Seeks Diversification," *Advertising Age,* June 25, 1984, p. 3.

2. PETER DRUCKER, *Age of Discontinuity* (New York: Harper & Row, 1969).

3. See ALVIN TOFFLER, *Future Shock* (New York: Bantam, 1970), p. 28.

4. The statistical data in this chapter are drawn from the *Statistical Abstract of the United States, 1984;* various Bureau of Census publications; and other sources.

5. See "The Greying of America," *Newsweek,* February 28, 1977, pp. 50–65; and DIANE HARRIS, "USA Tomorrow: The Demographic Factor," *Financial World,* September 15, 1983, pp. 16–20.

6. See "The Year 2000: A Demographic Profile of Consumer Market," *The Marketing News,* May 25, 1984, Sec. 1, pp. 8–10; and HARRIS, "USA Tomorrow," pp. 16, 18.

7. For more reading, see PAUL C. GLICK, "How American Families Are Changing," *American Demographics,* January 1984, pp. 21–25.

8. See ELLEN GRAHAM, "Advertisers Take Aim at a Neglected Market: The Working Woman," *Wall Street Journal,* July 5, 1977, p. 1.

9. See JUNE KRONHOLZ, "A Living-Alone Trend Affects Housing, Cars, and Other Industries," *Wall Street Journal,* November 16, 1977, p. 1.

10. Before 1983, the Bureau of the Census classified markets using SMSA (Standard Statistical Metropolitan Area) classifications. In June 1983, the bureau adopted the MSA (Metropolitan Statistical Area) concept, which classifies heavily populated areas as MSAs or PMSAs (Primary Metropolitan Statistical Areas). MSAs and PMSAs are defined in the same way, except that PMSAs are also components of larger "megalopolies" called CMSAs (Consolidated Metropolitan Statistical Areas). MSAs and PSMAs are areas consisting of (1) a city of at least 50,000 in population, or (2) an urbanized area of at least 50,000 with a total metropolitan area of at least 100,000.

11. "The Year 2000: A Demographic Profile," p. 10.

12. For more reading, see BRYANT ROBEY and CHERYL RUSSELL, "A Portrait of the American Worker," *American Demographics,* March 1984, pp. 17–21.

13. See WILLIAM LAZER, "How Rising Affluence Will Reshape Markets," *American Demographics,* February 1984, pp. 17–20; and "USA Tomorrow," p. 19.

14. DONELLA H. MEADOWS, DENNIS L. MEADOWS, JORGEN RANDERS, and WILLIAM W. BEHRENS III, *The Limits to Growth* (New York: New American Library, 1972), p. 41.

15. RACHEL CARSON, *Silent Spring* (Boston: Houghton Mifflin, 1962).

16. *First Annual Report of the Council on Environmental Quality* (Washington, DC: Government Printing Office, 1970), p. 158.

17. See "The Coming Boom in Solar Energy," *Business Week,* October 9, 1978, pp. 88–104.

18. See KARL E. HENION II, *Ecological Marketing* (Columbus, OH: Grid, 1976).

19. TOFFLER, *Future Shock,* pp. 25–30.

20. ALVIN TOFFLER, *The Third Wave* (New York: Bantam, 1980).

21. For an excellent and comprehensive list of future possible products, see DENNIS GABOR, *Innovations: Scientific, Technological, and Social* (London: Oxford University Press, 1970). Also see CHARLES PANAT, *Breakthroughs* (Boston: Houghton Mifflin, 1980); and "Technologies for the '80s," *Business Week,* July 6, 1981, pp. 48ff.

22. See M. F. WOLF, ed., "Perspectives," *Research Management,* September–October 1983, p. 2. See also "A Deepening Commitment to R&D," *Business Week,* July 9, 1984, pp. 64–78.

23. "Corporate Growth, R&D, and the Gap Between," *Technology Review,* March–April 1978, p. 39.

24. See BRO UTTAL, "Is IBM Playing Too Rough?" *Fortune,* December 10, 1984, pp. 34–37; and "Personal Computers: IBM Will Keep Knocking Heads," *Business Week,* January 10, 1985, p. 67.

25. LEO GREENLAND, "Advertisers Must Stop Conning Consumers," *Harvard Business Review,* July–August 1974, p. 18.

26. For a summary of legal developments in marketing, see LOUIS W. STERN and THOMAS L. EOVALDI, *Legal Aspects of Marketing Strategy: Antitrust and Consumer Protection Issues* (Englewood Cliffs, NJ: Prentice-Hall, 1984).

27. See EDWARD MEADOWS, "Bold Departures in Antitrust," *Fortune,* October 5, 1981, pp. 180–88.

28. Extracts from GERALD R. SALANCIK and GREGORY D. UPAH, "Directions for Interorganizational Marketing" (unpublished paper, School of Commerce, University of Illinois. Champaign, August 1978).

29. See BILL ABRAMS, "'Middle Generation' Growing More Concerned with Selves," *Wall Street Journal,* January 21, 1982, p. 25.

30. See RAYMOND A. BAUER and DAN H. FENN, JR., "What Is a Corporate Social Audit?" *Harvard Business Review,* January–February 1973, pp. 37–48.

31. LEONARD L. BERRY and JAMES S. HENSEL, "Public Relations: Opportunities in the New Society," *Arizona Business,* August–September 1973, pp. 14–21.

WHAT SORT OF MAN READS PLAYBOY?

Both musician and audiophile (PLAYBOY readers buy 28 percent of the stereo equipment sold in America), he's decided that a melody is like a pretty girl: composed of overtones, harmonies and rests. The woman who accompanies him appreciates his discipline and doesn't intrude on his work. She has her own. Still, she knows that when the lines are played out and the cover's turned down, he won't leave all his talents at the keyboard.

6
Consumer Markets: Influences on Consumer Behavior

Playboy magazine has passed its thirtieth anniversary. It has been a national institution ever since it was launched by a spunky young editor named Hugh Hefner. Hefner improved the formula for "girlie magazines" by encasing bottoms and bosoms between the pages of great fiction by Graham Greene and Vladimir Nabokov. Male readers could feel that they were buying a high-class literary magazine rather than a girlie magazine. *Playboy* marketed a life style—the hedonistic young male with good taste in girls, automobiles, electronic gadgetry, food, and clothing. Its success was so phenomenal that Hefner used the proceeds to build a large empire of hotels, clubs, and other ventures.

Playboy's galloping growth slowed down around 1972. Between 1972 and 1975 the magazine's circulation fell from 7.5 million copies to around 5 million, where it stabilized. A number of hungry competitors had invaded *Playboy's* market to share the loot. The most extreme was *Hustler,* which featured a vulgar sexuality and attracted 1.5 million readers, mainly blue-collar workers. But the main threat to *Playboy* was the newly launched *Penthouse,* a British magazine that was redone and launched in the United States. *Penthouse* incarnated a new and gusty hero in Bob Guccione, who said he was seeking nothing less than to displace *Playboy.* He called *Playboy* a tired old rabbit and made *Penthouse* more sexually explicit than *Playboy.* He packaged harder-hitting journalism and exposés. He offered higher margins to newsstand dealers and managed to get display space next to *Playboy,* whereas previous imitators were always in the back rack. *Penthouse* managed to build its circulation to over 4 million copies in a relatively brief period.

Playboy found itself in a dilemma. If it increased the magazine's sexual explicitness, it would lose a lot of loyal advertisers. If it held the line, it would lose some circulation. It opted for holding the line on its old formula despite the fact that the *Playboy* image was becoming more difficult to square with the new concerns and life style events taking place in the 1970s.

Since the mid-70s *Playboy* has been searching for a way to renew its old excitement and leadership in the male magazine market. One of *Playboy's* key needs is the ability to understand its readers better. Who reads *Playboy,* who reads the other magazines, and why?

In an average year, around 30 percent of the male population read one or more issues of *Playboy,* and only 16 percent buy one or more issues. Most males do not read *Playboy* or other male magazines. Nonreading males include those with strong religious convictions, or strong family orientations, or certain social or ethnic backgrounds.

Age also affects *Playboy's* readership. About 47 percent of the males under 25 years of age read one or more issues of *Playboy* in a year; the comparable numbers are 40 percent of males between 25 and 35, and 26 percent of males over 35. Another factor is social class in that *Playboy's* readers are largely middle class, as opposed to the lower-class readers of the more racy male magazines. Life style is another factor in that *Playboy* appeals to males who are upwardly mobile, better educated, and interested in a good time and affluent living. *Playboy* readers measure above-average on the following life style characteristics: self-confidence, partygoing, poker playing, sports interest, and grooming.

Playboy faces some hard choices. Should it move toward more sexual explicitness in order to attract younger readers and maybe more blue-collar readers, at the risk of alienating its older readers and losing its more conservative corporate advertisers? Should it start "aging" its women models and its articles to better match the interests of its aging readers?

The demographic outlook shows that the fastest-growing age groups in the next decade are the 35 to 54 group and the 64 + group. If Playboy does an image overhaul, how many new readers will it gain and how many old readers will it lose? *Playboy* knows that the key lies in understanding the factors that influence and motivate consumer behavior.[1]

Т

he *Playboy* example highlights how a person's buying behavior is influenced by culture, social class, life style, and other factors. Buying behavior is never simple—yet understanding it is the essential task of marketing management.

This chapter and the next will explore the dynamics of the consumer market:

The **consumer market** consists of **all the individuals and households who buy or acquire goods and services for personal consumption.**

In 1983 the American consumer market consisted of 234 million persons and over $2 trillion in personal consumption expenditures—the equivalent of almost $9,000 for every man, woman, and child. Each year this market grows by several million persons and over $100 billion, representing one of the most lucrative consumer markets in the world.[2] Figure 6-1 shows the annual food consumption of a family of four.

Consumers vary tremendously in age, income, education level, mobility patterns, and tastes. Marketers have found it worthwhile to distinguish different consumer groups and develop products and services tailored to their needs. If a market segment is large enough, some companies may set up special marketing programs to serve this market. Here are two examples of special consumer groups:

Black consumers. An important group in the United States are the 26 million black Americans with an aggregate personal income of almost $100 billion. Blacks spend proportionately more than whites on clothing, personal care, home furnishings, alcohol, and tobacco; and proportionately less on medical care, food, transportation, education, and recreation. Blacks do less "shopping around" than whites and patronize neighborhood and discount stores more. Blacks listen to radio more than whites, although they are less likely to listen to FM. Some companies run special marketing programs for black consumers. They advertise in *Ebony* and *Jet,* use blacks in commercials, and develop distinctive products (such as black cosmetics), packaging, and appeals. At the same time, these companies recognize that the black market contains several subsegments that may warrant different marketing approaches.[3]

Senior consumers. As the U.S population ages, "seniors"—people 65 and older—are becoming a very attractive market. Long the target of the makers of products such as laxatives, tonics, and denture products, this group is now attracting the

FIGURE 6-1 *Yearly Food Consumption of an American Family of Four* *Photo courtesy of the Du Pont Company.*

attention of other marketers. The seniors market is expected to grow to over 30 million consumers during the next decade. Seniors are better off financially—their average per capita after-tax income exceeds the national average by more than $330, and seniors' annual purchasing power has been estimated to be as high as $200 billion. Many marketers are realizing that seniors are not all poor and feeble. They have some special needs but most are healthy and active, and they have many of the same needs and wants as younger consumers. The "young-old" segment (under 75) identifies strongly with "middle-age" groups. Though they do buy proportionately more health-related products, they also offer attractive opportunities for marketers of other products and services previously targeted toward younger segments. For example, the fact that seniors have more leisure time and money makes them ideal targets for products such as travel, entertainment, eating out, and other leisure activities. Their desire to look as young as they feel makes seniors good candidates for specially designed products in areas such as cosmetics and personal care products, clothing, health foods, and home physical fitness products. Marketers must also recognize that the seniors market is not homogeneous—it consists of many different segments with diverse demographics, life styles, and other characteristics. As the seniors segment continues to grow in size and buying power, and as the stereotypes of seniors as doddering, creaky, and impoverished shut-ins fade, more and more marketers will develop special strategies for cultivating this important market.[4]

Other consumer submarkets—women,[5] Hispanics,[6] youths[7]—may also provide attractive opportunities for tailored marketing programs.

The 234 million American consumers buy an incredible variety of goods and services. We will look next at how consumers make their choices among these products.

A MODEL OF CONSUMER BEHAVIOR

In earlier times, marketers could arrive at a fair understanding of consumers through the daily experience of selling to them. But the growth in the size of firms and markets has removed many marketing decision makers from direct contact with their customers. Increasingly, managers have had to turn to consumer research. They are spending more money than ever to study consumers, trying to learn: Who buys? How do they buy? When do they buy? Where do they buy? Why do they buy?

The central question is this: How do consumers respond to various marketing stimuli the company might use? The company that really understands how consumers will respond to different product features, prices and advertising appeals has an enormous advantage over its competitors. Therefore companies and academics have invested much energy in researching the relationship between marketing stimuli and consumer response. Their starting point is the simple stimulus-response model shown in Figure 6-2. This figure shows marketing and other stimuli entering the consumer's "black box" and producing certain responses. The marketers must figure out what is in the buyer's "black box."

This model is expanded in Figure 6-3. On the left, marketing stimuli consists of the four Ps—product, price, place, and promotion. Other stimuli include major forces and events in the buyer's environment—economic, technological, political, and cultural. All these stimuli enter the buyer's black box, where they are turned into a set of observable buyer responses shown on the right—product choice, brand choice, dealer choice, purchase timing, and purchase amount.

The marketer's task is to understand how the stimuli are transformed into responses inside the consumer's black box. The black box has two components. First, the buyer's characteristics influence how he or she perceives and reacts to the stimuli. Second, the buyer's decision process itself influences outcomes. This chapter examines the first component—the influence of buyer characteristics on purchase behavior. The next chapter examines the second component—the influence of the buyer decision process.

MAJOR FACTORS INFLUENCING CONSUMER BEHAVIOR

Consumers do not make decisions in a vacuum. Their purchases are strongly influenced by cultural, social, personal, and psychological factors. These factors are shown in Figure 6-4. For the most part they are not controllable by the marketer, but must be taken into account. We want to examine the influence of each factor on a buyer's behavior. We will illustrate these characteristics for the case of a hypothetical consumer named Betty Smith:

FIGURE 6-2
Overall Model of Buyer Behavior

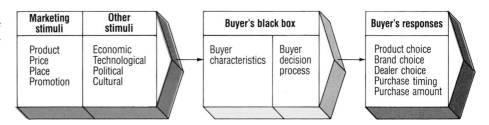

FIGURE 6-3 *Detailed Model of Buyer Behavior*

Betty Smith is a married college graduate who works as a brand manager in a leading consumer packaged-goods company. She is currently interested in finding a new leisure time activity that will offer some contrast to her working day. This need has led her to consider buying a camera and taking up photography. Many characteristics in her background will influence the way she goes about looking at cameras and choosing a brand.

Cultural Factors

Cultural factors exert the broadest and deepest influence on consumer behavior. We will look at the role played by the buyer's culture, subculture, and social class.

Culture

Culture is the most fundamental determinant of a person's wants and behavior (see Chapter 5). Whereas lower creatures are largely governed by instinct, human behavior is largely learned. The child growing up in a society learns a basic set of values, perceptions, preferences, and behaviors through a process of socialization involving the family and other key institutions. Thus a child growing up in America learns or is exposed to the following values: achievement and success, activity and involvement, efficiency and practicality, progress, material comfort, individualism, freedom, external comfort, humanitarianism, and youthfulness.[8]

Betty Smith's interest in cameras is a result of being raised in a modern society where camera technology and a whole set of consumer learnings and values have developed. Betty knows what cameras are. She knows how to read instructions on how to operate cameras, and her society has accepted the idea of women

FIGURE 6-4 *Detailed Model of Factors Influencing Behavior*

Cultural	Social	Personal	Psychological	Buyer
Culture	Reference groups	Age and life-cycle stage	Motivation	
		Occupation	Perception	
Subculture	Family	Economic circumstances	Learning	
		Lifestyle	Beliefs and attitudes	
Social class	Roles and statuses	Personality and self-concept		

photographers. In another culture, say a remote primitive tribe in central Australia, a camera would mean nothing. It would simply be a curiosity. International marketers know that cultures are at different stages of development with respect to buying cameras, and they concentrate on those where interest is highly developed.

Marketers are forever trying to spot cultural shifts in order to imagine new products that might be wanted. Here are some of today's major cultural themes:

1. *Leisure time.* People are seeking increased leisure time to spend in such activities as sports, vacationing, and camping. To increase their leisure time, they are adopting more time-saving products and services such as microwave ovens, automatic dishwashers, and fast-food restaurants.

2. *Health.* People are becoming more concerned about their health. They are putting more time into physical exercises such as jogging and weightlifting, eating lighter and more natural foods, and learning how to relax.

3. *Youthfulness.* Older people want to look and feel young. They are spending more money on physical exercise, youthful clothing, formulas to restore color to graying hair, and cosmetic surgery.

4. *Informality.* People want a more relaxed and informal style. They are choosing more casual clothing, furnishing their homes more simply, and entertaining with a lighter touch.

Subculture

Each culture contains smaller groups or **subcultures** that provide more specific identification and socialization for its members. Four types of subcultures can be distinguished. *Nationality groups* such as the Irish, Polish, Italians, and Puerto Ricans are found within large communities and exhibit distinct ethnic tastes and proclivities. *Religious groups* such as the Catholics, Mormons, Presbyterians, and Jews represent subcultures with specific preferences and taboos. *Racial groups* such as the blacks and Orientals have distinct culture styles and attitudes. *Geographical areas* such as the Deep South, California, and New England are distinct subcultures with characteristic life styles.

Betty Smith's interest in various goods will be influenced by her nationality, religion, race, and geographical background. These factors will influence her food preferences, clothing choices, recreation, and career aspirations. Subcultures attach different meanings to picture taking, and Betty's subculture identification may influence her interest in cameras and the brand she buys.

Social Class

Virtually all human societies exhibit social stratification. Stratification may take the form of a caste system where the members of different castes are reared for certain roles and cannot change their caste membership. More frequently, stratification takes the form of social classes.

> **Social classes** are relatively homogeneous and enduring divisions in a society which are hierarchically ordered and whose members share similar values, interests, and behaviors.

Social scientists have identified the six social classes, as shown in Table 6-1.[9]

TABLE 6-1

Characteristics of Six Major American Social Classes

1. **Upper Uppers (less than 1 percent).**
   Upper uppers are the social elite who live on inherited wealth and have a well-known family background. They give large sums to charity, run the debutante balls, maintain more than one home, and send their children to the finest schools. They are a market for jewelry, antiques, homes, and vacations. They often buy and dress conservatively, not being interested in ostentation. While small as a group, they serve as a reference group for others to the extent that their consumption decisions trickle down and are imitated by the other social classes.

2. **Lower Uppers (about 2 percent).**
   Lower uppers are persons who have earned high income or wealth through exceptional ability in the professions or business. They usually come from the middle class. They tend to be active in social and civic affairs and seek to buy the symbols of status for themselves and their children, such as expensive homes, schools, yachts, swimming pools, and automobiles. They include the *nouveaux riches,* whose pattern of conspicuous consumption is designed to impress those below them. The ambition of lower uppers is to be accepted in the upper-upper stratum, which is more likely to be achieved by their children than themselves.

3. **Upper Middles (12 percent).**
   Upper middles possess neither family status nor unusual wealth. They are primarily concerned with "career." They have attained positions as professionals, independent businesspersons, and corporate managers. They believe in education and want their children to develop professional or administrative skills so that they will not drop into a lower stratum. Members of this class like to deal in ideas and "high culture." They are joiners and highly civic-minded. They are the quality market for good homes, clothes, furniture, and appliances. They seek to run a gracious home, entertaining friends and clients.

4. **Lower Middles (30 percent).**
   Lower middles are primarily white-collar workers (office workers, small-business owners), "gray collars" (mailmen, firemen), and "aristocrat blue collars" (plumbers, factory foremen). They are concerned with "respectability." They exhibit conscientious work habits and adhere to culturally defined norms and standards, including going to church and obeying the law. The home is important, and lower middles like to keep it neat and "pretty." They buy conventional home furnishings and do a lot of their own work around the home. They prefer clothes that are neat and clean rather than high-styled.

5. **Upper Lowers (35 percent).**
   Upper lowers are the largest social class segment, the blue-collar working class of skilled and semiskilled factory workers. While they seek respectability, their main drive is security, "protecting what they have." The working-class husband has a strong "all-male" self-image, being a sports enthusiast, outdoorsman, and heavy smoker and beer drinker. The working-class wife spends most of her time in the house cooking, cleaning, and caring for her children. She sees being the mother of her children as her main vocation, and she has little time for organizations and social activity.

6. **Lower Lowers (20 percent).**
   Lower lowers are at the bottom of society and consist of poorly educated, unskilled laborers. They are often out of work and on some form of public assistance. Their housing is typically substandard and located in slum areas. They often reject middle-class standards of morality and behavior. They buy more impulsively. They often do not evaluate quality, and they pay too much for products and buy on credit. They are a large market for food, television sets, and used automobiles.

Source: Adapted from James F. Engel, Roger D. Blackwell, and David T. Kollat, *Consumer Behavior,* 3rd ed. (New York, Holt, Rinehart & Winston, 1978), pp. 127–28.

Social class is not indicated by a single factor such as income, but is measured as a combination of occupation, income, education, wealth, and other variables. People are ranked as occupying inferior or superior positions according to their social class. In the United States, the lines between social classes are not fixed and rigid; over their lifetimes, people can move into a higher social class or drop into a lower one. Marketers are interested in social class because people within a given social class tend to exhibit similar behavior—including buying behavior.

Social classes show distinct product and brand preferences in such areas as clothing, home furnishings, leisure activity, and automobiles (see Exhibit 6-1). Some marketers focus their effort on one social class. For example, certain stores appeal to the higher social classes; others to the lower social classes. Baker, a manufacturer of fine traditional furniture, designs furniture for higher social class consumers, whereas Kroehler designs most of its furniture for lower social class consumers. The social classes also differ in their media exposure, with higher social class consumers having greater exposure to magazines and newspapers. When lower-class consumers read magazines, they tend to be romance and movie magazines. The social classes differ in their television program preferences, with the higher social class members preferring current events and drama and the lower social class members preferring soap operas and quiz shows. There are also language differences between the social classes. The advertiser has to be skillful in composing words and dialogues that ring true to the target social class.

Betty Smith may have come from a higher social class background. In this case, her family probably owned an expensive camera and may have dabbled in

EXHIBIT 6-1

HOW SOCIAL CLASS INFLUENCES BUYING BEHAVIOR

Does money determine one's social class? Not by any means, as Michigan's first $1 million lottery winner shows.

In 1973 53-year-old Hermus Millsaps jumped up on the stage of the Lansing Civic Center, the proud holder of a $1 million lottery ticket entitling him to twenty annual installments of $50,000. That lucky ticket allowed him to quit his $4.68-per-hour job sawing wood for shipping crates.

What did Hermus do with his windfall? He happily described the improvements to his one-bedroom bungalow that helped whittle his first $50,000 installment to only a little over $10,000 in four short months. Among his new acquisitions: extensive aluminum siding along the lower half of the house, new storm windows, a twin-oven gas range, a sun porch, a new outdoor grill, and dark-green paneling and indirect lighting in the basement. There's also the $100,000 life insurance policy that calls for annual premiums of $5,000. And there's the new $1,000 electric guitar and amplifier that allow Hermus and his 47-year-old wife to enjoy their new-found free time singing away.

"I got to take it easy now," he told a reporter. "In fact I spent a little too much to start out with, but I put it to good cause . . . fixing up my house. That money really goes fast."

To escape the barrage of people seeking his financial assistance, Hermus took a vacation. He went back home to Emory Gap, Tennessee, to visit his mother. Wanting to share his new wealth, he bought her some new clothes, a stereo tape deck, and some flowers.

When asked about the possibility of moving, Hermus replied: "I could have gone out and bought a brick home in Bloomfield Hills . . . or a ranch home in Grosse Pointe, but we got our happiness in this place and there's no use moving out of the neighborhood." As content as he is with his household improvements, he does not regard them as an indication of happiness. "Money ain't everything," he says. "You can't take it and buy love. You can have all the money in the whole world, but if you ain't got love you ain't accomplished nothing."

Source: "First Lottery Millionaire Settles into Easy Living," *Detroit Free Press,* July 8, 1973, p. A3.

photography. The fact that she harbors the idea of "going professional" is also in line with a higher social class background.

Social Factors

A consumer's behavior is also influenced by social factors, such as the consumer's reference groups, family, and social roles and statuses.

Reference Groups

A person's behavior is strongly influenced by many groups.

> **Reference groups** are *those groups that have a direct (face-to-face) or indirect influence on the person's attitudes or behavior.*

Groups having a direct influence on a person are called *membership groups.* These are groups to which the person belongs and interacts. Some are *primary groups* with whom there is fairly continuous interaction, such as family, friends, neighbors, and co-workers. Primary groups tend to be informal. Some are *secondary groups,* which tend to be more formal and have less continuous interaction. They include social organizations such as religious organizations, professional associations, and trade unions.

People are also influenced by groups to which they do not belong. An *aspirational group* is one to which the individual wishes or aspires to belong. For example, a teenage football player may hope to play someday for the Dallas Cowboys, and he identifies with this group although there is no face-to-face contact. A *dissociative group* is one whose values or behavior an individual rejects. The same teenager may want to avoid any relationship with the Hare Krishna cult group.

Marketers try to identify the reference groups of the particular target market they are selling to. Reference groups influence a person in at least three ways. They expose the person to new behaviors and life styles. They also influence the person's attitudes and self-concept because he or she normally desires to "fit in." And they create pressures for conformity that may affect the person's actual product and brand choices (see Exhibit 6-2).

EXHIBIT 6-2

HOME-PARTY-PLAN SELLING—USING REFERENCE GROUPS TO SELL

An increasingly popular form of nonstore selling involves throwing sales parties in homes and inviting friends and acquaintances to see merchandise demonstrated. Companies such as Mary Kay Cosmetics and Tupperware Home Parties are masters at this form of selling and have enjoyed great growth in sales and profits. Here is how home-party selling works.

A Mary Kay "beauty consultant" (of which there are 46,000) will ask different neighbors to hold small beauty shows in their homes. The neighbor will invite her friends for a few hours of informal socializing and refreshment. Within this congenial atmosphere, the

Mary Kay consultant will give a two-hour beauty plan and free makeup lessons to the guests, hoping that the majority of guests will buy some of the cosmetics just demonstrated. The hostess receives a commission of approximately 15 percent on sales plus a discount on personal purchases. About 60 percent of the guests are likely to purchase something, partly because they want to look good in the other women's eyes.

Mary Kay sells cosmetics at home parties. *Courtesy of Mary Kay Cosmetics, Inc., Dallas, Texas.*

Home-party selling is being used to sell cosmetics, cookware, household products, dresses, shoes, and lingerie. Tupperware Home Parties, now thirty-two years old, handles 140 different products, has 80,000 independent salespeople, and has annual sales of approximately $200 million. Mary Kay Cosmetics, now twenty-two years old, uses a highly motivational approach, rewarding its saleswomen for recruiting new consultants—called "offspring"—and honoring the top saleswomen at the annual convention by naming them Queens of Personal Sales and giving them a pink Cadillac to drive for an entire year. Mary Kay's enterprise depends on her sharp understanding of Middle-American women and how they can influence each other in the buying process.

Sources: See "The Mary Kay Way," *Newsweek,* May 7, 1979, p. 75; and David D. Seltz, "The Party-Plan Concept," in *Handbook of Innovative Marketing Techniques* (Reading, Mass.: Addison-Wesley, 1981), chap. 1, pp. 3–11.

The importance of group influence varies among products and brands. Bearden and Etzel suggest that group influence will more strongly affect product and brand choices for conspicuous purchases.[10] A product or brand can be conspicuous for one of two reasons. First, a product may be noticeable because the buyer is one of few people who owns it—luxuries are more conspicuous than necessities because fewer people own the luxuries. Second, a brand can be conspicuous because it is consumed in public where it can be seen by others. Figure 6-5 suggests

FIGURE 6-5
Extent of Group Influence on Product and Brand Choice

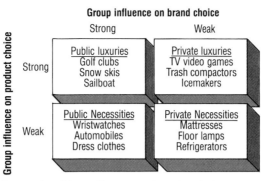

Group influence on brand choice

	Strong	Weak
Strong	Public luxuries Golf clubs Snow skis Sailboat	Private luxuries TV video games Trash compactors Icemakers
Weak	Public Necessities Wristwatches Automobiles Dress clothes	Private Necessities Mattresses Floor lamps Refrigerators

(vertical axis) Group influence on product choice

Source: Adapted from William O. Bearden and Michael J. Etzel, "Reference Group Influence on Product and Brand Purchase Decisions," *The Journal of Consumer Research,* September 1982, p. 185.

how group influence might affect product and brand choices for four categories of products—public luxuries, private luxuries, public necessities, and private necessities.

A person considering the purchase of a public luxury such as a sailboat is likely to be strongly influenced by others. The sailboat will be noticeable because few people own one. The brand will be noticeable because the boat is used in public. Thus both the product and the brand will be conspicuous, and both the decision about whether to own the product and what brand to buy will be strongly influenced by the opinions of others. At the other extreme, product and brand decisions for private necessities are not much affected by group influences because neither the product nor the brand will be noticed by others.

Manufacturers of products and brands where group influence is strong must figure out how to reach the opinion leaders in the relevant reference groups. At one time, sellers thought that *opinion leaders* were primarily community social leaders whom the mass market imitated because of "snob appeal." But opinion leaders are found in all strata of society, and a specific person may be an opinion leader in certain product areas and an opinion follower in other areas. The marketer tries to reach the opinion leaders by identifying certain personal characteristics associated with opinion leadership, determining the media read by the opinion leaders, and directing messages at the opinion leaders.

If Betty Smith buys a camera, both the product and the brand will be visible to others she respects, and her decision to buy the camera and her brand choice may be strongly influenced by some of her groups. Friends who belong to a photography club may influence her to buy a good camera. The more cohesive the group, the more effective its communication; and the more important the group, the more influential it will be in shaping Betty's product and brand choice.

Family

Members of the buyer's family can exercise a strong influence on the buyer's behavior. We can distinguish between two families in the buyer's life. The *family of orientation* consists of one's parents. From parents a person acquires an orientation toward religion, politics, and economics and a sense of personal ambition, self-worth, and love. Even if the buyer no longer interacts very much with his or her

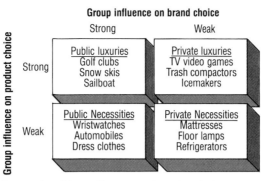

parents, the parent's influence on the buyer's unconscious behavior can be significant. In countries where parents continue to live with their children, their influence can be crucial.

The *family of procreation*—the buyer's spouse and children—have a more direct influence on everyday buying behavior. The family is the most important consumer-buying organization in society, and it has been researched extensively.[11] Marketers are interested in the roles and relative influence of the husband, wife, and children on the purchase of a large variety of products and services.

Husband-wife involvement varies widely by product category. The wife has traditionally been the main purchasing agent for the family, especially in the areas of food, sundries, and staple clothing items. This is changing with the increased number of working wives and the willingness of husbands to do more of the family purchasing. Marketers of staple products would therefore be making a mistake to continue to think of women as the main or only purchasers of their products.

In the case of expensive products and services, husbands and wives engage in more joint decision making. The marketer needs to determine which member normally has the greater influence on the purchase of a particular product or service. Either the husband is more dominant, or the wife, or they have equal influence. The following products and services fall under each:

- *Husband-dominant:* life insurance, automobiles, television
- *Wife-dominant:* washing machines, carpeting, non-living-room furniture, kitchenware.
- *Equal:* living-room furniture, vacation, housing, outside entertainment

At the same time, the dominance of a family member varies for different subdecisions within a product category. Davis found that the decision of "when to buy an automobile" was influenced primarily by the husband in 68 percent of the cases, primarily by the wife in 3 percent of the cases, and equally in 29 percent of the cases.[12] On the other hand, the decision of "what color of automobile to buy" was influenced primarily by the husband in 25 percent of the cases, by the wife in 25 percent of the cases, and equally in 50 percent of the cases. An automobile company would take these varying decision roles into account in designing and promoting its cars.

Table 6-2 shows the relative influence of husbands and wives in several other product categories. For example, husbands dominate in initiating the idea of buying automobile tires, gathering information on them, and making the final decision. In contrast, wives dominate in initiating the idea of buying broadloom carpeting, gathering information on it, and making the final decision. Thus automobile tire manufacturers must focus marketing programs primarily on husbands, while broadloom carpet manufacturers must focus their marketing programs primarily on wives. The other product categories, such as cameras and vacations, are more mixed in the relative influence of the two spouses, and marketing communications may have to be directed differently at different stages of the buying process.

In the case of Betty Smith buying a camera, her husband will play an influencer role. He may have an opinion about her buying a camera and the kind of

	INITIATION		INFORMATION GATHERING		PURCHASE DECISION INFLUENCE	
	H	W	H	W	H	W
Automobile tires	88	12	87	13	80	20
Life insurance	75	25	73	27	64	36
Clothes dryer	67	33	45	55	47	53
Color TV	62	38	59	41	54	46
Vacation (by air)	56	44	53	47	53	47
Camera (still)	46	54	53	47	50	50
Coffee maker	27	73	36	64	36	64
Broadloom carpet	18	82	28	72	40	60

Source: Purchase Influence: Measures of Husband/Wife Influence on Buying Decisions (New Canaan, CT: Haley, Overholser, and Associates, 1975), pp. 27–29.

camera to buy. At the same time, she will be the primary decider, purchaser, and user.

Roles and Statuses

A person participates in many groups—family, clubs, organizations. The person's position in each group can be defined in terms of *role* and *status*. With her parents, Betty Smith plays the role of daughter; in her family, she plays the role of wife; in her company, she plays the role of brand manager. A **role** consists of the activities a person is expected to perform according to the persons around him or her. Each of Betty's roles will influence some of her buying behavior.

Each role carries a **status** reflecting the general esteem accorded to it by society. The role of brand manager has more status in this society than the role of daughter. As a brand manager, Betty will buy the kind of clothing that reflects her role and status.

People often choose products to communicate their status in society. Thus company presidents will drive Mercedes and Cadillac automobiles, wear expensive, finely tailored clothes, and drink Cutty Sark scotch. Marketers are aware of products' potential for becoming *status symbols*. However, status symbols vary not only for different social classes, but also geographically. Status symbols that are "in" in New York are ownership of horses, season opera tickets, and an Ivy League college degree; those that are "in" in Chicago are sculpture in the home and a whirlpool bath; and those that are "in" in San Francisco are indoor plants, home winery, recreation vehicles, and involvement in est.[13]

Personal Factors A buyer's decisions are also influenced by personal outward characteristics, notably the buyer's age and life-cycle stage, occupation, economic circumstances, life style, and personality and self-concept.

Age and Life-Cycle Stage

People change the goods and services they buy over their lifetimes. They eat baby food in the early years, most foods in the growing and mature years, and special diets in the later years. People's taste in clothes, furniture, and recreation is also age-related.

Consumption is also shaped by the stage of the *family life cycle*. Nine stages of the family life cycle are listed in Table 6-3, along with the financial situation and

TABLE 6-3
An Overview of the Family Life Cycle and Buying Behavior

STAGE IN FAMILY LIFE CYCLE	BUYING OR BEHAVIORAL PATTERN
1. Bachelor stage: Young single people not living at home	Few financial burdens. Fashion opinion leaders. Recreation-oriented. Buy: basic kitchen equipment, basic furniture, cars, equipment for the mating game, vacations.
2. Newly married couples: Young, no children	Better off financially than they will be in near future. Highest purchase rate and highest average purchase of durables. Buy: cars, refrigerators, stoves, sensible and durable furniture, vacations.
3. Full nest I: Youngest child under six	Home purchasing at peak. Liquid assets low. Dissatisfied with financial position and amount of money saved. Interested in new products. Like advertised products. Buy: washers, dryers, TV, baby food, chest rubs and cough medicines, vitamins, dolls, wagons, sleds, skates.
4. Full nest II: Youngest child six or over	Financial position better. Some wives work. Less influenced by advertising. Buy larger-sized packages, multiple-unit deals. Buy: many foods, cleaning materials, bicycles, music lessons, pianos.
5. Full nest III: Older married couples with dependent children	Financial position still better. More wives work. Some children get jobs. Hard to influence with advertising. High average purchase of durables. Buy: new, more tasteful furniture, auto travel, nonnecessary appliances, boats, dental services, magazines.
6. Empty nest I: Older married couples, no children living with them, head in labor force	Home ownership at peak. Most satisfied with financial position and money saved. Interested in travel, recreation, self-education. Make gifts and contributions. Not interested in new products. Buy: vacations, luxuries, home improvements.
7. Empty nest II: Older married, no children living at home, head retired	Drastic cut in income. Keep home. Buy: medical appliances, medical-care products that aid health, sleep, and digestion.
8. Solitary survivor, in labor force	Income still good but likely to sell home.
9. Solitary survivor, retired	Same medical and product needs as other retired group; drastic cut in income. Special need for attention, affection, and security.

Sources: William D. Wells and George Gubar, "Life Cycle Concepts in Marketing Research," *Journal of Marketing Research,* November 1966, pp. 355–63, here p. 362. Also see Patrick E. Murphy and William A. Staples, "A Modernized Family Life Cycle," *Journal of Consumer Research,* June 1979, pp. 12–22; and Janet Wagner and Sherman Hanna, "The Effectiveness of Family Life Cycle Variables in Consumer Expenditure Research," *Journal of Consumer Research,* December 1983, pp. 281–91.

typical product interests of each group. Marketers often define their target markets in life-cycle stage terms and develop appropriate products and marketing plans.

Some recent work has identified *psychological life-cycle stages*. Adults experience certain *passages* or *transformations* as they go through life.[14] Thus Betty Smith may move from being a satisfied brand manager and wife to being an unsatisfied person searching for a new way to fulfill herself. This may have stimulated her strong interest in photography. Marketers should pay attention to the changing consumption interests that might be associated with these adult passages.

Occupation

A person's occupation has an influence on the goods and services bought. A blue-collar worker will buy work clothes, work shoes, lunch boxes, and bowling recreation. A company president will buy expensive clothes, air travel, country club membership, and a large sailboat. Marketers try to identify the occupational groups that have an above-average interest in their products and services. A company can even specialize in producing products needed by a particular occupational group.

Economic Circumstances

A person's economic circumstances will greatly affect product choice. People's economic circumstances consist of their *spendable income* (its level, stability, and time pattern), *savings and assets* (including the percentage that is liquid), *borrowing power,* and *attitude toward spending versus saving.*

Betty Smith can consider buying an expensive Nikon if she has enough spendable income, savings, or borrowing power and she prefers spending to saving. Marketers of income-sensitive goods pay continuous attention to trends in personal income, savings, and interest rates. If economic indicators point to a recession, marketers can take steps to redesign, reposition, and reprice their product; reduce their production and inventories; and do other things to protect their financial solvency.

Life Style

People coming from the same subculture, social class, and even occupation may have quite different life styles. Betty Smith, for example, can choose to live like a capable homemaker, a career woman, or a free spirit. She plays several roles, and her way of reconciling them expresses her life style. If she gravitates toward becoming a professional photographer, this has further life style implications, such as keeping odd hours and traveling a lot.

A person's **life style** refers to *the person's pattern of living in the world as expressed in his or her activities, interests, and opinions.* Life style portrays the "whole person" in interaction with his or her environment. Life style captures something more than the person's social class or personality alone. If we know what social class someone belongs to, we can infer several things about that person's likely behavior but fail to see him or her as an individual. If we know what kind of personality someone has, we can infer several things about that person's

TABLE 6-4
Life Style Dimensions

ACTIVITIES	INTERESTS	OPINIONS	DEMOGRAPHICS
Work	Family	Themselves	Age
Hobbies	Home	Social issues	Education
Social events	Job	Politics	Income
Vacation	Community	Business	Occupation
Entertainment	Recreation	Economics	Family size
Club membership	Fashion	Education	Dwelling
Community	Food	Products	Geography
Shopping	Media	Future	City size
Sports	Achievements	Culture	Stage in life cycle

Source: Joseph T. Plummer, "The Concept and Application of Life-Style Segmentation," *Journal of Marketing,* January 1974, p. 34.

distinguishing psychological characteristics but not much about his or her activities, interests, and opinions. Life style attempts to profile a person's whole pattern of acting and interacting in the world.

The technique of measuring life styles is known as *psychographics.*[15] It involves measuring the major dimensions shown in Table 6-4. The first three are known as the AIO dimensions (activities, interests, opinions), and the variables are listed under each dimension. Respondents are given lengthy questionnaires—sometimes as long as twenty-five pages—in which they are asked how strongly they agree or disagree with such statements as

- I would like to become an actor.
- I enjoy going to concerts.
- I usually dress for fashion, not for comfort.
- I often have a cocktail before dinner.

The data are then analyzed on a computer to find distinctive life style groups. Using this approach, the Chicago-based advertising agency of Needham, Harper, and Steers identified 10 life style types, such as "Scott, the successful professional" and "Candice, the chic suburbanite."

More recently, Arnold Mitchell developed the VALS (values and life styles) typology, which classifies the American public into nine life style groups.[16] These groups are described below, along with the percentage of the U.S. population in each.

- *Survivors* (4%) are people marked by poverty and little education who have given up on life. They find little satisfaction in life and concentrate on just making it from day to day. They tend to be conservative and are "despairing, depressed, and withdrawn."

- *Sustainers* (7%) are also marked by poverty but are striving to move ahead toward a better life. They are "angry, distrustful, rebellious, and combative," and have a deep distrust of the system. Despite their strong need for status and group acceptance, they see themselves as having less social status.

- *Belongers* (33%) are traditional, conforming, and family-oriented. They have a strong need for acceptance and would rather be followers than leaders. They prefer the status quo and tend to lead happy and contented lives.

- *Emulators* (10%) are "ambitious, competitive, and ostentatious," and are striving to move ahead by emulating the richer and more successful. They tend to be hard-working, less conservative, and fairly successful but less satisfied with life.
- *Achievers* (23%) are the "driving and driven" people who made the system and are now at the top. They are hard-working, successful, and self-confident, and they tend to feel good about the system, themselves, and their accomplishments.
- *I-am-mes* (5%) are typically young people in transition between the old and the new. They find life confusing, contradictory, and uncertain; experience emotional ups and downs; and live life "intensely, vividly, and experientially." They are seeking and finding new interests and new life goals.
- *Experientials* (7%) are seeking intense personal experiences and emotions. Action and interaction are the important things in their lives. They are politically and socially liberal, independent and self-reliant, and fairly happy with life. They appreciate nature and seek spiritual meaning in things.
- *Societally conscious* (9%) people are driven by social ideals—by concern with societal issues and events such as consumerism, conservation, pollution, and wildlife protection. They tend to be well-educated; "successful, influential, and mature"; and sophisticated and politically effective.
- *Integrateds* (2%) are mature and balanced people who have a broad perspective and can find solutions to opposing views. They combine inner directedness and outer directedness. They lead when action is called for, and they have high social status even though they do not seek it.

A person may progress through several of these life style groups over the course of a lifetime. In preparing a marketing strategy for a product, the marketer searches for relationships between the product or brand and life style groups. A yogurt manufacturer may find that because "experientials" have a deeper appreciation for natural things, they are heavier users of yogurt. The marketer can then aim the brand more directly at this life style group.

The life style concept, when used carefully,[17] can help the marketer gain an understanding of changing consumer values and how they affect buying behavior. The implications of the life style concept are well stated by Boyd and Levy:

> Marketing is a process of providing customers with parts of a potential mosaic from which they, as artists of their own life styles, can pick and choose to develop the composition that for the time seems the best. The marketer who thinks about his products in this way will seek to understand their potential settings and relationships to other parts of consumer life styles, and thereby to increase the number of ways they fit meaningfully into the pattern.[18]

Personality and Self-Concept

Each person has a distinct personality that will influence his or her buying behavior. By **personality,** we mean *the person's distinguishing psychological characteristics that lead to relatively consistent and enduring responses to his or her own environment.* A person's personality is usually described in terms of such traits as the following:[19]

Self-confidence	Ascendancy	Emotional stability
Dominance	Sociability	Achievement
Autonomy	Defensiveness	Order
Change	Affiliation	Adaptability
Deference	Aggressiveness	

This Michelob ad appeals to "achievers." *Courtesy of Anheuser-Busch Companies, Inc.*

Personality can be a useful variable in analyzing consumer behavior, providing that personality types can be classified and strong correlations exist between certain personality types and product or brand choices. For example, a beer company may discover that many heavy beer drinkers are high on sociability and aggressiveness. This suggests a possible brand image for the beer and the kinds of people to depict in the advertising. Some companies have been able to use personality segmentation to advantage (see Chapter 10).

Many marketers use a concept related to personality—a person's *self-concept* (also called self-image). All of us carry around a complex mental picture of ourselves. For example, Betty Smith may see herself as being extroverted, creative, and active. To that extent, she will favor a camera that projects the same qualities. If the Nikon is promoted as a camera for extroverted, creative, and active persons, then its brand image will match her self-image. Marketers should try to develop brand images that match the self-image of the target market.

The theory, admittedly, is not that simple. What if Betty's *actual self-concept* (how she views herself) differs from her *ideal self-concept* (how she would like to view herself) and from her *others self-concept* (how she thinks others see her). Which self will she try to satisfy with the choice of a camera? Some marketers feel that buyers' choices will correspond more to their actual self-concept; others to the ideal self-concept; and still others to the others self-concept. As a result, self-concept theory has had a mixed record of success in predicting consumer responses to brand images.[20]

Psychological Factors

A person's buying choices are also influenced by four major psychological factors—motivation, perception, learning, and beliefs and attitudes. We will explore each factor's role in the buying process.

Motivation

We saw that Betty Smith became interested in buying a camera. Why? What is she really seeking? What needs is she trying to satisfy?

A person has many needs at any point in time. Some needs are *biogenic*. They arise from physiological states of tension such as hunger, thirst, discomfort. Other needs are *psychogenic*. They arise from psychological states of tension such as the need for recognition, esteem, or belonging. Most of these needs will not be intense enough to motivate the person to act at a given point in time. A need becomes a motive when it is aroused to a sufficient level of intensity. A **motive** (or drive) is *a need that is sufficiently pressing to direct the person to seek satisfaction of the need*. Satisfying the need reduces the tension.

Psychologists have developed theories of human motivation. Two of the most popular—the theories of Sigmund Freud and Abraham Maslow—carry quite different implications for consumer analysis and marketing.

FREUD'S THEORY OF MOTIVATION. Freud assumes that people are largely unconscious about the real psychological forces shaping their behavior. He sees the person as growing up and repressing many urges. These urges are never eliminated or under perfect control; they emerge in dreams, in slips of the tongue, in neurotic and obsessive behavior, or ultimately in psychoses when the person's ego can no longer balance the impulsive power of the id with the oppressive power of the superego.

Thus a person does not fully understand his or her motivational mainsprings. If Betty Smith wants to purchase an expensive camera, she may describe her motive as wanting a hobby or career. At a deeper level, she may be purchasing the camera to impress others with her creative talent. At a still deeper level, she may be buying the camera to feel young and independent again.

When Betty looks at a camera, she will react not only to the camera's performance, but also to other cues. The camera's shape, size, weight, material, color, and case can all trigger certain emotions. A rugged-looking camera can arouse Betty's feelings about being independent, which she can either handle or avoid. In designing a camera, the manufacturer should be aware of the impact of visual and tactile elements in triggering consumer emotions that can stimulate or inhibit purchase.

The leading exponent of Freudian motivation theory in marketing is Ernest Dichter, who for over two decades has been interpreting buying situations and product choices in terms of underlying unconscious motives. Dichter calls his approach *motivational research,* and it consists of collecting "in-depth interviews" with a few dozen consumers to uncover the deeper motives triggered by the product. He uses various "projective techniques" to throw the ego off guard—techniques such as word association, sentence completion, picture interpretation, and role playing.[21]

Motivation researchers have produced some interesting and occasionally bizarre hypotheses as to what may be in the buyer's mind regarding certain purchases. They have suggested that:

- Consumers resist prunes because they are wrinkled-looking and remind people of old age.
- Men smoke cigars as an adult version of thumbsucking. They like their cigars to have a strong odor in order to prove their masculinity.
- Women prefer vegetable shortening to animal fats because the latter arouse a sense of guilt over killing animals.
- A woman is very serious when baking a cake because unconsciously she is going through the symbolic act of giving birth. She dislikes easy-to-use cake mixes because the easy life evokes a sense of guilt.

MASLOW'S THEORY OF MOTIVATION. Abraham Maslow sought to explain why people are driven by particular needs at particular times.[22] Why does one person spend considerable time and energy on personal safety and another on pursuing the esteem of others? His answer is that human needs are arranged in a hierarchy, from the most pressing to the least pressing. Maslow's hierarchy of needs is shown in Figure 6-6.

In their order of importance, they are *physiological* needs, *safety* needs, *social* needs, *esteem* needs, and *self-actualization* needs. A person will try to satisfy the most important needs first. When a person succeeds in satisfying an important need, it will cease being a motivator for the present time, and the person will be motivated to satisfy the next most important need.

For example, a starving man (need 1) will not take an interest in the latest happenings in the art world (need 5), nor in how he is seen or esteemed by others (need 3 or 4), nor even in whether he is breathing clean air (need 2). But as each important need is satisfied, the next most important need will come into play.

FIGURE 6-6
Maslow's Hierarchy of Needs

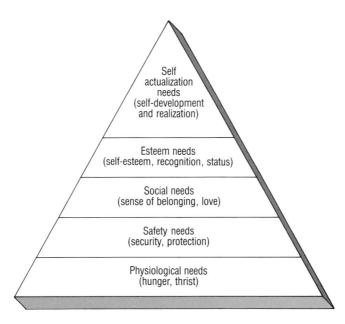

Self actualization needs (self-development and realization)

Esteem needs (self-esteem, recognition, status)

Social needs (sense of belonging, love)

Safety needs (security, protection)

Physiological needs (hunger, thrist)

What light does Maslow's theory throw on Betty Smith's interest in buying a camera? We can guess that Betty has satisfied her physiological, safety, and social needs; they do not motivate her interest in cameras. Her camera interest might come from a strong need for more esteem from others, or it might come from a need for self-actualization. She wants to actualize her potential as a creative person and express herself through photography.

Perception

A motivated person is ready to act. How the motivated person acts is influenced by his or her perception of the situation. Two people in the same motivated state and objective situation may act quite differently because they perceive the situation differently. Betty Smith might consider a fast-talking camera salesperson aggressive and insincere. Another camera buyer might consider the same salesperson intelligent and helpful.

Why do people have different perceptions of the same situation? All of us capture a stimulus through *sensations*—that is, flows of information through our five senses: sight, hearing, smell, touch and taste. However, each of us attends, organizes, and interprets this sensory information in an individual way. **Perception** can be defined as "the process by which an individual selects, organizes, and interprets information inputs to create a meaningful picture of the world."[23]

Perception depends not only on the character of the physical stimuli, but also on the relation of the stimuli to the surrounding field (the Gestalt idea) and on conditions within the individual. People can emerge with different perceptions of the same stimulus because of three perceptual processes: selective exposure, selective distortion, and selective retention.

SELECTIVE EXPOSURE.   People are exposed to a tremendous amount of stimuli every day of their lives. Even limiting this to commercial stimuli, the average person may be exposed to over fifteen hundred ads a day. It is impossible for a person to attend to all these stimuli, most will be screened out. The real challenge is to explain which stimuli people will notice.

1. People are more likely to notice stimuli that relate to a current need. Betty Smith will notice all kinds of ads about cameras because she is motivated to buy one; she will probably not notice ads about stereophonic equipment.

2. People are more likely to notice stimuli that they anticipate. Betty Smith is more likely to notice cameras in the camera store than a line of radios also carried by the store, because she did not expect the store to carry radios.

3. People are more likely to notice stimuli whose deviation is large in relation to the normal size of the stimuli. Betty Smith is more likely to notice an ad offering $100 off the list price of a Nikon than one offering $5 off the list price.[24]

Selective exposure means that marketers have to work especially hard to attract the consumer's attention. Their message will be lost on most people who are not in the market for the product. Even people who are in the market may not notice the message unless it stands out from the surrounding sea of stimuli. Ads that are larger in size, or use four colors where most ads are black and white, or are novel and provide contrast are more likely to be noticed.

SELECTIVE DISTORTION.   Even stimuli that consumers notice do not necessarily come across in the intended way. Each person attempts to fit incoming information into his or her existing mind set. Selective distortion describes the tendency of people to twist information into personal meanings. Betty Smith may hear the salesperson mention some good and bad points about a competing camera brand. Since she already has a strong leaning toward Nikon, she is likely to distort the points in order to conclude that Nikon is the better camera. People tend to interpret information in a way that will support rather than challenge their preconceptions.

SELECTIVE RETENTION.   People will forget much that they learn. They will tend to retain information that supports their attitudes and beliefs. Because of selective retention, Betty is likely to remember good points mentioned about the Nikon and forget good points mentioned about competing cameras. She remembers Nikon's good points because she "rehearses" them more whenever she thinks about choosing a camera.

These three perceptual factors—selective exposure, distortion, and retention—mean that marketers have to work hard to get their messages through. This explains why marketers use so much drama and repetition in sending messages to their market. (For an interesting sidelight on perception, see Exhibit 6-3.)

Learning

When people act, they learn. **Learning** describes *changes in an individual's behavior arising from experience.* Most human behavior is learned.

EXHIBIT 6-3

SUBLIMINAL PERCEPTION: CAN CONSUMERS BE PERSUADED WITHOUT KNOWING IT?

In 1957 the words "Eat popcorn" and "Drink Coca-Cola" were flashed on a screen in a New Jersey movie theater every five seconds for one three-hundredth of a second. The researchers reported that although the audience did not recognize these messages on the conscious level, they absorbed them on the unconscious level and purchased 58 percent more popcorn and 18 percent more Coca-Cola. Suddenly advertising agencies and consumer protection groups became intensely interested in this phenomenon called *subliminal perception*. People expressed their fears of being brainwashed, and California and Canada declared it illegal. However, the controversy lost a lot of its force when scientists failed to replicate these results. But the issue was not dead. In 1974 Wilson Bryan Key, in his *Subliminal Seduction*, claimed that consumers were still being manipulated by publishers and advertisers who hid messages in print ads, magazines, and TV commercials; and in 1979 Melvin Ross made the same claim.

Subliminal perception has since been studied by many psychologists and consumer researchers. None have been able to show that subliminal messages have any effect on consumer behavior. It appears that subliminal advertising simply doesn't have the power attributed to it by the critics. Further, most advertisers scoff at the notion of an industry conspiracy to manipulate consumers through "invisible" messages. As one advertising agency executive put it, "We have enough trouble persuading consumers with a series of up-front thirty-second ads—how could we do it in 1/300th of a second?"

Sources: Wilson Bryan Key, *Subliminal Seduction* (New York: NAL, 1974); Melvin H. Ross, "The Reappearance of Subliminal Persuasion," *Marketing Review*, October–November 1979, pp. 23ff; and Timothy E. Moore, "Subliminal Advertising: What You See Is What You Get," *Journal of Marketing*, Spring 1982, pp. 38–47.

Learning theorists say that a person's learning is produced through the interplay of drives, stimuli, cues, responses, and reinforcement.

We saw that Betty Smith has a drive toward self-actualization. *Drive* is defined as a strong internal stimulus-impelling action. Her drive becomes a *motive* when it is directed toward a particular drive-reducing *stimulus object,* in this case a camera. Betty's response to the idea of buying a camera is conditioned by the surrounding cues. *Cues* are minor stimuli that determine when, where, and how the person responds. Seeing cameras in a shop window, hearing of a special sales price, and being encouraged by her husband are all cues that can influence Betty's *response* to the impulse to buy a camera.

Suppose Betty buys the camera. If the experience is *rewarding,* the probability is that she will use the camera more and more. Her response to cameras will be reinforced.

Later on, Betty may want to buy binoculars. She notices several brands, including one by Nikon. Since she knows that Nikon makes good cameras, she infers that Nikon also makes good binoculars. We say that she *generalizes* her response to similar stimuli.

The reverse of generalization is *discrimination.* When Betty examines binoculars made by Olympus, she sees that they are lighter and more compact than

Nikon's binoculars. Discrimination means that she has learned to recognize differences in sets of stimuli and can adjust her response accordingly.

The practical significance of learning theory for marketers is that they can build up demand for a product by associating it with strong drives, using motivating cues, and providing positive reinforcement. A new company can enter the market by appealing to the same drives as competitors and providing similar cue configurations because buyers are more likely to transfer loyalty to similar brands than to dissimilar brands (generalization). Or it may design its brand to appeal to a different set of drives and offer strong cue inducements to switch (discrimination).

Beliefs and Attitudes

Through acting and learning, people acquire their beliefs and attitudes. These in turn influence their buying behavior.

A **belief** is *a descriptive thought that a person holds about something.* Betty Smith may believe that a Nikon takes great pictures, stands up well under rugged use, and costs $550. These beliefs may be based on real knowledge, opinion, or faith. They may or may not carry an emotional charge. For example, Betty Smith's belief that a Nikon camera is heavy may or may not matter to her decision.

Manufacturers, of course, are very interested in the beliefs that people carry in their heads about specific products and services. These beliefs make up product and brand images, and people act on their beliefs. If some of the beliefs are wrong and inhibit purchase, the manufacturer would want to launch a campaign to correct these beliefs.

An **attitude** describes *a person's enduring favorable or unfavorable cognitive evaluations, emotional feelings, and action tendencies toward some object or idea.*[25] People have attitudes regarding almost everything: religion, politics, clothes, music, food, and so on. Attitudes put them into a frame of mind of liking or disliking things, moving toward or away from them. Thus Betty Smith may hold such attitudes as "Buy the best," "The Japanese make the best products in the world," and "Creativity and self-expression are among the most important things in life." The Nikon camera is therefore salient to Betty because it fits well into her existing attitudes. A company would benefit greatly from researching the various attitudes people have that might bear on its product.

Attitudes lead people to behave in a fairly consistent way toward similar objects. People do not have to interpret and react to everything in a fresh way. Attitudes economize on energy and thought. For this very reason, attitudes are very difficult to change. A person's attitudes settle into a coherent pattern, and to change one may require difficult adjustments in many other attitudes.

Thus a company would be well advised to fit its products into existing attitudes, rather than to try to change people's attitudes. There are exceptions, of course, where the great cost of trying to change attitudes may pay off.

> Honda entered the U.S. motorcycle market facing a major decision. It could either sell its motorcycles to a small number of people already interested in motorcycles or try to increase the number interested in motorcycles. The latter would be more expensive because many people had negative attitudes toward motorcycles. They associated motorcycles with black leather jackets, switchblades, and crime.

Honda took the second course and launched a major campaign based on the theme. "You meet the nicest people on a Honda." Its campaign worked, and many people adopted a new attitude toward motorcycles.

We can now appreciate the many forces acting on consumer behavior. The person's choice is the result of the complex interplay of cultural, social, personal, and psychological factors. Many of these factors cannot be influenced by the marketer. However, they are useful in identifying the buyers who may be more interested in the product. Other factors are subject to marketer influence and give the marketer hints on how to develop the product, price, place, and promotion to attract strong consumer response.

■ *Summary*

Markets have to be understood before marketing strategies can be developed. The consumer market buys goods and services for personal consumption. It is the ultimate market for which economic activities are organized. The consumer market consists of many submarkets, such as blacks and seniors, which may require special marketing programs.

Marketers must understand how consumers transform marketing and other stimuli into buyer responses. Consumer behavior is influenced by the buyer's characteristics and by the buyer's decision process. Buyer characteristics include four major factors: cultural, social, personal, and psychological.

Culture is the most fundamental determinant of a person's wants and behavior. It includes basic values, perceptions, preferences, and behaviors the person learns from the family and other key institutions. Marketers try to track cultural shifts that might suggest new ways to serve consumers. *Subcultures* are "cultures within cultures"—nationality groups, religious groups, racial groups, and geographical groups that have distinct values and life styles. *Social classes* are subcultures whose members have similar social prestige based on similar patterns of occupation, income, education, wealth, and other variables. People with different cultural, subcultural, and social class characteristics have different product and brand preferences. Marketers may want to focus their marketing programs on the special needs of certain groups.

Social factors also influence a buyer's behavior. A person's reference groups—family, friends, social organizations, professional associations—strongly affect product and brand choices. The person's position within each group can be defined in terms of role and status. A buyer chooses products and brands that reflect his or her role and status.

The buyer's age, life-cycle stage, occupation, economic circumstances, life style, personality, and other *personal characteristics* influence his or her buying decisions. Young consumers have different needs and wants from older consumers; the needs of young married couples differ from those of retirees; consumers with higher incomes buy differently from those who have less to spend. Consumer life styles—the whole pattern of acting and interacting in the world—are also an important influence on buyers' choices.

Finally, consumer buying behavior is influenced by four major *psychological* factors—motivation, perception, learning, and attitudes. Each of these factors provides a different perspective for understanding the workings of the buyer's "black box."

A person's buyer behavior is the result of the complex interplay of all these cultural, social, personal, and psychological factors. Many of these factors cannot be controlled by marketers, but they are useful in identifying and understanding the particular consumer marketers are trying to influence.

■ Questions for Discussion

1. The Mondavi Winery of California has introduced a six-pack of 6.3-ounce cans of Chablis, with future plans to introduce six-packs of Rosé, Burgundy, and other varieties of wine. Based on your knowledge of cultural, social, personal, and psychological variables influencing consumer behavior, what factors would work for or against the success of such a product?

2. Using automobile ads as examples, show how car advertising stresses one or more of the major factors influencing consumer behavior.

3. In 1982 Seven-Up ran ads with the theme "crisp and clean with no caffeine." What consumer behavior factors were considered in the decision to run this ad?

4. Discuss the influence of cultural characteristics (culture, subculture, and social class) on the patronage of department stores.

5. Which social characteristics have the greatest effect on an individual's record album purchases?

6. Based on recent demographic trends, are any stages of a family life cycle *not* included in Table 6-3? Discuss the marketing implications.

7. *Self-concept* is synonymous with *personality.* Discuss.

8. What level of Maslow's hierarchy of needs are marketers of the following products primarily attempting to satisfy? (a) smoke detectors, (b) telephone long-distance dialing, (c) Seagram's VO, (d) life insurance, and (e) transcendental meditation.

9. Give an example of how VALS might be used by a marketer of consumer packaged goods.

■ References

1. Drawn from various sources.

2. *Statistical Abstract of the United States,* 1984.

3. For more reading, see THOMAS S. ROBERTSON, JOAN ZIELINSKI, and SCOTT WARD, *Consumer Behavior* (Glenview, IL: Scott, Foresman, 1984), pp. 536–51. Also see KEVIN A. WALL, "New Market: Among Blacks, the Haves Are Now Overtaking the Have-Nots," *Advertising Age,* February 11, 1974, pp. 35–36; MARY JANE SCHLINGER and JOSEPH T. PLUMMER, "Advertising in Black and White," *Journal of Marketing Research,* May 1972, pp. 149–53; RAYMOND A. BAUER, and SCOTT M. CUNNINGHAM, "The Negro Market," *Journal of Advertising Research,* April 1970, pp. 3–12; and HERBERT ALLEN, "Product Appeal: No Class Barrier," *Advertising Age,* May 18, 1981, p. S4.

4. See DANIEL BURSTEIN, "Maturity Market: Exploring New Images," *Advertising Age,* August 29, 1983, p. M9; and CHARLES D. SCHEWE, "Research Dispels Myths about Elderly; Suggests Marketing Opportunities," *Marketing News,* May 25, 1984, Sec. 1, p. 12.

5. See RENA BARTOS, "What Every Marketer Should Know about Women," *Harvard Business Review,* May–June 1978, pp. 73–85.

6. See "Marketing to Hispanics," *Advertising Age,* March 19, 1984, p. M10.

7. See MELVIN HELITZER and CARL HEYEL, *The Youth Market* (New York: Media Books, 1970), p. 58; and GEORGE W. SCHIELE, "How to Reach the Young Consumer," *Harvard Business Review,* March–April 1974, pp. 77–86.

8. See LEON G. SCHIFFMAN and LESLIE LAZAR KANUK, *Consumer Behavior,* 2d ed. (Englewood Cliffs, NJ: Prentice-Hall, 1983), pp. 404–20.

9. This classification was originally developed by W. LLOYD WARNER and PAUL S. LUNDT in *The Social Life of a Modern Community* (New Haven, CT: Yale University Press, 1941). For a summary of more recent classifications, see RICHARD P. COLEMAN, "The Continuing Significance of Social Class to Marketers," *Journal of Consumer Research,* December 1983, pp. 265–80.

10. WILLIAM O. BEARDEN and MICHAEL J. ETZEL, "Reference Group Influence on Product and Brand Purchase Decisions," *Journal of Consumer Research,* September 1982, p. 185.

11. See HARRY L. DAVIS, "Decision Making within the Household," *Journal of Consumer Research,* March 1976, pp. 241–60; HARRY L. DAVIS and BENNY P. RIGAUX, "Perception of Marital Roles in Decision Processes," *Journal of Consumer Research,* June 1974, pp. 51–60; and HARRY L. DAVIS, "Dimensions of Marital Roles in Consumer Decision Making," *Journal of Marketing Research,* May 1970, pp. 168–77.

12. See DAVIS, "Dimensions of Marital Roles."

13. See "Across the Nation—Thumbnail Guide to Americans' Tastes," *U.S. News and World Report,* February 14, 1977, p. 39.

14. GAIL SHEEHY, *Passages: Predictable Crises in Adult Life* (New York: Dutton, 1974); and ROGER GOULD, *Transformations* (New York: Simon and Schuster, 1978).

15. See WILLIAM D. WELLS, "Psychographics: A Critical Review," *Journal of Marketing Research,* May 1975, pp. 196–213; and PETER W. BERNSTEIN, "Psychographics Is Still an Issue on Madison Avenue," *Fortune,* January 16, 1978, pp. 78–84.

16. ARNOLD MITCHELL, *The Nine American Lifestyles* (New York: Macmillan, 1983). Used by permission of the author and the publisher.

17. For more reading on the pros and cons of using the life style concept, see SONIA YUSPEH, "Syndicated Values/Lifestyles Segmentation Schemes: Use Them as Descriptive Tools, Not to Select Targets," *Marketing News,* May 25, 1984, p. 1; and "SRI's Response to Yuspeh: Demographics Aren't Enough," *Marketing News,* May 25, 1984, p. 1.

18. HARPER W. BOYD, JR., and SIDNEY J. LEVY, *Promotion: A Behavioral View* (Englewood Cliffs, NJ: Prentice-Hall, 1967), p. 38.

19. See RAYMOND L. HORTON, "Some Relationships between Personality and Consumer Decision-Making," *Journal of Marketing Research,* May 1979, pp. 244–45.

20. For more reading, see EDWARD L. GRUBB and HARRISON L. GRATHWOHL, "Consumer Self-Concept, Symbolism, and Market Behavior: A Theoretical Approach," *Journal of Marketing,* October 1967, pp. 22–27; IRA J. DOLICH, "Congruence Relationships between Self-Images and Product Brands, *Journal of Marketing Research,* February 1969, pp. 40–47; E. LAIRD LANDON, JR., "The Differential Role of Self-Concept and Ideal Self-Concept in Consumer Purchase Behavior," *Journal of Consumer Research,* September 1974, pp. 44–51; and M. JOSEPH SIRGY, "Self-Concept in Consumer Behavior; A Critical Review," *Journal of Consumer Research,* December 1982, pp. 287–300.

21. See ERNEST DICHTER, *Handbook of Consumer Motivations* (New York: McGraw-Hill, 1964).

22. ABRAHAM H. MASLOW, *Motivation and Personality* (New York: Harper & Row, 1954), pp. 80–106.

23. BERNARD BERELSON and GARY A. STEINER, *Human Behavior: An Inventory of Scientific Findings* (New York: Harcourt Brace Jovanovich, 1964), p. 88.

24. This relationship is known as Weber's law and is one of the main laws in psychophysics. See Chapter 10.

25. See DAVID KRECH, RICHARD S. CRUTCHFIELD, and EGERTON L. BALLACHEY, *Individual in Society* (New York: McGraw-Hill, 1962), chap. 2.

7

Consumer Markets: Buyer Decision Processes

For decades AT&T monopolized the residential telephone market: Consumers had no choice but to lease whatever telephones the company chose to offer. But in the late 1970s, the Supreme Court opened the way for competition when it ruled that ·consumers could buy and attach their own phones to AT&T lines. And in the early 1980s, the breakup of AT&T and the advent of inexpensive, one-piece electronic phones threw the industry into competitive chaos. Suddenly, AT&T found itself competing with hundreds of other telephone suppliers for a piece of the exploding $1.5 billion residential telephone market. During the next few years, AT&T learned a great deal about consumer buying behavior.

AT&T and its competitors offered hundreds of new phone models designed to meet any conceivable consumer preference. At one extreme, they offered one-piece electronic phones at prices as low as $7 to $10. At the other extreme, they offered fancy phones selling for several hundred dollars— decorator phones in endless styles and colors, and phones with exotic features such as programmable memories for automatic dialing, last-number redial, cordless operation, mute and hold buttons, and speakers for hands-free conversations.

Despite huge R&D and marketing expenditures, the industry met with disaster. During 1983 and 1984, sales of home telephones boomed, but the companies lost hundreds of millions. By the end of 1984, more than half of all the telephone suppliers were out of the business. AT&T did better than most— but despite a 20 percent market share in 1984, the company made little money on its phone sales. Where did AT&T and the others go wrong? In their rush to grab a share of the rapidly growing market, they seriously miscalculated consumer wants and phone buying behavior.

For example, the telephone suppliers assumed that consumers would naturally want to buy rather than lease their phones, and overlooked the need to educate consumers about the benefits of phone ownership. But many consumers were still unaware that they could own their phones, or that it made economic sense to buy rather than lease. More than 120 million U.S. households still lease telephones.

Many sellers assumed that consumers would flock to buy inexpensive, one-piece phones, and that the number of phones per home would jump dramatically. Though consumers did buy carloads of cheap phones at first, they didn't like the flimsy designs and high failure rates. Demand soon turned back to more traditional and reliable phones. And the average number of phones per household increased only from 1.7 in 1982 to 1.9 in 1984.

The telephone marketers also believed that consumers would buy phones from just about any retailer—or even through catalogs or mail order—if the price was right. But it turned out that buyers preferred to deal with reputable retailers who helped them with purchase decisions and backed up the sale. One of the reasons for AT&T's relative success in this turbulent market was its recognition that consumers would return to higher-quality phones and retailers after trying cheaper phones from less dependable sources. Thus AT&T developed a solid retail network. In addition to its own 900 phone stores, it sold quality phones through over 10,000 retail outlets including Sears, Penney, K mart, Montgomery Ward, Target, and Ace Hardware.

AT&T, however, erred at the other extreme—it assumed that consumers wanted high-priced phones with fancy features. AT&T offered 215 different models with prices as high as $350. But telephone buyers still preferred good old basic telephones, in traditional styles and colors and at more moderate prices—phones like those they'd been leasing for years. And buyers weren't much interested in exotic "bells and whistles"—in fact, the new features confused many consumers. For these complicated phones, consumers needed more sales assistance than most retail stores were willing or able to provide. AT&T now has a training program to teach retail salespeople in non-AT&T stores how to demonstrate phone products and answer buyers' questions.

After the shakeout, the residential telephone market will settle into steady, long-term growth. And most experts agree that demand will shift to more sophisticated, high-tech phones as consumers grow accustomed to the new technologies. But the shift will involve gradual changes in consumer attitudes. To retain its leadership in the more competitive telephone industry, AT&T will have to develop a more thorough understanding of consumers and their telephone buying behavior.[1]

Marketers have to be extremely careful in analyzing consumer behavior. Consumers often turn down what appears to be a winning offer. If they do not vote for a product, the product loses. The new plant and equipment might as well have been built on quicksand. Du Pont found this out when it lost $100 million on its Corfam synthetic leather material. So did Ford when it launched the famous (or infamous) Edsel, losing a cool $350 million in the process.[2] And so did Brown-Forman Distillers Corporation when consumers decided not to drink its new Frost 8/80, a "dry, white" whisky, which it thought would be a smashing success.[3]

In the preceding chapter we looked at all the influences—cultural, social, personal, and psychological—that affect buyers. In this chapter we will look at how consumers make buying decisions. We will examine consumer buying roles and the types of decisions consumers face, the main steps in the buyer decision process, and the process by which consumers learn about and buy new products.

IDENTIFYING THE BUYERS AND BUYING DECISION PROCESS

A major task of the marketer is to identify correctly target buyers of a product. The marketer needs to know what people are involved in the buying decision and what role each person plays.

Buying Roles For many products, it is fairly easy to identify the decision maker. Men normally choose their cigars and women choose their pantyhose. Other products, however, involve a decision-making unit consisting of more than one person. Consider the selection of a family automobile. The suggestion to buy a new car might come from the oldest child. A friend might advise the family on the kind of car to buy. The husband might choose the make. The wife might have a definite opinion regarding the car's style. The husband might make the final decision with the wife approving. The wife might end up using the car more than her husband.

Thus we can distinguish several roles people might play in a buying decision:

Initiator. The initiator is the person who first suggests or thinks of the idea of buying the particular product or service.

Influencer. An influencer is a person whose views or advice carries some weight in making the final decision.

Decider. The decider is the person who ultimately determines the buying decision or any part of it—whether to buy, what to buy, how to buy, or where to buy.

Buyer. The buyer is the person who makes the actual purchase.

User. The user is the person(s) who consumes or uses the product or service.

A company needs to identify these roles because they have implications for designing the product, determining messages, and allocating the promotional budget. If the husband decides on the car's make, then the automobile company will direct most of the advertising to reach husbands. The automobile company might design certain car features to please the wife and place some ads in media reaching wives. Knowing the main participants and the roles they play helps the marketer fine-tune the marketing program.

Types of Buying Decision Behavior Consumer decision making varies with the type of buying decision. There are great differences between buying toothpaste, a tennis racket, an expensive camera, and a new car. The more complex decisions are likely to involve more buying participants and more buyer deliberation. Howard and Sheth have distinguished three types of buying behavior.[4]

Routinized Response Behavior

The simplest type of buying behavior occurs in the purchase of low-cost, frequently purchased items. Buyers have very few decisions to make—they are well acquainted with the product class, know the major brands, and have fairly clear preferences among the brands. They do not always buy the same brand because of stockouts, special deals, and a wish for variety. But in general buyers do not give much thought, search, or time to the purchase. The goods in this class are often called *low-involvement goods.*

The marketer has two tasks. The marketer must provide positive satisfaction for current customers by maintaining consistent quality, service, and value. The marketer must also try to attract new buyers by introducing new features and using point-of-purchase displays, price specials, and premiums.

Limited Problem Solving

Buying is more complex when buyers confront an unfamiliar brand in a familiar product class. For example, persons thinking about buying a new tennis racket may be shown a new brand with an offset handle or one made of boron or another new material. They may ask questions and watch ads to learn more about the new brand. This is described as limited problem solving because buyers are fully aware of the product class, but are not familiar with all the brands and their features.

The marketer recognizes that consumers are trying to reduce risk by gathering information. The marketer must design a communication program that will increase the buyer's brand comprehension and confidence.

Extensive Problem Solving

Buying reaches its greatest complexity when buyers face an unfamiliar product class and do not know what criteria to use. For example, a man may become interested in buying a citizen-band transceiver for the first time. He has heard such brand names as Cobra, Panasonic, and Midland, but lacks clear brand concepts. He does not even know what product class attributes to consider in choosing a good citizen-band transceiver. He is in a state of extensive problem solving.

The marketer of products in this class must understand the information-gathering and evaluation activities of prospective buyers. The marketer needs to facilitate the buyer's learning of the attributes of the product class, their relative importance, and the high standing of the marketer's brand on the more important attributes.

STAGES IN THE BUYER DECISION PROCESS

We are now ready to examine the stages the buyer passes through to reach a buying decision and outcome. We will use the model in Figure 7-1, which shows the consumer as passing through five stages: *problem recognition, information search, evaluation of alternatives, purchase decision,* and *postpurchase behavior.* This model emphasizes that the buying process starts long before the actual purchase and has consequences long after the purchase. It encourages the marketer to focus on the entire buying process, rather than just the purchase decision.[5]

This model seems to imply that consumers pass through all five stages with every purchase they make. But in more routine purchases, consumers skip or reverse some of these stages. A woman buying her regular brand of toothpaste would recognize the need and go right to the purchase decision, skipping information search and evaluation. However, we will use the model in Figure 7-1 because it shows the full range of considerations that arise when a consumer faces a new purchase situation, especially one involving extensive problem solving.

To illustrate this model, we will once again refer to Betty Smith and try to understand how she became interested in buying an expensive camera and the stages she went through to make the final choice.

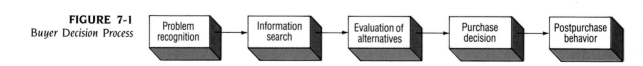

FIGURE 7-1
Buyer Decision Process

Problem recognition → Information search → Evaluation of alternatives → Purchase decision → Postpurchase behavior

Problem Recognition The buying process starts with the buyer recognizing a problem or need. The buyer senses a difference between his or her actual state and a desired state. The need can be triggered by internal or external stimuli. In the former case, one of the person's normal needs—hunger, thirst, sex—rises to a threshold level and becomes a drive. From previous experience, the person has learned how to cope with this drive and is motivated toward a class of objects that he or she knows will satisfy this drive.

Or a need can be aroused by an external stimulus. Betty Smith passes a bakery and the sight of freshly baked bread stimulates her hunger; she admires a neighbor's new car; or she watches a television commercial for a Jamaican vacation. All of these can lead her to recognize a problem or need.

The marketer at this stage needs to determine the circumstances that usually trigger consumer problem recognition. The marketer should research consumers to find out (a) what kinds of felt needs or problems arose, (b) what brought them about, and (c) how they led to this particular product.

Betty Smith might answer that she felt the need for a new hobby. This happened when her busy season at work slowed down, and she thought of cameras after talking to a friend about photography. By gathering such information, the marketer can identify the stimuli that most often trigger interest in the product category and develop marketing programs which capitalize on these stimuli.

Information Search An aroused consumer may or may not search for more information. If the consumer's drive is strong and a well-defined gratification object is near at hand, the consumer is likely to buy it then. If not, the consumer may simply store the need in memory. The consumer may undertake no further search, some further search, or very active search for information bearing on the need.

Assuming that the consumer undertakes some search, we distinguish between two levels. The milder search state is called *heightened attention*. Here Betty Smith simply becomes more receptive to information about cameras. She pays attention to camera ads, cameras used by friends, and camera conversations.

Or Betty may go into *active information search,* where she will look for reading material, phone friends, and engage in other search activities to gather product information. How much search she undertakes will depend upon the strength of her drive, the amount of information she initially has, the ease of obtaining additional information, the value she places on additional information, and the satisfaction she gets from search. Normally the amount of consumer search activity increases as the consumer moves from decision situations that involve limited problem solving to those that involve extensive problem solving.

Of key interest to the marketer are the major information sources the consumer will turn to and the relative influence each will have on the purchase decision. *Consumer information sources* fall into four groups:

- *Personal sources:* family, friends, neighbors, acquaintances
- *Commercial sources:* advertising, salespersons, dealers, packaging, displays
- *Public sources:* mass media, consumer-rating organizations
- *Experiential sources:* handling, examining, using the product

The relative influence of these information sources varies with the product cate-

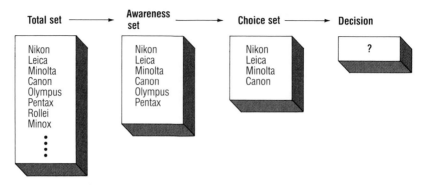

FIGURE 7-2
Successive Sets Involved in Consumer Decision Making

Total set	Awareness set	Choice set	Decision
Nikon	Nikon	Nikon	?
Leica	Leica	Leica	
Minolta	Minolta	Minolta	
Canon	Canon	Canon	
Olympus	Olympus		
Pentax	Pentax		
Rollei			
Minox			

gory and the buyer's characteristics. Generally speaking, the consumer receives the most information exposure about a product from commercial sources—that is, marketer-dominated sources. The most effective exposures, however, tend to come from personal sources. Each type of source may perform a different function in influencing the buying decision. Commercial information normally performs an *informing* function, and personal sources perform a *legitimizing* or *evaluating* function. For example, physicians normally learn of new drugs from commercial sources, but turn to other physicians for evaluation information.

As a result of gathering information, the consumer increases his or her awareness of the available brands and their features. Before looking for information, Betty Smith knew only a few camera brands out of the *total set* of available cameras shown at the far left of Figure 7-2. The camera brands she knew constituted her *awareness set.* The incoming information increased her awareness set, and further information helped her eliminate certain brands from consideration. The remaining brands that met her buying criteria constituted her *choice set.* Her final decision will be made from this set, based on the decision evaluation process she uses.[6]

A company must design its marketing mix to get its brand into the prospect's awareness set and choice set. If its brand fails to get into these sets, the company has lost its opportunity to sell to the customer. The company must also learn which other brands remain in the consumer's choice set, so that it knows its competition and can plan its appeals.

The marketer should carefully identify consumers' sources of information and the importance of each source. Consumers should be asked how they first heard about the brand, what information they received, and the importance they place on different information sources. This information is critical in preparing effective communication to target markets.

Evaluation of Alternatives

We have seen how the consumer uses information to arrive at a set of final brand choices. Now the question is: How does the consumer choose among the alternative brands in the choice set? The marketer needs to know how the consumer processes information to arrive at brand choices. Unfortunately, there is no simple and single evaluation process used by all consumers, or even by one consumer in all buying situations. There are several decision evaluation processes.

Certain basic concepts will help explain consumer evaluation processes. First, we assume that each consumer sees a product as a bundle of *product attributes.*

The following attributes are of interest to buyers in some familiar product classes:

- *Cameras:* picture quality, ease of use, camera size, price
- *Hotels:* location, cleanliness, atmosphere, cost
- *Mouthwash:* color, effectiveness, kills germs, price, taste/flavor
- *Brassieres:* comfort, fit, life, price, style
- *Lipstick:* color, container, creaminess, prestige factor, taste/flavor
- *Tires:* safety, tread life, ride quality, price

While the above attributes are of normal interest, consumers will vary as to which they consider relevant. Consumers will pay the most attention to those attributes connected with their needs. The market for a product can often be segmented according to the attributes that are of primary interest to different customer groups.

Second, the consumer will attach different *importance weights* to the relevant attributes. A distinction can be drawn between the importance of an attribute and its salience.[7] *Salient attributes* are those that come to the consumer's mind when he or she is asked to think of a product's attributes. The marketer must not conclude that these are necessarily the most important attributes. Some of them may be salient because the consumer has just been exposed to a commercial message mentioning them or has had a problem involving them, hence making these attributes "top-of-the-mind." Furthermore, in the class of nonsalient attributes may be some that the consumer forgot but whose importance would be recognized when they are mentioned. Marketers should be more concerned with attribute importance than attribute salience.

Third, the consumer is likely to develop a set of *brand beliefs* about where each brand stands on each attribute. The set of beliefs held about a particular brand is known as the *brand image.* The consumer's beliefs may be at variance with the true attributes due to his or her particular experience and the effect of selective perception, selective distortion, and selective retention.

Fourth, the consumer is assumed to have a *utility function* for each attribute. The utility function describes how the consumer expects product satisfaction to vary with alternative levels of each attribute. For example, Betty Smith may expect her satisfaction from a camera to increase with better picture quality; to peak with a medium-weight camera as opposed to a very light or very heavy one; to be higher for a 35-mm camera than for a 135-mm camera. If we combine the attribute levels where the utilities are highest, they make up Betty's ideal camera. The camera would also be her preferred camera if it were available and affordable.

Fifth, the consumer arrives at attitudes (judgments, preferences) toward the brand alternatives through some *evaluation procedure.* Consumers have been found to apply different evaluation procedures to make a choice among multiattribute objects.[8]

We will illustrate these concepts with Betty Smith's camera buying situation. Suppose Betty has narrowed her choice set to four cameras (A, B, C, D). Assume that she is primarily interested in four attributes—picture quality, ease of use, camera size, and price. Table 7-1 shows how she believes each brand rates on each attribute. Betty believes that brand A (say Nikon) will give her picture quality of 10 on a 10-point scale; is easy to use, 8; has medium size, 6; and is fairly expensive, 4.

TABLE 7-1
A Consumer's Brand
Beliefs about Cameras

CAMERA	ATTRIBUTE			
	Picture quality	Ease of use	Camera size	Price
A	10	8	6	4
B	8	9	8	3
C	6	8	10	5
D	4	3	7	8

Note: The number 10 represents the highest desirable score on that attribute. In the case of price, a high number means a low cost, which makes the camera more desirable.

Similarly, she has beliefs about how the other cameras rate on these attributes. The marketer would like to be able to predict which camera Betty will buy.

Clearly, if one camera rated best on all the criteria, we could predict that Betty would choose it. But the brands vary in appeal. If Betty wants picture quality above everything, she should buy A; if she wants the camera that is easiest to use, she should buy B; if she wants the best camera size, she should buy C; if she wants the lowest-price camera, she should buy D. Some buyers will buy on only one attribute, and their choices are easy to predict.

Most buyers consider several attributes, but assign different importance to each. If we knew the importance weights Betty assigns to the four attributes, we could predict her camera choice more reliably.

Suppose Betty assigns 40 percent of the importance to the camera's picture quality, 30 percent to ease of use, 20 percent to its size, and 10 percent to its price. To find Betty's perceived value for each camera, her weights are multiplied by her beliefs about each camera. This leads to the following perceived values:

$$\text{Camera A} = .4(10) + .3(8) + .2(6) + .1(4) = 8.0$$
$$\text{Camera B} = .4(8) + .3(9) + .2(8) + .1(3) = 7.8$$
$$\text{Camera C} = .4(6) + .3(8) + .2(10) + .1(5) = 7.3$$
$$\text{Camera D} = .4(4) + .3(3) + .2(7) + .1(8) = 4.7$$

We would predict that Betty will favor camera A.

This model is called the *expectancy value model* of consumer choice.[9] It is one of several possible models describing how consumers go about evaluating alternatives. We recognize that consumers might evaluate a set of alternatives in other ways, such as the following:[10]

1. Betty might decide that she should consider only cameras that satisfy a set of minimum attribute levels. She might decide that any camera she bought would have to offer a picture quality greater than 7 *and* ease of use greater than 8. In this case, we would predict that she would choose camera B because only camera B satisfies the minimum requirements. (This is called the *conjunctive model* of consumer choice.)

2. Betty might decide that she would settle for a camera that had a picture quality greater than 7 *or* ease of use greater than 8. In this case, A and B both remain in the evaluation set. (This is called the *disjunctive model* of consumer choice.)

Marketers should study buyers to find out how they actually evaluate brand alternatives. Suppose most camera buyers form their preferences by using the

Real repositioning: To rate higher with consumers, Minolta added autofocus, motorized film control, and other desirable features not offered on other 35mm cameras. *Courtesy of Minolta Corporation.*

expectancy value process. Knowing this, the marketer could take steps to influence the buyer's decision. Betty Smith was inclined to buy camera A. The marketer of camera C, for example, could use the following strategies to influence people like Betty:[11]

■ *Modifying the camera.* The marketer could redesign the camera so that it delivers better pictures or other characteristics that this type of buyer desires. This is called *real repositioning.*

- *Altering beliefs about the camera.* The marketer could try to alter buyers' beliefs of where the camera stands on key attributes. This is especially recommended if buyers underestimate camera C's qualities. This is not recommended if buyers are accurately evaluating camera C; exaggerated claims would lead to buyer dissatisfaction and bad word of mouth. Attempting to alter beliefs about the camera is called *psychological repositioning*.

- *Altering beliefs about the competitor's brands.* The marketer could try to change buyers' beliefs about where competitive brands stand on different attributes. This may make sense where buyers believe a competitor's brand has more quality than it actually has. This is called *competitive depositioning*.

- *Altering the importance weights.* The marketer could try to persuade buyers to attach more importance to attributes the brand excels in. The marketer of camera C can tout the benefits of buying the right-size camera, since C has superiority in this attribute.

- *Calling attention to neglected attributes.* The marketer could try to draw the buyer's attention to neglected attributes. If camera C offers a larger choice of lenses, the marketer might tout the benefits of this attribute to the market.

- *Shifting the buyer's ideals.* The marketer could try to persuade buyers to change their ideal levels for one or more attributes. The marketer of camera C might try to convince buyers that cameras which provide high-quality pictures are harder to use or that only an expert can see the differences in quality.

Purchase Decision

In the evaluation stage, the consumer ranks brands in the choice set and forms purchase intentions. Normally the consumer will buy the most preferred brand, but two factors can come between the purchase intention and the purchase decision. These factors are shown in Figure 7-3.[12]

The first is the *attitudes of others.* Suppose Betty Smith's husband feels strongly that Betty should buy the lowest-priced camera (D) to keep down expenses. Then Betty's *purchase probability* for camera A will be somewhat reduced. The extent to which another person's attitude will reduce Betty's preferred alternative depends upon two things: (1) the intensity of the other person's negative attitude toward her preferred alternative and (2) her motivation to comply with the other person's wishes.[13] The more intense the other person's negativism and the closer the other person is to Betty, the more she will revise downward her purchase intention.

Purchase intention is also influenced by *unanticipated situational factors.* The consumer forms a purchase intention based on such factors as expected family income, expected price, and expected benefits from the product. When the con-

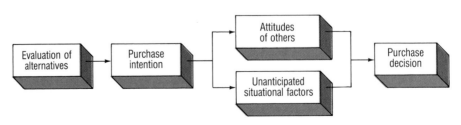

FIGURE 7-3
Steps between Evaluation of Alternatives and a Purchase Decision

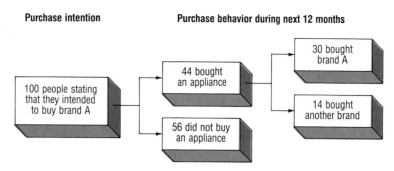

FIGURE 7-4
Consequences of Purchase Intentions and Purchase Decisions

Purchase intention

Purchase behavior during next 12 months

100 people stating that they intended to buy brand A

44 bought an appliance

56 did not buy an appliance

30 bought brand A

14 bought another brand

sumer is about to act, unanticipated situational factors may arise to change the purchase intention. Betty Smith may lose her job, some other purchase may become more urgent, or a friend may report being disappointed in that camera.

Thus preferences and even purchase intentions are not completely reliable predictors of actual purchase choice. They direct purchase behavior, but may not fully determine the outcome. Figure 7-4 shows a fairly typical outcome. In a study of one hundred people who stated an intention to buy brand A of an appliance within the next twelve months, only forty-four ended up buying the particular appliance, and only thirty (or 68 percent) purchased brand A.

A consumer's decision to modify, postpone, or avoid a purchase decision is heavily influenced by *perceived risk*. Many purchases involve some *risk taking*.[14] Consumers cannot be certain about the purchase outcome. This produces anxiety. The amount of perceived risk varies with the amount of money at stake, the amount of attribute uncertainty, and the amount of consumer self-confidence.

A consumer develops certain routines for reducing risk, such as decision avoidance, information gathering from friends, and preference for national brand names and warranties. The marketer must understand the factors that provoke a feeling of risk in consumers and provide information and support that will reduce the perceived risk.

Postpurchase Behavior

After purchasing the product, the consumer will experience some level of satisfaction or dissatisfaction. The consumer will also engage in postpurchase actions of interest to the marketer. The marketer's job does not end when the product is bought, but continues into the postpurchase period.

Postpurchase Satisfaction

What determines whether the buyer is satisfied or dissatisfied with a purchase? The answer lies in the relationship between the consumer's *expectations* and the product's *perceived performance*.[15] If the product matches expectations, the consumer is satisfied; if it exceeds them, the consumer is highly satisfied; if it falls short, the consumer is dissatisfied.

Consumers base their expectations on messages they receive from sellers, friends, and other information sources. If the seller exaggerates the product's performance, consumers will experience *disconfirmed expectations,* which lead to dissatisfaction. The larger the gap between expectations and performance, the greater the consumer's dissatisfaction. Here the consumer's coping style comes into play. Some consumers magnify the gap when the product is not perfect, and they are highly dissatisfied. Other consumers minimize the gap and are less dissatisfied.[16]

This theory suggests that the seller should make product claims that faithfully represent the product's likely performance so that buyers experience satisfaction. Some sellers might even understate performance levels so that consumers experience higher-than-expected satisfaction with the product.

Festinger and Bramel believe that most nonroutine purchases will unavoidably involve some postpurchase discomfort:

> When a person chooses between two or more alternatives, discomfort or dissonance will almost inevitably arise because of the person's knowledge that while the decision he has made has certain advantages, it also has some disadvantages. This dissonance arises after almost every decision, and further, the individual will invariably take steps to reduce this dissonance.[17]

Postpurchase Actions

Satisfaction with the product will affect subsequent behavior. A satisfied consumer is more likely to purchase the product the next time and will say good things about the product to others. According to marketers, "A satisfied customer is our best advertisement."

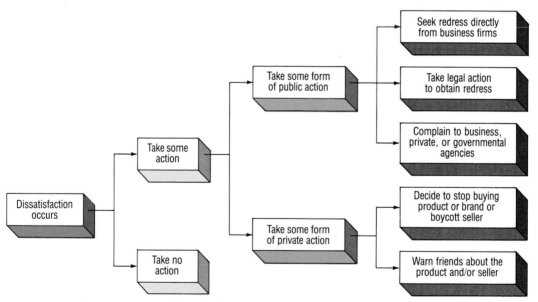

FIGURE 7-5 *How Customers Handle Dissatisfaction*

Source: Ralph L. Day and E. Laird Landon, Jr., "Toward a Theory of Consumer Complaining Behavior," in *Consumer and Industrial Buying Behavior,* ed. Arch G. Woodside, Jagdish N. Sheth, and Peter D. Bennett (New York: Elsevier North-Holland, 1977), p. 432.

The Coca-Cola Company encourages customers to voice problems and ask questions using its toll-free 1-800-GET COKE hotline. *Courtesy of Coca-Cola Company.*

A dissatisfied consumer responds differently. The dissatisfied consumer will try to reduce the dissonance because of a drive in the human organism "to establish internal harmony, consistency, or congruity among his opinions, knowledge, and values."[18] Dissonant consumers will resort to one of two courses of action. They may try to reduce the dissonance by *abandoning* or *returning* the product, or they may try to reduce the dissonance by seeking information that may *confirm* its high value (or avoiding information that may confirm its low value). In the case of Betty Smith, she may return the camera, or she may seek information that will make her feel better about the camera.

Marketers should be aware of the ways consumers handle dissatisfaction. Figure 7-5 outlines these ways. Consumers have a choice between taking and not taking any action. If they act, they can take public action or private action. Public actions include complaining to the company, going to a lawyer, or complaining to other groups that might help the buyer get satisfaction. Or the buyer may simply stop buying the product or bad-mouth it to friends and others. In all these cases, the seller loses something.

Marketers can take steps to minimize the amount of consumer postpurchase dissatisfaction and to help customers feel good about their purchase. Automobile companies can send a letter to new car owners congratulating them on having selected a fine car. They can place ads showing satisfied owners driving their new cars. They can solicit customer suggestions for improvements and list the location of available services. They can write instruction booklets that reduce dissonance. They can send owners a magazine containing articles describing the pleasures of owning the new car.

Postpurchase communications to buyers have been shown to result in fewer product returns and order cancellations.[19] In addition, they provide good channels for customer complaining and allow for speedy redress of customer grievances. Paying careful attention to the dissatisfactions of previous purchasers can help the

EXHIBIT 7-1

CUSTOMERS: P&G'S PIPELINE TO PRODUCT PROBLEMS

One of the first mass marketers to establish a broad service operation, Procter & Gamble Co. is celebrating the 10th anniversary of its 800-number service this year. While it has been a leader in consumer services—it hired its first expert in 1941—its current operation is not as fully computerized as some of the hard-goods makers. P&G first experimented with the phone-line idea in 1971, and by 1979 it began implementing a plan to have an 800 number on every P&G consumer product sold in the U.S.

Last year, P&G received 670,000 mail and phone contacts about its products—the overall figure this year is running 17% ahead of that. And according to G. Gibson Carey, P&G division manager for general advertising, the calls fall into three broad categories: requests for information, complaints, and testimonials.

P&G employs 75 people in its service department, 30 of whom handle calls; the rest answer letters and help collate information for other departments. Phones are manned weekdays from 9:30 a.m. to 7:30 p.m. Employees receive three to five weeks of training. Besides instruction on how to deal with people over the phone, the training includes the history of each product, the company's marketing and advertising strategy for it, and what happens if it is misused. Telephone representatives have reference manuals and access to technical staff but no computers to help answer questions. Information from P&G customers is tallied by hand and computerized later.

Most callers dial the company with the product package in hand. And every product has a code printed on it identifying the plant, the manufacturing date, and sometimes even the shift and the line on which it was made. Thus, if P&G has supplied defective packages, as happened not long ago with one product, it can trace the problem's source quickly and correct it.

Because of the calls it received on various products, P&G has:

- Included instructions for baking at high attitudes on the Duncan Hines brownies package.
- Added a recipe for making a wedding cake to the information on its white cake mix package.
- Told users what to do if Downy liquid fabric softener accidentally freezes (numerous customers had that problem during a cold spell).

"As a general rule, we don't look at [consumer service] as a source for new product ideas," Carey concedes. Information from the calls first goes to product-development personnel who track quality control. Each division and top management get a separate report. P&G also surveys customers to determine whether callers were satisfied with the treatment they received.

Carey says the 800-number service is "a distant, early-warning signal" of product problems. Without it, "we wouldn't find out about them for weeks or months." And, he points out: "There's a whole lot of enlightened self-interest in this."

Source: Reprinted from the June 11, 1984, issue of *Business Week* by special permission, © 1984 by McGraw-Hill, Inc.

company to spot and correct problems, resulting in increased postpurchase satisfaction for future buyers (see Exhibit 7-1).

There is one more step in the postpurchase behavior of buyers that sellers should watch—namely, what the buyers ultimately do with the product. The major

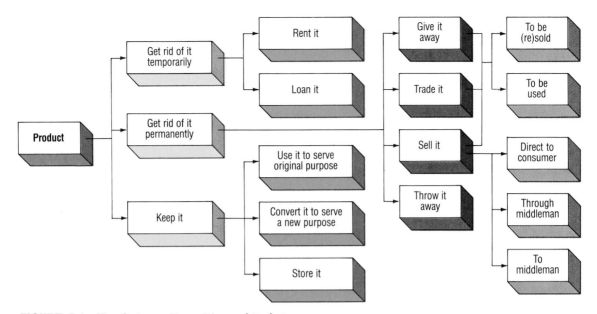

FIGURE 7-6 *How Customers Use or Dispose of Products*

Source: Jacob Jacoby, Carol K. Berning, and Thomas F. Dietvorst, "What about Disposition?" *Journal of Marketing,* July 1977, p. 23.

possibilities are shown in Figure 7-6. If consumers use the product to serve a new purpose, this should interest the seller because this purpose can be advertised. If consumers store the product and make little use or get rid of it, this indicates that the product is not very satisfying and word of mouth would not be strong. Of equal interest is how consumers ultimately dispose of the product. If they sell or trade the product, this will dampen new product sales. The seller needs to study how the product is used and disposed of for clues as to possible problems and opportunities.

Understanding the consumer's needs and buying power is the foundation of successful marketing. By understanding how buyers go through problem recognition, information search, evaluation of alternatives, the purchase decision, and postpurchase behavior, the marketer can pick up many clues as to how to meet the buyer's needs. By understanding the various participants in the buying process and the major influences on their buying behavior, the marketer can develop an effective marketing program to support an attractive offer to the target market.

BUYER DECISION PROCESSES TOWARD NEW PRODUCTS

We have examined the stages buyers go through in trying to satisfy a need. Buyers may pass quickly or slowly through these stages, and some of the stages may even be reversed.[20] Much depends on the nature of the buyer, the product, and the buying situation.

We will now consider how buyers approach the purchase of new products. Companies risk millions of dollars each year developing and launching new products. They are eager for guidance from studies of consumer new product adoption behavior. Much research has been done on this topic, and we will summarize it below.

We define **new product** as *a good, service, or idea that is perceived by some potential customers as new.* The new product may have been around for awhile, but our interest is in how consumers learn about products for the first time and make decisions on whether to adopt them. We define **adoption process** as "the mental process through which an individual passes from first hearing about an innovation to final adoption."[21] We define **adoption** as *the decision by an individual to become a regular user of the product.*

We are now ready to examine the main generalizations drawn from hundreds of studies of how people accept new ideas.

Stages in the Adoption Process

We notice that consumers go through a number of stages in the process of adopting a new product. Rogers identifies five:

1. *Awareness:* The consumer becomes aware of the innovation but lacks information about it.

2. *Interest:* The consumer is stimulated to seek information about the innovation.

3. *Evaluation:* The consumer considers whether it would make sense to try the innovation.

4. *Trial:* The consumer tries the innovation on a small scale to improve his or her estimate of its value.

5. *Adoption:* The consumer decides to make full and regular use of the innovation.

This suggests that the innovator should think about how to help consumers move through these stages. A manufacturer of microwave ovens may discover that many consumers are in the interest stage, but do not move to the trial stage because of uncertainty and the large investment. If these same consumers would be willing to use a microwave oven on a trial basis for a small fee, the manufacturer should consider offering a trial-use plan with an option to buy.

Individual Differences in Innovativeness

People differ markedly in their readiness to try new products. Rogers defines a person's *innovativeness* as "the degree to which an individual is relatively earlier in adopting new ideas than the other members of his social system." In each product area, there are apt to be "consumption pioneers" and early adopters. Some people are the first to adopt new clothing fashions or new appliances, such as the microwave oven. Other individuals adopt new products much later. This has led to a classification of people into the adopter categories shown in Figure 7-7.

The adoption process is represented as a normal distribution when plotted over time. After a slow start, an increasing number of people adopt the innovation,

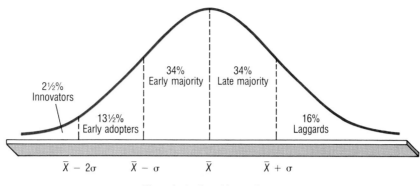

2½%
Innovators

13½%
Early adopters

34%
Early majority

34%
Late majority

16%
Laggards

$\bar{X} - 2\sigma$ $\bar{X} - \sigma$ $\bar{X}$ $\bar{X} + \sigma$

Time of adoption of innovations

Source: Redrawn from Everett M. Rogers, *Diffusion of Innovations* (New York: Free Press, 1962), p. 162.

the number reaches a peak, and then it diminishes as fewer nonadopters remain. Innovators are defined as the first 2.5 percent of the buyers to adopt a new idea; the early adopters are the next 13.5 percent who adopt the new idea; and so forth.

Rogers sees the five adopter groups as differing in values. Innovators are *venturesome;* they try new ideas at some risk. Early adopters are guided by *respect;* they are opinion leaders in their community and adopt new ideas early but carefully. The early majority are *deliberate;* they adopt new ideas before the average person, although they rarely are leaders. The late majority are *skeptical;* they adopt an innovation only after a majority of people have tried it. Finally, laggards are *tradition-bound;* they are suspicious of changes, mix with other tradition-bound people, and adopt the innovation only because it has now taken on a measure of tradition in itself.

This adopter classification suggests that an innovating firm should research the demographic, psychographic, and media characteristics of innovators and early adopters and should direct communications specifically to them. Identifying early adopters is not always easy. No one has demonstrated the existence of a general personality factor call innovativeness. Individuals tend to be innovators in certain areas and laggards in others. We can think of a businessperson who dresses conservatively, but who delights in trying unfamiliar cuisines.

The firm's problem is to identify the characteristics of those who are likely to be early adopters in its product area. For example, studies show that innovative housewives are more gregarious and usually higher in social status than noninnovative housewives. Home computer innovators are middle-aged, higher in income and education, and tend to be opinion leaders, though they tend to be more rational, more introverted, and less social.[22] Certain communities tend to have more people who are early adopters. Rogers offered the following hypotheses about early adopters:

> The relatively earlier adopters in a social system tend to be younger in age, have higher social status, a more favorable financial position, more specialized operations, and a different type of mental ability from later adopters. Earlier

adopters utilize information sources that are more impersonal and cosmopolite than later adopters and that are in closer contact with the origin of new ideas. Earlier adopters utilize a greater number of different information sources than do later adopters. The social relationships of earlier adopters are more cosmopolite than for later adopters, and earlier adopters have more opinion leadership.[23]

Role of Personal Influence

Personal influence plays a major role in the adoption of new products. Personal influence describes the effect of statements made by one person on another's attitude or probability of purchase. According to Katz and Lazarsfeld:

> About half of the women in our sample reported that they had recently made some change from a product or brand to which they were accustomed to something new. The fact that one third of these changes involved personal influences indicates that there is also considerable traffic in marketing advice. Women consult each other for opinions about new products, about the quality of different brands, about shopping economies and the like.[24]

Personal influence is more significant in some situations and for some individuals than for others. Personal influence is more important in the evaluation stage of the adoption process than in the other stages. It has more influence on later adopters than early adopters. And it is more important in risky than in safe situations.

Influence of Product Characteristics on Rate of Adoption

The characteristics of the innovation affect its rate of adoption. Some products catch on almost overnight (frisbees), whereas others take a long time to gain acceptance (diesel engine autos). Five characteristics are especially important in influencing an innovation's rate of adoption. We will consider the characteristics in relation to the rate of adoption of personal computers for home use.

The first characteristic is the innovation's *relative advantage*—the degree to which it appears superior to existing products. The greater the perceived relative advantage of using a personal computer, say in preparing income taxes and keeping financial records, the sooner the personal computers will be adopted.

The second characteristic is the innovation's *compatibility*—the degree to which it matches the values and experiences of the individuals in the community. Personal computers, for example, are highly compatible with the life styles found in upper-middle-class homes.

The third characteristic is the innovation's *complexity*—the degree to which it is relatively difficult to understand or use. Personal computers are complex and will therefore take a longer time to penetrate U.S. homes.

The fourth characteristic is the innovation's *divisibility*—the degree to which it may be tried on a limited basis. To the extent that people can rent personal computers with an option to buy, the product's rate of adoption will increase.

The fifth characteristic is the innovation's *communicability*—the degree to which the results can be observed or described to others. Because personal computers lend themselves to demonstration and description, this will help them diffuse faster in the social system.

Other characteristics influence the rate of adoption, such as initial costs, ongoing costs, risk and uncertainty, scientific credibility, and social approval. The new product marketer has to research all these factors and give the key ones maximum attention in developing the new product and marketing program.

■ Summary

Before planning its marketing strategy, a company needs to identify its target consumers and the types of decision processes they go through. Although many buying decisions involve only one decision maker, other decisions may involve several participants who play such roles as initiator, influencer, decider, buyer, and user. The marketer's job is to identify the other buying participants, their buying criteria, and their level of influence on the buyer. The marketing program should be designed to appeal to and reach the other key participants as well as the buyer.

The number of buying participants and the amount of buying deliberateness increase with the complexity of the buying situation. Howard and Sheth have distinguished three types of buying decision behavior: routinized response behavior, limited problem solving, and extensive problem solving.

In buying something, the buyer goes through a decision process consisting of problem recognition, information search, evaluation of alternatives, purchase decision, and postpurchase behavior. The marketer's job is to understand the buyer's behavior at each stage and what influences are operating. This understanding allows the marketer to develop a significant and effective marketing program for the target market.

With regard to new products, consumers respond at different rates, depending on the consumer's characteristics and the product's characteristics. Manufacturers try to bring their new products to the attention of potential early adopters, particularly those with opinion leader characteristics.

■ Questions for Discussion

1. A shopper is at the evaluation of alternatives stage of the buyer decision process when considering the choice of a supermarket in which to do "routine" shopping. What factors do you believe most consumers would consider "very important" in their choice of a supermarket? (List these factors in order of importance.)

2. Can an "impulse" purchase be explained by the buyer decision process described in this chapter?

3. What are the results of information search?

4. If you were given the task of developing a model of consumer behavior, what variables and/or relationships would you add to those discussed in this chapter?

5. Apply the five different roles in the decision process to your decision regarding college.

6. Explain which of the three classes of buying situations would probably apply to the purchase decision for (a) a European vacation, (b) a six-pack of beer, (c) a new suit, and (d) a museum to visit.

7. Relate the stages of the consumer buying process to your latest purchase of a pair of shoes.

8. Why is the postpurchase behavior stage included in the model of the buying process?

■ References

1. See Brian O'Reilly, "Lessons from the Home Phone Wars," *Fortune,* December 24, 1984, pp. 83–86; and Jules Abend, "Merchandising Home Telephones: Strategies for Grabbing More Market Share," *Stores,* June 1984, pp. 55–60.
2. See the opening vignette in Chapter 12.
3. Frederick C. Klein, "How a New Product Was Brought to Market Only to Flop Miserably," *Wall Street Journal,* January 5, 1973, pp. 1, 19.
4. John A. Howard and Jagdish N. Sheth, *The Theory of Buyer Behavior* (New York: Wiley, 1969), pp. 27–28.
5. Several models of the consumer buying process have been developed by marketing scholars. The most prominent models are those of Howard and Sheth, *The Theory of Buyer Behavior;* Francesco M. Nicosia, *Consumer Decision Processes* (Englewood Cliffs, NJ: Prentice-Hall, 1966); and James F. Engel, Roger D. Blackwell, and David T. Kollat, *Consumer Behavior,* 3rd ed. (New York: Holt, Rinehart & Winston, 1978); and James R. Bettman, *An Information Processing Theory of Consumer Choice* (Reading, MA: Addison-Wesley, 1979).
6. See Chem L. Narayana and Ron J. Markin, "Consumer Behavior and Product Performance: An Alternative Conceptualization," *Journal of Marketing,* October 1975, pp. 1–6. These various sets are an elaboration of the concept of an *evoked set,* which was originally proposed by Howard and Sheth, *Theory of Buyer Behavior,* p. 26. They defined *evoked set* as the set of brands "that become alternatives in the buyer's choice decision."
7. James H. Myers and Mark L. Alpert, "Semantic Confusion in Attitude Research: Salience vs. Importance vs. Determinance," in *Advances in Consumer Research* (Proceedings of the Seventh Annual Conference of the Association of Consumer Research, October 1976), IV, pp. 106–10.
8. See Paul E. Green and Yoram Wind, *Multiattribute Decisions in Marketing: A Measurement Approach* (Hinsdale, IL: Dryden Press, 1973), chap. 2.
9. This model was developed by Martin Fishbein in "Attitudes and Prediction of Behavior," in *Readings in Attitude Theory and Measurement,* Martin Fishbein, ed. (New York: Wiley, 1967), pp. 477–92. For a critical review of this model, see William L. Wilkie and Edgar A. Pessemier, "Issues in Marketing's Use of Multi-Attribute Attitude Models," *Journal of Marketing Research,* November 1973, pp. 428–41.
10. Other models are described in Green and Wind, *Multiattribute Decisions in Marketing,* chap. 2; Peter Wright, "Consumer Choice Strategies: Simplifying vs. Optimizing," *Journal of Marketing Research,* February 1975, pp. 60–67; and Bettman, *An Information Processing Theory of Consumer Choice.*
11. See Harper W. Boyd, Jr., Michael L. Ray, and Edward C. Strong, "An Attitudinal Framework for Advertising Strategy," *Journal of Marketing,* April 1972, pp. 27–33.
12. See Jagdish N. Sheth, "An Investigation of Relationships among Evaluative Beliefs, Affect, Behavioral Intention, and Behavior," in *Consumer Behavior: Theory and Application,* John U. Farley, John A. Howard, and L. Winston Ring, eds. (Boston: Allyn & Bacon, 1974), pp. 89–114.
13. See Fishbein, "Attitudes and Prediction of Behavior."
14. See Raymond A. Bauer, "Consumer Behavior as Risk Taking," in *Risk Taking and Information Handling in Consumer Behavior,* Donald F. Cox, ed. (Boston: Division of Research, Harvard Business School, 1967); and James W. Taylor, "The Role of Risk in Consumer Behavior," *Journal of Marketing,* April 1974, pp. 54–60.
15. See John E. Swan and Linda Jones Combs, "Product Performance and Consumer Satisfaction: A New Concept," *Journal of Marketing,* April 1976, pp. 25–33.
16. See Rolph E. Anderson, "Consumer Dissatisfaction: The Effect of Disconfirmed Expectancy on Perceived Product Performance," *Journal of Marketing Research,* February 1973, pp. 38–44.
17. Leon Festinger and Dana Bramel, "The Reactions of Humans to Cognitive Dissonance," in *Experimental Foundations of Clinical Psychology,* Arthur J. Bachrach, ed. (New York: Basic Books, 1962). pp. 251–62.
18. Leon Festinger, *A Theory of Cognitive Dissonance* (Stanford, CA: Stanford University Press, 1957), p. 260.
19. See James H. Donnelly, Jr., and John M. Ivancevich, "Post-Purchase Reinforcement and Back-Out Behavior," *Journal of Marketing Research,* August 1970, pp. 399–400.
20. The following discussion leans heavily on Everett M. Rogers, Diffusion of Innovations (New York: Free Press, 1962). Also see Thomas S. Robertson, *Innovative Behavior and Communication* (New York: Holt, Rinehart, & Winston, 1971).

21. ROGERS, *Diffusion of Innovations.*

22. MARY LEE DICKERSON and JAMES W. GENTRY, "Characteristics of Adopters and Non-Adopters of Home Computers," *Journal of Consumer Research,* September 1983, pp. 225–35.

23. ROGER, *Diffusion of Innovations,* p. 192.

24. ELIHU KATZ and PAUL F. LAZARSFELD, *Personal Influence* (New York: Free Press, 1955), p. 234.

8

Organizational Markets and Organizational Buying Behavior

Gulfstream Aerospace Corporation sells business jets with price tags as high as $16 million to corporate buyers. Locating potential buyers isn't a problem—the organizations that can afford to own and operate multimillion dollar business aircraft are easily identified. Gulfstream's more difficult problems involve reaching key decision makers, understanding their complex motivations and decision processes, figuring out what factors will be important in their decisions, and designing effective marketing approaches.

Gulfstream Aerospace recognizes the importance of *rational* motives and *objective* factors in buyers' decisions. A company buying a jet will evaluate Gulfstream aircraft on such things as quality and performance, prices and operating costs, and service. And these may appear to be the only things that drive the buying decision. But having a superior product isn't enough to land the sale; Gulfstream Aerospace must also pay attention to the more subtle *human factors* that affect the choice of a jet.

"The purchase process may be initiated by the chief executive officer, a board member (wishing to increase efficiency or security), the company's chief pilot, or through vendor efforts like advertising or a sales visit. The CEO will be central in deciding whether to buy the jet, but he or she will be heavily influenced by the company's pilot, financial officer, and perhaps by the board itself.

"Each party in the buying process has subtle roles and needs. The salesperson who tries to impress, for example, both the CEO with depreciation schedules and the chief pilot with minimum runway statistics will almost certainly not sell a plane if he overlooks the psychological and emotional components of the buying decision. 'For the chief executive,' observes one salesperson, 'you need all the numbers for support, but if you can't find the kid inside the CEO and excite him or her with the raw beauty of the new plane, you'll never sell the equipment. If you sell the excitement, you sell the jet.'

"The chief pilot, as an equipment expert, often has veto power over purchase decisions and may be able to stop the purchase of one or another brand of jet by simply expressing a negative opinion about, say, the plane's bad weather capabilities. In this sense, the pilot not only influences the decision but also serves as an information 'gatekeeper' by advising management on the equipment to select. Though the corporate legal staff will handle the purchase agreement and the purchasing department will acquire the jet, these parties may have little to say about whether or how the plane will be obtained, and which type. The users of the jet—middle and upper management of the buying company, important customers, and others—may have at least an indirect role in choosing the equipment.

"The involvement of many people in the purchase decision creates a group dynamic that the selling company must factor into its sales planning. Who makes up the buying group? How will the parties interact? Who will dominate and who submit? What priorities do the individuals have?"

In some ways, selling corporate jets to organizational buyers is like selling cars and kitchen appliances to families. Gulfstream Aerospace asks the same questions as consumer marketers. Who are the buyers, and what are their needs? How do buyers make their buying decisions, and what factors influence these decisions? What marketing program will be most effective? But the answers to these questions are usually different for the organizational buyer. Thus Gulfstream Aerospace faces many of the same challenges as consumer marketers—and some additional ones.[1]

I n one way or another most large companies sell to other organizations. Many industrial companies sell *most* of their products to organizations—companies such as Xerox, Du Pont, and countless other large and small firms. Even large consumer products companies do organizational marketing. For example, General Mills makes many familiar products for final consumers—Cheerios, Betty Crocker cake mixes, Gold Medal flour, Parker Brothers games. But to sell these products to final consumers, General Mills must first sell them to the wholesale and retail organizations that serve the consumer market. General Mills also makes products, such as specialty chemicals, that are sold only to other companies.

Organizations constitute a vast market. In fact, industrial markets involve many more dollars and items than consumer markets. Figure 8-1 shows the large volume of transactions needed to produce and sell a simple pair of shoes. Hide dealers sell to tanners, who sell leather to shoe manufacturers, who sell shoes to wholesalers, who in turn sell shoes to retailers, who finally sell them to consumers. Each party in the production and distribution chain buys many other goods and services as well. It is easy to see why there is more organizational buying than consumer buying—many sets of organizational purchases were made for only one set of consumer purchases.

Companies that sell to other organizations must do their best to understand organizational buying behavior and the buyer needs, resources, motivations, and buying processes that shape such behavior. In this chapter, we will discuss the nature of organizational markets and try to understand how industrial buyers make their purchasing decisions.

ORGANIZATIONAL MARKETS

Types of Organizational Markets We will examine three types of organizational markets: the industrial market, the reseller market, and the government market.

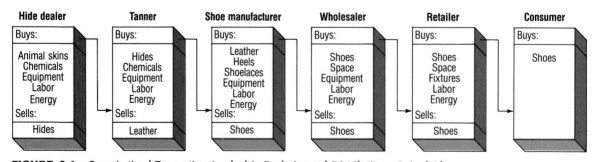

FIGURE 8-1 *Organizational Transactions Involved in Producing and Distributing a Pair of Shoes*

You can't be proud of your company when you're not proud of your company car.

After all, the cars in your company's fleet do reflect your company's image.

That's why more and more companies are adding the Buick Century to their fleets.

Your drivers are certain to be proud of the Century, with its aerodynamic shape, plush interior and the sumptuous appointments for which Buick is famous.

Yet, your accountants will also be proud of the Century. It costs little more than an ordinary car. And though it is indeed luxurious, it is a very efficient car to operate. It offers, in fact, an impressive EPA-estimated 25 MPG, 39 MPG estimated highway.

For a fleet that's both smart to own and smart to look at, contact your Buick fleet representative.

You'll be proud you did.

Wouldn't you really rather have a Buick?

Buick aims its familiar "Wouldn't you really rather have a Buick?" at the industrial market. *Courtesy of McCann-Erickson.*

The Industrial Market

The **industrial market** consists of *all the individuals and organizations that acquire goods and services which enter into the production of other products and services that are sold, rented, or supplied to others.* The industrial market includes buyers from many types of industries—manufacturing; construction; transportation; communication; banking, finance, and insurance; transportation; services; agricultural, forestry, and fisheries; mining; and public utilities. The industrial market is *huge:* It consists of over 13 million organizations which buy more than $3 *trillion* worth of goods and services each year. (That's more money than most of us can imagine—taped end to end, 3 trillion one dollar bills would wrap around the earth over 11,000 times!) Thus, the industrial market is the largest and most diverse organizational market.

The Reseller Market

The **reseller market** consists of *all the individuals and organizations that acquire goods for the purpose of reselling or renting them to others at a profit.* Where firms in the industrial market produce form utility, resellers produce time, place, and possession utility. The reseller market includes over 390,000 wholesaling firms and 1,800,000 retailing firms that combine to purchase over $2 trillion worth of goods and services a year. Resellers purchase goods for resale and goods and services for conducting their operations. In their role as purchasing agents for their own customers, resellers purchase a vast variety of goods for resale—indeed everything produced except for the few classes of goods that producers sell directly to customers.

The Government Market

The **government market** consists of *governmental units—federal, state, and local—that purchase or rent goods and services for carrying out the main functions of government.* In 1983, governments purchased about $690 billion worth of products and services. The federal government accounts for almost 40 percent of the total spent by governments at all levels, making it the nation's largest customer. Federal, state, and local government agencies buy an amazing range of products and services. They buy bombers, sculpture, chalkboards, furniture, toiletries, clothing, fire engines, vehicles, and fuel. In 1981 they spent approximately $175 billion for defense, $170 billion for education, $110 billion for public welfare, $54 billion for natural resources, $50 billion for health and hospitals, $45 billion for highways, and smaller sums for postal services, space research, and housing and urban renewal. No wonder governments represent a tremendous market for any producer or reseller.

Characteristics of *Organizational* *Markets* In some ways, organizational markets are similar to consumer markets—both involve people who assume buying roles and make purchase decisions to satisfy needs. But in many ways, organizational markets differ sharply from consumer markets. The major differences are in market structure and demand characteristics, the nature of the buying unit, and the types of decisions and the decision process.

Market Structure and Demand Characteristics

The organizational marketer normally deals with far *fewer, larger buyers* than the consumer marketer. The Goodyear Company's fate in the industrial market depends on getting orders from one of only a few large automakers. But when Goodyear sells replacement tires to consumers, its potential market includes the owners of 105 million American cars currently in use. Even in populous organizational markets, a few buyers normally account for most of the purchasing.

Organizational markets are also more *geographically concentrated.* More than half the nation's industrial buyers are concentrated in seven states: New York, Pennsylvania, Illinois, Ohio, New Jersey, and Michigan. Such industries as petroleum, rubber, and steel have even greater concentration. Most agricultural output comes from a relatively few states.

Organizational demand is *derived demand*—it ultimately comes from the demand for consumer goods. General Motors buys steel because consumers buy cars. If consumer demand for cars slackens, so will the demand for steel and all the other products used to make cars. Industrial marketers sometimes promote their products directly to final consumers to generate more industrial demand (see Exhibit 8-1).

EXHIBIT 8-1

YOU CAN'T BUY IT, BUT YOU'RE GOING TO LOVE IT

G.D. Searle & Co. is spending nearly $1 million on consumer advertising for a product consumers can't buy. The Skokie, IL, company is putting more marketing muscle behind its NutraSweet, the sugar substitute now available in dozens of commercial food and beverage products.

The unconventional advertising move was decided upon "to improve the product's public recognition factor," says Max Downham, vice-president for planning and administration for Searle's NutraSweet Goup. "We also wanted to augment the advertising being conducted by our customers," he adds.

NutraSweet is Searle's brand name for aspartame, a sweetener made from protein compounds. Searle, which hopes to generate sales of $1 billion for the product by 1988, is running ads that say, "Introducing NutraSweet. You can't buy it, but you're going to love it." Ogilvy & Mather/Chicago is the advertising agency. The print ads also feature a coupon that can be sent in for gum balls sweetened with NutraSweet. Later plans call for distribution of samples of products.

Aspartame was approved for dry foods in 1981 and in early July the Food and Drug Administration approved its use in soft drinks. Products already on the market with NutraSweet include Quaker Oats Halfsies cereal, Swiss Miss Sugar Free cocoa mix, Lipton ice tea mix, and D-Zerta low-calorie gelatin dessert. Two weeks ago, Searle signed a pact to sell about $50 million worth of NutraSweet annually for use in Coca-Cola drinks.

"Our advertising goal is to achieve a consumer recognition level for NutraSweet of at least 50%," Downham says.

Source: You Can't Buy It But You're Going to Love It," *Sales and Marketing Management,* August 15, 1983, pp. 11–12.

Many organizational markets are characterized by *inelastic demand.* Total demand for many industrial products is not much affected by price changes, especially in the short run. A drop in the price of leather will not cause shoe manufacturers to buy much more unless it results in lower show prices which increase consumer demand.

Finally, organizational markets have more *fluctuating demand.* The demand for many industrial goods and services tends to be more volatile than the demand for consumer goods and services. A small percentage increase in consumer demand can cause large increases in industrial demand. Economists call this the *acceleration principle.* Sometimes a rise of only 10 percent in consumer demand can cause as much as a 200 percent rise in industrial demand in the next period.

The Nature of the Buying Unit

As compared with consumer purchases, an organizational purchase usually involves *more buying participants* and *more professional purchasing.* Organizational purchasing is often done by professionally trained purchasing agents who spend their work lives learning how to buy better. The more complex the purchase, the more likely that several persons will participate in the decision-making process. Buying committees made up of technical experts and top management are common in the purchase of major goods. This means that organizational marketers must have well-trained sales representatives to deal with well-trained buyers.

Types of Decisions and the Decision Process

Organizational buyers usually face *more complex* purchasing decisions than consumer buyers. Purchases often involve large sums of money, complex technical and economic considerations, and complicated interactions among many people at many levels of the buyer's organization. Because the purchases are more complex, organizational buyers may take longer to make their decisions. A company buying a complex computer system may take many months or more than a year to select a supplier.

The organizational buying process tends to be *more formalized* than the consumer buying process. Large organizational purchases usually require detailed product specifications, written purchase requests, rigorous supplier searches, and formal approval. The purchase process may be spelled out in detail in policy manuals.

Finally, in the organizational buying process, buyer and seller are often much *more dependent* on each other. Consumer marketers usually remain at a distance from their customers. But organizational marketers may roll up their sleeves and work very closely with their customers during all stages of the buying process—from helping customers to define the problem, to finding solutions, to after-sale operation.

Other Characteristics

Here are some additional characteristics of organizational buying.

- *Direct purchasing.* Organizational buyers often buy directly from producers rather than through middlemen, especially for items that are technically complex or expensive.
- *Reciprocity.* Organizational buyers often select suppliers who also buy from them. An example of this reciprocity would be a paper manufacturer who buys needed chemicals from a chemical company that is buying a considerable amount of its paper.

Reciprocity is forbidden by the Federal Trade Commission and the Justice Department's antitrust division if it shuts out competition in an unfair manner. A buyer can still choose a supplier that it also sells something to, but the buyer should be able to show that it is getting competitive prices, quality, and service from that supplier.[2]

■ *Leasing.* Organizational buyers are increasingly turning to equipment leasing instead of outright purchase. This happens with computers, shoe machinery, packaging equipment, heavy construction equipment, delivery trucks, machine tools, and salesforce automobiles. The lessee gains a number of advantages, such as having more available capital, getting the seller's latest products, receiving better servicing, and gaining some tax advantages. The lessor often ends up with a larger net income and the chance to sell to customers who might not have been able to afford outright purchase.[3]

A MODEL OF ORGANIZATIONAL BUYER BEHAVIOR

Webster and Wind define **organizational buying** as "the decision-making process by which formal organizations establish the need for purchased products and services, and identify, evaluate, and choose among alternative brands and suppliers."[4] In trying to understand organizational buyer behavior, marketers must find answers to some difficult questions. What kinds of buying decisions do organizational buyers make? How do they choose among various suppliers? Who makes the decisions? What is the organizational buying decision process? What factors influence organizational buyers' purchase decisions?

At the most basic level, marketers want to know how organizational buyers will respond to various marketing stimuli. A simple model of organizational buyer behavior is shown in Figure 8–2.[5] The figure shows that marketing and other stimuli influence the organization and produce certain buyer responses. The marketing stimuli consist of the four Ps: product, price, place, and promotion. The other stimuli consist of major forces in the organization's environment: economic, technological, political, and cultural. All these stimuli enter the organization and

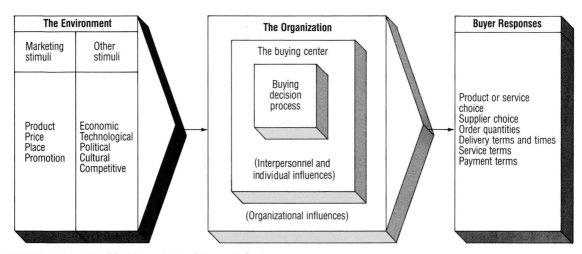

FIGURE 8-2 A Model of Organizational Buyer Behavior

are transformed into buyer responses: product or service choice, supplier choice, order quantities, delivery times and terms, service terms, and payment terms. To design effective marketing mix strategies, the marketer must understand what happens within the organization to turn the stimuli into purchase responses.

Within the organization, the buying activity consists of two major components—the buying center (made up of all the people involved in the buying decision) and the buying decision process. The figure shows that the buying center and the buying decision process—and hence the buying decision—are influenced by internal organizational, interpersonal, and individual factors as well as by external environmental factors.

We will examine the various elements suggested by this organizational buyer behavior model. For now we will focus on the largest and most important organizational market—the industrial market. Later in the chapter we will consider the special characteristics of reseller and government buyer behavior.

INDUSTRIAL BUYER BEHAVIOR

We will examine four questions about industrial buyer behavior:

- What buying decisions do industrial buyers make?
- Who participates in the buying process?
- What are the major influences on buyers?
- What is the industrial buying decision process?

What Buying Decisions Do Industrial Buyers Make? The industrial buyer faces a whole set of decisions in making a purchase. The number of decisions depends on the type of buying situation. Robinson and others distinguish three types of buying situations, which they call *buyclasses*,[6] based on the newness of the purchase, the amounts and types of information needed, and the number of new purchase alternatives being considered by the buyer.

Major Types of Buying Situations

At one extreme is the straight rebuy, which is a fairly routine decision; at the other extreme is the new task, which may call for thorough research; in the middle is the modified rebuy, which requires some research. (For examples, see Figure 8-3).

STRAIGHT REBUY. In a straight rebuy, the buyer reorders something without any modifications. It is usually handled on a routine basis by the purchasing department. The buyer chooses from suppliers on its "list," based on its past buying satisfaction with the various suppliers. The "in" suppliers make an effort to maintain product and service quality. They often propose automatic reordering systems so that the purchasing agent will save reordering time. The "out" suppliers attempt to offer something new or exploit dissatisfaction so that the buyer will consider them. Out-suppliers try to get their foot in the door with a small order and then enlarge their "purchase share" over time.

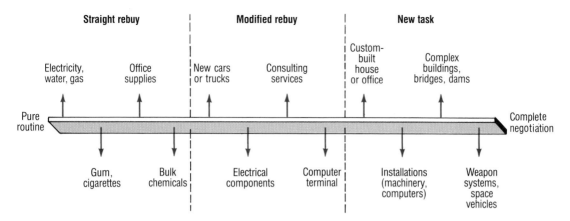

FIGURE 8-3 *Three Types of Industrial Buying Situations*

Source: From *Marketing Principles*, 3rd. ed. by Ben M. Enis. Copyright © 1980 Scott, Foresman and Company. Reprinted by permission.

MODIFIED REBUY. In a modified rebuy, the buyer wants to modify product specifications, prices, other terms, or suppliers. The modified rebuy usually expands the number of decision participants. The in-suppliers become nervous and have to put their best foot forward to protect the account. The out-suppliers see it as an opportunity to make a "better offer" to gain some new business.

NEW TASK. The new task faces a company buying a product or service for the first time. The greater the cost or risk, the larger the number of decision participants and the greater their information seeking. In the new-task situation, the buyer must obtain a great deal of information about alternative products and suppliers. The buyer has to determine product specifications, price limits, delivery terms and times, service terms, payment terms, order quantities, acceptable suppliers, and the selected supplier. Different decision participants influence each decision, and the order in which the decisions are made varies.

This situation arises infrequently, but it is very important to marketers because it leads to straight or modified rebuy situations later on. The new task situation is the marketer's greatest opportunity and challenge. The marketer not only tries to reach as many key buying influences as possible, but also provides information and assistance.

The Role of Systems Buying and Selling

Many buyers prefer to buy a whole solution to their problem and not make all the separate decisions involved. Called **systems buying,** it originated in government practices in buying major weapons and communication systems. Instead of purchasing and putting all the components together, the government would solicit bids from prime contractors who would assemble the package or system. The winning prime contractor would be responsible for bidding and assembling the subcomponents. The prime contractor would thus provide *a turnkey operation,* so called because the buyer simply had to turn one key to get everything necessary.

Sellers have increasingly recognized that buyers like to purchase in this way and have adopted the practice of **systems selling** as a marketing tool. Systems selling has two components. First, the supplier sells a group of interlocking products. For example, the supplier sells not only glue, but applicators and dryers as well. Second, the supplier sells a system of production, inventory control, distribution, and other services to meet the buyer's need for a smooth-running operation. Systems selling is a key industrial marketing strategy for winning and holding accounts.

Who Participates in the Industrial Buying Process?

Who participates in the buying decisions for the hundreds of billions of dollars worth of goods and services needed by the industrial market? Webster and Wind call the decision-making unit of a buying organization the **buying center,** defined as "all those individuals and groups who participate in the purchasing decision-making process, who share some common goals and the risks arising from the decisions."[7]

The buying center includes all members of the organization who play any of five roles in the purchase decision process.[8]

- *Users.* Users are the members of the organization who will use the product or service. In many cases, the users initiate the buying proposal and help define the product specifications.

- *Influencers.* Influencers are persons who affect the buying decision. They often help define specifications and also provide information for evaluating alternatives. Technical personnel are particularly important as influencers.

- *Buyers.* Buyers are persons with formal authority for selecting the supplier and arranging the terms of purchase. Buyers may help shape product specifications, but they play their major role in selecting vendors and negotiating. In more complex purchases, the buyers might include high-level officers participating in the negotiations.

- *Deciders.* Deciders are persons who have formal or informal power to select or approve the final suppliers. In routine buying, the buyers are often the deciders, or at least the approvers.

- *Gatekeepers.* Gatekeepers are persons who control the flow of information to others. For example, purchasing agents often have authority to prevent salespersons from seeing users or deciders. Other gatekeepers include technical personnel and even personal secretaries.

The buying center is not a fixed and formally identified unit within the buying organization; it is a set of buying roles assumed by different persons for different purchases. Within the organization, the size and composition of the buying center will vary for different classes of products and for different buying situations. For some routine purchases, one person—say a purchasing agent—may assume all the buying center roles and be the only person involved in the buying decision. For more complex purchases, the buying center may include twenty or thirty persons from different levels and departments in the organization. One study of organizational buying showed that the typical industrial equipment purchase involved seven persons from three management levels representing four different departments. Some equipment purchases involved as many as twenty-eight persons from six management levels and eight different departments.[9]

The buying center usually includes some obvious participants who are formally involved in the buying decision—the decision to buy a corporate jet will probably involve the company's chief pilot, a purchasing agent, some legal staff, a member of top management, and others formally charged with the buying decision. It may also involve informal, less obvious participants, some of whom may actually make or strongly influence the buying decision. Sometimes even the people in the buying center are not aware of all the buying participants. For example, the decision about which jet to buy may actually be made by a corporate board member who has an interest in flying and knows a lot about airplanes. This board member may be a behind-the-scenes influencer who ultimately sways the decision.

Each buying center member has unique views and objectives regarding a particular buying decision. Some members will have more influence than others. Thus many industrial buying decisions result from the complex interactions of continually changing buying center participants.

The buying center concept presents a substantial marketing challenge. The industrial marketer has to figure out: Who are the major decision participants? In what decisions do they exercise influence? What is their relative degree of influence? And what evaluation criteria does each decision participant use? Consider the following example:

> The American Hospital Supply Corporation sells nonwoven disposable surgical gowns to hospitals. It tries to identify the hospital personnel who participate in this buying decision. The decision participants turn out to be (1) the vice-president of purchasing, (2) the operating room administrator, and (3) the surgeons. Each party plays a different role. The vice-president of purchasing analyzes whether the hospital should buy disposable gowns or reusable gowns. If the findings favor disposable gowns, then the operating room administrator compares various competitors' products and prices and makes a choice. This administrator considers the gown's absorbency, antiseptic quality, design, and cost and normally buys the brand that meets the functional requirements at the lowest cost. Finally, surgeons influence the decision retroactively by reporting their satisfaction or dissatisfaction with the particular brand.

When a buying center includes many participants, the industrial marketer will not have the time or resources to reach all of them. Small companies concentrate on reaching the *key buying influences*. Large companies go for *multilevel in-depth selling* to reach as many decision participants as possible. Their salespeople virtually "live" with the customer when it is a major account with recurrent sales.

What Are the Major Influences on Industrial Buyers?

Industrial buyers are subject to many influences when they make their buying decisions. Some marketers assume that the major influences are economic. They see the buyers as favoring the supplier who offers the minimum price, or best product, or most service. This view suggests that industrial marketers should concentrate on offering strong economic benefits to buyers.

Other marketers see the buyers as responding to personal motives where they seek favors, or attention, or risk reduction. A study of buyers in ten large companies concluded that

> . . . corporate decision-makers remain human after they enter the office. They respond to "image"; they buy from companies to which they feel "close"; they favor suppliers who show them respect and personal consideration, and who do extra things "for them"; they "over-react" to real or imagined slights, tending to reject companies which fail to respond or delay in submitting requested bids.[10]

This view suggests that industrial marketers should concentrate mostly on the human and social factors in the buying situation.

Industrial buyers actually respond to both economic and personal factors. Where there is substantial similarity in supplier offers, industrial buyers have little basis for rational choice. Since they can meet organizational goals with any supplier, buyers can bring in personal factors. Where competing products differ substantially, industrial buyers are more accountable for their choice and pay more attention to economic factors.

Webster and Wind have classified the various influences on industrial buyers into four main groups: environmental, organizational, interpersonal, and individual.[11] These groups are listed in Figure 8-4 and described below.

Environmental Factors

Industrial buyers are heavily influenced by factors in the current and expected economic environment, such as the level of primary demand, the economic outlook, and the cost of money. As the level of economic uncertainty rises, industrial buyers cease making new investments in plant and equipment and attempt to reduce their inventories. Industrial marketers can do little to stimulate purchases in this environment.

An increasingly important environmental factor is imminent shortages in key materials. Companies are showing a greater willingness to buy and hold larger inventories of scarce materials. They are willing to sign long-term contracts to guarantee receiving these materials. Du Pont, Ford, Chrysler, and several other major companies have defined *supply planning* as a major responsibility of their purchasing executives.[12]

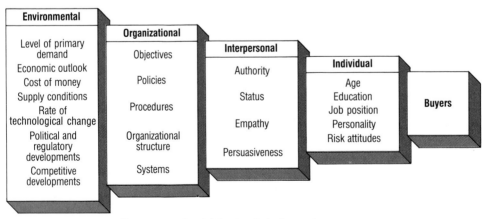

FIGURE 8-4 *Major Influences on Industrial Buying Behavior*

Industrial buyers are also affected by technological, political, and competitive developments in the environment. The industrial marketer has to monitor the same factors, determine how they will affect the buyer, and try to turn these problems into opportunities.

Organizational Factors

Each buying organization has its own objectives, policies, procedures, organizational structure, and systems. The industrial marketer has to know these as well as possible. Such questions as these arise: How many people are involved in the buying decision? Who are they? What are their evaluative criteria? and What are the company's policies and constraints on the buyers?

The industrial marketer should be aware of the following organizational trends in the purchasing area:

- ■ *Upgraded purchasing.* Purchasing departments have often occupied a low position in the management hierarchy, in spite of often being responsible for managing more than half of the company's costs. However, the recent combination of inflation and shortages has led many companies to upgrade their purchasing departments. Several large corporations have elevated the heads of purchasing to vice-presidential levels. Caterpillar and some other companies have combined several functions—such as purchasing, inventory control, production scheduling, and traffic—into a high-level function called *material management.* "New wave" materials managers are actively building new supply sources. Many companies are looking for top talent, hiring MBAs, and offering higher compensation. This means that industrial marketers must correspondingly upgrade their sales personnel to match the caliber of the new buyers.

- ■ *Centralized purchasing.* In multidivisional companies, much purchasing is carried out by the separate divisions because of their differing needs. But recently companies have tried to recentralize some of the purchasing. Headquarters identifies materials purchased by several divisions and considers buying them centrally. This gives the company more purchasing clout. The individual plants can buy from another source if they can get a better deal, but in general, centralized purchasing produces substantial savings for the company.[13] For the industrial marketer, this development means dealing with fewer and higher-level buyers. Instead of the seller's regional sales forces dealing with separate plants, the seller may use a national account sales force to deal with the buyer. National account selling is challenging and demands a sophisticated salesforce and marketing-planning effort.

- ■ *Long-term contracts.* Industrial buyers are increasingly seeking long-term contracts with suppliers. These contracts call for skillful negotiation, and buyers are adding negotiating specialists to their staffs. Industrial marketers, in turn, will have to add skilled negotiators to their staffs.

- ■ *Purchasing performance evaluation.* Some companies are setting up incentive systems to reward purchasing managers for especially good purchasing performance, in much the same way that sales personnel receive bonuses for especially good selling performance. These systems will lead purchasing managers to increase their pressure on sellers for the best terms.

Interpersonal Factors

The buying center usually includes many participants with different statuses, authority, empathy, and persuasiveness. Each influences and is influenced by the others. In many cases, the industrial marketer will not know what kinds of group dynamics take place during the buying process. As Bonoma points out:

Managers do not wear tags that say "decision maker" or "unimportant person." The powerful are often invisible, at least to vendor representatives.[14]

The buying center participant with the highest rank does not always have the most interpersonal influence. Participants may have influence in the buying decision because they control rewards and punishments, because they are well liked, because they have special knowledge or expertise relevant to the purchase decision, or because they are related by marriage to the company's president.

Interpersonal factors are often very subtle. Where possible, industrial marketers must observe the buyer's decision-making process, understand the personalities and interpersonal factors involved, and design strategies that take these factors into account.

Individual Factors

Each participant in the buying decision process brings in personal motivations, perceptions, and preferences. These are influenced by the participant's age, income, education, professional identification, personality, and attitudes toward risk. Buyers exhibit different buying styles. Some of the younger, higher-educated buyers are "computer freaks" and make rigorous analyses of competitive proposals before choosing a supplier. Other buyers are "tough guys" from the "old school" and play off the sellers:

> . . . A good example of a cagey buyer is [the] vice president in charge of purchasing for Rheingold's big New York brewery. . . . Using the leverage of hundreds of millions of cans a year, like many other buyers, he takes punitive action where one company slips in quality or fails to deliver. "At one point American started talking about a price rise," he recalls, "Continental kept its mouth shut. . . . American never did put the price rise into effect, but anyway, I punished them for talking about it." For a three-month period he cut the percentage of cans he bought from American.[15]

Industrial marketers must know their customers and adapt their tactics to specific environmental, organizational, interpersonal, and individual influences on the buying situation.

How Do Industrial Buyers Make Their Buying Decisions? We now come to the issue of how industrial buyers move through the purchasing process. Robinson and others identified eight stages of the industrial buying process and called them *buyphases*.[16] They are listed in Table 8-1. The table shows that buyers facing the new task buying situation will go through all the stages of the buying process. Buyers making modified or straight rebuys will skip some of the stages. We will examine these steps for the typical new task buying situation.

Problem Recognition

The buying process begins when someone in the company recognizes a problem or need that can be met by acquiring a good or a service. Problem recognition can occur as a result of internal or external stimuli. Internally, the most common events leading to problem recognition are the following:

TABLE 8-1

Major Stages (Buyphases) of the Industrial Buying Process in Relation to Major Buying Situations (Buyclasses)

STAGES OF THE BUYING PROCESS (BUYPHASES)	BUYING SITUATIONS (BUYCLASSES)		
	New task	Modified rebuy	Straight rebuy
1. Problem recognition	Yes	Maybe	No
2. General need description	Yes	Maybe	No
3. Product specification	Yes	Yes	Yes
4. Supplier search	Yes	Maybe	No
5. Proposal solicitation	Yes	Maybe	No
6. Supplier selection	Yes	Maybe	No
7. Order routine specification	Yes	Maybe	No
8. Performance review	Yes	Yes	Yes

Source: Adapted from Patrick J. Robinson, Charles W. Faris, and Yoram Wind, *Industrial Buying and Creative Marketing* (Boston: Allyn & Bacon, 1967), p. 14.

■ The company decides to launch a new product and needs new equipment and materials to produce this product.

■ A machine breaks down and requires replacement or new parts.

■ Some purchased material turns out to be unsatisfactory, and the company searches for another supplier.

■ A purchasing manager senses an opportunity to obtain better prices or quality.

Externally, the buyer may get some new ideas at a trade show, or see an ad, or receive a call from a sales representative who offers a better product or a lower price. Industrial marketers can therefore stimulate problem recognition by developing ads or calling on prospects.

General Need Description

Having recognized a need, the buyer proceeds to determine the general characteristics and quantity of the needed item. For standard items, this is not much of a problem. For complex items, the buyer will work with others—engineers, users, consultants—to define the general characteristics. They will want to rank the importance of reliability, durability, price, and other attributes desired in the item.

The industrial marketer can render assistance to the buying company in this phase. Often the buyer is not aware of the value of different product characteristics. An alert marketer can help the buyer define the company's needs.

Product Specification

The buying organization now proceeds to develop the item's technical specifications. A value analysis engineering team will be put to work on the problem. **Value analysis,** which General Electric pioneered in the late forties, is *an approach to cost reduction in which components are carefully studied to determine if they can be redesigned or standardized or made by cheaper methods of production.* The team will examine the high-cost components in a given product—usually 20 per-

TABLE 8-2

Questions Asked in Value Analysis

1. Does the use of the item contribute value?
2. Is its cost proportionate to its usefulness?
3. Does it need all its features?
4. Is there anything better for its intended use?
5. Can a usable part be made by a lower-cost method?
6. Can a standard product be found that will be usable?
7. Is the product made on proper tooling, considering the quantities that are used?
8. Do material, labor, overhead, and profit total its cost?
9. Will another dependable supplier provide it for less?
10. Is anyone buying it for less?

Source: Albert W. Frey, *Marketing Handbook,* 2d ed. (New York: Ronald Press, 1965), Sec. 27, p. 21. Copyright © 1985. Reprinted by permission of John Wiley & Sons, Inc.

cent of the parts account for 80 percent of the costs. They will also look for product components that are overdesigned in that these components will last longer than the product itself. Table 8-2 lists the major questions raised in the value analysis. The team will decide on the optimal product characteristics and specify them accordingly. Tightly written specifications will allow the buyer to refuse merchandise that fails to meet the intended standards.

Sellers too can use value analysis as a tool for breaking into an account. By demonstrating a better way to make an object, outside sellers can turn straight rebuy situations into a new task situations in which their company has a chance for business.

Supplier Search

The buyer now tries to identify the most appropriate vendors. The buyer can examine trade directories, do a computer search, or phone other companies for recommendations. Some of the vendors will be dropped from consideration because they are not large enough to supply the needed quantity or because they have a poor reputation for delivery and service. The buyer will end up with a small list of qualified suppliers.

The newer the buying task, and the more complex and expensive the item, the greater the amount of time spent in searching for and qualifying suppliers. The supplier's task is to get listed in major directories and build a good reputation in the marketplace. Sales representatives should watch for companies in the process of searching for suppliers and make certain that their firm is considered.

Proposal Solicitation

The buyer will now invite qualified suppliers to submit proposals. Some suppliers will send only a catalog or a sales representative. Where the item is complex or expensive, the buyer will require detailed written proposals from each potential supplier. The buyer will review the remaining suppliers when they make their formal presentations.

Industrial marketers must therefore be skilled in researching, writing, and presenting proposals. Their proposals should be marketing documents, not just technical documents. Their oral presentations should inspire confidence. They should position their company's capabilities and resources so that the company stands out from the competition.

Supplier Selection

In this stage the members of the buying center will review the proposals and move toward supplier selection. They will perform a *vendor analysis* to select supplier(s). They will consider not only the technical competence of the various suppliers, but also their ability to deliver the item on time and provide necessary services. The buying center will often draw up a list of the desired supplier attributes and their relative importance. In selecting a chemical supplier, a buying center listed the following attributes in order of importance:

1. Technical support services
2. Prompt delivery
3. Quick response to customer needs
4. Product quality
5. Supplier reputation
6. Product price
7. Complete product line
8. Sales representatives' caliber
9. Extension of credit
10. Personal relationships
11. Literature and manuals

The members of the buying center will rate the suppliers against these attributes and identify the most attractive suppliers. They often use a supplier evaluation model similar to the one shown in Table 8-3.

Lehmann and O'Shaughnessy found that the importance of various supplier attributes depends on the type of purchase situation the buyer faces.[17] They classi-

TABLE 8-3
An Example of Vendor Analysis

ATTRIBUTES	RATING SCALE				
	Unacceptable (0)	Poor (1)	Fair (2)	Good (3)	Excellent (4)
Technical and production capabilities					X
Financial strength			X		
Product reliability					X
Delivery reliability			X		
Service capability					X
4 + 2 + 4 + 2 + 4 = 16					
Average score:					
16/5 = 3.2					

Note: This vendor shows up as strong except on two attributes. The purchasing agent has to decide how important the two weaknesses are. The analysis could be redone using importance weights for the five attributes.
Source: Adapted from Richard Hill, Ralph Alexander, and James Cross, *Industrial Marketing.*, 4th ed. (Homewood, IL: Irwin, 1975), pp. 101–4.

fied buyers' choice criteria into five categories: *performance criteria* (How well will the supplier's product perform?), *economic criteria* (How much will it cost to buy and use the product?), *integrative criteria* (Is the supplier customer-oriented and cooperative?), *adaptive criteria* (Can the supplier adapt to the buyer's changing needs?), and *legalistic criteria* (What legal or policy constraints must be considered when buying the product?). Their study of 220 purchasing managers showed that economic criteria were most important in situations involving routine purchases of standard products. Performance criteria became more important in purchases of nonstandard, more complex products. Adaptive criteria were important for almost all types of purchases, while integrative criteria were rated as less important in most buying situations.

Buyers may attempt to negotiate with preferred suppliers for better prices and terms before making the final selections. In the end, they may select a single supplier or a few suppliers. Many buyers prefer multiple sources of supply so that they will not be totally dependent on one supplier in case something goes wrong and so that they will be able to compare the prices and performance of the various suppliers. The buyer will normally place most of the order with one supplier, and less with other suppliers. For example, a buyer using three suppliers may buy 60 percent of the needed quantity from the prime supplier and 30 to 10 percent from the two other suppliers.

The prime supplier will make an effort to protect its prime position, while the others will try to expand their supplier share. Out-suppliers in the meantime will attempt to get a foot in the door by making an especially good price offer and will thereafter try to work their way to being a larger supplier.

Order Routine Specification

The buyer now writes the final order with the chosen supplier(s) listing the technical specifications, quantity needed, expected time of delivery, return policies, warranties, and so on. In the case of MRO items (maintenance, repair, and operating items), buyers are increasingly moving toward *blanket contracts* rather than *periodic purchase orders*. Nor does the buyer want to write fewer and larger purchase orders because this means carrying more inventory.

A blanket contract establishes a long-term relationship where the supplier promises to resupply the buyer as needed on agreed price terms over a specified period of time. The stock is held by the seller; hence the name "stockless purchase plan." The buyer's computer automatically prints out or teletypes an order to the seller when stock is needed. Blanket contracting leads to more single-source buying and the buying of more items from that single source. This locks the supplier in tighter with the buyer and makes it difficult for out-suppliers to break in unless the buyer becomes dissatisfied with the supplier's prices or service.[18]

Performance Review

In this stage the buyer reviews suppliers' performance. The buyer may contact users and ask them to rate their satisfaction. The performance review may lead the buyer to continue, modify, or drop the seller. The seller's job is to monitor the same variables used by the buyer to make sure that the seller is delivering the expected satisfaction.

We have described the buying stages that would operate in a new task buying situation. In the modified rebuy or straight rebuy situation, some of these stages would be compressed or bypassed. Each stage represents a narrowing of the number of supplier alternatives. A seller should try to become part of the buyer's buying process in the earliest possible stage.

The eight-stage model provides a simple view of the industrial buying decision process. The actual process is usually much less straightforward and much more complex.[19] Each organization buys in its own way, and each buying situation has unique requirements. Different buying center participants may be involved at different stages of the process. Although certain buying process steps usually occur, buyers do not always follow them in the same order, and they may add other steps. Often, buyers repeat certain stages more than once.

The industrial marketer needs to model each important customer's buying process individually. Figure 8-5 shows a model of a company's buying decision process for a test stand for automotive engines. The figure shows that this buying decision involved five different company personnel. Two suppliers and several outside buying influences were also involved. Finally, thirteen different events led to placing an order with one of the suppliers. Such a model can help the marketer to locate key decision makers and buying influences and to design an effective marketing plan for selling and servicing the customer.

RESELLER BUYER BEHAVIOR

In most ways, reseller buyer behavior is similar to industrial buyer behavior. Reseller organizations have buying centers consisting of varying numbers of participants who interact to make a variety of buying decisions. They have a buying decision process that starts with problem recognition and ends with decisions about which products to buy from which suppliers and under what terms. The buyers are influenced by a wide range of environmental, organizational, interpersonal, and individual factors.

But there are some important differences between industrial and reseller buying behavior. Resellers differ in the types of buying decisions they make, who participates in the buying decision, and how they make their buying decisions.

What Buying Decisions Do Resellers Make? Resellers serve as purchasing agents for *their* customers, so they buy products and brands they think will appeal to their customers. They have to decide what product assortment to carry, what vendors to buy from, and what prices and terms to negotiate. The assortment decision is primary, and it positions the reseller in the marketplace. The reseller's assortment strategy will strongly influence its choice of which products to buy and which suppliers to buy from.

Resellers face three types of buying decisions. In the *new item situation,* the reseller is offered a new item and then gives a "yes-no" answer, depending on how good the item looks. This differs from the new task situation faced by producers who *have* to purchase the needed item from someone.

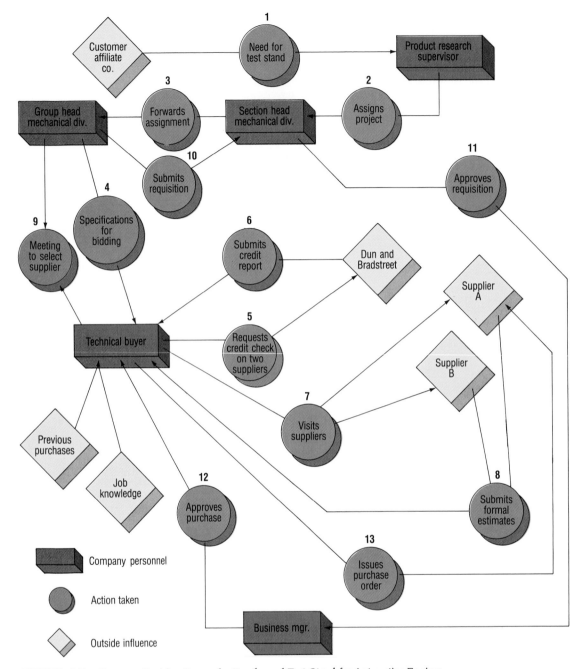

FIGURE 8-5 *Company Decision Process for Purchase of Test Stand for Automotive Engines*

Source: Murray Harding, "Who Really Makes the Purchasing Decision?" *Industrial Marketing,* September 1966, p. 77.

In the *best-vendor situation,* the reseller needs an item and must determine the best supplier. This situation occurs (1) when the reseller does not have the space to carry all the available brands or (2) when the reseller is seeking someone to produce a private brand. Resellers such as Sears and A&P sell a substantial number of items under their own names; therefore much of their buying operation consists of vendor selection.

In the *better-terms situation,* the reseller wants to obtain better terms from current suppliers. Legally suppliers are prevented, under the Robinson-Patman Act, from granting different terms to different resellers in the same reseller class unless these terms reflect cost differences, distress sales, or other special conditions. Nevertheless, resellers will press their suppliers for preferential treatment, such as more service, easier credit terms, and larger volume discounts.

Who Participates in the Reseller Buying Process?

Who does the buying for wholesale and retail organizations? The reseller's buying center may include one or many participants assuming roles of users, influencers, buyers, deciders, or gatekeepers. Some of these participants will have formal buying responsibility, and some will be behind-the-scenes influencers. In small "mom and pop" firms, the owner usually takes care of merchandising and buying decisions. In large reseller firms, buying is a specialized function and a full-time job. The buying center and its actions vary for different types of resellers, and differences can even be found within each type of enterprise.

Consider supermarkets. In the corporate headquarters of a supermarket chain, specialist buyers (sometimes called merchandise managers) will have the responsibility for developing brand assortments and listening to new brand presentations made by salespersons. In some chains these buyers have the authority to accept or reject new items. In many chains, however, they are limited to screening "obvious rejects" and "obvious accepts"; otherwise they must bring new items to the chain's *buying committee* for approval.

Even when an item is accepted by a buying committee, chain-store managers may not carry it. According to one supermarket chain executive: "No matter what the sales representatives sell or buyers buy, the person who has the greatest influence on the final sale of the new item is the store manager." In the nation's chain and independent supermarkets, two-thirds of the new items accepted at the warehouse are ordered on the store manager's own decision, and only one-third represent forced distribution.[20]

Thus producers face a major challenge in trying to get new items into stores. They offer the nation's supermarkets between 150 and 250 new items each week, and store space does not permit more than 10 percent to be accepted (see Exhibit 8-2).

How Do Resellers Make Their Buying Decisions?

For new items, resellers use roughly the same buying process described for the industrial buyer. For standard items, resellers simply reorder goods when the inventory gets low. The orders are placed with the same suppliers as long as their terms, goods, and services are satisfactory. Buyers will try to renegotiate prices if their margins erode due to rising operating costs. In many retail lines, the profit

EXHIBIT 8-2

THE GREAT COOKIE WARS: FOUGHT IN THE RESELLER MARKET

The mid-1980s may go down in food marketing history as the years of the great cookie wars. During the late 1970s and early 1980s, the $2.5 billion cookie industry slumbered, dominated by giants such as Nabisco, United Biscuits (Keebler), and American Brands (Sunshine). Then, in 1982, PepsiCo's Frito-Lay unit began to test Grandma's cookies—a "soft and chewy," moister cookie that was to be only the first in a quick succession of new "like-home-made" brands to hit the market. Grandma's captured a 15 to 20 percent share in test markets, and the war was on!

Frito-Lay backed Grandma's with a $70 million advertising budget (over five times the ad budget for the entire industry the previous year) and lured customers away from other brands with price discounts and free samples. The established producers counterattacked. Nabisco tried to protect its 35 to 40 percent market share by upping its ad budget from $8 to $30 million and discounting its prices. Number-two Keebler sponsored sweepstakes and expanded distribution. Sunshine increased its advertising from less than $500,000 to over $30 million.

In 1983 the war intensified when another marketing giant, Procter & Gamble, entered the fray with its "crunchy on the outside, chewy on the inside" Duncan Hines brand, backed by an estimated $100 million in advertising. And Nabisco followed with its "close to home-made" Almost Home brand. In the consumer market, the war of the cookie giants—PepsiCo, P&G, Nabisco, American Brands, and United Biscuits—is likely to rage for several years.

But the war is also being fought on a second front—in the reseller market—and many observers believe that the battle for reseller support will decide the winner of the war. The main objective is *shelf space* in over 300,000 supermarkets, convenience stores, and corner grocers across the country. More shelf space means more consumer exposure, resulting in more sales. Beyond awarding more shelf space, retailers can help a favored producer by using its displays, passing out its samples, and running ads featuring its brands.

Shelf space, floor space, and advertising space are precious commodities to retailers, and each cookie maker will have to work hard for its share (P&G asked Safeway for 30 percent of its cookie shelf space but got only 7.5 percent). Each producer must convince retailers that its cookie deserves more support. Thousands of sales reps, armed with research on consumer preferences and promises of huge consumer advertising and promotion programs for their products, will try to persuade retailers that supporting their brands will result in greater sales and profits. Retailers will be courted with trade discounts, cooperative advertising, attractive free-standing displays, liberal returns policies, and strong service.

The great cookie war will be a long and costly one for the cookie makers. In the end, consumers will decide the winners. But the cookie maker that best "sells" the reseller market will have powerful allies.

Sources: From information found in Al Urbanski, "On With the $2.1 Billion Cookie War," *Sales and Marketing Management,* June 6, 1983, pp. 37–40; Ann M. Morrison, "Cookies Are Frito-Lay's Bag," *Fortune,* August 9, 1982, pp. 64–67; "Products of the Year," *Fortune,* December 12, 1983, p. 76; and other sources.

---

margin is so low (1 to 2 percent on sales in supermarkets, for example) that a sudden drop in demand or rise in operating costs will drive profits into the red.

Resellers consider many factors besides costs when choosing products and suppliers. Several studies have attempted to rank the acceptance criteria used by buyers, buying committees, and store managers. A. C. Nielsen Company asked store managers to rank on a three-point scale the importance of different elements in influencing their decision to accept a new item.[21] The results were as follows:

Evidence of consumer acceptance	2.5
Advertising/promotion	2.2
Introductory terms and allowances	2.0
Why item was developed	1.9
Merchandising recommendations	1.8

Thus sellers stand the best chance when they can report strong evidence of consumer acceptance, present a well-designed advertising and sales promotion plan, and provide strong financial incentives to the retailer.[22]

Resellers are improving their buying skills over time. They are mastering the principles of demand forecasting, merchandise selection, stock control, space allocation, and display. They are learning to measure profit per cubic foot rather than only profit per product. They are making increased use of computers to keep current inventory figures, determine economic order quantities, prepare orders, and generate printouts of dollars spent on vendors and products.

Vendors are therefore facing increasingly sophisticated buying on the part of resellers. Vendors need to understand the resellers' changing requirements and to develop competitively attractive offers that help resellers serve their customers better. Table 8-4 lists several marketing tools used by vendors to make their offer to resellers more attractive.

GOVERNMENT BUYER BEHAVIOR

Government buying and industrial buying are similar in many ways. But there are also differences that must be understood by companies that wish to sell products and services to governments.[23] To achieve success in the government market, sell-

TABLE 8-4
Vendor Marketing Tools Used with Resellers

Cooperative advertising, where the vendor agrees to pay a portion of the reseller's advertising costs for the vendor's product.

Preticketing, where the vendor places a tag on each product listing its price, manufacturer, size, identification number, and color; these tags help the reseller reorder merchandise as it is being sold.

Stockless purchasing, where the vendor carries the inventory and delivers goods to the reseller on short notice.

Automatic reordering systems, where the vendor supplies forms and computer links for automatic reordering of merchandise by the reseller.

Advertising aids, such as glossy photos, broadcast scripts.

Special prices for storewide promotion.

Return and exchange privileges for the reseller.

Allowances for merchandise markdowns by the reseller.

Sponsorship of in-store demonstrations.

ers must locate key decision makers, identify the factors that influence buyer behavior, and understand the buying decision process.

Who Participates in the Government Buying Process? Who does the buying of the $690 billion of goods and services? Government buying organizations are found at the federal, state, and local levels. The federal level is the largest, and its buying units operate in the civilian and military sectors.

The *federal civilian buying* establishment consists of seven categories: departments (Commerce), administration (General Services Administration), agencies (Federal Aviation Agency), boards (Railroad Retirement Board), commissions (Federal Communications Commission), the executive office (Bureau of the Budget), and miscellaneous (Tennessee Valley Authority). "No single federal agency contracts for all the government's requirements and no single buyer in any agency purchases all that agency's needs for any single item of supplies, equipment or services."[24] Many agencies control a substantial percentage of their own buying, particularly for industrial products and specialized equipment. At the same time, the General Services Administration plays a major role in centralizing the buying of commonly used items in the civilian section (office furniture and equipment, vehicles, fuels) and in standardizing buying procedures for the other agencies.

Federal military buying is carried out by the Defense Department, largely through the Defense Supply Agency and the army, navy, and air force. The Defense Supply Agency was set up in 1961 to buy and distribute supplies used by all military services in an effort to reduce costly duplication. It operates six supply centers, which specialize in construction, electronics, fuel, personnel support, industrial, and general supplies. The trend has been toward "single managers" for major product classifications. Each service branch buys equipment and supplies in line with its own mission; for example, the Army Department operates offices for acquiring its own material, vehicles, medical supplies and services, and weaponry.

State and local buying agencies include school districts, highway departments, hospitals, housing agencies, and many others. Each has its own buying procedures that sellers have to master.

What Are the Major Influences on Government Buyers? Government buyers are influenced by environmental, organizational, interpersonal, and individual factors. A unique thing about government buying is that it is carefully monitored by outside publics. One watchdog is Congress, and certain congressmen have made a career out of exposing government extravagance and waste. Another watchdog is the Bureau of the Budget, which checks on government spending and seeks to improve efficiency. Many private groups also watch government agencies to monitor how they spend the public's money.

Because spending decisions are subject to public review, government organizations get involved in considerable paperwork. Elaborate forms must be filled out and signed before purchases are approved. The level of bureaucracy is high, and marketers have to find a way to "cut through the red tape."

Noneconomic criteria are playing a growing role in government buying. Government buyers are asked to favor depressed business firms and areas, small-business firms, and business firms that avoid racial, sex, or age discrimination. Sellers need to keep these factors in mind when deciding to pursue government business.

How Do Government Buyers Make Their Buying Decisions? Government buying practices often seem complex and frustrating to suppliers. In a recent survey, suppliers registered a variety of complaints about procedures. These included excessive paperwork, bureaucracy, needless regulations, emphasis on low bid prices, decision-making delays, frequent shifts in procurement personnel, and excessive policy changes.[25] Yet the "ins and outs" of selling to the government can be mastered in a short time. The government is generally helpful in providing information about its buying needs and procedures. Government is often as anxious to attract new suppliers as the suppliers are to find customers.

The Small Business Administration prints a booklet entitled *U.S. Government Purchasing, Specifications, and Sales Directory,* which lists thousands of items most frequently purchased by the government and is cross-referenced by the agencies most frequently buying them. The Government Printing Office issues the *Commerce Business Daily,* which lists major current defense and civilian agency procurements, as well as recent contract awards that can provide leads to subcontracting markets. The General Services Administration operates Business Service Centers in several major cities, whose staffs provide a complete education on the way government agencies buy and the steps that suppliers should follow. Various trade magazines and associations provide information on how to reach schools, hospitals, highway departments, and other government agencies.

Government buying procedures fall into two types: the *open bid* and the *negotiated contract.* Open bid buying means that the government office invites bids from qualified suppliers for carefully described items, generally awarding a contract to the lowest bidder. The supplier must consider whether it can meet the specifications and accept the terms. For commodities and standard items, such as fuel or school supplies, the specifications are not a hurdle. Specifications may, however, be a hurdle for nonstandard items. The government office is usually required to award the contract to the lowest bidder on a winner-take-all basis. In some cases, allowance is made for the supplier's superior product or reputation for completing contracts.

In negotiated contract buying, the agency works with one or more companies and negotiates a contract with one of them covering the project and terms. This occurs primarily in connection with complex projects—those involving major research and development cost and risk or those for which there is little effective competition. Contracts can have countless variations, such as *cost-plus pricing, fixed-pricing,* and *fixed price-and-incentive* (the supplier earns more if costs are reduced). Contract performance is open to review and renegotiation if the supplier's profits seem excessive.

Government contracts won by large companies give rise to substantial subcontracting opportunities for small companies. Thus government purchasing activity creates derived demand in the producer market. Subcontracting firms, however, must be willing to place performance bonds with the prime contractor, thereby assuming some of the risk.

Many companies that sell to the government have not been marketing-oriented—for a number of reasons. Total government spending is determined by elected officials rather than by marketing effort to develop this market. The government's procurement policies have emphasized price, leading suppliers to invest their effort in technology to bring costs down. Where the product's characteristics are carefully specified, product differentiation is not a marketing factor. Nor is advertising or personal selling of much consequence in winning bids on an open bid basis.

More companies are now establishing separate marketing departments to guide government-directed marketing efforts. J. I. Case, Eastman Kodak, and Goodyear are examples. These companies want to coordinate bids and prepare them more scientifically, to propose projects to meet government needs rather than just respond to government initiatives, to gather competitive intelligence, and to prepare stronger communications to describe the company's competence.

■ Summary

Organizations constitute a vast market. There are three major types of organizational markets—the industrial market, the reseller market, and the government market.

In many ways, organizational markets are similar to consumer markets, but in other ways they contrast sharply. Organizational markets usually have fewer and larger buyers who are more geographically concentrated. Organizational demand is derived, largely inelastic, and more fluctuating. More buyers are usually involved in the organizational buying decision, and organizational buyers are better trained and more professional than consumer buyers. Organizational purchasing decisions are more complex and the buying process is more formalized.

The *industrial market* consists of firms and individuals that buy goods and services in order to produce other goods and services for sale or rental to others. Industrial buyers make decisions that vary with the buying situation or buyclass. Buyclasses are of three types: straight rebuys, modified rebuys, and new tasks. The decision-making unit of a buying organization—the buying center—consists of persons who play any of five roles: users, influencers, buyers, deciders, and gatekeepers. The industrial marketer needs to know: Who are the major participants? In what decisions do they exercise influence? What is their relative degree of influence? and What evaluation criteria does each decision participant use? The industrial marketer also needs to understand the major environmental, organizational, interpersonal, and individual influences operating in the buying process. The buying process itself consists of eight stages called buyphases: problem recognition, general need description, product specification, supplier search, proposal solicitation, supplier selection, order routine specification, and performance review. As industrial buyers become more sophisticated, industrial marketers must upgrade their marketing capabilities.

The *reseller market* consists of individuals and organizations that acquire and resell goods produced by others. Resellers have to decide on their assortment, suppliers, prices, and terms. They face three types of buying situations: new items, new vendors, and new terms. In small wholesale and retail organizations, buying may be carried on by one or a few individuals; in large organizations, by an entire purchasing department. In a modern supermarket chain, the major participants include headquarters buyers, storewide buying committees, and individual store managers. With new items, the buyers go through a buying process similar to the one shown for industrial buyers; and with standard items, the buying process consists of routines for reordering and renegotiating contracts.

The *government market* is a vast one that annually purchases $690 billion of products and services—for the pursuit of defense, education, public welfare, and other public needs. Government buying practices are highly specialized and specified, with open bidding or negotiated contracts characterizing most of the buying. Government buyers operate under the watchful eye of Congress, the Bureau of the Budget, and several private watchdog groups. Hence they tend to fill out more forms, require more signatures, and respond more slowly in placing orders.

■ Questions for Discussion

1. It has been argued that a college of business administration is an industrial marketer. What characteristics of an industrial market does the demand for students (i.e., industrial products) exhibit?

2. Into which of the major types of buying situations would you classify the following? (a) United Airlines' purchase of an additional DC-10, (b) Caterpillar's purchase of diesel engine parts, and (c) Pacific Power and Electric's purchase of solar energy panels.

3. How would the participants in the producer buying process differ between a small machine tool shop and the U.S. Steel Corporation?

4. Discuss the major environmental factors that would influence Greyhound's purchase of buses.

5. Apply the buyphases to a farmer seeking to buy a large tractor.

6. The government market is not a significant one for most products. Comment.

7. How do the buying influences on the government buyer differ from those on the industrial or reseller buyer?

8. Companies are searching for "more able" purchasing executives. What abilities should a modern purchasing agent have?

■ References

1. The quoted material is reprinted by permission of *Harvard Business Review.* Excerpts from "Major Sales: Who Really Does the Buying?" by THOMAS V. BONOMA (May–June 1982). Copyright © 1982 by the President and Fellows of Harvard College; all rights reserved.

2. See REED MOYER, "Reciprocity: Retrospect and Prospect," *Journal of Marketing,* October 1970, pp. 47–54.

3. See LEONARD J. BERRY and KENNETH E. MARICLE, "Consumption Without Ownership: Marketing Opportunity for Today and Tomorrow," *MSU Business Topics,* Spring 1973, pp. 33–41.

4. FREDERICK E. WEBSTER, JR., and YORAM WIND, *Organizational Buying Behavior* (Englewood Cliffs, NJ: Prentice-Hall, 1972), p. 2.

5. For a discussion of other organizational buyer behavior models, see RAYMOND L. HORTON, *Buyer Behavior: A Decision-Making Approach* (Columbus, OH: Charles E. Merrill, 1984), chap. 16.

6. PATRICK J. ROBINSON, CHARLES W. FARIS, and YORAM WIND, *Industrial Buying Behavior and Creative Marketing* (Boston: Allyn & Bacon, 1967).

7. WEBSTER and WIND, *Organizational Buying Behavior,* p. 6. For more reading on buying centers, see BONOMA, "Major Sales: Who Really Does the Buying;" and WESLEY J. JOHNSON and THOMAS V. BONOMA, "Purchase Process for Capital Equipment and Services," *Industrial Marketing Management,* 10 (1981), pp. 253–64.

8. WEBSTER and WIND, *Organizational Buying Behavior,* pp. 78–80.

9. JOHNSTON and BONOMA, "Purchase Process," pp. 258–59.

10. See MURRAY HARDING, "Who Really Makes the Purchasing Decision," *Industrial Marketing,* September 1966, p. 76. This point of view is further developed in ERNEST DICHTER, "Industrial Buying Is Based on Same 'Only Human' Emotional Factors That Motivate Consumer Market's Housewife," *Industrial Marketing,* February 1973, pp. 14–16.

11. WEBSTER and WIND, *Organizational Buying Behavior,* pp. 33–37.

12. See "The Purchasing Agent Gains More Clout," *Business Week,* January 13, 1975, pp. 62–63.

13. Ibid.

14. BONOMA, "Major Sales," p. 114.

15. WALTER GUZZARDI, JR., "The Fight for 9/10 of a Cent," *Fortune,* April 1961, p. 152.

16. ROBINSON, FARIS, and WIND, *Industrial Buying.*

17. DONALD R. LEHMANN and JOHN O'SHAUGHNESSY, "Decision Criteria Used in Buying Different Categories of Products," *Journal of Purchasing and Materials Management,* Spring 1982, pp. 9–14.

18. See LEONARD GROENEVELD, "The Implications of Blanket Contracting for Industrial Purchasing and

Marketing," *Journal of Purchasing,* November 1972, pp. 51–58; and H. Lee Mathews, David T. Wilson, and Klaus Backhaus, "Selling to the Computer Assisted Buyer," *Industrial Marketing Management,* 6 (1977), 307–15.

19. Johnston and Bonoma, "Purchase Process," p. 261.

20. Robert W. Mueller and Franklin H. Graf, "New Items in the Food Industry, Their Problems and Opportunities" (Special report to the Annual Convention of the Supermarket Institute, Cleveland, May 20, 1968), p. 2.

21. Ibid., p. 5.

22. Also see David B. Montgomery, *New Product Distribution: An Analysis of Supermarket Buyer Decisions* (Cambridge, MA: Marketing Science Institute, March 1973). Montgomery found the two most important variables to be company reputation and the perceived newness of the product.

23. For more reading on similarities and differences, see Jagdish N. Sheth, Robert F. Williams, and Richard M. Hill, "Government and Business Buying: How Similar Are They?" *Journal of Purchasing and Materials Management,* Winter 1983, pp. 7-13.

24. Stanley E. Cohen, "Looking in the U.S. Government Market," *Industrial Marketing,* September 1964, pp. 129-38.

25. See "Out of the Maze," *Sales and Marketing Management,* April 9, 1979.

CASE 3

COMP-U-CARD INTERNATIONAL

Comp-U-Card was acquired in 1976 by Walter A. Forbes with the idea that consumers would soon be shopping from their living rooms, using TV sets tied to two-way cable systems to examine merchandise and order it from factories. The idea was to make Comp-U-Card the next Sears Roebuck by hooking into the system a central computer that would hold all sorts of items and handle ordering and billing automatically. But consumers lacked the necessary equipment, and even with equipment, possibly little inclination to use it. The change is taking longer than was originally thought. Comp-u-store, a much less sophisticated approach, is now offered. The company lost almost $14 million in its first six years and in 1983 showed a profit of $31,000. Offering several services, the company is said to be the largest shopping club for bargain hunters in the country.

The Comp-u-store service, currently being promoted by Comp-U-Card, is described in the following excerpts from its promotional material, with brand names omitted.

Introducing the electronic shopping mall

Let me show you how easy it is to shop the Comp-u-store way. Suppose you want to shop for a XXX VCR Model #2700. Here's how you do it:

- You call Comp-u-store's toll-free number, anytime between 8 a.m.–11 p.m. E.S.T., Monday–Friday; 9 a.m.–7 p.m. Saturdays; and 12 p.m.–5 p.m. Sundays.

- Tell your Shopping Consultant you'd like a price quote on a XXX Video Cassette Recorder Model #2700.

- You will be quoted the *lowest available price* (Comp-u-store's prices are updated every day). And that's the *total cost, delivered to your home.* There's nothing extra to pay.

- You can charge the item to your new SUPER CARD over the phone (remember, your SUPER CARD carries an instant line of credit.)

■ Or you can just shop. *You don't have to buy from Comp-u-store if you don't want to.* But you still save time and money by asking Comp-u-store for the latest, and the lowest, prices from all over the country.

Just think of Comp-u-store as your own electronic shopping mall: where your fingers do the walking!

Here's the secret of Comp-u-store's low prices

Comp-u-store is *not* like a regular store. They carry no stock (the suppliers do that) so there is no money tied up in inventory. Nor do they have retail expenses like high-rent locations or expensive advertising campaigns.

Because Comp-u-store gives you a *direct* link to suppliers, you typically may save up to 40% (sometimes more!) off the manufacturer's suggested list price. (That includes delivery. Remember, *Comp-u-store's price is the TOTAL price— delivered to your home.*)

Compare *that* to some retail markups of 100%!

The difference in price is yours to keep. And it can be substantial. Just look at these typical Comp-u-store prices (as of June 1984) and see how much money you save:

ITEM	MFS. SUGG. LIST PRICE	COMP-U-STORE PRICE*	YOU SAVE	
Brand A VCR #HRD120	$ 750.00	$499.00	$251.00	33%
Brand B Sewing Machine #600	$1,099.00	$598.00	$501.00	46%
Brand C 19″ Color TV #91C510A	$ 399.00	$248.00	$151.00	38%
Brand D Disk Drive #VIC1541	$ 399.00	$234.00	$165.00	41%
Brand E Flatware 20 pc. Set	$ 200.00	$ 99.00	$101.00	51%

*Minimal delivery and handling charges are additional and will vary depending on location. However, your shopping consultant will *always* quote you the *full delivered cost* of the item.

Of course, Comp-u-store won't *always* be able to offer you the lowest price on every item. (You might get a lower price from a store going out of business, or selling below cost.) But in most cases, Comp-u-store will save you plenty of dollars. A quick check in your local newspaper will confirm that.

With Comp-u-store it's as if you're the only person in the store

No matter how advanced shopping becomes, one thing will never change: people will always want good, personal service.

Call Comp-u-store and you talk one-on-one with a shopping consultant, committed to your total satisfaction. There is no other customer to push ahead of you. Instead you have your consultant's full attention . . . to give you prices . . . to arrange delivery to your home. Or, if you prefer, directly to the homes of your friends or business associates.

What's more, *you'll receive Comp-u-store's private newsletter.* It's packed with special buys on brand name items. These are limited-time-only prices you won't find listed anywhere else.

For an annual membership fee of $25 you have access to the service, which lists some 60,000 brand-name products that may be ordered, paid for by credit card, and delivered to your door, usually by United Parcel Service. The company now has about 700,000 members. They bought $20 million of merchandise in 1983, with orders expected to double in 1984.

The recent rapid growth is attributed to the heavy promotional efforts of the Super Visa Credit Card sponsor, Columbus, Ohio, based Bank One, and Comp-U-Card. Massive direct mailings have been sent to more than 22 million middle-class households offering the service and free Visa cards.

Competitive shopping opportunities are available, including the following (some in only a few areas):

- Retail stores

- Catalog mail order stores

- Catalog orders by phone

- Catalog orders by mail

- Computer-based via phone (Comp-u-store)

- Videodisc players, in-store for public use (Comp-u-card test)

- Computer-based, in store for public use (Electronistore by R. R. Donnelley)

- Videotex (text only)

- Videotex (text and graphics)

Comp-U-Card management is confident that electronic shopping is imminent. It is held that people are value-conscious and do not like to go shopping nearly as much as retailers think. The idea is being tested by putting "shopping machines" (kiosks equipped with video disc players) in dime and drug stores in the Midwest and Southeast. Customers can punch up demonstrations of merchandise they want and use the Comp-U-Card service to check prices and place orders.

R. R. Donnelley and Sons, the largest U.S. commercial printer, is marketing the Electronistore, a computer shopping terminal or an electronic kiosk to retailers for in-store use. Products will be displayed in color and information provided through a touch-control system. Payment will be accepted by credit card and merchandise shipped to an address designated by the customer. The "shopping machines" are seen by retailers as an opportunity to cut costs and as an intermediate step in the development of electronic shopping through home terminals. Electronic home shopping will generate sales of about $7 billion a year by the late 1980s, about 15 percent of 1984 mail-order and catalog business, according to a Booz, Allen & Hamilton study.

1. Evaluate, on a qualitative basis, the Comp-u-store computer-based telephone marketing system from the point of view of:
   a. A consumer buyer.
   b. A retailer solicited to participate.
   c. A distributor solicited to participate.
   d. A manufacturer solicited to participate.

2. Evaluate, on a qualitative basis, the in-store "shopping machine" from the point of view of:
   a. A consumer buyer.
   b. A retailer solicited to buy an Electronistore system.

CASE 4

LEVI STRAUSS & CO.

Levis Strauss & Co. has broadened its distribution to include J. C. Penney and Sears, Roebuck, thereby reducing its reliance on jean specialty chains, jean boutiques, and upscale department stores. This decision was triggered by a sustained slump in the apparel and retailing industries, a substantial drop in the company's earnings, and the apparent maturing of the market for jeans. The management found it difficult to make the change and keep in balance the best interests of its old retailer-customers, its new ones (Sears and Penney), and the company itself. The company now faces the problems of (1) whether to broaden its distribution even more to include discount and off-price outlets and (2) deciding what other changes, if any, should be made in its marketing efforts to improve profits on jeans.

Many retailers, manufacturers, and security analysts believe that the jeans business has finally matured. Reasons cited are the aging U.S. population and the declining interest in designer jeans and Western looks. People are buying dressier, more fashionable clothes; the preppy look is gaining acceptance; and chinos are considered a comfortable alternative to denim. Levi Strauss officials said they did not believe the jeans' popularity was declining. Instead, they felt that the increased interest in the dress-up look meant that people were expanding their wardrobes and thereby creating an opportunity for the company, the largest apparel company in the United States.

Levi's plan to sell through mass merchandisers has had an impact on several interest groups. Some of Levi's longtime retailers were shocked by the change the added competition it brought. Independent and chain specialty stores whose businesses were built around Levi's had mixed reactions. Upscale department stores were especially upset by the plan and many, including Macy's, dropped the line.

The head of a large jean specialty chain believes that the plan helped Levi Strauss and its retailers in geographic areas where they were weak. Others fear price competition. Sears and Penney, especially the latter, have been promoting their own brands of jeans against Levi's. It is not clear whether they want to stock Levi jeans as traffic builders, image builders, or direct contributors to profits. What they do is critical to Levi Strauss and its current retailers. Mass retailers carrying Levi jeans commonly make price comparisons between their own brands and Levi's in their advertising.

It was reported that Levi's executives acknowledged their debt to their retailer-customers, but made it clear that sentiment did not sway them. The proposal to expand distribution had been discussed a number of times over the years, and the management felt it was the right time to make the move. The company had experienced poor years; competition in the jean market was severe; consumer demand had weakened, especially for designer jeans and the Western look; and broadened distribution would expose Levi jeans to more potential consumers as well as increase sales to new retailers as they stocked their shelves.

Levi's management is planning to increase the advertising budget to help the retailers. It is also formulating criteria and guidelines for determining what types of goods it should sell through Sears and Penney and whether to shift more of its advertising attention to a few feature items in its line, such as the button-fly 501 brand blue jeans. The overall advertising budget has been increased by 13 percent, and it is reported that $35 million was earmarked for TV promotion of 501 blue jeans, including expenditures during the 1984 Olympic Games. Competitors believe Levi is overspending in TV advertising and are searching for other ways to improve profits on jeans. Murjani has been licensed to use the Coca-Cola brand name on its designer jeans and expects a significant increase in sales to result from the use of the name. In the past Levi did the opposite; it licensed the use of the Levi brand name by a shoe marketer.

Earlier, Levi's Canadian subsidiary had announced the 555, the limited-edition jean—limited to between 30,000 and 50,000 pairs. This jean carries a retail price a few dollars higher than the best-selling nonregistered Levi jeans. Distribution is exclusively through a Canadian specialty jean chain, Thrifty's Just Pants. The 555 is a straight-leg jean with a button-fly front and other details similar to the original 1849 gold rush blue jeans. Levi's two-horse trademark appears on a leather patch on the rear pocket. A small copper plate carries a five-digit serial number, which is registered in the company's archives when the buyer returns the postage-paid card provided at the time of purchase. Buyers will receive a certificate documenting their ownership and a token good for a 10 percent discount on the purchase of another Levi Strauss item. The subsidiary's director of marketing believes the "limited edition" idea will be as successful with apparel as it has been with books, works of art, and other collectibles. A museum director was quoted as saying that 555 could in time become a museum piece.

1. Should Levi Strauss expand its distribution of blue jeans to include discount and/or off-price retailers? What criteria should be used in selecting additional outlets?
2. What further use, if any, should the company make of the limited-edition jeans idea?
3. What other changes in Levi's marketing efforts do you recommend?

four

SELECTING TARGET MARKETS

Part Four of this book shows how successful companies evaluate and select market segments to enter and satisfy.

Chapter 9, MEASURING AND FORECASTING DEMAND

Chapter 10, MARKET SEGMENTATION, TARGETING, AND POSITIONING

This will lead us to Part Five, "Developing the Marketing Mix," where we will examine how companies develop each major component of the marketing mix—product, price, place, and promotion—to support their intended position in the target market.

9
Measuring and Forecasting Demand

In February 1981, RCA officially introduced its product of the decade—the SelectaVision videodisc player—backed by high hopes, 5,000 retail outlets, and over $22 million in advertising. RCA claimed its research showed that about 2.4 million people were ready to buy, and modestly forecast first-year sales at 200,000 units. The company set up facilities capable of producing more than 500,000 units a year and predicted it would sell all it could make.

The videodisc player is the visual counterpart of the phonograph. The buyer can hook the player up to a television set, pop in a videodisc, and watch a recent movie, a children's program, a cultural event, or a "how-to" such as Dr. Spock on baby care. The SelectaVision initially sold for about $500 and the discs were priced from $15 to $30. RCA was certain it had a winner.

But by the end of the first year, RCA had sold only 65,000 units; by mid-1984, even after a series of drastic price cuts, it had sold a total of only 500,000 units. In April 1984, RCA announced that it would withdraw from the videodisc market and swallow a staggering $580 million loss.

Where did RCA's forecasting go wrong? In part, the people at RCA fell into "better mousetrap" thinking—they got caught up in their own dreams and thought consumers would be as enamored of their invention as they were. This resulted in overly optimistic forecasts and kept RCA in the videodisc business long after later forecasts soured. Second, RCA based its forecasts on faulty assessments of consumer preferences. The videodisc featured playback only. Owners could not use it to record television programs or take pictures of the family. But SelectaVision's primary competitor—videocassette recorders—*did* offer these features.

RCA counted on consumers buying SelectaVision rather than VCRs because of its lower unit and disc prices (in 1981, VCRs were selling for $600 to $2,000, with tapes costing around $50 to $70). RCA's technological forecasts indicated that VCR unit and tape costs would fall slowly. That was RCA's third forecasting mistake—it incorrectly forecast future VCR technological improvements and competitive marketing strategies. By 1984, rapid improvements in technology had dropped VCR prices to under $500. And the rapid growth of the videotape rental market caught RCA by surprise. Videotape rental soon became commonplace—consumers could run to a nearby rental outlet, rent a tape of a favorite movie for $1 to $3, view it once, and return it without having to buy it. This put the software costs of videocassette recorders well below those of the videodisc player. When consumers cast their votes in the marketplace, VCRs became the clear winner. By 1984, Americans had purchased over 8 million VCRs to only 800,000 videodisc players.

Forecasting the size and growth rate of a new market is always hazardous. For videodisc players and other new technological products—personal computers, videorecorders, video games—forecasting is even more complex because consumers have no experience in using the products. The forecaster must consider possible consumer reactions to the product, competitor responses, future technological developments, environmental consequences, and many other factors. And as RCA and many other companies know only too well, forecasting mistakes can be very costly.[1]

$\mathbf{W}$hen a company such as RCA finds an attractive market, it must estimate its current size and future potential carefully. The company can lose a lot of profit by overestimating or underestimating the market. This chapter will present the principles and tools for measuring and forecasting market demand. The next chapter will look at the more qualitative aspects of markets, and at how markets can be further segmented and the most attractive segments selected.

Demand can be measured and forecasted on many levels. Figure 9-1 shows *ninety* different types of demand measurement! Demand can be measured for six different *product levels* (product item, product form, product line, company sales, industry sales, and total sales), five different *space levels* (customer, territory, region, USA, world), and three different *time levels* (short range, medium range, and long range).

Each type of demand measurement serves a specific purpose. Thus a company might make a short-range forecast of the total demand for a particular product item to provide a basis for ordering raw materials, planning production, and scheduling short-run financing. Or it might make a long-range forecast of regional demand for its major product line to provide a basis for considering market expansion.

DEFINING THE MARKET

Market demand measurement calls for a clear understanding of the market involved. The term *market* has acquired many meanings over the years.

1. In its original meaning, a market is a *physical place* where buyers and sellers gather to exchange goods and services. Medieval towns had market squares where sellers brought their goods and buyers shopped for goods. Today's transactions occur all over the city in what are called shopping areas rather than markets.

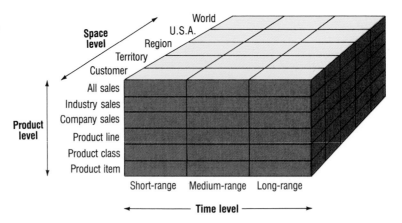

FIGURE 9-1
Ninety Types of Demand Measurement
(6 × 5 × 3)

2. To an economist, a market describes all the buyers and sellers who transact over some good or service. Thus the soft-drink market consists of major sellers such as Coca-Cola, Pepsi-Cola, and Seven-Up and all the consumers who buy soft drinks. The economist is interested in the *structure, conduct,* and *performance* of each market.

3. To a marketer, a market is *the set of all actual and potential buyers of a product.* A *market* is the set of buyers, and an *industry* is the set of sellers. Most of the things a marketer wants to know about a market are shown in Figure 9-2.

We will adopt the last definition of market. The size of a market, then, hinges on the number of buyers who might exist for a particular market offer. Those who are in the market for something have three characteristics: *interest, income,* and *access.*

FIGURE 9-2
What a Marketer Wants to Know about a Market

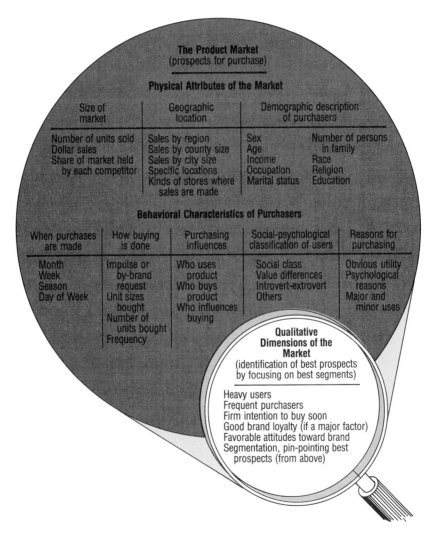

Source: Jack Z. Sissors, "What is a Market?" *Journal of Marketing,* 30, 3 (July 1966), p. 20.

Let us apply this to the market for motorcycles. We will leave aside companies that purchase motorcycles and concentrate on the consumer market. We must first estimate the number of consumers who have a potential *interest* in owning a motorcycle. To do this, we could contact a random sample of consumers and pose the following question: "Would you have a strong interest in owning a motorcycle?" If one person out of ten says yes, we can assume that 10 percent of the total number of consumers would constitute the potential market for motorcycles. The *potential market* is the set of consumers who profess some level of interest in a defined market offer.

Consumer interest is not enough to define a market. Potential consumers must have enough *income* to afford the product. They must be able to answer the following question positively: "Can you afford to purchase a motorcycle?" The higher the price, the fewer the number of people who can answer this question positively. The size of a market is a function of both interest and income.

Access barriers further reduce market size. If motorcycles are not distributed in a certain area because they are too costly to ship in, potential consumers in that area are not available to marketers. The *available market* is the set of consumers who have interest, income, and access to a particular market offer.

For some market offers, the company may restrict sales to certain groups. A particular state might ban the sale of motorcycles to anyone under 21 years of age. The remaining adults constitute the *qualified available market*—the set of consumers who have interest, income, access, and qualifications for the particular market offer.

The company now has the choice of going after the whole qualified available market or concentrating on certain segments. The *served market* (also called the *target market*) is the part of the qualified available market the company decides to pursue. The company, for example, may decide to concentrate its marketing and distribution effort on the East Coast. The East Coast becomes its served market.

The company and its competitors will end up selling a certain number of motorcycles in its served market. The *penetrated market* is the set of consumers who have already bought the product.

Figure 9-3 brings the preceding concepts together with some hypothetical numbers. The bar on the left of the figure illustrates the ratio of the potential market—all interested persons—to the total population, here 10 percent. The bar on the right illustrates several breakdowns of the potential market. The available market—those who have interest, income, and access—is 40 percent of the potential market. The qualified available market—those who can meet the legal requirements—is 20 percent of the potential market (or 50 percent of the available market). The company is concentrating its efforts on 10 percent of the potential market (or 50 percent of the qualified available market). Finally, the company and its competitors have already penetrated 5 percent of the potential market (or 50 percent of the served market).

These definitions of a market are a useful tool for marketing planning. If the company is not satisfied with current sales, it can consider a number of actions. It can try to attract a larger percentage of buyers from its served market. It can lower the qualifications of potential buyers. It can expand to other available markets, such as the West Coast. It can lower its price to expand the size of the available market.

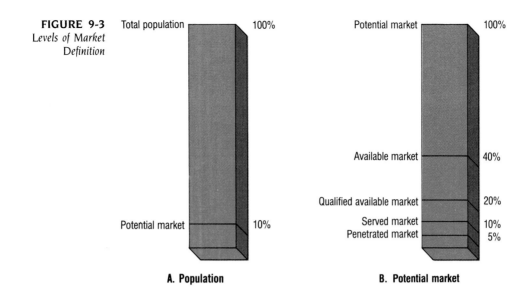

FIGURE 9-3
Levels of Market Definition

Total population   100%

Potential market   10%

A. Population

Potential market   100%

Available market   40%

Qualified available market   20%

Served market   10%
Penetrated market   5%

B. Potential market

Ultimately, the company can try to expand the potential market by a major advertising campaign to convert noninterested consumers into interested consumers. This is what Honda did when it ran its successful campaign on the theme "You meet the nicest people on a Honda."

MEASURING CURRENT MARKET DEMAND

We will now examine practical methods for estimating current market demand. Marketing executives will want to estimate *total market demand, area market demand,* and *actual sales and market shares.*

Estimating Total Market Demand

Total market demand is defined as follows:

> **Total market demand** for a product is the total volume that would be bought by a defined consumer group in a defined geographic area in a defined time period in a defined marketing environment under a defined level and mix of industry marketing effort.

The most important thing to realize about total market demand is that it is not a fixed number, but a function of the specified conditions. One of these conditions, for example, is the level and mix of industry marketing effort, and another is the state of the environment. The dependence of total market demand on these conditions is illustrated in Figure 9-4A. The horizontal axis shows different possible levels of industry marketing expenditure in a given time period. The vertical axis shows the resulting demand level. The curve represents the estimated level of market demand associated with varying levels of industry marketing expenditure. Some base sales (called the *market minimum*) would take place without any demand-stimulating expenditures. Greater marketing expenditures would yield higher levels of demand.

The distance between the market minimum and the market potential shows the overall *marketing sensitivity of demand.* We can think of two extreme types of markets, the *expansible* and the *nonexpansible.* An expansible market, such as the market for racquetball, is quite affected in its total size by the level of industry marketing expenditures. In terms of Figure 9-4A, the distance between Q_0 and Q_1 is relatively large. A nonexpansible market, such as the market for opera, is not much affected by the level of marketing expenditures; the distance between Q_0 and Q_1 is relatively small. Organizations selling in a nonexpansible market can take the market's size (the level of *primary demand*) for granted and concentrate their marketing resources on getting a desired market share (the level of *selective demand*).

The *industry market* forecast can now be derived. The market forecast shows the level of market demand corresponding to the planned level of industry marketing expenditure in the given environment.

If a different marketing environment is assumed, the market demand curve will have to be reestimated. For example, the market for motorcycles is stronger during prosperity than during recession. The dependence of market demand on the environment is illustrated in Figure 9-4B. The main point is that the marketer should carefully define the situation for which market demand is being estimated.

Companies have developed various practical methods for estimating total market demand. We will illustrate two here.

Suppose a phonograph record company wants to estimate the total annual sales of phonograph records. A common way to estimate this is as follows:

$$Q = n \times q \times p \qquad\qquad (9\text{-}1)$$

where

Q = total market demand
n = number of buyers in the market
q = quantity purchased by an average buyer per year
p = price of an average unit

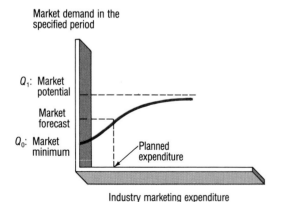

A. Market demand as a function of industry marketing expenditure (assumes a marketing environment of prosperity)

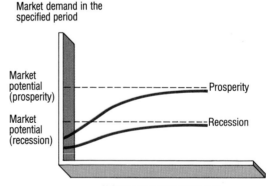

B. Market demand as a function of industry marketing expenditures (under prosperity vs. recession)

FIGURE 9-4 *Market Demand*

Thus if there are 100 million buyers of phonograph records each year, and the average buyer buys six records a year, and the average price is $5, then the total market demand for phonograph records is $3 billion (= 100,000,000 × 6 × $5).

A variation on Equation (9-1) is known as the *chain ratio method*. The chain ratio method involves multiplying a base number by several adjusting percentages. Here is an example:

The U.S. Navy wants to attract 112,000 new male recruits each year from American high schools. The question is whether this is a reasonable target in relation to the market potential. The market potential has been estimated by using the following method:

Total number of male high school graduating students	10,000,000
Percentage who are militarily qualified (no physical, emotional, or mental handicaps)	× .50
Percentage of those qualified who are potentially interested in military service	× .15
Percentage of those qualified and interested in military service who consider the Navy the preferred service	× .30

This chain of numbers shows the market potential to be 225,000 recruits. Since this exceeds the target number of recruits sought, the U.S. Navy should not have much trouble meeting its target if it does a reasonable job of marketing the Navy.

Estimating Area Market Demand Companies face the problem of selecting the best territories and allocating their marketing budget optimally among these territories. Therefore they need to estimate the market potential of different territories. Two major methods are available: the *market-buildup method,* which is used primarily by industrial goods firms, and the *market-factor index method,* which is used primarily by consumer goods firms.

Market-Buildup Method

The market-buildup method calls for identifying all the potential buyers in each market and estimating their potential purchases. Consider the following example.

A manufacturer of mining instruments developed an instrument for detecting "fool's gold." Fool's gold is an iron ore that is often confused with metallic gold. By detecting it, miners would not waste their time digging deposits of fool's gold. The manufacturer wants to price the instrument at $1,000. He sees each mine as buying one or more instruments, depending on the mine's size. His problem is to determine the market potential for this instrument in each mining state and whether to hire a sales representative to cover that state. He would place a sales representative in each state that has a market potential of over $300,000. He would like to start by estimating the market potential in Colorado.

To estimate the market potential in Colorado, the manufacturer can consult the Standard Industrial Classification (SIC) developed by the U.S. Bureau of the Census. The SIC classifies industries according to the *product produced* or *operation performed.* All industries fall into the ten major divisions shown in column 1 of Table 9-1. Each major industrial group is assigned to a two-digit code. Mining bears the code numbers 10 to 14. Metal mining bears the code number 10 (see column 2). Within metal mining are further breakdowns into three-digit SIC numbers (see column 3). The gold and silver ores category has the code number 104.

TABLE 9-1
The Standard Industrial Classification (SIC)

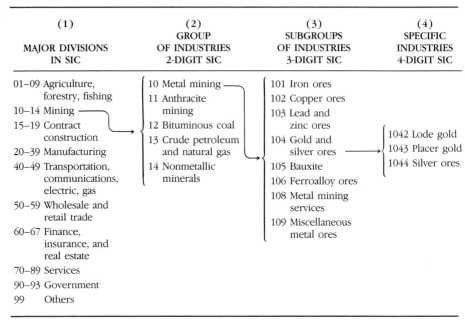

(1) MAJOR DIVISIONS IN SIC	(2) GROUP OF INDUSTRIES 2-DIGIT SIC	(3) SUBGROUPS OF INDUSTRIES 3-DIGIT SIC	(4) SPECIFIC INDUSTRIES 4-DIGIT SIC
01–09 Agriculture, forestry, fishing 10–14 Mining 15–19 Contract construction 20–39 Manufacturing 40–49 Transportation, communications, electric, gas 50–59 Wholesale and retail trade 60–67 Finance, insurance, and real estate 70–89 Services 90–93 Government 99 Others	10 Metal mining 11 Anthracite mining 12 Bituminous coal 13 Crude petroleum and natural gas 14 Nonmetallic minerals	101 Iron ores 102 Copper ores 103 Lead and zinc ores 104 Gold and silver ores 105 Bauxite 106 Ferroalloy ores 108 Metal mining services 109 Miscellaneous metal ores	1042 Lode gold 1043 Placer gold 1044 Silver ores

Source: The Standard Industrial Classification Manual (Washington, DC: U.S. Bureau of the Budget, 1967).

Finally, gold and silver ores are subdivided into further groups, with four-digit code numbers (see column 4). Thus lode gold has the code number 1042. Our manufacturer is interested in mines that mine lode deposits and placer deposits.

Next the manufacturer can turn to the Census of Mining to determine the number of gold-mining establishments in each state, their locations within the state, the number of employees, annual sales, and net worth. Using the data on Colorado, he prepares the market potential estimate shown in Table 9-2. Column 1 classifies mines into three groups based on the number of employees. Column 2 shows the number of mines in each group. Column 3 shows the potential number of instruments that mines in each size class might purchase. Column 4 shows the unit market potential (column 2 times column 3). Finally, column 5 shows the dollar market potential, given that each instrument sells for $1,000. Colorado has a dollar market potential of $370,000, and therefore one sales representative should be hired for Colorado.

Market-Factor Index Method

Consumer goods companies also have to estimate area market potentials. Consider the following example.

A shirt manufacturer was interested in starting a national system of franchised stores to sell T-shirts. Each store would carry several sizes and colors and would print an emblem chosen by the customer on each T-shirt. The customer could choose from hundreds of emblems. The manufacturer estimated that total national potential for T-shirts could reach $100 million annually. He would sell a franchise in any town where the store might sell more than $60,000 a year. He would advertise in the *Wall Street Journal* to attract potential franchisees, examine their business qualifications, and make sure that the town had enough buying potential to justify a store.

He received an application from a recent graduate of the University of Illinois at Champaign. This person wanted to buy a franchise with some inherited money. He had taken some marketing and business courses at the university. The manufacturer wondered whether a store in Champaign, Illinois, could gross enough sales to reward both the franchisee and the manufacturer.

The manufacturer wants to evaluate the market potential for T-shirt sales in Champaign. A common method is to identify market factors that are correlated with area market potential and combine them into a weighted index. An excellent example of this method is called the *buying power index,* which is published each year by *Sales and Marketing Management* magazine in its *Survey of Buying Power.*[2] This survey estimates the buying power for each region, state, and metropolitan area of the nation. The buying power index is based on three factors: the area's share of the nation's *disposable personal income, retail sales,* and *population.* The buying power index for a specific area is given by

$$B_i = .5y_i + .3r_i + .2p_i \tag{9-2}$$

where

B_i = percentage of total national buying power in area i
y_i = percentage of national disposable personal income in area i
r_i = percentage of national retail sales in area i
p_i = percentage of national population in area i

The three coefficients in the formula reflect the relative weight of the three factors.

The manufacturer looks up Champaign, Illinois, and finds that this market has .0764 percent of the nation's disposable personal income, .0900 percent of the

TABLE 9-2
Market-Buildup Method Using SIC: Instrument Market Potential in Colorado

SIC	(1) NUMBER OF EMPLOYEES	(2) NUMBER OF MINES	(3) POTENTIAL NUMBER OF INSTRUMENT SALES PER EMPLOYEE SIZE CLASS	(4) UNIT MARKET POTENTIAL (2×3)	(5) DOLLAR MARKET POTENTIAL (AT $1,000 PER INSTRUMENT)
1042	Under 10	80	1	80	
(lode deposits)	10–50	50	2	100	
	Over 50	20	4	80	
		150		260	$260,000
1043	Under 10	40	1	40	
(placer	10–50	20	2	40	
deposits)	Over 50	10	3	30	
		70		110	110,000
					$370,000

nation's retail sales, and .0070 percent of the nation's population. The buying power index for Champaign is therefore

$$B = .5(.0764) + .3(.0900) + .2(.0770) = .0806$$

That is, Champaign could account for .0806 percent of the nation's total potential demand for T-shirts. Since the total potential is $100 million nationally each year, this amounts to selling $80,600 (=$100,000,000 × .000806) in Champaign. Since a successful store sells over $60,000 annually, the manufacturer leans toward selling a franchise to this applicant. The manufacturer needs to make sure that other T-shirt companies are not already operating in the Champaign market and selling this volume of T-shirts.

The manufacturer recognizes that the weights used in the buying power index are somewhat arbitrary. They apply mainly to consumer goods that are neither low-priced staples nor high-priced luxury goods. Other weights can be assigned. Furthermore, the manufacturer would want to adjust the market potential for additional factors, such as competitors' presence in the market, local promotional costs, seasonal factors, and local market idiosyncrasies. For example, Champaign is a college town with over thirty thousand students, and this might make Champaign even more attractive.

Estimating Actual Sales and Market Shares Besides estimating total and area demand, a company will want to know the actual industry sales taking place in its market. This means that it must identify its competitors and estimate their sales.

The industry's trade association will often collect and publish total industry sales, although not listing individual company sales separately. In this way, each company can evaluate its performance against the industry as a whole. Suppose the company's sales are increasing at 5 percent a year and industry sales are increasing at 10 percent. This company is actually losing its relative standing in the industry.

Another way to estimate sales is to buy reports from a marketing research firm that audits total sales and brand sales. For example, the A. C. Nielsen Company audits the retail sales of various product categories in supermarkets and drugstores and sells this information to interested companies. A company can obtain data on total product category sales as well as brand sales. It can compare its performance with that of the total industry or any particular competitor to see whether it is gaining or losing in its relative standing.

FORECASTING FUTURE DEMAND

Having looked at ways to estimate current demand, we will now examine ways to forecast future demand. Very few products or services lend themselves to easy forecasting. These cases generally involve a product whose absolute level or trend is fairly constant and a situation where competitive relations are nonexistent (pub-

Using sales data for forecasting purposes. *Courtesy of Texas Instruments.*

lic utilities) or stable (pure oligopolies). In most markets, total demand and company demand are not stable, and good forecasting becomes a key factor in company success. Poor forecasting can lead to overly large inventories, costly price markdowns, or lost sales due to being out of stock. The more unstable the demand, the more critical is forecast accuracy and the more elaborate is forecasting procedure.

Companies commonly use a three-stage procedure to arrive at a sales forecast. First they make an *economic forecast,* then use it to make an *industry forecast,* and then use the industry forecast to make a *company sales forecast.* The economic forecast calls for projecting inflation, unemployment, interest rates, consumer spending and saving, business investment, government expenditures, net exports, and so on. The result is a forecast of gross national product, which is used along with other indicators to forecast industry sales. Then the company bases its sales forecast on the assumption of achieving a certain share of industry sales.

There are several specific techniques companies use to forecast their sales. These techniques are listed in Table 9-3 and described in the following paragraphs.

Survey of Buyers' Intentions

Forecasting is the art of anticipating what buyers are likely to do under a given set of conditions. This suggests that the buyers should be surveyed. Surveys are especially valuable if the buyers have clearly formulated intentions, will carry them out, and will describe them to interviewers.

For *major consumer durables,* several research organizations conduct peri-

TABLE 9-3
Some Common Sales Forecasting Techniques

Surveys of buyers' intentions	Time-series analysis
Composite of salesforce opinions	Leading indicators
Expert opinion	Statistical demand analysis
Market-test method	

odic surveys of buying intentions. These organizations ask questions like the following:

Do you intend to buy an automobile within the next six months?

.00	.10	.20	.30	.40	.50	.60	.70	.80	.90	1.00
No chance		Slight chance		Fair chance		Good chance		Strong chance		For certain

---

This is called a *purchase probability scale.* In addition, the various surveys ask about the consumer's present and future personal finances, and expectations about the economy. The various bits of information are combined into a *consumer sentiment measure* (Survey Research Center of the University of Michigan) or a *consumer confidence measure* (Sindlinger and Company). Consumer durable-goods producers subscribe to these indexes to help them anticipate major shifts in consumer buying intentions so that they can adjust their production and marketing plans accordingly.[3]

For *industrial buying,* various agencies carry out intention surveys regarding plant, equipment, and materials. The two best-known surveys are conducted by the U.S. Department of Commerce and by McGraw-Hill. Most of the estimates have been within 10 percent of the actual outcomes.

Composite of Salesforce Opinions

Where buyer interviewing is impractical, the company may ask its sales representatives for estimates. An example is the Pennwalt Corporation:[4]

> In August, the field sales personnel are provided with tabulating cards to prepare their sales forecasts for the coming year. Individual cards are prepared for each product sold to each major customer, showing the quantity shipped to the customer in the previous six months. Each card also provides space in which the field salesmen post their forecasts for the coming year. Additional tab cards are also supplied for those customers who were not sold in the current six-month period but who were customers in the prior year; and finally, blank cards are provided for submitting forecasts of sales to new customers. Salesmen fill in their forecasts (on the basis of current prices) using informed judgment; in some divisions, they are in a position to substantiate their forecasts by obtaining purchase estimates from their customers.

Few companies use their salesforce's estimates without some adjustments. Sales representatives are biased observers. They may be naturally pessimistic or optimistic, or they may go to one extreme or another because of recent sales setbacks or successes. Furthermore, they are often unaware of larger economic developments and do not know whether their company's marketing plans will influence future sales in their territories. They may understate demand so that the company will set a low sales quota.[5] They may not have the time to prepare careful estimates or may not consider it worthwhile.

Assuming these biases can be countered, a number of benefits can be gained by involving the salesforce in forecasting. Sales representatives may have better insight into developing trends than any other single group. Through participating in the forecasting process, the sales representatives may have greater confidence in their quotas, and more incentive to achieve them. Also, a "grassroots" forecasting procedure provides estimates broken down by product, territory, customer, and representative.

Expert Opinion Companies can also obtain forecasts by turning to experts. Experts include dealers, distributors, suppliers, marketing consultants, and trade associations. Thus auto companies survey their dealers periodically for their forecasts of short-term demand. Dealer estimates, however, are subject to the same strengths and weaknesses as salesforce estimates.

Many companies buy economic and industry forecasts from well-known firms such as Data Resources, Wharton Econometric, and Chase Econometric. These forecasting specialists are in a better position than the company to prepare economic forecasts because they have more data available and more forecasting expertise.

Reprinted with permission of Data Resources, Inc.

Occasionally companies will put together a special group of experts to make a particular kind of forecast. The experts may be assembled and asked to exchange views and come up with a group estimate (group discussion method). Or they may be asked to supply their estimates individually, and the analyst combines them into a single estimate (pooling of individual estimates). Or they may supply individual estimates and assumptions that are reviewed by a company analyst, revised, and followed by further rounds of estimation (Delphi method).[6]

Market-Test Method Where buyers do not plan their purchases carefully or are very erratic in carrying out their intentions, or where experts are not very good guessers, a direct market test is desirable. A direct market test is especially desirable in forecasting the sales of a new product or of an established product in a new channel of distribution or territory. (Market testing is discussed in Chapter 12.)

Time-Series Analysis Many firms prepare their forecasts on the basis of past sales. The assumption is that past data capture causal relations that can be uncovered through statistical analysis. These causal relations can be used to predict future sales. A time series of a product's past sales (Y) can be separated into four major components.

The first component, *trend* (T), is the long-term, underlying pattern of growth or decline in sales resulting from basic developments in population, capital formation, and technology. It is found by fitting a straight or curved line through past sales.

The second component, *cycle* (C), captures the intermediate-term, wavelike movement of sales resulting from changes in general economic and competitive activity. The cyclical component can be useful for intermediate-range forecasting. Cyclical swings, however, are difficult to predict because they do not occur on a regular basis.

The third component, *season* (S), refers to a consistent pattern of sales movements within the year. The term "season" describes any recurrent hourly, weekly, monthly, or quarterly sales pattern. The seasonal component may be related to weather factors, holidays, and trade customs. The seasonal pattern provides a norm for forecasting short-range sales.

The fourth component, *erratic events* (E), includes strikes, blizzards, fads, riots, fires, war scares, and other disturbances. These erratic components are by definition unpredictable and should be removed from past data to see the more normal behavior of sales.

Time-series analysis consists of decomposing the original sales series (Y) into the components, T, C, S, and E. Then these components are recombined to produce the sales forecast. Here is an example:

An insurance company sold 12,000 new ordinary life insurance policies this year. It would like to predict next year's December sales. The long-term trend shows a 5 percent sales growth rate per year. This alone suggests sales next year of 12,600 (= 12,000 × 1.05). However, a business recession is expected next year and will probably result in total sales achieving only 90 percent of the expected trend-adjusted sales. Sales next year will more likely be 11,340 (= 12,600 × .90). If sales were the same each month, monthly sales would be 945 (= 11,340/12). However, December is an above-average month for insurance policy sales, with a seasonal index standing at 1.30. Therefore December sales may be as high as 1,228.5 (= 945 × 1.3). No erratic events, such as strikes or new insurance regulations, are expected. Therefore the best estimate of new policy sales next December is 1,228.5.

Leading Indicators Many companies try to forecast their sales by finding one or more *leading indicators*—namely, other time series that change in the same direction but in advance of company sales. For example, a plumbing supply company might find that its sales lag the housing starts index by about four months. The housing starts index would then be a useful leading indicator. The National Bureau of Economic Research has identified twelve of the best leading indicators, and their values are published monthly in the *Survey of Current Business.*[7]

Statistical Demand Analysis Time-series analysis treats past and future sales as a function of time, rather than of any real demand factors. Numerous real factors affect the sales of any product. **Statistical demand analysis** is *a set of statistical procedures designed to discover the most important real factors affecting sales and their relative influence.* The factors most commonly analyzed are prices, income, population, and promotion.

Statistical demand analysis consists of expressing sales (Q) as a dependent variable and trying to explain sales as a function of a number of independent demand variables $X_1, X_2, \ldots, X_n$; that is,

$$Q = f(X_1, X_2, \ldots, X_n) \tag{9-3}$$

Using a technique called multiple-regression analysis, various equation forms can be statistically fitted to the data in the search for the best predicting factors and equation.[8]

As an illustration, a soft-drink company found that the per capita sales of soft drinks by state was well explained by[9]

$$Q = -145.5 + 6.46X_1 - 2.37X_2 \tag{9-4}$$

where

X_1 = *mean annual temperature of the state (farenheit)*
X_1 = *annual per capita income in the state (in hundreds)*

For example, New Jersey had a mean annual temperature of 54 and an annual per capita income of 24 (in hundreds). Using Equation (9-4), we would predict per capita soft-drink consumption in New Jersey to be

$$Q = -145.5 + 6.46(54) - 2.37(24) = 146.6$$

Actual per capita consumption was 143. To the extent that this equation predicted this well for other states, it would serve as a useful forecasting tool. Marketing management would predict next year's mean temperature and per capita income for each state and use Equation (9-4) to predict next year's sales.

■ Summary

To carry out their responsibilities, marketing managers need measures of current and future market size. We define *market* as the set of actual and potential consumers of a market offer. Being in the market means having interest, income, and access to the market offer. The marketer's task is to distinguish various levels of the market being investigated, such as the potential market, available market, qualified available market, served market, and penetrated market.

One task is to estimate current demand. Total demand can be estimated through the chain ratio method, which involves multiplying a base number by successive percentages. Area market demand can be estimated by the market-buildup method or the market-factor index method. Actual industry sales require identifying the relevant competitors and using some method of estimating the sales of each. Finally, companies are interested in estimating the market shares of competitors to judge their relative performance.

For estimating future demand, the company can use seven possible forecasting methods: buyers' intentions surveys, composite of salesforce opinions, expert opinion, market tests, time-series analysis, leading indicators, and statistical demand analysis. These methods vary in their appropriateness with the purpose of the forecast, the type of product, and the availability and reliability of data.

■ Questions for Discussion

1. The market for home-entertainment electronic equipment has grown tremendously in the past few years. What effect do you think this has had on the demand for LP records?

2. Sales of Izod-Lacoste apparel with the alligator emblem were $15 million in 1969. By 1981 sales were approximately $450 million. How could Lacoste, in 1969, know what extent of growth to anticipate when forecasting sales for a long-range strategic plan covering ten to fifteen years.

3. You are marketing manager for Cat's Pride cat litter and you notice that after years of relatively stable sales, the sales of this product have increased by 50 percent during the past year. How would you now forecast sales for the coming year?

4. Describe the difference between the *potential market, available market, target market,* and *penetrated market* for a Rolls Royce Silver Spirit.

5. List some expansible and nonexpansible markets. Can you think of any markets that may have been previously considered nonexpansible but have expanded? What caused the unexpected expansion to occur?

6. Discuss two market- and sales-forecasting techniques Wilson might use for a new line of tennis rackets.

7. Relate the concepts of market potential and company demand to Miller Lite beer.

8. What are the two major methods for estimating current company demand? Which one do you think a clothing manufacturer should use?

■ References

1. Based on "RCA's Slipped Disc," *Fortune,* April 30, 1984, pp. 7–8; "RCA's Biggest Gamble Ever," *Business Week,* March 9, 1981, pp. 79–80; "The Anatomy of RCA's Videodisc Failure," *Business Week,* April 23, 1984, pp. 89–90; and "Sales of RCA Videodisc System Fail to Live Up to Expectations," *Chicago Tribune,* January 15, 1982.

2. For more on using this survey, see "Putting the Four to Work," *Sales and Marketing Management,* October 28, 1974, pp. 13ff; for other examples of how firms use the buying power index, see RICHARD KERN, "Sharper Planning Puts Marketers Ahead of Change," *Sales and Marketing Management,* July 25, 1983, pp. A7–A14.

3. See "How Good Are Consumer Pollsters?" *Business Week,* November 9, 1969, pp. 108–10.

4. Adapted from *Forecasting Sales,* Business Policy Study No. 106 (New York: National Conference Board, 1963).

5. However, see Jacob Gonik, "Tie Salesmen's Bonuses to Their Forecasts," *Harvard Business Review,* May–June 1978, pp. 116–23.

6. See Kip D. Cassino, "Delphi Method: A Practical 'Crystal Ball' for Researchers," *Marketing News,* January 6, 1984, Section 2, pp. 10–11.

7. Geoffrey H. Moore and Julius Shiskin, *Indictors of Business Expansions and Contractions* (New York: Columbia University Press, Occasional Paper 103, 1967).

8. See Gilbert A. Churchill, *Marketing Research: Methodological Foundations* (Hinsdale, IL: Dryden Press, 1983), chap. 15.

9. See "The DuPort Company," in *Marketing Research: Text and Cases* (3rd ed.), Harper W. Boyd, Jr., Ralph Westfall, and Stanley Stasch, eds. (Homewood, IL: Irwin, 1977), pp. 498–500.

The Family of Quality Brands from Procter & Gamble

Soaps, Cleaners and Fabric Softeners

Laundry and Dishwashing Products

Paper and Personal Hygiene Products

Foods

Beverages

Beauty Care Products

Health and Personal Care Products

10
Market Segmentation, Targeting, and Positioning

Procter & Gamble makes ten different brands of laundry detergent—Tide, Cheer, Gain, Dash, Bold 3, Dreft, Ivory Snow, Oxydol, Era, and Solo. It also sells seven brands of hand soap (Zest, Coast, Ivory, Safeguard, Camay, Lava, and Kirk's Castile), three shampoos (Prell, Head & Shoulders, and Pert), three liquid dishwashing detergents (Joy, Ivory, and Dawn), and two brands each of toothpaste (Crest and Gleam), deodorant (Secret and Sure), coffee (Folger's and High Point), cooking oil (Crisco and Puritan), fabric softener (Downy and Bounce), floor cleaner (Spic & Span and Mr. Clean), and disposable diapers (Pampers and Luvs). Thus P&G brands compete with one another on the supermarket shelf. But why would P&G introduce several brands in one category instead of concentrating its resources on a single leading brand?

The answer lies in the fact that different people want different mixes of benefits from the products they buy. Take laundry detergents as an example. People use laundry detergents to get their clothes clean. But they also want other things from their detergents—things such as economy, bleaching power, fabric softening, fresh smell, strength or mildness, and lots of suds. We all want *some* of each of these benefits from our detergent, but we may have different priorities for each benefit. To some people, cleaning and bleaching power are most important; to others, fabric softening is most important; still others want a mild, fresh-scented detergent. Thus, there are groups—or segments—of laundry detergent buyers, and each segment seeks a special combination of benefits.

Procter & Gamble has identified at least ten important laundry detergent segments, and it has developed a different brand designed to meet the special needs of each segment. The ten P&G brands are positioned for different segments, as follows:

- *Tide* is the "extra action," all-purpose detergent for extra-tough laundry jobs. It is a family detergent—"it gets out the dirt kids get into. Tide's in, dirt's out."

- *Cheer* is specially formulated for use in hot, warm, or cold water. It's "all tempa-Cheer."

- *Gain* was originally P&G's "enzyme" detergent, but was repositioned as the detergent with a lingering fragrance—"for laundry so clean it's bursting with freshness."

- *Dash* is P&G's concentrated powdered detergent with "three powerful dirt dissolvers." It also makes less suds, so it won't clog "today's automatic washing machines."

- *Bold 3* originally "powered out dirt." Now it's the detergent plus fabric softener. It "cleans, softens, and controls static."

- *Ivory Snow* is "Ninety-nine and forty-four one hundreds percent pure." It's the "mild, gentle soap for diapers and baby clothes."

- *Dreft* is also formulated for baby's diapers and clothes, and it contains borax, nature's natural sweetener.
- *Oxydol* contains bleach. It's for "sparkling whites, a full-power detergent with color-safe bleach."
- *Era* is P&G's concentrated liquid detergent. It contains proteins to clean more stains.
- *Solo* is positioned as a heavy-duty liquid detergent with a fabric softener. "The convenience

of a liquid plus a softer wash that doesn't cling."

By segmenting the market and having several different detergent brands, P&G has an attractive offering for consumers in all important preference groups. All P&G brands combined hold more than a 50 percent share of the laundry detergent market—much more than any single brand could obtain by itself.

Organizations which sell to consumer and industrial markets recognize that they cannot appeal to all buyers in those markets, or at least not to all buyers in the same way. The buyers are too numerous, widely scattered, and varied in requirements and buying practices. Different companies will be in better positions to serve particular segments of the market. Each company has to identify the most attractive parts of the market that it can serve effectively.

Sellers have not always practiced this philosophy. Their thinking passed through three stages:

- *Mass marketing.* In mass marketing, the seller mass-produces, mass-distributes, and mass-promotes one product to all buyers. At one time Coca-Cola produced only one drink for the whole market, hoping it would appeal to everyone. The argument for mass marketing is that it should lead to the lowest costs and prices and create the largest potential market.

- *Product-differentiated marketing.* Here the seller produces two or more products that exhibit different features, styles, quality, sizes, and so on. Today Coca-Cola produces several soft drinks packaged in different sizes and containers. They are designed to offer variety to buyers rather than appeal to different market segments.

- *Target marketing.* Here the seller distinguishes between market segments, selects one or more of these segments, and develops products and marketing mixes tailored to each segment. For example, Coca-Cola developed Tab to meet the needs of diet-conscious drinkers.

Today's companies are moving away from mass marketing and product-differentiated marketing toward target marketing. Target marketing helps sellers identify marketing opportunities better. The sellers can develop the right product for each target market. They can adjust their prices, distribution channels, and advertising to reach the target market efficiently. Instead of scattering their marketing effort ("shotgun" approach), they can focus it on the buyers who have the greater purchase interest ("rifle" approach).

Target marketing calls for three major steps (Figure 10-1). The first is **market segmentation,** dividing a market into distinct groups of buyers who might re-

FIGURE 10-1 *Steps in Market Segmentation, Targeting, and Positioning*

Market segmentation

1. Identify bases for segmenting the market

2. Develop profiles of resulting segments

Market targeting

3. Develop measures of segment attractiveness

4. Select the target segment(s)

Market positioning

5. Develop positioning for each target segment

6. Develop marketing mix for each target segment

quire separate products or marketing mixes. The company identifies different ways to segment the market and develops profiles of the resulting market segments. The second step is **market targeting,** evaluating each segment's attractiveness and selecting one or more of the market segments to enter. The third step is **market positioning,** formulating a competitive positioning for the product and a detailed marketing mix. This chapter will describe the principles of market segmentation, market selection, and market positioning.

MARKET SEGMENTATION

Markets consist of buyers, and buyers differ in one or more respects. They may differ in their wants, resources, geographical locations, buying attitudes, and buying practices. Any of these variables can be used to segment a market.

The General Approach to Segmenting a Market

Figure 10-2A shows a market of six buyers. Each buyer is potentially a separate market because of unique needs and wants. Ideally, a seller might design a separate marketing program for each buyer. For example, air-frame producers such as Boeing and McDonnell-Douglas face only a few buyers and treat them as separate

FIGURE 10-2
Different Segmentations of a Market

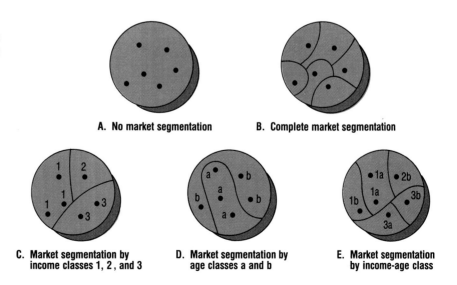

A. No market segmentation

B. Complete market segmentation

C. Market segmentation by income classes 1, 2, and 3

D. Market segmentation by age classes a and b

E. Market segmentation by income-age class

markets. This ultimate degree of market segmentation is illustrated in Figure 10-2B.

Most sellers will not find it worthwhile to "customize" their product to satisfy each specific buyer. Instead, the seller identifies broad classes of buyers who differ in their product requirements or marketing responses. For example, the seller may discover that income groups differ in their wants. In Figure 10-2C, a number (1, 2, or 3) is used to identify each buyer's income class. Lines are drawn around buyers in the same income class. Segmentation by income results in three segments, the most numerous segment being income class 1.

On the other hand, the seller may find pronounced differences between younger and older buyers. In Figure 10-2D, a letter (*a or b*) is used to indicate each buyer's age. Segmentation by age class results in two segments, each with three buyers.

Now income and age may both count heavily in influencing the buyer's behavior toward the product. In this case, the market can be divided into five segments: 1*a*, 1*b*, 2*b*, 3*a*, and 3*b*. Figure 10-2E shows that segment 1*a* contains two buyers and the other segments contain one buyer.

Using more characteristics to segment the market gives the seller finer precision, but at the price of multiplying the number of segments and thinning out the populations in each one.

Bases for Segmenting Consumer Markets There is no single way to segment a market. A marketer has to try different segmentation variables, singly and in combination, hoping to find an accurate way to view the market structure. Here we will examine the major geographic, demographic, psychographic, and behavior variables used in segmenting consumer markets (see Table 10-1).

Geographic Segmentation

Geographic segmentation calls for dividing the market into different geographical units such as nations, states, regions, counties, cities, or neighborhoods. The company decides to operate in one or a few geographical areas or to operate in all but pay attention to variations in geographical needs and preferences. For example, General Foods' Maxwell House ground coffee is sold nationally but is flavored regionally. People in the West prefer stronger coffee than people in the East.

Some companies even subdivide major cities into smaller geographical areas. R. J. Reynolds Company has subdivided Chicago into three distinct submarkets.[1] In the North Shore area, Reynolds promotes its low-tar brands because residents are better educated and more concerned about health. In the blue-collar Southeast area, Reynolds promotes Winston because this area is conservative. In the black South side, Reynolds promotes the high menthol content of Salem, using the black press and billboards heavily.

Demographic Segmentation

Demographic segmentation consists of dividing the market into groups on the basis of demographic variables such as age, sex, family size, family life cycle, income, occupation, education, religion, race, and nationality. Demographic varia-

TABLE 10-1

*Major Segmentation
Variables for Consumer
Markets*

VARIABLE	TYPICAL BREAKDOWNS
Geographic	
Region	Pacific, Mountain, West North Central, West South Central, East North Central, East South Central, South Atlantic, Middle Atlantic, New England
County size	A, B, C, D
City or MSA size	Under 5,000; 5,000–20,000; 20,000–50,000; 50,000–100,000; 100,000–250,000; 250,000–500,000; 500,000–1,000,000; 1,000,000–4,000,000; 4,000,000 or over
Density	Urban, suburban, rural
Climate	Northern, southern
Demographic	
Age	Under 6, 6–11, 12–19, 20–34, 35–49, 50–64, 65 +
Sex	Male, female
Family size	1–2, 3–4, 5 +
Family life cycle	Young, single; young, married, no children; young, married, youngest child under 6; young, married, youngest child 6 or over; older, married, with children; older, married, no children under 18; older, single; other
Income	Under $2,500; $2,500–$5,000; $5,000–$7,500; $7,500–$10,000; $10,000–$15,000; $15,000–$20,000; $20,000–$30,000; $30,000–$50,000; $50,000 and over
Occupation	Professional and technical; managers, officials, and proprietors; clerical, sales; craftsmen, foremen; operatives; farmers; retired; students; housewives; unemployed
Education	Grade school or less; some high school; high school graduate; some college; college graduate
Religion	Catholic, Protestant, Jewish, other
Race	White, black, oriental, Hispanic
Nationality	American, British, French, German, Scandinavian, Italian, Latin American, Middle Eastern, Japanese
Psychographic	
Social class	Lower lowers, upper lowers, lower middles, upper middles, lower uppers, upper uppers
Life style	Belongers, achievers, integrateds
Personality	Compulsive, gregarious, authoritarian, ambitious
Behavioristic	
Purchase occasion	Regular occasion, special occasion
Benefits sought	Quality, service, economy
User status	Nonuser, ex-user, potential user, first-time user, regular user
Usage rate	Light user, medium user, heavy user
Loyalty status	None, medium, strong, absolute
Readiness stage	Unaware, aware, informed, interested, desirous, intending to buy
Attitude toward product	Enthusiastic, positive, indifferent, negative, hostile

bles are the most popular bases for distinguishing customer groups. One reason is that consumer wants, preferences, and usage rates are often highly associated with demographic variables. Another is that demographic variables are easier to measure than most other types of variables. Even when the target market is described in nondemographic terms (say, a personality type), the link back to demographic characteristics is necessary in order to know the size of the target market and how to reach it efficiently.

Here we will illustrate how certain demographic variables have been applied to market segmentation.

AGE AND LIFE-CYCLE STAGE. Consumer wants and capacities change with age. Some companies offer different products or use different marketing approaches for different age and life-cycle segments. For example, Richardson-Vicks offers four variations of its Life Stage vitamins, each formulated for the special needs of specific age segments—chewable Children's Formula for children from 4 to 12 years old; Teens Formula for teenagers; and two adult versions (Men's Formula and Women's Formula). Johnson & Johnson developed Affinity Shampoo for women over 40 to counteract age-related hair changes.

Nevertheless, age and life cycle can be tricky variables. For example, the Ford Motor Company used buyers' age in developing its target market for its initial Mustang automobile; the car was designed to appeal to young people who wanted an inexpensive, sporty automobile. But Ford found that the car was being purchased by all age groups. It then realized that its target market was not the physically young but the psychologically young.

SEX. Sex segmentation has long been applied in clothing, hairdressing, cosmetics, and magazines. Occasionally other marketers will notice an opportunity for sex segmentation. The cigarette market provides an excellent example. Most cigarette brands are smoked by men and women alike. Increasingly, however, feminine brands like Eve and Virginia Slims have been introduced accompanied by appropriate flavor, packaging, and advertising cues to reinforce the female image. Today it is as unlikely to see men smoking Eve as it is to see women smoking Marlboros. Another industry that is beginning to recognize the potential for sex segmentation is the automobile industry. In the past, cars were designed to appeal to male and female family members. With more working women and women car owners, however, some manufacturers are studying the opportunity to design cars especially for women drivers.

INCOME. Income segmentation is another longstanding practice in such product and service categories as automobiles, boats, clothing, cosmetics, and travel. Other industries occasionally recognize its possibilities. For example, Suntory, the Japanese liquor company, introduced a scotch selling for $75 to attract drinkers who want the very best.

At the same time, income does not always predict the customers for a given product. One would think that manual workers would buy Chevrolets and managers would buy Cadillacs. Yet many Chevrolets are bought by managers (often as a second car), and some Cadillacs are bought by manual workers (such as high-paid plumbers and carpenters). Manual workers were among the first purchasers of color television sets; it was cheaper for them to buy these sets than go out to the movies and restaurants.

Coleman drew a distinction between the "underprivileged" segments and the "overprivileged" segments of *each* social class.[2] The most economical cars are not

If you think a woman's perspiration is the same as a man's...

This special pH paper shows that a woman's perspiration pH

(Simulated demonstration)
can actually be higher than a man's.

Notice the dramatic change in her paper.

And pH balanced Secret is made to accommodate a woman's chemistry, to help keep her dry all day.

...think again.

pH Balanced Secret.
Strong enough for a man...but made for a woman.

© 1984 Procter & Gamble Company

An example of sex segmentation; "Secret is made for a woman." *Courtesy of The Procter & Gamble Company.*

bought by the really poor, but rather by "those who think of themselves as poor relative to their status aspirations and to their needs for a certain level of clothing, furniture, and housing which they could not afford if they bought a more expensive car." On the other hand, medium-priced and expensive cars tend to be purchased by the overprivileged segments of each social class.

MULTIVARIABLE DEMOGRAPHIC SEGMENTATION. Most companies will segment a market by combining two or more demographic variables. The Charles Home for the

Blind (name disguised) serves the needs of blind persons for care, psychological counseling, and vocational training. However, it is not able to serve all types of blind people because of limited facilities. A multiple segmentation of blind persons is shown in Figure 10-3, where they are distinguished according to age, sex, and income. The Charles Home has chosen to serve low-income males of working age. It feels that it can do the best job for this group.

Psychographic Segmentation

In **psychographic segmentation,** buyers are divided into different groups on the basis of social class, life style, or personality characteristics. People within the same demographic group can exhibit very different psychographic profiles.

SOCIAL CLASS. We described the six American social classes in Chapter 6 and showed that social class has a strong influence on preferences in cars, clothes, home furnishings, leisure activities, reading habits, and retailers. Many companies design products or services for specific social classes, building in features that appeal to the target social class.

LIFE STYLE We saw in Chapter 6 that people's interest in various goods is influenced by their life styles and that the goods they consume express their life styles. Marketers of various products and brands are increasingly segmenting their markets by consumer life styles. For example, a manufacturer of men's blue jeans will want to design jeans for a specific male life style group: the "active achiever," the "self-indulgent pleasure seeker," the "traditional homebody," the "blue-collar outdoorsman," the "business leader," or the "successful traditionalist."[3] Each group would require different jean designs, prices, advertising copy, and outlets. Unless the company clarifies the primary life style group it is aiming at, its jeans may not appeal to any male life style group in particular.

Some researchers have identified life styles that are product-specific. Ruth Ziff identified the following product life styles that are specific to ethical drug users (percentage of each shown in parentheses):[4]

■ *Realists* (35 percent) are not health fatalists, nor excessively concerned with protection or germs. They view remedies positively, want something that is convenient and works, and do not feel the need for a doctor-recommended medicine.

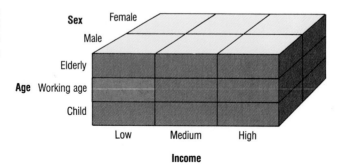

FIGURE 10-3
Segmentation of Blind Persons by Three Demographic Variables

- *Authority seekers* (31 percent) are doctor- and prescription-oriented, are neither fatalists nor stoics concerning health, but they prefer the stamp of authority on what they do take.

- *Skeptics* (23 percent) have a low health concern, are least likely to resort to medication, and are highly skeptical of cold remedies.

- *Hypochondriacs* (11 percent) have a high health concern, regard themselves as prone to any bug going around, and tend to take medication at the first symptom. They do not look for strength in what they take, but need some mild authority reassurance.

Drug firm marketing would be the most effective with hypochondriacs and the least effective with skeptics. If each life style group exhibits distinct demographic characteristics and media preferences, drug companies could do a better job of targeting.

PERSONALITY.   Marketers have also used personality variables to segment markets. They give their products *brand personalities* that correspond to *consumer personalities*. In the late fifties, Fords and Chevrolets were promoted as having different personalities. Ford buyers were thought to be "independent, impulsive, masculine, alert to change, and self-confident, while Chevrolet owners are conservative, thrifty, prestige-conscious, less masculine, and seeking to avoid extremes."[5] Evans investigated whether this was true by subjecting Ford and Chevrolet owners to the Edwards Personal Preference test, which measures needs for achievement, dominance, change, aggression, and so on. Except for slightly higher dominance scores, Ford owners' personalities were not significantly different from those of Chevy owners.

Other studies of a wide variety of products and brands, however, occasionally turn up personality differences. Shirley Young, the director of research for a leading advertising agency, reported developing successful market segmentation strategies based on personality traits in such product categories as women's cosmetics, cigarettes, insurance, and liquor.[6] Ackoff and Emshoff were able to identify four drinker-personality types (see Table 10-2) and help Anheuser-Busch develop specific messages and media exposure patterns to reach them.[7] Burnett found that blood donors are low in self-esteem, low risk takers, and more concerned about their health; nondonors tend to be the opposite on all these dimensions.[8] This suggests that social agencies should use different marketing approaches for retaining current donors and attracting new ones.

Behavior Segmentation

In **behavior segmentation,** buyers are divided into groups on the basis of their knowledge, attitude, use, or response to a product. Many marketers believe that behavior variables are the best starting point for constructing market segments.

OCCASIONS.   Buyers can be distinguished according to occasions when they get the idea, make a purchase, or use a product. For example, air travel is triggered by occasions related to business, vacation, or family. An airline can specialize in serv-

TABLE 10-2
Drinker-Personality
Segmentation

TYPE OF DRINKER	PERSONALITY TYPE	DRINKING PATTERN
Social drinker	Driven by his own needs, particularly to achieve, and attempts to manipulate others to get what he wants. Driven by a desire to get ahead. Usually a younger person.	Controlled drinker who may sometimes become high or drunk but is unlikely to be an alcoholic. Drinks primarily on weekends, holidays, and vacations, usually in a social setting with friends. Drinking is seen as a way to gain social acceptance.
Reparative drinker	Sensitive and responsive to the needs of others and adapts to their needs by sacrificing his own aspirations. Usually middle-aged.	Controlled drinker who infrequently becomes high or drunk. Drinks primarily at the end of the workday, usually with a few close friends. Views drinking as a reward for sacrifices made for others.
Oceanic drinker	Sensitive to the needs of others. Often a failure who blames himself for his nonachievement.	Drinks heavily, especially when under pressure to achieve. At times shows a lack of control over his drinking and is likely to become high, drunk, and even alcoholic. Drinking is a form of escape.
Indulgent drinker	Generally insensitive to others and places the blame for his failures on others' lack of sensitivity to him.	Like the oceanic drinker, he drinks heavily, often becomes high, drunk, or alcoholic. Drinks as a form of escape.

Source: Adapted from Russell L. Ackoff and James R. Emshoff, "Advertising Research at Anheuser-Busch, Inc. (1968–74)," *Sloan Management Review, 16, 3* (Spring 1975), pp. 1–15.

ing people for whom one of these occasions dominates. Thus charter airlines serve people whose vacation includes flying somewhere.

Occasion segmentation can help firms build up product usage. For example, orange juice is most commonly consumed at breakfast. An orange juice company can try to promote drinking orange juice at lunch or dinner. Certain holidays—Mother's Day and Father's Day for example—were promoted partly to increase the sale of candy and flowers. The Curtis Candy Company promoted the "trick-or-treat" custom at Halloween, with every home ready to dispense candy to eager little callers knocking at its door.

BENEFITS SOUGHT. A powerful form of segmentation is to classify buyers according to the different benefits that they seek from the product. Yankelovich applied benefit segmentation to the purchase of watches. He found that "approximately 23 percent of the buyers bought for lowest price, another 46 percent bought for durability and general product quality, and 31 percent bought watches as symbols of some important occasion."[9] The better-known watch companies at the time focused almost exclusively on the third segment by producing expensive watches, stressing prestige, and selling through jewelry stores. The U.S. Time Company

Occasion segmentation: Hallmark advertises gifts for Father's Day. *Courtesy of Hallmark Cards, Inc.*

decided to focus on the first two segments by creating Timex watches and selling them through mass merchandisers. Using this segmentation strategy, U.S. Time became the world's largest watch company.

Benefit segmentation requires determining the major benefits people look for in the product class, the kinds of people who look for each benefit, and the major brands that deliver each benefit. One of the most successful benefit segmentations was reported by Haley, who studied the toothpaste market (see Table 10-3). Haley's research uncovered four benefit segments: those seeking economy, protection, cosmetic, and taste benefits. Each benefit-seeking group had particular demographic, behavioristic, and psychographic characteristics. For example, decay pre-

TABLE 10-3
Benefit Segmentation of
the Toothpaste Market

BENEFIT SEGMENTS	DEMOGRAPHICS	BEHAVIOR	PSYCHOGRAPHICS	FAVORED BRANDS
Economy (low price)	Men	Heavy users	High autonomy, value oriented	Brands on sale
Medicinal (decay prevention)	Large families	Heavy users	Hypochondriac, conservative	Crest
Cosmetic (bright teeth)	Teens, young adults	Smokers	High sociability, active	Aqua-Fresh, Ultra Brite
Taste (good tasting)	Children	Spearmint lovers	High self-involvement, hedonistic	Colgate, Aim

Source: Adapted from Russell J. Haley, "Benefit Segmentation: A Decision Oriented Research Tool," *Journal of Marketing,* July 1963, pp. 30–35.

vention seekers had large families, were heavy toothpaste users, and were conservative. Each segment also favored certain brands. A toothpaste company can use these results to clarify which benefit segment it is appealing to, its characteristics, and the major competitive brands. The company can also search for a new benefit and launch a brand that delivers this benefit.[10]

USER STATUS. Many markets can be segmented into nonusers, ex-users, potential users, first-time users, and regular users of a product. High-market-share companies are particularly interested in attracting potential users, while smaller firms will try to attract regular users to their brand. Potential users and regular users require different kinds of marketing appeals.

Social marketing agencies pay close attention to user status. Drug rehabilitation agencies sponsor rehabilitation programs to help regular users quit the habit. They sponsor talks by ex-users to discourage young people from trying drugs.

USAGE RATE. Markets can also be segmented into light-, medium-, and heavy-user groups (called volume segmentation). Heavy users are often a small percentage of the market but account for a high percentage of total consumption. Some data on usage rates for popular consumer products are shown in Figure 10-4. Using beer as an example, the chart shows that 68 percent of the panel members did not drink beer. The 32 percent who did were divided into two groups. The lower 16 percent were light users and accounted for only 12 percent of total beer consumption. The heavy half accounted for 88 percent of the total consumption—over seven times as much consumption as the light users. Clearly a beer company would prefer to attract one heavy user to its brand over several light users. Most beer companies target the heavy beer drinker, using appeals such as Schaefer's "One beer to have when you're having more than one."

The heavy users of a product often have common demographics, psychographics, and media habits. In the case of heavy beer drinkers, their profile shows that more of them are in the working class compared with light beer drinkers and that they fall between the ages of 25 and 50 (instead of under 25 and over 50), watch television more than three and one-half hours per day (instead of under two

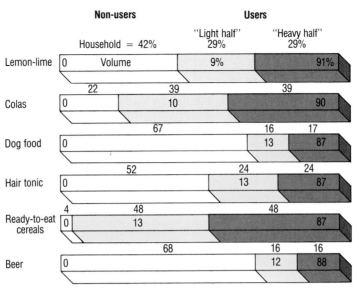

FIGURE 10-4
Annual Purchase Concentration in Several Product Categories

Source: Dik Warren Twedt, "How Important to Marketing Strategy Is the 'Heavy User'?" *Journal of Marketing,* January 1964, p. 72.

hours), and prefer to watch sports programs.[11] Profiles like this assist the marketer in developing price, message, and media strategies.

Social marketing agencies often face a heavy-user dilemma. A family planning agency would normally target families who would have the most children, but these families are also the most resistant to birth control messages. The National Safety Council would target unsafe drivers, but these drivers are the most resistant to safe-driving appeals. The agencies must consider whether to go after a few high-resistant heavy offenders or many less-resistant light offenders.

Loyalty status. A market can also be segmented by consumer loyalty patterns. Consumers can be loyal to brands (Tide), stores (Sears), and companies (Ford). We will deal here with brand loyalty. Suppose there are five brands: A, B, C, D, and E. Buyers can be divided into four groups according to their loyalty status:[12]

- *Hard-core loyals.* Consumers who buy one brand all the time. Thus a buying pattern of A,A,A,A,A,A represents a consumer with undivided loyalty to brand A.
- *Soft-core loyals.* Consumers who are loyal to two or three brands. The buying pattern A,A,B,B,A,B, represents a consumer with a divided loyalty between A and B.
- *Shifting loyals.* Consumers who shift from favoring one brand to another. The buying pattern A,A,A,B,B,B would suggest a consumer who is shifting brand loyalty from A to B.
- *Switchers.* Consumers who show no loyalty to any brand. The buying pattern A,C,E,B,D,B would suggest a nonloyal consumer who is either *deal-prone* (buys the brand on sale) or *variety-prone* (wants something different).

Each market is made up of different numbers of the four types of buyers. A brand-loyal market is one with a high percentage of buyers showing hard-core brand loyalty—the toothpaste market and the beer market seem to be fairly high brand-loyal markets. Companies selling in a brand-loyal market have a hard time gaining more market share, and companies trying to enter such a market have a hard time getting in.

A company can learn a great deal by analyzing loyalty patterns in its market. It should study the characteristics of its own hard-core loyals. Colgate finds that its hard-core loyals are more middle class, have larger-size families, and are more health conscious. This pinpoints the target market for Colgate.

By studying its soft-core loyals, the company can pinpoint which brands are most competitive with its own. If many Colgate buyers also buy Crest, Colgate can attempt to improve its positioning against Crest, possibly by using direct comparison advertising.

By looking at customers who are shifting away from its brand, the company can learn about its marketing weaknesses. As for nonloyals, the company can attract them by putting its brand on sale.

The company should be aware that what appear to be brand-loyal purchase patterns may reflect *habit, indifference,* a *low price,* or the *nonavailability* of other brands. The concept of brand loyalty has some ambiguities and must be used carefully.

BUYER READINESS STAGE. At any time, people are in different stages of readiness to buy a product. Some people are unaware of the product; some are aware; some are informed; some are interested; some are desirous; and some intend to buy. The relative numbers make a big difference in designing the marketing program. Suppose a health agency wants women to take an annual Pap test to detect cervical cancer. At the beginning, most women are unaware of the Pap test. The marketing effort should go into high-awareness-building advertising using a simple message. If successful, the advertising should then dramatize the benefits of the Pap test and the risks of not taking it, in order to move more women into the stage of desire. Facilities should be readied for handling the large number of women who may be motivated to take the examination. In general, the marketing program must be adjusted to the changing distribution of buyer readiness.

ATTITUDE. People in a market can be classified by their degree of enthusiasm for the product. Five attitude classes can be distinguished: enthusiastic, positive, indifferent, negative, and hostile. Door-to-door workers in a political campaign use the voter's attitude to determine how much time to spend with the voter. They thank enthusiastic voters and remind them to vote; they spend no time trying to change the attitudes of negative and hostile voters. They reinforce those who are positively disposed and try to win the vote of the indifferent voters. To the extent that attitudes are correlated with demographic descriptors, the organization can increase its efficiency in reaching the best prospects.[13]

Bases for Segmenting Industrial Markets Industrial markets can be segmented with many of the same variables used in consumer market segmentation. Industrial buyers can be segmented geographically and by several behavior variables: benefits sought, user status, usage rate, loyalty status, readiness stage, and attitudes.

A common way to segment industrial markets is by *end users*. Different end users often seek different benefits and can be approached with different marketing mixes. Consider the transistor market:

The market for transistors consists of three submarkets: military, industrial, and commercial.

The military buyer attaches great importance to the product's quality and availability. Firms selling transistors to the military market must make a considerable investment in R&D, use sales representatives who know military buying procedures, and specialize in limited-line products.

Industrial buyers, such as computer manufacturers, look for high quality and good service. Price is not critical unless it becomes exorbitant. In this market, transistor manufacturers make a modest investment in R&D, use sales representatives who have technical product knowledge, and offer a broad line.

Commercial buyers, such as pocket-radio manufacturers, buy their component largely on price and delivery. Transistor manufacturers selling in this market need little or no R&D effort, use aggressive sales representatives who are nontechnical, and offer the most common lines that can be mass-produced.

Customer size is another industrial segmentation variable. Many companies set up separate systems for dealing with major and minor customers. For example, Steelcase, a major manufacturer of office furniture, divides its customers into two groups:

- *Major accounts.* Accounts such as IBM, Prudential, and Standard Oil are handled by national account managers working with field district managers.
- *Dealer accounts.* Smaller accounts are handled by field sales personnel working with franchised dealers who sell Steelcase products.

Industrial companies typically define their target market opportunities by applying several segmentation variables. This is illustrated in Figure 10-5 for an aluminum company:[14]

The aluminum company first undertook *macrosegmentation,* consisting of three steps.[15] It looked at which end-use market to serve: automobile, residential, or beverage containers. Choosing the residential market, it determined the most attractive product application: semifinished material, building components, or aluminum mobile homes. Deciding to focus on building components, it next considered the best customer size to serve, and chose large customers.

The second stage consisted of *microsegmentation* within the large customer building components market. The company saw customers falling into three groups—those who bought on price, service, and quality. Because the aluminum company had a high service profile, it decided to concentrate on the service-motivated segment of the market.

Requirements for Effective Segmentation

Clearly, there are many ways to segment a market. Not all segmentations, however, are effective. For example, buyers of table salt could be divided into blond and brunette customers. But hair color is not relevant to the purchase of salt. Furthermore, if all salt buyers buy the same amount of salt each month, believe all salt is

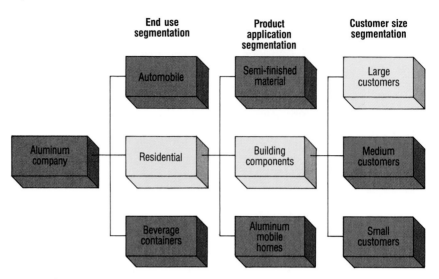

the same, and want to pay the same price, this market would be minimally segment-able from a marketing point of view.

To be useful, market segments must exhibit the following characteristics:

■ *Measurability,* the degree to which the size and purchasing power of the segments can be measured. Certain segmentation variables are difficult to measure. An illustration would be the size of the segment of teenage smokers who smoke primarily to rebel against their parents.

■ *Accessibility,* the degree to which the segments can be effectively reached and served. Suppose a perfume company finds that heavy users of its brand are single women who are out late at night and frequent bars. Unless this group lives or shops at certain places and is exposed to certain media, they will be difficult to reach.

■ *Substantiality,* the degree to which the segments are large or profitable enough. A segment should be the largest possible homogeneous group worth going after with a tailored marketing program. It would not pay, for example, for an automobile manu-facturer to develop cars for persons whose height is less than four feet.

■ *Actionability,* the degree to which effective programs can be formulated for attracting and serving the segments. A small airline, for example, identified seven market seg-ments, but its staff was too small to develop separate marketing programs for each segment.

MARKET TARGETING

Marketing segmentation reveals the market segment opportunities facing the firm. The firm now has to decide on (1) how many segments to cover and (2) how to identify the best segments. We will look at each decision in turn.

The firm can adopt one of three market-coverage strategies, known as undifferentiated marketing, differentiated marketing, and concentrated marketing. These strategies are illustrated in Figure 10-6 and discussed below.

Undifferentiated Marketing

The firm might decide to ignore market segment differences and go after the whole market with one market offer.[16] It focuses on what is common in the needs of consumers rather than on what is different. It designs a product and a marketing program that will appeal to the broadest number of buyers. It relies on mass distribution and mass advertising. It aims to endow the product with a superior image in people's minds. An example of undifferentiated marketing is the Hershey Company's marketing some years ago of only one chocolate candy bar for everyone.

Undifferentiated marketing is defended on the grounds of cost economies. It is seen as "the marketing counterpart to standardization and mass production in manufacturing."[17] The narrow product line keeps down production, inventory, and transportation costs. The undifferentiated advertising program keeps down adver-

FIGURE 10-6
Three Alternative Market Coverage Strategies

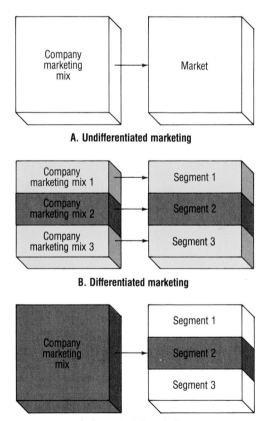

A. Undifferentiated marketing

B. Differentiated marketing

C. Concentrated marketing

tising costs. The absence of segment marketing research and planning lowers the costs of marketing research and product management.

Nevertheless, a growing number of marketers have expressed strong doubts about this strategy. Gardner and Levy, while acknowledging that "some brands have very skillfully built up reputations of being suitable for a wide variety of people," noted:

> In most areas audience groupings will differ, if only because there are deviants who refuse to consume the same way other people do. . . . It is not easy for a brand to appeal to stable lower middle-class people and at the same time to be interesting to sophisticated, intellectual upper middle-class buyers. . . . It is rarely possible for a product or brand to be all things to all people.[18]

The firm practicing undifferentiated marketing typically develops an offer aimed at the largest segments in the market. When several firms do this, the result is intense competition for the largest segments and undersatisfaction of the smaller ones. Thus the American auto industry for a long time produced only large automobiles. The result is that the larger segments may be less profitable because they attract disproportionately heavy competition. Kuehn and Day have called this the "majority fallacy."[19] The recognition of this fallacy has resulted in firms' being more interested in the smaller segments of the market.

Differentiated Marketing

Here the firm decides to operate in several segments of the market and designs separate offers to each. General Motors tries to produce a car for every "purse, purpose, and personality." By offering product and marketing variations, it hopes to attain higher sales and a deeper position within each market segment. It hopes that obtaining a deep position in several segments will strengthen consumers' overall identification of the company with the product category. Furthermore, it hopes for greater repeat purchasing because the firms' offer matches the customer's desire rather than the other way around.

A growing number of firms have adopted differentiated marketing. Here is an excellent example.[20]

> Edison Brothers operates nine hundred shoe stores that fall into four different chain categories, each appealing to a different market segment. Chandler's sells higher-priced shoes. Baker's sells moderate-priced shoes. Burt's sells shoes for budget shoppers, and Wild Pair is oriented to the shopper who wants very stylized shoes. Within three blocks on State Street in Chicago are found Burt's, Chandler's, and Baker's. Putting the stores near each other does not hurt them because they are aimed at different segments of the women's shoe market. This strategy has made Edison Brothers the country's largest retailer of women's shoes.

Differentiated marketing typically creates more total sales than undifferentiated marketing. "It is ordinarily demonstrable that total sales may be increased with a more diversified product line sold through more diversified channels."[21] However, it also increases the costs of doing business. The following costs are likely to be higher:

- *Product modification costs,* Modifying a product to meet different market segment requirements usually involves some R&D, engineering, or special tooling costs.
- *Production costs.* It is usually more expensive to produce, say, ten units of ten different products than one hundred units of one product. This is especially true the longer the production setup time for each product and the smaller the sales volume of each product. On the other hand, if each model is sold in sufficiently large volume, the higher costs of setup time may be quite small per unit.
- *Administrative costs.* The company has to develop separate marketing plans for the separate segments of the market. This requires extra marketing research, forecasting, sales analysis, promotion planning, and channel management.
- *Inventory costs.* It is generally more costly to manage inventories of differentiated products than an inventory of only one product. The extra costs arise because more records must be kept and more auditing must be done. Furthermore, each product must be carried at a level that reflects basic demand plus a safety factor to cover unexpected variations in demand. The sum of the safety stocks for several products will exceed the safety stock required for one product.
- *Promotion costs.* Differentiated marketing involves trying to reach different market segments with different advertising. This leads to lower usage rates of individual media and the loss of quantity discounts. Furthermore, since each segment may require separate creative advertising planning, promotion costs are increased.

Since differentiated marketing leads to higher sales and costs, nothing can be said in advance regarding the profitability of this strategy. Some firms find that they have *oversegmented* their market and offer too many brands. They would like to manage fewer brands, with each appealing to a broader customer group. Called "countersegmentation" or "broadening the base," they seek a larger volume for each brand.[22] Johnson & Johnson, for example, broadened its target market for its baby shampoo to include adults. And Beecham launched its AquaFresh toothpaste to attract two benefit segments, those seeking fresh breath and those seeking cavity protection.

Concentrated Marketing

Many firms see a third possibility that is especially appealing when company resources are limited. Instead of going after a small share of a large market, the firm goes after a large share of one or a few submarkets.

Several examples of concentrated marketing can be cited. Hewlett-Packard concentrated on the high-priced calculator market, Richard D. Irwin on the economics and business texts market, and Saab on the luxury sports car market (see Exhibit 10-1). Through concentrated marketing the firm achieves a strong market position in the segments it serves, owing to its greater knowledge of the segments' needs and the special reputation it acquires. Furthermore, it enjoys many operating economies because of specialization in production, distribution, and promotion. If the segment is chosen well, the firm can earn a high rate of return on its investment.

At the same time, concentrated marketing involves higher than normal risks. The particular market segment can turn sour; for example, when young women suddenly stopped buying sportswear, it caused Bobbie Brooks's earnings to go deeply into the red. Or a competitor may decide to enter the same segment. For these reasons, many companies prefer to diversify in several market segments.

EXHIBIT 10-1

SAAB FINDS A MARKET NICHE

Is there room for small fry along side the big fish in the auto industry? Saab thinks so. And so do thousands of consumers. Saab isn't afraid to compete in a market dominated by giants such as GM and Toyota—because it has chosen to compete on its own terms. Using a concentrated market-coverage strategy, Saab has found a profitable niche in the car market.

During World War II Saab made fighter planes. After the war, the company directed its aerospace engineers to design a small, inexpensive, fun-to-drive car, and they responded with an automobile which had many of the things pilots demand from airplanes—aerodynamic design, driver comfort, precise controls, and advanced safety features. The first Saab had surprisingly advanced features, many of which would not appear on other cars for another twenty years—a transverse engine with front-wheel drive, four-wheel disc brakes, rack-and-pinion steering, independent suspension, and flow-through ventilation.

Until the late 1970s, Saab was a moderately priced "Swedish Tinkertoy" with annual U.S. sales of about 10,000 cars. Saab became known as an "engineer's car," and Saab buyers consisted mostly of engineers, college professors, and road-rally buffs. Then in the late 1970s, Saab executives sought a segmentation strategy that would expand sales and profits. They had two major options in the compact-car market—the large economy segment or the smaller luxury segment. The major U.S. and Japanese automakers were aggressively attacking the economy segment, and Saab management estimated that it would have to sell 250,000 cars a year in that segment to turn a profit. Saab had neither the production capacity nor the distribution system needed to compete in such a mass market, so management opted to concentrate on the luxury/sports car segment, where it would sell fewer cars but make more profit on each one.

The upscale luxury/sports car segment is small but potentially profitable and much less competitive than other car buying segments. And it's a segment that will explode during this decade. It consists of upscale consumers aged 25 to 44, the fastest-growing age group. By 1990 this group will account for more than 45 percent of all households. And they will be the most affluent, with 62 percent of the 35 to 44 age group consisting of two-income families. Buyers in this segment demand a lot—high quality, performance, service,comfort—but they are willing and able to pay for what they get.

The luxury/sport segment is a particularly attractive target for Saab. The company's strengths fit very well with the market's needs. The segment is small and demands performance and quality. Saab has small capacity, prides itself on the quality of its production process, and has a solid reputation for advanced engineering. Upscale buyers in the segment can afford to buy the kind of car Saab makes best.

So beginning in 1979 the company introduced its new Saab 900 Turbo line (priced up to $20,000) as "the most intelligent car ever built" and targeted customers who were "willing to pay more for distinctive autos with performance, luxury, styling, and pure image." It backed this position with other things buyers in this segment were looking for. Upscale buyers want creature comforts—the Saab 900 Turbo comes with air conditioning, power disc brakes, AM/FM stereo cassette player, full instrumentation, power steering, tinted glass, window defoggers, electrically heated seats, and many other features as standard equipment. Sports car buyers want performance information—in the showroom, Saab distributes a 50-page "Engineering Features" book that explains every nuance of the car. Affluent buyers want service—salespeople are required to introduce every Saab buyer to the service manager, and dealers are given incentives to make certain each Saab is well "prepped" before delivery. Buyers receive mail questionnaires after delivery asking about dealer sales and service performance.

How did the new targeting strategy work? Saab appears to have hit the target. The average buyer of a new Saab is male, age 30 to 40, and well-educated (40 percent have attended graduate school). They are managers and professionals with average household incomes between $50,000 and $80,000. And they are loyal—over 75 percent intend to buy another Saab when the time comes. Since the new segmentation strategy began, sales have risen steadily. By 1983, the company was selling more than 25,000 Saabs annually in the United States, and demand outstripped supply (some dealers were auctioning Saabs off to the highest bidder). Saab's 42 percent increase in sales in 1983 was the best in the industry.

This Saab story has a happy ending—it shows how a company with less resources can succeed profitably against larger competitors by concentrating on a small, high-quality segment. Saab's competitive strategy is summed up by one Saab executive as follows: "GM is in the business of selling millions of hamburgers. We're just selling a few steaks here and there."

Source, Based on information found in Bernie Whalen, "'Tiny' Saab Drives Up Profits with Market-Niche Strategy, Repositioning," *Marketing News,* March 16, 1984, Sec. 1, pp. 14–16. Used with permission of *Marketing News,* published by the American Marketing Association. Also see "SAAB Hitches Star to Yuppie Market," *Business Week,* November 19, 1984, p. 62.

Choosing a Market-Coverage Strategy

The following factors need to be considered in choosing a market-coverage strategy:[23]

- *Company resources.* When the firm's resources are limited, concentrated marketing makes the most sense.
- *Product homogeneity.* Undifferentiated marketing is more suited for homogeneous products such as grapefruit or steel. Products that are capable of design variation, such as cameras and automobiles, are more suited to differentiation or concentration.
- *Product stage in the life cycle.* When a firm introduces a new product, it is practical to launch only one version, and undifferentiated marketing or concentrated marketing makes the most sense. In the mature stage of the product life cycle, differentiated marketing starts making more sense.
- *Market homogeneity.* If buyers have the same tastes, buy the same amounts per period, and react the same way to marketing stimuli, a strategy of undifferentiated marketing is appropriate.
- *Competitive marketing strategies.* When competitors practice active segmentation, undifferentiated marketing can be suicidal. Conversely, when competitors practice undifferentiated marketing, a firm can gain by pursuing differentiated or concentrated marketing.

Identifying Attractive Market Segments

Suppose the firm uses the preceding criteria for choosing a market-coverage strategy and decides on concentrated marketing. It must now identify the most attractive segment to enter. Consider the following situation:

A successful manufacturer of snow removal equipment is looking for a new product. Management reviews several opportunities and lands on the idea of producing snowmobiles. Management recognizes that it could manufacture any of three product types: gasoline, diesel, or electric. And it can design a snowmobile for any of three markets: consumer, industrial, or military. The nine product/

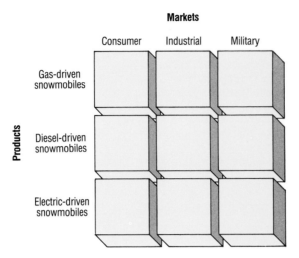

FIGURE 10-7
Product/Market Grid for Snowmobiles

Markets

Consumer   Industrial   Military

Products

Gas-driven snowmobiles

Diesel-driven snowmobiles

Electric-driven snowmobiles

market alternatives are shown in Figure 10-7. Assuming that the company wants to focus initially on a single segment, management has to decide on which one.

The company needs to collect data on the nine market segments—specifically, current dollar sales, projected sales-growth rates, estimated profit margins, competitive intensity, marketing channel requirements, and so on. The best segment would have large current sales, a high growth rate, a high profit margin, weak competition, and simple marketing channel requirements. Usually no segment would excel in all these dimensions, and tradeoffs would have to be made.

After the company identifies the more objectively attractive segments, it must ask which segments fit its business strengths best. For example, the military market may be highly attractive, but the company may have had no experience selling to the military. On the other hand, it may have distinctive competence when it comes to selling to the consumer market. Thus the company seeks a segment that is attractive in itself and for which it has the necessary business strengths to succeed. It wants to target the segments in which it has the greatest strategic advantage.

MARKET POSITIONING

Once a company has decided which segments of the market it will enter, it must decide what "positions" it wants to occupy in those segments. A product's **position** is the way the product is *defined by consumers* on important attributes—the place the product occupies in consumers' minds relative to competing products. Thus Tide is positioned as an all-purpose, family detergent; Era is positioned as a concentrated liquid; Cheer is positioned as the detergent for all temperatures. Datsun and Toyota are positioned on economy; Mercedes and Cadillac are positioned on luxury.[24]

Consumers are overloaded with information about products and services. They cannot reevaluate products every time they make a buying decision. To simplify buying decision making, they organize products into categories—they "position" products, services, and companies in their minds. A product's position is a complex set of consumer perceptions, impressions, and feelings consumers hold for the product compared with competing products. Consumers position products with or without the assistance of marketers. But marketers do not want to leave their products' positions to chance. They plan positions that will give their products the greatest competitive advantage in selected target markets, and they design marketing mixes to establish the planned positions.

The marketer can follow several positioning strategies.[25] It can position its product on specific *product attributes* (Datsun advertises its low price; Saab features technical and performance attributes). Alternatively, products can be positioned on the needs they fill or the *benefits* they offer (Crest reduces cavities; Aim tastes good). Or products can be positioned according to *usage occasions*. In the summer, Gatorade can be positioned as a beverage for replacing athletes' body fluids; in the winter, it can be positioned as the beverage to use when the doctor recommends drinking plenty of liquids. Another approach is to position the product for certain classes of *users*. Johnson & Johnson improved the market share for its baby shampoo from 3 to 14 percent by repositioning the product as one for adults who wash their hair often and need a gentle shampoo.

A product can be positioned directly *against a competitor*. In its "dare to compare" campaign, Texas Instruments asked consumers to make side-by-side comparisons of its personal computer with the IBM PC. It attempted to position its product as easier to use and more versatile. In its famous "We're number two, so we try harder" campaign, Avis successfully positioned itself against larger Hertz. A product may also be positioned *away from competitors*—7-Up became the number-three soft drink when it was positioned as the "un-cola," the fresh and thirst-quenching alternative to Coke and Pepsi.

Finally, the product can be positioned with respect to different *product classes*. For example, some margarines are positioned against butter, others against cooking oils. Camay hand soap is positioned with bath oils rather than with soap. Marketers often use a combination of these positioning strategies. Thus Johnson & Johnson's Affinity shampoo is positioned as a hair conditioner for women over 40 (product class and user). Arm & Hammer baking soda has been successfully positioned as a deodorizer for refrigerators or garbage disposals (product class and usage situation).

To plan a position for a current or new product, a company must first undertake a competitive analysis to identify the existing positions of its own and competing products. Suppose our snowmobile manufacturer learns that snowmobile buyers in its target segment are primarily interested in two attributes: size and speed. Potential customers and dealers can be asked where they see competitors' snowmobiles along these dimensions. The findings are shown in the *product position map* in Figure 10-8. Competitor A is seen as producing small/fast snowmobiles; B, medium-size/medium-speed snowmobiles; C, small-to-medium-size/slow snowmo-

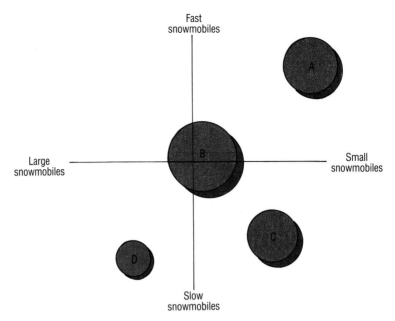

biles; and D, large/slow snowmobiles. The areas of the circles are proportional to the competitors' sales.[26]

Given these competitor positions, what position should the company seek? It has two choices. One is to position next to one of the existing competitors and fight for market share. The management might do this if it feels that (1) it can build a superior snowmobile, (2) the market is large enough for two competitors, (3) the company has more resources than the competitor, or (4) this position is the most consistent with the company's business strengths.

The other choice is to develop a snowmobile that is not currently being offered to this market, such as a large/fast snowmobile (see empty northwest quadrant of Figure 10-8). The company would win those customers seeking this type of snowmobile, since competitors are not offering it. But before making this decision, the management has to be sure that (1) it is technically feasible to build a large/fast snowmobile, (2) it is economically feasible to build a large/fast snowmobile at the planned price level, and (3) a sufficient number of buyers prefer a large/fast snowmobile. If the answers are all positive, the company has discovered a "hole" in the market and should move to fill it.

Suppose, however, management decides there is more profit potential and less risk in building a small/fast snowmobile to compete with competitor A. In this case, it would study A's snowmobile and seek a way to differentiate its offer in the eyes of potential buyers. It can develop its competitive positioning on product features, style, quality, price, and other dimensions.

Once management decides on its positioning strategy, it can turn to the task of developing its detailed marketing mix. If the company decides to take the high-price/high-quality position in this market segment, it must develop superior product features and quality, seek retailers who have an excellent reputation for service, develop advertising that appeals to affluent buyers, limit sales promotion to tasteful presentations, and so on.

The company's positioning decisions determine who its competitors will be. When setting its positioning strategy, the company should assess its competitive strengths and weaknesses relative to those of potential competitors, and select a position in which it can attain a strong competitive advantage. We will look more closely at competitive marketing strategies in Chapter 20.

■ Summary

Sellers can take three approaches to a market. *Mass marketing* is the decision to mass-produce and mass-distribute one product and attempt to attract all kinds of buyers. *Product differentiation* is the decision to produce two or more market offers differentiated in style, features, quality, sizes, and so on, designed to offer variety to the market and distinguish the seller's products from competitor's products. *Target marketing* is the decision to distinguish the different groups that make up a market and to develop appropriate products and marketing mixes for selected target markets. Sellers today are moving away from mass marketing and product differentiation toward target marketing because the latter is more helpful in spotting market opportunities and developing more effective products and marketing mixes.

The key steps in target marketing are market segmentation, market targeting, and market positioning. Market segmentation is the act of dividing a market into distinct groups of buyers who might merit separate products or marketing mixes. The marketer tries different variables to see which reveal the best segmentation opportunities. For consumer marketing, the major segmentation variables are geographic, demographic, psychographic, and behavioral. Industrial markets can be segmented by end use, customer size, geographic location, and product application. The effectiveness of the segmentation analysis depends upon arriving at segments that are measurable, accessible, substantial, and actionable.

Next, the seller has to target the best market segment(s). The first decision is how many segments to cover. The seller can ignore segment differences (undifferentiated marketing), develop different market offers for several segments (differentiated marketing), or go after one or a few market segments (concentrated marketing). Much depends on company resources, product and market homogeneity, product life-cycle stage, and competitive marketing strategies.

If the company decides to enter one segment, which one should it be? Market segments can be evaluated on their intrinsic attractiveness and on company business strengths needed to succeed in that market segment.

Market selection, then, defines the company's competitors and positioning possibilities. The company researches the competitors' positions and decides whether to take a position similar to that of some competitor or go after a hole in the market. If the company positions itself near another competitor, it must seek further differentiation through product features and price/quality differences. Its decision on positioning will then enable it to take the next step, planning the details of the marketing mix.

■ Questions for Discussion

1. When the Cadillac Cimarron was introduced, Cadillac officials said that even if they sold every car, they would consider the Cimarron a disaster if it had been sold only to traditional customers. The Cadillac merchandising director said: "Our salespeople will tell some buyers, 'This car isn't for you,'" Explain this sales rationale in terms of market segmentation.

2. What three stages do sellers move through in their approach to a market? Relate these to the Ford Motor Company.

3. After the market segmentation process has been completed, the organization should begin developing the marketing mix factors. Comment.

4. Besides age and sex, what other demographic segmentation variables are used by the brewery industry? Explain. Also, identify major benefit segments in the beer market.

5. If you were a manager of a mass transit company, how would you use benefit segmentation to appeal to potential riders?

6. Give specific examples of marketers who have been successful in segmenting their markets on each of the following bases: low price; high quality; and service.

7. Has Wendy's International hamburger chain met the requirements for effective segmentation? Why?

8. Differentiated marketing is always the best approach to target marketing. Comment.

9. If a clothing manufacturer were considering adding a new line of women's skirts for casual wear, how would it go about the market segmentation and target marketing process?

■ References

1. See "R. J. Reynolds Stops a Slide in Market Share," *Business Week,* January 26, 1976, p. 92.

2. RICHARD P. COLEMAN, "The Significance of Social Stratification in Selling," in *Marketing: A Maturing Discipline,* Martin L. Bell, ed. (Chicago: American Marketing Association, 1961), pp. 171–84.

3. JOSEPH T. PLUMMER, "Life Style Patterns: New Constraint for Mass Communications Research," *Journal of Broadcasting,* Winter 1971–72, pp. 79–89.

4. RUTH ZIFF, "Psychographics for Market Segmentation," *Journal of Advertising Research,* April 1971, p. 3–9.

5. Quoted in FRANKLIN B. EVANS, "Psychological and Objective Factors in the Prediction of Brand Choice; Ford versus Chevrolet," *Journal of Business,* October 1959, pp. 340–69.

6. SHIRLEY YOUNG, "The Dynamics of Measuring Unchange," in *Attitude Research in Transition,* Russell I. Haley, ed. (Chicago: American Marketing Association, 1972), pp. 61–82.

7. RUSSELL L. ACKOFF and JAMES R. EMSHOFF, "Advertising Research at Anheuser-Busch, Inc. (1968–74)," *Sloan Management Review,* Spring 1975, pp. 1–15.

8. JOHN J. BURNETT, "Psychographic and Demographic Characteristics of Blood Donors," *Journal of Consumer Research,* June 1981, pp. 62–66.

9. See DANIEL YANKELOVICH, "New Criteria for Market Segmentation," *Harvard Business Review,* March–April 1964, pp. 83–90, here p. 85.

10. For more reading on benefit segmentation, see RUSSELL I. HALEY, "Benefit Segmentation: Backwards and Forwards," *Journal of Advertising Research,* February–March 1984, pp. 19–25.

11. FRANK M. BASS, DOUGLAS J. TIGERT, and RONALD T. LONSDALE, "Market Segmentation: Group versus Individual Behavior," *Journal of Marketing Research,* August 1968, p. 276.

12. This classification was adapted from GEORGE H. BROWN, "Brand Loyalty—Fact or Fiction?" *Advertising Age,* June 1952–January 1953, a series.

13. For more on consumer segmentation variables, see RONALD FRANK, WILLIAM MASSEY, and YORAM WIND, *Marketing Segmentation* (Englewood Cliffs, NJ: Prentice-Hall, 1972); and YORAM WIND, "Issues and Advances in Segmentation Research," *Journal of Marketing Research,* August 1978, pp. 317–37.

14. The illustration is from E. RAYMOND COREY, "Key Options in Market Selection and Product Planning," *Harvard Business Review,* September–October 1975, pp. 119–28.

15. Wind and Cardozo suggest that industrial segmentation should proceed by first developing macrosegments and then microsegments. See YORAM WIND and RICHARD CARDOZO, "Industrial Market Segmentation," *Industrial Marketing Management,* 3(1974), 153–66.

16. See WENDELL R. SMITH, "Product Differentiation and Market Segmentation as Alternative Marketing Strategies," *Journal of Marketing,* July 1956, pp. 3–8; and ALAN A. ROBERTS, "Applying the Strategy of Market Segmentation," *Business Horizons,* Fall 1961, pp. 65–72.

17. SMITH, "Product Differentiation," p. 4.

18. BURLEIGH GARDNER and SIDNEY LEVY, "The Product and the Brand," *Harvard Business Review,* March–April 1955, p. 37.

19. ALFRED A. KUEHN and RALPH L. DAY, "Strategy of Product Quality," *Harvard Business Review,* November–December 1962, pp. 101–2.

20. NATALIE MCKELVY, "Shoes Make Edison Brothers a Big Name," *Chicago Tribune,* February 23, 1979, Sec. 5, p. 9.

21. ROBERTS, "Applying the Strategy of Market Segmentation," p. 66.

22. ALAN J. RESNIK, PETER B. B. TURNEY, and J. BARRY MASON, "Marketers Turn to 'Countersegmentation,'" *Harvard Business Review,* September–October 1979, pp. 100–6.

23. R. WILLIAM KOTRBA, "The Strategy Selection Chart," *Journal of Marketing,* July 1966, pp. 22–25.

24. For more reading on positioning, see YORUM WIND, "New Twists for Some Old Tricks," *The Wharton Magazine,* Spring 1980, pp. 34–39; and DAVID A. AAKER and J. GARY SHANSBY, "Positioning Your Product," *Business Horizons,* May–June 1982, pp. 56–62.

25. See WIND, "New Twists," p. 36; and AAKER and SHANSBY, "Positioning Your Product," pp. 57–58.

26. These maps must be interpreted with care. Not all customers share the same perceptions. The map shows the average perceptions. Attention should also be paid to the scatter of perceptions.

CASE 5

RCA: VIDEOCASSETTE PLAYERS

RCA, a leader in consumer electronics and home entertainment equipment, has a leading position in the sale of videocassette recorder (VCR) hardware and prerecorded VCR tapes. The company faces the question of whether it should market a videocassette player (VCP) in addition to its VCR line. General Electric Company, as well as Japanese and Korean companies, plan to sell VCPs in the United States for as little as $200.

The VCR is one of the electronic success stories of recent years. Nearly 20 percent of U.S. homes now have one, and the number is growing rapidly. But apparently there are some potential buyers who do not want the elaborate recording equipment that comes with the standard VCR. The "play only" market consists of (1) homes with no interest in recording, (2) VCR homes where a second set is wanted for "play only," (3) the rental market retail outlets that sell and rent equipment and tapes for overnight use, and (4) the industrial market for training and related purposes.

A major problem for consumers is the availability of incompatible formats, the principal ones being VHS and Beta. RCA uses the VHS format. Sony's BetaMax, once the leader, seems to be losing ground. Now, Kodak and others are bringing out still another format in their new smaller-width tape, which is 8mm versus the conventional ½ inch. This is an effort to develop a system with a camera, which will be better suited for home movies to be shown on a TV screen.

The one-set market consists of those who believe the play and record machines have more functions than they need. Also included are those who feel the VCR is too expensive, even though the price difference over the VCP may be as low as $150.

The second-set market could be huge, according to General Electric's VCR product manager. Reasoning by analogy, he suggests that since 50 percent of color-TV-owning households have at least one other color TV, VCP buying would follow the same patterns. He visualizes less expensive VCP units attached to TVs in bedrooms and children's rooms in addition to the VCR play and record machine already in the house.

Rental companies constitute a natural market. At present they mount their VCRs in holders so that borrowers cannot damage the devices in an attempt to record. Currently rental outlets buy only about 5 percent of VCRs sold, but that is growing fast. If present overnight rates, $10 or less, are continued, a higher profit margin would result from the rental of the lower-cost VCP. "Eighty percent of our customer's don't want the bells and whistles. They just want the playback unit," says William E. Mapes, president of National Video, Inc., a video sales and rental chain based in Portland, Oregon. The chain plans to have Japanese play-only units selling for $200 or less available in its stores in early 1985.

The commercial and industrial market is dominated by the laser-type videodisc players of Magnavox and Pioneer because of their higher fidelity and freeze-frame features, despite a considerably higher price. However, there may be marginal commercial and industrial uses for a VCP using less sophisticated technology and having lower-quality performance or fewer features.

RCA's SelectaVision videodisc player, using the CED or tongue-and-groove technology, had limited acceptance in the industrial market relative to the laser-type players. In the consumer market, RCA's SelectaVision videodisc players did not meet the company's sales expectations, causing it to be withdrawn and production stopped after selling over 500,000 players and investing over $580 million. The player sold for about $400.

Following RCA's announcement of discontinuance, the price dropped and units could be bought for as low as $99 at retail. The company stated it would continue to produce videodiscs for perhaps three years; about 10.9 million discs had been produced previously. Among the reasons given by analysts for the poor sales performance of RCA's videodisc player were: (1) high price relative to its features and functions and (2) scarcity of software. Had RCA continued production of its videodisc player, it would have had to compete with the new videocassette player (VCP).

Industry sources say that to obtain sales, VCP will probably have to be priced at least $200 below VCRs, which now sell for as little as $350. Private-label products and Sony's BetaMax have been aggressively promoting on a price basis. Price comparisons, however, are difficult to make because of the wide range of features available and the reputation and service support of the manufacturer and/or retailer of the product. The videodisc experience has caused RCA to be cautious about entering the VCP market. When competitors announced their VCP plans, RCA said it had no plans to enter.

One observer suggested that "In the end, it may well turn out that RCA had the right idea [play-only machine]—just the wrong product [videodisc]. And by introducing a VCP line, RCA would cut into VCR sales."

Should RCA market a VCP in addition to its existing line of VCRs? If so, what are your recommendations regarding a marketing plan for VCR players and RCA's role in software?

CASE 6

HENRY F. ORTLIEB BREWING COMPANY

An affable, well-dressed man walked into a restaurant one evening recently and ordered a bottle of Ortlieb's beer, a local brand. "I'm sorry," the waitress said. "We don't have any Ortlieb's."

"Then give me a bottle of birch beer," replied Joseph Ortlieb, owner of Henry F. Ortlieb Brewing Co., a small concern that has been making beer in Philadelphia since 1869. Mr. Ortlieb says that when dinner arrived, he swallowed his pride and "ordered a draft of Miller's."

As this incident suggests, life is sometimes frustrating for a small brewer, especially when giant national competitors, such as Anheuser-Busch Inc. and Miller Brewing Co., and large regional brewers have successfully established themselves in his own backyard. And the disappointments range, of course, beyond not being able to buy a bottle of his own beer. They include such far more serious setbacks as the loss of customers to slick, well-financed national and regional advertising campaigns.

"When you're an ant in a battle of elephants," one small brewer says, "you're going to get stomped on." "The years are numbered for small plants," says another, J. M. Magenau, Jr., who closed his ailing Erie, Pa., brewery in March after deciding he couldn't match the big companies' costly advertising programs.

Ferment in the Industry

Joe Ortlieb agrees that "we don't have the dollars like they (the big brewers) do." But we would rather fight than fold. And he is doing so with some success. Henry F. Ortlieb Brewing returned to profitability last year after sustaining losses from 1973 through 1976. And in May of this year the company's total production rose sharply, to 44,000 barrels from 31,300 a year earlier. The 49-year-old Mr. Ortlieb is jubilant about that figure—"more beer, I think, than we ever put out before," he says.

But no one denies that these are less than heady times for small breweries. Since 1960, about 125 of them have perished. Today, although there are still 45 brewing companies in business in this country, the industry is controlled by a handful of giants.

In 1960, total production of the five industry leaders at that time represented about 33% of all U.S. beer shipments. By 1968, that figure had increased to about 47%, and by last year, the figure for the current top five had risen to more than 70%. Some analysts believe that the battle for dominance may now be between the big two—Anheuser-Busch and the Miller Brewing unit of Phillip Morris, Inc.—as they slug it out with national advertising campaigns, new products, and increased capacity.

What Ortlieb Faces

In this area, Ortlieb faces competition from four of the top five national brands. In addition, Ortlieb battles for the hearts and throats of Philadelphians with two of the country's biggest regional brewers—F. & M. Schaefer Corp., which leads in sales in Philadelphia, and C. Schmidt & Sons, Inc. Two other firms—Carling National Breweries, Inc. and Genesee Brewing Co.—are also strong here.

Tiny Henry F. Ortlieb is at the bottom of the barrel. "Ortlieb is small enough in volume that they don't appear in any of our charts," a major beer distributor here says.

Still, Joe Ortlieb says that "things look good for us." His sales of 331,000 barrels last year may be tiny compared with Anheuser-Busch's national total of 36.6 million, but they represent a 2.7% rise for Ortlieb. And in the first five months of this year, Ortlieb's output rose to 164,000 barrels, up 25.8% from a year earlier.

Indeed, Mr. Ortlieb, a grandson of founder Trupert Ortlieb, has been moving with confidence since he became sole owner of the company two years ago. Mr. Ortlieb, whose title is president, has assembled a new management team, including a brewmaster recruited from Rheingold Breweries Inc. and a new sales manager from Schmidt & Sons, Philadelphia's other, and much larger, brewery. He also has begun modernizing and expanding his aging plant, the newest section of which was built in 1948.

"Willingness to Take Chances"

Beyond that, Mr. Ortlieb has begun a modest advertising campaign to remind Philadelphians that his little brewery is still afloat. He has also computerized the company's financial operations and added a new product, McSorley's ale.

"Joe seems willing to take chances," says Ross Heuer, editor of Brewers Digest, a trade journal. "There are probably a dozen small breweries that are resisting (the trend), and Ortlieb is one of the primary examples.

One factor that enables Ortlieb to resist is its loyal following in this area, at least among older quaffers. Charlie Lawn, a 55-year-old Philadelphia cab driver, says he has been drinking Ortlieb's for 30 years and doesn't intend to switch. A beer distributor here asserts that in Philadelphia's working-class neighborhoods, "there are pockets where Ortlieb's is so strong, nobody else can sell."

Mr. Ortlieb says that "people are amazing. The brand loyalty they've developed is just outstanding." Ortlieb's traditionally has been a strong seller within "the shadow of the smokestack." he says. His advertising, he adds, plays up the fact that "we're a local beer hoping for local support."

Joe Ortlieb is much involved in that advertising campaign. He stars in his own radio and television commercials, and in one TV spot, acknowledging that Ortlieb can be a difficult name to remember, he encouraged people to ask for "Joe's beer." Mr. Heuer, the Brewers Digest editor, calls Mr. Ortlieb's advertising "very imaginative" and adds that "the public knows he's a working brewery president—he's not an ivory-tower man."

Mr. Ortlieb spent a record $250,000 on advertising last year. This year he will spend about 25% less, he says, conceding that he can't compete with "the tremendous advertising that's carried on by the national breweries," such as Anheuser-Busch (its major brand is Budweiser) and Miller. Their advertising "just inundates the consumer," he says.

As a result of that advertising, beer distributors and retailers here say young drinkers prefer the national or regional brands to Ortlieb's hometown brew. Regular customers tend to be "the old-time drinkers who have been drinking Ortlieb's for 30 years," says Carmen Schick, manager of a local distributor.

So, believing the older drinker to be more price-conscious, Ortlieb retails a case of its standard canned beer for about $5.75, underpricing most major national brands by $1.20 to $1.40 a case. At the same time, Ortlieb is aiming its ad campaign at a "younger group," the men in their late 20s to late 40s, who drink the most beer, says Haven Babb, an account executive at Schaefer Advertising, Inc., a King of Prussia, Pa., agency that handles Mr. Ortlieb's advertising.

As for the under-25 drinker, Mr. Ortlieb sees him as "fickle," faddishly hopping from one highly promoted brand to another. However, the small brewer isn't forsaking that market, either. Last fall it acquired highly regarded McSorley's ale. "We think this will lead us to the youth market," Mr. Ortlieb says. He plans to test-market McSorley's along the south Jersey shore because "You get a lot of kids down there in the summer."

The Fight with Schaefer

Despite the local loyalty, the advertising campaign, and Mr. Ortlieb's personal involvement, Ortlieb's share of the market has declined over the years. Joseph Farrell, the company's sales manager, says the firm's share of beer sales in Philadelphia County has shrunk to about 11% from an estimated 15% to 16% five years ago. It has fallen even more in suburban regions, declining to an estimated 2% in one nearby county, he adds. Moreover, while the company's overall beer sales rose last year, its mainstay Ortlieb brand, on the skids for several years, slipped another 13% to 152,587 barrels, Mr. Farrell says.

But the sales manager insists that Ortlieb's major brand will rebound this year. One reason is that Ortlieb hopes to siphon business from Schaefer, the New York-based regional brewer that is No. 1 in the Philadelphia market. Mr. Farrell believes that Schaefer, an old foe that invaded Ortlieb territory in the mid-1960s, isn't competing as aggressively as it once did.

The contrast between the two companies could hardly be sharper. Schaefer's two breweries produced 4.6 million barrels of beer last year—14 times more than Ortlieb did at its only plant. Schaefer regards its Lehigh Valley plant, about 60 miles northwest of here, as "the most efficient" in the East.

The little Ortlieb brewery, actually a collection of old brick buildings dating back to the 19th Century, is in a deteriorated industrial section of Philadelphia. The plant's annual capacity is 500,000 barrels, and until recently it could operate at only 70% of capacity.

Still, the Ortlieb people assert that their old plant produces a better beer. At Schaefer, William J. Schoen, president, says that Ortlieb makes "a good product" but that the two brewers produce different types of beer.

Sprucing up the Plant

Mr. Ortlieb has been sprucing up his plant ever since he bought out his relatives in early 1976. Antiquated wood tubs, which were used to grow yeast (a plant that causes fermentation), have been replaced with shiny metal tanks. In the brewhouse, "we've started to automate," says Joseph Johnston, the spirited brewmaster who came from Rheingold. Beer production has increased, Mr. Ortlieb says, and "we waste less water."

Ortlieb officials report that the company has spent $800,000 on capital projects in the past two years and may spend an additional $1 million this year. "We're now making plans for a five-year program, all departments, to increase capacity by at least 25%," Mr. Johnston says.

He adds that Mr. Ortlieb frequently participates in the daily tasting sessions at which the brewmaster and his assistants sample beer that has been aged from six to eight weeks. If the clarity, odor and taste are deemed satisfactory, the brews are packaged the next day. "Beer tasting is an art," says Mr. Ortlieb, taking a mouthful of one of his brands.

He describes the main Ortlieb brand as having a "more full-bodied flavor" and as being a maltier, heavier brew with a slightly darker color than the national premium brands. "We decided to give our beer a different character than Bud or Schlitz," he explains, although the industry trend is away from heavier beers.

Is this difference an advantage to Ortlieb? "I'm not really sure," Mr. Ortlieb says. "Sometimes I think it might help us. Sometimes I think it might hurt us."

Low-Calorie Beers

Aware that the big brewers have successfully marketed low-calorie beers, Ortlieb has its own light beer "on the drawing board," the official says, adding that it may be introduced this year. Mr. Ortlieb says he previously tried to develop a beer with an extremely low calorie content (about a calorie per ounce, against regular beer's 12 or so per ounce). But the experimental brew had a "terrible" taste, and "I wouldn't dare sell it," he says.

Joe Ortlieb knows what his customers want. Because he often visits local taverns, "his marketing research is mostly firsthand," says Mr. Heuer, the Brewers Digest editor. When his company does something that Ortlieb consumers either like or dislike, Joe Ortlieb "will hear it directly from the man at the bar," Mr. Heuer adds.

Mr. Ortlieb is a shirt-sleeve executive who has worked at the brewery since his college days, beginning in the warehouse, where he loaded trucks. He studied business at Buckness University in Lewisburg, PA., and brewing at the United States Brewers Academy in Mount Vernon, N.Y. As head of the company, he has impressed subordinates as a hard worker who often spends Saturdays at the plant.

And that's the image he is trying to put across to the public, says Mr. Babb, the advertising man. "He's asking you to give (his product) a try because he's put his whole life into the brewery," Mr. Babb says.

Mr. Ortlieb is determined that his effort won't be in vain, despite the demise of so many other small beer firms. Jesting grimly, Mr. Ortlieb says that if enough others go down the drain, "someday I'll be the 10th-largest brewery in the nation."

Source: John L. Moore, "Squeezed by Nationals, A Local Brewery Keeps Its Head above Water," *Wall Street Journal,* July 10, 1978. Reprinted by permission of *The Wall Street Journal,* © Copyright Dow Jones & Company, Inc. 1978. All Rights Reserved.

1. Does Ortlieb Brewing Company have a market niche? If so, what is it and what is happening to it?

2. What could Ortlieb do to improve his *marketing* efforts?

3. What could Ortlieb do to improve his marketing *management* efforts?

4. Evaluate Joe Ortlieb's marketing research and marketing intelligence system.

5. How should Ortlieb react to a proposal that he join a group of small noncompeting breweries which would permit the use of selected common brand names on locally brewed beer to permit joint advertising or at least wider recognition for the jointly used brand names?

five

DEVELOPING THE MARKETING MIX

Part Five of this book describes the major decisions that companies make with respect to each marketing mix tool—product, price, place, and promotion.

11
Designing Products: Products, Brands, Packaging, and Services

Revlon each year sells more than $1 billion worth of cosmetics, toiletries, and fragrances to consumers around the world. Its many successful perfume products combine to make Revlon number one in the popular-price segment of the turbulent, highly fragmented, $300 billion fragrance market. In the strictest sense, Revlon's perfumes are no more than carefully formulated mixtures of natural oils and synthetic chemicals which produce pleasing scents. But Revlon knows that when it sells perfume, it sells much more than fragrant fluids—it sells what the fragrances will do for the women who use them.

Of course, a perfume's scent contributes to its success or failure. Fragrance marketers agree: "No smell; no sell." Perfumes are composed of "notes." There is a top note—the first fragrance to reach the nose. This top note soon gives way to more subtle middle and lower notes which may last for hours. In an average perfume, 80 to 90 different natural and synthetic ingredients produce the final composition. Most new aromas are developed by elite "perfumers"—highly paid experts who blend ingredients to produce unique and appealing scents—at one of 50 or so select "fragrance houses."

Perfume is shipped from the fragrance houses in big, ugly oil drums—hardly the stuff of which dreams are made! A $150-an-ounce perfume may cost no more than $3 to produce, but to perfume consumers the product is much more than a few dollars worth of tangible ingredients and a pleasing scent. As one fragrance industry expert asks, "Is fragrance really a product, or is its enduring appeal because it is the essence of passion built into the genes and senses of each of us?"

Many things beyond the ingredients and scent add to a perfume's allure. In fact, when Revlon designs a new perfume, the scent may be the last element developed. Revlon first researches women's attitudes and feelings about themselves and their relationships with others. It develops and tests new perfume concepts which better match women's changing values, desires, and life-styles. When Revlon finds a promising new concept, it creates a scent to fit the concept.

Revlon's marketing research in the early 1970s showed that women were feeling more competitive with men, and that they were striving to establish individual identities. For the new woman of the 1970s, Revlon created Charlie—the first of the "life-style" perfumes. Thousands of women adopted Charlie as a bold statement of independence, and it quickly became the world's best selling perfume. Charlie established a new trend in the fragrance market, and set off a flurry of me-too products which contributed to solid industry growth through the 1970s.

In the late 1970s, Revlon research indicated a shift in women's attitudes—". . . women had made the equality point, which Charlie addressed. Now women were hungering for an expression of femininity. They were ready to re-express themselves personally." Revlon subtly shifted Charlie away from its "life-style" position and toward one of "femininity and romance." It also successfully launched a new perfume, Jontue, positioned on a theme of romance.

A perfume's name is an important product attribute. Revlon uses such names as Charlie, Fleurs de Jontue, Ciara, and Scoundrel to create images that support each perfume's positioning. Competitors offer perfumes with such evocative names as Opium,

Joy, White Linen, Paloma Picasso, LeJardin, Youth Dew, and L'Air du Temps, which suggest that the perfumes will do more than just make you smell better. Oscar de la Renta's Ruffles perfume *began* as a name, chosen because it created images of whimsey, youth, glamour, and femininity—all well suited to the target market of young, stylish women. A scent was later selected to go with Ruffles' name and product positioning.

Revlon must also carefully package its perfumes. To consumers, the bottle and package are the most tangible symbol of the perfume and its image. Bottles must feel comfortable and be easy to handle, and they must display well in stores. Most importantly, they must be styled to support the perfume's product concept and image.

So when a woman buys perfume, she buys much, much more than a mixture of fragrant fluids. The perfume's image and personality, its promises, its scent, its name and package, the company that makes it, the stores that sell it—all become a part of the total perfume product. When Revlon sells perfume, it sells more than just the tangible product —it sells life-style, self-expression, and exclusivity; achievement, success, and status; femininity, romance, passion, and fantasy; memories, hopes, and dreams.[1]

Clearly, perfume is more than just perfume when Revlon sells it. Revlon's exceptional success in the rough-and-tumble fragrance world is based on developing an innovative product concept. Constructing an effective product concept is the first step in marketing mix planning.

The chapter begins with the question, What is a product? It turns out that "product" is a complex concept that has to be carefully defined. We will then look at ways to classify the multitude of products found in consumer and industrial markets, hoping to find links between appropriate marketing strategies and types of products. Next, we will recognize that each product can be turned into a brand, which involves several decisions. The product can also be packaged and labeled, and various customer services can be offered in addition. Finally, we will move from decisions about individual products to decisions the company must make in building its product lines and product mixes.

WHAT IS A PRODUCT?

A Wilson tennis racquet, a Vidal Sasoon haircut, a Rolling Stones concert, a Club Mediterranean vacation, a two-ton stake truck, Head skis, and a telephone answering service are all products. We define product as follows:

A **product** is anything that can be offered to a market for attention, acquisition, use, or consumption that might satisfy a want or need. It includes physical objects, services, persons, places, organizations, and ideas.

We also need to define product item:

A **product item** is a distinct unit that is distinguishable by size, price, appearance, or some other attribute. An item is sometimes called a stockkeeping unit or product variant.[2]

Core, Tangible, and Augmented Product

In developing a product, the product planner needs to think about the product on three levels. The most fundamental level is the *core product,* which answers the question, What is the buyer really buying? Every product is really the packaging of a problem-solving service. A woman buying lipstick buys more than lip color. Charles Revson of Revlon, Inc., recognized this early: "In the factory, we make cosmetics; in the store, we sell hope." Theodore Levitt pointed out that "purchasing agents do not buy quarter-inch drills; they buy quarter-inch holes." And supersalesman Elmer Wheeler would say, "Don't sell the steak—sell the sizzle." Marketers must uncover the needs hiding under every product and sell *benefits,* not *features.* The core product stands at the center of the total product, as illustrated in Figure 11-1.

The product planner has to turn the core product into a *tangible product.* Perfume, computers, educational seminars, and political candidates are all tangible products. Tangible products may have as many as five characteristics: *a quality level, features, styling, a brand name,* and *packaging.*

Finally, the product planner may offer additional services and benefits that make up *augmented product.* IBM's success is partly traceable to its skillful augmentation of its tangible product—the computer. While its competitors were busy selling computer features to buyers, IBM recognized that customers were more interested in solutions, not hardware. Customers wanted instruction, canned software programs, programming services, quick repairs, and guarantees. IBM sold a system, not just a computer.

Product augmentation leads the marketer to look at the buyer's total *consumption system:* "The way a purchaser of a product performs the total task of whatever it is that he or she is trying to accomplish when using the product."[3] In this way, the marketer will recognize many opportunities for augmenting its offer in a competitively effective way. According to Levitt:

FIGURE 11-1
Three Levels of Product

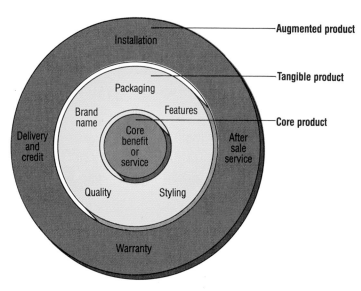

The *new* competition is not between what companies produce in their factories, but between what they add to their factory output in the form of packaging, services, advertising, customer advice, financing, delivery arrangements, warehousing, and other things that people value.[4]

Thus, broadly defined, a product is more than a simple set of tangible attributes. In fact, some products (a haircut or a doctor's examination) have no tangible features. Consumers perceive products as complex bundles of benefits that satisfy their needs. When developing products, marketers must first identify the core consumer needs the product will satisfy. They must then design the tangible product and search for ways to augment the product to create the bundle of benefits that will best satisfy consumer's desires.

PRODUCT CLASSIFICATION SCHEMES

In seeking marketing strategies for individual products, marketers have developed several product classification schemes based on product characteristics.

Durable Goods, Products can be classified into three groups according to their durability or tangi-
Nondurable Goods, bility:[5]
and Services

Nondurable goods. *Nondurable goods are tangible goods normally consumed in one or a few uses.* Examples include beer, soap, and salt. Since these goods are consumed fast and purchased frequently, the appropriate strategy is to make them available in many locations, charge only a small markup, and advertise heavily to induce trial and build preference.

Durable goods. *Durable goods are tangible goods that normally survive many uses.* Examples include refrigerators, machine tools, and clothing. Durable products normally require more personal selling and service, command a higher margin, and require more seller guarantees.

Services. *Services are activities, benefits, or satisfactions that are offered for sale.* Examples include haircuts and repairs. Services are intangible, inseparable, variable, and perishable. As a result, they normally require more quality control, supplier credibility, and adaptability. (Because of the growing importance of services in our society, their marketing will be examined in Chapter 23.)

Consumer Goods Consumer goods are those which are bought by final consumers for personal
Classification consumption. Marketers usually classify these goods on the basis of *consumer shopping habits* because the way consumers shop for products has direct implications for marketing strategy. We can distinguish among convenience, shopping, specialty, and unsought goods (see Figure 11-2A).[6]

Convenience goods. *Goods that the customer usually purchases frequently, immediately, and with the minimum of effort in comparison and buying.* Examples include tobacco products, soap, and newspapers.

Convenience goods can be further divided into staples, impulse goods, and emergency goods. *Staples* are goods that consumers purchase on a regular basis.

FIGURE 11-2
Classification of Consumer and Industrial Goods

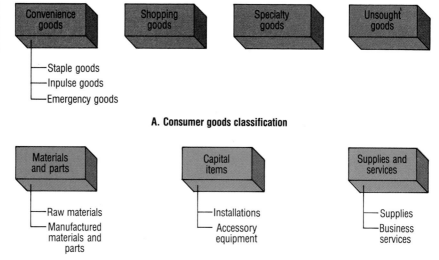

A. Consumer goods classification

B. Industrial goods classification

For example, one buyer might routinely purchase Heinz ketchup, Crest toothpaste, and Ritz crackers. *Impulse goods* are purchased without any planning or search effort. These goods are normally available in many places because consumers seldom look for them. Thus candy bars and magazines are placed next to checkout counters because shoppers may not have thought of buying them. *Emergency goods* are purchased when a need is urgent—umbrellas during a rainstorm, boots and shovels during the first winter snowstorm. Manufacturers of emergency goods will place them in many outlets to avoid losing the sale when the customer needs these goods.

> **Shopping goods.** *Goods that the customer, in the process of selection and purchase, characteristically compares on such bases as suitability, quality, price, and style.* Examples include furniture, clothing, used cars, and major appliances.

Shopping goods can be divided into homogeneous and heterogeneous goods. The buyer sees homogeneous shopping goods as being similar in quality but different enough in price to justify shopping comparisons. The seller has to "talk price" to the buyer. But in shopping for clothing, furniture, and more heterogeneous goods, product features are often more important to the consumer than the price. If the buyer wants a pin-striped suit, the cut, fit, and look are likely to be more important than small price differences. The seller of heterogeneous shopping goods must therefore carry a wide assortment to satisfy individual tastes and must have well-trained sales personnel to provide information and advice to customers.

> **Specialty goods.** *Goods with unique characteristics or brand identification for which a significant group of buyers is habitually willing to make a special purchase effort.* Examples include specific brands and types of fancy goods, cars, hi-fi components, photographic equipment, and men's suits.

A Mercedes, for example, is a specialty good because buyers are willing to travel a great distance to buy a Mercedes. Specialty goods do not involve the buyer's making comparisons; the buyer only invests time to reach the dealers carrying the wanted products. The dealers do not need convenient locations; however, they must let prospective buyers know their locations.

Unsought goods. *Goods that the consumer does not know about or knows about but does not normally think of buying.* New products such as smoke detectors and food processors are unsought goods until the consumer is made aware of them through advertising. The classic examples of known but unsought goods are life insurance, cemetery plots and gravestones, and encyclopedias.

By their very nature, unsought goods require a lot of marketing effort in the form of advertising and personal selling. Some of the most sophisticated personal selling techniques have developed out of the challenge of selling unsought goods.

Industrial Goods Classification

Industrial goods are those bought by individuals and organizations for further processing or for use in conducting a business. Thus the distinction between a consumer good and an industrial good is based on the purpose for which the product is purchased. A particular product might be a consumer or an industrial product depending on the buying situation. If a consumer buys a lawnmower for use around the home, the lawnmower is a consumer good. If the same consumer buys the same lawnmower for use in a landscaping business, the lawnmower is classified as an industrial good.

Industrial goods can be classified in terms of *how they enter the production process and their relative costliness.* We can distinguish three groups: materials and parts, capital items, and supplies and services (see Figure 11–2B).

Materials and parts. *Goods that enter the manufacturer's product completely.* They fall into two classes: raw materials and manufactured materials and parts.

Raw materials, in turn, fall into two major classes: *farm products* (wheat, cotton, livestock, fruits and vegetables) and *natural products* (fish, lumber, crude petroleum, iron ore). Each is marketed somewhat differently.

Farm products are supplied by many small producers who turn them over to marketing intermediaries who provide assembly, grading, storage, transportation, and selling services. Farm products are somewhat expandable in the long run, but not in the short run. Farm products' perishable and seasonal nature gives rise to special marketing practices. Their commodity character results in relatively little advertising and promotional activity, with some exceptions. From time to time, commodity groups will launch campaigns to promote the consumption of their product—such as potatoes, prunes, or milk. And some producers even brand their product—such as Sunkist oranges and Chiquita bananas.

Natural products are highly limited in supply. They usually have great bulk and low unit value and require substantial transportation in moving them from producer to user. There are fewer and larger producers, who tend to market them directly to industrial users. Because the users depend on these materials, long-term supply contracts are common. The homogeneity of natural materials limits the amount of demand creation activity. Price and delivery reliability are the major factors influencing the selection of suppliers.

Manufactured materials and parts include component materials (iron, yarn, cement, wires) and *component parts* (small motors, tires, castings). *Component materials* are usually processed further—for example, pig iron is made into steel and yarn is woven into cloth. The standardized nature of component materials usually means that price and supplier reliability are the most important purchase factors. *Component parts* enter the finished product completely with no further change in form, as when small motors are put into vacuum cleaners and tires are added on automobiles. Most manufactured materials and parts are sold directly to industrial users, with orders often placed a year or more in advance. Price and service are the major marketing considerations, and branding and advertising tend to be less important.

Capital items. *Goods that enter the finished product partly.* They include two groups: installations and accessory equipment.

Installations consist of *buildings* (factories, offices) and *fixed equipment* (generators, drill presses, computers, elevators). Installations are major purchases. They are usually bought directly from the producer, with the typical sale being preceded by a long negotiation period. The producers use a top-notch salesforce, which often includes sales engineers. The producers have to be willing to design to specification and to supply postsale services. Advertising is used but is much less important than personal selling.

Accessory equipment includes *portable factory equipment and tools* (hand tools, lift trucks) and *office equipment* (typewriters, desks). These types of equipment do not become part of the finished product. They simply aid in the production process. They have a shorter life than installations, but a longer life than operating supplies. Although some accessory equipment manufacturers sell direct, more often they use middlemen because the market is geographically dispersed, the buyers are numerous, and the orders are small. Quality, features, price, and service are major considerations in vendor selection. The salesforce tends to be more important than advertising, although advertising can be used effectively.

Supplies and services. *Items that do not enter the finished product at all.*

Supplies are of two kinds: *operating supplies* (lubricants, coal, typing paper, pencils) and *maintenance and repair items* (paint, nails, brooms). Supplies are the equivalent of convenience goods in the industrial field because they are usually purchased with a minimum effort on a straight rebuy basis. They are normally marketed through intermediaries because of the great number of customers, their geographical dispersion, and the low unit value of these goods. Price and service are important considerations because suppliers are quite standardized and brand preference is not high.

Business services include *maintenance and repair services* (window cleaning, typewriter repair) and *business advisory services* (legal, management consulting, advertising). Maintenance and repair services are usually supplied under contract.

Maintenance services are often provided by small producers, and repair services are often available from the manufacturers of the original equipment. Business advisory services are normally new task buying situations, and the industrial buyer will choose the supplier on the basis of the supplier's reputation and personnel.

Thus we see that a product's characteristics will have a major influence on marketing strategy. At the same time, marketing strategy will also depend on such factors as the product's stage in the life cycle, the number of competitors, the degree of market segmentation, and the condition of the economy.

BRAND DECISIONS

Consumers perceive a brand as an intrinsic part of the product, and branding can add value to the product. For example, most consumers would perceive a bottle of Chanel No. 5 as a high-quality, expensive perfume. But the same perfume presented in an unmarked bottle would be viewed as lower in quality even though the fragrance is identical. Thus branding decisions are an important aspect of product strategy.

First, we should become familiar with the language of branding. Here are some key definitions:[7]

Brand: A name, term, sign, symbol, or design, or a combination of them intended to identify the goods or services of one seller or group of sellers and to differentiate them from those of competitors.

Brand name: That part of a brand which can be vocalized—the utterable. Examples are Avon, Chevrolet, Disneyland, American Express, and UCLA.

Brand mark: That part of a brand which can be recognized but is not utterable, such as a symbol, design, or distinctive coloring or lettering. Examples are the Playboy bunny and the Metro-Goldwyn-Mayer lion.

Trademark: A brand or part of a brand that is given legal protection because it is capable of exclusive appropriation. A trademark protects the seller's exclusive rights to use the brand name and/or brand mark.

Copyright: The exclusive legal right to reproduce, publish, and sell the matter and form of a literary, musical, or artistic work.

Branding poses challenging decisions to the marketer. The key decisions are shown in Figure 11-3 and discussed below.

Branding Decision The company must first decide whether it should put a brand name on its product. Historically, most products went unbranded. Producers and middlemen sold their goods directly out of barrels, bins, and cases, without any supplier identification. The earliest signs of branding were in the efforts of medieval guilds to require craftsmen to put trademarks on their products to protect themselves and consumers against inferior quality. In the fine arts, too, branding began with artists signing their works.

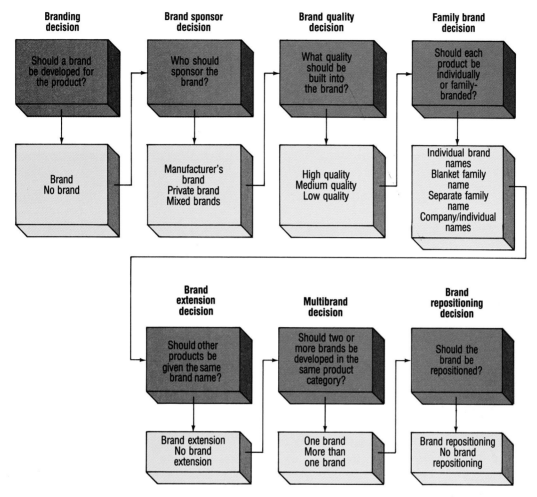

FIGURE 11-3 *An Overview of Branding Decisions*

In the United States the earliest brand promoters were the patent medicine makers. Branding's real growth occurred after the Civil War with the growth of national firms and national advertising media. Some of the early brands still survive, such as Borden's Condensed Milk, Quaker Oats, Vaseline, and Ivory Soap.

Branding has grown so strong that today hardly anything goes unbranded. Salt is packaged in distinctive manufacturers' containers, oranges are stamped with growers' names, common nuts and bolts are packaged in cellophane with a distributor's label, and automobile components—spark plugs, tires, filters—bear brand names that differ from those of the automakers. Even chicken has been branded successfully.[8]

Frank Perdue of Perdue Farms, Salisbury, Maryland, has converted a basic agricultural commodity into a branded product. Many consumers on the East Coast insist on a Perdue chicken. Perdue spends about $1 million annually on television and radio commercials where he touts the merits of his chickens. His theme is "It takes a tough man to make a tender chicken," and he offers a money-back guarantee to dissatisfied customers.

Recently there has been a return to "no branding" of certain staple consumer goods and pharmaceuticals. These "generics" are plainly packaged with no manufacturer identification (see Exhibit 11-1). The intent of generics is to bring down the cost to the consumer by saving on packaging and advertising. Thus the issue of branding versus no branding is very much alive today.

EXHIBIT 11-1

GENERICS: THE GROWTH OF "NO-BRAND, NO-FRILLS" PRODUCTS

In 1978 "generic" products began appearing on the shelves of U.S. drugstores and supermarkets, and sales of these products grew rapidly at the expense of national and store brands. Generics are unbranded, plainly packaged, less-expensive versions of common products purchased in supermarkets, such as spaghetti, paper towels, and canned peaches. They offer standard or lower quality at prices as much as 30 to 40 percent lower than national brands and 20 percent lower than store brands. The lower price is made possible by lower-quality ingredients, lower-cost packaging and labeling, and minimal advertising and promotion costs.

Generics took brand-name manufacturers by surprise. By 1982 nearly 80 percent of all supermarkets were selling generics, and consumers could purchase these no-brand products in three of every four product categories. Sales of generics reached $2.6 billion and accounted for over 11 percent of supermarket unit sales.

The price savings of generics have strong appeal to consumers, especially in hard economic times. And certain types of consumers are more attracted by generics than others. Demographic profiles of generic purchasers reveal larger households, middle or higher incomes, higher education levels, and an average age bracket of 35 to 45. Purchasers of generics have also been found to be less brand-loyal and more innovative.

Four out of five consumers believe that lower prices for generics result from reduced advertising and packaging costs. Though only one out of five consumers believes that generics cost less because of lower quality, product quality remains an important consideration in consumers' buying decisions. Generics have made greater inroads into product categories where consumers care less about quality or where they perceive little difference in quality between generics and national brands. Categories such as paper products, frozen foods, peanut butter, canned vegetables, plastic bags, disposable diapers, and dog food have been especially vulnerable to generics. Generics have had less success in categories such as health and beauty aids, where consumers are less willing to trade quality for price.

How far generics will penetrate the U.S. shopper's marketbasket is still an open question, but it appears that generics peaked in 1982. Since that time, the unit market share for generics has dropped to about 9 percent. This decline in share has resulted partly from an improved economy—consumers now have more discretionary income than they did when generics exploded in the late 1970s and early 1980s, and reduced inflation has helped to hold down the prices of national and store brands.

The decline of generics has also resulted from improved marketing strategies developed by brand-name manufacturers to counter the generics threat. These marketers have responded by emphasizing brand identification and quality. For example, when threatened by generic pet foods in 1982, Ralston-Purina increased its quality rather than reducing its price and targeted family pet owners who identified strongly with their pets and cared most about quality. Kraft countered the generic threat by using advertising showing taste tests in which children preferred the taste of Kraft macaroni and cheese to that of the generic brand.

Another strategy is to cut costs and pass the savings along to consumers in the form of lower prices and greater values. Or the brand-name manufacturer can introduce lower-quality, lower-priced products that compete more directly with generic products. Procter & Gamble, for example, introduced its line of Banner paper products. Though this line offered less quality than other P&G brands, when compared with generics it offered greater quality and a competitive price.

The brand-name marketers must convince consumers that their product's higher and more consistent quality is worth the extra cost. Branded products that provide a substantial quality difference will not be strongly threatened by generics. Those most threatened are weak national brands and lower-price store brands that offer little additional quality. Why pay 20 to 40 percent more for a branded item, when its quality is not noticeably different from that of its generic cousin?

Sources: "Generic Groceries Keep Adding Market Share," *Marketing News,* February 23, 1979, p. 16; "Buyers Mix Generics, Quality," *Advertising Age,* August 20, 1979, p. 3; Martha R. McEnally and Jon M. Hawes, "The Market for Generic Brand Grocery Products: A Review and Extension," *Journal of Marketing,* Winter 1984, pp. 75–83; and Jill Andresky Fraser, "Marketing: Generics Getting Back to Brands," *Madison Avenue,* February 1984, pp. 52–58.

This raises the questions: Why have branding in the first place? Who benefits? How do they benefit? At what cost? We have to look at branding from the buyer's viewpoint, the seller's viewpoint, and society's viewpoint.

Buyer's Viewpoint

Some buyers see branding as a device used by sellers to raise their prices. But most buyers want branding because it provides a number of benefits.

Brand names tell the buyer something about product quality. Suppose a buyer goes shopping for a television set and sees several different sets, none of them carrying brand names. The buyer could tell very little about the quality and reliability of the different sets. However, if they carried such names as Zenith, Sony, Sears, and Sanyo, they would conjure up different images of the probable quality and reliability. In the Soviet Union, where television sets are produced in different factories and not branded, Soviet consumers look for identification marks indicating which factories produced them because the factories have different reputations for reliability. Soviet consumers would welcome branding as an indicator of quality.

Brand names also increase the shopper's efficiency. Imagine the homemaker going into a supermarket and finding thousands of unlabeled products. The homemaker would probably want to touch, taste, or smell many of the products to be sure of their quality. If the homemaker asked another member of the family to do the shopping, she would have to communicate the quality desired in each product. It is far more efficient to communicate in brand names than in general product descriptions.

Finally, brand names help call consumers' attention to new products that might benefit them. They become the basis upon which a whole story can be built about the new product's distinctive qualities.

Familiar brands provide consumer information and recognition. *Courtesy of University of North Carolina Media Center.*

Seller's Viewpoint

But why should sellers resort to branding when it clearly involves a cost—packaging, labeling, legal protection—and a risk if the product should prove unsatisfying to the user? It turns out that branding gives the seller several advantages.

1. The brand name makes it easier for the seller to process orders and track down problems. Thus Anheuser-Busch receives an order for a hundred cases of Michelob eight-ounce beer instead of an order for "some of your better beer." Furthermore, the seller finds it easier to trace the order if it is misshipped or to find out why the beer was flat if consumers complain.

2. The seller's brand name and trademark provide legal protection of unique product features, which would otherwise be copied by competitors.

3. Branding gives the seller the opportunity to attract a loyal and profitable set of customers. Brand loyalty gives the seller some protection from competition and greater control in planning its marketing mix.

4. Branding helps the seller segment markets. Instead of P&G selling a simple detergent, it can offer ten detergent brands, each formulated somewhat differently and aimed at specific benefit-seeking segments.

5. Good brands help build the corporate image. By carrying the company's name, they help advertise the quality and size of the company.

Society's Viewpoint

Does branding benefit the society as a whole? How much branding is necessary or desirable in particular product categories? Those favoring branding offer the following arguments:

1. Branding leads to higher and more consistent product quality. A brand makes a promise to consumers about delivering certain satisfactions. The seller cannot easily tamper with the brand's quality or be careless about quality control because the consumers have certain expectations. Branding also makes it advantageous for some sellers to go after the high-quality end of the market.

2. Branding increases the rate of innovation in society. Branding gives producers an incentive to look for new features that could be protected against imitating competitors. Branding results in more product variety and choice for consumers.

3. Branding increases shopper efficiency, since it provides much more information about products and where to find them.

Others think branding is overdone. Their criticisms include the following:

1. Branding leads to false and unnecessary differentiation of goods, especially in homogeneous product categories.

2. Branding leads to higher consumer prices, since branding requires heavy advertising, packaging, and other costs which are ultimately passed on to consumers.

3. Branding increases the status consciousness of people who buy certain brands to "impress" others.

Overall, branding clearly adds net value to consumers and society, *and* it can also be overdone in some categories and lead to higher costs. The societal issues posed by branding will be examined in Chapter 24.

Brand Sponsor Decision   In deciding to brand a product, the manufacturer has three options with respect to brand sponsorship. The product may be launched as a *manufacturer's brand* (also called a national brand). Or the manufacturer may sell the product to middlemen who put on a *private brand* (also called middlemen brand, distributor brand, or dealer brand). Or the manufacturer may produce some output under its own brand names and some that is sold under private labels. Kellogg's, International Harvester, and IBM produce virtually all their output under their own brand names. Warwick Electronics produces virtually all its output under various distributors' names, such as Sears. Whirlpool produces output both under its own name and under distributor's names.

Manufacturers' brands tend to dominate the American scene. Consider such well-known brands as Campbell's soup and Heinz ketchup. While most manufacturers create their own brand names, some of them "rent" well-known brand names by paying a royalty for the use of the name (see Exhibit 11-2).

EXHIBIT 11-2

LICENSING BRAND NAMES ON A ROYALTY BASIS

A manufacturer or retailer may take years and spend millions to develop consumer preference for its brand. An alternative is to "rent" names that already hold magic for consumers. Names or symbols previously created by other manufacturers, the names of well-known celebrities, characters introduced in popular movies and books—for a fee, any of these can provide a manufacturer's product with an instant and proven brand name.

Name and character licensing has become a big business in recent years. Manufacturers pay out almost $1 billion annually for the right to use popular names and characters on their products, and these products generate almost $20 billion each year in retail sales.

Apparel and accessories sellers are the largest users of licensing. Producers and retailers pay sizable royalties to adorn their products with the names of such fashion innovators as Bill Blass, Calvin Klein, Pierre Cardin, Gucci, and Halston, who license their names or initials for items from blouses to ties and linens to luggage. Such arrangements can be expensive—in 1981 Pierre Cardin reaped a reported $50 million in royalties on products that generated about $1 billion in wholesale business for 540 licensees. In recent years, designer labels have become so common that many retailers are discarding them in favor of their own store brands in order to regain exclusivity, pricing freedom, and higher margins.

Sellers of children's toys, games, food, and other products also make extensive use of name and character licensing. The list of characters attached to children's clothing, toys, school supplies, linens, dolls, lunchboxes, cereals, and other items is almost endless—from such classics as Disney, Peanuts, and Flintstones characters to E.T., Gremlins, and the latest Star Wars heroes. From the venerable Raggedy Ann and Andy to Pac Man, the Smurfs, the Shirt Tales, and Cabbage Patch.

Licensed names or characters can add immediate distinction and familiarity to a new product, and can set it apart from competitor's products. Customers debating between two similar products will most likely reach for the one with a familiar name on it. In fact, consumers often seek out products that carry their favorite names or characters.

Almost everyone is getting into the licensing act these days, even Harley-Davidson, the motorcycle maker. Over the past 80 years, the Harley-Davidson name has developed a distinct image—some people even tattoo it on their bodies. And Harley-Davidson is now licensing its name for consumer products. One toy manufacturer is now marketing the Harley-Davidson Big Wheel tricycle, and Harley-Davidson is open to other products that meet appropriate standards of quality and taste—products ranging from chocolates to cologne.

Sources: Based on miscellaneous sources, including Kevin Higgins, "Marketers Embrace Licensing to Move Products Off Shelves," *Advertising Age,* October 15, 1982, pp. 1ff; "Why Designer Labels Are Fading," *Business Week,* February 21, 1983, pp. 70–75; and Carol Cain, "Licensed Characters Can Get Soggy Sales Fast," *Advertising Age,* September 27, 1984, pp. 34–36.

In recent times, however, large retailers and wholesalers have developed their own brands. The private-label tires of Sears and J. C. Penney are as well known today as the manufacturers' brands of Goodyear, Goodrich, and Firestone. Sears has created several names—Diehard batteries, Craftsman tools, Kenmore appliances—that command brand preference and even brand insistence; over 90 percent of Sear's products are sold under its own labels. A&P has created different private labels for its canned goods, and they account for over 25 percent of its sales.

An increasing number of department stores, supermarkets, service stations, clothiers, drugstores, and appliance dealers are launching private labels.

Why do middlemen bother with sponsoring their own brands? They have to hunt down qualified suppliers who can deliver consistent quality. They have to order large quantities and tie up their capital in inventories. They have to spend money promoting their private label; Sears spent $631 million on major advertising in 1983. They have to take the chance that if their private-label product is not good, the customer will develop a negative attitude toward their other products.

In spite of these potential disadvantages, middlemen develop private brands because they can be profitable. Middlemen can often locate manufacturers with excess capacity who will produce the private label at a low cost. Other costs, such as advertising and physical distribution, may also be low. This means that the private brander is able to charge a lower price and often make a higher profit margin.

Private brands also give middlemen exclusive products that cannot be purchased from competitors and allow them to build greater store traffic and loyalty. For example, if K mart successfully promotes Canon cameras, other stores that sell Canon products will also benefit. Further, if K mart drops the Canon brand, it loses the benefit of its previous promotion for Canon. But if K mart promotes its private brand of Focal cameras, K mart alone benefits from the promotion. And consumer loyalty to the Focal brand becomes loyalty to K mart.

The competition between manufacturers' and middlemen's brands is called *the battle of the brands*. In this confrontation, middlemen have many advantages. Retail shelf space is scarce, and many manufacturers, especially the newer and smaller ones, cannot introduce products into distribution under their own name. Middlemen take special care to maintain the quality of their brands, thus building consumer confidence. Many shoppers know that the private-label brand is often manufactured by one of the larger manufacturers anyway.

Middlemen's brands are often priced lower than comparable manufacturers' brands, thus appealing to budget-conscious shoppers, especially in times of inflation. Middlemen give more prominent display to their own brands and make sure they are better stocked. As a result, the former dominance of manufacturers' brands is weakening. Some marketing analysts predict that middlemen's brands will eventually knock out all but the strongest manufacturers' brands.

Manufacturers of national brands are very frustrated. They spend a lot of money on consumer-directed advertising and promotion to maintain strong brand preference. Their price has to be somewhat higher to cover this promotion. At the same time, the mass distributors exert considerable pressure on them to put more of their promotional money into trade allowances and deals if they want adequate shelf space. Once manufacturers start giving in, they have less to spend on consumer promotion, and their brand leadership starts slipping. This is the national brand manufacturers' dilemma.[9]

Brand Quality Decision In developing a brand, the manufacturer has to choose a quality level and other attributes that will support the brand's position in the target market. Quality is one of the marketer's major positioning tools. *Quality* stands for *the rated ability of the brand to perform its functions*. Quality is a summary term for the product's durability, reliability, precision, ease of operation and repair, and other valued attributes. Some of these attributes can be measured objectively. From a marketing point of view, quality should be measured in terms of buyers' perceptions.

Most brands are established initially at one of four quality levels: low, average, high, and superior. In one study investigators found that profitability rose with brand quality.[10] The curve in Figure 11-4A suggests that a company should aim at delivering high quality. Superior quality increases profitability only slightly over high quality, whereas inferior quality hurts profitability substantially. At the same time, if all competitors delivered high quality, this strategy would be less effective. Quality must be chosen with a target market segment in mind.

A company must also decide how to manage brand quality through time. Three strategies are illustrated in Figure 11-4B. The first, where the manufacturer invests in continuous research and development to improve the product, usually produces the highest return and market share. Procter & Gamble is a major practitioner of product improvement strategy, which, combined with the high initial product quality, helps explain its leading position in many markets. The second strategy is to maintain product quality. Many companies leave their quality unaltered after its initial formulation unless glaring faults or opportunities occur. The third strategy is to reduce product quality through time. Some companies cut the quality to offset rising costs, hoping buyers will not notice any difference. Others adulterate their products deliberately in order to increase their current profits, although often this hurts long-run profitability.

The theme of quality is now attracting stronger interest among consumers and companies. American consumers have been impressed with the product quality found in Japanese automobiles and electronics and in European automobiles, clothing, and food. Many consumers are favoring apparel that lasts and stays in style longer, instead of trendy apparel. They are showing more interest in fresh and nutritious foods, gourmet items, and cheeses and less interest in soft drinks, sweets,

FIGURE 11-4
Brand Quality Strategies and Profitability

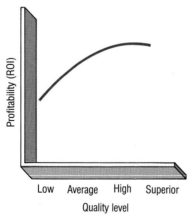

A. Relationship between product quality and profitability (return on investment - ROI)

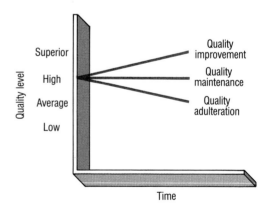

B. Three-strategies for managing product quality through time

and TV dinners. A number of companies are catering to this growing interest in quality, but much more can be done.[11]

Family Brand Decision Manufacturers who brand their product face several further choices. At least four brand-name strategies can be distinguished:

1. *Individual brand names.* This policy is followed by Procter & Gamble (Tide, Bold, Dash, Cheer, Gain, Oxydol, Solo) and Genesco, Inc. (Jarman, Mademoiselle, Johnson & Murphy, and Cover Girl).

2. *A blanket family name for all products.* This policy is followed by Heinz and General Electric.

3. *Separate family names for all products.* This policy is followed by Sears (Kenmore for appliances, Kerrybrook for women's clothing, and Homart for major home installations).

4. *Company trade name combined with individual product names.* This policy is followed by Kellogg's (Kellogg's Rice Krispies and Kellogg's Raisin Bran).

What are the advantages of an individual brand-names strategy? A major advantage is that the company does not tie its reputation to the product's acceptance. If the product fails, it does not compromise the manufacturer's name.

Using a blanket family name for all products also has some advantages. The cost of introducing the product will be less, because there is no need for "name" research, or for heavy advertising expenditures to create brand-name recognition and preference. Furthermore, sales will be strong if the manufacturer's name is good. Thus Campbell's introduces new soups under its brand name with extreme simplicity and instant recognition.

Where a company produces quite different products, it may not be appropriate to use one blanket family name. Swift & Company developed separate family names for its hams (Premium) and fertilizers (Vigoro). When Mead Johnson developed a diet supplement for *gaining* weight, it created a new family name, Nutriment, to avoid confusion with its family brand for weight-*reducing* products, Metrecal. Companies will often invent different family brand names for different quality lines within the same product class. Thus A&P sells a first-grade, second-grade, and third-grade set of brands—Ann Page, Sultana, and Iona, respectively.

Finally, some manufacturers want to associate their company name along with an individual brand name for each product. The company name legitimizes, and the individual name individualizes, the new product. Thus Quaker Oats in *Quaker Oats Cap'n Crunch* taps the company's reputation in the breakfast cereal field and Cap'n Crunch individualizes and dramatizes the new product.

Brand Extension Decision A **brand extension strategy** is any *effort to use a successful brand name to launch product modifications or new products.* After Quaker Oats' success with Cap'n Crunch dry breakfast cereal, it used the brand name and cartoon character to launch a line of ice-cream bars, T-shirts, and other products. Armour used its Dial brand name to launch a variety of new products that would not easily have obtained distribution without the strength of the Dial name. Honda Motor Company used its name to launch its new power lawnmower. Brand extension saves the manufac-

Del Monte ties its products together using a family brand; General Mills uses individual brand names for its different products—Betty Crocker, Nature Valley, Bisquick, Yoplait, Gorton's, Gold Medal, and many others. *Photos courtesy of Del Monte Corporation and General Mills, Inc.*

turer the high cost of promoting new names and creates instant brand recognition of the new product. At the same time, if the new product fails to satisfy, it may hurt consumers' attitudes toward the other products carrying the same brand name.[12]

Multibrand Decision

Multibrand strategy consists of the seller's developing two or more brands in the same product category. This marketing practice was pioneered by P&G when it introduced Cheer detergent as a competitor for its already successful Tide. Although Tide's sales dropped slightly, the combined sales of Cheer and Tide were higher. P&G now produces ten detergent brands.

Manufacturers adopt multibrand strategies for several reasons. First, manufacturers can gain more shelf space, thus increasing the retailer's dependence on their brands. Second, few consumers are so loyal to a brand that they will not try another. The only way to capture the "brand switchers" is to offer several brands. Third, creating new brands develops excitement and efficiency within the manufacturer's organization. Managers in P&G and General Motors compete to outperform each other. Fourth, a multibrand strategy positions the different benefits and appeals, and each brand can attract a separate following.[13]

Brand Repositioning Decision

However well a brand is initially positioned in a market, the company may have to reposition it later. A competitor may have launched a brand next to the company's brand and cut into its market share. Or customer preferences may have shifted, leaving the company's brand with less demand. Marketers should consider repositioning existing brands before introducing new ones. In this way they can capitalize on existing brand recognition and consumer loyalty created by past marketing efforts.

Respositioning may require changing both the product and its image. P&G repositioned Bold detergent by adding a fabric-softening ingredient. Or a brand can be repositioned by changing only the product's image. Ivory Soap was repositioned without reformulation from a "baby soap" to an "all natural soap" for adults who want healthy-looking skin. Kraft repositioned Velveeta from a "cooking cheese" to a "good tasting, natural, and nutritious" snack cheese—the product remained unchanged, but Kraft used new advertising appeals to change consumer perceptions of Velveeta. When repositioning a brand, the marketer must be careful not to foresake or confuse current loyal brand users. When shifting Velveeta's position, Kraft made certain that the product's new position was compatible with its old one. Thus it retained loyal customers while attempting to attract new users.[14]

Selecting a Brand Name

The brand name should not be a casual afterthought. Stern noted that a good brand name:

> . . . can save millions of dollars over the product's life because it carries its own meaning, describes the product's advantages, is instantly recognized and serves to differentiate the product significantly from competition . . . we should add that often millions of dollars are spent to develop a product and to see it just through its first year of public life. That is a lot of cash to bet on haphazard brand name development and vest-pocket testing.[15]

Most large marketing companies have developed a formal brand-name selection process. One study of large consumer product companies found that the typical selection process includes six steps.[16] First, the company identifies objectives or criteria for the brand name. Selecting a brand name begins with a careful review of the product and its benefits, the target market, and proposed marketing strategies. Second, the company generates a list of potential brand names. One expert recommends that this initial list should contain at least 100 names, and it may contain as many as 800.[17] Third, the candidate names are screened to select the 10 to 20 that are most appropriate for further testing. Often the company assigns a team to the task of generating and screening potential brand names. This team may include product managers and other company marketing people, advertising agency people, and outside brand-name consultants.

Fourth, the company obtains consumers' reactions to the remaining brand names. It may conduct surveys or focus group interviews to find out which names best project the desired product concept, and which are most easily understood, remembered, and linked. Fifth, the company conducts a trademark search to be sure that each remaining brand name can be registered and legally protected. Finally, the company selects one of the surviving names as the final brand name for the product.

Finding the best brand name is a difficult task. Among the desirable qualities for a brand name are these: (1) *It should suggest something about the product's benefits and qualities.* Examples: Beautyrest, Craftsman, Sunkist, Spic and Span, Firebird. (2) *It should be easy to pronounce, recognize, and remember.* Short names help. Examples: Tide, Crest, Puffs. But longer ones are sometimes effective. Examples: "Gee, Your Hair Smells Terrific" Shampoo, Better Business Bureau. (3) *It should be distinctive.* Examples: Mustang, Kodak, Exxon. (4) *It should translate easily into foreign languages.* Before spending $100 million to change its name to Exxon, Standard Oil of New Jersey tested the name in 54 languages in more than 150 foreign markets. It found that the name Enco referred to a stalled engine when pronounced phonetically in Japan.[18] (5) *It should be capable of registration and legal protection.* For example, the name should be unique—it cannot be registered if it infringes on existing brand names.

Once chosen, the brand name must be protected. Many firms strive to build a unique brand name that will eventually become identified with the product category. Such brand names as Frigidaire, Kleenex, Levi's, Jello, Scotch Tape, and Fiberglas have succeeded in this way. However, their very success may threaten the exclusive rights to the name. Cellophane and shredded wheat are now names in the common domain.

PACKAGING DECISIONS

Many physical products offered to the market have to be packaged. Packaging can play a minor role (inexpensive hardware items) or a major role (cosmetics). Some packages—such as the Coca Cola bottle and the L'eggs container—are world famous. Many marketers have called packaging a fifth P, along with price, product, place, and promotion. Most marketers, however, treat packaging as an element of product strategy.

We define **packaging** as *the activities of designing and producing the container or wrapper for a product.* The container or wrapper is called the package. The package may include up to three levels of material. The *primary package* is the product's immediate container. The bottle holding Old Spice After-Shave Lotion is

Each an original... all of them ours. One could be yours.

IMAGINATIVE PACKAGING LTD. 30 E. 60 St. NEW YORK, N.Y. 10022 212 758-3288

Packaging is an essential part of the product in perfume marketing. *Courtesy of Imaginative Packaging Ltd.*

the primary package. The *secondary package* refers to the material that protects the primary package and that is discarded when the product is about to be used. The cardboard box containing the bottle of after-shave lotion is a secondary package and provides additional protection and promotion opportunity. The *shipping package* refers to packaging necessary for storage, identification, or transportation. A corrugated box carrying six dozen Old Spice After-Shave Lotions is a shipping package. Finally, *labeling* is part of packaging and consists of printed information appearing on or with the package that describes the product.

Traditionally, packaging has been treated as an incidental marketing decision. Packaging decisions were based mostly on cost and production considerations; the primary function of the package was to contain and protect the product. In recent times, however, numerous factors have contributed to the increased use of packaging as an important marketing tool.

■ *Self-service.* An increase in self-service means that packages must now perform many sales tasks. Packages must attract consumers, describe product benefits, inspire confidence, and make a favorable overall impression. For example, a typical supermarket shopper is exposed to over 14,000 products in a single shopping trip, and research has shown that in-store decisions account for two-thirds of every dollar spent.[19] Thus the package may be an important last step in the marketer's attempts to obtain sales.

■ *Consumer affluence.* Rising consumer affluence means that consumers are willing to pay a little more for the convenience, appearance, dependability, and prestige of better packages.

■ *Company and brand image.* Companies are recognizing the power of well-designed packages to contribute to instant consumer recognition of the company or brand. Every film buyer immediately recognizes the familiar yellow packaging of Kodak film.

■ *Innovational opportunity.* Innovative packaging can bring large benefits to producers. Uneeda Biscuit's innovation in 1899 of a stay-fresh unit package (paperboard, inner paper wrap, and paper overwrap) managed to prolong the shelf life of crackers better than the old cracker boxes, bins, and barrels could. Kraft's development of processed cheese in tins extended cheese's shelf life and earned Kraft a reputation for reliability. Today Kraft is testing retort pouches, which are foil-and-plastic containers, as a successor to cans. The first companies to put their soft drinks in pop-top cans and their liquid sprays in aerosol cans attracted many new customers. Now wine makers are experimenting with pop-top cans and bag-in-the-carton forms of packaging.

Developing an effective package for a new product requires a large number of decisions. The first task is to establish the *packaging concept.* The packaging concept is a definition of what the package should basically *be* or *do* for the particular product. Should the main functions of the package be to offer superior product protection, introduce a novel dispensing method, suggest certain qualities about the product or the company, or something else?

General Foods developed a new dog-food product in the form of meatlike patties. Management decided that the unique and palatable appearance of these patties demanded maximum visibility. Visibility was defined as the basic packaging concept, and management considered alternatives in this light. It finally narrowed down the choice to a tray with a film covering.[20]

Decisions must be made on specific elements of the package—size, shape, materials, color, text, and brand mark. These various elements must be harmonized to maximize value added for consumers and support for the product's position and marketing strategy. The package must be consistent with the product's advertising, pricing, distribution, and other marketing strategies.

Companies usually consider several alternative package designs for a new product. To select the most effective package, the company must put these alternative designs through a number of tests. *Engineering tests* are conducted to ensure that the package stands up under normal conditions; *visual tests,* to ensure that the script is legible and the colors harmonious; *dealer tests,* to ensure that dealers find the package attractive and easy to handle; and *consumer tests,* to ensure favorable consumer response.

In spite of these precautions, a packaging design occasionally gets through with some basic flaw:

> Sizzl-Spray, a pressurized can of barbeque sauce developed by Heublein, . . . had a potential packaging disaster that was discovered in the market tests. . . . "We thought we had a good can, but fortunately we first test marketed the product in stores in Texas and California. It appears as soon as the cans got warm they began to explode. Because we hadn't gotten into national distribution, our loss was only $150,000 instead of a couple of million.[21]

After selecting and introducing the package, the company must reevaluate it regularly to see that it remains effective in the face of changing consumer preferences and advances in technology. In the past, a package design might last for fifteen years before requiring modifications. In today's rapidly changing environment, most companies must reappraise their packaging every two or three years.[22] Keeping a package up to date usually requires only minor but regular modifications—changes so subtle that they go unnoticed by most consumers. But some packaging changes involve complex decisions, drastic action, and high cost and risk (see Exhibit 11-3).

EXHIBIT 11-3

CANNING CAMPBELL'S CAN

Over the past 87 years, the venerable Campbell Soup Co. has marketed tens of billions of cans of soup adorned with its distinctive red-and-white label and gold medallion. But about a year ago, Campbell management came to the conclusion that the time had finally come to can the can as too expensive, too messy and too inconvenient in this day of fast-acting microwave ovens. Ever since then, the company has been engaged in a multimillion-dollar search for a new container.

For openers, Campbell next winter will begin test-marketing individual portions of soup in a sealed plastic soup bowl, which can be popped into a microwave oven to produce hot soup in a jiffy—with no can to open and no dishes to wash. The company also wants to incorporate into its design the "image of warmth" soup bowls convey, says Frank Terwilliger, Campbell's director of packing. But so far, Campbell hasn't come up with a bowl design whose color and shape it really likes.

Campbell's new package prototypes. *Photos courtesy of The Campbell Soup Company.*

The stakes in the search are huge, given Campbell's 80 percent share of the canned-soup market. (It also is the nation's third largest can maker behind American Can Co. and the Continental Group.) To come up with a permanent substitute for the can, Campbell researchers are experimenting with a number of different containers and conducting extensive market research. "We're constantly tracking consumers," says Herbert Baum, Campbell vice president for marketing. "We sit in homes with them. We talk to them in supermarkets."

At this point, Campbell designers are working with an assortment of plastic bags and boxes, all holding 10 ounces of a meatier, "upscale" soup—one with a clearer broth and ingredients of a higher quality than those in the can. The sales pitch on both the plastic bowls and the eventual successor to the tin can will be convenience: "Heat 'n Eat" and "Microready" are among the slogans being considered for the new bowls.

Campbell's move is being hailed by Wall Street analysts. "It's damn hard to open a can of soup, or a can of anything else," says John C. Maxwell of Lehman Brothers, who thinks that the new packaging could help boost overall soup consumption. George Novello of E.F. Hutton says the switch will have a very positive impact on the company's earnings; metals prices have been rising faster than plastics prices and the change should cut Campbell's packaging costs by as much as 15 percent. But achieving that goal will take a lot of time—and a lot of money. Company officials estimate that simply revamping production facilities could cost $100 million or more. Thus, the company estimates it will be five years at least before its soup can takes a final bow.

Source: "Canning Campbell's Can," *Newsweek,* April 9, 1984, p. 84.

Cost remains an important packaging consideration. Developing effective packaging for a new product may cost a few hundred thousand dollars and take from a few months to a year. Converting to a new package may cost millions, and implementing a new package design may take several years. Marketers must weigh packaging costs against consumer perceptions of value added by the packaging and against the role of packaging in helping to accomplish marketing objectives. In making packaging decisions, the company must also pay attention to growing societal concerns about packaging and make decisions that serve society's interests as well as immediate customer and company objectives (see Exhibit 11-4).

EXHIBIT 11-4

PACKAGING AND PUBLIC POLICY

Packaging is attracting increasing public attention. Marketers should heed the following issues in making their packaging decisions.

1. *Fair packaging and labeling.* The public is concerned about packaging and labeling that might be false and misleading. The Federal Trade Commission Act of 1914 held that false, misleading, or deceptive labels or packages would be considered unfair competition. Consumers have also been concerned about the confusing sizes and shapes of packages, which make price comparisons difficult. Congress passed the Fair Packaging and Labeling Act in 1967, which established mandatory labeling requirements, encouraged the adoption of additional voluntary industrywide packaging standards, and empowered federal agencies to set packaging regulations in specific industries. The Food and Drug Administration has required processed-food producers to include nutritional labeling clearly stating the amounts of protein, fat, carbohydrates, and calories contained in the contents of the package, as well as vitamin and mineral content expressed as a percentage of the recommended daily allowance. Consumerists have lobbied for additional labeling legislation to require open dating (to describe the freshness of the product), unit pricing (to describe the cost of the item in some standard measurement unit), grade labeling (to rate the A, B, C quality level of certain consumer goods), and percentage labeling (to describe the percentage of each important ingredient).

2. *Excessive cost.* Critics have called packaging excessive in many cases, charging that it raises prices. They point to secondary "throwaway" packaging and raise the question of its value to the consumer. They point to the fact that the package sometimes costs more than the contents; for example, Evian moisturizer consists of five ounces of natural spring water packaged in an aerosol spray selling for $5.50. Marketers retort that critics do not understand all the functions of the package and that marketers also want to keep packaging costs down.

3. *Scarce resources.* The growing concern over shortages of paper, aluminum, and other materials raises the question of whether industry should try harder to reduce its packaging. For example, the growth of nonreturnable glass containers has resulted in using up to seventeen times as much glass as with returnable containers. The throwaway bottle is also an energy waster, which cannot be afforded in this time of high energy costs. Some states have passed laws prohibiting or taxing nonreturnable containers.

4. *Pollution.* As much as 40 percent of the total solid waste in this country is made up of package material. Many packages end up in the form of broken bottles and bent cans littering the streets and countryside. All of this packaging creates a major problem in solid waste disposal that is a huge consumer of labor and energy.

These questionable aspects of packaging have mobilized public interest in new packaging laws. Marketers must be equally concerned and must attempt to design ecological packages for their products.

LABELING DECISIONS

Sellers may also design labels for their products, which may be a simple tag attached to the product or an elaborately designed graphic that is part of the package. The label might carry only the brand name or a great deal of information. Even if the seller prefers a simple label, the law may require additional information.

Labels perform several functions, and the seller has to decide which ones to use. At the very least, the label *identifies* the product or brand, such as the name Sunkist stamped on oranges. The label might also *grade* the product—canned peaches are grade-labeled A, B, and C. The label might *describe* several things about the product—who made it, where it was made, when it was made, its contents, how it is to be used, and how to use it safely. Finally, the label might *promote* the product through its attractive graphics. Some writers distinguish between identification labels, grade labels, descriptive labels, and promotional labels.

Labels of well-known brands seem old-fashioned after a while and need freshening up. The label on Ivory Soap has been redone eighteen times since the 1890s, with gradual changes in the letters' size and script. On the other hand, the label on Orange Crush soft drink was substantially changed when its competitors' labels began to picture fresh fruits and pull in more sales. Orange Crush developed a label with new symbols to suggest freshness and much stronger and deeper colors.

There has been a long history of legal concerns surrounding labels. Labels could mislead customers or fail to describe important ingredients or fail to include sufficient safety warnings. As a result, several federal and state laws regulate labeling, the most prominent being the Fair Packaging and Labeling Act of 1966. Labeling practices have been affected in recent times by *unit pricing* (stating the price per unit of standard measure), *open dating* (stating the expected shelf life of the product), and *nutritional labeling* (stating the nutritional values in the product). Sellers should make sure their labels contain all the required information before launching new products.

CUSTOMER SERVICE DECISIONS

Customer service is another element of product strategy. A company's offer to the marketplace usually includes some services. The service component can be a minor or a major part of the total offer. In fact, the offer can range from a pure good on the one hand to a pure service on the other.

For a *pure tangible good* such as soap, toothpaste, or salt, no services accompany the product. A *tangible good with accompanying services* consists of a tangible product with one or more services that enhance its consumer appeal. For example, an automobile manufacturer sells an automobile with a warranty, operating and maintenance instructions, delivery, and credit. An offer may consist of *a major service with accompanying minor goods and services*. For example, airline passengers are buying transportation service—they arrive at their destinations without anything tangible to show for their expenditure. But the trip includes some tangibles, such as food and drinks and an airline magazine. Finally, an offer might consist primarily of a *pure service*. Examples include psychotherapy and hair styling. The psychoanalyst gives a pure service, with the only tangible elements consisting of an office and a couch.

Thus the company's product can be a good or a service, and additional services might be included. Here we will focus on customer services accompanying the main offer. Services are further discussed in Chapter 23. The marketer faces three decisions with respect to customer services: (1) What customer services should be included in the customer services mix? (2) What level of service should be offered? (3) In what forms should the services be provided?

The Service Mix Decision The marketer needs to survey customers to identify the main services that might be offered and their relative importance. For example, Canadian buyers of industrial equipment ranked thirteen service elements in the following order of importance: (1) delivery reliability, (2) prompt quotation, (3) technical advice, (4) discounts, (5) after-sales service, (6) sales representation, (7) ease of contact, (8) replacement guarantee, (9) wide range of manufacturer, (10) pattern design, (11) credit, (12) test facilities, and (13) machining facilities.[23] These importance rankings suggest that the seller should at least match competition on delivery reliability, prompt quotation, technical advice, and other services deemed most important by the customers.

But the issue of which services to offer is more subtle than this. A service can be highly important to customers and yet not determine supplier selection if all the suppliers offer the service at the same level. Consider the following example:

> The Monsanto Company was seeking a way to improve its customer services mix. Customers were asked to rate Monsanto, Du Pont, and Union Carbide on several attributes. All three companies were seen by customers as offering high delivery reliability and having good sales representatives. However, none was viewed as rendering sufficient technical service. Monsanto carried out a study to determine how important technical service is to chemical buyers, and found out it had high importance. Monsanto then hired and trained additional technical people and launched a campaign describing itself as the leader in technical service. This gave Monsanto a differential advantage in the minds of buyers seeking technical service.

The Service Level Decision Customers not only want certain services, but also want them in the right amount and quality. If bank customers have to stand in long lines or face frowning bank tellers, they might switch to another bank.

Companies need to check on their own and competitors' service levels in relation to customers' expectations. The company can spot service deficiencies through a number of devices: *comparison shopping, periodic customer surveys, suggestion boxes,* and *complaint-handling systems.* The task is not to *minimize* complaining behavior, but to *maximize* the customer's opportunity to complain so that the company can know how it is doing and disappointed customers can obtain satisfaction.

A useful device is to survey customers periodically to find out how they feel about each service. Figure 11-5A shows how customers rated fourteen service elements of an automobile dealer's service department on importance and performance. Importance was rated on a four-point scale of "extremely important," "important," "slightly important," and "not important." Dealer performance was rated on a four-point scale of "excellent," "good," "fair," and "poor." For example, "Job done right the first time" received mean ratings of 3.83 and 2.63, indicating that customers felt it was highly important but was not being performed that well.

The ratings of the fourteen elements are shown in Figure 11-5B. The figure is divided into four sections. Quadrant A shows important service elements that are not being performed at the desired levels; they include elements 1, 2, and 9. The dealer should concentrate on improving the service department's performance on these elements. Quadrant B shows important service elements where the department is performing well; its job is to maintain the high performance. Quadrant C shows minor service elements that are being delivered in a mediocre way, but do not need any attention because they are not very important. Quadrant D shows that a minor service element, "Send out maintenance notices," is being performed in an excellent manner, a case of possible "overkill." Measuring service elements according to importance and performance tells marketers where to focus their efforts.

The Service Form Decision   Marketers must also decide on the forms in which to offer various services. The first question is, How should each service element be priced? For example, consider what Zenith should offer in repair services on its television sets. Zenith has three options. It could offer free repair service for a year with the sale of a set. It could sell a service contract. Or it could decide not to offer repair services at any price, leaving this to television repair specialists.

Another question is, How should the service be delivered? Zenith could provide repair services in several ways. It could hire and train its own service people and locate them across the country. It could arrange with distributors and dealers

Attribute number	Attribute description	Mean importance rating[a]	Mean performance rating[b]
1	Job done right the first time	3.83	2.63
2	Fast action on complaints	3.63	2.73
3	Prompt warranty work	3.60	3.15
4	Able to do any job needed	3.56	3.00
5	Service available when needed	3.41	3.05
6	Courteous and friendly service	3.41	3.29
7	Car ready when promised	3.38	3.03
8	Perform only necessary work	3.37	3.11
9	Low prices on service	3.29	2.00
10	Clean up after service work	3.27	3.02
11	Convenient to home	2.52	2.25
12	Convenient to work	2.43	2.49
13	Courtesy buses and rental cars	2.37	2.35
14	Send out maintenance notices	2.05	3.33

[a] Ratings obtained from a four-point scale of "extremely important," "important," "slightly important," "not important."

[b] Ratings obtained from a four-point scale of "excellent," "good," "fair," and "poor." A "no basis for judgment" category was also provided.

A.   B.

FIGURE 11-5 *Importance and Performance Ratings for Automobile Dealer's Service Department*

Source: John A. Martilla and John C. James, "Importance-Performance Analysis." *Journal of Marketing,* January 1977, pp. 77–79.

to provide repair services. Or it could leave it to independent companies to provide repair services.

For each service, various options exist. The company's decision depends on customer preferences as well as competitors' strategies.

The Customer Given the importance of customer service as a competitive tool, many companies *Service Department* have established strong customer service departments to handle the following customer services:[24]

- *Complaints and adjustments.* Procedures are established for handling complaints. Whirlpool, for example, has set up hot lines to facilitate consumer complaining. By keeping statistics on the types of complaints, the customer service department can press for desired changes in product design, quality control, high-pressure selling, and so on. It is less expensive to preserve the goodwill of existing customers than to attract new customers or woo back lost customers.

- *Credit service.* Companies can offer customers a number of credit options, including installment credit contracts, open-book credit, loans, and leasing options. The costs of extending credit are usually more than covered by the gross profit on the additional sales and the reduced cost of marketing expenditures to overcome customers' feelings that they can't afford the purchase.

- *Maintenance service.* Well-managed companies run a parts and service department that is effective, speedy, and reasonable in cost. Although maintenance service is often run by the production department, marketing should monitor customer satisfaction with this service.

- *Technical service.* Companies can provide customers who buy complex equipment with technical services such as custom design work, installation, customer training, applications research, and process improvement research.

- *Information service.* Companies can set up an information unit that answers customer inquiries and disseminates information on new products, features, processes, expected price changes, order backlog status, and new company policies.

All these services should be coordinated and used as tools in creating customer satisfaction and loyalty.[25]

PRODUCT LINE DECISIONS

We have looked at product strategy decisions—branding, packaging, and services—at the level of the individual product. But product strategy also calls for building a product line. We define product line as follows:

> A **product line** is a group of products that are closely related, either because they function in a similar manner, are sold to the same customer groups, are marketed through the same types of outlets, or fall within given price ranges.

Thus General Motors produces a line of cars, and Revlon produces a line of cosmetics.

Each product line needs a marketing strategy. Most companies assign a specific person to manage each product line. This person faces a number of tough decisions on product line length, product line modernization, and product line featuring.

Product Line Length Decision

Product line managers have to decide on product line length. The line is too short if the manager can increase profits by adding items; the line is too long if the manager can increase profits by dropping items.

The issue of product line length is influenced by company objectives. Companies that want to be positioned as full-line companies or are seeking high market share and market growth will carry longer lines. They are less concerned when some items fail to contribute to profits. Companies that are keen on high profitability will carry shorter lines consisting of "cherry-picked" items.

Product lines tend to lengthen over time.[26] Excess manufacturing capacity will put pressure on the product line manager to develop new items. The sales-force and distributors will also put pressure on the manager for a more complete product line to satisfy their customers. The product line manager will want to add items to the product line in pursuit of greater sales and profits.

But as items are added, several costs rise: design and engineering costs, inventory carrying costs, manufacturing changeover costs, order processing costs, transportation costs, and promotional costs to introduce new items. Eventually someone calls a halt to the mushrooming product line. Top management may freeze things because of insufficient funds or manufacturing capacity. Or the controller may question the line's profitability and call for a study. The study will probably show a large number of money-losing items, and they will be pruned from the line in a major effort to increase profitability. A pattern of undisciplined product line growth followed by massive pruning will repeat itself many times.

A company can systematically increase the length of its product line in two ways: by stretching its line and by filling its line.

Product Line Stretching Decision

Every company's product line covers a certain range of the products offered by the industry as a whole. For example, BMW automobiles are located in the medium-high price range of the automobile market. **Product line stretching** occurs when a company *lengthens its product line beyond its current range*. The company can stretch its line downward, upward, or both ways.

DOWNWARD STRETCH. Many companies initially locate at the high end of the market and subsequently stretch their lines downward. Beech Aircraft has historically produced expensive private aircraft but has recently added less expensive aircraft to meet a threat from Piper, which began to produce larger planes.

A company may stretch downward for any number of reasons. It may be attacked at the high end and counterattack by invading the low end. It may find that faster growth is taking place at the low end. The company may have initially entered the high end to establish a quality image and intended to roll downward. The company may add a low-end product to plug a market hole that would otherwise attract a new competitor.

In making a downward stretch, the company faces some risks. The new low-end item might "cannibalize" higher-end items, leaving the company worse off. Consider the following.[27]

> Ford introduced the small-size Falcon in 1959 to attract economy-car buyers. But many of its buyers were those who would have bought the standard-size Ford. In effect, Ford reduced its own profit margin by failing to design its car for a really different segment than loyal Ford buyers.

Or the low-end item may provoke competitors to counteract by moving into the higher end. Or the company's dealers may not be willing or able to handle the lower-end products.

One of the great miscalculations of several American companies has been their unwillingness to plug holes in the lower end of their markets. General Motors resisted building smaller cars; Xerox, smaller copying machines; and Harley Davidson, smaller motorcycles. In all these cases, Japanese companies found a major opening and moved in quickly and successfully.

UPWARD STRETCH. Companies at the lower end of the market may want to enter the higher end. They may be attracted by a faster growth rate or higher margins at the higher end, or they may simply want to position themselves as full-line manufacturers.

An upward stretch decision can be risky. The higher-end competitors not only are well entrenched, but may counterattack by entering the lower end of the market. Prospective customers may not believe that the newcomer can produce quality products. Finally, the company's sales representatives and distributors may lack the talent and training to serve the higher end of the market.

TWO-WAY STRETCH. Companies in the middle range of the market may decide to stretch their lines in both directions. Texas Instruments' strategy in the hand-calculator market illustrates this. Before Texas Instruments (TI) entered this market, the market was dominated primarily by Bowmar at the low-price/low-quality end and Hewlett-Packard at the high-price/high-quality end (see Figure 11-6). TI introduced its first calculators in the medium-price/medium-quality end of the market. Gradually it added more machines at each end. It offered better calculators at the same or lower prices than Bowmar, ultimately destroying it; and it designed high-quality calculators selling at lower prices than Hewlett-Packard calculators, taking away a good share of HP's sales at the high end. This two-way stretch won TI the market leadership in the hand-calculator market.

Product Line-Filling Decision

A product line can also be lengthened by adding more items within the present range of the line. There are several motives for **product line filling:** reaching for

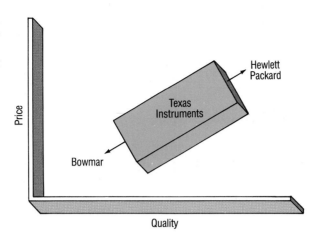

FIGURE 11-6
*Two-Way Product Line
Stretch in the Hand-
Calculator Market*

incremental profits, trying to satisfy dealers who complain about lost sales because of missing items in the line, trying to utilize excess capacity, trying to be the leading full-line company, and trying to plug holes to keep out competitors.

Line filling is overdone if it results in cannibalization and customer confusion. The company needs to differentiate each item in the consumer's mind. Each item should possess a *just noticeable difference*. According to Weber's law, customers are more attuned to relative than to absolute differences.[28] They will perceive the difference between boards two and three feet long and boards twenty and thirty feet long, but not between boards twenty-nine and thirty feet long. The company should make sure that new product items have a noticeable difference.

Product Line Modernization Decision
In some cases, product line length is adequate, but the line needs to be modernized. For example, a company's machine tools may have a 1920s look and lose out to better-styled competitors' lines.

The issue in **product line modernization** is whether to overhaul the line piecemeal or in one fell swoop. A piecemeal approach allows the company to see how customers and dealers take to the new style before changing the whole line. Piecemeal modernization causes less drain on the company's cash flow. A major disadvantage of piecemeal modernization is that it allows competitors to see changes and start redesigning their own lines.

Product Line Featuring Decision
The product line manager typically selects one or a few items in the line to feature. This is **product line featuring.** Sometimes managers feature promotional models at the low end of the line to serve as "traffic builders." Thus Sears will announce a special low-priced sewing machine to attract people. And Rolls Royce announced an economy model selling for only $49,000—in contrast to its high-end model selling for $108,000—to bring people into its showrooms. Once the customers arrive, salespeople may try to influence them to buy at the high end of the line.

At other times, managers will feature a high-end item to give the product line "class." Stetson promotes a man's hat selling for $150, which few people buy but which acts as a "flagship" to enhance the whole line.

PRODUCT MIX DECISIONS

An organization with several product lines has a product mix. We define product mix as follows.[29]

> A **product mix** (also called *product assortment*) is the set of all product lines and items that a particular seller offers for sale to buyers.

Avon's product mix consists of four major product lines: cosmetics, jewelry, fashions, and household items. Each product line consists of several sublines. For example, cosmetics breaks down into lipstick, rouge, powder, and so on. Each line and subline has many individual items. Altogether, Avon's product mix includes 1,300 items. A large supermarket handles as many as 14,000 items; a typical K mart stocks 15,000 items; and General Electric manufactures as many as 250,000 items.

A company's product mix can be described as having a certain width, length, depth, and consistency. These concepts are illustrated in Table 11-1 in connection with selected Procter & Gamble consumer products.

The *width* of P&G's product mix refers to how many different product lines the company carries. Table 11-1 shows a product mix width of six lines. (In fact, P&G produces many additional lines, including mouthwashes, toilet tissue, and others.)

The *length* of P&G's product mix refers to the total number of items the company carries. In Table 11-1, it is 32. We can also compute the average length of a line at P&G by dividing the total length (here 32) by the number of lines (here 6), or 5.3. The average P&G product line as represented in Table 11-1 consists of 5.3 brands.

TABLE 11-1 *Product Mix Width and Product Line Length Shown for Procter & Gamble Products*

	DETERGENTS	TOOTHPASTE	BAR SOAP	DEODORANTS	DISPOSABLE DIAPERS	COFFEE
	Ivory Snow	Gleem	Ivory	Secret	Pampers	Folger's
	Dreft	Crest	Camay	Sure	Luvs	Instant Folger's
	Tide		Lava			High Point Instant
	Joy		Kirk's			Folger's Flaked Coffee
Product	Cheer		Zest			
	Oxydol		Safeguard			
line	Dash		Coast			
	Cascade					
length	Ivory Liquid					
	Gain					
	Dawn					
	Era					
	Bold 3					
	Liquid Tide					
	Solo					

Product mix width (spanning across the top)

The *depth* of P&G's product mix refers to how many variants are offered of each product in the line. Thus if Crest comes in three sizes and two formulations (regular and mint), Crest has a depth of six. By counting the number of variants within each brand, the average depth of P&G's product mix can be calculated.

The *consistency* of the product mix refers to how closely related the various product lines are in end use, production requirements, distribution channels or in some other way. P&G's product lines are consistent insofar as they are consumer goods that go through the same distribution channels. The lines are less consistent insofar as they perform different functions for the buyers.

These four dimensions of the product mix provide the handles for defining the company's product strategy. The company can increase its business in four ways. The company can add new product lines, thus widening its product mix. In this way, its new lines capitalize on the company's reputation in its other lines. Or the company can lengthen its existing product lines to become a more full-line company. Or the company can add more product variants to each product and thus deepen its product mix. Finally, the company can pursue more product line consistency or less, depending upon whether it wants to acquire a strong reputation in a single field or participate in several fields.

Thus we see that product strategy is a multidimensional and complex subject calling for decisions on product mix, product line, branding, packaging, and service strategy. These decisions must be made not only with a full understanding of consumer wants and competitors' strategies, but also with increasing attention to the growing public policy affecting product decisions (see Exhibit 11-5).[30]

EXHIBIT 11-5

PRODUCT DECISIONS AND PUBLIC POLICY

Marketing managers must heed various laws and regulations when making their product decisions. The main areas of product concern are as follows.

Product additions and deletions. Decisions to add products, particularly through acquisitions, may be prevented under the Antimerger Act if the effect threatens to lessen competition. Decisions to drop old products must be made with an awareness that the firm has legal obligations, written or implied, to its suppliers, dealers, and customers who have a stake in the discontinued product.

Patent protection. The firm must heed the U.S. patent laws in developing new products. The firm is prevented from designing a product that is "illegally similar" to another company's established product. An example was Polaroid's suit trying to prevent Kodak from selling its new instant picture camera on the grounds that it infringed on Polaroid's instant camera patents.

Product quality and safety. Manufacturers of foods, drugs, cosmetics, and certain fibers must comply with specific laws regarding product quality and safety. The Federal Food, Drug, and Cosmetic Act protects consumers from unsafe and adulterated food, drugs, and cosmetics. Various acts provide for the inspection of sanitary conditions in the meat and poultry processing industries. Safety legislation has been passed to regulate fabrics, chemical substances, automobiles, toys, and drugs and poisons. The Consumer Product Safety Act of 1972 established a Consumer Product Safety Commission, which has the authority to ban or seize imminently hazardous products and set severe penalties for violation of the law. If consumers have been injured by a product that has been defectively designed, they can sue manufacturers or dealers. Product liability suits are now occurring at the rate of over one million per year, with awards running as high as $500,000. This has resulted in a substantial increase in product recalls. General Motors spent $3.5 million on postage alone when it had to notify 6.5 million car owners of defective motor mounts.

Product warranties. Many manufacturers offer written product warranties to convince customers of their product's quality. But these warranties are often subject to certain qualifications and written in a language the average consumer does not understand. Too often, consumers learn that they are not entitled to services, repairs, and replacements that seem to be implied. To protect consumers, Congress passed the Magnuson-Moss Warranty–Federal Trade Commission Improvement Act in 1975. The act requires that full warranties meet certain minimum standards, including repair "within a reasonable time and without charge" or a replacement or full refund if the product does not work "after a reasonable number of attempts" at repair. Otherwise the company must make it clear that it is offering only a limited warranty. The law has led several manufacturers to switch from full to limited warranties and others to drop warranties altogether as a marketing tool.

Sources: Howard C. Sorenson, "Products Liability: The Consumer's Revolt," *Best Review,* September 1974, p. 48; "Managing the Product Recall," *Business Week,* January 1975, pp. 46–48; Roger A. Kerin and Michael Harvey, "Contingency Planning for Product Recall," *MSU Business Topics,* Summer 1975, pp. 5–12; and "The Guesswork on Warranties," *Business Week,* July 14, 1975, p. 51.

■ Summary

Product is a complex concept that must be carefully defined. Product strategy calls for making coordinated decisions on product items, product lines, and the product mix.

Each product item offered to customers can be looked at on three levels. The *core product* is the essential service the buyer is really buying. The *tangible product* is the features, styling, quality, brand name, and packaging of the product offered for sale. The *augmented product* is the tangible product plus the various services accompanying it, such as warranty, installation, service maintenance, and free delivery.

Several schemes have been proposed for classifying products. For example, all products can be classified according to their durability (nondurable goods, durable goods, and services). Consumer goods are usually classified according to consumer shopping habits (convenience, shopping, specialty and unsought goods). Industrial goods are classified according to how they enter the production process (materials and parts, capital items, and supplies and services).

Companies have to develop brand policies for the product items in their lines. They must decide whether to brand at all, whether to do manufacturing or private branding, what quality they should build into the brand, whether to use family brand names or individual brand names, whether to extend the brand name to new products, whether to put out several competing brands, and whether to reposition any of the brands.

Physical products require packaging decisions to create such benefits as protection, economy, convenience, and promotion. Marketers have to develop a packaging concept and test it functionally and psychologically to make sure it achieves the desired objectives and is compatible with public policy.

Physical products also require labeling for identification and possible grading, description, and promotion of the product. U.S. laws require sellers to present certain minimum information on the label to inform and protect consumers.

Companies have to develop customer services that are desired by customers and effective against competitors. The company has to decide on the most important services to offer, the level at which each service should be provided, and the form of each service. The *service mix* can be coordinated by a customer service department that handles complaints and adjustments, credit, maintenance, technical service, and customer information.

Most companies produce not a single product but a product line. A *product line* is a group of products related in function, customer purchase needs, or distribution channels. Each product line requires a product strategy. *Line stretching* raises the question of whether a particular line should be extended downward, upward, or both ways. *Line filling* raises the question of whether additional items should be added within the present range of the line. *Line modernization* raises the question of whether the line needs a new look, and whether the new look should be installed piecemeal or all at once. *Line featuring* raises the question of which items to feature in promoting the line.

Product mix describes the set of product lines and items offered to customers by a particular seller. The product mix can be described as having a certain width, length, depth, and consistency. The four dimensions of the product mix are the tools for developing the company's product strategy.

■ Questions for Discussion

1. A Sony color TV would be grouped under which consumer product classification (convenience, shopping, specialty, or unsought goods)?

2. The latest buzzword on Madison Avenue is "brand personality," or how people feel about a brand rather than what the brand does. Timex wants to change its brand personality from utilitarian to something else. What would you suggest, and how should it go about accomplishing the change in brand personality?

3. Relate the concepts of product mix, product line, and product item to General Motors.

4. Discuss the core, tangible, and augmented product for your favorite brand of perfume or after-shave lotion.

5. In how many retail outlets must each type of consumer goods (convenience, shopping, specialty, and unsought) be distributed in a particular geographic area? Explain why.

6. Industrial goods always become part of the finished product. Comment.

7. Who benefits from the use of brand names? Explain briefly.

8. Two of the most expensive and widely discussed brand-name changes in recent years have been Enco (Esso) to Exxon and Bank Americard to Visa. Why, do you think, did these companies go to this expense?

9. Describe some of the service decisions the following marketers must make: (a) women's dress shop, (b) savings and loan, and (c) sporting goods store.

■ References

1. Based on information found in Bess Gallanis, "New Strategies Revive the Rose's Fading Bloom," *Advertising Age,* February 27, 1984, pp. M9–M11; Annette Green, "Passion Fits the Product Mix," *Advertising Age,* February 27, 1984, p. M12; "What Lies Behind the Sweet Smell of Success," *Business Week,* February 27, 1984, pp. 139–143; and other sources.

2. See *Marketing Definitions: A Glossary of Marketing Terms,* compiled by the Committee on Definitions of the American Marketing Association (Chicago: American Marketing Association, 1960).

3. See HARPER W. BOYD, JR., and SIDNEY J. LEVY, "New Dimensions in Consumer Analysis," *Harvard Business Review,* November–December 1963, pp. 129–40.

4. THEODORE LEVITT, *The Marketing Mode* (New York: McGraw-Hill, 1969), p. 2.

5. The three definitions can be found in *Marketing Definitions.*

6. The first three definitions can be found in *Marketing Definitions.* For further reading on this classification of goods, see RICHARD H. HOLTON, "The Distinction between Convenience Goods, Shopping Goods, and Specialty Goods," *Journal of Marketing,* July 1958, pp. 53–56; and GORDON E. MIRACLE, "Product Characteristics and Marketing Strategy," *Journal of Marketing,* January 1965, pp. 18–24.

7. The first four definitions can be found in *Marketing Definitions.*

8. See Bill Paul, "It Isn't Chicken Feed to Put Your Brand on 78 Million Birds," *Wall Street Journal,* May 13, 1974, p. 1.

9. See E. B. Weiss, "Private Label?" *Advertising Age,* September 30, 1974, pp. 27ff; and Frances Dunne, "Private Labels Are No Secret Anymore," *Advertising Age,* July 25, 1983, p. M30.

10. Sidney Schoeffler, Robert D. Buzzell, and Donald F. Heany, "Impact of Strategic Planning on Profit Performance," *Harvard Business Review,* March–April 1974, pp. 137–45.

11. "Research Suggests Consumers Will Increasingly Seek Quality," *Wall Street Journal,* October 15, 1981, p. 1.

12. See Theodore R. Gamble, "Brand Extension," in *Plotting Marketing Strategy,* Lee Adler, ed. (New York: Simon & Schuster, 1967), pp. 170–71. For several more recent examples, see "Name Game," *Time,* August 31, 1981, pp. 41–42.

13. See Robert W. Young, "Multibrand Entries," in Adler, *Plotting Marketing Strategy,* pp. 143–64.

14. See Bess Gallanis, "Positioning Old Products in New Niches," *Advertising Age,* May 3, 1984, p. M50; and "Marketers Should Consider Restaging Old Brands Before Launching New Ones," *Advertising Age,* December 10, 1982, p. 5.

15. Walter Stern, "A Good Name Could Mean a Brand of Fame," *Advertising Age,* January 17, 1983, pp. M53–M54.

16. James U. McNeal and Linda M. Zerin, "Brand Name Selection for Consumer Products," *MSU Business Topics,* Spring 1981, pp. 35–39.

17. Stern, "A Good Name," p. M53.

18. Ibid., p. M53.

19. Charles A. Moldenhauer, "Packaging Designers Must Be Cognizant of Right Cues If the Consumer Base Is to Expand," *Marketing News,* March 30, 1984, p. 14; and Elliot C. Young, "Judging a Package by Its Cover," *Madison Avenue,* August 1983, p. 17.

20. "General Foods—Post Division (B)," Case M-102, Harvard Business School, 1964.

21. "Product Tryouts: Sales Tests in Selected Cities Help Trim Risks of National Marketing," *Wall Street Journal,* August 10, 1962, p. 1.

22. Moldenhauer, "Packaging Designers," p. 14.

23. Peter G. Banting, "Customer Service in Industrial Marketing: A Comparative Study," *European Journal of Marketing,* 10, No. 3 (1976), 140.

24. See Ralph S. Alexander and Thomas L. Berg, *Dynamic Management in Marketing* (Homewood, IL: Irwin, 1965), pp. 419–28.

25. For more examples of how companies have used customer service as a marketing tool, see "Making Service a Potent Marketing Tool," *Business Week,* June 11, 1984, pp. 164–70.

26. See Benson P. Shapiro, *Industrial Product Policy: Managing the Existing Product Line* (Cambridge, MA: Marketing Science Institute, September 1977), pp. 9–10.

27. Mark Hanan, *Market Segmentation* (New York: American Management Association, 1968), pp. 24–26.

28. See Steuart Henderson Britt, "How Weber's Law Can Be Applied to Marketing," *Business Horizons,* February 1975, pp. 21–29.

29. This definition can be found in *Marketing Definitions.*

30. For more on product liability, see "Unsafe Products: The Great Debate over Blame and Punishment," *Business Week,* April 30, 1984, pp. 96–104.

12
Designing Products: New Product Development and Product Life-Cycle Strategies

One of the costliest new product failures in history was Ford's Edsel automobile, introduced in 1957. The Ford Motor Company in the early fifties began to feel the need for adding a new automobile to its product line. At that time, Fords and Chevrolets each had 25 percent of the auto market. But there was a difference. Chevrolet car owners, when they became more prosperous, moved up to the Pontiac-Buick-Oldsmobile class. Ford owners, as they moved to higher-priced cars, also favored Pontiacs, Buicks, and Oldsmobiles. They did not find Ford's Mercury appealing and could not afford the elegant Lincoln.

Ford needed to develop an attractive intermediate-price car for upwardly mobile Ford and Chevrolet owners. Ford's marketing research indicated that the growing middle class would be buying better cars. Ford studied car owner demographics, desires, and preferences and set about designing a car that would appeal to these buyers. The car's design was kept top secret, although Ford ran publicity to excite the public about the coming of a new and unique car. Ford decided, at tremendous cost, to establish a separate dealer system for Edsel. Edsel was to be sold by Edsel dealers exclusively. The company also considered over six thousand possible names for the new car, including several created by poetess Marianne Moore, such as Bullet Cloisonne, Mongoose Civique, and Andante Con Motor. Ignoring all these names, the car was named Edsel in honor of Henry Ford's only son.

Ford launched the Edsel with great fanfare on September 4, 1957. On that day sixty-five hundred cars were purchased or ordered. That day belonged to Edsel, but it was the only day. Although over 2 million people went to look at the car in showrooms, few bought it. By January 1958 the exclusive dealerships were discontinued, and Ford created a new Mercury-Edsel-Lincoln Division. In November 1959 Ford stopped producing Edsels.

Why did the Edsel fail? First, many consumers did not find the car attractive. The front of the car carried vertical lines and the back carried horizontal lines, suggesting that two design teams went to work on opposite ends of the car. Furthermore, the front grill was peculiar looking and became the butt of many Freudian jokes. Second, Ford advertised the Edsel as being a new kind of car. However, consumers did not see it this way; it seemed like another medium-priced car. Ford got itself into trouble by overpromising. Third, in Ford's rush to produce the car, quality control was careless and many Edsels were "lemons." Some owners and journalists spread bad word of mouth about the car.

Edsel's timing was also bad. Ford introduced the car in 1957 just as the economy started to dip into a major recession. People wanted cheaper cars and turned to the Volkswagen and American Motors' Rambler. There was a strong reaction against chrome and flashy cars like the Edsel. Yet nothing in the earlier research forecasted these changes in the economy and customer preferences. The Edsel was a victim of poor planning and timing, and this cost Ford $350 million.[1]

A company has to be good at developing new products. It also has to be good at managing them in the face of changing tastes, technologies, and competition. Every product seems to go through a life cycle—it is conceived and born, develops through several phases, and eventually dies as younger products come along that better serve consumer needs.

Figure 12-1 shows the hypothetical course of a product's sales and profits from inception to demise. The product life cycle begins when the company finds and develops a new product idea. During product development, the company accumulates increasing investment costs. After the company launches the product, sales pass through an introductory period, then through a period of strong growth, followed by maturity and eventual decline. Meanwhile profits go from negative to positive, peak in the growth or mature sales stages, and then decline.

The product life cycle presents companies with two major challenges. First, because all products eventually decline, the firm must develop a process for finding new products to replace aging ones (the problem of *new product development*.) Second, the firm must understand how its products age, and adapt its marketing strategies for products as they pass through different life-cycle stages (the problem of *product life-cycle strategies*.) Some companies put their energies into developing new products, sometimes to the detriment of skillfully managing existing products. Other companies concentrate on managing current products and fail to develop new products for the future. Companies need to strike a balance between these two extremes.

We will first look at the problem of finding and developing new products, and then at the problem of managing them successfully over their life cycles.

FIGURE 12-1
Sales and Profits over the Product's Life from Inception to Demise

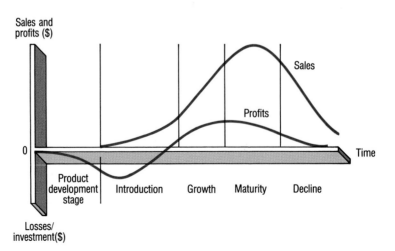

NEW PRODUCT DEVELOPMENT STRATEGY

Given the rapid changes in tastes, technology, and competition, a company cannot rely only on its existing products. Customers want and expect new and improved products. Competition will do its best to provide them. Every company needs a new product development program.

A company can obtain new products in two ways. One is through *acquisition,* by buying a whole company, a patent, or a license to produce someone else's product. The other is through *new product development,* by setting up its own research and development department.

We will concentrate on new product development—on *original products, product improvements, product modifications,* and *new brands* that the firm develops through its own R&D efforts. We will also be concerned with whether the consumer sees the item as "new," although this will not be our primary focus.

Innovation can be very risky. Ford lost an estimated $350 million on its Edsel automobile; RCA lost a staggering $580 million on its SelectaVision videodisc player; Xerox's venture into computers was a disaster; and the French Concorde aircraft will never recover its investment. And here are several consumer packaged-goods products, launched by sophisticated companies, that failed in the marketplace:

- Red Kettle soup (Campbell)
- Knorr soup (Best)
- Cue toothpaste (Colgate)
- Flavored ketchups (Hunt)
- Babyscott diapers (Scott)
- Nine Flags men's cologne (Gillette)
- Vim tablet detergent (Lever)
- Post dried fruit cereal (General Foods)
- Gablinger's beer (Rheingold)
- Resolve analgesic (Bristol-Myers)
- Mennen E deodorant (Mennen)

One study found that the new product failure rate was 40 percent for consumer products, 20 percent for industrial products, and 18 percent for services.[2] A recent study of 700 consumer and industrial firms by Booz, Allen & Hamilton found an overall success rate for new products of only 65 percent (see Exhibit 12-1 for a summary of other findings).

Why do many new products fail? There are several reasons. A high-level executive might push a favorite idea through in spite of negative marketing research findings. Or the idea is good, but the market size has been overestimated. Or the actual product has not been designed as well as it should have been. Or it has been incorrectly positioned in the market, not advertised effectively, or overpriced. Sometimes the costs of product development are higher than expected, or the competitors fight back harder than expected.

EXHIBIT 12-1

BOOZ, ALLEN & HAMILTON'S LATEST STUDY OF NEW PRODUCT MANAGEMENT ACTIVITY

The international management and technology consulting firm of Booz, Allen & Hamilton released in 1982 an updated study of new product management activity. Their study consisted of a mail survey of 700 consumer and industrial companies and lengthy interviews with 150 new product executives. Here are some of their key findings:

- Management reported an average new product success rate of 65 percent.
- Companies were able to develop one successful product out of every seven they researched, which is a substantial improvement over the 1968 rate of one out of every fifty-eight ideas.
- Only 10 percent of the new products were "new to the world," and only 20 percent were "new product lines," but these highest-risk products represented 60 percent of the "most successful" new products.
- New product spending has become more efficient, in that successful entries accounted for 54 percent of total new product expenditures, up from 30 percent in 1968.
- Successful new product companies don't spend more on R&D and marketing, as a percentage of sales, than unsuccessful ones.
- The median number of new products introduced between 1976 and 1981 was five; that number is expected to double over the next five years.
- Managers expect new products to increase company sales growth by one-third over the next five years, while the portion of total company profits generated by new products is expected to be 40 percent.

Source: New Products Management for the 1980s (New York: Booz, Allen & Hamilton, 1982).

Successful new product development may even be more difficult to achieve in the future for the following reasons:

- *Shortage of important new product ideas.* Some scientists think there is a shortage of important new technologies of the magnitude of the automobile, television, computers, xerography, and wonder drugs.
- *Fragmented markets.* Keen competition is leading to increasingly fragmented markets. Companies have to aim new products at smaller market segments rather than the mass market, and this means lower sales and profits for each product.
- *Growing social and governmental constraints.* New products have to increasingly satisfy public criteria such as consumer safety and ecological compatibility. Government requirements have slowed down innovation in the drug industry and have complicated product design and advertising decisions in such industries as industrial equipment, chemicals, automobiles, and toys.
- *Costliness of the new product development process.* Finding, developing, and launching new products can be very costly, and these costs will rise steadily due to inflation on manufacturing, media, and distribution costs.
- *Capital shortage.* Many companies cannot afford or cannot raise the funds needed for new product development. They emphasize product modification and imitation rather than true innovation.

1. *Product managers.* Many companies leave new product development to their product managers. In practice, this system has several faults. Product managers are usually so busy managing their product lines that they give little thought to new products other than brand modifications or extensions; they also lack the specific skills and knowledge needed to develop new products.

2. *New product managers.* General Foods and Johnson & Johnson have new product managers who report to group managers. This position professionalizes the new product function; on the other hand, new product managers tend to think in terms of product modifications and line extensions limited to their product market.

3. *New product committees.* Most companies have a high-level management committee charged with reviewing new product proposals. Consisting of representatives from marketing, manufacturing, finance, engineering, and other departments, its function is not development or coordination so much as reviewing and approving new product plans.

4. *New product departments.* Large companies often establish a new product department headed by a manager who has substantial authority and access to top management. The department's major responsibilities include generating and screening new ideas, directing and coordinating research and development work, and carrying out field testing and precommercialization work.

5. *New product venture teams.* Dow, Westinghouse, Monsanto, and General Mills assign major new product development work to venture teams. A *venture team* is a group brought together from various operating departments and charged with bringing a specific product or business into being.

Sources: This list relies on information in *Organization for New-Product Development* (New York: Conference Board, 1966); and David S. Hopkins, *Options in New-Product Organization* (New York: Conference Board, 1974).

■ *Shorter life spans of successful products.* When a new product is successful, rivals are so quick to follow suit that the new product is typically fated for only a short happy life. Alberto-Culver was so eager to follow P&G into the shampoo market that it devised a name and filmed a TV commercial before it had even developed its own product.

Thus companies face a dilemma—they must develop new products, but the odds weigh heavily against success. Companies can minimize this dilemma through stronger and more systematic planning. First, they can design effective *organizational arrangements* for nurturing and handling new products. The most common arrangements are described in Table 12-1. Then they can establish a systematic *new product process* for effectively finding and cultivating new products. The major steps in this development process are shown in Figure 12-2 and described below.

Idea Generation New product development starts with the search for new ideas. A company typically has to generate many ideas in order to find a few good ones. Booz, Allen & Hamilton summarized this in the form of a decay curve for new product ideas that shows how many ideas typically survive each stage of the development process (see Fig-

FIGURE 12-2
*Major Stages in New
Product Development*

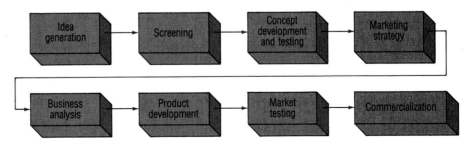

ure 12-3). In 1968 it took fifty-eight new product ideas to yield one good one. The latest study shows that companies are now able to turn one out of seven ideas into a successful new product. Booz, Allen & Hamilton concluded that many companies are prescreening and planning more effectively and are investing money only in the best ideas, rather than using a shotgun approach.

The search for new product ideas should be systematic rather than haphazard. Otherwise the company will find scores of ideas, most of which will not be appropriate for its type of business. One company spent more than a million dollars for research and development on a new product, only to have top management refuse final approval because it did not want to get into that type of business.

Top management can avoid this error by defining its new product development strategy carefully. It should state what products and markets to emphasize. It should state what the company wants to accomplish with the new products, whether it is high cash flow, market-share domination, or some other objective. It should state the relative effort to be devoted to developing original products, modifying existing products, and imitating competitors' products.

To generate a continuous flow of new product ideas, the company must aggressively cultivate many idea sources. Major sources of new product ideas include:

- *Internal sources.* One study found that over 55 percent of all new product ideas come from within the company.[3] The company can find new ideas through formal research and development. It can pick the brains of its scientists, engineers, and manufacturing personnel. Or company executives can brainstorm new product ideas. The company's salespeople are another good source because they are in daily contact with customers.

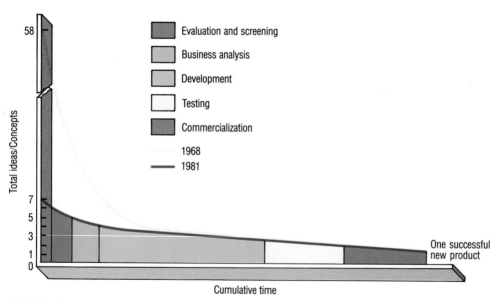

FIGURE 12-3 *Decay Curve of New Product Ideas*

Source: *New Products Management for the 1980s* (New York: Booz, Allen & Hamilton, 1982).

- *Customers.* Almost 28 percent of all new product ideas come from an analysis of customers. Consumer needs and wants can be monitored through consumer surveys and focus groups. The company can analyze customer inquiries and complaints to discover new products that can better solve consumer problems. Company engineers or salespeople can meet with customers to obtain suggestions or discover new technologies and applications. General Electric's Video Products Division has its design engineers talk directly with final consumers to get ideas for new electronics products for the home. National Steel has a product application center where company engineers work with automotive customers to discover specific customer needs that might require new products or applications.[4] Finally, consumers often create new products on their own to solve their problems, and companies can benefit by finding these products and commercializing them. Pillsbury obtains promising new recipes through its annual Bake-Off—one of Pillsbury's four cake-mix lines and several variations of another resulted directly from Bake-Off winners' recipes. IBM's Installed User Program finds and acquires user-developed software programs for its medium and large computers—about one-third of all the software IBM leases for these computers is developed by outside users.[5]

- *Competitors.* About 27 percent of new product ideas come from analyses of competitors' products. Companies regularly buy competing new products, take them apart to see how they work, analyze their market performance, and decide whether the company should respond with a new product of its own. The company can also monitor competitors' ads and other communications to obtain clues about their new product interests.

- *Distributors and Suppliers.* Resellers are close to the market and can pass along information about consumer problems and new product possibilities. Suppliers can tell the company about new concepts, techniques, and materials that can be used to develop new products.

- *Other sources.* Other idea sources include trade magazines, shows, and seminars; government agencies; new product consultants; advertising agencies; marketing research firms; university and commercial laboratories; and inventors (see Exhibit 12-2).

EXHIBIT 12-2

WILD NEW IDEAS—KEEP THEM COMING

There is no dearth of wild ideas. Burt Shulman, who works for IBM, has invented a number of things in his spare time: a gadget that blows smoke away from the noses of people who use soldering guns; an alarm-clock radio that senses when it is going to snow or rain and wakens the sleeper earlier than usual; a tiny machine that improves the circulation of desk-bound executives by continuously moving their feet up and down; a device that permits motorists to breath fresh air when they are caught in traffic jams; ultrasonic tweezers for the permanent removal of ingrown hairs; and a jogging machine strapped on the jogger's back to help the jogger run at twenty miles an hour. None of these, unfortunately, have been commercial successes.

Occasionally a wild idea works. Consider contact lenses for chickens! Robert Garrison invented them while working with the owner of a large chicken farm in Oregon. There were 470.8 million chickens in 1978, and the large farms had more than ten thousand birds each. Raising chickens for egg production is big business, and a device that saves chickens from pecking each other to death and makes them concentrate on eating and producing eggs is a needed product. The chicken's comb and way it holds its head signal the pecking order. If chickens cannot see the combs, cannibalism among chickens is greatly reduced. When the birds wear contact lenses, their perception is reduced to twelve inches, and they cannot recognize the comb of another chicken. The lens also solves the problem of the most submissive birds' having a hard time getting to the feeding trough. Since chicken farms already spend money debeaking birds in order to avoid cannibalism and debeaking often creates trauma, the expense of putting in lenses saves money in the long run.

Who knows what will be next? A contraceptive pet food to keep down the cat population? Don't laugh. The Carnation Company of Los Angeles is working on it.

Sources: "Burt Shulman" is described in Richard Severs, ". . . or Jogger Huff Puffing: It's a Gas," *Chicago Tribune,* January 7, 1979. "Contact lenses for chickens" is adapted from Darral G. Clarke, "Optical Distortion, Inc.," in *Problems in Marketing,* ed. Steven H. Star and others (New York: McGraw-Hill, 1977), pp. 530–50.

Idea Screening The purpose of idea generation is to create a large number of ideas. The purpose of the succeeding stages is to *reduce* the number of ideas. The first idea-pruning stage is *screening*.

In the screening stage, the company must avoid two types of errors. A DROP-error occurs when the company dismisses an otherwise good idea. Some companies shudder when they think of some of the ideas they dismissed:

> Xerox saw the novel promise of Chester Carlson's copying machine; IBM and Eastman Kodak did not see it at all. RCA was able to envision the innovative opportunity of radio; the Victor Talking Machine Company could not. Henry Ford recognized the promise of the automobile; yet only General Motors realized the need to segment the automobile market into price and performance categories, with a model for every classification, if the promise was to be fully achieved. Marshall Field understood the unique market development possibilities of installment buying; Endicott Johnson did not, calling it "the vilest system yet devised to create trouble." And so it has gone.[6]

If a company makes too many DROP-errors, its standards are too conservative.

A GO-error occurs when the company permits a poor idea to move into development and commercialization. This results in products which lose money or produce disappointing profits.

The purpose of screening is to spot and drop poor ideas as early as possible. Product development costs rise substantially at each successive stage. When products reach later stages, management often feels that it has invested so much in development that the product should be launched to recoup some of the investment. But this is letting good money chase bad, and the real solution is to not let poor product ideas get this far.

Most companies require their executives to write up new product ideas on a standard form that can be reviewed by a new product committee. They describe the product, the target market, and the competition and make some rough estimates of market size, product price, development time and costs, manufacturing costs, and rate of return.

Even if the idea looks good, the question arises, Is it appropriate for the particular company? Does it mesh well with the company's objectives, strategies, and resources? Table 12-2 shows a common type of rating form for this question. The first column lists factors required for the successful launching of the product in

TABLE 12-2 *Product-Idea Rating Device*

PRODUCT SUCCESS REQUIREMENTS	(A) RELATIVE WEIGHT	(B) COMPANY COMPETENCE LEVEL											RATING (A × B)
		.0	.1	.2	.3	.4	.5	.6	.7	.8	.9	1.0	
Company personality and goodwill	.20							✔					.120
Marketing	.20										✔		.180
Research and development	.20								✔				.140
Personnel	.15							✔					.090
Finance	.10										✔		.090
Production	.05									✔			.040
Location and facilities	.05				✔								.015
Purchasing and supplies	.05										✔		.045
Total	1.00												.720*

Adapted from Barry M. Richman, "A Rating Scale for Product Innovation," *Business Horizons,* Summer 1962, pp. 37–44.
*Rating scale: .00–.40 poor, .41–.75 fair; .76–1.00 good. Present minimum acceptance rate: .70.

the marketplace. In the next column, management assigns weights to these factors to reflect their relative importance. Thus management believes that marketing competence is very important (.20) and purchasing and supplies competence is of minor importance (.05).

The next task is to rate the company's competence on each factor on a scale from .0 to 1.0. Here management feels that its marketing competence is very high (.9) and its location and facilities competence is low (.3). The final step is to multiply the importance of each success factor by the company competence level to obtain an overall rating of ability to launch this product successfully. Thus, if marketing is an important success factor and this company is very good at marketing, this will increase the overall rating of the product idea. In the example, the product idea scored .72, which places it at the high end of the "fair idea" level.[7]

The checklist promotes a more systematic product idea evaluation and basis for discussion—it is not designed to make the decision for management.[8]

Concept Development and Testing

Surviving ideas must now be developed into product concepts. It is important to distinguish between a product idea, a product concept, and a product image. A *product idea* is an idea for a possible product that the company can see itself offering to the market. A *product concept* is an elaborated version of the idea expressed in meaningful consumer terms. A *product image* is the particular picture consumers acquire of an actual or potential product.

Concept Development

Suppose an automobile manufacturer discovers how to design an electric car that can go as fast as 50 miles an hour and as far as 100 miles before needing to be recharged. The manufacturer estimates that the electric car's operating costs will be about half of those of a conventional car.

This is a product idea. Customers, however, do not buy a product idea; they buy a product concept. The marketer's task is to develop this idea into some alternative product concepts, evaluate their relative attractiveness to customers, and choose the best one.

Among the product concepts that might be created for the electric car are the following:

- *Concept 1.* An inexpensive subcompact designed as a second family car to be used by the homemaker for short shopping trips. The car is ideal for loading groceries and transporting children, and it is easy to enter.
- *Concept 2.* A medium-cost, intermediate-size car designed as an all-purpose family car.
- *Concept 3.* A medium-cost sporty compact appealing to young people.
- *Concept 4.* An inexpensive subcompact appealing to the conscientious citizen who wants basic transportation, low fuel cost, and low ecological pollution.

Concept Testing

Concept testing calls for testing these concepts with an appropriate group of target consumers. The concepts may be presented symbolically or physically. At this stage a word or picture description suffices, although the more concrete and physical the stimulus, the greater the reliability of the concept test. The consumers are presented with an elaborated version of each concept. Here is concept 1:

> An efficient, fun-to-drive, electric-powered car in the subcompact class that seats four. Great for shopping trips and visits to friends. Costs half as much to operate as similar gasoline-driven cars. Goes up to 50 miles an hour and does not need to be recharged for 100 miles. Priced at $8,000.

Consumers are asked to react to this concept with the questions shown in Table 12-3. The responses will help the company determine which concept has the strongest appeal. For example, the last question in Table 12-3 goes after the consumer's *intention-to-buy* and usually reads: "Would you *definitely, probably, probably not, definitely not* buy this product?" Suppose 10 percent of the consumers said "definitely" and another 5 percent said "probably." The company would project these figures to the corresponding population size of this target group to estimate sales volume. Even then, the estimate is tentative because people do not always carry out their stated intentions.[9]

TABLE 12-3

Major Questions in a Concept Test for an Electric Car

1. Is the concept of an electric car clear to you?
2. What do you see as distinct benefits of an electric car compared with a conventional car?
3. Do you find the claims about the electric car's performance believable?
4. Would an electric car meet a real need of yours?
5. What improvements can you suggest in various features of the electric car?
6. Who would be involved in a possible purchase decision and who would use the car?
7. What do you think the price of the electric car should be?
8. Would you prefer an electric car to a conventional car? For what uses?
9. Would you buy an electric car? (Definitely, probably, probably not, definitely not)

Marketing Strategy Development Suppose the first-listed concept for the electric car tests out best. The next step calls for developing a preliminary marketing strategy for introducing this car into the market.

The marketing strategy statement consists of three parts. The first part describes the size, structure, and behavior of the target market, the planned product positioning and the sales, market share, and profit goals sought in the first few years. Thus:

> The target market is households that need a second car for shopping trips and visits to friends. The car will be positioned as more economical to buy and operate, and more fun to drive, than cars currently available to this market. The company will aim to sell five hundred thousand cars in the first year, at a loss not exceeding $3 million. The second year will aim for sales of seven hundred thousand cars with a planned profit of $5 million.

The second part of the marketing strategy statement outlines the product's planned price, distribution strategy, and marketing budget for the first year:

> The electric car will be offered in three colors and will have optional air-conditioning and power-drive features. It will sell at a retail price of $8,000, with 15 percent off the list price to dealers. Dealers who sell over ten cars per month will get an additional discount of 5 percent on each car sold that month. An advertising budget of $10 million will be split 50:50 between national and local advertising. Advertising copy will emphasize the car's economy and fun. During the first year, $100,000 will be spent on marketing research to monitor who is buying the car and their satisfaction levels.

The third part of the marketing strategy statement describes the planned long-run sales and profit goals and marketing mix strategy over time:

> The company intends to ultimately capture 6 percent of the total auto market and realize an after-tax return on investment of 15 percent. To achieve this, product quality will start high and be further improved over time through technical research. Price will be raised in the second and third years if competition permits. The total advertising budget will be boosted each year by about 10 percent. Marketing research will be reduced to $60,000 per year after the first year.

Business Analysis Once management has decided on the product concept and marketing strategy, it can evaluate the business attractiveness of the proposal. Management must review the sales, costs, and profit projections to determine whether they satisfy the company's objectives. If they do, the product can move to the product development stage.

Estimating Sales

Management needs to estimate whether sales will be high enough to return a satisfactory profit to the firm. Management should examine the sales history of similar products and should survey market opinion. Management should prepare estimates of minimum and maximum sales to learn the range of risk.

FIGURE 12-4
Product Life-Cycle Sales
for Three Types of
Products

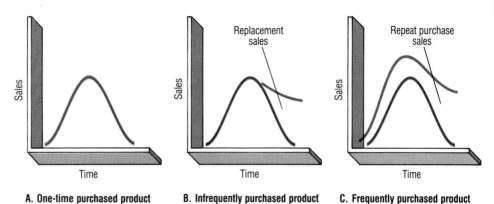

A. One-time purchased product   **B. Infrequently purchased product**   **C. Frequently purchased product**

Sales forecasting methods were described in Chapter 9. In forecasting the sales of a product, much depends on whether it is a one-time purchased product, an infrequently purchased product, or a frequently purchased product.

Figure 12-4A illustrates the product life-cycle sales that can be expected for one-time purchased products. Sales rise at the beginning, peak, and later approach zero as the number of potential buyers is exhausted. If new buyers keep entering the market, the curve will not quite go down to zero.

Infrequently purchased products such as automobiles, toasters, and industrial equipment exhibit replacement cycles, dictated by either their physical wearing out or their obsolescence associated with changing styles, features, and tastes.[10] Sales forecasting for this product category calls for separately estimating first-time sales and replacement sales (see Figure 12-4B).

Frequently purchased products, such as consumer and industrial nondurables, have product life-cycle sales resembling Figure 12-4C. The number of first-time buyers initially increases and then decreases as fewer are left (assuming a fixed population). Repeat purchases occur soon, providing that the product satisfies some fraction of the people who become steady customers. The sales curve eventually falls to a plateau representing a level of steady repeat-purchase volume; by this time the product is no longer in the class of new products.

Estimating Costs and Profits

After preparing the sales forecast, management can estimate the expected costs and profits of this venture. The costs are estimated by the R&D, manufacturing, accounting, and finance departments. The planned marketing costs are included in the analysis. The financial attractiveness of the proposal is estimated, using such techniques as breakeven analysis, payout period analysis, and risk-and-return analysis, all of which are described in standard finance textbooks.

Product   If the product concept passes the business test, it moves to R&D or engineering to
Development   be developed into a physical product. Up to now it existed only as a word descrip-

Design prototype for a new General Motors automobile. *Courtesy of General Motors Corporation.*

tion, a drawing, or a crude mockup. This step calls for a large jump in investment, which dwarfs the idea-evaluation costs incurred in the earlier stages. This stage will show whether the product idea can be translated into a technically and commercially feasible product. If not, the company's accumulated investment will be lost except for any useful information gained in the process.

The R&D department will develop one or more physical versions of the product concept. It hopes to find a prototype that satisfies the following criteria: (1) Consumers see it as embodying the key attributes described in the product concept statement; (2) the prototype performs safely under normal use and conditions; (3) the prototype can be produced for the budgeted manufacturing costs.

Developing a successful prototype can take days, weeks, months, or even years. The prototype must incorporate the required functional characteristics and also convey the intended psychological characteristics. The electric car, for example, should strike consumers as being well built and safe. Management must learn how consumers decide how well built a car is. One consumer practice is to slam the door to hear its "sound." If the car does not have "solid-sounding" doors, consumers will think it is poorly built.

When the prototypes are ready, they must be tested. *Functional tests* are conducted under laboratory and field conditions to make sure that the product performs safely and effectively. The new car must start well; its tires must not fall off; it must be able to maneuver corners without overturning. *Consumer tests* involve asking consumers to test-drive the car and rate the car and its attributes. (For an actual example of product development and testing, see Exhibit 12-3.)

EXHIBIT 12-3

BRUNSWICK GOES THROUGH THE RIGOR OF PRODUCT DEVELOPMENT AND TESTING

After World War II, Brunswick Corporation, the market leader in bowling and billiard equipment, searched for a new product area. The company wished to use its expertise in fabricating large wooden objects. Brunswick finally selected the school furniture market.

To identify the needs in the market, Brunswick interviewed three hundred educators. Many educators expressed dissatisfaction with the heavy furniture in the typical classroom. Brunswick decided to develop a line of light, movable classroom furniture. This furniture would facilitate team teaching, small-group learning, and the use of classroom television.

The initial step in the new product development process was to develop sketches of the new furniture. Educators and school officials were asked to react to these sketches. Some educators thought that the chairs looked flimsy, and others raised questions about the orthopedics of the chair. This led to a series of revised sketches. Then Brunswick produced a set of handmade prototypes that it tested in the company's offices.

A final prototype was then selected, and a limited number of chairs were produced for further testing. Educators and children were exposed to these chairs to see how the chairs would be used and would withstand various kinds of maltreatment. Children were placed in a room and photographed as they used the chairs with and without supervision. Model classrooms were constructed using the full Brunswick furniture line. These classrooms served as places to observe chair use as well as to display the furniture to educators.

When Brunswick determined that the furniture met educators' needs and would survive abuse, it introduced its chair line at the annual National Education Association convention. It sold out the entire first year's production capacity before the convention ended.

This was not, however, the end of product development and testing. As reports of field usage came back to Brunswick, the chair was modified to cope with unforeseen problems. For example, in California it became a craze among high school students to peel the desk arm away from the chair. The chair was redesigned to prevent this.

There were other inputs for chair modification. Many cost-cutting changes were initiated by manufacturing. The wooden chair gave way to fiberglass models, with the cost per chair dropping from $18 to $5.

Market Testing If the product passes functional and consumer tests, the next step is market testing.

Market testing is the stage where the product and marketing program are introduced into more realistic market settings.

Market testing allows the marketer to gain experience with marketing the product, to root out potential problems, and to find out where more information is needed before going to the enormous expense of full introduction. The basic purpose of market testing is to test the product itself in real market situations. But market testing also allows the company to test the entire marketing program for the product—product positioning strategy, advertising, distribution, pricing, branding and packaging, and budget levels. The company uses market testing to learn how consumers and dealers will react to handling, using, and repurchasing the product. Market testing results can be used to make more reliable sales and profit forecasts.

The amount of market testing needed varies with each new product. Market testing costs can be enormous, and market testing takes time during which competitors may gain an advantage. When the costs of developing and introducing the product are low or when management is already confident that the new product will succeed, the company may do little or no product testing. Minor modifications of current products or imitations of successful competitor products, for example, might not need testing. When introducing the new product requires a large investment, or when management is uncertain of the product or marketing program, the product may require extensive market testing. In fact, some products and marketing programs are tested, then withdrawn, modified, and retested many times over a period of several years before they are finally introduced. The costs of such market tests are high, but they are often insignificant compared with the costs of making a major mistake (see Exhibit 12-4).

EXHIBIT 12-4

TEST MARKETING SAVES A PRODUCT—DREAM WHIP

After conducting extensive product tests and consumer home-use tests, General Foods decided it was ready to put its Dream Whip whipped cream into several test markets to see how much consumer purchase would be generated under real market conditions. General Foods chose five sites for test marketing—Indianapolis, Huntington, Louisville, Columbus, and Cincinnati—because this number of cities would permit testing different marketing mixes and budgets. Furthermore, one or two cities might yield atypical results because of weather conditions, competitive maneuvers, and so on.

Dream Whip was introduced in October and the response was very positive. However, by the following June, inventory started building up. Mail from consumers started to come in about the product's failure to perform. General Foods' researchers examined the complaints and discovered that hot weather caused a high failure rate in whipping. Management decided to delay national introduction. Instead, management opened a few additional test markets in Boston, Detroit, and Pittsburgh during the cold weather months to collect more consumer response data and to trim inventories. Meanwhile, the research and development department searched for a solution, which it found a year later, and modified the formula. The new formula for Dream Whip was successful in the test markets during warm weather. The new product was finally ready for national introduction. The expense of test marketing was minor compared with the huge losses the company would have suffered had it gone straight into national marketing.

Thus whether or not testing is done, and the amount of testing, depend on the investment cost and risk of introducing the product on the one hand, and on the testing costs and time pressures on the other. Market-testing methods vary with the type of product and market situation, and each method has advantages and disadvantages. Table 12-4 describes the major market testing approaches.

Commercialization Market testing presumably gives management enough information to make a final decision about whether to launch the new product. If the company goes ahead with commercialization, it will face its largest costs to date. The company will have to

TABLE 12-4

*Methods of Market
Testing*

Consumer Packaged Goods

Standard test markets. Standard test markets test the new consumer product in a situation resembling the one it would face in a full-scale launch. The company locates a small number of representative test cities in which the company's salesforce tries to sell the trade on carrying the product and giving it good shelf exposure and other support. The company puts on a full advertising and promotion campaign in these markets similar to the one that would be used in national marketing. The company uses store or warehouse audits, consumer and distributor surveys, and other measures to gauge product performance. The results are used to forecast national sales and profits, to discover potential product problems, and to fine-tune the marketing program.

Standard market tests have some drawbacks. First, they take a long time to complete—usually from one to three years. If it turns out that the testing was unnecessary, the company will have lost many months of sales and profits. Second, extensive standard test markets may cost millions of dollars. Finally, standard test markets give competitors a look at the company's new product well before it is introduced nationally. Many competitors will buy and analyze the product. They will also monitor the company's test market results and may have time to develop defensive strategies. If the testing goes on too long, competing products may even beat the company's product to the market. Furthermore, competitors often try to distort test market results by cutting their prices in test cities, increasing their advertising and promotion, or even buying up the product being tested. Despite these disadvantages, standard market tests are the most widely used approach when major market testing is needed. They provide a wealth of information on product and marketing performance under actual market conditions.

Controlled test markets. Several research firms have arranged a controlled panel of stores which have agreed to carry new products for a fee. The company with the new product specifies the number of stores and geographical locations it wants. The research firm delivers the product to the participating stores and controls shelf location, number of facings, displays and point-of-purchase promotions, and pricing according to specified plans. Sales results are tracked to determine the impact of these factors on demand.

Test marketing companies like Behavior-Scan use information from electronic scanners at checkout counters to track test-market results. The company maintains a panel of about 2,500 shoppers in eight carefully selected small cities. These consumers buy from cooperating stores and show identification cards when making purchases. Detailed electronic scanner information on each consumer's purchase is fed into a central computer, where it is combined with the consumer's demographic information and reported daily. Thus Behavior-Scan can provide up-to-the-minute reports on the overall sales of new products being tested. And because the scanners record the specific purchases of individual consumers, the system can also provide information on repeat purchases and how different types of consumers are reacting to the new product and various elements of the marketing program.

Controlled test markets take less time than standard test markets (six months to a year) and usually cost less (a year-long Behavior-Scan test might cost from $200,000 to $600,000). However, some companies are concerned that the limited number of small cities and panel consumers used by the research services may not be representative of their products' markets or target consumers. And, as in standard test markets, controlled test markets allow competitors to get a look at the company's new product.

Simulated test markets. Here new products are tested in a simulated shopping environment. The company or research firm shows a sample of consumers ads and promotions for a variety of products, including the new product being tested. The consumers are given a small amount of money and are invited into a store where they may use the money to buy items or keep the money. The company notes how many consumers buy the new product and competing brands. This provides a measure of trial and the commercial's effectiveness against competing commercials. Consumers are then asked the reasons for their purchase or nonpurchase. Some weeks later they are interviewed by phone to determine product attitudes, usage, satisfaction, and repurchase intentions. Sophisticated computer models are used to project national sales from results of the simulated test market.

Simulated test markets overcome some of the disadvantages of standard and controlled test markets. They usually cost much less ($35,000 to $75,000) and can be run in eight weeks. And the new product is kept out of competitors' view. Yet, many marketers don't think that simulated market tests are as accurate or reliable as real-world tests.

Sales wave research. Here a sample of consumers try the new product in their homes at no cost. They are reoffered the product or competitive brands as many as three to five times (sales waves) at a reduced cost, with the company noting how many consumers selected the product again and their reported level of satisfaction. Sales wave research can be done inexpensively and privately and it allows for the collection of in-depth information on consumer reactions to the new product. The disadvantages result from small sample sizes and difficulties in generalizing results to larger groups of consumers.

Industrial Durable Goods

Product-use tests. The manufacturer selects a small group of potential customers who agree to use the new product for a limited period. The manufacturer's technical people observe how these customers use the product. This tells the manufacturer about customer training and servicing requirements. After the test, the customer is asked to express purchase intent and other reactions.

Trade shows. Trade shows draw a large number of buyers who view new products in a few concentrated days. The manufacturer can see how much interest buyers show in the new product, how they react to various features and terms, and how many express purchase intentions or place orders.

Distribution and dealer display rooms. The new industrial product can be tested in distributor and dealer display rooms, where it may stand next to the manufacturer's other products and possibly competitors' products. This method yields preference and pricing information in the normal selling atmosphere for the product.

Controlled or test marketing. Some manufacturers will produce a limited supply of the product and give it to the salesforce to sell in a limited number of geographical areas that will be given promotional support, printed catalog sheets, and so on.

Sources: For more on testing consumer products, see Edward M. Tauber, "Forecasting Sales Prior to Test Market," *Journal of Marketing,* January 1977, pp. 80–84; Jeremy Main, "Help and Hype in the New-Products Game," *Fortune,* February 7, 1983, pp. 60–64; "To Test or Not to Test Is Seldom the Question," *Advertising Age,* February 20, 1984, pp. M10ff; "Product Hopes Tied to Cities with Right Stuff," *Advertising Age,* February 20, 1984, pp. M10ff; and Eleanor Johnson Tracy, "Testing Time for Test Markets," *Fortune,* October 29, 1984, pp. 75–76. For more on testing industrial products, see Morgan B. McDonald, Jr., *Appraising the Market for New Industrial Products* (New York: Conference Board, 1967), chap. 2.

build or rent a full-scale manufacturing facility. And it may have to spend, in the case of a new consumer packaged good, between $10 million and $100 million for advertising and sales promotion alone in the first year.

In launching a new product, the company must make four decisions.

When (Timing)

The first decision is whether it is the right time to introduce the new product. If the electric car will cannibalize the company's other cars, its introduction may be delayed.[11] Or if the electric car can be improved further, the company may prefer to launch it next year. Or if the economy is depressed, the company may prefer to wait.

Where (Geographical Strategy)

The company must decide whether to launch the new product in a *single locality,* a *region, several regions,* the *national market,* or the *international market.* Few companies have the confidence, capital, and capacity to launch new products into full national distribution. They will develop a *planned market rollout* over time. Small companies, in particular, will select an attractive city and put on a blitz campaign to enter the market. They will enter other cities one at a time. Large companies will introduce their product into a whole region and then move to the next region. Companies with national distribution networks, such as auto companies, will launch their new models in the national market unless there are production shortages.

To Whom (Target Market Prospects)

Within the rollout markets, the company must target its distribution and promotion to the best prospect groups. Presumably the company has already profiled the prime prospects on the basis of earlier market testing. Prime prospects for a new consumer product would ideally have four characteristics:[12] (1) They would be early adopters; (2) they would be heavy users; (3) they would be opinion leaders and talk favorably about the product; (4) they could be reached at a low cost.

How (Introductory Marketing Strategy)

The company must develop an action plan for introducing the new product into the rollout markets. It must allocate the marketing budget among the marketing mix elements and sequence the various activities. Thus the electric car's launch may be preceded by a teaser publicity campaign after it arrives in the showrooms, and then by offers of gifts to draw more people to the showrooms. The company must prepare a separate marketing plan for each new market. The marketing plans should be guided by the findings in the theory of consumer adoption behavior described in Chapter 7.

PRODUCT LIFE-CYCLE STRATEGIES

After launching the new product, management wants the product to enjoy a long and happy life. Although under no illusion that the product will sell forever, management wants to earn a decent profit to cover all the effort and risk that went into it. Management hopes that sales will be high and last long. Management is aware that each product will exhibit a life cycle, although the exact shape and duration is not easily known in advance.

The typical product life cycle (PLC) is S-shaped (Figure 12-5A) and is marked by four distinct stages:

FIGURE 12-5 *Three Product Life-Cycle Patterns*

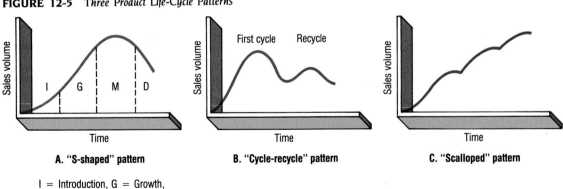

A. "S-shaped" pattern   B. "Cycle-recycle" pattern   C. "Scalloped" pattern

I = Introduction, G = Growth,
M = Maturity, D = Decline

1. *Introduction* is a period of slow sales growth as the product is being introduced in the market. Profits are nonexistent in this stage because of the heavy expenses of product introduction.

2. *Growth* is a period of rapid market acceptance and increasing profits.

3. *Maturity* is a period of slowdown in sales growth because the product has achieved acceptance by most of the potential buyers. Profits stabilize or decline because of increased marketing outlays to defend the product against competition.

4. *Decline* is the period when sales show a strong downward drift and profits erode.

Not all products exhibit an S-shaped product life cycle. Cox studied the sales histories of 754 ethical drug products and found six different product life-cycle patterns.[13] A typical form was a "cycle-recycle" pattern (Figure 12-5B). The second "hump" in sales was caused by a promotional push in the decline stage. Another common pattern was "scalloped" (Figure 12-5C), consisting of a succession of life cycles based on the discovery of new product characteristics, new uses, or new users. Nylon's sales, for example, show a scalloped pattern because of the many new uses—parachutes, hosiery, shirts, carpeting—discovered over time.

The PLC concept can describe a product class (gasoline-powered automobiles), a product form ("convertible top" automobiles), or a brand (Mustang). The PLC concept has a different degree of applicability in each case.

Product classes have the longest life cycles. The sales of many product classes stay in the mature stage for an indefinite duration, since they are highly population related (cars, perfume, refrigerators, and steel). *Product forms,* on the other hand, tend to exhibit the standard PLC histories more faithfully than do product classes. Product forms such as the "dial telephone" and "cream deodorants" pass through a regular history of introduction, rapid growth, maturity, and decline. As for *brands,* a

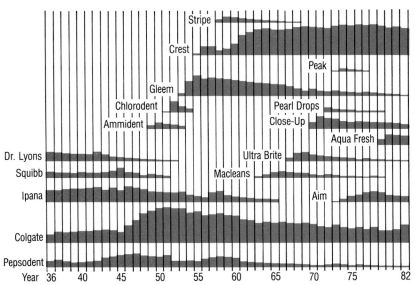

FIGURE 12-6 *Product Life Cycles for Selected Toothpaste Brands from 1936 to 1982*

Source: "Life Beyond the Life Cycle," *The Nielsen Researcher,* Number 1, 1984, p. 3.

brand's sales history can be erratic because of changing competitive attacks and counterattacks. The life cycles of several toothpaste brands are shown in Figure 12-6.

The PLC concept can also be applied to what are known as styles, fashions, and fads. Their special life-cycle features are described in Exhibit 12-5.

The PLC concept can be used by marketers as a useful conceptual framework for describing product-market dynamics. However, applying the PLC concept as a tool for forecasting product performance or for developing marketing strategies presents some practical problems.[14] For example, managers may have difficulty identifying a product's current life-cycle stage, when it moves into the next stage, and the factors that affect how the product will move through the stages. In practice, it is very difficult to forecast the sales level at each PLC stage, the duration of each stage, and the shape of the PLC curve.

Using the PLC concept to develop marketing strategy can be difficult because strategy is both a cause and result of the product's life cycle. The product's current PLC position suggests which marketing strategies will be most effective, and the resulting marketing strategies affect product performance in later life-cycle stages. Despite these and other problems, when used carefully the PLC concept can be a useful framework for developing effective marketing strategies for different stages of the product life cycle. We now turn to these stages and consider appropriate marketing strategies.

Introduction Stage

The **introduction stage** starts when the new product is first distributed and made available for purchase. Introduction takes time, and sales growth is apt to be slow. Such well-known products as instant coffee, frozen orange juice, and powdered coffee creamers lingered for many years before they entered a stage of rapid growth. Buzzell identified four causes for the slow growth of many processed food products: (1) delays in the expansion of production capacity; (2) technical problems ("working out the bugs"); (3) delays in making the product available to customers, especially in obtaining adequate distribution through retail outlets; (4) customer reluctance to change established behavior patterns.[15] In the case of expensive new products, sales growth is retarded by additional factors, such as the small number of buyers who can adopt and afford the new product.

In this stage, profits are negative or low because of the low sales and heavy distribution and promotion expenses. Much money is needed to attract distributors and "fill the pipelines." Promotional expenditures are at their highest ratio to sales "because of the need for a high level of promotional effort to inform potential consumers of the new and unknown product, induce trial of the product, and secure distribution in retail outlets."[16]

There are only a few competitors and they produce basic versions of the product, since the market is not ready for product refinements. The firms focus their selling on those buyers who are the readiest to buy, usually the higher-income groups. Prices tend to be on the high side because "costs are high due to relatively low output rates, technological problems in production may have not yet been fully mastered, and high margins are required to support the heavy promotional expenditures which are necessary to achieve growth."[17]

EXHIBIT 12-5

STYLE, FASHION, AND FAD CYCLES

In markets where style and fashion are influential, sales cycles take place, and marketers need to understand and predict them.

A *style* is a basic and distinctive mode of expression appearing in a field of human endeavor. For example, styles appear in homes (colonial, ranch, Cape Cod), clothing (formal, casual), and art (realistic, surrealistic, abstract). Once a style is invented, it may last for generations, coming in and out of vogue. A style exhibits a cycle showing several periods of renewed interest.

A *fashion* is a currently accepted or popular style in a given field. For example, jeans are a fashion in today's clothing. Fashions pass through four stages. In the *distinctiveness stage,* some consumers take an interest in something new to set themselves apart from other consumers. The product may be custom-made or produced in small quantities by some manufacturers. In the *emulation stage,* other consumers take an interest out of a desire to emulate the fashion leaders, and additional manufacturers begin to produce larger quantities of the product. In the *mass fashion stage,* the fashion has become extremely popular and manufacturers have geared up for mass production. Finally, in the *decline stage,* consumers start moving toward other fashions that are beginning to catch their eye.

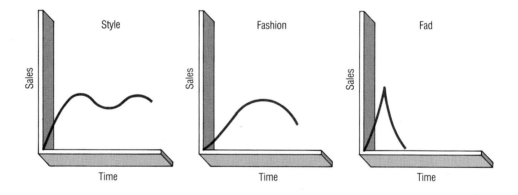

Thus fashions tend to grow slowly, remain popular for a while, and decline slowly. The length of a fashion cycle is hard to predict. Wasson believes that fashions come to an end because they represent a purchase compromise, and consumers start looking for missing attributes. For example, as automobiles get shorter, they get less comfortable, and then a growing number of buyers start wanting longer cars. Furthermore, too many consumers adopt the fashion, thus turning others away. Reynolds suggests that the length of a particular fashion cycle depends on the extent to which the fashion meets a genuine need, is consistent with other trends in the society, satisfies societal norms and values, and does not meet technological limits as it develops. Robinson, however, sees fashions as living out inexorable cycles regardless of economic, functional, or technological changes in society.

Fads are fashions that come quickly into the public eye, are adopted with great zeal, peak early, and decline very fast. Their acceptance cycle is short, and they tend to attract only a limited following. They often have a novel or capricious aspect, as when people start buying "pet rocks" or run naked and "streak." Fads appeal to people who are searching for excitement or who want to distinguish themselves from others or have something to talk excitement or who want to distinguish themselves from others or have something to talk about to others. Fads do not survive because they normally do not satisfy a strong need or satisfy it well. It is difficult to predict whether something will only be a fad, and if so, how long it will last—a few days, weeks, or months. The amount of media attention it receives, along with other factors, will influence its duration.

Sources: Chester R. Wasson, "How Predictable Are Fashion and Other Product Life Cycles?" *Journal of Marketing,* July 1968, pp. 36–43; William H. Reynolds, "Cars and Clothing: Understanding Fashion Trends," *Journal of Marketing,* July 1968, pp. 44–49; and Dwight E. Robinson, "Style Changes: Cyclical, Inexorable and Foreseeable," *Harvard Business Review,* November–December 1975, pp. 121–31. See also George B. Sproles, "Analyzing Fashion Life Cycles—Principles and Perspectives," *Journal of Marketing,* Fall 1981, pp. 116–24.

Growth Stage If the new product satisfies the market, sales will start climbing substantially. The early adopters will continue their purchasing and conventional consumers will start following their lead, especially if they hear favorable word of mouth. New competitors will enter the market attracted by the opportunities for large-scale production and profit. They will introduce new product features, and this will expand the market. The increased number of competitors leads to an increase in the number of distribution outlets, and factory sales jump just to fill the pipelines.

Prices remain where they are or fall only slightly insofar as demand is increasing quite rapidly. Companies maintain their promotional expenditures at the same or at a slightly raised level to meet competition and continue educating the market. Sales rise much faster, causing a decline in the promotion-sales ratio.

Profits increase during this **growth stage** as promotion costs are spread over a large volume, and unit manufacturing costs fall due to the "experience curve" effect (see Chapter 13). The firm uses several strategies to sustain rapid market growth as long as possible:

- The firm improves product quality and adds new product features and models.
- It enters new market segments.
- It enters new distribution channels.
- It shifts some advertising from building product awareness to bringing about product conviction and purchase.
- It lowers prices at the right time to attract the next layer of price-sensitive buyers.

The firm that pursues these market-expanding strategies will improve its competitive position. But this comes at an additional cost. The firm in the growth stage faces a tradeoff between high market share and high current profit. By spending a lot of money on product improvement, promotion, and distribution, it can capture a dominant position; but it forgoes maximum current profit in the hope of making this up in the next stage.

Maturity Stage At some point a product's rate of sales growth will slow down, and the product will enter a stage of relative maturity. This **maturity stage** normally lasts longer than the previous stages, and it poses formidable challenges to marketing management. *Most products are in the maturity stage of the life cycle, and therefore most of marketing management deals with the mature product.*

The slowdown in the rate of sales growth creates overcapacity in the industry. This overcapacity leads to intensified competition. Competitors engage more frequently in markdowns and off-list pricing. They increase their advertising and trade and consumer deals. They increase their R&D budgets to find better versions of the product. These steps mean some profit erosion. Some of the weaker competitors start dropping out. The industry eventually consists of well-entrenched competitors whose basic drive is to gain a competitive advantage.

The product manager should not simply defend the product. A good offense is the best defense. He or she should consider strategies of market, product, and marketing mix modification.

Market Modification

Here the manager tries to increase the consumption of the existing product. The manager looks for *new users* and *market segments.* The manager also looks for ways to stimulate *increased usage* among present customers. The manager may want to *reposition* the brand to appeal to a larger or faster-growing segment.

Product Modification

The product manager can also modify product characteristics—such as *product quality, features,* or *style*—to attract new users and more usage.

A strategy of *quality improvement* aims at increasing the functional performance of the product—its durability, reliability, speed, taste. This strategy is effective to the extent that the quality can be improved, buyers believe the claim of improved quality, and a sufficient number of buyers want higher quality.

A strategy of *feature improvement* aims at adding new features that expand the product's versatility, safety, or convenience. Feature improvement has been a successful strategy of Japanese makers of watches, calculators, and copying machines. For example, Sony keeps adding new playing features to its Walkman line of miniature stereo players. Stewart outlines five advantages of feature improvement.[18]

1. New features build a company image of progressiveness and leadership.
2. New features can be adapted quickly, dropped quickly, and often made optional at very little expense.

Sony keeps adding new features to its Walkman line. *Courtesy of Sony Corporation of America.*

3. New features can win the loyalty of certain market segments.
4. New features can bring the company free publicity.
5. New features generate salesforce and distributor enthusiasm.

A strategy of *style improvement* aims at increasing the esthetic appeal of the product. Thus car manufacturers restyle their cars periodically to attract buyers who want a new look.

Marketing Mix Modification

The product manager should also try to stimulate sales by modifying one or more marketing mix elements. Prices can be cut to attract new triers and competitors' customers. A more effective advertising campaign can be sought. Aggressive sales promotion—trade deals, cents-off, gifts, and contests—can be used. The company can move into higher-volume market channels, particularly mass merchandisers, if these channels are growing. The company can offer new or improved services to the buyers.

Decline Stage The sales of most product forms and brands eventually dip. The sales decline may be slow, as in the case of oatmeal cereal; or rapid, as in the case of the Edsel automobile. Sales may plunge to zero, or they may drop to a low level and continue for many years at that level. This is the **decline stage.**

Sales decline for a number of reasons, including technological advances, consumer shifts in tastes, and increased domestic and foreign competition. All lead to overcapacity, increased price cutting, and profit erosion.

As sales and profits decline, some firms withdraw from the market. Those remaining may reduce the number of their product offerings. They may drop smaller market segments and marginal trade channels. They may cut the promotion budget and reduce their prices further.

Carrying a weak product can be very costly to the firm. The cost is not just the amount of uncovered overhead or financial loss. Financial accounting cannot adequately convey all the hidden costs: The weak product may consume a disproportionate amount of management's time; it often requires frequent price and inventory adjustment; it generally involves short production runs in spite of expensive setup times; it requires both advertising and salesforce attention that might better be diverted to making the "healthy" products more profitable; its very unfitness can cause customer misgivings and cast a shadow on the company's image. The biggest cost may well lie in the future. By not being eliminated at the proper time, weak products delay the aggressive search for replacement products; they create a lopsided product mix, long on "yesterday's breadwinners" and short on "tomorrow's breadwinners"; they depress current profitability and weaken the company's foothold on the future.

For these reasons, companies need to pay more attention to their aging products. The first task is to identify those products in the declining stage by periodically reviewing the sales, market shares, cost, and profit trends on each of its products.[19] For each declining product, management has to decide whether to *maintain, harvest,* or *terminate* it. Management may decide to maintain its brand in the hope that

TABLE 12-5
*Product Life Cycle:
Characteristics and
Responses*

	INTRODUCTION	GROWTH	MATURITY	DECLINE
Characteristics				
Sales	Low	Fast growth	Slow growth	Decline
Profits	Negligible	Peak levels	Declining	Low or zero
Cash flow	Negative	Moderate	High	Low
Customers	Innovative	Mass market	Mass market	Laggards
Competitors	Few	Growing	Many rivals	Declining number
Responses				
Strategic focus	Expand market	Market penetration	Defend share	Productivity
Mktg. expenditures	High	High (declining %)	Falling	Low
Mktg. emphasis	Product awareness	Brand preference	Brand loyalty	Selective
Distribution	Patchy	Intensive	Intensive	Selective
Price	High	Lower	Lowest	Rising
Product	Basic	Improved	Differentiated	Rationalized

Source: Peter Doyle, "The Realities of the Product Life Cycle," *Quarterly Review of Marketing,* Summer 1976, p. 5.

competitors will leave the industry. For example, Procter & Gamble remained in the declining liquid-soap business as others withdrew, and it made good profits. Or management may decide to harvest the product, which means reducing various costs (plant and equipment, maintenance, R&D, advertising, sales force) and hoping that sales hold up fairly well for a while. If successful, harvesting will increase the company's profits in the short run. Or management may decide to drop the product from the line. It can sell it to another firm or simply liquidate it at salvage value. If the company plans to find a buyer, it will not want to run down the product through harvesting.

Large companies often dispose of brands that no longer meet their financial targets, although these brands might be profitable for a smaller company to handle. Here is a case in point.[20]

> Bristol-Myers marketed Ipana toothpaste until 1968 when its sales fell to a low level. Bristol-Myers sold the brand in early 1969 to two Minnesota businessmen. They modified the ingredients and packaged the product in Ipana tubes. Without any promotion, they continued to supply the retailers, and sales ran at $250,000 in the first seven months of operation.

The key characteristics of each stage of the product life cycle are summarized in Table 12-5. The table also lists the marketing responses made by companies in each stage.[21]

■ *Summary*

Organizations are increasingly recognizing the necessity and advantages of developing new products and services. Their current offerings face shortening life spans and must be replaced by newer products.

New products, however, can fail. The risks of innovation are as great as the rewards. The key to successful innovation lies in developing better organizational arrangements for handling new product ideas and developing sound research and decision procedures at each stage of the new product development process.

The new product development process consists of eight stages: idea generation, idea screening, concept development and testing, marketing strategy development, business analysis, product development, market testing, and commercialization. The purpose of each stage is to decide whether the idea should be further developed or dropped. The company wants to minimize the chances of poor ideas moving forward and good ideas being rejected.

Each commercialized product exhibits a life cycle marked by a changing set of problems and opportunities. The sales history of the typical product follows an S-shaped curve made up of four stages. The *introduc-* *tion stage* is marked by slow growth and minimal profits as the product is being pushed into distribution. If successful, the product enters a *growth stage* marked by rapid sales growth and increasing profits. During this stage the company attempts to improve the product, enter new market segments and distribution channels, and reduce its prices slightly. There follows a *maturity stage* in which sales growth slows down and profits stabilize. The company seeks innovative strategies to renew sales growth, including market, product, and marketing mix modification. Finally, the product enters a *decline stage* in which sales and profits deteriorate. The company's task during this stage is to identify the declining product and decide whether to maintain, harvest, or drop it. In the last case, the product can be sold to another firm or liquidated for salvage value.

■ Questions for Discussion

1. Polaroid, an acknowledged leader in photographic technology, introduced an "instant movie" system, Polavision, with substantial promotional expenditures to retailers and consumers. It lost $60 million the first two years after introduction, never gaining wide acceptance. Why, do you think, did Polavision fail, given Polaroid's previous record of new product successes?

2. The guiding principle in the idea generation stage is to limit the number of new product ideas that are proposed. Comment.

3. At what stage in the new product development process is the consumer first contacted? Explain briefly.

4. What type of market testing would you suggest for the following new products? (a) Clairol hair-care product, (b) American Motors line of trucks, and (c) Samsonite plastic suitcases.

5. Discuss the role and importance of promotional expenditures in each stage of the product life cycle.

6. Which one of the strategies discussed in the maturity stage did the following companies utilize? (a) Arm & Hammer baking soda, (b) State Farm insurance, and (c) Ford Mustang.

7. There is nothing the manager can do once a product reaches the decline stage. Comment.

■ References

1. William H. Reynolds, "The Edsel Ten Years Later," *Business Horizons,* Fall 1967, pp. 39–46; and John Brooks, *The Fate of the Edsel and Other Business Adventures* (New York: Hayes and Row, 1963).
2. David S. Hopkins and Earl L. Bailey, "New Product Pressures," *Conference Board Record,* June 1971, pp. 16–24.
3. See Leigh Lawton and A. Parasuraman, "So You Want Your New Product Planning to Be Productive," *Business Horizons,* December 1980, pp. 29–34.
4. See "Listening to the Voice of the Marketplace," *Business Week,* February 21, 1983, p. 90ff.
5. See Eric vonHipple, "Get New Products from Consumers," *Harvard Business Review,* March–April 1982, pp. 117–22.
6. Mark Hanan, "Corporate Growth through Venture Management," *Harvard Business Review,* January–February 1969, p. 44.
7. Refinements of this technique can be found in John T. O'Meara, Jr., "Selecting Profitable Products," *Harvard Business Review,* January–

February 1961, pp. 83–89; and John S. Harris, "New Product Profile Chart," *Chemical and Engineering News,* April 1969, pp. 110–18.

8. For more on idea screening, see Tom W. White, "Use Variety of Internal, External Sources to Gather and Screen New Product Ideas," *Marketing News,* September 16, 1983, Sec. 2, p. 12.

9. For more on product concept testing, see William L. Moore, "Concept Testing," *Journal of Business Research,* 10 (1982), pp. 279–94; and David A. Schwartz, "Concept Testing Can Be Improved— and Here's How," *Marketing News,* January 6, 1984, pp. 22–23.

10. The physical life expectancies (in years) of some major appliances are: freezer, 20.4; refrigerator, 15.2; electric range, 12.1; color TV, 12.0; and automatic washing machine, 10.8. See M. D. Ruffin and K. J. Tippett, "Service Life Expectancy of Household Appliances: New Estimates from the USDA," *Home Economics Research Journal,* 3 (1975), 159–70.

11. See Roger A. Kerin, Michael G. Harvey, and James T. Rothe, "Cannibalism and New Product Development," *Business Horizons,* October 1978, pp. 25–31.

12. Philip Kotler and Gerald Zaltman, "Targeting Prospects for a New Product," *Journal of Advertising Research,* February 1976, pp. 7–20.

13. William E. Cox, Jr., "Product Life Cycles as Marketing Models," *Journal of Business,* October 1967, pp. 375–84. See also John E. Swan and David R. Rink, "Fitting Market Strategy to Varying Product Life Cycles," *Business Horizons,* January–February 1982, pp. 72–76.

14. See George S. Day, "The Product Life Cycle: Analysis and Applications Issues," *Journal of Marketing,* Fall 1981, pp. 60–67.

15. Robert D. Buzzell, "Competitive Behavior and the Product Life Cycle," in *New Ideas for Successful Marketing,* John S. Wright and Jac L. Goldstucker, eds. (Chicago: American Marketing Association, 1966), pp. 46–68, here p. 51.

16. Ibid., p. 51.

17. Ibid., p. 52.

18. John B. Stewart, "Functional Features in Product Strategy," *Harvard Business Review,* March–April 1959, pp. 65–78.

19. Several systems are in use. See Philip Kotler, "Phasing Out Weak Products," *Harvard Business Review,* March–April 1965, pp. 107–18; and Paul W. Hamelman and Edward M. Mazze, "Improving Product Abandonment Decisions," *Journal of Marketing,* April 1972, pp. 20–26.

20. "Abandoned Trademark Turns a Tidy Profit for Two Minnesotans," *Wall Street Journal,* October 27, 1969, p. 1.

21. For further reading on the product life-cycle concept, see Theodore Levitt, "Exploit the Product Life Cycle," *Harvard Business Review,* November–December 1965, pp. 81–94; Nariman K. Dhalla and Sonia Yuspeh, "Forget the Product Life Cycle Concept!" *Harvard Business Review,* January–February 1976, pp. 102–12; and the special section of articles on the product life cycle in the Fall 1981 issue of the *Journal of Marketing.*

CASE 7

HANES CORPORATION: FROM L'EGGS TO CHILDREN'S BOOKS?

The outstanding success of L'eggs panty hose encouraged Hanes to launch other products using the L'eggs marketing ideas with the hope of duplicating the L'eggs success. For example, the article below discusses Hanes' foray into cosmetics. In another effort to broaden the Hanes product mix, the marketing director for new products is working on a plan for marketing high-quality children's paperback books under the name Starbooks. He has called a meeting of his staff to get their ideas and provide a training opportunity.

These books would be aimed at preschool readers, early readers, and readers up to 12 years of age and be retail priced from $0.60 to $1.69. The licensing rights to 200 titles from several publishers would be available. Children's books are sold through book and department stores, direct mail, book clubs, and other retail outlets, with supermarkets and drug outlets each accounting for 6 percent of total children's book sales. Milwaukee, Rochester,

New York, Kansas City, and Salt Lake City were considered possible test markets, if it is decided to go ahead.

The marketing director's reasons for focusing on children's books included the following:

A large market exists, $600 million a year.

Many competitors with small market shares. Western Publishing Company's Golden Books are probably the best known.

Absence of aggressive marketing efforts.

Trend toward one-store shopping favors supermarkets and large chain drug stores.

Supermarkets and drugstores already carry children's books.

Children's books carry a higher percentage gross margin than most items in supermarkets.

The L'eggs marketing plan seemed to fit children's books, at least in part. The L'eggs direct distribution network was already in place.

A few days before the meeting, it was learned that a new marketing plan for Golden Books was soon to be launched by Racine-based Western Publishing Company, a subsidiary of Mattel, Inc., the well-known toy and game marketer. Western Publishing had not been innovative or aggressive in the past, and the marketing director did not believe the new plan would change the competitive situation very much.

What recommendations would you make to the marketing director?

Appendix: A Hosiery Giant Jumps from L'eggs to Faces

Hanes Corp. plowed along for 57 years as a none-too-sparkling apparel producer until 1971, when it introduced L'eggs, a distinctively packaged line of women's pantyhose. The product rapidly propelled the company's sales and earnings upward and made Hanes the dominant force in the $1.2 billion women's hosiery market. This week, banking on the marketing and distribution expertise it gained from the L'eggs venture, Hanes will begin a foray into a market that is wholly new to it: the $1.6 billion cosmetics business.

In some 700 supermarkets and 300 drug and discount stores in Kansas City and Cincinnati, display racks will blossom with an 80-item line of Hane's cosmetics, called L'aura.[1] If the tests prove successful, Hanes will probably push the line into other markets by early next year. The cosmetics line, Hanes hopes, will give the company the same kind of boost that it got from L'eggs in 1971. Revenues that year were $176 million; they hit $372 million last year. And earnings are up more than fivefold since 1971, reaching $18.6 million last year.

The new venture takes Hanes into a segment of a crowded and ferociously competitive market. But the segment it has picked out—sales in supermarkets and discount drug stores—is one that giants of the cosmetics business, such as Revlon, Avon Products, and Cheseborough-Pond's, have yet to enter to any significant degree. Up to now two brands have been dominant in this market: Maybelline (a product of Schering-Plough Corp.) and Cover Girl (a Noxell Corp. product).

Hanes figures that a marketing and distribution strategy borrowed from its L'eggs venture will win it a substantial share of the market. Among the key elements in that strategy:

The cosmetics will be sold from open displays, appealing to the impulse shopper. The displays are being built by New York City's Howard Display, Inc., which

[1]The name *L'aura* was changed to L'erin at the request of Richardson-Merrell Co., which was already using it.

created the award-winning L'eggs displays. And Hanes is pushing to have them placed near checkout counters, just as it has done with its L'eggs displays.

The packaging will be distinct from any other cosmetics on supermarket shelves, just as the packaging for L'eggs set that product apart from the competition. Each cosmetics item will be packaged in a burgundy-colored box with small plastic windows; supermarket competitors usually use plastic-blister packaging.

Hanes's own sales force will keep the displays in proper shape and will replenish stocks. Bypassing the middleman and serving retailers directly in this fashion proved to be a major element in L'eggs' success, and Hanes is counting on the approach to work with L'aura.

But until Hanes begins a blitz of heavy TV and print advertising for the new line in Kansas City and Cincinnati toward the end of August, the company is being very cautious in talking about its new product. President Robert E. Elberson has said only: "This is one of the few times that a company has introduced an entire line of cosmetics at once. Usually one or two products are introduced and line extensions follow."

Behind the caution lies Elberson's disappointment with an earlier effort to transfer the L'eggs marketing concept to selling socks and men's underwear. That effort, begun two years ago, has not reached far beyond the initial test markets in half a dozen cities, and although Hanes has not scrapped the product lines, they are not expected to move into the national marketplace any time soon. One problem, Hanes found, was that competition from such widely known brands as Fruit of the Loom was deeply entrenched. And in order to carry a full range of colors and sizes, the company had to use much larger display racks than it needs for L'eggs or L'aura.

Each L'aura display rack takes up 4 sq. ft., which is a lot for today's crowded supermarkets to relinquish without fairly sure profits in sight. But Harry P. Knabb, manager of purchasing and package development for L'eggs New Ventures Div., says that stores in the two test markets are cooperating and "early indications are favorable." Larry Day, director of general merchandising for Great Atlantic & Pacific Tea Co. in the Kansas City area, adds: "All of our 30 stores in this area will carry the line. The products are attractively packaged, and I'm optimistic." The test market retailers will get a 40% markup on the cosmetics.

Tough Competition

It will probably cost Hanes heavily to establish an image for its new line and to take a slice out of the competition. When it started selling L'eggs in 1971, leadership in the hosiery business was conspicuously absent: Hundreds of companies sold some 600 different brands of stockings and pantyhose, and consumers generally saw their products as being all alike. Hanes's product, with its unique egg-shaped container, easily stood out and won the customer's attention.

Cosmetics, though, already has imaginative market leaders working hard to maintain the customer's loyalty. "Hanes will have to convince the consumer that its products are different," says Frank LeCates, and analyst at Donaldson, Lufkin & Jenrette Securities Corp., "and to do this it will have to pull its products through with heavy and expensive advertising," Hanes, maintaining its low profile before the test marketing of its new line begins, is keeping mum on its ad spending plans for its new cosmetics. But the company is no slouch when it comes to spending for advertising. Last year its ad budget was more than $27.1 million—only a shade behind the $29.7 spent by Revlon, a company almost three times its size.

CASE 8

CAMPBELL SOUP COMPANY

The Campbell Soup Company, a large, diversified branded food company, has been marketing canned soup with the familiar red and white label for almost 100 years and now holds over 80 percent of the U.S. market, with private-label brands supplied by the H. J. Heinz a distant second at about 10 percent. Recognizing that environmental and competitive changes may cause a decline in the size of the canned soup market and the company's share of market, Campbell's new marketing-minded management is aggressively seeking new market opportunities and new approaches for old product lines. The soup business is of particular interest because of its current and historical importance to the company.

Changes in life styles and other significant environmental changes, as well as changes internal to the company, present both threats and opportunities. The company is faced with the problem of how to increase the consumption of prepared soup and its share of the market in an environment vastly different from the one in which the long-time staple product was born and nurtured. A complete rethinking of Campbell's soup marketing is desired.

The short-run problem is to make canned soup more attractive. The company has recently characterized itself as the "well-being" company and promoted its foods as conducive to good health. One advertising campaign presented soup as health insurance. "Soup is good for you" has also been part of the company's advertising. Efforts by Campbell to increase the use of soup include promoting it for different occasions, such as breakfast; other uses, such as making sauces; and creative cookery, such as mixing two or more soups. Ready-to-eat chunky soup was created for those who want to make soup an entire meal. Most of Campbell's soups are condensed and must be diluted.

Also important now, because of the development time required, is the phasing in of new packages for soup to increase its attractiveness. Among the products being developed is a microwave soup. The concept being considered is a coextruded plastic bowl containing 9.5 ounces of chicken soup with broad egg noodles. It is a shelf-stable product with a plastic overcap to be slipped off for a heating time of three minutes. The plastic container is reusable if a person wants to save some of the soup for another time. This will be the first microwavable soup and is said to represent a packaging breakthrough. Also being considered is the instant dry soup market, in which Lipton is the leader and the company has no position at present.

Campbell's management believes that the future of food packaging lies in more attractive and more convenient containers like plastic, aseptic boxes, and microwavable dishes. It is searching for suitable new packages and a plan to phase them in alongside the familiar canned soup.

The company's director of marketing research says, "The can isn't as user friendly as it used to be." In consumer preference surveys, he continues, canned soup "is being battered and beaten" (*Wall Street Journal,* March 28, 1984). The director of packaging is quoted in the same source as saying, "Deep down everybody feels good about the can. We don't want to muck it up by changing that good solid conservation image." Offering a dud for the tin can could be disastrous.

A major objection against the soup can is the inconvenience of using the can opener, mixing with water if the soup is condensed, heating, and cleaning up.

Health-centered objections come from younger people who believe that artificial ingredients and preservatives are used. They also believe that the cooking process and cans do not preserve nutrients. Of the same nature is the contention that the salt content in canned soups is too high for good health. This claim is made by people and consumer watchdog groups in various age and interest groups, particularly the elderly, who represent a growing market and generally prefer lighter meals, including soup.

A third major objection to canned soup comes from the rapidly growing segment of U.S. households, now almost 40 percent, using microwave ovens, which are not designed for metal containers.

The outstanding advantage of the can has been extended shelf life, but this is being eroded by technological advances making plastic impervious to oxygen. A second advantage is that the rigid tin can protects its contents from physical damage better than almost any other package form.

The technological threat to the tin can, which is actually a tin-plated steel can, is not immediate. Improved can technology is gradually eliminating the potential health hazard associated with lead in the older soldered-seam process. Efforts to make cans lighter and less expensive are being made. In view of the rapidly changing frontier of packaging technology, major food processors, with a heavy investment in existing technology and faced with tremendously expensive new packaging systems, tend to be holding back on any major moves. The answer to the basic issue of what, where, when, and how to change packaging is dependent upon technical feasibility, economic soundness, and market acceptance, and of these market acceptance comes first.

It is generally held that metal and glass are the best oxygen barriers for packaging. It is also recognized that the economic attractiveness of plastic will justify compromises on such variables as shelf life, especially when products are "dated." Present estimates are that the plastic can, which will look very much like the metal can, will be one-third the weight and require half as much energy to produce. Some expect it to be the future workhorse of the food-packaging industry.

Long-term development as seen by one analyst is from cans to semi-rigid packages, such as aseptics used for fruit juices and milk, and then to flexible packages such as films and pouches, like Kraft's A La Carte retort pouch entrees. Their present use in upscale markets is just the beginning. In time they will severely reduce the use of tin cans. But "The can is going to be around for a long time," according to a company executive. Eventually, alternative packaging could capture as much as 80 percent or more of the canned soup market. High risks are involved in adjusting to change when uncertainty is high regarding technological capabilities, economic consideration, and market acceptance.

1. Describe the activities and circumstances involved in the preparation and consumption of soup, considering each of the different forms available in the marketplace, including soup from "scratch." What are the problems and opportunities of each from a consumer point of view?

2. What are your recommendations for increasing the consumption of canned prepared soup and Campbell's share of the market? Of soup in new forms of packaging?

13
Pricing Products: Pricing Considerations and Approaches

The Easy Rider Motor Company manufactures a recreational vehicle—specifically a truck camper—called the Free Spirit, which it sells through franchised dealers at a retail price of $12,000. The dealers have been pressuring the company to add a second recreational vehicle to the line at the higher end. In response, the company has designed the High Rise and is about to set its price to dealers and customers. Here are the major facts:

1. The company has enough plant capacity to produce up to five hundred units per year of the new model. Any more than this would require investing in new plant capacity.

2. The fixed costs of producing the High Rise are estimated at $500,000. The direct costs are estimated at $10,000 per unit.

3. There is a major competitor producing a high-quality recreational vehicle retailing for $14,000. The competitor charges its dealers $11,200, a 20 percent dealer discount off the list price. The company estimates that the competitor's profit margin is approximately $1,400 per unit. The competitor sells about six hundred units per year.

4. The company would like its High Rise to retail for at least $2,200 more than its Free Spirit.

5. The company displayed the High Rise at the latest retail trade show, and over two-thirds of the visitors reported that the High Rise seemed better designed than the competitor's model.

With this information, what dealer price and retail price should the Easy Rider Motor Company establish for the High Rise?

If the company is cost-oriented, it could start with the fact that each unit costs $10,000 to manufacture and add a markup for the profit it wants. If the company wants $1,400 gross profit per unit, dealers should be charged $11,400 and in turn mark it up for the profit they want. This approach ignores the competitor's price and the consumers' perceived value of the High Rise.

A market-oriented approach would start with buyers' perceptions of the value of the High Rise. For example, if market testing indicates that potential buyers think the High Rise is worth at least $500 more than the competitor's truck camper, then the company might consider a retail price of $14,500. It might offer dealers a 22 percent dealer discount to motivate them to outsell the competitor's models, which means that dealers would pay $11,310 and the company would make a gross profit of $1,310 per unit.

The company will also want to consider other pricing alternatives. The High Rise might be priced at the competitor's price of $14,000 so that the companies fight for market share on grounds other than price. Or the company might price the High Rise below the competitor's price in an effort to grab a higher market share. However, this violates the wish to price the High Rise at least $2,200 more than the Free Spirit; also, it could lead to a higher volume of orders than the company could fill, and this would require increased investment. On the other hand, the company might want to consider pricing the High Rise at $15,000 to suggest Cadillac quality (called prestige pricing). Even here, it might set the price at $14,999 so it sounds as if the price is in the $14,000 range (called odd pricing).

The Easy Rider Motor Company's pricing problem is even more complicated. The company can produce the High Rise with optional features (better heating, lighting, bedding, and so on) and will have to figure out a price structure for the different options. Price will also depend on the size of the planned promotion budget because this will make a difference in the company's ability to convince the market to pay a high price. The High Rise could cannibalize some of the sales of the Free Spirit, depending on how close their prices are. Or conversely, the High Rise could increase the sale of the Free Spirit, since dealers will be able to attract more traffic with the longer product line.[1]

All profit organizations and many nonprofit organizations face the task of setting a price on their products or services. Price goes by many names:

> Price is all around us. You pay *rent* for your apartment, *tuition* for your education, and a *fee* to your physician or dentist. The airline, railway, taxi, and bus companies charge you a *fare;* the local utilities call their price a *rate;* and the local bank charges you *interest* for the money you borrow. The price for driving your car on Florida's Sunshine Parkway is a *toll,* and the company that insures your car charges you a *premium.* The guest lecturer charges an *honorarium* to tell you about a government official who took a *bribe* to help a shady character steal *dues* collected by a trade association. Clubs or societies to which you belong may make a special *assessment* to pay unusual expenses. Your regular lawyer may ask for a *retainer* to cover her services. The "price" of an executive is a *salary,* the price of a salesperson may be a *commission,* and the price of a worker is a *wage.* Finally, although economists would disagree, many of us feel that *income taxes* are the price we pay for the privilege of making money.[2]

How are prices set? Historically, prices were set by buyers and sellers negotiating with each other. Sellers would ask for a higher price than they expected to receive, and buyers would offer less than they expected to pay. Through bargaining, they would arrive at an acceptable price.

Setting one price for all buyers is a relatively modern idea. It was given impetus by the development of large-scale retailing at the end of the nineteenth century. F. W. Woolworth, Tiffany and Co., John Wanamaker, J. L. Hudson, and others advertised a "strictly one-price policy" because they carried so many items and supervised so many employees.

Historically, price has operated as the major determinant of buyer choice. This is still true in poorer nations, among poorer groups, and with commodity-type products. However, nonprice factors have become relatively more important in buyer choice behavior in recent decades.

Price is the only element in the marketing mix that produces revenue; the other elements represent costs. Yet many companies do not handle pricing well. The most common mistakes are: Pricing is too cost-oriented; price is not revised often enough to capitalize on market changes; price is set independently of the rest of the marketing mix rather than as an intrinsic element of market-positioning strategy; and price is not varied enough for different product items and market segments.

In this and the next chapter, we will look at the problem of setting prices. This chapter will examine the factors marketers must consider when setting prices and look at general pricing approaches. In the next chapter, we will examine pricing strategies for new product pricing, product-mix pricing, initiating and responding to price changes, and adjusting prices for buyer and situational factors.

FACTORS TO CONSIDER WHEN SETTING PRICES

The company's pricing decisions are influenced by a number of internal company factors and external environmental considerations. These factors are shown in Figure 13-1. *Internal factors* include the company's marketing objectives, marketing mix strategy, costs, and organization. *External factors* include the nature of the market and demand, competition, and other environmental factors.

Internal Factors Affecting Pricing Decisions

Marketing Objectives

Before setting price, the company must decide what it wants to accomplish with the particular product. If the company has selected its target market and market positioning carefully, then its marketing mix strategy, including price, will be fairly straightforward. For example, if the Easy Rider Motor Company wants to produce a luxurious truck camper for the affluent customer segment, this implies charging a high price. Thus pricing strategy is largely determined by the prior decision on market positioning.

At the same time, the company may pursue additional objectives. The clearer a firm is about its objectives, the easier it is to set price. Examples of common objectives are survival, current profit maximization, market-share maximization, and product quality leadership.

SURVIVAL. Companies set survival as their major objective if plagued with overcapacity, intense competition, or changing consumer wants. To keep the plant going and the inventories turning over, companies must set a low price, hoping that the market is price-sensitive. Profits are less important than survival. In recent years, troubled companies such as Chrysler and International Harvester have resorted to large price rebate programs in order to survive. As long as their prices cover variable costs and some fixed costs, they can stay in business for a while.

FIGURE 13-1
Factors Affecting Price Decisions

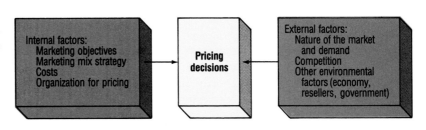

CURRENT PROFIT MAXIMIZATION.   Many companies want to set a price that will maximize current profits. They estimate the demand and costs associated with alternative prices and choose the price that will produce the maximum current profit, cash flow, or rate of return on investment. In all cases, the company is emphasizing current financial performance rather than long-run performance.

MARKET-SHARE LEADERSHIP.   Other companies want to achieve the dominant market share. They believe that the company owning the largest market share will enjoy the lowest costs and highest long-run profit. They go after market-share leadership by setting prices as low as possible. A variation of this objective is to pursue a specific market-share gain: Say the company wants to increase its market share from 10 percent to 15 percent in one year. It will search for the price and marketing program that will achieve this.

PRODUCT QUALITY LEADERSHIP.   A company might adopt the objective of being the product quality leader in the market. This normally calls for charging a high price to cover the high product quality and high cost of R&D. Michelin, the tire manufacturer, is a prime example of a firm pursuing product quality leadership. It keeps introducing new tire features and longer-lasting tires, and it prices its tires at a premium.

OTHER OBJECTIVES.   The company might use price to achieve other more specific objectives. It can set prices low to prevent competition from entering the market or set prices at competitors' levels to stabilize the market. Prices can be set to maintain the loyalty and support of resellers, or to avoid government intervention. Prices can be temporarily reduced to create excitement for a product or to draw more customers into a retail store. One product may be priced to help the sales of other products in the company's line. Thus pricing may play an important role in helping to accomplish the company's objectives at many levels.

Marketing Mix Strategy

Price is only one of the marketing mix tools that the company uses to achieve its marketing objectives. Price decisions must be coordinated with product design, distribution, and promotion decisions to form a consistent and effective marketing program. Decisions made for other marketing mix variables may affect pricing decisions. For example, producers who use many resellers and expect these resellers to support and promote their products may have to build larger reseller margins into their prices. The decision to develop a high-quality position will mean that the seller must charge a higher price to cover higher costs.

The company often makes its pricing decision first and then bases other marketing mix decisions on the price it wants to charge for the product. For example, Ford discovered through research that a market segment existed for an affordable sporty car and designed the Mustang to sell within the price range that this segment was willing to pay. Similarly, IBM designed the PC Jr. to sell at a price that was competitive with other moderately priced personal computers. In both cases,

Volkswagen positions its car on price and economy: Jaguar positions its car on quality, performance and other nonprice factors—its price adds prestige. *Courtesy of Volkswagen of America and Jaguar Cars Inc.*

price was a key product positioning factor that defined the product's market, competition, and design. The intended price determined what product features could be offered and what production costs could be incurred.

Thus the marketer must consider the total marketing mix when setting prices. If the product is positioned on nonprice factors, then decisions about quality, promotion, and distribution will strongly influence price. If price is a key positioning factor, then price will strongly influence decisions on the other marketing mix elements. In most cases, the company will consider all the marketing mix decisions together when developing the marketing program.

Costs

Costs set the floor for the price that the company can set for its product. The company wants to charge a price that covers all its costs for producing, distributing, and selling the product, including a fair rate of return for its effort and risk. The company must watch its costs carefully. If it costs the company more than competitors to produce and sell a comparable product, the company will have to charge a higher price than competitors or make less profit, putting it at a competitive disadvantage.

TYPES OF COSTS. A company's costs take two forms, fixed and variable. *Fixed costs* (also known as overhead) are costs that do not vary with production or sales revenue. Thus a company must pay bills each month for rent, heat, interest, and executive salaries, whatever the company's output. Fixed costs go on irrespective of the production level.

Variable costs vary directly with the level of production. Each hand calculator produced by Texas Instruments (TI) involves a cost of plastic, wires, packaging, and other inputs. These costs tend to be constant per unit produced. They are called variable because their total varies with the number of units produced.

Total costs are the sum of the fixed and variable costs for any given level of production. Management wants to charge a price that will at least cover the total production costs at a given level of production.

COST BEHAVIOR AT DIFFERENT LEVELS OF PRODUCTION PER PERIOD. To price intelligently, management needs to know how its costs vary with different levels of production.

First, take the case where TI has built a fixed-size plant to produce 1,000 hand calculators per day. Figure 13-2A shows the typical U-shaped behavior of the short-run average cost curve (SRAC). The cost per unit is high if few units are produced per day. As production approaches 1,000 units per day, average cost falls. The reason is that the fixed costs are spread over more units, with each one bearing a smaller fixed cost. TI can try to produce more than 1,000 units per day, but at increasing costs. Average cost increases after 1,000 units because the plant becomes inefficient: Workers have to wait for machines, machines break down more often, and workers get in each other's way.

If TI believed that it could sell 2,000 units a day, it should consider building a larger plant. The plant would use more efficient machinery and work arrangements, and the unit cost of producing 2,000 units per day would be less than that of 1,000 units per day. This is shown in the long-run average cost curve (see Figure 13-2B). In fact, a 3,000-capacity plant would even be more efficient, according to Figure 13-2B. But a 4,000 daily production plant would be less efficient because of increasing diseconomies of scale: There are too many workers to manage, paper-

FIGURE 13-2
Cost per Unit at Different Levels of Production per Period

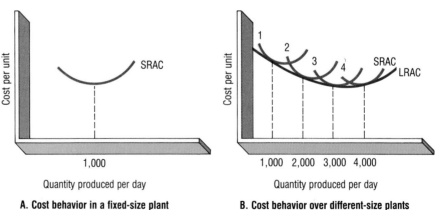

A. Cost behavior in a fixed-size plant

B. Cost behavior over different-size plants

work slows things down, and so on. Figure 13-2B indicates that a 3,000 daily production plant is the optimal size to build if demand is strong enough to support this level of production.

COST BEHAVIOR AS A FUNCTION OF ACCUMULATED PRODUCTION. Suppose TI runs a plant that produces 3,000 hand calculators per day. As TI gains experience in producing hand calculators, it learns how to do it better. Workers learn shortcuts and become more familiar with their equipment. With practice, the work becomes better organized, and improved equipment and better production processes are found. With higher volume, the company becomes more efficient and realizes economies of scale. The result is that average cost tends to fall with accumulated production experience. This is shown in Figure 13-3.[3] Thus the average cost of producing the first 100,000 calculators is $10 per calculator. When the company has produced the first 200,000 calculators, the average cost has fallen to $9. After its accumulated production experience doubles again to 400,000, the average cost is $8. This decline in the average cost with accumulated production experience is called the *experience curve* (sometimes *learning curve*).[4]

If a downward-sloping experience curve exists, this is highly significant for the company. Not only will the company's unit production cost fall, it will fall faster if the company makes and sells more during a given time period. But the market has to stand ready to buy the higher output. And to take advantage of the experience curve, TI must get a large market share early in the product's life cycle. This suggests the following pricing strategy. TI should price its calculators low; its sales will then increase, and its costs will decrease through gaining more experience, and then it can lower its prices further. This logic is used by Texas Instruments in its pricing. It prices very aggressively, gets a lion's share of the market, and finds that its costs continue to fall.[5]

Organizational Considerations

Management must decide who within the organization is responsible for setting price. Companies handle pricing in a variety of ways. In small companies, prices are often set by top management rather than by the marketing or sales department. In

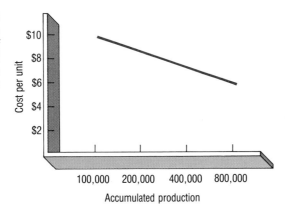

FIGURE 13-3
Cost per Unit as a Function of Accumulated Production: The Experience Curve

large companies, pricing is typically handled by divisional or product line managers. In industrial markets, salespeople may be allowed to negotiate with customers within certain price ranges. Even here, top management sets the pricing objectives and policies and often approves the prices proposed by lower-level management or salespeople.[6] In industries where pricing is a key factor (aerospace, railroads, oil companies), companies will often establish a pricing department to set prices or assist others in determining appropriate prices. This department reports to the marketing department or top management. Others who exert an influence on pricing include sales managers, production managers, finance managers, and accountants.

External Factors Affecting Pricing Decisions

The Market and Demand

Costs set the floor for prices, and the market and demand set the ceiling. Both consumer and industrial buyers balance the price of a product or service against the benefits of owning it. Thus, before setting prices, the marketer must understand the relationship between price and demand for its product.

In this section, we will look at how the price-demand relationship varies for different types of markets, and at how buyer perceptions of price affect the pricing decision. Then we will discuss methods for measuring the price-demand relationship.

PRICING IN DIFFERENT TYPES OF MARKETS. The seller's pricing latitude varies with different types of markets. Economists distinguish four types of markets, each presenting a different pricing challenge.

Under *pure competition,* the market consists of many buyers and sellers trading in a homogeneous commodity such as wheat, copper, or financial securities. No single buyer or seller has much influence on the going market price. A seller cannot charge more than the going price because buyers can obtain as much as they need at this price. Nor would sellers charge less than the market price because they can sell all they want at the market price. If the price and profits rise, new sellers can easily enter the market. Pure competitive markets are characterized by high mobility of resources and high information among buyers and sellers. In these markets, buyers and sellers are price-takers rather than price-makers. To the extent that sellers cannot establish any differential features in their offer, they cannot sell their goods for any more than the market price. Sellers in these markets do not spend much time on marketing strategy, since the role of marketing research, product development, pricing, advertising, and sales promotion is minimal as long as the market stays purely competitive.

Under *monopolistic competition,* the market consists of many buyers and sellers who transact over a range of prices rather than a single market price. The reason for the price range is that sellers are able to differentiate their offers to the buyers. Either the physical product can be varied in quality, features, or style, or the accompanying services can be varied. Buyers see different offers and will pay different amounts. Sellers try to develop differentiated offers for different customer segments and freely use branding, advertising, and personal selling, in addition to price, to distinguish their offers. Sellers who can maintain differentiated offers can earn above-average rates of return. Their continued success depends on barriers to entry, such as advertising, goodwill, patents, licensing procedures, and high capital requirements. Because there are many competitors, each firm is less affected by competitors' marketing strategies than in oligopolistic markets.

Under *oligopolistic competition,* the market consists of a few sellers who are highly sensitive to each other's pricing and marketing strategies. The product can be homogeneous (steel, aluminum) or heterogeneous (cars, computers). The reason for the few sellers is high barriers to entry in the form of patents, high capital requirements, control over raw materials, proprietary knowledge, scarce locations, and so on. Each seller is alert to competitors' strategies and moves. If a steel company slashes its price by 10 percent, buyers will quickly switch to this supplier. The other steelmakers will have to respond by lowering their prices or increasing their services. An oligopolist is never sure that it will gain anything permanent through a price cut. On the other hand, if the oligopolist raised the price, the competitors might not follow this lead. The oligopolist would have to retract its price increase or risk losing customers to competitors. Oligopolists, in developing their pricing and marketing strategies, must pay as much attention to competitors' behavior as to customers' behavior. We saw in the Easy Rider example that Easy Rider had to take account of its major competitor in deciding what price to charge for its recreational vehicle.

A *pure monopoly* consists of one seller. The seller may be a government monopoly (U.S. Postal Service), a private regulated monopoly (a power company), or a private nonregulated monopoly (Dupont when it introduced nylon). Pricing is handled differently in each case. A government monopoly can pursue a variety of pricing objectives. It might set a price below cost because the product is important to buyers and they cannot afford to pay full cost. Or the price might be set to cover costs or to produce good revenue—or even quite high, to discourage consumption. In a regulated monopoly, the government permits the company to set rates that will yield a "fair return," one that will enable the company to maintain and expand its plant as needed. Nonregulated monopolies are free to price at what the market will bear. However, they do not always charge the full price for a number of reasons: fear of government regulation, desire not to attract competition, desire to penetrate the market faster with a low price.

CONSUMER PERCEPTIONS OF PRICE AND VALUE. Ultimately, the consumer will decide whether a product's price is right. When setting prices, the company must consider consumer perceptions of price and how these perceptions affect consumers' buying decisions. Nagle emphasizes that pricing decisions, like other marketing mix decisions, must be buyer-oriented:

> . . . pricing requires more than mere technical expertise. It requires creative judgment and a keen awareness of buyers' motivations . . . the key to effective pricing is the same one that opens doors to efficacy in other marketing functions: a creative awareness of who buyers are, why they buy, and how they make their buying decisions. The recognition that buyers differ in these dimensions is as important for effective pricing as it is for effective promotion, distribution, or product development.[7]

The architecture of power.

Achievement
has its own rewards.

The promise of success; the freedom to pursue it. An American phenomenon symbolically expressed in the Corum Gold Coin Watch.

A watch steeped in the traditions of our country.

A watch that has a power and personality uniquely its own.

The case is an American $20 gold piece, literally halved. (The Eagle becomes the dial; the Goddess of Liberty the back of the case.)

Inside is cushioned an ultra-thin electronic quartz movement. Known for its accuracy, it also never needs winding.

The crystal is sapphire, one of the hardest substances known to man; the setting stem, a diamond. And the strap is imported lizard.

In addition, the Corum Gold Coin Watch is water-resistant. Each is hand-crafted, start to finish, by a single watchmaker in La Chaux-de-Fonds, Switzerland.

For brochure send $1.50 to Corum, 650 Fifth Ave., N.Y., N.Y. 10019. Also available in Canada.

CORUM®
An Investment in Time

An inexpensive watch keeps the time, but many consumers will pay much more for intangibles. *Courtesy of North American Watch Corp.*

When consumers buy a product, they exchange something of value (the price) to get something of value (the benefits of having or using the product). Effective, buyer-oriented pricing involves understanding what value consumers place on the benefits they receive from the product and setting a price consistent with this value. The benefits include both tangibles and intangibles. When a consumer buys a meal at a fancy restaurant, it is easy to calculate the value of the meal's ingredients. But it is very difficult, even for the consumer, to measure the value of other satisfactions such as taste, a plush environment, relaxation, conversation, and status. And these values will vary for different consumers and for different situations (see Exhibit 13-1). Thus the company will often find it difficult to measure the value customers will attach to its product. But the consumer consciously or subconsciously uses these values to evaluate a product's price. If the consumer perceives that the price is greater than the product's value, the consumer will not buy the product.

EXHIBIT 13-1

WHAT'S A HAMBURGER WORTH?

Is any hamburger worth $4? The answer seems to depend on what consumer you talk to and what they want from their burgers. Most people won't pay more than half a dollar, maybe a dollar and a half for a Big Mac or a Whopper with cheese. But there's a growing segment of consumers who seem almost eager to pay as much as $3.50 or $4.00 for a new class of burgers—gourmet burgers—served at restaurants with names like Chili's, Fuddruckers, Flakey Jake's, or J. J. Muggs.

Fuddruckers' gourmet burger. *Courtesy of Fuddruckers, Inc.*

What makes a hamburger worth $4 to some consumers? The burgers probably *are* better—bigger and cooked to order from fresh beef. But it's not just the hamburgers that attract customers. The upmarket burger places offer several less tangible benefits that some consumers value highly. They have tables and chairs instead of plastic benches; they sell beer, wine, and cocktails; some even provide table service.

The average cost for a hamburger, fries, and a beverage at Chili's runs about $6, compared to about $2.50 at a conventional fast-food restaurant. But when you add up all the values—of the hamburger, the amenities, and the atmosphere—the price of a gourmet burger at Chili's seems more reasonable to some consumers than the lower prices they'd pay at McDonald's or Burger King.

So, who would pay $4 for a hamburger? You'd be surprised just how many people would! There are now about 100 fancyburger restaurants with over $100 million in sales. And even conservative analysts estimate that the market will explode to over 3,000 restaurants selling $2 to $3 billion annually. Some estimate an eventual $8 billion market for $4 hamburgers.

Source: Based on information from Roger Neal, "Fancyburgers," *Forbes,* June 18, 1984, p. 92.

Marketers must try to analyze the consumer's motivations for buying the product, and set price according to consumer perceptions of the product's value. Because consumers vary in the values they assign to different product features, marketers often vary their pricing strategies for different price segments. They offer different combinations of product features at different prices. For example, jeans makers may offer lower-priced, rugged jeans for consumers who value utility and durability and higher-priced designer jeans for customers who value fashion and status.

Buyer-oriented pricing means that the marketer cannot design a product and marketing program and then set the price. Effective pricing begins with analyzing consumer needs and price perceptions. Price must be considered along with the other marketing mix variables before the marketing program is set.

ANALYZING THE PRICE-DEMAND RELATIONSHIP. Each price the company might charge will lead to a different level of demand. The relation between the price charged and the resulting demand level is captured in the familiar *demand schedule* shown in Figure 13-4A. The demand schedule shows the number of units the market will buy in a given time period at alternative prices that might be charged during the period. In the normal case, demand and price are inversely related, that is, the higher the price, the lower the demand (and conversely). Thus the company would sell less if it raised its price from P_1 to P_2. Presumably, consumers with limited budgets who face alternative products will buy less of something if its price is too high.

Most demand schedules slope downward in either a straight or a curved line. In the case of prestige goods, the demand curve is sometimes positively sloped, as in Figure 13-4B. A perfume company found that by raising its price from P_1 to P_2, it sold more perfume rather than less. Consumers interpreted the higher price as signifying a better or more desirable perfume. However, if too high a price is charged (P_3), the level of demand will be lower than at P_2.

An *estimate of demand schedules* is attempted by most companies. In researching the demand schedule, the investigator should make the assumptions about competition explicit. There is no problem when a monopolist is selling to

FIGURE 13-4
Two Hypothetical Demand Schedules

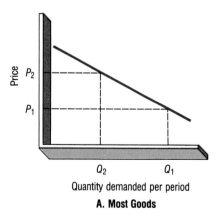

Quantity demanded per period

A. Most Goods

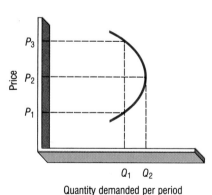

Quantity demanded per period

B. Prestige goods

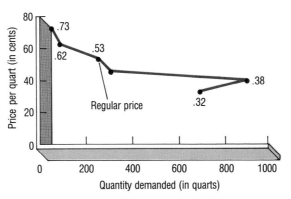

FIGURE 13-5
Demand Schedule for Quaker State Motor Oil

Source: Sidney Bennett and J. B. Wilkinson. "Price-Quantity Relationships and Price Elasticity Under In-Store Experimentation." *Journal of Business Research,* January 1974, pp. 30–34.

the market. The demand schedule shows the total market demand resulting from different prices. If the company faces competition, there are two ways to estimate demand. One is to assume that competitors' prices remain constant regardless of the price charged by the company. The other is to assume that competitors charge a different price for each price the company chooses. We will assume the former and defer the question of competitors' prices.

To measure a demand schedule requires varying the price. Pessemier developed a laboratory method for determining how many units of a product people will buy at different possible prices.[8] Wyner and others estimated demand for residential telephones by surveying consumers and obtaining their reactions to various prices in simulated purchasing situations.[9] Bennett and Wilkinson used an in-store method for estimating the demand schedule: They systematically varied the prices of several products sold in a discount store. Figure 13-5 shows the estimated demand schedule for Quaker State Motor oil. Demand rises as the price is lowered from 73 cents to 38 cents, then drops between 38 cents and 32 cents, possibly due to people thinking the oil is too cheap and may damage the car.

In measuring the price-demand relationship, the market researcher must not allow other factors affecting demand to vary. If Quaker State raised its advertising budget when it lowered its price, we would not know how much of the increased demand was due to the lower price and how much to the increased advertising. The same problem arises if a holiday weekend occurs when the lower price is established, because more travel and purchase of motor oil takes place on holidays.

Economists show the impact of nonprice factors on demand through shifts of the demand curve, rather than movements along the demand curve. Suppose the initial demand curve is D_1 in Figure 13-6. The seller is charging P and selling Q_1 units. Now suppose the economy suddenly improves, or the seller doubles its advertising budget. The higher demand generated is reflected through an upward shift of the demand curve from D_1 to D_2. Without changing the price P, the seller's demand is now Q_2.

FIGURE 13-6
*Effects of Promotion and
Other Nonprice
Variables on Demand
Shown through Shifts of
the Demand Curve*

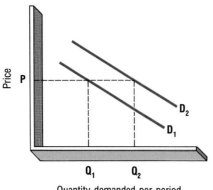

PRICE ELASTICITY OF DEMAND. *Price elasticity* must be determined by marketers: How responsive demand will be to a change in price. Consider the two demand curves in Figure 13-7. In Figure 13-7A a price increase from P_1 to P_2 leads to a relatively small decline in demand from Q_1 to Q_2. In Figure 13-7B the same price increase leads to a substantial drop in demand from Q'_1 to Q'_2. If demand hardly changes with a small change in price, we say the demand is inelastic. If demand changes considerably, we say the demand is elastic. The price elasticity of demand is given by the following formula:

$$\text{price elasticity of demand} = \frac{\%\ \text{change in quantity demanded}}{\%\ \text{change in price}}$$

Suppose demand falls by 10 percent when a seller raises its price by 2 percent. Price elasticity of demand is therefore −5 (the minus sign confirms the inverse relation between price and demand). If demand falls by 2 percent with a 2 percent increase in price, then elasticity is −1. In this case, the seller's total revenue stays the same: The seller sells fewer items but at a higher price that preserves the same total revenue. If demand falls by 1 percent when price is increased by 2 percent, then elasticity is −½. The less elastic the demand, the more it pays for the seller to raise the price.

FIGURE 13-7
*Inelastic and Elastic
Demand*

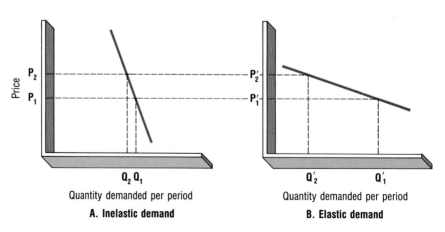

A. Inelastic demand　　　　**B. Elastic demand**

What determines the price elasticity of demand? Demand is likely to be less elastic under the following conditions: (1) there are few or no substitutes or competitors; (2) buyers do not readily notice the higher price; (3) buyers are slow to change their buying habits and search for lower prices; (4) buyers think the higher prices are justified by quality improvements, normal inflation, and so on.

If demand is elastic rather than inelastic, sellers will consider lowering their price. A lower price will produce more total revenue. This makes sense as long as the costs of producing and selling more do not increase disproportionately.

Various studies of price elasticity have been reported. For example, the price elasticity of housing is -0.5; refrigerators, -1.07 to -2.06; automobiles, -0.6 to -1.1; cereal, -1.4 to -1.7; and gasoline, about 0.[10] Elasticities will change over time and under different economic conditions and must therefore be reestimated each time.

Competitors' Prices and Offers

Another external factor influencing the company's pricing decisions is competitors' prices and their possible reactions to the company's pricing strategies. Consumers evaluate a product's price and value against the prices and values of comparable products. Also, the company's pricing strategy may affect the nature of the competition it faces—a high-price, high-margin strategy may attract competition, whereas a low-price, low-margin strategy may discourage competitors or drive them out of the market.

The company needs to learn the price and quality of each competitor's offer. This can be done in several ways. The firm can send out comparison shoppers to price and compare competitors' offers. The firm can acquire competitors' price lists and buy competitors' equipment and take it apart. The firm can ask buyers how they perceive the price and quality of each competitor's offer.

Once the company is aware of competitors' prices and offers, it can use them as an orienting point for its own pricing. If the firm's offer is similar to a major competitor's offer, the firm will have to price close to the competitor or lose sales. If the firm's offer is inferior, the firm will not be able to charge as much as the competitor. If the firm's offer is superior, the firm can charge more than the competitor. However, the firm must be aware that competitors might change their prices in response to the firm's price. Basically, the firm will use price to position its offer relative to competitors.

Other External Factors

When setting prices, the company must also consider other factors in its external environment. For example, *economic conditions* can have a dramatic impact on the effectiveness of different pricing strategies. Economic factors such as inflation, boom or recession, and interest rates influence pricing decisions because they affect both the costs of producing a product and consumer perceptions of the product's price and value.

The company must consider what impact its prices will have on other parties in its environment. How will *resellers* react to various prices? The company should set prices that allow resellers a fair profit, encourage their support, and help them to sell the product effectively. The *government* is another important external influence on pricing decisions. Marketers need to know the laws affecting price and make sure their pricing policies are defensible. The major laws affecting price are summarized in Exhibit 13-2.

EXHIBIT 13-2

PRICE DECISIONS AND PUBLIC POLICY

Sellers must understand the law in pricing their products. They must avoid the following practices.

Price fixing. Sellers must set prices without talking to competitors. Otherwise price collusion is suspected. Price fixing is illegal per se—that is, the government does not accept any excuses for price fixing. The only exception is where price agreements are carried out under the supervision of a government agency, as in many local milk industry agreements, in the regulated transportation industries, and in fruit and vegetable cooperatives.

Resale price maintenance. A manufacturer cannot require dealers to charge a specified retail price for its product. The seller can propose, however, a manufacturer's suggested retail price to the dealers. The manufacturer cannot refuse to sell to a dealer who takes independent pricing action, nor punish the dealer by shipping late or denying advertising allowances. However, the manufacturer can refuse to sell to a dealer on other grounds presumably not related to the dealer's pricing.

Price discrimination. The Robinson-Patman Act seeks to ensure that sellers offer the same price terms to a given level of trade. For example, every retailer is entitled to the same price terms whether the retailer is Sears or the local bicycle shop. However, price discrimination is allowed if the seller can prove its costs are different when selling to different retailers; for example, that it costs less to sell a large volume of bicycles to Sears than to sell a few bicycles to a local dealer. Or the seller can discriminate in its pricing if the seller manufactures different qualities of the same product for different retailers. The seller has to prove that these differences exist and that the price differences are proportional. Price differentials may also be used to "meet competition" in "good faith," providing the firm is trying to meet competitors at its own level of competition and that the price discrimination is temporary, localized, and defensive rather than offensive.

Minimum pricing. A seller is not allowed to sell below cost with the intention to destroy competition. Wholesalers and retailers in over half the states face laws requiring a minimum percentage markup over their cost of merchandise plus transportation. Called unfair trade practices, they attempt to protect small merchants from larger merchants who might sell items below cost to attract customers.

Price increases. Companies are free to increase their prices to any level except in times of price controls. The major exception to the freedom of pricing is regulated public utilities. Since utilities have monopoly power, their rates are regulated in the public interest. The government has used its influence from time to time to discourage major industry price hikes during periods of shortages or inflation.

Deceptive pricing. Deceptive pricing is more common in the sale of consumer goods than business goods, because consumers typically possess less information and buying acumen. In 1958 the Automobile Information Disclosure Act required auto manufacturers to affix on auto windshields a statement of the manufacturer's suggested retail price, the prices of optional equipment, and the dealer's transportation charges. In the same year, the FTC issued its Guides against Deceptive Pricing, warning sellers not to advertise a price reduction unless it is a saving from the usual retail price, not to advertise "factory" or "wholesale" prices unless this is true, not to advertise comparable value prices on imperfect goods, and so forth.

GENERAL PRICING APPROACHES

The price the company charges will be somewhere between one that is too low to produce a profit and one that is too high to produce any demand. Figure 13-8 summarizes the major considerations in setting price. Product costs set a floor to the price; consumer perceptions of the product's value establish the ceiling. The company must consider competitors' prices and other external and internal factors to find the best price between these two extremes.

Companies resolve the pricing issue by selecting a general pricing approach that includes one or more of these three sets of considerations. We will examine the following approaches: the cost-based approach (cost-plus pricing, breakeven analysis, and target profit pricing), the buyer-based approach (perceived-value pricing), and the competition-based approach (going-rate and sealed-bid pricing).

Cost-Based Pricing Cost-Plus Pricing

The most elementary pricing method is to add a standard markup to the cost of the product. An appliance retailer might pay a manufacturer $20 for a toaster and mark it up to sell at $30, which is a 50 percent markup on cost. The retailer's gross margin is $10. If the store's operating costs amount to $8 per toaster sold, the retailer's profit margin will be $2.[11]

The manufacturer who made the toaster also probably used cost-plus pricing. If the manufacturer's standard cost of producing the toaster was $16, it might have added a 25 percent markup, setting the price to the retailer at $20. Construction companies submit job bids by estimating the total project cost and adding a standard markup for profit. Lawyers and other professionals typically price by adding a standard markup to their costs. Some sellers tell their customers they will charge them cost plus a specified markup; for example, aerospace companies price this way to the government.

Markups vary considerably among different goods. Some common markups (on price, not cost) in department stores are 20 percent for tobacco goods, 28 percent for cameras, 34 percent for books, 41 percent for dresses, 46 percent for costume jewelry, and 50 percent for millinery.[12] In the retail grocery industry, coffee, canned milk, and sugar tend to have low markups, while frozen foods, jellies, and some canned products have high markups. Quite a lot of dispersion is found around the averages. Within the frozen foods category, for example, markups on retail price range from a low of 13 percent to a high of 53 percent.[13] Preston

FIGURE 13-8
Major Considerations in Setting Price

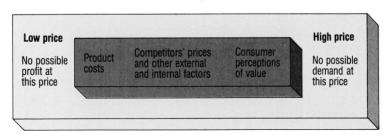

found that varying markups reflected differences in unit costs, sales, turnover, and manufacturers' versus private brands, but still a lot remained unexplained.[14]

Does the use of standard markups to set prices seem logical? Generally, no. Any pricing method that ignores current demand and competition is not likely to lead to the optimal price. The retail graveyard is full of merchants who insisted on using standard markups in the face of competitors who had gone into discount pricing.

Still, markup pricing remains popular for a number of reasons. First, sellers have more certainty about costs than about demand. By tying the price to cost, sellers simplify their own pricing task; they do not have to make frequent adjustments as demand changes. Second, where all firms in the industry use this pricing method, prices tend to be similar. Price competition is therefore minimized, which it would not be if firms paid attention to demand variations when they priced. Third, many people feel that cost-plus pricing is fairer to both buyers and sellers. Sellers do not take advantage of buyers when the latter's demand becomes acute, yet the sellers earn a fair return on their investment.

Breakeven Analysis and Target Profit Pricing

Another cost-oriented pricing approach is that of *target profit pricing*. The firm tries to determine the price that will produce the profit it is seeking. Target pricing is used by General Motors, which prices its automobiles to achieve a 15 to 20 percent profit on its investment. This pricing method is also used by public utilities, which are constrained to make a fair return on their investment.

Target pricing uses the concept of a *breakeven chart*. A breakeven chart shows the total cost and total revenue expected at different sales volume levels. Figure 13-9 shows a hypothetical breakeven chart. Fixed costs are $6 million regardless of sales volume. Variable costs are superimposed on the fixed costs and rise with volume. The total revenue curve starts at zero and rises with each unit sold. The slope of the total revenue curve reflects the price. Here the price is $15 (for example, the company's revenue is $12 million on 800,000 units, or $15 per unit).

FIGURE 13-9
Breakeven Chart for Determining Target Price

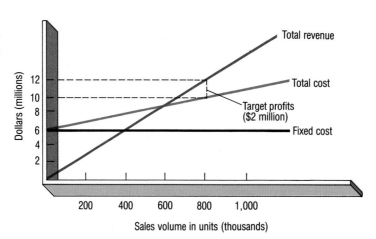

At $15, the company must sell at least 600,000 units to break even; that is, for total revenue to cover total cost. If the company seeks a target profit of $2 million, it must sell at least 800,000 units at a price of $15 each. If the company is willing to charge a higher price, say $20, it will not need to sell as many units to achieve its target profit. However, the market may not buy even this lower volume at the higher price: Much depends on the price elasticity of demand. This is not shown in the breakeven chart. This pricing method requires the company to consider different prices, their impact on the volume necessary to pass the breakeven point and realize target profits, and the likelihood that this will happen with each possible price.

Buyer-Based Pricing An increasing number of companies are basing their prices on the product's *perceived value*. They see the buyers' perception of value, not the seller's cost, as the key to pricing. They use the nonprice variables in the marketing mix to build up perceived value in the buyers' minds. Price is set to capture the perceived value.

Consider the various prices different restaurants charge for the identical items. A consumer who wants a cup of coffee and a slice of apple pie may pay $1.25 at a drugstore counter, $1.50 at a family restaurant, $1.75 at a hotel coffee shop, $3.00 for hotel room service, and $4.00 at an elegant restaurant. Each successive restaurateur can charge more because of the value added by the atmosphere.

The company using perceived-value pricing must establish the value in the buyers' minds concerning different competitive offers. In the previous example, consumers could be asked how much they would pay for the same coffee and pie in the different surroundings. Sometimes consumers could be asked how much they would pay for each benefit added to the offer. Exhibit 13-3 shows how Caterpillar uses the value of different benefits to price its construction equipment.

EXHIBIT 13-3

HOW CATERPILLAR USES PERCEIVED-VALUE PRICING

Caterpillar uses perceived value to set prices on its construction equipment. It might price a tractor at $24,000, although a similar competitor's tractor might be priced at $20,000. And Caterpillar will get more sales than the competitor! When a prospective customer asks a Caterpillar dealer why he should pay $4,000 more for the Caterpillar tractor, the dealer answers:

$20,000 is the tractor's price if it is only equivalent to the competitor's tractor
$3,000 is the price premium for superior durability
$2,000 is the price premium for superior reliability
$2,000 is the price for premium superior service
$1,000 is the price for the longer warranty on parts
$28,000 is the price to cover the value package
$4,000 discount
$24,000 final price

This stunned customer learns that although he is being asked to pay a $4,000 premium for the Caterpillar tractor, he is in fact getting a $4,000 discount! He ends up choosing the Caterpillar tractor because he is convinced that the lifetime operating costs of the Caterpillar tractor will be lower.

If the seller charges more than the buyer-recognized value, the company's sales will suffer relative to what they could be. Many companies overprice their products, and their products sell poorly. Other companies underprice. These products sell extremely well, but they produce less revenue than they would if price was raised to the perceived-value level.[15]

Competition-Based Pricing

Going-Rate Pricing

In *going-rate pricing,* the firm bases its price largely on competitors' prices, with less attention paid to its own costs or demand. The firm might charge the same, more, or less than its major competitor(s). In oligopolistic industries that sell a commodity such as steel, paper, or fertilizer, firms normally charge the same price. The smaller firms "follow the leader." They change their prices when the market leader's prices change, rather than when their own demand or cost changes. Some firms may charge a slight premium or slight discount, but they preserve the amount of difference. Thus minor gasoline retailers usually charge a few cents less than the major oil companies, without letting the difference increase or decrease.

Going-rate pricing is quite popular. Where demand elasticity is difficult to measure, firms feel that the going price represents the collective wisdom of the industry concerning the price that will yield a fair return. They also feel that conforming to the going price will preserve industry harmony.

Sealed-Bid Pricing

Competition-based pricing also dominates where firms bid for jobs. The firm bases its price on expectations of how competitors will price rather than on a rigid relation to the firm's costs or demand. The firm wants to win the contract, and this requires pricing lower than the other firms.

Yet the firm cannot set its price below a certain level. It cannot price below cost without worsening its position. On the other hand, the higher it sets it price above its costs, the lower its chance of getting the contract.

The net effect of the two opposite pulls can be described in terms of the *expected profit* of the particular bid (see Table 13-1). Suppose a bid of $9,500 would yield a high chance of getting the contract, say .81, but only a low profit, say $100. The expected profit with this bid is therefore $81. If the firm bid $11,000, its profit would be $1,600, but its chance of getting the contract might be reduced, say to .01. The expected profit would be only $16. One logical bidding criterion would be to bid the price that would maximize the expected profit. According to Table 13-1, the best bid would be $10,000, for which the expected profit is $216.

TABLE 13-1
Effect of Different Bids
on Expected Profit

COMPANY'S BID	COMPANY'S PROFIT	PROBABILITY OF WINNING WITH THIS BID (ASSUMED)	EXPECTED PROFIT
$ 9,500	$ 100	.81	$ 81
10,000	600	.36	216
10,500	1,100	.09	99
11,000	1,600	.01	16

Using expected profit as a criterion for setting price makes sense for the large firm that makes many bids. In playing the odds, the firm will achieve maximum profits in the long run. The firm that bids only occasionally or needs a particular contract badly will not find it advantageous to use the expected-profit criterion. The criterion, for example, does not distinguish between a $1,000 profit with a .10 probability and a $125 profit with an .80 probability. Yet the firm that wants to keep production going would prefer the second contract to the first.

■ Summary

In spite of the increased role of nonprice factors in the modern marketing process, price remains an important element in the marketing mix. Many internal and external factors influence the company's pricing decisions. Internal factors include the firm's marketing objectives, marketing mix strategy, costs, and organization for pricing.

The pricing strategy is largely determined by the company's target market and positioning objectives. Common pricing objectives include survival, current profit maximization, market-share leadership, and product quality leadership.

Price is only one of the marketing mix tools the company uses to accomplish its objectives, and pricing decisions affect and are affected by product design, distribution, and promotion decisions. Price decisions must be carefully coordinated with the other marketing mix decisions when designing the marketing program.

Costs set the floor for the company's price—the price must cover all the costs of making and selling the product, plus a fair rate of return. The company must analyze how costs vary at different output levels and with different levels of accumulated production experience.

Management must decide who within the organization is responsible for setting price. In large companies,

some pricing authority may be delegated to lower-level managers and salespeople, but top management usually sets pricing policies and approves proposed prices. Production, finance, and accounting managers also influence pricing.

External factors that influence pricing decisions include the nature of the market and demand, competitors' prices and offers, and other external factors such as the economy, reseller needs, and government actions. The seller's pricing latitude varies with different types of markets. Pricing is especially challenging in markets characterized by monopolistic competition or oligopoly.

Ultimately, the consumer decides whether the company has set the right price. The consumer weighs the price against the perceived values of using the product—if the price exceeds the sum of the values, consumers will not buy the product. Consumers differ in the values they assign to different product features, and marketers often vary their pricing strategies for different price segments. When assessing the market and demand, the company estimates the demand schedule, which shows the probable quantity purchased per period at alternative price levels. The more inelastic the demand, the higher the company can set its price. Demand and consumer value perceptions set the ceiling for prices.

Consumers evaluate a product's price against the prices of competitors' products. The company must learn the price and quality of competitors' offers and use them as an orienting point for its own pricing.

The company can select one or a combination of three general pricing approaches: the cost-based approach (cost-plus or breakeven analysis and target profit pricing), the buyer-based (perceived-value) approach, and the competition-based (going-rate or sealed-bid pricing) approach.

■ Questions for Discussion

1. What are the most influential factors affecting the setting of price in each of the four market types discussed in this chapter?

2. If product A's price elasticity of demand is −5 and product B's elasticity is −2, which would lose less from a price increase?

3. If you had a chance to open a car wash where annual fixed costs were $100,000, variable costs were $0.50 per car washed, and you determined that a "competitive" price would be $1.50 per car, would you invest in this business?

4. In setting prices, it is essential to establish only target market objectives. Comment.

5. Relate the essential factors in developing pricing policies and constraints to Adidas's decision to price a new line of shoes.

6. What are the major types of cost-oriented pricing strategies? Give a company example of each.

7. If a company is to respond accurately to price changes, it must thoroughly understand its competitors. Comment.

8. Public policy makers are charged with overseeing what major pricing issues?

■ References

1. This example is adapted from an example found in DAVID J. SCHWARTZ, *Marketing Today: A Basic Approach* (3rd ed.) (New York: Harcourt Brace Jovanovich, 1981), pp. 270–73.

2. Ibid., p. 271.

3. Accumulated production is drawn on a semi-log scale so that equal distances represent the same percentage increase in output.

4. For more on experience curves, see GEORGE S. DAY and DAVID B. MONTGOMERY, "Diagnosing the Experience Curve," *Journal of Marketing,* Spring 1983, pp. 44–58.

5. See "Selling Business and Theory of Economics," *Business Week,* September 8, 1973, pp. 86–88; and ALAN R. BECKENSTEIN and H. LANDIS GABEL, "Experience Curve Pricing Strategy: The Next Target of Antitrust?" *Business Horizons,* September–October 1982, pp. 71–77.

6. See P. RONALD STEPHENSON, WILLIAM L. CRON, and GARY L. FRAZIER, "Delegating Pricing Authority to the Sales Force: The Effects on Sales and Profit Performance," *Journal of Marketing,* Spring 1979, pp. 21–28.

7. THOMAS NAGLE, "Pricing as Creative Marketing," *Business Horizons,* July–August 1981, p. 19.

8. EDGAR A. PESSEMIER, "An Experimental Method for Estimating Demand," *Journal of Business,* October 1980, pp. 373–83.

9. GORDAN A. WYNER, LOIS H. BENEDETTI, and BART M. TRAPP, "Measuring Quantity and Mix of Product Demand," *Journal of Marketing,* Winter 1984, pp. 101–9.

10. ARNOLD C. HARBERGER, *The Demand for Durable Goods* (Chicago: University of Chicago Press, 1960), pp. 3–14; and SCOTT A. NESLIN and ROBERT W. SHOEMAKER, "Using a Natural Experiment to

Estimate Price Elasticity: The 1974 Sugar Shortage and the Ready-to-Eat Cereal Market," *Journal of Marketing,* Winter 1983, pp. 44–57.

11. The arithmetic of markups and margins is discussed in Appendix 1, "Marketing Arithmetic."

12. *Departmental Merchandising and Operating Results of 1965* (New York: National Retail Merchants Association, 1965).

13. See LEE E. PRESTON, *Profits, Competition, and Rules of Thumb in Retail Food Pricing* (Berkeley: University of California Institute of Business and Economic Research, 1963), p. 31.

14. Ibid., pp. 29–40.

15. See DANIEL A. NIMER, "Pricing the Profitable Sale Has a Lot to Do with Perception," *Sales Management,* May 19, 1975, pp. 13–14. For more on value-based pricing, see BENSON P. SHAPIRO and BARBARA B. JACKSON, "Industrial Pricing to Meet Customer Needs," *Harvard Business Review,* November–December 1978, pp. 119–27; and JOHN L. FORBIS and NITIN T. MEHTA, "Value-Based Strategies for Industrial Products," *Business Horizons,* May–June 1981, pp. 32–42.

14

Pricing Products: Pricing Strategies

Heublein, Inc., produces Smirnoff, the leading brand of vodka, with 23 percent of the American market. In the 1960s Smirnoff was attacked by another brand, Wolfschmidt, priced at one dollar less a bottle and claiming to be of the same quality. Heublein saw a real danger of customers switching to Wolfschmidt. Heublein considered the following possible counter-strategies:

1. Lower Smirnoff's price by one dollar to hold on to market share.

2. Maintain Smirnoff's price but increase advertising and promotion expenditures.

3. Maintain Smirnoff's price and let its market share fall.

All three strategies would lead to lower profits. It seemed that Heublein faced a no-win situation.

At this point a fourth strategy occurred to Heublein's marketers, and it was brilliant. Heublein raised the price of Smirnoff by one dollar! It introduced a new brand, Relska, to compete with Wolfschmidt. And it introduced another brand, Popov, at a lower price than Wolfschmidt. This product-line pricing strategy positioned Smirnoff as the elite brand and Wolfschmidt as an ordinary brand. Heublein's adroit maneuvers produced a substantial increase in its overall profits.

The irony is that Heublein's three brands are pretty much the same in their taste and cost of manufacture. Heublein has learned how to sell substantially the same product at different prices by building effective concepts for each.

In this chapter, we will look at pricing dynamics. Companies do not set a single price, but a pricing structure that covers different items in its line. This pricing structure changes over time as products move through their life cycles. The company adjusts product prices to reflect changing costs and demand, and to account for variations in buyers and situations. As the competitive environment changes, the company considers initiating price changes at times and responding to them at other times. This chapter will examine the major dynamic pricing strategies available to management. We will look at *new product pricing strategies* for products in the introductory stage of the product life cycle; *product-mix pricing strategies* for related products in the product mix; *price-adjustment strategies* that account for customer differences and changing situations; and *strategies for initiating and responding to price changes*.

NEW PRODUCT PRICING STRATEGIES

Pricing strategies usually change as the product passes through the product life cycle. The introductory stage is especially challenging. We can distinguish between pricing a genuine product innovation that is patent-protected and pricing a product that imitates existing products.

Pricing an Innovative Product Companies launching a patent-protected innovative product can choose between market-skimming pricing and market penetration pricing.

Market-Skimming Pricing

Many companies that invent new patent-protected products set high prices initially to "skim" the market. Du Pont is a prime user of market skimming. On its new discoveries—cellophane, nylon—it estimates the highest price it can charge given the comparative benefits of its new product versus the available substitutes. Du Pont sets a price that makes it just worthwhile for some segments of the market to adopt the new material. After the initial sales slow down, it lowers the price to draw in the next price-sensitive layer of customers. In this way, Du Pont skims a maximum amount of revenue from the various segments of the market. Polaroid also practices market skimming: It first introduces an expensive version of a new camera and gradually introduces simpler, lower-priced models to draw in new segments.

Market skimming makes sense under the following conditions: (1) A sufficient number of buyers have a high current demand; (2) the unit costs of producing a small volume are not so much higher that they cancel the advantage of charging what the traffic will bear; (3) the high initial price will not attract more competitors; (4) the high price supports the image of a superior product.

Market Penetration Pricing

Other companies set a relatively low price on their innovative product, hoping to attract a large number of buyers and win a large market share. Texas Instruments (TI) is a prime user of market penetration pricing. TI will build a large plant, sets its price as low as possible, win a large market share, experience falling costs, and cut its price further as costs fall.

The following conditions favor setting a low price:[1] (1) the market is highly price-sensitive, and a low price stimulates more market growth; (2) production and distribution costs fall with accumulated production experience; and (3) a low price discourages actual and potential competition.

Pricing an Imitative New Product A company that plans to develop an imitative new product faces a product-position-ing problem. It must decide where to position the product on quality and price. Figure 14-1 shows nine possible price-quality strategies. If the existing market leader has preempted cell 1 by producing the premium product and charging the highest price, the newcomer might prefer to use one of the other strategies. The newcomer could design a high-quality product and charge a medium price (cell 2), design an average-quality product and charge an average price (cell 5), and so on. The newcomer must consider the size and growth rate of the market in each cell and the particular competitors.

PRODUCT-MIX PRICING STRATEGIES

The logic of setting a price on a product has to be modified when the product is part of a product mix. In this case, the firm searches for a mutual set of prices that maximize the profits on the total product mix. Pricing is difficult because the various products have demand and cost interrelationships and are subject to different degrees of competition. We will distinguish four situations.

FIGURE 14-1
Nine Marketing Mix Strategies on Price/Quality

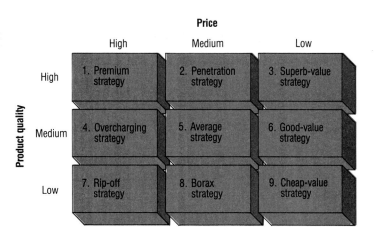

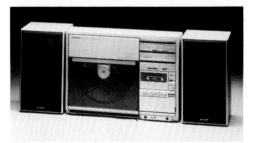

Product line pricing: These three stereo radio and cassette recorders sell for $99.95, 129.95, and $399.95, respectively. *Courtesy of Sharp Electronics Corp.*

Product-Line Pricing Companies normally develop product lines rather than single products. For example, Panasonic offers five different color video sound cameras, ranging from a simple one weighing 4.6 pounds to a complex one weighing 6.3 pounds that includes automatic focusing, fade control, and two-speed zoom lens. Each successive camera in the line offers additional features. Management must decide on the price steps to establish between the various cameras.

The price steps should take into account cost differences between the cameras, customer evaluations of the different features, and competitors' prices. If the price difference between two successive cameras is small, buyers will buy the more advanced camera, and this will increase company profits if the cost difference is smaller than the price difference. If the price difference is large, customers will buy the less advanced cameras.

In many lines of trade, sellers use well-established price points for the products in their line. Thus men's clothing stores might carry men's suits at three price levels: $150, $220, and $310. The customers will associate low-, average-, and high-quality suits with the three price "points." Even if the three prices are raised moderately, men will normally buy suits at their preferred price point. The seller's task is to establish perceived quality differences that lend support to the price differences.

Optional Product Pricing Many companies offer to sell optional or accessory products along with their main product. The automobile buyer can order electric window controls, defoggers, and light dimmers. Pricing these options is a sticky problem. Automobile companies have to decide which items to build into the price and which ones to offer as options. General Motors' normal pricing strategy is to advertise a stripped-down model for $8,000 to pull people into showrooms and devote most of the showroom space to displaying loaded cars at $10,000 or $12,000.

The economy model is stripped of so many comforts and conveniences that most buyers reject it. When GM launched its new front-wheel drive J-cars in the spring of 1981, it took a clue from the Japanese automakers and included in the sticker price a number of useful items previously sold only as options. Now the advertised price represented a well-equipped car. Unfortunately, however, the price was high and many car shoppers balked.

Captive Product Pricing Companies in certain industries produce products that must be used with the main product. Examples of captive products are razor blades and camera film. Manufacturers of the main products (razors and cameras) often price them low and set high markups on the supplies. Thus Kodak prices its cameras low because it makes its money on selling film. Those camera makers who do not sell film have to price their cameras higher in order to make the same overall profit.

By-Product Pricing In producing processed meats, petroleum products, and other chemicals, there are often by-products. If the by-products have no value and disposing of them is in fact costly, this will affect the pricing of the main product. The manufacturer will seek a market for these by-products and should accept any price that covers more than the cost of storing and delivering them. This will enable the seller to reduce the main product's price to make it more competitive.

PRICE-ADJUSTMENT STRATEGIES

Companies adjust their basic price to account for various customer differences and changing situational factors. We will examine the following adjustment strategies: discount pricing and allowances, discriminatory pricing, psychological pricing, promotional pricing, and geographical pricing.

Discount Pricing and Allowances Most companies will adjust their basic price to reward customers for certain acts, such as early payment of bills, volume purchases, and buying off season. These price adjustments—called discounts and allowances—are described below.

Cash Discounts

A cash discount is a price reduction to buyers who pay their bills promptly. A typical example is "2/10, net 30," which means that payment is due within thirty days, but the buyer can deduct 2 percent from the cost by paying the bill within ten days. The discount must be granted to all buyers meeting these terms. Such discounts are customary in many industries and serve the purpose of improving the sellers' liquidity and reducing credit collection costs and bad debts.

Quantity Discounts

A quantity discount is a price reduction to buyers who buy large volumes. A typical example is "$10 per unit for less than 100 units; $9 per unit for 100 or more units."

Quantity discounts must be offered to all customers and must not exceed the cost savings to the seller associated with selling large quantities. These savings include reduced expenses of selling, inventory, and transportation. They may be offered on a noncumulative basis (on each order placed) or a cumulative basis (on the number of units ordered over a given period). Discounts provide an incentive to the customer to buy more from a given seller rather than buying from multiple sources.

Functional Discounts

Functional discounts (also called trade discounts) are offered by the manufacturer to trade channel members who perform certain functions such as selling, storing, and recordkeeping. Manufacturers may offer different functional discounts to different trade channels because of the varying services they perform, but manufacturers must offer the same functional discounts within each trade channel.

Seasonal Discounts

A seasonal discount is a price reduction to buyers who buy merchandise or services out of season. Seasonal discounts allow the seller to maintain steadier production during the year. Ski manufacturers will offer seasonal discounts to retailers in the spring and summer to encourage early ordering. Hotels, motels, and airlines will offer seasonal discounts in their slower selling periods.

Allowances

Allowances are other types of reductions from the list price. For example, *trade-in allowances* are price reductions granted for turning in an old item when buying a new one. Trade-in allowances are most common in the automobile industry and are also found in some other durable-goods categories. *Promotional allowances* are payments or price reductions to reward dealers for participating in advertising and sales-support programs.

Discriminatory Pricing

Companies will often modify their basic prices to accommodate differences in customers, products, and locations. In *discriminatory pricing,* the company sells a product or service at two or more prices that do not reflect a proportional difference in costs. Discriminatory pricing takes several forms:

1. *Customer basis.* Here different customers pay different amounts for the same product or service. Museums will charge a lower admission fee to students and senior citizens.
2. *Product-form basis.* Here different versions of the product are priced differently but not proportionately to their respective costs. SCM Corporation prices its most expensive Proctor-Silex fabric iron at $54.95, which is five dollars more than its next most expensive iron. The top model has a light that signals when the iron is ready to use. Yet the extra feature costs less than one dollar to make.
3. *Place basis.* Here different locations are priced differently even though the cost of offering each location is the same. A theatre varies its seat prices because of audience preferences for certain locations.

4. *Time basis.* Here prices are varied seasonally, by the day, and even by the hour. Public utilities vary their prices to commercial users by time of day and weekend versus weekday.

If price discrimination is to work, certain conditions must exist.[2] First, the market must be segmentable, and the segments must show different intensities of demand. Second, members of the segment paying the lower price should not be able to turn around and resell the product to the segment paying the higher price. Third, competitors should not be able to undersell the firm in the segment being charged the higher price. Fourth, the cost of segmenting and policing the market should not exceed the extra revenue derived from price discrimination. Fifth, the practice should not breed customer resentment and ill will. Sixth, the particular form of price discrimination should not be considered illegal under the law.

With the current deregulation taking place in certain industries, such as airlines and trucks, companies in these industries have increased their use of discriminatory pricing. Consider the price discrimination introduced by airlines:

> The passengers on a plane bound from Raleigh to Los Angeles may pay as many as thirteen different round-trip fares for the same flight! Those who check carefully benefit from the intense competition between different carriers flying this route. The thirteen fares are: first class, $1,092; first class—night, $956; first class—youth, $819; coach, $910; coach—night, $637; coach—youth, 683; tour fare, $637; youth with parent, $368; 60-day Super-Saver, $619; 14-day Super-Saver, $519; family plan, $860 for first dependent, $208 for additional dependents; military personnel, $341; and Visit USA (for foreigners traveling in the U.S.), $473.

Psychological Pricing Price communicates something about the product. For example, many consumers use price as an indicator of quality. A $100 bottle of perfume may contain only $3 worth of scent, but people are willing to pay $100 because this indicates something special. Sellers should consider the psychology of prices and not simply the economics.

Even small differences in price can communicate product differences to consumers. Consider a stereo amplifier priced at $300 compared to one priced at $299.95. The actual price difference is only 5 cents, but the psychological difference can be much greater. For example, some consumers will see the $299.95 as a price in the $200 range rather than the $300 range. The $299.95 will more likely be perceived as a bargain price, and the $300 price conveys more quality. Some psychologists argue that each digit has symbolic and visual qualities that should be considered in pricing. Thus 8 is symmetrical and creates a soothing effect, and 7 is angular and creates a jarring effect.

Promotional Pricing Under certain circumstances, companies will temporarily price their products below the list price, and sometimes even below cost. Promotional pricing takes several forms:

1. Supermarkets and department stores will price a few products as *loss leaders* to attract customers to the store in the hope that they will buy other things at normal markups.

Carvel uses promotional pricing. *Courtesy of Carvel Corp.*

2. Sellers will also use *special-event pricing* in certain seasons to draw in more customers. Thus linens are promotionally priced every January to attract shopping-weary customers into the stores.
3. Manufacturers will sometimes offer *cash rebates* to consumers who buy the product from dealers within a specified time period. The manufacturer sends the rebate directly to the customer. Rebates are a flexible tool for trimming inventories during difficult selling periods without cutting list prices. They have recently been popular with Chrysler and other automakers, and also with other big-ticket item sellers such as Fedders, Polaroid, and Minolta.
4. *Psychological discounting* is another promotion-pricing technique, where the seller puts an artificially high price on a product and offers it at substantial savings; for example, "Was $359, Is $299." Psychological discounting is specifically prohibited by the Federal Trade Commission and Better Business Bureau. On the other hand, discounts from normal prices are a legitimate form of promotional pricing (see Exhibit 14-1).

EXHIBIT 14-1

MOVING MINK COATS THROUGH PROMOTIONAL DISCOUNTING

Irwin and Carol Ware lease and operate the fur salon in the posh I. Magnin department store on North Michigan Avenue in Chicago. To move the sluggish inventory of fur coats, they decided to run a one-day sale. Fur coats were marked down from 50 to 70 percent. They loaded the racks with furs, with one rack bearing the sign "Everything on this rack below $2,000." To announce the sale, hype-type television advertising was used, as well as newspaper ads touting this as the sale of a lifetime. Customers learned that they could take twenty-four months to pay.

Did this hard-sell, bargain-basement hawking work? No question about it. Carol Ware handled over two hundred customers that day, with 50 percent leaving the store with newly purchased fur coats. The average salon sale: $4,500.

Source: Adapted from "Sale of Mink Coats Strays a Fur Piece from the Expected," *Wall Street Journal,* March 20, 1980, p. 1.

Geographical The company must decide how to price its products to customers located in differ-
Pricing ent parts of the country. Should the company charge higher prices to distant customers to cover the higher shipping costs and thereby risk losing their business?
Or should the company charge the same to all customers regardless of location? We
will examine five major geographical pricing strategies in connection with the
following hypothetical situation:

> The Peerless Paper Company is located in Atlanta, Georgia, and sells paper
> products to customers all over the United States. The cost of freight is high and
> affects the companies from whom customers buy their paper. Peerless wants to
> establish a geographical pricing policy. Management is trying to determine how to
> price a $100 order to three specific customers: customer A (Atlanta); customer B
> (Bloomington, Indiana); and customer C (Compton, California).

FOB Origin Pricing

Peerless can ask each customer to pay the shipping cost from the Atlanta factory to
the customer's specific destination. All three customers would pay the same factory
price of $100, with customer A paying, say, $10 for shipping, customer B paying
$15, and customer C paying $25. Called *FOB origin pricing,* it means that the goods
are placed free on board a carrier, at which point the title and responsibility pass to
the customer, who pays the freight from the factory to the destination.

Advocates of FOB pricing feel that this is the most equitable way to allocate
freight charges, because each customer picks up its own cost. The disadvantage,
however, is that Peerless will be a high-cost firm to distant customers. If Peerless's
main competitor is in California, this competitor would outsell Peerless in California. In fact, the competitor would outsell Peerless in most of the West, while Peerless would dominate the East. A vertical line could be drawn on a map connecting
the cities where the two companies' price plus freight would just be equal. Peerless
would have the price advantage east of this line, and its competitor would have the
price advantage west of this line.

Uniform Delivered Pricing

Uniform delivered pricing is the exact opposite of FOB pricing. Here the company
charges the same price plus freight to all customers regardless of their location. It
is also called "postage stamp pricing," based on the fact that the U.S. government
sets a uniform delivered price on first-class mail anywhere in the country. The
freight charge is set at the average freight cost. Suppose this is $15. Uniform deliv-
ered pricing therefore results in a high charge to the Atlanta customer (who pays
$15 freight instead of $10) and a subsidized charge to the Compton customer (who
pays $15 instead of $25). The Atlanta customer would prefer to buy paper from
another local paper company that uses FOB origin pricing. On the other hand,
Peerless has a better chance to win the California customer. Other advantages are
that uniform delivered pricing is relatively easy to administer and allows the firm to
maintain a nationally advertised price.

Zone Pricing

Zone pricing falls between FOB origin pricing and uniform delivered pricing. The
company establishes two or more zones. All customers within a zone pay the same

total price; and this price is higher in the more distant zones. Peerless might set up an East zone and charge $10 freight to all customers in this zone; a Midwest zone and charge $15; and a West zone and charge $25. In this way, the customers within a given price zone receive no price advantage from the company. A customer in Atlanta and Boston pay the same total price to Peerless. The complaint, however, is that the Atlanta customer is subsidizing the Boston customer's freight cost. In addition, a customer just on the west side of the line dividing the East and Midwest pays substantially more than one just on the east side of the line, although they may be within a few miles of each other.

Basing-Point Pricing

Basing-point pricing allows the seller to designate some city as a basing point and charge all customers the freight cost from that city to the customer location regardless of the city from which the goods are actually shipped. For example, Peerless might establish Chicago as the basing point and charge all customers $100 plus the appropriate freight from Chicago to the destination. This means that an Atlanta customer pays the freight cost from Chicago to Atlanta even though the goods may be shipped from Atlanta. This customer is paying a "phantom charge." In its favor, using a basing-point location other than the factory raises the total price to customers near the factory and lowers the total price to customers far from the factory.

If all the sellers used the same basing-point city, delivered prices would be the same for all customers, and price competition would be eliminated. Such industries as sugar, cement, steel, and automobiles used basing-point pricing for years, but this method is less popular today because of adverse court rulings charging collusive pricing by competitors. Some companies establish multiple basing points to create more flexibility. They would quote freight charges from the basing-point city nearest to the customer.

Freight Absorption Pricing

The seller who is anxious to do business with a particular customer or geographical area might absorb all or part of the actual freight charges in order to get the business. The seller might reason that if it can get more business, its average costs will fall and more than compensate for the extra freight cost. Freight absorption pricing is used for market penetration and also to hold on to increasingly competitive markets.

PRICE CHANGES

Initiating Price Changes After developing their price structures and strategies, companies will face occasions when they will want to cut or raise prices.

Initiating Price Cuts

Several circumstances may lead a firm to consider cutting its price, even though this might provoke a price war. One circumstance is *excess capacity*. Here the firm needs additional business and cannot generate it through increased sales effort, product improvement, or other measures. In the late 1970s various companies abandoned "follow-the-leader pricing" and turned to "flexible pricing" to boost their sales.[3]

Another circumstance is *falling market share* in the face of vigorous price competition. Several American industries—automobiles, consumer electronics, cameras, watches, and steel—have been losing market share to Japanese competitors whose high-quality products carry lower prices than American products. Zenith, General Motors, and other American companies have resorted to more aggressive pricing action. General Motors, for example, cut its subcompact car prices by 10 percent on the West Coast, where Japanese competition is strongest.

Companies will also initiate price cuts in a *drive to dominate the market through lower costs.* Either the company starts with lower costs than its competitors, or it initiates price cuts in the hope of gaining market share that will lead to falling costs through larger volume.

Initiating Price Increases

Many companies have had to raise prices in recent years. They do this knowing that the price increases will be resented by customers, dealers, and the company's own salesforce. Yet a successful price increase can increase profits considerably. For example, if the company's profit margin is 3 percent of sales, a 1 percent price increase will increase profits by 33 percent if sales volume is unaffected.

A major circumstance provoking price increases is the persistent worldwide *cost inflation.*[4] Rising costs unmatched by productivity gains squeeze profit margins and lead companies to regular rounds of price increases. Companies often raise their prices by more than the cost increase in anticipation of further inflation or government price controls. Companies hesitate to make long-run price commitments to customers—they fear that cost inflation will erode their profit margins. Companies are able to increase their prices in a number of ways to fight inflation (see Exhibit 14-2).[5]

EXHIBIT 14-2

PRICE STRATEGIES FOR MEETING INFLATION

Here are several ways in which companies are adjusting their prices to meet inflation:

1. *Adoption of delayed quotation pricing.* The company decides not to set its final price until the product is finished or delivered. Delayed quotation pricing is prevalent in industries with long production lead times, such as industrial construction and heavy equipment manufacture.

2. *Use of escalator clauses.* The company requires the customer to pay today's price and all or part of any inflation increase that takes place before delivery. An escalator clause in the contract bases price increases on some specified price index, such as the cost-of-living index. Escalator clauses are found in many contracts involving industrial projects of long duration.

3. *Unbundling of goods and services.* The company maintains its price but eliminates one or more elements that were part of the former offer. These elements are offered

optionally and priced separately. For example, IBM decides to offer training services as a separately priced item rather than as part of the former offer. This amounts to increasing the price of the former total offer. Companies have increasingly unbundled their product offers in recent years.

4. *Reduction of discounts.* The company reduces its normal cash and quantity discounts and limits its salesforce from offering off-list pricing to get the business.

5. *Elimination of low-margin products, orders, and customers.* The company eliminates low-profit products, orders, and customers. Or the company raises the price or adds special charges for their handling.

6. *Reduction of product quality, features, and service.* The company can preserve its profit margin by reducing the quality, features, or services it offers. With these policies, the company risks losing its loyal customers.

Another factor leading to price increases is *overdemand.* When a company cannot supply all its customers' needs, it can raise its prices, put customers on allocation, or both. Prices can be raised almost invisibly by dropping discounts and adding higher-priced units to the line. Or prices can be pushed up boldly.

In passing price increases on to customers, the company should avoid acquiring the image of price gouger. The price increases should be supported with a company communication program telling customers why prices are being increased. The company salesforce should help customers find ways to economize.

Buyer Reactions to Price Changes

Whether the price is raised or lowered, the action will surely affect buyers, competitors, distributors, and suppliers and may interest government as well.

Customers do not always put a straightforward interpretation on price changes.[6] A price cut can be interpreted in the following ways:[7] The item is about to be replaced by a later model; the item has some fault and is not selling well; the firm is in financial trouble and may not stay in business to supply future parts; the price will come down even further, and it pays to wait; or the quality has been reduced.

A price increase, which would normally deter sales, may carry some positive meanings to the buyers: The item is very "hot" and may be unobtainable unless it is bought soon; the item represents an unusually good value; or the seller is greedy and is charging what the traffic will bear.

Competitor Reactions to Price Changes

A firm contemplating a price change has to worry about competitors' as well as customers' reactions. Competitors are very likely to react where the number of firms is small, the product is homogeneous, and the buyers are highly informed.

How can the firm anticipate the likely reactions of its competitors? Assume that the firm faces one large competitor. The competitor's reaction can be estimated from two vantage points. One is to assume that the competitor reacts in a set way to price changes. In this case, the competitor's reaction can be anticipated. The other is to assume that the competitor treats each price change as a fresh challenge and reacts according to self-interest at the time. In this case, the company will have to determine what constitutes the competitor's self-interest at the time.

The problem is complicated because the competitor can put different interpretations on, say, a company price cut, such as the company is trying to steal the market; or the company is doing poorly and is trying to boost its sales; or the company wants the whole industry to reduce prices to stimulate total demand.

When there are several competitors, the company must estimate each competitor's likely reaction. If all competitors behave alike, this amounts to analyzing only a typical competitor. If the competitors do not behave alike because of critical differences in size, market shares, or policies, then separate analyses are necessary. If some competitors will match the price change, there is good reason to expect that the rest will also match it.

Responding to Price Changes Here we reverse the question and ask how a firm should respond to a price change initiated by a competitor. The firm needs to consider the following issues: (1) Why did the competitor change the price? Is it to steal the market, to utilize excess capacity, to meet changing cost conditions, or to lead an industry-wide price change? (2) Does the competitor plan to make the price change temporary or permanent? (3) What will happen to the company's market share and profits if it doesn't respond? Are other companies going to respond? and (4) What are the competitor's and other firms' responses likely to be to each possible reaction?

Besides these issues, the company must make a broader analysis. The company has to consider the product's stage in the life cycle, its importance in the company's product portfolio, the intentions and resources of the competitor, the price and value sensitivity of the market, the behavior of costs with volume, and the company's alternative opportunities.

FIGURE 14-2
Price Reaction Program for Meeting a Competitor's Price Cut

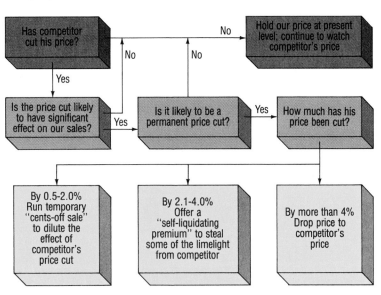

Source: Redrawn, with permission, from an unpublished paper by Raymond J. Trapp, Northwestern University, 1964.

An extended analysis of company alternatives is not always feasible at the time of a price change. The competitor may have spent considerable time preparing this decision, but the company may have to react decisively within hours or days. About the only way to cut down price reaction decision time is to anticipate possible competitor's price changes and prepare contingent responses. Figure 14-2 shows a company's price reaction program for meeting a competitor's possible price cut. Reaction programs for meeting price changes find their greatest application in industries where price changes occur with some frequency and where it is important to react quickly. Examples can be found in the meatpacking, lumber, and oil industries.[8]

■ Summary

Pricing is a dynamic process. Companies design a pricing structure that covers all their products, change it over time, and adjust it to account for different customers and situations.

Pricing strategies usually change as a product passes through its life cycle. In pricing innovative new products, the company can follow a skimming policy by setting prices high initially to "skim" the maximum amount of revenue from various segments of the market. Or it can use penetration pricing by setting a low initial price to win a large market share. The company can decide on one of nine price-quality strategies for introducing an imitative product.

When the product is part of a product mix, the firm searches for a set of prices that will maximize the profits from the total mix. The company decides on the price zones for items in its product line and on the pricing of optional products, captive products, and by-products.

Companies apply a variety of price-adjustment strategies to account for differences in consumer segments and situations. One is geographical pricing, where the company decides how to price to distant customers, choosing from such alternatives as FOB pricing, uniform delivered pricing, zone pricing, basing-point pric-

ing, and freight absorption pricing. A second is discount pricing and allowances, where the company establishes cash discounts, quantity discounts, functional discounts, seasonal discounts, and allowances. A third is discriminatory pricing, where the company establishes different prices for different customers, product forms, places, or times. A fourth is psychological pricing, where the company adjusts the price to better communicate a product's intended position. A fifth is promotional pricing, where the company decides on loss-leader pricing, special-event pricing, and psychological discounting.

When a firm considers initiating a price change, it must consider customers' and competitors' reactions. Customers' reactions are influenced by the meaning customers see in the price change. Competitors' reactions flow from a set reaction policy or a fresh appraisal of each situation. The firm initiating the price change must also anticipate the probable reactions of suppliers, middlemen, and government.

The firm that faces a price change initiated by a competitor must try to understand the competitor's intent and the likely duration of the change. If swiftness of reaction is desirable, the firm should preplan its reactions to different possible price actions by competitors.

■ Questions for Discussion

1. Armco, a major steel company, has developed a new process for galvanizing steel sheets so that they can be painted (previously not possible) and used in car-body parts to prevent rust. What factors should Armco consider in setting a price for this product?

2. GE has invented a revolutionary new household bulb that will last five times longer than the typical 1,000-hour life of ordinary incandescent bulbs and use only one-third as much electricity. It is thinking of pricing the bulb at $10 (this will save $20 over the bulb's rated life in lower electric bills). What problems might GE have with this pricing policy? What suggestions would you make?

3. A company has decided to increase its prices because of cost inflation. It is about to announce the price increase to its customers. It is trying to decide how to explain the price increases. What are two different approaches, and which would you favor?

4. In 1981 and 1982, auto manufacturers resorted to aggressive rebate programs in an attempt to sell more cars. What dangers exist with this pricing strategy?

5. Do the following companies practice market penetration or market skimming in pricing their products? (a) McDonald's, (b) Curtis Mathes television sets, and (c) Bic Corporation. Why?

6. Discuss the two major discount pricing tactics Head Skis might employ in dealing with the retail outlets that carry its products.

7. In recent years the majority of price changes made by marketers have been price increases. Why?

■ References

1. See JOEL DEAN, *Managerial Economics* (Englewood Cliffs, NJ: Prentice-Hall, 1951), pp. 420ff.
2. See GEORGE STIGLER, *The Theory and Practice of Price* (rev. ed.) (New York: Macmillan, 1952), pp. 215ff.
3. See "Flexible Pricing," *Business Week,* December 12, 1977, pp. 78–88.
4. See "Pricing Strategy in an Inflation Economy," *Business Week,* April 6, 1974, pp. 43–49.
5. NORMAN H. FUSS, JR., "How to Raise Prices—Judiciously—to Meet Today's Conditions," *Harvard Business Review,* May–June 1975, pp. 10ff; and MARY LOUISE HATTEN, "Don't Get Caught with Your Prices Down," *Business Horizons,* March–April 1982, pp. 23–28.
6. For an excellent review, see KENT B. MONROE, "Buyers' Subjective Perceptions of Price," *Journal of Marketing Research,* February 1973, pp. 70–80.
7. See ALFRED R. OXENFELDT, *Pricing for Marketing Executives* (San Francisco: Wadsworth, 1961), p. 28.
8. See, for example, WILLIAM M. MORGENROTH, "A Method for Understanding Price Determinants," *Journal of Marketing Research,* August 1964, pp. 17–26.

CASE 9

TEXAS INSTRUMENTS, INC.: SPEAKING LEARNING-AID PRODUCTS

Texas Instruments' drive into consumer markets has been changed in the past few years by (1) discontinuing digital watches and home computers, and (2) introducing several new hand-held learning-aid products (LAPs) at relatively low prices. The Little Professor, Dataman, and First Watch have numerical memories and displays. The first two teach math, and the third teaches how to tell time. The Spelling B and Speak & Spell teach how to spell, and they have both numerical and alphabetical memories and displays. Speak & Spell is further distinguished by its voice capability. Recent additions are Speak & Read and Speak & Math.

Although the LAPs differ significantly in both form and function from earlier TI consumer products (calculators, personal computers, and watches) and are in the introductory and growth stages of the product life cycle, the marketing strategy that has been pursued to date is virtually identical to that employed earlier for the company's more mature products. Their educational value suggests that they could be marketed to schools as a supplementary learning aid. Only a limited effort has been made to develop either the educational or the home entertainment markets. As with any new product introduction, TI is faced with assessing market potential and familiarizing potential customers with a previously unheard-of product. These problems are particularly acute in this case, because the products were developed as an outgrowth of technological innovation, rather than in response to expressed consumer needs.

The company is at the point where it must decide what strategies and action programs it should use to ensure successful participation in the market for small electronic learning-aid products. A major aspect is the pricing strategy.

The learning aids began in 1972 when TI, along with such firms as Bowmar, National Semiconductor, and Commodore, packaged inexpensive calculators with game books. By 1975 National Semiconductor had introduced the Quiz Kid, an owl-shaped, hand-held machine in which the user inputted simple math problems, and what he or she believed to be the correct answer. The device then indicated with a green or a red light whether the answer was correct or incorrect. TI's Little Professor and Dataman machines were distinguished by the preprogramming of specific math problems within each machine's memory. The Dataman extended the Little Professor's capability by adding game-playing capabilities and a fluorescent "stadium scoreboard" display for correct answers.

Later Spelling B and Speak & Spell were introduced. These products are noteworthy for their alphabetic capabilities. Speak & Spell uses TI's voice synthesizer technology. It contains 230 of the most commonly misspelled words in order of difficulty. It asks you to spell a word that it clearly pronounces. When you finish spelling you press a button; if you were right, it says: "That is correct, now spell *treasure*." If you had misspelled the word, it would have said: "Wrong, try again." You would then have had another chance. If you missed again, the unit would have said: "The correct spelling is T-R-E-A-S-U-R-E." The unit also automatically displays the number of right and wrong answers at the end of a block of ten words. Speak & Spell can be used as a pronunciation guide and as the basis for a number of games, and it will accept additional small memory modules that raise the spelling difficulty.

The new technology involved holds enormous potential, since voice-command control will eventually be an important aspect of life. The speech synthesis chip, which has brought such wide attention to Speak & Spell, is a far more advanced (and compact) version of the circuit and chip systems that have been used for almost two decades in commercial and industrial "talking machines," such as in banking systems and disconnected and new-number messages by telephone companies. The memory capability of Speak & Spell is more than twice that of any previous portable voice memory system. The speech synthesis capability of Speak & Spell was almost universally hailed as a major innovation, and as a result received a great deal of attention.

The company's talking products store individual words on semiconductor chips packaged in snap-in modules. The buyer must purchase additional modules to expand the vocabulary. The high levels of consumer interest and user involvement, along with the company's leading technological position, have indicated a strong basis for a well-planned line of voice-synthesized learning aids to be aggressively marketed the year round. This would be in contrast to past efforts involving year-end promotion of two or three items.

Now Texas Instruments has developed an educational tool that brings the teaching of reading into the electronics age. By combining two new technologies and building on its Speak & Spell learning aid, TI has produced what it calls the Magic Wand Speaking Reader. With it, preschool children can help teach themselves to read by sliding a handheld "wand" across a strip of bars printed under the words in special books.

The plastic wand, about the size of a fat pen, uses a tiny beam of infrared light to decipher vocal instructions contained in the bar-code strips. It operates much as checkout scanners in supermarkets decode product identification data from the bar codes printed on grocery items, but TI's wand costs about a fourth as much as existing systems. The Magic Wand is said to be the first of a family of learning aids and portable computing products using bar-code storage. The company will put the battery-operated device on the market for a list price of $120.

The Magic Wand may also be the key to low-cost electronic publishing because it requires no change in the printing techniques and equipment now in use. TI plans to capitalize on the "razor-blade" side of this new market by encouraging publishing houses to turn out their own books. Publishers will supply the text, and TI, using a computerized "bar-code factory," will translate the words into bars and spaces the Magic Wand can read. Mattel Inc.'s Western Publishing, publisher of Little Golden Books, is using a similar approach in developing a talking reader.

Several future uses have been proposed for voice synthesis chips, including foreign language education and electronic games. An example of the potential is the electronic dictionary, already being offered by at least two firms. It can translate as many as 1,500 English words and phrases into a foreign language, such as French, German, Spanish, Russian, and Japanese. Languages can be changed by switching modules available at $25 to $50 each. Both the Lexicon and the Craig are pocket-size and sell for about $200.

TI's Consumer Products Group's direct salesforce sells LAPs as well as calculators, and until recently also digital watches, to major retail chains. Smaller stores place their orders directly with TI or purchase through distributors. In a recent year, advertising amounted to about $1 million for learning-aid products and was confined to the four weeks following Thanksgiving. The sole advertising medium used was television (prime and fringe time), with heavy exposure. The company used some trade magazine advertising, but the program was not extensive. Cooperative advertising was offered to retailers, with a specified percentage of total purchase available to dealers for co-op advertising purposes.

TI achieved its dominant position in hand-held calculator and digital watches sales by using a low-margin, high-volume strategy. Relatively low prices were established on a few models in the anticipation that large production volumes, coupled with accumulated experience in manufacturing and marketing, would result in a series of unit cost decreases. This in turn would permit still lower prices and thereby result in the dominant market share and presumably profit for Texas Instruments.

On numerous occasions, Speak & Spell has been in short supply. Moreover, there are no close substitutes. The retail price for Speak & Spell has varied considerably by year and by type of retail outlet. The range has been from less than $45 to over $60. This has raised the question of whether the company's learning-curve pricing strategy, basic to the nonconsumer business, was appropriate for the consumer-oriented products.

1. For the learning-aid products line, should the company use the low-price strategy it used for digital watches and hand-held calculators and home computers?

2. What are your recommendations concerning the company's opportunity to develop and aggressively market a line of learning aids featuring the company's speech synthesis technology?

A NEW TI PRODUCT: VOCAID

VOCAID is designed to provide speech capabilities for the voiceless. It consists of a keyboard, with each key identified by a word or expression. By depressing the appropriate keys, the VOCAID emits a synthesized voice expression of the selected message. Additional modules and matching keyboard templates, purchased separately, can be used to expand VOCAID's capability. Pricing the VOCAID hardware and the additional cartridges and templates is a problem. There is some uncertainty as to what retail prices should be suggested by

Texas Instruments. It has been suggested the company should price the items according to their value to the buyer, rather than start with cost. Questions were raised about how potential user/buyers can be identified and how the value to user/buyers can be determined.

1. Should VOCAID be marketed along with learning-aid products? Why? Why not?
2. What recommendations would you as a consultant give management concerning the pricing of this product? How it should be marketed?

CASE 10

LOCTITE CORPORATION

Loctite is a highly profitable and rapidly growing manufacturer and marketer of adhesives, sealants, and related specialty chemicals, with annual sales of almost $200 million. The company's growth has been in the "wonder glues," specifically in the anaerobic type, which cures quickly in absence of air, and the "crazy glues" (cyanoacrylates), which cure instantly upon exposure to moisture present in trace amounts on surfaces to be bonded. In the industrial market this product sells for over $60 per pound. A pound contains roughly 30,000 drops and is generally applied a few drops at a time. Consumer packages are much smaller, containing about one-tenth of an ounce and selling for up $2 per tube, or about $20 or more per ounce.

The company's phenomenal success in the industrial market has attracted competitors, including some large and aggressive ones, such as Esmark and the 3M Company. Competitive anaerobic and cyanoacrylate products are being marketed in most countries where the company conducts business. The company has patent protection on its anaerobics in the United States and, to a lesser extent, in a number of foreign countries. Nearly all competitive anaerobic sealants and adhesives are sold at prices lower than Loctite's. Although the company has selectively reduced prices to meet competition from time to time, it believes that attention to technical service and customer needs has generally enabled it to maintain its market position without significant price reductions.

The company plans to intensify its "application engineering" approach, which helped it overtake Eastman Kodak in the more competitive "crazy glue," or cyanoacrylates, market. This approach casts well-trained, technical service personnel as customer problem solvers using Loctite's products, often especially formulated for the customer's application. The company has three principal user markets for its products: the industrial market, the consumer market, and the automotive aftermarket. In the Industrial Products Group, approximately 60 percent of sales are made through independent distributors, some of which sell adhesives and sealants made by others. The remainder of sales are made directly to end users. The company maintains close and continued contact with its distributors and major end users to provide technical assistance and support for its products. In the United States and Canada, sales are made through approximately 120 technically trained district managers and sales engineers, and through approximately 2,800 independent industrial distributors.

Hoping to improve profitability, Loctite decided to try consumer goods marketing techniques in marketing RC 601, a puttylike adhesive for repairing worn machine parts. After going to the field to determine what potential customers wanted and studying the product from the customers' point of view, changes were made. The before and after contrast is as follows:

	BEFORE	AFTER
Market target	Design engineers[a]	Maintenance workers[b]
Product	Thin liquid	Gel
Package	Bottle (red)	Tube (silver)
Name	RC 601	Quick Metal
Price	Cost-based	Value-based
Promotion	Technical description[c]	"Keeps machines running until parts arrive"
Sales effort	Routine	Special promotions and incentives at all levels
Sales results		700% increase after changes

[a]Reluctant to try unproved products.
[b]Able to buy anything anywhere he needs to make machine operate.
[c]Nonmigrating thoxotropic anaerobic gel.

The Industrial Products Division faces the problem of pricing three new products. The details are as follows:

- **Bond-a-matic.** This is an instant glue applicator for assembly lines and is targeted at small and medium-sized manufacturers that put a lot of parts together. The product avoids "adhesive clog," a common and costly problem. The company is so confident of the product's performance that it will mail a demonstration kit for a thirty-day free trial. It should be priced low enough so that it can be bought by production managers without approval for a capital expenditure.
- **Quick Repair Kit.** This includes an assortment of materials to make quick minor repairs requiring fast-curing adhesive and/or sealants to keep equipment running and minimize waste of materials in small shops and factories. The kit includes a pair of Vice-Grip pliers as a premium.
- **Quick-Metal.** This is a puttylike adhesive for temporary repair of worn metal bearings and other machine parts. Equipment is ready to run in one hour compared with twelve hours for "metalizers," the most commonly used alternative method. Loctite claims that the product can save the user of $4,000 in time and labor. It is packaged in 50cc tubes.

All these products are to be sold through the Industrial Products Division's distributors. In determining the suggested price to be charged by the distributors for each product, assume the following hypothetical data:

LOCTITE:

	BOND-A-MATIC	QUICK REPAIR KIT	QUICK-METAL
Cost to make	$27.00	$ 6.25	$1.50
All other costs	23.00	5.75	3.50
Total cost per unit	$50.00	$12.00	$5.00

DISTRIBUTOR:
Usual gross margin on this type of product, 33⅓% of selling price.

1. What factors should be considered in determining the price Loctite should suggest its distributors charge their customers?
2. What price would you recommend Loctite suggest its distributors charge?
3. How would you use the problem-solving approach when selling through distributors and retailers?

15

Placing Products: Distribution Channels and Physical Distribution

A quarter of a century ago Dr Pepper was little more than a small Texas concentrate company. But by the early 1980s, Dr Pepper was the largest-selling noncola soft drink in the country—and the third largest seller overall behind Coke and Pepsi. By 1982, sales of Dr Pepper and the company's other brands (which include Canada Dry and Welch's) exceeded $500 million, and the company had enjoyed 27 straight years of profits.

Dr Pepper makes a good product and uses national advertising to create strong consumer preference. But successful soft-drink marketing requires much more. Much of the marketing battle is fought in the distribution channels—by bottlers' salesforces and on retailers' shelves. The company sells Dr Pepper concentrate to bottlers who carbonate, bottle, promote, and sell it to retailers. In turn, the retailers stock, promote, and sell Dr Pepper to consumers. Dr Pepper relies heavily on its distribution channels to help create demand and get the product into the hands of consumers. Over the years, the company has carefully developed a loyal corps of more than 500 bottlers who sell the Dr Pepper brand in their local markets. Though most Dr Pepper bottlers have another major soft drink brand (usually Coke or Pepsi) they depend on for most of their sales, Dr Pepper earned the position of the "top" second brand for most of its bottlers.

Strong bottler support is essential to Dr Pepper's success. Dr Pepper can generate some brand preference through national advertising, but consumer soft-drink choices are heavily influenced by the actions of retailers. And bottlers strongly influ-ence retailers. The bottler's salesforce makes regular calls on retailers and uses local promotional pro-grams to encourage retailers to give Dr Pepper better shelf position, feature Dr Pepper in their weekly newspaper ads, and promote Dr Pepper with price specials, displays, coupons, and samples. The bottlers understand local market conditions and retailers' needs, and they can often help the company design marketing programs that more effectively tap local markets.

Traditionally, Dr Pepper has followed a "local" marketing approach. The company has given its bot-tlers considerable autonomy with Dr Pepper advertis-ing and promotion, allowing bottlers to adapt the brand's marketing programs to local market condi-tions. But in the early 1980s, management decided to turn Dr Pepper from a large regional brand, with sales concentrated in the South and West, into a truly national brand. The company shifted from its local marketing approach to a national approach using company-controlled, national marketing activities rather than dealer-adapted, local programs. Dr Pep-per cut back its field salesforce, resulting in less service to bottlers. It took ad placement out of the hands of bottlers and began to put most of its adver-tising and promotional dollars into national advertis-ing placed by the company. Under the new ap-proach, bottlers had much less to say about how Dr Pepper would be sold in their local market areas.

Dr Pepper counted on its centralized market-ing program to increase consumer demand and pull more of the product through the channel. The new national advertising was popular with consumers, but it didn't create a nation full of Peppers. Instead, the new approach alienated Dr Pepper bottlers. When the company tried to force-feed bottlers with the new national marketing program, many were offended and laid back on Dr Pepper. The company lost its special status as the top second brand and became just another second brand to most bottlers. Dr Pepper lost market share and watched the fizz go out of its profits. In 1982, Dr Pepper unit sales dropped 3 percent, and the company's fourth-quarter loss of $4 million was the first in 27 years. Dr Pepper dropped to fourth behind 7-Up.

In 1983, the company abandoned its national marketing approach, returned to its local approach, and tried to mend fences with its bottlers. Whether it will successfully win back favor in its distribution channels remains to be seen. But the lesson is clear—to sell final consumers on Dr Pepper, the company must first sell its bottlers. As one bottler noted: "They can make it if they capture the imaginations of bottlers first, and the public second." That, it appears, is exactly what Dr Pepper is trying to do.[1]

M arketing channel decisions are among the most critical facing management. The company's chosen channels intimately affect every other marketing decision. The company's pricing depends upon whether it uses large and high-quality dealers or medium-size, medium-quality dealers. The firm's salesforce decisions depend upon how much selling and training the dealers will need. In addition, the company's channel decisions involve relatively long-term commitments to other firms. When a truck manufacturer signs up independent dealers, it cannot easily replace them with company-owned branches if conditions change. Therefore management must choose channels with an eye on tomorrow's likely selling environment as well as today's.

In this chapter we will examine four major issues: (1) What is the nature of marketing channels, and what trends are taking place? (2) How do channel firms interact and organize to do the work of the channel? (3) What problems do companies face in designing, managing, and evaluating their channels? (4) What role do physical distribution decisions play in attracting and satisfying customers? In the next chapter we will examine marketing channel issues from the perspective of retailers and wholesalers.

THE NATURE OF MARKETING CHANNELS

Most producers work with marketing intermediaries to bring their products to market. They try to forge a distribution channel. We define **distribution channel** as *the set of firms and individuals that take title, or assist in transferring title, to the particular good or service as it moves from the producer to the consumer.*

Why Are Marketing Intermediaries Used? Why do producers delegate some of the selling job to intermediaries? The delegation means relinquishing some control over how and to whom the products are sold. The producer appears to be placing the firm's destiny in the hands of intermediaries.

Since producers could sell directly to final customers, they must feel they gain certain advantages in using middlemen. These advantages are described below.

Many producers lack the financial resources to carry out direct marketing. For example, General Motors sells its automobiles through over 28,000 independent dealers; even General Motors would be hard pressed to raise the cash to buy out its dealers.

Direct marketing would require many producers to become middlemen for the complementary products for other producers in order to achieve mass-distribution economies. For example, the Wm. Wrigley Jr. Company would not find it practical to establish small retail gum shops throughout the country or to sell gum door to door or by mail order. It would have to sell gum along with many other small products and would end up in the drugstore and foodstore business. Wrigley finds it easier to work through the extensive network of privately owned distribution institutions.

Producers who can afford to establish their own channels can often earn a greater return by increasing their investment in their main business. If a company earns a 20 percent rate of return on manufacturing and foresees only a 10 percent return on retailing, it will not want to undertake its own retailing.

The use of middlemen largely boils down to their superior efficiency in making goods widely available and accessible to target markets. Marketing intermediaries, through their contacts, experience, specialization, and scale of operation, offer the firm more than it can usually achieve on its own.

From the economic system's point of view, the basic role of marketing intermediaries is to transform the heterogeneous supplies found in nature into meaningful goods assortments desired by people. According to Alderson:

> The materials which are useful to man occur in nature in heterogeneous mixtures which might be called conglomerations since these mixtures have only random relationship to human needs and activities. The collection of goods in the possession of a household or an individual also constitutes a heterogeneous supply, but it might be called an assortment since it is related to anticipated patterns of future behavior. The whole economic process may be described as a series of transformations from meaningless to meaningful heterogeneity.[2]

Alderson adds: "The goal of marketing is the matching of segments of supply and demand."[3]

Figure 15-1 shows one major source of the economies effected by the use of middlemen. Part A shows three producers each using direct marketing to reach three customers. This system requires nine different contacts. Part B shows the three producers working through one distributor, who contacts the three customers. This system requires only six contacts. In this way, middlemen reduce the amount of work that must be done.

Marketing Channel Functions

A **marketing channel** performs the work of moving goods from producers to consumers. It overcomes the major time, place, and possession gaps that separate goods and services from those who would use them. Members of the marketing channel perform a number of key functions:[4]

FIGURE 15-1
*How a Distributor
Effects an Economy of
Effort*

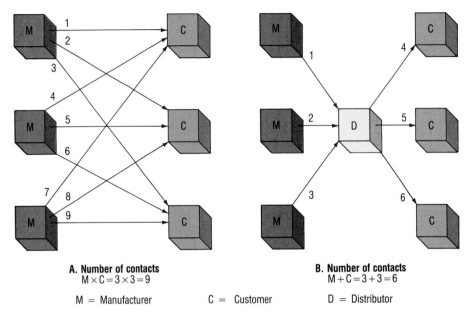

A. Number of contacts
M×C=3×3=9

B. Number of contacts
M+C=3+3=6

M = Manufacturer   C = Customer   D = Distributor

- *Research*—gathering of information necessary for planning and facilitating exchange.
- *Promotion*—development and dissemination of persuasive communications about the offer.
- *Contact*—searching out and communicating with prospective buyers.
- *Matching*—shaping and fitting the offer to the buyer's requirements. This includes such activities as manufacturing, grading, assembling, and packaging.
- *Negotiation*—the attempt to reach final agreement on price and other terms of the offer so that transfer of ownership or possession can be effected.
- *Physical distribution*—transporting and storing of the goods.
- *Financing*—acquisition and dispersal of funds to cover the costs of the channel work.
- *Risk taking*—assumption of risks in connection with carrying out the channel work.

The first five functions help consummate transactions; the last three help fulfill the completed transactions.

The question is not *whether* these functions need to be performed—they must be—but rather *who* is to perform them. All the functions have three things in common: They use up scarce resources, they can often be performed better through specialization, and they are shiftable among channel members. To the extent that the manufacturer performs them, its costs go up and its prices have to be higher. When some functions are shifted to middlemen, the producer's costs and prices are lower, but the middlemen must add a charge to cover their work. The issue of who should perform various channel tasks is one of relative efficiency and effectiveness.

Marketing functions, then, are more basic than the institutions that at any given time perform them. Changes in channel institutions largely reflect the discovery of more efficient ways to combine or separate economic functions that must be carried out to provide satisfactory assortments of goods to target customers.

Number of Channel Levels Marketing channels can be characterized by the number of channel levels. Each middleman that performs some work in bringing the product and its ownership closer to the final buyer constitutes a *channel level*. Since the producer and the final consumer both perform some work, they are part of every channel. We will use the number of *intermediary levels* to designate the *length* of a channel. Figure 15-2 illustrates several marketing channels of different lengths.

- A *zero-level channel* (also called a *direct marketing channel*) consists of a manufacturer selling directly to consumers. The three major ways of direct selling are door to door, mail order, and manufacturer-owned stores. Avon's sales representatives sell cosmetics to homemakers on a door-to-door basis; Franklin Mint sells collectible objects through mail order; and Singer sells its sewing machines through its own stores.

- A *one-level channel* contains one selling intermediary. In consumer markets this intermediary is typically a retailer; in industrial markets it is often a sales agent or a broker.

- A *two-level channel* contains two intermediaries. In consumer markets they are typically a wholesaler and a retailer; in industrial markets they may be an industrial distributor and dealers.

- A *three-level channel* contains three intermediaries. For example, in the meatpacking industry a jobber usually intervenes between the wholesalers and the retailers. The jobber buys from wholesalers and sells to the smaller retailers, who generally are not serviced by the large wholesalers.

Higher-level marketing channels are also found, but with less frequency. From the producer's point of view, the problem of control increases with the number of channel levels, even though the manufacturer typically deals only with the adjacent level.

Types of Channel Flows The institutions that make up a marketing channel are connected by several types of flows. The most important are the physical flow, title flow, payment flow, infor-

FIGURE 15-2 *Examples of Different-Level Channels*

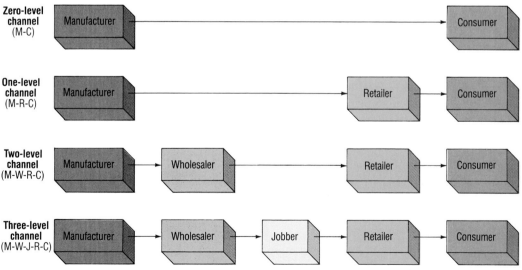

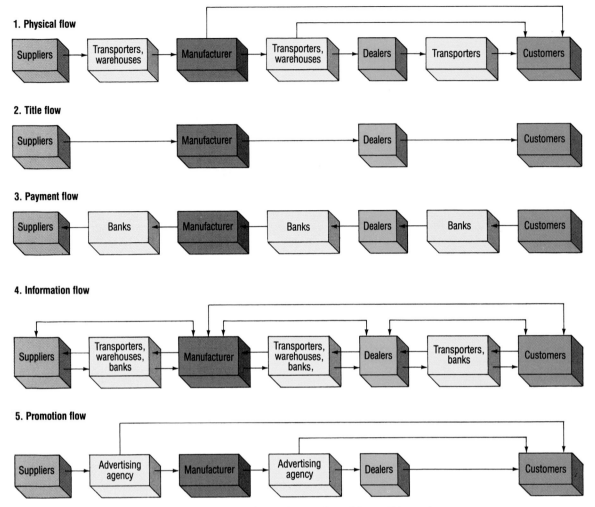

FIGURE 15-3   *Five Different Marketing Flows in the Marketing Channel for Forklift Trucks*

mation flow, and promotion flow. These are illustrated in Figure 15-3 for the marketing of forklift trucks.

The *physical flow* describes the movement of physical products from raw materials to final customers. In the case of a forklift truck manufacturer such as Clark Equipment, raw materials, subassemblies, parts, and engines flow from suppliers via transportation companies (transporters) to the manufacturer's warehouses and plants. The finished trucks are warehoused and later shipped to dealers in response to orders. The dealers sell and ship them to customers. Large orders may be shipped directly from the company warehouses or plant. One or more modes of shipment may be used, including railroads, trucks, and airfreight.

The *title flow* describes the passage of ownership from one marketing institution to another. In the case of forklift trucks, title to the raw materials and components passes from the suppliers to the manufacturer. Title to the finished trucks passes from the manufacturer to the dealers and then to the customers. If the dealers hold the trucks on *consignment,* they will not be included in the title flow.

The *payment flow* shows customers paying their bills through banks and other financial institutions to the dealers, the dealers paying the manufacturer, and the manufacturer paying various suppliers. Payments are also made to transporters and independent warehouses (not shown).

The *information flow* shows how channel organizations exchange information. Each adjacent pair exchanges information, and there are also information exchanges between nonadjacent pairs.

Finally, the *promotion flow* describes directed flows of influence (advertising, personal selling, sales promotion, and publicity) from one party to other parties in the system. Suppliers promote their names and products to the manufacturer, and also to final customers in the hope of influencing the manufacturer to adopt their products. Manufacturers direct a promotion flow to dealers (trade promotion) and final customers (end-user promotion).

If all these flows were superimposed on one diagram, they would emphasize the tremendous complexity of even simple marketing channels. This complexity goes even further, once we start distinguishing among different types of retailers, wholesalers, and others (see Chapter 16).

Channels in the Service Sector   The concept of marketing channels is not limited to the distribution of physical goods. Producers of services and ideas also face the problem of making their output *available* and *accessible* to target populations. They develop "educational dissemination systems" and "health delivery systems." They must figure out agencies and locations for reaching a geographically distributed population:

> Hospitals must be located in geographic space to serve the people with complete medical care, and we must build schools close to the children who have to learn. Fire stations must be located to give rapid access to potential conflagrations, and voting booths must be placed so that people can cast their ballots without expending unreasonable amounts of time, effort, or money to reach the polling stations. Many of our states face the problem of locating branch campuses to serve a burgeoning and increasingly well educated population. In the cities we must create and locate playgrounds for the children. Many overpopulated countries must assign birth control clinics to reach the people with contraceptive and family planning information.[5]

Marketing channels also are used in "person" marketing. Before 1940, professional comedians could reach audiences through vaudeville houses, special events, nightclubs, radio, movies, carnivals, and theaters. In the 1950s television emerged as a strong channel and vaudeville disappeared. Politicians also must find cost-effective channels—mass media, rallies, coffee hours—for distributing their messages to voters.

Channels normally describe a forward movement of products. We can also talk about *backward channels.* According to Zikmund and Stanton:

> The recycling of solid wastes is a major ecological goal. Although recycling is technologically feasible, reversing the flow of materials in the channel of distribution—marketing trash through a "backward" channel—presents a

challenge. Existing backward channels are primitive, and financial incentives are inadequate. The consumer must be motivated to undergo a role change and become a producer—the initiating force in the reverse distribution process.[6]

The authors identify several middlemen that can play a role in "backward channels," including manufacturers' redemption centers, "Clean-up Days" community groups, traditional middlemen such as soft-drink middlemen, trash-collection specialists, recycling centers, modernized "rag and junk men," trash-recycling brokers, and central-processing warehousing.

CHANNEL BEHAVIOR AND ORGANIZATION

Distribution channels are more than static collections of firms tied together by various flows. They are complex behavioral systems in which people and companies interact to accomplish individual, company, and channel goals. Some channel systems consist of only informal interactions among loosely organized firms; others consist of formal interactions guided by highly specified organizational structures. And channel systems do not stand still: New institutions emerge and whole new channel systems evolve. Here we will look at the dynamics of channel behavior and at the ways channel members organize to do the work of the channel.

Channel Behavior A distribution channel is a coalition of dissimilar firms that have banded together for mutual benefit. Each channel member is dependent on the other channel members. A Ford dealer depends on the Ford Motor Company to design cars that meet consumer needs; Ford depends on the dealer to attract consumers, persuade them to buy Ford automobiles, and service these automobiles after the sale. The Ford dealer also depends on other dealers to provide good sales and service that will uphold the reputation of Ford and its dealer body. In fact, the success of individual Ford dealers will depend on how well the entire Ford distribution channel competes with the channels of other auto manufacturers.

Each channel member plays a specific role in the channel and specializes in performing one or more functions. IBM's role is to produce personal computers that will be attractive to consumers and to create demand through national advertising; Computerland's role is to display these computers in convenient locations, answer the questions of potential buyers, close sales, and provide service. The channel will be most effective when each member is assigned the tasks it can do best.

Ideally, because the success of individual channel members depends on overall channel success, all firms in the channel should understand and accept their specific roles, coordinate their goals and activities with those of other channel members, and cooperate to accomplish overall channel goals. Each firm should consider how its actions affect total channel performance. Manufacturers, wholesalers, and retailers should complement one another's needs and cooperate to produce greater profits than each participant could obtain individually. By cooperating, they can more effectively sense, serve, and satisfy the target market.

From the Coca-Cola Company, to the Coke bottler, to the retailer, to the consumer—channel members must all work together to make Coke successful. *Courtesy of Coca-Cola Company.*

But individual channel members rarely take such a global view. They are usually more concerned with their own short-run goals and their dealings with firms next to them in the channel. Cooperating to achieve overall channel goals sometimes means giving up individual company goals. Though channel members are dependent on one another, they often act independently in their own short-run best interests. They often disagree on the roles each should play—on who should do what and for what compensation. Such disagreements over goals and roles generate *channel conflict.*

Horizontal conflict describes conflict occurring between firms at the same level of the channel. Some Ford dealers in Chicago complain about other dealers in the city stealing sales from them by being too aggressive in their pricing and advertising or by selling outside their assigned territories. Some Pizza Inn franchisees complain about other Pizza Inn franchisees cheating on ingredients, maintaining poor service, and hurting the overall Pizza Inn image.

Vertical conflict is even more common and refers to conflicts between different levels of the same channel. For example, General Motors came into conflict with its dealers some years ago when trying to enforce policies on service, pricing, and advertising. And Coca-Cola came into conflict with its bottlers who agreed to bottle Dr Pepper. A large chain saw company caused conflict when it decided to bypass its wholesale distributors and sell directly to large retailers such as J. C. Penney and K mart, which then competed directly with its smaller retailers.

Some conflict in the channel takes the form of healthy competition. This competition can be good for the channel—without it, the channel could become passive and noninnovative. But sometimes conflict can damage the channel. Stern provides the following example:[7]

> When retail druggists were pressing manufacturers to maintain retail prices on their brands through policing of Fair Trade laws, Lever Brothers found it difficult to control the pricing behavior of "pine board" (cut rate) drug stores relative to Pepsodent, the best-selling brand of toothpaste at the time. In retaliation, the druggists removed the brand from their shelves, thereby forcing consumers to request packages each time they wanted to replenish their household supplies. Surely this was a pathological move in a conflict situation, for in the process of "hurting" Lever Brothers, the druggists hurt themselves by foregoing sales volume and by inconveniencing their customers. The entire system suffered as a result of the boycott.

For the channel as a whole to perform effectively, each channel member's role must be specified, and channel conflict must be managed effectively. Cooperation, role specification, and conflict management in the channel are accomplished through strong channel leadership. The channel will perform better if it contains a firm, agency, or administrative mechanism that has the power to allocate resources efficiently within the channel system and to assign roles and manage conflict.

In a large, single company, the formal organization structure assigns roles and provides for the leadership necessary to ensure cooperation and manage conflict among organization members. But in a distribution channel made up of independent firms, leadership and power are not formally established. Traditionally, distribution channels have lacked effective leadership and effective administrative mechanisms for assigning roles and managing conflict. In recent years, however, new types of channel organizations have evolved that provide stronger leadership and improved performance. We will look now at these organizations.[8]

Channel Organization Historically, distribution channels have been haphazard collections of independently owned and managed companies, each showing little concern for overall channel performance. These *conventional marketing channels* have lacked strong leadership and have been characterized by damaging conflict and poor performance.

Growth of Vertical Marketing Systems

One of the most significant recent developments has been the *vertical marketing systems* that have emerged to challenge conventional marketing channels. Figure 15-4 contrasts the two types of channel arrangements.

A conventional marketing channel consists of an independent producer(s), wholesaler(s), and retailer(s). Each is a separate business entity seeking to maxi-

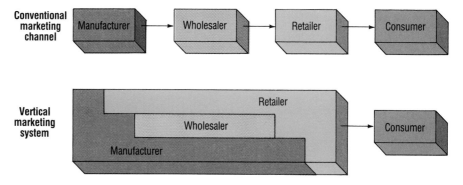

mize its own profits, even at the expense of maximizing the profits for the system as a whole. No channel member has complete or substantial control over the other members, and there are no formal mechanisms for assigning roles and resolving channel conflict. McCammon characterizes conventional channels as "highly fragmented networks in which loosely aligned manufacturers, wholesalers, and retailers have bargained with each other at arms' length, negotiated aggressively over terms of sale, and otherwise behaved autonomously."[9]

A vertical marketing system (VMS), by contrast, consists of the producer, wholesaler(s), and retailer(s) acting as a unified system. Either one channel member owns the others, or franchises them, or has so much power that they all cooperate. The vertical marketing system can be dominated by the producer, wholesaler, or retailer. McCammon characterizes VMSs as "professionally managed and centrally programmed networks, preengineered to achieve operating economies and maximum market impact."[10] The VMSs came into being to control channel behavior and manage the conflict that results from independent channel members pursuing their own objectives. They achieve economies through size, bargaining power, and elimination of duplicated services. VMSs have become the dominant mode of distribution in consumer marketing, serving as much as 64 percent of the total market.

We will now examine the three major types of VMSs shown in Figure 15-5. Each type employs a different mechanism for establishing or using leadership and power in the channel. In a corporate VMS, coordination and conflict management are achieved through common ownership at different levels of the channel. In a contractual VMS, roles and administrative mechanisms are established through contractual agreements among channel members. In an administered VMS, leadership is assumed by one or a few dominant channel members.

Corporate VMS. A **corporate VMS** combines successive stages of production and distribution under single ownership. As examples:

> . . . Sherwin-Williams currently owns and operates over 2,000 retail outlets . . . Sears reportedly obtains 50 percent of its throughput from manufacturing facilities in which it has an equity interest . . . Holiday Inn is evolving into a self-supply network that includes a carpet mill, a furniture manufacturing plant, and numerous captive redistribution facilities. In short, these and other organizations are massive, vertically integrated systems. To describe them as "retailers,"

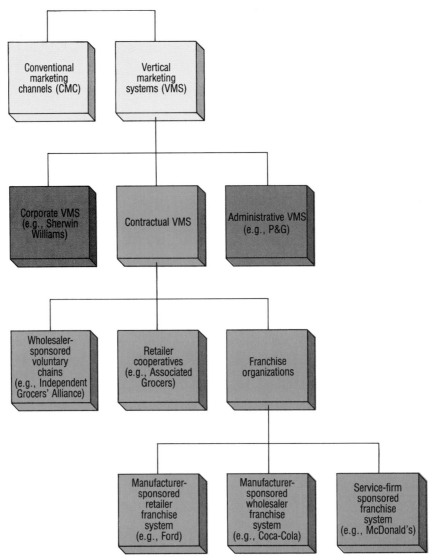

FIGURE 15-5 *Conventional Marketing Channels and Vertical Marketing Systems*

"manufacturers," or "motel operators" oversimplifies their operating complexities and ignores the realities of the marketplace.[11]

In such integrated corporate systems, cooperation and conflict management are handled through regular organizational channels.

CONTRACTUAL VMS. A **contractual VMS** consists of independent firms at different levels of production and distribution integrating their programs on a contractual basis to obtain more economies or sales impact than they could achieve alone. Contractual VMSs have expanded the most in recent years and constitute one of the most significant developments in the economy. Contractual VMSs are of three types.

■ *Wholesaler-sponsored voluntary chains.* Wholesalers organize voluntary chains of independent retailers to help them compete with large chain organizations. The wholesaler develops a program in which independent retailers standardize their selling practices and achieve buying economies that enable the group to compete effectively with chain organizations. Examples include the Independent Grocers Alliance and Sentry Hardwares.

■ *Retailer cooperatives.* Retailers may take the initiative and organize a new, jointly owned business entity to carry on wholesaling and possibly production. Members concentrate their purchases through the retailer co-op and plan their advertising jointly. Profits are passed back to members in proportion to their purchases. Nonmember retailers may also buy through the co-op but do not share in the profits. Examples include Certified Grocers and Ace Hardwares.

■ *Franchise organizations.* A channel member called a franchiser might link several successive stages in the production-distribution process. Franchising has been the fastest-growing and most interesting retailing development in recent years. Although the basic idea is an old one, some forms of franchising are quite new. Three forms of franchises can be distinguished.

The first is the *manufacturer-sponsored retailer franchise system,* exemplified by the automobile industry. Ford, for example, licenses dealers to sell its cars, the dealers being independent businesspeople who agree to meet various conditions of sales and service.

The second is the *manufacturer-sponsored wholesaler franchise system,* which is found in the soft-drink industry. Coca-Cola, for example, licenses bottlers (wholesalers) in various markets who buy its syrup concentrate and then carbonate, bottle, and sell it to retailers in local markets.

The third is the *service-firm-sponsored retailer franchise system.* Here a service firm organizes a whole system for bringing its service efficiently to consumers. Examples are found in the auto rental business (Hertz, Avis), fast-food service business (McDonald's, Burger King), and motel business (Howard Johnson, Ramada Inn).

The fact that most consumers cannot distinguish between contractual and corporate VMSs is evidence of how successful the contractual organizations have been in competing with corporate chains. The various contractual VMSs are discussed further in Chapter 16.

ADMINISTERED VMS. An **administered VMS** coordinates successive stages of production and distribution, not through common ownership or contractual ties, but through the size and power of one of the parties. Manufacturers of a dominant brand are able to secure strong trade cooperation and support from resellers. Thus General Electric, Procter & Gamble, Kraftco, and Campbell Soup are able to command unusual cooperation from resellers in connection with displays, shelf space, promotions, and price policies.

Many independent retailers, if they have not joined VMSs, have developed specialty stores that serve market segments not attractive to the mass merchandisers. The result is a polarization in retailing between large vertical marketing organizations on the one hand and specialty independent stores on the other. This development creates a problem for manufacturers. They are strongly tied to independent middlemen whom they cannot easily give up. But they must eventually realign themselves with the high-growth vertical marketing systems and have to accept less attractive terms. Vertical marketing systems constantly threaten to bypass large manufacturers and set up their own manufacturing. *The new competition in retailing is no longer between independent business units, but between whole systems of centrally programmed networks (corporate, administered, and contractual) competing to achieve the best cost economies and customer response.*

Growth of Horizontal Marketing Systems

Another channel organization development is the readiness of two or more companies at one level to join together to exploit an emerging marketing opportunity. Each company lacks the capital, knowhow, production, or marketing resources to venture alone; or it is afraid of the risk; or it sees a substantial synergy in joining with another company. The companies may work with each other on a temporary or permanent basis, or create a separate company. Adler calls this *symbiotic marketing.*[12] For example, Dr Pepper lacked bottlers for its soft drink and decided to license Coca-Cola bottlers to bottle Dr Pepper. And Freightliner entered a marketing agreement with the White Motor Company to use the latter's dealers to sell Freightliner trucks.

Growth of Multichannel Marketing Systems

Companies are increasingly adopting multichannel systems to reach the same or different markets. For example, the John Smythe Company, a Chicago-based furniture retailer, sells a full line of furniture through its company-owned conventional furniture stores as well as through its Homemakers Division, which operates furniture warehouse showrooms. Furniture shoppers can spot many similar items in both channels, usually finding lower prices at the latter. J. C. Penney operates department stores, mass-merchandising stores (called The Treasury), and specialty stores. Tillman has labeled multichannel retailing organizations *merchandising conglomerates* and defined them as "a multiline merchandising empire under central ownership, usually combining several styles of retailing with behind-the-scenes integration of some distribution and management functions."[13]

Many companies operate multichannels that serve two different customer levels. Called *dual distribution,* this can breed conflicts for the sponsoring company.[14] For example, General Electric sells large home appliances through independent dealers (department stores, discount houses, catalog retailers) and also directly to large housing tract builders. The independent dealers would like General Electric to get out of the business of selling to tract builders. General Electric defends its position by pointing out that builders and retailers need very different marketing approaches.

CHANNEL DESIGN DECISIONS

We will now examine several channel decision problems facing manufacturers. In designing marketing channels, manufacturers have to struggle between what is ideal and what is available. A new firm typically starts as a local or regional operation selling in a limited market. Since it has limited capital, it usually uses existing middlemen. The number of middlemen in any local market is apt to be limited: a few manufacturers sales agents, a few wholesalers, several established retailers, a few trucking companies, and a few warehouses. Deciding on the best channels might not be a problem. The problem might be to convince one or a few available middlemen to handle the line.

If the new firm is successful, it might branch out to new markets. Again, the manufacturer will tend to work through the existing intermediaries, although this might mean using different types of marketing channels in different areas. In the smaller markets the firm might sell directly to retailers; in the larger markets it might sell through distributors. In rural areas it might work with general-goods merchants; in urban areas, with limited-line merchants. In one part of the country it might grant exclusive franchises because the merchants normally work this way; in another, it might sell through all outlets willing to handle the merchandise. The manufacturer's channel system thus evolves in response to local opportunities and conditions.

Designing a channel system calls for establishing the channel objectives and constraints, identifying the major channel alternatives, and evaluating them.

Establishing the Channel Objectives and Constraints   Effective channel planning begins with a determination of which markets are to be reached with what objectives. The objectives include the desired level of customer service and the desired functions intermediaries should perform. Each producer develops its objectives in the context of constraints stemming from customers, products, intermediaries, competitors, company policies, and the environment.

- *Customer characteristics.* Channel design is greatly influenced by customer characteristics. When trying to reach a large or widely dispersed customer population, long channels are needed. If customers buy small amounts frequently, long channels are needed because of the high cost of filling small and frequent orders.

- *Product characteristics. Perishable* products require more direct marketing because of the dangers associated with delays and repeated handling. *Bulky* products, such as building materials or soft drinks, require channel arrangements that minimize the shipping distance and the number of handlings in the movement from producer to consumers. *Nonstandardized* products, such as custom-built machinery and specialized business forms, are sold directly by company sales representatives because middlemen lack the requisite knowledge. Products requiring installation or maintenance services are usually sold and maintained by the company or exclusively franchised dealers. *High unit value* products are often sold through a company salesforce rather than through middlemen.

- *Middlemen characteristics.* Channel design reflects the strengths and weaknesses of different types of intermediaries in handling various tasks. For example, manufacturers' representatives are able to contact customers at a low cost per customer because the total cost is shared by several clients. But the selling effort per customer is less intense than if the company's sales representatives did the selling. In general, marketing intermediaries differ in their aptitude for handling promotion, negotiation, storage, contact, and credit.

- *Competitive characteristics.* Channel design is influenced by competitors' channels. Producers may want to compete in or near the same outlets carrying the competitors' products. Thus food processors want their brands to be displayed next to competitive brands; and Burger King wants to locate next to McDonald's. In other industries, producers may want to avoid the channels used by competitors. Avon decided not to compete with other cosmetics manufacturers for scarce positions in retail stores and established instead a profitable door-to-door selling operation.

- *Company characteristics.* Company characteristics play an important role in channel selection. The company's *size* determines the size of its markets and its ability to secure desired dealers. Its *financial resources* determine which marketing functions it can handle and which to delegate to intermediaries. The company's *product mix* influences its channel pattern. The wider its product mix, the greater the company's ability to deal with customers directly. The greater the depth of the company's product mix, the more it might favor exclusive or selective dealers. The more consistent the company's product mix, the greater the homogeneity of its marketing channels. The company's *marketing strategy* will influence channel design. Thus a policy of speedy customer delivery affects the functions the producer wants intermediaries to perform, the number of final-stage outlets and stocking points, and the choice of transportation carriers.

■ *Environmental characteristics.* When *economic conditions* are depressed, producers want to move their goods to market in the most economical way. This means using shorter channels and dispensing with nonessential services that add to the final price of the goods. *Legal regulations and restrictions* also affect channel design. The law has sought to prevent channel arrangements that "may tend to substantially lessen competition or tend to create a monopoly."

Identifying the Major Alternatives

Suppose a manufacturing company has defined its target market and desired positioning. It should next identify its major channel alternatives. A channel alternative is described by three elements: (1) the types of business intermediaries, (2) the number of intermediaries, and (3) the terms and mutual responsibilities of each participant.

Types of Intermediaries

The firm should identify the types of intermediaries available to carry on its channel work. Consider the following example:

> A manufacturer of test equipment developed an audio device for detecting poor mechanical connections in any machine with moving parts. The company executives felt that this product would have a market in all industries where electric, combustion, or steam engines were used or manufactured. This meant such industries as aviation, automobile, railroad, food canning, construction, and oil. The company's salesforce was small, and the problem was how to reach these diverse industries effectively. The following channel alternatives came out of management discussion:
>
> *Company salesforce.* Expand the company's direct salesforce. Assign representatives to territories and give them responsibility for contacting all prospects in the area. Or develop separate company salesforces for the different industries.
>
> *Manufacturer's agency.* Hire manufacturer's agencies in different regions or end-use industries to sell the new test equipment.
>
> *Industrial distributors.*[15] Find distributors in the different regions or end-use industries who will buy and carry the new line. Give them exclusive distribution, adequate margins, product training, and promotional support.

Companies should also search for more innovative marketing channels. This happened when the Conn Organ Company decided to merchandise organs through department and discount stores, thus drawing more attention than organs had ever enjoyed in small music stores. A daring new channel was exploited when the Book-of-the-Month Club decided to merchandise books through the mails. Other sellers followed soon after with Record-of-the-Month clubs, Candy-of-the-Month clubs, and dozens of others.

Sometimes a company has to develop a channel other than the one it prefers because of the difficulty or cost of breaking into the preferred channel. The decision sometimes turns out extremely well. For example, the U.S. Time Company originally tried to sell its inexpensive Timex watches through regular jewelry stores. But most jewelry stores refused to carry them. The company looked for other channels and managed to get its watches into mass-merchandise outlets. This turned out to be a wise decision because of the rapid growth of mass merchandising.

Number of Intermediaries

Companies have to decide on the number of middlemen to use at each level. Three strategies are available.

INTENSIVE DISTRIBUTION.   Producers of convenience goods and common raw materials typically seek *intensive distribution*—that is, stocking their product in as many outlets as possible. These goods must have place utility. Cigarettes, for example, sell in over one million outlets to create maximum brand exposure and convenience.

EXCLUSIVE DISTRIBUTION.   Some producers deliberately limit the number of intermediaries handling their products. The extreme form of this is *exclusive distribution,* where a limited number of dealers are granted the exclusive right to distribute the company's products in their respective territories. It often goes with *exclusive dealing,* where the manufacturer requires these dealers not to carry competing lines. Exclusive distribution is found to some extent in the distribution of new automobiles, some major appliances, and some women's apparel brands. Through granting exclusive distribution, the manufacturer hopes for more aggressive and knowledgeable selling and more control over intermediaries' policies on prices, promotion, credit, and various services. Exclusive distribution tends to enhance the product's image and allow higher markups.

SELECTIVE DISTRIBUTION.   Between intensive and exclusive distribution stands *selective distribution*—the use of more than one but less than all the intermediaries who are willing to carry a particular product. It is used by established companies and by new companies seeking to obtain distributors by promising them selective distribution. The company does not have to dissipate its efforts over many outlets, including many marginal ones. It can develop a good working relationship with the selected middlemen and expect a better than average selling effort. Selective distribution enables the producer to gain adequate market coverage with more control and less cost than intensive distribution.

Terms and Responsibilities of Channel Members

The producer must determine the conditions and responsibilities of the participating channel members. The main elements in the "trade-relations mix" are the price policies, the conditions of sale, the territorial rights, and the specific services to be performed by each party.

- *Price policy* calls for the producer's establishing a list price and schedule of discounts. The producer must be sure discounts strike the middleman as being equitable and sufficient.

- *Conditions of sale* refer to the payment terms and to producer guarantees. Most producers grant cash discounts to their distributors for early payment. Producers may also extend guarantees to distributors regarding defective merchandise or price declines. A guarantee against price declines is used to induce distributors to buy larger quantities.

- *Distributors' territorial rights* are another element in the trade-relations mix. Distributors want to know where the producer will set up other distributors. They would also like to receive full credit for all sales taking place in their territory, whether or not these sales occurred through their personal efforts.

- *Mutual services and responsibilities* must be carefully spelled out, especially in franchised- and exclusive-agency channels. For example, the Howard Johnson Company provides restaurant leaseholders with a building, promotional support, a recordkeeping system, training, and general administrative and technical assistance. In turn, leaseholders are expected to satisfy company standards regarding physical facilities, cooperate with new promotional programs, furnish requested information, and buy specified food products.

Evaluating the Major Channel Alternatives

Suppose a producer has identified several channel alternatives and wants to select the one that will best satisfy the firm's long-run objectives. Each alternative needs to be evaluated against economic, control, and adaptive criteria. Consider the following situation:

A Memphis furniture manufacturer wants to sell its line through retailers on the West Coast. The manufacturer is trying to decide between two alternatives.

1. One alternative calls for hiring ten new sales representatives who would operate out of a sales office in San Francisco. They would receive a base salary plus commission based on their sales.

2. The other alternative would use a San Francisco *manufacturer's sales agency* that has extensive contacts with retailers. The agency has thirty sales representatives who would receive a commission based on their sales.

Economic Criteria

Each channel alternative will produce a different level of sales and costs. The first issue is whether more sales will be produced through a company salesforce or a sales agency. Most marketing managers believe that a company salesforce will sell more. Company sales representatives concentrate on the company's products; they are better trained to sell the company's products; they are more aggressive because their future depends on the company; they are more successful because customers prefer to deal directly with the company.

On the other hand, the sales agency could conceivably sell more than a company salesforce. First, the sales agency has thirty sales representatives, not just ten. Second, the agency salesforce may be just as aggressive as a direct salesforce. This depends on how much commission the line offers in relation to other lines carried. Third, some customers prefer dealing with agents who represent several manufacturers rather than with salespersons from one company. Fourth, the agency has extensive contacts, whereas a company salesforce would have to build them from scratch.

The next step is to estimate the costs of selling different volumes through each channel. The cost schedules are shown in Figure 15-6. The fixed costs of engaging a sales agency are lower than those of establishing a company sales office. But costs rise faster through a sales agency because sales agents get a larger commission than company salespeople.

There is one sales level (S_B) at which selling costs are the same for the two channels. The sales agency would be the preferred channel at any sales volume below S_B, and the company sales branch would be preferred at any volume higher than S_B. In general, sales agents tend to be used by smaller firms, or by larger firms in smaller territories where the sales volume is too low to warrant a company salesforce.

Control Criteria

The evaluation must be broadened to consider control issues with the two channels. Using a sales agency poses more of a control problem. A sales agency is an independent business firm interested in maximizing its profits. The agent may concentrate on the customers who are the most important in terms of the assortment they buy rather than their level of interest in the particular manufacturer's goods. Furthermore, the agency's salesforce may not master the technical details concerning the company's product or handle its promotion materials effectively.

Adaptive Criteria

Each channel involves some duration of commitment and loss of flexibility. A manufacturer using a sales agency may have to offer a five-year contract. During this

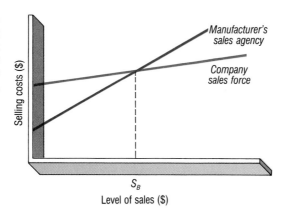

FIGURE 15-6
Breakeven Cost Chart for the Choice between a Company Salesforce and a Manufacturer's Sales Agency.

Selling costs ($)

Manufacturer's sales agency

Company sales force

S_B

Level of sales ($)

period, other means of selling, such as direct mail, may become more effective, but the manufacturer is not free to drop the sales agency. To be considered, a channel involving a long commitment should be greatly superior on economic or control grounds.

CHANNEL MANAGEMENT DECISIONS

As a result of reviewing its alternatives, the company will decide on the most effective channel design. Now it must implement and manage the chosen channel. Channel management calls for selecting and motivating individual middlemen and evaluating their performance through time.

Selecting Channel Members Producers vary in their ability to attract qualified middlemen for the proposed channel. Some producers have no trouble recruiting middlemen. For example, Ford was able to attract twelve hundred new dealers for its ill-fated Edsel. In some cases, the promise of exclusive or selective distribution will draw a sufficient number of applicants.

At the other extreme are producers who have to work hard to line up the desired number of qualified middlemen. When Polaroid started, it could not get photographic equipment stores to carry its new cameras and was forced to go to mass-merchandising outlets. Small food producers normally find it hard to get grocery stores to carry their products.

Whether producers find it easy or difficult to recruit middlemen, they should at least determine what characteristics distinguish the better middlemen. They will want to evaluate the middlemen's number of years in business, the other lines carried, growth and profit record, solvency, cooperativeness, and reputation. If the middlemen are sales agents, producers will want to evaluate the number and character of other lines carried and the size and quality of the salesforce. If the middleman is a department store that wants exclusive distribution, the producer will want to evaluate the store's location, future growth potential, and type of clientele.

Motivating Channel Members Middlemen must be continuously motivated to do their best. The terms that lead them to join the channel provide some of the motivation, but these must be supplemented by continuous supervision and encouragement from the producer. The producer must sell not only through the middlemen, but to them.

Stimulating channel members to top performance must start with the manufacturer's attempting to understand the needs and wants of the particular middlemen. According to McVey, manufacturers often criticize middlemen "for failure to stress a given brand, or for the poor quality of his salesman's product knowledge, his disuse of supplier's advertising materials, his neglect of certain customers (who may be good prospects for individual items but not for the assortment), and even for his unrefined systems of record keeping, in which brand designations may be lost."[16] However, these shortcomings from the manufacturer's point of view may be understandable from the middleman's point of view. McVey listed the following propositions to help understand middlemen:

Frigidaire informs and motivates its retailers at a dealer sales meeting. *Courtesy of Frigidaire.*

The middleman is not a hired link in a chain forged by a manufacturer, but rather an independent market. . . . After some experimentation, he settles upon a method of operation, performing those functions he deems inescapable in the light of his own objectives, forming policies for himself wherever he has freedom to do so. . . .

[The middleman often acts] as a purchasing agent for his customers and only secondarily as a selling agent for his suppliers. . . . He is interested in selling any product which these customers desire to buy from him. . . .

The middleman attempts to weld all of his offerings into a family of items which he can sell in combination, as a packaged assortment, to individual customers. His selling efforts are directed primarily at obtaining orders for the assortment, rather than for individual items. . . .

Unless given incentive to do so, middlemen will not maintain separate sales records by brands sold. . . . Information that could be used in product development, pricing, packaging, or promotion-planning is buried in nonstandard records of middlemen, and sometimes purposely secreted from suppliers.[17]

Producers vary greatly in how they handle their distributor relations. We can distinguish three approaches: *cooperation, partnership,* and *distribution programming.*[18]

Most producers see the problem as finding ways to gain *cooperation.* They will use the carrot-and-stick approach. They will use such positive motivators as higher margins, special deals, premiums, cooperative advertising allowances, display allowances, and sales contests. At times they will apply negative sanctions such as threatening to reduce the margins, slow down delivery, or terminate the relationship. The weakness of this approach is that the producer has not really studied the needs, problems, strengths, and weaknesses of the distributors. Instead, the producer applies miscellaneous motivators based on crude stimulus-response thinking. McCammon notes that many manufacturer programs "consist of hastily improvised trade deals, uninspired dealer contests, and unexamined discount structures."[19]

More sophisticated companies try to forge a long-term *partnership* with their distributors. The manufacturer develops a clear sense of what it wants from its distributors and what its distributors can expect in terms of market coverage, product availability, market development, account solicitation, technical advice and services, and market information. The manufacturer seeks an agreement from its distributors on these policies and may base compensation on their adhering to these policies.

Distribution programming is the most advanced arrangement. McCammon defines this as building a planned, professionally managed, vertical marketing system that incorporates the needs of both the manufacturer and the distributors.[20] The manufacturer establishes a department within the marketing department called *distributor relations planning,* and its job is to identify the distributors' needs and build up merchandising programs to help each distributor operate as optimally as possible. This department and the distributors jointly plan the merchandising goals, inventory levels, space and visual merchandising plans, sales-training requirements, and advertising and promotion plans. The aim is to convert the distributors from thinking that they make their money primarily on the buying side (through an adversary relation with the supplier) to seeing that they make their money on the selling side by being part of a sophisticated vertical marketing system.

Evaluating Channel Members The producer must periodically evaluate middlemen's performance against such standards as sales quota attainment, average inventory levels, customer delivery time, treatment of damaged and lost goods, cooperation in company promotional and training programs, and middleman services owed to the customer.

The producer typically sets sales quotas for the middlemen. After each period, the producer might circulate a list showing the sales performance of each middleman. This list should motivate middlemen at the bottom to do better and middlemen at the top to maintain their performance. Each middleman's sales performance can be compared with his performance in the preceding period. The average percentage improvement for the group can be used as a norm.

Manufacturers need to be sensitive to their dealers. Manufacturers who treat their dealers lightly risk not only losing their support, but also causing some legal actions. Exhibit 15-1 describes various rights and duties pertaining to manufacturers and their channel members.

PHYSICAL DISTRIBUTION DECISIONS

We are now ready to examine the physical side of distribution, that is, how companies store, handle, and move goods so that they will be available to customers at the right time and place. Customer attraction and satisfaction are highly influenced by the seller's physical distribution capabilities. Here we will consider the nature, objectives, systems, and organizational aspects of physical distribution.

EXHIBIT 15-1

DISTRIBUTION DECISIONS AND PUBLIC POLICY

For the most part, manufacturers are free under the law to develop whatever channel arrangements suit them. In fact, the law affecting channels seeks to make sure that manufacturers are not prevented from using channels as the result of the exclusionary tactics of others. But this places them under obligation to proceed cautiously in their own possible use of exclusionary tactics. Most of the law is concerned with mutual rights and duties of the manufacturer and channel members once they have formed a relationship.

Exclusive dealing. Many manufacturers and wholesalers like to develop exclusive channels for their products. The policy is called *exclusive distribution* when the seller enfranchises only certain outlets to carry its products. It is called *exclusive dealing* when the seller requires these outlets not to handle competitors' products. Both parties draw benefits from exclusive dealing, the seller achieving more dependable outlets without having to invest capital in them, and the distributors gaining a steady source of supply and seller support. However, the result is that other manufacturers are excluded from selling to these dealers. This has brought exclusive dealing contracts under the purview of the Clayton Act. They are legal as long as they do not substantially lessen competition, or tend to create a monopoly, and both partners enter into the agreement voluntarily.

Exclusive territorial distributorships. Exclusive dealing often includes exclusive territorial agreements. The seller may agree not to sell to other distributors in the area, or the buyer may agree to confine sales to its own territory. The first practice is fairly normal under franchise systems as a way to increase dealer enthusiasm and investment in the area. A seller is under no legal compulsion to sell through more outlets than it wishes. The second practice, where the manufacturer tries to restrain each dealer to sell only in its own territory, has become a major legal issue.

Tying agreements. Manufacturers of a strongly demanded brand occasionally sell it to dealers on condition that the dealers take some or all of the rest of the line. This practice is called *full-line forcing.* Such tying arrangements are not illegal per se, but they do run afoul of the Clayton Act if they tend to lessen competition substantially. Buyers are being prevented from freely choosing among competing suppliers of these other brands.

Dealers' rights. Sellers are free to select their dealers, but their right to terminate dealerships is somewhat qualified. In general, sellers can drop dealers "for cause." But they cannot drop dealers, for example, if the dealers refuse to cooperate in a dubious legal arrangement, such as exclusive dealing or tying agreements.

Nature of Physical Distribution

Physical distribution comprises the tasks involved in planning, implementing, and controlling the physical flows of materials and final goods from points of origin to points of use to meet the needs of customers at a profit. The main elements of the physical distribution mix are shown in Figure 15-7. The major physical distribution cost is transportation, followed by warehousing, inventory carrying, receiving and shipping, packaging, administration, and order processing.

Management has become concerned about the total cost of physical distribution, which amounts to 13.6 percent of sales for manufacturing companies and 25.6 percent for reseller companies.[21] Experts believe that substantial savings can be gained in the physical distribution area, which has been described as "the last frontier for cost economies"[22] and "the economy's dark continent."[23] Physical distribution decisions, when uncoordinated, result in high costs. Not enough use is

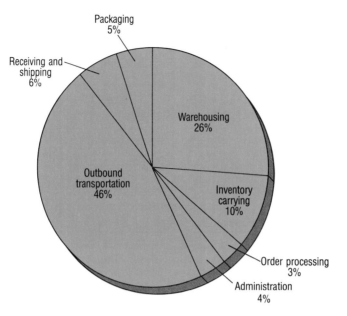

FIGURE 15-7
Cost of Physical Distribution Elements as a Percent of Total Physical Distribution Cost

Packaging
5%

Receiving and shipping
6%

Warehousing
26%

Outbound transportation
46%

Inventory carrying
10%

Order processing
3%

Administration
4%

Source: Based on B. J. LaLonde and P. H. Zinszer, *Customer Service: Meaning and Measurement* (Chicago: National Council of Physical Distribution Management, 1976).

being made of modern decision tools for coordinating inventory levels, transportation modes, and plant, warehouse, and store locations.

Physical distribution is not only a cost, it is a potent tool in demand creation. Companies can attract additional customers by offering better service or lower prices through physical distribution improvements. Companies lose customers when they fail to supply goods on time. In the summer of 1976 Kodak launched its national advertising campaign for its new instant camera before it had delivered enough cameras to the stores. Customers found that it was not available and bought a Polaroid instead.

Traditional thinking starts with goods at the plant and tries to find low-cost solutions to get them to customers. Marketers prefer *market logistics* thinking that starts with the marketplace and works backward to the factory. Here is an example of market logistics thinking:

> German consumers typically purchase separate bottles of soft drinks. A soft-drink manufacturer decided to design and test a six-pack. Consumers responded positively to the convenience aspect of carrying a six-pack home. Retailers responded positively because the bottles could be loaded faster on the shelves and more bottles would be purchased per occasion. The manufacturer designed the six-packs to fit comfortably on the store shelves. Then cases and pallets were designed for bringing these six-packs efficiently to the store's receiving rooms. Factory operations were redesigned to produce the new six-packs. The purchasing department let out bids for the new needed materials. Once implemented, this new packaging of soft drinks was an instant hit with consumers, and the manufacturer's market share rose substantially.

The Physical Distribution Objective

Many companies state their objective as *getting the right goods to the right places at the right time for the least cost*. Unfortunately, this provides little actual guidance. No physical distribution system can simultaneously maximize customer service and minimize distribution cost. Maximum customer service implies large inventories, premium transportation, and multiple warehouses, all of which raise distribution cost. Minimum distribution cost implies cheap transportation, low stocks, and few warehouses.

A company cannot achieve physical distribution efficiency by letting each physical distribution manager keep down his or her own costs. Physical distribution costs interact, often in an inverse way:

- The traffic manager favors rail shipment over air shipment whenever possible. This reduces the company's freight bill. However, because the railroads are slower, this ties up working capital longer, delays customer payment, and may cause customers to buy from competitors offering faster service.
- The shipping department uses cheap containers to minimize shipping costs. This leads to a high rate of damaged goods in transit and customer ill will.
- The inventory manager favors low inventories to reduce inventory cost. However, this increases stockouts, back orders, paperwork, special production runs, and high-cost fast-freight shipments.

Given that physical distribution activities involve strong tradeoffs, decisions must be made on a total system basis.

The starting point for designing the system is to study what customers want and what competitors are offering. Customers are interested in several things: on-time delivery, supplier willingness to meet emergency needs, careful handling of merchandise, supplier willingness to take back defective goods and resupply them quickly, and supplier willingness to carry inventory for the customer.

The company has to research the relative importance of these services to customers. For example, service repair time is very important to buyers of copying equipment. Xerox therefore developed a service delivery standard that can "put a disabled machine anywhere in the continental United States back into operation within three hours after receiving the service request." Xerox runs a service division consisting of 12,000 service and parts personnel.

The company must look at competitors' service standards in setting its own. It will normally want to offer at least the same level of service as competitors. But the objective is to maximize profits, not sales. The company has to look at the costs of providing higher levels of service. Some companies offer less service and charge a lower price. Other companies offer more service than competitors and charge a premium price to cover their higher costs.

The company ultimately has to establish physical distribution objectives to guide its planning. For example, Coca-Cola wants "to put Coke within an arm's length of desire." Companies go further and define standards for each service factor. One appliance manufacturer has established the following service standards: to deliver at least 95 percent of the dealer's orders within seven days of order receipt, to fill the dealer's order with 99 percent accuracy, to answer dealer inquiries on order status within three hours, and to ensure that damage to merchandise in transit does not exceed 1 percent.

Given a set of objectives, the company is ready to design a physical distribution system that will minimize the cost of achieving these objectives. The major decision issues are: (1) How should orders be handled? (*order processing*) (2) Where should stocks be located? (*warehousing*) (3) How much stock should be kept on hand? (*inventory*) and (4) How should goods be shipped? (*transportation*). We will now examine these four elements and their implications for marketing.

Order Processing

Physical distribution begins with a customer order. The order department prepares multicopy invoices and dispatches them to various departments. Items out of stock are back-ordered. Shipped items are accompanied by shipping and billing documents with copies going to various departments.

The company and customers benefit when these steps are carried out quickly and accurately. Ideally, sales representatives send in their orders every evening, in some cases phoning them in. The order department processes these quickly. The warehouse sends the goods out as soon as possible. Bills go out as soon as possible. The computer is used to expedite the order-shipping-billing cycle.

Industrial engineering studies of how sales orders are processed can help shorten this cycle. Some of the key questions are: What happens after receiving a customer purchase order? How long does the customer credit check take? What procedures are used to check inventory and how long does it take? How soon does manufacturing hear of new stock requirements? How long does this take for sales managers to get a complete picture of current sales?

Ringer and Howell reported a study in which a company cut down the time between the receipt and the issuance of an order from sixty-two hours to thirty hours without any change in costs.[24] General Electric operates a computer-oriented system which, upon receipt of a customer's order, checks the customer's credit standing and whether and where the items are in stock. The computer issues an order to ship, bills the customer, updates the inventory records, sends a production order for new stock, and relays the message back to the sales representative that the customer's order is on its way, all in less than fifteen seconds.

Warehousing

Every company has to store its goods while they wait to be sold. A storage function is necessary because production and consumption cycles rarely match. Many agricultural commodities are produced seasonally, but demand is continuous. The storage function overcomes discrepancies in desired quantities and timing.

The company must decide on a desirable number of stocking locations. More stocking locations mean that goods can be delivered to customers more quickly. However, warehousing costs go up. The number of stocking locations must strike a balance between the level of customer service and distribution costs.

Some company stock is kept at or near the plant, and the rest is located in warehouses around the country. The company might own *private warehouses* and rent space in *public warehouses*. Companies have more control in owned warehouses, but they tie up their capital and face some inflexibility if desired locations change. Public warehouses, on the other hand, charge for the rented space and provide additional services (at a cost) for inspecting goods, packaging them, shipping them, and invoicing them. In using public warehouses, companies have a wide choice of locations and warehouse types, including those specializing in cold storage, commodities only, and other requirements.

Companies use storage warehouses and distribution warehouses. *Storage warehouses* store goods for moderate to long periods of time. *Distribution warehouses* receive goods from various plants and suppliers and move them out as soon as possible. For example, Wal-Mart Stores, Inc., a regional discount chain, operates four distribution centers. One center covers 400,000 square feet on a 93-acre site. The shipping department loads fifty to sixty trucks daily, delivering merchandise on a twice-weekly basis to its retail outlets. This is less expensive than supplying each retail outlet directly from each plant.

The older multistoried warehouses with slow elevators and inefficient materials-handling procedures are receiving competition from newer single-storied *automated warehouses* with advanced materials-handling systems under the control of a central computer. In these automated warehouses costing $10 to $20 million each, only a few employees are necessary. The computer reads store orders and directs lift trucks and electric hoists to gather goods, move them to loading docks, and issue invoices. These warehouses have reduced worker injuries, labor costs, pilferage, and breakage and have improved inventory control.

Inventory

Inventory levels represent another physical distribution decision affecting customer satisfaction. Marketers would like their companies to carry enough stock to fill all customer orders immediately. However, it is not cost-effective for a company to carry this much inventory. *Inventory cost increases at an increasing rate as the customer service level approaches 100 percent.* Management would need to know whether sales and profits would increase enough to justify higher inventories.

Inventory decision making involves knowing when to order, and how much to order. As inventory draws down, management must know at what stock level to

This Xerox automated warehouse is a high-rise storage facility which uses robots for automatic storage and retrieval. *Courtesy of Xerox Corporation.*

place a new order. This stock level is called the *order* (or *reorder*) *point*. An order point of 20 means ordering when the stock of the item falls to 20 units. The order point should be higher the higher the order lead time, the usage rate, and service standard. If order lead time and customer usage rate are variable, the order point should be set higher to provide a *safety stock*. The final order point should balance the risks of stockout against the costs of overstock.

The other inventory decision is how much to order. The larger the quantity ordered, the less frequently an order has to be placed. The company needs to balance order-processing costs and inventory carrying costs. Order-processing costs for a manufacturer consist of *setup costs* and *running costs* for the item. If setup costs are low, the manufacturer can produce the item often and the cost per item is pretty constant and equal to the running costs. However, if setup costs are high, the manufacturer can reduce the average cost per unit by producing a long run and carrying more inventory.

Order-processing costs must be compared with inventory carrying costs. The larger the average stock carried, the higher the inventory carrying costs. These carrying costs include storage charges, cost of capital, taxes and insurance, and depreciation and obsolescence. Inventory carrying costs may run as high as 30 percent of inventory value. This means that marketing managers who want their companies to carry larger inventories need to show that the larger inventories will produce incremental gross profit that will exceed incremental inventory carrying costs.

The optimal order quantity can be determined by observing how order-processing costs and inventory carrying costs sum up at different possible order levels. Figure 15-8 shows that the order-processing cost per unit decreases with the number of units ordered, because the order costs are spread over more units. Inventory carrying charges per unit increase with the number of units ordered, because each total cost curve. The lowest point on the total cost curve is projected down on the unit remains longer in inventory. The two costs curves are summed vertically into a horizontal axis to find the optimal order quantity Q^*.

FIGURE 15-8
Determining Optimal
Order Quantity

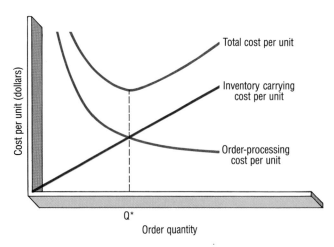

Total cost per unit

Inventory carrying
cost per unit

Order-processing
cost per unit

Cost per unit (dollars)

Q^*

Order quantity

Transportation Marketers need to take an interest in their company's transportation decisions. The choice of transportation carriers will affect the pricing of the products, on-time delivery performance, and the condition of the goods when they arrive, all of which will affect customer satisfaction.

In shipping goods to its warehouses, dealers, and customers, the company can choose among five transportation modes: rail, water, truck, pipeline, and air. Each transportation mode's characteristics are summarized in Table 15-1 and discussed in the following paragraphs.

RAIL. In spite of a shrinking share of total transportation, railroads remain the nation's largest transportation carrier, accounting for 30 percent of the nation's total cargo ton-miles. Railroads are one of the most cost-effective modes for shipping carload quantities of bulk products—coal, sand, minerals, farm and forest products—over long land distances. The rate costs for shipping merchandise are quite complex. The lowest rate comes from shipping carload rather than less-than-carload quantities. Manufacturers will attempt to combine shipments to common destinations to take advantage of lower carload rates. Railroads have recently begun to increase customer-oriented services. They have designed new equipment to handle special categories of merchandise more efficiently, provided flatcars for carrying truck trailers by rail (piggyback), and provided in-transit services such as diversion of shipped goods to other destinations en route and processing of goods en route.

WATER. A substantial amount of goods moves by ships and barges on coastal and inland waterways. The cost of water transportation is very low for shipping bulky, low-value, nonperishable products such as sand, coal, grain, oil, and metallic ores. On the other hand, water transportation is the slowest transportation mode and is dependent on climatic conditions.

TRUCK. Motor trucks have steadily increased their share of transportation and now account for 21 percent of total cargo ton-miles. They account for the largest portion of intracity as opposed to intercity transportation. Trucks are highly flexible in their

TABLE 15-1
Characteristics of Major Transportation Modes

TRANSPORTATION MODE	1980 CARGO TON-MILES (billions)	PERCENTAGE OF TOTAL	TYPICAL SHIPPED PRODUCTS
Rail	858.1	30.0%	Farm products, minerals, sand, chemicals, autos
Water	827.2	28.7	Oil, grain, sand, gravel, metallic ores, coal
Truck	602.0	21.0	Clothing, books, computers, paper goods
Pipeline	585.2	20.2	Petroleum, coal, chemicals
Air	4.6	00.1	Technical instruments, perishable food

Source: U.S. Department of Transportation, *National Transportation Statistics*, DOT-TSC-RSPA-81-8, September 1981.

routing and time schedules. They can move merchandise door to door, saving shippers the need to transfer goods from truck to rail and back again at a loss of time and risk of theft or damage. Trucks are an efficient mode of transportation for short hauls of high-value merchandise. Their rates are competitive with railway rates in many cases, and trucks can usually offer faster services.

PIPELINE. Pipelines are a specialized means of shipping petroleum, coal, and chemicals from sources to markets. Pipeline shipment of petroleum products is less expensive than rail shipment, although more expensive than water shipment. Most pipelines are used by their owners to ship their own products, although they are technically available for use by any shipper.

AIR. Air carriers transport less than 1 percent of the nation's goods but are becoming more important as a transportation mode. Although air freight rates are considerably higher than rail or truck freight rates, air freight is ideal where speed is essential or distant markets have to be reached. Among the most frequently air-freighted products are perishables (fresh fish, cut flowers) and high-value, low-bulk items (technical instruments, jewelry). Companies find that air freight reduces their required inventory levels, number of warehouses, and costs of packaging.

Choosing Transportation Modes In choosing a transportation mode for a particular product, shippers consider as many as six criteria. Table 15-2 ranks the various transportation modes according to these criteria. Thus if a shipper seeks speed, air and truck are the prime contenders. If the goal is low cost, then water and pipeline are the prime contenders. Trucks appear to offer the most advantages, thus explaining their growing share.

Shippers are increasingly combining two or more transportation modes, thanks to containerization. **Containerization** consists of putting the goods in boxes or trailers that are easy to transfer between two transportation modes. *Piggyback* describes the use of rail and trucks; *fishyback,* water and trucks; *trainship,* water and rail; and *airtruck,* air and trucks. Each coordinated mode of transportation offers specific advantages to the shipper. For example, piggyback is cheaper than trucking alone and yet provides flexibility and convenience.

TABLE 15-2 *Transportation Modes Ranked according to Major Shipper Criteria (1 = Highest Rank)*

	SPEED (door-to-door delivery time)	FREQUENCY (scheduled shipments per day)	DEPENDABILITY (meeting schedules on time)	CAPABILITY (ability to handle various products)	AVAILABILITY (no. of geographic points served)	COST (per ton-mile)
Rail	3	4	3	2	2	3
Water	4	5	4	1	4	1
Truck	2	2	2	3	1	4
Pipeline	5	1	1	5	5	2
Air	1	3	5	4	3	5

Source: Adapted from James L. Heskett, Robert J. Ivie, and Nicholas A. Glaskowsky, *Business Logistics* (New York: Ronald Press, 1964), pp. 71ff. Reprinted by permission of John Wiley & Sons, Inc.

In choosing transportation modes, shippers can decide between private, contract, and common carriers. If the shipper owns its own truck or air fleet, the shipper becomes a *private carrier*. A *contract carrier* is an independent organization selling transportation services to others on a contract basis. *A common carrier* provides services between predetermined points on a schedule basis and is available to all shippers at standard rates.

Transportation decisions must consider the complex tradeoffs between various transportation modes and their implications for other distribution elements such as warehousing and inventory. As the relative costs of different transportation modes change over time, companies need to reanalyze their options in the search for optimal physical distribution arrangements.

Organizational Responsibility for Physical Distribution

We see that decisions on warehousing, inventory, and transportation require the highest degree of coordination. A growing number of companies have set up a permanent committee composed of managers responsible for different physical distribution activities. This committee meets periodically to develop policies for improving overall distribution efficiency. Some companies have appointed a vice-president of physical distribution, who reports to the marketing vice-president or manufacturing vice-president in most cases, or to the president. The location of the physical distribution department within the company is a secondary concern. The important thing is that the company coordinate its physical distribution and marketing activities in order to create high market satisfaction at a reasonable cost.

■ *Summary*

Marketing channel decisions are among the most complex and challenging decisions facing the firm. Each channel system creates a different level of sales and costs. Once a particular marketing channel has been chosen, the firm must usually adhere to it for a substantial period. The chosen channel will significantly affect and be affected by the other elements in the marketing mix.

Each firm needs to identify alternative ways to reach the market. They vary from direct selling to using one, two, three, or more intermediary channel levels. The organizations making up the marketing channel are connected by physical, title, payment, information, and promotion flows. Marketing channels are characterized by continuous and sometimes dramatic change. Three of the most significant trends are the growth of vertical, horizontal, and multichannel marketing systems. These trends have important implications for channel cooperation, conflict, and competition.

Channel design calls for identifying the major channel alternatives in terms of the types of intermediaries, the number of intermediaries, and the channel terms and responsibilities. Each channel alternative has to be evaluated according to economic, control, and adaptive criteria.

Channel management calls for selecting particular middlemen and motivating them with a cost-effective trade-relations mix. Individual channel members must be periodically evaluated against their own past sales and other channel members' sales.

Just as the marketing concept is receiving increasing recognition, more business firms are heeding the physical distribution concept. Physical distribution is an area of potentially high cost savings and improved customer satisfaction. When order processors, warehouse planners, inventory managers, and transportation managers make decisions, they affect each other's costs and demand-creation capacity. The physical distribution concept calls for treating all these decisions within a unified framework. The task becomes that of designing physical distribution arrangements which minimize the total cost of providing a desired level of customer services.

■ Questions for Discussion

1. "In a battle between giants like Procter & Gamble and Safeway [supermarket chain] five years ago, P&G would have prevailed. Now Safeway can call the tune." What has caused the change in power?

2. Why are marketing intermediaries used? Explain by using a concrete example.

3. How many channel levels are commonly used by the following companies? (a) Sears, (b) Fuller Brush, and (c) A&P.

4. Channels of distribution do not differ for services and physical products. Comment.

5. Distinguish among the three major types of vertical marketing systems. Give an example of each.

6. There is no way to alleviate channel conflict. Comment.

7. Which of the following products would intensively, exclusively, and selectively be distributed, and why? (a) Rolex watches, (b) Volkswagen automobiles, (c) Gillette blades, and (d) Estée Lauder perfume.

8. How do *physical distribution decisions* differ from *channel decisions?* What is the overriding objective of physical distribution?

9. In what ways has the computer facilitated physical distribution?

10. Which mode of transportation would probably be used to distribute the following products? (a) beer, (b) expensive jewelry, (c) natural gas, and (d) farm machinery.

■ References

1. Adapted from AL URBANSKI, "Dr Pepper Heals Itself," *Sales & Marketing Management,* March 14, 1983, pp. 33–36.
2. WROE ALDERSON, "The Analytical Framework for Marketing," *Proceedings—Conference of Marketing Teachers from Far Western States* (Berkeley: University of California Press, 1958).
3. WROE ALDERSON, *Marketing Behavior and Executive Action: A Functionalist Approach to Marketing Theory* (Homewood, IL: Irwin, 1957), p. 199.
4. For other lists, see EDMUND D. MCGARRY, "Some Functions of Marketing Reconsidered," in *Theory in Marketing,* Reavis Cox and Wroe Alderson, eds. (Homewood, IL: Irwin, 1950), pp. 269–73; and LOUIS P. BUCKLIN, *A Theory of Distribution Channel Structure* (Berkeley: Institute of Business and Economic Research, University of California, 1966), pp. 10–11.
5. RONALD ABLER, JOHN S. ADAMS, and PETER GOULD, *Spatial Organizations: The Geographer's View of the World* (Englewood Cliffs, NJ: Prentice-Hall, 1971), pp. 531–32.
6. WILLIAM G. ZIKMUND and WILLIAM J. STANTON, "Recycling Solid Wastes: A Channels-of-Distribution Problem," *Journal of Marketing,* July 1971, p. 34.
7. LOUIS W. STERN and ADEL I. EL-ANSARY, *Marketing Channels* (2d ed.) (Englewood Cliffs, NJ: Prentice-Hall, 1982), pp. 291–92.
8. For an excellent summary of channel conflict and power, see STERN and EL-ANSARY, *Marketing Channels,* chaps. 6 and 7.
9. BERT C. MCCAMMON, JR., "Perspectives for Distribution Programming," in *Vertical Marketing Systems,* Louis P. Bucklin, ed. (Glenview, IL: Scott Foresman, 1970), pp. 32–51.
10. Ibid.
11. Ibid., p. 45.
12. LEE ADLER, "Symbiotic Marketing," *Harvard Business Review,* November–December 1966, pp. 59–71.
13. ROLLIE TILLMAN, "Rise of the Conglomerchant," *Harvard Business Review,* November–December 1971, pp. 44–51.
14. See ROBERT E. WEIGAND, "Fit Products and Channels to Your Markets," *Harvard Business Review,* January–February 1977, pp. 95–105.
15. For reading on industrial distributors, see FREDERICK E. WEBSTER, JR., "The Role of the Industrial Distributor," *Journal of Marketing,* July 1976, pp. 10–16; and JAMES D. HLAVACEK and TOMMY J. MCCUISTON, "Industrial Distributors—When, Who, and How?" *Harvard Business Review,* March–April 1983, pp. 96–101.
16. PHILLIP MCVEY, "Are Channels of Distribution What the Textbooks Say?" *Journal of Marketing,* January 1960, pp. 61–64.

17. Ibid.
18. See BERT ROSENBLOOM, *Marketing Channels: A Management View* (Hinsdale, IL: Dryden Press, 1978), pp. 192–203.
19. MCCAMMON, "Perspectives for Distribution Programming," p. 32.
20. Ibid., p. 43.
21. B. J. LALONDE and P. H. ZINSZER, *Customer Service: Meaning and Measurement* (Chicago: National Council of Physical Distribution Management, 1976).
22. DONALD D. PARKER, "Improved Efficiency and Reduced Cost in Marketing," *Journal of Marketing,* April 1962, pp. 15–21.
23. PETER DRUCKER, "The Economy's Dark Continent," *Fortune,* April 1962, pp. 103ff.
24. JURGEN F. RINGER and CHARLES D. HOWELL, "The Industrial Engineer and Marketing," in *Industrial Engineering Handbook* (2d ed.), Harold Bright Maynard, ed. (New York: McGraw-Hill, 1963) pp. 10, 102–3.

16
Placing Products: Retailing and Wholesaling

Store managers across the country increasingly are studying the phenomenal success of Federated Department Stores and especially its crown jewel, Bloomingdale's. Not every store, of course, can emulate Bloomingdale's specific techniques: Ice-cream made from Himalayan mangoes might not sell as well in the suburbs of Spokane as it does on Manhattan's East Side. But any store can follow Bloomingdale's essential formula: first, know your customers, their ages, incomes, customs, habits, tastes. Then set out to woo them with distinctive merchandise, exciting displays, and a general adventure—in fact, fun.

Headquarters has allowed Bloomingdale's full rein to exploit what it has long seen as its major market: young, affluent, fashion-conscious, traveled, professional people. They are attuned less to refrigerators and washing machines ("Bloomies" sells neither), more to clothes of fashion and quality, stereo equipment and wacky gadgetry for the compact Manhattan society of small apartments, crowded schedules, and casual relationships. These consumers go for such baubles as yogurt makers and peanut-butter-making machines on the one hand, and promotional extravaganzas featuring France's top ten fashion designers on the other.

This market, Bloomingdale's has learned, enjoys tasting but does not stand still long enough to savor. It thrives on variety and excitement.

Thus Bloomingdale's does not merely display merchandise; it showcases it, turning the store into an adult Disneyland. Bloomies does everything in the biggest way possible and prides itself on being like no other store in the world. On any given day, the store is likely to play host to celebrities ranging from actors and authors to sports figures to visiting royalty—further enhancing its allure.

Behind the glitter lies a coolly calculated merchandising strategy. The flashy goods are a kind of patina on a store that also stocks many basic items: The customer—not necessarily young or particularly fashionable—who is willing to settle for a $15 lamp can find one, but is more likely to come in to look at the latest in $250 lamps. So Bloomingdale's seeks to make itself a trend-setter, sensing the farthest-out ideas its market is ready for (or might be persuaded to accept), then moving in with appropriate goods and heavy promotion.

The method is not unique. All stores promote themselves, but Bloomingdale's does it louder, more frequently, and in unusual ways. As a result, Bloomingdale's sales per square foot of floor space is four times the average for all U.S. department stores.[1]

Bloomingdale's has a magic that keeps customers coming back. It puts drama into the ordinary act of shopping and sells excitement to its target market. But not all shoppers want this. Some want to walk in, find quality products at low prices, get good service, and get out fast. Stores serving these mass markets must operate efficiently and offer lower prices. Sears became the world's largest retailer using sophisticated buying and merchandising methods that give customers good value and service.

At the other end of the size spectrum is the "mom and pop" store. These small retailers are important because they are everywhere and offer customers more convenience and personal service. They adapt more easily and often create new retailing forms that larger stores later copy. Also, these smaller businesses give people a chance to be their own bosses.

Whether large or small, whether selling to a class or mass market, all retailers operate in a fast-changing environment. They must watch for signs of change and be ready to shift their strategies quickly. Many retailing giants have paid dearly for not changing. W. T. Grant, one of the oldest and largest variety chains, went bankrupt. So did Food Fair, once the eighth-largest supermarket chain. Others such as A&P and Montgomery Ward are looking for strategies to regain their former glory. Even Sears has had trouble:

> During the 1970s Sears painfully discovered the risks of a changing environment. Its strategies for each decade since its founding in 1886 were right on target, and it took over the number-one spot from the older Montgomery Ward's in the 1940s. [Sears] prospered through the early 1970s when it decided to change its strategy from expansion to upgrading. It decided to pursue affluent consumers by adding higher-quality lines and even designer merchandise. But its timing was bad. The boom turned into bust, and Sears customers were in no mood to pay higher prices. They shifted their shopping to K mart and other discount merchandisers. Nor did the new strategy attract more affluent consumers. In 1974, Sears experienced its first profit slump in thirteen years, a 24.8% decline. After its retailing profits peaked in 1976 at $441.2 million, they fell to $363.9 million for 1977 and $330.7 million for 1978. In the 1980s, Sears is still looking for the strategy which will help it regain the ground it lost.[2]

Small retailers are also vulnerable to the changing environment—as many as 75 percent of new small retailers fail within five years. Many people who start these small businesses lack the management skills needed to succeed.

This chapter looks at retailing and wholesaling institutions from the manager's viewpoint. In the first section we examine retailing's nature and importance, major types of retailers, decisions retailers make, and the future of retailing. In the second section, we discuss the same topics for wholesalers.

RETAILING

Retailing is *all activities involved in selling goods or services directly to final consumers for their personal, nonbusiness use.* Many institutions—manufacturers, wholesalers, retailers—do retailing. But most is done through **retailers** or **retail stores,** *businesses whose sales come primarily from retailing.* Retailing can be done by person, mail, telephone, or vending machine in stores, on the street, or in the consumer's home. We know that Sears and K mart are retailers, but so are the Avon lady, the local Holiday Inn, and a doctor seeing patients.

Retailing is a major industry. Retail stores make up 18 percent of all U.S. businesses. They outnumber manufacturers and wholesalers by more than seven to one and are the third largest source of the nation's jobs. U.S. retailers generated more than $1.2 trillion in sales in 1984. And some retailers are true giants. For example, the ten largest retailers and their 1983 sales in billions were Sears ($35.9), K mart ($18.6), Safeway ($18.5), Kroger ($15.2), J. C. Penney ($12.1), Southland ($8.8), Federated Department Stores ($8.7), Lucky Stores ($8.4), American Stores ($8.0), and Household International ($7.9).[3] The largest retailers are primarily department store chains and supermarket chains.

TYPES OF RETAILERS

Retailers come in all shapes and sizes, and new retailing forms keep emerging. The distribution functions performed by retailers can be combined in different ways to create new types of retailing institutions. For example, a modern K mart combines the features of a supermarket and discount store.

Retailers can be classified by one or more of several characteristics: amount of service, product line sold, relative price emphasis, nature of business premises, control of outlets, and type of store cluster. These classification schemes, and the corresponding retailer types, are shown in Table 16-1 and discussed below.

Amount of Service Different products have different service requirements, and customers' service preferences vary. Some customers will pay retailers for additional service, others would rather have fewer services and pay a lower price. Thus several types of retailers have evolved offering different levels of service. Table 16-2 shows three levels of service and the retailing institutions typically employing them.

TABLE 16-1 *Different Ways to Classify Retail Outlets*

AMOUNT SERVICE	PRODUCT LINE SOLD	RELATIVE PRICE EMPHASIS	NATURE OF BUSINESS PREMISES	CONTROL OF OUTLETS	TYPE OF STORE CLUSTER
Self-service Limited service Full service	Specialty store Department store Supermarket Convenience store Combination store, superstore, and hypermarche Service business	Discount store Warehouse Catalog showroom	Mail and telephone order retailing Automatic vending Buying service Door-to-door retailing	Corporate chain Voluntary chain and retailer cooperative Consumer cooperative Franchise organization Merchandising conglomerate	Central business district Regional shopping center Community shopping center Neighborhood shopping center

DECREASING SERVICES ←		→ INCREASING SERVICES
Self-service	**Limited service**	**Full service**
Very few services	Small variety of services	Wide variety of services
Price appeal	Shopping goods	Fashion merchandise
Staple goods		Specialty merchandise
Convenience goods		
Warehouse retailing	Door-to-door sales	Specialty stores
Grocery stores	Department stores	Department stores
Discount retailing	Telephone sales	
Variety stores	Variety stores	
Mail-order retailing		
Automatic vending		

The left group of rows is labeled **Attributes** and the lower group **Examples**.

Source: Adapted from Larry D. Redinbaugh, *Retailing Management: A Planning Approach* (New York: McGraw-Hill, 1976), p.12.

Self-service retailing in this country grew rapidly in the Great Depression of the 1930s. Customers were willing to carry out their own "locate-compare-select" process to save money. Today self-service is the cornerstone of all discount operations and is typically used by sellers of convenience goods and nationally branded, fast-moving shopping goods.

Limited-service retailers such as Sears or J. C. Penney provide more sales assistance because they carry more shopping goods for which customers need more information. They also offer additional services such as credit and merchandise return not usually offered by low-service stores. Their increased operating costs result in higher prices.

In *full-service retailing,* found in specialty stores and first-class department stores, salespeople assist customers in every phase of the locate-compare-select process. Full-service stores typically carry a higher proportion of specialty goods and slower-moving items such as cameras, jewelry, and fashions, for which customers like to be "waited on." They provide more liberal returns policies, various credit plans, free delivery, home servicing, and facilities such as lounges and restaurants. More services result in much higher operating costs, which are passed along to customers as higher prices. It is not surprising that full-service retailing has been declining relative to other types of retailing for several years.

Product Line Sold

Retailers can be classified by the length and breadth of their product assortments. Among the most important types are the specialty store, department store, supermarket, convenience store, and superstore.

Specialty Store

A specialty store carries a narrow product line with a deep assortment within that line. Examples include apparel stores, sporting goods stores, furniture stores, florists, and bookstores. Specialty stores can be further classified by the narrowness of their product lines. A clothing store is a *single-line store,* a men's clothing store is a *limited-line store,* and a men's custom shirt store is a *superspecialty store.* The increasing use of market segmentation, market targeting, and product specialization have resulted in the rapid growth of superspecialty stores such as Athlete's

Computers at a computer store and at a department store. The specialty store offers depth of assortment; the department store provides less depth in computers but offers many other lines of products. *Photos courtesy of Hewlett-Packard and Sears, Roebuck & Co.*

Foot (sport shoes), Tall Men (tall men's clothing), The Gap (jeans), and Computerland (personal computers).

The shopping center boom has also contributed to the recent growth of specialty stores; specialty stores occupy 60 to 70 percent of the total shopping center space. Though most specialty stores are independently owned, chain specialty stores are showing the strongest growth. The most successful chain specialty stores zero in on specific target market needs.

> The Limited specializes in high-fashion clothes for women 18 to 35 years old who are willing to pay more to get just the right look. The store has a contemporary atmosphere, displays coordinated outfits, and uses fashionably dressed salespeople who are the same age as target customers. The Limited carefully studies the fashion interests of its target market, pretests new fashion ideas, aims its advertising carefully, and builds a unique image.

Department Store

A department store carries a wide variety of product lines—typically clothing, home furnishings, and household goods. Each line is operated as a separate department managed by specialist buyers or merchandisers. Examples of well-known department stores include Bloomingdale's (New York), Marshall Field (Chicago), and Filene's (Boston).

The first department store, Bon Marché, was established in Paris in 1852.[4] It introduced four innovative principles: (1) low markups and rapid turnover, (2) marking and displaying merchandise prices, (3) encouraging shoppers to look around without pressure to purchase, and (4) a liberal complaint policy. Several other department stores followed—Whiteley's in Britain (1870s), reputed to carry "everything from a pin to an elephant," and Lewis (1870), the first to set up branches and employ central buying. The earliest American department stores included Jordan Marsh, Macy's, Wanamaker's, and Stewart's. These stores were housed in impressive buildings in fashionable central locations and sold the concept of "shopping for enjoyment." They were far different from specialty stores of the period, which displayed few items and discouraged looking around.

Through the first half of the century, fueled by urban growth, department stores became the major retailing institution in downtown areas. *Specialty department stores* such as Saks Fifth Avenue and I. Magnin emerged, carrying only clothing, shoes, cosmetics, gift items, and luggage. But after World War II, department stores moved into the declining stage of the retail life cycle. Several factors contributed to this decline. Competition among department stores increased, raising operating costs. Department stores faced greater competition from other types of retailers, particularly discount houses, specialty store chains, and warehouse retailers. And the heavy traffic, poor parking, and deterioration of central cities made downtown shopping less appealing. As a result, many department stores closed or merged with others.

Department stores are today waging a "comeback war" that is taking many forms. Many have opened suburban branches that offer better facilities and parking to faster-growing populations of higher-income consumers. Others have added "bargain basements" to meet the discount threat. Still others have remodeled their stores or set up "boutiques" that compete with specialty stores. Some are experimenting with mail order and telephone shopping. Others, like Dayton-Hudson, have become merchandising conglomerates by diversifying into discount and specialty stores. Some department stores are cutting back on employees, services, and product lines, but this may eliminate their major strategic advantages—assortment and service. Department stores need to find better ways to increase their falling profit margins.

Supermarket

Supermarkets are large, low-cost, low-margin, high-volume, self-service stores which "serve the customer's total needs for food, laundry, and household maintenance products."[5] Most supermarket stores are owned by supermarket chains like Safeway, Kroger, A&P, Winn-Dixie, and Jewel.

Supermarket retailing began in 1912 with the cash-and-carry Great Atlantic and Pacific Tea Company (A&P) food stores, and in Piggly Wiggly stores (1916), which introduced the concepts of self-service, customer turnstiles, and checkout counters. But supermarkets did not achieve great popularity until the 1930s. Michael "King" Kullen is credited with starting the first successful supermarket in 1930, a self-service, cash-and-carry grocery store over seven times the size of conventional food stores of that day. Kullen operated profitably with a gross margin half that of other food stores. Three hundred supermarkets were opened within the next two years, and by 1939 over 5,000 supermarkets accounted for over 20 percent of total grocery sales. Today over 37,000 supermarkets take in 76 percent of all grocery sales.

The supermarket takeoff in the 1930s resulted from several factors. The Great Depression made consumers more price conscious and allowed retailers to obtain merchandise at low prices and large buildings at low rentals. Mass automobile ownership reduced the need for small neighborhood stores. Advances in refrigeration let supermarkets and consumers store perishables longer. With new packaging technology, food could be sold in storable, consumer-sized packages rather than barrels and crates, and this stimulated brand preselling through advertising that reduced the need for salesclerks. Finally, the integration of grocery, meat, and produce departments fostered one-stop shopping and attracted consumers from greater distances, giving supermarkets the volume needed to offset their lower margins.

Over the years, supermarkets have found new ways to build their sales volumes further. Most chains now operate fewer but larger stores—the average store today is more than 50 percent larger than stores of the mid-1950s. Supermarkets now carry a larger number and variety of items. A typical supermarket today carries around 8,000 items, compared to 3,000 in 1946. The most significant change has been in the number of nonfood items carried—nonprescription drugs, beauty aids, housewares, magazines, books, toys—by companies pursuing "scrambled merchandising" strategies. Today many supermarkets are also selling prescriptions, appliances, records, sporting goods, hardware, garden supplies, and even cameras, hoping to find high-margin lines to improve profits.

Supermarkets are also upgrading their facilities and services to attract more customers—more expensive locations, better architecture and decor, longer store hours, check-cashing services, delivery, and even childcare centers. Supermarkets are increasing their promotion activities with more and better advertising and stronger sales promotions. Chains are selling more store brands to increase their margins and reduce their dependence on national brands.

Facing rising costs and changing markets, supermarkets have become increasingly vulnerable to innovative competition. Supermarkets now earn an operating profit of only about 1 percent of sales. The market has become more segmented, and domination by one type of food retailer is no longer likely. Supermarkets have been hit hard by new types of competitors—"box" stores, food discounters, superstores, and hypermarches. Another challenge has been the rapid growth of away-from-home eating—Americans now spend nearly 40 percent of their food budgets outside the food stores.

According to McCammon, the supermarket concept involves (1) self-service and self-selection displays; (2) centralization of customer services, usually at the checkout counter; (3) large-scale facilities; (4) a strong price emphasis; and (5) a

A convenience store, a supermarket, and a superstore. *Courtesy of 7-Eleven Corporation and Safeway Stores.*

broad assortment and wide variety of merchandise.[6] This concept has recently spread from food retailing to the retailing of other goods such as drugs (Walgreen's), home improvements (Lowe's, Hechinger's), and toys (Toys "R" Us).

Convenience Store

Convenience food stores are small stores which carry a limited line of high-turn-over convenience goods. Examples include 7-Elevens and White Hen Pantries. These stores locate near residential areas and remain open long hours and seven days a week. Convenience stores must charge high prices to make up for higher operating costs and lower sales volume. But they satisfy an important consumer need. Consumers use convenience stores for "fill-in" purchases at off hours or when time is short, and they are willing to pay for the convenience. The number of convenience stores increased from about 2,000 in 1957 to almost 39,000 stores with sales of $15.1 billion in 1982.[7]

Convenience food retailing has recently spread to the food-gasoline store. At these stores, customers can get gas, select from about one hundred convenience items—bread, milk, cigarettes, and soft drinks—and charge the purchase to their oil credit cards.

Superstore, Combination Store, and Hypermarche

These three types of stores are larger than the conventional supermarket.

Superstores are almost twice the size of conventional supermarkets (30,000 versus 18,000 square feet) and aim to meet all the consumer's needs for routinely purchased food and nonfood items. They offer such services as laundry, dry cleaning, shoe repair, check cashing, bill paying, and bargain lunch counters.[8] Because of their wider assortment, superstore prices are 5 to 6 percent higher than those of conventional supermarkets. Many leading chains are moving toward superstores. For example, Kroger plans to build 114 superstores averaging 30,000 square feet in size. Safeway is moving in with Pak 'N Save superstores, and A&P has opened Super Plus stores in Chicago and other locations.[9]

Combination stores are combined food and drug stores. They have an average selling space of about 55,000 square feet (about one and a half football fields). Three basic designs are used. Kroger locates its supermarkets and its Super X discount drugstores side by side, and each store can be run as a separate operation. The Jewel Company uses a single store with drugs on one side and food on the other. This offers consumers easier access and greater convenience, and probably generates more sales "synergy" than the side-by-side design. Borman's in Detroit sandwiches the drugs between supermarket items to generate more cross-shopping.

Hypermarches are even bigger than combination stores, ranging in size from 80,000 to 220,000 square feet (about *six* football fields). The hypermarche combines supermarket, discount, and warehouse retailing principles. Its product assortment goes beyond routinely purchased goods and includes furniture, heavy and light appliances, clothing, and many other things. The hypermarche offers discount prices and operates like a warehouse. Many products come direct from the manufacturer prepacked in wire "baskets" stacked twelve to fifteen feet high on metal racks. Forklifts move through aisles during selling hours to restock shelves. Customers select items from bulk displays, and the store gives discounts to customers who carry their own heavy appliances and furniture out of the store.

The first hypermarche, opened in Paris by Carrefour, was immediately successful. The real boom occurred in the late 1960s and early 1970s, especially in France and Germany, where several hundred now operate. American chains are proceeding more cautiously. Though a few operations—J. C. Penney's The Treasury and Jewel's Grand Bazaar—have adopted some hypermarche principles, most American chains prefer to open superstores instead.

Service Business

For some businesses, the "product line" is actually a service. Service retailers include hotels and motels, banks, airlines, colleges, hospitals, movie theaters, tennis clubs, bowling alleys, restaurants, repair services, barber and beauty shops, dry cleaners, and funeral homes. Service retailers in the United States are growing faster than product retailers, and each service industry has its own retailing drama. Banks look for new ways to distribute their services efficiently, including automatic tellers, direct deposit, and telephone banking. Health maintenance organizations (HMOs) are revolutionizing the ways consumers get and pay for health services. The amusement industry has spawned Disney World and other theme parks, and such groups as Transcendental Meditation, est, and Silva Mind Control have applied franchising and chain store principles to mass-distribute personal growth services. H&R Block has built a franchise network to help consumers pay as little as possible to Uncle Sam. (For more on services, see Chapter 23).

Relative Price Emphasis Retailers can also be classified according to their prices. Most retailers offer medium prices and normal levels of quality and customer services. Some offer higher-quality goods and service at higher prices—Gucci's justifies its high prices by saying, "You will remember the goods long after the prices are forgotten." Discount stores run lower-cost, lower-service operations and sell goods for less than regular prices (called "off-list" pricing or "off-price" retailing). Here we will look at discount stores and two offshoots, warehouse stores and catalog showrooms.

Discount Store

A discount store sells standard merchandise at lower prices by accepting lower margins and selling higher volume. The use of occasional discounts or specials does not make a discount store. Nor does selling inferior goods at low prices. A true discount store has five characteristics: (1) It regularly sells its merchandise at lower prices; (2) it emphasizes national brands, not inferior goods at low prices; (3) it operates on a self-service, minimum facilities basis; (4) it locates in a low-rent area and draws customers from fairly long distances; and (5) it has spartan and functional fixtures.[10] In 1981 there were an estimated 8,164 discount department stores, with almost $67 billion in sales.[11]

Discount retailing began before World War II, but its real growth took place in the late 1940s when it moved from soft goods (clothing, toiletries) to hard goods (refrigerators, washing machines, air conditioners, furnishings, sporting goods). Early discounters such as Masters, Korvette, and Two Guys succeeded for many reasons. After the war, many hard goods became more standardized and reliable, allowing more preselling and reducing the need for in-store selling. And a vast new group of price-conscious but affluent consumers emerged. The early discount stores operated warehouselike facilities in low-rent but heavily traveled districts. They slashed prices, advertised widely, and carried a reasonable width and depth of products. They cut expense levels to half those incurred by department and specialty stores, and their average stock turnover of fourteen times per year was almost four times that of a conventional department store. By 1960, discount stores accounted for one-third of all sales of household appliances.

In recent years, facing intense competition from other discounters and department stores, many discount retailers have traded up; they have improved decor, added new lines and services, and opened suburban branches—leading to higher costs and prices. And as some department stores have cut their prices to compete with discounters, the distinction between many discount and department stores has blurred. As a result, several major discount stores folded in the 1970s because they lost their price advantage. And many department store retailers have upgraded their stores and services to maintain the distinction between themselves and improved discounters.

When the major discount stores traded up, a new wave of "off-price" retailers moved in to fill the low-price, high-volume gap. These new discounters have moved heavily into special merchandise areas such as discount sporting goods, discount furniture and appliances, and discount electronics products (see Exhibit 16-1).

EXHIBIT 16-1

"OFF-PRICE" RETAILING AT 47TH STREET PHOTO

On the surface, 47th Street Photo doesn't look like much of a retailing operation. Its main store is a small, dingy affair located above Kaplan's Delicatessen on New York's West 47th Street. Its second store, a small computer outlet located a few blocks away, is only slightly more attractive. But beneath the surface, 47th Street Photo represents the state of the art in "off-price" retailing—selling quality, branded merchandise at large discounts. In business for only fifteen years, 47th Street's two tiny stores annually sell more than $100 million worth of electronics products, and its sales are growing at 25 percent a year.

47th Street Photo is typical of the new discounters that emerged at retailing's low end to fill the gap created when more mature discount institutions began to trade up their merchandise, services, and prices. 47th Street maintains a low-cost, low-margin, high-volume philosophy. It carries a huge inventory of over 25,000 fast-moving, branded electronics products—including such items as cameras and camera equipment (only 30 percent of its business), personal computers, calculators, typewriters, telephones, answering machines, and videotape machines. It keeps its costs down through low-cost, no-frills facilities, efficient operations, and smart buying. Then it offers customers the lowest prices and turns its inventory quickly.

47th Street Photo's customers endure more abrupt treatment and enjoy fewer services than they would at plusher specialty stores. Like a well-run restaurant, 47th Street gets 'em in, feeds 'em, and gets 'em out. Customers line up at the sales counter to be waited on by efficient but curt salespeople who prefer that customers know what they want before coming in. In-store product inspections and comparisons are discouraged, and salespeople offer little information or assistance.

But the price is right! 47th Street Photo regularly monitors competitor prices to be certain that its own prices support its "lowest-price" position. Price examples: Suggested retail price of the Canon PC-20 copier, $1,295; at 47th Street Photo, it's $880. Macy's offers a Brother typewriter for $400, and on a recent Sunday it's out of stock. At 47th Street the same model is $289 and, of course, in stock.

Half of 47th Street Photo's sales come from mail order and telephone customers. Its 224-page catalog, toll-free telephone numbers, and packed ads in the *New York Times, Wall Street Journal,* and several other business and special interest magazines make New York's "only dopes pay retail" shopping style available to the rest of the country. Over the years, 47th Street has built a solid reputation for trustworthiness. A price is a price, no bait-and-switch, no haggling or hidden prices.

So on the surface, 47th Street Photo doesn't look like much of a retailing operation. But behind its low-overhead exterior is a gutsy, finely tuned merchandising machine.

Source: Adapted from John Merwin, "The Source," *Forbes,* April 9, 1984, pp. 74–78.

Food retailers have also adopted discount retailing. A recent example is the "box" store, pioneered by Aldi Discount Food. In these warehouselike operations, services are slashed to the minimum and customers pay cash and bring their own bags. Aldi carries only about 450 high-turnover items—and none are perishable, eliminating the need for costly refrigeration. Prices are posted on signs rather than on the merchandise, saving marking costs. The lower costs are passed along to consumers in the form of reduced prices. Such box stores have not been very successful. Consumers enjoy the savings, but the lack of variety and absence of frozen and refrigerated foods forces consumers to go to additional stores to complete their food shopping. As a result, some box stores have closed in recent years and others are moving toward more conventional supermarkets by increasing their product assortments and adding services.[12]

Warehouse Store

A warehouse store is a no-frills, reduced-service operation that seeks high volume through low prices. In its broad form, it includes hypermarches and box stores. One of its most interesting forms is the *furniture showroom warehouse.* Conventional furniture stores have run warehouse sales for years to clear out old stock. But Ralph and Leon Levitz developed it into a new retailing concept in 1953. By 1977 they had built sixty-one furniture warehouse showrooms. Shoppers enter a football-field-size warehouse located in a low-rent suburban area. They first pass through the warehouse section, where they see some 52,000 items worth about $2 million stacked in neat tiers. Then they enter the showroom section, consisting of about 200 rooms of attractively displayed furniture. Customers select goods and place orders with salespeople. By the time the customer pays, leaves, and drives to the loading dock, the merchandise is ready. Heavy goods can be delivered within a few days, or customers can save money by providing their own delivery.

The Levitz operation targets buyers of medium-priced brand-name furniture who want discount prices and immediate availability. Shoppers enjoy low prices and wide brand assortment, but they must settle for limited customer service. Levitz stores have a mixed profit picture. They generate high volume, but are saddled with high inventory costs, large promotional expenditures, and often too many competitors.[13]

Catalog Showroom

A catalog showroom sells a wide selection of high-markup, fast-moving, brand-name goods at discount prices, goods such as jewelry, power tools, cameras, luggage, small appliances, toys, and sporting goods. Emerging in the late 1960s, these stores have become one of retailing's hottest new forms, even threatening traditional discounters who have traded up to more service, higher markups, and higher prices. The industry is dominated by publicly owned companies such as Best Products and Service Merchandise. By the late 1970s, some 470 companies operated about 1,700 catalog showrooms in the United States.[14]

The catalog showrooms provide lengthy color catalogs showing each item's list price and discount price. Best Products publishes a 500-page color catalog displaying 8,500 items that is mailed free to 10 million prospective customers each year.[15] Customers can order by phone and pay delivery charges, or examine items in one of Best's 196 showrooms and buy them out of stock. Catalog showrooms make their money by cutting costs and margins to provide low prices that will attract a higher volume of sales.

They carry presold, branded goods, lease stores in low-rent areas, hire a third fewer salespeople, use case displays to minimize shoplifting, and operate largely on a cash basis. Customers must put up with certain inconveniences, such as driving some distance, standing in line to see some items (many are in locked cases), waiting for items to be supplied from the back room, and finding little service when they have problems. But the rapid growth of catalog showrooms suggests that many consumers are willing to accept less service to save money.

Nature of Business Premises Most goods and services are sold through stores, but *nonstore retailing* has been growing much faster than store retailing. Nonstore retailing accounts for 14 percent of all retail purchases. As much as a third of all general merchandise may be sold through nonstore channels by the end of the century.[16] Some experts envision *remote retailing,* where customers will order goods using home computers and receive them without stepping into stores.[17] Here we examine four forms of nonstore retailing: mail and telephone order retailing, vending machines, buying services, and door-to-door selling and in-house parties.

Mail and Telephone Order Retailing

Mail and telephone order retailing uses the mail or telephone to get orders or to facilitate delivery. After the Civil War, merchants began sending catalogs to people living in rural areas. A. Montgomery Ward was established in 1872, followed by Sears and Roebuck in 1886. By 1918 these two firms conducted giant mail order businesses, and there were some 2,500 other mail order houses. In the 1930s and 1940s, as chain stores opened branches in smaller towns, many retailers discontinued their mail order operations. But today, far from declining, the mail and telephone order business is booming.

More than 11,000 mail and telephone order houses in the United States generate sales of over $8 billion. These businesses take several forms.

MAIL-ORDER CATALOG. Here the seller mails a catalog to a select group of customers and makes it available on the premises. This approach is used by general merchandise mail order houses carrying a full line of goods. Sears is the industry giant—it sends out over 300 million catalogs each year and generates over $3.7 billion of catalog sales. J. C. Penney sells over $1.6 billion a year from its catalog operation.[18] These giant merchandisers also operate in-store catalog counters and catalog offices in small communities where customers can look at catalogs, place orders, and pick up purchases when they arrive from the central warehouse.

Catalogers include such huge general merchandisers as Sears and J.C. Penney and smaller specialty retailers such as L.L. Bean. *Courtesy of L.L. Bean.*

The huge general merchandise retailers are joined by over 4,000 other catalogers now in the market, with combined sales of about $40 billion a year. Consumers can buy just about anything from catalogs. Hanover House distributes 22 different catalogs selling everything from shoes to decorative lawn birds. L. L. Bean sells camping gear and outdoor wear, Spiegel offers designer fashions and furniture, and Sharper Image sells $2,400 jet-propelled surfboards.[19]

Recently, specialty department stores such as Neiman-Marcus and Saks Fifth Avenue have begun using catalogs to cultivate upper-class markets for high-priced, often exotic merchandise such as "his and her" bathrobes, designer jewelry, and gourmet foods. Several major corporations have also acquired mail order divisions. Xerox offers children's books; Avon sells women's apparel; American Airlines markets luggage; General Foods offers needlework kits; General Mills sells shirts; and American Express markets fox coats.

DIRECT RESPONSE. Here the direct marketer runs a newspaper, magazine, radio, or television ad describing some product, and the customer can write or phone for it. The direct marketer selects the media vehicles that maximize the number of orders for a given advertising expenditure. This strategy works well with such products as records and tapes, books, and small appliances.

DIRECT MAIL. Here the marketer sends single mail pieces—letters, flyers, foldouts—to prospects whose names are on special mailing lists of high-potential buyers of the product category. The mailing lists are leased or purchased from mailing-list brokerage houses. Direct mail has proved very successful in selling books, magazine subscriptions, and insurance, and is increasingly being used to sell novelty items, clothing, and even gourmet foods. The major charities have used direct mail to raise over $21.4 billion, or over 80 percent of their contributions.[20]

TELEMARKETING. Direct marketers use the telephone to sell everything from home repair services to newspaper subscriptions to zoo memberships. Some telephone marketers have developed computerized phoning systems where households are dialed automatically and computerized messages presented. Telephone selling has been opposed by many groups who are proposing laws to ban or limit it.

Several factors have caused the increase in mail and telephone order retailing. Working women have less shopping time. In-store shopping has become less appealing because of higher driving costs, traffic and parking headaches, crime in urban shopping areas, less in-store service, and longer checkout lines. Also, many chain stores have dropped slower-moving specialty items, creating an opportunity for direct marketers to promote these items. Finally, the development of toll-free lines and the willingness of telephone retailers to accept orders at night or on Sundays has boosted this form of retailing.

Automatic Vending

Automatic vending through coin-operated machines grew rapidly after World War II, and total sales soared to $13 billion by 1979. Automatic vending is not new—in 215 B.C. Egyptians could buy sacrificial water from coin-actuated devices.[21] In the 1880s, the Tutti-Frutti Company installed chewing gum machines in train stations. Today's machines employ space-age and computer technology and are used to sell a considerable variety of impulse goods with high convenience value—cigarettes, beverages, candy, newspapers, foods and snacks, hosiery, cosmetics, paperbacks, records and tapes, T-shirts, insurance policies, and even shoeshines and fishing worms.

Vending machines are found in factories, offices, lobbies, retail stores, gasoline stations, and railway cars. Vending machine owners rent space in good locations and service the machines. Vending machines are increasingly supplying entertainment services—pinball machines, jukeboxes, and electronic computer games. Automatic teller machines provide bank customers with twenty-four-hour checking, savings, withdrawals, and funds-transfer services.

Vending machines offer twenty-four-hour selling, self-service, and less damaged goods. But automatic vending is a more costly channel, and prices of vended goods are often 15 to 20 percent higher. The vendor must bear the high costs of frequent restocking of widely scattered machines, frequent machine breakdowns, and high pilferage in some locations. Customers must put up with machine breakdowns, out-of-stocks, and the fact that merchandise cannot be returned.

Some predict that automatic vending will eventually develop into the fully automated store where all items are purchased from machines, with a few attendants present. But several experiments conducted in the 1950s and 1960s produced little success. Only one type of automatic store has succeeded—the coin-operated laundry. The real revolution in automatic vending might come from "in-home" shopping through interactive telecommunication systems and highly automated order-processing, billing, and warehouse facilities.

Buying Service

A buying service is a storeless retailer serving a specific clientele—usually the employees of large organizations such as schools, hospitals, unions, and government agencies. Buying service members are entitled to buy from a selective list of retailers that have agreed to give discounts to the members. A customer seeking a videorecorder would get a form from the buying service, take it to an approved retailer, and buy the appliance at a discount. The retailer would then pay a small fee to the buying service. For example, United Buying Service offers its 900,000 members the opportunity to buy merchandise at "cost plus 8 percent."

Door-to-Door Retailing

This form of selling—which started centuries ago with roving peddlers—has burgeoned into a $6 billion industry. More than 600 companies sell either door-to-door, office-to-office, or at home sales parties. One pioneer, the Fuller Brush Company, still employs about 10,000 salespeople to sell its brushes, brooms, and other products. Others include vacuum cleaner companies like Electrolux and book-selling companies like Southwestern. Encyclopedia companies have sold door-to-door for years—World Book became the leader by enlisting schoolteachers to sell its encyclopedias part time.

Door-to-door selling's image improved considerably when Avon entered the industry with its Avon lady—the homemaker's friend and beauty consultant. In 1983, its army of over 425,000 U.S. representatives sold $1.2 billion worth of products in more than 50 million homes, making Avon the world's largest cosmetics firm and the number one door-to-door marketer. Tupperware helped to popularize home sales parties, in which several friends and neighbors attend a party in someone's home where Tupperware is demonstrated and sold. Tupperware handles about 140 different products, and in 1983 its force of over 300,000 independent representatives generated sales of more than $775 million dollars.[22]

Door-to-door selling meets the convenience and personal attention needs of consumers, but the high costs of hiring, training, paying, and motivating the salesforce result in higher prices to the consumer. Door-to-door selling has a somewhat uncertain future. The increase in the number of single-person and working-couple households decreases the chances of finding anyone at home. And with the recent proliferation of interactive telecommunication technologies, the door-to-door salesperson may well be replaced in the future by the household television or home computer.

Control of Outlets

Retailing institutions can be classified by form of ownership. About 80 percent of all retail stores are independents, and they account for two-thirds of all retail sales. Here we will look at several other forms of ownership—the corporate chain, voluntary chain and retailer cooperative, consumer cooperative, franchise organization, and merchandising conglomerate.

Corporate Chain

The chain store is one of the most important retail developments of this century. One of the first chains in America, The Great Atlantic and Pacific Tea Company (A&P) started in 1859 with one store importing tea directly from the Orient and grew to twenty-five stores by 1869. Another pioneer chain, Woolworth's, began by selling variety goods through a low-price, high-volume approach. But little chain store growth took place until the turn of the century.

Gist defines a *chain store* as *two or more outlets that are commonly owned and controlled, sell similar lines of merchandise, have central buying and merchandising, and may use a similar architectural motif.*[23] Each characteristic deserves comment. The U.S. Bureau of the Census classifies chains in seven groups ranging from a two-to-three-unit class to an over-one-hundred-unit class, but experts disagree on how few units constitute a chain.

Common ownership and control is the characteristic that distinguishes corporate chains from voluntary chains and franchise operations. The fact that corporate chains sell similar lines of merchandise distinguishes them from merchandising conglomerates, which combine several chains under common ownership. Central buying and merchandising means that headquarters largely decides on the chain's product assortment, places bulk orders to get quantity discounts, distributes goods to individual units, and sets pricing, promotion, and other standard policies for the units. Finally, chains develop a consistent architectural style to make their units more visible and identifiable to consumers.

Corporate chains appear in all types of retail operations—supermarket, discount, variety, specialty, and department stores. In terms of product lines, corporate chains (when defined as having eleven or more units) are strongest in department stores (94 percent of total 1979 sales volume), variety stores (80 percent), food stores (54 percent), drugstores (50 percent), shoe stores (48 percent), and women's apparel stores (37 percent).

Corporate chains gain an advantage over independents through efficiencies that allow them to charge lower prices and achieve higher sales volume. Chains achieve their efficiency in many ways. First, their size allows them to buy in large quantities at lower prices. Second, chains can afford to hire corporate-level specialists to deal with such areas as pricing, promotion, merchandising, inventory control, and sales forecasting. Third, chains can integrate retailing and wholesaling functions, while independent retailers must deal with many wholesalers. Fourth, chains gain promotional economies because their advertising costs are spread over many stores and a large sales volume.

Voluntary Chain and Retailer Cooperative

The great success of corporate chains brought two reactions. First, it inspired the passage of antichain legislation at the state level (fair trade laws) and federal level (Robinson-Patman Act). These laws attempted to prevent the chains from competing with independents by charging lower prices achieved through centralized buying power. Second, the success of chains caused many independents to band together in one of two forms of associations. One is the *voluntary chain*—a wholesaler-sponsored group of independent retailers that engage in group buying and common merchandising. Examples include the Independent Grocers Alliance (IGA), Sentry Hardwares, and Western Auto. The other is the *retailer cooperative*—a group of independent retailers that band together and set up a jointly owned central buying organization (wholesale operation) and conduct joint merchandising and promotion efforts. Examples include Associated Grocers and Ace Hardware. Through these organizations, independents can achieve buying and promotion economies that allow them to meet the price challenge of corporate chains.

Consumer Cooperative

A consumer cooperative is a retail firm owned by its customers. Residents of a community may start a consumer co-op when they feel local retailers are charging too high prices or providing poor product assortment or quality. The residents contribute money to open their own store, and they vote on its policies and elect managers. The store may set low prices, or it may set normal prices and give members patronage dividends based on their purchase levels.

Many successful co-ops are ideological, and several are found in college communities. Although there are a few thousand cooperatives in the United States, they have never become an important retailing force. The opposite is true in some European countries, especially in the Scandinavian countries and Switzerland.

> A striking example is Migros in Switzerland, a consumer cooperative that accounts for 11 percent of the entire Swiss retail volume! Migros was founded in 1925 by Gottlieb Duttweiler as a corporate grocery chain dedicated to challenging high-markup competitors in the grocery field. He was so successful that in 1946 he turned Migros into a consumer cooperative by selling one share of stock to each of his 85,000 registered customers. Today, Migros is a huge federation of 440 branch stores, 74 specialty stores, and numerous other enterprises essentially owned by its customers.

Franchise Organization

A *franchise organization is a contractual association between a franchiser (manu-facturer, wholesaler, service organization) and franchisees (independent business-people who buy the right to own and operate one or more units in the franchise system).* The main distinction between a franchise organization and other contractual systems (voluntary chains and retail cooperatives) is that franchise organizations are normally based on some unique product or service; method of doing business; or trade name, goodwill, or patent that the franchiser has developed. In 1983 there were an estimated 465,000 franchise outlets, with sales of $436 billion. Their heaviest concentration in terms of numbers of units is in gasoline service stations (29.9 percent) and fast-food restaurants. (15.1 percent).

The compensation the franchiser receives may include an initial fee, a royalty on gross sales, rental and lease fees for equipment and fixtures supplied by the franchiser, a share of the profits, and sometimes a regular license fee. Some franchisers also charge management consulting fees, but these are usually included as part of the package deal. McDonald's charges an initial fee of $150,000 for a franchise and receives a 3 percent royalty fee and a rental charge of 8.5 percent of the franchisee's volume. It also requires franchisees to go to Hamburger University for three weeks to learn how to manage the business.

The franchiser usually sets specific requirements on how the franchised "product" can be used or dispensed. McDonald's required that all franchisees' equipment and many supplies be obtained from McDonald's or authorized suppliers. But this type of requirement was challenged, and a federal court ruling held that the clause must be dropped from franchising contracts. Franchisees can buy from whatever sources they wish, as long as they meet strict quality standards.

Merchandising Conglomerate

Merchandising conglomerates are free-form corporations that combine several diversified retailing forms under central ownership, along with some integration of their distribution and management functions.[24] Major examples include Federated Department Stores, Allied Stores, Dayton-Hudson, and J. C. Penney. One of the most profitable of the diversified retailers, Melville Corporation, operates Thom McAn, Miles, and Vanguard shoe chains; Chess King, a string of 326 young men's fashion stores; Foxmoor, a women's apparel store; Clothes Bin, a chain of discount women's apparel stores; CVS, a chain of health and beauty aid stores; and Marshall, Inc., a regional chain that carries all kinds of name-brand clothing.[25] Diversified retailing is likely to increase through the 1980s and 1990s. The major question is whether diversified retailing produces management systems and economies that benefit all the separate retailing units in the conglomerate.

Type of Store Cluster

Most stores today cluster together to increase their customer pulling power and to provide consumers with the convenience of one-stop shopping. The four main types of store clusters are the central business district, the regional shopping center, the community shopping center, and the neighborhood shopping center.

Central Business District

Central business districts were the dominant form of retail cluster until the 1950s. Every large city and town had a central business district containing department stores, specialty stores, banks, and movie theaters. Smaller business districts could be found in outlying areas. When people began to migrate to the suburbs in the 1950s, these central business districts, with their traffic, parking, and crime problems, began to lose business. Downtown merchants began to open branches in suburban shopping centers, and the decline of the central business districts continued. Only recently have the cities joined with merchants to try to revitalize downtown shopping areas by building malls and underground parking. Some central business districts have made a comeback; others remain in a slow and possibly irreversible decline.

Regional Shopping Center

A *shopping center* is "a group of commercial establishments planned, developed, owned, and managed as a unit related in location, size, and type of shop to the trade area that it services, and providing on-site parking in definite relationship to the types and sizes of stores it contains."[26] The regional shopping center is the largest and most dramatic of the shopping centers.

A regional shopping center is like a mini-downtown. It contains from 40 to 100 stores and serves from 100,000 to 1,000,000 customers living within 30 minutes' driving time. In its early form, the regional shopping center had two strong department stores "anchoring" the ends, with a set of specialty stores in between. This arrangement encouraged comparison shopping—consumers could easily compare similar lines at various specialty and department stores. A customer wishing to buy jeans could compare at Sears, Lord & Taylor, Just Jeans, The Gap, and the County Seat. Regional centers have added new types of retailers over the years—dentists, health clubs, and even branch libraries. Larger regional malls now have several department stores and several shopping levels. Most newer malls are enclosed to provide comfortable shopping in any weather conditions.

Community Shopping Center

A community shopping center contains 15 to 50 retail stores serving 20,000 to 100,000 people living mostly within one and one-half miles of the center. The

Federated Department Stores, Inc., a diversified corporation, consists of all these retailers. *Courtesy of Federated Department Stores, Inc.*

center normally contains a primary store, usually a branch of a department or variety store, and a supermarket, specialty stores, convenience goods stores, professional offices, and sometimes a bank. The primary store usually locates at the corner of the L in L-shaped shopping centers or in the center of line-shaped centers. The stores nearest the primary store usually sell shopping goods, and the more distant stores sell convenience goods.

Neighborhood Shopping Center

Most shopping centers are neighborhood centers that contain 5 to 15 stores and serve populations of less than 20,000 people. They are close and convenient for consumers. They usually contain a supermarket as the anchor store and several service establishments—a dry cleaner, self-service laundry, drugstore, barber or beauty shop, a hardware, or other stores located in an unplanned strip.

All shopping centers combined now account for about one-third of all retail sales, but they may be reaching their saturation point. Many areas contain too many malls, and sales per square foot are dropping, vacancy rates are climbing, and some bankruptcies have occurred. The current trend is toward smaller malls located in medium-size and smaller cities in fast-growing areas such as the Southwest.

RETAILER MARKETING DECISIONS

We will now examine the major marketing decisions retailers must make about their target markets, product assortment and services, price, promotion, and place.

Target Market Decision

Retailers must first define and profile the target market, and decide how their operations will be positioned in the target market. The positioning decision guides all other retailer marketing decisions—product assortment, services, pricing, advertising, store decor, and other decisions must all consistently support the retailer's position in its market segment.

Some stores define their target market and position quite well. A women's apparel store in Palm Springs positions itself as "fashions for the discriminating woman" and targets upper-income women between the ages of 30 and 35 living within 30 minutes' driving time from the store. We saw earlier that Bloomingdale's has clearly identified its target market and positioning.

But too many retailers fail to clarify their target markets and positions. They try to have "something for everyone" and end up satisfying no market well. Even large department stores like Sears must define their major target markets so that they can design effective strategies for serving these markets.

A retailer should carry out periodic marketing research to check that it is satisfying its target customers. Consider a store that has targeted affluent consumers, but whose store image is shown by the solid line in Figure 16-1. The store does not currently appeal to its target market—it must change its target market or redesign itself into a "classier" store. Suppose the store now upgrades its products, services, and salespeople and raises its prices. Some time later, a second customer survey reveals the image shown by the dashed line in Figure 16-1. The store has established a position that is consistent with its target market choice.

Product Assortment and Services Decision

Retailers have to decide on three major product variables: product assortment, services mix, and store atmosphere.

The retailer's *product assortment* must match the shopping expectations of the target market. In fact, it becomes a key element in the competitive battle among similar retailers. The retailer has to decide on product assortment *width* (narrow or wide) and *depth* (shallow or deep). Thus a restaurant can offer a narrow and shallow assortment (small lunch counter), a narrow and deep assortment (delicatessen), a wide and shallow assortment (cafeteria), or a wide and deep assortment (large restaurant). Another product assortment dimension is the quality of the goods. The customer is interested not only in the range of choice, but also in the quality of the products.

Retailers also must decide on the *services mix* to offer customers. The old "mom and pop" grocery stores offered home delivery, credit, and conversation,

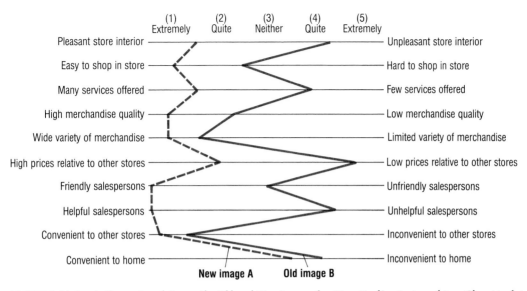

	(1) Extremely	(2) Quite	(3) Neither	(4) Quite	(5) Extremely	
Pleasant store interior						Unpleasant store interior
Easy to shop in store						Hard to shop in store
Many services offered						Few services offered
High merchandise quality						Low merchandise quality
Wide variety of merchandise						Limited variety of merchandise
High prices relative to other stores						Low prices relative to other stores
Friendly salespersons						Unfriendly salespersons
Helpful salespersons						Unhelpful salespersons
Convenient to other stores						Inconvenient to other stores
Convenient to home						Inconvenient to home

New image A   Old image B

FIGURE 16-1   A Comparison between the Old and New Image of a Store Seeking to Appeal to a Class Market

Source: Adapted from David W. Cravens, Gerald E. Hills, and Robert B. Woodruff, *Marketing Decision Making: Concepts and Strategy* (Homewood, IL: Irwin, 1976), p. 234.

services that today's supermarkets have eliminated. Table 16-3 lists some of the major services full-service retailers can offer. The services mix is one of the key tools of nonprice competition for differentiating one store from another.

The *store's atmospherics* is a third element in its product arsenal. Every store has a physical layout that makes moving around hard or easy. Every store has a "feel"; one store is dirty, another is charming, a third is palatial, a fourth is somber. The store must embody a planned atmosphere that suits the target market and moves them toward purchase. A funeral parlor should be quiet, somber, and peaceful, and a discothèque should be bright, loud, and vibrating. The atmosphere is designed by creative people who know how to combine visual, aural, olfactory, and tactile stimuli to achieve the desired effect.[27]

Price Decision   Retailer's prices are a key competitive factor and reflect the quality of goods carried and services offered. Retail prices are based on the cost of merchandise, and intelligent buying is a key ingredient in successful retailing. Retailers can often make as much money through smart buying as through smart selling. Beyond this, they must price carefully in a number of other ways.

Low markups can be set on some items that can work as *traffic builders* or *loss leaders,* in the hope that customers will buy additional items with higher markups once they are in the store. In addition, retail management has to be adept in its use of markdowns on slower-moving merchandise. Shoe retailers, for example, expect

TABLE 16-3
Typical Retail Services

PREPURCHASE SERVICES	POSTPURCHASE SERVICES	ANCILLARY SERVICES
1. Accepting telephone orders	1. Delivery	1. Check cashing
2. Accepting mail orders (or purchases)	2. Regular wrapping (or bagging)	2. General information
3. Advertising	3. Gift wrapping	3. Free parking
4. Window display	4. Adjustments	4. Restaurants
5. Interior display	5. Returns	5. Repairs
6. Fitting rooms	6. Alterations	6. Interior decorating
7. Shopping hours	7. Tailoring	7. Credit
8. Fashion shows	8. Installations	8. Restrooms
9. Trade-ins	9. Engraving	9. Baby attendant service
	10. COD delivery	

Source: Carl M. Larson, Robert E. Weigand, and John S. Wright, *Basic Retailing* (Englewood Cliffs, NJ: Prentice-Hall, 1976), p. 364.

to sell 50 percent of their shoes at a 60 percent markup, 25 percent at a 40 percent markup, and the remaining 25 percent at cost. Their initial pricing anticipates these expected markdowns.

Promotion Decision Retailers use the normal promotional tools—advertising, personal selling, sales promotion, and publicity—to reach consumers. Retailers advertise in newspapers, magazines, radio, and television. The advertising may be supplemented by hand-delivered circulars and direct mail pieces. Personal selling requires careful training of the salespeople in how to greet customers, meet their needs, and handle their doubts and complaints. Sales promotion may take the form of in-store demonstrations, trading stamps, grand prizes, and visiting celebrities. Publicity is always available to retailers who have something interesting to say. Consider the range of promotional styles available to three art galleries that opened in Chicago:

> The (Seaberg-Isthmus Gallery) edged quietly into the local art world last month with a model of promotional-making-with-words, when a simple and informative letter announced (its opening). . . . Our second example is Origin, which received a lurid public-relations blast that embarrassed the young artist (Matt) and is enough to scare off the very people he would like to see in his studio-gallery. Somehow the hard sell and art mix poorly. . . . Our third example is a prime instance of non-sell. With no name but the address, 1017 Armitage, the workshop of Julian Frederick Harr has a tidy gallery up front (and) behind is a cluttered, chip-and-shaving sculptor's studio . . . In the long run, Harr, quietly building his people-traps, is better off than Matt, who will have to live down his own well-intentioned publicity. But the Seaberg-Isthmus soft sell is by far the most effective.[28]

Place Decision The choice of location is a key competitive factor in the retailer's ability to attract customers. And the costs of building or leasing facilities have a major impact on the retailer's profits. Thus site location decisions are among the most important the retailer makes. Small retailers may have to settle for locations that are available and affordable. Large retailers usually employ specialists who select locations using advanced site-location methods.[29]

THE FUTURE OF RETAILING

Several trends will affect the future of retailing. The slowdown in population and economic growth means that retailers will no longer achieve sales and profit growth through natural expansion in current and new markets. Growth will have to come from increasing their shares of current markets. But increasing competition from new retailers and retailing forms will make it harder for retailers to hold onto or improve their market shares. Consumer demographics, life styles, and shopping patterns are changing rapidly, and retail markets are becoming more fragmented. To be successful, retailers will have to choose target segments carefully and position themselves strongly.

The increasing costs of capital, labor, energy, and merchandise will make more efficient operation and smarter buying essential to successful retailing. New technologies in such areas as computerized checkout and inventory control will increase efficiency and provide new ways to serve consumers better. Finally, increased social and environmental concerns will lead to increased state and federal regulation of retailing. Retailers must run their operations with an eye toward long-run consumer welfare.

Many retailing innovations result from the search for greater productivity, and as solutions to high-cost, high-priced retailing. Such innovations are partially explained by the *wheel of retailing* concept.[30] According to this concept, many new types of retailing institutions begin as low-margin, low-price, low-status operations. They challenge established retailers that have become "fat" over the years by letting their costs and margins increase. The new retailers' success leads them gradually to upgrade their facilities and offer additional services. This increases their costs and forces them to increase their prices. Eventually, the new retailing institutions resemble the conventional retailers they replaced.

The cycle begins again when still newer types of retailing institutions evolve featuring lower costs and prices (see Exhibit 16-2). The wheel of retailing concept seems to explain the initial success and later troubles of department stores, supermarkets, and more recently, discount stores. On the other hand, the concept does not explain the growth of suburban shopping centers and automatic vending, both of which started out as high-margin, high-cost operations.

Marketers are continually seeking new ways to retail their products and services. Here are some interesting examples:

A soft-drink manufacturer opened a chain of soft-drink stores which offered large savings to the take-home market. American Bakeries started Hippopotamus Food Store outlets that feature institutional-sized packages at 10 to 30 percent savings. One large New York bank instituted "house-call loans" where it will qualify a customer over the phone and deliver the money in person. Adelphi University in Garden City, New York, developed a "commuter-train classroom"—executives who commute daily between Long Island and Manhattan can earn MBAs by sitting in on fifty-minute classes held in specially reserved cars on the commuter train.

EXHIBIT 16-2

THE WHEEL OF RETAILING TURNS AT K MART

Over the past two decades, K mart has been the model for discount department stores and has held unswervingly to the principles of discount merchandising. But like many other discount retailers, K mart is now moving away from the formula that made it the No. 2 retailer in the country (with 1983 sales of $18.6 billion vs. Sears $35.9 billion). Over the next several years, K mart will trade up and away from its no-frills, low-price strategy toward an upscale philosophy emphasizing quality and value rather than low prices. With this new strategy, K mart hopes to get more business from the increasing numbers of more affluent consumers, consumers who currently shop at K mart only to "cherry-pick" sales items.

To establish the new image, K mart is making gradual but sweeping changes in its merchandise assortment and store facilities. Its broadened and upgraded product assortment will include more well-known national brands and higher-quality store brands. More store space will be devoted to fashions, sporting goods, electronics, and other higher-margin goods. K mart advertising will feature fewer sales, more branded products, and more "lifestyle" appeals.

K mart is spending a whopping $450 million to modernize and upgrade its more than 2,000 stores. The plain fixtures and long rows of pipe racks are being replaced, and store space is being modularized into special departments—a Kitchen Korner, home electronics center, nutrition center, hardcover books section, and others—to provide a more pleasing shopping environment for more discriminating shoppers.

Thus, the wheel of retailing turns at K mart. The new, upgraded K mart stores will more closely resemble Sears' or Penney's stores than discount stores. And the new strategy could be risky—while K mart attempts to woo more upscale consumers, other discounters will emerge and try to lure away the core of price-conscious, lower-scale consumers that made K mart so successful in the first place.

But K mart understands the wheel of retailing, and is taking steps to assure that it won't be displaced at the bottom of the retailing ladder. At the same time that it is upgrading its K mart stores, the company is also moving into "off-price" and other new forms of discount retailing to pick up the low-end business that might be lost under the new upscale strategy. In recent years, K mart has developed or acquired a number of discount specialty chains—Designer Depot (designer label clothing at large discounts), Garment Rack (lower-quality clothing), Accent (quality gifts and housewares at discount prices), Bishop Buffets and Furr's Cafeterias (inexpensive food), and other businesses that combine for $600 million in annual sales outside the K mart stores. And the company is considering additional discount operations in such areas as toys, sporting goods, hardware, jewelry, books, and drugs. Rather than falling victim to the wheel of retailing, K mart appears to be using it to advantage.

Sources: "K Mart's Plan to be Born Again, Again," *Fortune,* September 21, 1981, pp. 74–85; Jesse Snyder, "K Mart Moves to Sell 'Store of the '90s' Idea," *Advertising Age,* March 12, 1984, pp. 52–53; "K Mart: The No. 2 Retailer Starts to Make an Up-Scale Move—At Last," *Business Week,* June 4, 1984, pp. 50–51.

New retail forms will continue to emerge to meet new consumer needs and new situations.[31] But the life cycle of new retail forms is getting shorter. Table 16-4 shows the life cycles of some major retailing institutions. Department stores took about 100 years to reach the mature stage of the life cycle; more recent forms reach maturity in about 10 years. Retailers can no longer sit back with a successful formula. To remain successful, they must continually adapt to new retailing environments.

TABLE 16-4
Life Cycles of Retail Institutions

RETAIL INSTITUTION	EARLY GROWTH	MATURITY	APPROXIMATE TIME TO REACH MATURITY
Department stores	Mid-1860s	Mid-1960s	100 years
Variety stores	Early 1900s	Early 1960s	60 years
Supermarkets	Mid-1930s	Mid-1960s	30 years
Discount department stores	Mid-1950s	Mid-1970s	20 years
Fast-food service outlets	Early 1960s	Mid-1970s	15 years
Home improvement centers	Mid-1960s	Late 1970s	15 years
Furniture warehouse showrooms	Late 1960s	Late 1970s	10 years
Catalog showrooms	Late 1960s	Late 1970s	10 years

Source: Bert C. McCammon, Jr., "The Future of Catalog Showrooms: Growth and Its Challenges to Management" (Marketing Science Institute working paper, 1973), p. 3.

WHOLESALING

Wholesaling includes *all activities involved in selling goods and services to those buying for resale or business use.* A retail bakery engages in wholesaling when it sells pastry to the local hotel. But we will call *wholesalers* firms engaged *primarily* in wholesaling activity.

Wholesalers differ from retailers in several ways. First, because they deal mostly with business customers rather than final consumers, wholesalers pay less attention to promotion, atmosphere, and location. Second, wholesalers usually cover larger trade areas and have larger transactions than retailers. Third, wholesalers are subject to different legal regulations and taxes.

Wholesalers buy primarily from manufacturers and sell mostly to retailers, industrial consumers, and other wholesalers. But why are wholesalers used at all? For example, why would a manufacturer use wholesalers rather than selling directly to retailers or consumers? The answer is that wholesalers are often more efficient in performing one or more of the following channel functions:

1. *Selling and promoting.* Wholesalers provide salesforces enabling manufacturers to reach many small customers at a relatively low cost. The wholesaler has more contacts and is often more trusted by the buyer than the distant manufacturer.

2. *Buying and assortment building.* Wholesalers can select items and build assortments needed by their customers, thus saving the consumers considerable work.

3. *Bulk-breaking.* Wholesalers achieve savings for their customers by buying in carload lots and breaking bulk.

4. *Warehousing.* Wholesalers hold inventories, thereby reducing the inventory costs and risks to suppliers and customers.

5. *Transportation.* Wholesalers provide quicker delivery to buyers because they are closer.

6. *Financing.* Wholesalers finance their customers by granting credit, and they finance their suppliers by ordering early and paying bills on time.

7. *Risk bearing.* Wholesalers absorb risk by taking title and bearing the cost of theft, damage, spoilage, and obsolescence.

8. *Market information.* Wholesalers supply information to suppliers and customers about competitors' activities, new products, and price developments.

9. *Management services and counseling.* Wholesalers often help retailers improve their operations by training their salesclerks, helping with store layouts and displays, and setting up accounting and inventory control systems.

A number of major economic developments have contributed to wholesaling's growth over the years. They include (1) the growth of mass production in large factories located far from major buyers; (2) the growth of production in advance of orders rather than in response to specific orders; (3) an increase in the number of levels of intermediate producers and users; and (4) the increasing need for adapting products to the needs of intermediate and final users in terms of quantities, packages, and forms.[32]

TYPES OF WHOLESALERS

Wholesalers fall into four major groups (see Table 16-5): merchant wholesalers, brokers and agents, manufacturers' sales branches and offices, and miscellaneous wholesalers. We will now examine each of these groups of wholesalers.

TABLE 16-5 *Classification of Wholesalers*

MERCHANT WHOLESALERS	BROKERS AND AGENTS	MANUFACTURERS' AND RETAILERS' BRANCHES AND OFFICES	MISCELLANEOUS WHOLESALERS
Full-service wholesalers	Brokers	Sales branches and offices	Agricultural assemblers
Wholesale merchants	Agents	Purchasing offices	Petroleum bulk plants and terminals
Industrial distributors			Auction companies
Limited-service wholesalers			
Cash-and-carry wholesalers			
Truck wholesalers			
Drop shippers			
Rack jobbers			
Producers' cooperatives			
Mail order wholesalers			

Merchant Wholesalers

Merchant wholesalers are independently owned businesses that take title to the merchandise they handle. In different trades they may be called jobbers, distributors, or mill supply houses. They are the largest single group of wholesalers, accounting for roughly 50 percent of all wholesaling. Merchant wholesalers can be subclassified into two broad types: full-service wholesalers and limited-service wholesalers.

Full-Service Wholesalers

Full-service wholesalers provide a full set of services such as carrying stock, using a salesforce, offering credit, making deliveries, and providing management assistance. They include two types: wholesale merchants and industrial distributors.

WHOLESALE MERCHANTS. Wholesale merchants sell primarily to retailers and provide a full range of services. They vary mainly in the width of their product line. *General merchandise wholesalers* carry several merchandise lines to meet the needs of both general merchandise retailers and single-line retailers. *General-line wholesalers* carry one or two lines of merchandise in a greater depth of assortment. Major examples are hardware wholesalers, drug wholesalers, and clothing wholesalers. *Specialty wholesalers* carry only part of a line in great depth. Examples are health food wholesalers, seafood wholesalers, and automotive parts wholesalers. They offer customers the advantage of deeper choice and greater product knowledge.

INDUSTRIAL DISTRIBUTORS. Industrial distributors are merchant wholesalers who sell to manufacturers rather than to retailers. They provide such services as carrying stock, offering credit, and providing delivery. They may carry a broad range of merchandise (often called a mill supply house), a general line, or a specialty line. Industrial distributors may concentrate on such lines as MRO items (maintenance, repair, and operating supplies), OEM items (original equipment supplies such as ball bearings, motors), or equipment (such as hand and power tools, and fork trucks).

Limited-Service Wholesalers

Limited-service wholesalers offer fewer services to their suppliers and customers. There are several types of limited-service wholesalers.

CASH-AND-CARRY WHOLESALERS. Cash-and-carry wholesalers have a limited line of fast-moving goods, sell to small retailers for cash, and normally do not deliver. A small fish store retailer, for example, normally drives at dawn to a cash-and-carry fish wholesaler and buys several crates of fish, pays on the spot, and drives the merchandise back to the store and unloads it.

TRUCK WHOLESALERS. Truck wholesalers (also called truck jobbers) perform a selling and delivery function primarily. They carry a limited line of semiperishable merchandise (such as milk, bread, snack foods), which they sell for cash as they make their rounds of supermarkets, small groceries, hospitals, restaurants, factory cafeterias, and hotels.

DROP SHIPPERS. Drop shippers operate in bulk industries such as coal, lumber, and heavy equipment. They do not carry inventory or handle the product. Once an order is received, they find a manufacturer who ships the merchandise directly to the customer on the agreed terms and time of delivery. The drop shipper assumes title and risk from the time the order is accepted to the time it is delivered to the customer. Because drop shippers do not carry inventory, their costs are lower and they can pass on some savings to customers.

RACK JOBBERS. Rack jobbers serve grocery and drug retailers, mostly in the area of nonfood items. These retailers do not want to order and maintain displays of hun-

A typical Fleming Companies, Inc. wholesale food distribution center. The average Fleming warehouse contains 500,000 square feet of floor space (with 30-foot high ceilings), carries 16,000 different food items, and serves 150 to 200 retailers within a 500-mile radius. *Courtesy of Fleming Companies, Inc. Oklahoma City, OK.*

dreds of nonfood items. The rack jobbers send delivery trucks to stores, and the delivery person sets up racks of toys, paperbacks, hardware items, health and beauty aids, or other items. They price the goods, keep them fresh, set up point-of-purchase displays, and keep inventory records. Rack jobbers sell on consignment, which means that they retain title to the goods and bill the retailers only for the goods sold to consumers. Thus they provide such services as delivery, shelving, inventory carrying, and financing. They do little promotion because they carry many branded items that are highly advertised.

PRODUCERS' COOPERATIVES. Producers' cooperatives, owned by farmer-members, assemble farm produce to sell in local markets. Their profits are distributed to members at the end of the year. They often attempt to improve product quality and promote a co-op brand name, such as Sun Maid raisins, Sunkist oranges, or Diamond walnuts.

MAIL-ORDER WHOLESALERS. Mail-order wholesalers send catalogs to retail, industrial, and institutional customers featuring jewelry, cosmetics, specialty foods, and other small items. Their main customers are businesses in small outlying areas. No salesforce is maintained to call on customers. The orders are filled and sent by mail, truck, or other efficient means of transportation.

Brokers and Agents Brokers and agents differ from merchant wholesalers in two ways: They do not take title to goods, and they perform only a few functions. Their main function is to facilitate buying and selling, and for this they earn a commission ranging from 2 to 6 percent of the selling price. Like merchant wholesalers, they generally specialize by product line or customer types. They account for 10 percent of the total wholesale volume.

Brokers

The chief function of a broker is to bring buyers and sellers together, and assist in negotiation. Brokers are paid by the party that hired them. They do not carry inventory, get involved in financing, or assume risk. The most familiar examples are food brokers, real estate brokers, insurance brokers, and security brokers.

Agents

Agents represent either buyers or sellers on a more permanent basis. There are several types.

Manufacturers' agents (also called manufacturers' representatives) are more numerous than the other types of agent wholesalers. They represent two or more manufacturers of complementary lines. They enter into a formal written agreement with each manufacturer covering pricing policy, territories, order-handling procedures, delivery service and warranties, and commission rates. They know each manufacturer's product line and use their wide contacts to sell the manufacturer's products. Manufacturers' agents are used in such lines as apparel, furniture, and electrical goods. Most manufacturers' agents are small businesses, with only a few employees who are skilled salespeople. They are hired by small manufacturers who cannot afford to maintain their own field salesforces and by large manufacturers who want to use agents to open new territories or to represent them in territories that cannot support a full-time salesperson.

Selling agents are given contractual authority to sell a manufacturer's entire output. The manufacturer either is not interested in the selling function or feels unqualified. The selling agent serves as a sales department and has significant influence over prices, terms, and conditions of sale. The selling agent normally has no territorial limits. Selling agents are found in such product areas as textiles, industrial machinery and equipment, coal and coke, chemicals, and metals.

Purchasing agents generally have a long-term relationship with buyers and make purchases for them, often receiving, inspecting, warehousing, and shipping the merchandise to the buyers. One type consists of *resident buyers* in major apparel markets, who look for suitable lines of apparel that can be carried by small retailers located in small cities. They are knowledgeable and provide helpful market information to clients as well as obtaining the best goods and prices available.

Commission merchants (or houses) are agents that take physical possession of products and negotiate sales. They are not normally employed on a long-term basis. They are used most often in agricultural marketing by farmers who do not want to sell their own output and do not belong to producers' cooperatives. A commission merchant would take a truckload of commodities to a central market, sell it for the best price, deduct a commission and expenses, and pay the balance to the producer.

Manufacturers' and Retailers' Branches and Offices The third major type of wholesaling consists of wholesaling operations conducted by sellers or buyers themselves, rather than through independent wholesalers. There are two types.

Sales Branches and Offices

Manufacturers often set up their own sales branches and offices to improve inventory control, selling, and promotion. *Sales branches* carry inventory and are found in such industries as lumber and automotive equipment and parts. *Sales offices* do not carry inventory and are most often found in dry goods and notion industries. Sales branches and offices account for about 11 percent of all wholesale establishments and 36 percent of all wholesale volume.

Purchasing Offices

Many retailers set up purchasing offices in major market centers such as New York and Chicago. These purchasing offices perform a role similar to that of brokers or agents, but are part of the buyer's organization.

Miscellaneous Wholesalers A few specialized types of wholesalers have evolved to meet special needs in certain sectors of the economy. For example, *agricultural assemblers* gather farm products from farmers and build them into larger lots for shipment to food processors, bakers, and government buying agencies. *Petroleum bulk plants and terminals* sell and deliver petroleum products to filling stations. *Auction companies* are important in such industries as tobacco and livestock, where buyers want to inspect goods prior to purchase. Such specialized wholesalers are very important in certain industries, but they account for only a small proportion of total wholesale volume.

WHOLESALER MARKETING DECISIONS

Wholesalers also make decisions about target markets, product assortments and services, pricing, promotion, and place.

Target Market Decision Wholesalers, like retailers, need to define their target market and not try to serve everyone. They can choose a target group of customers according to size criteria (only large retailers), type of customer (convenience food stores only), need for service (customers who need credit), or other criteria. Within the target group, they can identify the more profitable customers and design stronger offers and build better relationships with them. They can propose automatic reordering systems, set up management training and advisory systems, and even sponsor a voluntary chain. They can discourage less profitable customers by requiring larger orders or adding surcharges to smaller ones.

Product Assortment and Services Decision The wholesalers' "product" is their assortment. Wholesalers are under great pressure to carry a full line and maintain sufficient stock for immediate delivery. But this can damage profits. Wholesalers today are reexamining how many lines to carry and are choosing to carry only the more profitable ones. They are grouping their items on an ABC basis, with A standing for the most profitable items and C for the least profitable. Inventory-carrying levels are varied for the three groups.

Wholesalers are also reexamining which services count most in building strong customer relationships and which should be dropped or charged for. The key is to find a distinct mix of services valued by their target customers.

Pricing Decision Wholesalers usually mark up the cost of goods by a standard percentage, say 20 percent to cover their expenses. Expenses may run 17 percent of the gross margin, leaving a profit margin of approximately 3 percent. In grocery wholesaling the average profit margin is often less than 2 percent. Wholesalers are beginning to experiment with new approaches to pricing. They may cut their margin on some lines in order to win important new customers. They will ask suppliers for a special price break when they can turn it into an opportunity to increase the supplier's sales.

Promotion Decision Most wholesalers are not promotion-minded. Their use of trade advertising, sales promotion, publicity, and personal selling is largely haphazard. Many are behind the times in personal selling—they still see selling as a single salesperson talking to a single customer instead of a team effort to sell, build, and service major accounts. As for nonpersonal promotion, wholesalers would benefit from adopting some of the image-making techniques used by retailers. They need to develop an overall promotional strategy and to make greater use of supplier promotion materials and programs.

Place Decision Wholesalers typically locate in low-rent, low-tax areas and put little money into their physical setting and offices. Often the materials-handling and order-processing systems lag behind the available technologies. To meet rising costs, progressive wholesalers have been making time and motion studies of materials-handling procedures. The ultimate development is the automated warehouse where orders are fed into a computer. The items are picked up by mechanical devices and automatically conveyed to the shipping platform, where they are assembled. This type of mechanization is progressing rapidly, and so is the mechanization of many office activities. Many wholesalers are turning to computers and word-processing machines to carry out accounting, billing, inventory control, and forecasting.

THE FUTURE OF WHOLESALING

Changes in wholesaling have been less dramatic than in retailing, but no less important. In the nineteenth century, wholesalers held the dominant position in marketing channels. Most manufacturers were small and depended on major wholesalers to distribute their products to the many small retailers who dotted the land. Wholesaler power began to diminish in the twentieth century as manufacturers grew larger and giant retailing chains and franchise systems emerged. Large manufacturers sought ways to sell direct to the major retailers, and the major retailers sought ways to buy direct from the manufacturers.

The opportunity to go direct, even though not used most of the time, increased manufacturer and retailer power and forced wholesalers to become more efficient. Wholesalers declined in relative importance in the 1930s and 1940s and did not regain their position until the mid-1950s. Wholesale sales volume has continued to grow, but in relative terms wholesalers have just about held their own.

Manufacturers always have the option of bypassing wholesalers, or replacing an inefficient wholesaler with a more dynamic one. Manufacturers' major complaints against wholesalers are as follows: (1) They do not aggressively promote the manufacturer's product line, acting more like order takers; (2) they do not carry enough inventory and fail to fill customers' orders fast enough; (3) they do not supply the manufacturer with up-to-date market and competitive information; (4) they do not attract high-caliber managers and bring down their own costs; and (5) they charge too much for their services.

These complaints are justified in many cases. Wholesalers must adapt to a rapidly changing environment. According to Lopata:

> Technological advances, product line proliferation, changing retail structures, and social adjustments are only a few of the real problems that complicate the wholesaler's life. Each improved product passing through the wholesale level generates a new demand for investments in warehouse space, market analysis, and sales training, and for myriad adjustments in the wholesaler's information systems. Each major retailing shift designed to satisfy customer needs obliges him to adjust his selling patterns, to review his customer service levels, to study product assortments, and to revise his strategies.[33]

Progressive wholesalers are those who are willing to change their ways to meet the challenges of chain organizations, discount houses, and rising labor costs. They are adapting their services to the needs of target customers and finding cost-reducing methods of transacting business.

■ Summary

Retailing and wholesaling consist of many organizations doing the work of bringing goods and services from the point of production to the point of use.

Retailing includes all the activities involved in selling goods or services directly to final consumers for their personal, nonbusiness use. Retailing is one of the major industries in the United States. Retailers can be classified in several ways: by the amount of service they provide (self-service, self-selection, limited service, or full service); product line sold (specialty stores, department stores, supermarkets, convenience stores, combination stores, superstores, hypermarches, and service businesses); relative price emphasis (discount stores, warehouse stores, and catalog showrooms); nature of the business premises (mail and telephone order retailing, automatic vending, buying services, and door-to-door retailing); control of outlets (corporate chains, voluntary chains and retailer cooperatives, consumer cooperatives, franchise organizations, and merchandising conglomerates); and type of store cluster (central business districts, regional shopping centers, community shopping centers, and neighborhood shopping centers). Retailers make decisions on their target market, product assortment and services, pricing, promotion, and place. Retailers need to find ways to improve their professional management and increase their productivity.

Wholesaling includes all the activities involved in selling goods or services to those who are buying for the purpose of resale or for business use. Wholesalers help manufacturers deliver their products efficiently to the many retailers and industrial users across the nation. Wholesalers perform many functions, including selling and promoting, buying and assortment building, bulk-breaking, warehousing, transporting, financing, risk bearing, supplying market information, and providing management services and counseling. Wholesalers fall into four groups. Merchant wholesalers take possession of the goods. They can be subclassified as full-service wholesalers (wholesale merchants, industrial distributors) and limited-service wholesalers (cash-and-carry wholesalers, truck wholesalers, drop shippers, rack jobbers, producers' cooperatives, and mail order wholesalers). Agents and brokers do not take possession of the goods but are paid a commission for facilitating buying and selling. Manufacturers' and retailers' branches and offices are wholesaling operations conducted by nonwholesalers to bypass the wholesalers. Miscellaneous wholesalers include agricultural assemblers, petroleum bulk plants and terminals, and auction companies. Wholesaling is holding its own in the economy. Progressive wholesalers are adapting their services to the needs of target customers and are seeking cost-reducing methods of transacting business.

■ Questions for Discussion

1. In two of its San Diego outlets, Montgomery Ward opened "Law Store" booths that provide a one-shot consultation for a $10 fee. Customers are ushered to an enclosure like a telephone booth where operators connect them to a central office of lawyers who respond to queries over the telephone. Discuss the retailer marketing decisions for the "Law Store."

2. What is the major difference between *retailers* and *wholesalers?* Explain by using an example of each.

3. Analyze the major differences between a *warehouse store* and a *catalog showroom.* What factors contributed to their growth?

4. Door-to-door selling will decline in the late 1980s. Comment.

5. If friends of yours were planning to open a card shop, which type of store cluster would you recommend that they select? Why?

6. Is there a difference between the approach taken in *retailer marketing decisions* and that taken in *product marketing decisions?* Explain.

7. The major distinction between *merchant wholesalers* and *agents/brokers* is that the former offer more services to the buyer. Comment.

8. Would a small manufacturer of lawn and garden tools seek a manufacturer's agent or a selling agent to handle the merchandise? Why?

9. Why do you think the promotion area of marketing strategy traditionally has been weak for wholesalers?

■ References

1. See "Leading Toward a Green Christmas," *Time,* December 1, 1975, pp. 74–80; RICHARD L. GORDON and STUART EMMRICH, "Bloomingdale's Future in Expanding Its Mystique," *Advertising Age,* October 3, 1983, p. 3ff; and LAUREL BUXBAUM, "Bye Bye, Broadway; Hello, Bloomies," *Advertising Age,* September 5, 1983, pp. M18–M19.

2. For more details, see PHYLLIS BERMAN, "Two Big for Miracles," *Forbes,* June 15, 1977, pp. 26–29.

3. See "The Largest Retailers Ranked by Sales," *Fortune,* June 11, 1984, p. 186.

4. ERNEST SAMHABER, *Merchants Make History* (New York: Harper & Row, 1964), pp. 345–48.

5. The quoted part of the definition is from WALTER J. SALMON, ROBERT D. BUZZELL, STANTON G. CORT, and MICHAEL R. PEARCE, *The Super Store: Strategic Implications for the Seventies* (Cambridge, MA: Marketing Science Institute, 1972), p. 83.

6. See BERT MCCAMMON, "High Performance Marketing Systems" (unpublished paper).

7. See "1982 Grocery Store Sales," *Progressive Grocer,* April 1983, p. 58.

8. SALMON et al., *Super Store,* p. 4.

9. See "Super Warehouses Chomp into the Food Business," *Business Week,* April 16, 1984, p. 72.

10. RONALD R. GIST, *Retailing Concepts and Decisions* (New York: Wiley, 1968), pp. 45–46. This list of elements is slightly modified from Gist's.

11. Standard and Poor's Industry Surveys, *Retailing,* November 16, 1981.

12. See THEODORE J. GAGE, "No Thrills for the No Frills," *Advertising Age,* March 15, 1982, p. M36.

13. See JONATHON N. GOODRICH and JO ANN HOFFMAN, "Warehouse Retailing: The Trend of the Future?" *Business Horizons,* April 1979, pp. 45–50.

14. "Catalog Showroom Hot Retailer," *Chicago Tribune,* December 6, 1978, Sec. 4, p. 12.

15. See "Best Products: Too Much Too Soon at the Nation's No. 1 Catalog Showroom," *Business Week,* July 23, 1984, pp. 136–38.

16. See LEO BOGART, "The Future of Retailing," *Harvard Business Review,* November–December 1973, p. 26; and RICHARD GREEN, "A Boutique in Your Living Room," *Forbes,* May 7, 1984, pp. 86–94.

17. BELDEN MENKUS, "Remote Retailing a Reality by 1985?" *Chain Store Age Executive,* September 1975, p. 42.

18. See GREEN, "A Boutique," p. 90; and WENDY KIMBALL and LEWIS LAZARE, "Sears Book Gets Breezy Look," *Advertising Age,* July 9, 1984, p. 24.

19. See GREEN, "A Boutique," p. 88.

20. For an excellent book on direct mail techniques, see BOB STONE, *Successful Direct Marketing Methods* (2d ed.) (Chicago: Crain Books, 1979).

21. G. R. SCHREIBER, *A Concise History of Vending in the U.S.A.* (Chicago: Vend, 1961), p. 9.

22. See Avon Annual Reports and Dart & Kraft 1983 annual report.

23. See RONALD R. GIST, *Marketing and Society: Text and Cases* (2d ed.) (Hinsdale, IL: Dryden Press, 1974), p. 334.

24. See ROLLIE TILLMAN, "Rise of the Conglomerchant," *Harvard Business Review,* November–December 1971, pp. 44–51.

25. See PHYLLIS BERMAN, "Melville Corp.: Discounting with a Difference," *Forbes,* April 16, 1979, pp. 93–94.

26. This definition is from the Urban Land Institute and can be found in ROGER A. DICKINSON, *Retail Management: A Channels Approach* (Belmont, CA: Wadsworth, 1974), p. 9.

27. For more discussion, see PHILLIP KOTLER, "Atmospherics as a Marketing Tool," *Journal of Retailing,* Winter 1973–74, pp. 48–64.

28. HAROLD HAYDON, "Galleries: A Little Push Is Better Than Too Much or No Promotion at All," *Chicago Sun-Times,* October 30, 1970, p. 55.

29. For more on retail site location, see LEWIS A. SPAULDING, "Beating the Bushes for New Store Locations," *Stores,* October 1980, pp. 30–35; and "How to Use Foresight in Site Selection," *Discount Store News,* November 5, 1979.

30. MALCOLM P. MCNAIR, "Significant Trends and Developments in the Postwar Period," in *Competitive Distribution in a Free, High-Level Economy and Its Implications for the University,* A. B. Smith, ed. (Pittsburgh: University of Pittsburgh Press, 1958), pp. 1–25. Also see the critical discussion by STANLEY C. HOLLANDER, "The Wheel of Retailing," *Journal of Marketing,* July 1960, pp. 37–42. For other theories of retail change, see RONALD R. GIST, *Retailing Concepts and Decisions* (New York: Wiley, 1968), chap. 4.

31. For additional articles on the future of retailing, see WILLIAM R. DAVIDSON, ALBERT D. BATES, and STEPHEN J. BASS, "The Retail Life Cycle," *Harvard Business Review,* November–December 1976, pp. 89–96; ALBERT D. BATES, "The Troubled Future of Retailing," *Business Horizons,* August 1976, pp. 22–28; and MALCOLM P. MCNAIR and ELEANOR G. MAY, "The Next Revolution of the Retailing Wheel," *Harvard Business Review,* September–October 1978, pp. 81–91.

32. DAVID A. REVZAN, *Wholesaling in Marketing Organization* (New York: Wiley, 1961) pp. 10–11.

33. RICHARD S. LOPATA, "Faster Pace in Wholesaling," *Harvard Business Review,* July–August 1969, p. 131.

CASE 11

GOULD, INC.: FOCUS 800 BAT-TERY

Gould, Inc., a diversified manufacturer of electrical equipment, is launching a major test of an innovative plan for direct consumer sales to help it gain a larger share of the sagging $2.5 billion replacement automobile battery market. Gould invented the maintenance-free battery and makes about one out of seven car batteries made in the United States, but almost all its batteries are sold under private labels, mostly through oil companies and mass merchandisers. The new direct marketing plan will bring the company into competition with some of its own biggest private-label customers, such as J. C. Penney, K mart, and Mobil's Montgomery Ward. The plan is now being tested in the seven-county Chicago area.

The 800 BAT-TERY plan calls for the establishment of a roadside service for stranded motorists by maintaining a fleet of leased "Rover" vans in the Chicago area and equipping them with a stock of fresh batteries. A motorist unable to start his car can dial the 800

BAT-TERY number toll free between 6 A.M. and 10 P.M. seven days a week. If the dispatcher, after a diagnostic dialogue with the caller, believes it is a battery problem, a van is dispatched and will usually arrive within an hour. If roadside tests show a battery is needed, one is sold and installed by the van driver at a price ranging from $49.50 to $69.50. If the battery is not faulty and the car can be started, the charge is $15 payable to the van driver by cash, check, or credit card (credit risk is verified by the dispatcher when the call is first received). If the car cannot be started, there is no charge. The plan is believed to be quite attractive to consumers because it offers greater convenience at no higher cost compared with batteries purchased in traditional outlets.

Most replacement batteries are purchased at a national retail chain (such as Sears, K mart, and Penney's) or through a gasoline station. Gould supplies both types of retailers as well as some vehicle manufacturers, but its batteries are always sold under their brand name rather than the Gould name. Consequently, a dissatisfied retailer can easily switch to another supplier without affecting consumer demand. Since there is overcapacity in the industry, all manufacturers are anxious to supply retailers. This puts the battery manufacturers in a difficult bargaining position, which has resulted in battery sales being more profitable for the retailers than the manufacturers.

Gould could have decided to develop a chain of retail outlets, as has been done by the big tire manufacturers, e.g., Goodyear, Firestone, and General. However, it was unlikely that batteries would draw as well as tires because they are usually purchased on an emergency basis and less frequently. To attract motorists, other merchandise or services would have to be offered. Even then, the stores would have little to distinguish them from competing stores. Moreover, if the capital investment in each store were $200,000 and the interest rate 15 percent per year, the interest charge alone would be $30,000 per year per store. Considering the number of stores necessary to service adequately the seven-county Chicago area (not to mention the entire country!), the retail store option requires a substantial capital investment.

An examination of the experience of Federal Express revealed that a leased van fleet could be operated for much less money and more time and space flexibility than retail stores. In fact, the cost of leasing 24 vans in the Chicago area was estimated to be $7,000 a month (*Business Week,* June 15, 1981, p. 82). There are other costs associated with entering the retail battery market, such as advertising to establish consumer awareness, but these costs would be approximately the same for the van or store plan.

Before establishing this system, Gould undertook consumer research to determine the demand. There are approximately 47 million replacement battery sales per year with the possibility of even more as new-car price increases encourage drivers to keep and maintain their existing cars. Replacement sales can be categorized as *anticipatory* or *distress.* Anticipatory sales are those in which serviceable batteries are replaced because the owner feels that the battery may fail under tough starting conditions. Anticipatory sales are about 20 percent of total replacement sales but are highly seasonal. They represent 50 percent of replacement sales in September. Distress sales make up 80 percent of replacement sales and are also highly seasonal. Automobiles require extra starting power in cold weather and batteries deliver less power as the temperatures drop. Peak demand is experienced on extremely cold mornings.

Gould tested the new approach in Wilkes-Barre, Pa., and raised its market share by five percentage points. That area was used because it could be serviced by one of the company's nearby battery plants. If the Chicago area test is successful, Gould will eventually extend it to 42 markets.

This case was prepared by Professor Richard Yalch, School of Business Administration, University of Washington, Seattle, 98195. Although all the case information was taken from published news stories, the casewriter benefited from a class presentation at Northwestern University by Richard Melrose of Gould, Inc.

What opportunities and threats does the plan face and how should the management deal with them?

CASE 12

FOTOMAT CORPORATION

Fotomat Corporation is principally engaged in the sale of film processing services and photographic merchandise. It was the leader in film processing through the 1970s and early 1980s. In addition to Fox-Stanley, it was the only real "national" chain in the very fragmented photo finishing industry. Fotomat competed very effectively by stressing quality and convenience. Slowed growth of the photo finishing industry, coupled with the influx of "minilabs" into the United States, has put Fotomat in a difficult position. Minilabs match its quality and convenience, but in one hour opposed to Fotomat's one day. Drugstores and other retail outlets further eroded Fotomat's competitive edge by offering similar processing services at cut-rate prices. The low entry and exit costs for minilabs allow many smaller entrepreneurs to enter the business. In light of the above, Fotomat must reassess its competitive position in the marketplace and develop a marketing plan for survival and growth.

Fox-Stanley is Fotomat's top competitor in photo finishing. It markets its services through kiosk-type outlets across the country. Fox has also been hit with troubled times, a major problem being the one-hour minilabs. They have "upstaged" the kiosks. But unlike Fotomat, Fox Photo has begun to adapt. It has closed 340 of its 965 kiosks, while it has added 4 one-hour minilab photo stores per month to its present base of nearly 100.

Fotomat must decide whether it too will develop its own network of minilabs; go into mail order; and/or increase its wholesale business. Moreover, can the kiosks be made more profitable by (1) Offering services and merchandise in addition to photo processing services? (2) Changing some of them into small stores with even more services and merchandise than the kiosks? or (3) Should they be eliminated as a retail concept whose time has passed, at least for this industry? The company is at a critical stage in its life.

When Fotomat was founded in 1968, Kodak had well over 90 percent of the market. How could Fotomat hope to compete with a very large firm that manufactures cameras, film, processing chemicals, and supplies and provides processing, printing, and enlarging services? Richard D. Irwin, Fotomat president, answered this question as follows:

> By building a better mousetrap. The key to this business is that it is a service-oriented industry and you have to offer people convenience. So we locate our kiosks where people can trade with us easily, and on a drive-thru basis. We put our kiosks near high-traffic areas like shopping centers and offer quality service. We do not necessarily try to be lowest priced. (*Commercial and Financial Chronicle,* June 6, 1975)

Kiosks were staffed by part-time "Fotomates," usually housewives or high school students who were paid the minimum wage. The company favored this system, since the labor costs were low and part-time help was difficult to unionize. But here, Fotomat fell victim to rising minimum wage requirements that have recently increased labor costs and cut into profit margins. Prime kiosk locations became scarce, as did part-time labor in urban areas. Competitive price cutting is common, and sales per kiosk have been falling in recent years. All this translates into lower profit margins for Fotomat. Despite this situation, Fotomat continued to open more kiosks at a rapid rate.

In the early years the company found its strength in convenience, reliability, speedy service, and a guarantee. Fotomat offers to replace free of charge any film that does not turn out properly—even if due to customer negligence. The company focused on the "instamatic" photographer, who was not as concerned with picture quality as with speed and convenience in getting back prints or slides.

Contributing to Fotomat's problems was the shift in demand from instamatic cameras and films, which made up approximately 90 percent of its business at the time, to 35mm cameras and film. The shift, which Fotomat missed, was fueled by the new technologies in 35mm cameras that enabled amateur photographers to take better pictures more easily, and at a lower cost. This amateur photography market, which consisted of 18- to 49-year-olds, of which 53 percent were female, was more concerned with quality and bought more prints, enlargements, and accessories than the instamatic users. In addition, the number of polaroid cameras, which use film that does not need processing, is on the rise. Because of these changes, Fotomat lost its niche in the market and had to solve the problem of how to compete in the increasingly competitive photo processing industry.

Fotomat's president, Richard D. Irwin, belatedly recognized that the company had missed the significant shift from the instamatic cameras and films, which he said "made up around 90 percent of the business" in the early 1970s to 35mm film, which represents over 50 percent of the exposures today. Forecasts call for it to rise to 80 to 90 percent by 1990. To correct the damage done by its myopia, in late 1978 Fotomat introduced the Series 35, a merchandising effort to capture the 35mm market by stressing higher-quality processing and larger prints. The program brought an increase in 35mm work and helped to improve the image of Fotomat among serious photographers. By 1985, 35mm exposures represented over 50 percent of Fotomat's total film processing business.

In addition to this program, Fotomat opened specialty camera stores selling camera and photography accessories in hopes of further penetrating this growing market segment.

In the period of 1975 to 1978, the availability of photo finishing services in pharmacies, supermarkets, and discount stores increased greatly. In many locations, these outlets would be very close to the kiosks. During this period, sales per store fell 12 percent and net income declined more than 40 percent. In addition, Fotomat added almost 500 stores per year. In the rush to create more outlets, management did more of the same, rather than make improvements. New kiosks were put up near existing ones, which cannibalized sales.

Fotomat could not maintain its competitive edge due to the increased availability of photo services offered by new retail outlets that offered the same convenience at cut-rate prices. Further complicating the situation was the introduction of one-hour minilabs in the late seventies.

It is difficult to say whether the recession of 1979–1982 had a big impact on the photo finishing industry. Though the recession did reduce consumers' discretionary spending in areas such as photography, people still take pictures, especially for special occasions such as birthdays and parties. Further, picture taking, a hobby that grew at 12 percent during the seventies, is currently growing at less than 5 percent a year.

As of 1983, the photo finishing industry had sales of $3.5 billion. The industry as a whole is very fragmented and is characterized by low profit margins. Seventy-five percent of the outlets use a wholesale processing facility. Only minilabs and mail order operations have their own facilities. As mentioned above, most of these retail outlets contract their processing to wholesale processing plants.

Mail order is also a growing segment of the industry. It is characterized by the lowest prices, low distribution costs, and low profit margins. Processing time is usually 4 to 7 days. This segment has become increasingly fragmented due to low entry and exit barrier costs.

The minilab segment is the fastest-growing segment of the industry. The number of outlets increased from 600 in 1980 to over 3,000 by the end of 1983. Minilabs seem to have sprung up in many high-traffic areas once dominated by kiosks. They have processing capabilities to develop film in one hour for a price approximately 25 percent higher than normal one-day service, yet offer the same quality. This segment is very fragmented, with no clear industry leader or national chain. Eugene Glazer, photo finishing analyst for Dean Witter in New York says: "By lowering the entry level into the business (minilabs), we will reach a saturation point and there will be a shakeout in the industry in the next two to three years."

Retail outlets without a minilab on site require wholesale laboratories to process the film. This enables retail competitors to offer the same service as Fotomat, which they do at cut-rate prices because they are using developing as a "loss leader" to get the consumer into the store, whereas Fotomat's processing is its main source of income.

The relative importance and price levels of retailers of photo processing in a recent year are as follows:

TYPE OF OUTLET	SALES $(Millions)	%	PRICE LEVEL
Drug stores	945	27	Low
Kiosks	490	14	Medium
Specialty camera stores	420	12	High
Mail order	420	12	Lowest
Minilabs	385	11	Very High
Discount stores	350	10	Low
Department stores	350	10	Low
Others, e.g., supermarkets	175	5	Low

Fotomat's major problems with its kiosks in the 1970s caused it to explore the sales of different products and services to supplement sales at the kiosks. These early attempts included pantyhose, key making, shoe repair, and instant printing. They proved to be less than promising, prompting one astute observer to quip: "The only common thread throughout the product line is desperation."

In 1978 it began selling blank videocassette tape and a service that transfers 8-millimeter home movies to videotape cassettes. The transfer business, while profitable, has grown slowly. On the other hand, blank tape sales are growing rapidly and have been profitable. Rental movies were discontinued when they were found to be unprofitable.

Fotomat's annual report for the year ended January 31, 1984, indicates the following:

1. Continued negative earning with some improvement
2. Heavy debt
3. Aggressive cost reduction program
4. Sales of all 45 specialty camera stores
5. Consolidation of retail stores, mostly kiosk type, into 40 profitable markets located near processing plants and resulting in the elimination of 1,182 of the company's 3,779 retail outlets
6. Signed agreements with several large retail establishments to service their photo finishing needs in company plants in 10 locations across the country
7. Acquisition of Portrait World, Inc., a firm that specializes in pictures of schoolchildren and has an excellent reputation with school leaders, students, and parents
8. Launching of two major programs aimed at key customers: a Preferred Customer card and a New Mothers club. Both are ongoing programs and have been well received.
9. New emphasis on videotape transfer service, allowing slides or movies to be reproduced in videotape format in the belief that the booming sales of VCRs should create a large and growing market for this Fotomat service

In late 1984, Fotomat's board of directors approved a plan that would infuse new capital into the company, refinance its debt, and increase to 60 percent the ownership stake of Koneshiroku Photo Industry Company, a Japanese company that makes Konica cameras and other photo products. Koneshiroku already owned 20 percent of Fotomat, bought in 1979.

The videocassette recorder/player business is in a period of rapid growth. With more than 20 percent of U.S homes having VCR equipment, it represents a huge potential market for both programs and equipment. How and where Fotomat should try to take advantage of this great market opportunity is yet to be determined. It may be a limited opportunity, and the company might be better advised to develop a network of one-hour minilabs. Also the company must decide how best to use its ten photo processing plants. Is it better advised to give priority to providing wholesale service to drugstores and other retailers that simply serve as a film drop or target the mail order business? What are your recommendations?

17

Promoting Products: Communication and Promotion Strategy

Apple Computer grew explosively through the late 1970s and early 1980s. But by mid-1983, Apple was a troubled company. The major source of the trouble was IBM, which entered the personal computer market late but soon dominated. By 1983 IBM had captured about a third of all personal computer sales, and its share was growing rapidly. IBM's astounding success triggered an industry "shakeout"—dozens of large and small companies swallowed their losses and abandoned their personal computer lines. Most of the remaining competitors repositioned their machines as "IBM-compatibles" and sought market niches in which they could compete against IBM.

By 1983 Apple's once formidable share of the personal computer market had eroded to less than 20 percent. Its previously steady Apple IIe line was slipping, and its new and larger Lisa and Apple III models had flopped. The days of Apple's glorious growth had passed; the company streamlined operations, retrenched, and set a goal of simply trying to survive the shakeout.

But rather than becoming just another maker of IBM-compatible machines, Apple took a risky gamble. It bet its future on an innovative new product, the Macintosh, which Apple boldly positioned as an alternative to IBM. The Macintosh was an outstanding product—a powerful machine with revolutionary graphics capabilities, yet exceptionally easy to understand and use. Apple knew that consumers who got to know the powerful but friendly little Macintosh would like it. Experienced personal computer users would adopt it as an exciting alternative to IBM. Less experienced home and business users who were still intimidated by personal computers would appreciate

the ease with which they could apply the Macintosh's considerable power.

The folks at Apple knew they had a good thing, but they still had to convince others. Apple's recent product failures and eroding market position made consumers, retailers, financial analysts, the media, and other important publics skeptical about Apple's ability to compete with IBM. The dramatically new Macintosh would need an exceptional promotion program to convince these skeptics—and it got one.

Apple reshaped all its promotion tools to tell consumers about the exciting new Macintosh—its advertising, salesforce, retail network, sales promotions, and publicity. Apple set up a new 65-person national accounts salesforce to win over large corporate customers, and a restructured, 350-person salesforce worked to obtain reseller support (over 80 percent of all personal computers are sold by retailers). An expanded, newly inspired network of over 2,000 retail dealers carried the Macintosh story to millions of consumers. Apple even had the Macintosh speak for itself—the innovative "Test Drive a Macintosh" promotion encouraged customers to borrow a Macintosh from the dealer for 24 hours to test for themselves Apple's claim that Macintosh was the first personal computer anyone can learn to use overnight.

But the heart of Apple's landmark program to tell the Macintosh story was its bold and innovative advertising. Apple kicked off 1984 with $2 million worth of Super Bowl advertising that featured a startling, futuristic "1984" ad. The ad set the tone for Macintosh's bold positioning and for the advertising yet to come. This advertising was credited with selling more than $100 million of Macintoshes within the next ten days.

The Super Bowl ads were reinforced by dramatic 20-page advertising inserts in major newsweeklies and business publications. And for the rest of the year, Apple extolled the virtues of the Macintosh to potential buyers with over $100 million worth of fresh and exciting advertising. As noted in an *Advertising Age* editorial, ". . . while the startling event of the now-classic commercial on last January's Super Bowl telecast is most often cited, Apple's flamboyant use of media and its advertising throughout the year were equally dramatic: Ads with bold, clean, simple illustrations and clear direct text. They stood out from the crowd, the clutter." To cap off the 1984

campaign in style, Apple spent $3 million to purchase *all* the advertising space—about 40 pages—in the special postelection edition of *Newsweek*.

This attention-grabbing campaign won Apple's President and CEO, John Sculley, honors as *Advertising Age's* "Adman of the Year." And Apple did better than simply survive the industry shakeout. In 1984 Apple sold an estimated 383,000 Macintoshes, and total company sales reached $1.5 billion, a 50 percent increase over 1983. Apple still faces an uphill battle as it moves against IBM to hold market share. But for the time being, the company has returned from the brink. Credit goes to innovative product development, a unique positioning strategy, and a bold and imaginative promotion and communication program.[1]

Modern marketing calls for more than developing a good product, pricing it attractively, and making it accessible to target customers. Companies must also communicate with their customers. What is communicated, however, should not be left to chance.

To communicate effectively, companies hire advertising agencies to develop effective ads; sales promotion specialists to design sales incentive programs; and public relations firms to develop the corporate image. They train their salespeople to be friendly and knowledgeable. For most companies the question is not whether to communicate, but how much to spend and in what ways.

A modern company manages a complex marketing communications system (see Figure 17-1). The company communicates with its middlemen, consumers, and various publics. Its middlemen communicate with their consumers and various

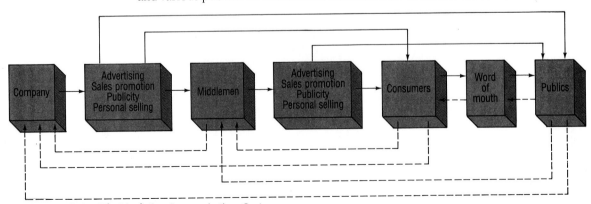

FIGURE 17-1 *The Marketing Communications System*

publics. Consumers engage in word-of-mouth communication with each other and with other publics. Meanwhile each group provides communication feedback to every other group.

The marketing communications mix (also called the promotion mix) consists of four major tools:

Advertising: Any paid form of nonpersonal presentation and promotion of ideas, goods, or services by an identified sponsor

Sales promotion: Short-term incentives to encourage purchase or sales of a product or service

Publicity: Nonpersonal stimulation of demand for a product, service, or business unit by planting commercially significant news about it in a published medium or obtaining favorable presentation of it upon radio, television, or stage that is not paid for by the sponsor

Personal selling: Oral presentation in a conversation with one or more prospective purchasers for the purpose of making sales.[2]

Within each category are specific tools such as sales presentations, point-of-purchase displays, specialty advertising, trade shows, fairs, demonstrations, catalogs, literature, press kits, posters, contests, premiums, coupons, and trading stamps. At the same time, communication goes beyond these specific tools. The product's styling, its price, the package's shape and color, the salesperson's manner and dress all communicate something to buyers. The whole marketing mix, not just the promotional mix, must be orchestrated for maximum communication impact.

This chapter examines two major questions: What are the major steps in developing effective marketing communication? How should the promotion budget and mix be determined? Chapter 18 will focus on mass communication tools—advertising, sales promotion, and publicity. Chapter 19 will focus on the salesforce as a communication and promotion tool.

STEPS IN DEVELOPING EFFECTIVE COMMUNICATION

Marketers need to understand how communication works. Communication involves the nine elements shown in Figure 17-2. Two elements represent the major parties in a communication—*sender* and *receiver.* Another two represent the major communication tools—*message* and *media.* Four represent major communication functions—*encoding, decoding, response,* and *feedback.* The last element represents *noise* in the system. These elements are defined as follows:

- *Sender:* The party sending the message to another party (also called the *source* or *communicator*)
- *Encoding:* The process of putting thought into symbolic form
- *Message:* The set of symbols that the sender transmits

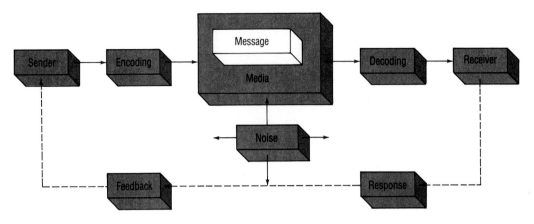

FIGURE 17-2 *Elements in the Communication Process*

- *Media:* The communication channels through which the message moves from sender to receiver
- *Decoding:* The process by which the receiver assigns meaning to the symbols transmitted by the sender
- *Receiver:* The party receiving the message sent by another party (also called the *audience* or *destination*)
- *Response:* The set of reactions the receiver has after being exposed to the message
- *Feedback:* The part of the receiver's response that the receiver communicates back to the sender
- *Noise:* The occurrence of unplanned static or distortion during the communication process resulting in the receiver's receiving a different message than the sender sent

The model underscores the key factors in effective communication. Senders must know what audiences they want to reach and what responses they want. They must be skillful in encoding messages that take into account how the target audience tends to decode messages. They must transmit the message through efficient media that reach the target audience. They must develop feedback channels so that they can know the audience's response to the message.

We will examine the elements in the communication model mainly in terms of the *planning flow* (from target audience back to the communicator). The marketing communicator must make the following decisions: (1) identify the target audience, (2) determine the response sought, (3) choose a message, (4) choose the media, (5) select source attributes, and (6) collect feedback.

Identifying the Target Audience A targeting communicator must start with a clear target audience in mind. The audience may be potential buyers of the company's products, current users, deciders, or influencers. The audience may be individuals, groups, particular publics, or the general public. The target audience will critically influence the communicator's decisions on *what* is to be said, *how* it is to be said, *when* it is to be said, *where* it is to be said, and *who* is to say it.

Determining the Response Sought   Once the target audience has been identified, the marketing communicator must determine what response is sought. The ultimate response, of course, is purchase. But purchase behavior is the result of a long process of consumer decision making. The marketing communicator needs to know where the target audience now stands and to which state it needs to be moved.

The target audience may be in any of the six *buyer readiness states—awareness, knowledge, liking, preference, conviction,* or *purchase.* These states are described in the following paragraphs.

Awareness

The communicator must first know how aware the target audience is of the product or organization. The audience may be unaware of the entity, know only its name, or know one or a few things about it. If most of the target audience is unaware, the communicator's task is to build awareness, perhaps just name recognition. This can be accomplished with simple messages repeating the name. Even then, building awareness takes time.

> Suppose a small Iowa college called Pottsville seeks applicants from Nebraska but has no name recognition in Nebraska. And suppose there are thirty thousand high school seniors in Nebraska who may potentially be interested in Pottsville College. The college might set the objective of making 70 percent of these students aware of Pottsville's name within one year.

Knowledge

The target audience might have company or product awareness, but not know much more. Pottsville may want its target audience to know that it is a private four-year college in eastern Iowa with excellent programs in ornithology and thanatology. Pottsville College needs to learn how many people in the target audience have little, some, and much knowledge about Pottsville. The college may decide to build up product knowledge as its immediate communication objective.

Liking

If the target audience knows the product, how do they feel about it? We can develop a scale covering *dislike very much, dislike somewhat, indifferent, like somewhat, like very much.* If the audience looks unfavorably on Pottsville College, the communicator has to find out why and then develop a communications campaign to build up favorable feeling. If the unfavorable view is rooted in real inadequacies of the college, then a communications campaign will not do the job. The task would require improving the college and then communicating its quality. Good public relations call for "good deeds followed by good words."

Preference

The target audience might like the product, but not prefer it to others. In this case, the communicator will try to build consumer preference. The communicator will tout the product's quality, value, performance, and other attributes. The communicator can check on the campaign's success by remeasuring the audience's preferences after the campaign.

Conviction

A target audience might prefer a particular product but not develop a conviction about buying it. Thus some high school seniors may prefer Pottsville, but may not be sure they want to go to college. The communicator's job is to build conviction that going to college is the right thing to do.

Purchase

Some members of the target audience might have conviction, but not quite get around to making the purchase. They may wait for additional information or plan to act later. The communicator must lead these consumers to take the final step. Among purchase-producing devices are offering the product at a low price, offering a premium, offering an opportunity to try it on a limited basis, or indicating that it will soon be unavailable.

These six states reduce into three stages known as the *cognitive,* (awareness, knowledge), *affective* (liking, preference, conviction), and *behavioral* (purchase). Buyers normally pass through these stages on their way to purchase. The communicator's task is to identify the stage most consumers are in and develop a communication campaign that will move them to the next stage.

Some marketing scholars have challenged the idea that consumers pass through *cognition, affect,* and *behavior,* in that order. Ray has suggested that some consumers pass from *cognition* to *behavior* to *affect.*[3] An example would be a student who hears of Pottsville, enrolls there, and then develops a strong liking. Ray also suggested that some consumers pass from *behavior* to *affect* to *cognition.* A student may sign up for a course blindly, develop a liking, and finally begin to understand the subject. Each assumed sequence of the three stages would lead to a different communications strategy.

Choosing a Message   Having defined the desired audience response, the communicator moves to developing an effective message. Ideally, the message should get *Attention,* hold *Interest,* arouse *Desire,* and obtain *Action* (known as the AIDA model). In practice, few messages take the consumer all the way from awareness through purchase, but the AIDA framework suggests the desirable qualities.

Formulating the message will require solving three problems: what to say (*message content*), how to say it logically (*message structure*), and how to say it symbolically (*message format*).

Message Content

The communicator has to figure out an appeal or theme that will produce the desired response. Three types of appeals can be distinguished. *Rational appeals* relate to the audience's self-interest. They show that the product will produce the claimed benefits. Examples would be messages demonstrating a product's quality, economy, value, or performance.

Emotional appeals attempt to stir up some negative or positive emotion that will motivate purchase. Communicators have worked with fear, guilt, and shame appeals in getting people to do things they should (brushing their teeth, having an annual health checkup) or stop doing things they shouldn't (smoking, overimbibing, drug abuse, overeating). Fear appeals are effective up to a point, but if the audience anticipates too much fear in the message, the audience may avoid it.[4] Communicators also use positive emotional appeals such as love, humor, pride, and joy. Evidence has not established that a humorous message, for example, is necessarily more effective than a straight version of the same message.[5]

Moral appeals are directed to the audience's sense of what is right and proper. They are often used to urge people to support social causes such as a cleaner environment, better race relations, equal rights for women, and aid to the disadvantaged. An example is the March of Dimes appeal: "God made you whole. Give to help those He didn't." Moral appeals are less often used in connection with everyday products.

Message Structure

A message's effectiveness also depends on its structure. The communicator has to decide on three issues. The first is whether to draw a definite conclusion or leave it to the audience. Drawing a conclusion is usually more effective.[6] The second is whether to present a one-sided or two-sided argument. Usually a one-sided argument is more effective in sales presentations, except where the audiences are highly educated and negatively disposed.[7] The third is whether to present the strongest arguments first or last. Presenting them first establishes strong attention, but may lead to an anticlimactic ending.[8]

Message Format

The communicator must develop a strong format for the message. In a print ad, the communicator has to decide on the headline, copy, illustration, and color. To attract attention, advertisers use such devices as *novelty and contrast, arresting pictures and headlines, distinctive formats, message size and position,* and *color, shape, and movement.*[9] If the message is to be carried over the radio, the communicator has to choose words, voice qualities (speech rate, rhythm, pitch, articulation), and vocalizations (pauses, sighs, yawns). The "sound" of an announcer promoting a used automobile has to be different from one promoting a quality bed mattress.

If the message is to be carried on television or in person, then all these elements plus body language (nonverbal clues) have to planned. Presenters have to pay attention to facial expressions, gestures, dress, posture, and hair style. If the message is carried by the product or its packaging, the communicator has to pay attention to texture, scent, color, size, and shape.

> Color plays a major communication role in food preferences. When housewives sampled four cups of coffee that had been placed next to brown, blue, red, and yellow containers (all the coffee was identical, but this was unknown to the housewives), 75 percent felt that the coffee next to the brown container tasted too strong; nearly 85 percent judged the coffee next to the red container to be the

This innovative outdoor ad attracts attention. *Courtesy of Chevrolet Motor Division, General Motors Corporation.*

richest; nearly everyone felt that the coffee next to the blue container was mild and the coffee next to the yellow container was weak.

Choosing Media The communicator must now select efficient channels of communication. Communication channels are of two broad types, personal and nonpersonal.

Personal Communication Channels

In personal communication channels, two or more persons communicate directly with each other. They might communicate face to face, person to audience, over the telephone, or even through the mails on a personal correspondence basis. Personal communication channels are effective because they provide opportunities for personal addressing and feedback.

A further distinction can be drawn between advocate, expert, and social channels of communication. *Advocate channels* consist of company salespeople contacting buyers in the target market. *Expert channels* consist of independent persons with expertise making statements to target buyers. *Social channels* consist of neighbors, friends, family members, and associates talking to target buyers. This last channel, known as *word-of-mouth influence,* is the most persuasive in many product areas.

Personal influence carries great weight in product categories that are expensive or risky. Buyers of automobiles and major appliances go beyond mass-media sources to seek the opinions of knowledgeable people. Personal influence is also influential for products with high social visibility.

Companies can take several steps to stimulate personal influence channels to work on their behalf. They can identify influential individuals and companies and devote extra effort to them. Or they can create opinion leaders by supplying certain people with the product on attractive terms. Companies can work through community influentials such as disc jockeys, class presidents, and presidents of women's organizations; or use influential people in testimonial advertising; or develop advertising that has high "conversation value."[10]

Nonpersonal Communication Channels

Nonpersonal communication channels are media that carry messages without personal contact or feedback. They include mass and selective media, atmospheres, and events. *Mass and selective media* consist of print media (newspapers, magazines, direct mail), electronic media (radio, television), and display media (billboards, signs, posters). Mass media are aimed at large, often undifferentiated, audiences; selective media are aimed at specialized audiences. *Atmospheres* are designed environments that create or reinforce the buyer's leanings toward purchase or consumption of the product. Thus lawyers' offices and banks are designed to communicate confidence and other things that might be valued by the clients.[11] *Events* are designed occurrences to communicate particular messages to target audiences. Public relations departments arrange news conferences or grand openings to achieve specific communication effects on an audience.

Although personal communication is often more effective than mass communication, mass media may be the major way to stimulate personal communication. Mass communications affect personal attitudes and behavior through a *two-step-flow-of-communication process.* "Ideas often flow from radio and print to opinion leaders and from these to the less active sections of the population."[12]

This two-step flow has several implications. First, the influence of mass media on public opinion is not as direct, powerful, and automatic as supposed. It is mediated by *opinion leaders,* persons who belong to primary groups and whose opinions are sought in one or more product areas. Opinion leaders are more exposed to mass media than those they influence. They carry messages to people who are less exposed to media, thus extending the influence of the mass media; or they may carry altered or no messages, thus acting as *gatekeepers*.

Second, the hypothesis challenges the notion that people's consumption styles are primarily influenced by a "trickle-down" effect from higher-status classes. Since people primarily interact within their own social class, they pick up their fashion and other ideas from people like themselves who are opinion leaders.

A third implication is that mass communicators would be more efficient by directing their message specifically to opinion leaders, letting them carry the message to others. Thus pharmaceutical firms first try to promote their new drugs to the most influential physicians.

Selecting Source Attributes   The message's impact on the audience is influenced by how the audience perceives the sender. Messages delivered by highly credible sources are more persuasive. Pharmaceutical companies want doctors to testify about their products' benefits because doctors have high credibility. Antidrug crusaders will use ex-drug addicts to warn high school students against drugs because ex-addicts have higher credibility than teachers. Marketers will hire well-known personalities such as newscasters or athletes to deliver their messages.

But what factors underlie source credibility? The three factors most often identified are expertise, trustworthiness, and likability.[13] *Expertise* is the degree to which the communicator appears to possess the necessary authority to back the claim. Doctors, scientists, and professors rank high on expertise in their respective fields. *Trustworthiness* is related to how objective and honest the source is perceived to be. Friends are trusted more than strangers or salespeople. *Likability* describes the source's attractiveness to the audience. Such qualities as candor, humor, and naturalness make a source more likable. The most highly credible source, then, would be a person who scored high on all three dimensions.[14]

Collecting Feedback   After disseminating the message, the communicator must research its effect on the target audience. This involves asking the target audience whether they recognize or recall the message; how many times they saw it; what points they recall; how they felt about the message; and their previous and current attitudes toward the product and company. The communicator would also like to collect behavioral measures of audience response, such as how many people bought the product, liked it, and talked to others about it.

Figure 17-3 provides an example of feedback measurement. Looking at brand A, we find that 80 percent of the total market are aware of brand A, 60 percent of those who are aware have tried it, and only 20 percent of those who have tried it are satisfied. This indicates that the communication program is effective in creating awareness, but that the product fails to meet consumer expectations. On the other hand, only 40 percent of the total market are aware of brand B, only 30 percent of those aware have tried it, but 80 percent of those who have tried it are satisfied. In this case, the communication program needs to be strengthened to take advantage of the brand's satisfaction-generating power.

FIGURE 17-3
*Current Consumer
States for Two Brands*

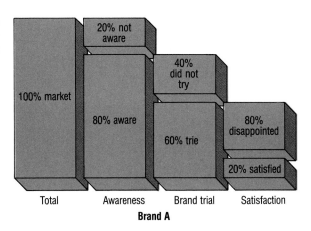

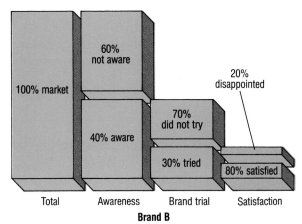

SETTING THE TOTAL PROMOTION BUDGET AND MIX

We have looked at the steps involved in planning and directing communications to a specific target audience. But how does the company decide on (1) the total promotion budget and (2) its division among the major promotional tools? We will examine these questions in that order, although a company can start with either one.

*Establishing the
Total Promotion
Budget*

One of the most difficult marketing decisions facing companies is how much to spend on promotion. John Wanamaker, the department store magnate, said: "I know that half of my advertising is wasted, but I don't know which half. I spent $2 million for advertising, and I don't know if that is half enough or twice too much."

Thus it is not surprising that industries and companies vary considerably in how much they spend on promotion. Promotion spending may amount to 20 to 30 percent of sales in the cosmetics industry and only 5 to 10 percent in the industrial machinery industry. Within a given industry, low- and high-spending companies can be found. Philip Morris is a high spender. When it acquired the Miller Brewing Company, and later the Seven-Up Company, it substantially increased total promotion spending. The additional spending at Miller's helped raise its market share from 4 to 19 percent within a few years.

How do companies decide on their promotion budget? We will describe four common methods used to set the total budget for any component, such as advertising.

Affordable Method

Many companies set the promotion budget at what they think the company can afford. One executive explained this method as follows: "Why it's simple. First, I go upstairs to the controller and ask how much they can afford to give this year. He says a million and a half. Later, the boss comes to me and asks how much we should spend and I say 'Oh, about a million and a half.'"[15]

This method of setting budgets completely ignores the impact of promotion on sales volume. It leads to an uncertain annual promotion budget, which makes long-range market planning difficult.

Percentage-of-Sales Method

Many companies set their promotion expenditures at a specified percentage of current or forecasted sales or of the sales price. A railroad company executive said: "We set our appropriation for each year on December 1 of the preceding year. On that date we add our passenger revenue for the next month, and then take 2% of the total for our advertising appropriation for the new year."[16] Automobile companies typically budget a fixed percentage for promotion based on the planned car price. Oil companies set the appropriation at some fraction of a cent for each gallon of gasoline sold under their label.

A number of advantages are claimed for this method. First, the percentage-of-sales method means that promotion expenditures are likely to vary with what the company can "afford." This satisfies the financial managers who feel that expenses should bear a close relation to the movement of corporate sales over the business cycle. Second, this method encourages management to think in terms of the relationship between promotion cost, selling price, and profit per unit. Third, this method encourages competitive stability to the extent that competing firms spend approximately the same percentage of their sales on promotion.

In spite of these advantages, the percentage-of-sales method has little to justify it. It uses circular reasoning in viewing sales as the cause of promotion rather than as the result. It leads to an appropriation set by the availability of funds rather than by the opportunities. It discourages experimenting with countercyclical promotion or aggressive spending. The promotion budget's dependence on year-to-year sales fluctuations interferes with long-range planning. The method does not provide a logical basis for choosing the specific percentage, except what has been done in the past or what competitors are doing. Finally, it does not encourage building up the promotion budget by determining what each product and territory deserves.

Competitive-Parity Method

Some companies set their promotion budget to match competitors' outlays. This thinking is illustrated by the executive who asked a trade source: "Do you have any figures which other companies in the builders' specialties field have used which would indicate what proportion of gross sales should be given over to advertising?"[17]

Two arguments are advanced for this method. One is the competitors' expenditures represent the collective wisdom of the industry. The other is that maintaining a competitive parity helps prevent promotion wars.

Neither argument is valid. There are no grounds for believing that the competition has a better idea of what a company should be spending on promotion. Company reputations, resources, opportunities, and objectives differ so much that their promotion budgets are hardly a guide. Furthermore, there is no evidence that budgets based on competitive parity discourage promotion wars.

Objective-and-Task Method

The objective-and-task method calls upon marketers to develop their promotion budget by (1) defining their specific objectives, (2) determining the tasks that must be performed to achieve these objectives, and (3) estimating the costs of performing these tasks. The sum of these costs is the proposed promotion budget.

Ule showed how the objective-and-task method could be used to establish an advertising budget for a new cigarette, Sputnik (*name fictitious*).[18] The steps are as follows:

1. *Establish the market-share goal.* The advertiser wants 8 percent of the market. Since there are 50 million cigarette smokers, the company wants to switch 4 million smokers to Sputnik.

2. *Determine the percent of the market that should be reached by Sputnik advertising.* The advertiser hopes to reach 80 percent (40 million smokers) with its advertising.

3. *Determine the percent of aware smokers that should be persuaded to try the brand.* The advertiser would be pleased if 25 percent of aware smokers, or 10 million smokers, tried Sputnik. This is because the advertiser estimates that 40 percent of all triers, or 4 million persons, would become loyal users. This is the market goal.

4. *Determine the number of advertising impressions per 1 percent trial rate.* The advertiser estimates that 40 advertising impressions (exposures) for every 1 percent of the population would bring about a 25 percent trial rate.

5. *Determine the number of gross rating points that would have to be purchased.* A gross rating point is one exposure to 1 percent of the target population. Since the company wants to achieve 40 exposures to 80 percent of the population, it will want to buy 3,200 gross rating points.

6. *Determine the necessary advertising budget on the basis of the average cost of buying a gross rating point.* To expose 1 percent of the target population to one impression costs an average of $3,277. Therefore, 3,200 gross rating points would cost $10,486,400 ($=\$3,277 \times 3,200$) in the introductory year.

This method has the advantage of requiring management to spell out its assumptions about the relationship between dollars spent, exposure levels, trial rates, and regular usage.

The overall answer to how much weight promotion should receive in the total marketing mix (as opposed to product improvement, lower prices, more services, and so on) depends on where the company's products are in their life cycle, whether they are commodities or highly differentiable, whether they are routinely needed or have to be "sold," and other considerations. In theory, the total promotional budget should be established where the marginal profit from the last promotional dollar just equals the marginal profit from the last dollar in the best nonpromotional use. Implementing this principle, however, is not easy.

Establishing the Promotion Mix

Companies within the same industry differ considerably in how they divide their promotional budgets. Avon concentrates its promotional funds on personal selling (its advertising is only 1.5 percent of sales), while Revlon spends heavily on advertising (about 7 percent of sales). In selling vacuum cleaners, Electrolux spends heavily on a door-to-door salesforce, while Hoover relies more on advertising. Thus it is possible to achieve a given sales level with various mixes of advertising, personal selling, sales promotion, and publicity.

Companies are always searching for ways to gain efficiency by substituting one promotional tool for another as its economics become more favorable. Many companies have replaced some field sales activity with telephone sales and direct mail. Other companies have increased their sales promotion expenditures in relation to advertising to gain quicker sales. The substitutability among promotional tools explains why marketing functions need to be coordinated into a single marketing department.

Designing the promotion mix is even more complicated when one tool can be used to promote another. Thus when McDonald's decides to run Million Dollar Sweepstakes in its fast-food outlets (a form of sales promotion), it has to take out newspaper ads to inform the public. When General Mills develops a consumer advertising/sales promotion campaign to back a new cake mix, it has to set aside money to promote this campaign to the resellers to win their support.

Many factors influence the marketer's choice of promotional tools. We will examine these factors in the following paragraphs.

Nature of Each Promotion Tool

Each promotion tool—advertising, personal selling, sales promotion, and publicity—has unique characteristics and costs. Marketers have to understand these characteristics in selecting the tools.

ADVERTISING. Because of the many forms and uses of advertising, it is difficult to make generalizations about its distinctive qualities as a component of the promotion mix. Yet the following qualities can be noted:[19]

- *Public presentation.* Advertising is a highly public mode of communication. Its public nature confers a kind of legitimacy on the product and also suggests a standardized offering. Because many persons receive the same message, buyers know that their motives for purchasing the product will be publicly understood.
- *Pervasiveness.* Advertising is a pervasive medium that permits the seller to repeat a message many times. It also allows the buyer to receive and compare the messages of

various competitors. Large-scale advertising by a seller says something positive about the seller's size, popularity, and success.

■ *Amplified expressiveness.* Advertising provides opportunities for dramatizing the company and its products through the artful use of print, sound, and color. Sometimes the tool's very success at expressiveness may, however, dilute or distract from the message.

■ *Impersonality.* Advertising cannot be as compelling as a company sales representative. The audience does not feel obligated to pay attention or respond. Advertising is only able to carry on a monologue, not a dialogue, with the audience.

On the one hand, advertising can be used to build up a long-term image for a product (such as Coca-Cola ads), and, on the other, to trigger quick sales (as in Sears advertising a weekend sale). Advertising is an efficient way to reach numerous geographically dispersed buyers at a low cost per exposure. Certain forms of advertising, such as TV advertising, can require a large budget; other forms, such as newspaper advertising, can be done on a small budget.

PERSONAL SELLING. Personal selling is the most effective tool at certain stages of the buying process, particularly in building up buyers' preference, conviction, and action. The reason is that personal selling, when compared with advertising, has three distinctive qualities:[20]

■ *Personal confrontation.* Personal selling involves an alive, immediate, and interactive relationship between two or more persons. Each party can observe each other's needs and characteristics at close hand and make immediate adjustments.

■ *Cultivation.* Personal selling permits all kinds of relationships to spring up, ranging from a matter-of-fact selling relationship to a deep personal friendship. The effective sales representative will normally keep the customer's interests at heart if he wants a long-run relationship.

■ *Response.* Personal selling makes the buyer feel under some obligation for having listened to the sales talk. The buyer has a greater need to attend and respond, even if the response is a polite "thank you."

These distinctive qualities come at a cost. Personal selling is the company's most expensive contact tool, costing companies an average of $205 a sales call in 1983.[21] In 1981, American firms spent over $150 billion on personal selling compared with $61 billion on advertising. This money supported over 6.4 million Americans who are engaged in sales work.[22]

SALES PROMOTION. Although sales promotion involves a diverse collection of tools—coupons, contests, premiums, and others—these tools have three distinctive characteristics:

■ *Communication.* They gain attention and usually provide information that may lead the consumer to the product.

■ *Incentive.* They incorporate some concession, inducement, or contribution that gives value to the consumer.

■ *Invitation.* They include a distinct invitation to buy quickly.

Companies use sales promotion tools to create a stronger and quicker response. Sales promotion can be used to dramatize product offers and to boost sagging sales. Sales promotion effects are usually short-lived, however, and are not effective in building long-run brand preference.

PUBLICITY. Publicity's appeal is based on its three distinctive qualities:

- *High credibility.* News stories and features seem more authentic and credible to readers than ads.
- *Off guard.* Publicity can reach many prospects who may avoid salespeople and advertisements. The message gets to the buyers as news rather than as a sales-directed communication.
- *Dramatization.* Like advertising, publicity has a potential for dramatizing a company or product.

Marketers tend to underuse publicity or use it as an afterthought. Yet a well-thought-out publicity campaign coordinated with the other promotion mix elements can be extremely effective and much less costly.

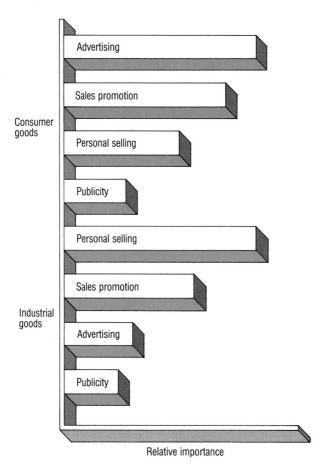

FIGURE 17-4
Relative Importance of Promotion Tools in Consumer versus Industrial Markets

Factors in Setting the Promotion Mix

Companies consider several factors in developing their promotion mixes. These factors are examined below.

TYPE OF PRODUCT/MARKET.   The effectiveness of promotional tools varies between consumer and industrial markets. The differences are shown in Figure 17-4. Consumer goods companies normally devote most of their funds to advertising, followed by sales promotion, personal selling, and, finally, publicity. Industrial goods companies devote most of their funds to personal selling, followed by sales promo-

FIGURE 17-5

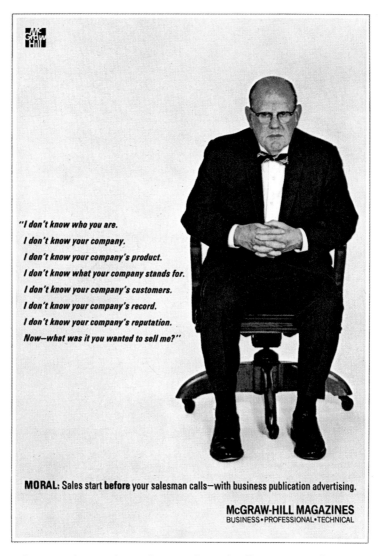

"*I don't know who you are.
I don't know your company.
I don't know your company's product.
I don't know what your company stands for.
I don't know your company's customers.
I don't know your company's record.
I don't know your company's reputation.
Now—what was it you wanted to sell me?*"

MORAL: Sales start **before** your salesman calls—with business publication advertising.

McGRAW-HILL MAGAZINES
BUSINESS•PROFESSIONAL•TECHNICAL

Advertising has a role to play in industrial selling. *Courtesy of McGraw-Hill, Inc.*

tion, advertising, and publicity. In general, personal selling is more heavily used with expensive and risky goods and in markets with fewer and larger sellers (hence, industrial markets).

Although advertising is less important than sales calls in industrial markets, it still plays a significant role. Advertising can build product awareness and comprehension, develop sales leads, offer legitimation, and reassure buyers. Advertising's role in industrial marketing is dramatically conveyed in a McGraw-Hill ad (see Figure 17-5). Advertising could have prevented most of the statements the buyer made in that ad. Morrill showed, in his study of industrial commodity marketing, that advertising combined with personal selling increased sales 23 percent over what they were with no advertising. The total promotional cost as a percent of sales was reduced by 20 percent.[23] Levitt's research also showed the important role that advertising can play in industrial marketing (see Exhibit 17-1).

EXHIBIT 17-1

ROLE OF CORPORATE ADVERTISING IN INDUSTRIAL MARKETING

Theodore Levitt sought to determine the relative contribution of the company's reputation (built mainly by advertising) and the company's sales presentation (personal selling) in producing industrial sales. Purchasing agents were shown filmed sales presentations of a new, but fictitious, technical product for use as an ingredient in making paint. The variables were the quality of the sales presentation and whether the salesperson came from a well-known company, a less-known but creditable company, or an unknown company. Purchasing-agent reactions were collected after seeing the films and again five weeks later. The findings were as follows:

1. A company's reputation improves the chances of getting a favorable first hearing and an early adoption of the product. Therefore, corporate advertising that can build up the company's reputation (other factors also shape its reputation) will help the company's sales representatives.

2. Sales representatives from well-known companies have an edge in getting the sale if their sales presentation is adequate. If a sales representative from a lesser-known company makes a highly effective presentation, this can overcome the disadvantage. Smaller companies should use their limited funds to select and train good representatives, rather than spend these funds on advertising.

3. Company reputations have the most effect where the product is complex, the risk is high, and the purchasing agent is less professionally trained.

Source: Theodore Levitt, *Industrial Purchasing Behavior: A Study in Communication Effects* (Boston: Division of Research, Harvard Business School, 1965). Copyright © 1965 by the President and Fellows of Harvard College; all rights reserved.

Conversely, personal selling can make a strong contribution in consumer goods marketing. It is not simply the case that "salesmen put products on shelves and advertising takes them off." Well-trained consumer goods salespeople can sign

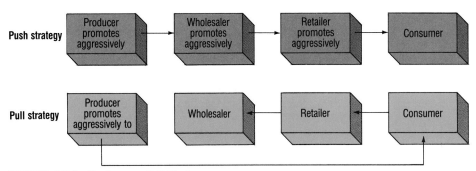

FIGURE 17-6 *Push versus Pull Strategy*

up more dealers to carry the brand, influence them to devote more shelf space to the brand, and encourage them to cooperate in special promotions.

PUSH VERSUS PULL STRATEGY. The promotional mix is heavily influenced by whether the company chooses a push or a pull strategy to create sales. The two strategies are contrasted in Figure 17-6. A **push strategy** calls for using the salesforce and trade promotion to push the product through the channels. The producer aggressively promotes the product to wholesalers, the wholesalers aggressively promote the product to retailers, and the retailers aggressively promote the product to consumers.[24] A **pull strategy** calls for spending a lot of money on advertising and consumer promotion to build up consumer demand. If effective, consumers will ask their retailers for the product, the retailers will ask the wholesalers for the product, and the wholesalers will ask the producers for the product.

Some small industrial goods companies use only push strategies; some direct marketing companies use only pull. Most large companies use some combination of push and pull. For example, Procter & Gamble uses mass-media advertising to pull its products and a large salesforce and trade promotions to push its products through the channels.

BUYER READINESS STAGE. Promotional tools vary in their cost-effectiveness at different stages of buyer readiness. Figure 17-7 shows the relative effectiveness of four promotional tools.[25] Advertising, along with publicity, plays the major role in the awareness stage, more important than that played by "cold calls" from sales representatives. Customer comprehension is primarily influenced by education, with advertising and personal selling playing secondary roles. Customer conviction is primarily influenced by personal selling, followed closely by advertising. Finally, closing the sale is predominantly a function of the sales call. Clearly, personal selling, given its expensiveness, should be focused on the later stages of the customer buying process.

PRODUCT LIFE-CYCLE STAGE. Promotional tools vary in their effectiveness at different stages of the product life cycle. In the introduction stage, advertising and publicity are cost-effective in producing high awareness, and sales promotion is useful in

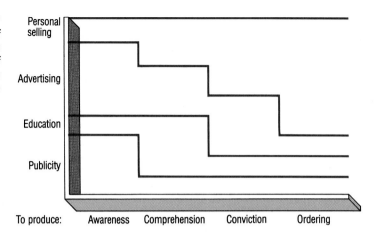

FIGURE 17-7
Relative Effectiveness of Four Promotional Tools at Different Stages of the Customer Buying Process

To produce: Awareness Comprehension Conviction Ordering

promoting early trial. Personal selling is relatively expensive, although it must be used to get the trade to carry the product.

In the growth stage, advertising and publicity continue to be potent, while sales promotion can be reduced because fewer incentives are needed.

In the mature stage, sales promotion resumes its importance relative to advertising. Buyers know the brands and need only a reminder level of advertising.

In the decline stage, advertising is kept at a reminder level, publicity is eliminated, and salespeople give the product only minimal attention. Sales promotion, however, might continue strong.[26]

Responsibility for Marketing Communications Planning Members of the marketing department often have different views on how to split the promotion budget. The sales manager would prefer to hire two extra sales representatives rather than spend $80,000 on one single television commercial. The public relations manager feels that he or she can do wonders with some money transferred from advertising to publicity.

Historically, companies left these decisions to different people. No one was responsible for thinking through the roles of the various promotion tools and coordinating them. Today, companies are moving toward the concept of *integrated marketing communications*. This concept calls for (1) appointing a marketing communications director who has overall responsibility for the company's marketing communications; (2) developing policies on the use of the different promotion tools; (3) keeping track of all promotional expenditures by product, tool, stage of product life cycle, and observed effect; and (4) coordinating the promotional activities when major campaigns take place.

These steps will go a long way in improving the impact of the company's promotional program.

■ Summary

Promotion is one of the four major elements of the company's marketing mix. The main promotional tools—advertising, sales promotion, publicity, and personal selling—have separate and overlapping capabilities, and their effective coordination requires careful definition of communication objectives.

In preparing specific marketing communications, the communicator has to understand the nine elements of any communication process: sender, receiver, encoding, decoding, message, media, response, feedback, and noise. The communicator's first task is to identify the target audience and its characteristics. Next, the communicator has to define the sought response, whether it be awareness, knowledge, liking, preference, conviction, or purchase. Then a message should be constructed containing an effective content, structure, and format. Media must be selected, both for personal communication and nonpersonal communication. The message must be delivered by someone with good source credibility—someone who is an expert, trustworthy, and likable. Finally, the communicator must monitor how much of the market becomes aware, tries the product, and is satisfied in the process.

The company has to decide how much to spend for promotion. The most popular approaches are to spend what the company can afford, use a percentage of sales, base promotion on competitors' expenditures, or base it on an analysis and costing of the communication objectives and tasks.

The company has to split the promotional budget among the major tools. Companies are guided by the characteristics of each promotional tool, the type of product/market, whether the company prefers a push or a pull strategy, the buyer's readiness stage, and the product life-cycle stage. The interactions of the different promotion activities require organizational coordination for maximum impact.

■ Questions for Discussion

1. Apply the four major tools in the marketing communication mix to professional sports teams.

2. What two communication parties are used in marketing communication? Discuss how they relate to McDonald's.

3. How would the six buyer readiness states relate to your last purchase of beer or a soft drink?

4. Which type of message content is used by the following marketers? (a) AT&T, (b) Toyota, (c) American Lung Association, and (d) General Electric.

5. What major types of communication channels can an organization utilize? When should each be used?

6. State whether the following individuals are credible sources for market communication: (a) the President, (b) Neil Armstrong, and (c) Mary Lou Retton. Why?

7. How might a company set its promotional budget? Discuss the advantages of each approach.

8. The type of product being marketed has no relationship to the communication mix employed by the marketer. Comment.

9. Who should have responsibility for marketing communications planning? Why?

■ References

1. Based on material found in BRIAN MORAN and CLEVELAND HORTON, "John Scully: Marketing Methods Bring Back Apple," *Advertising Age,* December 31, 1984, pp. 1+. Also see DEBORAH WISE and CATHERINE HARRIS, "Apple's New Crusade: A Bold Plan to Take on IBM in the Office," *Business Week,* November 26, 1984, pp. 146–54.

2. These definitions, except for *sales promotion,* are from *Marketing Definitions: A Glossary of Marketing Terms* (Chicago: American Marketing Association, 1960). The AMA definition of *sales promotion* covers, in addition to incentives, such marketing media as displays, shows and exhibitions, and demonstrations that can better be classified as forms of advertising, personal selling, or publicity. Some marketing scholars have also suggested adding *packaging* as a fifth element of the promotion mix, although others classify it as a product element.

3. MICHAEL L. RAY, *Marketing Communication and the Hierarchy-of-Effects* (Cambridge, MA: Marketing Science Institute, November 1973). Also see ROBERT E. SMITH and WILLIAM R. SWINYARD, "Information Response Models: An Integrated Approach," *Journal of Marketing,* Winter 1982, pp. 81–93.

4. MICHAEL L. RAY and WILLIAM L. WILKIE, "Fear: The Potential of an Appeal Neglected by Marketing," *Journal of Marketing,* January 1970, pp. 55–56; and BRIAN STERNTHAL and C. SAMUEL CRAIG, "Fear Appeals: Revisited and Revised," *Journal of Consumer Research,* December 1974, pp. 22–34.

5. See BRIAN STERNTHAL and C. SAMUEL CRAIG, "Humor in Advertising," *Journal of Marketing,* October 1973, pp. 12–18.

6. CARL I. HOVLAND and WALLACE MANDELL, "An Experimental Comparison of Conclusion-Drawing by the Communication and by the Audience," *Journal of Abnormal and Social Psychology,* July 1952, pp. 581–88.

7. See C. I. HOVLAND, A. A. LUMSDAINE, and F. D. SHEFFIELD, *Experiments on Mass Communication* (Princeton, NJ: Princeton University Press, 1948), vol. III, chap. 8.

8. For more on message content and structure, see LEON G. SCHIFFMAN and LESLIE LAZAR KANUK, *Consumer Behavior* (2d ed.) (Englewood Cliffs, NJ: Prentice-Hall, 1983), pp. 270–77.

9. For a discussion of these devices, see JAMES F. ENGEL, ROGER D. BLACKWELL, and DAVID T. KOLLAT, *Consumer Behavior* (3rd ed.) (Hinsdale, IL: Dryden Press, 1978), pp. 346–48.

10. These and other points are discussed in THOMAS S. ROBERTSON, *Innovative Behavior and Communication* (New York: Holt, Rinehart & Winston, 1971), chap. 9.

11. See PHILIP KOTLER, "Atmospherics as a Marketing Tool," *Journal of Retailing,* Winter 1973–74, pp. 48–64.

12. P. F. LAZARSFELD, B. BERELSON, and H. GAUDET, *The People's Choice* (2d ed.) (New York: Columbia University Press, 1948), p. 151.

13. HERBERT C. KELMAN and CARL I. HOVLAND, "Reinstatement of the Communication in Delayed Measurement of Opinion Change," *Journal of Abnormal and Social Psychology,* 48 (1953), 327–35.

14. For more on source credibility, see SCHIFFMAN and KANUK, *Consumer Behavior,* pp. 258–67.

15. Quoted in DANIEL SELIGMAN, "How Much for Advertising?" *Fortune,* December 1956, p. 123.

16. ALBERT WESLEY FREY, *How Many Dollars for Advertising?* (New York: Ronald Press, 1955), p. 65.

17. Ibid., p. 49.

18. G. MAXWELL ULE, "A Media Plan for 'Sputnik' Cigarettes," *How to Plan Media Strategy* (American Association of Advertising Agencies, 1957 Regional Convention), pp.41–52.

19. See SIDNEY J. LEVY, *Promotional Behavior* (Glenview, IL: Scott, Foresman, 1971), chap. 4.

20. Ibid.

21. See "Average Cost Shatters $200 Mark for Industrial Sales Call, But Moderation Seen in 1984 Hikes," *Marketing News,* August 17, 1984, p. 16.

22. *Sales and Marketing Management,* February 21, 1983, p. 36.

23. *How Advertising Works in Today's Marketplace: The Morrill Study* (New York: McGraw-Hill, 1971), p. 4.

24. For more on push strategies, see MICHAEL LEVY, JOHN WEBSTER, and ROGER KERIN, "Formulating Push Marketing Strategies: A Method and Application," *Journal of Marketing,* Winter 1983, pp. 25–34.

25. "What IBM Found about Ways to Influence Selling," *Business Week,* December 5, 1959, pp. 69–70. Also see HAROLD C. CASH and WILLIAM J. CRISSY, "Comparison of Advertising and Selling," in *The Psychology of Selling* (Flushing, NY: Personal Development Associates, 1965), vol. 12.

26. For more on advertising and the product life cycle, see JOHN E. SWAN and DAVID R. RINK, "Fitting Market Strategy to Product Life Cycles," *Business Horizons,* January–February 1982, pp. 60–67.

18

Promoting Products: Advertising, Sales Promotion, and Publicity

PepsiCo is a large and diversified company, with sales of more than $8 billion. Its divisions and brands are household words to consumers— Pepsi-Cola (Pepsi, Diet Pepsi, Pepsi-Free, Mountain Dew, Teem); Frito-Lay (Lays, O'Grady's, Ruffles, Fritos, Cheetos, Doritos, Grandma's cookies); Pizza Hut and Taco Bell restaurants; Wilson Sporting Goods. All are among the market leaders in their categories.

PepsiCo has developed an extensive array of mass-promotion tools to communicate with its many publics. Hundreds of PepsiCo employees in numerous advertising, sales promotion, publicity, and public relations units scattered throughout the company work with more than a dozen large advertising agencies and other firms to develop communications targeted toward consumers, bottlers and retailers, stockholders, the financial community, employees, and the general public.

PepsiCo uses massive doses of advertising to build and maintain market share for its brands. In 1983, PepsiCo spent more than $472 million worldwide on advertising and promotion, making it the country's twelfth largest advertiser. Pepsi's soft-drink products held a 1983 market share of 26 percent (behind Coca-Cola's 35 percent)—the advertising bill for these products was more than $65 million. In 1984, PepsiCo was expected to spend more than $40 million on its Pepsi brand alone. In 1983, the company gave Pizza Hut $47 million in advertising support and chipped in another $19 million for Taco Bell. Other products are supported by amounts ranging from a few to many millions of dollars.

But PepsiCo uses more than just advertising to communicate with consumers and other publics. Over a third of its 1983 advertising expenditures—

some $133 million—went to "unmeasured media," such things as coupons, premiums, contests and sweepstakes, special events, trade shows, and other sales promotions. For several years Pepsi has conducted the "Pepsi Challenge," a taste preference promotion urging consumers to compare Pepsi's taste to Coke's. Consumers are continually coaxed with PepsiCo coupons and premiums; retailers are enticed with allowances and displays. New products and ad campaigns are introduced to bottlers and the press during extravagantly staged events.

In 1984, Pepsi used a combination of advertising, sales promotion, and publicity to help establish its new "Pepsi—The choice of a new generation" campaign, a campaign designed to replace the aging "Pepsi generation" with a new and younger generation of Pepsi consumers. The new campaign departed dramatically from Pepsi's traditional low-keyed, nostalgic "slice of life" advertising approach. It employed hype and humor, and created a light-hearted excitement Pepsi believed would attract and appeal to the younger generation. Pepsi signed Lionel Richie (for a reported $8 million) and the Jackson Brothers (for a reported $10 million) as spokespersons for the new promotional thrust. To start the campaign, the company created seven new commercials, including two 60-second Jackson commercials that cost Pepsi $2 million to produce. Michael Jackson and his brothers were also used in a variety of sales promotion events, including a Pepsi-sponsored "Victory Tour" of concerts across the United States.

Pepsi took advantage of the excitement surrounding the Jackson campaign through a concentrated publicity effort. It held press conferences and issued press releases on the signing of the Jacksons, details of the ads and concert tour, and related activities. It prescreened the ads to bottlers and the press. The campaign became a media event—it was discussed in countless newspaper and magazine articles and television features. MTV: Music Television, despite its policy against product identifications, ran a special program providing first-ever showings of the Jackson commercials and an interview with the commercials' director. The commercials helped improve the ratings of CBS's Grammy Awards show, the first program to carry the ads. Thus Pepsi's skillful blending of all the mass promotion got the company's "new generation" campaign off to a fast start.

In addition to direct forms of advertising and sales promotion communication, PepsiCo communicates corporate responsibility through several public relations activities. It joined with Boys Club of America to establish the SuperFit All-Stars Program for youth physical fitness education. Its PepsiCo Fellows program supports research on the relationship between exercise and fitness. It supports the arts through the PepsiCo Summerfare, a leading performing arts festival. And its Awards to Volunteers program provides funds to nonprofit organizations and recognizes and supports employee volunteer activities.

PepsiCo owes much of its success to the development of quality products with strong appeal to millions of consumers around the world. But success also depends on PepsiCo's skill in telling its publics about the company and its products through a carefully planned communications effort.[1]

M

any new consumer products fail each year not because they are weak, but because they arrive on the market without distinction or excitement. Companies must do more than make good products—they must carefully position products in the consumer's mind.[2] To do this they must skillfully orchestrate the mass-promotion tools of advertising, sales promotion, and publicity. These tools are examined in this chapter.

ADVERTISING

Advertising consists of *nonpersonal forms of communication conducted through paid sponsorship*. In 1983, advertising ran up a bill of $75.9 billion. The spenders included not only commercial firms, but museums, fundraisers, professionals, and various social action organizations that advertise their causes to various target publics. In fact, the 28th largest advertising spender is a nonprofit organization—the U.S. government.

Within the commercial sector, the top 100 national advertisers account for about one-fourth of all advertising.[3] Table 18-1 lists the top 10 advertisers in 1983. Procter & Gamble is the leader with $774 million, or 8.1 percent of its total U.S. sales of $9.6 billion. The other major spenders are found in the auto, food, retailing, drug, and tobacco industries. Advertising as a percentage of sales is low in the automobile industry and high in food, drugs, toiletries, and cosmetics, followed by gum, candy, and soaps. Companies spending the largest percentages of their sales on advertising were Sterling Drug (24.4 percent), Noxell (22.8 percent), Richardson-Vicks (22.6 percent), and Mattel (21.4 percent).

RANK	COMPANY	TOTAL U.S. ADVERTISING (millions)	TOTAL U.S. SALES (millions)	ADVERTISING AS A PERCENT OF SALES
1	Procter & Gamble	$773.6	$ 9,554	8.1%
2	Sears	732.5	32,637	2.2
3	Beatrice	602.8	13,443*	4.5
4	General Motors	595.1	66,160	0.9
5	R. J. Reynolds	593.4	10,769	5.5
6	Philip Morris	527.5	9,303	5.7
7	Ford	479.1	33,000	1.5
8	AT&T	463.1	67,648	0.7
9	K mart	400.0	17,786	2.2
10	General Foods	386.1	6,408	6.0

*Sales for Beatrice are worldwide—U.S. sales not available.

Source: Reprinted with permission from September 14, 1984, issue of *Advertising Age.* Copyright 1984, Crain Communications, Inc.

The advertising dollars go into various media: magazine and newspaper space; radio and television; outdoor displays (posters, signs, skywriting); direct mail; novelties (matchboxes, blotters, calendars); cards (car, bus); catalogs; directories; and circulars. And advertising has many uses: long-term buildup of the organization's image *(institutional advertising),* long-term buildup of a particular brand *(brand advertising),* information dissemination about a sale, service, or event *(classified advertising),* announcement of a special sale *(sale advertising),* and advocacy of a particular cause *(advocacy advertising).*

Advertising's roots can be traced back to early history (see Exhibit 18-1). Although advertising is primarily a private enterprise marketing tool, it is used in all the countries of the world, including socialist countries (see Exhibit 18-2). Advertising is a cost-effective way to disseminate messages, whether it be to build brand preference for Coca-Cola all over the world or to motivate a developing nation's consumers to drink milk or practice birth control.

EXHIBIT 18-1

HISTORICAL MILESTONES IN ADVERTISING

Advertising practice goes back to the very beginnings of recorded history. Archeologists in the countries rimming the Mediterranean Sea have dug up signs announcing various events and offers. The Romans painted walls to announce gladiator contests and the Phoenicians painted murals on prominent rocks along parade routes extolling their wares, a precursor of modern outdoor advertising. A Pompeii wall painting praised a politician and asked for the people's votes.

Another early form of advertising was the *town crier.* During the Golden Age in Greece, town criers circulated through Athens announcing the sale of slaves, cattle, and other goods. An early Athenian "singing commercial" went as follows: "For eyes that are shining, for cheeks like the dawn/For beauty that lasts after girlhood is gone/For prices in reason, the woman who knows/Will buy her cosmetics of Aesclyptos." These town criers foreshadowed radio as an advertising medium and the car loudspeakers used by politicians.

Another early advertising form was the *mark* placed by artisans on their individual goods, such as pottery. As an artisan's reputation spread through word of mouth, buyers began to look for his distinctive mark just as trademarks and brand names are used today. Osnabrück linen was carefully controlled for quality and commanded a price 20 percent higher than unbranded Westphalian linens. As production became more centralized and markets became more distant, the mark took on more significance.

The turning point in the history of advertising came in the year 1450 when Gutenberg invented the printing press. Advertisers no longer had to produce extra copies of a sign by hand. The first printed advertisement in the English language appeared in 1478.

In 1622, advertising received a substantial boost with the launching of the first English newspaper, *The Weekly Newes.* Later Addison and Steele published the *Tatler* and became devotees of advertising. Addison included this advice to copy writers: "The great art in writing advertising is the finding out the proper method to catch the reader, without which a good thing may pass unobserved, or be lost among commissions of bankrupts." The September 14, 1710, issue of the *Tatler* contained ads for razor strops, patent medicine, and other consumer products.

Advertising had its greatest growth in the United States. Ben Franklin has been called the father of American advertising because his *Gazette,* first published in 1729, attained the largest circulation and advertising volume of any paper in colonial America. Several factors contributed to America's becoming the cradle of advertising. First, American industry led in the mechanization of production, which created surpluses and the need to convince consumers to buy more. Second, the development of a fine network of waterways, highways, and roads made the transportation of goods and advertising media to the countryside feasible. Third, the establishment in 1813 of compulsory public education increased literacy and the growth of newspapers and magazines. The invention of radio and later television created two more amazing media for the dissemination of advertising.

EXHIBIT 18-2

ADVERTISING IN THE SOVIET UNION AND CHINA

There are more than one hundred advertising agencies operating today in the Soviet Union, notwithstanding the Marxist-Leninist doctrine that advertising is a tool of capitalistic exploitation.

These agencies were initially established to build demand for Soviet exports in other countries. But many advertisements also appear in print and broadcast media reaching Russian consumers. The 1957 Prague Conference of Advertising Workers of Socialist Countries made three points on how advertising was to be used: (1) to educate people's tastes, develop their requirements, and thus actively form demand; (2) to help the consumer by providing information about the most rational means of consumption; and (3) to help to raise the culture of trade. Furthermore, Soviet advertising was to be ideological, truthful, concrete, and functional. The Soviets claim that their advertising does not indulge in devices used in the West. Their ads will not use celebrities—only experts. They will not use mood advertising. They will not create brand differentiation when none exists. A major use of Soviet advertising today is to stimulate demand for products in excess supply when the companies choose not to do the logical thing—cut prices.

China opened its doors to Western advertising in 1978. The advertising volume is still small—foreign marketers spent only about $17 million on advertising in 1983 to reach China's population of almost 1 billion. But the ad market is beginning to surge as the Chinese consumer market grows.

Now Chinese workers, with a little cash in their pockets, are being urged by Western advertisers to buy Esso gasoline, Kodak film, and Coca-Cola. Colorful billboards line the streets of large cities, neon signs flash Japanese company names, and foreign-made commercials enliven local television.

Source: Information on advertising in China from "Billings Are Up in China, of All Places," *Business Week,* June 4, 1984, p. 36.

Organizations obtain their advertising in different ways. In small companies, advertising is handled by someone in the sales department, who will occasionally work with an advertising agency. Large companies set up advertising departments, whose managers report to vice-presidents of marketing. The advertising department's job is to develop the total budget, approve agency ads and campaigns, and handle direct mail advertising, dealer displays, and other forms of advertising not ordinarily performed by the agency. Most companies use an outside advertising agency because it offers several advantages (see Exhibit 18-3).

EXHIBIT 18-3

HOW DOES AN ADVERTISING AGENCY WORK?

Madison Avenue, USA, is a name familiar to most Americans. It's an avenue in New York City where some major advertising agencies are headquartered. But most of the nation's ten thousand agencies are found outside New York, and there are few cities that do not have at least one agency, even if it is a one-person shop. The six largest U.S. agencies in terms of world billings in 1983 were Young & Rubicam, Ted Bates, J. Walter Thompson, Ogilvy & Mather, McCann-Erickson, and BBDO. Young and Rubicam had billings of over $2.7 billion.

Advertising agencies were started in the last half of the nineteenth century by salespeople and brokers who worked for various media and received a commission for selling advertising space to companies. As media competition for advertising increased, the salespeople began to offer help to customers in preparing their ads. Eventually they formed agencies and grew closer to the advertisers than to the media. These agencies offered an increasing range of advertising and, in some cases, marketing services, to their clients.

Even companies with a strong advertising department will use advertising agencies. Agencies employ creative and technical specialists who often can perform advertising tasks better and more efficiently than the company's staff. Agencies also bring an outside perspective to bear on the company's problems, as well as a broad range of experience from working with different clients and situations. Agencies are paid from media discounts and therefore cost the firm very little. In addition, since the firm can cancel its agency contract at any time, an agency has a strong incentive to perform effectively.

Advertising agencies are typically organized around four departments: *creative,* which handles the development and production of ads; *media,* which selects media and places ads; *research,* which determines audience characteristics and wants; and *business,* which handles the agency's business activities. Each account is supervised by an account executive, and personnel in each department are assigned to work on one or more accounts.

Agencies often attract new business through their reputation or size. Generally, however, a client invites a few agencies to make a competitive presentation for its business and then selects one of them.

Ad agencies receive compensation in the form of commissions and some fees. Typically, the agency receives 15 percent of the media cost as a rebate. Suppose the agency buys $60,000 of magazine space for a client. The magazine bills the advertising agency for $51,000 ($60,000 less 15 percent), and the agency bills the client for $60,000, keeping the $9,000 commission. If the client bought space directly from the magazine, it would have paid $60,000 because these commissions are only paid to accredited advertising agencies.

Both advertisers and agencies are becoming more and more dissatisfied with the commission system. Larger advertisers complain that they pay more for the same services received by smaller ones simply because they place more advertising. Advertisers also believe that the commission system drives agencies away from low-cost media and short advertising campaigns. Agencies are unhappy because they perform extra services for an account without receiving additional compensation. The trend today is toward compensation on either a straight fee basis or a combination commission and fee.

Other trends are also buffeting the advertising agency business. Full-service agencies are facing increasing competition from limited-service agencies specializing in media buying, or advertising copy writing, or advertising production. Business managers in agencies are getting more power and demanding more profit-mindedness from the creative staff. Some advertisers have opened in-house agencies, thus abandoning a longstanding relationship with their agency. Finally, the Federal Trade Commission wants agencies to share responsibility with the client for deceptive advertising. These trends will effect some changes in the industry, but agencies that do a good job will endure.

Sources: For advertising agency statistics, see John J. O'Conner, "Agency Income Tops $6.5 Billion in 1983," *Advertising Age,* March 28, 1984, p. 1; and "Census Sees Steep Rise in Shop Growth," *Advertising Age,* May 7, 1984, p. 68.

MAJOR DECISIONS IN ADVERTISING

Marketing management must make five important decisions in developing an advertising program. These decisions are listed in Figure 18-1 and are examined in the following sections.

Objectives Setting The first step in developing an advertising program is to set the advertising objectives. These objectives must flow from prior decisions on the target market, marketing positioning, and marketing mix. The marketing positioning and mix strategy defines the job that advertising must do in the total marketing program.

Many specific communication and sales objectives can be assigned to advertising. Colley lists fifty-two possible advertising objectives in his well-known *Defining Advertising Goals for Measured Advertising Results.*[4] He outlines a method called DAGMAR (after the book's title) for turning advertising objectives into specific measurable goals. An *advertising goal* is a specific communication task to be accomplished with a specific audience in a specific period of time. DAGMAR outlines an approach to measuring whether advertising goals have been achieved.

Advertising objectives can be classified as to whether their aim is to inform, persuade, or remind. Table 18-2 lists examples of these objectives.

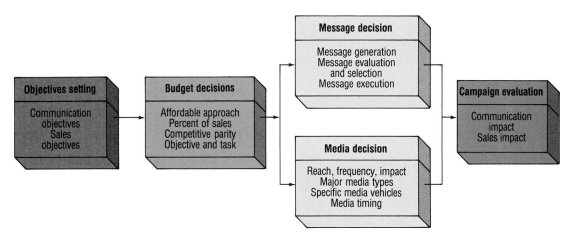

FIGURE 18-1 *Major Decisions in Advertising*

Informative advertising figures heavily in the pioneering stage of a product category, where the objective is to build *primary demand.* Thus the yogurt industry initially had to inform consumers of yogurt's nutritional benefits and many uses.

Persuasive advertising becomes important in the competitive stage, where a company's objective is to build *selective demand.* For example, Chivas Regal attempts to persuade consumers that Chivas Regal delivers status like no other brand of Scotch. It seeks to build a "very best" position for Chivas Regal in the consumer's mind.

Some persuasive advertising has moved into the category of *comparison advertising,* which seeks to establish the superiority of one brand by comparing it directly or indirectly to one or more other brands. In its classic comparison campaign, Avis positioned itself against market-leading Hertz by claiming, "We're number two, but we try harder." Procter & Gamble positioned Scope against Listerine, claiming that minty-fresh Scope "fights bad breath and doesn't give medicine

TABLE 18-2
Possible Advertising Objectives

To inform:	
Telling the market about a new product	Describing available services
Suggesting new uses for a product	Correcting false impressions
Informing the market of a price change	Reducing consumers' fears
Explaining how the product works	Building a company image

To persuade:	
Building brand preference	Persuading customer to purchase now
Encouraging switching to your brand	Persuading customer to receive a sales call
Changing customer's perception of product attributes	

To remind:	
Reminding consumers that the product may be needed in the near future	Keeping it in their minds during off seasons
Reminding them where to buy it	Maintaining its top-of-mind awareness

breath." In its "dare to compare" campaign, Texas Instruments invited consumers to compare its Texas Instruments Professional Computer against the IBM personal computer. Comparison advertising has been used in such product categories as deodorants, toothpastes, automobiles, wines, and pain relievers.[5]

Reminder advertising is highly important in the mature stage to keep the consumer thinking about the product. The purpose of expensive four-color Coca-Cola ads in magazines is to remind people about Coca-Cola, not to inform or persuade them. A related form of advertising is *reinforcement advertising,* which seeks to assure current purchasers that they have made the right choice. Automobile ads will often depict satisfied customers enjoying some special feature of the car they bought.

Budget Decision

After determining advertising objectives, the company can proceed to establish its advertising budget for each product. The role of advertising is to shift the product's demand curve upward. The company wants to spend the amount required to achieve the sales goal. Four commonly used methods for setting the advertising budget were described in Chapter 17. The theoretically correct method for setting the advertising budget (or any other marketing budget) was described in Chapter 3. Companies such as Du Pont and Anheuser-Busch run advertising experiments as part of their advertising budgeting process. Thus Anheuser-Busch will spend higher-than-normal amounts in some territories and lower-than-normal amounts in others and will check the results against control territories to measure what it gains or loses with higher or lower expenditures. Its findings enabled Anheuser-Busch to cut its advertising expenditures per case with no loss in market share.[6]

Message Decision

Given the advertising objectives and budget, management has to develop a creative strategy. Advertisers go through three steps: message generation, message evaluation and selection, and message execution.

Message Generation

Creative people use different methods to generate advertising ideas to carry out the advertising objectives. Many creative people proceed *inductively* by talking to consumers, dealers, experts, and competitors. The Schlitz campaign "When you are out of Schlitz you are out of beer" came about because the advertising agency executive overheard a customer say this to a bartender when the latter said he was out of Schlitz.

Some creative people use a *deductive* framework for generating advertising messages. Maloney proposed one framework (see Table 18-3).[7] He saw buyers as expecting one of four types of reward from a product: *rational, sensory, social,* or *ego satisfaction.* And buyers may visualize these rewards from *results-of-use experience, product-in-use experience,* or *incidental-to-use experience.* Crossing the four types of rewards with the three types of experience generates twelve types of advertising messages.

Message Evaluation and Selection

The advertiser needs to evaluate the possible messages. Twedt suggested that mes-

TABLE 18-3 *Examples of Twelve Types of Messages*

TYPES OF POTENTIALLY REWARDING EXPERIENCE WITH A PRODUCT	POTENTIAL TYPE OF REWARD			
	Rational	Sensory	Social	Ego satisfaction
Results-of-use experience	1. Get clothes cleaner	2. Settles stomach upset completely	3. When you care enough to serve the best	4. For the skin you deserve to have
Product-in-use experience	5. The flour that needs no sifting	6. Real gusto in a great light beer	7. A deodorant to guarantee social acceptance	8. The shoe for the young executive
Incidental-to-use experience	9. The plastic pack keeps the cigarette fresh	10. The portable television that's lighter in weight, easier to lift	11. The furniture that identifies the home of modern people	12. Stereo for the man with discriminating taste

Source: Adapted from John C. Maloney, "Marketing Decisions and Attitude Research," in *Effective Marketing Coordination*, ed. George L. Baker, Jr. (Chicago: American Marketing Association, 1961).

sages be rated on *desirability, exclusiveness,* and *believability*.[8] The message must first say something desirable or interesting about the product. The message must also say something exclusive or distinctive that does not apply to other brands in the product category. Finally, the message must be believable. Believability may be hard to achieve—many consumers are skeptical about the truth of advertising in general. One recent study found that, on average, consumers rate advertising messages as "somewhat unbelievable."[9]

Advertisers should evaluate the desirability, exclusiveness, and believability of their advertising messages. For example, The March of Dimes searched for an advertising theme to raise money for its fight against birth defects.[10] Twenty possible messages came out of a brainstorming session. A group of young parents were asked to rate each message for interest, distinctiveness, and believability, assigning up to 100 points for each. For example, "Five hundred thousand unborn babies die each year from birth defects" scored 70, 60, and 80 on interest, distinctiveness, and believability, while "Your next baby could be born with a birth defect" scored 58, 50, and 70. The first message outperformed the second and was preferred for advertising purposes.

Message Execution

The message's impact depends not only on what is said, but also on how it is said. Message execution can be decisive for products that are highly similar, such as detergents, cigarettes, coffee, and beer. The advertiser has to put the message across in a way that wins the target audience's attention and interest.

The advertiser usually prepares a *copy strategy statement* describing the objective, content, support, and tone of the desired ad. Here is a copy strategy statement for a Pillsbury product called 1869 Brand Biscuits:

> The *objective* of the advertising is to convince biscuit users that now they can buy a canned biscuit that's as good as homemade—Pillsbury's 1869 Brand Biscuits. The *content* consists of emphasizing the following product characteristics: (1) they

look like homemade biscuits, (2) they have the same texture as homemade biscuits, and (3) they taste like homemade biscuits. *Support* for the "good as homemade" promise will be twofold: (1) 1869 Brand Biscuits are made from a special kind of flour (soft wheat flour) used to make homemade biscuits but never before used in making canned biscuits, and (2) the use of traditional American biscuit recipes. The *tone* of the advertising will be a news announcement, tempered by a warm, reflective mood emanating from a look back at traditional American baking quality.

Creative people must now find a *style, tone, words,* and *format* for executing the message.

Any message can be presented in different *execution styles,* such as

1. *Slice-of-life.* This shows one or more persons using the product in a normal setting. A family seated at the dinner table might express satisfaction with a new biscuit brand.
2. *Life style.* This emphasizes how a product fits in with a life style. A scotch ad shows a handsome middle-aged man holding a glass of scotch in one hand and steering his yacht with the other.
3. *Fantasy.* This creates a fantasy around the product or its use. Revlon's initial ad for Jontue featured a barefoot woman wearing a chiffon dress and coming out of an old

Life style: The National Dairy Board shows how milk contributes to a healthy, active life sytle. *Courtesy of National Dairy Board.*

Personality symbols: Marlboro created this famous personality symbol. *Reprinted by permission of Philip Morris, Incorporated.*

French barn, crossing a meadow, and confronting a handsome young man on a white steed, who carries her away.

4. *Mood or image.* This builds an evocative mood or image around the product, such as beauty, love, or serenity. No claim is made about the product except through suggestion. Many cigarette ads, such as those for Salem and Newport cigarettes, create moods.

5. *Musical.* This shows one or more persons or cartoon characters singing a song involving the product. Many cola ads have used this format.

6. *Personality symbol.* This creates a character that personifies the product. The character might be *animated* (Green Giant, Cap'n Crunch, Mr. Clean) or *real* (Marlboro man, Morris the Cat).

7. *Technical expertise.* This shows the company's expertise and experience in making the product. Thus Hills Brothers shows one of its buyers carefully selecting the coffee beans, and Italian Swiss Colony emphasizes its many years of experience in wine-making.

8. *Scientific evidence.* This presents survey or scientific evidence that the brand is preferred to or outperforms one or more other brands. For years, Crest toothpaste has featured scientific evidence to convince toothpaste buyers of Crest's superior anticavity-fighting properties.

9. *Testimonial evidence.* This features a highly credible or likable source endorsing the product. It could be a celebrity like Bill Cosby (Jello Pudding) or ordinary people saying how much they like the product.

The communicator must also choose an appropriate *tone* for the ad. Procter & Gamble is consistently positive in its tone: Its ads say something superlatively positive about the product. Humor is avoided so as not to take attention away from the message. On the other hand, Volkswagen's classic ads for its famous Beetle typically took on a humorous and self-deprecating tone ("the Ugly Bug").

Memorable and attention-getting *words* must be found. The themes listed below on the left would have had much less impact without the creative phrasing on the right:[11]

THEME	CREATIVE COPY
7-Up is not a cola.	"The Un-Cola."
Let us drive you in our bus instead of driving your car.	"Take the bus, and leave the driving to us."
Shop by turning the pages of the telephone directory.	"Let your fingers do the walking."
If you drink a beer, Schaefer is a good beer to drink.	"The beer to have when you're having more than one."
We don't rent as many cars, so we have to do more for our customers.	"We try harder."

Creativity is especially required for headlines. There are six basic types of headlines: *news* ("New Boom and More Inflation Ahead . . . and What You Can Do about It"); *question* ("Have You Had It Lately?"); *narrative* ("They Laughed When I Sat

Down at the Piano, But When I Started to Play!"); *command* ("Don't Buy Until You Try All Three"); 1-2-3 *ways* ("12 Ways to Save on Your Income Tax"); and *how-what-why* ("Why They Can't Stop Buying"). Look at the care the airlines exercise to find the right way to describe their airline as safe without mentioning safety: "The Friendly Skies of United" (United); "The Wings of Man" (Eastern); and "The World's Most Experienced Airline" (Pan American).

Format elements such as ad size, color, and illustration will make a difference in an ad's impact as well as cost. A minor rearrangement of mechanical elements within the ad can improve its attention-gaining power by several points. Larger-size ads gain more attention, though not necessarily by as much as their difference in cost. Four-color illustrations instead of black and white increase ad effectiveness and ad cost.[12]

Media Decision The advertiser's next task is to choose advertising media to carry the advertising message. The steps are (1) deciding on reach, frequency, and impact; (2) choosing among major media types; (3) selecting specific media vehicles; and (4) deciding on media timing.

Deciding on Reach, Frequency, and Impact

In order to select media, the advertiser must determine the desired reach, frequency, and impact needed to achieve the advertising objectives:

1. *Reach.* The advertiser must decide how many persons in the target audience should be exposed to the ad campaign during the specified period of time. For example, the advertiser might seek to reach 70 percent of the target audience during the first year.

2. *Frequency.* The advertiser must also decide how many times the average person in the target audience should be exposed to the message during the specified time period. For example, the advertiser might seek an average exposure frequency of three. Krugman has argued that fewer than three exposures to a message may be insufficient to have an effect, and more than three exposures may be wasteful.[13]

3. *Impact.* The advertiser must also decide on the impact that the exposure should have. Messages on television typically have more impact than messages on radio because television combines sight and sound, not just sound. Within a media form such as magazines, the same message in one magazine (say, *Newsweek*) may deliver more credibility than in another (say, *Police Gazette*). For example, the advertiser may seek an impact of 1.5 where 1.0 is the impact of an ad in an average medium.

Now suppose the advertiser's product might appeal to a market of 1 million consumers. The goal is to reach 700,000 consumers (=1,000,000 × .7). Since the average consumer will receive three exposures, 2,100,000 exposures (=700,000 × 3) must be bought. Since high-impact exposures of 1.5 are desired, a rated number of exposures of 3,150,000 (=2,100,000 × 1.5) must be bought. If a thousand exposures with this impact cost $10, the advertising budget will have to be $31,500 (=3,150 × $10). In general, the more reach, frequency, and impact the advertiser seeks, the higher the advertising budget will have to be.

Choosing Among Major Media Types

The media planner has to know the capacity of the major media types to deliver reach, frequency, and impact. The major advertising media are profiled in Table 18-4. The major media types, in order of their advertising volume, are *newspapers, television, direct mail, radio, magazines,* and *outdoor.* Each medium has certain advantages and limitations. Media planners make their choices among these media categories by considering several variables, the most important ones being

1. *Target audience media habits.* For example, radio and television are the most effective media for reaching teenagers.
2. *Product.* Women's dresses are best shown in color magazines, and Polaroid cameras are best demonstrated on television. Media types have different potentials for demonstration, visualization, explanation, believability, and color.
3. *Message.* A message announcing a major sale tomorrow will require radio or newspapers. A message containing a great deal of technical data might require specialized magazines or mailings.
4. *Cost.* Television is very expensive, while newspaper advertising is inexpensive. What counts is the cost per thousand exposures rather than the total cost.

Ideas about media impact and cost must be reexamined regularly. For a long time, television enjoyed the dominant position in the media mix, and other media were neglected. Then media researchers began to notice television's reduced effectiveness due to increased commercial clutter. Advertisers beamed shorter and more numerous commercials at the television audience, resulting in poorer attention and impact. Furthermore, television advertising costs rose faster than other media costs. Several companies found that a combination of print ads and television commercials often did a better job than television commercials alone. This illustrates that advertisers must periodically review the different media to determine their best buys.

Given the media characteristics, the media planner must decide how to allocate the budget to the major media types. For example, in launching its new biscuit, Pillsbury might decide to allocate $3 million to daytime network television, $2 million to women's magazines, and $1 million to daily newspapers in twenty major markets.

Selecting Specific Media Vehicles

The media planner now chooses the specific media vehicles that will be most cost-effective. The media planner turns to several volumes published by Standard Rate and Data that provide circulation and costs for different ad sizes, color options, ad positions, and quantities of insertions in different women's magazines. The media planner evaluates the magazines on qualitative characteristics such as credibility, prestige, geographic editioning, occupational editioning, reproduction quality, editorial climate, lead time, and psychological impact. The media planner decides which specific vehicles deliver the best reach, frequency, and impact for the money.

TABLE 18-4 *Profiles of Major Media Types*

MEDIUM	VOLUME IN BILLIONS (1983)	PERCENTAGE (1983)	EXAMPLE OF COST (1984)	ADVANTAGES	LIMITATIONS
Newspapers	$20.6	27.1%	$20,974 for one page, weekday *Chicago Tribune*	Flexibility; timeliness; good local market coverage; broad acceptance; high believability	Short life; poor reproduction quality; small "pass-along" audience
Television	16.1	21.2	$6,000 for thirty seconds of prime time in Chicago	Combines sight, sound, and motion; appealing to the senses; high attention; high reach	High absolute cost; high clutter; fleeting exposure; less audience selectivity
Direct mail	11.8	15.5	$1,280 for the names and addresses of 36,650 veterinarians	Audience selectivity; flexibility; no ad competition within the same medium; personalization	Relatively high cost; "junk mail" image
Radio	5.2	6.8	$500 for one minute of prime time in Chicago	Mass use; high geographic and demographic selectivity; low cost	Audio presentation only; lower attention than television; nonstandardized rate structures; fleeting exposure
Magazines	4.2	5.6	$73,710 one page, four color in *Newsweek*	High geographic and demographic selectivity; credibility and prestige; high-quality reproduction; long life; good pass-along readership	Long ad purchase lead time; some waste circulation; no guarantee of position
Outdoor	0.8	1.1	$21,960 per month for 71 billboards in metropolitan Chicago	Flexibility, high repeat exposure; low cost; low competition	No audience selectivity; creative limitations
Other	17.2	22.7			
Total	75.9	100.0%			

Source: Columns 2 and 3 are from *Advertising Age,* May 28, 1984, p. 50. Printed with permission. Copyright © 1984, Crain Communications, Inc.

Media planners calculate the *cost per thousand persons reached* by a particular vehicle. If a full-page, four-color advertisement in *Newsweek* costs $74,000 and *Newsweek's* estimated readership is 3 million persons, the cost of reaching each one thousand persons is approximately $25. The same advertisement in *Business Week* may cost $30,000 but reach only 775,000 persons, at a cost per thousand of $39. The media planner would rank the various magazines according to cost per thousand and favor those magazines with the lower cost per thousand.

The media planner must also consider the costs of producing ads for each medium. Newspaper ads may cost very little to produce, but the costs of flashy television ads may run as high as $1 million. Apple paid $400,000 to produce one futuristic television commercial introducing its Macintosh computer. Midas Muffler paid over $480,000 for six 30-second ads. On average, advertisers must pay more than $85,000 to produce a single 30-second television commercial.[14] The media planner must add in production costs when evaluating the cost effectiveness of each medium.

Several adjustments have to be applied to these initial cost measures. First, the measures should be adjusted for *audience quality*. For a baby lotion advertisement, a magazine read by one million young mothers would have an exposure value of one million, but if read by one million old men would have a zero exposure value. Second, the exposure value should be adjusted for the *audience attention probability*. Readers of *Vogue*, for example, pay more attention to ads than readers of *Newsweek*. Third, the exposure value should be adjusted for the *editorial quality* (prestige and believability) one magazine might have over another.

Media planners increasingly use more sophisticated measures of media effectiveness and employ them in mathematical models for arriving at the best media mix. Many advertising agencies use a computer program to select the initial media, and then make further improvements based on subjective factors omitted in the model.[15]

Deciding on Media Timing

The advertiser has to decide how to schedule the advertising over the year in relation to seasonality and expected economic developments. Suppose sales of a particular product peak in December and wane in March. The seller has three options. The firm can vary its advertising expenditures to follow the seasonal pattern, to oppose the seasonal pattern, or to be constant throughout the year. Most firms pursue a policy of seasonal advertising. Even here, the firm has to decide whether its advertising expenditures should lead or coincide with seasonal sales. It also has to decide whether its advertising expenditures should be more intense, proportional, or less intense than the seasonal amplitude of sales.

The advertiser also has to choose between ad continuity and ad pulsing. *Continuity* is achieved by scheduling exposures evenly within a given period. *Pulsing* refers to scheduling exposures unevenly over the same time period. Thus fifty-two exposures could be scheduled continuously at one per week throughout the year, or flighted in several concentrated bursts. Those who favor pulsing feel that the audience will learn the message more thoroughly and money can be saved. Anheuser-Busch's research indicated that Budweiser could suspend advertising in a particular market and experience no adverse sales effect for at least a year and a half.[16] Then the company could introduce a six-month burst of advertising and restore the previous growth rate. This analysis led Budweiser to adopt a pulsing strategy.

New Advertising Media

New communications technologies developed during the past several years have spawned a variety of new electronic media. The use of these new media has grown dramatically, especially by direct marketers and others trying to reach special target segments. Several of these media are described in Exhibit 18-4.

EXHIBIT 18-4

THE NEW ELECTRONIC MEDIA

Marketers using selective targeting strategies need media that zero in on selected segments of consumers. In recent years, advances in communication technologies have given rise to some exciting new electronic media marketers can use to reach selected target markets. Some of these new media are described here.

Telemarketing. Telemarketing (telephone marketing) has become the major direct marketing tool. In 1983, marketers spent more than $13.6 billion on telephone calls to help sell their products and services. Telemarketing blossomed in the late 1960s with the introduction of inward and outward Wide Area Telephone Service (WATS). With IN WATS, marketers can use toll-free 800 numbers to handle customer service and complaints, or to receive orders from television and radio ads, direct mail, or catalogs. With OUT WATS, they can use the phone to sell directly to consumers and businesses, generate or qualify sales leads, reach more distant buyers, or service current customers or accounts. An astonishing 1.6 billion 800-number calls were made in 1981. During January 1982 more than 700 people dialed an 800 number every minute in response to television commercials. The average household receives 19 telephone sales calls each year and makes 16 calls to place an order. Marketers also use 900 numbers to promote or sell products and services. The consumer dials a 900 number, receives promotional information, and can be forwarded to a different number for direct communication with the marketer's salespeople. For example, 900-210-RICK was used to promote a new Rick Springfield album—the caller heard some of the new album and listened to Rick talk about it.

Some telemarketing systems are fully automated. For example, automatic dialing and recorded message players (ADRMPs) self-dial numbers, play a voice-activated advertising message and take orders from interested customers on an answering-machine device or by forwarding the call to an operator.

Telemarketing is used by large and small consumer and industrial companies. Here are some examples:

- Quaker Oats built a sweepstakes for one of its cereals around a toll-free 800 number—the number received more than 15 million calls in a four-month period and increased sales by more than 30 percent.

- C'est Croissant uses a catalog and toll-free number to sell mail order croissants across the country. The company receives up to 500 calls a month and ships out about 15,000 dozen croissants a year to its nearly 13,000 customers.

- Raleigh Bicycles used telemarketing to reduce the amount of personal selling needed for contacting its dealers. In the first year, salesforce travel costs were reduced by 50 percent and sales in a single quarter were up 34 percent.

- Avis uses computer-assisted telemarketing programs in its fleet-leasing operations to locate and qualify prospects, and to generate good leads for its salespeople. The program cuts salesforce costs, substantially improves the salesforce's available selling time, and reduces the time required to close a sale by one month.

Cable Television. Today more than 70 million households subscribe to one of more than 4,200 cable television systems. Cable systems allow "narrowcasting"—narrow program formats such as all sports, all news, nutrition programs, arts programs, and others targeted at select population segments. Using cable television, advertisers can more effectively target their advertising messages to special market segments, rather than using the shotgun approach offered by network television and other mass media.

new items and higher levels of inventory, encouraging off-season buying, encouraging stocking of related items, and gaining entry into new retail outlets. For the *salesforce,* objectives include encouraging support of a new product or model, encouraging more prospecting, and stimulating sales in off-season.

Selecting the Sales Promotion Tools

Many tools are available to accomplish the sales promotion objectives. The promotion planner should take into account the type of market, sales promotion objectives, competitive conditions, and cost effectiveness of each tool. The main tools are described below.

Samples, Coupons, Price Packs, Premiums, and Trading Stamps

These tools make up the bulk of consumer promotions. *Samples* are offers of a small amount or trial of a product to consumers.[25] Some samples are free; others are self-liquidating—the company charges a small amount to offset sampling costs. Samples might be delivered door-to-door, sent in the mail, picked up in the store, found attached to another product, or featured in an advertising offer. Sampling is the most effective and most expensive way to introduce a new product. To introduce Finesse shampoo and conditioner, Helene Curtis spent millions of dollars distributing more than 70 million samples.[26]

Coupons are certificates entitling the bearer to a stated saving on the purchase of a specific product. Over 100 billion coupons are distributed each year, and about 4 percent are redeemed.[27] Coupons can be mailed, enclosed in other products, or inserted in ads. They can be effective in stimulating sales of a mature brand and inducing early trial of a new brand. Experts believe they should provide a 15 to 20 percent saving to be effective.

Price packs (also called cents-off deals) are offers to consumers of savings off the regular price of a product, flagged on the label or package. They may take the form of a *reduced-price pack,* which is single packages sold at a reduced price (such as two for the price of one); or a *banded pack,* which is two related products banded together (such as a toothbrush and toothpaste). Price packs are very effective in stimulating short-term sales, even more than coupons.

Premiums are merchandise offered free or at low cost as an incentive to purchase a particular product. Expenditures on premiums reached more than $10 billion in 1983.[28] A *with-pack premium* accompanies the product inside (in-pack) or outside (on-pack) the package. The package itself, if a *reusable container,* may serve as a premium. A *free-in-the-mail premium* is an item mailed to consumers who send in a proof of purchase, such as a boxtop. A *self-liquidating premium* is an item sold below its normal retail price to consumers who request it. Manufacturers now offer consumers all kinds of premiums bearing the company's name: Budweiser fans can order T-shirts, hot-air balloons, and hundreds of other items with Bud's name on them.[29]

Trading Stamps are a special type of premium consumers can redeem for merchandise at stamp redemption centers. Trading stamps were widely used in the 1950s and 1960s, but during the economic downturn of the 1970s many merchants decided to drop them and offer lower prices instead. Trading stamps have made a comeback in the last several years, and increasing numbers of retailers are using them to generate store loyalty. Today, more than 100 companies offer trading stamps through supermarkets, gas stations, drugstores, and motels.[30]

Point-of-Purchase Displays and Demonstrations

POP displays and demonstrations take place at the point of purchase or sale. A five-foot-high cardboard display of Cap'n Crunch next to Cap'n Crunch cereal boxes is an example. Unfortunately, many retailers do not like to handle the hundreds of displays, signs, and posters they receive from manufacturers each year. Manufacturers are responding by creating better POP materials, tying them in with television or print messages, and offering to set them up. The L'eggs panty hose display is one of the most creative in the history of POP materials and a major factor in the success of this brand.[31] Another example is Pepsi's "tipping can" display, which was selected as the Display of the Year in 1983 by the Point-of-Purchase Advertising Institute:

> From a display of ordinary Pepsi six-packs on the retail shelf, a mechanically rigged six-pack begins to tilt forward, grabbing the attention of passing shoppers who think the six-pack will fall from the rack. A sign on the tilting six-pack urges shoppers, "Don't forget the Pepsi!" In test market stores, the display helped get more trade support and increased Pepsi sales by 14 cases per week.[32]

Trade Promotion

Manufacturers use a number of techniques to secure the cooperation of wholesalers and retailers. Manufacturers may offer a *buying allowance,* which is an offer of money off on each case purchased during a stated period of time. The offer encourages dealers to buy a quantity or carry a new item they might not ordinarily buy. The dealers can use the buying allowances for immediate profit, advertising, or price redemptions.

Manufacturers may offer a *merchandise allowance* to compensate dealers for featuring the manufacturer's products. An *advertising allowance* compensates dealers for advertising the manufacturer's product. A *display allowance* compensates them for carrying special displays of the product.

Manufacturers may offer *free goods* which are extra cases of merchandise to middlemen who buy a certain quantity. They may offer *push money,* which is cash or gifts to dealers or their salesforces to push the manufacturer's goods. Manufacturers may offer free *specialty advertising* items that carry the company's name, such as pens, pencils, calendars, paperweights, matchbooks, memo pads, ashtrays, and yardsticks.[33]

Business Conventions and Trade Shows

Industry associations organize annual conventions and typically sponsor a trade show at the same time. Firms selling to the particular industry display and demonstrate their products at the trade show. Over 5,600 trade shows take place every year, drawing approximately 80 million people. The participating vendors expect

TIPPERS STOP TRAFFIC!

The bottle or 6-pack that asks to be put in the shopping cart!

PEPSI

Every 30 seconds this self-contained tipper display will appear to fall from the shelf and then slowly return to its place.

Display occupies the space of two 2-liter bottles or four 6-packs of cans.

Operates for 6 to 8 weeks on one 6-volt battery.

Works on the shelf or a rack. For a super visual effect, use multiple units on a mass display.

AND THERE'S MORE...

Pepsi's tipping can and tipping bottle display grab shopper attention.
Courtesy of Pepsi-Cola.

several benefits, including generating new sales leads, maintaining customer contacts, introducing new products, meeting new customers, and selling more to present customers.[34]

Contests, Sweepstakes, and Games

These devices present to consumers, dealers, or salesforces the chance to win something—such as cash, trips, or goods—as a result of luck or extra effort. A *contest* calls for consumers to submit an entry—a jingle, estimate, suggestion—to be examined by a panel of judges who will select the best entries. A *sweepstake* calls for consumers to submit their names in a drawing. A *game* presents something to consumers every time they buy—bingo numbers, missing letters—which may or may not help them win a prize. A *sales contest* is a contest involving dealers or the salesforce to induce them to redouble their efforts over a stated period, with prizes going to the top performers.

Developing the Sales Promotion Program

The marketer must make some additional decisions to define the full promotion program—how much incentive to offer, who can participate, how to advertise the sales promotion, how long it should last, when it should start, and how much to budget.

Size of Incentive

The marketer has to determine how much to offer. A certain minimum incentive is necessary if the promotion is to succeed. A higher incentive level will produce more sales response, but at a diminishing rate. Some of the large consumer packaged-goods firms have a sales promotion manager who studies the effectiveness of past promotions and recommends appropriate incentives to brand managers.

Conditions for Participation

Incentives might be offered to everyone or to select groups. A premium might be offered only to those who turn in boxtops. Sweepstakes might not be offered in certain states, or to families of company personnel, or to persons under a certain age.

Distribution Vehicle for Promotion

The marketer must decide how to promote and distribute the promotion program. A fifteen-cents-off coupon could be distributed in the package, store, mail, or advertising media. Each distribution method involves a different level of reach and cost.

Duration of Promotion

If the sales promotion period is too short, many prospects will not be able to take advantage, since they may not be repurchasing at the time. If the promotion runs too long, the deal will lose some of its "act now" force. According to one researcher, the optimal frequency is about three weeks per quarter, and optimal duration is the length of the average purchase cycle.[35]

Timing of Promotion

Brand managers need to develop calendar dates for the promotions. The dates will be used by production, sales, and distribution. Some unplanned promotions will also be needed and require cooperation on short notice.

Total Sales Promotion Budget

The sales promotion budget can be developed in two ways. The marketer can choose the promotions and estimate their total cost. The more common way is to take a conventional percentage of the total budget to use for sales promotion.

Strang found three major planning inadequacies in how companies handle sales promotion: (1) lack of consideration of cost effectiveness; (2) use of simplistic decision rules, such as extensions of last year's spending, percentage of expected sales, maintenance of a fixed ratio to advertising, and the "leftover approach"; and (3) advertising and sales promotion budgets being prepared independently.[36]

Pretesting Sales promotion tools should be pretested when possible to determine if they are appropriate and of the right incentive size. Yet fewer than 42 percent of premium offers are ever tested.[37]

Implementing Companies should establish implementation plans for each promotion covering lead time and sell-off time. *Lead time* is the time necessary to prepare the program prior to launching it. *Sell-off time* begins with the launch and ends when the deal closes.

Evaluating *the Results* Evaluation is a crucial requirement, and yet, according to Strang, "evaluation of promotion programs receives . . . little attention. Even where an attempt is made to evaluate a promotion, it is likely to be superficial. . . . Evaluation in terms of profitability is even less common.[38]

Manufacturers can use four methods to measure effectiveness. The most common method is to compare sales before, during, and after a promotion. Suppose a company has a 6 percent market share in the prepromotion period, which jumps to 10 percent during the promotion, falls to 5 percent immediately after, and rises to 7 percent after some time. The promotion evidently attracted new triers as well as more purchasing by existing customers. After the promotion, sales fell as consumers worked down their inventories. The long-run rise to 7 percent indicates that the company gained some new users. If the brand's share returned to the prepromotion level, then the promotion only altered the time pattern of demand rather than the total demand.

Consumer panel data would reveal the kinds of people who responded to the promotion and what they did after the promotion. If more information is needed, *consumer surveys* can be conducted to learn how many recall the promotion, what they thought of it, how many took advantage of it, and how it affected their subsequent brand choice behavior. Sales promotions can also be evaluated through *experiments* that vary such attributes as incentive value, duration, and distribution media.

Clearly, sales promotion plays an important role in the total promotion mix. Its systematic use requires defining the sales promotion objectives, selecting the appropriate tools, constructing the sales promotion program, pretesting it, implementing it, and evaluating the results. Exhibit 18-6 describes several award-winning sales promotion campaigns.

EXHIBIT 18-6

AWARD-WINNING SALES PROMOTIONS

Each year *Advertising Age* selects the "Best Promotions of the Year"—those that obtain outstanding results relative to budgets through innovative applications of sales promotion techniques to traditional consumer product lines. Some of the 1983 "Best Promotions" are described below.

Wheaties "Search for Champions" Contest

This national contest selected amateur athletes to be featured on Wheaties cereal boxes. General Mills invited local schools, churches, and community organizations to cast official ballots (found inside Wheaties boxes) for their local sports heroes. The organizations sponsoring the top fifty vote getters received $1 per ballot; those sponsoring one of the six winners received an additional $1,000. The contest was supported by 30-second television spots and 39.3 million free-standing inserts offering 25-cents-off coupons. "Vote-drive kits" were sent to several thousand nonprofit organizations. Publicity was generated through national TV programs and local media. Winners were announced at a special media event in New York's Central Park and in ads in *Sports Illustrated.* The promotion cost only $100,000 more than normal trade promotion for the period, but the contest successfully tapped grassroots spirit and moved Wheaties off the shelf. Consumers redeemed 6.7 percent of the coupons (compared with an average redemption rate of 2.4 percent for grocery products). General Mills received more than 50,000 entries, and Wheaties sales increased significantly.

9-Lives "Free Health Exam for Your Cat" Offer

In this unusual premium promotion, Star-Kist Foods teamed with the American Animal Hospital Association to offer cat owners a free $15 cat physical in exchange for proofs of purchase from 9-Lives cat food products. The 1500 AAHA members donated their services to get cat owners into the habit of regular pet checkups. Star-Kist supported the premium offer with 40 million coupons distributed through free-standing inserts, 23 million coupons delivered through magazine advertising, and trade discounts to encourage reseller participation. The promotion cost about $600,000 (excluding media). Consumers redeemed 5.1 percent of the coupons (40 percent higher than normal), and Star-Kist distributed more than 50,000 free exam certificates. During the promotion, 9-Lives canned products achieved their highest share of the market in two years.

The "Boodles and Dine" Sweepstakes

General Wine & Spirits Company used this sweepstakes to gain on-premise trade support, and to establish Boodles gin (third behind Tanqueray and Beefeater) as a "call" brand, a brand ordered by name. Consumers simply mailed in an entry form to become eligible for three grand prizes of dinner for two each week for a year, three first prizes of dinner for two every two weeks for a year, and three second prizes of dinner for two each month for a year. Entry forms were distributed through ads in *Esquire, Gentlemen's Quarterly, Gourmet, Penthouse,* and other magazines. Where legal, counter card entry forms, table tents, and other point-of-sale materials were also used. The budget: $120,000 for the sales promotion and $226,000 for media. The results: 428,000 entries! During the two months of the promotion, sales were four times greater than normal. In markets surveyed after the promotion, on-premise distribution had doubled.

The "Free Pair of L'eggs" Promotion

L'eggs gave the tried-and-true coupon format a new twist by distributing about 40 million variable-value, instant-winner, ruboff coupons for its regular and control top pantyhose. About 80 percent of the coupons gave 50 cents off, 15 percent gave 75 cents off, and 5 percent gave $1 off. Another 50,000 coupons gave free pantyhose. The total budget, including media, was $1 to $1.3 million. Consumers redeemed 1.5 million coupons, and the promotion generated additional sales of almost 2.9 million pairs of pantyhose. During the six months of the promotion, L'eggs share of the control top market increased 5.2 percent; its share of the regular pantyhose market grew 2.3 percent.

"The Red Baron Fly-In" Promotion

Red Baron Pizza Service used an imaginative combination of special events, couponing, and charitable activities to boost sales of its frozen pizza. The company re-created World War I flying ace Barton Manfred von Richtofen—complete with traditional flying gear and open-cockpit Stearman biplanes—as its company spokesperson. Red Baron pilots barnstormed thirteen markets, exhibited the plane, performed stunts, distributed coupons, and invited consumers to "come fly with the Red Baron." The company donated $500 to a local youth organization in each market and urged consumers to match the gift through fundraising events keyed to the Red Baron's appearance. Trade support was obtained through trade promotions and local tie-in promotions. The total budget: about $1 million. The results: For the four-week period during and after the fly-ins, unit sales in the thirteen markets jumped an average of 100 percent. In the 90 days following the fly-in, sales in some markets increased as much as 400 percent.

Source: Adapted from William A. Robinson, "The Best Promotions of 1983," *Advertising Age,* May 31, 1984, pp. 10–12. Reprinted with permission. Copyright 1984 by Crain Communications, Inc.

PUBLICITY

Another major promotion tool is publicity. **Publicity** involves "securing editorial space, as divorced from paid space, in all media read, viewed, or heard by a company's customers or prospects, for the specific purpose of assisting in the meeting of sales goals."[39] Publicity's results can sometimes be spectacular. Consider the case of Cabbage Patch dolls:

> Publicity played a major role in making Coleco's Cabbage Patch dolls the sensation of the 1983 Christmas season. The dolls were formally introduced at a Boston press conference where local school children performed a mass adoption ceremony for the press. Thanks to Coleco's publicity machine, child psychologists publicly endorsed the Cabbage Patch Kids, and Dr. Joyce Brothers and other newspaper columnists proclaimed that the Kids were healthy playthings. Major women's magazines featured the dolls as ideal Christmas gifts, and after a 5-minute feature on the "Today" show, the Kids made the complete talk-show circuit. Marketers of other products used the hard-to-get Cabbage Patch dolls as premiums, and retailers used them to lure customers into their stores. The word spread, and every child just *had* to have one. The dolls were sold out by Thanksgiving, and the great "Cabbage Patch Panic" began.[40]

The great "Cabbage Patch Panic." *Courtesy of Coleco.*

Publicity is used to promote brands, products, persons, places, ideas, activities, organizations, and even nations. Trade associations have used publicity to rebuild interest in declining commodities such as eggs, milk, and potatoes. Organizations have used publicity to attract attention or counter a poor image. Nations have used publicity to attract more tourists, foreign investment, and international support.

Publicity is part of a larger concept, that of **public relations.** Company public relations has several objectives, including obtaining favorable publicity for the company, building up a good "corporate citizen" image for the company, and handling adverse rumors and stories that break out. Public relations departments use several tools to carry out these objectives:[41]

■ *Press relations.* The aim of press relations is to place newsworthy information into the news media to attract attention to a person, product, or service.

■ *Product publicity.* Product publicity involves various efforts to publicize specific products.

■ *Corporate communications.* This activity covers internal and external communications to promote understanding of the institution.

■ *Lobbying.* Lobbying involves dealing with legislators and government officials to promote or defeat legislation and regulation.

- *Counseling.* Counseling involves advising management about public issues and company positions and image.

Those skilled in publicity are usually found in the company's public relations department. The public relations department is typically located at corporate headquarters; and its staff is so busy dealing with various publics—stockholders, employees, legislators, city officials—that publicity to support product marketing objectives may be neglected. One solution is to add a publicity specialist to the marketing department.

Publicity is often described as a marketing stepchild because of its limited and sporadic use. Yet publicity can create a memorable impact on public awareness at a fraction of the cost of advertising. The company does not pay for the space or time in the media. It pays for a staff to develop and circulate the stories. If the company develops an interesting story, it could be picked by all the media and be worth millions of dollars in equivalent advertising. Furthermore, it would have more credibility than advertising. Exhibit 18-7 describes two publicity campaigns that cost little but achieved substantial results.

EXHIBIT 18-7

TWO EXAMPLES OF SUCCESSFUL PUBLICITY CAMPAIGNS

A publicist is able to find or create stories around even mundane products. Some years ago the Potato Board decided to finance a publicity campaign to encourage more potato consumption. A national attitude and usage study indicated that many consumers perceived potatoes as too fattening, not nutritious enough, and not a good source of vitamins and minerals. These attitudes were disseminated by various opinion leaders, such as food editors, diet advocates, and doctors. Actually potatoes have far fewer calories than most people imagine, and they contain several important vitamins and minerals. The Potato Board decided to develop separate publicity programs for consumers, doctors and dieticians, nutritionists, home economists, and food editors. The consumer program consisted of disseminating many stories about the potato for network television and women's magazines, developing and distributing *The Potato Lover's Diet Cookbook,* and placing articles and recipes in food editors' columns. The food editors' program consisted of food editor seminars conducted by nutrition experts.

Publicity can be highly effective in brand promotion. One of the top brands of cat food is Star-Kist Foods' 9-Lives. Its brand image revolves around Morris the Cat. The advertising agency of Leo Burnett, which created Morris for its ads, wanted to make him more of a living, breathing, real-life feline to whom cat owners and cat lovers could relate. It hired a public relations firm, which then proposed and carried out the following ideas: (1) launch a Morris "Look-Alike" contest in nine major markets, with Morris booked for personal appearances and extensive stories appearing about the search for a look-alike; (2) write a book called *Morris, An Intimate Biography,* describing the adventures of this famous feline; (3) establish a coveted award called "The Morris," a bronze statuette given to the owners of award-winning cats selected at local cat shows; (4) sponsor an "Adopt-a-Cat Month," with Morris as the official "spokescat" urging people to adopt stray cats as Morris once was; and (5) distribute a booklet called "The Morris Method" on cat care. These publicity steps strengthened the brand's market share in the cat food market.

Major Decisions in Publicity In considering when and how to use product publicity, management should establish the publicity objectives, choose the publicity messages and vehicles, implement the publicity plan, and evaluate the publicity results.

Establishing the Publicity Objectives The first task is to set specific objectives for the publicity. The Wine Growers of California hired the public relations firm of Daniel J. Edelman, Inc., in 1966 to develop a publicity program to support two major marketing objectives: Convince Americans that wine drinking is a pleasurable part of good living and improve the image and market share of California wines among all wines. The following publicity objectives were established: Develop magazine stories about wine and get them placed in top magazines (*Time, House Beautiful*) and in newspapers (food columns, feature sections); develop stories about wine's many health values and direct them to the medical profession, and develop specific publicity for the young adult market, college market, governmental bodies, and various ethnic communities. These objectives were fashioned into specific goals so that final results could be evaluated.

Choosing the Publicity Messages and Vehicles The publicist next identifies interesting stories to tell about the product. Suppose a relatively unknown college wants more public recognition. The publicist will search for possible stories. Do any faculty members have unusual backgrounds or are any working on unusual projects? Are any new and unusual courses being taught? Are any interesting events taking place on campus? Usually this search will uncover hundreds of stories that can be fed to the press. The stories chosen should reflect the image this college wants.

If the number of stories is insufficient, the publicist should propose newsworthy events that the college could sponsor. Here the publicist gets into *creating news* rather than *finding news*. The ideas include hosting major academic conventions, inviting celebrity speakers, and developing news conferences. Each event is an opportunity to develop a multitude of stories directed at different audiences.

Event creation is a particularly important skill in publicizing fundraising drives for nonprofit organizations. Fundraisers have developed a large repertoire of special events, including *anniversary celebrations, art exhibits, auctions, benefit evenings, bingo games, book sales, cake sales, contests, dances, dinners, fairs, fashion shows, parties in unusual places, phonothons, rummage sales, tours,* and *walkathons.* No sooner is one type of event created, such as a walkathon, than competitors spawn new versions such as readathons, bikeathons, and jogathons.

Implementing the Publicity Plan Implementing publicity requires care. Take the matter of placing stories in the media. A great story is easy to place. But most stories are less than great and may not get past busy editors. One of the chief assets of publicists is their personal relationship with media editors. Publicists are often ex-journalists who know many media editors and know what they want. Publicists look at media editors as a market to satisfy so that these editors will continue to use their stories.

Evaluating the Publicity Results Publicity's contribution is difficult to measure because it is used with other promotional tools. If it is used before the other tools come into action, its contribution is easier to evaluate.

The easiest measure of publicity effectiveness is the number of *exposures* created in the media. Publicists supply the client with a "clippings book" showing all the media that carried news about the product and a summary statement such as the following:

> Media coverage included 3,500 column inches of news and photographs in 350 publications with a combined circulation of 79.4 million; 2,500 minutes of air time on 290 radio stations and an estimated audience of 65 million; and 660 minutes of air time on 160 television stations with an estimated audience of 91 million. If this time and space had been purchased at advertising rates, it would have amounted to $1,047,000.[42]

This exposure measure is not very satisfying. There is no indication of how many people actually read or heard the message, and what they thought afterward. There is no information on the net audience reached, since publications overlap in readership.

A better measure is the change in product *awareness/comprehension/attitude* resulting from the publicity campaign (after allowing for the impact of other promotional tools). This requires surveying the before-and-after levels of these variables. The Potato Board learned, for example, that the number of people who agreed with the statement "Potatoes are rich in vitamins and minerals" went from 36 percent before the campaign to 67 percent after the campaign, a significant improvement in product comprehension.

Sales and profit impact is the most satisfactory measure if obtainable. For example, 9-Lives sales increased 43 percent at the end of the "Morris the Cat" publicity campaign. However, advertising and sales promotion had been stepped up, and their contribution has to be considered.

■ Summary

Three major tools of mass-promotion are advertising, sales promotion, and publicity. They are mass-marketing tools as opposed to personal selling, which targets specific buyers.

Advertising—the use of paid media by a seller to communicate persuasive information about its products, services, or organization—is a potent promotional tool. American marketers spend over $75 billion annually on advertising, and it takes many forms (national, regional, local; consumer, industrial, retail; product, brand, institutional, and so on). Advertising decision making is a five-step process consisting of objectives setting, budget decision, message decision, media decision, and campaign evaluation. Advertisers should establish clear goals as to whether the advertising is supposed to inform, persuade, or remind buyers. The advertising budget can be established on the basis of what is afford-

able, as a percentage of sales, on the basis of competitors' expenditures, or on the basis of objectives and tasks. The message decision calls for generating messages, evaluating and selecting among them, and executing them effectively. The media decision calls for defining the reach, frequency, and impact goals; choosing among major media types; selecting specific media vehicles; and scheduling the media. Finally, campaign evaluation calls for evaluating the communication and sales effects of advertising, before, during, and after the advertising.

Sales promotion covers a wide variety of short-term incentive tools—coupons, premiums, contests, buying allowances—designed to stimulate consumer markets, the trade, and the organization's own salesforce. Sales promotion expenditures have been growing at a faster rate than advertising in recent years. Sales promotion calls for establishing the sales promotion objectives; selecting the tools; developing, pretesting, and implementing the sales promotion program; and evaluating the results.

Publicity—which is the securing of free editorial space or time—is the least utilized of the major promotional tools, although it has great potential for building awareness and preference in the marketplace. Publicity involves establishing the publicity objectives; choosing the publicity messages and vehicles; implementing the publicity plan; and evaluating the publicity results.

■ Questions for Discussion

1. List the advantages and disadvantages of each of the "new media" and discuss when each could be best used. What other new media might appear in the next fifteen years?

2. Many firms have had to contend with negative rumors about their products in recent years—K mart coats from Taiwan with poisonous snakes nesting in them, McDonald's using worms in its hamburger meat, Pop Rocks candy making your stomach explode, Bubble Gum containing spider eggs. How can the company best deal with these rumors when using public relations and advertising?

3. The major objective of advertising is to inform. Comment.

4. Explain the major aspects of the message decision and relate them to a specific product.

5. Sales promotion tools are only effective when used for consumer promotion. Comment.

6. Which sales promotion tools are the most widely utilized for supermarket products? Why?

7. How might a manufacturer of consumer package goods evaluate whether its national sales promotion campaign was successful?

8. Discuss how you would develop a publicity campaign for the American Cancer Society.

■ References

1. Based on PepsiCo annual reports; *Advertising Age*'s special issue on top 100 advertisers, September 14, 1984; JOHN J. O'CONNOR, "New Pepsi Ads Turn to Humor," *Advertising Age,* February 27, 1984, p. 1; NANCY GIGES, "Soft-Drink Marketing: It's All Showmanship," *Advertising Age,* March 12, 1984, p. 3; "No More Aftertaste," *Barron's,* May 28, 1984, pp. 35–36; and miscellaneous sources.

2. See AL RIES and JACK TROUT, *Positioning: The Battle for Your Mind* (New York: Warner Books, 1981).

3. Statistical information in this section on advertising's size and composition draws on the special issue of *Advertising Age* on the 100 leading national advertisers, September 14, 1984.

4. See RUSSEL H. COLLEY, *Defining Advertising Goals for Measured Advertising Results* (New York: Association of National Advertisers, 1961).

5. See WILLIAM L. WILKE and PAUL W. FARRIS, "Comparison Advertising: Problem and Potential," *Journal of Marketing,* October 1975, pp. 7–15; and NANCY GIGES, "Comparison Ads: Battles That Wrote Dos and Don'ts," *Advertising Age,* September 19, 1980, pp. 59–64.

6. See RUSSELL L. ACKOFF and JAMES R. EMSHOFF, "Advertising Research at Anheuser-Busch, Inc. (1963–68)," *Sloan Management Review,* Winter 1975, pp. 1–15.

7. JOHN C. MALONEY, "Marketing Decisons and Attitude Research," in *Effective Marketing Coordina-*

tion George L. Baker, Jr., ed. (Chicago: American Marketing Association, 1961), pp. 595–618.

8. DIK WARREN TWEDT, "How to Plan New Products, Improve Old Ones, and Create Better Advertising," *Journal of Marketing,* January 1969, pp. 53–57.

9. See "Ad Quality Good, Believability Low," *Advertising Age,* May 31, 1984, p. 3.

10. See WILLIAM A. MINDAK and H. MALCOLM BYBEE, "Marketing's Application to Fund Raising," *Journal of Marketing,* July 1971, pp. 13–18.

11. L. GREENLAND, "Is This the Era of Positioning?" *Advertising Age,* May 19, 1972.

12. For more on copy approaches, see DAVID OGILVY and JOEL RAPHAELSON, "Research on Advertising Techniques that Work—and Don't Work," *Harvard Business Review,* July–August 1982, pp. 14–18.

13. See HERBERT E. KRUGMAN, "What Makes Advertising Effective?" *Harvard Business Review,* March–April 1975, pp. 96–103, here p. 98.

14. See "Goodbye, Mr. Whipple," *Newsweek,* March 28, 1984, pp. 62–64.

15. See DENNIS H. GENSCH, *Advertising Planning* (New York: Elsevier, 1973).

16. PHILIP H. DOUGHERTY, "Bud 'Pulses' the Market," *New York Times,* February 18, 1975, p. 40.

17. JOHN ROSSITER, "Predicting Starch Scores," *Journal of Advertising Research,* October 1981, pp. 63–68.

18. DAVID B. MONTGOMERY and ALVIN J. SILK, "Estimating Dynamic Effects of Market Communications Expenditures," *Management Science,* June 1972, pp. 485–501.

19. See ROBERT D. BUZZELL, "E. I. Du Pont de Nemours & Co.: Measurement of Effects of Advertising," in his *Mathematical Models and Marketing Management* (Boston: Division of Research, Graduate School of Business Administration, Harvard University, 1964), pp. 157–79.

20. For more on the legal aspects of advertising and sales promotion, see LOUIS W. STERN and THOMAS L. EOVALDI, *Legal Aspects of Marketing Strategy* (Englewood Cliffs, NJ: Prentice-Hall, 1984), chaps. 7 and 8.

21. See "$60 Billion Can't Be Wrong," *Marketing Communications,* January 1983, p. 48.

22. ROGER A. STRANG, "Sales Promotion—Fast Growth, Faulty Management," *Harvard Business Review,* July–August 1976, pp. 115–24, here pp. 116–17.

23. See ROGER STRANG, ROBERT M. PRENTICE, and ALDEN G. CLAYTON, *The Relationship between Advertising and Promotion in Brand Strategy* (Cambridge, MA: Marketing Science Institute, 1975), chap. 5.

24. STRANG, "Sales Promotion," p. 124.

25. Most of the definitions in this section have been adapted from JOHN F. LUCK and WILLIAM LEE SIEGLER, *Sales Promotion and Modern Merchandising* (New York: McGraw-Hill, 1968).

26. EILEEN NORRIS, "Curtis Samples Success in Small Packets," *Advertising Age,* November 28, 1983, p. M36.

27. OTTO KLEPPNER, THOMAS RUSSELL, and GLEN VERRILL, *Advertising Procedure* (Englewood Cliffs, NJ: Prentice-Hall, 1983), p. 299.

28. ED FITCH, "Without a Plan, the Carrots Just Dangle," *Advertising Age,* May 10, 1984, p. M15.

29. For more reading, see CARL-MAGNUS SEIPEL, "Premiums—Forgotten by Theory," *Journal of Marketing,* April 1971, pp. 26–34; and FITCH, "Without a Plan."

30. BETSY GILBERT, "Retailers Stamp Out Loyalty Problems," *Advertising Age,* May 10, 1984, p. M34.

31. "Our L'eggs Fit Your Legs," *Business Week,* March 27, 1972.

32. "Pepsi Tops Honor Role of 1983's Best Point-of-Purchase Displays," *Marketing News,* April 27, 1984, pp. 14–15.

33. For more on trade promotion, see JOHN A. QUELCH, "It's Time to Make Trade Promotion More Effective," *Harvard Business Review,* May–June 1983, pp. 130–36.

34. See SUZETTE CAVANAUGH, "Setting Objectives and Evaluating the Effectiveness of Trade Show Exhibits," *Journal of Marketing,* October 1976, pp. 100–5.

35. ARTHUR STERN, "Measuring the Effectiveness of Package Goods Promotion Strategies" (Paper presented to the Association of National Advertisers, Glen Cove, February 1978).

36. STRANG, "Sales Promotion," p. 119.

37. RUSSEL D. BOWMAN, "Merchandising and Promotion Grow Big in Marketing World" *Advertising Age,* December 1974, p. 21.

38. STRANG, "Sales Promotion," p. 120.

39. GEORGE BLACK, *Planned Industrial Publicity* (Chicago: Putnam, 1952), p. 3.

40. See LYNN LANGWAY, "Harvesting the Cabbage," *Newsweek,* December 12, 1983, pp. 81–85.

41. Adapted from SCOTT M. CUTLIP and ALLEN H. CENTER, *Effective Public Relations* (3rd ed.) (Englewood Cliffs, NJ: Prentice-Hall, 1964), pp. 10–14.

42. ARTHUR M. MERIMS, "Marketing's Stepchild: Product Publicity," *Harvard Business Review,* November–December 1972, pp. 111–12.

19
Promoting Products: Personal Selling and Sales Management

At the age of 29, Kim Kelley is already something of a legend around Honeywell Inc. "He's the one who cried when he made his sale, isn't he?" a fellow Honeywell salesperson asks with a chuckle.

Indeed he is. Kim stood there in his customer's office last June and bawled like a baby. And for good reason. Kim had just shaken hands on an $8.1 million computer sale to the State of Illinois. He had gambled his whole career on making that sale. He had spent three years laying the groundwork for it, and for three solid months he had been working six days a week, often 14 hours a day, competing against salespeople from four other computer companies.

It was a make-or-break situation for Kim Kelley, and, standing there with tears of joy and relief streaming down his cheeks, he knew he had it made. A bright future with Honeywell was assured, and he had just made an $80,000 commission—more money than he had earned in all four of his previous years with the company.

. . . Such is the life of the "big-ticket" salesperson who pursues multimillion-dollar contracts while others sell in bits and drabs. Lured by fat commissions (1 percent of the equipment's total value in Honeywell's case), they devote months to delicate planning and months more to the heat of battle, all to make one big sale.

He was sent to Springfield in 1970 and was told to keep four or five big sales simmering but to put only one at a time "on the front burner." Kim wasted little time picking his target, the state government, the biggest potential customer in his region. His long-range strategy was to devote at least half his time to pursuing the state, and to use the balance to scratch out small sales elsewhere to meet his annual quota of $500,000 worth of new equipment.

For three years, he patiently made daily rounds of key state offices, pausing a few minutes in each one to drop off technical documents or just to chat. He pursued the bureaucrats further at after-hours hangouts like the American Legion hall. "People don't buy products, they buy relationships," Kim believes.

Toward the end of 1972, the Illinois Secretary of State asked for bids for a massive new computer system. Five manufacturers responded: Honeywell, Burroughs, Univac division of Sperry Rand, Control Data, and International Business Machines.

In the ensuing three-month scramble, Control Data was eliminated because of "high cost," according the Noel Sexton, head of a technical committee assigned by the state to evaluate the bids. IBM was never in strong contention, says Hank Malkus, who was then division administrator in the secretary's office. "IBM doesn't tailor its equipment to a customer's need. They just say, 'Here's our equipment, you make your system fit it,'" Mr. Malkus contends.

That made the contest a three-horse race between Honeywell, Burroughs, and Univac. "The equipment was close," says Patrick Halperin, executive assistant to the secretary of state. "But the staff felt far more comfortable with Honeywell because they felt Kim had been more thorough in his marketing."

Indeed he was. Kim dealt solely with the committee. "Some of the other vendors put more emphasis on selling to the front office and tried to play on previous friendships," Mr. Sexton recalls.

Kim fed the committee information, not persuasion. "When we asked to see customers," says Mr. Malkus, "Kim just gave us a list of Honeywell users and said, choose." Univac, on the other hand, annoyed committee members by discouraging them from interviewing users.

Kim flew in Honeywell experts and top marketing officials from Boston, Minneapolis, Phoenix, and Chicago to answer technical questions on engineering, financing, installation, and service. "He showed the ability of his firm to cooperate," says Mr. Halperin.

"Incredible attention to detail" helped, too, Kim thinks. The committee was asking few new bits of information daily—things like how much air conditioning his equipment would need. Kim answered every question within two days, always hand-delivering replies to each committee member. "That gave me five minutes more selling time with each one," he explains.

When Hank Malkus gruffly ordered him down to the state capitol last June, Kim knew it was "decision day," but he didn't know who had won. Minutes later, Mr. Malkus was grinning, his secretary was hugging Kim, and Kim was crying.[1]

Robert Louis Stevenson observed that "everyone lives by selling something." Salesforces are found in nonprofit as well as profit organizations. College recruiters are the college's salesforce arm for attracting students. Churches use membership committees to attract new members. The U.S. Agricultural Extension Service sends agricultural specialists to sell farmers on using new farming methods. Hospitals and museums use fundraisers to contact and raise money from donors.

The people who do the selling are called by various names: sales representatives, salespersons, account executives, sales consultants, sales engineers, field representatives, agents, service representatives, and marketing representatives. Selling is one of the oldest professions in the world (see Exhibit 19-1).

EXHIBIT 19-1

MILESTONES IN THE HISTORY OF SELLING AND SALESMANSHIP

Selling goes back to the dawn of history. Paul Hermann described a Bronze Age traveling salesman's sample case: ". . . a solid wooden box, 26 inches in length, containing in specially hollowed compartments various types of axe, sword blades, buttons, etc." Early sellers and traders were not held in high esteem. The Roman word for salesman meant "cheater," and Mercury, the god of cunning and barter, was regarded as the patron deity of merchants and traders.

The buying and selling of commodities flourished over the centuries and centered in market towns. Itinerant peddlers carried goods to the homes of prospective customers who were unable to get to the market towns.

The first salesmen in the United States were Yankee peddlers (pack peddlers), who carried clothing, spices, household wares, and notions in backpacks from East Coast manufacturing centers to settlers in the western frontier regions. The pack peddlers also traded with the Indians, exchanging knives, beads, and ornaments for furs. Many traders came to be viewed as shrewd, unprincipled tricksters who would not think twice about putting sand in the sugar, dust in the pepper, and chicory in the coffee. They often sold colored sugar water as "medicine" guaranteed to cure all possible ills.

In the early 1800s some of the peddlers began to use horse-drawn wagons and to stock heavier goods such as furniture, clocks, dishes, weapons, and ammunition. Some of these wagon peddlers settled in frontier villages and opened the first general stores and trading posts.

The larger retailers traveled once or twice a year to the nearest major city to replenish their stocks. Eventually wholesalers and manufacturers hired greeters, or drummers, who would seek out and invite retailers to visit the displays of their employers. The drummers would meet incoming trains and ships to beat their competitors. In time the drummers traveled to their customers' places of business. Prior to 1860 there were fewer than one thousand traveling salesmen, many of whom were credit investigators who also took orders for goods. By 1870 there were seven thousand, by 1880 twenty-eight thousand, and by 1900 ninety-three thousand traveling salesmen.

Modern selling and sales management techniques were refined by John Henry Patterson (1844–1922), widely regarded as the father of modern salesmanship. Patterson ran the National Cash Register Company (NCR). He asked his best salesmen to demonstrate their sales approaches to the other salesmen. The best sales approach was printed in a "Sales Primer" and distributed to all NCR salesmen to be followed to the letter. This was the beginning of the canned sales approach. In addition, Patterson assigned his salesmen exclusive territories and sales quotas to stretch their effort. He held frequent sales meetings that served the double purpose of sales training and sociability. He sent his salesmen regular communications on how to sell. One of the young men trained by Patterson was Thomas J. Watson, who later founded IBM. Patterson showed other companies the way to turn their salesforces into effective tools for building sales and profit.

Sources: Based on various sources, including Paul Hermann, *Conquest by Man* (New York: Harper & Row, Pub., 1954), p. 38; Frederic Russell, Frank Beach, and Richard Buskirk, *Textbook of Salesmanship* (New York: McGraw-Hill, 1969), pp. 8–10; Bertrand Canfield, *Salesmanship: Practices and Principles* (New York: McGraw-Hill, 1950), p. 6; and Thomas and Marva Belden, *The Lengthening Shadow* (Boston: Little, Brown, 1962), p. 44.

There are many stereotypes of sales representatives. "Salesmen" may conjure up an image of Arthur Miller's pitiable Willy Loman in *Death of a Salesman* or Meredith Willson's cigar-smoking, back-slapping, joke-telling Harold Hill in *The Music Man*. Sales representatives are typically pictured as loving sociability—although many sales representatives actually dislike it. They are criticized for foisting goods on people—although buyers often search out sales representatives.

Actually the term *sales representative* covers a broad range of positions in our economy, where the differences are often greater than the similarities. McMurry devised the following classification of sales positions:

- Positions where the salesperson's job is largely to deliver the product—milk, bread, fuel, oil.

- Positions where the salesperson is largely an inside order taker—the haberdashery salesperson standing behind the counter.

- Positions where the salesperson is also largely an order taker but works in the field, as the packing house, soap, or spice salesperson does.

- Positions where the salesperson is not expected or permitted to take an order but only builds goodwill or educates the actual or potential user—the distiller's "missionary person" or the medical "detailer" representing an ethical pharmaceutical house.

- Positions where the major emphasis is placed on technical knowledge—the engineering salesperson who is primarily a consultant to the client companies.
- Positions that demand the creative sale of tangible products like vacuum cleaners, refrigerators, siding, and encyclopedias.
- Positions requiring the creative sales of intangibles, such as insurance, advertising services, or education.[2]

This list ranges from the least to the most creative types of selling. The earlier jobs call for maintaining accounts and taking orders, while the latter require hunting down prospects and influencing them to buy. Our discussion will focus on the more creative types of selling.

> **Salesforce management** is the analysis, planning, implementation and control of sales force activities. It includes setting salesforce objectives; designing salesforce strategy; and recruiting, selecting, training, supervising, and evaluating the firm's sales representatives.

The major decisions companies face in building and managing an effective sales force are shown in Figure 19-1 and discussed in the following sections.

ESTABLISHING SALESFORCE OBJECTIVES

Companies set different objectives for their salesforces. IBM's sales representatives are responsible for "selling, installing, and upgrading" customer computer equipment; AT&T sales representatives are responsible for "developing, selling, and protecting" accounts. Sales representatives perform one or more of the following tasks for their companies:

- *Prospecting.* Sales representatives find and cultivate new customers.
- *Communicating.* Sales representatives skillfully communicate information about the company's products and services.
- *Selling.* Sales representatives know the art of "salesmanship"—approaching, presenting, answering objections, and closing sales.

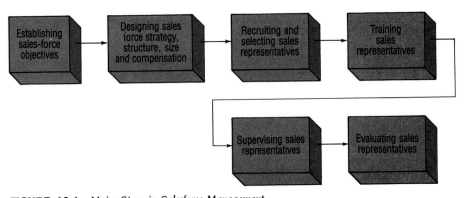

FIGURE 19-1   *Major Steps in Salesforce Management*

- *Servicing.* Sales representatives provide services to customers—consulting on their problems, rendering technical assistance, arranging financing, and expediting delivery.
- *Information gathering.* Sales representatives carry out market research and intelligence work and fill in call reports.
- *Allocating.* Sales representatives evaluate customer quality and allocate scarce products during product shortages.

Companies become more specific about their salesforce objectives and activities. One company advises its sales representatives to spend 80 percent of their time with current customers and 20 percent with prospects; and 85 percent of their time on established products and 15 percent on new products.[3] If norms are not established, sales representatives tend to spend most of their time selling established products to current accounts and neglect new products and new prospects.

As companies increase their market orientation, their salesforces need to become more market-oriented. The traditional view is that salespeople should worry about volume and the company should worry about profit. The newer view is that salespeople should know how to produce customer satisfaction and company profit. They should know how to analyze sales data, measure market potential, gather market intelligence, and develop marketing strategies and plans. Sales representatives need analytical marketing skills, and this becomes especially critical at the higher levels of sales management. Marketers believe that a market-oriented rather than a sales-oriented salesforce will be more effective in the long run.

DESIGNING SALESFORCE STRATEGY

Once the company has established its salesforce objectives, it is ready to face questions of salesforce strategy, structure, size, and compensation.

SalesForce Strategy The company will be competing with others to get orders from customers. It must ground its strategy in an understanding of the customer buying process. It can use one or more of five sales contact approaches to customers:

- *Sales representative to buyer.* A sales representative talks to a prospect or customer in person or over the phone.
- *Sales representative to buyer group.* A sales representative makes a sales presentation to a buying group.
- *Sales team to buyer group.* A sales team (such as a company officer, a sales representative, and a sales engineer) makes a sales presentation to a buying group.
- *Conference selling.* The sales representative brings resource people from the company to meet with one or more buyers to discuss problems and mutual opportunities.
- *Seminar selling.* A company team conducts an educational seminar for a technical group in a customer company about state-of-the-art developments.

Thus the salesperson often acts as an "account manager" who arranges contacts between people in the buying and selling organizations. Selling increasingly calls for teamwork. Salespeople need help from others in the company—from top management, especially when selling to national accounts[4] or when major sales[5] are at stake; from technical people who provide customer services such as installation or maintenance; from office staff such as sales analysts, order processors, and secretaries.

Once the company has decided on a desirable selling approach, it can use either a direct or a contractual salesforce. A *direct* (or *company*) *salesforce* consists of full- or part-time paid employees who work exclusively for the company. This salesforce includes *inside sales personnel,* who conduct business from their office using the telephone and receiving visits from prospective buyers, and *field sales personnel,* who travel and visit customers. A *contractual salesforce* consists of manufacturer's reps, sales agents, or brokers, who are paid a commission based on their sales.

Salesforce Structure

Salesforce strategy also involves structuring the salesforce to have maximum effectiveness in the marketplace. This is simple if the company sells one product line to one end-using industry with customers in many locations; here the company would use a territorial-structured salesforce. If the company sells many products to many types of customers, it might need a product-structured or customer-structured salesforce. These alternative structures are discussed below.

Territorial-Structured Salesforce

In the simplest sales organization, each sales representative is assigned an exclusive territory in which to represent the company's full line. This sales structure has a number of advantages. First, it results in a clear definition of the salesperson's responsibilities. To the extent that personal selling makes the difference, the salesperson receives the credit or blame for territory sales. Second, territorial responsibility increases the sales representative's incentive to cultivate local business and personal ties. These ties contribute to the sales representative's selling effectiveness and personal life. Third, travel expenses are relatively small, since each sales representative travels within a small geographical area.

Territorial sales organization is supported by a hierarchy of sales management positions. Several territories will be supervised by a *district sales manager,* several districts will be supervised by a *regional sales manager,* and several regions will be supervised by a *national sales manager* or *sales vice-president.* Each higher-level sales manager takes on increasing marketing and administrative work in relation to the time available for selling. In fact, sales managers are paid for their management skills rather than their selling skills. The new sales trainee, in looking ahead at the career path, will become a sales representative, then a district manager, and depending on his or her ability and motivation may move to higher levels of sales or general management.

Product-Structured Salesforce

The importance of sales representatives' knowing their products, together with the development of product divisions and product management, has led many companies to structure their salesforces along product lines. Product specialization is warranted where the products are numerous, technically complex, or highly unrelated.

The existence of different company products, however, is not a sufficient argument for specializing the salesforce by product. Problems may occur if the company's separate product lines are bought by the same customers. For example, the American Hospital Supply Corporation has several product divisions, each with its own salesforce. It is possible that several sales representatives from the American Hospital Supply Corporation could call on the same hospital on the same day. This means that company sales personnel travel over the same routes, and each waits to see the customer's purchasing agents. These extra costs must be weighed against the benefits of more knowledgeable product representation.

Customer-Structured Salesforce

Companies often specialize their salesforces along customer lines. Separate salesforces may be set up for different industries, for major versus regular accounts, and for current versus new business development. The most obvious advantage of customer specialization is that each salesforce can become knowledgeable about specific customer needs. At one time General Electric structured its salesforce by products (fan motors, switches). But because different customers perceived these products in terms of their own industry applications, GE changed to specialization by markets. A customer-structured salesforce can sometimes reduce total salesforce costs. At one time a pump manufacturer used highly trained sales engineers to sell to all its customers—to original equipment manufacturers who needed highly technical assistance and to jobbers who did not. Later the company split its salesforce and used lower-paid, less technical salespeople to deal with jobbers.

The major disadvantage of customer-structured salesforces arises when the various types of customers are scattered throughout the country. This means extensive travel by each of the company's salesforces.

Complex Salesforce Structures

When a company sells a wide variety of products to many types of customers over a broad geographical area, it often combines several types of salesforce structure. Sales representatives may be specialized by territory-product, territory-customer, product-customer, or ultimately by territory-product-customer. A sales representative may then report to one or more line or staff managers.

Salesforce Size Once the company has set its strategy and structure, it is ready to consider salesforce size. Sales representatives are one of the company's most productive and expensive assets. Increasing their number will increase both sales and costs.

Many companies use the *workload approach* to establish salesforce size.[6] This method consists of the following steps:

1. Customers are grouped into size classes by their annual sales volume.

2. Call frequencies (number of sales calls on an account per year) are established for each class. They reflect how much call intensity the company seeks in relation to competitors.

3. The number of accounts in each size class is multiplied by the corresponding call frequency to arrive at the total workload (in sales calls per year) for the country.

4. The average number of calls a sales representative can make per year is determined.

5. The number of sales representatives needed is determined by dividing the total annual calls required by the average annual calls made by a sales representative.

Suppose the company estimates that there are one thousand A accounts and two thousand B accounts in the nation; and A accounts require thirty-six calls a year and B accounts twelve calls a year. This means the company needs a salesforce that can make sixty thousand calls a year. Suppose the average sales representative can make one thousand calls a year. The company would need sixty full-time sales representatives.

Salesforce Compensation

To attract the desired number of sales representatives, the company has to develop an attractive compensation plan. Sales representatives like income regularity, reward for above-average performance, and fair payment for experience and longevity. On the other hand, management emphasizes control, economy, and simplicity. Management objectives, such as economy, will conflict with sales representatives' objectives, such as financial security. It is understandable why compensation plans vary tremendously not only among industries, but among companies within the same industry.

Management must determine the level and components of an effective compensation plan. The *level of compensation* must bear some relation to the "going market price" for the type of sales job and abilities required. For example, the average earnings of an experienced industrial salesperson in 1983 amounted to $36,900.[7] If the market price for salespeople is well defined, the firm will have to pay the going rate. To pay less will attract too few quality applicants; to pay more is unnecessary. But the market price for sales manpower is seldom well defined. For one thing, company plans vary on the importance of fixed and variable salary elements, fringe benefits, and expense allowances. And data on the average take-home pay of sales representatives working for competing firms can be misleading because of significant variations in the average seniority and ability levels of competitors' salesforces. Published data on industry salesforce compensation levels are infrequent and generally lack sufficient detail.

The company must determine the *components of compensation*—a fixed amount, a variable amount, expenses, and fringe benefits. The *fixed amount,* which might be salary or a drawing account, satisfies the sales representative's need for some stability of income. The *variable amount,* which might be commissions, a bonus, or profit sharing, stimulates and rewards greater effort. *Expense allowances* enable the sales representatives to undertake selling efforts that are considered necessary or desirable. And *fringe benefits,* such as paid vacations, sickness or accident benefits, pensions, and life insurance, provide security and job satisfaction.

Top sales management must decide on the relative importance of these components in the compensation plan. A popular rule favors making about 70 percent of the salesperson's total income fixed and allocating the remaining 30 percent among the other elements. But the variations around this average are so large that it can hardly serve as a guide. Fixed compensation should receive more emphasis in jobs with a high ratio of nonselling to selling duties and in jobs where the selling task is technically complex. Variable compensation should have more emphasis in jobs where sales are cyclical or depend on initiative.

Fixed and variable compensation give rise to three basic types of compensation plans—straight salary, straight commission, and combination salary and commissions. One study of consumer and industrial companies showed that 20 percent paid straight salary, 5 percent paid straight commission, and 75 percent paid salary plus commission or bonus.[8]

RECRUITING AND SELECTING SALES REPRESENTATIVES

Having established the strategy, structure, size, and compensation of the salesforce, the company now has to make a number of operational sales management decisions. Specifically, the company has to set up systems for recruiting and selecting, training, supervising, and evaluating.

Importance of Careful Selection At the heart of a successful salesforce operation is the selection of effective salespeople. The performance differences between top and average salespeople can be large, and careful selection can substantially increase overall salesforce performance. A survey of over 500 companies revealed that, in a typical salesforce, 27 percent of the salespeople bring in over 52 percent of the sales.[9]

Poor salesperson selection can also result in costly turnover. One study found an average annual salesforce turnover rate for all industries of almost 20 percent.[10] The costs of high turnover can be great. The company must spend more to hire and train replacements, and a salesforce containing a high proportion of new people is less productive. New salespeople often have a harder time generating enough sales to cover their costs. Direct income averages only about half of salesperson's direct selling costs. If a salesperson receives $30,000 a year in income, another $30,000 may go into fringe benefits, expenses, supervision, office space, supplies, and secretarial assistance. Thus the salesperson must produce sales on which the gross margin covers at least the $60,000 in selling expenses. If the gross margin is 10 percent, the salesperson must sell $600,000 for the company to break even.

What Makes a Good Sales Representative? Selecting sales representatives would not be a problem if one knew what traits to look for. If effective sales representatives are outgoing, aggressive, and energetic, these characteristics could be checked in applicants. But many successful sales representatives are also introverted, mild mannered, and far from energetic. Successful sales representatives include men and women who are tall and short, articulate and inarticulate, well groomed and slovenly.

Nevertheless, the search continues for the magic combination of traits that spells sure-fire sales ability. Numerous lists have been drawn up. McMurry wrote: "It is my conviction that the possessor of an *effective* sales personality is a *habitual 'wooer,' an individual who has a compulsive need to win and hold the affection of others.*"[11] McMurry listed five additional traits of the super-salesperson: "A high level of energy, abounding self-confidence, a chronic hunger for money, a well-established habit of industry, and a state of mind that regards each objection, resistance, or obstacle as a challenge."[12] Charles Garfield found that successful salespeople are goal-directed risk takers who identify strongly with their customers (see Exhibit 19-2).

EXHIBIT 19-2

WHAT MAKES A SUPERSALESPERSON?

Charles Garfield, clinical professor of psychology at the Univ. of California, San Francisco School of Medicine, claims his 20-year analysis of more than 1,500 superachievers in every field of endeavor is the longest running to date. *Peak Performance—Mental Training Techniques of the World's Greatest Athletes,* the first book Garfield wrote about his findings, was published June 1. Although he says it will be followed shortly by a book on business which will cover supersalespeople, many companies (such as IBM, which took 3,000) have ordered the current book for their sales forces. Garfield says that the complexity and speed of change in today's business world means that to be a peak performer in sales requires greater mastery of different fields than to be one in science, sports, or the arts. The following are the most common characteristics he has found in peak sales performance:

- Supersalespeople are always taking risks and making innovations. Unlike most people, they stay out of the "comfort zone" and try to surpass their previous levels of performance.

- Supersalespeople have a powerful sense of mission and set the short-, intermediate-, and long-term goals necessary to fulfill that mission. Their personal goals are always higher than the sales quotas set by their managers. Supersalespeople also work well with managers, especially if the managers also are interested in peak performance.

- Supersalespeople are more interested in solving problems than in placing blame or bluffing their way out of situations. Because they view themselves as professionals in training, they are always upgrading their skills.

- Supersalespeople see themselves as partners with their customers, and as team players rather than adversaries. Peak performers believe their task is to communicate with people, while mediocre salespeople psychologically change their customers into objects and talk about the number of calls and closes they made as if it had nothing to do with human beings.

- Supersalespeople take each rejection as information they can learn from, whereas mediocre people personalize rejection.

- The most surprising finding is that, like peak performers in sports and the arts, supersalespeople use mental rehearsal. Before every sale they review it in their mind's eye, from shaking the customer's hand when they walk in to discussing his problems and asking for the order.

Source: "What Makes a Supersalesperson?" *Sales and Marketing Management,* August 13, 1984, p. 86.

How can a company determine the characteristics that sales representatives should possess in its industry? The job duties suggest some of the characteristics to look for. Is there a lot of paper work? Does the job call for much travel? Will the salesperson confront a high proportion of rejections? The company should also examine the traits of its most successful representatives for possible clues.

Recruitment Procedures After management has developed selection criteria, it must recruit. The personnel department seeks applicants by various means, including soliciting names from current sales representatives, using employment agencies, placing job ads, and contacting college students. Companies have sometimes found it hard to sell college students on selling. A survey of one thousand male college students indicated that only one in seventeen showed an interest in selling.[13] The reluctant ones gave such reasons as "Selling is a job and not a profession," "It calls for deceit if the person wants to succeed," and "There is insecurity and too much travel." Some women believe that selling "is a man's career." To counter these objections, company recruiters emphasize starting salaries, income opportunities, and the fact that one-fourth of the presidents of large U.S. corporations started out in marketing and sales. They point out that more than 21 percent of the people selling manufactured products are women (see Exhibit 19-3).

Applicant-Rating Procedures Recruitment procedures, if successful, will attract many applicants. The company will need to select the best ones. The selection procedures can vary from a single informal interview to prolonged testing and interviewing not only of the applicant, but of the applicant's family.

Many companies give formal tests to sales applicants. Although test scores are only one information element in a set that includes personal characteristics, references, past employment history, and interviewer reactions, they are weighted quite heavily by such companies as IBM, Prudential, Procter & Gamble, and Gillette. Gillette claims that tests have reduced turnover by 42 percent and have correlated well with the subsequent progress of new sales representatives in the sales organization.

TRAINING SALES REPRESENTATIVES

Many companies used to send their new representatives into the field almost immediately after hiring them. They would be supplied with samples, order books, and instructions to sell west of the Mississippi. Training programs were luxuries. A training program meant making large outlays for instructors, materials, and space; paying a person who was not yet selling; and losing opportunities because he or she was not in the field.

Today's new sales representatives may spend a few weeks to several months in training. The median training period is twenty weeks in industrial products and service companies, and eighteen in consumer products companies.[14] At IBM, new sales representatives are not on their own for two years! And IBM expects its sales representatives to spend 15 percent of their time each year in additional training.

The annual training bill for major U.S. corporations runs into millions of dollars. Yet sales management sees training as adding more value than cost. Today's sales representatives are selling to more cost- and value-conscious buyers. Further-

EXHIBIT 19-3

ON THE JOB WITH A SUCCESSFUL XEROX SALESWOMAN

The word "salesman" is beginning to have an archaic ring. The entry of women into what was once a male bastion has been swift and dramatic. More than 21 percent of people selling manufactured products are women, vs. 7 percent a decade ago. And women are making special strides selling high-tech equipment. At Xerox, for example, they are 39 percent of the sales force.

Nancy Reck doing business despite the weather. *Photo © by Rebecca Chao, used with permission.*

Nancy Reck decided that sales offered the best opportunity when she and her husband, Miles, moved from Jacksonville, Florida, to Chapel Hill, North Carolina, 3½ years ago so he could work on a doctorate. They were holding down five jobs between them to make ends meet when Nancy, 30, found what she had been looking for: a single job that paid enough to support both of them. Sales, says the former schoolteacher, "is a field where compensation is related to performance. You write your own ticket."

Reck signed up with Xerox as a sales representative and quickly made her mark. In each of the last three years, she has qualified for the President's Club, which means she exceeded all of her sales goals, an honor won by only one of every five members of the sales force last year. Her income, which she won't discuss, is probably about $50,000 a year.

A native of tiny Seaboard, North Carolina, Reck earned her spurs on the "low volume" beat, selling Xerox copiers and electronic typewriters door to door to small businesses in 17 counties in her home state. Recently she was promoted to a new job that is a stepping stone to management.

Reck worried she would have to develop an artificial personality to succeed in sales. Instead she found she could just be herself: "I treat every customer as if he were my father, my brother, or my best friend."

more, they are selling more technically complex products. The company wants and needs mature and knowledgeable sales representation.

The training programs have several goals:

1. *Sales representatives need to know and identify with the company.* Most companies devote the first part of the training program to describing the company's history and objectives, the organization and lines of authority, the chief officers, the company's financial structure and facilities, and the chief products and sales volume.

2. *Sales representatives need to know the company's products.* Sales trainees are shown how products are produced and how they function in various uses.

3. *Sales representatives need to know customers' and competitors' characteristics.* Sales representatives learn about the different types of customers and their needs, buying motives, and buying habits. They learn about the company's and competitors' strategies and policies.

4. *Sales representatives need to know how to make effective presentations.* Sales representatives receive training in the principles of salesmanship. In addition, the company outlines the major sales arguments for each product, and some provide a sales script.

5. *Sales representatives need to understand field procedures and responsibilities.* Sales representatives learn how to divide time between active and potential accounts; and how to use the expense account, prepare reports, and route effectively.

Principles of Salesmanship

Many sales representatives do not know how to sell (see Exhibit 19-4). One of the major objectives of training programs is to train sales representatives in the art of selling. Companies spend hundreds of millions of dollars on seminars, books, cassettes, and other materials. Almost a million copies of books on selling are purchased every year, with such tantalizing titles as *How to Outsell the Born Salesman, How to Sell Anything to Anybody, The Power of Enthusiastic Selling, How*

Power Selling Brought Me Success in 6 Hours, Where Do You Go from No. 1, and *1000 Ways a Salesman Can Increase His Sales.* One of the most enduring books is Dale Carnegie's *How to Win Friends and Influence People.*

EXHIBIT 19-4

HOW WELL TRAINED ARE SALES REPS?

A vice-president of a major food company spent one week watching fifty sales presentations to a busy buyer for a major supermarket chain. Here are some of his reactions:

> I watched a soap company representative come in to the buyer. He had three separate new promotional deals to talk about with six different dates. He had nothing in writing . . . . After the salesman left, the buyer looked at me and said, "It will take me 15 minutes to get this straightened out."

> I watched another salesman walk in to the buyer and say, "Well, I was in the area, and I want you to know that we have a great new promotion coming up next week." The buyer said, "That's fine. What is it?" He said, "I don't know . . . . I'm coming in next week to tell you about it." The buyer asked him what he was doing there today. He said, "Well, I was in the area."

> Another salesman came and said, "Well, it's time for us to write that order now . . . . getting ready for the summer business." The buyer said, "Well, fine, George, how much did I buy last year in total?" The salesman looked a little dumbfounded and said, "Well, I'll be damned if I know . . . . "

> The majority of salesmen were ill-prepared, unable to answer basic questions, uncertain as to what they wanted to accomplish during the call. They did not think of the call as a studied, professional presentation. They didn't have a real idea of the busy retailer's needs and wants.

Source: From an address given by Donald R. Keough at the Twenty-seventh Annual Conference of the Super-Market Institute in Chicago, April 26–29, 1964.

All of the training approaches try to convert a salesperson from being a passive *order taker* to being an active *order getter. Order takers* operate on the following assumptions: (1) Customers know their needs; (2) they would resent any attempt at influence; and (3) they prefer salespersons who are courteous and self-effacing. An example of an order-taking mentality would be a salesperson who calls on a dozen customers each day, simply asking if the customer needs anything.

In training salespersons to be *order getters,* there are two basic approaches, a *sales-oriented approach* and a *customer-oriented approach.* The first one trains the salesperson in *high-pressure selling techniques,* such as those used in selling encyclopedias or automobiles. The techniques include overstating the product's merits, criticizing competitive products, using a slick canned presentation, selling yourself, and offering some concession to get the order on the spot. This form of selling assumes the customers are not likely to buy except under pressure; they are influenced by a slick presentation and ingratiating manner; and they will not be sorry after signing the order, or if they are, it doesn't matter.

The other approach trains sales personnel in *customer problem solving*. The salesperson learns how to identify customer needs and propose effective solutions. This approach assumes (1) Customers have latent needs that constitute company opportunities; (2) they appreciate good suggestions; and (3) they will be loyal to sales representatives who have their long-term interests at heart. The problem solver is a more compatible image for the salesperson under the marketing concept than the hard seller or order taker.

Most training programs view the selling process as consisting of several steps that the salesperson must master. These steps are shown in Figure 19-2 and discussed below.[15]

Prospecting and Qualifying

The first step in the selling process is to identify prospects. The salesperson must approach many prospects to get a few sales. In one segment of the insurance industry, only one out of nine prospects becomes a customer; in the computer hardware/software business, 125 phone calls result in 25 interviews leading to 5 demonstrations and 1 sale.[16] Although the company supplies leads, sales representatives need skill in developing their own leads. Leads can be developed in the following ways: (1) asking current customers for the names of prospects; (2) cultivating other referral sources, such as suppliers, dealers, noncompeting sales representatives, bankers, and trade association executives; (3) joining organizations to which prospects belong; (4) engaging in speaking and writing activities that will draw attention; (5) examining data sources (newspapers, directories) in search of names; (6) using the telephone and mail to track down leads; and (7) dropping in unannounced on various offices (cold canvassing).

Sales representatives need to know how to screen out poor leads. Prospects can be qualified by examining their financial ability, volume of business, special requirements, location, and likelihood of continuous business. The salesperson should phone or write to prospects to see if they are worth pursuing.

Preapproach

Before calling on a prospect, the salesperson should learn as much as possible about the prospect company (what it needs, who is involved in the purchase decision) and its buyers (their personal characteristics and buying styles). The salesper-

FIGURE 19-2
Major Steps in Effective Selling

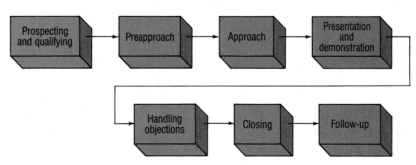

son can consult standard sources (*Moody's, Standard and Poor, Dun and Bradstreet*), acquaintances, and others to learn about the company. The salesperson should set *call objectives,* which might be to qualify the prospect, or gather information, or make an immediate sale. Another task is to decide on the best *approach,* which might be a personal visit, a phone call, or a letter. The best *timing* should be thought out because many prospects are busy at certain times. Finally, the salesperson should give thought to an *overall sales strategy* for the account.

Approach

The salesperson should know how to meet and greet the buyer to get the relationship off to a good start. This involves the salesperson's appearance, the opening lines, and the follow-up remarks. The salesperson should wear clothes similar to what the buyer wears; show courtesy and attention to the buyer; and avoid distracting mannerisms, such as pacing the floor or staring at the customer. The opening lines should be positive, such as "Mr. Smith, I am Bill Jones from the ABC Company. My company and I appreciate your willingness to see me. I will do my best to make this visit profitable and worthwhile for you and your company." This might be followed by some key questions or the showing of a display or sample to attract the buyer's attention and curiosity.

Presentation and Demonstration

The salesperson now tells the product "story" to the buyer, showing how the product will make or save money. The salesperson describes the *product features* but concentrates on selling the *customer benefits.* The salesperson will follow the AIDA formula of getting *attention,* holding *interest,* arousing *desire,* and obtaining *action.*

Companies use three styles of sales presentation. The oldest is the *canned approach,* which is a memorized sales talk covering the main points. It is based on stimulus-response thinking—that the buyer is passive and can be moved to purchase by the use of the right stimulus words, pictures, terms, and actions. An encyclopedia salesperson might describe the encyclopedia as "a once-in-a-lifetime buying opportunity" and focus on some beautiful four-color pages of sports pictures, hoping to trigger desire for the encyclopedia. Canned presentations are used primarily in door-to-door and telephone selling.

The *formulated approach* is also based on stimulus-response thinking but first identifies the buyer's needs and buying style. The salesperson initially draws the buyer into the discussion that reveals the buyer's needs and attitudes. Then the salesperson moves into a formulated presentation that shows how the product will satisfy that buyer's needs. It is not canned but follows a general plan.

The *need-satisfaction approach* starts with a search for the customer's real needs by encouraging the customer to do most of the talking. This approach calls for good listening and problem-solving skills. It is well described by an IBM sales representative: "I get inside the business of my key accounts. I uncover their key problems. I prescribe solutions for them, using my company's systems and even, at times, components from other suppliers. I prove beforehand that my systems will

Sales representatives make a presentation. *Courtesy of Hewlett-Packard.*

save money or make money for my accounts. Then I work with the account to install the system and make it prove out."[17]

Sales presentations can be improved with demonstration aids such as booklets, flip charts, slides, movies, and actual product samples. To the extent that the buyer can see or handle the product, he or she will better remember its features and benefits.

Handling Objections

Customers almost always pose objections during the presentation or when asked to place an order. Their resistance can be psychological or logical. *Psychological resistance* includes resistance to interference, preference for established habits, apathy, reluctance to giving up something, unpleasant associations about the other person, tendency to resist domination, predetermined ideas, dislike of making decisions, and neurotic attitude toward money.[18] *Logical resistance* might consist of objections to the price, delivery schedule, or certain product or company characteristics. To handle these objections, the salesperson maintains a positive approach, asks the buyer to clarify the objection, questions the buyer in such a way that the buyer has to answer his or her own objection, denies the validity of the objection, or turns the objection into a reason for buying. The salesperson needs training in the broader skills of negotiation, of which handling objections is a part.[19]

Closing

The salesperson now attempts to close the sale. Some salespeople do not get to this stage or do not handle it well. They lack confidence, or feel guilty about asking for the order, or do not recognize the right psychological moment to close the sale. Salespersons need to know how to recognize closing signals from the buyer, including physical actions, statements or comments, and questions. Salespersons can use one of several closing techniques. They can ask for the order, review the points of agreement, offer to help write up the order, ask whether the buyer wants A or B, get the buyer to make minor choices such as the color or size, or indicate what the buyer will lose if the order is not placed now. The salesperson may offer the buyer specific inducements to close, such as a special price or an extra quantity at no charge.

Follow-Up

This last step is necessary if the salesperson wants to ensure customer satisfaction and repeat business. Immediately after closing, the salesperson should complete any necessary details on delivery time, purchase terms, and other matters. The salesperson should schedule a follow-up call when the initial order is received to make sure there is proper installation, instruction, and servicing. This visit would detect any problems, assure the buyer of the salesperson's interest, and reduce any cognitive dissonance that might have arisen.

SUPERVISING SALES REPRESENTATIVES

New sales representatives need more than a territory, a compensation package, and training—they need supervision. Through supervision, employers hope to direct and motivate the salesforce to do a better job. Exhibit 19-5 indicates that much work still needs to be done.

Directing Sales Representatives Companies vary in how closely they supervise their sales representatives. Sales representatives who are paid mostly on commission and who are expected to hunt down their own prospects are generally left on their own. Those who are salaried and must cover definite accounts are likely to receive substantial supervision.

Developing Customer Targets and Call Norms

Most companies classify customers into A, B, and C accounts, reflecting the account's sales volume, profit potential, and growth potential. They establish the desired number of calls per period on each account class. Thus A accounts may receive nine calls a year; B, six calls; and C, three calls. The call norms depend upon competitive call norms and expected account profitability.

EXHIBIT 19-5

HOW EFFICIENTLY DO COMPANIES MANAGE THEIR
SALESFORCES?

There is much evidence of inefficiency in the way companies manage their salesforces. A survey of 257 Fortune "500" companies revealed the following:

- 54% have not conducted an organized study of the sales representatives' use of time, even though most respondents felt that time ultilization represents an area for improvement.
- 25% do not have a system for classifying accounts according to potential.
- 30% do not use call schedules for their salesforce.
- 51% do not determine the number of calls it is economical to make on an account.
- 83% do not determine an approximate duration for each call.
- 51% do not use a planned sales presentation.
- 24% do not set sales objectives for accounts.
- 72% do not set profit objectives for accounts.
- 19% do not use a call report system.
- 63% do not use a prescribed routing pattern in covering territories.
- 77% do not use the computer to assist in time and territorial management.

Source: Robert Vizza, "Managing Time and Territories for Maximum Sales Success," *Sales Management*, July 15, 1971, pp. 31–36.

The real issue is how much sales volume can be expected from a particular account as a function of the annual number of calls. Magee described an experiment where similar accounts were randomly split into three sets.[20] Sales representatives were asked to spend less than five hours a month with accounts in the first set, five to nine hours a month with those in the second set, and more than nine hours a month with those in the third set. The results demonstrated that additional calls produced more sales, leaving only the question of whether the magnitude of sales increase justified the additional cost.

Developing Prospect Targets and Call Norms

Companies often specify how much time their salesforce should spend prospecting for new accounts. Spector Freight wants its sales representatives to spend 25 percent of their time prospecting, and to stop calling on a prospect after three unsuccessful calls.

Companies set up prospecting standards for a number of reasons. If left alone, many sales representatives will spend most of their time with current customers. Current customers are better-known quantities. Sales representatives can depend upon them for some business, whereas a prospect may never deliver any business. Unless sales representatives are rewarded for opening new accounts, they may avoid new account development. Some companies rely on a missionary sales-force to open new accounts.

Using Sales Time Efficiently

Sales representatives need to know how to use their time efficiently. One tool is the *annual call schedule* showing which customers and prospects to call on in which months, and which activities to carry out. The activities include participating in trade shows, attending sales meetings, and carrying out marketing research projects.

The other tool is *time-and-duty* analysis. The sales representative spends time in the following ways:

- *Travel.* In some jobs, travel time amounts to over 50 percent of total time. Travel time can be cut down by using faster means of transportation—recognizing, however, that this will increase costs. More companies are encouraging air travel for their salesforce to increase their ratio of selling to total time.
- *Food and breaks.* Some portion of the salesforce's workday is spent in eating and taking breaks.
- *Waiting.* Waiting consists of time spent in the buyer's outer office. This is dead time unless the sales representative uses it to plan or to fill out reports.
- *Selling.* Selling is the time spent with the buyer in person or on the phone. It breaks down into "social talk" (the time spent discussing other things) and "selling talk" (the time spent discussing the company's products).
- *Administration.* This is a miscellaneous category consisting of the time spent in report writing and billing, attending sales meetings, and talking to others in the company about production, delivery, billing, sales performance, and other matters.

No wonder actual selling time may amount to as little as 15 percent of total working time! If it could be raised from 15 to 20 percent, this would be a 33 percent improvement. Companies are constantly seeking more time-efficient methods—using "phone power," simplifying recordkeeping forms, developing better call and routing plans, and supplying more and better customer information. Many companies are computerizing their call report and sales information systems to make salespeople more efficient.[21]

Motivating Sales Representatives

Some sales representatives will do their best without any special urging from management. To them, selling is the most fascinating job in the world. They are ambitious and self-starters. But most sales representatives require encouragement and special incentives to work at their best level. This is especially true of field selling for the following reasons:

- *The nature of the job.* The selling job involves frequent frustration. Sales representatives usually work alone; their hours are irregular; and they are often away from home. They confront aggressive, competing sales representatives; they have an inferior status relative to the buyer; they often do not have the authority to do what is necessary to win an account; they lose large orders they have worked hard to obtain.
- *Human nature.* Most people operate below capacity in the absence of special incentives, such as financial gain or social recognition.

- *Personal problems.* Sales representatives are occasionally preoccupied with personal problems, such as sickness in the family, marital discord, or debt.

Management can influence salesforce morale and performance through its organizational climate, sales quotas, and positive incentives.

Organizational Climate

Organizational climate describes the feeling that the sales representatives get regarding their opportunities, value, and rewards for a good performance. Some companies treat sales representatives as if they were of minor importance. Other companies treat their sales representatives as the prime movers and allow unlimited opportunity for income and promotion. The company's attitude toward its representatives acts as a self-fulfilling prophecy. If they are held in low esteem, there is much turnover and poor performance; if they are held in high esteem, there is little turnover and high performance.

The personal treatment from the sales representative's immediate superior is an important aspect of organizational climate. An effective sales manager keeps in touch with the salesforce through correspondence and phone calls, personal visits in the field, and evaluation sessions in the home office. At different times the sales manager acts as the salesperson's boss, companion, coach, and confessor.

Sales Quotas

Many companies set quotas for their sales representatives specifying what they should sell during the year and by product. Their compensation is often related to their degree of quota fulfillment.

Sales quotas are set when developing the annual marketing plan. The company first decides on a sales forecast that is reasonably achievable. This becomes the basis of planning production, workforce size, and financial requirements. Then management establishes sales quotas for its regions and territories which typically add up to more than the sales forecast. Sales quotas are set higher than the sales forecast in order to stretch sales managers and salespeople to their best effort. If they fail to make their quotas, the company may still make its sales forecast.

Each area sales manager divides the area's quota among the area's representatives. There are three schools of thought on quota setting. The *high-quota school* sets quotas higher than what most representatives will achieve but that are nevertheless attainable. Its adherents believe that high quotas spur extra effort. The *modest-quota school* sets quotas that a majority of the salesforce can achieve. Its adherents feel that the salesforce will accept the quotas as fair, attain them, and gain confidence. The *variable-quota school* thinks that individual differences among sales representatives warrant high quotas for some, modest quotas for others. According to Heckert:

> Actual experience with sale quotas, as with all standards, will reveal that sales representatives react to them somewhat differently, particularly at first. Some are stimulated to their highest efficiency, others are discouraged. Some sales executives place considerable emphasis upon this human element in setting their

quotas. In general, however, good men will in the long run respond favorably to intelligently devised quotas, particularly when compensation is fairly adjusted to performance.[22]

Positive Incentives

Companies use several motivators to stimulate salesforce effort. Periodic *sales meetings* provide a social occasion, a break from routine, a chance to meet and talk with "company brass," and a chance to air feelings and to identify with a larger group. Companies also sponsor *sales contests* to spur the salesforce to a special selling effort above what would normally be expected. Other motivators include honors, awards, and profit-sharing plans.

EVALUATING SALES REPRESENTATIVES

We have described how management communicates what the sales representatives should be doing and motivates them to do it. But this requires good feedback. And good feedback means getting regular information from representatives to evaluate their performance.

Sources of Information Management obtains information about its sales representatives in several ways. The most important source is sales reports. Additional information comes through personal observation, customers' letters and complaints, customer surveys, and conversations with other sales representatives.

Sales reports are divided into *plans for future activities* and *writeups of completed activities.* The best example of the former is the *salesperson's work plan,* which sales representatives submit a week or month in advance. The plan describes intended calls and routing. This report leads the salesforce to plan and schedule activities, informs management of their whereabouts, and provides a basis for comparing plans and accomplishments. Sales representatives can be evaluated on their ability to "plan their work and work their plan." Occasionally, management contacts individual sales representatives after receiving their plans to suggest improvements.

Companies are beginning to require their representatives to draft an annual *territory marketing plan* in which they outline their programs for developing new accounts and increasing business from existing accounts. The formats vary considerably—some ask for general ideas on territory development and others ask for detailed volume and profit estimates. This type of report casts representatives into the role of marketing managers and profit centers. Their managers study these plans, make suggestions, and use them to develop sales quotas.

Sales representatives write up their completed activities on *call reports.* Call reports keep sales management informed of the salesperson's activities, indicate the status of the customers' accounts, and provide information that might be useful in subsequent calls. Sales representatives also submit expense reports for which they are partly or wholly reimbursed. Some companies also require reports on new business, reports on lost business, and reports on local business and economic conditions.

These reports supply the raw data from which sales management can extract key indicators of sales performance. The key indicators are (1) average number of sales calls per salesperson per day, (2) average sales call time per contact, (3) average revenue per sales call, (4) average cost per sales call, (5) entertainment cost per sales call, (6) percentage of orders per hundred sales calls, (7) number of new customers per period, (8) number of lost customers per period, and (9) salesforce cost as a percentage of total sales. These indicators answer several useful questions: Are sales representatives making too few calls per day? Are they spending too much time per call? Are they spending too much on entertainment? Are they closing enough orders per hundred calls? Are they producing enough new customers and holding on to the old customers?

Formal Evaluation of Performance
The salesforce's reports along with other reports and observations supply the raw materials for evaluating members of the salesforce. Formal evaluation produces at least three benefits. First, management has to develop and communicate clear standards for judging performance. Second, management is motivated to gather well-rounded information about each salesperson. And third, representatives know they will have to sit down one morning with the sales manager and explain their performance or failure to achieve certain goals.

Salesperson-to-Salesperson Comparisons

One type of evaluation is to compare and rank the sales performance of the various sales representatives. Such comparisons, however, can be misleading. Relative sales performances are significant only if there are no variations in factors such as territory market potential, workload, degree of competition, and company promotional effort. Furthermore, sales are not usually the best indicator of achievement. Management should be more interested in how much each representative contributes to net profits. And this requires examining each representative's sales mix and sales expenses.

Current-to-Past Sales Comparisons

A second type of evaluation is to compare a sales representative's current performance with past performance. This should provide a direct indication of progress. An example is shown in Table 19-1.

The sales manager can learn many things about John Smith from this table. Smith's total sales increased every year (line 3). This does not necessarily mean that Smith is doing a better job. The product breakdown shows that he has been able to push the sales of product B further than those of product A (lines 1 and 2). According to his quotas for the two products (lines 4 and 5), his success in increasing product B sales may be at the expense of product A sales. According to gross profits (lines 6 and 7), the company earns twice as much gross profit (as a ratio to sales) on A as it does on B. Smith may be pushing the higher-volume, lower-margin product at the expense of the more profitable product. Although he increased total sales by $1,100 between 1984 and 1985 (line 3), the gross profits on his total sales actually decreased by $580 (line 8).

TABLE 19-1 *Form for Evaluating Sales Representative's Performance*

	TERRITORY: MIDLAND		SALES REPRESENTATIVE: JOHN SMITH	
	1982	1983	1984	1985
1. Net sales product A	$251,300	$253,200	$270,000	$263,100
2. Net sales product B	$423,200	$439,200	$553,900	$561,900
3. Net sales total	$674,500	$692,400	$823,900	$825,000
4. Percent of quota product A	95.6	92.0	88.0	84.7
5. Percent of quota product B	120.4	122.3	134.9	130.8
6. Gross profits product A	$ 50,260	$ 50,640	$ 54,000	$ 52,620
7. Gross profits product B	$ 42,320	$ 43,920	$ 53,390	$ 56,190
8. Gross profits total	$ 92,580	$ 94,560	$109,390	$108,810
9. Sales expense	$ 10,200	$ 11,100	$ 11,600	$ 13,200
10. Sales expense to total sales (%)	1.5	1.6	1.4	1.6
11. Number of calls	1,675	1,700	1,680	1,660
12. Cost per call	$ 6.09	$ 6.53	$ 6.90	$ 7.95
13. Average number of customers	320	324	328	334
14. Number of new customers	13	14	15	20
15. Number of lost customers	8	10	11	14
16. Average sales per customer	$ 2,108	$ 2,137	$ 2,512	$ 2,470
17. Average gross profit per customer	$ 289	$ 292	$ 334	$ 326

Sales expense (line 9) shows a steady increase, although total expense as a percentage of total sales seems to be under control (line 10). The upward trend in Smith's total dollar expense does not seem to be explained by any increase in the number of calls (line 11), although it may be related to his success in acquiring new customers (line 14). However, there is a possibility that in prospecting for new customers, he is neglecting present customers, as indicated by an upward trend in the annual number of lost customers (line 15).

The last two lines in the table show the level and trend in Smith's sales and gross profits per customer. These figures become more meaningful when they are compared with overall company averages. If John Smith's average gross profit per customer is lower than the company's average, he may be concentrating on the wrong customers or may not be spending enough time with each customer. Looking back at his annual number of calls (line 11), Smith may be making fewer annual calls than the average salesperson. If distances in his territory are not much different, this may mean he is not putting in a full workday, he is poor at planning his routing or minimizing his waiting, or he spends too much time with certain accounts.

Qualitative Evaluation of Sales Representatives

The evaluation usually includes the salesperson's knowledge of the company, products, customers, competitors, territory, and responsibilities. Personality characteristics can be rated, such as general manner, appearance, speech, and temperament. The sales manager can also review any problems in motivation or compliance. The sales manager should check to make sure that the representative knows the law (see Exhibit 19-6). Each company must decide what would be most useful to know. It should communicate these criteria to the representatives so that they understand how their performance is evaluated and can make an effort to improve it.

EXHIBIT 19-6

PERSONAL SELLING AND PUBLIC POLICY

Sales representatives must follow the rules of "fair competition" in trying to obtain orders. Certain activities are illegal or heavily regulated. Sales representatives are to refrain from offering bribes to buyers, purchasing agents, or other influence sources. It is illegal to procure technical or trade secrets of competitors through espionage or bribery. They must not disparage competitors or their products by suggesting things that are not true. They must not sell used items as new or mislead the customer about the buying advantages. They must inform customers of their rights, such as the seventy-two-hour "cooling-off" period in which customers can return the merchandise and receive their money back. They must not discriminate against buyers on the basis of their race, sex, or creed.

Source: Adapted from Ovid Riso, ed., *The Dartnell Sales Manager's Handbook,* 11th ed. (Chicago: Dartnell Corporation, 1968), pp. 320–22.

■ *Summary*

Most companies use sales representatives, and many companies assign them the pivotal role in the marketing mix. The high cost of this resource calls for an effective sales management process consisting of six steps: establishing salesforce objectives; designing salesforce strategy, structure, size, and compensation; recruiting and selecting; training; supervising; and evaluating.

As an element of the marketing mix, the salesforce is very effective in achieving certain marketing objectives and carrying on certain activities such as prospecting, communicating, selling and servicing, information gathering, and allocating. Under the marketing concept, the salesforce needs skills in marketing analysis and planning in addition to the traditional selling skills.

Once the salesforce objectives have been decided, strategy answers the questions of what type of selling would be most effective (solo selling, team selling) what type of salesforce structure would work best (territorial, product, or customer structured), how large the salesforce should be, and how the salesforce should be compensated in terms of pay level and pay components such as salary, commission, bonus, expenses, and fringe benefits.

Sales representatives must be recruited and selected carefully to hold down the high costs of hiring the wrong persons. Training programs familiarize new salespeople with the company's history, its products and policies, the characteristics of the market and competitors, and the art of selling. The art of selling involves a seven-step sales process: prospecting and qualifying, preapproach, approach, presentation and demonstration, handling objections, closing, and follow-up. Salespeople need supervision and continuous encouragement because they must make many decisions and are subject to many frustrations. Periodically, the company must evaluate their performance to help them do a better job.

■ Questions for Discussion

1. How does *personal selling* differ from *advertising*?
2. Relate the six tasks of selling to an automobile sales representative.
3. In what alternative ways can a salesforce be structured? Relate each to a specific company that sells industrial products.
4. A combination of straight salary and commission is probably the best way to compensate a salesforce. Comment.
5. What two personal qualities do you think are most important to a successful sales representative? Why?

6. You have just been hired by the World Book Encyclopedia Company to be a salesperson for the summer. Discuss how you would progress through the steps in effective selling.
7. What major tasks must those who supervise sales representatives undertake?
8. How would your manager in question 6 go about evaluating your selling job for World Book at the end of the summer?

■ References

1. Excerpts from THOMAS EHRICH, "To Computer Salesmen, the "Bit-Ticket" Deal Is the One to Look For," *Wall Street Journal*, January 22, 1974, p. 1.
2. ROBERT N. McMURRY, "The Mystique of Super-Salesmanship," *Harvard Business Review*, March–April 1961, p. 114.
3. See WILLIAM R. DIXON, "Redetermining the Size of the Sales Force: A Case Study," in *Changing Perspectives in Marketing Management*, Martin R. Warshaw (Ann Arbor: University of Michigan, Michigan Business Reports, 1962), No. 37, p. 58.
4. See ROGER M. PEGRAM, *Selling and Servicing the National Account* (New York: Conference Board, 1972); and BENSON P. SHAPIRO and ROWLAND MORIARTY, "National Account Management," Marketing Science Institute, 1980.

5. WILLIAM H. KAVEN, *Managing the Major Sale* (New York: American Management Association, 1971); and BENSON P. SHAPIRO and RONALD S. POSNER, "Making the Major Sale," *Harvard Business Review*, March–April 1976, pp. 68–78.
6. For more on the workload and other approaches, see WALTER J. TALLEY, "How to Design Sales Territories," *Journal of Marketing*, January 1961, pp. 7–13; and GILBERT A. CHURCHILL, JR., NEIL M. FORD, and ORVILLE C. WALKER, JR., *Sales Force Management* (Homewood, IL: Irwin, 1981), pp. 160–67.
7. "1984 Survey of Selling Costs," *Sales and Marketing Management*, February 20, 1984, p. 60.
8. Ibid., p. 61.
9. The survey was conducted for the Sales Executives Club of New York and was reported in *Business Week*, February 1, 1964, p. 52.

10. "1984 Survey of Selling Costs," p. 67.
11. MCMURRY, "Mystique of Super-Salesmanship," p. 117.
12. Ibid., p. 118
13. "Youth Continues to Snub Selling," *Sales Management,* January 15, 1965, p. 69. Also see DONALD L. THOMPSON, "Stereotype of the Salesman," *Harvard Business Review,* January–February 1972, p. 21.
14. "1984 Survey of Selling Costs," p. 73.
15. Some of the following discussion is based on W. J. E. CRISSY, WILLIAM H. CUNNINGHAM, and ISABELLA C. M. CUNNINGHAM, *Selling: The Personal Force in Marketing* (New York: Wiley, 1977), pp. 119–29.
16. VINCENT L. ZIRPOLI, "You Can't 'Control' the Prospect, So Manage the Presale Activities to Increase Performance," *Marketing News,* March 16, 1984, p. 1.
17. MARK HANAN, "Join the Systems Sell and You Can't Be Beat," *Sales and Marketing Management,* August 21, 1972, p. 44. Also see MARK HANAN, JAMES CRIBBIN, and HERMAN HEISER, *Consultative Selling* (New York: American Management Association, 1970).
18. CRISSY, CUNNINGHAM, and CUNNINGHAM, *Selling,* pp. 289–94.
19. See GERALD I. NIERENBERG, *The Art of Negotiation* (New York: Hawthorn, 1968); and CHESTER L. KARRASS, *Give and Take: The Complete Guide to Negotiating Strategies* (New York: Crowell, 1974).
20. See JOHN F. MAGEE, "Determining the Optimum Allocation of Expenditures for Promotional Effort with Operations Research Methods," in *The Frontiers of Marketing Thought and Science,* Frank M. Bass, ed. (Chicago: American Marketing Association, 1958), pp. 140–56.
21. For examples, see "S&MM's Special Computers in Marketing Section," *Sales and Marketing Management,* December 5, 1983, pp. 52–63.
22. J. B. HECKERT, *Business Budgeting and Control* (New York: Ronald Press, 1946), p. 138.

CASE 13

THE PILLSBURY CO.: TOTINO'S PIZZA

Totino's, Inc., a Minneapolis-based frozen pizza company, was acquired by the Pillsbury Co. in 1975 when the annual sales growth rate was 20 percent. Within two years, Totino's revolutionary crisp crust technology had been developed and the company was ready to put into action an aggressive marketing plan designed to make it the leader in consumer frozen pizza. The key aspects of the plan were product improvement, aggressive promotional efforts, and the three basic segments of the market: high, medium, and low price.

The plan was successful and within three years Totino's was the leading brand of frozen pizza in the United States despite the new competitive entries sponsored by General Mills (Saluto), H. J. Heinz (La Pizzeria), Nestlé (Stouffers), Quaker Oats (Celeste) and more vigorous competition from over 100 smaller regional firms. (Additional industry information is found in the appendix.)

In 1976 Pillsbury acquired Fox De Luxe Pizza, which at the time was a small manufacturer of frozen pizza distributed primarily in the southeastern part of the country. Fox De Luxe was different in product formulation, utilizing a nonfried (baked) crust. It also normally sold at a slightly lower retail price than Totino's regular Party Pizza.

More recently, in 1984, Pillsbury has introduced a frozen pizza designed exclusively to be prepared in microwave ovens. This product was introduced under the Pillsbury Microwave brand name. Pillsbury also sells several other microwave-specific frozen products, including pancakes and popcorn.

Jeno's, Inc., of Duluth, Minnesota, the former leader in the frozen pizza market and more recently second, sought to regain leadership by attempting to nullify Totino's advantage in the crisp crust and distinctive package. Jeno's followed Totino's by two years in introducing its "Crisp and Tasty Crust." The package for its "regular" size (about 10 oz) could be confused with Totino's package for the same size. After some legal action, Jeno's changed its packaging design. Subsequently, in the early 1980s, Jeno's increased its share through acquisition of Chef Saluto from General Mills and two regional brands, John's and Gino's, but remained in second place.

In general, the food industry is showing trends toward more upscale and healthful food products. Perhaps because of more women in the workforce, consumers are demanding higher-quality, more nutritious foods and are willing to pay for them. Within the pizza industry the products coming the closest to answering this need are the delivered store door (DSD) brands and deli pizzas, made fresh on the premises of some large supermarkets. Totino's My Classic Pizza competes in this higher-priced segment.

Advertising expenditures for the industry amount to about 2 percent of sales, among the lowest for food products and a level usually associated with commodity-type products. On the other hand, a considerable amount is spent at the retail level in the form of display, advertising, and other types of allowances as sales incentives. Consumers are also offered incentives. Promotional price specials and coupons have been the principal ones. *Hardly a week goes by without some special promotion for items in the frozen pizza case.*

Retailers favor profit-producing brands. With limited freezer cabinet space, they favor the seller who spends the most on advertising and promotion, especially trade allowances which directly improve profitability. On the other hand, Totino and other manufacturers recognize that such allowances and most types of sales promotion efforts are only short-term sales stimulators that build little consumer loyalty. Totino's management wants to spend its advertising and promotional dollars effectively to build customer loyalty—a strong consumer franchise. Yet competitors spend for immediate sales stimulation. This is especially true of marginal manufacturers.

Totino's management must now reconsider its marketing objectives and activities in view of the new competitive situation and changing life styles of the consumer, especially with regard to advertising and promotion aspects. What recommendations would you give Totino's management concerning the marketing of the product, particularly advertising and sales promotion?

Appendix: Additional Industry Information

1. Frozen pizza sales amounted to about $950 million in 1983 compared with pizzeria sales of almost $5 billion—many times more than frozen pizza sales. While frozen pizza represents about 30 percent of all pizza consumed, over 70 percent of all pizza, including pizzeria pizza, is eaten at home.

2. Frozen pizza is growing in dollar volume, but more slowly than other frozen prepared foods.

	DOLLAR GROWTH
Total frozen foods	+10.7
Frozen prepared foods	+21.3
Frozen single dish	+19.9
Frozen dinners	+48.3
Frozen hors d'oeuvres	+34.9
Frozen pizza	+ 3.1

3. Regional taste differences are wide, and the variety makes it difficult for fast-food chains to customize, which makes it easier for small regional pizza chains to survive. Pizza is more fragmented and less chain-dominated than the hamburger segment of the fast-food chain business. Regional taste differences were also a reason why, until recently, the frozen pizza industry was highly fragmented—no strong national brands.

4. Frozen pizza categories and trade estimates of case shares and growth rates for a recent year are:

	PERCENT OF TOTAL	GROWTH RATE
Single serve 6–8 oz	6.6%	+16.8
Regular 9–12 oz	53.4	+ 0.7
Mid-size 13–17 oz	11.9	+ 9.5
Deluxe 18 + oz	12.4	+ 7.9
French bread	7.4	+16.7

Pillsbury's pizza line includes the following:

NAME	DESCRIPTION	CATEGORY	WEIGHT (OZ)
Totino Party	Crisp crust	Regular	9–10.85
Totino Extra	Extra topping	Mid-size	13–14.3
Totino My Classic	Thin crust	De luxe	20–24.5
Totino Heat & Eat (M/W)	Microwave	Single serve	3.5–?
Pillsbury Microwave	Microwave	Single serve	6–9.9
Fox De Luxe	Crisp crust	Economy	10

5. The popularity of pizza crosses market segments. *Chain Institutions Magazine* found that in a recent year over 48 percent of the service operations surveyed reported that pizza is a "good seller" when it is on the menu. They included full-service restaurants, fast-food restaurants, hotels/motels, hospitals, nursing homes, schools, colleges/universities, and employee feeding facilities.

6. A number of large food processors are in the frozen pizza business:

MANUFACTURER	BRANDS
Pillsbury	Totino's, Fox De Luxe, Pillsbury Microwave
Quaker Oats	Celeste
Nestlé	Stouffer
American Home Products	Chef-Boy-Ar-Dee

The major independents are as follows:

MANUFACTURER	BRANDS
Jeno's, Inc.	Jeno's, Mr. P's, John's, Gino's, Chef Saluto
United Products*	La Pizzeria
Tony's	Tony's, Red Baron
Tombstone	Tombstone

*Purchased La Pizzeria from H. J. Heinz in 1984.

Shares of these seven manufacturers are estimated as follows:

MANUFACTURER	SHARE OF FROZEN PIZZA CASES (%)
Pillsbury	30
Jeno's, Inc.	25
Quaker Oats	8
Nestlé	8
Tony's	7
Tombstone	3
United Products	1
Chef-Boy-Ar-Dee	1

7. Totino's pizza is distributed in virtually all geographic areas. Totino's has a very strong brand position, especially in the regular (Party Pizza) segment, in many areas. However, in some markets local brands or strongly entrenched brands of major consumer goods companies have the dominant market share.

8. Frozen-food brokers and a frozen warehouse distribution system are commonly used to sell the product. Tony's and Tombstone are said to be the only firms with direct store delivery systems.

9. Trade deals are a major marketing tool for the industry. They are designed to encourage low-price promotions by the retailer to the consumer. The warfare for market share keeps prices low and cuts potentially high margins. In the trade, it is said that no one is making a lot of money yet from frozen pizzas. *"There isn't space in the cabinet for everybody and you go with the guys who are spending money* (advertising and promotional dollars)," stated a food retailer.

10. Until the recent introduction of Pillsbury's Microwave Pizza (a single serve size), microwave ovens produced an undesirably limp crust. Pillsbury's product uses technologically advanced packaging which includes a cooking device that allows the crust to stay crisp. Because of the costliness of this packaging, it would not make sense to use it on large-size pizzas or on those purchased by conventional oven users.

11. Some retailers indicate that deli/refrigerated pizza sales have caused a sizable increase in total pizza volume. It appears that deli/refrigerated pizza is a high impulse purchase item.

CASE 14

PUREX INDUSTRIES, INC.

Purex is a manufacturer and marketer of industrial and consumer products, primarily price-promoted items in both the branded and nonbranded categories. The company is the fourth largest maker of household cleaning products and the largest producer and distributor of private-label household cleaning products. Purex has a 25 percent share of the home liquid bleach market, second only to Clorox; and it claims a substantial share of the clothes dryer fabric softener market, second only to Procter & Gamble.

The following internal and external developments have recently brought about a new competitive situation that may call for changes in Purex's consumer products' marketing efforts, especially those relating to the household cleaning products.

1. Private-label and generic products now represent a significant and growing share of industry sales, particularly in the paper goods and household cleaning categories. Consumers are showing greater acceptance as a result of economic conditions and other influences, but acceptance varies by product, retail outlet, and area.

   According to the 1984 Generics Survey of the top 150 U.S. grocery retailers and wholesalers, generic brands increased to 10 percent of sales, despite their no-frills packaging and lack of marketing support. Because generics were priced at an average of 27.8 percent below national brands, and an average of 12.8 percent below private labels, according to the survey, operators estimated the national brands were the hardest hit by the growing popularity of generics.

2. Retailers, eager to attract price-conscious consumers and improve their profits, are moving toward nonbranded products and "no-frill" retailing in conventional supermarkets. New types of "no-frill" retail food stores, such as Aldi, A&P's Plus, and Jewel's T Box, as well as warehouse stores, placing great emphasis on value, are becoming more numerous. Some outlets have reduced the number of categories of goods stocked, while others carry only the two or three leading brands in each category.

3. Nationally advertised brand manufacturers, suffering from the inroads made by generics and private labels, are bringing out more price-oriented brands. Scott Paper Company, the leading producer of toilet paper, has products at both ends of the price spectrum. Procter & Gamble has launched an economy-priced unadvertised line of paper products under the name Summit. P&G has also introduced an economy-priced Ivory shampoo, but in test markets did not stress price as a selling point. It is not clear how much advertising support is planned.

4. Purex itself has taken several steps toward adjusting to changing conditions:

   a. Purchased the Decatur, Illinois, based A. E. Staley Company's assets and business in household products and retail food products, which gave Purex additional laundry products, fabric softeners, corn starch and syrup products, and four manufacturing facilities in the United States.

   b. Purchased the New York based Witco Chemical Company's two strategically located low-cost spray-drying detergent manufacturing plants, thus increasing Purex's capacity to five such units.

   c. Sold some of its losing or marginal industrial and agricultural businesses and shifted, on a royalty basis, the manufacture and sale of its drugstore products to Jeffrey Martin, Inc., an international marketing firm, which scored a great success with its Porcelana skin spot fade cream. The brands shifted include Ayds appetite-suppressant products, Doan's pills, and Cuticura medicated skin-care products. These actions have increased Purex's available cash, allowing reallocation of assets.

d. Realigned its operations to give separate worldwide organizations to consumer and industrial products and services.

Historically, Purex's first product was household liquid bleach, and its principal competition was and is Clorox. Each company sought to differentiate in the minds of consumers its brand of this commodity-type product through advertising, packaging, and product labels. The product itself was and is chemically the same. Over the years Purex acquired a number of well-known brand products, sometimes after they had passed their peak. Among them were Old Dutch scouring cleanser, Bo-Peep ammonia, LaFrance bluing, Cameo copper cleanser, Fels Naptha laundry bar soap, Sweetheart soap products, Dobie cleaning pads, Brillo soap pads, Ellio's Pizza, Pope brand tomatoes, and other Italian products. The company also developed products to give it a full line of household cleaning items.

Purex's management has attributed much of the company's success with its branded products to (1) its "key account" selling plan aimed at retailers and (2) its "price/value" concept aimed at consumers and retailers.

The "key account" concept involves working effectively with a limited number of large retail chains that account for a disproportionately large share of Purex's consumer product sales. By working closely with these "key accounts," learning their needs, coordinating activities, and fulfilling these needs, the company's key account representatives have been highly successful with the retailers. This successful Purex approach—cultivating mutually beneficial relationships with selected large retailers—has become more widely accepted by competitors, thereby decreasing one of Purex's earlier advantages.

The Purex "price/value" marketing concept elements are: competitive quality at lower prices, relatively light advertising support, and heavy retailer incentives. Purex has claimed that the retailers' gross profit margin on Purex products is significantly higher than on competitors' products. The company's "Symbol of Value" logo, consisting of a circle around an outstretched hand holding a bar of Purex soap above the words "Symbol of Value," appears in almost all advertisements and on product packages. Such value is somewhat difficult to demonstrate. Procter & Gamble, on the other hand, has claimed that its products provide superior product performance that can be perceived by consumers.

Purex sold price-promoted products under the "price/value" concept through the 1960s, but in the 1970s it pushed the concept more aggressively by adjusting the price downward even more sharply. Purex-branded bleaches and detergents were priced at 30 percent below top-selling brands. Trade observers now believe that competition will become even more severe for Purex if generics become more accepted and economy-priced branded products are proliferated by major premium branded goods manufacturers. The success of the "price/value" concept depends upon whether consumers believe they are getting a good value at a low price.

Household liquid bleach, a commodity-type product, is a case in point. The active ingredient in all liquid bleaches sold for household use in the United States is sodium hypochlorite in the amount of 5.25 percent. The remaining 94.75 percent is water. Yet the following prices for various branded and nonbranded bleaches have been observed in a large chain supermarket.

SIZE	NATIONAL	REGIONAL	PRIVATE LABEL	GENERIC
1 qt	$ .55			
2 qt	.79		$ .66	
4 qt	.94	$ .89	.79	$ .58
6 qt	1.65			

Price differences of this type exist in most outlets where liquid bleach is sold, even though all the bottles contain essentially the same bleach solution. Whether these price differences continue will depend on whether sellers are able to make meaningful differentiations in the minds of consumers. At one time Purex tried to differentiate its product by increasing the active ingredient to 5.75 percent, thus allowing it to claim a stronger, more effective product. Later the 5.25 percent formulation was restored and has continued. Clorox has developed a convenient nondrip bottle.

It is estimated that nonbranded products, including the private-label and generics, now account for almost 35 percent of Purex's household cleaning product sales. Some observers consider this a potential problem because this price-sensitive business comes in large orders with no consumer loyalty. Purex and other nonbranded product suppliers recognize the strong bargaining power of large retail chain buyers, especially when a supplier becomes overly dependent on one or a few buyers.

For many years Purex has enjoyed the advantage of its "value/price" marketing concept. In view of the new competitive situation, the question is whether the concept and marketing plans based on it will be sufficient for Purex to maintain its reasonably good growth and earnings record. What recommendations would you make to the Purex management?

six

MANAGING THE MARKETING EFFORT

Part Six of this book examines how companies design and implement sound competitive marketing strategies using the marketing mix tools.

EVEN THE MOST SKILLED DRIVER IS ONLY AS GOOD AS HIS TIRES.

EAGLE. ENGINEERED FOR CARS WITH THE PROPER QUALIFICATIONS

Ultimately, a car's contact with the road will either enhance or hinder a driver's ability to control it.

Which may be why a majority of professional drivers race on Goodyear racing Eagles.

This ongoing participation in racing is also the best way we know to push our tires to their limits.

The technology we've developed from those endeavors goes into every tire we make. As a result, our high-performance Eagle VR "Gatorback" is regarded as one of the best handling tires in the world.

So you might want to consider adding a set of Eagle VR radials to your own car. We think you'll find you're in very good company.

You'll find the complete line of Eagle high-performance tires only at the Eagle Qualification Center at your Goodyear retailer.

GOOD YEAR

20
Competitive Marketing Strategies

In recent years, the tire market has become intensely competitive, experiencing slow growth, overcapacity, and price wars. Each major tire producer has the same overall goal—to exist profitably in this industry. But each uses a vastly different competitive marketing strategy.

Goodyear Tire & Rubber, the world's largest tiremaker, is pouring money into this industry to protect its position as the market leader. Goodyear is investing heavily in plant modernization to lower costs and improve quality, in research and development to design more advanced tires, and in marketing and advertising to build up consumer and dealer preference. Through this strategy, Goodyear has increased its market share, but it will take a long time for this higher market share to translate into profits.

Goodyear is looking over its shoulder at Michelin, the No. 2 tiremaker and leading market challenger. Michelin rose to its high position by leading the industry in innovation. It introduced the steel-belted radial tire, a tire that lasted longer than competitors' tires. Michelin's continuous innovation of better tires won it a "Cadillac" reputation for high quality which allowed it to charge a premium price. Although Michelin has lowered its prices lately to gain market share, it still seeks market leadership through technological innovation.

Uniroyal, the fourth-ranked company in the tire industry, has chosen a diversification strategy to reduce its dependence on the slow-growth tire business. It is pushing into two nontire businesses—

agricultural chemicals and fabricated plastic products—which together account for 33 percent of its sales, but over 75 percent of its earnings. Uniroyal has divested its business units making golf balls, inner tubes, and fire hoses, but still must figure out what to do with its core tire business, which hangs like an albatross around its neck. Uniroyal is a major supplier of original equipment tires to General Motors, but because of the less than 2 percent growth in the tire industry and the intense price cutting, Uniroyal would be ready to sell its tire business if it could find a buyer.

Armstrong Rubber Company, sixth among U.S. tiremakers, has chosen to specialize in making tires almost entirely for the replacement market. It has shown great skill in picking and exploiting specialized market niches, such as tires for recreational vehicles and farm equipment. Armstrong selects smaller but potentially profitable market segments and pursues leadership in each chosen market segment by specializing in serving that segment's needs.

Each of these companies has adopted a competitive marketing strategy it believes is best suited to the company's position in the industry and to the highly competitive and rapidly changing industry environment. Goodyear focuses on cost reduction; Michelin pursues innovation; Uniroyal has chosen diversification; and Armstrong practices a market-niching strategy by entering small but highly profitable markets.[1]

M

anaging the marketing effort involves *analyzing* the marketing environment and possible marketing actions, *planning* marketing strategies and programs that best exploit market opportunities, *implementing* these strategies and programs through an effective marketing organization, and *controlling* marketing efforts to ensure that the company operates efficiently and effectively.

In Part Two of this book we examined the strategic and marketing planning processes to see how marketers plan their activities under the company's overall strategic plan. In Parts Three and Four we looked at how marketers analyze consumers and the marketing environment to select the most promising target markets. And in Part Five we looked closely at the marketing mix variables—the tools marketers can assemble into programs that will effectively achieve company and marketing objectives. We are ready now to examine the broad marketing strategies that might result from the company's analysis and planning, how these strategies are adapted to changing competitive situations, and how strategies are implemented and controlled.

In this chapter we discuss broad competitive strategies marketers use depending on their resources, industry position, and the competitive environment. In the next chapter we will examine how companies implement marketing strategies and programs, and how they organize and control their marketing efforts.

COMPETITIVE STRATEGIES

Marketers must design strategies that best match company resources to environmental opportunities. But what broad marketing strategies might the company use? Which ones are best for a particular company, or for the company's different divisions and products?

The marketing concept states that to be successful, marketers must determine the needs and wants of target consumers and deliver the desired satisfactions more efficiently and effectively than competitors. Thus marketing strategy must be adapted not only to target consumers, but also to the strategies of competitors who are serving the same target consumers. To succeed, marketers must formulate strategies that strongly position their offerings against competitors' offerings in the minds of consumers—strategies that give the company, business unit, or product the strongest possible *strategic advantage*.

No one strategy is best for all companies. Each company must determine what makes the most sense in light of its position in the industry and its objectives, opportunities, and resources. Even within a company, different strategies may be required for different businesses or products. Johnson & Johnson uses one marketing strategy for its leading brands in stable consumer markets, and a different marketing strategy for its new high-tech health care businesses and products. In the remainder of this chapter, we will look at broad *competitive marketing strategies* marketers can use for their companies, business units, or brands.

Competitive Positions Marketers must constantly adapt their strategies to the rapidly changing competitive environment. In the fast-growth economic environment of the 1960s, companies paid less attention than today to their competitors. The economic pie was growing fast enough for everyone to succeed. In the seventies and eighties, lackluster economic growth brought about intensified competition. Companies began to pay close attention to competitors' strengths and weaknesses and often launched aggressive attacks on competitors' positions. Companies increasingly based their marketing strategies on the logic of both consumers' wants and competitors' positions.[2]

Each firm's size and industry position will determine its marketing strategy. Large firms with dominant positions in an industry can practice certain strategies not affordable to small firms. But being large is not enough. There are winning strategies for large firms; there are also losing strategies for large firms. And small firms can often find strategies to achieve as good or better rates of return than large firms. Both large and small firms must design strategies that effectively position them against competitors in their market. Michael Porter, in his *Competitive Strategy*, suggests four generic positioning strategies that companies could follow—three winning strategies and one losing one.[3]

- ◼ **Overall cost leadership.** Here the company works hard to achieve the lowest costs of production and distribution so that it can price lower than its competitors and win a large market share. Firms pursuing this strategy must be good at engineering, purchasing, manufacturing, and physical distribution and need less skill in marketing. Texas Instruments is a leading practitioner of this strategy.
- ◼ **Differentiation.** Here the company concentrates on creating a highly differentiated product line and marketing program so that is comes across as the class leader in the industry. Most customers would prefer to own this brand if its price is not too high. Companies pursuing this strategy have major strengths in research and development, design, quality control, and marketing. IBM and Caterpillar enjoy the differentiation position in computers and heavy construction equipment, respectively.
- ◼ **Focus.** Here the company focuses its effort on serving a few market segments well rather than going after the whole market. The company gets to know the needs of these segments and pursues cost leadership, product differentiation, or both, within each segment. Thus Armstrong Rubber has specialized in making superior tires for farm equipment vehicles and recreational vehicles, and keeps looking for other niches to serve.

According to Porter, companies that pursue a clear strategy—one of the above—are likely to perform well. Those firms pursuing the same strategy constitute a *strategic group*. The firm that carries off that strategy best will make the most profits. Thus the lowest-cost firm among those firms pursuing a low-cost strategy will do the best. Porter suggests that firms that do not pursue a clear strategy—*middle-of-the-roaders*—do the worst. Chrysler and International Harvester both came upon difficult times because neither stood out in their respective industries as lowest in cost, highest in perceived value, or best in serving some market segment. Middle-of-the-roaders try to be good on all strategic dimensions, but since strategic dimensions require different and often inconsistent ways to organize the firm, these companies end up being not particularly excellent at anything (see Exhibit 20-1).

EXHIBIT 20-1

COMPETITIVE POSITIONS IN THE HEAVY-DUTY TRUCK
INDUSTRY

Companies that achieve cost leadership, high product differentiation, or market focusing can enjoy high rates of return. Those that pursue middle-of-the-road strategies usually earn only average or below average rates of return. Some research by William Hall illustrates how these competitive positions relate to profitability in the truck manufacturing industry. The figure below shows the competitive positions in the late 1970s of seven truck manufacturers according to their *relative delivered cost* (being a low-cost firm) and their *relative performance* (offering the most differentiated or desirable product or service). The percentages in the figure represent each manufacturer's return on investment in this industry.

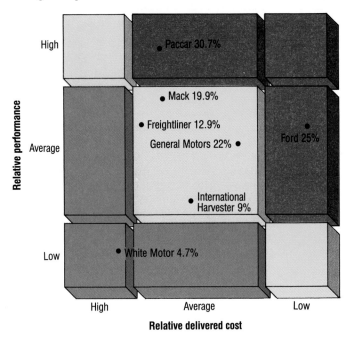

Ford has the lowest relative delivered cost. Its trucks show only average performance, but Ford's low-cost position gives it a higher margin and one of the industry's highest rates of return. Paccar is the industry leader in high-performance trucks (its Peterbilt and Kenworth trucks are considered the Cadillacs of the industry), and this high-performance leadership earns Paccar a 31 percent return on investment, the highest in the industry.

At the other extreme is White, whose trucks are below average in performance and high in delivered cost. Not surprisingly, White's rate of return was only 4.7 percent, lowest in the industry. The company was later bought by Volvo, which hoped to improve White's competitive performance.

The four companies in the middle box are "middle-of-the-roaders" that try to be good at performance and cost, but are not especially good at either. As it turns out, Freightliner was later purchased by Mercedes, and International Harvester's truck line is in serious trouble.

To improve their profitabilities, the middle-of-the-roaders must commit more strongly to one of Porter's three winning strategies. For example, International Harvester has three options. It can invest in more modern production facilities to become a low-cost firm, and compete with Ford and General Motors in the strategic group pursuing cost leadership. Or International Harvester could try to improve quality and more strongly differentiate its trucks so that it competes with Paccar and Mack in the strategic group pursuing product differentiation. This would be a harder strategy—it takes years to build a better product and reputation, and Paccar is too well established in this position. Finally, International Harvester might choose to go after certain niches in the truck market—to become a leader in each niche through low costs or product differentiation or through both. But if International Harvester stays in its current competitive position of trying to do a little of everything, its future will be difficult.

Source: The figure is reprinted by permission of the *Harvard Business Review.* An exhibit from "Survival Strategies in a Hostile Environment," by William K. Hall (September–October 1980). Copyright © 1980 by the President and Fellows of Harvard College; all rights reserved.

We will develop a different classification of competitive positions in this chapter. Companies, company divisions, or products can be classified by their behavior in an industry—that of leading, challenging, following, or niching. Suppose that an industry has the market structure shown in Figure 20-1. Forty percent of the market is in the hands of the *market leader,* the firm whose products hold the largest market share. Another 30 percent is in the hands of a *market challenger,* a runner-up that is fighting hard to increase its share of this market. Another 20 percent is in the hands of a *market follower,* another runner-up that wants to maintain its share without rocking the boat. The remaining 10 percent is in the hands of *market nichers,* firms whose products serve small segments not being pursued by firms with larger shares of the market.

We will now examine specific marketing strategies that are available to market leaders, challengers, followers, and nichers. In the sections that follow, it is important to remember that the classifications of competitive positions often do not apply to a whole company, but only to its position in a specific industry. For example, large and diversified companies such as IBM, Sears, or General Mills—or their individual businesses, divisions, or products—might be leaders in some markets and nichers in others. Such companies often use different competitive marketing strategies for different business units, depending on the competitive situations of each.

MARKET-LEADER STRATEGIES

Most industries contain one firm that is acknowledged as the market leader. This firm has the largest market share in the relevant product market. It usually leads the

FIGURE 20-1
Hypothetical Market Structure

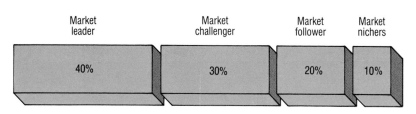

Market leader	Market challenger	Market follower	Market nichers
40%	30%	20%	10%

other firms in price changes, new product introductions, distribution coverage, and promotional intensity. The leader may or may not be admired or respected, but other firms acknowledge its dominance. The leader is an orientation point for competitors, a company to challenge, imitate, or avoid. Some of the best-known market leaders are General Motors (autos), Kodak (photography), U.S. Steel (steel), IBM (computers), Xerox (copying), Procter & Gamble (consumer packaged goods), Caterpillar (earth-moving equipment), Coca-Cola (soft drinks), Sears (retailing), McDonald's (fast food), and Gillette (razor blades).

A dominant firm's life is not altogether easy. It must maintain a constant vigilance. Other firms keep challenging its strengths or trying to take advantage of its weaknesses. The market leader can easily miss a turn in the market and plunge into second or third place. A product innovation may come along and hurt the leader (such as Tylenol's nonaspirin painkiller taking over the lead from Bayer Aspirin). The leader might spend conservatively, expecting hard times, while a challenger spends liberally (Montgomery Ward's loss of its retail dominance to Sears after World War II). The dominant firm might look old-fashioned against new and peppier rivals (*Playboy* magazine's fall to second place in newsstand circulation after *Penthouse*). The dominant firm's costs might rise excessively and hurt its profits (Food Fair's decline, resulting from poor cost control).

Dominant firms want to remain number one. This calls for action on three fronts. First, the firm must find ways to expand total demand. Second, the firm must protect its current market share through good defensive and offensive actions. Third, the firm can try to expand its market share further, even if market size remains constant.

Expanding the Total Market   All firms in an industry may benefit when the total market is expanded, but the dominant firm normally gains the most. If Americans buy 10 million cars instead of 8 million, General Motors stands to gain the most because it produces over half of the domestic cars sold in the U.S. If General Motors can convince more Americans to own cars, or own more cars per household, or replace them more often, it will benefit. In general, the leader should look for new users, new uses, and more usage of its products.

New Users

Every product class has the potential of attracting buyers who are unaware of the product or who are resisting it because of its price or lack of certain features. A manufacturer can search for new users among three groups. For example, a perfume manufacturer can try to convince women who do not use perfume to use perfume *(market penetration strategy)*, or convince men to start using perfume *(new market strategy)*, or sell perfume in other countries *(geographical expansion strategy)*.

One of the great success stories in developing a new class of users is that of Johnson & Johnson's baby shampoo, the leading brand of baby shampoo. The company became concerned about future sales growth when the birth rate slowed down. Their marketers noticed that other family members occasionally used the baby shampoo for their own hair. Management decided to develop an advertising

Market leader Campbell attempts to expand the total market by convincing consumers that "soup is good food." *Courtesy of Campbell Soup Company.*

campaign aimed at adults. In a short time, Johnson & Johnson baby shampoo became a leading brand in the total shampoo market.

New Uses

The marketer can expand markets by discovering and promoting new uses for the product. Here are some examples:

- Du Pont's nylon provides a classic example of new-use expansion. Every time nylon became a mature product, some new use was discovered. Nylon was first used as a fiber for parachutes; then for women's stockings; later as a major material in shirts and blouses; and still later in automobile tires, upholstery, and carpeting.[4] Each new use started nylon on a new life cycle. Credit goes to Du Pont's continuous research and development program to find new uses.

- Sales of Arm & Hammer baking soda stayed level for 125 years. The product had many uses, but no single use was advertised. When the company discovered that consumers were using baking soda as a refrigerator deodorizer, it launched a heavy advertising and publicity campaign focusing on this single use and succeeded in getting consumers in half of America's homes to place an open box of baking soda in their refrigerators. A few years later, Arm & Hammer discovered that some consumers used baking soda to put out kitchen grease fires, and promoted this use with great success.

- In many cases, consumers deserve the credit for discovering new uses. Vaseline petroleum jelly began as a simple machine lubricant. But over the years consumers have reported numerous new uses, including use as a skin ointment, a healing agent, and a hair dressing.

More Usage

A third market expansion strategy is to convince people to use more of the product per use occasion. If a cereal manufacturer convinces consumers to eat a full bowl of cereal instead of half a bowl, total sales will increase. Procter & Gamble advises users that its Head and Shoulders shampoo is more effective with two applications instead of one per shampoo.

A creative example of a company stimulating higher usage per occasion is the Michelin Tire Company (French). Michelin wanted French car owners to drive their cars more miles per year—thus leading to more tire replacement. They conceived the idea of rating French restaurants on a three-star system. They reported that many of the best restaurants were in the south of France, leading many Parisians to consider weekend drives to the south of France. Michelin also published guidebooks with maps and sights along the way to further entice travel.

Protecting Market Share While trying to expand total market size, the leading firm must also constantly protect its current business against competitor attacks. Coca-Cola must constantly guard against Pepsi-Cola; Gillette against Bic; Kodak against Fuji; McDonald's against Burger King; General Motors against Ford.

What can the market leader do to protect its position? The best response is *continuous innovation*. The leader refuses to be content with the way things are and leads the industry in new product ideas, customer services, distribution effectiveness, and cost cutting. It keeps increasing its competitive effectiveness and value to customers. It takes the offensive and exercises initiative, sets the pace, and exploits competitor's weaknesses. The best defense is a good offense.

The dominant firm, even when it does not launch offensives, must at least guard all its fronts and not leave any exposed flanks. It must keep its costs down, and its prices must be consistent with the value the customers see in the brand. The leader must "plug holes" so that competitors don't jump in. Thus a consumer packaged goods leader will produce its brands in several sizes and forms to meet varying consumer preferences and hold on to as much scarce dealer shelf space as possible.

Intensified competition in domestic and world markets in recent years has sparked management's interest in models of military warfare.[5] Leader companies have been advised to protect their market positions with competitive strategies patterned after successful military defense strategies. There are, in fact, six defense strategies that a market leader can use. They are illustrated in Figure 20-2 and described below.[6]

Position Defense

The most basic form of defense is to build fortifications around one's position. But simply defending one's current position or products is a form of *marketing myopia*. Henry Ford's myopia about his Model-T brought an enviably healthy company with $1 billion in cash reserves at its peak to the brink of financial ruin. Even such enduring brands as Coca-Cola and Bayer Aspirin cannot be relied upon by their companies as the main sources of future growth and profitability. Coca-Cola today, in spite of producing nearly half the soft drinks of the world, has aggressively moved into the wine market, has acquired fruit-drink companies, and has diversi-

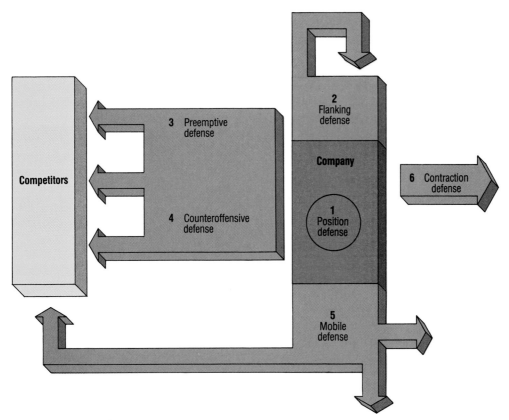

FIGURE 20-2 *Defense Strategies*

fied into desalinization equipment and plastics. Clearly leaders under attack would be foolish to put all their resources into building fortifications around their current products.

Flanking Defense

When guarding its overall position, the market leader should pay particular attention to its weaker flanks. Smart competitors will normally attack the company's weaknesses. Thus the Japanese successfully entered the small car market because U.S. automakers left a gaping hole in that submarket. The company must carefully check its flanks and protect the more vulnerable ones.

Many examples of flanking defenses are found in the business world.

> Chicago-based Jewel Food Stores believes that the supermarket will continue to remain a dominant force but is flanking its position by strengthening its food-retailing-assortment mix to meet new challenges. The fast-food boom has been met by offering a wide assortment of instant and frozen meals and the discount-food challenge by promoting generic lines. Jewel's various supermarkets are being tailored to suit local demands for such items as fresh bakery products and ethnic foods. And the company is taking no chances with some institutional developments. It has set up the Jewel-T division, which is a network of "box" discount stores patterned after pioneer Aldi. Watching a sudden turnaround in the competitive position of "independents" in 1977, Jewel's Star Market division in New England promptly began moving into franchising the following year. To hedge the "combination store" challenge, it integrated a large number of its supermarkets with its Osco Drug stores, using both side-by-side and fully integrated designs.

Preemptive Defense

A more aggressive defense is to launch an offense against competitors *before* they start their offense against the company. The company cuts down competitors before they can strike. Preemptive defense assumes that an ounce of prevention is worth a pound of cure. For example, a company could launch an attack against a competitor whose market share is approaching some dangerous level. When Chrysler's market share began rising from 12 to 18 percent some years ago, one rival marketing executive was heard to say, "If they [Chrysler] go to 20 percent, it will be over our dead bodies."

The preemptive defense might consist of "guerrilla actions"—hitting one competitor here, another there—to keep everyone off balance. Or it might consist of sustained frontal attacks aimed at retaining the initiative and keeping competitors always on the defensive.

Counteroffensive Defense

When a market leader is attacked despite its flanking or preemptive efforts, it must counterattack. The leader cannot remain passive when facing a competitor's price cuts, promotion blitz, product improvement, or sales territory invasion. The leader has the choice of meeting the competitor's attack head-on or moving against the competitor's weak points.

Sometimes market-share erosion is so rapid that a head-on counterattack is necessary. But to a company enjoying some strategic depth, it may be worth some minor setbacks to allow the offensive to develop fully (and be understood) before countering. This may seem a dangerous strategy of "wait and see," but there are sound reasons for not barreling into a counteroffensive. By waiting, the company can identify a weakness in the competitor's offense—a gap through which a successful counteroffensive can be launched. Cadillac designed its Seville as an alternative to the Mercedes and pinned its hopes on offering a smoother ride and more creature comforts than Mercedes was willing to design.

When a market leader's position is attacked, an effective counterattack may be to target the competitor's main territory so that it will have to pull back some of its resources to defend its own position. One of Northwest Airline's most profitable routes is Minneapolis to Atlanta. A small carrier announced a deep fare cut and advertised it heavily to expand its share in this market. Northwest retaliated by cutting its fares on the Minneapolis-Chicago route, which the other airline depended upon for its major revenue. With its major revenue source hurting, the other airline restored its Minneapolis-Atlanta fare to a normal level.

Mobile Defense

Mobile defense involves more than the leader's aggressively defending its current market position. Mobile defense consists of the leader's stretching to new markets that can serve as future bases for defense and offense. It spreads to these new markets not so much through normal brand proliferation as through innovation on two fronts—market broadening and market diversification. These moves generate "strategic depth" for the firm, which enables it to weather continual attacks and to launch counterstrikes.

In *market broadening,* the company shifts its focus from the current product to the broader underlying consumer need. For example, Armstrong Cork used a successful market-broadening strategy of redefining its focus from "floor covering" to "decorative room covering" (including walls and ceilings). By recognizing the consumer's need to create a pleasant interior through various covering materials, Armstrong Cork expanded into neighboring businesses that were balanced for growth and defense. But a broadening strategy should not be carried too far. Too much broadening would spread the company's resources too thin so that it would have trouble concentrating enough resources in any of its markets to compete effectively.

Market diversification into unrelated industries is the other alternative for generating "strategic depth." When U.S. tobacco companies like Reynolds and Philip Morris faced growing curbs on cigarette smoking, they were not content with position defense or even with looking for new substitutes for the cigarette; instead they moved quickly into new industries such as beer, liquor, soft drinks, and frozen foods.

Contraction Defense

Large companies sometimes find they can no longer defend all of their positions. Their resources are spread too thin, and competitors are nibbling away on several fronts. The best course of action then appears to be planned contraction (also called strategic withdrawal). Planned contraction is not market abandonment, but rather giving up the weaker positions and reassigning resources to stronger ones. Planned contraction consolidates competitive strength in the market and concentrates mass at pivotal positions.

In the slow-growth 1980s, an increasing opportunity seems to be emerging for profitable strategies of eliminating or fusing fragmented market segments. Westinghouse cut its number of refrigerator models from forty to the thirty that accounted for 85 percent of sales. General Motors standardized its auto engines and now offers fewer options. Campell's Soup, Heinz, General Mills, Del Monte, and Georgia-Pacific are among those companies that have significantly pruned their product lines in recent years.

Expanding Market Share   Market leaders can also grow by increasing their market shares further. The well-publicized Profit Impact of Management Strategies (PIMS) studies indicate that *profitability* rises with increasing *market share*.[7] The relationship is shown in Figure 20-3A.[8] According to the PIMS studies, businesses with very large relative market shares average three times the return on investment of firms with relative market shares of less than 20 percent.

These findings have led many companies to the objective of expanding their market shares to improve profitability. For example, General Electric has declared that it wants to be at least number one or two in each of its markets or else get out. GE has shed its computer business and its air-conditioning business because it could not achieve top-dog position in these industries.

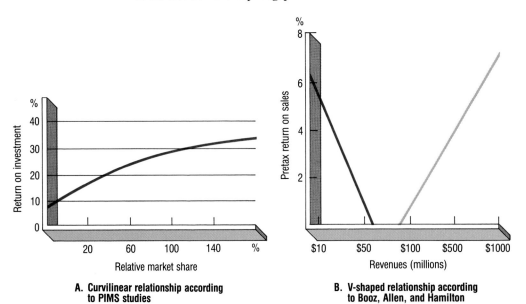

A. Curvilinear relationship according to PIMS studies

B. V-shaped relationship according to Booz, Allen, and Hamilton

FIGURE 20-3 *Relationships between Market Share and Profitability*

Sources: (A) Bradley T. Gale and Ben Branch, *Beating the Cost of Capital,* PIMSLETTER No. 32, (Cambridge, MA: The Strategic Planning Institute), p. 12. (B) "From Strategic Planning to Strategic Performance: Closing the Achievement Gap," *Outlook* published by Booz, Allen & Hamilton, New York, Spring 1981, p. 22.

Other studies have found a V-shaped relationship between market share and profitability in many industries (see Figure 20-3B).[9] Such industries have one or a few highly profitable large firms, several profitable and more-focused firms, and a large number of medium-sized firms with poorer profit performance. According to Roach:

> The large firms on the V-curve tend to address the entire market, achieving cost advantages and high market share by realizing economies of scale. The small competitors reap high profits by focusing on some narrower segment of the business and by developing specialized approaches to production, marketing, and distribution for that segment. Ironically, the medium-sized competitors at the trough of the V-curve are unable to realize any competitive advantage and often show the poorest profit performance. Trapped in a strategic "No Man's Land," they are too large to reap the benefits of more focused competition, yet too small to benefit from the economies of scale that their larger competitors enjoy.[10]

The message is that medium-sized firms need to figure out how to break into the big leagues or else settle for some special niches where they can do outstanding work.

Medium-sized companies must not think, however, that gaining increased market share will automatically improve profitability. Much depends on their strategy. Business analysts have cited many high market share companies with low profitability, and many low market share companies with high profitability. The cost of buying higher market share may far exceed the returns.[11] Higher shares tend to produce higher profits under two conditions:

- *Unit costs fall with increased market share.* Unit costs fall both because the leader enjoys cost economies of scale by running larger plants and goes down the cost experience curve faster. This means that one effective marketing strategy for gaining profitable increases in market share is to attain the lowest costs in the industry and pass the cost savings on to customers through lower prices. That was Henry Ford's strategy for selling autos in the 1920s and Texas Instruments' strategy for selling transistors in the 1960s.

- *The company offers a superior-quality product and charges a premium price that more than covers the cost of offering higher quality.* Crosby, in his book *Quality Is Free,* claims that building more quality into a product does not cost the company much more because the company saves in less scrappage, after-sales servicing, and so on.[12] But its products are so desired that consumers pay a large premium that results in a higher profit margin. This strategy for profitable market share growth is pursued by IBM, Caterpillar, and Michelin, among others.

All said, market leaders who stay on top have learned the art of expanding the total market, defending their current market position, and increasing their market share profitably. Exhibit 20-2 details the specific principles that Procter & Gamble uses to maintain and expand leadership in its market.

MARKET-CHALLENGER STRATEGIES

Firms that are second, third, or lower in an industry are sometimes quite large, such as Colgate, Ford, K mart, Avis, Westinghouse, Miller, and Pepsi-Cola. These runner-up firms can adopt one of two competitive strategies. They can attack the leader and other competitors in an aggressive bid for more market share (market challengers). Or they can play along with competitors and not rock the boat (market followers). We will now examine the competitive strategies available to market challengers.[13]

Defining the Strategic Objective and Competitor
A market challenger must first define its strategic objective. Most market challengers seek to increase their profitability by increasing their market shares. But the strategic objective chosen depends on who the competitor is. In most cases, the company can choose which competitors it will challenge, and it may choose one of three types of firms:

- *It can attack the market leader.* This is a high-risk but potentially high-gain strategy which makes good sense if the leader is not serving the market well. The company examines consumer needs or dissatisfaction, and if a sizable segment is unserved or poorly served, it offers a great strategic target. Miller successfully challenged Budweiser when it discovered the unfilled need for a "lighter" beer. An alternative strategy is to out-innovate the competitor across the entire market. Xerox took the copy market away from 3M by developing a better copying process (dry copying instead of wet copying).

- *It can attack firms its own size.* Here the company closely examines the market for similar-sized firms which are not doing the job or are underfinanced. When it finds such a competitor, it moves in to take away some of the competitor's market share. Even a broad frontal attack can work if the competitor's resources are limited.

- *It can attack small local and regional firms.* Many of these firms are underfinanced and will not be serving their customers well. Several of the major beer companies grew to their present size not by attacking large competitors, but by gobbling up small local or regional competitors.

EXHIBIT 20-2

HOW PROCTER & GAMBLE MAINTAINS MARKET LEADERSHIP

P&G is widely regarded as the nation's most skilled marketer of consumer packaged goods. It sells the number one brand in each of eight important categories: disposable diapers (Pampers), detergents (Tide), toilet tissue (Charmin), paper towels (Bounty), fabric softeners (Downy), toothpaste (Crest), shampoo (Head & Shoulders), and mouthwash (Scope). (See "P&G Up Against Its Wall," *Fortune*, February 23, 1981, pp. 49-54). Its market leadership rests on several principles.

Product innovation. P&G is an active product innovator and benefit segmentor. It launches brands offering new consumer benefits rather than me-too brands backed by heavy advertising. P&G spent ten years researching and developing the first effective anticavity toothpaste, Crest. It spent several years researching the first effective over-the-counter antidandruff shampoo, Head & Shoulders. The company thoroughly tests its new products with consumers, and only when real preference is indicated does it launch them in the national market.

Quality strategy. P&G designs products of above-average quality. Once launched, it makes a continuous effort to improve the product's quality over time. When they announce "new and improved," they mean it. This is in contrast to some companies that, after establishing the quality level, rarely improve it, and to other companies that deliberately reduce the quality in an effort to squeeze out more profit.

Product flanking. P&G produces its brands in several sizes and forms to satisfy varying consumer preferences. This gives its brand more shelf space and prevents competitors from moving in to satisfy unmet needs in the market.

Multibrand strategy. P&G is the originator of the art of marketing several brands in the same product category. For example, it produces ten brands of laundry detergents, each positioned somewhat differently in the consumer's mind. The trick is to design brands that meet different consumer wants and that compete against specific competitors' brands. Each brand manager runs the brand independently of the other brand managers and competes for company resources. Having several brands on the shelf, the company "locks up" shelf space and gains more clout with distributors.

Brand-extension strategy. P&G will often use its strong brand names to launch new products. For example, the Ivory brand has been extended from a soap to include liquid soap and a detergent. Launching a new product under a strong existing brand name gives it more instant recognition and credibility with much less advertising outlay.

Heavy advertising. P&G is the nation's largest consumer packaged goods advertiser, spending over $770 million per year. It never stints on spending money to create strong consumer awareness and preference.

Aggressive salesforce. P&G has a top-flight field salesforce, which is very effective in gaining shelf space and retailer cooperation in point-of-purchase displays and promotions.

Effective sales promotion. P&G has a sales promotion department to counsel its brand managers on the most effective promotions to achieve particular objectives. The department studies the results of consumer and trade deals and develops an expert sense of their effectiveness under varying circumstances. At the same time, P&G prefers to minimize the use of sales promotion, preferring to rely on advertising to build long-term consumer preference.

Competitive toughness. P&G carries a big stick when it comes to constraining aggressors. P&G is willing to spend large sums of money to outpromote new competitive brands and prevent them from getting a foothold in the market.

Manufacturing efficiency. P&G's reputation as a great marketing company is matched by its greatness as a manufacturing company. P&G spends large sums of money developing and improving production operations to keep its costs among the lowest in the industry.

Brand-management system. P&G originated the brand-management system, in which one executive is responsible for each brand. The system has been copied by many competitors, but frequently without the success P&G has achieved through perfecting its system over the years.

Thus P&G's market leadership is not based on doing one thing well, but on the successful orchestration of all the factors that count in market leadership.

Thus the challenger's strategic objective depends on which competitor it chooses to attack. If the attacker goes after the market leader, its objective may be to wrest a certain market share. Bic knows that it can't topple Gillette in the razor market—it is simply seeking a larger share. Or the challenger's goal might be to take over market leadership. IBM entered the personal computer market late, as a challenger, but quickly became the market leader. If the company goes after a small

Texas Instrument and COMPAQ challenge market leader IBM. (COMPAQ® is a registered trademark of COMPAQ Computer Corporation; IBM® is a registered trademark of International Business Machines Corporation.) *Courtesy of Texas Instruments Incorporated, COMPAQ Computer Corporation and International Business Machines Corporation.*

local company, its objective may be to put that company out of business. The important point remains: The company must choose its opponents carefully and have a clearly defined, decisive, and attainable objective.

Critical to choosing opponents and objectives is the need for systematic competitive analysis. Each company must collect up-to-date information on competitors. Its competitive information and analysis system must answer the following questions:[14]

- Who are our competitors?
- What are each competitor's sales, market share, and financial standing?
- What are each competitor's goals and assumptions?
- What is each competitor's strengths and weaknesses?
- What changes is each competitor likely to make in its future strategy in response to environmental, competitive, and internal developments?

Choosing an Attack Strategy How can the market challenger best attack the chosen competitor and achieve its strategic objectives? Five possible attack strategies are shown in Figure 20-4 and discussed below.

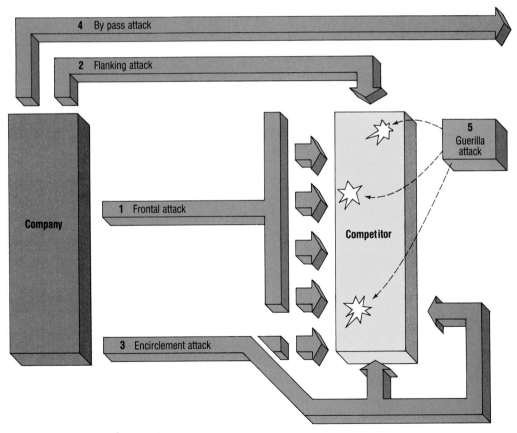

FIGURE 20-4 *Attack Strategies*

Frontal Attack

The company can launch a frontal (or head-on) attack by massing its resources right up against those of its competitor. It attacks the competitor's strengths rather than its weaknesses. The outcome depends on who has the greater strength and endurance. To succeed in a pure frontal attack, the challenger must match the competitor's product, advertising, price, and distribution efforts. Recently, the second-place manufacturer in Brazil decided to go after market leader Gillette. But when asked if it was offering the consumer a better blade, management replied, "no." "A lower price?" "No." "A better package?" "No." "A cleverer advertising campaign?" "No." "Better allowances to the trade?" "No." "Then how do you expect to take share away from Gillette?" "Sheer determination!" was the reply. Needless to say, the offensive failed.

For its frontal attack to succeed, the company needs a strength advantage over the competitor. The stronger and more entrenched the competitor, the greater the strength advantage needed by the challenger. If the market challenger has fewer resources than the competitor, a frontal attack becomes a suicide mission. RCA, GE, and Xerox learned this the hard way when they launched frontal attacks on IBM, overlooking its superior defensive position.[15]

An example of a successful pure frontal attack is S. C. Johnson and Son's entry into the shampoo market with the Agree brand: [16]

> In 1977, with what Forbes described as "almost Japanese-like thoroughness," S. C. Johnson first raided Colgate and others for experienced executives. Then it blitzed the market with a $14 million promotion that included 30 million sample bottles of its new hair conditioner, Agree. That about equaled the industry's total promotion on hair conditioners. It grabbed 15 percent of the market in its first year, wrested from such giants as Gillette's Toni, Breck, and Clairol. (By 1979, its share was 20 percent.) Then, in 1978, it invaded the shampoo market, reportedly spending $30 million in marketing costs in the summer of that year. It ended up with a 6 percent share of that market.

Flank Attack

The competitor expects to be attacked at the front and usually concentrates its resources to protect its strongest positions. But it usually has some weaker flanks, and these are natural points for the challenger's attack. These weak spots allow the challenger to concentrate its strength against the competitor's weakness. The challenger attacks the competitor's strong front to tie up its resources, but catches the competitor off guard by launching the real attack at the side or rear. Flank attacks make good sense when the company has fewer resources than the competitor.

A flank attack can be geographic or segmental. In a geographic attack, the company spots areas in the country or world where the competitor is performing at lower levels. For example, IBM's rivals chose to set up branches in medium- and smaller-sized cities that are relatively neglected by IBM. According to a Honeywell field sales manager:

> Out in the rural areas, we are relatively better off than in the cities. We have been quite successful in these areas because our sales force does not meet the ten plus to one ratio it hits in the cities where IBM concentrates its people. Thus, ours must be a concentration game.[17]

The other, and potentially more powerful, flanking strategy is to spot uncovered market needs not being served by the leaders:

German and Japanese automakers chose not to compete with American automakers by producing large, flashy, gas-guzzling automobiles, even though these were supposedly the preference of American buyers. Instead they recognized an unserved consumer segment that wanted small, fuel-efficient cars. They moved vigorously to fill this hole in the market, and to their satisfaction and Detroit's surprise, American taste for smaller, fuel-efficient cars grew to be a substantial part of the market.

A flanking strategy involves identifying market shifts that are causing gaps which are not being served by the industry's products, and rushing in to fill the gaps and develop them into strong segments. Instead of a bloody battle between two or more companies trying to serve the same market, flanking leads to a fuller coverage of the varied needs of the whole market. Flanking is in the best tradition of the modern marketing philosophy, which holds that the purpose of marketing is to "discover needs and serve them."

Encirclement Attack

Flanking involves finding gaps in the existing market coverage of competitors. Encirclement, on the other hand, involves launching an offensive on several fronts, so that the competitor must protect its front, sides, and rear simultaneously. The challenger may offer consumers everything the competitor offers and more, so that the offer is unrefusable. The encirclement strategy makes sense when the challenger has superior resources and believes that the encirclement will be swift and complete enough to break the competitor's hold on the market. Here is an example:

Seiko's attack on the watch market illustrates an encirclement strategy.[18] For several years, Seiko has been acquiring distribution in every major watch outlet and overwhelming its competitors and consumers with an enormous variety of constantly changing models. In the United States, it offers some four hundred models, but its marketing clout is backed by the some twenty-three hundred models it makes and sells worldwide. "They hit the mark on fashion, features, user preferences, and everything else that might motivate the consumer," says an admiring vice-president of a U.S. competitor.

Bypass Attack

The bypass is an indirect competitive strategy that avoids a direct move against the competitor. The challenger bypasses the competitor and targets easier markets to broaden its resources base. There are three bypass approaches—diversifying into *unrelated products,* diversifying into *new geographic markets,* and leapfrogging into *new technologies* to replace existing products.

Colgate's impressive turnaround utilized the first two principles.[19] In the United States, Colgate has always struggled in Procter & Gamble's shadow. In heavy-duty detergents, P&G's Tide routed Colgate's Fab by almost 5:1. In dishwashing liquids, P&G had almost twice Colgate's share. In soaps, too, Colgate trailed far behind.

When David Foster took over as CEO in 1971, despite it's $1.3 billion in sales, Colgate sill had the reputation as a stodgy marketer of soap and detergent. By 1979 Foster had transformed the company into a $4.3 billion conglomerate, capable of challenging P&G if necessary. Foster's real achievement was in recognizing that any head-on battle with P&G was futile. "They outgunned us 3 to 1 at the store level," said Foster, "and had three research people to our one." Foster's strategy was simple—increase Colgate's lead abroad and bypass P&G at home by diversifying into non-P&G markets. A string of acquisitions followed in textiles and hospital products, cosmetics, and a range of sporting goods and food products. The outcome: In 1971, Colgate was underdog to P&G in about half of its business. By 1976, in three-fourths of its business, it was either comfortably placed against P&G or didn't face it at all.

Technological leapfrogging is a bypass strategy used often in high-technology industries. Instead of imitating the competitor's product and mounting a costly frontal attack, the challenger patiently researches and develops the next technology. When satisfied with its superiority, it lauches an attack where it has an advantage. In the videogame market, Intellivision bypassed Atari's state-of-the-art technology and attacked when it had superior technology.

Guerrilla Attack

Guerrilla attack is another option available to market challengers, especially smaller or undercapitalized ones. The challenger makes small, periodic attacks to harass and demoralize the competitor, hoping eventually to establish permanent footholds.

In a guerrilla attack, the company can use both conventional and unconventional means to harass the competitor. These might include selective price cuts, executive raids, intense promotional outbursts, or assorted legal actions. The last, legal actions, is becoming one of the most common.

A Seattle-based beer distributor who had been supplying beer to Alaska by ship was upset when the Oetker Group of West Germany obtained a 75 percent tax credit for ten years from the Alaska legislature to establish beer production in Alaska. The Seattle distributor slapped a lawsuit on Oetker, charging the tax incentive was unconstitutional. Oetker eventually won in the courts, but four years of delay crippled its hope of capitalizing on the oil pipeline construction boom. After operating just thirty months, Oetker closed its Anchorage brewery.[20]

Normally, guerrilla actions are taken by smaller firms against larger ones. Not able to mount a frontal or even an effective flank attack, the smaller firm uses a barrage of short promotional and price attacks on random corners of the larger competitor's market in an attempt to weaken the competitor's market power. But continuous guerrilla campaigns can be expensive, and they must ultimately be followed up by a stronger attack if the challenger wishes to "beat" the competitor. Hence in terms of resources, guerrilla campaigns are not necessarily cheap operations.

The preceding attack strategies are very broad. The market challenger must put together a total strategy consisting of several specific strategies. Exhibit 20-3 shows how a well-known challenger company, Yamaha, attacked the leader in its industry.

EXHIBIT 20-3

HOW YAMAHA CHALLENGED HONDA FOR MARKET SHARE

In the early 1960s, Honda had established itself as the number one motorcycle brand in the United States. Its lightweight machines with their great eye appeal, the slogan, "You Meet the Nicest People on a Honda," and an aggressive sales organization and distribution network combined to greatly expand the total motorcycle market. Yamaha, another Japanese manufacturer, decided to enter the market against Honda. Its first step was to study Honda's major weaknesses, which included several dealers who had grown rich and lazy, abrupt management changes, discouragement of franchise-seeking dealers, and failure to promote the mechanical features of the motorcycles. Yamaha offered franchises to the best of the Honda-rejected franchises and used an enthusiastic salesforce to train and motivate these dealers. It improved its motorcycle to the point that it could claim and demonstrate mechanical superiority. It spent liberally on advertising and sales promotion programs to build buyer awareness and dealer enthusiasm. When motorcycle safety became a big issue, it designed superior safety features and advertised them extensively. These strategies propelled Yamaha into a clear second position in an industry swarming with over fifty manufacturers.

MARKET-FOLLOWER STRATEGIES

Not all runner-up companies will challenge the market leader. The effort to draw away the leader's customers is never taken lightly by the leader. If the challenger's lure is lower prices, improved service, or additional product features, the leader can quickly match these to diffuse the attack. The leader probably has more staying power in an all-out battle. A hard fight might leave both firms worse off, and this means the challenger must think twice before attacking. Unless the challenger can launch a preemptive strike—in the form of a substantial product innovation or distribution breakthrough—it often prefers to follow rather than attack the leader.

Patterns of "conscious parallelism" are common in capital-intensive homogeneous-product industries, such as steel, fertilizers, and chemicals. The opportunities for product and image differentiation are low; service quality is often comparable; price sensitivity runs high. Price wars can erupt at any time. The mood in these industries is against short-run grabs for market share because that strategy only provokes retaliation. Most firms decide against stealing each other's customers. Instead they present similar offers to buyers, usually by copying the leader. Market shares show a high stability.

This is not to say that market followers are without strategies. A market follower must know how to hold current customers and win a fair share of new customers. Each follower tries to bring distinctive advantages to its target market—location, services, financing. The follower is a major target of attack by challengers. Therefore the market follower must keep its manufacturing costs low and its product quality and services high. It must also enter new markets as they open up. Following is not the same as being passive or a carbon copy of the leader. The follower has to define a growth path, but one that does not create competitive retaliation. Three broad follower strategies can be distinguished:

- *Following closely.* Here the follower emulates the leader in as many market-segmentation and marketing-mix areas as possible. The follower almost appears to be a challenger, but if it does not radically block the leader, no direct conflict will occur. Some followers may even put very little into stimulating the market, hoping to live off the market leader's investments.
- *Following at a distance.* Here the follower maintains some differentiation, but follows the leader in terms of major market and product innovations, general price levels, and distribution. This follower is quite acceptable to the market leader, who may see little interference with its market plans and may be pleased that the follower's market share helps the leader avoid charges of monopolization. The distant follower may achieve its growth through acquiring smaller firms in the industry.
- *Following selectively.* This company follows the leader quite closely in some ways and sometimes goes its own way. The company may be quite innovative, and yet it avoids direct competition and follows many strategies of the leader where advantages are apparent. This company often grows into the future challenger.

Market followers, although they have lower market shares than the leader, may be as profitable or even more profitable. A recent study reported that many companies with less than half the market share of the leader had a five-year average return on equity that surpassed the industry median.[21] Crown Cork & Seal (metal containers) and Union Camp Corporation (paper) were among the successful market followers. The keys to their success were conscious market segmentation and concentration, effective research and development, profit emphasis rather than market-share emphasis, and strong top management.

MARKET-NICHER STRATEGIES

Almost every industry includes minor firms that specialize in parts of the market where they avoid clashes with the majors. These smaller firms occupy market niches that they serve effectively through specialization and that the majors are likely to overlook or ignore. These firms go by various names: market nichers, market specialists, threshold firms, or foothold firms. Market niching is of interest not only to small companies, but also to smaller divisions of larger companies that are not able to achieve major standing in that industry.

These firms try to find one or more market niches that are safe and profitable. An ideal market niche would have the following characteristics:

- The niche is of sufficient size and purchasing power to be profitable.
- The niche has growth potential.
- The niche is of negligible interest to major competitors.
- The firm has the required skills and resources to serve the niche effectively.
- The firm can defend itself against an attacking major competitor through the customer goodwill it has built up.

The key idea in nichemanship is specialization. The firm has to specialize along market, customer, product, or marketing mix lines. Here are several specialist roles open to a market nicher:

- *End-use specialist.* The firm specializes in serving one type of end-use customer. For example, a law firm can specialize in the criminal, civil, or business law markets.

Market nicher Saab targets the growing luxury-sport car segment. *Courtesy of Saab-Scania of America.*

- *Vertical-level specialist.* The firm specializes at some vertical level of the production-distribution cycle. For example, a copper firm may concentrate on producing raw copper, copper components, or finished copper products.

- *Customer-size specialist.* The firm concentrates on selling to either small-, medium- or large-size customers. Many nichers specialize in serving small customers who are neglected by the majors.

- *Specific-customer specialist.* The firm limits its selling to one or a few major customers. Many firms sell their entire output to a single company, such as Sears or General Motors.

- *Geographic specialist.* The firm sells only in a certain locality, region, or area of the world.

- *Product or product-line specialist.* The firm produces only one product line or product. Within the laboratory equipment industry are firms that produce only microscopes, or even more narrowly, only lenses for microscopes.
- *Product or feature specialist.* The firm specializes in producing a certain type of product or product feature. Rent-a-Wreck, for example, is a car-rental agency that rents only "beat-up" cars.
- *Job-shop specialist.* The firm manufacturers customized products as ordered by the customer.
- *Quality/price specialist.* The firm operates at the low or high end of the market. For example, Hewlett-Packard specializes in the high-quality, high-price end of the hand-calculator market.
- *Service specialist.* The firm offers one or more services not available from other firms. An example would be a bank that takes loan requests over the phone and hand delivers the money to the customer.

Niching carries a major risk in that the market niche may dry up or be attacked. That is why *multiple niching* is preferable to *single niching.* By developing strength in two or more niches, the company increases its chances for survival. Even some large firms prefer a multiple-niche strategy to serving the total market. One large law firm has developed a national reputation in the three areas of mergers and acquisitions, bankruptcies, and prospectus development, and does little else.

The main point is that low-share firms can be profitable too, and smart niching is one of the main answers. It is not all that is involved, however. Woo and Cooper studied the strategies of high-performing versus low-performing, low-share businesses to see what made the former do so well. They found that:[22]

- Many profitable low-share businesses are found in low-growth markets that are fairly stable. Most of them make industrial components or supplies that are purchased frequently. These firms don't change their products often. Most of their products are standardized, and the companies provide few extra services. The businesses tend to be found in high-value-added industries.
- These firms are strongly focused, not trying to do everything.
- They normally have a reputation for high quality and medium-to-low prices relative to high quality.
- They often have lower unit costs because they concentrate on a narrower product line and spend less on product R&D, new product introduction, advertising, sales promotion, and salesforce support.

We can see that small firms have many opportunities to serve customers in profitable ways. Many small firms discover good niches through blind luck, although good opportunities can be detected and developed in a more systematic manner.

Whether a company is a market leader, challenger, follower, or nicher in an industry, it must find the competitive marketing strategy that positions it most effectively against its competitors. And it must continually adapt its strategies to the fast-changing competitive environment. But in the increasingly competitive marketing environment, the company can become too "competitor-centered"—it can spend too much time watching and reacting to competitors' activities and lose sight of the consumer needs it seeks to satisfy. The company must work to remain "consumer-centered." When designing competitive marketing strategies, it must consider competitors' positions and actions—but the underlying goal is to succeed against competitors by finding better ways to satisfy consumer needs.

■ Summary

To be successful, a company must develop competitive marketing strategies that effectively position it against competitors and give it the strongest possible competitive advantage. Which strategy makes the most sense depends on the company's competitive position in its industry, and its objectives, opportunities, and resources. The company's competitive marketing strategy depends on whether it is a market leader, challenger, follower, or nicher.

A market leader faces three challenges: expanding the total market, protecting market share, and expanding market share. The market leader is interested in finding ways to expand the total market because it is the chief beneficiary of any increased sales. To expand market size, the leader looks for new users of the product, new uses, and more usage. To protect its existing market share, the market leader has several defenses: position defense, flanking defense, preemptive defense, counteroffensive defense, mobile defense, and contraction defense. The most sophisticated leaders cover themselves by doing everything right, leaving no openings for competitive attack. Leaders can also try to increase their market share. This makes sense if profitability increases at higher market-share levels and the company's tactics won't invite antitrust action.

A market challenger is a firm that aggressively tries to expand its market share by attacking the leader, other runner-up firms, or smaller firms in the industry. The challenger can choose from a variety of attack strategies, including a frontal attack, flanking attack, encirclement attack, bypass attack, and guerrilla attack.

A market follower is a runner-up firm that chooses not to rock the boat, usually out of fear that it stands to lose more than it might gain. The follower is not without a strategy, however, and seeks to use its particular competences to participate actively in the growth of the market. Some followers enjoy a higher rate of return on equity than the leaders in their industry.

A market nicher is a smaller firm that chooses to operate in some part of the market that is specialized and not likely to attract the larger firms. Market nichers often become specialists in some end use, vertical level, customer size, specific customer, geographic area, product or product line, product feature, or service.

■ Questions for Discussion

1. Suggest a strategy for a new small firm entering the photocopying market.

2. What might a "harassment" strategy look like for a dominant firm trying to protect its market share from challengers?

3. Hewlett-Packard, a market leader in the top end of the hand-held calculator market, found itself in a squeeze between aggressively promoted portable computers and less expensive calculators with increasingly sophisticated features. What market-leader strategy would you recommend for Hewlett-Packard?

4. Comment on the following statements made about the appropriate marketing strategy of

smaller firms: (a) "The smaller firm should concentrate on pulling away the larger firm's customers, while the larger firm should concentrate on stimulating new customers to enter the market." (b) "Larger firms should pioneer new products, and smaller ones should copy them."

5. Although Caterpillar is an extremely strong company, it has some vulnerabilities. Name some potential threats to Caterpillar.

6. What are some of the marketing principles General Motors used to maintain its four decades of leadership in the U.S. auto industry?

7. Briefly critique the following marketing strategy statement: "The company will offer the best product and best service at the lowest price."

■ *References*

1. See "Goodyear: Will Staying No. 1 in Tires Pump Up Profits?" *Business Week,* July 12, 1982, pp. 85–88; "Michelin: Spinning Its Wheels in the Competitive U.S. Market," *Business Week,* December 1, 1980, pp. 119–24; "Uniroyal: Narrowing the Choices As It Clings to the Tire Business," *Business Week,* June 11, 1979, pp. 74–76; and "The Niche Pickers at Armstrong Rubber," *Fortune,* September 6, 1982, pp. 100–4.

2. See Alfred R. Oxenfeld and William L. Moore, "Customer or Competitor: Which Guidelines for Marketing?" *Management Review,* August 1978, pp. 43–48.

3. Michael E. Porter, *Competitive Strategy: Techniques for Analyzing Industries and Competitors* (New York: Free Press, 1980), chap. 2.

4. See Jordan P. Yale, "The Strategy of Nylon's Growth," *Modern Textiles Magazine,* February 1964, pp. 32ff. Also see Theodore Levitt, "Exploit the Product Life Cycle," *Harvard Business Review,* November–December 1965, pp. 81–94.

5. Sun Tsu, *The Art of War* (London: Oxford University Press, 1963); Miyamoto Musashi, *A Book of Five Rings* (Woodstock, NY: Overlook Press, 1974); Carl von Clausewitz, *On War* (London: Routledge & Kegan Paul, 1908); and B. H. Liddell Hart, *Strategy* (New York: Praeger, 1967).

6. These six defense strategies, as well as the five attack strategies described later in the chapter, are taken from Philip Kotler and Ravi Singh, "Marketing Warfare in the 1980s," *Journal of Business Strategy,* Winter 1982, pp. 30–41.

7. Sidney Schoeffler, Robert D. Buzzell, and Donald F. Heany, "Impact of Strategic Planning on Profit Performance," *Harvard Business Review,* March–April 1974, pp. 137–45; and Robert D. Buzzell, Bradley T. Gale, and Ralph G. M. Sultan, "Market Share—the Key to Profitability," *Harvard Business Review,* January–February 1975, pp. 97–106.

8. See Buzzell, et al., "Market Share," pp. 97–106. The results should be interpreted cautiously because that data came from a limited number of industries and there was some variance around the main line of relationship.

9. John D. C. Roach, "From Strategic Planning to Strategic Performance: Closing the Achievement Gap," *Outlook,* published by Booz, Allen & Hamilton, New York, Spring 1981, p. 22. This curve assumes that pretax return on sales is highly correlated with profitability and that company revenue is a surrogate for market share. Michael Porter, in his *Competitive Strategy,* shows a similar V-shaped curve that makes the same point.

10. Roach, "Strategic Planning," p. 21.

11. Philip Kotler and Paul N. Bloom, "Strategies for High Market-Share Companies," *Harvard Business Review,* November–December 1975, pp. 63–72.

12. Philip B. Crosby, *Quality Is Free* (New York: McGraw-Hill, 1979).

13. For additional reading, see C. David Fogg, "Planning Gains in Market Share," *Journal of Marketing,* July 1974, pp. 30–38; and Bernard Catry and Michel Chevalier, "Market Share Strategy and the Product Life Cycle," *Journal of Marketing,* October 1974, pp. 29–34.

14. For more on competitive analysis, see Porter, *Competitive Strategy,* chap. 3.

15. "The 250 Million Dollar Disaster That Hit RCA," *Business Week,* September 25, 1971.

16. See "Stopping the Greasies," *Forbes,* July 9, 1979, p. 121.

17. Quoted in "Honeywell Information Systems," case available from the Intercollegiate Case Clearing House, Soldiers Field, Boston, 1975), pp. 7–8.

18. See "Seiko's Smash," *Business Week,* June 5, 1978, p. 89.

19. See "The Changing of the Guard," *Fortune,* September 29, 1979; and "How to Be Happy Though No. Two," *Forbes,* July 15, 1976, p. 36.
20. "Alaska Chills a German Beer," *Business Week,* April 23, 1979, p. 42.
21. R. G. Hamermesh, M. J. Anderson, Jr., and J. E. Harris, "Strategies for Low Market Share Businesses," *Harvard Business Review,* May–June 1978, pp. 95–102.
22. Carolyn Y. Woo and Arnold C. Cooper, "The Surprising Case for Low Market Share," *Harvard Business Review,* November–December 1982, pp. 106–13.

21
Implementing, Organizing, and Controlling Marketing Programs

During the 1970s, IBM became stodgy and bureaucratic. The $50-billion giant's sales were growing at 13 percent a year, and it still dominated the large computer segment, but the highly structured and tradition-bound IBM organization had trouble competing effectively against smaller, more flexible, entrepreneurial competitors in fast-changing, high-growth segments. IBM's share of the total information-processing market fell from a whopping 60 percent in the late sixties to less than 40 percent in 1980.

Thus when IBM decided in the early 1980s to enter the personal computer market, industry analysts were skeptical, and even many IBM executives were worried. The strategy was sound enough—to carry the IBM name and the company's established reputation for quality and service into the fastest-growing segment of the computer market. But with personal computers, the company would have to operate in unfamiliar marketing territory, selling a very different product, to very different customers, in a very different competitive environment. Could IBM—large and strongly wedded to traditional methods—successfully *implement* a new strategy that differed so dramatically from previous strategies? Despite its formidable size and power, few expected IBM to have much of an immediate impact on the personal computer market.

But in developing and marketing its new IBM PC, IBM pulled some surprises. It swept aside traditional operating methods and broke several long-held rules. It set up a "special operating unit" called Entry Systems with complete responsibility to design, make, and sell the IBM PC. IBM gave Entry Systems free rein over the project and shielded the unit from bureaucratic tangles. This independent "company

within a company" developed a culture and operating style similar to those of its entrepreneurial competitors. Free of the heavy-handed control IBM usually imposed on its operating units, Entry Systems ignored IBM traditions and did many "non-IBM-like" things. For example:

1. IBM had *always* constructed its computers from the ground up, using only IBM-designed and produced electronic components. But to get the PC to the market more quickly, Entry Systems assembled it from readily available components obtained from outside suppliers. For example, the heart of the PC was an advanced 16-bit microprocessor made by Intel Corporation.

2. IBM had *always* carefully guarded its computer designs and developed its own software. Not so for the PC! To encourage rapid acceptance and sales expansion, Entry Systems published the PC's technical specifications to show how the machine was built and how it operated. This made it easier for outside companies to design PC-compatible software programs, and the resulting wealth of available software made the PC even more attractive to consumers. IBM machines soon became the industry standard for software producers.

3. IBM had *always* sold its products directly to end users through its large and tightly controlled salesforce. But for the PC, Entry Systems developed a large network of independent retailers, including such heavyweights as Sears and Computerland. To overcome its lack

of retail distribution experience, Entry Systems copied its competitors' distribution techniques. For example, it patterned its dealer support and consumer education programs after those offered by Apple.

4. Until the late 1970s, IBM had *always* relied on slow-but-sure product innovation and price stability. But the company had recently invested billions to renovate its plants and equipment in a drive to become the industry's low-cost producer, and it had begun to use price as a major competitive weapon. Entry Systems followed suit for the PC—it spent millions to build modern production facilities that could turn out PCs at low cost, then followed an aggressive pricing policy to keep competitors off balance.

Thus to implement its strategy to enter the personal computer market, IBM made several tradition-shattering changes in its structure, operations, and tactics. And the new approach paid off—even IBM executives were amazed at how quickly and completely the IBM PC dominated. After only two and a half years, it held a 35 percent market share (60 to 70 percent in the corporate segment). IBM's successful entry caused an industry shakeout that drove out dozens of competitors. The new approach worked so well that since 1981 IBM has set up more than a dozen additional special business units to develop opportunities in software, robotics, high-tech health care, and other fast-growing markets.[1]

Analyzing the marketing environment and planning good strategies are only a start toward successfully managing the marketing effort. The company must also develop an effective marketing organization that carries out the activities needed to implement the strategy. And it must continually evaluate its activities and performance to ensure that strategic objectives are attained. In this chapter we will look at how marketing strategies are implemented and how marketing efforts are organized and controlled in the modern organization.

IMPLEMENTATION

A brilliant marketing strategy will count for little if the company fails to implement it properly.

> **Marketing implementation** is the process that turns marketing strategies and plans into marketing actions in order to accomplish strategic marketing objectives.

Implementation involves mobilizing the company's people and resources into day-to-day, month-to-month activities that effectively put the strategic plan to work. Where analysis and strategy planning address the *what* and *why* of marketing activities, implementation addresses the *who, where, when,* and *how*.

Strategy and implementation are closely related. First, the strategy determines the implementation activities needed. For example, top management's decision to "harvest" a product must be translated into specific actions such as allocating fewer funds to the product, directing salespeople to change their selling emphasis, perhaps raising prices, and reassigning ad agency efforts to other products. A decision to "build" a product would require different implementation activities. Second, the company's implementation capabilities influence management's choice of strategy. For example, management would avoid a broad frontal attack against a well-entrenched competitor if it lacked the resources to implement this strategy.

Implementation is difficult and complex—it is often easier to think up good marketing strategies than to carry them out. In one study, 90 percent of the planners surveyed felt that their strategies were not succeeding because they were being poorly implemented.[2] And managers often have trouble diagnosing implementation problems. Poor performance can result from poor strategies or from good strategies that are poorly implemented. It is usually hard to determine whether poor performance was caused by poor strategy, poor implementation, or both.[3]

Reasons for Poor Implementation What causes implementation failures? Why are many companies unable to successfully bridge the gap between marketing strategy and performance? Several factors cause implementation problems.

Isolated Planning

The company's strategic plan is often prepared by corporate-level "professional planners" who communicate poorly with the marketing managers who must implement the strategy. This leads to several problems. Staff planners who are concerned with broad strategy often do not worry about implementation details and may produce plans that are too superficial or too general. Planners who do not understand the practical problems faced by line managers may call for strategies that are unrealistic or too ambitious. Isolated planners may not adequately communicate their strategies to line marketing managers, and the managers may have trouble implementing the strategies because they do not fully understand them. Finally, isolated planning can lead to hostilities between planners and line marketing managers. Managers who face day-to-day operations may resent or oppose what they see as unrealistic strategies made up by "ivory-tower" planners.

Many companies have realized that professional corporate-level planners cannot prepare strategies *for* marketing managers—instead, planners must help the marketing managers find their own strategies. The line managers better understand operations and market conditions, and if they are included in the planning process, managers will be more willing and able to implement strategies. Many companies are now cutting down their large, centralized planning staffs and are doing strategic planning at operating levels. For example, after several unsuccessful attempts to create a strategic planning system at headquarters, General Motors decentralized the process and made strategic planning the responsibility of its line managers. Eaton cut its central planning group from 35 to 16, and General Electric reduced its corporate planning staff from 58 to 33.[4] In these and other companies, planners are not isolated—they work directly with line managers to design more workable strategies.

Tradeoffs between Long-Term and Short-Term Objectives

Companies design marketing strategies that will lead to *long-run* competitive advantage—strategic plans often cover activities for the next three to five years. But the marketing managers who implement these strategies are usually rewarded for *short-run* sales, growth, or profits. When faced with a choice between long-run strategy and short-run performance, managers usually trade off in favor of the short run. One study of major companies found numerous examples of such harmful tradeoffs.[5] For example, one company's long-term product development strategy failed because division marketing managers, who were rewarded for annual profits, often postponed small product development expenses and favored established products in order to improve current earnings and boost their bonuses. Another company designed a marketing strategy that stressed product availability and customer service. But under pressures for short-term profit performance, operating managers cut costs by minimizing inventories and reducing technical service staff. These managers met short-run performance goals and received high evaluations, but their actions hurt the company's long-run strategy and position.

Some companies are taking steps to identify such tradeoff problems and to encourage a better balance between short- and long-run goals. This involves making managers more aware of strategic goals, evaluating managers on both long-run and short-run performance, and rewarding managers for attaining long-run strategic objectives.[6]

Resistance to Change

The company's current operations have all been designed to implement previous strategies. New strategies not consistent with established company patterns and habits will be resisted. And the more different the new strategy from the old, the greater the resistance to implementing it. For dramatically new strategies, implementation may cut across traditional organization lines within the company, and across established operating patterns of suppliers and channel firms. For example, in order to implement a strategy of developing new markets for an old product line, one company had to create an entirely new sales division.[7] In another case, a company that specialized in industrial lighting products decided to brand its light bulbs and sell them through grocery stores.[8] The company was the country's largest producer of private-brand bulbs, but it had no experience in consumer marketing or in marketing to retailers. Two years and millions of dollars later, the brand had only a 0.3 percent market share. The company could not implement the new consumer-focused strategy because it could not change its long-held private-brand and industrial orientation.

Lack of Specific Implementation Plans

Some strategic plans are poorly implemented because the planners fail to develop detailed implementation plans. They leave the details to individual managers, and the result is poor implementation or no implementation at all. Hobbs and Heany describe a consumer appliance company that decided to improve profitability by filling out its product line:[9]

The company communicated the broad intent of the new strategy to its engineering and manufacturing units, authorized manufacturing to design a new appliance, and asked engineering to prepare for an initial production run of 2000 units. Later data showed that the failure rate for the new models was much higher than for older models. It turns out that the company's design engineers considered the first 2000 units to be "test models"—they planned to look at field results before setting final quality standards. But manufacturing thought the designs for the new appliance were final and invested millions of dollars in a new production line for the initial units. If the original product design was changed, much of this investment would have to be written off. Further, top management was counting on a fast and profitable introduction of the new product—if the product had to be redesigned, these goals could not be met. The company arrived at this difficult situation because it failed to put together a comprehensive program for implementing the new strategy.

Management cannot simply assume that its strategies will be implemented. It must prepare a detailed implementation plan that identifies and coordinates the specific activities needed to put the strategy into place. It must develop timetables for reaching specific objectives, and assign responsibility for major implementation tasks to individual managers.

The Implementation Process

People at all levels of the marketing system must cooperate to implement marketing strategies. Within the marketing department, people in advertising, sales, marketing research, and product development must carry out activities that support the strategic plan. These marketing people must coordinate their actions with people in other company departments—research and development, manufacturing, purchasing, finance, and legal. Many people and organizations in the company's external marketing system must also contribute to strategy implementation. The company's suppliers, wholesalers, and retailers; advertising agencies, marketing research firms, and outside consultants; financial publics, the media, citizen action groups, the government—all can help or hinder the company's attempts to implement its marketing strategies. The company must develop effective structures and systems that coordinate all these activities into an effective course of action.

According to McKinsey & Company, a leading consulting firm, a clear and well-planned strategy is only one of seven elements leading to successful performance. The McKinsey 7-S framework is shown in Figure 21-1.[10] The first three elements—strategy, structure, and systems—are the "hardware" of success. They involve hard analytical tools and judgments. The next four elements—skills, staff, style, and values—are the "software." They involve the people and people interactions needed for successful performance.

Thus a successful company first designs an appropriate *strategy* to reach its goals. It then builds an organization *structure* and information, planning, control, and reward *systems* to carry out this strategy. But McKinsey consultants argue that in recent decades management has been biased toward the hard analytical elements. This bias has diverted attention away from the important people-related elements. The company's strengths go beyond strategy, structure, and systems. Success also depends on having the right people (*staff*) doing the right things (*skills*) under an appropriate managerial and organizational climate (*style* and *shared values*).

FIGURE 21-1
McKinsey 7-S
Framework

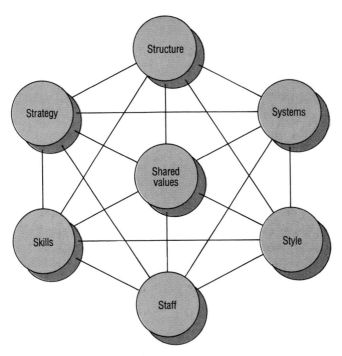

Source: Thomas J. Peters and Robert H. Waterman, Jr., *In Search of Excellence: Lessons from America's Best Run Companies.* Copyright © 1982 by Thomas J. Peters and Robert H. Waterman, Jr. Reprinted by permission of Harper & Row, Publishers.

The implementation process is shown in Figure 21-2.[11] The figure shows that marketing strategy and marketing performance are linked by an implementation system consisting of five interrelated activities: developing action programs, constructing an organization structure, designing decision and reward systems, developing human resources, and establishing a managerial climate and company culture.

Developing an Action Program

To implement marketing strategies, people at all levels of the marketing system must make specific decisions and perform specific tasks. At Procter & Gamble, implementation of top management's strategy of introducing a stream of high-quality new products requires well-planned and coordinated day-to-day decisions and actions by thousands of people inside and outside the organization. Within the marketing organization, marketing researchers test new product concepts and scan the marketplace for feasible new product ideas. For each new product, marketing managers make decisions about target segments and product positions, branding, packaging, pricing, promoting, and distributing. Salespeople are selected, trained and retrained, directed, and motivated.

Marketing managers work with other company managers to get resources and support for promising new products. They talk with engineering about product design; manufacturing about quality, production, and inventory levels; finance about project funding and cash flows; the legal staff about patents and product safety issues; and personnel about staffing and training needs. Marketing managers also work with people in outside organizations. They meet with advertising agency people to plan and launch ad campaigns, and with the media to obtain publicity support. The salesforce urges retailers to give new products local advertising support, provide adequate shelf space, and use company displays. Failures at any implementation level can affect the success of the new product.

To successfully implement strategies, the company must develop a detailed *action program*. This program identifies critical *decisions and tasks* required to turn marketing strategies into marketplace realities. The action program also assigns *responsibility* for decisions and tasks to specific people and units in the company. Finally, the action program includes a *timetable* which states when decisions must be made, when actions must be taken, and when strategic milestones must be

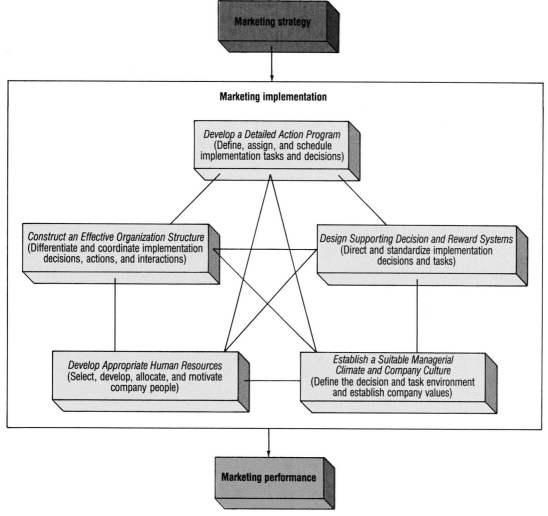

FIGURE 21-2 *The Marketing Implementation Process*

reached. The action program identifies what must be done, who will do it, and how decisions and actions will be coordinated to reach the company's strategic objectives.

Constructing an Effective Organization Structure

The company's formal organization structure plays an important role in implementing marketing strategy. The structure defines and assigns tasks to specific departments and people, establishes lines of authority and communication, and coordinates decisions and actions across the firm.

Companies with different strategies need different structures—the company should design a structure that fits and supports its strategy, its characteristics, and its competitive environment. The structure provides *differentiation*—it breaks up the work of the firm up into well-defined and manageable tasks, assigns these tasks to departments and people, and allows efficiency through specialization. The structure then provides *integration*—it coordinates these specialized decisions and actions by defining formal relationships among people and units, and by creating lines of authority and communication.

A company's structure evolves as the firm's strategies and environment change. A small firm developing new products in a fast-changing industry might need a flexible structure that encourages entrepreneurial activities—a decentralized structure with loose role specification and high levels of informal communication. A more established company in more stable markets might need a structure that provides more integration—a more centralized structure with well-defined roles, routine tasks, and communication "through proper channels."

In their study of forty-three successful companies, Peters and Waterman found the companies had several common structural characteristics that lead to successful strategy implementation.[12] For example, their structures had high levels of *informality*—United Airline's MBWA (management by walking around), IBM's "open-door" policy, 3M's "clubs" to create small-group interaction. The successful companies' structures were *decentralized,* with small autonomous divisions or entrepreneurial groups to foster innovation, and temporary task forces to integrate decisions and actions. The structures also tended to be *simple and lean.* Most of the excellent companies designed their structures around a single dimension, such as product divisions. These simple, decentralized structures are more flexible and fluid, and allow the companies to adapt more quickly to changing conditions. Johnson & Johnson provides an excellent example of structural simplicity. This $5 billion company is divided into 150 independent divisions that average about $30 million in size. Each division handles its own marketing decisions and activities. This structure puts control in the hands of operating managers and leads to more effective strategy development and implementation.

In addition to simple structures, the excellent companies have lean staffs, especially at higher levels. According to Peters and Waterman:[13]

> Indeed, it appears that most of our excellent companies have comparatively few people at the corporate level, and that what staff there is tends to be out in the field solving problems rather than in the home office checking on things. The bottom line is fewer administrators, more operators.

Some of the Peters and Waterman study conclusions have been questioned because the study focused on high-technology and consumer goods companies operating in rapidly changing environments.[14] The structures used by these companies may not be appropriate for other types of firms in different environments. Further, many of the study's excellent companies will need to change their structures as their strategies and situations evolve. For example, the decentralized and informal structure that made Hewlett-Packard so successful at the time of the study has caused problems for HP in recent years. The company has recently moved toward a more centralized structure (see Exhibit 21-1).

EXHIBIT 21-1

HEWLETT-PACKARD'S STRUCTURE EVOLVES

In 1939 two engineers—Bill Hewlett and Dave Packard—started Hewlett-Packard in a Palo Alto garage to build test equipment. At the start, Bill and Dave did everything themselves, from designing and building their equipment to marketing it. As the firm grew out of the garage and began to build more and different types of test equipment, Hewlett and Packard could no longer make all the necessary operating decisions by themselves. They assumed roles as top managers and hired functional managers to run various company activities. These managers were relatively autonomous, but still closely tied to the owners.

By the mid-1970s, Hewlett-Packard's 42 divisions employed more than 1,200 people. The company's structure evolved to support its heavy emphasis on innovation and autonomy. The structure was loose and decentralized. Each division operated as an autonomous unit, and was responsible for its own strategic planning, product development, marketing programs, and implementation.

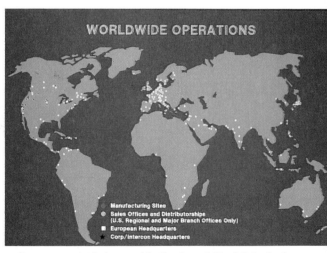

Hewlett-Packard began in this garage in 1939; it now operates around the world. *Courtesy of Hewlett-Packard.*

In 1982 Peters and Waterman, in their *In Search of Excellence,* cited HP's informal and decentralized structure as a major reason for the company's continued excellence. They praise HP's unrestrictive structure and high degree of informal communication (its MBWA style—management by walking around). Peters and Waterman note that the HP structure decentralizes decision making and responsibility. In the words of one HP manager:

> Hewlett-Packard [should not] have a tight, military-type organization, but rather . . . give people the freedom to work toward [overall objectives] in ways they determine best for their own areas of responsibility.

The structure also decentralizes authority and fosters autonomy:

> The sales force does not have to accept a product developed by a division unless it wants it. The company cites numerous instances in which several million dollars of development funds were spent by a division, at which point the sales force said, "No thanks."

But in recent years, though still profitable, Hewlett-Packard has met with some problems in the fast-changing microcomputer and minicomputer markets. According to *Business Week*:

> Hewlett-Packard's famed innovative culture and decentralization spawned such enormously successful products as its 3000 minicomputer, the handheld scientific calculator, and the ThinkJet nonimpact printer. But when a new climate required its fiercely autonomous divisions to cooperate in product development and marketing, HP's passionate devotion to the "autonomy and entrepreneurship" that Peters and Waterman advocate became a hindrance.

Thus Hewlett-Packard is finding that it must change its structure and culture to bring them in line with its changing situation. As *Business Week* puts it:

> To regain its stride, HP is being forced to abandon attributes of excellence for which it was praised. Its technology-driven, engineering-oriented culture, in which decentralization and innovation were a religion and entrepreneurs were the gods, is giving way to a marketing culture and growing centralization.

Sources: Based on information in Donald F. Harvey, *Business Policy and Strategic Management* (Columbus, OH: Charles E. Merrill, 1982), pp. 269–70; "Who's Excellent Now?" *Business Week,* November 5, 1984, pp. 76–78; and Thomas J. Peters and Robert H. Waterman, Jr., *In Search of Excellence: Lessons from America's Best-Run Companies* (New York: Harper & Row, 1982).

Designing Decision and Reward Systems

The company must also design decision and reward systems that support its marketing strategies. Systems include formal and informal operating procedures that guide and standardize such activities as planning, information gathering and distribution, money and manpower budgeting, recruiting and training, performance measurement and control, and personnel evaluation and rewards.

Poorly designed systems can work against strategy implementation; well-designed systems can encourage good implementation. Consider a company's management evaluation and rewards system. If the system compensates managers for short-run operating and profit results, managers will have little incentive to work toward long-run strategic objectives. Many companies are designing compensation systems that encourage managers to strike a better balance between short-run operating results and long-run strategic performance. Here are two examples:[15]

One large company operating in a slow-growth industry and threatened by low-cost imports decided on a new, two-pronged strategy. First, it would control costs and strengthen marketing activities to retrench in its current core business. Second, it would venture into new technologies by acquiring existing small, entrepreneurial companies in faster-growing markets. The company realized that the old and new businesses had very different strategies which would require different management systems—including different compensation plans. The company pays new-venture managers a base salary lower than that of comparable core-business managers. But at the same time, it gives new-business managers four times the potential bonus money available to the higher-salaried core-business managers. Thus the compensation system encourages core-business managers to focus on productivity and market consolidation, consistent with the core-business retrenchment strategy. The system encourages new-venture managers to take greater risks for higher potential returns, consistent with the venture-business strategy of innovation and market development.

Another company in a more stable competitive environment was concerned that its annual bonus system encouraged managers to ignore long-run strategies and focus on annual performance targets. To correct this, the company changed its bonus system to include rewards for both annual performance and the attainment of "strategic milestones." Under the new plan, each manager works with strategic planners to set two or three strategic objectives upon which he or she will be measured each year. At the end of the year, the manager's bonus is based on both operating performance and on the attainment of the strategic objectives. The bonus mix varies by the manager's organizational level. Top-level executives and staff planners, who are inclined to focus too heavily on broad strategy issues, have bonuses more heavily weighted toward annual operating results. Functional managers, who are inclined to favor current operations over long-run strategy, have their bonuses more heavily based on the attainment of strategic objectives. Thus the bonus system encourages managers at both levels to achieve more balance of the company's long- and short-run needs.

Developing Human Resources

Marketing strategies are implemented by people in the company and in outside organizations. Successful implementation requires careful human resources planning. At all levels, the company must fill out its structure and systems with people who have the skills, motivation, and personal characteristics needed for strategy implementation.[16]

Human resources must be recruited, allocated, developed, and maintained. . . . questions about recruitment [include] . . . Will the necessary work force be available? Where do the workers come from? Can we afford the cost? Personnel development is correlated with the "make versus buy" issue in the sense that policies of internal promotion and training may be preferred to recruiting from outside the organization. The allocation issue involves making sure that the tasks and resources distributed to various parts of the organization include the right people—those with appropriate skills and abilities to carry out the tasks effectively. . . . With respect to maintaining the work force, policies regarding levels of pay, supplemental benefits, and systems for performance appraisal need to be established. Such policies can be critical . . . to the ability to carry out a strategy and compete effectively.

The company must also make decisions about the proportion of managers and workers in line and staff positions. Many companies have begun to cut back on corporate level and other staff positions to reduce overhead and put decision making back in the hands of the implementers.

The company's selection and development of executives and other managers are especially crucial to strategy implementation. Different strategies call for managers with different personalities and skills. New venture strategies need managers with entrepreneurial skills; maintenance strategies require managers with organizational and administrative skills; and retrenchment strategies call for managers with cost-cutting skills. Thus the company must carefully match its managers to the requirements of the strategies to be implemented.

Establishing Managerial Climate and Company Culture

The company's managerial climate and company culture affect the way people in the firm go about making decisions and carrying out tasks. These informal organization factors can make or break strategy implementation. *Managerial climate* involves the way company managers work with others in the company. Some managers are "autocratic"—they take command, delegate little authority, keep tight controls, and insist on communication through formal channels. Others are "participative"—they delegate tasks and authority, coordinate rather than command, encourage subordinates to take initiative, and communicate informally. No one managerial style is best for all situations. Different strategies may require different leadership styles, and which style is best varies with the company's structure, tasks, people, and environment.

Company culture is a system of values and beliefs shared by people in an organization. It is the company's collective identity and meaning. The culture informally guides the behavior of people at all company levels. Peters and Waterman found that excellent companies have strong and clearly defined cultures.[17]

> Without exception, the dominance and coherence of culture proved to be an essential quality of the excellent companies. Moreover, the stronger the culture and the more it was directed toward the marketplace, the less need there was for policy manuals, organization charts, or detailed procedures and rules. In these companies, people way down the line know what they are supposed to do in most situations because the handful of guiding values is crystal clear. . . .
> Everyone at Hewlett-Packard knows that he or she is supposed to be innovative. Everyone at Procter & Gamble knows that product quality is the sine qua non.

They found that the cultures of excellent companies are based on just a few basic values, such as being the "best," paying attention to the details of execution, treating people as individuals, providing superior quality and service, encouraging innovation and being willing to support failure, and encouraging informal communication.[18]

Managerial style and company culture guide and motivate the decisions and actions of people in the company. Strategies that do not fit the company's style and culture will be difficult to implement. For example, a decision by Procter & Gamble to increase market penetration by reducing product quality and prices would meet resistance from company people at all levels who identify strongly with the company's reputation for quality. Because managerial style and culture are so difficult to change, companies usually design strategies that fit their current cultures rather than trying to change their styles and cultures to fit new and different strategies.

Relationships among Tasks, Structure, Systems, People, and Culture

For successful implementation, all the activities of the implementation system must support the strategy being implemented. But the action program, organization structure, decision and reward systems, people, and company style and culture must also be consistent with one another. The people in the company must have the skills needed to make the decisions and perform the tasks required to implement the strategy. The reward system must motivate people to carry out tasks critical to the strategy. The people will work more effectively if they identify with the managerial style and company culture.

Table 21-1 contains a list of questions companies should ask about each component of the implementation system. Successful implementation depends on how well the company blends the five activities into a cohesive program that supports its strategies.

TABLE 21-1
Questions about the Marketing Implementation System

Structure
What is the organization's structure?
What are the lines of authority and communication?
What is the role of task forces, committees, or similar mechanisms?

Systems
What are the important systems?
What are the key control variables?
How do product and information flow?

Tasks
What are the tasks to be performed and which are critical?
How are they accomplished, with what technology?
What strengths does the organization have?

People
What are their skills, knowledge, and experience?
What are their expectations?
What are their attitudes toward the firm and their jobs?

Culture
Are there shared values that are visible and accepted?
What are the shared values and how are they communicated?
What are the dominant management styles?
How is conflict resolved?

Fit
Does each component above support marketing strategy?
Do the various components fit together well to form a cohesive framework for implementing strategy?

Source: Adapted from David L. Aaker, *Strategic Market Management,* (New York: Wiley, 1984), p. 151. © 1984, John Wiley & Sons, Inc.

MARKETING DEPARTMENT ORGANIZATION

In the previous section, we looked at how the company's formal and informal organization supports strategy and its implementation. In this section, we will focus on the organization of the marketing department—how marketing departments evolve within companies and how they are organized.

Evolution of the Marketing Department The modern marketing department is the product of a long evolution. At least five stages can be distinguished, and companies can be found today in each stage of evolution.

Simple Sales Department

All companies start out with four simple functions. Someone must raise and manage capital (finance), produce the product or service (operations), sell it (sales), and keep the books (accounting). The selling function is headed by a sales vice-president who manages a salesforce and also does some selling. When the company needs some marketing research or advertising, the sales vice-president also handles this. This stage is illustrated in Figure 21-3A.

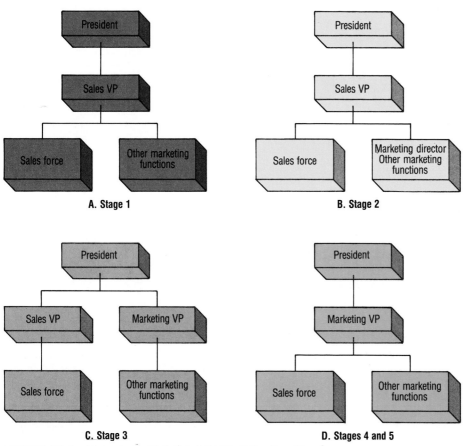

FIGURE 21-3 *Stages in the Evolution of the Marketing Department*

Sales Department with Ancillary Functions

As the company expands, it needs marketing research, advertising, and customer service on a more continuous and expert basis. The sales vice-president hires specialists to perform these functions. The sales vice-president may also hire a marketing director to plan and control the nonselling functions (see Figure 21-3B).

Separate Marketing Department

The continued growth of the company increases the importance of other marketing functions—marketing research, new product development, advertising and sales promotion, customer service—relative to salesforce activity. Nevertheless, the sales vice-president continues to give disproportionate time and attention to the salesforce. The marketing director will argue that more budget should go into the other marketing functions.

The company president will eventually see the advantage of establishing a marketing department that is relatively independent of the sales vice-president (see Figure 21-3C). The marketing department will be headed by a marketing vice-president who reports, along with the sales vice-president, to the president or executive vice-president. At this stage, sales and marketing are separate and equal functions and are supposed to work closely together.

Modern Marketing Department

Although the sales and marketing vice-presidents are supposed to work harmoniously, their relationship is often characterized by rivalry and distrust. The sales vice-president resists letting the salesforce become less important in the marketing mix; the marketing vice-president seeks more power for the non-salesforce functions. The sales vice-president tends to be short-run-oriented and preoccupied with achieving current sales. The marketing vice-president tends to be long-run-oriented and preoccupied with planning the right products and marketing strategy to meet customers' long-run needs.

If there is too much conflict between sales and marketing, the company president may place marketing activities back under the sales vice-president, instruct the executive vice-president to handle conflicts that arise, or place the marketing vice-president in charge of everything, including the salesforce. The last solution forms the basis of the modern marketing department, a department headed by a marketing vice-president with subordinates reporting from every marketing function (see Figure 21-3D).

Modern Marketing Company

A company can have a modern marketing department and yet not operate as a modern marketing company. The latter depends upon how the other company officers view the marketing function. If they view marketing as primarily a selling function, they are missing the point. Only when they see that all the departments are "working for the customer," and that marketing is the name not of a department but of a company philosophy, will they become a modern marketing company.

Ways of Organizing the Marketing Department

Modern marketing departments show numerous arrangements. Each arrangement, however, must permit the marketing organization to accommodate to four basic dimensions of marketing activity: functions, geographic areas, products, and customer markets.

Functional Organization

The most common form of marketing organization consists of functional marketing specialists reporting to a marketing vice-president who coordinates their activities. Figure 21-4 shows five specialists: marketing administration manager, advertising and sales promotion manager, sales manager, marketing research manager, and new products manager. Additional functional specialists might include a customer service manager, a marketing-planning manager, and a physical distribution manager.

The main advantage of a functional marketing organization is its administrative simplicity. On the other hand, this form loses effectiveness as the company's products and markets grow. First, there is inadequate planning for specific products and markets, since no one has full responsibility for any product or market. Products that are not favorites of various functional specialists get neglected. Second, each functional group competes to gain more budget and status relative to the other functions. The marketing vice-president has to constantly sift the claims of competing functional specialists and faces a difficult problem in coordination.

Geographic Organization

A company selling in a national market often organizes its salesforce (and sometimes other functions) along geographic lines. Figure 21-5 shows 1 national sales manager, 4 regional sales managers, 24 zone sales managers, 192 district sales managers, and 1,920 salespersons. The span of control increases as we move from the national sales manager down toward the district sales manager. Shorter spans allow managers to give more time to subordinates and are warranted when the sales task is complex, the salespersons are highly paid, and the salesperson's impact on profits is substantial.

Product Management Organization

Companies producing a variety of products or brands often establish a product or

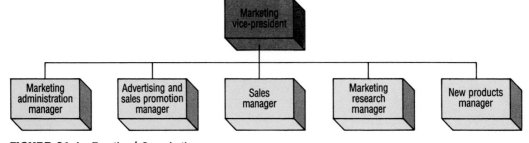

FIGURE 21-4 *Functional Organization*

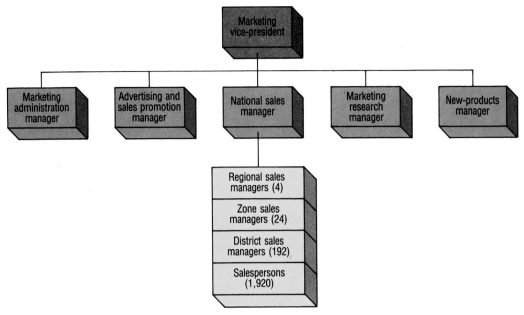

FIGURE 21-5 *Geographic Organization*

brand management organization. The product management organization does not replace the functional management organization, but serves as another layer of management. The product management organization is headed by a products manager who supervises several product group managers who supervise product managers in charge of specific products (see Figure 21-6).

A product management organization makes sense if the products are quite different, or if the sheer number of products is beyond the capacity of a functional marketing organization to handle.

Product management first appeared in the Procter & Gamble Company in 1927. A new company soap, Camay, was not doing well, and one of the young executives, Neil H. McElroy (later president of P&G), was assigned to give his exclusive attention to developing and promoting this product. He did this successfully, and the company soon added other product managers.

Since then, many firms, especially in the food, soap, toiletries, and chemical industries, have established product management organizations. General Foods, for example, uses a product management organization in its Post Division. There are separate product group managers in charge of cereals, pet food, and beverages. Within the cereal product group, there are separate product managers for nutritional cereals, children's presweetened cereals, family cereals, and miscellaneous cereals. In turn, the nutritional cereal product manager supervises brand managers.[19]

The product manager's role is to develop product plans, see that they are implemented, monitor results, and take corrective action. The manager develops a competitive strategy for the product, prepares a marketing plan and sales forecast, works with advertising agencies to develop promotion campaigns, stimulates sales-force and distributor support for the product, analyzes the product's performance,

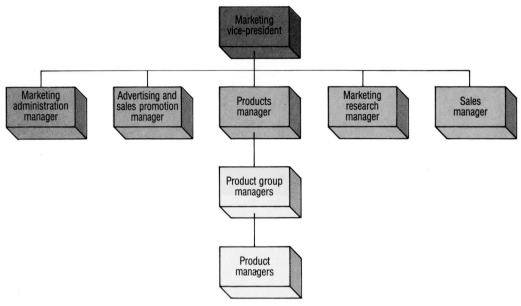

FIGURE 21-6 *Product Management Organization*

and initiates product improvements to meet changing market needs.

The product management organization introduces several advantages. First, the product manager harmonizes the marketing mix for the product. Second, the product manager can react more quickly to problems in the marketplace than a committee of specialists. Third, smaller brands are less neglected because they have a product advocate. Fourth, product management is an excellent training ground for young executives, for it involves them in almost every area of company operations (see Figure 21-7).

But a price is paid for these advantages. First, product management creates some conflict and frustration.[20] Product managers are typically not given enough authority to carry out their responsibilities effectively. They have to rely on persuasion to get the cooperation of advertising, sales, manufacturing, and other departments. They are told they are "mini-presidents" but are often treated as low-level coordinators.

Second, product managers become experts in their product but rarely become experts in any functions. They waver between posing as experts and being cowed by real experts. This is unfortunate when the product depends on a specific type of expertise, such as advertising.

Third, the product management system often turns out to be costlier than anticipated. Originally, one person is appointed to manage each major product. Soon product managers are appointed to manage even minor products. Each product manager, usually overworked, pleads and gets an *assistant brand manager*. Later they both are overworked and persuade management to given them a *brand assistant*. With all these personnel, payroll costs climb. In the meantime the company continues to increase its functional specialists in promotion, marketing re-

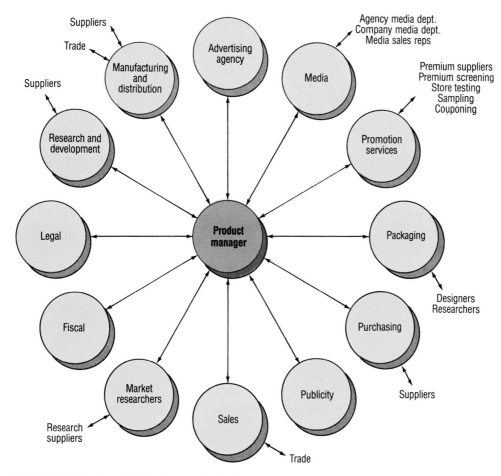

FIGURE 21-7 *The Product Manager's Interactions*

Source: Adapted from "Product Managers: Just What Do They Think?" *Printer's Ink,* October 28, 1966, p. 15.

search, information systems, and other areas. The company becomes saddled with a costly structure of product management people and functional specialists.

Pearson and Wilson have suggested five steps to make the product management system work better.[21]

1. Clearly state the limits of the product manager's role and responsibility for the management of a product.
2. Build a strategy development and review process to provide an agreed-to framework for the product manager's operations.
3. Consider areas of potential conflict between product managers and functional specialists when defining their respective roles.
4. Set up a formal process that forces to the top all conflict-of-interest situations between product management and functional line management.
5. Establish a system for measuring results that is consistent with the product manager's responsibilities.

Market Management Organization

Many companies will sell a product line to a highly diverse set of markets. For example, Smith Corona sells its electric typewriters to consumer, business, and government markets. U.S. Steel sells its steel to the railroad, construction, and public utility industries. Where the customers fall into groups with distinct buying practices or product preferences, a market management organization is desirable.

A market management organization is similar to the product management organization shown in Figure 21-6. A *markets manager* supervises several *market managers* (also called *market development managers, market specialists,* or *industry specialists*). Market managers are responsible for developing long-range and annual plans for the sales and profits in their markets. They have to coax help from marketing research, advertising, sales, and other functions. This system's main advantage is that the company is organized around the needs of specific customer segments.

Many companies are reorganizing along market lines. Hanan calls these *market-centered organizations* and argues that "the only way to ensure being market-oriented is to put a company's organizational structure together so that its major markets become the centers around which its divisions are built."[22] Xerox has converted from geographic selling to selling by industry. The Heinz Company split its marketing organization into three groups: groceries, commercial restaurants, and institutions. Each group contains further market specialists. For example, the institutional division contains separate market specialists who plan for schools, colleges, hospitals, and prisons.

Product Management/Market Management Organization

Companies that produce many products flowing into many markets face a dilemma. They could use a product management system, which requires product managers to be familiar with highly divergent markets. Or they could use a market management system, which means that market managers would have to be familiar with highly divergent products bought by their markets. Or they could install both product and market managers in a *matrix organization.*

The rub, however, is that this system is costly and generates conflict. Here are two of the many dilemmas:

■ How should the salesforce be organized? In the Du Pont example in Exhibit 21-2, should there be separate salesforces for rayon, nylon, and each of the other fibers? Or should the salesforce be organized according to men's wear, women's wear, and other markets? Or should the salesforce not be specialized?

■ Who should set the prices for a particular product market? In the Du Pont example, should the nylon product manager have final authority for setting nylon prices in all markets? What happens if the men's wear market manager feels that nylon will lose out in this market unless special price concessions are made on nylon?

Most managers feel that only the more important products and markets would justify separate managers. Some are not upset about the conflicts and costs and believe that the benefits of product and market specialization outweigh the costs.[23]

EXHIBIT 21-2

DU PONT USES A PRODUCT MANAGEMENT/MARKET
MANAGEMENT SYSTEM

Du Pont's textile fibers division consists of both product managers and market managers:

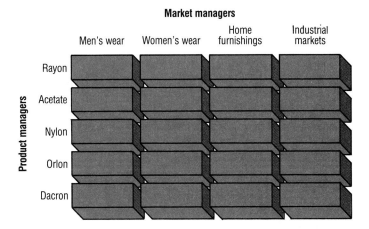

The product managers have the responsibility for planning the sales and profits of their respective fibers. These managers are primarily focused on short-run performance and uses of their fiber. Their job is to contact each market manager and ask for an estimate of how much material can be sold in each market. The market managers, on the other hand, have the responsibility for developing profitable markets for existing and potential Du Pont fibers. They take a long view of market needs and care more about evolving the right products for their market than pushing specific fibers. In preparing their market plan, they contact each product manager to learn about planned prices and availabilities of different materials. The final sales forecasts of the market managers and the product managers should add to the same grand total.

MARKETING CONTROL

The marketing department's job is to plan, implement, and control marketing activity. Because many surprises will occur during the implementation of marketing plans, the marketing department has to engage in continuous marketing control. Marketing control systems are essential in making sure that the company operates efficiently and effectively.

Marketing control, however, is far from being a single process. Three types of marketing control can be distinguished (see Table 21-2).

Annual plan control consists of marketing personnel checking ongoing performance against the annual plan, and taking corrective action when necessary. *Profitability control* consists of efforts to determine the actual profitability of different products, territories, end-use markets, and trade channels. *Strategic control*

TABLE 21-2
Types of Marketing Control

TYPE OF CONTROL	PRIME RESPONSIBILITY	PURPOSE OF CONTROL	APPROACHES
I. Annual plan control	Top management Middle management	To examine whether the planned results are being achieved	Sales analysis Market-share analysis Marketing expense-to-sales ratios Customer attitude tracking
II. Profitability control	Marketing controller	To examine where the company is making and losing money	Profitability by: Product Territory Market segment Trade channel Order size
III. Strategic control	Top management Marketing auditor	To examine whether the company is pursuing its best marketing opportunities and doing this efficiently	Marketing audit

consists of periodically examining whether the company's basic strategies are well matched to its opportunities.

Annual Plan Control

The purpose of annual plan control is to ensure that the company achieves the sales, profits, and other goals established in its annual plan. Four steps are involved (see Figure 21-8). First, management must state monthly or quarterly goals in the annual plan as benchmarks. Second, management must monitor its performance in the marketplace. Third, management must determine the causes of any serious performance deviations. Fourth, management must take corrective action to close the gaps between its goals and its performance. This may require changing the action programs, or even changing the goals.

What specific control tools are used by management to check on plan performance? The four main tools are sales analysis, market-share analysis, marketing expense-to-sales analysis, and customer attitude tracking.

Sales Analysis

Sales analysis consists of measuring and evaluating actual sales in relation to sales goals. There are two specific tools.

FIGURE 21-8
The Control Process

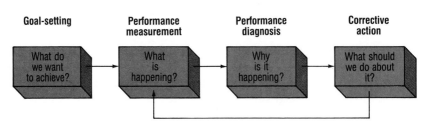

Goal-setting — What do we want to achieve? → Performance measurement — What is happening? → Performance diagnosis — Why is it happening? → Corrective action — What should we do about it?

Sales variance analysis measures the relative contributions of different factors to a gap in sales performance. Suppose the annual plan called for selling 4,000 widgets in the first quarter at $1 a widget, or $4,000. At quarter's end, only 3,000 widgets were sold at $0.80 a widget, or $2,400. The sales performance variance is $1,600, or 40 percent of expected sales. How much of this underperformance is due to the price decline and how much to the volume decline? The following calculation answers this question:

$$
\begin{aligned}
\text{Variance due to price decline} &= (\$1.00 - \$0.80)(3,000) = \$\ \ 600 \quad 37.5\% \\
\text{Variance due to volume decline} &= (\$1.00)(4,000 - 3,000) = \underline{\$1,000} \quad \underline{62.5\%} \\
& \$1,600 \quad 100.0\%
\end{aligned}
$$

Almost two-thirds of the sales variance is due to a failure to achieve the volume target. The company should look closely into why its expected sales volume was not achieved.[24]

Micro sales analysis may provide the answer. Micro sales analysis looks at specific products and territories that failed to produce their expected share of sales. Suppose the company sells in three territories and expected sales were 1,500 units, 500 units, and 2,000 units, respectively, adding up to 4,000 widgets. The actual sales volume was 1,400 units, 525 units, and 1,075 units, respectively. Thus territory one showed a 7 percent shortfall in expected sales; territory two, a 5 percent surplus; and territory three, a 46 percent shortfall! Territory three is causing most of the trouble. The sales vice-president can check into territory three to see why performance is poor.

Market-Share Analysis

Company sales do not reveal how well the company is doing relative to competitors. Suppose a company's sales increase. This could be due to improved economic conditions where all companies gained. Or it could be due to improved company performance in relation to its competitors. Management needs to track the company's market share. If the company's market share goes up, it is gaining on competitors; if its market share goes down, it is losing relative to competitors.

These conclusions from market-share analysis, however, are subject to certain qualifications.[25]

■ The assumption that outside forces affect all companies in the same way is not always valid.

■ The assumption that a company's performance should be judged against the average performance of all companies also is not always valid.

■ If a new firm enters the industry, then every existing firm's market share may fall.

■ Sometimes the decline in a company's market share is the result of a deliberate policy to improve profits.

Marketing Expense-to-Sales Analysis

Annual plan control requires making sure that the company is not overspending to achieve its sales goals. The key ratio to watch is *marketing expense-to-sales.* In one company this ratio was 30 percent and consisted of five component expense-to-

Keeping track of sales and expenses. *Courtesy of Hewlett-Packard.*

sales ratios: *salesforce-to-sales* (15 percent); *advertising-to-sales* (5 percent); *sales promotion-to-sales* (6 percent); *marketing research-to-sales* (1 percent); and *sales administration-to-sales* (3 percent).

Management needs to monitor these ratios. They will exhibit small fluctuations that can well be ignored. But fluctuations in excess of the normal range are a cause for concern. The period-to-period fluctuations in each ratio can be tracked on a *control chart,* as in Figure 21-9. This chart shows that the advertising expense-to-sales ratio normally fluctuates between 8 and 12 percent. In the fifteenth period, however, the ratio exceeded the upper control limit. This could be a rare chance event, or it might indicate that the company has lost control over this expense and should find the cause.

The behavior of successive observations even within the control limits should be watched. Note that the level of the expense-to-sales ratio rose steadily from the ninth period onward. The probability of encountering six successive increases by chance is low. Management should have investigated this pattern before the fifteenth period.

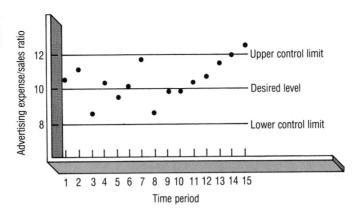

FIGURE 21-9
The Control Chart Model

Customer Attitude Tracking

Alert companies use systems to track the attitudes of customers, dealers, and other marketing system participants. By monitoring changing customer attitudes before they affect sales, management can take earlier action. The main customer attitude tracking systems are

- *Complaint and suggestion systems.* Market-oriented companies record, analyze, and respond to written and oral complaints that come from customers. Management attempts to correct whatever is causing the most frequent types of complaints. Many retailers, such as hotels, restaurants, and banks, provide suggestion cards to encourage customer feedback. Market-oriented companies try to maximize the opportunities for consumer complaining so that management can get a more complete picture of customer reactions to their products and services.
- *Customer panels.* Some companies run panels consisting of customers who have agreed to communicate their attitudes periodically through phone calls or mail questionnaires. These panels uncover a more representative range of customer attitudes than customer complaint and suggestion systems.
- *Customer survey.* Some companies periodically send out questionnaires to random samples of customers to evaluate the friendliness of the staff, the quality of the service, and other factors.[26]

Corrective Action

When actual performance deviates too much from the annual plan goals, companies take corrective actions. They might adjust their goals to make them more realistic and attainable. If the goals are sound, changes in strategy might be required. If strategy and goals remain appropriate, the company will have to change some of the elements of its implementation plan.

Profitability Control Besides annual plan control, companies also need to measure the profitability of their various products, territories, customer groups, trade channels, and order sizes. This information will help management determine whether any products or marketing activities should be expanded, reduced or eliminated.[27]

Marketing Profitability Analysis

We will illustrate the steps in marketing profitability analysis with the following example:

> The marketing vice-president of a lawnmower company wants to determine the profitability of selling its lawnmower through three types of retail channels: hardware stores, garden supply shops, and department stores. Its profit and loss statement is shown in Table 21-3A.

Step 1: *Identifying the functional expenses.* Assume that the expenses listed in Table 21-3A are incurred to sell the product, advertise it, pack and deliver it, and bill and collect for it. The first task is to measure how much of each expense was incurred for each activity.

TABLE 21-3A
A Simplified Profit and Loss Statement

Sales		$60,000
Cost of goods sold		39,000
Gross margin		$21,000
Expenses		
Salaries	$9,300	
Rent	3,000	
Supplies	3,500	
		15,800
Net profit		$5,200

TABLE 21-3B
Mapping Natural Expenses into Functional Expenses

NATURAL ACCOUNTS	TOTAL	SELLING	ADVERTISING	PACKING AND DELIVERY	BILLING AND COLLECTING
Salaries	$ 9,300	$5,100	$1,200	$1,400	$1,600
Rent	3,000	—	400	2,000	600
Supplies	3,500	400	1,500	1,400	200
	$15,800	$5,500	$3,100	$4,800	$2,400

TABLE 21-3C
Bases for Allocating Functional Expenses to Channels

CHANNEL TYPE		SELLING	ADVERTISING	PACKING AND DELIVERY	BILLING AND COLLECTING
		No. of Sales Calls in Period	No. of Advertisements	No. of Orders Placed in Period	No. of Orders Placed in Period
Hardware		200	50	50	50
Garden supply		65	20	21	21
Department stores		10	30	9	9
		275	100	80	80
Functional expense	=	$5,500	$3,100	$4,800	$2,400
No. of units		275	100	80	80
Cost per unit	=	$20	$31	$60	$30

TABLE 21-3D
*Profit and Loss
Statements for
Channels*

	HARDWARE	GARDEN SUPPLY	DEPT. STORES	WHOLE COMPANY
Sales	$30,000	$10,000	$20,000	$60,000
Cost of goods sold	19,500	6,500	13,000	39,000
Gross margin	$10,500	$ 3,500	$ 7,000	$21,000
Expenses				
Selling ($20 per call)	$ 4,000	$ 1,300	$ 200	$ 5,500
Advertising ($31 per advertisement)	1,550	620	930	3,100
Packing and delivery ($60 per order)	3,000	1,260	540	4,800
Billing ($30 per order)	1,500	630	270	2,400
Total expenses	$10,050	$ 3,810	$ 1,940	$15,800
Net profit (or loss)	$ 450	$ (310)	$ 5,060	$ 5,200

Suppose that most of the $9,300 in salary expense went to sales representatives ($5,100) and the rest went to an advertising manager ($1,200), packing and delivery help ($1,400), and an office accountant ($1,600). Table 21-3B shows the allocation of the salary expense to these four activities.

Table 21-3B also shows the rent of $3,000 as allocated to the four activities. Since the sales representatives work away from the office, none of the building's rent expense is assigned to selling. Most of the floor space and equipment rented are for packing and delivery. A small portion of the floor space is used by the advertising manager and office accountant.

Finally, the supplies expense covers promotional materials, packing materials, fuel purchases for delivery, and home-office stationary. The $3,500 in this account is reassigned to the function. Thus Table 21-3B summarizes how the natural expenses of $15,800 were translated into functional expenses.

Step 2: Assigning the functional expenses to the channels. The next task is to measure how much functional expense was associated with selling through each type of channel. Consider the selling effort, as indicated by the number of sales made in each channel. This is found in the Selling column of Table 21-3C. Altogether 275 sales calls were made during the period. Since the total selling expense amounted to $5,500 (see Table 21-3B), the selling expense per call averaged $20.

Advertising expense can be allocated according to the number of ads addressed to the different channels. Since there were 100 ads altogether, the average ad cost $31.

The packing and delivery expense is allocated according to the number of orders placed by each type of channel; this same basis was used for allocating billing and collection expense.

Step 3: Preparing a profit and loss statement for each channel. A profit and loss statement can now be prepared for each type of channel. The results are shown in Table 21-3D. Since hardware stores accounted for one-half of total sales ($30,000 out of $60,000), this channel is charged with half the cost of goods sold ($19,500 out of $39,000). This leaves a gross margin from hardware stores of $10,500. From this we must deduct the proportions of the functional expenses for hardware stores.

According to Table 21-3C, hardware stores received 200 out of 275 total sales calls. At $20 a call, hardware stores have to be charged with $4,000 selling expense.

Table 21-3C also shows that hardware stores were the target of 50 ads. At $31 an ad, the hardware stores are charged with $1,550 of advertising. The same reasoning applies in computing the share of the other functional expenses to charge to hardware stores. The result is that hardware stores gave rise to $10,050 of the total expenses. Subtracting this from the gross margin, the profit of selling through hardware stores is only $450.

This analysis is repeated for the other channels. The company is losing money in selling through garden supply shops and makes virtually all its profits in selling through department stores. Note that the gross sales through each channel are not a reliable indicator of the net profits being made in each channel.

Determining the Best Corrective Action

It would be naive to conclude that garden supply shops and possibly hardware stores should be dropped in order to concentrate on department stores. Several questions would need to be answered first. To what extent do buyers buy on the basis of store type versus brand—would garden supply and hardware store buyers seek out the brand in the remaining channel? What are the trends with respect to the importance of the three channels? Have company marketing strategies directed at the three channels been optimal?

Based on the answers, marketing management might take a number of alternative actions. It might do nothing. It might abandon only the weakest retailers in each channel. The company could establish a special charge for small orders to encourage larger orders. Or it could increase or decrease the number of sales calls and promotional aid going to garden supply shops and hardware stores.

To help evaluate marketing activities and actions, some companies have established a new job position called *marketing controller.* Marketing controllers are trained in finance and marketing and can perform a sophisticated financial analysis of past and planned marketing expenditures.[28]

Strategic Control

From time to time, companies must critically review their overall marketing effectiveness. In marketing, rapid obsolescence of strategies and programs is a constant possibility. Each company should periodically reassess its overall approach to the marketplace, using a tool known as the marketing audit.[29]

The Marketing Audit

We define marketing audit as follows:

> A **marketing audit** is a *comprehensive, systematic, independent,* and *periodic* examination of a company's—or business unit's—marketing environment, objectives, strategies, and activities with a view to determining problem areas and opportunities and recommending a plan of action to improve the company's marketing performance.

The marketing audit covers all major marketing dimensions of a business, not just a few troublespots. It involves an orderly sequence of diagnostic steps covering the organization's marketing environment, internal marketing system, and specific marketing activities. The diagnosis is followed by short-run and long-run corrective action plans to improve the company's overall effectiveness.

The marketing audit is normally conducted by an objective and experienced outside party that is relatively independent of the marketing department. The marketing audit should be carried out periodically instead of only when there is a crisis. It promises benefits for the company that is successful as well as for the company in trouble.

The marketing auditor should be given free rein to interview managers, customers, dealers, salespeople, and others who might throw light on the organization's marketing performance. Table 21-4 is a guide to the kinds of questions the marketing auditor will ask. Not all these questions are important in every situation. The auditor will develop a set of findings and recommendations based on this information. The findings may come as a surprise, and sometimes a shock, to management. Management decides which recommendations make sense, and how and when to implement them.

TABLE 21-4
Components of a
Marketing Audit

PART I. MARKETING ENVIRONMENT AUDIT

Macroenvironment

A. **Demographic**
1. What major demographic developments and trends pose opportunities or threats to this company?
2. What actions has the company taken in response to these developments and trends?

B. **Economic**
1. What major developments in income, prices, savings, and credit will affect the company?
2. What actions has the company been taking in response to these developments and trends?

C. **Natural**
1. What is the outlook for the cost and availability of natural resources and energy needed by the company?
2. What concerns have been expressed about the company's role in pollution and conservation and what steps has the company taken?

D. **Technological**
1. What major changes are occurring in product technology? In process technology? What is the company's position in these technologies?
2. What major generic substitutes might replace this product?

E. **Political**
1. What laws now being proposed could affect marketing strategy and tactics?
2. What federal, state, and local actions should be watched? What is happening in the areas of pollution control, equal employment opportunity, product safety, advertising, price control, and so forth, that affects marketing strategy?

F. **Cultural**
1. What is the public's attitude toward business and toward the products produced by the company?
2. What changes in consumer and business life styles and values have a bearing on the company?

Task Environment

A. **Markets**
1. What is happening to market size, growth, geographical distribution, and profits?
2. What are the major market segments?

B. **Customers**
1. How do customers and prospects rate the company and its competitors on reputation, product quality, service, salesforce, and price?
2. How do different customer segments make their buying decisions?

C. **Competitors**
1. Who are the major competitors? What are their objectives and strategies, their strengths and weaknesses, their sizes and market shares?
2. What trends will affect future competition and substitutes for this product?

TABLE 21-4 (Cont.)

*Components of a
Marketing Audit*

D. **Distribution and Dealers**
  1. What are the main trade channels for bringing products to customers?
  2. What are the efficiency levels and growth potentials of the different trade channels?

E. **Suppliers**
  1. What is the outlook for the availability of key resources used in production?
  2. What trends are occurring among suppliers in their pattern of selling?

F. **Facilitators and Marketing Firms**
  1. What is the cost and availability outlook for transportation services?
  2. What is the cost and availability outlook for warehousing facilities?
  3. What is the cost and availability outlook for financial resources?
  4. How effectively is the advertising agency performing?

G. **Publics**
  1. What publics represent particular opportunities or problems for the company?
  2. What steps has the company taken to deal effectively with each public?

PART II. MARKETING STRATEGY AUDIT

A. **Business Mission**
  1. Is the business mission clearly stated in market-oriented terms? Is it feasible?

B. **Marketing Objectives and Goals**
  1. Are the corporate and marketing objectives stated in the form of clear goals to guide marketing planning and performance measurement?
  2. Are the marketing objectives appropriate, given the company's competitive position, resources, and opportunities?

C. **Strategy**
  1. What is the core marketing strategy for achieving the objectives? Is it sound?
  2. Are enough resources (or too much resources) budgeted to accomplish the marketing objectives?
  3. Are the marketing resources allocated optimally to market segments, territories, and products?
  4. Are the marketing resources allocated optimally to the major elements of the marketing mix— i.e., product quality, service, salesforce, advertising, promotion, and distribution?

PART III. MARKETING ORGANIZATION AUDIT

A. **Formal Structure**
  1. Does the marketing officer have adequate authority and responsibility over company activities that affect the customer's satisfaction?
  2. Are the marketing activities optimally structured along functional, product, end user, and territorial lines?

B. **Functional Efficiency**
  1. Are there good communication and working relations between marketing and sales?
  2. Is the product management system working effectively? Are product managers able to plan profits or only sales volume?
  3. Are there any groups in marketing that need more training, motivation, supervision, or evaluation?

C. **Interface Efficiency**
  1. Are there any problems between marketing and manufacturing, R&D, purchasing, or financial management that need attention?

PART IV. MARKETING SYSTEMS AUDIT

A. **Marketing Information System**
  1. Is the marketing intelligence system producing accurate, sufficient, and timely information about market place developments?
  2. Is marketing research being adequately used by company decision makers?

B. **Marketing Planning System**
  1. Is the marketing planning system well conceived and effective?
  2. Is sales forecasting and market potential measurement soundly carried out?
  3. Are sales quotas set on a proper basis?

TABLE 21-4 (Cont.)
Components of a Marketing Audit

C. **Marketing Control System**
   1. Are the control procedures adequate to ensure that the annual plan objectives are being achieved?
   2. Does management periodically analyze the profitability of products, markets, territories, and channels of distribution?
   3. Are marketing costs being periodically examined?

D. **New Product Development System**
   1. Is the company well organized to gather, generate, and screen new product ideas?
   2. Does the company do adequate concept research and business analysis before investing in new ideas?
   3. Does the company carry out adequate product and market testing before launching new products?

PART V. MARKETING PRODUCTIVITY AUDIT

A. **Profitability Analysis**
   1. What is the profitability of the company's different products, markets, territories, and channels of distribution?
   2. Should the company enter, expand, contract, or withdraw from any business segments and what would be the short- and long-run profit consequences?

B. **Cost-Effectiveness Analysis**
   1. Do any marketing activities seem to have excessive costs? Can cost-reducing steps be taken?

PART VI. MARKETING FUNCTION AUDITS

A. **Products**
   1. What are the product line objectives? Are these objectives sound? Is the current product line meeting the objectives?
   2. Are there products that should be phased out?
   3. Are there new products that are worth adding?
   4. Would any products benefit from quality, feature, or style modifications?

B. **Price**
   1. What are the pricing objectives, policies, strategies, and procedures? To what extent are prices set on cost, demand, and competitive criteria?
   2. Do the customers see the company's prices as being in line with the value of its offer?
   3. Does the company use price promotions effectively?

C. **Distribution**
   1. What are the distribution objectives and strategies?
   2. Is there adequate market coverage and service?
   3. Should the company consider changing its degree of reliance on distributors, sales reps, and direct selling?

D. **Advertising, Sales Promotion, and Publicity**
   1. What are the organization's advertising objectives? Are they sound?
   2. Is the right amount being spent on advertising? How is the budget determined?
   3. Are the ad themes and copy effective? What do customers and the public think about the advertising?
   4. Are the advertising media well chosen?
   5. Is sales promotion used effectively?
   6. Is there a well-conceived publicity program?

E. **Salesforce**
   1. What are the organization's salesforce objectives?
   2. Is the salesforce large enough to accomplish the company's objectives?
   3. Is the salesforce organized along the proper principles of specialization (territory, market, product)?
   4. Does the salesforce show high morale, ability, and effort?
   5. Are the procedures adequate for setting quotas and evaluating performances?
   6. How is the company's salesforce rated in relation to competitors' salesforces?

■ *Summary*

This chapter examines how marketing strategies are implemented, and how marketing efforts are organized and controlled.

It is often easier to design good strategies than to carry them out. To be successful, companies must implement the strategies effectively. *Implementation* is the process that turns marketing strategies into marketing actions. Several factors can cause implementation failures— isolated planning, tradeoffs between long-term and short-term objectives, the company's natural resistance to change, and a failure to prepare detailed implementation plans.

The implementation process links marketing strategy with marketing performance. The process consists of five interrelated elements. The *action program* identifies crucial tasks and decisions needed to implement the strategy, assigns responsibility for implementation to specific people, and sets a timetable for the completion of implementation tasks. The *organization structure* differentiates tasks and assignments, and coordinates the efforts of the company's people and units. The company's structure evolves to fit the firm's strategy and situation. The company's *decision and reward systems* must also support marketing strategy. These systems guide activities such as planning, information, budgeting, training, control, and personnel evaluation and rewards. Well-designed systems can encourage good implementation.

Successful implementation also requires careful *human resources* planning. The company must recruit, allocate, develop, and maintain good people. It must carefully match its managers to the requirements of the strategies being implemented. The company's *managerial climate and company culture* can make or break implementation. Different strategies require different leadership styles. And company culture guides the behavior of people in the company—good implementation relies on strong and clearly defined cultures that fit the chosen strategy.

Each element of the implementation system must fit company strategy. Moreover, successful implementation depends on how well the company blends the five elements into a cohesive program that supports its strategies.

Most of the responsibility for implementation goes to the company's marketing department. The modern marketing department evolved through several stages. It started as a sales department, and later this department took on some ancillary functions, such as advertising and marketing research. As the ancillary functions grew in importance, many companies created a separate marketing department to manage these other marketing activities. But the heads of sales and marketing often disagreed, and eventually the two departments were merged into a modern marketing department headed by the marketing vice-president. A modern marketing department, however, does not automatically create a modern marketing company unless the other officers accept and practice a customer orientation.

Modern marketing departments are organized in a number of ways. The most common form is the functional marketing organization in which marketing functions are headed by separate managers reporting to the marketing vice-president. Another form is the product management organization in which products are assigned to product managers who work with functional specialists to develop and achieve their plans. Another form is the market management organization in which major markets are assigned to market managers who work with functional specialists to develop and achieve their plans. Some large companies use a product management and market management organization.

Marketing organizations carry out three types of marketing control.

Annual plan control consists of monitoring the current marketing effort and results to make sure that the annual sales and profit goals will be achieved. The main tools are sales analysis, market-share analysis, marketing expense-to-sales analysis, and customer attitude tracking. If underperformance is detected, the company can implement several corrective measures, including cutting production, changing prices, increasing salesforce pressure, and cutting fringe expenditures.

Profitability control calls for determining the actual profitability of the firm's products, territories, market segments, and trade channels. Marketing profitability analysis reveals the weaker marketing entities, although it does not indicate whether the weaker units should be bolstered or phased out.

Strategic control is the task of making sure that the company's marketing objectives, strategies, and systems are optimally adapted to the current and forecasted marketing environment. It uses the marketing audit, which is a comprehensive, systematic, independent, and periodic examination of the organization's marketing environment, objectives, strategies and activities. The purpose of the marketing audit is to determine marketing opportunity and problem areas and recommend short-run and long-run actions to improve the organization's overall marketing performance.

■ Questions for Discussion

1. Select a consumer service company and discuss how each of the seven "S's" of the McKinsey Framework are managed by that company.

2. Apple Computer has targeted the office market, first with the Lisa computer and then with the "Macintosh Office." What changes in the corporate culture at Apple were necessary to go from marketing computers primarily to the home and school markets to targeting the office market?

3. Discuss the pros and cons of instituting the product management organization for International Harvester's line of farm equipment (i.e., tractors, combines, and implements such as plows and harrows).

4. How does the *product management/market management organization* differ from the *corporate-divisional organization?*

5. A marketing controller is well versed in both marketing and finance. Would this individual be helpful in the latter stages of marketing planning? Why?

6. A friend of yours is planning to open a discothèque. He realizes that marketing "control" is essential for success. How would you advise him on the options he has for exercising marketing control in his new venture?

7. What are the relative advantages and disadvantages of customer attitude tracking when compared with the other annual plan control approaches?

8. The heart of the strategic control process is the marketing audit. Briefly discuss the characteristics and purpose of this concept.

■ References

1. Based on information found in Peter D. Petre, "Meet the Lean New IBM," *Fortune,* June 13, 1983, pp. 69–82; "Personal Computers: And the Winner Is IBM," *Business Week,* October 3, 1983, pp. 76–83; and "How the PC Project Changed the Way IBM Thinks," *Business Week,* October 3, 1983, pp. 86–90.

2. See George S. Day, *Strategic Market Planning: The Pursuit of Competitive Advantage* (New York: West, 1984), p. 205.

3. For more on diagnosing implementation problems, see Thomas V. Bonoma, "Making Your Marketing Strategy Work," *Harvard Business Review,* March–April 1984, pp. 70–71.

4. See "The New Breed of Strategic Planner: Number-Crunching Professionals Are Giving Way to Line Managers," *Business Week,* September 17, 1984, p. 62.

5. These and other examples can be found in Robert L. Banks and Steven C. Wheelwright, "Opera-tions vs. Strategy: Trading Tomorrow for Today," *Harvard Business Review,* May–June 1979, pp. 112–20.

6. See Ray Stata and Modesto A. Maidique, "Bonus System for Balanced Strategy," *Harvard Business Review,* November–December 1980, pp. 156–63.

7. See Banks and Wheelwright, "Operations vs. Strategy," p. 115.

8. See Bonoma, "Making Your Marketing Strategy Work," p. 73.

9. See John M. Hobbs and Donald F. Heany, "Coupling Strategy to Operating Plans," *Harvard Business Review,* May–June 1977, p. 121.

10. See Thomas J. Peters and Robert H. Waterman, Jr., *In Search of Excellence: Lessons from America's Best-Run Companies* (New York: Harper & Row, 1982), p. 10.

11. This figure is styled after several models of organizational design components. For examples, see Jay R. Galbraith, *Organizational Design* (Read-

ing, MA: Addison-Wesley, 1977); PETER LORANGE, *Implementation of Strategic Planning* (Englewood Cliffs, NJ: Prentice-Hall, 1982), p. 95; DAVID L. AAKER, *Strategic Market Management* (New York: Wiley, 1984), Chap. 9; and CARL R. ANDERSON, *Management: Skills, Functions, and Organization Performance* (Dubuque, IA: Wm. C. Brown, 1984), pp. 409–13.

12. See PETERS and WATERMAN, *In Search of Excellence.* For an excellent summary of the study's findings on structure, see AAKER, *Strategic Market Management,* pp. 154–57.

13. PETERS and WATERMAN, *In Search of Excellence,* p. 311.

14. See "Who's Excellent Now?" *Business Week,* November 5, 1984, pp. 76–78; and DANIEL T. CARROLL, "A Disappointing Search for Excellence," *Harvard Business Review,* November–December 1983, pp. 78–79ff.

15. These examples are adapted from those found in ROBERT M. TOMASKO, "Focusing Company Reward Systems to Help Achieve Business Objectives," *Management Review,* (New York: AMA Membership Publications Division, American Management Associations, October 1982), pp. 8–12.

16. WILLIAM F. GLUECK and LAWRENCE R. JAUCH, *Business Policy and Strategic Management* (New York: McGraw-Hill, 1984), p. 358.

17. PETERS and WATERMAN, *In Search of Excellence,* pp. 75–76.

18. Ibid., p. 285.

19. For details, see "General Foods Corporation: Post Division," in *Organization Strategy: A Marketing Approach,* E. Raymond Corey and Steven H. Star, eds. (Boston: Division of Research, Graduate School of Business Administration, Harvard University, 1971), pp. 201–30.

20. See DAVID J. LUCK, "Interfaces of a Product Manager," *Journal of Marketing,* October 1969, pp 32–36.

21. ANDRALL E. PEARSON and THOMAS W. WILSON, JR., *Making Your Organization Work* (New York: As-

sociation of National Advertisers, 1967), pp. 8–13. For further reading, see RICHARD M. CLEWETT and STANLEY F. STASCH, "Shifting Role of the Product Manager," *Harvard Business Review,* January–February 1975, pp. 65–73; VICTOR P. BUELL, "The Changing Role of the Product Manager in Consumer Goods Companies," *Journal of Marketing,* July 1973, pp. 3–11; "The Brand Manager: No Longer King," *Business Week,* June 9, 1973; and JOSEPH A. MOREIN, "Shift from Brand to Product Line Marketing," *Harvard Business Review,* September–October 1975, pp. 56–64.

22. MARK HANAN, "Reorganize Your Company around Its Markets," *Harvard Business Review,* November–December 1974, pp. 63–74.

23. See B. CHARLES AMES, "Dilemma of Product/Market Management," *Harvard Business Review,* March–April 1971, pp. 66–74.

24. For further discussion, see JAMES M. HULBERT and NORMAN E. TOY, "A Strategic Framework for Marketing Control," *Journal of Marketing,* April 1977, pp. 12–20.

25. See ALFRED R. OXENFELDT, "How to Use Market-Share Measurement," *Harvard Business Review,* January–February 1959, pp. 59–68.

26. For an application to a hotel chain, see ARTHUR J. DALTAS, "Protecting Service Markets with Consumer Feedback," *Cornell Hotel and Restaurant Administration Quarterly,* May 1977, pp. 73–77.

27. For a basic text, see DONALD R. LONGMAN and MICHAEL SCHIFF, *Practical Distribution Cost Analysis* (Homewood, IL: Irwin, 1955).

28. See SAM R. GOODMAN, *Techniques of Profitability Analysis* (New York: Wiley, 1970).

29. For details, see PHILIP KOTLER, WILLIAM GREGOR, and WILLIAM RODGERS, "The Marketing Audit Comes of Age," *Sloan Management Review,* Winter 1977, pp. 25–43. A preliminary marketing audit tool is described in PHILIP KOTLER, "From Sales Obsession to Marketing Effectiveness," *Harvard Business Review,* November–December 1977, pp. 67–75.

CASE 15

INTERNATIONAL BUSINESS MACHINE CORPORATION: PC HOME AND EDUCATIONAL MARKETS

International Business Machine Corporation dominates the overall computer market and has earned a 35 percent market share for the personal computer which was introduced in 1981 and is considered the industry standard. In January, 1984, IBM introduced the PCjr into the home computer market. Orders had already been taken for the PCjr before actual product introduction, but sales quickly waned. In response to complaints, the company replaced PCjr's keyboard, developed optional equipment which significantly expanded its memory, adapted business software for it, increased advertising and promotional support, and, finally, drastically reduced prices while also offering easier payment terms to dealers. By November computer and color monitor packages which had sold for $1,698 were available for less than $900. Sales rose dramatically. Market share increased from 11 percent to 17 percent in December. But when the discounts were withdrawn, sales declined. Market share dropped to 4 percent in February, and in late March, 1985, IBM announced it would stop making the PCjr.

The company now faces the question of what PC products and marketing efforts it should plan for the home and educational markets. Two major considerations are:

1. The existing PCjr equipment, user base, and retailers.
2. The growing business- and professional-related part-time after-hours business use of computers in the home, which requires compatibility of home and job-site or office computers.

The background of the present situation is as follows:

1. Speculation that the product was being developed and about to be launched persisted over an extended period, leading to all kinds of rumors and subjecting IBM and its dealers to pressure. Months before PCjr's official unveiling, dealers were taking nonrefundable deposits and even fighting back potential customers. All this resulted in high expectations.
2. The timing of PCjr's introduction was poor. Announced in November, 1983, PCjr was not shipped until mid-January. According to IBM, this premature introduction was forced by the media hype surrounding the product. What resulted was dealer dissatisfaction, and increased non-IBM home computer sales during the 1983 Christmas season. (About 40 percent of annual home computer sales are bought during the Christmas season.)
3. When the PCjr finally came to market in January, 1984, it proved to be a great disappointment. It was coolly received by end-users for three major reasons: the toy-like keyboard was difficult to use; the upper-end machine had insufficient power for doing business work; and less expensive machines were readily available from other manufacturers. In essence, it seemed that IBM had designed the PCjr as a deliberately crippled machine, so as not to cannibalize higher-end IBM personal computer sales. The home computer market turned out to be more demanding than had been expected.
4. The positioning of the product seemed unclear. PCjr was initially positioned toward the home and educational markets, as a computer any family member could use. Later, this positioning was extended to include business use. The approach seemed rather general and confusing to many.
5. Limited compatibility with the PC caused potential business and professional buyers not to buy the PCjr. Apparently IBM did not resolve the question of what role the PCjr should play in relation to its PC line in the business market.
6. In April of 1984, due to lower-than-expected PCjr sales and widespread dealer dissatisfaction, IBM launched an intensive advertising blitz, spending over $20 million. However, the problems persisted. Dealers slashed prices, cut back orders, used the PCjr as a bonus for customers buying higher-end IBM computers, and often chose to sell the Apple IIe over the PCjr.

7. After regrouping, major price cuts were announced for the PCjr. A new standard type keyboard, and a greatly expanded memory (512K) were made available. These changes were explained as responses to negative publicity, and consumer and dealer pressure. IBM wanted the PCjr to qualify as a machine used for business work at home, more sophisticated uses for education, and home applications.

8. August, 1984, brought significant advertising support for the PCjr; the first since April. In addition, IBM rolled out its "Writing to Read" system for schools around the country, offering eight new software programs and special school prices for the PCjr. IBM also participated in major joint promotions with consumer-product marketing giants such as Procter & Gamble and General Foods, offering PCjrs as sweepstakes prizes for children.

The home computer market, which consists of units priced under $1,500 and used primarily in the home, is expected to grow at an annual rate of 24 percent through the 1980s. It is estimated that one-third of U.S. households currently own a computer and that 80 percent will have one by the year 2000.

The projected uses of home computers in the years to come reads like science fiction. Electronic home transactions including shopping and banking as well as control of household equipment are suggested. The most common present uses of home computers are for word processing, home finances, and games.

Home computer buyers in the past were technicians and hobbyists, and sales were technology driven. Now, sales are increasingly driven by traditional marketing methods. New home computer buyers are not interested in how the machine operates; they want a high-performance, user-friendly computer, and they make purchase decisions based on price, service, compatability, distribution, corporate identity and image, and ease of use. Because of this new consumer orientation, advertising has become extremely important for creating awareness and providing marketing support to dealers. TV spending for hardware and software combined increased about one-third in 1984. IBM was the leading advertiser of personal computer systems in 1984. Apple holds second place, spending $16 million in 1983, $80 million in 1984, and much more in 1985. Both dealers and software companies welcome this trend toward increased consumer advertising and promotions.

Home computers have been distributed through specialty stores such as Computerland, and through direct sales to educational institutions. Recently, however, mass merchandisers have become an important channel of distribution. Some analysts contend that home computers must be sold through mass market channels to compete effectively. Commodore is the only major competitor presently utilizing mass merchandisers. Atari and Coleco, originally selling machines for game playing, also used them. Analysts considered the low-end Apple IIc and the PCjr as ideal for this channel because of their low prices and simple applications. It was rumored, but denied, that IBM had opened discussions with K mart. Large scale distribution agreements between the retail and computer giants "...could have broad implications ranging from price cuts to renewed sales and competition in the home computer market" according to the *The Wall Street Journal* (September 25, 1984).

Unlike the personal computer market, which includes the over-$1,500 machines, there is little standardization in the less-than-$1,500 home computer market. IBM, Apple, and Commodore do not use compatible software, and even the PCjr and IBM PC have limited compatability. IBM's encouragement to outside software writers was expected to make the PCjr's technical specifications the most widely used in what has been a fragmented business. Other product-related trends include built-in software, bundling (packing more elements on each chip), and networking between home computers and PCs or mainframes. These developments are in response to consumers who demand increased utility and sophistication, yet require a "transparent" system in which the user is virtually unaware of how the computer operates.

The home computer industry is in a turbulent state. In 1983, competitors were plagued by cutthroat price wars, oversupply, and heavy profit losses. The January, 1984,

Consumer Electronics Show was characterized by caution. The *New York Times* (January 9, 1984) reported that the industry was "more sober and wiser...Gone are the emphasis on cut-rate prices and the flurry of dazzling product introductions." Instead, the emphasis now is on profits, with trends toward more expensive machines and less emphasis on price as a basis for competition. As a result, some expect IBM's entry into the home market to cause a shift toward utility, rather than price-based, marketing: in this case user-friendly features and options become the key selling points. IBM's presence in the home computer industry lends credibility to and creates confidence in the market. IBM's entry is expected to improve overall sales. The PCjr was expected to expand the home computer market, to stabilize pricing, and to create a price umbrella for competitors, ending the days of heavy price slashing. This never materialized and prices for PCjr and competitive Apple products were advertised extensively at the retail level.

The home computer market continues to experience a consolidation of competitors and product lines. Texas Instruments' withdrawal from the market, the decline of Atari, and Coleco's withdrawal of Adam signal the trend toward "survival of the fittest"—IBM, Apple, and Commodore. Only the strongest can afford to implement high-powered marketing strategies and are able to reduce manufacturing costs in the hopes of curbing the squeeze on profits.

Major competitors in the home computer industry include IBM, Apple, Commodore, Tandy, and to a lesser extent Coleco, Atari, and the Japanese.

Apple

Apple is the second largest personal computer manufacturer with a market share of 9.5 percent in 1984. Traditionally, Apple has focused on the home and educational markets, but the business market has long been the apple of its eye. Until late 1983, Apple's main product to compete with the PCjr was the Apple IIe introduced at $1,500 and later reduced in price. Other Apple products include the Apple IIc, a portable computer, and the more sophisticated Macintosh which is positioned between IBM's PC and PCjr. The introduction of the Mac was an attempt to bridge the home and business markets. The Mac is easy to use, yet is a versatile machine. The computer has the following attributes: transportable, more memory than the basic PC, pop-up menu, graphics, windowing capability, a hand-held mouse, and other features. Industry estimates are that the Mac will sell between 200,000 and 500,000 units a year. Over 100 companies were called in to produce software for the Mac. Software was especially crucial because the Mac is unable to run programs designed for its sister computers. And the operating system of the Mac is not compatible with either the IBM (MS-DOS) or ATT (UNIX) operating systems.

Since John Sculley moved from Pepsico to Apple as president, advertising has become bold, both in spending and in message content. Spending is up from $2 million, before Sculley arrived, to $80 million in 1984 and is estimated to be over $200 million in 1985. In an effort to spur Christmas sales in 1984, Apple's advertising campaign focused on "Test drive a Macintosh." The premise is that if people take a Mac home, they will find out how easy it is to use. Apple spent $10 million on the campaign in the hopes of generating sales of 100,000 units in three months.

Commodore

The Commodore 64 is a low-priced computer (originally $595, discounted to less than $200) and is used for game playing and word processing. In the under $500 market, over 50 percent of the units sold are Commodore 64s. In 1983, Commodore 64 sales topped one million units but sales are slowing. In the Fall of 1984, sales fell 10 to 30 percent below year-ago levels at a time when sales should be speeding up for Christmas. Another sign of the slowdown of first-time customers is that disk drives, parts of the machines that allow the running of more complicated programs, were selling more quickly than the computers themselves. This may be a sign that customers are becoming more sophisticated in their uses and therefore might think about trading up.

In manufacturing and marketing, Commodore has distinguished itself in a number of ways. First, it is a low-cost manufacturer with its own semiconductor manufacturing operations. Second, it has been one of the leading price cutters in the industry. Finally, Commodore has utilized mass merchandisers for distribution. Over one-half of Commodore 64 sales are by six leading mass merchandisers, including K mart.

Commodore advertising during the first half of 1984 was down by 24 percent to $10.3 million versus the same period a year ago but up in the second half and directed against IBM and Apple.

Tandy

Despite its early lead in home computers and a strong distribution system, Tandy's market share has been eroding. In an effort to reverse this trend, Tandy has recently introduced TRS-80 Model 1000, the third in its line of 100 percent IBM compatibles, priced at $1,200. This price is about half that of the IBM PC and comparable with the PCjr. The advertising concept is "Tandy. Clearly superior."

Coleco

Coleco's Adam, originally $600 and later substantially reduced in price, recently was the fourth largest selling home computer, but like TI it withdrew from the market. Signs that Coleco may be exiting from this market include cancellation of a printer contract, price reduction, and clearing of inventories. It is estimated that 200,000 units had been sold by the end of 1984. Initially, the Adam showed poor sales results because equipment arrived late and in small quantities, and was unreliable. In an attempt to bolster sales, Coleco made heavy use of radio advertising and promotional devices such as contests, premiums of free Cabbage Patch dolls, and $500 scholarships, but these were of little use.

Atari

Atari is another computer maker whose future is questionable. Having been sold by Warner Communications to Jack Tramiel, founder of Commodore International, Atari continues to have pricing and inventory problems. Also, cash flow problems plague the company. Whether all of these factors will be too much for Atari is the subject of industry speculation. Despite problems the company announced in mid-1985 two new computers, one intended to be a match for Apple Computer's Macintosh.

Japanese Competitors

The Japanese are significant competitors in the total computer industry, having close to a monopoly in the production of printers. Further, the manufacturing of computers and their components is subcontracted to the Japanese by many U.S. companies. However, the Japanese have yet to achieve a significant entry in the home computer market. Significant barriers to entry include distribution and software. Speculation is that the Japanese are waiting for the industry to settle down before entering.

The once volatile computer market, as characterized by numerous competitors, price wars, oversupply, and heavy losses, is beginning to show signs of nearing stability. Emerging trends are (1) away from games toward serious home uses; (2) aggressive advertising and promotion; and (3) more effective use of channels of distribution. These forces will sustain those companies able to reduce their manufacturing costs and improve their marketing strategies. As the leading marketer of computers, IBM needs to develop fully a careful plan to support its efforts in the home computer market and to give careful consideration to the possible use of mass distribution methods to reach the home market.

Based upon a case prepared by Jennifer Bates, Andrea Fein, Emily Gales, and Lucretia Hadden

What PC product(s) and marketing efforts should IBM plan for the home and educational markets?

CASE 16

MINNETONKA, INC.

In 1978 Minnetonka, Inc., a Chaska, Minnesota, firm dealing primarily in bath products for the gift markets, introduced Softsoap, an inexpensive, pump-dispensed liquid hand soap. One industry analyst asserted that Softsoap was the "first major innovation in the hand soap market since Procter and Gamble introduced Ivory, 'the soap that floats,' a century ago." In 1982, the company put its hopes and dollars into the launch of ShowerMate, a liquid soap for the shower, which proved a disappointment. The following year it introduced Check-Up, a pump-dispensed toothpaste. The meteoric rise of Softsoap with almost an 8 percent market share in its first year and of Check-Up with a 5 percent share of the $1 billion dentifrice market attracted the interest of such marketing giants as Procter & Gamble, Colgate Palmolive, Lever Brothers, and Armour-Dial. Initially slow to react, these slumbering goliaths with a substantial stake in the bar soap and dentifrice markets launched their own brands, supported with heavy advertising and promotional efforts. Minnetonka must decide how to respond to this serious threat to its two largest revenue-generating products.

Starting out with a $3,000 investment in 1964, Robert Taylor, a Stanford MBA, began manufacturing scented soaps in attractive packages in his basement. In subsequent years he expanded his line into bubble baths, fruit shampoos, and fancy bar soap; moved out of his basement; and formed Minnetonka. By 1968 Taylor's initial investment had grown into a $650,000 business. Flushed with his early success, he diversified Minnetonka outside the bath-related products with lines ranging from candles and cosmetics to real estate. Taylor optimistically hoped to boost sales over the $100 million mark.

Problems quickly arose in managing such a diverse portfolio. With the added difficulties brought on by the 1974 economic recession, Taylor was faced with a $1.6 million loss. He responded by retrenching, divesting most of the bath-unrelated lines, and concentrating once again on innovative, attractively packaged soap products primarily for the gift market. Back on familiar ground, Taylor managed to turn Minnetonka around while successfully expanding his existing lines—Village Bath, Dirty Kids—and acquiring Claire Burke, Inc. Minnetonka, in 1976, was a growing firm dealing mostly in specialty bath products for the gift market. Utilizing a highly creative approach to manufacturing and packaging, Minnetonka developed such products as fruit shampoos, "War Paint" bubble baths, the "Incredible Soap Machine" liquid-soap pump-dispenser, and fancy bar soaps. Its products were primarily distributed through specialty stores.

In 1978, working from information garnered in focus group sessions on the Incredible Soap Machine, a Village Bath entry in the liquid/fancy soap category, Taylor set out to offer a liquid soap product positioned against the bar soaps. The focus groups had indicated a favorable reaction to the convenience and neatness of the Incredible Soap Machine, but the price, $4.94, was considered too high for regular use.

In response, Minnetonka came out with Softsoap at $1.59 for 10.5 ounces and retailed it through grocery and food outlets and drugstores, primarily using food brokers. Softsoap was attractively packaged in a plastic, pump-dispensing bottle with a clear plastic overcap. The package came in four colors: yellow, brown, blue, and green, and all colors featured a decorative wicker motif.

The sales rollout in April 1980 was supported by a heavy national television advertising schedule, plus magazine and Sunday supplement coupon offers. Softsoap was so successful that within days many stores were completely sold out of their initial order.

Beyond having an appealing and effective product that answered a need for some consumers, the key to Softsoap's success has been extremely strong distribution in grocery, drug, and mass-merchandising outlets. By the end of 1980, Softsoap was being sold in nearly all the supermarkets in the United States.

The successful advertising campaign that began in 1980 was expanded in 1981, bringing the "Soap without the soapy mess" message to consumers through television, magazines, newspapers, and outdoor advertising. Softsoap was the number-one advertiser in its product category during 1981.

The success of Softsoap boosted Minnetonka's sales to over $95 million in 1981, and euphoric sales forecasts for liquid soap brought an onslaught of competition. The company's sales fell by nearly 50 percent in two years.

By early 1982 there were more than forty competitors eager to capture a portion of the estimated $80 million liquid soap market. The ultimate threat was in the hands of the four major soapers—Armour-Dial, Procter & Gamble, Colgate Palmolive, and Lever Brothers. Each was reportedly in the research and development stage on products for the liquid soap class. In late 1981 the long-anticipated test marketing of both Procter & Gamble's Rejoice and Armour-Dial's Liqua 4 took place. Rejoice was positioned for use "instead of a bar" and claimed to "condition your skin as it cleans, leaving it soft and smooth." Liqua 4 came in a 5-ounce soap-shaped squeezable plastic container and was touted as a "liquid formula" that replaces bar soap with "complete skin care." In addition to the advertised brands, retailer-sponsored private-label brands and generic liquid soap in quite similar pump-dispenser bottles appeared at much lower prices.

Softsoap was distributed to retailers with a suggested retail price of $1.59 for 10.5 ounces. Actual shelf prices ranged between $1.29 and $1.77, not including deals or coupon offers, which at times reduced the price to as little as $0.99. The retailer received a 30 percent markup, compared with an industry average markup on bar soaps of around 15 percent. Private labels and generics sold for as little as $1. Procter & Gamble withdrew Rejoice and launched Liquid Ivory, priced at less than $1, presumably to take advantage of the well-known Ivory name in a market believed too small, roughly $100 million, to launch and profitably sustain a new brand.

At the time skeptics in the industry claimed that liquid soap was a small specialty market which was approaching its upper limit on a per capita basis; that liquid soap was not suited for shower or bath; that its importance would diminish after initial purchases prove disappointing; and that beyond a small segment, it would be a novelty item suitable for the gift market or for display in the home when there are guests.

The primary use of Softsoap is as a hand soap, usually in the place of bar soap at the bathroom and kitchen sinks. It is against this primary use category that product positioning and promotions are based. The product is broadly targeted to housewives. The target segment is currently defined by the distribution channels and, in an encompassing sense, includes all consumers who use those retail outlets where the product appears.

Research indicated that liquid soap was being used in the home primarily as a hand soap at a wash basin or sink, whereas almost 75 percent of the $1 billion bar soap sales was being used in showers or bathtubs. Seeking to gain an early competitive edge in this virtually untapped market segment for liquid soap, Minnetonka launched ShowerMate, its liquid soap product in a squeeze tube with a hook on one end, which could be hung on a shower head or on a towel bar during use. In 1982, the company introduced ShowerMate in a few markets and soon thereafter announced that it would be rolling out nationally with advertising support at a level of $10 to $15 million a year. Initial markets were Houston; Orlando and

Jacksonville, Florida; Denver; Portland, Oregon; Seattle; and Minneapolis–St. Paul. A number of competitive shower/tub liquid products were already available. Among them were Shower of Capri from S. C. Johnson & Co., and Shower Up from Jo Go Industries. Both Armour/Dial and Procter & Gamble had products in test markets.

ShowerMate, in a 12-ounce squeeze bottle with built-in hook, sold for about $2 retail, whereas Shower Up and Shower of Capri, in 8-ounce and 11-ounce squeeze bottles, respectively, sold for about $1.50 and $1.70. All were backed with extensive advertising and sold through grocery, drug, general, and mass-merchandise outlets. Price cutting became widespread.

ShowerMate was well received by the trade in 1982. It looked like a repeat of the Softsoap success. But despite the shift of advertising money from Softsoap to ShowerMate and the heavy volume of sales during the initial sell-in period, factory sales began to fall off. The product was in trouble. Robert Taylor later said: "The old bar-soap habit is difficult to crack. We felt it would be easy to transfer the halo of Softsoap. Maybe we underestimated the difficulty of breaking the habit." Two years after its introduction, ShowerMate had weak distribution and a declining sales volume. Most observers consider it a dead item.

Check-Up, a toothpaste in a pump-dispenser package, was introduced in 1983 and within one year had national distribution with an estimated 5 percent market share. Again the success of a Minnetonka fast-start product threatened large entrenched competitors. Soon Colgate introduced its Colgate brand toothpaste in a pump-dispenser package as well as its Dentguard brand, a plaque fighter. Check-Up was being promoted as a plaque fighter with no emphasis on the pump feature. Other established brands were made available in the pump-dispenser package. They included Crest (P&G), Aim (Lever Bros.), and Aqua-Fresh (Beecham). The importance of this $1 billion market to competitors is indicated by the shares held by each of the brands, which were estimated to be as follows: Crest, 33 percent; Colgate, 22 percent; Aqua-Fresh, 11 percent; Aim, 10 percent. Trade sources indicated that as the above competitors entered the pump market, Check-Up was being promoted heavily at about $17 million on an annualized basis, including advertising and merchandising.

According to *Forbes Magazine* (November 19, 1984) Robert Taylor thinks Check-Up will do better than Softsoap, despite the similarity of their fast starts. His reasons are as follows:

1. Minnetonka distributes Check-Up and splits the profits with Henkel, KG&A, the $3.3 billion West German consumer products and chemicals company. Henkel makes Check-Up in West Germany and has agreed to cover one-half the $17 million marketing budget for the U.S. brand. Henkel sell its Thera-Med brand of pump-dispensed toothpaste in several Western European countries with market shares ranging from 6 to 12 percent.

2. Product distinctiveness will be stressed, which for Check-Up is its plaque-fighting power. In the case of Softsoap, the slogan "soap without the soapy mess" promoted liquid soap and helped competitors', not just the sponsor's own product.

3. The overoptimism and euphoric sales forecasts associated with Softsoap's early success led to overbuilding. When sales fell, the company could not cut back quickly enough to prevent large losses. Taylor plans to avoid this trap.

4. The company will not be so heavily dependent on one product. It has a broader line ranging from Roger & Gallet soaps and Calvin Klein fragrances to Village Bath body paint for lovers.

Yet there are some similarities to the Softsoap experience, as pointed out in the *Forbes* article. Big competitors are coming into the market. Research done by Minnetonka indicates that many consumers are buying Check-Up for its unique package rather than its plaque-fighting power. Taylor is quoted as saying, "The risk is that we cannot hold on to the share of market we've attained, which means we could ultimately lose money."

As a market leader, Softsoap is now targeted at the middle or mainstream of the market; that is, it is a moderate-quality soap at a moderate price appealing to the market generally. Competitors have already started to fragment the liquid soap market with products designed for (1) those who want a higher-priced cleansing and a skin-care product (Yardley's and Jovan), (2) the baby-care market (Yardley's), and (3) the shower/bath market. Minnetonka could try to discourage further competition by entering liquid-soap products in these and other segments ahead of major competition.

In addition to, or in place of, segmenting the market, Minnetonka could launch a line of personal-care products based on the pump-dispensing bottle idea, such as hand lotions and shampoo, as it did for toothpaste with Check-Up. But the fundamental decision is whether or not Minnetonka should continue in the mass market competing against major soap companies, or sell specialty products in smaller markets. It could sell its mass-market products—Softsoap, ShowerMate and Check-Up—to another company as a going business and return to its original business, personal specialty products for the gift market. Henkel is interested in the United States market and has a 23 percent ownership interest in Clorox, a former Procter & Gamble subsidiary. Trade sources indicate the two companies have a cooperative arrangement regarding products and research. One of these might be a possible buyer or partner. If Minnetonka does get out of the mass market, it needs to reformulate its strategy for operating the rest of its business. If Minnetonka decides to compete against the major soap companies, then a plan for doing so must be formulated. Should the company compete head-on, or is some other strategy more promising? A logical approach would be built on the strengths of the company relative to market opportunities and competitive strengths and weaknesses.

What changes should Minnetonka make in its marketing objectives and strategy, if any?

CASE 17

MAYTAG CO.

The Maytag Co., a limited-line appliance manufacturer, has been one of the most profitable firms in the appliance business in recent years, with annual sales of over $500 million. Its basic strategy has been to make the best product and charge for it accordingly. Its sales have been primarily to the upper end of the replacement market. Neither the newly formed household market nor the builder's market has been targeted. Maytag's laundry equipment has the reputation of being trouble-free and the company has featured "Ol' Lonely," the Maytag repairman, in its advertising. Changing conditions make it desirable for the company to consider whether its strategy should be changed, especially in view of its recent acquisition of two cooking equipment manufacturers. In the past it has focused on premium-priced washers, dryers, and dishwashers for the replacement market.

Maytag acquired, for $28 million, the Cleveland, Tennessee, based Hardwick Stove Co., makers and marketers of gas and electric ranges and microwave ovens sold through conventional outlets in medium- and low-price brackets. It also acquired, for an estimated $75 million, Jenn-Air, a leading manufacturer of indoor electric barbecue grills and stove-top ventilation systems with sales of more than $100 million. These acquisitions gave Maytag the following:

1. A cooking equipment product line, but under two non-Maytag brand names.

2. A network of independent distributors used by the two acquired companies to supplement Maytag's distribution system, which sells product directly to 10,000 dealers.

3. Jenn-Air's strong customer identity among the same high-end consumers who buy Maytag appliances.

4. The opportunity to develop unique combination products that incorporate Hardwick conventional and microwave technologies and Jenn-Air's electric grill and ventilation strengths.

5. Hardwick's less than 2 percent market share in the countertop microwave market sold through conventional outlets in the medium- and low-price brackets.

6. Manufacturing capabilities of the acquired product lines.

Maytag's president explained that while "cooking equipment is a mature market, it is an exciting one because product innovation is changing the traditional way people cook and broadening sales opportunities." At the same time, Maytag's entry into the cooking equipment industry is a gamble that some of its success in washers, dryers, and dishwashers can rub off on ranges and ovens. Not long after Maytag entered the major kitchen appliance market, rival Hobart Corp., makers of Kitchen-Aid dishwashers, entered also by acquiring most of the Chambers Cooking equipment line from Rangaire.

Maytag's laundry equipment is regarded as the top of the line, but despite much effort and favorable ratings in *Consumer Reports,* many consumers and members of the industry still consider its dishwasher to be second to Hobart's Kitchen-Aid, long the leader in the high-quality, high-price niche. Maytag is, however, narrowing the gap. It has launched an extensive comparative advertising campaign aimed at Kitchen-Aid. The headline of one ad asks, "Which of these two great dishwashers is best—Kitchen-Aid or Maytag? The message gives a detailed point-by-point comparison and was delivered in fifty-eight major markets using spot TV and newspapers.

The premium-quality niche for laundry and kitchen appliances targeted by both Maytag and Kitchen-Aid may be eroding. Although there is no solid evidence of this, there is an increasingly prevalent feeling in the trade and among consumers that the quality difference between high-priced and medium-priced major laundry and kitchen appliances is becoming smaller and the price difference relatively larger.

Microwave ovens for the home first caught on in the 1950s, but their growth was slow until the early 1970s. At that time the problems involved in microwave cooking included uneven cooking; meats could not be browned; foil-wrapped foods could not be put in the oven; few cookbooks were available; and real or imagined personal radiation danger associated with microwaves.

As soon as these problems were overcome, sales took off. By the late 1970s the countertop microwave ovens were no longer considered a luxury. With more and more working women, the oven's appeal became stronger, and microwaves are now being used in over 40 percent of U.S. households, as compared with 45 percent for dishwashers. Microwave ovens, which range in price from $150 to $600, have been one of the hottest items in the appliance business. Industry forecasters foresee a penetration of these cooking units comparable to that of color television sets. Price competition and discounting are heavy. Premium prices are difficult to maintain.

Five of the forty or so producers of microwave ovens have well over 50 percent of the consumer market. Litton and Amana have been the leaders, but Sears, General Electric, and Sharp have been closing the gap.

Some of the major developments in the industry are as follows:

1. The structure of the major appliance industry is changing, through mergers and acquisitions, with a few large, full-line companies producing most of the industry output. Design and Manufacturing Co. of Connerville, Indiana, produces dishwashers that account for over half the dollars spent without selling a single unit under its own

name. It supplies such buyers as Sears, Magic Chef, Roper, Western Auto, Gambles, and Tappan.

2. Competition, always keen in this industry, has become even more so.
   a. Low-cost producers, such as White Consolidated Industries, are constantly driving for lower costs.
   b. General Electric has undertaken major projects focused on its dishwashers and refrigerators to improve product quality and reliability, but at the same time reduce production costs through the increased use of industrial robots.
   c. Marketing efforts have been intensified, with greater emphasis being given to quick sales stimulants such as factory rebates, special factory-authorized sales, and additional incentives for consumers and dealers. Advertising also has an important role.

3. Products are being designed with fewer electromechanical and more electronic components to control operations. Microprocessors and other advanced technology require greater technological resources not only for the design and manufacture of equipment, but also for service and repair.

4. Service is becoming a major problem. Special tools and more sophisticated service personnel are required for major repairs. Service calls are costly to make. The need for, and cost of, service calls are resented by consumers, especially when repairs are minor. Most companies would rather not be bothered with them. Few make a profit, although it is believed that in the appliance industry, the Sears service operation is profitable because of its large volume of maintenance contracts. GE and Whirlpool also have large service fleets and offer maintenance contracts.

5. General Electric hopes to reduce the problem by starting a "Quick Fix System" offered through franchised dealers. Customers can purchase detailed repair manuals for GE appliances and commonly needed replacement parts at a special display. GE surveys show that 40 percent of the appliance repairs are currently being done by consumers who get little help from makers. Moreover, 25 percent of the consumer repairs are made by women.

   Help by phone is also available. Whirlpool was an early user of an 800 number for consumer calls. The "GE Answer Center 800.626.2000" (a registered trademark) is open at all hours throughout the year to answer questions about the operation or repair of GE appliances and the selection or purchase of new ones.

The most significant technological development is the rapid movement toward electronic controls and readouts, including touch-pad controls instead of the less convenient knobs and dials, digital readouts indicating type and time of operation in progress, and flashing diagnostic readouts to minimize visits by the repairman. To the surprise of many in the industry, consumers—especially younger, more affluent buyers—have enthusiastically responded to these offerings. It now appears that digital appliances will take over in the upperend of the market and be increasingly popular in the middle range as the price premium for electronics, now about $50 on the GE dishwasher, is reduced. GE, Whirlpool, and KitchenAid are aggressively incorporating electronics, whereas White Consolidated Industries, one of the largest marketers in the business, appears to be quite cautious. Maytag appears to be on the fence or moving slowly.

Microwave ovens were among the first appliances to incorporate electronics and have been well received by consumers. Long a part of the kitchen equipment in California, they are now beginning to sweep the Northeast. Maytag has a minor position in the fast-moving microwave market. Its recent acquisition of Hardwick provided no real help against such competition. Unless it can find a niche in which it has some competitive advantage, it is not likely that it will make a profit from marketing microwave ovens.

Fast becoming a mass-market appliance, microwave sales are surging upward and prices are falling. The market is undergoing a familiar evolution: U.S. and Japanese manufacturers, long dominant, are facing competition from others, this time South Korea, including the Samsung Group and The Lucky-Goldstar Group, which introduced low-priced compact models to fit smaller living quarters and have done so well that they are establishing manufacturing facilities in the United States. Competitors claim the products are of inferior quality, but this has not been verified.

Developments following the acquisitions were:

1. Broader Maytag line including stoves and microwave ovens.
2. Continuance of the Jenn-Air and Hardwick lines.
3. Broader retail distribution of Maytag products by adding mass-merchandising outlets such as Montgomery-Ward.
4. Continuance of the same advertising theme, "Ol' Lonely," to emphasis reliability.
5. Continuance of the premium-price selling policy.

Some top-level issues involving major changes need attention. They are in addition to issues arising from periodic marketing audits designed to do more effectively what is already being done. Strategic issues include:

1. Should the company change its market target emphasis and include the replacement market? The builders' market? If so, what priorities should be assigned each market segment?
2. Should the company round out its kitchen line by adding refrigerators to compete more effectively with full-line marketers?
3. Should the company plan a trial run of a new distribution plan to reduce transport and inventory costs? Dealers would sell as they do now, but delivery and service products would be handled by Maytag from centrally located distribution points.

Maytag's marketing strategy has worked well for its laundry equipment but less well for its dishwasher, although this seems to be improving. However, the basic demographic and industry changes now occurring suggest that the old strategy may not fit current and near-term external and internal developments.

1. Should Maytag change its basic marketing strategy of premium products to replacement next? What are your recommendations and reasons?
2. What changes should Maytag make in its basic marketing strategy, which now focuses on premium products for the replacement market?

seven

EXTENDING MARKETING

Part Seven of this book examines how marketing applies in international, service, and nonprofit markets and discusses its impact on society as a whole. Specifically:

Chapter 22, INTERNATIONAL MARKETING.

Chapter 23, SERVICES MARKETING AND NONPROFIT MARKETING.

Chapter 24, MARKETING AND SOCIETY.

22
International Marketing

Campbell Soup Company is clearly America's soup market leader, with over 80 percent of the wet-soup sales in this country. But when it has ventured abroad, its performance has often been much less impressive.

One of Campbell's early calamitous experiences abroad occurred in Great Britain. It introduced its famous small red-and-white label cans of condensed soup in that country in the 1960s and used U.S. advertising themes. Campbell eventually lost $30 million on this venture. The reason: The consumers saw the small-size cans next to the large-size cans of the British soups and thought Campbell soup was expensive. What they failed to appreciate was that Campbell's soup was condensed and, with the addition of a cup of water, was really less expensive than the other soups.

In 1978 Campbell entered the Brazilian market in a joint venture with a Brazilian company. Campbell invested $6 million. This time Campbell's offerings consisted mainly of vegetable-and-beef combinations packed in extra-large cans bearing the familiar red-and-white label. Initial sales were satisfactory, but then they went flat. After three years and $2 million worth of advertising campaigns, Campbell decided to close down its consumer soup business in Brazil.

What went wrong this time? In belated interviews with Brazilian housewives, Campbell learned that these women felt that they were failing to fulfill their roles as homemakers by not serving their family a soup that they had made themselves. They preferred buying the dehydrated products of Knorr and Maggi to start a soup and add their own ingredients and flair. Households bought Campbell soup only to have around as an emergency soup in case they needed something quickly. Apparently Campbell had not done much in-depth marketing research before coming to Brazil. And it had confined its market tests to one temperate southern city, Curitiba, and did not test in Brazil's subtropical areas.

Campbell's inability to read a foreign market correctly has been repeated by many American firms. A few months following Campbell's failure in Brazil, Gerber announced that it was closing down its baby-food operation in Brazil after an eight-year struggle to make it pay off. Apparently Brazilian housewives did not consider prepared baby food a good substitute for fresh food made by themselves or their live-in maids. They might buy some prepackaged baby food on those occasions when they visit their family or go on vacation.[1]

Because of the large size of the U.S. market and some bad marketing experiences abroad, many American companies have avoided aggressive international marketing. Most American firms prefer domestic to foreign marketing because it is simpler and safer. Managers do not have to learn another language, deal with a different currency, face political and legal uncertainties, or adapt the product to different customer needs and expectations.

Two factors draw American companies into international marketing. First, they might be *pushed* by a weakening of marketing opportunities at home. GNP growth might slow down; government might become antibusiness; the tax burden might become too heavy; the government might push business into expanding abroad in order to earn more foreign exchange and reduce the U.S. trade deficit.[2] Second, American companies might be *pulled* into foreign trade by growing opportunities for their products in other countries. Without abandoning the domestic market, they might find other markets attractive even allowing for the extra costs and problems they face in operating abroad.

American exports amounted to over $200 billion—about 6 percent of the U.S. gross national product in 1979. This makes the United States the world's largest exporting nation in absolute dollars. Other countries are more involved in world trade. The United Kingdom, Belgium, the Netherlands, and New Zealand have to sell more than half their output abroad in order to have high employment and pay for imported goods. International marketing is second nature to companies in these countries.

Some companies here and abroad have gone into world marketing on such a large scale that they can be called *multinational companies*. Among American companies deriving more than 60 percent of their revenue from abroad in 1981 were Pan Am World Airways (92 percent), Exxon (72 percent), Citicorp (67 percent), Texaco (62 percent), Mobil (60 percent), and Colgate-Palmolive (60 percent).[3] Caterpillar, Coca-Cola, Dow Chemical, Ford, Gillette, Gulf Oil, IBM, ITT, Kodak, Pfizer, and Xerox earn more than 50 percent of their profits abroad, and their foreign operations are growing faster than their domestic operations. American companies face formidable multinational competitors such as Royal Dutch/ Shell, British Petroleum, Unilever, Philips, Volkswagenwerk, Nippon Steel, Siemens, Toyota Motor, and Nestlé.

While some American companies have expanded abroad aggressively, many foreign companies have entered the American market. Their names and brands have become household words, such as Sony, Honda, Nissan, Nestlé, Norelco, Mercedes Benz, and Volkswagen, with many Americans showing a preference for these brands over domestic brands. Many other products that appear to be produced by American firms are really produced by foreign multinationals. This group includes Bantam Books, Baskin-Robbins Ice Cream, Capitol Records, Kiwi Shoe Polish, Lipton Tea, and Saks Fifth Avenue. America is also attracting huge foreign investments in tourist and real estate ventures, notably Japanese land purchases in Hawaii, Kuwait's resort development off the South Carolina coast, and Arab purchases of Manhattan office buildings—and one offer by a Saudi Arabian sheik to buy the Alamo for his son.

As international competition intensifies, American companies have to increase their sophistication in handling international marketing operations. Some of America's most successful marketers fumbled when they went abroad. Kentucky Fried Chicken opened eleven outlets in Hong Kong, and all failed within two years. McDonald's located its first European outlet in an Amsterdam suburb, but sales were disappointing. However, McDonald's learned quickly how to locate and adapt and now operates numerous successful outlets around the world.

One might ask whether international marketing involves any new principles. Obviously the principles of setting marketing objectives, choosing target markets, developing marketing positions and mixes, and carrying out marketing control apply. The principles are not new, but the differences between nations can be so great that the international marketer needs to understand foreign environments and institutions and be prepared to revise basic assumptions about how people respond to marketing stimuli.

We will now examine the six basic decisions that a company faces in considering international marketing. (See Figure 22-1.)

APPRAISING THE INTERNATIONAL MARKETING ENVIRONMENT

A company has to learn many things before deciding whether to sell abroad. The company has to acquire a thorough understanding of the international marketing environment. That environment has undergone significant changes since 1945, creating both new opportunities and new problems. The most significant changes are (1) the internationalization of the world economy reflected in the rapid growth of world trade and investment; (2) the gradual erosion of the United States's dominant position and its attendant problems of an unfavorable balance of trade and the fluctuating value of the dollar in world markets; (3) the rising economic power of Japan in world markets (see Exhibit 22-1); (4) the establishment of an international financial system offering improved currency convertibility; (5) the shift in world income since 1973 to the oil-producing countries; (6) the increasing trade barriers

FIGURE 22-1
Major Decisions in International Marketing

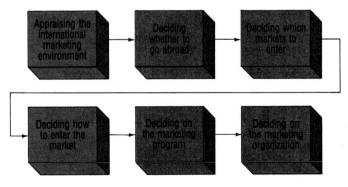

put up to protect domestic markets against foreign competition; and (7) the gradual opening up of major new markets—China, the USSR, and the Arab countries.[4]

EXHIBIT 22-1

THE WORLD'S CHAMPION MARKETERS: THE JAPANESE?

Few dispute that the Japanese have performed an economic miracle since World War II. In a relatively short time, they have achieved global market leadership in industries thought to be dominated by impregnable giants: autos, motorcycles, watches, cameras, optical instruments, steel, shipbuilding, pianos, zippers, radios, television, video recorders, hand calculators, and so on. Japanese firms are currently moving into the number-two position in computers and construction equipment and making strong inroads into the chemical, pharmaceutical, and machine-tool industries.

Many theories have been offered to explain Japan's global success. Some point to their unique business practices, such as lifetime employment, quality circles, consensus management, and just-in-time delivery. Others point to the supportive role of government policies and subsidies, the existence of powerful trading companies, and businesses' easy access to bank financing. Still others view Japan's success as based on low wage rates and unfair dumping policies.

One of the main keys to Japan's performance is its skill in marketing-strategy formulation and implementation. The Japanese came to the United States to study marketing and went home understanding its principles better than many U.S. companies did. The Japanese know how to select a market, enter it in the right way, build their market share, and protect their leadership position against competitors' attacks.

Selecting Markets

The Japanese government and companies work hard to identify attractive global markets. They favor industries that require high skills, high labor intensity, and only small quantities of natural resources: candidates include consumer electronics, cameras, watches, motorcycles, and pharmaceuticals. They prefer product markets that are in a state of technological evolution. They like product markets where consumers around the world would be willing to buy the same product designs. They look for industries where the market leaders are complacent or underfinanced.

Entering Markets

The Japanese send study teams into the target country to spend several months evaluating the market and figuring out a strategy. The teams search for niches to enter that are not being satisfied by any current offerings. Sometimes they establish their beachhead with a low-price stripped-down version of a product, sometimes with a product that is as good as the competitions' but priced lower, sometimes with a product exhibiting higher quality or new features or designs. The Japanese proceed to line up good distribution in order to provide quick service to their customers. They rely on advertising to bring their products to the public's attention. A key characteristic of their entry strategy is to build market share rather than early profits. The Japanese are patient capitalists who are willing to wait even a decade before realizing their profits.

Building Market Share

Once Japanese firms gain a market foothold, they direct their energies toward expanding their market share. They rely on product-development strategies and market-development strategies. They pour money into product improvement, product upgrading, and product proliferation, so that they can offer more and better things than the competition. They spot new opportunities through market segmentation, and sequence market development across a number of countries, pushing toward building a network of world markets and production locations.

Protecting Market Share

Once the Japanese achieve market domination, they find themselves in the role of defenders rather than attackers. U.S. firms such as IBM, Xerox, Motorola, and Texas Instruments are mounting counterattacks. The Japanese defense strategy is a good offense through continuous product development and refined market segmentation. Their aim is to fill holes in the market before their competition can.

Source: Philip Kotler and Liam Fahey, "The World's Champion Marketers: The Japanese," *Journal of Business Strategy,* Summer 1982, pp. 3–13.

The International Trade System

The American company looking abroad must start by understanding the international trade system. In attempting to sell to another country, the American firm will face various trade restrictions. The most common is the **tariff,** which is *a tax levied by the foreign government against certain imported products.* The tariff may be designed to raise revenue (revenue tariff) or to protect domestic firms (protective tariff). The exporter may also face a **quota,** which sets *limits on the amount of goods that the importing country will accept in certain product categories.* The purpose of the quota is to conserve on foreign exchange and protect local industry and employment. An **embargo** is the *ultimate form of quota in that imports in prescribed categories are totally banned.*

Trade is also discouraged by *exchange control,* which regulates the amount of available foreign exchange and its exchange rate against other currencies. The American company may also confront a set of *nontariff barriers,* such as discrimination against American company bids, and product standards that discriminate against American product features. For example, the Dutch government bars tractors that run faster than 10 miles an hour, which means that most American-made tractors are barred.

At the same time, certain forces liberalize and foster trade between nations, or at least between some nations. The General Agreement on Tariffs and Trade (GATT) is an international agreement that has reduced the level of tariffs throughout the world on six different occasions. Certain countries have formed *economic communities,* the most important of which is the European Economic Community (EEC, also known as the Common Market). The EEC's members are the major Western European nations, and they are striving to reduce tariffs within the community, reduce prices, and expand employment and investment. EEC has taken the form of a *customs union,* which is a *free trade area* (no tariffs facing the members) that imposes a uniform tariff for trade with nonmember nations. The next move would be an *economic union* in which all members would operate under the same trade policies.

Since EEC's formation, other economic communities have been formed, notably the Latin American Free Trade Association (LAFTA), the Central American

Common Market (CACM), and the Council for Mutual Economic Assistance (CMEA) (Eastern European countries).

Each nation has unique features that must be grasped. A nation's readiness for different products and services, and its attractiveness as a market to foreign firms, depend on its economic, political-legal, cultural, and business environments.

Economic Environment

In considering foreign markets, the international marketer must study each country's economy. Two economic characteristics reflect the country's attractiveness as an export market.

The first is the country's *industrial structure*. The country's industrial structure shapes its product and service requirements, income levels, and employment levels. Four types of industrial structures can be distinguished:

1. *Subsistence economies.* In a subsistence economy the vast majority of people engage in simple agriculture. They consume most of their output and barter the rest for simple goods and services. They offer few opportunities for exporters.

2. *Raw-material-exporting economies.* These economies are rich in one or more natural resources but poor in other respects. Much of their revenue comes from exporting these resources. Examples are Chile (tin and copper), Congo (rubber), and Saudi Arabia (oil). These countries are good markets for extractive equipment, tools and supplies, materials-handling equipment, and trucks. Depending on the number of foreign residents and wealthy native rulers and landholders, they are also a market for Western-style commodities and luxury goods.

3. *Industrializing economies.* In an industrializing economy, manufacturing begins to account for between 10 and 20 percent of the country's gross national product. Examples include Egypt, the Philippines, India, and Brazil. As manufacturing increases, the country relies more on imports of textile raw materials, steel, and heavy machinery, and less on imports of finished textiles, paper products, and automobiles. The industrialization creates a new rich class and a small but growing middle class, both demanding new types of goods, some of which can be provided only by imports.

4. *Industrial economies.* Industrial economies are major exporters of manufactured goods and investment funds. They trade manufactured goods among themselves and also export them to other types of economies in exchange for raw materials and semifinished goods. The large and varied manufacturing activities of these industrial nations and their sizable middle class make them rich markets for all sorts of goods.

The second economic characteristic is the country's *income distribution*. Income distribution is related to a country's industrial structure, but is also affected by the political system. The international marketer distinguishes countries with five different income-distribution patterns: (1) very low family incomes, (2) mostly low family incomes, (3) very low, very high family incomes, (4) low, medium, high family incomes, and (5) mostly medium family incomes. Consider the market for Lamborghinis, an automobile costing more than $50,000. The market would be very small in countries with type 1 or type 2 income patterns. The largest single market for Lamborghinis turns out to be Portugal (income pattern 3), the poorest country in Europe, but one with enough wealthy, status-conscious families to afford them.

Political-Legal Environment Nations differ greatly in their political-legal environments. At least four factors should be considered in deciding whether to do business in a particular country.

Attitudes toward International Buying

Some nations are very receptive, indeed encouraging, to foreign firms, and others are very hostile. As an example of the former, Mexico for a number of years has been attracting foreign investment by offering investment incentives, and site-location services. On the other hand, India has required the exporter to deal with import quotas, blocked currencies, and stipulations that a high percentage of the management team be nationals. IBM and Coca-Cola made the decision to leave India because of all the difficulties.

Political Stability

Stability is another issue. Governments change hands, sometimes violently. Even without a change, a regime may decide to respond to new popular feelings. The foreign company's property may be expropriated; or its currency holdings may be blocked; or import quotas or new duties may be imposed. Where political instability is high, international marketers may still find it profitable to do business in that country, but the situation will affect their mode of entry. They will prefer export marketing to direct foreign investment. They will keep their foreign stocks low. They will convert their currency rapidly. As a result, the people in the host country pay higher prices, have fewer jobs, and get less satisfactory products.[5]

Monetary Regulations

Sellers want to realize profits in a currency of value to them. In the best situation, the importer can pay in the seller's currency or in hard world currencies. Short of this, sellers might accept a blocked currency if they can buy other goods in that country that they need or can sell elsewhere for a needed currency. In the worst case they have to take their money out of the host country in the form of relatively unmarketable products that they can sell elsewhere only at a loss. Besides currency restrictions, a fluctuating exchange rate also creates high risks for the exporter.

Government Bureaucracy

A fourth factor is the extent to which the host government runs an efficient system for assisting foreign companies: efficient customs handling, adequate market information, and other factors conducive to doing business. A common shock to Americans is the extent to which impediments to trade disappear if a suitable payment (bribe) is made to some official(s).

Cultural Environment Each country has its own folkways, norms, and taboos. The way foreign consumers think about and use certain products must be checked by the seller before planning the marketing program. Here is a sampling of some of the surprises in the consumer market:

- The average Frenchman uses almost twice as many cosmetics and beauty aids as does his wife.
- The Germans and the French eat more packaged, branded spaghetti than the Italians.
- Italian children like to eat a bar of chocolate between two slices of bread as a snack.
- Women in Tanzania will not give their children eggs for fear of making them bald or impotent.

Business norms and behavior also vary from country to country. U.S. business executives need to be briefed on these before negotiating in another country. Here are some examples of foreign business behavior at variance with U.S. business behavior:

- South Americans are accustomed to talking business in close physical proximity with other persons—in fact, almost nose to nose. The American business executive retreats, but the South American pursues. And both end up being offended.
- In face-to-face communications, Japanese business executives rarely say no to an American business executive. Americans are frustrated and don't know where they stand. Americans come to the point quickly. Japanese business executives find this offensive.
- In France, wholesalers don't care to promote a product. They ask their retailers what they want, and deliver it. If an American company builds its strategy around the French wholesaler's cooperating in promotions, it is likely to fail.

Each country (and even regional groups within each country) has cultural traditions, preferences, and taboos that the marketer must study.[6]

DECIDING WHETHER TO GO ABROAD

Companies get involved in international marketing in one of two ways. Someone—a domestic exporter, a foreign importer, a foreign government— solicits the company to sell abroad. Or the company starts to think on its own about going abroad. It might face overcapacity or see better marketing opportunities in other countries than at home.

Before going abroad, the company should try to define its *international marketing objectives and policies.* First, it should decide *what proportion of foreign to total sales* it will seek. Most companies start small when they venture abroad. Some plan to stay small, seeing foreign operations as a small part of their business. Other companies have more grandiose plans, seeing foreign business as ultimately equal to or even more important than their domestic business.

Second, the company must choose between marketing in a *few countries* and marketing in *many countries.* The Bulova Watch Company made the latter choice and expanded into over one hundred countries. It spread itself too thin, made profits in only two countries, and lost around $40 million.[7]

Third, the company must decide on the *types of countries* to consider. The countries that are attractive will depend on the product, geographical factors, income and population, political climate, and other factors. The seller may have a preference for certain country groups or parts of the world.

DECIDING WHICH MARKETS TO ENTER

After developing a list of possible export markets, the company will have to screen and rank them. Consider the following example:

> CMC's market research in the computer field revealed that England, France, West Germany, and Italy offer us significant markets. England, France, and Germany are about equal-size markets, while Italy represents about two thirds the potential of any one of those countries. . . . Taking everything into consideration, we decided to set up first in England because its market for our products is as large as any and its language and laws are similar to ours. England is different enough to get your feet wet, yet similar enough to the familiar U.S. business environment so that you do not get in over your head.[8]

The market choice seems relatively simple and straightforward. Yet one can question whether the reason for selecting England—the compatibility of its language and culture—should have been given this prominence. The candidate countries should be ranked on several criteria, such as market size, market growth, cost of doing business, competitive advantage, and risk level.

The company should estimate the probable rate of return on investment in each market. Five steps are involved:[9]

1. *Estimate of current market potential.* The first step is to estimate current market potential in each market, using a checklist of indicators such as the one shown in Table 22-1. This task calls for using published data and primary data collected through company surveys.

2. *Forecast of future market potential.* The firm also needs to forecast future market potential, a difficult task.

3. *Forecast of sales potential.* Estimating the company's sales potential requires forecasting its probable market share, another difficult task.

4. *Forecast of costs and profits.* Costs will depend on the company's contemplated entry strategy. If it exports or licenses, its costs will be spelled out in the contracts. If it locates manufacturing facilities abroad, its cost estimation will require understanding

TABLE 22-1
Indicators of Market Potential

1. **Demographic Characteristics**	4. **Technological Factors**
Size of population	Level of technological skill
Rate of population growth	Existing production technology
Degree of urbanization	Existing consumption technology
Population density	Education levels
Age structure and composition of the population	
	5. **Socio-Cultural Factors**
2. **Geographic Characteristics**	Dominant values
Physical size of a country	Life style patterns
Topographical characteristics	Ethnic groups
Climate conditions	Linguistic fragmentation
3. **Economic Factors**	6. **National Goals and Plans**
GNP per capita	Industry priorities
Income distribution	Infrastructure investment plans
Rate of growth of GNP	
Ratio of investment to GNP	

Source: Susan P. Douglas, C. Samual Craig, and Warren Keegan, "Approaches to Assessing International Marketing Opportunities for Small and Medium-Sized Business," *Columbia Journal of World Business,* Fall 1982, pp. 26–32.

local labor conditions, taxes, trade practices, and so on. The company subtracts estimated costs from estimated sales to find company profits for each year of the planning horizon.

5. *Estimate of rate of return on investment.* The forecasted income stream should be related to the investment stream to derive the implicit rate of return. This should be high enough to cover (1) the company's normal target return on its investment and (2) the risk and uncertainty of marketing in that country.

DECIDING HOW TO ENTER THE MARKET

Once a company has decided to sell to a particular country, it must determine the best mode of entry. Its choices are *exporting, joint venturing,* and *direct investment abroad.*[10] Each succeeding strategy involves more commitment, risk, and possible profits. The three market entry strategies are shown in Figure 22-2, along with the various options under each.

Export The simplest way to get involved in a foreign market is through export. *Occasional exporting* is a passive level of involvement where the company exports surpluses from time to time and sells goods to resident buyers representing foreign companies. *Active exporting* takes place when the company makes a commitment to expand exports to a particular market. In either case the company produces all its goods in the home country. It may or may not modify them for the export market. Exporting involves the least change in the company's product lines, organization, investments, or mission.

A company can export its product in two ways. It can hire independent international marketing middlemen (indirect export) or handle its own exporting (direct export).

Indirect Export

Indirect export is more common in companies just beginning their exporting. First, it involves less investment. The firm does not have to develop an overseas sales-

FIGURE 22-2
Market Entry Strategies

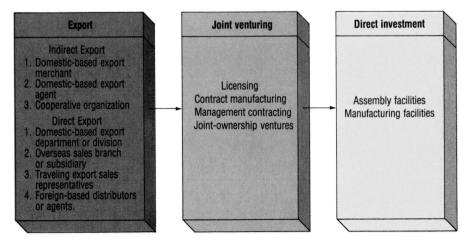

Export

Indirect Export
1. Domestic-based export merchant
2. Domestic-based export agent
3. Cooperative organization

Direct Export
1. Domestic-based export department or division
2. Overseas sales branch or subsidiary
3. Traveling export sales representatives
4. Foreign-based distributors or agents.

Joint venturing

Licensing
Contract manufacturing
Management contracting
Joint-ownership ventures

Direct investment

Assembly facilities
Manufacturing facilities

force or a set of contacts. Second, it involves less risk. International marketing middlemen bring knowhow and services to the relationship, and the seller normally makes fewer mistakes.

Three types of domestic middlemen are available to the exporting company:

1. *Domestic-based export merchant.* This middleman buys the manufacturer's product and sells it abroad on its own account.
2. *Domestic-based export agent.* The agent simply agrees to seek foreign buyers for a commission.
3. *Cooperative organization.* A cooperative organization carries on export activities on behalf of several producers and is partly under their administrative control. This form is often used by producers of primary products such as fruits and nuts.

Direct Export

Sellers approached by foreign buyers are likely to use direct export. So will sellers whose exporters have grown sufficiently large to undertake their own exporting. The investment and risk are somewhat greater, but so is the potential return.

The company can carry on direct exporting in several ways:

1. *Domestic-based export department or division.* An export sales manager with some clerical assistants carry on the actual selling and draw on marketing assistance as needed. It might evolve into a self-contained export department or sales subsidiary carrying out all export activities and possibly operating as a profit center.
2. *Overseas sales branch or subsidiary.* An overseas sales branch allows the manufacturer to achieve greater presence and program control in the foreign market. The sales branch handles sales distribution and may handle warehousing and promotion as well. It often serves as a display center and customer service center.
3. *Traveling export sales representatives.* The company can send home-based sales representatives abroad at certain times to find business.
4. *Foreign-based distributors or agents.* Foreign-based distributors would buy and own the goods; foreign-based agents would sell the goods on behalf of the company. They may be given exclusive rights to represent the manufacturer in that country or only general rights.

Joint Venturing A second broad method of entering a foreign market is to join with foreign companies to set up production and marketing facilities. Joint venturing differs from exporting in that a partnership is formed that leads to some production facilities abroad, and it differs from direct investment in that an association is formed with someone in that country. Four types of joint venture can be distinguished.

Licensing

Licensing represents a simple way for a manufacturer to become involved in international marketing. The licensor enters an agreement with a licensee in the foreign market, offering the right to use a manufacturing process, trademark, patent, trade secret, or other item of value for a fee or royalty. The licensor gains entry into the market at little risk; the licensee gains production expertise, or a well-known product or name, without having to start from scratch. Gerber introduced its baby foods in the Japanese market through a licensing arrangement. Coca-Cola carried out its international marketing by licensing bottlers around the world—or, more techni-cally, *franchising* bottlers—because it supplies the syrup needed to produce the product.

Licensing has potential disadvantages. The firm has less control over the li-censee than if it had set up its own production facilities. Furthermore, if the li-censee is very successful, the firm has forgone these profits, and if and when the contract ends, it may find it has created a competitor. To avoid these dangers, the licensor must establish a mutual advantage for the licensee. A key to doing this is to remain innovative so that the licensee continues to depend on the licensor.[11]

Contract Manufacturing

Another option is to contract with local manufacturers to produce the product. Sears used this method in opening up department stores in Mexico and Spain. Sears found qualified local manufacturers to produce many of the products it sells.

Contract manufacturing has the drawback of less control over the manufactur-ing process and the loss of potential profits on manufacturing. On the other hand, it offers the company a chance to start faster, with less risk, and with the opportunity to form a partnership with or buy out the local manufacturer later.

Management Contracting

Here the domestic firm supplies the management knowhow to a foreign company that supplies the capital. The domestic firm is exporting management services rather than products. Hilton uses this arrangement in managing hotels around the world.

Management contracting is a low-risk method of getting into a foreign market, and it yields income from the beginning. The arrangement is especially attractive if the contracting firm is given an option to purchase some share in the managed company within a stated period. On the other hand, the arrangement is not sensi-ble if the company can put its scarce management talent to better uses or if it can make greater profits by undertaking the whole venture. Management contracting prevents the company from setting up its own operations for a period of time.

Joint Ownership Ventures

Joint ownership ventures consist of foreign investors joining with local investors to create a local business in which they share joint ownership and control. The for-eign investor may buy an interest in a local company, a local company may buy an interest in an existing operation of a foreign company, or the two parties may form a new business venture.

A jointly owned venture may be necessary or desirable for economic or political reasons. The firm may lack the financial, physical, or managerial resources to undertake the venture alone. Or the foreign government may require joint ownership as a condition for entry.

Joint ownership has certain drawbacks. The partners may disagree over in-vestment, marketing, or other policies. Where many American firms like to reinvest earnings for growth, local firms often like to take out these earnings. Where American firms accord a large role to marketing, local investors may rely on selling. Furthermore, joint ownership can hamper a multinational company from carrying out specific manufacturing and marketing policies on a worldwide basis.[12]

Direct Investment The ultimate involvement in a foreign market is investment in foreign-based assembly or manufacturing facilities. As a company gains experience in export, and if the foreign market appears large enough, foreign production facilities offer distinct advantages. First, the firm may secure cost economies in the form of cheaper labor or raw materials, foreign government investment incentives, and freight savings. Second, the firm will gain a better image in the host country because it creates jobs. Third, the firm develops a deeper relationship with government, customers, local suppliers, and distributors, enabling it to adapt its products better to the local marketing environment. Fourth, the firm retains full control over the investment and can therefore develop manufacturing and marketing policies that serve its long-term international objectives.

The main disadvantage is that the firm exposes a large investment to risks, such as blocked or devalued currencies, worsening markets, or expropriation. In some cases, the firm has no choice but to accept these risks if it wants to operate in the host country.

DECIDING ON THE MARKETING PROGRAM

Companies that operate in one or more foreign markets must decide how much, if at all, to adapt their marketing mixes to local conditions. At one extreme are companies that use a *standardized marketing mix* worldwide. Standardization of the product, advertising, distribution channels, and other elements of the marketing mix promises the lowest costs because no major changes have been introduced. This thinking is behind the idea that Coca-Cola should taste the same around the world and that General Motors should produce a "world car" which suits the needs of most consumers in most countries.

At the other extreme is a *customized marketing mix.* The producer adjusts the marketing mix elements to each target market, bearing more costs but hoping for a larger market share and return. Nestlé, for example, varies its product line and its advertising in different countries. Between these two extremes, many possibilities exist. Thus Levi Strauss can sell the same jeans worldwide but can vary the advertising theme in each country (see Exhibit 22-2).

A recent survey of leading consumer packaged goods multinationals concluded: "To the successful multinational, it is not really important whether marketing programs are internationally standardized or differentiated; the important thing is that the *process* through which these programs are developed is standardized."[13]

For example, many multinational marketers are centralizing their advertising and other marketing decision processes. A survey by Grey Advertising of 50 multinational marketers revealed that 76 percent believe they should use the same advertising agency worldwide, with some local deviation in advertising strategies if justified. Only 21 percent currently run their ad programs centrally, but another 41 percent are moving toward centralized advertising decision making.[14]

EXHIBIT 22-2

CUSTOMIZATION OR GLOBALIZATION?

The degree to which companies should standardize their products and marketing programs has become the subject of recent controversy. On the one hand are companies that customize their offerings to better meet the varied needs of consumers in different international markets. On the other hand are companies seeking to globalize their products and to sell them the same way worldwide. Let's explore each side's position.

On the One Hand . . .

More traditional international marketers hold that consumers in different countries vary widely in their needs and wants and that marketing programs will be more effective if they are tailored to specific market needs. Weir states:

> There is no "international" market . . . from a marketing standpoint. Instead there are literally dozens of countries in which U.S. products and services can be sold. All of these are different from one another in their economies, politics, traditions, cultures, and customer habits . . . and ingrained consumer habits are hard to change.

Those who support customized marketing programs provide an unending list of examples showing how international markets differ from the United States and from each other. Countries differ in their economic, political, legal, and cultural development and institutions. Consumers in different countries have varied geographic, demographic, economic, and cultural characteristics, resulting in distinctive motivations, spending power, product preferences, and shopping patterns. Most international marketers think that such differences across cultures call for customized products, prices, distribution channels, and promotion strategies.

Eric Haueter of CPC International (which sells more than 2,000 products in 36 countries, including such brands as Hellman's, Best Foods, Knorr, Mazzola, and Skippy) suggests that firms should "think globally but act locally to give the individual consumer more to say in what he or she wants." To meet diverse individual demands, it should "market module by module, bit by small bit, rather than trying to gobble the whole globe in a gulp." The corporate level gives strategic direction; local units focus on the individual. Haueter believes that preoccupation with standardization makes a company inflexible and places it at a disadvantage against competitors who produce the goods that consumers want.

> It's the height of arrogance to assume that you can standardize a product and sell it to people all around the world; to assume that if it works here it can be imposed there. That's what is often done in the name of international marketing. . . . What is required is a network of local units operating autonomously and independently on the spot but under a common set of global strategic, financial, and ethical guidelines. . . . We determined that there were considerable business opportunities . . . if you search sensitively, then adapt and tailor your approach in many different ways . . . we found success by producing a greater variety of products in smaller batches and learned to minimize the effects of reduced scale economies by the application of new technologies.

Thus most companies recognize differences in consumer needs and wants in different countries, assume that these differences are difficult to change, and customize their products and marketing programs to more effectively serve consumers in each country.

On the Other Hand . . .

Recently, many companies have moved toward *globalization*—the creation of "world brands," standardized products that are manufactured, positioned, and marketed in much the same way worldwide. Theodore Levitt, a leading proponent of global marketing, asserts:

> The world is becoming a common marketplace in which people—no matter where they live—desire the same products and lifestyles. Global companies must forget the idiosyncratic differences between countries and cultures and instead concentrate on satisfying universal drives.

Levitt believes that new communication, transportation, and travel technologies have created a more homogeneous world market. People around the world want the same basic things—things that make life easier and increase their discretionary time and buying power. This convergence of needs and wants has created global markets for standardized products.

According to Levitt, traditional multinational corporations focus on differences between specific markets and falsely assume that the marketing concept means giving people what they say they want. They cater to superficial or even entrenched differences and produce a proliferation of highly customized products rather than questioning whether differing preferences can be changed to accept standardized products. Customization results in less efficiency and higher prices to consumers.

In contrast, the global corporation sells more or less the same product the same way to all consumers to take advantage of the lower costs resulting from standardization. It focuses on similarities across world markets and aggressively works to "sensibly force suitably standardized products and services on the entire globe." It customizes products and marketing programs to meet local preferences only when these preferences cannot be changed or avoided. These global marketers realize substantial economies through standardization of production, distribution, marketing, and management. Thus they can translate efficiencies from standardization into greater value for consumers by offering high quality and more reliable products at lower prices.

Levitt concedes that there *are* differences in consumer preferences, shopping and spending patterns, customs, promotional practices, and cultural institutions in different markets, and that these differences cannot be entirely ignored. But he thinks the preferences and patterns are changeable. According to Levitt, despite what consumers *say* they want, all consumers want good products at lower prices. The global company accepts or adjusts to differences only after aggressively trying to reshape or avoid them. And companies can capitalize on global need similarities and still make minor adjustments in different markets. Levitt thinks that consumers will accept high-quality, lower-priced standardized products even if they are not entirely suitable.

> If the price is low enough, they will take highly standardized world products, even if these aren't exactly what mother said was suitable, what immemorial custom decreed was right, or what market research fabulists asserted was preferred.

So which approach is best—customization or globalization? The answer is different for each company; it depends on the nature of each firm's products, markets, market position, financial resources, and other factors. But for most companies, the answer probably lies somewhere between the two extremes.

Sources: Based on Edward L. Weir, "Avoiding the Pitfalls of International Marketing," *Marketing and Media Decisions,* March 1983, pp. 80–82; "Modular Marketing Cracks International Markets," *Marketing News,* April 27, 1984, p. 10; Mitchell Lynch, "Harvard's Levitt Called Global Marketing 'Guru,'" *Advertising Age,* June 25, 1984, pp. 49–50; Theodore Levitt, "The Globalization of Markets," *Harvard Business Review,* May–June 1983, pp. 92–102. Excerpt reprinted by permission of the *Harvard Business Review.* Copyright © 1983 by the President and Fellows of Harvard College; all rights reserved.

We will now examine possible adaptations of a company's product, promotion, price, and distribution as it goes abroad.

Product Keegan distinguished five adaptation strategies of product and promotion to a foreign market (see Figure 22-3).[15] Here we will examine the three product strategies, and later look at the two promotion strategies.

Straight extension means introducing the product in the foreign market without any change. Top management instructs its marketing people: "Take the product as is and find customers for it." The first step, however, should be to determine whether the foreign consumers use that product. Deodorant usage among men ranges from 80 percent in the United States to 55 percent in Sweden, 28 percent in Italy, and 8 percent in the Philippines. Many Spaniards do not use such common products as butter and cheese.

Straight extension has been successful in some cases but a disaster in others. General Foods introduced its standard powdered Jell-O in the British market only to find that British consumers prefer the solid-wafer or cake form. Straight extension is tempting because it involves no additional R&D expense, manufacturing retooling, or promotion modification. But it can be costly in the long run.

Product adaptation involves altering the product to meet local conditions or preferences. Heinz varies its baby-food products: In Australia it sells a baby food made from strained lamb brains; and in the Netherlands, a baby food made from strained brown beans. General Foods blends different coffees for the British (who drink their coffee with milk), the French (who drink their coffee black), and Latin Americans (who want a chicory taste).

Product invention consists of creating something new. This can take two forms. *Backward invention* is the reintroducing of earlier product forms that happen to be well adapted to the needs of that country. The National Cash Register Company reintroduced its crank-operated cash register that could sell at half the cost of a modern cash register and sold substantial numbers in the Orient, Latin America, and Spain. This illustrates the existence of *international product life cycles;* countries are at different stages of readiness to accept a particular product.[16] *Forward invention* is creating a brand new product to meet a need in another country. There is an enormous need in less-developed countries for low-cost, high-

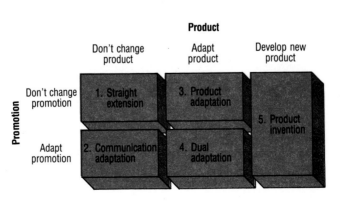

FIGURE 22-3
Five International Product and Promotion Strategies

protein foods. Companies such as Quaker Oats, Swift, and Monsanto are researching the nutrition needs of these countries, formulating new foods, and developing advertising campaigns to gain product trial and acceptance. Product invention appears to be a costly strategy, but the payoffs might make it worthwhile.

Promotion Companies can adopt the same promotion strategy they used in the home market or change it for each local market.

Consider the message. Many multinational companies use a standardized advertising theme around the world. Exxon used "Put a tiger in your tank" and gained international recognition. The copy is varied in a minor way, such as changing the colors to avoid taboos in other countries. Purple is associated with death in most of Latin America; white is a mourning color in Japan; and green is associated with jungle sickness in Malaysia. Even names have to be modified. In Germany, *scotch* (scotch tape) means "schmuck." In Sweden, Helene Curtis renamed Every Night Shampoo to Every Day because Swedes wash their hair in the morning (see Exhibit 22-3).

Other companies encourage their international divisions to develop their own ads. The Schwinn Bicycle Company might use a pleasure theme in the United States and a safety theme in Scandinavia.

EXHIBIT 22-3

WATCH YOUR LANGUAGE!

Many U.S. multinationals have had difficulty crossing the language barrier, with results ranging from mild embarrassment to outright failure. Seemingly innocuous brand names and advertising phrases can take on unintended or hidden meanings when translated into other languages. And careless translations can make a marketer look downright foolish to foreign consumers. We've all run across examples when buying products from foreign countries—here's one from a firm in Taiwan attempting to instruct children on how to install a ramp on a garage for toy cars.

> Before you play with, please fix the waiting plate by yourself as per below diagram. But after you once fixed it, you can play with as is and no necessary to fix off again.

Many U.S. firms are guilty of similar atrocities when marketing abroad.

The classic language blunders involve standardized brand names that do not translate well. When Coca-Cola first marketed Coke in China in the 1920s, it developed a group of Chinese characters which, when pronounced, sounded like the product name. Unfortunately, the characters actually translated to mean "bite the wax tadpole." Today, the characters on Chinese Coke bottles translate to "happiness in the mouth."

Several car makers have had similar problems when their brand names crashed into the language barrier. Chevy's Nova translated into Spanish as *no va*—"It doesn't go." GM changed the name to Caribe and sales increased. Ford introduced its Fiera truck only to discover that the name means "ugly old woman" in Spanish. And it introduced its Comet car in Mexico as the Caliente—slang for "streetwalker." Rolls Royce avoided the name Silver

Mist in German markets, where "mist" means "manure." Sunbeam, however, entered the German market with its Mist-Stick hair curling iron. As should have been expected, the Germans had little use for a "manure wand."

One well-intentioned firm sold its shampoo in Brazil under the name Evitol. It soon realized it was claiming to sell a "dandruff contraceptive." An American company reportedly had trouble marketing Pet milk in French-speaking areas. It seems that the word "pet" in French means, among other things, "to break wind."

Such classic boo-boos are soon discovered and corrected, and they may result in little more than embarrassment for the marketer. But countless other more subtle blunders may go undetected and damage product performance in less obvious ways. The multinational company must carefully screen its brand names and advertising messages to guard against those that might damage sales, make it look silly, or offend consumers in specific international markets.

Source: Some of these and many other examples of language blunders are found in David A. Ricks, "Products That Crashed into the Language Barrier," *Business and Society Review,* Spring 1983, pp. 46–50.

Media also require international adaptation because media availability varies from country to country. Commercial TV time is available for one hour each evening in Germany, and advertisers must buy time months in advance. In Sweden, commercial TV time is nonexistent. Commercial radio is nonexistent in France and Scandinavia. Magazines are a major medium in Italy and a minor one in Austria. Newspapers are national in the United Kingdom and local in Spain.

Price Manufacturers often price their products lower in foreign markets. Incomes may be low, and a low price is necessary to sell the goods. The manufacturer may set low prices to build a market share. Or the manufacturer may want to dump goods that have no market at home. If the manufacturer charges less in the foreign market than in the home market, this is called *dumping.* The Zenith Company accused

Using a standardized advertising message: Coca-Cola used Mean Joe Greene in the United States, other sports heros in other countries. *Courtesy of Coca-Cola Company.*

Japanese television manufacturers of dumping their TV sets on the U.S. market. If the U.S. Customs Bureau finds dumping, it can levy a dumping tariff.

Manufacturers have little control over the retail prices charged by foreign middlemen who carry their products. Many foreign middlemen use high markups, even though this means selling fewer units. They also like to buy on credit, and this increases the manufacturer's cost and risk.

Distribution Channels The international company must take a *whole-channel* view of the problem of distributing products to final consumers.[17] Figure 22-4 shows the three major links between the seller and the ultimate buyer. The first link, *seller's headquarters organization,* supervises the channels and is part of the channel itself. The second link, *channels between nations,* gets the products to the borders of the foreign nations. The third link, *channels within nations,* gets the products from their foreign entry point to the ultimate consumers. Too many American manufacturers think their job is done once the product leaves their hands. They should pay more attention to how it is handled within the foreign country.

Within-country channels of distribution vary considerably from country to country. There are striking differences in the *numbers and types of middlemen* serving each foreign market. To get soap into Japan, Procter & Gamble has to work through what is probably the most complicated distribution system in the world. It must sell to a *general wholesaler* who sells to a *basic product specialty wholesaler* who sells to a *specialty wholesaler* who sells to a *regional wholesaler* who sells to a *local wholesaler* who finally sells to *retailers.* All these distribution levels may result in a doubling or tripling of the consumer's price over the importer's price.[18] If P&G takes the same soap to tropical Africa, the company sells to an *import wholesaler* who sells to a *mammy* who sells to a *petty mammy* who sells the soap *door to door.*[19]

Another difference lies in the *size and character of retail units* abroad. Where large-scale retail chains dominate the U.S. scene, most foreign retailing is in the hands of many small independent retailers. In India, millions of retailers operate tiny shops or sell in open markets. Their markups are high, but the real price is brought down through price haggling. Supermarkets could conceivably bring down prices, but they are difficult to start because of many economic and cultural barriers.[20] People's incomes are low, and they prefer to shop daily for small amounts rather than weekly for large amounts. They lack storage and refrigeration space to keep food for several days. Packaging is not well developed because it

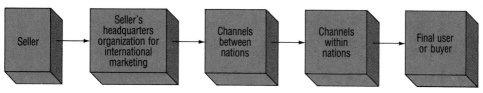

FIGURE 22-4 *Whole-Channel Concept for International Marketing*

would add too much to the cost. These factors have kept large-scale retailing from spreading rapidly in developing countries.

DECIDING ON THE MARKETING ORGANIZATION

Companies manage their international marketing activities in at least three different ways. Most companies first organize an export department, then create an international division, and ultimately become a multinational organization.

Export Department A firm normally gets into international marketing by simply shipping out the goods. If its international sales expand, the company organizes an export department consisting of a sales manager and a few assistants. As sales increase, the export department is expanded to include various marketing services so that it can go after business more aggressively. If the firm moves into joint ventures or direct investment, the export department will no longer be adequate.

International Division Many companies get involved in several international markets and ventures. A company may export to one country, license to another, have a joint ownership venture in a third, and own a subsidiary in a fourth. Sooner or later it will create an international division or subsidiary to handle all its international activity. The international division is headed by an international division president, who sets goals and budgets and is responsible for the company's growth in the international market.

International divisions are organized in a variety of ways. The international division's corporate staff consists of specialists in marketing, manufacturing, research, finance, planning, and personnel; they will plan for, and provide services to, various operating units. The operating units may be organized according to one or more of three principles.

They may be *geographical organizations.* Reporting to the international division president may be vice-presidents for North America, Latin America, Europe, Africa, and the Far East. These area vice-presidents are responsible for a salesforce, sales branches, distributors, and licensees in their respective areas. Or the operating units may be *product-group organizations,* with a vice-president responsible for worldwide sales of each product group. The vice-presidents may draw on corporate staff area specialists for expertise on different geographical areas. Finally, the operating units may be *international subsidiaries,* each headed by a president. The various subsidiary presidents report to the president of the international division.

A major disadvantage of the international division concept is that the corporation's top management may think of it as just another division and never get involved enough to appreciate and plan for global marketing.

Multinational Organization Several firms have passed beyond the international division stage and become truly multinational organizations. They stop thinking of themselves as national marketers who venture abroad and start thinking of themselves as global marketers. The top corporate management and staff are involved in the planning of worldwide manufacturing facilities, marketing policies, financial flows, and logistical systems. The global operating units report directly to the chief executive or executive committee, not to the head of an international division. Executives are trained in worldwide operations, not just domestic *or* international. Management is recruited from many countries; components and supplies are purchased where they can be obtained at the least cost; and investments are made where the anticipated returns are greatest.

Major companies must go more multinational in the 1980s and 1990s if they are going to grow. As foreign companies successfully invade the domestic market, U.S. companies will have to move more aggressively into foreign markets. They will have to evolve from *ethnocentric* companies treating their foreign operations as secondary to *geocentric* companies viewing the entire world as a single market.[21]

■ *Summary*

Companies undertake international marketing for a variety of reasons. Some are pushed by poor opportunities in the home market, and some are pulled by superior opportunities abroad. Given the risk of international marketing, companies need a systematic way to make their international-marketing decisions.

The first step is to understand the international marketing environment, particularly the international trade system. In considering a particular foreign market, its economic, political-legal, and cultural characteristics must be assessed. Second, the company must consider what proportion of foreign to total sales it will seek, whether it will do business in a few or many countries, and what types of countries it wants to market in. The third step is to decide which particular markets to enter, and this calls for evaluating the probable rate of return on investment against the level of risk. Fourth, the company has to decide how to enter each attractive market, whether through exporting, joint venturing, or direct investment. Many companies start as exporters, move to joint venturing, and finally undertake direct investment. Companies must next decide on the extent to which their products, promotion, price, and distribution should be adapted to individual foreign markets. Finally, the company must develop an effective organization for pursuing international marketing. Most firms start with an export department and graduate to an international division. A few pass to a multinational organization, which means that worldwide marketing is planned and managed by the top officers of the company.

■ Questions for Discussion

1. In appraising the international marketing environment, the economic environment of the country is the most important consideration for the firm. Comment.

2. Discuss the relevant aspects of the political-legal environment that might affect K mart's decision to open retail outlets in Italy.

3. What steps are involved in deciding which markets to enter? Relate these steps to a consumer product example.

4. Briefly discuss the three major strategies that a firm might use to enter a foreign market.

5. How does licensing differ from the other joint venture possibilities?

6. What product strategy possibilities might Hershey's consider in marketing its chocolate bars in South American countries?

7. The price of products sold in foreign markets is usually lower than in the domestic market. Why?

8. Which type of international marketing organization would you suggest for the following companies? (a) Huffy bicycles is planning to sell three models in the Far East; (b) a small manufacturer of toys is going to market its products in Europe; and (c) Dodge is contemplating selling its full line of cars and trucks in Kuwait.

■ References

1. Based on "Brazil: Campbell Soup Fails to Make It to the Table," *Business Week,* October 12, 1981; and "Brazil: Gerber Abandons a Baby-Food Market," *Business Week,* February 8, 1982.

2. See "The Reluctant Exporter," *Business Week,* April 10, 1978, pp. 54–66.

3. See "The Top 1500 Companies," published by Economic Information Systems, New York, 1982.

4. See WARREN J. KEEGAN, "Multinational Product Planning: New Myths and Old Realities," in *Multinational Product Management* (Cambridge, MA: Marketing Science Institute, 1976), pp. 1–8.

5. For a system of rating the political stability of different nations, see F. T. HANER, "Rating Investment Risks Abroad," *Business Horizons,* April 1979, pp. 18–23.

6. For further examples, see DAVID A. RICKS, MARILYN Y. C. FU, and JEFFERY S. ARPAN, *International Business Blunders* (Columbus, OH: Grid, 1974).

7. IGAL AYAL and JEHIEL ZIF, "Market Expansion Strategies in Multinational Marketing," *Journal of Marketing,* Spring 1979, pp. 84–94.

8. JAMES K. SWEENEY, "A Small Company Enters the European Market," *Harvard Business Review,* September–October 1970, pp. 127–28.

9. See DAVID S. R. LEIGHTON, "Deciding When to Enter International Markets," in *Handbook of Modern Marketing,* Victor P. Buell, ed. (New York: McGraw-Hill, 1970), Sec. 20, pp. 23–28.

10. The discussion of entry strategies in this section is based on the discussion in GORDON E. MIRACLE and GERALD S. ALBAUM, *International Marketing Management* (Homewood, IL: Irwin, 1970), chaps. 14–16.

11. For more on licensing, see ALLAN C. REDDY, "International Licensing May Be Best for Companies Seeking Foreign Markets," *Marketing News,* November 12, 1982, pp. 6–7.

12. For more on joint ventures, see "Are Foreign Partners Good for U.S. Companies?" *Business Week,* May 28, 1984, pp. 58–60.

13. RALPH Z. SORENSON and ULRICH E. WIECHMANN, "How Multinationals View Marketing Standardization," *Harvard Business Review,* May–June 1975, pp. 38–54.

14. DENNIS CHASE, "Global Marketing: The New Wave," *Advertising Age,* June 25, 1984, p. 49.

15. WARREN J. KEEGAN, "Multinational Product Planning: Strategic Alternatives," *Journal of Marketing,* January 1969, pp. 58–62.

16. LOUIS T. WELLS, JR., "A Product Life Cycle for International Trade?" *Journal of Marketing,* July 1968, pp. 1–6.
17. See MIRACLE and ALBAUM, *International Marketing Management,* pp. 317–19.
18. See WILLIAM D. HARTLEY, "How Not to Do It: Cumbersome Japanese Distribution System Stumps U.S. Concerns," *Wall Street Journal,* March 2, 1972, pp. 1, 8.
19. For a description of the distribution systems in selected countries, see WADI-NAMBIARATCHI, "Channels of Distribution in Developing Economies," *Business Quarterly,* Winter 1965, pp. 74–82.
20. However, see ARIEH GOLDMAN, "Outreach of Consumers and the Modernization of Urban Food Retailing in Developing Countries," *Journal of Marketing,* October 1974, pp. 8–16.
21. See YORAM WIND, SUSAN P. DOUGLAS, and HOWARD V. PERLMUTTER, "Guidelines for Developing International Marketing Strategies," *Journal of Marketing,* April 1973, pp. 14–23.

Unique ad strategy increases use of Sunrise Hospital on weekends

23
Services Marketing and Nonprofit Marketing

The Evanston Hospital, serving the North Shore area of Chicago, appointed Dr. John McLaren as its first vice-president of marketing. Hospitals have had vice-presidents of development and public relations, but this appointment raised a number of eyebrows both inside and outside the hospital.

Before 1970, hospitals had the problem of too many patients. The situation turned around drastically in the 1970s, and hospitals experienced declining admissions and patient-days. Given the high fixed costs and rising labor costs, their declining patient census could spell the difference between being in the black and being in the red.

Hospitals began to scramble for ways to get a larger share of the available patients. Since most patients go to their own physician's hospital, the key market target was physicians. Every hospital began to ponder how it could attract more of the "high-yield" physicians to its staff. The key was in knowing what physicians want—things like the latest equipment, good colleagues and nursing staffs, a good hospital image, and good parking.

The more hospitals looked at the problem, the more complex the marketing challenges appeared. Hospitals had to research the community's health needs, images of competing hospitals, and how patients felt about hospital services. Individual hospitals began to realize that they could no longer offer every kind of medical service; this led to expensive duplication of equipment and services and underutilized capacity. Hospitals began to pick and choose medical specialties—heart, pediatrics, burn treatment, psychiatry.

Meanwhile some hospitals went overboard in making a pitch for patients.

Sunrise Hospital in Las Vegas ran a large ad showing a ship with the caption "Introducing the Sunrise Cruise. Win a Once-in-a-Lifetime Cruise Simply by Entering Sunrise Hospital on Any Friday or Saturday: Recuperative Mediterranean Cruise for Two." St. Luke's Hospital in Pheonix introduced nightly bingo games for all patients (except cardiac cases), producing immense patient interest and an annual profit of $60,000. A Philadelphia hospital served candlelight dinners with steak and champagne to parents of newborn children.

Then what was Dr. John McLaren's job at the Evanston Hospital? His job was to promote particular hospital services (services marketing), the hospital itself (organization), some key physicians (person marketing), Evanston as an attractive community (place marketing), and ideas on better health (idea marketing).

Marketing as a discipline developed initially for selling physical products such as toothpaste, cars, steel, and equipment. In previous chapters we defined products broadly to include the tangible and intangible offerings of both profit and nonprofit organizations. But the traditional marketing focus on physical products may cause people to overlook the many other types of entities that are marketed. In this chapter we will examine the special characteristics and marketing requirements of services, organizations, persons, places, and ideas.

SERVICES MARKETING

American service industries have grown phenomenally since the mid-1940s. Service businesses generate over two-thirds of the U.S. gross national product and employ more than seven out of ten U.S. workers.[1] In contrast, Germany has 41 percent of its workforce in the service sector, and Italy has 35 percent. As a result of rising affluence, more leisure, and the growing complexity of its products, the United States has become the world's first service economy.

Service industries are quite varied. The government sector offers services with its courts, employment services, hospitals, loan agencies, military services, police and fire departments, postal service, regulatory agencies, and schools. The private nonprofit sector offers services with its museums, charities, churches, colleges, foundations, and hospitals. A good part of the business sector offers services with its airlines, banks, hotels, insurance companies, consulting firms, medical and law practices, entertainment companies, real estate firms, advertising and research agencies, and retailers.

Not only are there traditional service industries, but new types keep popping up all the time:

> For a fee, there are now companies that will balance your budget, baby-sit your philodendron, wake you up in the morning, drive you to work, or find you a new home, job, car, wife, clairvoyant, cat feeder, or gypsy violinist. Or perhaps you want to rent a garden tractor? A few cattle? Some original paintings? Or maybe [someone] to decorate your next cocktail party? If it is business services you need, other companies will plan your conventions and sales meetings, design your products, handle your data processing, or supply temporary secretaries or even executives.[2]

Some service businesses are very large, with sales and assets in the billions. Table 23-1 shows the five largest service companies in each of seven service categories. In 1983, *Fortune* magazine's 500 largest service companies totaled almost $1 trillion in revenues. But there are also tens of thousands of smaller service providers that contributed another $1 trillion or more.

TABLE 23-1 *The Largest U.S. Service Companies*

COMMERCIAL BANKING	DIVERSIFIED FINANCIAL	LIFE INSURANCE	RETAILING	TRANSPORTATION	UTILITIES	DIVERSIFIED SERVICES
Citicorp	Federal National Mortgage Association	Prudential	Sears	Santa Fe Southern Pacific	AT&T	Philbro-Solomon
BankAmerica	Aetna	Metropolitan	K mart	UAL	GTE	RCA
Chase Manhattan	American Express	Equitable	Safeway	United Parcel Service	Pacific Gas & Electric	City Investing
Manufacturers Hanover	CIGNA	Aetna	Kroger	CSX	Commonwealth Edison	Halliburton
J. P. Morgan	Travelers Corp.	New York Life	J. C. Penney	AMR	Southern Company	Fluor

Source: "The Service 500," *Fortune,* June 11, 1984, pp. 170–91. © 1984 Time, Inc. All rights reserved.

Nature and Characteristics of a Service

We define service as follows:

A **service** is any activity or benefit that one party can offer to another that is essentially intangible and does not result in the ownership of anything. Its production may or may not be tied to a physical product.

Renting a hotel room, depositing money in a bank, traveling on an airplane, visiting a psychiatrist, having a haircut, having a car repaired, watching a professional sport, seeing a movie, having clothes cleaned in a dry-cleaning establishment, getting advice from a lawyer—all involve buying a service.

Services have four characteristics that must be considered when designing marketing programs.

Intangibility

Services are intangible. They cannot be seen, tasted, felt, heard, or smelled before they are bought. The person getting a face lift cannot see the result before the purchase, and the patient in the psychiatrist's office cannot know the outcome in advance. The buyer has to have faith in the service provider.

Service providers can do certain things to improve the client's confidence. First, they can increase the service's tangibility. A plastic surgeon can make a drawing showing how the patient's face will look after the surgery. Second, service providers can emphasize the service's benefits rather than just describing its features. A college admissions officer can talk to prospective students about the great jobs its alumni have found instead of describing life on the campus. Third, service providers can develop brand names for their service to increase confidence, such as Magikist cleaning, United Airlines' Red Carpet service, and Transcendental Meditation. Fourth, service providers can use a celebrity to create confidence in the service, as American Express did in an advertising campaign featuring numerous people with well-known names but lesser-known faces.

Inseparability

A service cannot exist separately from its providers, whether they are persons or machines. A service cannot be put on a shelf and bought by the consumer whenever needed. The service requires the presence of the service provider. Surgery requires the presence of doctors and their equipment; verifying the accuracy of a company's records requires the presence of an auditor.

Several strategies exist for getting around this limitation. The service provider can learn to work with larger groups. Psychotherapists have moved from one-on-one therapy to small-group therapy to groups of over three hundred people in a larger hotel ballroom getting "therapized." The service provider can learn to work faster—the psychotherapist can spend thirty minutes with each patient instead of fifty minutes and can see more patients. The service organization can train more service providers and build up client confidence, as H & R Block has done with its national network of trained tax consultants.

Variability

Services are highly variable—they depend on who provides them and when and where they are provided. A Dr. Christiaan Barnard heart transplant is likely to be of higher quality than one performed by a recent M.D. And Dr. Barnard's heart transplants will vary with his energy and mental set at the time of each operation. Service buyers are frequently aware of this high variability and talk to others before selecting a provider.

Service firms can take two steps toward quality control. The first is investing in good personnel selection and training. Airlines, banks, and hotels spend substantial sums to train their employees in providing good service. One should find the same friendly and helpful personnel in every Marriott Hotel. The second step is monitoring customer satisfaction through suggestion and complaint systems, customer surveys, and comparison shopping so that poor service can be detected and corrected.[3]

Perishability

Services cannot be stored. The reason many doctors charge patients for missed appointments is that the service value only existed at that point when the patients did not show up. The perishability of services is not a problem when demand is steady, because it is easy to staff the services in advance. When demand fluctuates, service firms have difficult problems. For example, public transportation companies have to own much more equipment because of rush hour demand than they would if demand were even throughout the day.

Sasser has described several strategies for producing a better match between demand and supply in a service business.[4]

On the demand side:

- *Differential pricing* will shift some demand from peak to off-peak periods. Examples include low early-evening movie prices and weekend discount prices for car rentals.
- *Nonpeak demand can be cultivated.* McDonald's opened its Egg McMuffin breakfast service and hotels developed their mini-vacation weekend.

- *Complementary services* can be developed during peak time to provide alternatives to waiting customers, such as cocktail lounges to sit in while waiting for a table and automatic tellers in banks.
- *Reservation systems* are a way to manage the demand level. Airlines, hotels, and physicians employ them extensively.

On the supply side:

- *Part-time employees* can be hired to serve peak demand. Colleges add part-time teachers when enrollment goes up, and restaurants call in part-time waiters and waitresses when needed.
- *Peak-time efficiency routines* can be introduced. Employees perform only essential tasks during peak periods. Paramedics assist physicians during busy periods.
- *Increased consumer participation* in the tasks can be encouraged, as when consumers fill out their own medical records or bag their own groceries.
- *Shared services* can be developed, as when several hospitals share medical equipment purchases.
- *Facilities making potential expansion possible* can be developed, as when an amusement park buys surrounding land for later development.

Classification of Services

It is difficult to generalize about services marketing because services vary considerably. Services can be classified in a number of ways. First, is the service *people-based* or *equipment-based* (see Figure 23-1). A psychiatrist needs virtually no equipment, but a pilot needs an airplane. Within people-based services, we can distinguish between those involving professionals (accounting, management consulting), skilled labor (plumbing, car repair), and unskilled labor (janitorial service, lawn care). In equipment-based services, we can distinguish between those involving automated equipment (automated car washes, vending machines), equipment operated by relatively unskilled labor (taxis, motion picture theaters), and equipment operated by skilled labor (airplanes, computers). Even within a specific service industry, different service providers vary in the amount of equipment they use. Sometimes the equipment adds value to the service (stereo amplification), and sometimes it exists to reduce the amount of labor needed (automated car washes).

Second, is the *client's presence* necessary to the service? Brain surgery involves the client's presence, but a car repair does not. If the client must be present, the service provider has to be considerate of his or her needs. Thus beauty shop operators will invest in their shop's decor, play background music, and engage in light conversation with the client.

Third, what about the *client's purchase motive*? Does the service meet a *personal* need (personal services) or a *business* need (business services)? Physicians may price physical examinations for private patients differently from those for company employees on a retainer. Service providers typically develop different marketing programs for personal and business markets.

Fourth, what about the *service provider's motives (profit* or *nonprofit)* and *form (private* or *public)*? These two characteristics, when crossed, produce four quite different types of service organizations. Clearly the marketing programs of a private investor hospital will differ from those of a private charity hospital or a Veterans Administration hospital.[5]

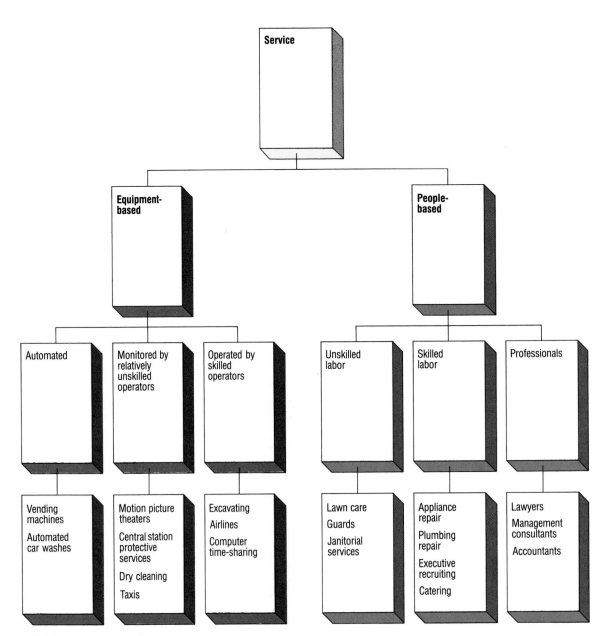

FIGURE 23-1 *Types of Service Businesses*

Source: Reprinted by permission of the *Harvard Business Review.* An exhibit from "Strategy is Different in Service Businesses," by Dan R. E. Thomas (July–August 1978). Copyright © 1978 by The President and Fellows of Harvard College; all rights reserved.

The Extent and Importance of Marketing in the Service Sector

Service firms typically lag behind manufacturing firms in their use of marketing. George and Barksdale surveyed four hundred service and manufacturing firms and concluded that

> in comparison to manufacturing firms, service firms appear to be: (1) generally less likely to have marketing mix activities carried out in the marketing

department, (2) less likely to perform analysis in the offering area, (3) more likely to handle their advertising internally rather than go to outside agencies, (4) less likely to have an overall sales plan, (5) less likely to develop sales training programs, (6) less likely to use marketing research firms and marketing consultants, and (7) less likely to spend as much on marketing when expressed as a percentage of gross sales.[6]

There are several reasons why service firms have neglected marketing. Many service businesses are small (shoe repair, barbershops) and do not use management techniques such as marketing, which they think would be expensive or irrelevant. There are also service businesses (law and accounting firms) that believe that it is unprofessional to use marketing. Other service businesses (colleges, hospitals) had so much former demand that they had no need for marketing until recently.

Today, as competition intensifies, as costs rise, as productivity stagnates, and as service quality deteriorates, more service firms are taking an interest in marketing. Airlines were one of the first service industries to study their consumers and competition and take positive steps to make travelers' trips easier and more pleasant. Banks are another industry that moved toward more active use of marketing in a relatively short period of time. At first banks thought of marketing as consisting mainly of promotion and friendliness, but they have now set up marketing organization, information, planning, and control systems.[7] In stock brokerage, insurance, and lodging, the marketing concept has come in unevenly, with some leaders

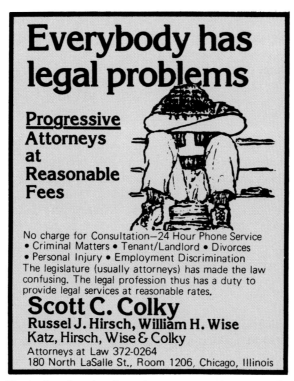

Firm advertises legal services. *Courtesy of Katz, Hirsch, Wise & Colky, Chicago, Ill.*

taking major marketing steps (Merrill Lynch, Hyatt Regency) and most firms lagging behind.

As service competition intensifies, more marketing sophistication will be needed. One of the main agents of change will be product marketers who move into service industries. Sears moved into services marketing years ago—insurance, banking, income tax consulting, car rentals. Xerox Corporation operates a major sales-training business (Xerox Learning), and Gerber Products runs nursery schools and sells insurance.

Service firms are under great pressure to increase productivity. Since the service business is highly labor-intensive, costs have been rising rapidly. Service providers can improve productivity in several ways. They can work harder or more skillfully for the same pay. Or they can increase the quantity of service by giving up some quality. For example, doctors could treat more patients by giving less time to each patient. Service providers can add equipment to increase service capacities. Levitt recommended that companies adopt a "manufacturing attitude" toward producing services, as represented by the McDonald's assembly-line approach to fast-food retailing, resulting in the "technological hamburger."[8] Commercial dishwashing, jumbo jets, multiple-unit motion picture theaters—all represent technological expansions of service.

Service firms can also reduce or replace the need for a service by inventing a product solution, the way television substituted for out-of-home entertainment, the wash-and-wear shirt for the commercial laundry, and penicillin for tuberculosis sanitariums. Finally, service providers can improve productivity by producing more effective services. Nonsmoking clinics and jogging may reduce the need for expensive medical services later on. Hiring paralegal workers reduces the need for expensive legal professionals.

ORGANIZATION MARKETING

We will use the term **organization marketing** to describe *activities undertaken to create, maintain, or alter attitudes and behavior of target audiences toward particular organizations.* We do not mean the marketing activities to sell the organization's products, but those undertaken to "sell" the organization itself. Organization marketing has traditionally been handled by the public relations department. This is evident from the following definition of public relations:

> **Public relations** is the management function that evaluates public attitudes, identifies the policies and procedures of an individual or an organization with the public interest, and plans and executes a program of action to earn public understanding and acceptance.[9]

Public relations is essentially marketing management shifted from a product or service to an organization.[10] The same skills are needed: knowledge of audience needs, desires, and psychology; communication skill; and ability to design and execute influence programs. The similarities between marketing and public relations have led some companies to combine both functions under single control. General Electric appointed a vice-president of marketing and public affairs who "will be responsible for all corporate activities in advertising, public affairs, and public relations. He will also handle corporate marketing, including research and personnel development."

Organization marketing calls for assessing the organization's current image and developing a marketing plan to improve its image.

Image Assessment The first step in image assessment is to research the organization's current image among key publics. The *way an individual or a group sees an object* is called its **image.** Different individuals can have different images of the same object. The organization might be pleased with its public image or might find that it has serious image problems.

Figure 23-2A shows the results of measuring the images of five management consulting firms, using the two dimensions of visibility and favorability. Firm 1 is in the best position; it is highly visible and enjoys the highest repute. Firm 2 is well regarded but less well known; it needs to increase its visibility. Firm 3 is less well regarded, but fortunately not many people know about it. This firm should maintain a low profile and improve its quality. If effective, Firm 3 will move to quadrant II, at which point it will seek more publicity. Firm 4 is in the worst position: It is seen as a poor service provider *and* everyone knows this. The firm's best course of action is to reduce its visibility (which would move it to quadrant III) and then plan to move eventually to quadrants II and I. This would take some years—if the firm ever accomplished it at all. Thus a firm's initial position in the visibility-favorability space defines the basic type of strategy it needs.

One of the major tools for measuring the detailed content of an image is the *semantic differential*.[11] The semantic differential involves developing an appropriate list of attributes describing the object. People place a mark on each scale according to their impression of the degree to which the object possesses that attribute. The image researcher averages the responses on each scale and represents this by a point. The points on the various scales are connected, forming an image

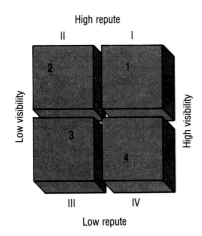

A. Visibility-favorability image space

FIGURE 23-2 *Image Assessment Tools*

High integrity ——— Low integrity
Innovative ——— Noninnovative
Friendly ——— Unfriendly
Knowledgeable ——— Superficial
Large ——— Small
Desired   Actual

B. Content image space

profile of the object. Suppose a firm finds its image to be that shown by the solid line in Figure 23-2B. The firm is seen as high in integrity but not particularly innovative, friendly, knowledgeable, or large.

Image Planning and Control The next step calls for the organization to identify the image that it would like to have. It must not aim for the "impossible." Assume that the firm decides that a feasible and desirable image is shown by the dashed line in Figure 23-2B. The firm would like to be seen as more innovative, more friendly, more knowledgeable, and larger.

The firm now develops a marketing plan to shift its actual image toward the desired one. Suppose it wants to put the most emphasis on increasing its reputation as a knowledgeable firm. The key step, of course, is to hire better consultants. If the firm has highly knowledgeable consultants but they are not visible, it needs to give them more exposure. Its knowledgeable consultants should be encouraged to join business and trade associations, give speeches, write articles, and develop public seminars on "hot" new topics.[12]

The firm must resurvey its publics periodically to see whether its activities are improving its image. Image modification cannot be accomplished overnight because of limited funds and the "stickiness" of public images. If the firm is making no progress, either its substance or its communications are deficient.

PERSON MARKETING

Persons are also marketed. *Person marketing* consists of *activities undertaken to create, maintain, or alter attitudes or behavior toward particular persons.* Two common forms of person marketing are celebrity marketing and political candidate marketing. A third form, personal marketing, is described in Appendix 2, "Careers in Marketing."

Celebrity Marketing Although celebrity marketing has a long history going back to the Caesars, in recent times it has been associated with the buildup of Hollywood stars and entertainers. Hollywood actors and actresses would hire *press agents* to promote their stardom. The press agent would place news about the star in the mass media and also schedule appearances in highly visible locations. One of the great promoters was the late Brian Epstein, who managed the Beatles' rise to stardom and received a larger share of the money than any Beatle. Today celebrities are promoted by entire organizations. Bucky Dent of the Yankees phoned the William Morris Agency and asked Lee Salomon to manage his public life.[13] The agency lined him up to visit children's hospitals, Little Leagues, and conventions; to co-host "A.M. New York" and appear on the Merv Griffin show; to have posters made and marketed; to make a commercial for a car manufacturer; and to get spreads in *Playboy* and other magazines.

Celebrity marketers cannot work miracles; much depends on the star. If the star is a born promoter, there is no limit. Elton John, who has made more money than the Beatles or Elvis Presley, wears one of over two hundred pairs of glasses,

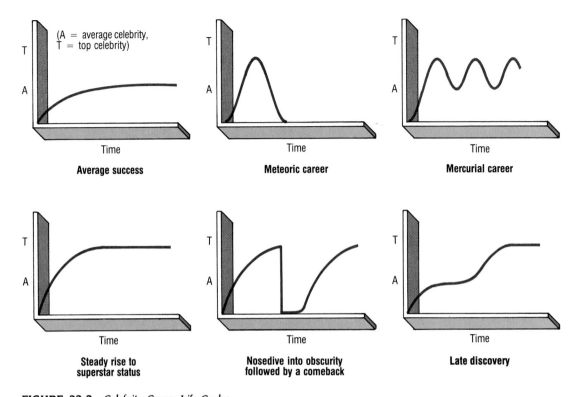

FIGURE 23-3 *Celebrity Career Life Cycles*

Source: Charles Seton, "The Marketing of a Free Lance Fashion Photographer" (unpublished student paper, January 20, 1978).

pounds the piano with his feet, bats tennis balls into the crowd, and hires actors to wander around the stage dressed as Frankenstein or Queen Elizabeth. Whether these are his ideas or his manager's, he carries them off well.

Celebrity marketers recognize that celebrity life cycles are quite varied and often short (see Figure 23-3). The head of marketing for Polygram, a major record firm, likens a performer's career to a crate of strawberries that must be packaged, brought to the market, and sold before they spoil and become worthless. Mike Gormley, national publicity director for Mercury Records, describes a typical meeting: "We get together every six weeks. We'll go down our sales figures. If we decide a group is getting 'no action'—meaning no airplay or sales—we'll drop them. If promotion doesn't get results, you don't just throw away more money."[14] Some "has-been" celebrities, such as Eddie Fisher, will try to relaunch, but they find it difficult to get back to the top.[15]

Political Candidate Marketing

Political candidate marketing has become a major industry and area of specialization.[16] Every few years the public is treated to numerous campaigns for local, state, and national offices. Political campaigns consist of the candidate's going into the voter market and using marketing research and commercial advertising to maximize voter "purchase."

Interest in the marketing aspects of elections has been stimulated by the spectacular growth in *political advertising, scientific opinion polling, computer analysis of voting patterns,* and *professional campaign management firms.*

> The personal handshake, the local fund-raising dinner, the neighborhood tea, the rally, the precinct captain and the car pool to the polls are still very much with us . . . the new campaign has provided a carefully coordinated strategic framework within which the traditional activities are carried out in keeping with a Master Plan. It centers on a shift from the candidate-controlled, loosely knit, often haphazard "play-it-by-ear" approach to that of a precise, centralized "team" strategy for winning or keeping office. Its hallmarks include the formal strategic blueprint, the coordinated use of specialized propaganda skills, and a more subtle approach to opinion measurement and manipulation. And, though there is a world of difference between selling a candidate and merchandising soap or razor blades, some of the attributes of commercial advertising have been grafted onto the political process.[17]

PLACE MARKETING

Place marketing involves *activities undertaken to create, maintain, or alter attitudes or behavior toward particular places.* Four types of places marketing can be distinguished.

Domicile Marketing Domicile marketing involves developing or promoting the sale or rental of single-family dwellings, apartments, and other types of housing units. It has traditionally relied on classified want ads and real estate agents. Advanced marketing has emerged in connection with condominium selling and the development of total communities.[18] Large builders research housing needs and develop housing products aimed at the price ranges and preferences of specific market segments. Some high-rise apartments have been built for the jet set, others for the geriatric set, filled with the features, symbols, and services appropriate to each. Entire housing communities have been designed for specific life-cycle or life-style groups.

Business Site Marketing Business site marketing involves developing, selling, or renting business sites or properties such as factories, stores, offices, and warehouses. Large developers research companies' land needs and respond with real estate solutions, such as industrial parks, shopping centers, and new office buildings. Most states operate industrial development offices that try to sell companies on the advantages of locating new plants in their states (see Exhibit 23-1). They spend large sums on advertising and offer to fly prospects to the site at no cost. Troubled cities, such as New York, Detroit, and Atlanta, have appointed task forces to refurbish the city's image and draw new business to the area. Foreign nations, such as Ireland, Greece, and Turkey, have marketed their homeland as a good location for business investment.

Land Investment Marketing Land investment marketing involves developing and selling for investment. The buyers—corporations, doctors, small investors, speculators—hope to sell the land when it rises sufficiently in value. Land investment marketing has been instrumental in developing large parts of Florida and the Far West. Land developers have designed elaborate marketing programs involving mass-media advertising and publicity, direct mail, personal sales calls, free dinner meetings, and even free flights to the site.

EXHIBIT 23-1

"THE GOODLIEST LAND": BUSINESS SITE MARKETING IN NORTH CAROLINA

In 1854 two English explorers returned to their homeland with news of "The Goodliest Land Under the Cope of Heaven"—they were describing what is now North Carolina. In recent years, numerous American and foreign companies have come to share this opinion of the Tar Heel state. In three successive *Business Week* surveys, North Carolina was named as first choice of the nation's top business executives for new plant location. The state does offer a number of economic and cultural advantages, but much credit for the state's popularity goes to the North Carolina Department of Commerce's Division of Industrial Development. The division employs a high-quality marketing program—including advertising, publicity, and

North Carolina advertises to attract new business to the state. *Courtesy of North Carolina Dept. of Commerce, Industrial Development Division.*

personal selling—to convince targeted firms and industries to come to North Carolina.

The division's 24 industrial development representatives coordinate efforts with development professionals in more than 300 individual North Carolina communities. And the division provides extensive information to firms considering locating in the state—in-depth profiles of more than 325 communities, a computerized inventory of available industrial sites and buildings, estimates of state and local taxes for specific sites, analyses of labor costs and fringe benefits, details of transportation convenient to sites, and estimates of construction costs.

But the Division of Industrial Development does more than simply provide information—it aggressively seeks out firms and effectively persuades them to locate in North Carolina. It invites groups of business executives to tour the state and hear presentations, and it sets up booths at industry trade fairs. Its representatives (sometimes including the state's governor) travel to other states to carry the North Carolina story to executives in attractive businesses and industries. The division also communicates and persuades through informational and promotional brochures delivered by mail, and through mass-media advertising. Ads and brochures such as those shown here tout North Carolina's benefits: a large and productive laborforce, numerous educational and technical training institutions, low taxes, a good transportation network, low energy and construction costs, a good living environment, and plentiful government support and assistance.

The division's total budget runs only about $2 million a year, but the returns are great. From 1977 through 1983, new and expanding businesses announced investments of more than $13 billion in North Carolina, creating more than 200,000 new jobs.

Source: Based on information supplied by the North Carolina Department of Commerce, Division of Industrial Development.

Vacation Marketing

Vacation marketing involves attracting vacationers to spas, resorts, cities, states, and even entire nations. The effort is carried on by travel agents, airlines, motor clubs, oil companies, hotels, motels, and governmental agencies. The power of place marketing was demonstrated in the career of the late Steve Hannagan: "He built monuments to his skill and the power of press-agentry in making the Memorial Day auto races at Indianapolis a national event and in making Miami Beach and Sun Valley into nationally known resorts."[19]

Today almost every city and state publicizes its tourist attractions. Miami Beach is considering making gambling legal in order to attract more tourists; and the Virgin Islands is trying to "repopularize" the islands after some bad tourist incidents. Some places, however, are trying to demarket themselves. Palm Beach, Florida, is letting its beach erode to discourage tourists; Oregon has publicized its bad weather; Yosemite National Park may ban snowmobiling, conventions, and private cars; and Finland wants to discourage tourists from vacationing in certain areas where they feel the ravages of mass tourism exceed the revenues.

IDEA MARKETING

Ideas can also be marketed. In one sense, all marketing is the marketing of an idea, whether it be the idea of brushing one's teeth, the idea that Crest is the most effective decay preventer, or anything else. Here we will confine our discussion to the marketing of social ideas, such as public health campaigns to reduce smoking, alcoholism, drug abuse, and overeating; environmental campaigns to promote wilderness protection, clean air, and conservation; and other campaigns such as family planning, women's rights, and racial equality. This area has been called social marketing.[20]

> **Social marketing** is the design, implementation, and control of programs seeking to increase the acceptability of a social idea, cause, or practice in a target group(s). It utilizes market segmentation, consumer research, concept development, communications, facilitation, incentives, and exchange theory to maximize target group response.

Social marketers can pursue different objectives: produce *understanding* (knowing the nutritional value of different foods); trigger a *one-time action* (participating in a mass immunization campaign); attempt to *change behavior* (auto seatbelt campaign); change a *basic belief* (convincing anti-abortion adherents to believe in a woman's right to abortion).

The Advertising Council of America has carried out dozens of social advertising campaigns, including "Smokey the Bear," "Keep America Beautiful," "Join the Peace Corps," "Buy Bonds," and "Go to College." But social marketing is much broader. Many public advertising campaigns fail because they assign advertising the primary role and fail to develop and use all the marketing mix tools.

Wiebe, in his study of four social campaigns, showed how their differential success was related to how closely they resembled selling a normal product or service.[21] The great success of the Kate Smith radio marathon to sell bonds one evening was due to the presence of force (patriotism), direction (buy bonds), mechanism (banks, post offices, telephone orders), adequacy and compatibility (many centers to purchase the bonds), and distance (ease of purchase). The other three social campaigns met with less success because the other marketing mix variables were ignored.

In designing social change strategies, social marketers go through a normal marketing planning process. First, they define the social change objective—for example, "to reduce the percentage of teenagers who smoke from 60 percent to 40 percent within five years." Next they analyze the attitudes, beliefs, values, and behavior of teenagers and the forces that support teenage smoking. They consider alternative communication and distribution approaches that might dissuade teenagers from smoking (see Exhibit 23-2), develop a marketing plan, and build a marketing organization to carry out the plan. Finally, they evaluate and adjust the ongoing program to make it more effective.

Social marketing is new, and its effectiveness relative to other social change strategies is hard to evaluate. It is difficult to produce social change with any strategy, let alone one that relies on voluntary response. Social marketing has mainly been applied to family planning,[22] environmental protection,[23] energy conservation, improved nutrition, auto driver safety, and public transportation—and there have been some encouraging successes. But more applications are needed before we can fully assess social marketing's potential for producing social change.

EXHIBIT 23-2

CAN SOCIAL MARKETING REDUCE CIGARETTE
SMOKING?

The weight of scientific evidence demonstrates a link between cigarette smoking and lung cancer, heart disease, and emphysema. Most cigarette smokers are aware of the bad effects of cigarette smoking. The problem is to give them the means or the will to reduce their cigarette consumption. The four Ps suggest several possible approaches:

1. *Product*
   a. Require manufacturers to add a tart or bitter ingredient to the tobacco.
   b. Cut down further on the tar and nicotine in cigarettes.
   c. Find a new type of tobacco for cigarettes that tastes as good but is safe.
   d. Promote other products that will help people relieve their tensions, such as chewing gum.

2. *Promotion*
   a. Increase fear of early death among smokers.
   b. Create guilt or shame among cigarette users.
   c. Strengthen other goals of smokers that surpass their satisfaction from smoking.
   d. Urge smokers to cut down the number of cigarettes they smoke or to smoke only the first half of the cigarette.

3. *Place*
   a. Make cigarettes harder to obtain or unavailable.
   b. Make it easier for cigarette smokers to attend antismoking clinics.
   c. Make it harder to find public places that allow cigarette smoking.

4. *Price*
   a. Raise substantially the price of cigarettes.
   b. Raise the cost of life and health insurance to smokers.
   c. Offer a monetary or nonmonetary reward to smokers for each period they forgo smoking.

Antismoking campaigns appear to be worthwhile. However, social marketers should note some secondary consequences. People who stop smoking tend to eat more and gain weight. Overweight shortens people's lives by approximately fourteen years, whereas smoking shortens people's lives by seven years. Liquor shortens people's lives by four years. This might suggest that the social marketer should leave the smoker alone or encourage the smoker to drink instead of smoke.

■ *Summary*

Marketing has been broadened in recent years to cover "marketable" entities other than products—namely, services, organizations, persons, places, and ideas.

The United States is the world's first service economy in that most Americans work in service industries. *Services* are activities or benefits that one party can offer to another that are essentially intangible and do not result in the ownership of anything. Services are intangible, inseparable, variable, and perishable. Services can be classified according to whether they are people- or equipment-based, whether the client's presence is necessary, whether the client is a consumer or business, and whether the service provider is a profit or nonprofit firm in the private or public sector. Service industries lag behind manufacturing firms in adopting and using marketing concepts. Yet rising costs and increasing competition are forcing service industries to search for ways to increase their productivity. Marketing makes a contribution by calling for more systematic planning of service concepts and their pricing, distribution, and promotion.

Organizations can also be marketed. *Organization marketing* is undertaken to create, maintain, or alter attitudes or behavior of target audiences toward particular organizations. It calls for assessing the organization's current image and developing a marketing plan for bringing about an improved image.

Person marketing consists of activities undertaken to create, maintain, or alter attitudes or behavior toward particular persons. Two common forms are celebrity marketing and political candidate marketing.

Place marketing involves activities to create, maintain, or alter attitudes or behavior toward particular places. The four most common types are domicile marketing, business site marketing, land investment marketing, and vacation marketing.

Idea marketing involves efforts to market ideas. In the case of social ideas it is called *social marketing* and consists of the design, implementation, and control of programs seeking to increase the acceptability of a social idea, cause, or practice in a target group. Social marketing goes further than public advertising in coordinating advertising with the other elements of the marketing mix. The social marketer proceeds by defining the social change objective, analyzing consumer attitudes and competitive forces, developing and testing alternative concepts, developing appropriate channels for the idea's communication and distribution, and finally, monitoring the results. Social marketing has been applied to family planning, environmental protection, antismoking campaigns, and other public issues.

■ Questions for Discussion

1. In 1983 the U.S. government was ranked twenty-eighth among the leading advertisers based on total expenditures, while the Canadian government was the leading advertiser in that country, spending twice as much as General Foods, the second-ranked advertiser. Why, do you think, was there such a difference between the relative rankings of these two governments in advertising expenditures?

2. Many banks have been hiring marketing executives with consumer packaged goods marketing experience. Why, do you think, has this trend occurred and what problems, if any, might result from this hiring practice?

3. Relate the four distinctive characteristics of services to the purchase of a ticket to a movie.

4. Producers of services have historically been more marketing-oriented than producers of products. Comment.

5. Explain how the distribution channel is important to the following service marketers: (a) Coopers and Lybrand ("Big 8" accounting firm), (b) Paramount Pictures, (c) Joe's Repair Shop, and (d) the local repertory theater.

6. What is the primary purpose of the individual charged with organization marketing? Explain.

7. The only places that can be marketed effectively are those people enjoy visiting. Comment.

8. What distinguishes *social marketing* from *social advertising?* Explain.

■ References

1. James Cook, "You Mean We've Been Speaking Prose All These Years?" *Forbes,* April 11, 1983, pp. 142–49.

2. "Services Grow While the Quality Shrinks," *Business Week,* October 1971, p. 50.

3. For a good discussion of quality control systems at the Marriott Hotel chain, see G. M. Hostage, "Quality Control in a Service Business," *Harvard Business Review,* July–August 1975, pp. 98–106.

4. See W. Earl Sasser, "Match Supply and Demand in Service Industries," *Harvard Business Review,* November–December 1976, pp. 133–40.

5. For more on classifying services, see Christopher H. Lovelock, "Classifying Services to Gain Strategic Marketing Insights," *Journal of Marketing,* Summer 1983, pp. 9–20.

6. William R. George and Hiram C. Barksdale, "Marketing Activities in the Service Industries," *Journal of Marketing,* October 1974, p. 65. Also see A. Parasuraman, Leonard L. Berry, and Valerie A. Zeithaml, "Service Firms Need More Marketing," *Business Horizons,* November–December 1983, pp. 28–31.

7. See Daniel T. Carroll, "Ten Commandments for Bank Marketing," *Bankers Magazine,* Autumn 1970, pp. 74–80. Also see G. Lynn Shostack, "Banks Sell Services—Not Things," *Bankers Magazine,* Winter 1977, pp. 40–45; and Steven Mintz, "Banking on Marketing," *Sales and Marketing Management,* June 6, 1983, pp. 43–48.

8. Theodore Levitt, "Product-Line Approach to Service," *Harvard Business Review,* September–October 1972, pp. 41–52; also see his "The Industrialization of Service," *Harvard Business Review,* September–October 1976, pp. 63–74.

9. *Public Relations News,* October 27, 1947.

10. For this argument, see Philip Kotler and William Mindak, "Marketing and Public Relations," *Journal of Marketing,* October 1978, pp. 13–20.

11. The semantic differential technique was originally presented in C. E. Osgood, C. J. Suci, and P. H. Tannenbaum, *The Measurement of Meaning* (Urbana: University of Illinois Press, 1957).

12. For additional ways to market the services of a professional service firm, see Philip Kotler and Paul N. Bloom, *Marketing Professional Services* (Englewood Cliffs, NJ: Prentice-Hall, 1984).

13. Carol Oppenheim, "Bucky Dent: The Selling of a Sudden Superstar," *Chicago Tribune,* December 16, 1978, Sec. 2, p. 1.

14. "In the Groove at Mercury Records," *Chicago Daily News,* Panorama magazine, October 16, 1976.

15. John E. Cooney, "Eddie Fisher Discovers That Regaining Fame Is a Daunting Goal," *Wall Street Journal,* February 20, 1978, p. 1.

16. See Theodore White, *The Making of a President 1960* (New York: Atheneum, 1961); Joe McGinness, *The Selling of a President 1968* (New York: Trident Press, 1969); and Daniel Burstein, "Presidential Timbre: Grooming the Candidates," *Advertising Age,* March 12, 1984, p. M4.

17. See E. Glick, *The New Methodology* (Washington, DC: American Institute for Political Communication, 1967), p. 1. Also see Philip Kotler and Neil Kotler, "Business Marketing for Political Candidates," *Campaigns and Elections,* Summer 1981, pp. 24–33.

18. For a description of the marketing of a "new town" in Texas called The Woodlands, see Betsy D. Gelb and Ben M. Enis, "Marketing a City of the

Future," in *Marketing Is Everybody's Business* (Santa Monica, CA: Goodyear, 1977).

19. See SCOTT CUTLIP and ALLEN H. CENTER, *Effective Public Relations* (3rd ed.) (Englewood Cliffs, NJ: Prentice-Hall, 1964), p. 10.

20. See PHILIP KOTLER and GERALD ZALTMAN, "Social Marketing: An Approach to Planned Social Change," *Journal of Marketing,* July 1971, pp. 3–12.

21. G. D. WIEBE, "Merchandising Commodities and Citizenship on Television," *Public Opinion Quarterly,* Winter 1951–52, pp. 679–91.

22. See EDUARDO ROBERTO, *Strategic Decision-Making in a Social Program: The Case of Family-Planning Diffusion* (Lexington, MA: Lexington Books, 1975).

23. See KARL E. HENION II, *Ecological Marketing* (Columbus, OH: Grid, 1976).

24
Marketing and Society

Giant Foods, Inc., is a leading supermarket chain in the Washington, DC, area. In 1970 the company adopted, in response to the growing consumer movement, a new concept of its business. The typical food chain is content to carry those food products that manufacturers want to sell and buyers want to buy, without making any judgments or offering consumers any advice. Giant, however, adopted a different view: "We are the customer's channel for food. We should strive to help the customer obtain the best value possible, not only in his pocketbook but also in his/her food intake. Our store should be an instrument to help the customer know how to buy good food value."

This consumer orientation has been implemented through a series of specific measures:

1. The chain would not carry any "rip-off" foods.
2. The chain would try to carry low-, medium-, and high-priced versions of basic food to give the consumer a real choice.
3. The chain would occasionally point out that some food item is expensive and that a substitute item would cost less and give the same benefit.
4. The chain would post the prices of each brand clearly and in unit terms (pounds, pints, etc.) so that consumers could make price comparisons.
5. The chain would date perishable products so that consumers would know their freshness.
6. The chain would employ full-time home economists to answer consumer questions about food values, recipes, and other problems.
7. The chain would make it easy for consumers to register complaints.
8. The chain would appoint a well-known consumer advocate to its board of directors so that management would always be aware of the consumer's point of view.

Through these measures, Giant moved from being a distributor acting in the sellers' interests to being an agent acting in the customers' interests. Did the consumer orientation pay? According to a spokesman for the company: "These actions have improved Giant's goodwill immeasurably and have earned the admiration of leaders of the consumer movement."

iant Foods took a responsible and creative approach to marketing. Responsible marketers interpret buyer wants and respond with appropriate products, priced to yield good value to the buyers and profit to the producer. The *marketing concept* is a philosophy of service and mutual gain. Its practice leads the economy by an invisible hand to satisfy the diverse and changing needs of millions of consumers.

Not all marketers practice the marketing concept. Some individuals and companies engage in questionable marketing practices. And certain private marketing transactions, seemingly innocent in themselves, have profound implications for the larger society. Consider the sale of cigarettes. Ordinarily, companies should be free to sell cigarettes, and smokers should be free to buy them. However, this transaction affects the public interest. First, the smoker may be shortening his or her own life. Second, smoking places a burden on the smoker's family, and on society at large. Third, other people in the presence of the smoker may have to inhale the smoke and may experience discomfort and harm. This is not to say that cigarettes should be banned. Rather, it shows that private transactions may involve larger questions of public policy.

The businessperson can counter such criticisms by pointing to the great wealth created in America by its mass-production and mass-consumption philosophy. Surely a few excesses, abuses, and wastes are a small price to pay for the endless supply of material goods enjoyed in this country.

But this attitude is dangerous. If the public *thinks* there are things wrong with marketing, it is folly to ignore these concerns. For reasons of self-interest and conscience, marketers should examine their role in society.

This chapter examines the social consequences of private marketing practices. It addresses the following questions: (1) What are the most frequent social criticisms of marketing? (2) What steps have private citizens taken to curb marketing ills? (3) What steps have legislators and government agencies taken to curb marketing ills? (4) What steps have enlightened companies taken to carry out socially responsible marketing? (5) What principles might guide future policy toward marketing?

SOCIAL CRITICISMS OF MARKETING

Social criticisms of marketing can be classified into those alleged to hurt individual consumers, society as a whole, and other business firms.

Marketing's Impact on Individual Welfare Consumers have many concerns about how well the American marketing system serves their interests. A recent consumer survey conducted by Louis Harris and Associates for Atlantic Richfield Company found that consumers are worried about high prices, poor-quality products, dangerous products, exaggerated advertising claims, and several other problems associated with marketing practices (see Figure

FIGURE 24-1
*Survey of Consumer
Concerns, 1982 versus
1976*

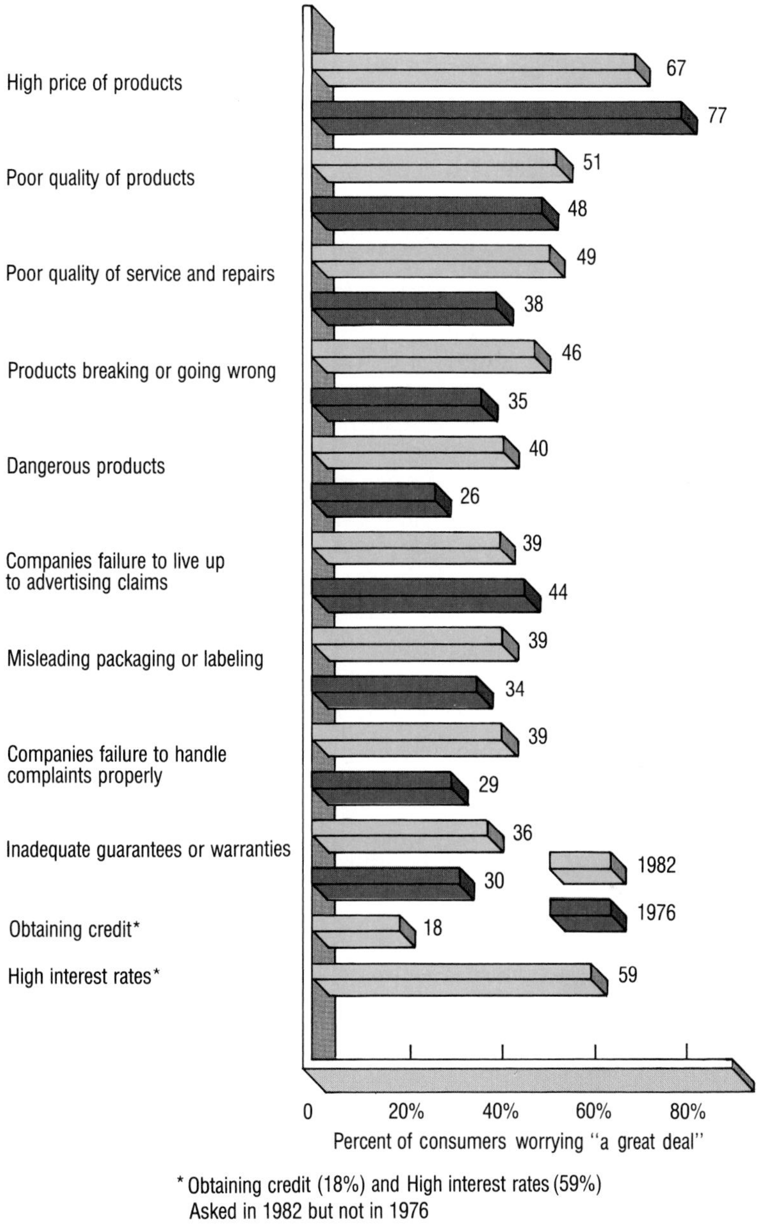

High price of products — 67 / 77

Poor quality of products — 51 / 48

Poor quality of service and repairs — 49 / 38

Products breaking or going wrong — 46 / 35

Dangerous products — 40 / 26

Companies failure to live up to advertising claims — 39 / 44

Misleading packaging or labeling — 39 / 34

Companies failure to handle complaints properly — 39 / 29

Inadequate guarantees or warranties — 36 / 30

1982
1976

Obtaining credit* — 18

High interest rates* — 59

0   20%   40%   60%   80%

Percent of consumers worrying "a great deal"

* Obtaining credit (18%) and High interest rates (59%)
Asked in 1982 but not in 1976

Source: Consumerism in the eighties, poll of 1,252 adults October 15–26, 1982, conducted by Louis Harris and Associates for ARCO. See Myrlie Evers, "Consumerism in the Eighties," *Public Relations Journal,* August 1983, pp. 24–26.

24-1). Consumer advocates, government agencies, and other critics have accused marketing of harming consumers through high prices, deceptive practices, high-pressure selling, shoddy or unsafe products, planned obsolescence, and poor service to disadvantaged consumers. We will now examine these criticisms.

High Prices

Many critics charge that the American marketing system causes prices to be higher than they would be under "sensible" arrangements. They point to three factors.

HIGH COSTS OF DISTRIBUTION. A longstanding charge is that greedy middlemen mark up prices beyond the value of their services. This criticism is an ancient one. Plato held that shopkeepers practiced the acquisitive arts and brought nothing new into existence. Aristotle condemned shopkeepers for making their profit at the expense of the buyers. In the Middle Ages, the Church placed restrictions on middlemen.

One of the most thorough studies of distribution costs appeared in *Does Distribution Cost Too Much?*[1] The study was undertaken after observing that selling and distribution costs rose from 20 percent of product costs in 1850 to 50 percent of product costs in 1920. The authors concluded that distribution cost too much and pointed their finger at " . . . duplication of sales efforts, multiplicity of sales outlets, excessive services, multitudes of brands, and unnecessary advertising . . . misinformed buying on the part of consumers . . . and, among distributors themselves, lack of a proper knowledge of costs, too great zeal for volume, poor management and planning, and unwise prices policies."[2]

How do retailers answer these charges? They argue as follows: First, middlemen perform work that would otherwise have to be performed by manufacturers or consumers. Second, the rising markup reflects improved services that consumers want: more convenience, larger stores and assortment, longer store hours, return privileges, and others. Third, the costs of operating stores keep rising and force retailers to raise their prices. Fourth, retail competition is so intense that margins are actually quite low. For example, supermarket chains are left with barely 1 percent profit on their sales after taxes.

HIGH ADVERTISING AND PROMOTION COSTS. Modern marketing is also accused of pushing up prices because of heavy advertising and sales promotion. For example, a dozen tablets of a heavily-promoted brand of aspirin sell for the same price as one hundred tablets of less-promoted brands. Critics feel that if "commodity" products were sold in bulk, their prices would be much lower. Differentiated products—cosmetics, detergents, toiletries—include costs of packaging and promotion that can amount to 40 percent or more of the manufacturer's price to the retailer. Much of the packaging and promotion adds only psychological rather than functional value to the product. Retailers use additional promotion—advertising, trading stamps, games of chance—adding several cents more to retail prices.

Businesspeople respond in several ways. First, consumers are interested in more than the functional qualities of products. They also seek psychological benefits such as feeling affluent, beautiful, or special. Consumers can usually buy functional versions of products at lower prices, but they often are willing to pay more for products that also provide these psychological benefits. Second, branding gives buyers confidence. A brand name signifies a certain quality, and consumers are willing to pay for well-known brands even if they cost a little more. Third, heavy advertising is a necessary, cost-effective way to inform the millions of potential buyers of the existence and merits of a brand. If consumers want to know what is available on the market, they must expect manufacturers to spend large sums of money on advertising. Fourth, heavy advertising and promotion are necessary for the firm when competitors are doing it. The individual enterprise would lose "share of mind" if it did not match competitive expenditures. At the same time, companies are very cost conscious about promotion and try to spend their money wisely. And fifth, heavy sales promotion is necessary from time to time because goods are produced ahead of demand in a mass-production economy. Special incentives have to be offered to buyers to clear excess inventories.

EXCESSIVE MARKUPS. Critics charge that certain industries are particularly guilty of marking up goods excessively. They point to the drug industry, where a pill costing 5 cents to manufacture may cost the consumer 40 cents; they point to the pricing tactics of funeral homes that prey on the emotions of bereaved relatives;[3] they point to the high charges of television and auto repair people. The alleged exploitation is dramatized in books with such provocative titles as *The Poor Pay More, The Hucksters, The Permissible Lie, The Innocent Consumer vs. the Exploiters, The Thumb on the Scale or the Supermarket Shell Game,* and *100,000,000 Guinea Pigs.*

Marketers respond that most businesses try to deal fairly with consumers because they want repeat business. Most consumer abuses are unintentional. When unscrupulous marketers do take advantage of consumers, they should be reported to Better Business Bureaus and other consumer protection groups. Marketers also respond that consumers often do not understand the reason for high markups. For example, pharmaceutical markups must cover the costs of purchasing, promoting, and distributing existing medicines and the high research and development costs of searching for new medicines.

Deceptive Practices

Businesspeople are often accused of deceptive practices that lead consumers to believe they will get more value than they actually do. Certain industries draw a disproportionate number of complaints. Among the worst offenders are insurance companies (alleging that policies are "guaranteed renewable" or underwritten by the government), publishing companies (approaching subscribers under false pretenses), mail order land sales organizations (misrepresenting land tracts or improvement costs), home improvement contractors (using bait-and-switch tactics), automotive repair shops (advertising ultra-low repair prices and then "discovering" a necessary major repair), home freezer plans (falsely representing the savings), correspondence schools (overstating employment opportunities after course completion), vending machine companies (falsely guaranteeing top locations), studios offering dance instruction (signing up elderly people for lessons beyond their life expectancy), and companies selling medical devices (exaggerating therapeutic claims).

Deceptive practices fall into three groups. *Deceptive pricing* includes such practices as falsely advertising "factory" or "wholesale" prices or advertising a large price reduction from an artificially high list price. *Deceptive promotion* includes overstating the product's attributes, misrepresenting the guarantees, falsely demonstrating the product's performance, luring the customer to the store for a bargain that is out of stock or downgraded by the salesperson, and running rigged contests. *Deceptive packaging* includes exaggerating the apparent package contents through subtle design, not filling the package to the top, using misleading labeling, and describing the size in misleading terms.

Deceptive practices have given rise to legislative and administrative remedies. In 1938 the Wheeler-Lea Act gave the FTC power to regulate "unfair or deceptive acts or practices." The FTC has published several guidelines listing deceptive practices. The toughest problem is distinguishing between *puffery* and *deception* in advertising. Shell Oil advertised that Super Shell with platformate consistently gave more mileage than the same gasoline without platformate. Now this was true, but what Shell did not say is that almost all automotive gasoline includes platformate. Its defense was that it had never claimed that platformate was an exclusive Shell feature. But even though the message was literally true, the FTC felt that the ad's intent was to deceive.

Marketers argue that most businesspeople avoid deceptive practices because such practices harm their businesses in the long run. If consumers do not get what they expect, they will switch to more reliable products. Also, consumers usually protect themselves from deception or exaggeration. Most consumers recognize the marketer's selling intent and exercise a healthy skepticism when they buy, sometimes to the point of not believing legitimate product claims. Levitt claims that some advertising puffery is inevitable, and even desirable:

> There is hardly a company that would not go down in ruin if it refused to provide fluff, because nobody will buy pure functionality. . . . Worse, it denies . . . man's honest needs and values. If religion must be architectured, packaged, lyricized, and musicized to attract and hold its audience, and if sex must be perfumed, powdered, sprayed, and shaped in order to command attention, it is ridiculous to deny the legitimacy of more modest, and similar, embellishments to the world of commerce. . . . Many of the so-called distortions of advertising, product design, and packaging may be viewed as a paradigm of the many responses that man makes to the conditions of survival in the environment. Without distortion, embellishment, and elaboration, life would be drab, dull, anguished, and at its existential worst. . . . I shall argue that embellishment and distortion are among advertising's legitimate and socially desirable purposes; and that illegitimacy in advertising consists only of falsification with larcenous intent.[4]

High-Pressure Selling

Salespeople in certain industries are accused of applying high-pressure selling techniques that induce people to buy goods they had no thought of buying. It is often said that encyclopedias, insurance, real estate, and jewelry are sold, not bought. The salespeople are trained to deliver smooth canned talks to entice purchase. They sell hard because sales contests promise big prizes to those who sell the most. The following pep talk was given to salespeople by a sales manager:

> One thought this morning—high pressure. . . . Everybody's afraid of the word! Been so easy selling last couple of years everybody's squeamish about doing any

work. . . . Order takers, that's what we've become. . . . What's the answer? Pressure, brother, high pressure and lemme tell you the guys that don't wise up are going to get left behind, and fast.[5]

Businesspeople recognize that buyers can often be talked into buying unwanted or unneeded things. Recent legislation requires door-to-door salespeople to announce their purpose to sell the product. Buyers are also allowed a "three-day cooling-off period" in which they can cancel a contract after rethinking it. In addition, consumers can complain to Better Business Bureaus when they feel that undue selling pressure was applied.

Shoddy or Unsafe Products

Another criticism is that products lack the quality they should have. One complaint is that products are not made well. "If (the consumer) somehow escapes rattles, pings, loose buttons, or missing knobs there probably will be dents, mismatched sizes, static fluttering, leaking, or creaking,"[6] Automobiles receive a disproportionate number of complaints. Consumers Union, an independent testing agency that publishes *Consumer Reports,* tested thirty-two cars and found something wrong with all of them. "Cars were delivered with rain leaks, fender dents, nonaligned windows, broken distributor caps, ignition locks that wouldn't lock."[7] Complaints have also been lodged against home and auto repair services, various appliances, and clothing.

A second complaint is that certain products deliver little benefit. Consumers got a shock on hearing that dry breakfast cereal may have little nutritional value. Robert B. Choate, a nutritional specialist, told a Senate subcommittee: "In short, (the cereals) fatten but do little to prevent malnutrition. . . . The average cereal. . . . fails as a complete meal even with milk added."[8] Choate added that consumers could often get more nutrition by eating the cereal package than the contents.

A third complaint concerns products' safety characteristics. For years, Consumers Union has reported various hazards in tested products—electrical dangers in appliances, carbon monoxide poisoning from room heaters, finger risks in lawn-mowers, and faulty steering in automobiles. Product quality has been a problem for several reasons, including occasional manufacturer indifference, increased production complexity, poorly trained labor, and insufficient quality control.

On the other hand, most manufacturers want to produce good quality. Consumers who are disappointed with one of their products may avoid their other products and influence other consumers to do the same. The way a company deals with product quality and safety problems can damage or enhance its reputation (see Exhibit 24-1). Companies selling poor-quality or unsafe products risk damaging confrontations with consumer groups. For example, Ralph Nader's *Unsafe at Any Speed* exposed safety defects in General Motor's Corvair that led to the car's demise. In addition to consumer groups, various laws mandate local, state, and federal government agencies to protect consumers against poor or unsafe products.

EXHIBIT 24-1

A CONTRAST IN COMPANY RESPONSES TO UNSAFE PRODUCTS

This is the story of two companies, one that moved too slowly after its tire failures allegedly killed twenty-nine people and injured fifty, and another that moved swiftly when its toy killed two children.

Concern over the performance of the Firestone 500 radial tire was first indicated in 1976 when a Ralph Nadar group started receiving consumer complaints. The National Highway Traffic Safety Administration (NHTSA) investigated after receiving more than five hundred complaints. Over fourteen thousand consumer complaints were compiled. Then Firestone sought an injunction against release of the NHTSA report. The Firestone Company waited until it was forced by the government to recall 13 million Firestone radial tires.

Parker Brothers Toy Company, a subsidiary of General Mills, voluntarily recalled a spectacularly successful toy called Riviton, a kit consisting of plastic parts, rubber rivets, and a riveting tool. When Parker Brothers heard of the first death, it was assumed to be a freak accident. When the second death was caused by the same part of the toy, "the decision was very simple. Were we supposed to sit back and wait for death No. 3?" said Randolph Barton, president of Parker Brothers. In support of Parker Brothers' swift behavior, Susan King, chairman of the Consumer Product Safety Commission, stated that the company was "a model of social responsibility."

Planned Obsolescence

Critics have charged that producers in certain industries cause their products to become obsolete before they actually need replacement. Three types of obsolescence can be distinguished.

Planned style obsolescence is a producer strategy to change users' concepts of acceptable appearance. Manufacturers of women's apparel, men's apparel, automobiles, furniture, and even homes have been accused of this. The annual style change of Detroit automobiles is an example.

Planned functional obsolescence means a deliberate policy by manufacturers to "withhold fully developed attractive features whose present absence and subsequent introduction may be used to encourage an earlier replacement of the product. . . . "[9] An example would be the withholding by automobile manufacturers of a whole set of safety, pollution reduction, and gasoline economy improvements.

Planned material obsolescence means that manufacturers choose materials and components that are subject to higher breakage, wear, rot, or corrosion. For example, many drapery manufacturers are using a higher percentage of rayon in their drapes. They argue that rayon reduces the price of the drapes and has better holding power. Critics assert that rayon will cause the drapes to fall apart in two cleanings instead of four.

Businesspeople respond that consumers like style changes. They get tired of the old goods and want a new look in fashion or a new-styled automobile. No one has to buy the new look and if enough people do not like it, it will fail. Companies withhold new functional features when they are not adequately tested, when they add more cost to the product than consumers are willing to pay, and for other good reasons. But they do this at the risk of having a competitor introduce the new feature and steal the market. Also, companies often substitute new materials in order to lower their costs and prices. They do not design their products to break down earlier because they would lose their customers to other brands. Thus much of so-called planned obsolescence is the working out of dynamic competitive and technological forces in a free society, leading to ever-improving goods and services.

Poor Service to the Disadvantaged

The American marketing system has been accused of poorly serving disadvantaged consumers. According to David Caplovitz in his *The Poor Pay More,* the urban poor often have to shop in smaller stores that carry inferior goods and charge higher prices.[10] The former chairman of the FTC, Paul Rand Dixon, summarized a Washington, DC, study:

> The poor pay more—nearly twice as much—for appliances and furniture sold in Washington's low-income area stores. . . . Goods purchased for $100 at wholesale sold for $225 in the low-income stores compared with $159 in the general market stores. . . . Installment credit is a major marketing factor in selling to the poor . . . some low-income market retailers imposed effective annual finance charges as high as 33 percent. . . . [11]

Yet ironically, the merchants' profits were not exorbitant:

> Low income market retailers have markedly higher costs, partly because of bad debt expenses, but to greater extent because of higher selling, wage, and commission costs. These expenses reflect in part greater use of home demonstration selling, and expenses associated with the collection and processing of installment contracts. Thus, although their markups are often two or three times higher than general market retailers, on the average low-income market retailers do not make particularly high profits.[12]

Clearly, better marketing systems must be built in low-income areas, and low-income people need consumer protection. The FTC has taken action against merchants who advertise false values, sell old merchandise as new, or charge too much for credit. It is trying to make it harder for merchants to win court judgments and garnishments against low-income people who were wheedled into buying something. Another hope is to encourage large-scale retailers to open outlets in low-income areas.[13]

Marketing's Impact on Society as a Whole The American marketing system has been accused of contributing to several "evils" in American society. Advertising has been a special target—so much so that the American Association of Advertising Agencies recently launched a campaign to defend advertising against what it felt are common but unjustified criticisms (see Exhibit 24-2). Here we will examine claims that marketing contributes to excessive materialism, false wants, insufficient social goods, cultural pollution, and excessive political power.

EXHIBIT 24-2

ADVERTISING: ANOTHER WORD FOR FREEDOM OF CHOICE

In 1984, the American Association of Advertising Agencies launched an advertising campaign featuring ads such as these to counter common criticisms of advertising. The association is concerned about research findings of negative public attitudes toward advertising. Two-thirds of the public recognizes that advertising provides helpful buying information, but a significant portion feels that advertising is exaggerated or misleading. The association believes that the ad campaign will increase general advertising credibility and make advertisers' messages more effective. Several media agreed to run the ads as a public service.

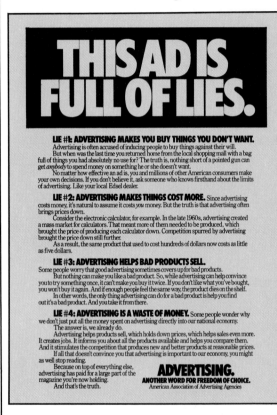

Reproduced with permission of American Association of Advertising Agencies

Excessive Materialism

Critics have charged that the marketing system encourages excessive interest in material possessions. People are judged by what they own rather than by what they are. People are not considered successful unless they own a suburban home, two cars, and the latest clothes and appliances.

Most people enter the materialistic race with great vigor, but few win the big prizes. Many drop out along the way, some repudiate the system, and the emphasis on material accumulation leaves many unhappy or frustrated.

Some of this may be changing. Dominant value systems breed their opposites, and some Americans are losing their drive for possessions. They are relaxing more, playing more, and learning to get along with less. "Small is beautiful" and "less is more" describe this ideology. More emphasis is being placed on cultivating close relationships and simple pleasures than on being "hooked on things."

False Wants

The interest in things is not seen as a natural state of mind but rather as one created by marketing. Business hires Madison Avenue to stimulate people's desires for goods, and Madison Avenue uses the mass media to create materialistic models of the good life. Conspicuous consumption on the part of some creates envy in others. People work harder to earn the necessary money, their purchases increase the output and productive capacity of the Industrial State, and the Industrial State in turn makes greater use of Madison Avenue to stimulate desire for the industrial output. Thus people are seen as the manipulated link between production and consumption. Wants come to depend on output. Galbraith calls this the "dependence effect":

> The control or management of demand is, in fact, a vast and rapidly growing industry in itself. It embraces a huge network of communications, a great array of merchandising and selling organizations, nearly the entire advertising industry, numerous ancillary research, training and other related services and much more. In everyday parlance this great machine, and the demanding and varied talents that it employs, are said to be engaged in selling goods. In less ambiguous language it means that it is engaged in the management of those who buy goods.[14]

And Marcuse suggests:

> "False" (needs) are those which are superimposed upon the individual by particular social interests. Most of the prevailing needs to relax, to have fun, to behave and consume in accordance with the advertisements, to love and hate what others love and hate, belong to this category of false needs.[15]

These quotations probably exaggerate the power of business to stimulate wants. Under normal social conditions, people choose among conflicting life styles, and they have normal defenses against the mass media—selective attention, perception, distortion, and retention. The mass media are most effective when they appeal to existing needs rather than attempt to create new ones. Furthermore, people seek information when making important purchases and do not rely on single sources of information. Even minor purchases, which may be influenced by advertising messages, lead to repeat purchases only if the product meets performance expectations. Finally, the high failure rate of new products belies the claim that companies are able to control demand.

On a deeper level, our wants and values are influenced not only by marketers, but also by family, peer groups, religion, ethnic backround, and education. If Americans are highly materialistic, this value system arose out of basic socialization processes that go much deeper than business and mass media could produce alone.

Insufficient Social Goods

Business has been accused of overstimulating demand for private goods at the expense of public goods. As private goods increase, they require a complement of public services that is usually not forthcoming. According to Galbraith:

> An increase in the consumption of automobiles requires a facilitating supply of streets, highways, traffic control, and parking space. The protective services of the police and the highway patrols must also be available, as must those of the hospitals. Although the need for balance here is extraordinarily clear, our use of privately produced vehicles has, on occasion, got far out of line with the supply of the related public services. The result has been hideous road congestion, an annual massacre of impressive proportions, and chronic colitis in the cities.[16]

Thus Galbraith sees private consumption leading to a "social imbalance" and "social costs" that neither producers nor consumers appear willing to pay for. A way must be found to restore a social balance between private and public goods. Manufacturing firms could be required to bear the full social costs of their operations. In this way, they would build these costs into the price. Where buyers did not find the private goods worth the price, those firms would disappear and resources would move to those uses that could support the sum of the private and social costs.

Cultural Pollution

Critics charge the marketing system with creating *cultural pollution*. People's senses are constantly being assaulted by advertising. Serious programs are interrupted by commercials; printed matter is lost between pages of ads; magnificent landscapes are marred by billboards. These interruptions intrude sex, power, or status continuously into people's consciousnesses.

Yet the flood of advertising strikes people in different ways. In a study of consumer attitudes toward advertising, Bauer and Greyser found that advertising was a low-salience topic, something like the daily weather.[17] Although people occasionally complain about it, they do not complain about it seriously. Only 15 percent of those interviewed thought advertising needed change, and they were people who wanted many institutions changed. The average respondent "paid some attention" to about seventy-six ads during an average day and did not find more than 16 percent of them annoying or offensive. Some people thought that the best part of television programming was the ads!

Businesspeople answer the charges of commercial noise with these arguments: First, they hope that their ads primarily reach the target audience. Because of mass-communication channels, some ads are bound to reach people who have no interest in the product and are therefore bored or irritated. People who buy magazines addressed to their interests—such as *Vogue* or *Fortune*—rarely complain about the ads because they advertise products of interest. Second, the ads make radio and television a free medium and keep down the costs of magazines and newspapers. Most people think commercials are a small price to pay.

Excessive Political Power

Another criticism is that business wields too much political power. There are "oil," "cigarette," and "auto" senators who advance particular industries' interests against the public interest. Advertisers are accused of holding too much power over the mass media, constraining its freedom to report independently and objectively. One critic said: "How can *Life, Post,* and *Reader's Digest* afford to tell the truth about the scandalously low nutritional value of most packaged foods . . . when these magazines are being subsidized by such advertisers as General Foods, Kellogg's, Nabisco, and General Mills? . . . The answer is *they cannot and do not.*"[18]

American industries do promote and protect their interests. They have a right to representation in Congress and the mass media, although their influence could become too extensive. Fortunately, many powerful business interests thought to be untouchable have been tamed in the public interest. Standard Oil was dismantled in 1911, and the meatpacking industry was disciplined after the exposures of Upton Sinclair. Ralph Nader inspired legislation requiring the automobile industry to build more safety into its vehicles, and the Surgeon General's Report required cigarette companies to include a health warning on their packages. The media are becoming more courageous in featuring editorial material designed to interest different market segments. Excessive business power tends to breed countervailing forces to check and offset these powerful interests.

Marketing's Impact on Other Businesses Critics also charge that many companies ride roughshod over other companies. Three problems are involved: anticompetitive mergers, artificial barriers to entry, and predatory competition.

Anticompetitive Acquisition

A recurrent accusation is that many firms expand by acquiring other firms rather than by internally developing new and needed products. Within a certain time period, the nine leading ethical drug companies developed eight new businesses internally and acquired sixteen other businesses.[19] As another example, P&G acquired Clorox, the major producer of household liquid bleach.[20] The Supreme Court ruled that P&G's acquisition would deprive the industry of potential competition not only from P&G, had it entered the market on its own, but also from smaller firms that might now be discouraged from entering this market.

Acquisition is a complicated subject. Acquisitions can be beneficial to the society in certain circumstances: when the acquiring company gains economies of scale leading to lower costs and lower prices; when a well-managed company takes over a poorly managed company and improves its efficiency; when an industry that was noncompetitive becomes competitive after the acquisition. Acquisitions can also be harmful, particularly when a vigorous young competitor is absorbed and fewer firms dominate the industry.

Barriers to Entry

Critics have charged that marketing practices add substantial barriers to entry. These barriers take the form of patents, substantial promotion requirements, and tie-ups of suppliers or dealers.

Antitrust people recognize that some barriers are associated with real economies of large-scale enterprise. Other barriers could be challenged by existing and new laws. For example, some critics have proposed a progressive tax on advertising expenditures to reduce the role of selling costs as a major barrier to entry.

Predatory Competition

Some firms have been known to go after other firms with the intention of hurting or destroying them. They may set their prices below costs, threaten to cut off business with suppliers, or disparage the competitor's products.

Various laws have been designed to prevent predatory competition. The difficulty is to establish that the intent or action was really predatory. In the classic A&P case, this large retailer was able to charge lower prices than small "mom and pop" grocery stores. The question is whether this was predatory competition or the healthy competition of a more efficient retailing institution against the less efficient.[21]

CITIZEN ACTIONS TO REGULATE MARKETING

Because some people have viewed business as the cause of many economic and social ills, grassroots movements have arisen from time to time to discipline business. The two major antibusiness movements have been *consumerism* and *environmentalism*.

Consumerism American business firms have been the target of an organized consumer movement on three occasions. The first consumer movement took place in the early 1900s and was fueled by rising prices, Upton Sinclair's exposés of conditions in the meat industry, and ethical drug scandals. The second consumer movement, in the mid-1930s, was sparked by an upturn in consumer prices in the midst of the Depression and another drug scandal.

The third movement began in the 1960s. Consumers had become better educated; products had become increasingly complex and hazardous; discontent with American institutions was widespread; influential writings by John Kenneth Galbraith, Vance Packard, and Rachel Carson accused big business of wasteful and manipulative practices; a 1962 presidential message of John F. Kennedy declared that consumers have the right to safety, to be informed, to choose, and to be heard; there were congressional investigations of certain industries; and finally, Ralph Nader appeared on the scene to crystallize many of the issues.[22]

Since then many consumer groups have been organized and several consumer laws have been passed. The consumer movement has spread internationally and has become very strong in Scandinavia and the Low Countries.

But what is the consumer movement? **Consumerism** is an *organized movement of citizens and government to enhance the rights and power of buyers in relation to sellers.* The traditional sellers' rights include

1. The right to introduce any product in any size and style, provided it is not hazardous to personal health or safety; or, if it is, to introduce it with the proper warning and controls
2. The right to price the product at any level, provided there is no discrimination among similar classes of buyers
3. The right to spend any amount of money to promote the product, provided it is not defined as unfair competition
4. The right to formulate any product message, provided it is not misleading or dishonest in content or execution
5. The right to introduce any buying incentive schemes they wish

The traditional buyers' rights include

1. The right not to buy a product that is offered for sale
2. The right to expect the product to be safe
3. The right to expect the product to perform as claimed

Comparing these rights, many believe that the balance of power lies on the sellers' side. True, the buyer can refuse to buy. But critics feel that the buyer has insufficient information, education, and protection to make wise decisions when facing highly sophisticated sellers. Consumer advocates call for the following additional consumer rights:

4. The right to be adequately informed about the more important aspects of the product
5. The right to be protected against questionable products and marketing practices
6. The right to influence products and marketing practices in directions that will enhance the "quality of life"

Each proposed right leads to specific proposals by consumerists. The right to be informed includes the right to know the true interest cost of a loan *(truth-in-lending),* the true cost per standard unit of competing brands *(unit pricing),* the basic ingredients in a product *(ingredient labeling),* the nutritional quality of foods *(nutritional labeling),* the freshness of products *(open dating),* and the true benefits of a product *(truth-in-advertising).*

The proposals related to *consumer protection* include the strengthening of consumers' position in cases of business fraud, the requiring of more safety in products, and the issuing of greater powers to government agencies.

The proposals relating to *quality of life* include regulating the ingredients that go into certain products (detergents) and packaging (soft-drink containers), reducing the level of advertising and promotional "noise," and placing consumer representatives on company boards to introduce consumer considerations in business decision making.

Consumers have not only rights but responsibilities to protect themselves instead of leaving this to someone else. Consumers who feel they got a bad deal have several remedies available, including writing to the company president or to the media; contacting federal, state, or local agencies; and filing claims in small-claims courts.

Environmentalism

Where consumerists focus on whether the marketing system is efficiently serving consumer wants, environmentalists focus on marketing's impact on the environment and the costs of serving these needs and wants. In 1962 Rachel Carson's *Silent Spring* presented a documented case of pesticide pollution of the environment.[23] It was no longer a matter of wasted resources, but of human survival. In 1970 the Ehrlichs coined the term "eco-catastrophe" to symbolize the harmful impact of certain American business practices on the environment.[24] And in 1972 the Meadowses published *The Limits to Growth,* which warned people that the quality of life would inevitably decline in the face of unchecked population growth, spreading pollution, and continued exploitation of natural resources.[25]

These concerns underpin environmentalism. **Environmentalism** is *an organized movement of concerned citizens and government to protect and enhance people's living environment.* Environmentalists are concerned with strip mining, forest depletion, factory smoke, billboards, and litter; with the loss of recreational opportunity; and with the increase in health problems due to bad air, water, and chemically sprayed food.

Environmentalists are not against marketing and consumption; they simply want them to operate on more ecological principles. They do not think the marketing system's goal should be to maximize *consumption, consumer choice,* or *consumer satisfaction.* The marketing system's goal should be to maximize *life quality.* And life quality means not only the quantity and quality of consumer goods and services, but also the quality of the environment.

Environmentalists want environmental cost included in producer and consumer decision making. They favor using taxes and regulations to impose the true social costs of anti-environmental behavior. Requiring business to invest in antipollution devices, taxing nonreturnable bottles, and banning high-phosphate detergents are viewed as necessary to lead businesses and consumers to move in environmentally sound directions.

Environmentalists are more critical of marketing than consumerists. They complain of too much wasteful packaging, where consumerists like the convenience of modern packaging. Environmentalists feel that advertising leads people to buy more than they need, but consumerists worry more about deception in advertising. Environmentalists dislike shopping centers, but consumerists welcome more stores.

Environmentalism has hit certain industries hard. Steel companies and public utilities have had to invest billions of dollars in pollution-control equipment and costlier fuels. The auto industry has had to introduce expensive emission controls in cars. The soap industry has had to develop low-phosphate detergents. The packaging industry has had to develop ways to reduce litter and increase biodegradability in its products. The gasoline industry has had to formulate new low-lead and no-lead gasolines. These industries resent environmental regulations, especially

Photographed by Luiz Claudio Marigo. *Seven-colored Tanager:* *Genus: Tangara Species: fastuosa*
Adult size: Average length, 14cm Adult weight: Unknown
Habitat: Tropical coastal forests of northeastern Brazil Surviving number: Unknown

Wildlife as Canon sees it:
A photographic heritage for all generations.

Once abundant in the tropical forests of Brazil, the stunningly beautiful seven-colored tanager has seriously declined in the past 30 years. Continually sought after as a cage bird because of its fanciful plumage and threatened with the loss of its habitat, this species of tanager today faces an uncertain future.

Nothing could bring the seven-colored tanager back should it vanish completely. And while photography can record it for posterity, more importantly photography can help save it and the rest of wildlife.

Photography is an invaluable research tool that can assist in efforts to save the seven-colored tanager. Continued protection from the pet trade and the preservation of its natural habitat are needed to ensure the survival of the species. Also through photography, one can better appreciate and understand this exotic and fabulous denizen of tropical forests.

And understanding is perhaps the single most important factor in saving the seven-colored tanager and all of wildlife.

FD 150-600mm f/5.6L

Canon
Images for all time

Canon shows societal concern by discussing the role of photography in creating long-run environmental benefits. *Courtesy of Canon, Inc.*

when imposed too rapidly to allow the companies to make the proper adjustments. These companies have absorbed large costs and have passed them on to buyers.

Marketers' lives have become more complicated. Marketers have to check into the ecological properties of the product and its packaging. They have to raise prices to cover environmental costs, knowing that the product will be harder to sell. Yet there is no turning back to the "cowboy" economy of the past when few managers worried about the effect of product and marketing decisions on environmental quality. It was partly this indifference that led to environmentalism in the first place.[26]

PUBLIC ACTIONS TO REGULATE MARKETING

Citizen agitation against specific marketing practices will usually stimulate public debate and lead to legislative proposals. The bills will be debated, many will be defeated, others will be modified and sometimes made "toothless," and a few will emerge in really workable form.

We listed many of the laws bearing on marketing in Chapter 5. The task is to translate these laws into understandings that marketing executives have as they make decisions in the areas of competitive relations, products, price, promotion, and channels of distribution. Figure 24-2 summarizes the major issues facing marketing management when making decisions. The specific dos and don'ts have already been reviewed in the appropriate chapters.

BUSINESS ACTIONS TOWARD SOCIALLY RESPONSIBLE MARKETING

Initially, many companies opposed consumerism and environmentalism. They thought the criticisms were either unjustified or unimportant. They resented consumer leaders who pointed an accusing finger and caused their sales to plummet. Companies resented consumer proposals that increased business costs more than

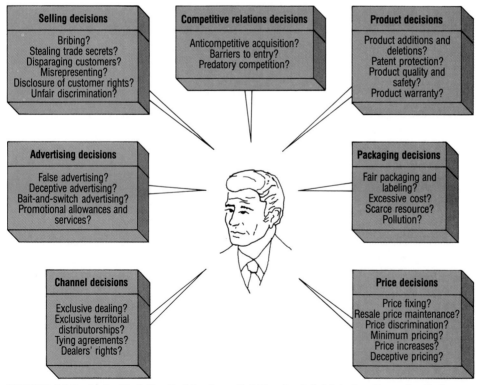

FIGURE 24-2 *Major Marketing Decision Areas that May Be Called into Question under the Law*

they helped the consumer. They felt that most consumers would not pay attention to unit pricing or ingredient labeling and that the proposals of advertising substantiation, corrective advertising, and counteradvertising would stifle advertising creativity. They felt that consumers were better off than ever, that large companies developed safe products and promoted them honestly, and that new consumer laws would lead to higher seller costs which would be passed on to consumers in higher prices.

At the present time most companies have come around to accepting the new consumer rights in principle. They might oppose specific pieces of legislation as not being the best way to solve particular consumer problems, but they recognize the consumer's right to information and protection. Many of these companies have developed constructive responses to consumerism and environmentalism in order to better serve consumer needs (see Exhibit 24-3).

Here we will examine responsible and creative business responses to the changing marketing environment. We first outline a concept of enlightened marketing and then consider marketing ethics.

A Concept of Enlightened Marketing

A concept of enlightened marketing grows out of the concept of enlightened capitalism. Two centuries ago Adam Smith, in his *Wealth of Nations,* attempted to show

---

EXHIBIT 24-3

CONSTRUCTIVE RESPONSES TO CONSUMERISM

In 1974 Professors Greyser and Diamond surveyed major companies to learn what steps they were taking to respond to consumerism. They found that 51 percent upgraded product quality and performance standards; 26 percent established industry product standards; 24 percent increased research commitments to better identify consumer wants and needs; 23 percent modified products for greater safety, ease of use, and repair; 22 percent made postsale follow-up calls on consumers; 20 percent supported industry self-regulation efforts; 19 percent made advertisements more informative; 16 percent developed owner's manuals on product use, care, and safety; 15 percent created new organizational positions to deal with consumer affairs; and 14 percent provided more informative product labeling.

In developing constructive responses, a major issue is how to bring consumer influence into the company decision-making process. In addition to consumer surveys and suggestion and complaint systems, further steps can be taken. The Stop and Shop Companies in Boston appointed a *consumer advisory board* consisting of twenty-five women shoppers who hold monthly meetings with the food chain's high-level managers. Several manufacturers have created a *consumer affairs unit* that handles customer inquiries and complaints, disseminates information to the customers, deals with consumer interest groups, and acts as a consumer ombudsman. The consumer affairs unit also carries out a *consumer affairs audit* to determine how well the company is serving customers and reports its findings to management.

Sources: Stephen A. Greyser and Steven L. Diamond, "Business Is Adapting to Consumerism," *Harvard Business Review,* September–October 1974, p. 57; and E. Patrick McGuire, *The Consumer Affairs Department: Organization and Functions* (New York: Conference Board, 1973).

that freedom of enterprise and private property would result in a dynamic and progressive economy. People pursue their self-interest and, if given the freedom to do this, they and the society will benefit. Entrepreneurs will put their resources into the areas of highest profit opportunity. Profits are usually high where needs must be met. As resources move in, costs are brought down through healthy competition. The system would be characterized by efficiency and flexibility. It would be guided by the "invisible hand" of the price system to produce needed goods without resort to government bureaucracy and direction.

This system, of course, can be abused. Companies that try to destroy competitors, raise barriers to entry, and gain the protection and favors of legislators are not competing fairly. The concept of enlightened capitalism calls upon businesspeople to recognize that their long-run interests are best served by self-reliant and honest activity within the rules of the system. Enlightened marketing holds that the company's marketing should support the best long-run performance of the marketing system. Enlightened marketing embodies five principles.

Consumer Oriented Marketing

The company should view and organize its marketing activities from the consumers' point of view. It should strive effectively and efficiently to sense, serve, and satisfy a defined set of needs of a defined group of customers. Consider the following example:

> Barat College, a women's college in Lake Forest, Illinois, published a college catalog that candidly spelled out Barat College's strong and weak points. Among the weak points it shared with applicants were the following: "An exceptionally talented student musician or mathematician . . . might be advised to look further for a college with top faculty and facilities in that field. . . . The full range of advanced specialized courses offered in a university will be absent. . . . The library collection is average for a small college, but low in comparison with other high-quality institutions."

The effect of "telling it like it is" is to build confidence so that applicants really know what they will find at Barat College, and to emphasize that Barat College will strive to improve its consumer value as rapidly as time and funds permit.

Innovative Marketing

The company should continuously seek real product and marketing improvements. The company that overlooks new and better ways to do things will eventually be challenged by a company that has found a better way. One of the best examples of an innovative marketer is Procter & Gamble:

> P&G invests heavily in research and development to find innovative solutions to consumer problems. As a result, most of its new products quickly become market leaders. P&G spent years developing a toothpaste that would effectively reduce tooth decay. When introduced, Crest quickly outdistanced less effective competitors, and with constant improvement, Crest has remained the market leader for over twenty years. P&G examined the shampoo market and found a benefit that many consumers wanted but no brand provided—dandruff control. Years of research produced Head and Shoulders, an instant market leader. Then

P&G looked at the paper products business. It found that new parents needed relief from the chores of handling and washing diapers. Again, after years of research, P&G found an innovative solution—a disposable paper diaper that most families could afford. The product—Pampers—immediately won market leadership.

Value Marketing

The company should put most of its resources into value-building marketing investments. A number of things marketers do—one-shot sales promotions, minor packaging changes, advertising puffery—may raise sales in the short run, but add less value than improvements in the product's quality, features, or convenience. Consider the following example of value marketing:

> Kundenkreditbank is a large and profitable chain of consumer banks in Germany. Its chairman, Stefan Kaminsky, decided that the bank should serve working-class customers and help them increase their total assets so they could enjoy a higher standard of living. Kaminsky's bank offers a high level of customer service and advice. Branches are kept small and employees are well trained. Employees know their customers as well as lawyers or doctors know their clients or patients. Customers can phone their banker at home in the evening if they have a pressing problem. When Kaminsky hires branch managers, he tells them: "I want you to understand that you will be in this branch for thirty years. These employees are your family. You will be rewarded for good performance through salary increases and bonus participation in the income earned by your branch." Since the branch managers are not rewarded by being moved to headquarters, they dig deep roots in their communities. The bank branch operates like a club—in one section is a table with consumer reports and cassettes to help consumers buy goods more carefully. Bank employees do everything possible to help consumers increase their wealth.

Sense-of-Mission Marketing

The company should define its mission in broad social terms rather than narrow product terms. When a company defines a social mission, company personnel feel better about their work and have a clearer sense of direction. Consider the mission statement of the International Minerals and Chemical Corporation:

> We're not merely in the business of selling our brand of fertilizer. We have a sense of purpose, a sense of where we are going. The first function of corporate planning is to decide what kind of business the company is in. Our business is *agricultural productivity*. We are interested in anything that affects plant growth, now and in the future.[27]

Societal Marketing

An enlightened company makes marketing decisions by considering *consumers' wants,* the *company's requirements, consumers' long-run interests,* and *society's long-run interests.* The company is aware that neglecting the last two considerations is a disservice to consumers and society.

Alert companies have recognized societal problems as presenting opportunities. As Drucker states: "Consumerism actually should be, must be, and I hope will be, the opportunity of marketing. This is what we in marketing have been waiting for."[28]

A societally oriented marketer wants to design not only pleasing but salutary products. The distinction is shown in Figure 24-3. Current products can be classified according to their degree of *immediate consumer satisfaction* and *long-run consumer benefit. Desirable products* combine high immediate satisfaction and high long-run benefits, such as tasty, nutritious breakfast foods. *Pleasing products* give high immediate satisfaction but may hurt consumers in the long run, such as cigarettes. *Salutary products* have low appeal but benefit consumers in the long run, such as low-phosphate detergents. Finally, *deficient products* have neither immediate appeal nor salutary qualities, such as bad-tasting patent medicine.

The challenge posed by pleasing products is that they sell extremely well, but may ultimately hurt the consumer. The product opportunity, therefore, is to add salutary qualities without diminishing the product's pleasing qualities. For example, Sears developed a phosphate-free laundry detergent that was very effective. The challenge posed by salutary products is to add some pleasing qualities so that they will become more desirable in the consumers' minds.

Marketing Ethics

Even conscientious marketers face many moral dilemmas. The best thing to do is often unclear. Since not all executives have fine moral sensitivity, companies need to develop corporate marketing policies. *Policies* are "broad, fixed guidelines that everyone in the organization must adhere to, and that are not subject to exception."[29] They cover distributor relations, advertising standards, customer service, pricing, product development, and general ethical standards.

The finest guidelines cannot anticipate or resolve all the difficult ethical situations confronting the marketer. Consider Howard Bowen's classic questions about the marketer's responsibilities:

> Should he conduct selling in ways that intrude on the privacy of people, for example, by door-to-door selling . . . ? Should he use methods involving ballyhoo, chances, prizes, hawking, and other tactics which are at least of doubtful good taste? Should he employ "high pressure" tactics in persuading people to buy? Should he try to hasten the obsolescence of goods by bringing out an endless succession of new models and new styles? Should he appeal to and attempt to strengthen the motives of materialism, invidious consumption, and "keeping up the the Joneses"?[30]

FIGURE 24-3
Classification of New Product Opportunities

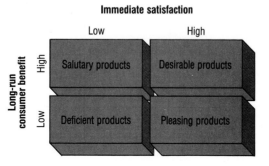

720   Seven   Extending Marketing

Table 24-1 lists fourteen difficult ethical situations marketers could face during their careers. If marketers favor the immediate sales-producing actions in all fourteen cases, their marketing behavior might well be described as immoral or

1. You work for a cigarette company and up to now have not been convinced that cigarettes cause cancer. A recent report has come across your desk that clearly establishes the connection between cigarette smoking and cancer. What would you do?

2. Your R&D department has modernized one of your products. It is not really "new and improved," but you know that putting this statement on the package and in the advertising will increase sales. What would you do?

3. You have been asked to add a stripped-down model to the low end of your line that could be advertised to attract customers. The product won't be very good, but the sales representatives could be depended upon to persuade buyers to buy the higher-priced units. You are asked to give the green light for developing this stripped-down version. What would you do?

4. You are interviewing a former product manager who just left a competitor's company. You are thinking of hiring him. He would be more than happy to tell you all the competitor's plans for the coming year. What would you do?

5. One of your dealers in an important territory has had family troubles recently and his sales have slipped. He was one of the company's top producers in the past. It is not clear how long it will take before his family trouble straightens out. In the meantime, many sales are being lost. There is a legal way to terminate the dealer's franchise and replace him. What would you do?

6. You have a chance to win a big account that will mean a lot to you and your company. The purchasing agent hinted that he would be influenced by a "gift." Your assistant recommends sending a fine color television set to his home. What would you do?

7. You have heard that a competitor has a new product feature that will make a big difference in sales. He will have a hospitality suite at the annual trade show and unveil this feature at a party thrown for his dealers. You can easily send a snooper to this meeting to learn what the new feature is. What would you do?

8. You are eager to win a big contract, and during sales negotiations you learn that the buyer is looking for a better job. You have no intention of hiring him, but if you hinted that you might, he would probably give you the order. What would you do?

9. You have to choose between three ad campaigns outlined by your agency for your new product. The first (A) is a soft-sell, honest information campaign. The second (B) uses sex-loaded emotional appeals and exaggerates the product's benefits. The third (C) involves a noisy, irritating commercial that is sure to gain audience attention. Preliminary tests show that the commercials are effective in the following order: C, B, and A. What would you do?

10. You are a marketing vice-president working for a beer company, and you have learned that a particularly lucrative state is planning to raise the minimum legal drinking age from 18 to 21. You have been asked to join other breweries in lobbying against this bill and make contributions. What would you do?

11. You want to interview a sample of customers about their reactions to a competitive product. It has been suggested that you invent an innocuous name like Marketing Research Institute and interview people. What would you do?

12. You produce an antidandruff shampoo that is effective with one application. Your assistant says that the product would turn over faster if the instructions on the label recommended two applications. What would you do?

13. You are interviewing a capable woman applicant for a job as sales representative. She is better qualified than the men just interviewed. At the same time, you suspect that some of your current salesmen will react negatively to her hiring, and you also know that some important customers may be ruffled. What would you do?

14. You are a sales manager in an encyclopedia company. A common way for encyclopedia representatives to get into homes is to pretend they are taking a survey. After they finish the survey, they switch to their sales pitch. This technique seems to be very effective and is used by most of your competitors. What would you do?

amoral. If they refuse to go along with *any* of the actions, they might be ineffective as marketing managers and unhappy because of the constant moral tension. Managers need a set of principles that will help them determine the moral gravity of each situation and how far they can go in good conscience.

But what principle should guide companies and marketing managers on issues of ethics and social responsibility? Goodpaster and Matthews describe three frames of reference for corporate responsibility.[31]

- *The Invisible Hand.* Under this framework, "the true and only social responsibilities of business organizations are to make profits and obey the laws . . . the common good is best served when each of us and our economic institutions pursue not the common good or moral purpose . . . but competitive advantage. Morality, responsibility, and conscience reside in the invisible hand of the free market system, not in the hands of the organizations within the system, much less the hands of managers within the system."

- *The Hand of Government.* Under this framework, "the corporation would have no moral responsibility beyond political and legal obedience . . . corporations are to seek objectives that are rational and purely economic. The regulatory hands of the law and the political process rather than the invisible hand of the marketplace turn these objectives to the common good."

- *The Hand of Management.* This framework "encourages corporations to exercise independent, noneconomic judgment over matters [of morals and ethics] that face them in their short- and long-term plans and operations." It calls for "moral reasoning and intent" from the corporation, and for managers to apply their individual morality to corporate decisions.

The first two philosophies suggest that issues of morality, ethics, responsibility, and conscience are decided by the free market or legal system, and that companies and their managers are not responsible for independent moral judgments. Companies can in good conscience do whatever the system allows. The third philosophy places responsibility not with the system, but in the hands of individual companies and mangers.

This more enlightened hand-of-management philosophy suggests that a corporation should have a "social conscience," and that companies and managers should apply high standards of ethics and morality when making corporate decisions, regardless of "what the system allows." History provides an endless list of examples of company actions which, though strictly legal and allowed by the market system, were blatantly irresponsible. Consider the following example:

> Prior to the Pure Food and Drug Act, the advertising for a diet pill promised that a person taking this pill could eat virtually anything at any time and still lose weight. Too good to be true? Actually the claim was quite true; the product lived up to its billing with frightening efficiency. It seems that the primary active ingredient in this "diet supplement" was tapeworm larvae. These larvae would develop in the intestinal tract and, of course, be well fed; the pill taker would in time, quite literally, starve to death.[32]

Each company and marketing manager must work out a philosophy of socially responsible and ethical behavior. Under the societal marketing concept, each manager must look beyond what is legal and allowed, and develop standards based on personal integrity, corporate conscience, and long-run consumer welfare. A clear and responsible philosophy will help the marketing manager deal with the many knotty questions posed by marketing and other human activities.

Marketing executives of the 1980s and 1990s will face many challenges. They will have abundant marketing opportunities because of technological advances in solar energy, home computers and robots, cable television, modern medicine, and new forms of transportation, recreation, and communication. At the same time, forces in the socioeconomic environment will increase the constraints under which marketing can be carried out. Those companies that are able to create new values and practice societally responsible marketing will have a world to conquer.

PRINCIPLES FOR PUBLIC POLICY TOWARD MARKETING

Finally, we want to propose several principles that might guide the formulation of public policy toward marketing. These principles represent the implicit assumptions underlying much of contemporary American marketing theory and practice.

The Principle of Consumer and Producer Freedom

To the maximum extent possible, marketing decisions should be made by consumers and producers under relative freedom.

This principle states that a high level of marketing freedom is important if a marketing system is to deliver a high standard of living. People are able to achieve satisfaction in *their* terms rather than in terms defined by someone else. It leads to a closer matching of products to desires and therefore the chance of greater fulfillment. Freedom for producers and consumers is the cornerstone of a dynamic marketing system. But further propositions are necessary to implement this freedom and prevent abuses.

The Principle of Curbing Potential Harm

The political system intervenes in producer or consumer freedom only if serious harm would occur in the absence of intervention.

To the extent possible, transactions freely entered into by producers and consumers are their private business, not the concern of third parties. The exception is transactions that *harm or threaten to harm one or both of the parties or a third party.* The principle of transactional harm is widely recognized as grounds for government intervention. The major issue is whether there is real and sufficient actual or potential harm to justify the intervention.

The Principle of Meeting Basic Needs

The marketing system should serve disadvantaged consumers as well as affluent consumers.

In a free-enterprise system, producers produce goods for markets that are willing and able to buy. If certain groups lack purchasing power, they may go without essential goods and services, causing harm to their physical or psychological well-being.

The solution calls for preserving the principle of producer and consumer freedom but using economic and political interventions to bring social output closer into line with need priorities. Through progressive income taxes, the surplus incomes of the rich are transferred to the poor through welfare payments and improved social services. The system reduces extremes of incomes. Most people would have basic amenities and look forward to more goods and services as something everyone would share to some extent.

The Principle of Economic Efficiency

The marketing system strives to supply goods and services efficiently and at low prices.

Every society is characterized by scarce resources in relation to the population's needs and wants. The extent to which these needs and wants can be satisfied depends upon the efficiency with which the scarce resources are used. Inefficiency or waste exists if the society could produce the same output with fewer resources or more output with the same resources. The cost of the inefficiency is measured by the satisfaction consumers would have enjoyed from the goods that were not produced because of the inefficiency.

Free economies rely on active producer competition and informed buyers to make a market efficient. Competitors are profit maximizers who develop products, prices, and marketing programs attuned to buyer needs and watch their costs carefully. Buyers are utility maximizers who are aware of competitive products, prices, and qualities and choose carefully. The presence of active competition and well-informed buyers keeps quality high and prices low.

The Principle of Innovation

The marketing system encourages authentic innovation.

An effective marketing system invests in continuous process and product innovation. Process innovation seeks to bring down the costs of production and distribution. Product innovation seeks to formulate new products to meet changing consumer needs and desires.

A distinction can be drawn between authentic and trivial innovation. Marketers are more concerned with the market's acceptance of new features and styles than with whether the innovation represents a genuine contribution to human welfare. Much innovation is really *imitation* of other brands, with a slight difference to provide a talking point. The consumer may face ten brands in a product class that are very similar. This disproportion between the number of brands and the number of really different products is known as the problem of *brand proliferation*. An effective marketing system encourages real product innovation and differentiation to meet the preferences of different market segments.

The Principle of Consumer Education and Information

The marketing system invests heavily in consumer education and information to increase long-run consumer satisfaction and welfare.

The principle of economic efficiency requires public investment in consumer education and information. This is particularly important where goods and brands are confusing because of their plentifulness and conflicting claims.

Ideally, manufacturers would provide adequate information about their products. Private consumer groups and the government would disseminate product information and evaluation and would lean hard on manufacturers to provide better information. Students in public schools would take courses in consumer education to acquire better buying skills.

The Principle of Consumer Protection

The marketing system must supplement consumer education and information with consumer protection in certain product and market practice areas.

Consumer education and information cannot do the whole job of protecting consumers. Modern products are so complex that even trained consumers cannot buy them with confidence. Consumers do not know whether a color television set has too much radiation, whether a new automobile is designed with adequate safety, and whether a new drug product is without dangerous side effects. A government agency has to review and judge the safety levels of various foods, drugs, toys, appliances, fabrics, automobiles, and housing.

Consumer protection also covers production and marketing activities that are environmentally destructive. The consumers may buy the products but fail to understand the environmental consequences. Consumer protection also covers the prevention of deceptive practices and certain high-pressure selling techniques where consumers would be defenseless.

The assumption behind these seven principles is that the goal of the marketing system is not to maximize producers' profits or total consumption or consumer choice, but rather to maximize life quality. *Life quality* means meeting basic needs, having available varied and good-quality products, and enjoying the physical and cultural environment. Since the marketing system has a major impact on the quality of life, it must be managed on principles consistent with improving the quality of life.

■ Summary

A marketing system should function to sense, serve, and satisfy consumer needs and enhance the quality of consumers' lives. In endeavoring to meet consumer needs, businesspeople may take certain actions that are not to everyone's liking or benefit. Marketing executives should be aware of the main criticisms.

Marketing's impact on consumer welfare has been criticized for high prices, deceptive practices, high-pressure selling, shoddy or unsafe products, planned obsolescence, and poor service to disadvantaged consumers. Marketing's impact on society has been criticized for excessive materialism, false wants, insufficient social goods, cultural pollution, and excessive political power.

Marketing's impact on business competition has been criticized for anticompetitive acquisition, high barriers to entry, and predatory competition.

These felt abuses of the marketing system have given rise to citizen action movements, specifically consumerism and environmentalism. *Consumerism* is an organized social movement seeking to strengthen the rights and power of consumers relative to sellers. Resourceful marketers will recognize it as an opportunity to serve consumers better by providing more consumer information, education, and protection. *Environmentalism* is an organized social movement seeking to minimize the harm done by marketing practices to the environment and quality of life. It calls for intervening in consumer wants when their satisfaction would create too much environmental cost.

Citizen action has led to the passage of many laws to protect consumers in the area of product safety, truth-in-packaging, truth-in-lending, and truth-in-advertising.

Although many businesses initially opposed these social movements and laws, most of them now recognize a need for positive consumer information, education, and protection. Some companies have pursued a policy of enlightened marketing based on the principles of consumer orientation, innovation, value creation, social mission, and societal orientation. These companies have formulated company policies and guidelines to help their executives deal with moral dilemmas.

Future public policy must be guided by a set of principles that will improve the marketing system's contribution to the quality of life. The set of principles calls for relative consumer and producer freedom, intervention only where there is potential harm, arrangements to meet basic consumer needs adequately, the practice of economic efficiency, emphasis on authentic innovation, and the provision of consumer education, information, and protection.

■ Questions for Discussion

1. Which two criticisms of marketing's impact on individual consumer welfare are the most legitimate? Briefly defend your position.

2. Those critics of marketing's impact on society are really condemning our American business system rather than just the area of marketing. Comment.

3. The Federal Trade Commission is proposing to restrict mergers between large (over $2 billion in sales) corporations. Which criticisms of market-

ing's impact on other businesses would this help to alleviate? Why?

4. How does *consumerism* differ from *environmentalism?* Which poses the greater threat to marketing? Explain.

5. Discuss the five principles of enlightened marketing.

6. Ethical issues facing marketing will decrease in the 1990s. Comment.

7. If you were the marketing manager at Dow Chemical Company, how would you deal with the principle of curbing potential harm with regard to water pollution?

8. How might the scarcity of natural resources including energy affect the principles of economic efficiency and innovation in the future?

9. What relationship exists between the principle of consumer education and information and the principle of consumer protection. Which will be the dominant one in the next ten years? Why?

■ *References*

1. PAUL W. STEWART and J. FREDERICK DEWHURST with LOUIS FIELD, *Does Distribution Cost Too Much?* (New York: Twentieth Century Fund, 1939).

2. Ibid., p. 348.

3. JESSICA MITFORD, *The American Way of Death* (New York: Simon & Schuster, 1963).

4. Excerpts from THEORDORE LEVIT, "The Morality (?) of Advertising," *Harvard Business Review,* July–August 1970, pp. 84–92.

5. "Confessions of a Diaper Salesman," *Fortune,* March 1949.

6. "Rattles, Pings, Dents, Leaks, Creaks–And Costs," *Newsweek,* November 25, 1968, p. 92.

7. Ibid.

8. "The Breakfast of Fatties?" *Chicago Today,* July 24, 1970.

9. GERALD B. TALLMAN, "Planned Obsolescence as a Marketing and Economic Policy," in *Advancing Marketing Efficiency,* L. H. Stockman, ed. (Chicago: American Marketing Association, 1958), pp. 27–39.

10. DAVID CAPLOVITZ, *The Poor Pay More* (New York: Free Press, 1963).

11. A speech delivered at Vanderbilt University Law School, reported in *Marketing News,* August 1, 1968, pp. 11, 15.

12. Ibid.

13. For further reading, see ALAN R. ANDREASEN, *The Disadvantaged Consumer* (New York: Free Press, 1975).

14. JOHN KENNETH GALBRAITH, *The New Industrial State* (Boston: Houghton Mifflin, 1967), p. 200.

15. HERBERT MARCUSE, *One Dimensional Man* (Boston: Beacon Press, 1964), pp. 4–5.

16. JOHN KENNETH GALBRAITH, *The Affluent Society* (Boston: Houghton Mifflin, 1958), p. 255.

17. RAYMOND A. BAUER and STEPHEN A. GREYSER, *Advertising in America: The Consumer View* (Boston: Graduate School of Business Administration, Harvard University, 1968).

18. From an advertisement for *Fact* magazine, which does not carry advertisements.

19. MARK HANAN, "Corporate Growth through Venture Management," *Harvard Business Review,* January–February 1969, p. 44.

20. FTC v. Procter & Gamble, 386 U.S. 568 (1967).

21. See MORRIS ADELMAN, "The A & P Case: A Study in Applied Economic Theory," *Quarterly Journal of Economics,* May 1949, p. 238.

22. For more details, see PHILIP KOTLER, "What Consumerism Means for Marketers," *Harvard Business Review,* May–June 1972, pp. 48–57. Also see PAUL N. BLOOM and STEPHEN A. GREYSER, "The Maturing of Consumerism," *Harvard Business Review,* November–December 1981, pp. 130–39.

23. RACHEL CARSON, *Silent Spring* (Boston: Houghton Mifflin, 1962).

24. PAUL R. EHRLICH and ANN H. EHRLICH, *Population, Resources, Environment: Issues in Human Ecology* (San Francisco: W. H. Freeman, 1970).

25. DONNELLA H. MEADOWS, DENNIS L. MEADOWS, JORGEN RANDERS, and WILLIAM W. BEHRENS III, *The Limits to Growth* (New York: Universe Books, 1972).

26. See NORMAN KANGUN, "Environmental Problems and Marketing: Saint or Sinner?" in *Marketing Analysis for Societal Problems,* Jagdish N. Sheth and Peter L. Wright, eds. (Urbana: University of Illinois, 1974).

27. GORDON O. PEHRSON, quoted in "Flavored Algae from the Sea?" *Chicago Sun-Times,* February 3, 1965, p. 54.

28. PETER DRUCKER, "The Shame of Marketing," *Marketing/Communications,* August 1969, pp. 60, 64.

29. EARL L. BAILEY, *Formulating the Company's Marketing Policies: A Survey* (New York: Conference Board, Experiences in Marketing Management, No. 19, 1968), p. 3.

30. HOWARD R. BOWEN, *Social Responsibilities of the Businessman* (New York: Harper & Row, Pub., 1953), p. 215.

31. KENNETH E. GOODPASTER and JOHN B. MATTHEWS, JR., "Can a Corporation Have a Conscience?" *Harvard Business Review,* January–February 1982, pp. 132–41.

32. DAN R. DALTON and RICHARD A. COSIER, "The Four Faces of Social Responsibility," *Business Horizons,* May–June 1982, pp. 19–27.

CASE 18

NIKE, INC.

The meteoric rise of Nike, named for the Greek goddess of Victory, to America's number-one running shoe marketer was built on the jogging boom. Its entrepreneurial managers operated rather informally in trying to keep up with the demand for athletic shoes and apparel. In 1985, following this period of rapid growth, annual sales volume approaches $1 billion and the jogging boom appears to have peaked. More formal planning and management based on analysis of the worldwide athletic shoe and apparel market are needed to help the company catch its second wind and hold its position in the race.

As the baby boomers mature in the 1980s and 1990s, the 25- to 45-year-old population group will grow and create demand changes for the quality athletic shoe industry. Baby boomers grew up wearing gym shoes as everyday leisure wear. However, as adults they may be less inclined to purchase these shoes for everyday wear. At the same time, baby boomers are associated with growing upscale tastes, higher disposable income, and a concern for physical fitness. This trend could expand the potential market for upscale athletic shoes, apparel, and equipment.

Consumer attitudes towards physical fitness are changing. Running has been displaced to a certain extent by aerobics and health clubs. Physcial fitness is becoming a group activity, which could cause a decline in the solitary sport of running. Consumers are looking for more diverse fitness programs. There are increasing numbers of participants in sports and exercise programs such as aerobics, raquetball, Nautilus machines, and cycling. Reebok and other smaller shoe companies have capitalized on the popularity of aerobics by introducing a new shoe designed especially for aerobics. Nike has been slow to develop specialty shoes. Nike's late entry into the aerobics segment was unsuccessful.

Along with these changes in physical fitness habits has come a change in athletic apparel needs, an important market segment for Nike. In five years this segment is expected to equal Nike's sales in the shoe segment. Currently apparel sales account for 8 percent of Nike's total sales. Children's shoes, largely a fashion segment, account for 15 percent. Nike may be able to transfer its high-quality image from shoes to apparel.

Nike's success was built on the running shoes. Nike started in 1962 as the exclusive United States distributor for Tiger, an inexpensive Japanese running shoe. Robert Knight, a former miler at the University of Oregon, began his business career by selling Tiger shoes out of the trunk of his car at high school track meets. He soon broke with Tiger over a disputed franchise, but began to have specialized shoes of his own design made in factories in Taiwan and South Korea.

With the advent of the jogging explosion, athletic shoes like Nike's became part of the uniform of the "Me Decade" of the 1970s. Nike's image and culture fit the period. Nike's advertising showed the solitary runner against the backdrop of clogged city traffic. This advertising appealed especially to the youth market. With the tremendous increase in popularity came a tremendous increase in sales. Nike's annual sales growth averaged 100 percent throughout most of the 1970s until they reached $694 million in 1981, with Nike replacing Adidas as the largest-selling quality athletic shoe.

The athletic shoe market is maturing and becoming more competitive. In 1983, domestic market growth rate per year slowed to 8 percent versus 14 percent for each of the three preceding years. The running "boom" that originated in the 1970s has peaked. The heart attack death of Jim Fixx, author of the *Joy of Running,* may have signaled the peak of the jogging fad.

Predicting that "We see only a couple of more years of strong growth for [running] shoes in the U.S.," Nike began to diversify. In 1981, Nike introduced a line of wearing apparel and children's wear. It also launched an effort to enter the international market, opening offices in West Germany and Japan. All three efforts experienced rapid sales growth, with the new ventures making up 39 percent of Nike's sales.

Sales of both adult and children's shoes in 1984 showed little growth over the previous year. Nike's new ventures were not entirely successful. While apparel sales had grown 50 percent in 1984, profits were below average. Nike found the international markets increasingly difficult to penetrate. In Europe, Nike had to compete with West German based Adidas and Puma, which between them had 95 percent of the European market. In both Europe and Japan, Nike had to contend with cultures where jogging had not become a popular pastime. The results were 1984's disappointing performance.

Nike is best known for its running shoes, which are specially designed with the aid of professional athletes in Nike's sport laboratory. Nike is considered the shoe for the serious runner, although it is often worn as part of leisure wear, especially by teenagers. Nike also has a line of tennis and gym shoes, which make up a major portion of its sales. The firm has also had great success in its line of children's shoes and in leisure apparel. However, it is Nike's running shoes that have maintained the firm's image of high quality. Within the running shoe segments, Nike's primary competition has come from specialized firms such as New Balance and Puma. Nike currently sells more than 500 different types of shoes.

Nike's current channels of distribution are mostly smaller specialty sporting goods stores such as Athlete's Feet and Footlocker. On-premise expertise by salespeople is a major factor in the sale of athletic shoes because of the wide variety of styles and brands. Currently, Nike makes little use of larger retailers such as Sears, although it does sell some of its less expensive brands through J. C. Penney.

Competitive distribution channels are concentrated in the same specialty sporting goods stores as Nike. Converse is an exception. It sells 30 percent of its products through nonspecialty outlets. Specialty athletic stores, department stores, shoe stores, and discount stores all sell quality athletic shoes, with the specialty stores carrying the high-end shoes. Most of the outlets sell athletic apparel as well.

Retailers have had little channel power because the products are sold through a variety of different outlet types. Specialty outlets are beginning to exercise greater influence as competition for limited shelf space increases, and the size of most retailers will increase their influence as competition becomes more intense.

Nike uses professional athletes to endorse its product. Nike signed the few major running stars, and the endorsements were a major factor in Nike's success in its first ten years. Nike has continued this practice in other segments, using tennis star John McEnroe to endorse its tennis shoe, and basketball star Michael Jordan to endorse its basketball shoe.

Nike's current promotional budget is concentrated in endorsements by athletes and sponsorship of sporting events. Of the $18 million budget, $16 million goes toward endorsement and sponsorships. It does not have a strong advertising campaign for its products. Nike had developed a high awareness for its "swoosh" logo, but not for its specific products.

Nike's previous advertising campaigns emphasized the solitary, self-involved individual versus the impersonal, machine-centered society. This theme appealed to runners. It had also a broad appeal to the "rebellious youth" of the 1970s.

Nike's main competitors in the quality *athletic shoe market* are Converse and Adidas. Nike currently holds 32 percent of the $1.9 billion U.S. market, with Converse and Adidas holding 9 percent each. Nike had approximately $614 million in sales, while the other two have around $180 million. All three firms compete within every market segment of the athletic shoe market, and offer a line of wearing apparel. There are also numerous smaller competitors, who compete in specialized market niches. These smaller firms have grown rapidly; seven of them had recent sales in excess of $50 million.

Converse specializes in basketball, tennis, and gym shoes. It has great appeal for teenagers with products including a rainbow-colored "break-dancing" shoe. Converse recently entered the running shoe segment with a new line of high-quality shoes but has had difficulty in establishing a high-quality image.

Adidas is the world's largest quality athletic shoe company, with sales of all product lines exceeding $2 billion in 1983. It competes in every segment, although it is also best known for its gym shoes. Adidas is also the largest seller of athletic apparel and is the largest firm in the international market. Apparel and international sales together make up 80 percent of Adidas' sales, versus 24 percent for Nike.

In terms of pricing, all the major firms have a wide range. The prices for Nike products range from $15.95 to $125. Smaller firms tend to have comparable pricing for all their products and also have a wide range.

Industry rivalry is currently relatively moderate. This has come about because of the strong brand identification needed to be successful within this industry. As the athletic shoe market matures, firms will begin competing outside their current niches. This competition will lead to greater competition for market share and shelf space.

The industry holds little attraction for new firms of significant size because of its mature stage and the need to build a consumer franchise. However, smaller firms currently within the industry could grow at the expense of the established large firms, if market and fashion trends continue away from running and other current fitness sports. Competition in the athletic shoe market is currently moderate because of the relatively high barriers to entry as well as rapid growth. However, as the athletic segments mature and fashion trends become more conservative, competition is likely to become much more intense as firms seek to expand their current market niches.

The competitive environment in Europe is less favorable for Nike than in the domestic market. Adidas and Puma dominate the athletic shoe market in Europe, with a market share in West Germany of 95 percent. Nike must also compete with a number of U.S. firms such as Pony and New Balance, which are also seeking to enter the European market. Nike has had to make large investments in distributors and manufacturing plants just to achieve its current modest penetration into the European market. There are tariffs and other barriers to entry within the Common Market. The "jogging boom" that carried Nike's sales in the United States never materialized in Europe. Nike is betting that such a boom will take place.

The competitive environment in Asia is somewhat more favorable. Japan's Tiger athletic shoe is the only major Asian competitor. It does not dominate the market as Adidas does in Europe. Ninety-five percent of Nike's shoes are already produced in Asia. Nike could save transportation cost. Nike Japan is a joint venture between Nike and Japan's sixth-largest trading company. This joint venture gives Nike instant recognition and contacts within Japan. Nike has a high-quality image due to its strong identification with major U.S. sports such as tennis, baseball, and golf. There is a growing jogging trend in Japan. This follows other sports that have moved from the United States into Japan.

How should Nike change its product line? Why?

Should Nike make an aggressive effort to develop the Asian market?

What should it do about the European market?

CASE 19

SEARS ROEBUCK & CO.: SEARS FINANCIAL NETWORK

Sears Financial Network is offering a broad range of consumer financial services through its financial network centers in nearly 300 Sears stores, with another 200 or more to be opened in the next few years. Sears is counting on attracting many of the nearly 40 million households that regularly shop at Sears to its in-store financial centers, which bring together in one location representatives of the Allstate Insurance Group, Coldwell Banker Real Estate Group, and Dean Witter Financial Services Group. In California, Sears Savings Bank is also represented. While store hours are observed, the center and its representatives operate independently of the store management, as Allstate in-store agents and concession operators, much like the optical departments have done in the past.

Management now needs to determine potential customer groups; what consumer financial services it should offer and how they should be packaged; and how the centers and individual services should be promoted. Prudent planning calls for initially determining what would be sound for Sears before being overly concerned with legal restrictions and requirements because they vary from area to area and are subject to change. This is especially important in this turbulent industry where changes are in the offing, yet planning is for the long haul.

Sears sees financial services as a growth opportunity suited to its capabilities and competitive strengths. It is also attractive because it goes beyond but builds upon the current business. Historically, Sears has continued to grow for over a hundred years by finding new major growth opportunities that took the company *beyond* but did not abandon the existing business. In each case it took an outsider to provide the vision needed to see the new growth opportunity.

In the 1890s, when Richard Sears was having difficulty in keeping his retail business afloat, Julius Rosenwald, a supplier of apparel to whom Sears owed money, saw an opportunity to become "buyer for the American Farmer." He became a part of Sears Roebuck, and the mail order concept launched the company on an era of tremendous prosperity. By the 1920s America's economic and social structure had again changed drastically. The new growth opportunity seen by General Wood, another outsider, lay in the rapidly growing urban areas populated by an increasingly prosperous working class and newly emerging white-collar middle class. To serve these new consumers, Wood developed a nationwide system of retail stores using the mail order plants as jobbers and the catalog as a supplement to retail selling. A second enormously prosperous period ensued for Sears.

The American economy in its present stage is characterized by the inability of existing institutions to serve the country's growing needs for more efficient, more accessible, and more adequate financial and real estate services. This was seen by Arthur Wood, still another outsider who joined the firm as legal counsel and served as chairman just prior to Edward R. Telling. It was Mr. Telling who was responsible for working out the financial services concept and its implementation. The confidence in which Sears is held by the American people is perhaps its greatest asset, one that will serve it well in fields where trust and confidence are essential.

Customers now find the Sears Financial Network centers to be a group of three separate but contiguous offices, each handling its own service—insurance, real estate, or stock and bond investments. Discounts on store merchandise are offered by Coldwell Banker in some situations. Consumer bank services are available in some California stores, and Sears is making every effort to acquire "consumer banks" and make this service available in other states where the legality is now in question.

J. C. Penney and K mart are in various stages of planning and offering financial centers.

K mart is considering adding several banking and brokerage services to a broad range of insurance offerings it tested in 15 Texas and Florida stores. The exact mix of K mart in-store investment services is still being determined but "will look pretty similar to Sears," the executive VP-finance of K mart is reported to have said. Ten "financial marts" in K mart stores were opened in the San Diego area in early 1985 jointly with First Nationwide, the nation's sixth-largest savings and loan. It was approved by the Federal Home Loan Board to operate "limited service" branches in K mart stores. The branches offer money-market accounts, individual-retirement accounts, and short-term certificates of deposit.

In developing the full potential of the financial services opportunity, the first step is to develop each financial service independently, except for common location, common advertising, and legally permissible cross-promotions. In this connection, Allstate's strategy should be considered for possible use by Coldwell Banker and Dean Witter in building business through their financial center activities.

The nucleus of the financial network is Allstate Insurance Company's strong customer base in life, home, and auto insurance, which was developed through a strategy centered on in-store company agents, who after building a list or "book" of clients, moved out into more widely disbursed new Allstate neighborhood sales offices, taking their clients with them. This opened the way for newly recruited agents who went through the process and thereby continued to expand the company's customer base. Presently it is not clear whether this process could or should be used with the stock brokerage or real estate services.

Financial services Sears might consider offering or inviting concessionaires such as H&R Block to operate are tax preparation, legal, financial planning and asset management. Clustering these affords a one-stop or financial supermarket arrangement that may be more convenient for customers and increase the frequency of visit to the financial center because of the breadth of services available. Where no Sears bank is available, "Cash Stations" or automatic tellers could be included by arrangement with a bank network, which again may increase customer convenience and frequency of visits.

While possible long-term benefits from "bundling" the financial services into a package, maybe including merchandise, must wait until the individual services are firmly established and the legal, competitive, and operational problems are clarified, it is important to develop several scenarios or views of what the future will be like and how Sears can provide the needed individual and integrated services to consumers at a profit.

Transition plans are also necessary. Here is one possible plan. Consumers in the Sears target group for the most part decide specific financial transactions one at a time, with only a rough idea of an overall plan. They may seek advice from friends, relatives, lawyers, and others, but make the decisions and administer their affairs themselves. There is an opportunity to develop a financial planning service to help customers coordinate their financial transactions. Trust and confidence are essential. A *single service-based planner* such as an insurance agent or a stockbroker is inclined to overemphasize his or her specific service and is frequently suspected of giving biased advice. Financial planning lends itself to leading customers to services. If Sears can organize such a service so that customer and company interest are *mutually benefitted,* it could use the service as the core of its consumer financial services business. Ignoring for the moment the legal aspects and thinking of what would be economically sound for Sears and its customers, possible plans must be offered and analyzed as a basis for moving into the future.

1. What are the strengths and weaknesses of the present and suggested Sears Financial Network plan?

2. What is the underlying marketing strategy being used? Try to state it in as few words as possible.

3. What changes in the marketing aspects of the program would you recommend? Why?

CASE 20

DART & KRAFT INC.: TUPPERWARE

The Tupperware division, one of the company's star performers in the 1970s, with an annual growth rate of 17 percent, was slowed down by economic and social changes in the early 1980s. It now faces the problem of formulating a marketing plan to avoid the threat and capitalize on the opportunities created by environmental change.

Since its establishment in 1945 by Earl Tupper, a Du Pont chemist, Tupperware has emerged as the leading manufacturer of plastic housewares. Originally marketing a line of plastic bowls with exceptional seals through supermarkets and department stores, Tupper had minimal success until he adopted the home party plan method of distribution, first developed by Stanley Home Products in the 1930s. Demonstration was the key to making the products' unique composition and seal discernible to the consumer. Tupperware grew rapidly and was acquired by Dart Industries in 1958. Tupperware accounted for 9 percent of its parent's sales and 26 percent of its profits in 1982, but recent results have been much less impressive. International sales account for 57 percent of Tupperware's revenues and are projected to grow at 16 percent per year, versus 12 percent for the domestic market. Tupperware has specifically targeted those countries where growth in disposable income will support increasing refrigeration purchases. The company offers two reasons for its recent less than satisfactory performance: the effect of translating foreign results into U.S. dollars, and the increasing difficulty of recruiting independent sales personnel.

Domestically, the tightening of retail shelf space together with low barriers to entry have caused the direct selling industry to experience a sharp rise in the number of companies vying for a slower-growing pool of individuals willing to work as independent contractors. Despite the tendency for representatives to take on the products of more than one firm, direct sellers are faced with a dealer shortage. The ability to attract new recruits is the primary determinant of growth in direct sales. Consequently, competition for competent salespeople is intensifying, threatening Tupperware's position as one of the most attractive direct sales employers. Mary Kay Cosmetics and Avon are stepping up incentives and compensation packages. A similar response by Tupperware would certainly lower its profit margins. These developments cast doubt on the wisdom of continuing exclusively with party plan marketing. Some industry observers fear that the party plan is nearing saturation as an effective means of distribution. While the influx of new direct sale enterprises has been rapid, some competitors, like Rubbermaid, have shifted to selling through stores.

Underlying demographic and economic shifts are complicating the challenges Tupperware faces. A strengthening economy is: (1) depressing the need for women to supplement the family income and (2) offering more opportunities for full-time employment. Fewer women are home during the day or are willing to devote spare time to direct sale parties. In addition, Tupperware's family-user base is a shrinking percentage of the population.

Tupperware manufactures high-quality plastics that carry a lifetime guarantee. The primary Tupperware line is containers for storing and serving food, but Tupperware has also introduced toys and other household products, including planters and decorative shelving units. The low repurchase rate implied by the lifetime guarantee, coupled with the high percentage of sales made to repeat customers, indicates the necessity for continual improvement and change in the product line. New products are introduced every 60 days as older, slower-moving products are phased out with corresponding frequency. The total product line remains constant at 125 products. New product ideas come from three sources: Tupperware's own research and development laboratories, independent inventors, and dealers and hostesses. Dealers and hostesses are also asked for suggestions on new colors, sizes, or uses for current products. Product improvements are also important. The development of a new polymer in 1979, making Tupperware products dishwasher-safe, and the adoption of the "instant seal" technology developed by MIT in 1970 give Tupperware a quality advantage over its competition. In 1984 Modular Mates were introduced. This is a line of compact, stackable containers aimed at smaller families that have less space to live in. Cookware for microwave ovens was being developed and plans made to tap this fast-growing market.

All sales are made at parties on a cash basis only. Because most customers pay by check, Tupperware has been able to keep an accurate record of exactly who its consumers are and how frequently they purchase. There is seldom an across-the-board change in the product line prices; the majority of products remain priced close to the original price, which is set with a high margin, typically much higher than those of competing products.

Tupperware's sole channel of distribution is its multilevel field sales organization. There are four levels in the Tupperware sales pyramid: dealers, unit managers, distributors, and regional vice presidents. *Dealers* form the broad base of the sales structure, and are the most fundamental element of the party system; they are almost entirely women. Dealers recruit friends and acquaintances to hostess Tupperware Home Parties, where they perform product demonstrations and take orders. Hostesses are compensated with a gift. In addition to a 35 percent sales commission, dealers also earn prizes for recruiting new dealers. Because most women have several distinct groups of friends, each party introduces the dealer to new users and paves the way to future parties and new recruits. When friendship networks are exhausted, dealers recruit hostesses through "friend finding," the door-to-door dating of parties.

Promotion to *unit manager* requires additional sales training as well as achievement of specified levels of sales and recruitment. Managers work full-time running parties, training dealers, and keeping records. The ratio of unit managers to dealers is roughly 1:12. They receive a commission of 3 to 5 percent of retail sales in their unit and are supplied with a new car every two years.

Distributors are the third level of the organization and are hand-picked from the ranks of unit managers. They are typically a husband-wife team. Distributorship requires a substantial investment in inventory and warehouse rental, which Tupperware helps to finance. Distributors oversee several units and are responsible for the costs associated with shipping, weekly rallies, and incentive gifts for their "territories." As compensation they receive a 20 percent commission on the retail sales in their area. Tupperware sets sales goals for its distributors, who in turn are allowed considerable latitude in designing incentives to encourage dealers and managers to meet these figures. Distribution costs account for over 50 percent of retail sales.

On the highest level of the Tupperware sales hierarchy are its twelve *regional vice-presidents,* the only members of the sales organization who are company employees. The RVP are men; they receive annual salaries of over $100,000.

Salesforce recruitment and motivation are essential to the execution of Tupperware's marketing strategy. At each level of the sales organization, the corporation employs state-of-the-art training and motivational techniques based on recognition and reward. The system encourages both sales and recruitment volume. Though turnover in direct selling operations is high, Tupperware turnover is considerably below the industry average. The company attributes its success to a family approach, which attempts to involve the dealers' husbands in the social and remunerative aspects of the business. In addition to being a channel of distribution, the salesforce provides Tupperware with a largely effective and efficient management information system. Unit managers and distributors prepare weekly reports to be phoned into regional vice-presidents, giving top management timely sales information. Promotions are then tailored to current market conditions.

Tupperware currently uses no advertising directed at the consumer. Management believes that one of the benefits of direct selling is that it precludes the need for advertising to support consumer awareness. The strength of the Tupperware brand name supports this view. However, advertising and promotion directed at prospective and current dealers, managers, and distributors are used heavily. In addition to media advertising (television, women's magazines) designed to increase recruiting levels, promotional efforts include sweepstakes, free trips for dealers, sales rallies, the Tupperware Jubilee, prizes for meeting sales and recruiting quotas, and hostess gifts.

Tupperware competes for both direct selling recruits and consumers for its products. As with many direct selling enterprises, there is considerable overlap between these groups. Only the larger direct sellers have the resources to compete with Tupperware's compensation and incentive schemes; these include Avon, Mary Kay, and Amway. The shortage of independent contractors is causing major sellers to compete more vigorously for recruits. Mary Kay's entire 1984 advertising and promotion budget was funneled into recruit-oriented programs. Avon recently overhauled its compensation system to allow sales leaders to earn commissions on the sales of the representatives they manage.

To the extent that Tupperware is placed in the broadly defined food storage category, its products compete with a wide range of substitutes: aluminum foil, plastic wrap, and the reusable containers in which various food processors package their products. There are few national brand names in the plastic housewares market with its estimated annual sales of $2.2 billion, of which one-half is in the dinnerware/tableware/kitchenware category. Tupperware is the leader with 17 percent, followed by Rubbermaid with 8 percent of the market and Eagle with an even smaller share. The remainder is divided among small regional producers, many of them in the private label or generic business. Rubbermaid's switch to selling through supermarkets leaves Tupperware virtually alone as a party plan marketer of plastic housewares. Moreover, Rubbermaid, Eagle, and other competitors have become even more competitive by stepping up their efforts to sell expanded lines in supermarkets.

Tupperware's options in meeting the present situation include one or more of the following:

1. Improve the effectiveness of the present party plan approach.
2. Sell through one or more types of retail stores, such as supermarkets, mass merchandising outlets, department stores, or specialty housewares stores.
3. Mail order marketing to selected segments through company direct mail campaigns, specialty catalogs by the company, specialty catalogs of other companies.
4. Telephone or telemarketing program.
5. Electronic home shopping program through an interactive system now available in some sections of the United States but more widely used in Great Britain.

In considering the various options, you have been asked to study the underlying forces leading to Tupperware's present situation and trends with respect to them as a basis for recommendations to management.

1. What recommendations would you make to the Tupperware management for improvement of marketing in the United States?
2. What methods of retailing should Tupperware use? How? Why?
3. What problems and opportunities would you expect Tupperware to face in its use of the party plan in international markets?

APPENDIX: THE DIRECT SELLING INDUSTRY

Over 400 firms utilize the direct sales channel of distribution, bypassing retail outlets with in-home placement by direct salespeople. This channel encompasses a wide variety of items, including cosmetics, books, plastic housewares, jewelry, toys, and vitamins, and some notable firms—Tupperware, Avon, Mary Kay, Stanley Home Products. Three forms of direct sales are used: repetitive, nonrepetitive, and the party plan. Repetitive sales include all products that are consumed on a regular basis and thus have a high purchase frequency. Nonrepetitive sales include consumer durables, such as vacuum cleaners. The third form (party plan) is used in 15 percent of all direct selling. Each year three-quarters of all U.S. households are contacted by direct salespeople; about 50 percent of those calls result in purchases. For some products, such as housewares, 83 percent of contacts result in purchases. The party plan is particularly effective because it is designed to fit the schedule of both dealer and hostess. This overcomes the major objection to other direct selling methods—that sales calls are often made at inconvenient times. Some consumers, however, are still reluctant to participate in party plans; they feel that attendance at a party is a commitment to purchase.

Companies are attracted to direct selling for its lower operating costs and greater flexibility relative to conventional mass merchandising. Distributors and salespeople are independent contractors. Therefore a large percentage of the company's promotional and distribution costs are variable, tied directly to sales in the form of commissions and incentives. Fixed costs are low. There are no pension or insurance expenses, paperwork is limited, and advertising is primarily word-of-mouth.

The number of direct selling firms has risen from 250 in 1980 to over 400 firms in 1983, an increase of 30 to 35 percent. This growth can be attributed to a number of factors. Shelf space in retail stores has become increasingly limited due to product proliferation, and store managers give preference to "proven products." The rising costs of capital and operating expenses such as advertising have made direct selling operations relatively attractive. Last, retail firms are using direct sales to supplement store sales. This recent growth in direct selling firms has resulted in mounting competition between direct sales companies for effective long-term salespeople. Productivity gains per rep are difficult to attain and maintain. New recruits tend to be more productive, but are also harder to find. Turnover among direct salespeople exceeds 100 percent.

When consumers compare direct selling with other methods of shopping, one out of four indicates an interest in direct selling. Direct purchase is most attractive to suburban/ rural residents, women, families, and to some extent blacks. But the public holds certain reservations about direct selling. Consumers believe that they end up buying things they do not really need, that prices are much higher than for similar products purchased at retail, and that in-home presentations do not permit the prospective purchaser to comparison shop.

The success of direct selling companies is directly related to the number and productivity of their salespeople. Therefore, a crucial element in any direct selling company's strategy is an incentive program that rewards salespeople for recruiting in addition to offering commissions on their own sales. The objective is to have a system in which recruiting is self-perpetuating, attracting an ever-widening circle of productive, long-term salespeople.

Over 80 percent of direct salespeople are women. They tend to have slightly higher than average incomes and high school educations. They are typically young, religious, and politically conservative. About half have worked in direct sales for less than two years, with 35 percent having more than five years experience. Two-thirds work less than ten hours per week. Direct selling is particularly attractive to women because the independence provides flexibility that appeals to housewives with children.

The motivation behind an individual's decision to enter direct sales has strong implications for his or her productivity. Women who take the job for purely financial considerations tend to be short term, working toward a predetermined monetary goal and then quitting. Women who sell for the sense of accomplishment are far more likely to be long term. The first year of selling is the most critical. If an individual stays through the first year, the chances that she will remain increase dramatically. The most common reason for quitting is dissatisfaction with the compensation.

Top 14 Domestic Direct Selling Companies

COMPANY	ESTIMATED YEAR-END 1982 U.S. SALESFORCE	ESTIMATED 1982 U.S. RETAIL SALES (millions)
Avon Products	440,000A	$1,262A
Amway	675,000	900
Tupperware (Dart & Kraft)	140,000	245
Encyclopedia Britannica	N/AV	400
Shaklee	8,880*	360
Electrolux (Consolidated Foods)	8,500	300
Mary Kay	177,000A	578A
Home Interiors	40,000	200
World Book (Scott & Fetzer)	15,000	190
Princess House (Colgate-Palmolive)	20,000	85
Kirby (Scott & Fertzer)	10,000	65
Stanhome	37,000	62
Jafra (Gillette)	60,000	51
Fuller Brush (Consolidated Foods)	15,000	60

*Only reps who buy directly and, in turn, sell to salespeople who merchandise the wares.
A = actual;   N/AV = not available.

Source: Morgan Stanley Research Estimates.

APPENDIX 1

Marketing Arithmetic

One aspect of marketing not discussed within the text is marketing arithmetic. The calculation of sales, costs, and certain ratios is important for many marketing decisions. The purpose of this appendix is to describe three major areas of marketing arithmetic: the operating statement, analytic ratios, and markups and markdowns.

OPERATING STATEMENT

The operating statement and the balance sheet are the two main financial statements used by companies. The balance sheet shows the assets, liabilities, and net worth of a company at a given point in time. The operating statement (also called profit and loss statement or income statement) is the more important of the two for marketing information. It shows company sales, cost of goods sold, and expenses during the given time period. By examining the operating statement from one time period to the next, the firm can spot favorable or unfavorable trends and take the appropriate action.

Table A.1-1 shows the 1985 operating statement for Dale Parsons, a small men's wear specialty store in the Midwest. This statement is for a retailer; the operating statement for a manufacturer would be somewhat different. Specifically, the section on purchases within the "cost of goods sold" area would be replaced by "cost of goods manufactured."

The operating statement's outline follows a logical sequence of steps to arrive at this firm's $5,000 net profit figure:

Net sales	$60,000
Cost of goods sold	−35,000
Gross margin	$25,000
Expenses	−20,000
Net profit	$ 5,000

Gross Sales			$65,000
Less: Sales returns and allowances			5,000
Net Sales			$60,000
Cost of Goods Sold:			
Beginning inventory, January 1, at cost		$12,000	
Gross purchases	$33,000		
Less: Purchase discounts	3,000		
Net purchases	$30,000		
Plus: Freight-in	2,000		
Net cost of delivered purchases		32,000	
Costs of goods available for sale		$44,000	
Less: Ending inventory, December 31, at cost		9,000	
Cost of goods sold			35,000
Gross Margin			$25,000
Expenses:			
Selling expenses			
Sales, salaries, and commissions	$ 8,000		
Advertising	1,000		
Delivery	1,000		
Total selling expenses		$10,000	
Administrative expenses			
Office salaries	$ 4,000		
Office supplies	1,000		
Miscellaneous (outside consultant)	1,000		
Total administrative expenses		$ 6,000	
General expenses			
Rent	$ 2,000		
Heat, light, and telephone	1,000		
Miscellaneous (insurance, depreciation)	1,000		
Total general expenses		$ 4,000	
Total expenses			$20,000
Net Profit			$ 5,000

Let us examine the major elements of the operating statement separately.

The first element of the operating statement details the amount that Parsons received for the goods he sold during the year. The sales figures consist of three items: gross sales, returns and allowances, and net sales. Gross sales is the total amount charged to customers during the year for merchandise purchased in Parson's store. As expected, some customers returned merchandise because of damage or a change of mind. If the customer receives a full refund or full credit on another purchase, we refer to this exchange as a "return." The customer may decide to keep the item if Parsons will reduce the price to reflect damage done to the good. This is called an "allowance." By reducing the gross sales figure by the returns and allowances we arrive at net sales—what Parsons earned in revenue after a year of selling merchandise:

Gross sales	$65,000
Returns and allowances	−5,000
Net sales	$60,000

The cost of goods sold for Dale Parsons in 1985 merits discussion. Of course, the stock of inventory in the store at the beginning of the year must be included. During the year, $33,000 worth of suits, slacks, shirts, ties, jeans, and so forth, was purchased. One company provided a discount of $3,000 to the store, and thus net purchases were $30,000. Since the store is located in a small town and requires a special delivery route, Parsons had to pay an additional $2,000 to get the products delivered to him, giving him a net cost of $32,000. When the beginning inventory was added to this figure, the cost of goods available for sale amounted to $44,000. The $9,000 ending inventory of clothes in the store on December 31 was then subtracted to come up with the $35,000 "cost of goods sold" figure. Here again we follow a logical series of steps to arrive at the cost of goods sold:

Amount we started with (beginning inventory)	$12,000
Net amount we purchased	+30,000
Any added costs to obtain these purchases	+ 2,000
Total cost of goods we had available for sale during year	$44,000
Amount we had left over (ending inventory)	− 9,000
Cost of merchandise that was actually sold	$35,000

The difference between what Parsons paid for the merchandise ($35,000) and what he received ($60,000) is called the gross margin ($25,000).

In order to show what Parsons "cleared" at the end of the year, the gross margin must be reduced by the "expenses" incurred in generating that volume of business. The selling expenses for Dale Parsons included two part-time employees; local newspaper, radio, and television advertising; and the cost of delivering merchandise to customers after alterations. Selling expenses amounted to $10,000 for the year. Administrative expenses included the salary for a part-time bookkeeper, office supplies such as stationery and business cards, and a miscellaneous expense of an administrative audit conducted by an outside consultant. Administrative expenses were $6,000 in 1985. Finally, the general expenses of rent, utilities, insurance, and depreciation came to $4,000. Total expenses were therefore $20,000 for the year. By subtracting expenses ($20,000) from gross margin ($25,000), we arrive at the net profit of $5,000 for Parsons during 1985.

ANALYTIC RATIOS

The operating statement supplies the data needed for deriving several key ratios. Typically these ratios are referred to as operating ratios—the ratio of selected items on the operating statement to net sales—and allow marketers to compare their performance in one year with that in previous years (or industry standards and competitors in the same year) in order to determine the overall success of the firm. The most commonly computed operating ratios are the gross margin percentage, the net profit percentage, the operating expense percentage, and the returns and allowances percentage.

RATIO	FORMULA	COMPUTATION FROM TABLE A.1-1
Gross margin percentage	$= \dfrac{\text{Gross margin}}{\text{Net sales}}$	$= \dfrac{\$25,000}{\$60,000} = 42\%$
Net profit percentage	$= \dfrac{\text{Net Profit}}{\text{Net Sales}}$	$= \dfrac{\$5,000}{\$60,000} = 8\%$
Operating expense percentage	$= \dfrac{\text{Total expenses}}{\text{Net sales}}$	$= \dfrac{\$20,000}{\$60,000} = 33\%$
Returns and allowances percentages	$= \dfrac{\text{Returns and allowances}}{\text{Net sales}}$	$= \dfrac{\$5,000}{\$60,000} = 8\%$

Another ratio that is useful for analytical purposes is the stockturn rate. The stockturn rate is the number of times an inventory turns over or is sold during a specified time period (often one year). It may be computed on a cost, selling, or unit price basis. Thus the formula can be

$$\text{stockturn rate} = \frac{\text{cost of goods sold}}{\text{average inventory at cost}}$$

or

$$\text{stockturn rate} = \frac{\text{selling price of goods sold}}{\text{average selling price of inventory}}$$

or

$$\text{stockturn rate} = \frac{\text{sales in units}}{\text{average inventory in units}}$$

We will use the first formula:

$$\frac{\$35,000}{\dfrac{\$12,000 + \$9,000}{2}} = \frac{\$35,000}{\$10,500} = 3.3$$

That is, Parsons's inventory turned over 3.3 times in 1985. Normally the higher the stockturn rate, the higher the management efficiency and company profitability.

Return on investment (ROI) is a frequently used measure of managerial effectiveness which uses data from the firm's operating statement and balance sheet. A commonly used formula for computing ROI is as follows:

$$\text{ROI} = \frac{\text{net profit}}{\text{sales}} \times \frac{\text{sales}}{\text{investment}}$$

Two questions may arise when looking at this formula: Why use a two-step process when ROI could be computed simply as net profit over investment, and What exactly is "investment"?

Insight for answering the first question can be gained by observing how each component of the formula can affect the ROI. Suppose Dale Parsons computed his ROI as follows:

$$\text{ROI} = \frac{\text{net profit } \$5,000}{\text{sales } \$60,000} \times \frac{\text{sales } \$60,000}{\text{investment } \$30,000}$$

$$8.3\% \quad \times \quad 2 \quad = 16.6\%$$

If Parsons had believed that increasing his share of the clothing market had certain marketing advantages, he might have generated the same ROI if his sales had doubled and profit and investment remained the same (accepting a lower profit ratio but generating a higher turnover and market share):

$$\text{ROI} = \frac{\text{net profit } \$5,000}{\text{sales } \$120,000} \times \frac{\text{sales } \$120,000}{\text{investment } \$30,000}$$

$$4.16\% \quad \times \quad 4 \quad = 16.6\%$$

Parsons might have increased his ROI by generating a higher net profit figure through more efficient marketing planning, implementation, and control:

$$\text{ROI} = \frac{\text{net profit } \$10,000}{\text{sales } \$60,000} \times \frac{\text{sales } \$60,000}{\text{investment } \$30,000}$$

$$16.6\% \quad \times \quad 2 \quad = 33.2\%$$

Another way to increase ROI is to find some way to generate the same levels of sales and profits while decreasing investment (perhaps by cutting the size of Parson's average inventory):

$$ROI = \frac{\text{net profit } \$5,000}{\text{sales } \$60,000} \times \frac{\text{sales } \$60,000}{\text{investment } \$15,000}$$

$$8.3\% \quad \times \quad 4 \quad = 33.2\%$$

What is "investment" in the ROI formula? Investment is often thought of as the total assets of the firm. However, many analysts have now turned to other measures of return to assess managerial performance. Some of these measures are return on net assets (RONA), return on stockholders equity (ROE), or return on assets managed (ROAM). Since investment is measured at a particular point in time, it is usual for ROI to be computed as the average investment between two time periods (e.g., January 1 and December 31 of the same year). ROI can also be measured as an "internal rate of return" by using discounted cash flow analysis (see any financial textbook dealing with this technique). The objective in using any of these measures is to determine how effectively the company has been in utilizing its resources. As inflation, competitive pressures, and cost of capital show greater upward movement, these measures become increasingly important barometers of marketing and corporate management performance.

MARKUPS AND MARKDOWNS

For retailers and wholesalers, an understanding of the concepts of markup and markdown is essential. The marketer must make a profit to stay in business, and thus the markup percentage is an important strategic consideration. Both markups and markdowns are expressed in percentage terms.

There are two different ways to compute markups—on cost or on selling price:

$$\text{markup percentage on cost} = \frac{\text{dollar markup}}{\text{cost}}$$

$$\text{markup percentage on selling price} = \frac{\text{dollar markup}}{\text{selling price}}$$

Dale Parsons must decide which formula to use; otherwise much confusion may result. If Parsons bought shirts for $8 and wanted to mark them up $4, his markup percentage on cost would be $4/$8 = 50%. If he based markup on selling price, the percentage would be $4/$12 = 33.3%. In figuring markup percentage, most retailers use the selling price rather than the cost.

Suppose Parsons knew his cost ($10) and desired margin (25%) for a man's tie and wanted to compute the selling price, using the markup as a percentage of selling price formula. The formula is

selling price = cost + (margin × selling price)
selling price = $10 + .25 selling price
.75 selling price = $10
selling price = $13.33

As a product moves through the channel of distribution, each channel member adds his markup to the product before selling it to the next member. This "markup chain" is illustrated for a suit purchased by a Parsons customer for $200:

		$ AMOUNT	% OF SELLING PRICE	
	Cost	$108	90%	
Manufacturer	Markup	12	10	markup
	Selling price	$120	100%	
	Cost	$120	80%	
Wholesaler	Markup	30	20	markup
	Selling price	$150	100%	
	Cost	$150	75%	
Retailer	Markup	50	25	markup
	Selling price	$200	100%	

The retailer whose markup is 25 percent does not necessarily enjoy more profit than a manufacturer whose markup is 10 percent. Profit also depends on how many items with that profit margin can be sold (stockturn rate), and on operating efficiency (expenses, etc.).

Sometimes a retailer would like to be able to convert markups based on selling price to cost, and vice versa. The formulas are

$$\text{markup percentage on selling price} = \frac{\text{markup percentage on cost}}{100\% + \text{markup percentage on cost}}$$

$$\text{markup percentage on cost} = \frac{\text{markup percentage on selling price}}{100\% - \text{markup percentage on selling price}}$$

Suppose Parsons found out that his competitor was using a markup percentage of 30 percent based on cost and he wanted to know what this would be on a percentage of selling price. The calculation would be

$$\frac{30\%}{100\% + 30\%} = \frac{30\%}{130\%} = 23\%$$

Since Parsons was using a 25 percent markup on the selling price for suits, he felt that his markup was compatible with that of his competitor.

Near the end of the summer Parsons found that he had an inventory of summer slacks in stock. Thus he knew that a markdown, a reduction from the original selling price, was necessary. He had purchased twenty pairs originally at $10 each and had sold ten pairs at $20 each. He marked down the other pairs to $15 and sold five pairs. His markdown ratio (percentage) is computed as follows:

$$\text{markdown percentage} = \frac{\text{dollar markdown}}{\text{total net sales in dollars}}$$

The dollar markdown is $25 (5 pairs × $5 each) and total net sales are $275, that is, (10 pairs × $20) + (5 pairs × $15). The ratio, then, is $25/$275 = 9%.

Markdown ratios are typically computed for each department, rather than for individual items, so that a measure of relative marketing efficiency for that department can be calculated and compared over time. Parsons will use markdown ratios to gauge the relative efficiency of the buyers and salespersons in the store's various departments.

APPENDIX 2

Careers in Marketing

Now that you have completed your first course in marketing, you have some knowledge of what this field entails. You may have decided that marketing has what you are seeking in a career—constant challenge, stimulating problems, working with people, and almost unlimited advancement opportunities. Marketing is a very broad field with a wide variety of tasks involving the analysis, planning, implementation, and control of marketing programs. Marketing positions are available in all types and sizes of institutions. This appendix will acquaint you with entry-level and higher-level marketing opportunities and suggest steps you might follow in selecting a career path and marketing yourself.

DESCRIPTION OF MARKETING JOBS

Between one-fourth and one-third of the civilian labor force is employed in marketing-related positions. Consequently, the number of marketing careers is enormous. Positions in marketing are thought to be excellent training for the highest levels in the organization because of the knowledge of products and consumers gained in these jobs. A 1976 profile of the *Fortune 500* chief executives showed more CEOs with a background in marketing and distribution than any other career emphasis.

Marketing salaries vary by company and position. Starting marketing salaries usually rank slightly below those for engineering and chemistry but equal or exceed those for economics/finance, accounting, general business, and the liberal arts. In 1984, marketing jobs for people with bachelor's degrees paid an average starting salary of $18,000. If you succeed in an entry-level marketing position, you will quickly be promoted to higher levels of responsibility and salary. Table A.2-1 shows the average 1983 salaries for various marketing positions.

POSITION	SALARY
Sales Management, Vice President	$61,375
Advertising Agency, Vice President	$59,233
Marketing Management, Vice President	$56,686
Sales Manager	$45,851
Marketing Planning Manager	$44,527
Marketing Research Manager	$42,403
Marketing Manager	$40,841
Advertising/Sales Promotion Manager	$40,428
Brand Manager	$38,525
Sales Persons	$36,706
Marketing Planning Staff	$35,033
Marketing Research Staff	$33,292
Advertising/Sales Promotion Staff	$30,792

Source: Gordon McAleer, *The 1984 American Marketing Association Marketing Compensation Report* (Chicago: American Marketing Association, 1984), p. 18.

Marketing has become an attractive career for some individuals who have not traditionally considered this field. One trend is the growing number of women entering marketing. Women have historically been employed in the retail sector of marketing. They are now moving into all types of sales and marketing positions. According to *Business Week,* women accounted for 2 percent of sales recruits in the insurance industry in 1971 and 12 percent in 1978. Women are very successful in sales careers in pharmaceutical companies, publishing companies, banks, and an increasing number of industrial selling jobs. Their ranks are also growing in product and brand manager positions.

Another trend is the growing acceptance of marketing by nonprofit organizations. Colleges, arts organizations, libraries, and hospitals are increasingly applying marketing to their problems. They are beginning to hire marketing directors and marketing vice-presidents to manage their varied marketing activities.

Here are brief descriptions of important marketing jobs.

Advertising

Advertising is an important business activity that requires skill in planning, fact gathering, and creativity. Although compensation for advertising personnel is comparable with that in other business fields, opportunities for rapid advancement in advertising are usually greater than in other fields because of less emphasis on age or length of employment. Typical jobs in advertising agencies are described below.[1]

Copywriters produce the concepts that become written words and visual images of advertisements. They dig for facts, read voraciously, borrow ideas. They talk to customers, suppliers, and *anybody* who can possibly give them a clue about how to attract the target audience's attention and interest.

[1]Description of advertising positions is based on Jack Engel, *Advertising: The Process and Practice* (New York: McGraw-Hill, 1980), pp. 429–34.

Artists are the other part of the creative team. Their major function is to translate copywriters' ideas into dramatic visuals called "layouts." Ad agency artists develop print layouts, package designs, television layouts (called "storyboards"), corporate logotypes, trademarks, and symbols. They specify style and size of typography, paste the type in place, and arrange all details of the ad so that it can be reproduced by engravers and printers. A particularly perceptive art director or copy chief becomes the agency's creative director and oversees all the agency's advertising. The creative director is high in the ad agency's structure.

Account executives are the liaison between client and agency. Their major responsibility is to know marketing and its components. They explain client plans and objectives to their creative teams and supervise the development of the total advertising plan for their accounts. Their main task is to keep the client happy with the agency! Because "account work" is essentially a job of personal relationships, account executives are usually personable, diplomatic, and bright.

Media buyers have the task of selecting the best media for clients. Media representatives flock to the buyer's office whenever they hear that a buy is under consideration. They come armed with statistics to prove that *their* numbers are better, *their* costs per thousand are less, and *their* medium delivers more ripe audiences than competitive media. Media buyers have to evaluate these claims. Media buyers also bargain with the broadcast media for best rates and make deals with the print media for good ad positions.

Large ad agencies maintain an active marketing research department to provide market information for the development of new ad campaigns and to assess current campaigns. Those interested in marketing research should consider possible employment in ad agencies.

Brand and Product Management

Brand and product managers plan, direct, and control business and marketing effort for their products. They are concerned with research and development, packaging, manufacturing, sales and distribution, advertising, promotion, market research, and business analysis and forecasting. In consumer goods companies, the newcomer (who usually needs an MBA) joins a brand team and learns the ropes by doing numerical analyses and watching the senior brand people. This person, if competent, eventually heads the team and is later assigned a larger brand to manage. Several industrial goods companies also have product managers. Product management is considered one of the best training grounds for future corporate officers.

Customer Affairs

Some large consumer-goods companies have established the position of customer affairs representative to act as a liaison between the customer and the firm. The representatives handle complaints, suggestions, and problems concerning the company's products, determine what action is required, and coordinate the activities required to solve the problem. The position requires a person who is empathetic, diplomatic, and capable of working with a wide range of people inside and outside the firm.

Industrial Marketing People interested in industrial marketing careers can go into sales, service, product design, marketing research, and so on. They usually need a technical background. Most people start in sales and spend time in training and making calls with senior salespeople. If they stay in sales, they may advance to district, regional, and higher sales positions. Or they may go into product management and work closely with customers, suppliers, manufacturing, and sales engineering.

International Marketing As U.S. firms increase their international business, they seek qualified persons who have some foreign language fluency and are willing to travel to and/or relocate in foreign cities. For such assignments, most companies select experienced personnel who have proved themselves in domestic operations. An MBA is often an asset but not always a requirement.

Marketing Management Science and Systems Analysis Individuals who have been trained in management science, quantitative methods, and systems analysis will tend to act as consultants to managers facing difficult marketing problems such as demand measurement and forecasting, market structure analysis, and new product evaluation. Career opportunities exist primarily within larger marketing-oriented firms, management consulting firms, and public institutions concerned with health, education, or transportation. An MBA or an MS is usually required.

Marketing Research Marketing researchers get involved with the managers in defining problems and identifying the information needed to resolve the problem. They will design the research project, including the questionnaires and samples, and will handle data tabulation, analysis, report preparation, and presentation of findings with recommendations to management. An understanding of statistics, psychology, and sociology is desirable at a master's degree level. Career opportunities exist with manufacturers, retailers, some wholesalers, trade and industry associations, marketing research firms, advertising agencies, and governmental and private nonprofit agencies.

New Product Planning Persons interested in new product planning can find opportunities in a large variety of organizations. They usually need a good background in marketing, marketing research, and sales forecasting; they need organizational skills to motivate and coordinate others; and they may need a technical background. Usually the person works first in some other marketing positions before joining the new product department.

Physical Distribution Physical distribution is a large and dynamic field, with many career opportunities. Major transportation carriers, manufacturers, wholesalers, and retailers all employ physical distribution specialists. Coursework in quantitative methods, finance, accounting, and marketing will provide students with the necessary skills for entering the field.

Public Relations Most organizations have a public relations person or staff to anticipate public problems, handle complaints, deal with media, build the corporate image, and so on. Persons interested in public relations should be able to speak and write clearly and persuasively and should preferably have a background in journalism, communications, or the liberal arts. The challenges in this job are highly varied and very people-oriented.

Purchasing Purchasing agents are playing a growing role in firms' profitability during periods of rising material costs and shortages. In retail organizations, being a "buyer" has frequently been a route to the top. Purchasing agents in industrial concerns play a key role in holding down the costs of manufacturing. A technical background is useful in some purchasing positions, along with a knowledge of credit, finance, and physical distribution.

Retailing Management Retailing companies provide people with an early opportunity to take on marketing responsibilities. The market growth of large-scale retailing has brought increased emphasis on "professional training" as part of the preparation for a career in retailing. Although historically retail starting salaries and job assignments have been at lower levels than in manufacturing or advertising, the gap is narrowing. The major routes to top management in retailing are merchandise management and store management. The progression in merchandise management is from buyer trainee to assistant buyer to buyer to merchandise division manager. In store management, the progression is from management trainee to assistant department (sales) manager to department manager to store (branch) manager. Whereas buyers are primarily concerned with assortment selection and promotion, department managers are concerned with salesforce management and display. Large-scale retailing offers the new recruit an opportunity to move in a few years into the management of a branch or part of a store doing as much as $5 million in sales.

Sales and Sales Management Sales and sales management opportunities exist in a wide range of profit and nonprofit organizations and in product and service organizations, including financial, insurance, consulting, and government. People have to carefully match their backgrounds, interests, technical skills, and academic training with available sales opportunities. Training programs vary greatly in form and length, ranging from a few weeks to two years. Career paths lead from salesperson to district, regional, and higher levels of sales management, and in many cases, the top management of the firm.

Other Marketing Careers We have excluded descriptions of many other marketing-related jobs such as sales promotion, wholesaling, packaging, pricing, and credit management. But information on these positions can be gathered through the same library sources.

CHOOSING AND GETTING A JOB

Here we want to describe how to go about choosing and getting a job. This calls for the application of marketing skills, particularly marketing analysis and planning. Following are eight suggested steps for choosing a career and finding that first job.

Make Self-Assessment Self-assessment is the most important part of a job search. Unless you have some very specific notion of what you want—be it a mild climate, a city with an opera company, a firm that is no bigger than the school you got your BA from, or a job in France—you are likely to end up with something that is suboptimal. Self-assessment is largely a process of clarifying and articulating ideas you may already hold in fuzzy or ambiguous form. To assist in self-assessment, you might look at the following books, which raise many questions you should consider:

1. *What Color Is Your Parachute?,* by Richard Bolles
2. *Three Boxes in Life and How to Get Out of Them,* by Richard Bolles
3. *Guerrilla Tactics in the Job Market,* by Tom Jackson

Also avail yourself of the counseling service at your school. Tests such as the Strong-Campbell Interest Inventory will help profile your interests.

Examine Job Description Now examine various job descriptions to see what positions best match your interests, desires, and abilities. Descriptions can be found in the *Occupation Outlook Handbook* and the *Dictionary of Occupational Titles* published by the U.S. Department of Labor. These volumes describe what workers in various occupations do, the specific training and education needed, and the availability of jobs in each field in the years ahead as well as possibilities for advancement and probable earnings.

Develop Job-Search Objectives Your initial career "shopping" list should be broad and flexible. Do not make the mistake of being narrow in your concept of ways to achieve your objectives. For example, if marketing research is your goal, consider the public as well as the private sector, and regional as well as national firms. Only after exploring many options should you begin to focus on specific sectors of industries and initial job assignments that may be right for you. You need to set down a list of basic goals. Your list might say: a job in a small company, in a large city, in the Sunbelt, doing marketing research, with an electronic data-processing firm.

Examine Job Market and Assess Opportunities You must now examine the market for those positions to get an idea of how many openings you can expect to be available. For an up-to-date listing of marketing-related job openings, refer to the latest edition of the *College Placement Annual* available at school placement offices. This publication is revised annually to show current job openings for hundreds of companies seeking college graduates for entry-level positions. Companies seeking experienced or advanced-degree personnel are also listed. Use the services of your placement office to the fullest extent at this stage to discover openings and set up interviews with firms looking to fill marketing positions that are of interest to you. Take the time to analyze the industries and companies in which you are interested. Some suggested information sources are business magazines, annual reports, business reference books, faculty members, and fellow students. Try to analyze the future growth and profit pattern of the company and industry, chances for advancement, salary levels, entry positions, amount of travel, and so on.

Develop Search Strategies You might use one or more strategies to contact the firm. Strategy possibilities include (1) on-campus interviews, (2) phoning or writing, or (3) asking marketing professors and/or school alumni or alumnae for possible contacts.

Develop Résumé and Cover Letter Your résumé should capture your abilities, education, background, training, work experience, and personal qualifications—but it should also be brief, usually one page. The goal is to gain a positive response from potential employers.

The cover letter is, in some ways, more difficult to write than the résumé. The cover letter must be persuasive, professional, and interesting. Ideally, it should set you above and apart from the other candidates for the position. Each letter should look and sound original, that is, individually typed and tailored to the specific organization being contacted. It should describe the position you are applying for, arouse interest, describe your qualifications, and indicate how you can be contacted. Cover letters should be addressed to an individual rather than a title. The letter should be followed up with a telephone call.

Obtain Interviews Here is some advice to follow before, during, and after your interviews. Preparation for interview:

1. Interviewers have extremely diverse styles—e.g., the "chit chat" let's-get-to-know-each-other style; the quasi-interrogation style of question after question; and the tough-probing why, why, why style, to name a few. Be ready for anything.
2. Practice being interviewed with a friend, and ask for a critique.
3. Ask at least five good questions that are not readily answered in the company literature.
4. Anticipate possible interview questions and frame suitable answers.
5. Avoid "back-to-back" interviews, as they can be exhausting.
6. Dress for the interview in conservative style rather than fashionable taste.
7. Plan to arrive about ten minutes early to collect your thoughts before being called. Check your name on the interview schedule, noting the name of the interviewer and the room number.
8. Review the major points you intend to cover.

During the interview:

1. Give a firm handshake in greeting the interviewer. Introduce yourself using the same form the interviewer has used. Make a good initial impression.
2. Retain your poise. Relax. Smile occasionally. Maintain enthusiasm throughout the interview.

3. Good eye contact, good posture, and distinct speech are musts. Don't clasp your hands or fiddle with jewelry, hair, etc. Sit comfortably in your chair. Do not smoke, even if asked.

4. Have extra copies of your résumé with you.

5. Have your story down pat. Present your selling points. Answer questions directly. Avoid one-word answers, but don't be wordy.

6. Most times, let the interviewer take the initiative, but don't be passive. Find an appropriate opportunity to direct the conversation to those things you want the interviewer to hear.

7. The latter part of the interview is the best time to make your most important point or to ask a pertinent question, in order to end the session on a high note.

8. Don't be afraid "to close": You might say, "I'm very interested in the position and I have enjoyed this interview."

After the interview:

1. Upon leaving, record the key points. Be sure to record who is to follow up on the interview and when a decision can be expected.

2. Objectively analyze the interview with regard to the questions asked, the answers given, your overall interview presentation, and the interviewer's response (interest, boredom, etc.) to specific points.

3. Send a thank-you letter mentioning any additional things and your availability to supply further information.

4. If you do not hear with the time specified, write or call the interviewer to determine your status.

Follow-up If you are successful, you will be invited to visit the organization. The in-company interview will run from a few hours to a whole day. Your interest, maturity, enthusiasm, assertiveness, logic, and company and functional knowledge will all be scrutinized. You should be asking questions that are important to you. Find out about the environment, job role, responsibilities, opportunity, current industrial issues, and the "firm's personality." If all goes well, you may be working in this organization at some future time. You can avoid embarrassment later if you remember the names of the people you meet.

Glossary

Administered vertical marketing system. Coordinates successive stages of production and distribution not through common ownership but through the size and power of one of the parties.

Adoption. The decision by an individual to become a regular user of the product.

Adoption process. The mental process through which an individual passes from first hearing about an innovation to final adoption.

Advertising. Any paid form of nonpersonal presentation and promotion of ideas, goods, or services by an identified sponsor.

Agent middlemen. Firms such as brokers and manufacturer's representatives that find customers or negotiate contracts but do not take title to the merchandise.

Attitude. A person's enduring favorable or unfavorable cognitive evaluations, emotional feelings, and action tendencies toward some object or idea.

Backward integration. The term refers to the company's seeking ownership or increased control of its supply systems.

Behavior segmentation. Dividing buyers into groups on the basis of their knowledge, attitude, use, or response to a product.

Belief. A descriptive thought that a person holds about something.

*Brand. A name, term, sign, symbol, or design, or a combination of them which is intended to identify the goods or services of one seller or group of sellers and to differentiate them from those of competitors.

Brand extension strategy. Any effort to use a successful brand name to launch product modifications or new products.

*Brand mark. That part of a brand which can be recognized but is not utterable, such as a symbol, design, or distinctive coloring or lettering.

*Brand name. That part of a brand which can be vocalized—the utterable.

Buyer. The person who makes the actual purchase.

*The definitions preceded by an asterisk are from *Marketing Definitions: A Glossary of Marketing Terms* (Chicago: American Marketing Association, 1960).

†Buying center. All those individuals and groups who participate in the purchasing decision-making process, who share some common goals and the risks arising from the decisions.

Capital items. Goods that enter the finished market partly.

Closed-end questions. Questions that include all the possible answers, and the respondent makes a choice among them.

Cognitive dissonance theory. Almost every purchase is likely to lead to some postpurchase discomfort, and the issues are how much discomfort and what will the consumer do about it.

Company demand. The company's sales resulting from its share of market demand.

Company marketing opportunity. An attractive arena for company marketing action in which the particular company would enjoy a competitive advantage.

Company sales forecast. The level of company sales based on the assumption of achieving a certain share of industry sales.

Company's marketing environment. Consists of the actors and forces that are external to the marketing management function of the firm and that impinge on the marketing management's ability to develop and maintain successful transactions with its target customers.

Concentric diversification. The term refers to the company's seeking to add new products that have technological or marketing synergies with the existing product line; these products will normally appeal to new classes of customers.

Conglomerate diversification. The term refers to the company's seeking to add new products that have no relationship to the company's current technology, products, or markets; these products will normally appeal to new classes of customers.

Consumerism. An organized movement of citizens and government to enhance the rights and power of buyers in relation to sellers.

Consumer market. All the individuals and households who buy or acquire goods and services for personal consumption.

Containerization. The putting of goods in boxes or trailers that are easy to transfer between two transportation modes.

Contractual vertical marketing system. A system in which independent firms at different levels of production and distribution integrate their programs on a contractual basis to obtain more economies and/or sales impact than they could achieve alone.

*Convenience goods. Goods that the customer usually purchases frequently, immediately, and with the minimum of effort in comparison and buying.

Copyright. The exclusive legal right to reproduce, publish, and sell the matter and form of a literary, musical, or artistic work.

Corporate vertical marketing system. A system that combines successive stages of production and distribution under single ownership.

Cues. Minor stimuli that determine when, where, and how the person responds.

Decider. The person who ultimately determines any part of the entire buying decision: whether to buy, what to buy, how to buy, or where to buy.

Decline stage. The product life-cycle stage in which sales and profits deteriorate.

Demands. People's wants that are backed by purchasing power.

Demographic segmentation. Dividing the market into groups on the basis of demographic variables such as age, sex, family size, family life cycle, income, occupation, education, religion, race, and nationality.

†The definitions preceded by a dagger are from Frederick E. Webster, Jr., and Yoram Wind, *Organizational Buying Behavior* (Englewood Cliffs, N.J.: Prentice-Hall, 1972).

Differentiated marketing. The firm decides to operate in several segments of the market and designs separate offers to each.

Discretionary income. The amount of money that people have left after paying for their basic food, clothing, shelter, insurance, and other necessaries.

Disposable personal income. The amount of money that people have left after paying taxes.

Distribution channel. The set of firms and individuals that take title, or assist in transferring title, to the particular good or service as it moves from the producer to the consumer.

Diversification growth opportunities. Those opportunities lying outside the current marketing channel system.

Drive. A strong internal stimulus impelling action. A drive becomes a motive when it is directed toward a particular drive-reducing stimulus object.

DROP-error. Occurs when the company dismisses an otherwise good product idea.

Durable goods. Tangible goods that normally survive many uses.

Embargo. The ultimate form of quota in that imports in prescribed categories are totally banned.

Environmentalism. An organized movement of concerned citizens and government to protect and enhance people's living environment.

Environmental threat. A challenge posed by an unfavorable trend or specific disturbance in the environment which would lead, in the absence of purposeful marketing action, to the stagnation or demise of a company, product, or brand.

Exchange. The act of obtaining a desired object from someone by offering something in return.

Expectations-performance theory. A consumer's satisfaction is a function of the consumer's product expectations and the product's perceived performance.

Facilitators. Business firms—such as transportation companies, warehouses, banks, and insurance companies—that assist in the logistical and financial tasks of distribution but do not take title to goods or negotiate purchases or sales.

Fads. Particular fashions that come quickly into the public eye, are adopted with great zeal, peak early, and decline very fast.

Fashion. A currently accepted or popular style in a given field. Fashions tend to pass through four stages: distinctiveness, emulation, mass fashion, and decline.

Forecasting. The art of anticipating what buyers are likely to do under a given set of conditions.

Forward integration. The term refers to the company's seeking ownership or increased control of some of its competitors.

Functional marketing organization. A form of marketing organization in which the various marketing functions are headed by separate managers who report to the marketing vice-president.

Gatekeepers. Persons who control the flow of information to others.

Geographic segmentation. Dividing the market into different geographical units such as nations, states, regions, counties, cities, or neighborhoods.

GO-error. Occurs when the company permits a poor product idea to move into development and commercialization.

Government market. Governmental units—federal, state, and local—that purchase or rent goods for carrying out the main functions of government.

Growth stage. The product life-cycle stage that is marked by rapid market acceptance and increasing profits.

Harvesting strategy. A marketing strategy in which the firm sharply reduces its expenses to increase its current profits, knowing that this will accelerate the rate of sales decline and ultimate demise of the product.

Horizontal diversification. The term refers to the company's seeking to add new products that could appeal to its current customers though technologically unrelated to its current product line.

Horizontal integration. The term refers to the company's seeking ownership or increased control of some of its competitors.

Human need. A state of felt deprivation in a person.

Human wants. The form that human needs take as shaped by a person's culture and individuality.

Image. The way an individual or group sees an object.

Image persistence. The result of people's continuing to see what they expect to see, rather than what is.

Industrial market. All the individuals and organizations who acquire goods and services that enter into the production of other products or services that are sold, rented, or supplied to others.

Influencer. A person whose views or advice carries some weight in making the final decision.

Initiator. The person who first suggests or thinks of the idea of buying the particular product or service.

Internal reports system. Provides current data on sales, costs, inventories, cash flows, and accounts receivable and payable.

International markets. Buyers found abroad, including foreign consumers, producers, resellers, and governments.

Introduction stage. The product life-cycle stage that is marked by slow growth and minimal profits as the product is being introduced in the market.

Learning. Changes in an individual's behavior arising from experience.

Life style. The person's pattern of living in the world as expressed in his or her activities, interests, and opinions.

Macroenvironment. The larger societal forces that affect all the actors in the company's microenvironment—namely, the demographic, economic, natural, technological, political, and cultural forces.

Market. The set of all actual and potential buyers of a product.

Market demand. The term refers to the *total volume* that would be *bought* by a defined *customer group* in a defined *geographical area* in a defined *time period* in a defined *marketing environment* under a defined *marketing program*.

Market development. The term refers to the company's seeking increased sales by taking its current products into new markets.

Market forecast. The expected level of market demand corresponding to the planned level of industry marketing expenditure in the given environment.

Market management organization. A form of marketing organization in which major markets are the responsibility of market managers who work with the various functional specialists to develop and achieve their plans for the market.

Market penetration. More sales to a company's present target group of buyers, without changing the product in any way.

Market positioning. Formulating a competitive positioning for the product and a detailed marketing mix.

Market potential. The limit approached by market demand as industry marketing expenditure goes to infinity, for a given set of competitive prices and a given environment.

Market segment. Customers who respond in a similar way to a given set of marketing stimuli.

Market segmentation. Dividing a market into distinct groups of buyers who might require separate products or marketing mixes.

Market targeting. Evaluating each segment's attractiveness and selecting one or more of the market segments to enter.

Market testing. The stage where the product and marketing program are introduced into more realistic market settings.

Marketing. Human activity directed at satisfying needs and wants through exchange processes.

Marketing audit. A comprehensive, systematic, independent, and periodic examination of a company's—or a business unit's—marketing environment, objectives, strategies, and activities with a view to determining problem areas and opportunities and recommending a plan of action to improve the company's marketing performance.

Marketing channel. Performs the work of selling and bringing goods from producers to consumers.

Marketing concept. A management orientation that holds that the key to achieving organizational goals consists of determining the needs and wants of target markets and delivering the desired satisfactions more effectively and efficiently than competitors.

Marketing implementation. The process that turns marketing strategies and plans into marketing actions in order to accomplish strategic marketing objectives.

Marketing information system. A continuing and interacting structure of people, equipment, and procedures to gather, sort, analyze, evaluate, and distribute pertinent, timely, and accurate information for use by marketing decision makers to improve their marketing planning, execution, and control.

Marketing intelligence system. The set of sources and procedures by which executives obtain their everyday information about developments in the commercial environment.

Marketing intermediaries. Firms that aid the company in promoting, selling, and distributing its goods to final buyers.

Marketing management. The analysis, planning, implementation, and control of programs designed to create, build, and maintain mutually beneficial exchanges with target buyers for the purpose of achieving organizational objectives.

Marketing management process. Consists of (1) organizing the marketing planning process, (2) analyzing marketing opportunities, (3) selecting target markets, (4) developing the marketing mix, and (5) managing the marketing effort.

Marketing managers. Personnel within the company who are involved in marketing analysis, planning, implementation, and/or control activities.

Marketing mix. The set of controllable marketing variables that the firm blends to produce the response it wants in the target market.

Marketing research. The systematic design, collection, analysis, and reporting of data and findings relevant to a specific marketing situation facing the company.

Marketing strategy. The marketing logic by which the business unit hopes to achieve its marketing objectives. Marketing strategy consists of specific strategies bearing on target markets, marketing mix, and marketing expenditure level.

Mass marketing. A style of marketing in which the seller mass-produces, mass-distributes, and mass-promotes one product to all buyers.

Materials and parts. Goods that enter the manufacturer's product completely.

Maturity stage. The product life-cycle stage in which sales growth slows down and profits stabilize.

Merchant middlemen. Firms such as wholesalers and retailers that buy, take title to, and resell merchandise.

Microenvironment. The actors in the company's immediate environment that affect its ability to serve its customers—namely, the company, market channel firms, customer markets, competitors, and publics.

Motive. A need that is sufficiently pressing to direct the person to seek satisfaction of the need. Satisfying the need reduces the felt tension.

New product. A good, service, or idea that is perceived by some potential customers as new.

*Nondurable goods. Tangible goods normally consumed in one or a few uses.

Open-end question. A question that allows the respondent to answer in his or her own words.

Organization. A social unit characterized by explicit goals, definite rules and regulations, a formal status structure, and clear lines of communication and authority.

†Organizational buying. The decision-making process by which formal organizations establish the need for purchased products and services, and identify, evaluate and choose among alternative brands and suppliers.

Organization marketing. Those activities undertaken to create, maintain, or alter attitudes and/or behavior of target audiences toward particular organizations.

Packaging. The activities of designing and producing the container or wrapper for a product.

‡Perception. The process by which an individual selects, organizes, and interprets information inputs to create a meaningful picture of the world.

Personality. The person's distinguishing psychological characteristics that lead to relatively consistent and enduring responses to his or her own environment.

*Personal selling. Oral presentation in a conversation with one or more prospective purchasers for the purpose of making sales.

Physical distribution. The tasks involved in planning, implementing, and controlling the physical flows of materials and final goods from points of origin to points of use to meet the needs of customers at a profit.

Political system. The term refers to the forms and institutions by which a nation is governed. It consists of an interacting set of laws, government agencies, and pressure groups that influence and constrain the conduct of various organizations and individuals in the society.

Position. The way a product is defined by consumers.

Price leader. A product that is priced below its normal markup or even below cost. It is used to attract customers to the store in the hope that they will buy other things at normal markups.

Pricing strategy. The task of defining the rough initial price range and planned price movement through time that the company will use to achieve its marketing objectives in the target market.

Primary data. Information that is originally collected for the specific purpose at hand.

Product. Anything that can be offered to a market for attention, acquisition, use, or consumption that might satisfy a want or need.

---

‡This definition is from Bernard Berelson and Gary A. Steiner, *Human Behavior: An Inventory of Scientific Findings* (New York: Harcourt Brace Jovanovich, 1964), p. 88.

Product concept. A management orientation that holds that consumers will favor those products that offer the most quality, performance, and features, and therefore the organization should devote its energy to making continuous product improvements.

Product development. The term refers to the company's seeking increased sales by developing new or improved products for its current markets.

Product-differentiated marketing. A style of marketing in which the seller produces two or more products that exhibit different features, styles, quality, sizes, and so on.

Product idea. An idea for a possible product that the company can see itself offering to the market.

Product image. The particular·picture consumers acquire of an actual or potential product.

Production concept. A management orientation that holds that consumers will favor those products that are available and highly affordable, and therefore management should concentrate on improving production and distribution efficiency.

*Product item.** A distinct unit that is distinguishable by size, price, appearance, or some other attribute. An item is sometimes called a stockkeeping unit or product variant.

*Product line.** A group of products that are closely related, either because they function in a similar manner, are sold to the same customer groups, are marketed through the same types of outlets, or fall within given price ranges.

Product line featuring. Raises the question of which product to feature in promoting the line.

Product line filling. Lengthening a product line by adding more products within the present range of the line.

Product line modernization. Deciding whether the line needs a new look and whether to overhaul the line piecemeal or in one fell swoop.

Product line stretching. Lengthening the company's product line beyond its current range.

Product management organization. A form of marketing in which products are the responsibility of product managers who work with the various functional specialists in the company to develop and achieve their plans for the product.

*Product mix.** The set of all product lines and items that a particular seller offers for sale to buyers.

Psychographics. The technique of measuring life styles.

Psychographic segmentation. Dividing the buyers into different groups on the basis of their social class, life style, and/or personality characteristics.

Public. Any group that has an actual or potential interest in or impact on an organization's ability to achieve its objectives.

*Publicity.** Nonpersonal stimulation of demand for a product, service, or business unit by planting commercially significant news about it in a published medium or obtaining favorable presentation of it upon radio, television, or stage that is not paid for by the sponsor.

Public relations. The management function that evaluates public attitudes, identifies the policies and procedures of an individual or an organization with the public interest, and plans and executes a program of action to earn public understanding and acceptance.

Pull strategy. A strategy that calls for spending a lot of money on advertising and consumer promotion to build up consumer demand.

Push strategy. A strategy that calls for using the salesforce and trade promotion to push the product through the channels.

Quota. A limitation on the amount of goals that an importing country will accept in certain product categories.

Reference groups. Those groups that have a direct (face-to-face) or indirect influence on the person's attitudes or behavior.

Reseller market. All the individuals and organizations who acquire goods for the purpose of reselling or renting to others at a profit.

Resellers. See Merchant middlemen.

Retailer/Retail store. Any business enterprise whose sales volume primarily comes from retailing.

Retailing. All the activities involved in selling goods or services directly to final consumers for their personal, nonbusiness use.

Role. The activities that a person is expected to perform according to the persons around him or her.

Sales analysis. The act of determining where the company's sales are coming from by product, customer, territory, and so on.

Sales budget. A conservative estimate of the expected volume of sales. It is used primarily for making current purchasing, production, and cash-flow decisions.

Sales potential. The limit approached by company demand as company marketing expenditure increases in relation to competition.

Sales promotion. Short-term incentives to encourage purchase or sale of a product or service.

Sales quota. A sales goal set for a product line, company division, or sales representative. It is primarily a management tool for defining and stimulating sales effort.

Sales-response function. Forecasts the likely sales volume during a specified time period associated with different possible levels of one or more marketing mix elements.

Sales variance analysis. An attempt to determine the relative contribution of different factors to a gap in sales performance.

Secondary data. Information that already exists somewhere, having been collected for another purpose.

Selling concept. A management orientation that holds that consumers will not buy enough of the organization's products unless the organization undertakes a substantial selling and promotion effort.

Service. Any activity or benefit that one party can offer to another that is essentially intangible and does not result in the ownership of anything. Its production may or may not be tied to a physical product.

*Shopping goods. Goods that the customer, in the process of selection and purchase, characteristically compares on such bases as suitability, quality, price, and style.

Social classes. Relatively homogeneous and enduring divisions in a society which are hierarchically ordered and whose members share similar values, interests, and behavior.

Social marketing. The design, implementation, and control of programs seeking to increase the acceptability of a social idea, cause, or practice in a target group(s). It utilizes market segmentation, consumer research, concept development, communications, facilitation, incentives, and exchange theory to maximize target group response.

Societal marketing concept. A management orientation that holds that the organization's task is to determine the needs, wants, and interests of target markets and to deliver the desired satisfactions more effectively and efficiently than competitors in a way that preserves or enhances the consumer's and the society's well-being.

Specialty goods. Goods with unique characteristics and/or brand identification for which a significant group of buyers are habitually willing to make a special purchasing effort.

Standard Industrial Classification (SIC). A U.S. Bureau of the Census classification of industries based on the product produced or operation performed by the industry.

Statistical demand analysis. A set of statistical procedures designed to discover the most important real factors affecting sales and their relative influence.

Status. The general esteem that each role is accorded by society.

Strategic business unit (SBU). Any business making up the company.

Strategic planning. The managerial process of developing and maintaining a strategic fit between the organization's goals and its changing market opportunities. It relies on developing a clear company mission, supporting objectives and goals, a sound business portfolio, and coordinated functional strategies.

Subcultures. Groups of people with shared value systems emerging from their common life experience or circumstances.

Suppliers. Business firms and individuals that provide the resources needed by the company and its competitors to produce the particular goods and services.

Supplies and services. Items that do not enter the finished product at all.

Systems buying. The act of buying a whole solution to a problem and not making all the separate decisions involved.

Systems selling. A key industrial marketing strategy for winning and holding accounts.

Target market. A well-defined set of customers whose needs the company plans to satisfy.

Target marketing. A style of marketing in which the seller distinguishes between market segments, selects one or more of these segments, and develops products and marketing mixes tailored to each segment.

Tariff. A tax levied by the foreign government against designated imported products.

Test marketing. Selecting one or more markets in which to introduce a new product and marketing program to see how well they perform and what revisions are needed, if any.

Time-series analysis. A company forecast prepared on the basis of a statistical-mathematical analysis of past data.

Total market demand. The total volume that would be bought by a defined consumer group in a defined geographic area in a defined time period in a defined marketing environment under a defined level and mix of industry marketing effort.

Total market potential. The maximum amount of sales (in units or dollars) that might be available to all the firms in an industry during a given period under a given level of industry marketing expenditures and given environmental conditions.

*Trademark. A brand or part of a brand that is given legal protection because it is capable of exclusive appropriation. A trademark protects the seller's exclusive rights to use the brand name and/or brand mark.

Transaction. A trade of values between two parties.

Undifferentiated marketing. The firm decides to ignore marketing differences and go after the whole market with one market offer.

*Unsought goods. Goods that the customer does not know about or knows about but does not normally think of buying.

User. The person(s) who consumes or uses the product or service.

Value analysis. An approach to cost reduction in which components are carefully studied to determine if they can be redesigned or standardized or made by cheaper methods of production.

Wholesaling. All the activities involved in selling goods and services to those buying for resale or business use.

Author Index

A

Aaker, David A., 282, 283, 287
Aaker, David L., 612, 614, 640
Abell, Derek F., 35, 52, 66, 82
Abend, Jules, 188, 206
Abler, Ronald, 415, 440
Abrams, Bill, 151, 154, 157
Ackoff, Russell L., 79, 82, 269, 286, 516, 540
Adelman, Morris, 712, 727
Adler, Lee, 422, 440
Albaum, Gerald S., 663, 673, 676, 677
Alderson, Wroe, 10, 27, 411, 440
Alexander, Ralph S., 323, 331
Allen, Herbert, 160, 184
Alpert, Mark L., 193, 206
Ames, B. Charles, 626, 640
Anderson, Carl R., 612, 640
Anderson, M. J., Jr., 600, 605
Anderson, Paul F., 70, 82
Anderson, Rolph E., 198, 206
Andreasen, Alan R., 112n, 707, 727
Ansoff, H. Igor, 34, 52, 67
Arpan, Jeffrey S., 662, 676
Ayal, Igal, 662, 676

B

Backhaus, Klaus, 226, 236
Bagozzi, Richard P., 8, 27
Bailey, Earl L., 335, 358, 720, 727
Ballachey, Egerton L., 182, 185
Bank, Seymour, 102, 117
Banks, Robert L., 610, 639
Banting, Peter M., 16, 27, 321, 331
Barksdale, Hiram C., 685, 696
Bartos, Rena, 161, 184
Bass, Frank M., 273, 286

Bass, Stephen J., 468, 478
Bates, Albert D., 468, 478
Bauer, Raymond A., 154, 157, 160, 184, 197, 206, 710, 727
Bearden, William O., 168, 184
Beckenstein, Alan R., 371, 386
Behrens, William W., III, 141, 157, 714, 727
Bell, Martin L., 17, 27
Belshaw, Cyril S., 8, 27
Benedetti, Lois H., 377, 386
Benson, Lisa, 18, 27
Berelson, Bernard, 179, 185, 493, 506
Berg, Thomas L., 323, 331
Berman, Phyllis, 444, 462, 477, 478
Bernstein, Peter W., 174, 185
Berry, Leonard L., 151, 154, 215, 235, 685, 696
Bettman, James R., 190, 194, 206
Black, George, 535, 541
Blackwell, Roger D., 109, 117, 190, 206, 491, 506
Bloom, Paul N., 591, 604, 688, 696, 712, 727
Bogart, Leo, 455, 478
Bonoma, Thomas V., 209, 218, 221–22, 235, 236, 609, 610, 639
Borch, Fred J., 13, 27
Bowen, Howard R., 720, 727
Bowman, Russel D., 533, 541
Boyd, Harper W., Jr., 175, 185, 195, 206, 297, 330
Bramel, Dana, 198, 206
Branch, Melville C., 58, 82
Britt, Steuart Henderson, 326, 331
Brooks, John, 333, 358
Brown, George H., 273, 286
Bucklin, Louis P., 411, 440
Buell, Victor P., 625, 640

Burnett, John J., 269, 286
Burstein, Daniel, 161, 184, 689, 696
Buzzell, Robert D., 310, 331, 352, 359, 449, 451, 477, 527, 541, 590, 604
Bybee, H. Malcolm, 517, 541

C

Calder, Bobby J., 104, 117
Caplovitz, David, 707, 727
Cardozo, Richard, 275, 286
Carroll, Daniel T., 615, 640, 685, 696
Carson, Rachel, 141, 157, 714, 727
Cash, Harold C., 503, 506
Cassino, Kip D., 255, 259
Catry, Bernard, 592, 604
Cavanaugh, Suzette, 531, 541
Center, Allen H., 536, 541, 692, 697
Chase, Dennis, 667, 676
Chevalier, Michel, 592, 604
Choate, Robert B., 705
Churchill, Gilbert A., Jr., 257, 259, 549, 568
Churchill, Winston, 19, 27
Clausewitz, Carl von, 587, 604
Clayton, Alden G., 528, 541
Clewett, Richard M., 625, 640
Cohen, Stanley E., 232, 236
Coleman, Richard P., 164, 184, 266, 286
Colley, Russel H., 514, 540
Combs, Linda Jones, 197, 206
Cook, James, 680, 696
Cooney, John E., 689, 696
Cooper, Arnold C., 602, 605
Corey, E. Raymond, 275, 286
Cort, Stanton G., 449, 451, 477
Cosier, Richard A., 722, 727
Cox, Donald F., 197, 206

Subject Index

Goods cost, operating statement, 737–39

Goods with services accompanying, tangible, 320–23

Goodwill, customer, 36

Goodyear Tire & Rubber, 579, 604

Gould, Inc., 479

Government agencies, 148–51

Government buyer behavior, 231–34

Government markets, 128, 212

Government natural resource management, 143

Government publics, 131

Government regulation, 19–20, 147–51, 380, 722

Government service sector, 680

Gross-profit curve, 79

Gross-profit function, 79

Growth strategies, 66–68

Gulfstream Aerospace Corporation, 209

H

Hanes Corporation, 359–61

Harvesting, SBU, 64, 65

Health factors, 164

Helene Curtis Industries, market management, 30–49 passim

Heublein, Inc., 389

Hewlett-Packard, 615–16

Hold, SBU, 64

Home improvement centers, 469

Honeywell, Inc., 543–44

Horizontal marketing systems, 422

House marketing, 690

Households, nonfamily, 135–36

Human resources planning, 47, 617–18

Hypermarche, 445, 450–52

I

IBM, 607–8, 639, 640–45

Idea marketing, 692–94

Image, organization, 687–88

Income, 139–41, 165, 246, 264, 266

Income distribution, foreign, 660

Industrial buyer behavior, 216–27

Industrial distributors, 470, 471

Industrial goods, classified, 300–302, 599

Industrial marketing careers, 748

Industrial markets, 128, 211–12, 216, 502

  buyer behavior, 216–27

  segmentation, 274–75

Industrial structure, foreign, 660

Industry and population mix, 138–39

Industry attractiveness, 64–65

Information, marketing:

  on competitors, 90–92

distribution, 113–15

for marketing plans, 33

primary data collection, 98–100

secondary data surveys, 97–98

sources of supply, 86

specific needs, 96–97

Information analysis, 112–13

Information cost, MIS, 88

Information management from sales reports, 547, 564–66

Information managers, 87–88

Information networks, 114–15

Information search, consumer, 191–92, 201, 724–25

Informative advertising, 515

Innovativeness and product adoption, 202–4

Institutional advertising, 511

Institutional loyalty, 154

Institutional markets, 22–24, 34

Intelligence bulletins, company, 92–93

Intermediaries, marketing channel, 410–11, 423–25 (*see also* Middlemen)

Internal publics, 131

Internal records, 89–90

International division, company, 674

International marketing careers, 748

International marketing-environment appraisal, 657–62

International markets, 128, 655–75

International trends, 22, 656–58

Interstate Commerce Commission (ICC), 150, 151

Interviewing, research, 103–5

Inventory, channel, 433–36

Investment, foreign market, 666, 667

J

Japan, global marketing, 657–59, 665

Job finding, 750–52

Job follow-up, 752

Job interviews, 751–52

Job résumé, 751, 752

Joint ownership ventures abroad, 666–67

Joint venturing, 665–67

K

K Mart, 467, 681

Kullen, "King" (Michael), 449

L

Labeling deception, 704, 717

Labeling decisions, 319–20

Labeling regulation, 150

Land marketing, 690–92

Law environments, 148–51

Leading indicators, 257

Learning and buying behavior, 180–82

Learning curve, portfolio plan, 65

Legislation, U.S. milestone, 149–50

Leisure, 164

Levi Strauss, 123, 239–40

Licensing, international, 665–66

Life-cycle stage, family, 172–73, 266

Life expectancy, 132, 133

Life quality maximization, 21

Life style, 518, 709

  buying behavior and, 173–75

  market segmentation, 268–69

Limits to Growth, The (Meadows et al.), 714

Local publics, 131

Loctite Corporation, 406

Logistics thinking, 432

Loss leaders, 465

Luxury goods, 140

M

Macroenvironment, company, 124, 132–56

Magazine advertising, 521–22, 710–11

Magnuson-Moss Warranty/FTC Improvement Act of 1975, 150, 329

Mail-order catalog, 456–57

Mail-order retailing, 445, 446, 455–56, 526

Mail-order wholesaling, 470, 472

Mail questionnaires, 102–3

Management (*see* Brand management; Channel management; Information management; Management by objectives; Market management; Marketing dept. managers; Marketing management; Product manager; Salesforce management)

Management by objectives, 60

Management contracting, 666

Managerial climate, 618

Managers, marketing, 13, 47–48

  strategic planning, 609–13, 627

Managers, sales, 548, 549, 563, 565, 567

Manufacturer-intermediary (middlemen) channels, 416–24, 427–28, 431

Manufacturers' agents (representatives), 473

Manufacturing branch/office, 470

Markdowns, 466

  arithmetic for, 742–44

Market:

  concepts, 10–11, 244–45

  expansion, 584–86, 711, 712

Market analysis and management, 44

Maslow's motivation theory, 178–79
Mass marketing, 262, 263, 425, 444
Mass media, 493
Materialism in America, 708–10, 720
Matrix portfolio planning (SBU), 62–68
Maytag Company, 648–51
McDonald's Corporation, 498, 657, 682
   experimental research, 102
   franchise operation, 61
   marketing concept, 17, 686
   See also following two entries; Fast food service
Meat Act, Wholesome, 1967, 151
Meat Inspection Act of 1906, 149
Media, 488, 520–25
   costs of specific vehicles, 521–23
   timing of, 523
Media publics, 131
Merchandising conglomerate, 422, 445, 461–62
Merchant middlemen, 127
Merchant wholesalers, 470–73
Message (advertising), 516–20
   execution styles, 518–19
   format, 491–92, 520
Message (promo), 487, 490–91, 494
   tone, 519
Message source credibility, 494
Metropolitan Statistical Areas (MSAs), 136, 138
Microenvironment, company, 124–31, 155–56
Midas Touch, The (Pohl), 20
Middle age in population, 133
Middle class income, 140
Middlemen, 126–27, 411–31, 665
   channel management, 428–31
   indirect export, 664–65
Middlemen's brands, 307–9
Miller Brewing Company, 29–30
Miller-Tydings Act of 1937, 150
Mineral supply, 142–43
Minnetonka, Inc., 645–48
Minolta camera, 195
Model bank, 113, 117
Monetary regulation, international, 661
Monopolistic markets, pricing, 372–73
Montgomery Ward, 456
Mothers, working, 135
Motivation, buying, 177–79, 181
Motivational research (Ernest Dichter), 178, 219–20
Motor Vehicle Safety Act of 1962, 151
Multinational corporations, 656, 667–69, 671–72, 674–75

N

NASA, 146–47

National Traffic & Safety Act of 1958, 150
Nature, cultural value, 155
Needs, human, 4–8
   Maslow's order of, 178–79
Neighborhood shopping center, 445, 463
Net-profit curve, profit-optimization, 79
New product ideas, 337–41, 586
   screening, 340–41
   sources, 338–39
New product planning, careers, 748
New products:
   pricing, 390–91
   sales objectives, 547
   strategies, 334–57, 390–91, 584–85
   success/failure, 335–38, 341, 510, 709
New products manager, 622
Newspaper advertising, 521–22, 711
Nielsen Company, A. C., Retail Index, 94, 98, 99
Nike, Inc., 728–30
Noise, message, 488
Nonprofit organizations, 22–24
   marketing research in, 11–12

O

Obsolescence, planned, 706–7
Occupation and buying behavior, 173
Oil supply, 142, 143
Oligopolistic pricing, 373
Open-end questions, 108–9
Operating statement arithmetic, 737–42
Opinion leaders, 169, 203, 493–94
Opportunities, company competitive, 73–74, 124, 132
Order getting and taking, 556
Order (reorder) point, 436
Order processing, 216, 434–35
Organization marketing, 686–88
Organization structure:
   action programs and, 46–47, 612–15, 628
   implementation system and, 619
Organizational buyer behavior, 215–27
Organizational buying, 214–16
Organizational climate, 47, 616, 618–19, 624–25
Organizational markets, 210–34
Organizational survival, 367
Ortlieb Brewing Co., Henry F., 288–91
Outdoor advertising, 521–22
Outlets, retail, 445–58
   control of, 459–62

P

Packaging, 7, 19, 21, 142, 143, 314–19, 673–74, 715
Packaging concept, 316–17
Packaging decisions, 314–15
Patent protection, 328, 665
Patriotism in culture, 154–55
PepsiCo, 230, 509–10, 540
Perceived-value pricing, 383–84
Perception, 179–80
Person-marketing, 688–90
Personal communication channel, 492–93
Personal factors influencing consumer behavior, 162, 171–77, 183
Personal interviewing, 103–5
Personal selling, 487, 498, 499, 501–4, 554–67
   history, 544–45
Personality:
   buying behavior and, 173, 175–77
   market segmentation, 269, 270
Persuasive advertising, 515
Physical distribution, 127, 412, 414, 430–39
Physical distribution manager, 627, 748
Pillsbury Co., 569–72
Pipelines shipment, 438
Place, marketing, 43, 475
Place marketing, 690–92
Planned obsolescence, 706–7
Planning, annual, 57
Planning, isolated, 609
Planning, long-range, 57
Planning, marketing, 72–80
Planning, strategic, 58–72
   marketing's role, 69–70
Planning-benefits, 56
Planning system need, 56–57
Playboy, 159, 160
Pleasure seekers, 154
Point-of-purchase displays, 530
Political candidate marketing, 689–90
Political-legal environment, foreign, 661
Political power, business, 711, 723
Pollution control, 143, 144, 148, 149, 714
Poor Pay More, The (Caplovitz), 707
Population:
   demographic environment and, 132–33
   geographic shifts in, 136–39
Portfolio matrix, strategic business unit, 61–64, 66
Portfolio planning, business, 61–68
Position, product, 282
Positioning (*see* Market positioning)
Postpurchase consumer behavior, 197–201

Purchasing power, 6
Purex Industries, Inc., 573–75
Push strategy, promotional, 503

Q

Quaker Oats Company and Gatorade, 119
Quality choice, 19, 591
Quality improvement, 355, 592–93
Quantity, output-need, 127
Question mark, SBU, 63, 64
Questionnaires, 101–2, 105–9
  for MIS, 87–88
Questions, research, 100–109
Quotas, import, 659, 661
Quotas, sales, 563–64

R

Rack jobbers, 470–72
Radio advertising, 491, 493, 521–22, 524, 711
Rail carrier, 437, 438
Raw material shortages, 141–43, 300–301
RCA, 243
  VCPs and VCRs, 287–88
Real estate marketing, 690–92
Real income, 139–40
Rebuy, 216–17, 222, 227
Receiver (audience), 488
Recycling, 415–16
Reference group, 167–69
Regional shopping center, 445, 462
Regulatory legislation, 19, 20, 147–51, 380, 722
Reinforcement advertising, 516
Relationships, people's, 154–55
Repair (after-sales) service, 322–23
Resale (see Resellers)
Research, experimental, 101, 102
Research, observational, 100
Research and development, (R&D);
  expenditures on, 145–48, 152, 336, 338, 344, 355
  marketing department and, 72, 125–26
  of new products, 336, 338, 344–45, 357
Research instruments, 105–9
Research plan:
  development, 95, 96–109
  implementation, 109–10
  interpreting and reporting, 110–11
  presentation, 109
Researchers and marketing department, 95–96, 109–10, 112–15
Reseller market, 212, 432
Resellers, 127, 128, 129, 150, 227–31
  buyer behavior of, 227–31, 379–80
Resources, renewable, 141–43, 319

Response, message, 488–90, 499, 500
Retail stores, types and classes, 445–59
Retailer branches, 470
Retailer cooperatives, 421
Retailers, 123, 127, 129, 444–68, 470
  in marketing channel, 416–19, 421–22
  marketing decisions, 464–66
  outlet types, 445–58
Retailing, 419, 444–68, 465
  careers, 749
  future of, 467–68
  wheel of, 467, 468
Retirees in population, 133
Revlon, 295
Robinson-Patman Act of 1936, 149–50, 229, 380
Role, 171

S

Saab, 280–81
Safety needs, 178, 179
Sales, net, analytic ratio arithmetic, 740–42
Sales, net, operating statement arithmetic, 737–39
Sales agency vs. salesforce, 426–29
Sales analysis, 628–29
Sales branches/offices, 474
Sales decline, new product, 356–57
Sales department, simple, 620–21
Sales effect, advertising research, 526–27
Sales effectiveness, 65
Sales forecasting, 244, 252–57
  of new product, 343–44
Sales manager, 622
  career as, 749
Sales positions, classified, 545–46
  careers, 749
Sales presentations, 558–59
Sales promotion, 466, 486, 487, 498–504, 527–33, 593
  objectives, 528–29
Sales quotas, 563–64
Sales reports information, 564–66
Sales representatives, 544–67
  evaluation, 564–67
  as forecasters, 254–55
  good traits, 551–53
  motivation, 562–64
  promotion, 499, 502
  selection, 551–53
  supervision, 560–64
  training, 553–60
  See also Salesforce; Salespeople
Sales-response function, 78–79
Sales time efficiency, 562
Sales variance analysis, 629
Sales vice-president, tasks, 620–21

Sales volume, 561
  in sales response function, 78–79, 563–65
Salesforce:
  compensation, 550–51
  evaluation, 565–67
  information from 89, 90
  intermediaries from, 424, 426, 427
  managing, 47–48, 546–64, 620–27
  in marketing department, 620–26
  objectives set, 546–47
  as promotional tool, 487, 498–500, 502–4, 528, 529, 531, 593
  size needed, 549–50
  strategy design, 547–51
  structures, 548–49
Salesforce management, 47–48, 546, 548, 549, 560–64
Salesmanship, 555–60
Salespeople, marketing department, 47–48
  See also Sales representatives; Salesforce
Sampling, market research, 105
Savings and purchasing, 140
Scale economics, 65
Schaefer beer, 272, 290–91
Searle, G. D., & Co., 213
Sears Roebuck & Co., 444, 456, 681, 731–32
Seasonality, portfolio planning, 65
Segments, target-marketing, 39–41, 262–63, 276–79, 281–82 (see also Market segments; Market segmentation)
Selective perceptual processes, 179–80
Self-concept (-image), 177
Self-esteem, 178, 179
Self-realization, 154
Self-service retailing, 446, 450, 451
Seller's market, 11
Sellers and buyers, 11, 18–19, 214, 217
Selling, 546–48, 555–60, 562
  marketing vs., 15–16, 22, 25
Selling, high-pressure, 701, 704–5
Selling agents, 473
Selling and buying (see Buying and selling)
Semantic differential, image, 687–88
Sender (communicator), 487, 494
Seniors:
  consumer market, 160–61
  See also Elderly; Retirees
Service, defined, 681
Service business, retailers, 445, 452
Service firms, 21–22, 682, 684, 686–88
Service sector:
  distribution channels, 415–16
  firms and providers, 21–22
  marketing, 684–86